Oxford
School
German
Dictionary

Editorial Manager: Valerie Grundy
New Edition: Nicholas Rollin
with the assistance of Marie-Louise Wasmeier

OXFORD
UNIVERSITY PRESS

OXFORD

UNIVERSITY PRESS

Great Clarendon Street, Oxford OX2 6DP

Oxford University Press is a department of the University of Oxford.
It furthers the University's objective of excellence in research, scholarship,
and education by publishing worldwide in

Oxford New York

Auckland Cape Town Dar es Salaam Hong Kong Karachi
Kuala Lumpur Madrid Melbourne Mexico City Nairobi New Delhi
Shanghai Taipei Toronto

with offices in

Argentina Austria Brazil Chile Czech Republic France Greece
Guatemala Hungary Italy Japan Poland Portugal Singapore
South Korea Switzerland Thailand Turkey Ukraine Vietnam

Oxford is a registered trade mark of Oxford University Press
in the UK and in certain other countries

© Oxford University Press 2007

First edition 1998
Revised edition 2002
Second edition 2004
Third edition 2005
This edition 2007

Database right Oxford University Press (maker)

All rights reserved. No part of this publication may be reproduced, stored in
a retrieval system, or transmitted, in any form or by any means, without the
prior permission in writing of Oxford University Press, or as expressly
permitted by law, or under terms agreed with the appropriate reprographic
rights organization. Enquiries concerning reproduction outside the scope of
the above should be sent to the Rights Department, Oxford University Press,
at the address above

You must not circulate this book in any other binding or cover and you
must impose this same condition on any other acquirer

British Library cataloguing in Publication Data available

ISBN 978-0-19-911530-3

10 9 8 7 6 5 4 3 2 1

Typeset in Arial MT and Nimrod MT

Printed in Italy by Rotolito Lombarda

INTRODUCTION

This dictionary has been specially written for students who are in their first years of learning German all the way through to preparing for exams. We have paid particular attention to making the dictionary user-friendly. With the help of colour headwords, alphabet tabs, easy-to-follow signposts and examples, the right translation can quickly be found. The things students need to know about words in German are clearly shown. These include main parts of irregular verbs, noun plurals, and the case taken by prepositions.

Throughout the writing of this dictionary we have worked in close consultation with students, teachers, and examining boards. We gratefully acknowledge the examining boards AQA (formerly NEAB and SEG), OCR, and EDEXCEL, who have read and commented on the dictionary text.

Since the first edition of this dictionary there have been many changes in German life. Not least has been the introduction of the euro. This new edition of the dictionary takes full account of these changes and many new words and examples have been included in order to provide the best possible learner's dictionary of German at this level.

HOW A BILINGUAL DICTIONARY WORKS

A bilingual dictionary contains two languages. When you look up a word in one of the languages, it gives the translation for that word in the other language. This dictionary is divided into two halves which are separated by a section of blue-edged pages. In the first half you look up German words, which are in alphabetical order, to find out what they mean in English and in the second half you look up English words, also in alphabetical order, to find out how to say them in German.

At the entry, you will find not only **translations** but also other information that will help you get the right word and use it correctly. Here is a guide to the different things you will find in an entry:

headword	a word you look up in the dictionary
translation	translations are the only things that are in 'ordinary' type in the dictionary. They are always typed like this, and something which is typed in a different way can never be a translation
noun	word class (part of speech): tells you whether the word you are looking up is a noun, a verb, an adjective, or some other part of speech. A headword can be more than one part of speech. For instance, book can be a noun (she was reading a book) or a verb (I've booked the seats)
(*signpost*)	helpful information: to guide you to the right translation, to show you how to use the translation, or to give you extra information about either the headword or the translation
example	a phrase or sentence using the word you have looked up. You should read through them carefully to see if they are close to what you want to understand or say
der/die/das	gender: after a German noun to tell you whether it is masculine (der), feminine (die), or neuter (das)
(PL *die*........)	shows the plural form of a German noun
●	indicates a phrasal verb such as to carry on
★	shows an idiomatic expression such as over the moon
[27]	verb number – tells you which verb pattern to look at in the blue-edged of the dictionary
✧	indicates an irregular German verb
SEP	indicates that a German verb is separable such as ablenken (PERF lenkt ab)

USING THE DICTIONARY

To find out what a German word means

Suppose you want to find out what the German word **Tor** means. You need to use the first half of the dictionary to find the German word that you are looking for. To help you do this, the guide words at the top of each page show the alphabetical range of words on the pages you have open. You will know that all German nouns start with a capital letter. Notice that this makes no difference to the alphabetical order, nor do accented letters like **ü**.

When you find the entry for **Tor** you will find the translation but you will also see what the gender of **Tor** is. Nouns in German are either masculine, feminine, or neuter. These are shown in the dictionary as *der, die,* or *das*. You can see that **Tor** says *das* so it is neuter.

However, it often happens that a German word has more than one translation in English so you will see that the translation for **Tor** is divided into sections numbered **1** and **2**.

Tor *das* (PL *die* **Tore**) **1** gate; **2** goal;
  mit 3 zu 2 Toren gewinnen to win
  by 3 goals to 2.

The first translation is **gate** and the second is **goal**. You will need to look at both translations and see which fits best in the German sentence you are trying to understand, so:

Uli hat das Tor geöffnet *means* Uli opened the gate

BUT

Uli steht im Tor *means* Uli's in goal

In English, the plural of most nouns is formed by adding -s. In German there are quite a lot of ways of forming the plural and these are not always easy to recognize. To help you with this, we show the plural form after every noun headword. For instance, if you are trying to find out what the German word **Häuser** means, you can see immediately that it is the plural of **Haus** and so it means **houses**.

Haus *das* (PL *die* **Häuser**) **1** house;
  2 nach Hause home; **zu Hause** at
  home.

German like English has certain words that you would use when chatting with friends but not in more formal situations. German words like this are marked (*informal*) like **flitzen** here:

flitzen *verb* (*informal*) (PERF **ist**
  geflitzt) **1** to dash; **2** to whizz.

You can think of a dictionary entry as being made out of different sorts of building bricks. In the entries below you can see how they fit together to help you find what you need. The more you use your dictionary the more confident you will feel about finding your way around it.

GERMAN-ENGLISH

headword in colour for easy look-up

abergläubisch *adjective* superstitious.

word class (part of speech)

abfahren ✧*verb* (PRES **fährt ab**, IMPERF **fuhr ab**, PERF **ist abgefahren**) to leave; **Peter fährt morgen ganz früh ab** Peter is leaving very early tomorrow morning; **wann fährt der Zug nach Berlin ab?** when does the Berlin train leave?

main forms of iregular verbs

gender

Abfahrt *die* (PL *die* **Abfahrten**) **1** departure; **2** run (*on a ski slope*); **3** exit (*on a motorway*).

noun plurals in colour for easy look-up

Abfall *der* (PL *die* **Abfälle**) rubbish.

Abfalleimer *der* (PL *die* **Abfalleimer**) rubbish bin.

typical examples to show German in context

abfliegen ✧*verb* (IMPERF **flog ab**, PERF **ist abgeflogen**) **1** to take off; **die Maschine ist mit zehn Minuten Verspätung abgeflogen** the plane took off ten minutes late; **2** to leave (*by plane*); **ich fliege um elf Uhr ab** my plane leaves at 11 o'clock.

Abflug *der* (PL *die* **Abflüge**) departure.

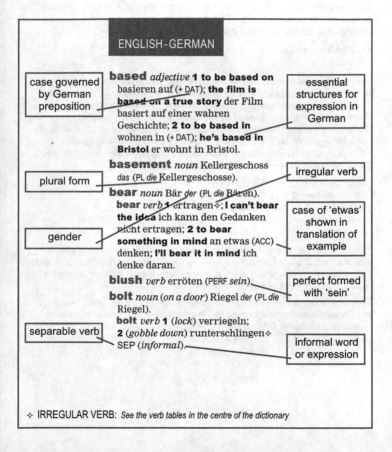

ENGLISH-GERMAN

case governed by German preposition

based *adjective* **1 to be based on** basieren auf (+ DAT); **the film is based on a true story** der Film basiert auf einer wahren Geschichte; **2 to be based in** wohnen in (+ DAT); **he's based in Bristol** er wohnt in Bristol.

essential structures for expression in German

basement *noun* Kellergeschoss *das* (PL *die* Kellergeschosse).

plural form

bear *noun* Bär *der* (PL *die* Bären). **bear** *verb* **1** ertragen ◇; **I can't bear the idea** ich kann den Gedanken nicht ertragen; **2 to bear something in mind** an etwas (ACC) denken; **I'll bear it in mind** ich denke daran.

irregular verb

gender

case of 'etwas' shown in translation of example

blush *verb* erröten (PERF *sein*).

bolt *noun* (*on a door*) Riegel *der* (PL *die* Riegel).

perfect formed with 'sein'

bolt *verb* **1** (*lock*) verriegeln; **2** (*gobble down*) runterschlingen ◇ SEP (*informal*).

separable verb

informal word or expression

◇ **IRREGULAR VERB:** *See the verb tables in the centre of the dictionary*

Finding an English word and how to say it in German

You can see that it is quite easy once you know how the dictionary works to look up a German word and find out what it means. Students usually find it harder to use the dictionary to find out how to say something in German. This dictionary is written specially to help you do this and to make it easy to find the right way of saying things in German.

Suppose you want to know how to say **garden** in German. Look up the word in the second part of the dictionary. If you follow the same method of going through the alphabetical order of the headwords as you did when you were looking up a German word, you will find **garden** on page 434.

garden *noun* Garten *der* (PL *die*
Gärten).

Now you can see that the German word for **garden** is **Garten**. But if you want to make a sentence using a noun like **Garten** you need to know its gender. The dictionary shows you that it is *der* **Garten** so in the garden will be **im Garten**. It is not always as easy as this to know which German word you need. Sometimes there will be more than one German word for the English word you are looking up. When the dictionary entry gives you more than just one translation, it is very important to take the time to read through the whole entry. If you look up plug the entry looks like this:

plug *noun* **1** (*electrical*) Stecker *der*
(PL *die* Stecker); **2** (*in a bath or sink*)
Stöpsel *der* (PL *die* Stöpsel); **to pull
out the plug** den Stöpsel
herausziehen.

You can see that **1** tells you that the German word for an electrical plug is **Stecker** and **2** tells you that the word for a **plug** in a bath or a sink is **Stöpsel**. Remember that information which is either in brackets or italics or both is there to help you, but it will never be the translation itself.

Wherever there is more than one translation, depending on what meaning of the English word you are looking for, the dictionary will always help you to choose the right one. Often it is not enough to find the translation of one word.

In the case of more common words the dictionary also gives you a selection of phrases you will often want to use. In the entry for **hair** below you can find out how to use the translation **Haare** in different expressions:

hair *noun* **1** Haare (*plural*); **to comb your hair** sich (DAT) die Haare kämmen; **to wash your hair** sich (DAT) die Haare waschen; **to have your hair cut** sich (DAT) die Haare schneiden lassen; **she's had her hair cut** sie hat sich die Haare schneiden lassen; **2 a hair** ein Haar.

Note on the German Spelling Reform

The German spelling reform was adopted by German-speaking countries in July 1996. You will find all the new spellings in this dictionary. However, since you may come across old spellings if you are reading pre-reform German material, we have also given all the most frequent old spellings as headwords to help you locate the entry. These are cross-referred to the new spellings. Thus **As** is cross-referred to **Ass** but the old spelling of **Ausschuss** (**Ausschuß**) is not shown.

Note on the German Spelling Reform

Aa

Aal *der* (PL *die* **Aale**) eel.

ab *preposition* (+ DAT) from; **ab Montag** from Monday; **Kinder ab sechs Jahren** children from the age of six.

ab *adverb* **1** off; **der Henkel ist ab** the handle has come off; **ab ins Bett!** (*informal*) off (you go) to bed!; **2 ab und zu** now and again.

abbiegen ◇*verb* (IMPERF **bog ab**, PERF **ist abgebogen**) **1** to turn off; **nach rechts abbiegen** to turn off to the right; **2 biegen Sie an der Ampel (nach) links ab** turn left at the lights.

Abbildung *die* (PL *die* **Abbildungen**) illustration.

abbrechen ◇*verb* (PRES **bricht ab**, IMPERF **brach ab**, PERF **hat abgebrochen**) **1** to break off (*a branch, negotiations*); **Ruth brach ein paar Zweige ab** Ruth broke off a few branches; **2** to pull down (*a building*); **3** to cut short; **leider mussten wir unsere Ferien vorzeitig abbrechen** unfortunately we had to cut short our holidays; **er hat sein Studium aus finanziellen Gründen abgebrochen** he left university for financial reasons; **4** (PERF **ist abgebrochen**) **der Ast ist abgebrochen** the branch has broken off.

Abend *der* (PL *die* **Abende**) evening; **am Abend** in the evening; **heute Abend** this evening, tonight; **gestern Abend** yesterday evening,

last night; **wann esst ihr zu Abend?** when do you have dinner?

Abendbrot *das* evening meal.

Abendessen *das* (PL *die* **Abendessen**) supper, dinner (*in the evening*); **was gibt es zum Abendessen?** what are we having for supper?

Abendkurs *der* (PL *die* **Abendkurse**) evening course.

abends *adverb* in the evening.

Abenteurfilm *der* (PL *die* **Abenteuerfilme**) adventure film.

Abenteuer *das* (PL *die* **Abenteuer**) adventure.

aber *conjunction* but; **es ist zwar nützlich, aber zu teuer** it's useful, but too expensive.

aber *adverb* really; **das ist aber sehr nett von dir** that's really nice of you; **du bist aber groß!** aren't you tall!; **aber ja!** but of course!; **jetzt ist aber Schluss!** that's it now!

abergläubisch *adjective* superstitious.

abfahren ◇*verb* (PRES **fährt ab**, IMPERF **fuhr ab**, PERF **ist abgefahren**) to leave; **Peter fährt morgen ganz früh ab** Peter is leaving very early tomorrow morning; **wann fährt der Zug nach Berlin ab?** when does the Berlin train leave?

Abfahrt *die* (PL *die* **Abfahrten**) **1** departure; **2** run (*on a ski slope*); **3** exit (*on a motorway*).

Abfall *der* (PL *die* **Abfälle**) rubbish.

Abfalleimer *der* (PL *die* **Abfalleimer**) rubbish bin.

abfliegen ⋄*verb* (IMPERF **flog ab**, PERF **ist abgeflogen**) **1** to take off; **die Maschine ist mit zehn Minuten Verspätung abgeflogen** the plane took off ten minutes late; **2** to leave (*by plane*); **ich fliege um elf Uhr ab** my plane leaves at 11 o'clock.

Abflug *der* (PL *die* **Abflüge**) departure.

Abflussrohr *das* (PL *die* **Abflussrohre**) outlet, drain.

abfragen *verb* (PERF **hat abgefragt**) **1** to test; **sie fragt ihn Vokabeln ab** she's testing him on his vocabulary; **2** to call up (*on a computer*); **Adressen am Computer abfragen** to call up addresses on the computer.

Abgase (*plural noun*) exhaust fumes.

abgeben ⋄*verb* (PRES **gibt ab**, IMPERF **gab ab**, PERF **hat abgegeben**) **1** to hand in (*homework, an application, lost property*); **2** to pass (*in football*); **den Ball abgeben** to pass the ball; **3 sich mit etwas abgeben** to spend time on something; **mit solchen Typen würde ich mich nicht abgeben** I wouldn't associate with blokes like that; **4 jemandem etwas abgeben** to give someone something; **gib mir ein Stück von deiner Schokolade** give me a piece of your chocolate; **5 er wird einen guten Lehrer abgeben** he'll make a good teacher.

abgelegen *adjective* remote.

abgemacht *adjective* agreed.

Abgeordnete *der/die* (PL *die* **Abgeordneten**) member of parliament.

abgießen *verb* (IMPERF **goss ab**, PERF **hat abgegossen**) **1** to pour away; **2** to drain (*vegetables*).

Abhang *der* (PL *die* **Abhänge**) slope.

abhängen[1] ⋄*verb* (IMPERF **hing ab**, PERF **hat abgehangen**) **von jemandem abhängen** to depend on somebody; **von etwas abhängen** to depend on something; **es hängt vom Wetter ab, ob wir am Wochenende nach Wales fahren** whether or not we are going to Wales at the weekend depends on the weather.

abhängen[2] *verb* (PERF **hat abgehängt**) **1** to unhitch (*a trailer*); **2** to uncouple (*a train carriage*); **3** (*informal*) to shake off; **die Einbrecher hängten die Polizei schnell ab** the burglars soon shook off the police.

abhängig *adjective* dependent.

abheben ⋄*verb* (IMPERF **hob ab**, PERF **hat abgehoben**) **1** to lift off; **2** to withdraw (*money*); **3** to answer the phone; **ich habe schon zweimal angerufen, aber niemand hat abgehoben** I've rung twice before, but nobody answered.

abholen *verb* (PERF **hat abgeholt**) **1** to collect; **2** to pick up; **ich hole dich am Bahnhof ab** I'll pick you up at the station.

Abitur *das* (PL *die* **Abiture**) A levels (*German students usually take Abitur at 19, sitting exams in four subjects, which they have to pass to* go on to university); **sein Abitur machen** to do your A levels.

Abiturient der (PL die Abiturienten) A-level student.

Abiturientin die (PL die Abiturientinnen) A-level student.

Abkommen das (PL die Abkommen) agreement.

abkürzen verb (PERF hat abgekürzt) **1** to abbreviate; **wie kürzt man das Wort ab?** how do you abbreviate that word?; **2 den Weg abkürzen** to take a short cut.

Abkürzung die (PL die Abkürzungen) **1** abbreviation; **die Abkürzung für Europäische Union is EU** the abbreviation for European Union is EU; **2** short cut.

abladen ◇verb (PRES lädt ab, IMPERF lud ab, PERF hat abgeladen) to unload.

ablaufen ◇verb (PRES läuft ab, IMPERF lief ab, PERF ist abgelaufen) **1** to expire (passport, contract); **2** to drain off; **das Badewasser ablaufen lassen** to let the bathwater out; **3** to go off; **wie ist die Besprechung abgelaufen?** how did the meeting go?

Ablaufdatum der (PL die Ablaufdaten) expiry date.

ablegen verb (PERF hat abgelegt) **1** to take off; **2 abgelegte Kleidung** cast-offs.

ablehnen verb (PERF hat abgelehnt) **1** to turn down (a position, money, an invitation); **2** to reject (an applicant, a suggestion).

ablenken verb (PERF hat abgelenkt) **1** to distract; **jemanden von seiner Arbeit ablenken** to distract somebody from their work; **2 jemanden von seinen Sorgen ablenken** to take somebody's mind off their worries; **3** to divert (attention, suspicion); **vom Thema ablenken** to change the subject.

abliefern verb (PERF hat abgeliefert) **1** to deliver; **2** to hand in (an essay, a form, lost property); **3** to drop off; **die Kinder abliefern** to drop the children off.

abmachen verb (PERF hat abgemacht) **1** to take off; **kannst du den Deckel abmachen?** can you take off the lid?; **2** to agree; **wir müssen noch einen Termin für unser nächstes Treffen abmachen** we still have to agree on a date for our next meeting; **abgemacht!** agreed!; **3** to sort out; **das müsst ihr untereinander abmachen** you'll have to sort that out amongst yourselves.

Abmachung die (PL die Abmachungen) agreement.

abnehmen ◇verb (PRES nimmt ab, IMPERF nahm ab, PERF hat abgenommen) **1** to take off (remove); **2 kann ich dir etwas abnehmen?** (carry) can I take something (for you)?; (help) can I do anything for you?; **3 jemandem etwas abnehmen** to take something off somebody; **sie nehmen einem schnell zwanzig Euro ab** they'll soon take 20 euros off you; **4** to buy; **5** to decrease (in

3

a
b
c
d
e
f
g
h
i
j
k
l
m
n
o
p
q
r
s
t
u
v
w
x
y
z

number); **6** to diminish; **7** to lose weight; **er hat schon vier Kilo abgenommen** he's already lost four kilos; **8** to answer the phone; **9 das nehme ich dir nicht ab** (*informal*) I don't buy that.

Abonnement *das* (PL *die* **Abonnements**) subscription.

abonnieren *verb* (PERF **hat abonniert**) to subscribe to.

abraten ⋄*verb* (PRES **rät ab**, IMPERF **riet ab**, PERF **hat abgeraten**) **jemandem von etwas abraten** to advise somebody against something.

abräumen *verb* (PERF **hat abgeräumt**) to clear away; **den Tisch abräumen** to clear the table.

abreagieren *verb* (PERF **hat abreagiert**) **1 seine Wut an jemandem abreagieren** to take your anger out on somebody; **2 sich abreagieren** to calm down.

Abreise *die* departure.

abreisen *verb* (PERF **ist abgereist**) to leave.

abreißen ⋄*verb* (IMPERF **riss ab**, PERF **hat abgerissen**) **1** to tear down (*a poster, notice*); **2** to demolish (*a building*); **3** (PERF **ist abgerissen**) to come off (*a button, for example*).

Absage *die* (PL *die* **Absagen**) refusal.

absagen *verb* (PERF **hat abgesagt**) **1** to cancel; **2 eine Einladung absagen** to turn down an invitation.

Absatz *der* (PL *die* **Absätze**) **1** heel (*of a shoe*); **2** paragraph.

abschaffen *verb* (PERF **hat abgeschafft**) **1** to abolish (*a regulation, capital punishment*); **2** to get rid of; **wir haben unseren Hund abgeschafft** we got rid of our dog.

abscheulich *adjective* horrible.

abschicken *verb* (PERF **hat abgeschickt**) to send off.

Abschied *der* (PL *die* **Abschiede**) **1** parting; **2** farewell; **3 Abschied nehmen** to say goodbye.

Abschleppdienst *der* breakdown service.

abschleppen *verb* (PERF **hat abgeschleppt**) **1** to tow away; **2 sich mit den Koffern abschleppen** (*informal*) to struggle along with the suitcases; **3 jemanden abschleppen** (*informal*) to pick somebody up.

Abschleppwagen *der* (PL *die* **Abschleppwagen**) breakdown truck.

abschließen ⋄*verb* (IMPERF **schloss ab**, PERF **hat abgeschlossen**) to lock.

Abschlussprüfung *die* (PL *die* **Abschlussprüfungen**) final exam.

abschneiden ⋄*verb* (IMPERF **schnitt ab**, PERF **hat abgeschnitten**) **1** to cut off; **ich schneide dir eine Scheibe Brot ab** I'll cut you a slice of bread; **2 gut/ schlecht abschneiden** to do well/ badly.

abschrecken *verb* (PERF **hat abgeschreckt**) to deter.

abschreiben ◇*verb* (IMPERF schrieb ab, PERF hat abgeschrieben) to copy.

Abseilen *das* abseiling.

abseits *adverb* **1** far away; **etwas abseits** a little way away; **2** offside (*in soccer*).

Absender *der* (PL *die* **Absender**) sender.

absetzen *verb* (PERF hat abgesetzt) **1** to take off (*your hat, glasses*); **2** to put down (*a bag, suitcase*); **3** to drop off; **ich setze euch am Bahnhof ab** I'll drop you off at the station; **4 die Pille absetzen** to stop taking the pill.

Absicht *die* (PL *die* **Absichten**) intention.

absichtlich *adverb* intentionally.

absolut *adjective* absolute. **absolut** *adverb* absolutely; **das ist absolut unmöglich** that's absolutely impossible.

abspülen *verb* (PERF hat abgespült) **1** to rinse, to rinse off; **2** to do the washing up.

Abstand *der* (PL *die* **Abstände**) **1** distance; **in zwanzig Meter Abstand** at a distance of 20 metres; **Abstand halten** to keep your distance; **2** interval.

abstauben *verb* (PERF hat abgestaubt) to dust.

abstellen *verb* (PERF hat abgestellt) **1** to turn off (*the radio, a tap*); **2** to put down (*a suitcase, the shopping*); **3** to park (*the car*).

Abstimmung *die* (PL *die* **Abstimmungen**) vote.

abstreiten ◇*verb* (IMPERF stritt ab, PERF hat abgestritten) to deny.

abstürzen *verb* (PERF ist abgestürzt) **1** to fall; **2** to crash (*a plane*).

Abszess *der* (PL *die* **Abszesse**) abscess.

abtauen *verb* (PERF hat abgetaut) to defrost (*the fridge*).

Abteil *das* (PL *die* **Abteile**) compartment.

abteilen *verb* (PERF hat abgeteilt) **1** to divide up; **2** to divide off.

Abteilung *die* (PL *die* **Abteilungen**) department.

Abtreibung *die* (PL *die* **Abtreibungen**) abortion.

abtrocknen *verb* (PERF hat abgetrocknet) **1** to dry up; **2 sich abtrocknen** to dry yourself.

abwägen *verb* (IMPERF wog ab, PERF hat abgewogen) to weigh up.

abwärts *adverb* down.

Abwasch *der* washing-up.

abwaschen ◇*verb* (PRES wäscht ab, IMPERF wusch ab, PERF hat abgewaschen) **1** to wash up (*the dishes*); **2** to wash off (*dirt, marks*).

Abwasser *das* (PL *die* **Abwässer**) sewage.

Abwechslung *die* (PL *die* **Abwechslungen**) change; **zur Abwechslung** for a change.

abwerten *verb* (PERF hat abgewertet) to devalue.

abwertend *adjective* pejorative.

abwesend *adjective* absent.

a
b
c
d
e
f
g
h
i
j
k
l
m
n
o
p
q
r
s
t
u
v
w
x
y
z

Abwesenheit *die* absence.

abwischen *verb* (PERF **hat abgewischt**) to wipe.

abzählen *verb* (PERF **hat abgezählt**) to count.

Abzeichen *das* (PL **die Abzeichen**) badge.

abziehen ⋄*verb* (IMPERF **zog ab**, PERF **hat abgezogen**) **1** to take off (*a sheet, backing*); **die Betten abziehen** to strip the beds; **2** to take out (*a key*); **3** to deduct, to take away; **4** to withdraw (*troops*); **5** (PERF **ist abgezogen**) to escape (*steam or smoke, for example*); **6** (PERF **ist abgezogen**) **sie sind gleich nach dem Essen abgezogen** (*informal*) they pushed off straight after the meal.

abzielen *verb* (PERF **hat abgezielt**) **etwas zielt auf etwas ab** something is aimed at something.

Abzweigung *die* (PL **die Abzweigungen**) turning.

ach *exclamation* oh!

Achsel *die* (PL **die Achseln**) shoulder.

Acht¹ *die* (PL **die Achten**) eight; **eine Acht schreiben** to write an eight.

Acht² *die* **1 Acht geben** to pay attention; **er sollte in der Schule besser Acht geben** he should pay more attention at school; **2 auf etwas/jemanden Acht geben** to look after something/somebody; **3 gib Acht!** watch out!; **4 sich in Acht nehmen** to be careful; **5 etwas außer Acht lassen** to disregard something.

acht *number* eight; **um acht (Uhr)** at eight (o'clock); **um halb acht** at half past seven.

Achtel *das* (PL **die Achtel**) eighth.

achten *verb* (PERF **hat geachtet**) **1** to respect (*a person, an opinion*); **2 auf etwas achten** to pay attention to something; **3 auf jemanden achten** to look after somebody; **4 achte nicht darauf!** don't take any notice of it!

achter, achte, achtes *adjective* eighth; **jede achte Kiste** every eighth crate; **mein achter Geburtstag** my eighth birthday; **sie ging als Achte durchs Ziel** she finished eighth.

Achterbahn *die* (PL **die Achterbahnen**) roller coaster.

achtgeben SEE **Acht**².

achthundert *number* eight hundred.

achtmal *adverb* eight times.

Achtung *die* **1** respect; **Achtung vor jemandem haben** to have respect for somebody; **2 Achtung!** look out!; **Achtung, fertig, los!** on your marks, get set, go!; **'Achtung Stufe'** 'mind the step'.

achtzehn *number* eighteen.

achtzig *number* eighty.

Acker *der* (PL **die Äcker**) field.

addieren *verb* (PERF **hat addiert**) to add.

Ader *die* (PL **die Adern**) vein.

Adjektiv *das* (PL **die Adjektive**) adjective.

Adler *der* (PL **die Adler**) eagle.

adoptieren *verb* (PERF **hat adoptiert**) to adopt.

Adoption *die* (PL *die* **Adoptionen**) adoption.

Adoptiveltern *plural noun* adoptive parents.

Adoptivkind *das* (PL *die* **Adoptivkinder**) adopted child.

Adresse *die* (PL *die* **Adressen**) address.

adressieren *verb* (PERF **hat adressiert**) to address; **an wen soll ich den Brief adressieren?** who shall I address the letter to?

Advent *der* Advent.

Adventskalender *der* (PL *die* **Adventskalender**) Advent calendar.

Adventskranz *der* (PL *die* **Adventskränze**) Advent wreath.

Adverb *das* (PL *die* **Adverbien**) adverb.

Aerobic *das* aerobics.

Affe *der* (PL *die* **Affen**) **1** monkey; **2** ape.

Afrika *das* Africa; **aus Afrika** from Africa; **nach Afrika** to Africa.

Afrikaner *der* (PL *die* **Afrikaner**) African.

Afrikanerin *die* (PL *die* **Afrikanerinnen**) African.

afrikanisch *adjective* African.

AG¹ *die* (PL *die* **AGs**) (*Aktiengesellschaft*) Plc (*Public limited company*).

AG² *die* (PL *die* **AGs**) **1** work group; **2** school club.

Agentur *die* (PL *die* **Agenturen**) agency.

aggressiv *adjective* aggressive.

ähneln *verb* (PERF **hat geähnelt**) **1** to resemble; **er ähnelt seinem Vater sehr** he's very like his father; **2 sich ähneln** to be alike.

ahnen *verb* (PERF **hat geahnt**) **1** to know; **das konnte ich wirklich nicht ahnen** I had no way of knowing that; **wer soll denn ahnen, dass ...?** who would know that ...?; **2** to suspect; **so etwas habe ich doch schon geahnt** I did suspect something like that.

ähnlich *adjective* **1** similar; **2 jemandem ähnlich sein** to be like somebody; **jemandem ähnlich sehen** to look like somebody; **3 ähnlich wie** like; **4 das sieht dir ähnlich!** (*informal*) that's just like you!

Ähnlichkeit *die* (PL *die* **Ähnlichkeiten**) similarity.

Ahnung *die* **1** idea; **hast du eine Ahnung, wie er heißt?** have you got any idea what he's called?; **2 keine Ahnung!** no idea!; **er hat von Mode absolut keine Ahnung** he doesn't know a thing about fashion; **3** premonition.

ahnungslos *adjective* unsuspecting.

Ahorn *der* (PL *die* **Ahorne**) maple.

Aids *das* Aids.

Akademiker *der* (PL *die* **Akademiker**) university graduate.

a
b
c
d
e
f
g
h
i
j
k
l
m
n
o
p
q
r
s
t
u
v
w
x
y
z

a
b
c
d
e
f
g
h
i
j
k
l
m
n
o
p
q
r
s
t
u
v
w
x
y
z

Akademikerin die (PL die Akademikerinnen) university graduate.

akademisch adjective academic.

Akkusativ der (PL die Akkusative) accusative.

Akne die acne.

Akte die (PL die Akten) file.

Aktentasche die (PL die Aktentaschen) briefcase.

Aktion die (PL die Aktionen)
1 action; **in Aktion treten** to go into action; 2 campaign.

Aktiv das active.

aktiv adjective active.

Aktualisierung die (PL die Aktualisierungen) 1 up-date; 2 updating.

aktuell adjective 1 topical; **ein aktuelles Thema** a topical issue; 2 **nicht mehr aktuell** no longer relevant; 3 current; **eine aktuelle Sendung** a current-affairs programme.

Akzent der (PL die Akzente)
1 accent; **mit starkem Akzent sprechen** to speak with a strong accent; 2 accent (on a letter); 3 stress; **den Akzent auf etwas legen** to stress something.

albern adjective silly.
albern adverb in a silly way.

Albtraum der (PL die Albträume) nightmare.

Album das (PL die Alben) album.

Algebra die algebra.

Alkohol der alcohol.

alkoholfrei adjective non-alcoholic.

Alkoholiker der (PL die Alkoholiker) alcoholic.

Alkoholikerin die (PL die Alkoholikerinnen) alcoholic.

alkoholisch adjective alcoholic.

All das space; **einen Satelliten ins All schicken** to send a satellite into space.

alle SEE **aller**.

Allee die (PL die Alleen) avenue.

allein adjective, adverb alone 1 **sie waren allein im Zimmer** they were alone in the room; **jemanden allein lassen** to leave somebody alone; 2 on your own; **sie hat das ganz allein gezeichnet** she drew it all on her own; 3 **von allein** by yourself, by itself (automatically); 4 **allein stehend** single; 5 **eine allein erziehende Mutter** a single mother; **der/die allein Erziehende** single parent; 6 **nicht allein** not only; 7 **allein der Gedanke** the mere thought.

alleinerziehend,
alleinstehend SEE **allein**.

aller, alle, alles pronoun 1 all; **alle meine Freunde** all my friends; **alles Geld** all the money; **alle miteinander** all together; 2 **alle Jungen in der Schule** all the boys in the school; **alle Bewohner der Stadt sind dagegen** all the people of the town are against it; **alles Gute!** all the best!; **Getränke aller Art** all kinds of drinks; 3 **alle** (plural) all; **alle waren da** they were

8

all there; **wir alle** all of us; **wir haben alle gesehen** we saw all of them; **4 ohne allen Grund** without any reason; **5 alle beide** both of them; **6** every; **alle Tage** every day; **alle fünf Minuten** every five minutes; **7 alles** everything, everybody (*people*).
alle *adjective* **alle sein** (*informal*) to be all gone.

allerbester, **allerbeste**, **allerbestes** *adjective* **1** very best; **2 am allerbesten** best of all.

allerdings *adverb* **1** though; **das Essen ist gut, allerdings ziemlich teuer** the food's good, though rather expensive; **2** certainly (*yes*); **'tut das weh?'** – **'allerdings!'** 'does it hurt?' – 'it certainly does!'.

Allergie *die* (PL **die Allergien**) allergy.

allergisch *adjective* allergic.

Allerheiligen *das* All Saints' Day.

allerlei *adjective* all sorts of; **allerlei Ausreden** all sorts of excuses.

allerletzter, **allerletzte**, **allerletztes** *adjective* very last.

alles SEE **aller**.

allgemein *adjective* **1** general; **2 im Allgemeinen** in general.
allgemein *adverb* **1** generally; **2 es ist allgemein bekannt, dass** ... it is common knowledge that ....

allmählich *adjective* gradual.
allmählich *adverb* gradually; **wir sollten allmählich gehen** it's time we got going.

Alltag *der* **1** daily routine; **2** weekday.

alltäglich *adjective* everyday (*event, sight*).

alltags *adverb* on weekdays.

Alpen *plural noun* **die Alpen** the Alps.

Alphabet *das* (PL **die Alphabete**) alphabet.

alphabetisch *adjective* alphabetical.

als *conjunction* **1** when; **als meine Freundin hier war** when my friend was here; **erst als** only when; **2** than (*as a comparison*); **er ist jünger als sie** he's younger than her; **3 lieber** ... **als** ... rather ... than ...; **ich würde lieber ins Kino gehen, als zum Essen** I'd rather go to the cinema than for a meal; **4** as; **als Frau kann ich das verstehen** as a woman, I can sympathize; **gerade als ich gehen wollte** just as I was about to leave; **5 als ob** as if; **als ob ich das nicht wüsste!** as if I didn't know that!

also *adverb, conjunction* **1** so; **ich konnte ihn telefonisch nicht erreichen, also habe ich ihm ein Fax geschickt** I couldn't get through to him on the phone, so I sent him a fax; **2** then; **also kommst du mit?** you're coming too, then?; **also gut** all right then; **3** well; **also, wie gesagt** well, as I said before; **4 na also!** there you are!

alt *adjective* **1** old; **wie alt bist du?** how old are you?; **alt werden** to grow old; **2 alles beim Alten lassen** to leave everything as it was.

a

Altar der (PL die **Altäre**) altar.

b

Alter das (PL die **Alter**) **1** age; **in deinem Alter** at your age; **im Alter von zwanzig** at the age of twenty; **2** old age; **im Alter** in old age.

c

d

älter adjective **1** older; **mein Rad ist älter als deins** my bike is older than yours; **2** elder; **mein älterer Bruder** my elder brother; **3** elderly.

e

f

g

altern verb (PERF **ist gealtert**) to age.

h

Alternative die (PL die **Alternativen**) alternative.

i

Altersgenosse der (PL die **Altersgenossen**) person of one's own age.

j

k

Altersgenossin der (PL die **Altersgenossinnen**) person of one's own age.

l

m

Altersgrenze die (PL die **Altersgrenzen**) age limit.

n

Altersheim das (PL die **Altersheime**) old people's home.

o

p

ältester, älteste, ältestes adjective **1** oldest; **2** eldest; **der älteste Sohn** the eldest son.

q

Altglas das used glass.

r

Altglascontainer der (PL die **Altglascontainer**) bottle bank.

s

t

altmodisch adjective old-fashioned.

u

Altpapier das waste paper.

v

Altstadt die (PL die **Altstädte**) old town.

w

Alufolie die tin foil.

x

Aluminium das aluminium.

y

am = **an dem**; **1 am Freitag** on Friday; **2 am besten** the best; **3 am**

z

teuersten (the) most expensive; **4 am höchsten** the highest; **5 am Abend** in the evening.

Ameise die (PL die **Ameisen**) ant.

Amerika das America.

Amerikaner der (PL die **Amerikaner**) American.

Amerikanerin die (PL die **Amerikanerinnen**) American.

amerikanisch adjective American.

Ampel die (PL die **Ampeln**) traffic lights.

Amsel die (PL die **Amseln**) blackbird.

Amt das (PL die **Ämter**) **1** office; **2** exchange (telephone).

amtlich adjective official.

amüsant adjective amusing.

amüsieren verb (PERF **hat amüsiert**) **1** to amuse; **2 sich amüsieren** to enjoy oneself; **amüsier dich gut!** enjoy yourself!; **3 sich über etwas amüsieren** to find something funny.

an preposition (+ DAT or + ACC) (the dative is used when talking about position; the accusative shows movement or a change of place) **1** at; **an der Spitze** at the top; **sich an den Tisch setzen** to sit down at the table; **er arbeitet an der Schule** he works at the school; **2** on (attached to, when talking about time); **das Bild hängt an der Wand** the picture is on the wall; **an dem Tag** on that day; **ich habe am fünften März Geburtstag** my birthday is on the fifth of March; **3** to; **einen Brief an jemanden schicken** to send a letter to somebody; **4 an einer Krankheit sterben** to die of a disease; **5 an jemanden denken** to think of somebody; **6 sich an etwas erinnern** to remember something; **7 an (und für) sich** actually; **an sich ist das kein Problem** actually, it's no problem; **8 es liegt an dir, jetzt etwas zu unternehmen** it's up to you to do something now.

an *adverb* **1** on; **das Licht ist an** the light's on; **2 ohne etwas an** with nothing on; **3 an die dreißig Euro** about thirty euros; **4 von heute an** from today.

analysieren *verb* (PERF **hat analysiert**) to analyse.

Ananas *die* (PL *die* **Ananas**) pineapple.

Anästhetikum *das* (PL *die* **Anästhetika**) anaesthetic.

anbieten ◇*verb* (IMPERF **bot an**, PERF **hat angeboten**) to offer; **Anna bot mir an, mich nach Hause zu bringen** Anna offered to take me home.

Anblick *der* (PL *die* **Anblicke**) sight.

anbrennen ◇*verb* (IMPERF **brannte an**, PERF **ist angebrannt**) to burn; **das Essen ist angebrannt** the food's burnt.

Andenken *das* (PL *die* **Andenken**) **1** souvenir; **2 zum Andenken an unsere Ferien** to remind us of our holiday.

anderer, andere, anderes *adjective* **1** other; **ich nehme das andere T-Shirt** I'll have the other T-shirt; **2** different; **3 ein anderer/ eine andere/ ein anderes** another;

ein anderes Mal another time.

andere *pronoun* **1 der/die/das andere** the other one; **nicht dieses Buch, sondern das andere** not that book, but the other one; **die anderen** the others; **die anderen kommen später** the others are coming later; **2 andere** other ones (*things, toys, etc.*); **3 ein anderer/ eine andere/ein anderes** a different one (*thing*), someone else (*person*); **4 kein anderer** no one else; **5 unter anderem** among other things; **6 etwas anderes** something else; **7 alles andere** everything else.

andererseits *adverb* on the other hand.

andermal *adverb* **ein andermal** another time.

ändern *verb* (PERF **hat geändert**) **1** to change; **2** to alter (*a garment*); **3 sich ändern** to change; **sie hat sich sehr geändert** she's changed a lot.

anders *adverb* **1** differently; **2 anders aussehen** to look different; **3 niemand anders** nobody else; **jemand anders** somebody else; **4 anders als** different from; **du bist ganz anders als ich** you're quite different from me; **5 irgendwo anders** somewhere else.

anderthalb *number* one and a half.

Anerkennung *die* **1** appreciation; **2** recognition (*of a king, state*).

Anfall *der* (PL *die* **Anfälle**) fit.

Anfang *der* (PL *die* **Anfänge**) **1** beginning, start; **am Anfang** at

a
b
c
d
e
f
g
h
i
j
k
l
m
n
o
p
q
r
s
t
u
v
w
x
y
z

the beginning; **von Anfang an** from the start; **2 zu Anfang** at first.

anfangen ⋄*verb* (PRES **fängt an**, IMPERF **fing an**, PERF **hat angefangen**) **1** to begin, to start; **die Schule fängt um acht an** school starts at eight; **mit etwas anfangen** to start (on) something; **2 bei einer Firma anfangen** to start working for a firm; **3 was soll ich damit anfangen?** what am I supposed to do with that?; **4 damit kann ich nichts anfangen** that's no good to me (*it's no use*), it doesn't mean anything to me (*I don't understand it*).

Anfänger *der* (PL **die Anfänger**) beginner.

Anfängerin *die* (PL **die Anfängerinnen**) beginner.

anfassen *verb* (PERF **hat angefasst**) **1** to touch; **2** to tackle (*a problem, a task*); **3** to treat (*a person*); **4 mit anfassen** to lend a hand; **5 sich anfassen** to feel; **es fasst sich weich an** it feels soft; **6 jemanden anfassen** to take somebody's hand; **sie hat ihre Mutter angefasst** she took her mother's hand; **fasst euch an!** hold hands!

anfragen *verb* (PERF **hat angefragt**) to enquire, to ask.

anfreunden *verb* (PERF **hat sich angefreundet**) **1 sich anfreunden** to make friends; **sie freundet sich mit allen möglichen Leuten an** she makes friends with all sorts of people; **2 sich anfreunden** to become friends; **wir haben uns**

angefreundet we've become friends.

Anführungszeichen *plural noun* inverted commas.

Angabe *die* (PL **die Angaben**) **1** piece of information; **2** serve (*in tennis*); **3** showing off; **das ist nur Angabe** he is/she is/they are only showing off.

angeben ⋄*verb* (PRES **gibt an**, IMPERF **gab an**, PERF **hat angegeben**) **1** to give (*your name, a reason*); **2** to show off; **3** to indicate (*on a map*); **4** to serve (*in tennis*).

Angeber *der* (PL **die Angeber**) show-off.

Angeberin *die* (PL **die Angeberinnen**) show-off.

Angebot *das* (PL **die Angebote**) offer.

angehen ⋄*verb* (IMPERF **ging an**, PERF **ist angegangen**) **1** to come on (*a radio, heating, a light*); **2** to concern; **das geht auch dich etwas an** it concerns you too; **das geht dich nichts an** it's none of your business; **3** (PERF **hat angegangen**) to tackle (*problems, difficulty, work*).

Angehörige *der/die* (PL **die Angehörigen**) relative.

Angel *die* (PL **die Angeln**) fishing rod.

Angelegenheit *die* (PL **die Angelegenheiten**) **1** matter; **2** business; **das ist meine Angelegenheit** that's my business.

angeln *verb* (PERF **hat geangelt**) **1** to fish; **angeln gehen** to go fishing; **2** to catch (*a fish*).

Angelrute *die* (PL *die* **Angelruten**) fishing rod.

angemessen *adjective* adequate.

angenehm *adjective* pleasant. **angenehm** *exclamation* pleased to meet you! (*when introduced to somebody*).

Angestellte *der/die* (PL *die* **Angestellten**) employee.

angewiesen *adjective* dependent; **auf etwas angewiesen sein** to be dependent on something; **auf jemanden angewiesen sein** to be dependent on somebody.

angewöhnen *verb* (PERF **hat angewöhnt**) **1 jemandem etwas angewöhnen** to get somebody used to something; **2 sich etwas angewöhnen** to get into the habit of doing something; **ich habe es mir angewöhnt, früh aufzustehen** I've got into the habit of getting up early.

Angewohnheit *die* (PL *die* **Angewohnheiten**) habit.

angreifen *verb* (IMPERF **griff an**, PERF **hat angegriffen**) **1** to attack; **2** to affect (*your health, voice*).

Angriff *der* (PL *die* **Angriffe**) attack.

Angst *die* (PL *die* **Ängste**) **1** fear; **2 Angst haben** to be afraid; **vor jemandem Angst haben** to be afraid of somebody; **mir ist Angst** I'm afraid; **3 jemandem Angst machen** to frighten somebody; **4 Angst vor einer Prüfung haben** to be worried about an exam; **Angst um jemanden haben** to be worried about somebody.

ängstlich *adjective* **1** nervous; **2** frightened; **3** anxious.

anhaben ◇*verb* (*informal*) (PRES **hat an**, IMPERF **hatte an**, PERF **hat angehabt**) to have on; **sie hat heute das neue Kleid an** she's got her new dress on today.

anhalten ◇*verb* (PRES **hält an**, IMPERF **hielt an**, PERF **hat angehalten**) **1** to stop; **2 den Atem anhalten** to hold your breath; **3** to last; **das schöne Wetter wird nicht lange anhalten** the nice weather won't last long; **4 jemanden zur Arbeit anhalten** to urge somebody to work.

Anhalter *der* (PL *die* **Anhalter**) hitchhiker; **per Anhalter fahren** to hitchhike.

Anhalterin *die* (PL *die* **Anhalterinnen**) hitchhiker.

Anhang *der* (PL *die* **Anhänge**) appendix.

Anhänger *der* (PL *die* **Anhänger**) **1** supporter; **2** trailer; **3** label (*on a suitcase*); **4** pendant; **5** loop (*for hanging up*).

Anhängerin *die* (PL *die* **Anhängerinnen**) supporter.

anhören *verb* (PERF **hat angehört**) **1** to listen to (*music, a CD*); **sich etwas anhören** to listen to something; **ich kann ihn mir nicht länger anhören** I can't listen to him any longer; **2 sich anhören** to sound; **sich gut anhören** to sound good; **3 jemandem etwas anhören** to hear something in somebody's voice; **man hörte ihr die**

a
b
c
d
e
f
g
h
i
j
k
l
m
n
o
p
q
r
s
t
u
v
w
x
y
z

Verzweiflung an you could hear the despair in her voice.

anklagen verb (PERF **hat angeklagt**) to accuse.

Ankleidekabine die (PL die **Ankleidekabinen**) changing cubicle.

anklicken verb (PERF **hat angeklickt**) **etwas anklicken** to click on something; **das Icon anklicken** to click on the icon.

ankommen ◊verb (IMPERF **kam an**, PERF **ist angekommen**) **1** to arrive; **gut ankommen** to arrive safely; **2 (bei jemandem) gut ankommen** (informal) to go down well (with somebody); **3 ankommen auf** to depend on; **es kommt ganz darauf an** it all depends; **4 es drauf ankommen lassen** (informal) to take a chance; **5 auf ein paar Minuten kommt es nicht an** a few minutes don't matter.

ankündigen verb (PERF **hat angekündigt**) to announce.

Ankunft die (PL die **Ankünfte**) arrival.

Ankunftstafel die (PL die **Ankunftstafeln**) arrivals board.

Ankunftszeit die (PL die **Ankunftszeiten**) time of arrival.

Anlage die (PL die **Anlagen**) **1** gardens; **2** investment; **das Haus ist eine gute Anlage** the house is a good investment; **3** plant (industrial, for recycling, for example); **4** enclosure; **als Anlage** enclosed; **5** system (music,

loudspeakers, etc.); **6** installation (military).

Anlass der (PL die **Anlässe**) **1** cause; **der Anlass ihres Streits** the cause of their row; **Anlass zu etwas geben** to give cause for something; **2** occasion; **ein festlicher Anlass** a festive occasion; **aus Anlass ihres Geburtstags** on the occasion of her birthday.

Anleitung die (PL die **Anleitungen**) instructions.

anmachen verb (PERF **hat angemacht**) **1** to turn on (the light, radio, TV); **2** to light (a fire); **3** to dress (salad); **4** (informal) to chat up (a person).

Anmeldeformular das (PL die **Anmeldeformulare**) registration form.

anmelden verb (PERF **hat angemeldet**) **1** to register (a car, change of address); **2 jemanden anmelden** to enrol somebody; **3 jemanden anmelden** to make an appointment for somebody; **sind Sie angemeldet?** do you have an appointment?; **4 ein Gespräch anmelden** to book a call (on the phone); **5 sich anmelden** to say that you're coming; **6 sich anmelden** to register your new address (in Germany a change of address has to be registered at the 'Einwohnermeldeamt'); **sich polizeilich anmelden** to register with the police; **7 sich anmelden** to make an appointment; **sich beim Arzt anmelden** to make an appointment with the doctor; **8 sich**

anmelden to check in (*at a hotel*); **9 sich anmelden** to enrol; **sich zu einem Abendkurs anmelden** to enrol for an evening course.

Anmeldung *die* (PL *die* **Anmeldungen**) **1** registration; **2** appointment.

annehmbar *adjective* acceptable.

annehmen ◇*verb* (PRES **nimmt an**, IMPERF **nahm an**, PERF **hat angenommen**) **1** to accept (*an invitation, help, a verdict*); **2** to take (*a call, name*); **3** to adopt (*a child, habit*); **4** to assume; **angenommen, dass** ... assuming that ...; **5** to suppose.

Annonce *die* (PL *die* **Annoncen**) (small) ad.

Anorak *der* (PL *die* **Anoraks**) **1** anorak; **2** cagoule.

anordnen *verb* (PERF **hat angeordnet**) **1** to arrange; **2** to order.

anpassen *verb* (PERF **hat sich angepasst**) **sich anpassen** to adapt.

anpassungsfähig *adjective* adaptable.

anprobieren *verb* (PERF **hat anprobiert**) to try on.

Anruf *der* (PL *die* **Anrufe**) (phone) call.

Anrufbeantworter *der* (PL *die* **Anrufbeantworter**) answering machine.

anrufen ◇*verb* (IMPERF **rief an**, PERF **hat angerufen**) **1** to ring, to phone; **ich rufe schnell mal meine Mutter an** I'll just quickly ring my mother; **2** to call to (*a passer-by*).

ans = **an das**; **ans Telefon gehen** to answer the phone.

Ansage *die* (PL *die* **Ansagen**) announcement.

Ansager *der* (PL *die* **Ansager**) announcer.

Ansagerin *die* (PL *die* **Ansagerinnen**) announcer.

anschalten *verb* (PERF **hat angeschaltet**) to switch on.

anschauen *verb* (PERF **hat angeschaut**) **1** to look at; **2 sich etwas anschauen** to look at something, to watch something (*on TV*); **sie schauten sich den neuen Film an** they saw the new film.

anscheinend *adverb* apparently.

Anschlag *der* (PL *die* **Anschläge**) **1** notice; **2** attack; **ein Anschlag auf den Präsidenten** an attack on the president.

Anschlagbrett *das* (PL *die* **Anschlagbretter**) notice board.

anschlagen ◇*verb* (PRES **schlägt an**, IMPERF **schlug an**, PERF **hat angeschlagen**) **1** to put up (*a notice, an announcement*); **2** to chip.

anschließen ◇*verb* (IMPERF **schloss an**, PERF **hat angeschlossen**) **1** to connect; **2 sich an etwas anschließen** to follow something; **an den Vortrag schließt sich eine Diskussion an** the talk will be followed by a discussion; **3 sich jemandem anschließen** to join somebody; **sich**

15

a
b
c
d
e
f
g
h
i
j
k
l
m
n
o
p
q
r
s
t
u
v
w
x
y
z

einer Gruppe anschließen to join a group.

anschließend *adverb*
1 afterwards; **2 anschließend an das Essen** after the meal.

Anschluss *der* (PL *die* **Anschlüsse**)
1 connection; **2 Anschluss finden** to make friends; **3 den Anschluss verlieren** to lose contact; **4 im Anschluss an** after.

anschnallen *verb* (PERF **hat sich angeschnallt**) **sich anschnallen** to fasten your seat belt.

Anschrift *die* (PL *die* **Anschriften**) address.

Anschuldigung *die* (PL *die* **Anschuldigungen**) accusation.

ansehen ⋄*verb* (PRES **sieht an**, IMPERF **sah an**, PERF **hat angesehen**)
1 to look at; **sie sah mich nicht an** she didn't look at me; **2 sich etwas ansehen** to look at something(*on TV*) to watch something; **sich einen Film ansehen** to see a film; **3 sich eine Stadt ansehen** to look round a town; **4** to regard; **ich sehe ihn als meinen Freund an** I regard him as a friend.

Ansehen *das* **1** respect; **2** reputation.

Ansicht *die* (PL *die* **Ansichten**) view; **meiner Ansicht nach** in my view.

Ansichtskarte *die* (PL *die* **Ansichtskarten**) picture postcard.

ansprechen ⋄*verb* (PRES **spricht an**, IMPERF **sprach an**, PERF **hat angesprochen**) **1** to speak to; **2** to appeal to; **die Musik spricht mich an** the music appeals to me; **3** to

mention; **er hat den Skandal, in den sie verwickelt war, angesprochen** he mentioned the scandal she was involved in; **4 auf etwas ansprechen** to respond to something (*a treatment, for example*).

Anspruch *der* (PL *die* **Ansprüche**)
1 demand; **keine Ansprüche stellen** to make no demands; **2** claim (*for compensation*); **3 Anspruch auf etwas haben** to be entitled to something; **4 viel Zeit in Anspruch nehmen** to take up a lot of time; **5 etwas in Anspruch nehmen** to take advantage of something (*an offer, for example*).

anständig *adjective* **1** decent; **2** respectable.

anstarren *verb* (PERF **hat angestarrt**) to stare at.

anstatt *preposition* (+ GEN) instead of.
anstatt *conjunction* **anstatt zu arbeiten** instead of working.

ansteckend *adjective* infectious.

anstelle *preposition* (+ GEN) instead of.

anstellen *verb* (PERF **hat angestellt**) **1** to employ; **2** to turn on (*the TV, radio*); **3** (*informal*) to do; **was stellt ihr heute Abend noch an?** what are you doing tonight?; **wie kann ich es nur anstellen, dass** ...? what can I do to ...?; **4 sich anstellen** to queue; **5 sich anstellen** to make a fuss; **stell dich nicht so an!** don't make such a fuss!

Anstieg *der* (PL *die* **Anstiege**)
1 increase; **2** way up, ascent.

anstreichen ◇*verb* (IMPERF **strich an**, PERF **hat angestrichen**) to paint.

anstrengen *verb* (PERF **hat angestrengt**) **1** to tire; **ihr Besuch hat mich sehr angestrengt** their visit tired me out; **2 sich anstrengen** to make an effort.

anstrengend *adjective* tiring.

Anstrengung *die* (PL *die* **Anstrengungen**) effort.

Antarktis *die* **die Antarktis** the Antarctic.

Anteil *der* (PL *die* **Anteile**) **1** share; **mein Anteil an dem Gewinn** my share of the profit; **2 Anteil nehmen** to sympathize; **3 Anteil nehmen an** to take an interest in.

Antenne *die* (PL *die* **Antennen**) aerial.

Antibiotikum *das* (PL *die* **Antibiotika**) antibiotic.

antik *adjective* antique.

Antiquitäten *plural noun* antiques.

Antiseptikum *das* (PL *die* **Antiseptika**) antiseptic.

Antivirenprogramm *das* (PL *die* **Antivirenprogramme**) anti-virus software.

Antrag *der* (PL *die* **Anträge**) application; **einen Antrag stellen** to make an application.

Antragsformular *das* (PL *die* **Antragsformulare**) application form.

Antwort *die* (PL *die* **Antworten**) answer, reply; **jemandem eine**

Antwort geben to give somebody an answer.

antworten *verb* (PERF **hat geantwortet**) to answer, to reply; **auf etwas antworten** to answer something; **jemandem antworten** to reply to somebody.

Anwalt *der* (PL *die* **Anwälte**) lawyer.

Anwältin *die* (PL *die* **Anwältinnen**) lawyer.

Anweisung *die* (PL *die* **Anweisungen**) instruction.

anwenden *verb* (PERF **hat angewendet**) **1** to use (*a method, process, medicine*); **2** to apply (*a rule, law*).

anwesend *adjective* present.

Anwesenheit *die* presence; **er gab es in meiner Anwesenheit zu** he admitted it in my presence.

Anzahl *die* number.

anzahlen *verb* (PERF **hat angezahlt**) to pay a deposit; **hundert Euro anzahlen** to pay a deposit of a hundred euros; **ein Auto anzahlen** to pay a deposit on a car.

Anzahlung *die* (PL *die* **Anzahlungen**) deposit.

Anzeichen *das* (PL *die* **Anzeichen**) sign.

Anzeige *die* (PL *die* **Anzeigen**) **1** advertisement; **2** report (*to the police*); **(eine) Anzeige gegen jemanden erstatten** to report somebody to the police.

anzeigen *verb* (PERF **hat angezeigt**) **1** to report; **jemanden**

anzeigen to report somebody to the police; **2** to show (*the time, a date*).

anziehen ⋄*verb* (IMPERF **zog an**, PERF **hat angezogen**) **1** to attract; **2** to put on (*clothes, the brakes*); **3** to dress (*a child or doll*); **gut angezogen** well dressed; **4** to tighten (*a knot, a screw*); **5 sich anziehen** to get dressed; **6 was soll ich anziehen?** what shall I wear?

Anzug *der* (PL *die* **Anzüge**) suit.

anzünden *verb* (PERF **hat angezündet**) to light.

Apfel *der* (PL *die* **Äpfel**) apple.

Apfelsaft *der* (PL *die* **Apfelsäfte**) apple juice.

Apfelsine *die* (PL *die* **Apfelsinen**) orange.

Apotheke *die* (PL *die* **Apotheken**) chemist's, pharmacy.

Apotheker *der* (PL *die* **Apotheker**) chemist, pharmacist.

Apothekerin *die* (PL *die* **Apothekerinnen**) chemist, pharmacist.

Apparat *der* (PL *die* **Apparate**) **1** set (*TV, radio*); **2** camera; **3** phone; **am Apparat!** speaking!; **4** gadget.

Appartement *das* (PL *die* **Appartements**) flat.

Appetit *der* appetite; **guten Appetit!** enjoy your meal!

Aprikose *die* (PL *die* **Aprikosen**) apricot.

April *der* April; **am ersten April** on the first of April; **April, April!** April fool!; **jemanden in den April**

schicken to play an April fool trick on somebody.

Aquarium *das* (PL *die* **Aquarien**) **1** aquarium; **2** tank (*for fish*).

Äquator *der* equator.

Araber *der* (PL *die* **Araber**) Arab.

Araberin *die* (PL *die* **Araberinnen**) Arab.

arabisch *adjective* **1** Arab; **die arabischen Länder** the Arab countries; **2** Arabian; **3** Arabic (*number*); **die arabische Sprache** Arabic.

Arbeit *die* (PL *die* **Arbeiten**) **1** work; **viel Arbeit haben** to have a lot of work; **von der Arbeit kommen** to come from work; **2** job; **3** test (*at school*); **4 sich viel Arbeit machen** to go to a lot of trouble.

arbeiten *verb* (PERF **hat gearbeitet**) to work.

Arbeiter *der* (PL *die* **Arbeiter**) worker.

Arbeiterin *die* (PL *die* **Arbeiterinnen**) worker.

Arbeitgeber *der* (PL *die* **Arbeitgeber**) employer.

Arbeitnehmer *der* (PL *die* **Arbeitnehmer**) employee.

Arbeitsamt *das* (PL *die* **Arbeitsämter**) job centre.

arbeitslos *adjective* unemployed.

Arbeitslose *der/die* (PL *die* **Arbeitslosen**) unemployed person; **die Arbeitslosen** the unemployed.

Arbeitslosigkeit *die* unemployment.

18

Arbeitsplatz der (PL die Arbeitsplätze) **1** job; **2** desk.

Arbeitspraktikum das (PL die Arbeitspraktika) work experience.

Arbeitsstunde die (PL die Arbeitsstunden) working hour.

Arbeitszimmer das (PL die Arbeitszimmer) study.

Architekt der (PL die Architekten) architect.

Architektin die (PL die Architektinnen) architect.

Architektur die architecture.

Ärger der **1** annoyance; **2** trouble; **Ärger mit dem Auto haben** to have trouble with the car.

ärgerlich adjective **1** annoying; **2** annoyed; **er war darüber sehr ärgerlich** he was very annoyed about it.

ärgern verb (PERF hat geärgert) **1** to annoy; **2 sich ärgern** to be annoyed, to get annoyed; **ich habe mich darüber geärgert** I was annoyed about it; **sich über jemanden ärgern** to get annoyed with somebody.

Arktis die **die Arktis** the Arctic; **in der Arktis** in the Arctic.

Arm der (PL die Arme) arm; **jemanden auf den Arm nehmen** (*informal*) to pull somebody's leg.

arm adjective poor.

Armband das (PL die Armbänder) bracelet.

Armbanduhr die (PL die Armbanduhren) wrist-watch.

Armee die (PL die Armeen) army.

Ärmel der (PL die Ärmel) sleeve.

Ärmelkanal der (English) Channel.

Armut die poverty.

arrangieren verb (PERF hat arrangiert) **1** to arrange; **2 sich arrangieren** to come to an arrangement.

Art die (PL die Arten) **1** way; **auf diese Art** in this way; **auf seine Art** in his own way; **2** kind; **diese Art (von) Buch** this kind of book; **Bücher aller Art** books of all kinds; **3** species; **eine gefährdete Art** an endangered species; **4** nature; **es ist nicht seine Art, das zu tun** it's not (in) his nature to do that.

Arterie die (PL die Arterien) artery.

artig adjective well-behaved.

Artikel der (PL die Artikel) article; **der bestimmte/unbestimmte Artikel** the definite/indefinite article.

Arznei die (PL die Arzneien) medicine.

Arzneimittel das (PL die Arzneimittel) drug.

Arzt der (PL die Ärzte) doctor.

Ärztin die (PL die Ärztinnen) doctor.

ärztlich adjective medical. **ärztlich** adverb **sich ärztlich behandeln lassen** to have medical treatment.

As SEE **Ass**.

Asche die (PL die Aschen) ash.

Aschenbecher der (PL die Aschenbecher) ashtray.

a
b
c
d
e
f
g
h
i
j
k
l
m
n
o
p
q
r
s
t
u
v
w
x
y
z

19

Aschermittwoch *der* Ash Wednesday.

Asiat *der* (PL *die* **Asiaten**) Asian.

Asiatin *die* (PL *die* **Asiatinnen**) Asian.

asiatisch *adjective* Asian.

Asien *das* Asia; **nach Asien** to Asia.

Ass *das* (PL *die* **Asse**) ace.

aß SEE **essen**.

Assistent *der* (PL *die* **Assistenten**) assistant.

Assistentin *die* (PL *die* **Assistentinnen**) assistant.

Ast *der* (PL *die* **Äste**) branch.

Asthma *das* asthma.

Astrologie *die* astrology.

Astronaut *der* (PL *die* **Astronauten**) astronaut.

Astronomie *die* astronomy.

Asyl *das* **1** asylum; **um politisches Asyl bitten** to apply for political asylum; **2** hostel (*for the homeless*).

Asylant *der* (PL *die* **Asylanten**) asylum-seeker.

Atelier *das* (PL *die* **Ateliers**) (*artist's*) studio.

Atem *der* breath; **außer Atem sein** to be out of breath.

atemlos *adjective* breathless.

Atemlosigkeit *die* breathlessness.

Athlet *der* (PL *die* **Athleten**) athlete.

Athletin *die* (PL *die* **Athletinnen**) athlete.

Atlantik *der* **der Atlantik** the Atlantic (Ocean); **im Atlantik** in the Atlantic.

Atlas *der* (PL *die* **Atlanten**) atlas.

atmen *verb* (PERF **hat geatmet**) to breathe.

Atmosphäre *die* (PL *die* **Atmosphären**) atmosphere.

Atom *das* (PL *die* **Atome**) atom.

atomar *adjective* atomic.

Atombombe *die* (PL *die* **Atombomben**) atomic bomb.

Atomwaffen *plural noun* nuclear weapons.

atomwaffenfrei *adjective* nuclear-free.

attraktiv *adjective* attractive.

ätzend *adjective* **1** corrosive; **2** caustic (*wit, remark*).

au *exclamation* **1** ouch!; **2** oh! (*when surprised or enthusiastic*); **au ja!** oh yes!

auch *adverb* **1** also, too; **Sophie war auch dabei** Sophie was also there, Sophie was there too; **ich auch** me too; **nicht nur ... sondern auch ...** not only ... but also ...; **2** '**ich gehe jetzt**' – '**ich auch**' 'I'm going now' – 'so am I'; '**er schläft**' – '**sie auch**' 'he's asleep' – 'so is she'; **3** '**ich bin nicht müde**' - '**ich auch nicht**' 'I'm not tired'-'neither am I'; **das weiß ich auch nicht** I don't know either; **4 auch wenn** even if; **5 wann auch** whenever; **was auch** whatever; **wo auch** wherever; **wer auch** whoever; **6 wie dem auch sei** however that may be; **7 lügst du auch nicht?** you're not lying, are you?

auf *preposition* (+ DAT *or* + ACC) (*the dative is used when talking about position; the accusative shows movement or a change of place*) **1** on; **das Buch liegt auf dem Tisch** the book's on the table; **er hat das Buch auf den Tisch gelegt** he put the book on the table; **2 ich war auf der Party** I was at the party; **ich gehe auf eine Party** I'm going to a party; **ich war auf der Post** I was at the post office; **er ist auf die Post gegangen** he went to the post office; **3 auf der Straße** in the street; **4 auf diese Art** in this way; **auf Deutsch** in German; **5** for (*indicating time or distance*); **er ist auf ein paar Tage verreist** he's gone away for a few days; **6 auf seinen Rat hin** on his advice; **7 auf Wiedersehen!** goodbye!

auf *adverb* **1** open; **die Tür ist auf** the door is open; **Mund auf!** open your mouth!; **2** up (*out of bed*); **auf sein** to be up; **er ist schon auf** he's already up; **3 auf einmal** suddenly; **4 auf einmal** at once (*at the same time*); **5 auf und ab** up and down; **6 sich auf und davon machen** to make off.

aufbekommen *verb* (IMPERF **bekam auf**, PERF **hat aufbekommen**) **1** to get open; **2 Hausaufgaben aufbekommen** to be given homework.

aufbewahren *verb* (PERF **hat aufbewahrt**) to keep.

aufblasen *verb* (PRES **bläst auf**, IMPERF **blies auf**, PERF **hat aufgeblasen**) to blow up.

aufbleiben *verb* (IMPERF **blieb auf**, PERF **ist aufgeblieben**) **1** to stay open; **wie lange bleiben die Geschäfte auf?** how long do the shops stay open?; **2** to stay up (*not go to bed*).

aufbringen *verb* (IMPERF **brachte auf**, PERF **hat aufgebracht**) **1** to raise (*money*); **2** to find (*patience, strength*); **3** to open; **ich bringe die Tür nicht auf** I can't open the door; **4 jemanden aufbringen** to make somebody angry; **5 Verständnis für etwas aufbringen** to be able to understand something.

aufeinander *adverb* **1** one on top of the other; **die Bretter aufeinander legen** to put the planks one on top of the other; **2 aufeinander liegen** to lie on top of each other; **3 aufeinander folgen** to follow one another; **4 aufeinander warten** to wait for each other; **5 aufeinander schießen** to shoot at each other; **6 aufeinander fahren** to collide with each other.

Aufenthalt *der* (PL **die Aufenthalte**) **1** stay; **2** stop (*pause in a journey*); **zehn Minuten Aufenthalt haben** to stop for ten minutes.

Aufenthaltsraum *der* (PL **die Aufenthaltsräume**) **1** lounge; **2** recreation room.

Auffahrt *die* (PL **die Auffahrten**) **1** drive; **2** slip road.

auffallend *adjective* striking.

auffangen *verb* (PRES **fängt auf**, IMPERF **fing auf**, PERF **hat aufgefangen**) to catch.

a b c d e f g h i j k l m n o p q r s t u v w x y z

aufführen verb (PERF hat
aufgeführt) **1** to perform (a play);
2 to list (words, items); **3 sich
aufführen** to behave.

Aufführung die (PL die
Aufführungen) performance.

auffüllen verb (PERF hat
aufgefüllt) **1** to fill up; **2** to stock up.

Aufgabe die (PL die Aufgaben)
1 task; **2** exercise (at school);
3 question (in a test or an exam);
4 Aufgaben homework.

aufgeben ◇verb (PRES gibt auf,
IMPERF gab auf, PERF hat
aufgegeben) **1** to give up; **ich gebe
auf!**; **2** to post; **3** to check
in (luggage); **4** to place (an
advertisement, order);
5 Hausaufgaben aufgeben to set
homework.

aufgehen ◇verb (IMPERF ging auf,
PERF ist aufgegangen) **1** to open (of
a door or flower, for example); **2** to
come undone (of a knot or zip, for
example); **3** to rise (of the sun,
moon); **4** to realize; **es ist mir
aufgegangen, dass** ... I've realized
that ...; **5** to work out (in maths);
zehn durch drei geht nicht auf
three into ten won't go.

aufgeregt adjective excited.

aufgeschlossen adjective open-
minded.

aufgrund preposition (+ GEN)
1 because of; **2** on the strength of.

aufhaben ◇verb (PRES hat auf,
IMPERF hatte auf, PERF hat
aufgehabt) **1** to have on (a hat);
2 den Mund aufhaben to have your

mouth open; **3 etwas aufhaben** to
have homework to do; **viel
aufhaben** to have a lot of homework;
4 to be open; **der Laden hat abends
auf** the shop is open in the evening.

aufhalten ◇verb (PRES hält auf,
IMPERF hielt auf, PERF hat
aufgehalten) **1** to hold open (a
door); **2** to hold up, to keep
(somebody from doing something);
3 die Hand aufhalten to hold out
your hand; **4 die Augen aufhalten**
to keep your eyes open; **5** to check
(inflation, an advance,
unemployment); **6 sich aufhalten** to
stay; **7 sich mit etwas aufhalten** to
spend your time on something.

aufhängen verb (PERF hat
aufgehängt) **1** to hang up
(washing); **2 sich aufhängen** to
hang yourself.

aufheben ◇verb (IMPERF hob auf,
PERF hat aufgehoben) **1** to pick up
(from the ground); **2** to keep; **3** to
abolish (a law); **4 gut aufgehoben
sein** to be well looked after.

aufheitern verb (PERF hat
aufgeheitert) **1** to cheer up; **2 sich
aufheitern** to brighten up (of the
weather).

aufhören verb (PERF hat
aufgehört) to stop; **aufhören zu
arbeiten** to stop working.

aufklären verb (PERF hat
aufgeklärt) **1** to solve (a crime); **2** to
explain (an event, incident); **3 ein
Kind aufklären** to tell a child the
facts of life; **4 sich aufklären** to be
solved (a misunderstanding or
mystery); **5 sich aufklären** to clear

up; **das Wetter klärt sich auf** the weather is clearing up.

Aufkleber *der* (PL *die* **Aufkleber**) sticker.

auflegen *verb* (PERF **hat aufgelegt**) **1** to put on; **2** to hang up (*when phoning*); **3** to lay; **noch ein Gedeck auflegen** to lay another place (*at table*); **4** to publish; **ein Buch neu auflegen** to reprint a book.

auflösen *verb* (PERF **hat aufgelöst**) **1** to dissolve; **2** to close (*an account*); **3 sich auflösen** to dissolve; **4 sich auflösen** to break up (*of a crowd, demonstration*); **5 der Nebel hat sich aufgelöst** the fog has lifted; **6 in Tränen aufgelöst sein** to be in floods of tears.

aufmachen *verb* (PERF **hat aufgemacht**) **1** to open; **2 jemandem aufmachen** to open the door to somebody; **3** to undo (*a zip, knot*); **4 sich aufmachen** to set out.

aufmerksam *adjective* **1** attentive; **2 auf etwas aufmerksam werden** to notice something; **3 jemanden auf etwas aufmerksam machen** to draw somebody's attention to something.

aufmuntern *verb* (PERF **hat aufgemuntert**) to cheer up.

Aufnahme *die* (PL *die* **Aufnahmen**) **1** photograph; **2** recording; **3** admission (*to hospital, to a club*); **4** welcome.

Aufnahmeprüfung *die* (PL *die* **Aufnahmeprüfungen**) entrance exam.

Aufnahmetaste *die* (PL *die* **Aufnahmetasten**) record button.

aufnehmen ✧*verb* (PRES **nimmt auf**, IMPERF **nahm auf**, PERF **hat aufgenommen**) **1** to receive (*guests*); **2** to take up (*an idea, activity, a theme*); **3** to admit (*to hospital, to a club*); **4** to photograph; **5** to film; **6** to record (*a song, a programme, a film*); **7 es mit jemandem aufnehmen können** to be a match for somebody; **8** to take (*food, news*); **etwas gelassen aufnehmen** to take something calmly.

aufpassen *verb* (PERF **hat aufgepasst**) **1** to pay attention; **2** to watch out; **3 auf jemanden aufpassen** to look after somebody; **4 auf etwas aufpassen** to keep an eye on something; **pass auf meine Tasche auf** keep an eye on my bag.

aufräumen *verb* (PERF **hat aufgeräumt**) to tidy up.

aufrecht *adjective* upright.

aufregen *verb* (PERF **hat aufgeregt**) **1** to excite; **2** to annoy; **3 sich aufregen** to get worked up.

aufregend *adjective* exciting.

aufs = **auf das**.

Aufsatz *der* (PL *die* **Aufsätze**) essay.

aufschieben ✧*verb* (IMPERF **schob auf**, PERF **hat aufgeschoben**) **1** to put off (*an arrangement*); **2** to slide open.

aufschlagen *verb* (PRES **schlägt auf**, IMPERF **schlug auf**, PERF **hat aufgeschlagen**) to open.

23

a b c d e f g h i j k l m n o p q r s t u v w x y z

aufschließen ◇*verb* (IMPERF **schloss auf**, PERF **hat aufgeschlossen**) to unlock.

Aufschnitt *der* sliced cold meat and cheese.

aufschreiben ◇*verb* (IMPERF **schrieb auf**, PERF **hat aufgeschrieben**) to write down.

aufsehen ◇*verb* (PRES **sieht auf**, IMPERF **sah auf**, PERF **hat aufgesehen**) to look up.

Aufsehen *das* sensation, stir; **Aufsehen erregen** to cause a stir.

Aufseher *der* (PL **die Aufseher**) **1** supervisor; **2** warder (*in a prison*); **3** attendant (*in a museum*).

Aufseherin *die* (PL **die Aufseherinnen**) **1** supervisor; **2** warder (*in a prison*); **3** attendant (*in a museum*).

aufsetzen *verb* (PERF **hat aufgesetzt**) **1** to put on; **2** to draft; **3 sich aufsetzen** to sit up.

Aufsicht *die* **1** supervision; **2** supervisor.

Aufstand *der* (PL **die Aufstände**) rebellion.

aufstehen ◇*verb* (IMPERF **stand auf**, PERF **ist aufgestanden**) **1** to get up; **2** (PERF **hat aufgestanden**) to be open.

aufstellen *verb* (PERF **hat aufgestellt**) **1** to put up; **2** to set up (*skittles, chess pieces*); **3 eine Mannschaft aufstellen** to pick a team; **4 eine Liste aufstellen** to draw up a list; **5 sich aufstellen** to line up.

auftauen *verb* (PERF **ist aufgetaut**) **1** to thaw; **2** to defrost; **die Erdbeeren sind aufgetaut** the strawberries have defrosted; **3** (PERF **hat aufgetaut**) to defrost; **ich habe die Erbeeren aufgetaut** I've defrosted the strawberries.

aufteilen *verb* (PERF **hat aufgeteilt**) to divide up.

Auftrag *der* (PL **die Aufträge**) **1** job; **2** order (*in business*); **etwas in Auftrag geben** to order something; **3** instructions; **einen Auftrag ausführen** to carry out an instruction; **4 im Auftrag von** on behalf of.

auftreten ◇*verb* (PRES **tritt auf**, IMPERF **trat auf**, PERF **ist aufgetreten**) **1** to appear (*on stage*); **2** to arise (*a problem, difficulty*); **3** to behave; **4** to tread.

aufwachen *verb* (PERF **ist aufgewacht**) to wake up.

aufwachsen ◇*verb* (PRES **wächst auf**, IMPERF **wuchs auf**, PERF **ist aufgewachsen**) to grow up.

aufwecken *verb* (PERF **hat aufgeweckt**) to wake up.

aufziehen ◇*verb* (IMPERF **zog auf**, PERF **hat aufgezogen**) **1** to wind up (*a clock or toy*); **2** to draw (*curtains*); **3 jemanden aufziehen** (*informal*) to tease somebody; **4** to bring up (*a child*).

Aufzug *der* (PL **die Aufzüge**) lift; **ich fahre mit dem Aufzug runter** I'm going down in the lift.

Auge *das* (PL **die Augen**) **1** eye; **2 unter vier Augen** in private.

Augenarzt *der* (PL *die* **Augenärzte**) ophthalmologist.

Augenärztin *die* (PL *die* **Augenärztinnen**) ophthalmologist.

Augenblick *der* (PL *die* **Augenblicke**) moment; **im Augenblick** at the moment.

Augenbraue *die* (PL *die* **Augenbrauen**) eyebrow.

August *der* August.

aus *preposition* (+ DAT) **1** out of; **er hat es aus dem Fenster geworfen** he threw it out of the window; **2** from; **aus Spanien** from Spain; **aus Erfahrung** from experience; **3** made of; **aus Holz** made of wood; **4 aus Spaß** for fun; **5 aus der Mode** out of fashion; **6 aus Versehen** by mistake; **7 aus welchem Grund?** for what reason?; **8 aus ihr ist eine gute Rechtsanwältin geworden** she made a good lawyer; **aus ihm ist nichts geworden** he never made anything of his life.
aus *adverb* **1** off (*of a TV, radio*); **das Licht ist aus** the light is off; **Licht aus!** lights out!; **2** finished; **wenn das Spiel aus ist** when the game has finished; **3 von mir aus** as far as I'm concerned; **4 von sich aus** of your own accord.

ausbauen *verb* (PERF hat **ausgebaut**) **1** to extend (*a building*); **2** to build up.

ausbeuten *verb* (PERF hat **ausgebeutet**) to exploit.

ausbilden *verb* (PERF hat **ausgebildet**) to train.

Ausbildung *die* **1** training; **2** education.

ausbreiten *verb* (PERF hat **ausgebreitet**) **1** to unfold; **2** to spread; **3** to stretch (*one's arms etc*).

ausbuhen *verb* (PERF hat **ausgebuht**) to boo; **die Menge buhte den Schiedsrichter aus** the crowd booed the referee.

ausdehnen *verb* (PERF hat **ausgedehnt**) **1** to extend, to prolong; **2** to expand.

Ausdruck¹ *der* (PL *die* **Ausdrücke**) expression; **etwas zum Ausdruck bringen** to express something.

Ausdruck² *der* (PL *die* **Ausdrucke**) print-out.

ausdrucken *verb* (PERF hat **ausgedruckt**) to print out.

ausdrücken *verb* (PERF hat **ausgedrückt**) **1** to squeeze (*oranges, lemons*); **2** to express; **3 sich ausdrücken** to express oneself.

auseinander *adverb* **1** apart; **etwas auseinander nehmen** to take something apart; **auseinander halten** to tell apart; **2 auseinander gehen** to part; **3 auseinander schreiben** to write as separate words; **4 sich mit einem Problem auseinander setzen** to come to grips with a problem; **5 sich mit jemandem auseinander setzen** to have it out with somebody.

Ausfahrt *die* (PL *die* **Ausfahrten**) **1** exit; **2 'Ausfahrt freihalten'** 'keep clear'.

a
b
c
d
e
f
g
h
i
j
k
l
m
n
o
p
q
r
s
t
u
v
w
x
y
z

Ausfall der (PL die **Ausfälle**)
1 result; **2** failure, breakdown;
3 loss (of hair, teeth); **4** cancellation.

ausfallen ◇verb (PRES **fällt aus**,
IMPERF **fiel aus**, PERF **ist**
ausgefallen) **1** to be cancelled;
etwas ausfallen lassen to cancel
something; **2** to fall out (hair); **3** to
fail (an engine, brakes, a signal); **4** to
break down (a machine, a car,
heating); **5** to turn out; **gut**
ausfallen to turn out well.

Ausflug der (PL die **Ausflüge**)
outing, trip; **einen Ausflug machen**
to go on an outing.

Ausfuhr die export.

ausführen verb (PERF **hat**
ausgeführt) **1** to carry out (a plan);
2 to export (goods); **3** to take out; **er**
hat seine Freundin zum Essen
ausgeführt he took his girlfriend
out for a meal; **4** den Hund
ausführen to take the dog for a walk.

ausführlich adjective detailed.
ausführlich adverb in detail.

ausfüllen verb (PERF **hat**
ausgefüllt) **1** to fill in; **ein Formular**
ausfüllen to fill in a form; **2** ihr
Beruf als Lehrerin füllt sie ganz
aus teaching gives her great
satisfaction.

Ausgabe die (PL die **Ausgaben**)
1 edition; **2** issue; **3 Ausgaben**
expenditure.

Ausgang der (PL die **Ausgänge**)
1 exit; **'kein Ausgang'** 'no exit';
2 end, ending; **3** result (of a game,
discussion).

ausgeben ◇verb (PRES **gibt aus**,
IMPERF **gab aus**, PERF **hat**
ausgegeben) **1** to spend; **2** to hand
out; **3 Fahrkarten ausgeben** to
issue tickets; **4** to serve (food);
5 sich ausgeben als to pretend to
be; **6 einen ausgeben** (informal) to
treat everybody (to a round of drinks
for example).

ausgebucht adjective fully booked.

ausgehen ◇verb (PRES **geht aus**,
IMPERF **ging aus**, PERF **ist**
ausgegangen) **1** to go out; **mit**
Freunden ausgehen to go out with
friends; **2** to run out (of supplies);
3 to end; **schlecht ausgehen** to end
badly; **4 davon ausgehen, dass** ...
to assume that ...

ausgerechnet adverb
1 ausgerechnet heute today of all
days; **2 ausgerechnet sie** she of all
people.

ausgeschlossen adjective out
of the question.

ausgestorben adjective **1** dead;
2 extinct.

ausgewogen adjective balanced.

ausgezeichnet adjective
excellent.

ausgleichen verb (IMPERF **glich**
aus, PERF **hat ausgeglichen**) to
equalize; **sie haben in der letzten**
Minute ausgeglichen they
equalized in the last minute.

aushalten ◇verb (PRES **hält aus**,
IMPERF **hielt aus**, PERF **hat**
ausgehalten) **1** to stand; **2 es ist**
nicht zum Aushalten it's
unbearable.

Aushilfe die (PL die Aushilfen) temporary assistant, temp.

aushöhlen verb (PERF hat ausgehöhlt) to hollow out.

auskennen ⬦verb (IMPERF kannte sich aus, PERF hat sich ausgekannt) **1** sich auskennen to know your way around; **2** sich gut mit etwas auskennen to know a lot about something.

auskommen ⬦verb (IMPERF kam aus, PERF ist ausgekommen) **1** to manage; mit fünfzig Euro auskommen to manage on fifty euros; **2** mit jemandem gut auskommen to get on well with somebody.

Auskunft die (PL die Auskünfte) **1** information; **2** information desk; **3** enquiries (when phoning).

auslachen verb (PERF hat ausgelacht) to laugh at.

ausladen ⬦verb (PRES lädt aus, IMPERF lud aus, PERF hat ausgeladen) **1** to unload; **2** jemanden ausladen (informal) to put somebody off.

Ausland das im Ausland abroad; ins Ausland reisen to travel abroad.

Ausländer der (PL die Ausländer) foreigner.

Ausländerin die (PL die Ausländerinnen) foreigner.

ausländisch adjective foreign.

Auslandsgespräch das (PL die Auslandsgespräche) international call.

ausleeren verb (PERF hat ausgeleert) to empty.

ausleihen ⬦verb (IMPERF lieh aus, PERF hat ausgeliehen) **1** to lend; **2** sich etwas ausleihen to borrow something.

ausmachen verb (PERF hat ausgemacht) **1** to turn off; **2** to put out; **3** to arrange; wir haben ausgemacht, dass wir uns heute Abend treffen we've arranged to meet up this evening; **4** das macht mir nichts aus I don't mind; macht es Ihnen etwas aus, wenn ...? would you mind if ...?; **5** viel ausmachen to make a great difference.

Ausnahme die (PL die Ausnahmen) exception.

ausnutzen verb (PERF hat ausgenutzt) **1** to use; **2** to take advantage of; **3** to exploit.

auspacken verb (PERF hat ausgepackt) to unpack.

Auspuff der (PL die Auspuffe) exhaust.

ausrechnen verb (PERF hat ausgerechnet) to work out.

Ausrede die (PL die Ausreden) excuse.

ausreichend adjective **1** sufficient; **2** fair, pass (as a mark at school).

Ausreise die (PL die Ausreisen) departure (from a country).

ausrichten verb (PERF hat ausgerichtet) jemandem etwas ausrichten to tell somebody something.

ausrufen verb (IMPERF rief aus, PERF hat ausgerufen) **1** to call out;

a
b
c
d
e
f
g
h
i
j
k
l
m
n
o
p
q
r
s
t
u
v
w
x
y
z

2 to call, to declare; **allgemeine Wahlen ausrufen** to call a general election.

Ausrufezeichen *das* (PL *die Ausrufezeichen*) exclamation mark.

ausruhen *verb* (PERF **hat sich ausgeruht**) **sich ausruhen** to have a rest.

ausrüsten *verb* (PERF **hat ausgerüstet**) to equip.

Ausrüstung *die* equipment.

ausschalten *verb* (PERF **hat ausgeschaltet**) **1** to switch off; **2** to eliminate.

ausschneiden ⋄*verb* (IMPERF **schnitt aus**, PERF **hat ausgeschnitten**) to cut out.

Ausschuss *der* (PL *die Ausschüsse*) committee.

aussehen ⋄*verb* (PRES **sieht aus**, IMPERF **sah aus**, PERF **hat ausgesehen**) to look.

Aussehen *das* appearance.

außen *adverb* **1** (on the) outside; **von außen** from the outside; **2 nach außen** outwards.

Außenminister *der* (PL *die Außenminister*) Foreign Secretary, Foreign Minister.

außer *preposition* (+ DAT) **1** apart from, except (for); **alle außer ihm** everyone except (for) him; **2** out of; **außer Sicht** out of sight; **außer Betrieb** out of order; **3 außer Haus** out; **4 außer sich sein** to be beside yourself.

außer *conjunction* **1** except; **außer**

sonntags except Sundays; **2 außer wenn** unless.

außerdem *adverb* **1** as well; **2** besides.

äußerer, äußere, äußeres *adjective* **1** external (*injury, circumstances*); **2** outer (*layer, circle*); **3** outward (*appearance, effect*).

außergewöhnlich *adjective* unusual.

außerhalb *preposition* (+ GEN) outside.
außerhalb *adverb* **außerhalb wohnen** to live out of town.

Außerirdische *der/die* (PL *die Außerirdischen*) alien (*from outer space*).

äußerlich *adjective* **1** external; **2** outward (*appearance*).

außerordentlich *adjective* extraordinary.

äußerst *adverb* extremely.

Äußerung *die* (PL *die Äußerungen*) remark.

Aussicht *die* (PL *die Aussichten*) **1** prospect; **etwas in Aussicht haben** to have the prospect of something; **keine Aussichten auf Erfolg haben** to have no chance of success; **2** view; **ein Zimmer mit Aussicht aufs Meer** a room with a view of the sea.

Aussprache *die* (PL *die Aussprachen*) **1** pronunciation; **2** talk.

aussprechen ◇*verb* (PRES spricht aus, IMPERF sprach aus, PERF hat ausgesprochen) **1** to pronounce; **2** to express; **3 lassen Sie ihn aussprechen** let him finish (*speaking*); **4 sich aussprechen** to talk; **sich mit jemandem aussprechen** to have a talk with somebody; **5 sich gegen etwas aussprechen** to come out against something; **sich für etwas aussprechen** to come out in favour of something; **6 sich lobend über jemanden aussprechen** to speak highly of somebody.

aussteigen ◇*verb* (IMPERF stieg aus, PERF ist ausgestiegen) **1** to get out; **2** to get off.

ausstellen *verb* (PERF hat ausgestellt) **1** to display (*in a shop*); **2** to exhibit; **3** to make out (*a certificate, bill*); **4** to issue (*a passport*); **5** to switch off.

Ausstellung die (PL die Ausstellungen) exhibition.

ausstreichen ◇*verb* (IMPERF strich aus, PERF hat ausgestrichen) to cross out.

aussuchen *verb* (PERF hat ausgesucht) **1** to choose; **2 sich etwas aussuchen** to choose something.

Austausch der exchange.

austauschen *verb* (PERF hat ausgetauscht) **1** to exchange; **2** to replace; **3** to substitute (*a player*).

Auster die (PL die Austern) oyster.

austragen ◇*verb* (PRES trägt aus, IMPERF trug aus, PERF hat ausgetragen) **1** to deliver (*post, newspapers*); **2** to hold (*a race*).

Australien das Australia; **aus Australien** from Australia.

Australier der (PL die Australier) Australian.

Australierin die (PL die Australierinnen) Australian.

australisch *adjective* Australian.

austreten ◇*verb* (PRES tritt aus, IMPERF trat aus, PERF hat ausgetreten) **1** to stamp out (*a cigarette or fire*); **2** to wear out (*shoes*); **3** (PERF ist ausgetreten) **aus einem Klub austreten** to leave a club; **ich trete aus** I'm leaving; **4** (*informal*) (PERF ist ausgetreten) to go to the loo.

austrinken ◇*verb* (IMPERF trank aus, PERF hat ausgetrunken) to drink up.

Ausverkauf der (PL die Ausverkäufe) sale.

ausverkauft *adjective* **1** sold out; **2 ein ausverkauftes Haus** a full house (*at the cinema or theatre*).

Auswahl die (PL die Auswahlen) choice, selection; **wenig Auswahl haben** to have a limited selection.

Auswanderer der (PL die Auswanderer) emigrant.

Auswanderin die (PL die Auswanderinnen) emigrant.

auswandern *verb* (PERF ist ausgewandert) to emigrate; **nach Amerika auswandern** to emigrate to America.

Auswanderung die emigration.

auswärts *adverb* **1** away (*in sport*); **auswärts spielen** to play away; **2 auswärts essen** to eat out; **3 sie arbeitet auswärts** she doesn't work locally.

Auswärtsspiel das (PL die **Auswärtsspiele**) away game.

Ausweg der (PL die **Auswege**) way out.

Ausweis der (PL die **Ausweise**) **1** identity card; **2** card (*for students or members*); **3** pass.

auswendig *adverb* by heart.

auswirken *verb* (PERF **hat sich ausgewirkt**) **sich auf etwas auswirken** to have an effect on something.

ausziehen ◇*verb* (IMPERF **zog aus**, PERF **hat ausgezogen**) **1** to take off (*clothes*); **2** to undress; **3 sich ausziehen** to get undressed; **4** (PERF **ist ausgezogen**) to move out (*move house*); **wir ziehen nächste Woche aus** we're moving out next week.

Auszubildende der/die (PL die **Auszubildenden**) trainee.

Auto das (PL die **Autos**) car; **Auto fahren** to drive; **das Auto waschen** to wash the car.

Autobahn die (PL die **Autobahnen**) motorway.

Autobahnraststätte die (PL die **Autobahnraststätten**) motorway service area.

Autofahrer der (PL die **Autofahrer**) motorist.

Autogramm das (PL die **Autogramme**) autograph.

Automat der (PL die **Automaten**) machine.

automatisch *adjective* automatic.

Autor der (PL die **Autoren**) author.

Autorin die (PL die **Autorinnen**) authoress.

Autorität die authority.

Autoskooter der (PL die **Autoskooter**) bumper car, dodgem car.

Autostopp der **per Autostopp fahren** to hitchhike.

Autotelefon das (PL die **Autotelefone**) car phone.

Autounfall der (PL die **Autounfälle**) car accident.

Autoverleih der (PL die **Autoverleihe**) car hire (firm).

Axt die (PL die **Äxte**) axe.

Bb

Baby das (PL die **Babys**) baby.

Babysitting das babysitting; **Babysitting machen** to babysit.

Bach der (PL die **Bäche**) stream.

Backe die (PL die **Backen**) cheek.

backen ◇*verb* (PRES **bäckt**, IMPERF **backte**, PERF **hat gebacken**) to bake.

Bäcker der (PL die **Bäcker**) **1** baker; **2 beim Bäcker** at the baker's.

Bäckerei die (PL die Bäckereien) baker's.

Backofen der (PL die Backöfen) oven.

Backpflaume die (PL die Backpflaumen) prune.

Bad das (PL die Bäder) **1** bath; **2** bathroom; **3** pool (for swimming).

Badeanzug der (PL die Badeanzüge) swimsuit.

Badehose die (PL die Badehosen) swimming trunks.

Bademeister der (PL die Bademeister) swimming-pool attendant.

Bademeisterin die (PL die Bademeisterinnen) swimming-pool attendant.

Bademütze die (PL die Bademützen) bathing cap.

baden verb (PERF hat gebadet) **1** to have a bath; **2** to bathe (in the sea); **3** to bath (wash somebody).

Badetuch das (PL die Badetücher) bath towel.

Badewanne die (PL die Badewannen) bath (tub).

Badezimmer das (PL die Badezimmer) bathroom.

Bahn die (PL die Bahnen) **1** railway; **2** train; **mit der Bahn fahren** to go by train; **3** tram; **4** track (in sport); **5** lane (on a track); **6** path; **auf die schiefe Bahn geraten** to go off the rails.

Bahnhof der (PL die Bahnhöfe) (railway) station.

Bahnsteig der (PL die Bahnsteige) platform.

Bahnübergang der (PL die Bahnübergänge) level crossing.

bald adverb **1** soon; **bis bald!** see you soon!; **2** wird's bald!** (informal) get a move on!; **3** almost; **ich hätte bald vergessen, ihn anzurufen** I almost forgot to ring him.

baldig adjective speedy.

Balken der (PL die Balken) beam.

Balkon der (PL die Balkons) balcony.

Ball der (PL die Bälle) **1** ball; **Ball spielen** to play ball; **2** ball; **auf dem Ball** at the ball.

Ballett das (PL die Ballette) ballet.

Balletttänzer der (PL die Balletttänzer) ballet dancer.

Balletttänzerin die (PL die Balletttänzerinnen) ballet dancer.

Ballon der (PL die Ballons) balloon.

Banane die (PL die Bananen) banana.

Band[1] das (PL die Bänder) **1** ribbon; **2** tape (for recording); **etwas auf Band aufnehmen** to tape something; **3** production line; **am Band arbeiten** to work on the production line; **4** am laufenden Band (informal) nonstop.

Band[2] der (PL die Bände) volume.

Band[3] die (PL die Bands) band.

band SEE **binden**.

Bank[1] die (PL die Bänke) bench.

Bank[2] die (PL die Banken) bank; **ich muss erst zur Bank gehen** I have to go to the bank first.

a
b
c
d
e
f
g
h
i
j
k
l
m
n
o
p
q
r
s
t
u
v
w
x
y
z

a
b
c
d
e
f
g
h
i
j
k
l
m
n
o
p
q
r
s
t
u
v
w
x
y
z

Bankkauffrau die (PL die Bankkauffrauen) bank clerk.

Bankkaufmann der (PL die Bankkaufleute) bank clerk.

Bankkonto das (PL die Bankkonten) bank account.

Banknote die (PL die Banknoten) banknote.

bankrott adjective bankrupt; **bankrott gehen/machen** to go bankrupt.

Bär der (PL die Bären) bear.

Bar die (PL die Bars) bar.

bar adjective (in) cash.

Bardame die (PL die Bardamen) barmaid.

barfuß adjective barefoot.

Bargeld das cash.

Barkeeper der (PL die Barkeeper) barman.

Barren der (PL die Barren) **1** bar; **2** parallel bars.

Bart der (PL die Bärte) beard.

bärtig adjective bearded.

Basel das Basle.

Basis die (PL die Basen) basis.

Bass der (PL die Bässe) bass.

basta exclamation and that's that!

basteln verb (PERF hat gebastelt) **1** to make (things); **2 sie bastelt gern** she likes making things.

bat SEE **bitten**.

Batterie die (PL die Batterien) battery.

Bau der (PL die Bauten) **1** construction; **im Bau sein** to be

under construction; **2** building; **3** building site; **auf dem Bau arbeiten** to work on a building site.

Bauarbeiten plural noun building work.

Bauarbeiter der (PL die Bauarbeiter) builder.

Bauarbeiterin die (PL die Bauarbeiterinnen) builder.

Bauch der (PL die Bäuche) stomach, belly.

Bauchschmerzen plural noun stomachache.

bauen verb (PERF hat gebaut) **1** to build; **2 einen Unfall bauen** (informal) to have an accident.

Bauer der (PL die Bauern) **1** farmer; **2** pawn (in chess).

Bäuerin die (PL die Bäuerinnen) **1** farmer; **2** farmer's wife.

Bauernhof der (PL die Bauernhöfe) farm.

Baum der (PL die Bäume) tree.

Baumwolle die cotton.

Bausparkasse die (PL die Bausparkassen) building society.

Baustelle die (PL die Baustellen) building site.

Bayer der (PL die Bayern) Bavarian.

Bayerin die (PL die Bayerinnen) Bavarian.

Bayern das Bavaria; **aus Bayern** from Bavaria.

bay(e)risch adjective Bavarian.

beabsichtigen verb (PERF hat beabsichtigt) to intend.

beachten *verb* (PERF **hat beachtet**) **1** to take notice of; **beachte ihn einfach nicht** just don't take any notice of him; **2** to observe; **3** to follow (*a rule, advice*); **4** to obey; **die Verkehrsregeln beachten** to obey traffic regulations.

Beamte *der* (PL *die* **Beamten**) **1** civil servant (*in Germany all public employees, such as teachers and policemen, are 'Beamte'*); **2** official.

Beamtin *die* (PL *die* **Beamtinnen**) **1** civil servant; **2** official.

beanspruchen *verb* (PERF **hat beansprucht**) **1** to claim (*benefit*); **2** to take up (*time, space*); **jemanden beanspruchen** to take up somebody's time; **3** to demand (*energy, attention*); **die Arbeit beansprucht sie sehr** her work is very demanding; **4** to take advantage of (*hospitality, services, help*); **ich möchte Ihre Geduld nicht zu sehr beanspruchen** I don't want to try your patience.

Beanstandung *die* (PL *die* **Beanstandungen**) complaint.

beantragen *verb* (PERF **hat beantragt**) to apply for.

beantworten *verb* (PERF **hat beantwortet**) to answer.

bearbeiten *verb* (PERF **hat bearbeitet**) **1** to deal with; **einen Antrag bearbeiten** to deal with an application; **2** to adapt (*a play*); **3** to treat (*wood, for example*); **er hat die Oberfläche mit Wachs bearbeitet** he's treated the surface with wax; **4 jemanden bearbeiten, dass er**

etwas macht (*informal*) to work on somebody so that he does something (*persuade*).

beaufsichtigen *verb* (PERF **hat beaufsichtigt**) to supervise.

Becher *der* (PL *die* **Becher**) **1** beaker, mug; **2** pot, carton (*of yoghurt, cream*).

Becherglas *das* (PL *die* **Bechergläser**) tumbler.

Becken *das* (PL *die* **Becken**) **1** basin; **2** pool (*for swimming*); **3** pelvis.

bedanken *verb* (PERF **hat sich bedankt**) **sich bedanken** to say thank you; **vergiss nicht, dich zu bedanken** don't forget to say thank you; **ich habe mich bei ihm bedankt** I thanked him.

Bedarf *der* **1** need; **2 bei Bedarf** if required; **3** demand; **je nach Bedarf** according to demand.

bedauerlicherweise *adverb* unfortunately.

bedauern *verb* (PERF **hat bedauert**) **1** to regret; **ich bedaure kein Wort** I don't regret a single word; **2 ich bedaure sehr, dass du nicht kommen kannst** I'm very sorry that you can't come; **bedaure!** sorry!; **3 jemanden bedauern** to feel sorry for somebody.

bedecken *verb* (PERF **hat bedeckt**) to cover.

bedeckt *adjective* **1** covered; **2** overcast (*weather*); **gestern war es den ganzen Tag bedeckt** it was overcast all day yesterday.

bedenken ◇*verb* (IMPERF **bedachte**, PERF **hat bedacht**) to consider.

Bedenken *plual noun* **1** doubts; **Bedenken haben** to have doubts; **2 ohne Bedenken** without hesitation.

bedenklich *adjective* **1** worrying; **die Situation ist sehr bedenklich** the situation is very worrying; **2** dubious; **er hat bedenkliche Mittel angewendet, um sein Ziel zu erreichen** he's used dubious methods to achieve his aims; **3** serious.

bedeuten *verb* (PERF **hat bedeutet**) to mean.

bedeutend *adjective* **1** important; **2** considerable.

Bedeutung die (PL die **Bedeutungen**) **1** meaning; **2** importance.

bedienen *verb* (PERF **hat bedient**) **1** to serve; **hier wird man sehr schnell bedient** you get served very quickly here; **2** to operate; **3 sich bedienen** to help oneself.

Bedienstete der/die (PL die **Bediensteten**) servant.

Bedienung die (PL die **Bedienungen**) **1** service; **Bedienung inbegriffen** service included; **2** waiter, waitress; **3** shop assistant; **4** operation (*of a machine*).

Bedingung die (PL die **Bedingungen**) condition; **nur unter der Bedingung, dass du**

mitkommst only on condition that you're coming with us.

bedrohen *verb* (PERF **hat bedroht**) to threaten.

bedroht *adjective* endangered.

Bedrohung die (PL die **Bedrohungen**) threat.

beeilen *verb* (PERF **hat sich beeilt**) **sich beeilen** to hurry (up); **beeilt euch!** hurry up!

beeindrucken *verb* (PERF **hat beeindruckt**) to impress.

beeinflussen *verb* (PERF **hat beeinflusst**) to influence.

beenden *verb* (PERF **hat beendet**) to end.

Beerdigung die (PL die **Beerdigungen**) funeral.

Beere die (PL die **Beeren**) berry.

Beet das (PL die **Beete**) **1** bed (*of flowers*); **2** patch (*of vegetables*).

befahl SEE **befehlen**.

Befehl der (PL die **Befehle**) **1** order; **2** command; **den Befehl über etwas haben** to be in command of something.

befehlen ◇*verb* (PRES **befiehlt**, IMPERF **befahl**, PERF **hat befohlen**) **1 jemandem befehlen, etwas zu tun** to order somebody to do something; **2** to give orders.

befestigen *verb* (PERF **hat befestigt**) **1** to fix; **etwas an der Wand befestigen** to fix something to the wall; **2** to fasten.

befinden ◇*verb* (IMPERF **befand sich**, PERF **hat sich befunden**) **sich befinden** to be; **sie befindet sich**

zur Zeit in Deutschland she's in Germany at the moment.

befolgen *verb* (PERF **hat befolgt**) to follow.

befördern *verb* (PERF **hat befördert**) **1** to carry (*people by bus or train*); **2** to transport (*goods by train or lorry*); **3** to promote; **er ist zum Kommissar befördert worden** he's been promoted to superintendent.

befragen *verb* (PERF **hat befragt**) to question.

befreien *verb* (PERF **hat befreit**) **1** to free; **2** to exempt; **jemanden vom Wehrdienst befreien** to exempt somebody from military service; **3 sich befreien** to free oneself.

Befreiung *die* liberation.

befreunden *verb* (PERF **hat sich befreundet**) **sich befreunden** to make friends.

befreundet *adjective* **mit jemandem befreundet sein** to be friends with somebody; **wir sind schon lange gut befreundet** we've been close friends for a long time.

befriedigen *verb* (PERF **hat befriedigt**) to satisfy.

befriedigend *adjective* satisfactory.

Befugnis *die* (PL *die* **Befugnisse**) authority.

begabt *adjective* gifted, talented.

Begabung *die* gift, talent.

begann SEE **beginnen**.

begegnen *verb* (PERF **ist begegnet**) **1 jemandem begegnen** to meet somebody; **etwas begegnen** to meet something; **2 sich begegnen** to meet (each other).

Begegnung *die* (PL *die* **Begegnungen**) meeting.

begehen ◇*verb* (IMPERF **beging**, PERF **hat begangen**) to commit.

begeistern *verb* (PERF **hat begeistert**) **1 jemanden für etwas begeistern** to fill somebody with enthusiasm for something; **2 sich begeistern** to get enthusiastic.

begeistert *adjective* enthusiastic.

Begeisterung *die* enthusiasm.

Beginn *der* beginning; **zu Beginn** at the beginning.

beginnen ◇*verb* (IMPERF **begann**, PERF **hat begonnen**) to begin, to start.

begleiten *verb* (PERF **hat begleitet**) to accompany; **jemanden begleiten** to accompany somebody; **er hat mich nach Hause begleitet** he took me home.

beglückwünschen *verb* (PERF **hat beglückwünscht**) to congratulate.

begonnen SEE **beginnen**.

begraben ◇*verb* (PRES **begräbt**, IMPERF **begrub**, PERF **hat begraben**) to bury.

begreifen ◇*verb* (IMPERF **begriff**, PERF **hat begriffen**) to understand.

begrenzen *verb* (PERF **hat begrenzt**) to limit.

a
b
c
d
e
f
g
h
i
j
k
l
m
n
o
p
q
r
s
t
u
v
w
x
y
z

a
b
c
d
e
f
g
h
i
j
k
l
m
n
o
p
q
r
s
t
u
v
w
x
y
z

Begriff *der* (PL *die* **Begriffe**)
1 concept; **davon kann ich mir keinen Begriff machen** I can't imagine that; 2 term; **ein Begriff aus der Malerei** a painting term;
3 **im Begriff sein, etwas zu tun** to be about to do something; 4 **für meine Begriffe** to my mind;
5 **schwer von Begriff** (*informal*) slow on the uptake.

Begründung *die* (PL *die* **Begründungen**) reason.

begrüßen *verb* (PERF **hat begrüßt**)
1 to greet; 2 to welcome.

Begrüßung *die* welcome.

begünstigen *verb* (PERF **hat begünstigt**) to favour.

behaart *adjective* hairy.

behaglich *adjective* cosy.

behalten ◇*verb* (PRES **behält**, IMPERF **behielt**, PERF **hat behalten**)
1 to keep; **du kannst die CD behalten** you can keep the CD; 2 to remember (*a name*).

Behälter *der* (PL *die* **Behälter**) container.

behandeln *verb* (PERF **hat behandelt**) 1 to treat; **er ist sehr schlecht behandelt worden** he's been treated very badly; **einen Patienten behandeln** to treat a patient; 2 to deal with (*a subject, question*).

Behandlung *die* (PL *die* **Behandlungen**) treatment.

behaupten *verb* (PERF **hat behauptet**) 1 to claim; 2 **sich behaupten** to assert oneself.

Behauptung *die* (PL *die* **Behauptungen**) claim.

beherrschen *verb* (PERF **hat beherrscht**) 1 to rule over (*a country, people*); 2 to control; 3 to know; 4 **sich beherrschen** to control oneself.

behilflich *adjective* **jemandem behilflich sein** to help somebody.

behindert *adjective* disabled, handicapped; **ist er behindert?** does he have a disability?

Behinderte *der/die* (PL *die* **Behinderten**) disabled person, handicapped person.

Behindertenheim *das* (PL *die* **Behindertenheime**) home for handicapped people.

Behinderung *die* 1 obstruction; 2 handicap, disability.

Behörde *die* (PL *die* **Behörden**) authority, authorities.

behüten *verb* (PERF **hat behütet**) to protect.

bei *preposition* (+ DAT) 1 near; **die Diskothek beim Bahnhof** the disco near the station; 2 at (*indicating a place or time*); **bei mir** at my place; **beim Arzt** at the doctor's; **bei Beginn** at the beginning; 3 **bei seinen Eltern wohnen** to live with your parents; 4 **bei uns in der Firma** in our firm; **bei guter Gesundheit** in good health; 5 **bei einem Verlag arbeiten** to work for a publisher; 6 **bei Regen** if it rains; **bei Nebel** in fog; **bei Tag** by day; 7 **etwas bei sich haben** to have something on you; 8 **bei Morris** c/o

Morris; **9 sich bei jemandem entschuldigen** to apologize to somebody; **10 bei der hohen Miete** with the high rent; **11 beim Fahren** while driving; **beim Lesen sein** to be reading; **beim Frühstück** at breakfast; **12 bei der Ankunft** on arrival.

beibringen ◇*verb* (PRES **bringt bei**, IMPERF **brachte bei**, PERF **hat beigebracht**) **jemandem etwas beibringen** to teach somebody something.

Beichte *die* (PL *die* **Beichten**) confession.

beichten *verb* (PERF **hat gebeichtet**) to confess.

beide *adjective, pronoun* **1** both; **ihr beide** both of you; **er hat seine beiden Eltern verloren** he has lost both his parents; **2 die ersten beiden** the first two; **eins von beiden** one of the two; **3 keiner von beiden** neither (of them); **4 beides** both; **er kann beides - Klavier und Gitarre spielen** he can do both - play the piano and the guitar; **5 dreißig beide** thirty all (*in tennis*).

beieinander *adverb* together.

Beifahrer *der* (PL *die* **Beifahrer**) passenger.

Beifahrerin *die* (PL *die* **Beifahrerinnen**) passenger.

Beifall *der* applause.

Beil *das* (PL *die* **Beile**) axe.

Beilage *die* (PL *die* **Beilagen**) **1** supplement (*to a paper*); **2** side-dish; **als Beilage Reis und Spinat** served with rice and spinach.

beiläufig *adjective* casual.

beilegen *verb* (PERF **hat beigelegt**) to enclose.

Beileid *das* condolences; **jemandem sein Beileid aussprechen** to offer your condolences to somebody.

beiliegen ◇*verb* (PRES **liegt bei**, IMPERF **lag bei**, PERF **hat beigelegen**) to be enclosed; **ein Scheck liegt bei** please find enclosed a cheque.

beiliegend *adjective* enclosed.

beim = **bei dem**.

Bein *das* (PL *die* **Beine**) leg.

beinahe *adverb* almost.

Beinbruch *der* (PL *die* **Beinbrüche**) broken leg; **das ist doch kein Beinbruch** (*informal*) it's not the end of the world.

beisammen *adverb* together.

beiseite *adverb* **1** aside; **etwas beiseite schieben** to push something aside; **2 etwas beiseite legen** to put something by; **3 das Geld beiseite schaffen** to hide the money away.

Beispiel *das* (PL *die* **Beispiele**) example; **zum Beispiel** for example; **mit gutem Beispiel vorangehen** to set a good example.

beispielsweise *adverb* for example.

beißen ◇*verb* (IMPERF **biss**, PERF **hat gebissen**) **1** to bite; **2** to sting (*of smoke, for example*); **3 sich beißen** to clash; **die Farben beißen sich** the colours clash.

a
b
c
d
e
f
g
h
i
j
k
l
m
n
o
p
q
r
s
t
u
v
w
x
y
z

Beitrag der (PL die Beiträge)
1 contribution; **2** subscription;
3 premium (*insurance fee*); **4** article
(*in a newspaper*).

beitragen ⋄verb (PRES **trägt bei**,
IMPERF **trug bei**, PERF **hat**
beigetragen) **zu etwas beitragen**
to contribute to something.

beitreten ⋄verb (PRES **tritt bei**,
IMPERF **trat bei**, PERF **ist**
beigetreten) to join; **ich trete dem**
Fußballverein bei I'm joining the
football club.

bekam SEE **bekommen**.

bekämpfen verb (PERF **hat**
bekämpft) **1** to fight; **2 sich**
bekämpfen to fight.

bekannt adjective **1** well known;
2 familiar; **das kommt mir**
bekannt vor that seems familiar;
3 mit jemandem bekannt sein to
know somebody; **4 für etwas**
bekannt sein to be (well) known for
something; **5 jemanden bekannt**
machen to introduce somebody;
6 das ist mir bekannt I know that;
7 etwas bekannt geben/machen
to announce something; **sie gab**
ihre Verlobung bekannt she
announced her engagement;
8 bekannt werden to become
known.

Bekannte der/die (PL die
Bekannten) **1** acquaintance;
2 friend.

bekannt geben verb (PRES **gibt**
bekannt, IMPERF **gab bekannt**, PERF
hat bekannt gegeben) to announce
SEE **bekannt**.

bekanntlich adverb **Rauchen ist**
bekanntlich schädlich as you
know, smoking is bad for you.

beklagen verb (PERF **hat sich**
beklagt) **sich beklagen** to
complain.

Bekleidung die clothes, clothing.

bekommen ⋄verb (IMPERF **bekam**,
PERF **hat bekommen**) **1** to get;
Angst bekommen to get frightened;
2 to catch (*a cold, the train*); **3 ein**
Kind bekommen to have a baby;
4 was bekommen Sie? (*in a shop*)
can I help you? (*in a restaurant*)
what would you like?; **5 was**
bekommen Sie dafür? how much is
it?; **6** (PERF **ist bekommen**) **fettes**
Essen bekommt mir nicht fatty
food doesn't agree with me; **7** (PERF
ist bekommen) **die Ferien sind mir**
gut bekommen the holiday did me
good.

Belag der (PL die Beläge) **1** covering;
2 coating; **3** topping (*on bread*);
4 lining (*of brakes*).

belasten verb (PERF **hat belastet**)
1 to burden; **2** to put weight on
(*foot*); **3** to pollute (*the atmosphere*);
4 to debit (*an account*); **5** to
incriminate.

belästigen verb (PERF **hat**
belästigt) **1** to bother; **2** to harass.

Belastung die **1** strain; **2** load;
3 burden; **4** pollution.

belaufen ⋄verb (PRES **beläuft**,
IMPERF **belief**, PERF **belaufen**) **sich**
auf etwas belaufen to amount to
something; **die Rechnung beläuft**
sich auf fünfhundert Euro the bill
amounts to five hundred euros.

belegen *verb* (PERF **hat belegt**)
1 to cover; **2 eine Scheibe Brot mit Käse belegen** to put some cheese on a slice of bread; **3** to enrol for (*a course*); **4** to reserve (*a seat*); **5 den ersten Platz belegen** to come first; **6** to prove (*facts*).

belegt *adjective* **1** occupied; **2 der Platz ist belegt** this seat is taken; **3 ein belegtes Brot** an open sandwich; **4 die Nummer ist belegt** (*when phoning*) the number's engaged.

beleidigen *verb* (PERF **hat beleidigt**) to insult.

Beleidigung *die* (PL *die* **Beleidigungen**) insult.

Beleuchtung *die* lighting.

Belgien *das* Belgium.

Belgier *der* (PL *die* **Belgier**) Belgian.

Belgierin *die* (PL *die* **Belgierinnen**) Belgian.

belgisch *adjective* Belgian.

Belichtung *die* exposure.

beliebig *adjective* any; **eine beliebige Zahl** any number you like.
beliebig *adverb* **beliebig lange** as long as you like; **beliebig viele** as many as you like.

beliebt *adjective* popular.

Beliebtheit *die* popularity.

bellen *verb* (PERF **hat gebellt**) to bark.

belohnen *verb* (PERF **hat belohnt**) to reward.

Belohnung *die* (PL *die* **Belohnungen**) reward.

belügen *verb* (IMPERF **belog**, PERF **hat belogen**) to lie to.

bemerkbar *adjective* **sich bemerkbar machen** to attract attention, to become noticeable.

bemerken *verb* (PERF **hat bemerkt**) **1** to notice; **2** to remark; **3 nebenbei bemerkt** by the way.

Bemerkung *die* (PL *die* **Bemerkungen**) remark.

bemitleiden *verb* (PERF **hat bemitleidet**) to pity.

bemühen *verb* (PERF **hat sich bemüht**) **1 sich bemühen** to try; **sich sehr bemühen** to try hard; **er bemüht sich um eine Stelle** he's trying to get a job; **2 sich um jemanden bemühen** to try to help somebody; **3 bitte, bemühen Sie sich nicht** please don't trouble yourself.

Bemühung *die* (PL *die* **Bemühungen**) effort.

benachrichtigen *verb* (PERF **hat benachrichtigt**) **1** to inform; **2** to notify (*officially*).

benachteiligt *adjective* disadvantaged.

benehmen ⋄*verb* (PRES **benimmt sich**, IMPERF **benahm sich**, PERF **hat sich benommen**) **sich benehmen** to behave; **benimm dich!** behave yourself!

Benehmen *das* behaviour.

beneiden *verb* (PERF **hat beneidet**) to envy; **jemanden um etwas beneiden** to envy somebody something.

a
b
c
d
e
f
g
h
i
j
k
l
m
n
o
p
q
r
s
t
u
v
w
x
y
z

benoten *verb* (PERF **hat benotet**) to mark.

benutzen *verb* (PERF **hat benutzt**) to use.

Benutzer *der* (PL *die* **Benutzer**) user.

Benutzerin *die* (PL *die* **Benutzerinnen**) user.

Benutzung *die* use.

Benzin *das* petrol.

beobachten *verb* (PERF **hat beobachtet**) to observe, to watch; **Vögel beobachten** to watch birds.

bequem *adjective* **1** comfortable; **2 machen Sie es sich bequem** make yourself at home; **3** lazy; **4** easy; **eine bequeme Lösung finden** to find an easy way out.

beraten ◇*verb* (PRES **berät**, IMPERF **beriet**, PERF **hat beraten**) **1** to advise; **2 jemanden gut/schlecht beraten** to give somebody good/bad advice; **3 sich beraten lassen** to get advice; **4 gut beraten sein** to be well advised; **5** to discuss (*a plan, matter*); **6 sich über etwas beraten** to discuss something.

Berater *der* (PL *die* **Berater**) adviser.

Beratung *die* (PL *die* **Beratungen**) **1** advice; **2** discussion; **3** consultation (*with a doctor*).

berauben *verb* (PERF **hat beraubt**) to rob.

berechnen *verb* (PERF **hat berechnet**) **1** to charge; **jemandem zehn Euro für etwas berechnen** to charge somebody ten euros for something; **2 jemandem zu viel berechnen** to overcharge somebody; **3** to calculate.

berechtigen *verb* (PERF **hat berechtigt**) **jemanden berechtigen, etwas zu tun** to give someone the right to do something.

berechtigt *adjective* justified.

Bereich *der* (PL *die* **Bereiche**) **1** area; **2** field (*in a profession*); **im Bereich Tourismus** in the field of tourism.

bereit *adjective* ready.

bereiten *verb* (PERF **hat bereitet**) **1** to make (*coffee, tea*); **2** to cause (*trouble, difficulty*); **leider hat es uns Schwierigkeiten bereitet** unfortunately it caused us some trouble; **3** to give (*a surprise, pleasure*).

bereits *adverb* already.

bereuen *verb* (PERF **hat bereut**) to regret.

Berg *der* (PL *die* **Berge**) **1** mountain; **2** hill.

bergab *adverb* downhill.

Bergarbeiter *der* (PL *die* **Bergarbeiter**) miner.

bergauf *adverb* uphill.

bergen ◇*verb* (PRES **birgt**, IMPERF **barg**, PERF **hat geborgen**) to rescue.

Bergsteigen *das* mountaineering.

Bergsteiger *der* (PL *die* **Bergsteiger**) mountaineer, climber.

Bergsteigerin *die* (PL *die* **Bergsteigerinnen**) mountaineer, climber.

Bergwacht *die* mountain rescue.

Bergwerk *das* (PL *die* **Bergwerke**) mine.

Bericht *der* (PL *die* **Berichte**) report.

berichten *verb* (PERF **hat berichtet**) **1** to report; **die Zeitungen haben nichts davon berichtet** the newspapers didn't report anything about it; **2 jemandem über etwas berichten** to tell somebody about something; **er hat mir über seine Ferien in Amerika berichtet** he told me about his holiday in America.

berücksichtigen *verb* (PERF **hat berücksichtigt**) to take into account.

Beruf *der* (PL *die* **Berufe**) **1** occupation; **2** profession; **ich bin Lehrerin von Beruf** I'm a teacher by profession; **3** trade; **4 was sind Sie von Beruf?** what do you do for a living?

beruflich *adjective* **1** professional; **2** vocational (*training*).
beruflich *adverb* **1 beruflich erfolgreich sein** to be successful in your career; **2 viel beruflich unterwegs sein** to be away a lot on business.

Berufsberatung *die* careers advice.

Berufsschule *die* (PL *die* **Berufsschulen**) technical college.

berufstätig *adjective* working.

Berufsverkehr *der* rush-hour traffic.

beruhigen *verb* (PERF **hat beruhigt**) **1** to calm down; **2** to reassure; **3 sich beruhigen** to calm down.

Beruhigungsmittel *das* (PL *die* **Beruhigungsmittel**) sedative, tranquillizer.

berühmt *adjective* famous.

berühren *verb* (PERF **hat berührt**) **1** to touch; **2** to touch on (*a topic, an issue*); **3** to affect; **ihre Geschichte berührte ihn seltsam** he was strangely affected by her story; **4 sich berühren** to touch.

besaß SEE **besitzen**.

beschädigen *verb* (PERF **hat beschädigt**) to damage.

Beschädigung *die* (PL *die* **Beschädigungen**) damage; **der Sturm verursachte zahlreiche Beschädigungen** the storm caused considerable damage.

beschaffen[1] *verb* (PERF **hat beschafft**) to get; **kannst du mir nicht einen Job beschaffen?** can't you get me a job?

beschaffen[2] *adjective* **so beschaffen sein, dass ...** to be such that ...

beschäftigen *verb* (PERF **hat beschäftigt**) **1** to occupy (*keep busy*); **2** to employ (*people*); **3 sich beschäftigen** to occupy yourself; **4 ich beschäftige mich mit den Kindern** I'm busy with the children; **5 sich mit einem Fall beschäftigen** to deal with a case; **sein Aufsatz beschäftigt sich mit der Umweltverschmutzung** his essay deals with environmental pollution.

a
b
c
d
e
f
g
h
i
j
k
l
m
n
o
p
q
r
s
t
u
v
w
x
y
z

beschäftigt *adjective* **1** busy;
2 employed.

Beschäftigung *die* (PL *die*
Beschäftigungen) **1** occupation;
2 activity.

Bescheid *der* (PL *die* Bescheide)
1 information; **2 jemandem
Bescheid sagen** to let somebody
know; **3 über etwas Bescheid
wissen** to know about something.

bescheiden *adjective* modest.

Bescheinigung *die* (PL *die*
Bescheinigungen) **1** certificate;
eine Bescheinigung des Arztes a
doctor's certificate; **2** (written)
confirmation.

beschimpfen *verb* (PERF **hat**
beschimpft) to abuse.

beschlagnahmen *verb* (PERF
hat beschlagnahmt) to confiscate.

beschleunigen *verb* (PERF **hat**
beschleunigt) **1** to speed up; **2** to
accelerate; **der Lastwagen hinter
uns hat plötzlich beschleunigt** the
lorry behind us suddenly
accelerated.

beschließen ⬦*verb* (IMPERF
beschloss, PERF **hat beschlossen**)
to decide.

Beschluss *der* (PL *die* Beschlüsse)
decision.

beschränken *verb* (PERF **hat**
beschränkt) to limit.

beschränkt *adjective* **1** narrow-
minded; **2** dim; **sie ist ein bisschen
beschränkt** she's a bit dim.

beschreiben ⬦*verb* (IMPERF
beschrieb, PERF **hat beschrieben**)
to describe.

Beschreibung *die* (PL *die*
Beschreibungen) description.

beschuldigen *verb* (PERF **hat**
beschuldigt) to accuse.

Beschuldigung *die* (PL *die*
Beschuldigungen) accusation.

beschützen *verb* (PERF **hat**
beschützt) to protect.

Beschwerde *die* (PL *die*
Beschwerden) complaint.

beschweren *verb* (PERF **hat sich
beschwert**) **sich beschweren** to
complain; **ich habe mich bei den
Nachbarn über ihn beschwert** I've
complained to the neighbours about
him.

beschwipst *adjective* tipsy.

beseitigen *verb* (PERF **hat**
beseitigt) to remove.

Besen *der* (PL *die* Besen) broom.

besetzen *verb* (PERF **hat besetzt**)
1 to occupy; **2** to fill (*a post, role*);
3 to trim, to edge (*with lace or fur*).

besetzt *adjective* **1** occupied;
2 besetzt sein to be engaged (*a
phone, toilet*); **3** taken (*a table, seat*);
der Platz ist besetzt this seat is
taken; **4** full (*of a train, bus*); **der
Zug ist voll besetzt** the train is full
up.

Besetztzeichen *das* (PL *die*
Besetztzeichen) engaged tone.

Besetzung *die* (PL *die*
Besetzungen) **1** cast; **2** team;
3 occupation.

besichtigen *verb* (PERF **hat**
besichtigt) **1** to look round (*a town,
museum*); **2** to see (*sights, a house*).

Besichtigung *die* (PL *die* Besichtigungen) visit.

besinnungslos *adjective* unconscious.

Besitz *der* **1** property; **2 im Besitz einer Sache sein** to be in possession of something.

besitzen ◇*verb* (IMPERF **besaß**, PERF **hat besessen**) **1** to own; **sie besitzen ein Haus in Italien** they own a house in Italy; **2** to have (*talent, a quality*).

Besitzer *der* (PL *die* **Besitzer**) owner.

Besitzerin *die* (PL *die* **Besitzerinnen**) owner.

besonderer, besondere, besonderes *adjective* **1** special; **unter besonderen Umständen** in special circumstances; **2** particular; **ohne besondere Begeisterung** without any particular enthusiasm; **3 keine besonderen Kennzeichen** no distinguishing features.

Besonderheit *die* (PL *die* **Besonderheiten**) **1** special feature; **2** peculiarity.

besonders *adverb* particularly.

besorgen *verb* (PERF **hat besorgt**) to get; **ich kann dir Karten besorgen** I can get you tickets.

besorgt *adjective* worried.

besprechen ◇*verb* (PRES **bespricht**, IMPERF **besprach**, PERF **hat besprochen**) **1** to discuss; **ich muss es erst mit meinen Eltern besprechen** I'll have to discuss it with my parents first; **2** to review (*a book, film*).

Besprechung *die* (PL *die* Besprechungen) **1** meeting (*at work*); **2** discussion; **3** review (*of a film, play*).

besser *adjective, adverb* better; **alles besser wissen** to know better.

Besserung *die* **1** improvement; **2 gute Besserung!** get well soon!

beständig *adjective* **1** constant; **2** settled (*weather*).

Bestandteil *der* (PL *die* Bestandteile) component.

bestätigen *verb* (PERF **hat bestätigt**) **1** to confirm; **2** to acknowledge (*receipt*); **3 sich bestätigen** to be confirmed, to prove to be true.

beste SEE **bester**.

bestechen ◇*verb* (PRES **besticht**, IMPERF **bestach**, PERF **hat bestochen**) **1** to bribe; **2** to win over.

Bestechung *die* (PL *die* Bestechungen) bribery.

Besteck *das* (PL *die* **Bestecke**) cutlery.

bestehen ◇*verb* (IMPERF **bestand**, PERF **hat bestanden**) **1** to exist; **2 es besteht die Gefahr, dass** ... there is a danger that ...; **noch besteht die Hoffnung, dass** ... there is still hope that ...; **3** to pass; **eine Prüfung bestehen** to pass an exam; **4 auf etwas bestehen** to insist on something; **5 aus etwas bestehen** to consist of something; **6 aus etwas bestehen** to be made of something.

a
b
c
d
e
f
g
h
i
j
k
l
m
n
o
p
q
r
s
t
u
v
w
x
y
z

bestellen *verb* (PERF **hat bestellt**)
1 to order (*goods*); **2** to reserve
(*tickets*); **3** to tell; **jemandem etwas**
bestellen to tell somebody
something; **4 bestell ihm schöne**
Grüße give him my regards; **5 kann**
ich etwas bestellen? can I take a
message?; **6** to send for; **jemanden**
zu sich bestellen to send for
somebody.

Bestellung *die* (PL *die*
Bestellungen) **1** order (*for goods*);
2 reservation (*for tickets*).

bestens *adverb* very well; **das hat**
ja bestens geklappt that worked
out very well.

bester,beste,bestes *adjective*
1 best; **sein bestes Buch** his best
book; **2 ich halte es für das Beste,**
wenn ... I think it would be best if
...; **sein Bestes tun** to do your best;
3 einen Witz zum Besten geben to
tell a joke; **4 jemanden zum Besten**
halten to pull somebody's leg.
am besten *adverb* best; **du bleibst**
am besten zu Hause you'd best
stay at home; **es ist am besten,**
wenn wir gleich anfangen it's best
if we get started straight away.

bestimmen *verb* (PERF **hat**
bestimmt) **1** to fix (*a time, price*);
2 to decide (on); **etwas allein**
bestimmen to decide (on)
something on your own; **er**
bestimmt immer, was wir machen
he always decides what we're going
to do; **3** to be in charge; **4 für**
jemanden bestimmt sein to be
meant for somebody; **5 für etwas**
bestimmt sein to be intended for

something (*a donation for a good*
cause, for example).

bestimmt *adjective* **1** certain; **zu**
einer bestimmten Zeit at a certain
time; **2** particular; **suchen Sie**
etwas Bestimmtes? are you
looking for anything in particular?;
3 definite.
bestimmt *adverb* **1** certainly,
definitely; **ich komme ganz**
bestimmt I'm definitely coming;
2 er hat es bestimmt vergessen
he's bound to have forgotten; **3 du**
weißt es doch bestimmt noch
surely you must remember it.

Bestimmung *die* (PL *die*
Bestimmungen) regulation.

bestrafen *verb* (PERF **hat bestraft**)
to punish.

bestreiten ◇*verb* (IMPERF **bestritt**,
PERF **hat bestritten**) **1** to deny; **2** to
dispute; **das möchte ich nicht**
bestreiten I'm not disputing it; **3** to
pay for.

bestürzt *adjective* upset.

Besuch *der* (PL *die* Besuche) **1** visit;
2 attendance (*at school*); **3 Besuch**
haben to have visitors/a visitor;
4 bei Freunden zu Besuch sein to
be staying with friends; **zu Besuch**
kommen to be visiting.

besuchen *verb* (PERF **hat**
besucht) **1** to visit; **2** to go to (*an*
exhibition, the theatre); **die Schule**
besuchen to go to school; **3** to
attend (*a lecture*).

Besucher *der* (PL *die* Besucher)
visitor.

Besucherin *die* (PL *die* Besucherinnen) visitor.

betätigen *verb* (PERF hat betätigt) **1** to operate; **2 die Bremse betätigen** to apply the brakes; **3 sich politisch betätigen** to be involved in politics; **4 sich künstlerisch betätigen** to do art; **5 sich als Reporter betätigen** to work as a reporter.

Betäubungsmittel *das* (PL *die* Betäubungsmittel) anaesthetic.

Bete *die* **Rote Bete** beetroot.

beteiligen *verb* (PERF hat beteiligt) **1** to give a share to; **jemanden mit zehn Prozent an einem Geschäft beteiligen** to give somebody a ten percent share of a business; **2 sich an etwas beteiligen** to take part in something; **3 kann ich mich an eurem Spiel beteiligen?** can I join in your game?

beten *verb* (PERF hat gebetet) to pray.

Beton *der* concrete.

betonen *verb* (PERF hat betont) to stress.

Betonung *die* (PL *die* Betonungen) stress.

Betrag *der* (PL *die* Beträge) amount.

betragen ◇*verb* (PRES beträgt, IMPERF betrug, PERF hat betragen) **1** to amount to, to come to; **2 sich betragen** to behave; **haben sich die Kinder gut betragen?** did the children behave well?

Betragen *das* behaviour.

betreffen ◇*verb* (PRES betrifft, IMPERF betraf, PERF hat betroffen) to concern; **was mich betrifft** as far as I'm concerned.

betreten ◇*verb* (PRES betritt, IMPERF betrat, PERF hat betreten) **1** to enter; **2 'Betreten verboten'** 'keep out', 'keep off' (*the grass, for example*).

Betrieb *der* (PL *die* Betriebe) **1** business, firm; **2** activity; **es war viel Betrieb** it was very busy; **3 in Betrieb sein** to be working (*of a machine*); **4 außer Betrieb sein** to be out of order; **5 eine Maschine in Betrieb setzen** to start up a machine.

Betriebsferien *plural noun* firm's holiday; **'Betriebsferien'** 'closed for the holidays'.

Betriebspraktikum *das* (PL *die* Betriebspraktika) training course.

betrinken ◇*verb* (IMPERF betrank sich, PERF hat sich betrunken) **sich betrinken** to get drunk.

betrog SEE **betrügen**.

Betrug *der* **1** deception; **2** fraud; **was für ein Betrug** what a swindle!

betrügen ◇*verb* (IMPERF betrog, PERF hat betrogen) **1** to cheat; **jemanden um tausend Euro betrügen** to cheat somebody out of a thousand euros; **2** to be unfaithful to, to cheat on; **sie hat ihren Mann betrogen** she's been unfaithful to her husband.

betrunken *adjective* drunk.

a
b
c
d
e
f
g
h
i
j
k
l
m
n
o
p
q
r
s
t
u
v
w
x
y
z

Bett *das* (PL *die* **Betten**) bed; **ins Bett gehen** to go to bed; **das Bett machen** to make the bed.

Bettbezug *der* (PL *die* **Bettbezüge**) duvet cover.

betteln *verb* (PERF **hat gebettelt**) to beg.

Bettlaken *das* (PL *die* **Bettlaken**) sheet.

Bettler *der* (PL *die* **Bettler**) beggar.

Bettlerin *die* (PL *die* **Bettlerinnen**) beggar.

Bettwäsche *die* bed linen.

Bettzeug *das* bedding.

beugen *verb* (PERF **hat gebeugt**) 1 to bend; 2 to decline, to conjugate (*in grammar*); 3 **sich nach vorn beugen** to bend forwards; **sich über etwas beugen** to bend over something; 4 **sich aus dem Fenster beugen** to lean out of the window; 5 **sich beugen** to submit.

Beule *die* (PL *die* **Beulen**) 1 bump; 2 lump; 3 dent.

beurteilen *verb* (PERF **hat beurteilt**) to judge.

Beutel *der* (PL *die* **Beutel**) bag.

Bevölkerung *die* (PL *die* **Bevölkerungen**) population.

bevor *conjunction* 1 before; 2 **bevor nicht** until; **bevor er nicht unterschrieben hat** until he has signed.

bevorzugen *verb* (PERF **hat bevorzugt**) to prefer.

bewachen *verb* (PERF **hat bewacht**) to guard.

bewaffnen *verb* (PERF **hat bewaffnet**) to arm.

bewahren *verb* (PERF **hat bewahrt**) **jemandem vor etwas bewahren** to protect someone from something.

bewaffnet *adjective* armed.

bewährt *adjective* 1 reliable; 2 proven (*method, design*); 3 **ein bewährtes Rezept** a well-tried recipe.

bewegen[1] *verb* (PERF **hat bewegt**) 1 to move; 2 **sich bewegen** to take exercise; 3 **sich bewegen** to move.

bewegen[2] ◇*verb* (IMPERF **bewog**, PERF **hat bewogen**) **jemanden dazu bewegen, etwas zu tun** to persuade somebody to do something.

bewegt *adjective* eventful.

Bewegung *die* (PL *die* **Bewegungen**) 1 movement; 2 exercise; 3 **eine Maschine in Bewegung setzen** to start (up) a machine; 4 **sich in Bewegung setzen** to start to move.

Beweis *der* (PL *die* **Beweise**) 1 proof; 2 **belastende Beweise** incriminating evidence; 3 token, sign.

beweisen ◇*verb* (IMPERF **bewies**, PERF **hat bewiesen**) 1 to prove; 2 to show.

bewerben ◇*verb* (PRES **bewirbt sich**, IMPERF **bewarb sich**, PERF **hat sich beworben**) **sich bewerben** to apply; **sich um eine Stelle bewerben** to apply for a job.

Bewerber *der* (PL *die* **Bewerber**) applicant.

Bewerberin *die* (PL *die* Bewerberinnen) applicant.

Bewerbung *die* (PL *die* Bewerbungen) application.

bewohnen *verb* (PERF **hat bewohnt**) to live in.

Bewohner *der* (PL *die* **Bewohner**) 1 resident; 2 inhabitant (*of a region*).

Bewohnerin *die* (PL *die* Bewohnerinnen) 1 resident; 2 inhabitant (*of a region*).

bewölkt *adjective* cloudy.

Bewölkung *die* clouds.

bewundern *verb* (PERF **hat bewundert**) to admire.

Bewunderung *die* admiration.

bewusst *adjective* 1 conscious; 2 deliberate; 3 **sich etwas bewusst sein** to be aware of something; **ich war mir der Folgen bewusst** I was aware of the consequences.

bewusstlos *adjective* unconscious.

Bewusstsein *das* 1 consciousness; 2 **bei vollem Bewusstsein sein** to be fully conscious; 3 **mir kam zu(m) Bewusstsein, dass** ... I realized that ....

bezahlbar *adjective* affordable.

bezahlen *verb* (PERF **hat bezahlt**) 1 to pay; **für etwas 10 Euro bezahlen** to pay 10 euros for something; 2 to pay for (*goods, food*); **er hat das Essen bezahlt** he paid for the meal.

Bezahlung *die* payment.

bezeichnend *adjective* typical.

beziehen ⬦*verb* (IMPERF **bezog**, PERF **hat bezogen**) 1 to cover; 2 **das Bett frisch beziehen** to put clean sheets on the bed; 3 to move into; **wann kannst du die neue Wohnung beziehen?** when will you be able to move into the new flat?; 4 to get (*goods, a pension*); 5 to take (*a newspaper*); 6 **sich auf etwas/ jemanden beziehen** to refer to something/somebody; 7 **es bezieht sich** it's clouding over.

Beziehung *die* (PL *die* Beziehungen) 1 connection; 2 relationship; 3 **Beziehungen** contacts; **Anna hat gute Beziehungen** Anna has good contacts; 4 **diplomatische Beziehungen** diplomatic relations; 5 **in dieser Beziehung** in this respect; 6 **eine Beziehung zu etwas haben** to be able to relate to something (*to art, pop music, for example*).

beziehungsweise *conjunction* 1 or rather; 2 respectively.

Bezirk *der* (PL *die* Bezirke) district.

Bezug *der* (PL *die* Bezüge) 1 cover (*of a cushion, duvet, etc.*); 2 connection; **keinen Bezug zu etwas haben** to be unable to relate to something; 3 **auf etwas Bezug nehmen** to refer to something; 4 **in Bezug auf** regarding; 5 **mit Bezug auf Ihr Angebot** with reference to your offer.

bezweifeln *verb* (PERF **hat bezweifelt**) to doubt.

BH *der* (PL *die* BHs) bra.

a
b
c
d
e
f
g
h
i
j
k
l
m
n
o
p
q
r
s
t
u
v
w
x
y
z

Bibel *die* (PL *die* Bibeln) bible; **die Bibel** the Bible.

Bibliothek *die* (PL *die* Bibliotheken) library.

Bibliothekar *der* (PL *die* Bibliothekare) librarian.

Bibliothekarin *die* (PL *die* Bibliothekarinnen) librarian.

biegen ⬦*verb* (IMPERF **bog**, PERF **hat gebogen**) **1** to bend; **2 sich biegen** to bend; **3** (PERF **ist gebogen**) to turn; **um die Ecke biegen** to turn the corner.

Biene *die* (PL *die* Bienen) bee.

Bier *das* (PL *die* Biere) beer.

Bierdeckel *der* (PL *die* Bierdeckel) beer mat.

bieten ⬦*verb* (IMPERF **bot**, PERF **hat geboten**) **1** to offer; **2** to bid (*at an auction*); **3 es bietet sich die Möglichkeit** there is a possibility; **4** to present (*a sight*); **5 das lasse ich mir nicht bieten!** I won't put up with it!

Bikini *der* (PL *die* Bikinis) bikini.

Bild *das* (PL *die* Bilder) **1** picture; **jemanden ins Bild setzen** to put somebody in the picture; **2** scene.

bilden *verb* (PERF **hat gebildet**) **1** to form; **2 sich bilden** to form; **3 sich bilden** to educate yourself.

Bildschirm *der* (PL *die* Bildschirme) screen.

bildschön *adjective* (very) beautiful.

Bildung *die* **1** formation; **2** education.

billig *adjective* cheap.

Billion *die* (PL *die* Billionen) billion (*a million million*); **drei Billionen Euro** three Billion euros.

bin SEE **sein**.

Binde *die* (PL *die* Binden) **1** bandage; **2** sanitary towel.

binden ⬦*verb* (IMPERF **band**, PERF **hat gebunden**) **1** to tie; **2** to bind (*a book*); **3** to make up (*a bouquet*); **4** to thicken (*a sauce*); **5 sich binden** to commit oneself.

Bindestrich *der* (PL *die* Bindestriche) hyphen.

Bindfaden *der* (PL *die* Bindfäden) (piece of) string.

Bindung *die* (PL *die* Bindungen) **1** tie; **2** relationship; **3** binding (*on a ski*).

Biokost *die* health food.

Biologie *die* biology.

biologisch *adjective* biological.

Birke *die* (PL *die* Birken) birch tree.

Birne *die* (PL *die* Birnen) **1** pear; **2** bulb.

bis *preposition* (+ ACC) **1** as far as; **dieser Zug fährt nur bis Passau** this train only goes as far as Passau; **2** up to; **Kinder bis zehn zahlen die Hälfte** children up to ten pay half; **bis jetzt** up to now; **bis zu** up to; **3** until, till (*with time*); **4** by; **bis dahin** by then; **5 bis auf** except for; **alle sind durchgefallen bis auf die zwei Mädchen** everyone failed except for the two girls; **6 bis bald!** see you soon!; **7 von München bis Salzburg** from Munich to Salzburg; **von Montag bis Freitag** from Monday to Friday; **zwei bis drei**

Euro two to three euros.

bis *conjunction* until, till; **sie bleibt, bis es dunkel wird** she's staying until it gets dark.

Bischof *der* (PL *die* **Bischöfe**) bishop.

bisher *adverb* so far.

bisherig *adjective* previous.

Biss *der* (PL *die* **Bisse**) bite.

biss SEE **beißen**.

bisschen *pronoun* **1 ein bisschen** a bit; ; **ein bisschen Brot** a bit of bread; **2 kein bisschen** not a bit.

bissig *adjective* **1** vicious; **'Vorsicht bissiger Hund!'** 'beware of the dog!'; **2** cutting (*remark, tone*).

bist SEE **sein**.

Bitte *die* (PL *die* **Bitten**) request.

bitte *adverb* **1** please; **'möchten Sie Kuchen?' – 'ja bitte'** 'would you like some cake?' – 'yes please'; **2** you're welcome (*in reply to thanks*); **3** come in (*after a knock on the door*); **4** (*in a shop*) **bitte?** yes, please?; **5 wie bitte?** sorry?

bitten *verb* (IMPERF **bat**, PERF **hat gebeten**) to ask; **jemanden um etwas bitten** to ask somebody for something.

bitter *adjective* bitter.

blamieren *verb* (PERF **hat blamiert**) **1** to disgrace; **2 jemanden blamieren** to embarrass somebody; **3 sich blamieren** to make a fool of yourself.

Blase *die* (PL *die* **Blasen**) **1** bubble; **2** blister; **3** bladder.

blasen *verb* (PRES **bläst**, IMPERF **blies**, PERF **hat geblasen**) to blow.

Blasinstrument *das* (PL *die* **Blasinstrumente**) wind instrument.

Blaskapelle *die* (PL *die* **Blaskapellen**) brass band.

blass *adjective* pale.

Blatt *das* (PL *die* **Blätter**) **1** leaf; **2** sheet; **ein Blatt Papier** a sheet of paper; **3** page; **4** newspaper.

blau *adjective* **1** blue; **ein blau gestreiftes Kleid** a dress with blue stripes; **2 ein blaues Auge haben** to have a black eye; **3 ein blauer Fleck** a bruise; **4 blau sein** (*informal*) to be tight; **5 eine Fahrt ins Blaue** a mystery tour.

Blech *das* (PL *die* **Bleche**) **1** sheet metal; **2** tin; **3** baking tray; **4** brass (*in music*).

Blei *das* lead.

bleiben *verb* (IMPERF **blieb**, PERF **ist geblieben**) **1** to stay, to remain; **2** to be left; **3 bleiben Sie am Apparat** hold the line; **4 bei etwas bleiben** to stick to something; **5 ruhig bleiben** to keep calm; **6 wo bleibt er so lange?** where has he got to?; **7 etwas bleiben lassen** to not do something; **wenn du nicht mitkommen willst, dann lass es eben bleiben** if you don't want to come, then don't.

bleich *adjective* pale.

Bleichmittel *das* (PL *die* **Bleichmittel**) bleach.

bleifrei *adjective* unleaded.

a
b
c
d
e
f
g
h
i
j
k
l
m
n
o
p
q
r
s
t
u
v
w
x
y
z

Bleistift der (PL die **Bleistifte**) pencil.

Bleistiftspitzer der (PL die **Bleistiftspitzer**) pencil sharpener.

blenden verb (PERF **hat geblendet**) **1** to dazzle; **2** to blind.

blendend adjective **1** marvellous; **2 es geht mir blendend** I feel great; **wir haben uns blendend amüsiert** we had a great time.

Blick der (PL die **Blicke**) **1** look; **2** glance; **3 auf den ersten Blick** at first sight; **4** view; **ein Zimmer mit Blick aufs Meer** a room with a sea view.

blicken verb (PERF **hat geblickt**) **1** to look; **2 sich blicken lassen** to show your face.

blieb SEE **bleiben**.

blies SEE **blasen**.

blind adjective blind.

Blinddarm der (PL die **Blinddärme**) appendix.

Blinddarmentzündung die (PL die **Blinddarmentzündungen**) appendicitis.

Blinde der/die (PL die **Blinden**) blind person, blind man/woman.

blinken verb (PERF **hat geblinkt**) **1** to flash; **2** to indicate (of a car).

Blinker der (PL die **Blinker**) indicator.

blinzeln verb (PERF **hat geblinzelt**) to blink.

Blitz der (PL die **Blitze**) **1** (flash of) lightning; **2** flash.

blitzen verb (PERF **hat geblitzt**) **1** to flash; **2** to sparkle; **3 es hat geblitzt** there was a flash of lightning.

Block der (PL die **Blöcke**) **1** pad (for writing on); **2** (PL die **Blocks**) block (of flats).

Blockflöte die (PL die **Blockflöten**) recorder.

blöd adjective stupid.

Blödsinn der nonsense.

blond adjective blonde, fair-haired.

bloß adverb **1** only; **es kostet bloß fünf Euro** it's only five euros; **2 warum hat er das bloß gemacht?** why on earth did he do it?; **3 was mache ich bloß?** whatever shall I do?; **4 fass das bloß nicht an!** don't touch it!
bloß adjective **1** bare (feet); **mit bloßem Auge** with the naked eye; **2** mere (words, suspicion); **der bloße Gedanke daran** the mere thought of it.

Blume die (PL die **Blumen**) flower.

Blumenkohl der cauliflower.

Bluse die (PL die **Blusen**) blouse.

Blut das blood.

Blutdruck der blood pressure.

Blüte die (PL die **Blüten**) blossom.

bluten verb (PERF **hat geblutet**) to bleed.

Blutgefäß das (PL die **Blutgefäße**) bloodvessel.

Blutprobe die (PL die **Blutproben**) blood test.

Blutwurst die (PL die **Blutwürste**) black pudding.

50

Bock *der* (PL *die* **Böcke**) **1** buck;
2 billy-goat; **3** ram; **4 Bock auf
etwas haben** (*informal*) to fancy
something; **5 einen Bock schießen**
(*informal*) to make a blunder.

Bockwurst *die* (PL *die*
Bockwürste) frankfurter.

Boden *der* (PL *die* **Böden**) **1** ground;
2 floor; **3** bottom (*of a container*);
4 loft, attic.

Bodensee *der* Lake Constance.

bog SEE **biegen**.

Bogen *der* (PL *die* **Bögen**) **1** curve;
2 arch; **3** turn (*in skiing*).

Bohne *die* (PL *die* **Bohnen**) bean.

bohren *verb* (PERF **hat gebohrt**) to
drill.

Bohrer *der* (PL *die* **Bohrer**) drill.

Bohrinsel *die* (PL *die* **Bohrinseln**)
oil rig.

Bohrmaschine *die* (PL *die*
Bohrmaschinen) electric drill.

Bombe *die* (PL *die* **Bomben**) bomb.

Bonbon *der* (PL *die* **Bonbons**) sweet.

Boot *das* (PL *die* **Boote**) boat.

Bord[1] *das* (PL *die* **Borde**) shelf.

Bord[2] *der* **an Bord** on board; **über
Bord** overboard.

Bordkarte *die* (PL *die* **Bordkarten**)
boarding card.

borgen (PERF **hat geborgt**) **1** to
borrow; **2 sich etwas borgen** to
borrow something; **ich habe es mir
von ihr geborgt** I borrowed it from
her; **3 jemandem etwas borgen** to
lend somebody something; **Evi hat
mir ihr Buch geborgt** Evi lent me
her book.

Börse *die* (PL *die* **Börsen**) stock
exchange.

Börsenmakler *der* (PL *die*
Börsenmakler) stock broker.

Borste *die* (PL *die* **Borsten**) bristle.

böse *adjective* **1** bad; **2** wicked;
3 naughty (*child*); **4** angry; **böse
werden** to get angry; **ich bin ihm
böse** I'm angry with him; **5 auf
jemanden böse sein** to be cross
with somebody.

boshaft *adjective* malicious.

bot SEE **bieten**.

Bote *der* (PL *die* **Boten**) messenger.

Botin *die* (PL *die* **Botinnen**)
messenger.

Botschaft *die* (PL *die* **Botschaften**)
1 message; **2** embassy; **die
britische Botschaft** the British
Embassy.

Botschafter *der* (PL *die*
Botschafter) ambassador.

Botschafterin *die* (PL *die*
Botschafterinnen) ambassador.

Bowle *die* (PL *die* **Bowlen**) punch (*for
drinking*).

boxen *verb* (PERF **hat geboxt**) **1** to
box; **2** to punch.

Boxer *der* (PL *die* **Boxer**) boxer.

brach SEE **brechen**.

brachte SEE **bringen**.

Branche *die* (PL *die* **Branchen**) (line
of) business.

Branchenverzeichnis *das* (PL
die **Branchenverzeichnisse**)
classified directory.

Brand *der* (PL *die* **Brände**) fire.

Brandung *die* surf.

brannte SEE **brennen**.

Brasilianer *der* (PL *die* Brasilianer) Brazilian.

Brasilianerin *die* (PL *die* Brasilianerinnen) Brazilian.

braten ◇*verb* (PRES **brät**, IMPERF **briet**, PERF **hat gebraten**) **1** to fry; **2** to roast.

Braten *der* (PL *die* Braten) **1** roast; **2** joint.

Brathähnchen *das* (PL *die* Brathähnchen) roast chicken.

Bratkartoffeln *plural noun* fried potatoes.

Bratpfanne *die* (PL *die* Bratpfannen) frying pan.

Bratwurst *die* (PL *die* Bratwürste) fried sausage.

Brauch *der* (PL *die* Bräuche) custom.

brauchbar *adjective* **1** usable; **2** useful.

brauchen *verb* (PERF **hat gebraucht**) **1** need; **ich brauche eine neue Birne für meine Lampe** I need a new bulb for my light; **du brauchst nur auf den Knopf zu drücken** all you need to do is press the button; **du brauchst nicht zu gehen** you needn't go; **2 sie braucht es nur zu sagen** she only has to say; **3** to take (*time*); **wie lange brauchst du mit dem Auto?** how long does it take you by car?; **4 ich könnte es gut brauchen** I could do with it.

brauen *verb* (PERF **hat gebraut**) to brew.

Brauerei *die* (PL *die* Brauereien) brewery.

braun *adjective* **1** brown; **2 braun werden** to get a tan; **braun (gebrannt) sein** to be tanned.

Bräune *die* tan.

Brause *die* (PL *die* Brausen) fizzy drink.

Braut *die* (PL *die* Bräute) bride.

Bräutigam *der* (PL *die* Bräutigame) bridegroom.

Brautjungfer *die* (PL *die* Brautjungfern) bridesmaid.

Brautpaar *das* (PL *die* Brautpaare) bride and groom.

brav *adjective* good.

BRD *die* (*Bundesrepublik Deutschland*) FRG (*Federal Republic of Germany*).

brechen ◇*verb* (PRES **bricht**, IMPERF **brach**, PERF **hat gebrochen**) **1** to break (*an agreement, a record*); **2 sich den Arm brechen** to break your arm; **3** to vomit; **4** (PERF **ist gebrochen**) to break; **der Ast ist gebrochen** the branch broke.

breit *adjective* **1** wide; **2** broad; **3 die breite Masse** the general public.

Breite *die* (PL *die* Breiten) width.

Bremse *die* (PL *die* Bremsen) **1** brake; **2** horsefly.

bremsen *verb* (PERF **hat gebremst**) **1** to brake; **2** to slow down (*development, production*); **3 jemanden bremsen** (*informal*) to stop somebody; **er ist nicht mehr zu bremsen** there's no stopping him.

Bremslicht *das* (PL *die* Bremslichter) brake light.

Bremspedal *das* (PL *die* Bremspedale) brake pedal.

brennen ⋄*verb* (IMPERF **brannte**, PERF **hat gebrannt**) **1** to burn; **2** to be on (*of a light*); **das Licht brennen lassen** to leave the light on; **3** to sting (*of a wound or sore*); **4 das Haus brennt** the house is on fire; **es brennt!** fire!; **5 darauf brennen, etwas zu tun** to be dying to do something.

Brennnessel *die* (PL *die* Brennnesseln) stinging nettle.

Brennpunkt *der* (PL *die* Brennpunkte) focus.

Brett *das* (PL *die* Bretter) **1** board; **2** plank; **3** shelf.

Brezel *die* (PL *die* Brezeln) pretzel.

bricht SEE **brechen**.

Brief *der* (PL *die* Briefe) letter.

Brieffreund *der* (PL *die* Brieffreunde) pen friend.

Brieffreundin *die* (PL *die* Brieffreundinnen) pen friend.

Briefkasten *der* (PL *die* Briefkästen) **1** letterbox; **2** postbox.

Briefmarke *die* (PL *die* Briefmarken) stamp.

Brieftasche *die* (PL *die* Brieftaschen) wallet.

Briefträger *der* (PL *die* Briefträger) postman.

Briefträgerin *die* (PL *die* Briefträgerinnen) postwoman.

Briefumschlag *der* (PL *die* Briefumschläge) envelope.

Briefwechsel *der* correspondence.

briet SEE **braten**.

Brillant *der* (PL *die* Brillanten) diamond.

Brille *die* (PL *die* Brillen) glasses, spectacles.

bringen ⋄*verb* (IMPERF **brachte**, PERF **hat gebracht**) **1** to bring; **2** to take; **Peter bringt dich nach Hause** Peter will take you home; **3 die Kinder ins Bett bringen** to put the children to bed; **4 einen Film im Fernsehen bringen** to show a film on television; **5** to publish (*an article*); **6** to yield (*interest, a profit*); **7 jemanden dazu bringen, etwas zu tun** to get somebody to do something; **8 mit sich bringen** to entail; **9 etwas hinter sich bringen** to get something over and done with; **10 es weit bringen** to go far; **11 jemanden auf eine Idee bringen** to give somebody an idea; **12 es zu nichts bringen** to get nowhere; **13 das bringt's nicht!** (*informal*) that's no use!

Brise *die* (PL *die* Brisen) breeze.

Brite *der* (PL *die* Briten) Briton; **die Briten** the British.

Britin *die* (PL *die* Britinnen) Briton.

britisch *adjective* British.

Brokkoli *der* broccoli.

Brombeere *die* (PL *die* Brombeeren) blackberry.

Brosche *die* (PL *die* Broschen) brooch.

Broschüre *die* (PL *die* Broschüren) brochure.

Brot *das* (PL *die* Brote) **1** bread; **ein Brot** a loaf of bread; **2 ein Brot** a slice of bread.

Brötchen *das* (PL *die* Brötchen) roll.

Bruch *der* (PL *die* Brüche) **1** break; **2** fracture; **3** hernia; **4** fraction.

Bruchteil *der* (PL *die* Bruchteile) fraction.

Brücke *die* (PL *die* Brücken) bridge.

Bruder *der* (PL *die* Brüder) brother.

Brühe *die* (PL *die* Brühen) **1** broth; **2** stock (*for cooking*).

Brühwürfel *der* (PL *die* Brühwürfel) stock cube.

brüllen *verb* (PERF **hat gebrüllt**) to roar.

brummen *verb* (PERF **hat gebrummt**) **1** to buzz; **2** to growl (*of a bear*); **3** to hum (*of an engine*).

Brunnen *der* (PL *die* Brunnen) **1** well; **2** fountain.

Brüssel *das* Brussels.

Brust *die* (PL *die* Brüste) **1** chest; **2** breast.

Brustschwimmen *das* breaststroke.

brutto *adverb* gross.

BSE *das* (*bovine spongiforme Enzephalopathie*) BSE.

Bub *der* (PL *die* Buben) boy.

Buch *das* (PL *die* Bücher) book.

Buche *die* (PL *die* Buchen) beech.

buchen *verb* (PERF **hat gebucht**) to book.

Bücherei *die* (PL *die* Büchereien) library.

Bücherregal *das* (PL *die* Bücherregale) bookcase.

Buchhalter *der* (PL *die* Buchhalter) accountant, bookkeeper.

Buchhalterin *die* (PL *die* Buchhalterinnen) accountant, bookkeeper.

Buchhandlung *die* (PL *die* Buchhandlungen) bookshop.

Büchse *die* (PL *die* Büchsen) tin, can.

Büchsenöffner *der* (PL *die* Büchsenöffner) tin opener.

Buchstabe *der* (PL *die* Buchstaben) letter (*of the alphabet*); **ein großer Buchstabe** a capital letter; **ein kleiner Buchstabe** a small letter.

buchstabieren *verb* (PERF **hat buchstabiert**) to spell.

Bucht *die* (PL *die* Buchten) bay.

Buchung *die* (PL *die* Buchungen) booking, reservation.

bücken (PERF **hat sich gebückt**) **sich bücken** to bend down.

Buddhismus *der* Buddhism.

Bude *die* (PL *die* Buden) **1** hut; **2** stall; **3 meine Bude** (*informal*) my room, my pad.

Büfett *das* (PL *die* Büfetts) buffet.

Bügel *der* (PL *die* Bügel) hanger.

Bügeleisen *das* (PL *die* Bügeleisen) iron.

bügeln *verb* (PERF **hat gebügelt**) to iron.

Bühne *die* (PL *die* Bühnen) stage.

Bulle der (PL die Bullen) **1** bull; **2** (*informal*) cop.

Bummel der (PL die Bummel) stroll (*around town*).

bummeln verb (PERF ist gebummelt) **1** to stroll; **wir sind durch die Stadt gebummelt** we strolled around town; **2** (PERF hat gebummelt) to dawdle.

Bund[1] der (PL die Bünde) **1** association; **2** waistband.

Bund[2] das (PL die Bunde) bunch.

Bundesbürger der (PL die Bundesbürger) German citizen.

Bundeskanzler der (PL die Bundeskanzler) Federal Chancellor.

Bundesland das (PL die Bundesländer) (federal) state.

Bundesliga die (German) national football league.

Bundesrat der Upper House (*of the German Parliament*).

Bundesrepublik die Federal Republic.

Bundesstraße die (PL die Bundesstraßen) A road, major road.

Bundestag der Lower House (*of the German Parliament*).

Bundeswehr die (German) Army.

Bungalow der (PL die Bungalows) bungalow.

bunt adjective colourful.

Buntstift der (PL die Buntstifte) coloured pencil.

Burg die (PL die Burgen) castle.

Bürger der (PL die Bürger) citizen.

Bürgerin die (PL die Bürgerinnen) citizen.

Bürgermeister der (PL die Bürgermeister) mayor.

Bürgersteig der (PL die Bürgersteige) pavement.

Büro das (PL die Büros) office.

Büroklammer die (PL die Büroklammern) paper clip.

Bürste die (PL die Bürsten) brush.

bürsten verb (PERF hat gebürstet) to brush.

Bus der (PL die Busse) bus; **ich fahre mit dem Bus** I'm going by bus.

Busbahnhof der (PL die Busbahnhöfe) bus station.

Busch der (PL die Büsche) bush.

Busen der (PL die Busen) bosom.

Busfahrer der (PL die Busfahrer) bus driver.

Busfahrerin die (PL die Busfahrerinnen) bus driver.

Busfahrkarte die (PL die Busfahrkarten) bus ticket.

Bushaltestelle die (PL die Bushaltestellen) bus stop.

Buslinie die (PL die Buslinien) bus route.

Bussard der (PL die Bussarde) buzzard.

Bußgeld das (PL die Bußgelder) fine.

Büstenhalter der (PL die Büstenhalter) bra.

a
b
c
d
e
f
g
h
i
j
k
l
m
n
o
p
q
r
s
t
u
v
w
x
y
z

Busverbindung *die* (PL *die* Busverbindungen) **1** bus connection; **2** bus line.

Butter *die* butter.

Butterbrot *das* (PL *die* Butterbrote) sandwich, bread and butter.

bzw. SEE **beziehungsweise**.

Cc

Café *das* (PL *die* Cafés) cafe.

Cafeteria *die* (PL *die* Cafeterias) cafeteria.

campen *verb* (PERF **hat gecampt**) to camp.

Camper *der* (PL *die* Camper) camper.

Camperin *die* (PL *die* Camperinnen) camper.

Camping *das* camping.

Campingbus *der* (PL *die* Campingbusse) camper (*vehicle*).

Campingkocher *der* (PL *die* Campingkocher) camping stove.

Campingplatz *der* (PL *die* Campingplätze) campsite.

CD *die* (PL *die* CDs) CD.

CD-Spieler *der* (PL *die* CD-Spieler) CD player.

Cello *das* (PL *die* Cellos) cello.

Cent *der* (PL *die* Cents) cent (*in euro and dollar systems*); **25 Cent** 25 cents.

Champignon *der* (PL *die* Champignons) mushroom.

Chance *die* (PL *die* Chancen) chance.

Chaos *das* chaos.

chaotisch *adjective* chaotic.

Charakter *der* (PL *die* Charaktere) character.

charmant *adjective* charming.

Charterflug *der* (PL *die* Charterflüge) charter flight.

Chatroom *der* (PL *die* Chatrooms) chatroom.

Chauvinist *der* (PL *die* Chauvinisten) chauvinist.

Chef *der* (PL *die* Chefs) **1** head (*of a firm*); **2** boss.

Chefin *die* (PL *die* Chefinnen) **1** head (*of a firm*); **2** boss.

Chemie *die* chemistry.

Chemikalie *die* (PL *die* Chemikalien) chemical.

Chemiker *der* (PL *die* Chemiker) chemist.

Chemikerin *die* (PL *die* Chemikerinnen) chemist.

chemisch *adjective* **1** chemical; **2 chemische Reinigung** dry-cleaning, dry-cleaner's.

Chicorée *der* chicory.

China *das* China.

Chinese *der* (PL *die* Chinesen) Chinese; **die Chinesen** the Chinese.

Chinesin *die* (PL *die* Chinesinnen) Chinese.

chinesisch *adjective* Chinese.

Chipkarte die (PL die Chipkarten) smart card.

Chips plural noun crisps.

Chirurg der (PL die Chirurgen) surgeon.

Chirurgin die (PL die Chirurginnen) surgeon.

Chlor das chlorine.

Chor der (PL die Chöre) choir.

Christ der (PL die Christen) Christian.

Christentum das Christianity.

Christin die (PL die Christinnen) Christian.

christlich adjective Christian.

Christus der Christ.

circa adverb approximately.

Clown der (PL die Clowns) clown.

Cola™ die (PL die Colas) Coke™.

Comic der (PL die Comics) cartoon.

Comicheft das (PL die Comichefte) comic.

Computer der (PL die Computer) computer; **ich spiele am Computer** I'm playing on the computer.

Computerprogramm das (PL die Computerprogramme) computer program.

Computerspiel das (PL die Computerspiele) computer game.

Container der (PL die Container) 1 container; 2 skip.

Cordsamt der corduroy.

Couch die (PL die Couchs) sofa.

Couchtisch der (PL die Couchtische) coffee table.

Cousin der (PL die Cousins) cousin.

Cousine die (PL die Cousinen) cousin SEE **Kusine**.

Creme die (PL die Cremes) 1 cream; 2 cream dessert.

Curry das 1 curry; 2 curry powder.

Currywurst die (PL die Currywürste) curried sausage.

Cursor der (PL die Cursors) cursor.

Dd

da adverb 1 there; **da draußen** out there; **da drüben** over there; **da sein** to be there; **man muss pünktlich da sein** you have to be there on time; **2 ist noch Brot da?** is there any bread left?; **3** here; **sind alle da?** is everyone here?; **da sind deine Handschuhe** here are your gloves; **4 ist Sabine da?** is Sabine about?; **5 von da an** from then on; **6 ich bin wieder da** I'm back; **7** so (therefore); **der Bus war weg, da bin ich gelaufen** the bus had gone, so I walked; **8 da kann man nichts machen** there's nothing you can do about it; **9 da, wo die Straße nach Stuttgart abzweigt** at the turning for Stuttgart.

da conjunction as, since; **da es gerade regnet** as it's raining.

dabei adverb 1 (included or next to) with it/him/her/them; **sie hatten die Kinder dabei** they had the children with them; **2 dicht dabei** close by; **3** (referring to something already mentioned) about it; **das**

a
b
c
d
e
f
g
h
i
j
k
l
m
n
o
p
q
r
s
t
u
v
w
x
y
z

Wichtigste dabei the most important thing about it; **4** at the same time; **er malte ein Bild und sang dabei** he painted a picture and sang at the same time; **5** during this; **6 jemandem dabei helfen, etwas zu tun** to help somebody do something; **7 was hast du dir denn dabei gedacht?** what were you thinking of?; **8 dabei sein** to be there; **er ist dabei gewesen** he was there; **9 was ist denn dabei?** so what?; **10 dabei sein, etwas zu tun** to be just doing something; **ich war gerade dabei zu gehen** I was just about to leave; **11 dabei bleiben** to stick with it (*an opinion, for example*); **12** and yet, even though.

dabeibleiben ◇*verb* (IMPERF **blieb dabei**, PERF **ist dabeigeblieben**) **1** to stay on (*at an organisation*); **2 er hat mit dem Training begonnen, ist aber nicht dabeigeblieben** he started training, but didn't keep it up.

dabeisein SEE **dabei**.

Dach *das* (PL **die Dächer**) roof.

Dachboden *der* (PL **die Dachböden**) loft, attic.

Dachgeschoss *das* (PL **die Dachgeschosse**) attic.

Dachrinne *die* (PL **die Dachrinnen**) gutter (*on roof edge*).

dachte SEE **denken**.

Dackel *der* (PL **die Dackel**) dachshund.

dadurch *adverb* **1** through it/them; **das Wasser muss dadurch gelaufen sein** the water must have run through it; **2** as a result; **3** in this way; **ich nehme die U-Bahn, dadurch bin ich eine halbe Stunde eher da** I'll take the tube, that way I'll be there half an hour earlier. **dadurch** *conjunction* **dadurch, dass** because.

dafür *adverb* **1** for it/them; **dafür kriegt man nicht viel** you won't get much for it/them; **2** instead; **wenn er schon nicht auf die Party gehen will, kann er dich dafür zum Essen einladen** if he doesn't want to go to the party he can take you for a meal instead; **3** but then (*on the other hand*); **4 dafür, dass** considering (that); **5 ich kann nichts dafür** it's not my fault.

dagegen *adverb* **1** against it/them; **ich bin dagegen** I'm against it; **2** for it/them (*when swapping*); **3** into it; **das Auto ist dagegen gefahren** the car drove into it; **4** by comparison; **5 hast du was dagegen?** do you mind?; **6** however.

daheim *adverb* at home.

daher *adverb* **1** from there; **2** that's why.

dahin *adverb* **1** there; **2 bis dahin** (*in the past*) until then, (*in the future*) by then; **3 jemanden dahin bringen, dass er etwas tut** to get somebody to do something.

dahinten *adverb* over there.

dahinter *adverb* **1** behind it/them; **2 dahinter kommen** to get to the bottom of it; **ich bin endlich dahinter gekommen** I finally got to the bottom of it.

dalassen ✧*verb* (PRES **lässt da**, IMPERF **ließ da**, PERF **hat dagelassen**) to leave there.

damals *adverb* at that time, then; **wir wohnten damals in Berlin** we were then living in Berlin.

Dame *die* (PL *die* **Damen**) **1** lady; **2** queen (*in chess or cards*); **3** draughts.

Damenbinde *die* (PL *die* **Damenbinden**) sanitary towel.

damit *adverb* **1** with it/them; **ich will damit spielen** I want to play with it; **hör auf damit!** stop it!; **2** by it; **was meinst du damit?** what do you mean by that?; **3 damit hat es noch Zeit** there's no hurry (about that); **4** therefore, because of that; **sie hat den zweiten Satz verloren und damit das Spiel** she lost the second set and because of it the match.

damit *conjunction* so that; **ich habe es aufgeschrieben, damit du es nicht vergisst** I wrote it down so that you won't forget.

Damm *der* (PL *die* **Dämme**) **1** dam; **2** embankment.

dämmern *verb* (PERF **hat gedämmert**) **es dämmert** it is getting light, it is getting dark.

Dämmerung *die* **1** dawn; **2** dusk.

Dampf *der* (PL *die* **Dämpfe**) steam.

dämpfen *verb* (PERF **hat gedämpft**) **1** to steam (*in cooking*); **2** to muffle (*a sound*); **3** to dampen (*somebody's enthusiasm*).

dampfen *verb* (PERF **hat gedampft**) to steam.

Dampfer *der* (PL *die* **Dampfer**) steamer.

danach *adverb* **1** after it/them; **2** afterwards; **kurz danach** shortly afterwards; **3 danach suchen** to look for it/them; **4 danach riechen** to smell of it; **5** accordingly; **6 es sieht danach aus** it looks like it.

Däne *der* (PL *die* **Dänen**) Dane.

daneben *adverb* **1** next to it/them; **2** by comparison.

Dänemark *das* Denmark.

Dänin *die* (PL *die* **Däninnen**) Dane.

dänisch *adjective* Danish.

Dank *der* **1** thanks; **mit Dank zurück** thanks for the loan; **2 vielen Dank** thank you very much.

dank *preposition* (+ GEN *or* + DAT) thanks to.

dankbar *adjective* **1** grateful; **2** rewarding.

danke *exclamation* thank you, thanks; **danke schön** thank you very much; **(nein) danke** no thank you, no thanks.

danken *verb* (PERF **hat gedankt**) **1** to thank; **2 nichts zu danken** don't mention it.

dann *adverb* then.

daran *adverb* **1** on it/them; **2 daran denken** to think of it/them; **3 dicht daran** close to it/them; **4 nahe daran sein, etwas zu tun** to be on the point of doing something; **5** about it/them; **daran ist nichts zu machen** there is nothing you can do about it; **6 es liegt daran, dass**

... it is because ...; **7 er ist daran gestorben** he died of it.

darauf *adverb* **1** on it/them; **2 darauf warten** to wait for it; **3 darauf antworten** to reply to it; **4** after that; **kurz darauf** shortly after that; **5 am Tag darauf** the day after; **6 am darauf folgenden Tag** the following day; **7 es kommt darauf an, ob** ... it depends whether ....

daraufhin *adverb* as a result.

daraus *adverb* **1** out of it/them, from it/them; **2 was ist daraus geworden?** what has become of it/them?; **3 mach dir nichts daraus** don't worry about it.

darf, **darfst** SEE **dürfen**.

darin *adverb* **1** in it/them; **2** in that respect; **der Unterschied liegt darin, dass** ... the difference is that ...

Darm *der* (PL **die Därme**) intestine(s).

darstellen *verb* (PERF **hat dargestellt**) **1** to represent; **2** to portray; **dieses Gemälde stellt Szenen aus dem Bürgerkrieg dar** this painting portrays scenes from the civil war; **3** to describe; **er stellt es so dar, als sei es meine Schuld** the way he describes it, it's all my fault; **4** to play (*in the theatre*).

Darsteller *der* (PL **die Darsteller**) actor.

Darstellerin *die* (PL **die Darstellerinnen**) actress.

darüber *adverb* **1** over it/them; **2** about it; **darüber sprechen** to talk about it; **3** more; **dreißig Euro oder darüber** thirty euros or more.

darum *adverb* **1** round it/them; **2 darum bitten** to ask for it; **3** that's why; **darum komme ich nicht** that's why I'm not coming; **4 ich sorge mich darum** I worry about it; **5 es geht darum, zu gewinnen** the main thing is to win; **6 darum geht es nicht** that's not the point; **7** because of that; **darum, weil** because.

darunter *adverb* **1** under it/them; **2 im Stock darunter** on the floor below; **3** among them; **mehrere Schüler, darunter zwei Zehnjährige** a number of pupils, among them two ten year olds; **4** less; **dreißig Euro oder darunter** thirty euros or less; **5 was verstehen Sie darunter?** what do you understand by that?

das *article* (*neuter*) **1** the; **das Haus** the house; **2** that; **das Mädchen war es** it was that girl; **das da** that one.

das *pronoun* **1** which, that; **das Kleid, das ich im Schaufenster gesehen habe** the dress which I saw in the window; **2 das mit der Spitze** the one with the lace; **3** who; **das Mädchen, das gegenüber wohnt** the girl who lives opposite; **4** that; **das wusste ich nicht** I didn't know that; **das geht** that's all right.

Dasein *das* existence.

dasein SEE **da**.

dass *conjunction* **1** that; **ich freue mich, dass** ... I'm very pleased that

...; **2 ich verstehe nicht, dass Karin ihn mag** I don't understand why Karin likes him.

dasselbe *pronoun* the same, the same one.

Daten *plural noun* data.

Datenbank *die* (PL *die* **Datenbanken**) database.

Datenverarbeitung *die* data processing.

datieren *verb* (PERF **hat datiert**) to date.

Dativ *der* (PL *die* **Dative**) dative.

Datum *das* (PL *die* **Daten**) date.

Dauer *die* **1** duration; **2** length; **3 für die Dauer von fünf Jahren** for (a period of) five years; **4 von Dauer sein** to last; **5 auf die Dauer** in the long run; **auf Dauer** permanently.

Dauerkarte *die* (PL *die* **Dauerkarten**) season ticket.

dauern *verb* (PERF **hat gedauert**) **1** to last; **2 lange dauern** to take a long time; **es hat vier Wochen gedauert, bis der Brief hier ankam** it took four weeks for the letter to arrive.

dauernd *adjective* constant.
dauernd *adverb* constantly.

Dauerwelle *die* (PL *die* **Dauerwellen**) perm.

Daumen *der* (PL *die* **Daumen**) thumb.

Daunendecke *die* (PL *die* **Daunendecken**) duvet.

davon *adverb* **1** from it/them; **2** about it; **ich weiß nichts davon** I don't know anything about it; **3** of it/them; **die Hälfte davon** half of it/them; **4 das kommt davon** (*informal*) it serves you right; **5 was habe ich davon?** what's the point?; **6 abgesehen davon** apart from that.

davor *adverb* **1** in front of it/them; **2** beforehand; **3 Angst davor haben** to be frightened of it/them; **4 kurz davor sein, etwas zu tun** to be on the point of doing something.

dazu *adverb* **1** to it/them; **2** in addition; **noch dazu** in addition (to it); **3** with it; **was isst du dazu?** what are you having with it?; **4 ich habe keine Lust dazu** I don't feel like it; **5 jemanden dazu bringen, etwas zu tun** to get somebody to do something; **6 ich bin nicht dazu gekommen** I didn't get round to it; **7 er ist nicht dazu bereit** he's not prepared to do it.

dazugeben ◇*verb* (PRES **gibt dazu**, IMPERF **gab dazu**, PERF **hat dazugegeben**) to add.

dazugehören *verb* (PERF **hat dazugehört**) **1** to belong to it/them; **2** to go with it/them (*of accessories*); **alles, was dazugehört** everything that goes with it.

dazukommen ◇*verb* (IMPERF **kam dazu**, PERF **ist dazugekommen**) **1** to arrive; **2** to be added; **3 kommt noch etwas dazu?** would you like anything else?

dazwischen *adverb* **1** in between; **2** between them; **der Unterschied dazwischen** the difference between them.

a
b
c
d
e
f
g
h
i
j
k
l
m
n
o
p
q
r
s
t
u
v
w
x
y
z

dazwischenkommen ◇*verb* (PRES **kommt dazwischen**, IMPERF **kam dazwischen**, PERF **ist dazwischengekommen**) to crop up.

DB *die* (*Deutsche Bundesbahn*) German railways.

DDR *die* (*Deutsche Demokratische Republik*) GDR, East Germany; **in der ehemaligen DDR** in the former East Germany.

Debatte *die* (PL *die* **Debatten**) debate.

Decke *die* (PL *die* **Decken**) **1** blanket, cover; **2** (table)cloth; **ich habe eine neue Decke aufgelegt** I've put on a new tablecloth; **3** ceiling.

Deckel *der* (PL *die* **Deckel**) **1** lid; **2** top.

decken *verb* (PERF **hat gedeckt**) **1** to cover; **2 ein Tuch über etwas decken** to spread a cloth over something; **3 den Tisch decken** to lay the table; **4 jemanden decken** to cover up for somebody; **5 einen Spieler decken** to mark a player (*in sport*).

definieren *verb* (PERF **hat definiert**) to define.

Definition *die* (PL *die* **Definitionen**) definition.

dehnbar *adjective* elastic.

dehnen *verb* (PERF **hat gedehnt**) to stretch.

dein *adjective* your.

deiner, **deine**, **deins** *pronoun* yours; **meine Uhr ist kaputt, kann ich deine haben?** my watch is broken, can I take yours?

deinetwegen *adverb* **1** because of you; **2** for your sake.

deins SEE **deiner**.

deklinieren *verb* (PERF **hat dekliniert**) to decline.

Delfin *der* (PL *die* **Delfine**) dolphin.

Delle *die* (PL *die* **Dellen**) dent.

Delphin *der* (PL *die* **Delphine**) dolphin.

dem *article* (*dative*) **1** (to) the; **2 es liegt auf dem Tisch** it's on the table. **dem** *pronoun* **1** to him; **gib es dem** give it to him; **2** to it, to that one; **3** to whom; **der Mann, dem ich das Geld gegeben habe** the man I gave the money to; **4** which; **das Messer, mit dem ich Zwiebeln schneide** the knife that I cut onions with.

demnächst *adverb* shortly.

Demokratie *die* (PL *die* **Demokratien**) democracy.

demokratisch *adjective* democratic.

Demonstrant *der* (PL *die* **Demonstranten**) demonstrator.

Demonstrantin *die* (PL *die* **Demonstrantinnen**) demonstrator.

Demonstration *die* (PL *die* **Demonstrationen**) demonstration.

demonstrieren *verb* (PERF **hat demonstriert**) to demonstrate.

den *article* (*accusative*) **1** the; **2 ich habe mir den Arm gebrochen** I've broken my arm.
den *pronoun* **1** him; **kennst du den?** do you know him?; **2** it, that one; **den kannst du gerne haben** you're welcome to it; **ich nehme**

den I'll take that one; **3** who(m); **4** which; **der Mantel, den ich mir gekauft habe** the coat I bought.

denen *pronoun* (*dative plural*) **1** (to) them; **2** that, (to) whom; **die Menschen, denen sie geholfen hat** the people she helped.

denkbar *adjective* conceivable.

denken ◇*verb* (IMPERF **dachte**, PERF **hat gedacht**) **1** to think; **ich denke oft an dich** I often think of you; **2 das kann ich mir denken** I can imagine.

Denkmal *das* (PL *die* **Denkmäler**) monument.

denn *conjunction* **1** because, for; **2 mehr denn je** more than ever. **denn** *adverb* **1 wo denn?** where?; **2 was ist denn los?** so what's the matter?; **3 warum denn nicht?** why ever not?; **4 es sei denn** unless.

dennoch *conjunction* nevertheless.

deprimierend *adjective* depressing.

deprimiert *adjective* depressed.

der *article* **1** (*masculine*) the; **der Mann** the man; **2** (*feminine and plural genitive*) of the; **die Katze der Frau** the woman's cat; **der Ball der Kinder** the children's ball; **3** (*dative*) (to) the; **ich gab es der Frau** I gave it to the woman.
der *pronoun* **1** who; **der Mann, der hier wohnt** the man who lives here; **2** which; **der Regenschirm, der mir gehört** the umbrella which is mine; **3 der da** that one; **4** him, he.

deren *pronoun* **1** their; **die Kinder und deren Hund** the children and their dog; **2** whose; **3** of which.

derselbe *pronoun* the same, the same one.

des *article* **1** (*masculine and neuter genetive singular*) of the; **das Klingeln des Telefons** the ringing of the phone; **2 der Ball des Jungen** the boy's ball.

deshalb *adverb* **1** therefore; **2** that's why.

Desinfektionsmittel *das* (PL *die* **Desinfektionsmittel**) disinfectant.

desinfizieren *verb* (PERF **hat desinfiziert**) to disinfect.

dessen *pronoun* **1** his; **2** its; **3** whose; **der Junge, dessen Mutter weint** the boy whose mother is crying; **4** of which.

desto *adverb* the; **je mehr, desto besser** the more the better.

deswegen *conjunction* **1** therefore; **2** that's why.

Detektiv *der* (PL *die* **Detektive**) detective.

deutlich *adjective* clear. **deutlich** *adverb* **ich konnte ihn deutlich sehen** I could clearly see him.

Deutsch *das* German; **auf Deutsch** in German; **fließend Deutsch sprechen** to speak fluent German.

deutsch *adjective* German.

Deutsche *der/die* (PL *die* **Deutschen**) German; **er ist Deutscher** he's German.

a
b
c
d
e
f
g
h
i
j
k
l
m
n
o
p
q
r
s
t
u
v
w
x
y
z

Deutschland *das* Germany; **nach Deutschland** to Germany.

Devisen *plural noun* foreign currency.

Dezember *der* December; **am ersten Dezember** on the first of December; **im Dezember** in December.

Dezimalzahl *die* (PL *die* Dezimalzahlen) decimal (number).

d. h. (*das heißt*) i.e.

Dia *das* (PL *die* Dias) slide.

Diagnose *die* (PL *die* Diagnosen) diagnosis.

diagonal *adjective* diagonal.

Diagramm *das* (PL *die* Diagramme) diagram.

Dialekt *der* (PL *die* Dialekte) dialect.

Dialog *der* (PL *die* Dialoge) dialogue.

Diamant *der* (PL *die* Diamanten) diamond.

Diät *die* (PL *die* Diäten) diet; **jemanden auf Diät setzen** to put somebody on a diet.

dich *pronoun* **1** you; **2** yourself.

dicht *adjective* **1** thick (*fog*); **2** dense; **3** watertight; **4** airtight; **5 er ist nicht ganz dicht** (*informal*) he's off his head.
dicht *adverb* **1** densely; **2** tightly; **3** close; **geh nicht so dicht an den Käfig** don't go so close to the cage; **dicht bei** close to.

Dichter *der* (PL *die* Dichter) poet.

Dichterin *die* (PL *die* Dichterinnen) poet.

Dichtung *die* (PL *die* Dichtungen) **1** poetry; **2** seal, washer.

dick *adjective* **1** thick; **2** swollen (*ankle, tonsils*); **3** fat (*person*).

Dickkopf *der* (PL *die* Dickköpfe) **1** stubborn person; **2 einen Dickkopf haben** to be stubborn.

die *article* (*feminine and plural*) the; **die Frau** the woman; **die Bücher** the books.
die *pronoun* (*feminine and plural*) **1** who; **die Frau, die hier wohnt** the woman who lives here; **die Frau, die ich kenne** the woman I know; **die Kinder, die ich gefragt habe** the children I asked; **2** which; **die Tasche, die ich gekauft habe** the bag I bought; **3** she, her; **4** them; **ich meine die** I mean them; **5 die da** that one, (*plural*) those.

Dieb *der* (PL *die* Diebe) thief.

Diebin *die* (PL *die* Diebinnen) thief.

Diebstahl *der* (PL *die* Diebstähle) theft.

Diele *die* (PL *die* Dielen) **1** hall; **2** floorboard.

dienen *verb* (PERF **hat gedient**) to serve.

Dienst *der* (PL *die* Dienste) service; **Dienst haben** to work, to be on duty (*of a soldier or doctor*).

Dienstag *der* (PL *die* Dienstage) Tuesday; **am Dienstag** on Tuesday.

dienstags *adverb* on Tuesdays.

dienstfrei *adjective* **1 ein dienstfreier Tag** a day off; **2 dienstfrei haben** to have time off, to be off duty.

dienstlich *adverb* on business.

Dienstreise *die* (PL *die* **Dienstreisen**) business trip.

diese SEE **dieser**.

Diesel *der* diesel.

dieselbe *pronoun* the same, the same one.

dieser, **diese**, **dieses** *adjective* **1** this; **2** these; **diese Äpfel** these apples.
dieses *pronoun* **1** this one; **mir gefällt dieses am besten** I like this one best; **2** these ones.

diesmal *adverb* this time.

Digitaluhr *die* (PL *die* **Digitaluhren**) **1** digital watch; **2** digital clock.

Diktat *das* (PL *die* **Diktate**) dictation.

Ding *das* (PL *die* **Dinge**) thing; **vor allen Dingen** above all; **das war ein Ding** (*informal*) that was quite something.

Dings *der/die/das* thingummy.

Dinosaurier *der* (PL *die* **Dinosaurier**) dinosaur.

Diplom *das* (PL *die* **Diplome**) diploma.

dir *pronoun* **1** you, to you; **sie hat es dir gegeben** she gave it to you; **ich verspreche dir, dass** ... I promise you that ...; **2 Freunde von dir** friends of yours; **3** yourself.

direkt *adjective* direct.
direkt *adverb* direct; **der Bus fährt direkt zum Flughafen** the bus goes direct to the airport.

Direktor *der* (PL *die* **Direktoren**) **1** director; **2** headmaster, principal; **3** manager (*of a bank, theatre*).

Direktorin *die* (PL *die* **Direktorinnen**) **1** director; **2** headmistress, principal; **3** manager (*of a bank, theatre*).

Direktübertragung *die* (PL *die* **Direktübertragungen**) live transmission.

Dirigent *der* (PL *die* **Dirigenten**) conductor.

dirigieren *verb* (PERF **hat dirigiert**) to conduct.

Diskette *die* (PL *die* **Disketten**) floppy disk.

Diskettenlaufwerk *das* (PL *die* **Diskettenlaufwerke**) disk drive.

Disko *die* (PL *die* **Diskos**) disco.

Diskothek *die* (PL *die* **Diskotheken**) disco, discotheque.

Diskriminierung *die* discrimination; **die Diskriminierung von Frauen** discrimination against women.

Diskussion *die* (PL *die* **Diskussionen**) discussion; **zur Diskussion stehen** to be under discussion.

diskutieren *verb* (PERF **hat diskutiert**) to discuss.

Disziplin *die* (PL *die* **Disziplinen**) discipline.

DJH *die* (*Deutsche Jugendherberge*) German youth hostel (association).

DM *die* (*Deutsche Mark*) DM, Deutschmark SEE **Mark**.

D-Mark *die* (PL *die* **D-Mark**) Deutschmark, German mark SEE **Mark**.

doch *adverb* **1** yes (*when you are contradicting somebody*); **'hast du keinen Hunger?' – 'doch!'** 'aren't you hungry?' – 'yes, I am!'; **2** after all; **sie hat ihn doch eingeladen** she invited him after all; **sie ist doch nicht gekommen** she hasn't come after all; **3 er hat doch meinen Brief bekommen?** he did get my letter, didn't he?; **sie kommt doch?** she's coming, isn't she?; **4** anyway; **du hörst ja doch nicht auf mich** you won't listen to me anyway; **5 pass doch auf!** do be careful!
doch *conjunction* but.

Doktor *der* (PL *die* **Doktoren**) doctor; **den Doktor machen** to do a doctorate.

Dokument *das* (PL *die* **Dokumente**) document.

Dokumentarfilm *der* (PL *die* **Dokumentarfilme**) documentary.

Dokumentarsendung *die* (PL *die* **Dokumentarsendungen**) documentary (programme).

dolmetschen *verb* (PERF **hat gedolmetscht**) to interpret.

Dolmetscher *der* (PL *die* **Dolmetscher**) interpreter.

Dolmetscherin *die* (PL *die* **Dolmetscherinnen**) interpreter.

Dom *der* (PL *die* **Dome**) cathedral.

Donau *die* Danube.

Donner *der* thunder.

donnern *verb* (PERF **hat gedonnert**) to thunder.

Donnerstag *der* (PL *die* **Donnerstage**) Thursday; **am Donnerstag** on Thursday.

donnerstags *adverb* on Thursdays.

doof *adjective* (*informal*) stupid.

Doppel *das* (PL *die* **Doppel**) **1** duplicate; **2** doubles (*in sport*).

Doppelbett *das* (PL *die* **Doppelbetten**) double bed.

Doppelfenster *das* (PL *die* **Doppelfenster**) double-glazed window; **wir haben Doppelfenster** we've got double glazing.

Doppelhaus *das* (PL *die* **Doppelhäuser**) semi-detached house.

Doppelklick *der* (PL *die* **Doppelklicks**) double-click (*with mouse*).

Doppelpunkt *der* (PL *die* **Doppelpunkte**) colon.

doppelt *adjective* **1** double; **2 in doppelter Ausführung** in duplicate; **3 die doppelte Menge** twice the amount.
doppelt *adverb* **1** doubly; **2** twice; **doppelt so viel** twice as much; **sich doppelt anstrengen** to try twice as hard.

Doppelzimmer *das* (PL *die* **Doppelzimmer**) double room.

Dorf *das* (PL *die* **Dörfer**) village.

Dorn *der* (PL *die* **Dornen**) thorn.

dort *adverb* there; **dort drüben** over there.

dorther *adverb* from there.

dorthin *adverb* there; **geht ihr jetzt dorthin?** are you going there now?

Dose *die* (PL *die* **Dosen**) tin, can.

dösen *verb* (PERF **hat gedöst**) to doze.

Dosenöffner *der* (PL *die* **Dosenöffner**) tin opener.

Dosierung *die* (PL *die* **Dosierungen**) dose.

Dosis *die* (PL *die* **Dosen**) dose.

Dotter *der* (PL *die* **Dotter**) yolk.

Dozent *der* (PL *die* **Dozenten**) lecturer.

Dozentin *die* (PL *die* **Dozentinnen**) lecturer.

Drache *der* (PL *die* **Drachen**) dragon.

Drachen *der* (PL *die* **Drachen**) kite.

Drachenfliegen *das* hang-gliding; **Drachenfliegen gehen** to go hang-gliding.

Draht *der* (PL *die* **Drähte**) **1** wire; **2 er ist auf Draht** (*informal*) he's on the ball.

Drama *das* (PL *die* **Dramen**) drama.

Dramatik *die* drama.

dran *adverb* SEE **daran 1 ich bin dran** it's my turn; **wer ist dran?** whose turn is it?; **2 gut dran sein** to be well off; **3 arm dran sein** to be in a bad way; **4 spät dran sein** to be late.

drängen *verb* (PERF **hat gedrängt**) **1** to push; **2** to press, to urge (*somebody*); **3 sich drängen** to crowd; **die Leute drängten sich vor der Kasse** people crowded around the box-office.

drankommen ⋄*verb* (IMPERF **kam dran**, PERF **ist drangekommen**) to have your turn; **wer kommt dran?** whose turn is it?

drauf *adverb* SEE **darauf 1 drauf und dran sein, etwas zu tun** to be on the point of doing something; **2 gut drauf sein** (*informal*) to be in a good mood.

draußen *adverb* outside.

Dreck *der* dirt.

dreckig *adjective* dirty, filthy.

Drehbuch *das* (PL *die* **Drehbücher**) **1** screenplay; **2** script.

drehen *verb* (PERF **hat gedreht**) **1** to turn; **an etwas drehen** to turn something; **2** to shoot (*a film*); **3 sich drehen** to turn; **4 sich im Kreis drehen** to rotate; **5 es dreht sich um ihr Taschengeld** it's about her pocket money.

Drei *die* (PL *die* **Dreien**) three.

drei *number* three.

Dreieck *das* (PL *die* **Dreiecke**) triangle.

dreieckig *adjective* triangular.

dreifach *adjective* triple.

dreihundert *number* three hundred.

dreimal *adverb* three times.

Dreirad *das* (PL *die* **Dreiräder**) tricycle.

dreißig *number* thirty.

drei viertel *number* three-quarters.

Dreiviertelstunde *die* (PL *die* **Dreiviertelstunden**) three-quarters of an hour.

a
b
c
d
e
f
g
h
i
j
k
l
m
n
o
p
q
r
s
t
u
v
w
x
y
z

dreizehn *number* thirteen.

drin *adverb* SEE **darin**; **drin sein** to be inside.

dringend *adjective* urgent.

drinnen *adverb* **1** inside; **2** indoors.

dritt *adverb* **sie sind zu dritt** there are three of them.

dritte SEE **dritter**.

Drittel *das* (PL die **Drittel**) third.

drittens *adverb* thirdly.

dritter, dritte, drittes *adjective* third; **zum dritten Mal** for the third time; **ein Dritter** a third person; **jeder Dritte, der mitwollte** every third person who wanted to come; **die Dritte Welt** the Third World.

Droge *die* (PL die **Drogen**) drug.

drogenabhängig *adjective* addicted to drugs.

Drogenabhängige *der/die* (PL die **Drogenabhängigen**) drug addict.

Drogenabhängigkeit *die* drug addiction.

drogensüchtig *adjective* addicted to drugs.

Drogensüchtige *der/die* (PL die **Drogensüchtigen**) drug addict.

Drogerie *die* (PL die **Drogerien**) chemist's.

Drogist *der* (PL die **Drogisten**) chemist.

Drogistin *die* (PL die **Drogistinnen**) chemist.

drohen *verb* (PERF **hat gedroht**) to threaten; **jemandem drohen** to threaten somebody.

Drohung *die* (PL die **Drohungen**) threat.

Drossel *die* (PL die **Drosseln**) **1** thrush (*bird*); **2** throttle.

drüben *adverb* over there.

Druck *der* **1** pressure; **jemanden unter Druck setzen** to put pressure on somebody; **2** printing; **3** (PL die **Drucke**) print.

drücken *verb* (PERF **hat gedrückt**) **1** to press; **2** **an der Tür drücken** to push the door; **'bitte drücken'** 'push'; **3** to hug; **4** to pinch (*of shoes*); **5** **die Preise drücken** to force down prices; **6** **sich vor etwas drücken** (*informal*) to get out of something; **du hast dich mal wieder vor dem Aufräumen gedrückt** you've got out of tidying up again.

drucken *verb* (PERF **hat gedruckt**) to print.

Drucker *der* (PL die **Drucker**) printer.

Druckknopf *der* (PL die **Druckknöpfe**) press stud.

Druckluftmesser *der* (PL die **Druckluftmesser**) pressure gauge.

Drucksache *die* (PL die **Drucksachen**) printed matter.

Druckschrift *die* (PL die **Druckschriften**) **1** block letters; **2** type; **3** pamphlet.

Drüse *die* (PL die **Drüsen**) gland.

Dschungel *der* (PL die **Dschungel**) jungle.

du *pronoun* **1** you; **2** **du sagen** to say 'du' (to each other); **per du sein** to be on familiar terms (*'du' is used when talking to family members, close friends, or people of your own age; otherwise 'Sie' is used*).

Dudelsack *der* (PL *die* **Dudelsäcke**) bagpipes.

Duft *der* (PL *die* **Düfte**) fragrance, scent.

duften *verb* (PERF **hat geduftet**) to smell; **nach Lavendel duften** to smell of lavender.

dumm *adjective* 1 stupid; 2 **das wird mir jetzt zu dumm** (*informal*) I've had enough of it; 3 **so etwas Dummes!** how annoying!; 4 **der Dumme sein** to draw the short straw.

dummerweise *adverb* stupidly.

Dummheit *die* (PL *die* **Dummheiten**) 1 stupidity; 2 stupid thing; **mach keine Dummheiten** don't do anything stupid.

Dummkopf *der* (PL *die* **Dummköpfe**) fool.

Dünger *der* (PL *die* **Dünger**) fertilizer.

dunkel *adjective* 1 dark; **ein dunkler Anzug** a dark suit; 2 **im Dunkeln** in the dark; 3 vague (*idea*); 4 shady (*business*); 5 deep (*voice*).

Dunkelheit *die* darkness, dark; **bei Einbruch der Dunkelheit** at dusk.

dünn *adjective* 1 thin; 2 weak (*coffee, tea*).

Dunst *der* (PL *die* **Dünste**) haze.

Duo *das* (PL *die* **Duos**) duet.

durch *preposition* (+ACC) 1 through; **er ist durch das Fernsehen**

bekannt geworden he's become famous through television; 2 by; **durch Boten** by courier; 3 **acht durch zwei ist vier** eight divided by two is four; 4 due to.

durch *adverb* 1 through; **die ganze Nacht durch** all through the night; 2 **den Winter durch** throughout the winter; 3 **durch und durch** completely; 4 **es war acht Uhr durch** (*informal*) it was gone eight o'clock.

durcharbeiten *verb* (PERF **hat durchgearbeitet**) 1 to work through; **die Nacht durcharbeiten** to work through the night; 2 **sich durch etwas durcharbeiten** to work your way through something.

durchaus *adverb* absolutely.

durchblicken *verb* (PERF **hat durchgeblickt**) 1 (*informal*) to understand; 2 **durchblicken lassen, dass** ... to hint that ....

durchbrechen ⋄*verb* (PRES **bricht durch**, IMPERF **brach durch**, PERF **hat durchgebrochen**) 1 to snap, to break in two; 2 (PERF **ist durchgebrochen**) **das Brett ist durchgebrochen** the board has snapped.

Durcheinander *das* 1 muddle; 2 mess; **in der Wohnung herrschte ein fürchterliches Durcheinander** the flat was a terrible mess; 3 confusion; **im allgemeinen Durcheinander** in the general confusion.

durcheinander *adverb* 1 in a mess; **mein Zimmer ist durcheinander** my room is (in) a

a
b
c
d
e
f
g
h
i
j
k
l
m
n
o
p
q
r
s
t
u
v
w
x
y
z

mess; **2 die Akten durcheinander bringen** to muddle up the files; **Karl hat ihre Namen durcheinander gebracht** Karl got their names mixed up; **3** confused; **bring mich nicht durcheinander** don't confuse me; **4 sie haben alle durcheinander geredet** they all talked at once.

durcheinanderbringen SEE **durcheinander**.

durchfahren ◇*verb* (PRES **fährt durch**, IMPERF **fuhr durch**, PERF **ist durchgefahren**) **1** to drive through; **2** to go through; **3 der Zug fährt (in Stuttgart) durch** the train doesn't stop (in Stuttgart).

Durchfall *der* diarrhoea.

durchfallen ◇*verb* (PRES **fällt durch**, IMPERF **fiel durch**, PERF **ist durchgefallen**) **1** to fall through; **2** to fail (*an exam*).

durchführen *verb* (PERF **hat durchgeführt**) to carry out.

Durchgang *der* (PL **die Durchgänge**) **1** passage; **2 'Durchgang verboten'** 'no entry'; **3** round (*in sport*).

Durchgangsverkehr *der* through traffic.

durchgehen ◇*verb* (IMPERF **ging durch**, PERF **ist durchgegangen**) **1** to go through; **2** (*informal*) to escape; **3 jemandem etwas durchgehen lassen** to let somebody get away with something.

durchkommen ◇*verb* (IMPERF **kam durch**, PERF **ist durchgekommen**) **1** to come

through; **2** to get through (*on the phone, in an exam*); **3** to pull through (*after an illness*).

durchlassen ◇*verb* (PRES **lässt durch**, IMPERF **ließ durch**, PERF **hat durchgelassen**) **1** to let through; **2** to let in.

durchmachen *verb* (PERF **hat durchgemacht**) **1** to go through; **2** to work through (*your lunch break, for example*); **3 wir haben die Nacht durchgemacht** we made a night of it.

Durchmesser *der* (PL **die Durchmesser**) diameter.

durchnehmen ◇*verb* (PRES **nimmt durch**, IMPERF **nahm durch**, PERF **hat durchgenommen**) to do (*a topic at school*).

durchs = **durch das.**

Durchsage *die* (PL **die Durchsagen**) announcement.

Durchschnitt *der* (PL **die Durchschnitte**) average; **im Durchschnitt** on average.

durchschnittlich *adjective* average.
durchschnittlich *adverb* on average.

durchsetzen *verb* (PERF **hat durchgesetzt**) **1** to carry through; **2 sich durchsetzen** to assert yourself; **3 sich durchsetzen** to catch on (*of a fashion, an idea*).

durchsichtig *adjective* transparent.

durchstreichen ◇*verb* (IMPERF **strich durch**, PERF **hat durchgestrichen**) to cross out.

Durchzug *der* draught.

dürfen ✧*verb* (PRES **darf**, IMPERF **durfte**, PERF **hat gedurft** or **hat dürfen**) **1** to be allowed; **sie darf das nicht** she's not allowed to do that; **er hat nicht gedurft** he wasn't allowed to; **2 Klaus hat sie im Krankenhaus besuchen dürfen** Klaus was allowed to visit her in hospital; **3 darf ich?** may I?; **4 das dürfen Sie nicht vergessen** you mustn't forget that; **du darfst es nicht alles so ernst nehmen** you mustn't take it all so seriously; **5 du darfst froh sein, dass sonst nichts passiert ist** you should be glad that nothing else happened; **das darf einfach nicht passieren** that just shouldn't happen; **das dürfte nicht schwierig sein** that shouldn't be difficult; **6 das darf nicht wahr sein!** I don't believe it!; **7 was darf es sein?** can I help you?; **8 das dürfte der Grund sein** that's probably the reason.

durfte, **durften**, **durftest**, **durftet** SEE **dürfen**.

dürftig *adjective* poor, meagre.

Dürre *die* (PL *die* **Dürren**) drought.

Durst *der* thirst; **Durst haben** to be thirsty.

durstig *adjective* thirsty.

Dusche *die* (PL *die* **Duschen**) shower.

duschen *verb* (PERF **hat geduscht**) **1** to have a shower; **2 sich duschen** to have a shower.

Düsenflugzeug *das* (PL *die* **Düsenflugzeuge**) jet (plane).

düster *adjective* **1** gloomy (*future, thoughts*); **2** dark.

Dutzend *das* (PL *die* **Dutzende**) dozen.

duzen *verb* (PERF **hat geduzt**) to call somebody 'du'; **wollen wir uns duzen?** shall we say 'du' to each other? (*'du' is used when talking to family members, close friends, or people of your own age*).

dynamisch *adjective* dynamic.

D-Zug *der* (PL *die* **D-Züge**) fast train, express.

Ee

Ebbe *die* (PL *die* **Ebben**) low tide; **es ist Ebbe** the tide is out.

eben *adjective* **1** flat; **2** level. **eben** *adverb* **1** just; **Gabi war eben hier** Gabi was just here; **eben noch** just now; **2 eben!** exactly!

Ebene *die* (PL *die* **Ebenen**) **1** plain; **2** level; **3** plane (*in geometry*).

ebenso *adverb* just as; **Ulla hat den Film ebenso oft gesehen wie du** Ulla's seen the film just as often as you; **ich habe ebenso viel Arbeit wie du** I've got just as much work as you.

Echo *das* (PL *die* **Echos**) echo.

echt *adjective* real, genuine; **die Kette ist aus echtem Gold** the necklace is real gold. **echt** *adverb* (*informal*) really; **das ist echt gut** that's really good.

Eckball der (PL die Eckbälle) corner (kick).

Ecke die (PL die Ecken) corner; **um die Ecke** round the corner.

eckig adjective square.

Edelstein der (PL die Edelsteine) precious stone.

EDV die (*elektronische Datenverarbeitung*) electronic data processing, EDP.

Efeu der (PL die Efeus) ivy.

Effekt der (PL die Effekte) effect.

effektiv adjective effective.
effektiv adverb really, actually.

EG die (*Europäische Gemeinschaft*) EC.

egal adjective **1 das ist mir egal** it's all the same to me; **2 egal, wie groß** no matter how big; **egal, ob er es will oder nicht** (it doesn't matter) whether he wants to or not.

egoistisch adjective selfish.

Ehe die (PL die Ehen) marriage.

ehe conjunction before; **ehe ich nicht weiß, was er will, mache ich nichts** I won't do anything before I know what he wants.

Ehefrau die (PL die Ehefrauen) wife.

ehemalig adjective former.

Ehemann der (PL die Ehemänner) husband.

Ehepaar das (PL die Ehepaare) married couple.

eher adverb **1** earlier, sooner; **je eher, desto besser** the sooner the better; **2** rather; **eher gehe ich zu Fuß, als Geld für ein Taxi auszugeben** I'd rather walk than pay for a taxi; **3** more; **das ist schon eher möglich** that's more likely.

Ehre die (PL die Ehren) honour.

ehrenamtlich adjective honorary.

Ehrgeiz der ambition.

ehrgeizig adjective ambitious.

ehrlich adjective honest.

Ehrlichkeit die honesty.

Ei das (PL die Eier) egg.

Eiche die (PL die Eichen) oak.

Eichhörnchen das (PL die Eichhörnchen) squirrel.

Eid der (PL die Eide) oath.

Eidechse die (PL die Eidechsen) lizard.

Eidotter das (PL die Eidotter) egg yolk.

Eierbecher der (PL die Eierbecher) egg-cup.

Eierschale die (PL die Eierschalen) eggshell.

Eifer der eagerness.

Eifersucht die jealousy.

eifersüchtig adjective jealous; **auf jemanden eifersüchtig sein** to be jealous of somebody.

eifrig adjective eager.

Eigelb das (PL die Eigelb(e)) egg yolk.

eigen adjective own; **sie ist erst siebzehn und hat schon ihr eigenes Auto** she's only seventeen and she's already got her own car.

Eigenart die (PL die Eigenarten) peculiarity.

eigenartig *adjective* peculiar.

Eigenschaft *die* (PL *die* Eigenschaften) **1** quality; **2** characteristic.

eigensinnig *adjective* obstinate.

eigentlich *adjective* actual. **eigentlich** *adverb* actually; **eigentlich habe ich keine Lust, heute ins Kino zu gehen** actually I don't fancy going to the cinema today.

Eigentum *das* property.

Eigentümer *der* (PL *die* Eigentümer) owner.

eignen *verb* (PERF hat sich geeignet) **sich eignen** to be suitable.

Eile *die* hurry.

eilen *verb* **1** (PERF ist geeilt) to hurry; **2** (PERF hat geeilt) to be urgent; **das eilt nicht** it's not urgent.

eilig *adjective* **1** urgent; **2** hurried; **3 es eilig haben** to be in a hurry.

Eilzug *der* (PL *die* Eilzüge) fast stopping train.

Eimer *der* (PL *die* Eimer) bucket.

ein, eine, ein *article* a, an; **ein Haus** a house; **eine Allergie** an allergy; **ein bisschen mehr** a bit more; **was für ein Kleid hast du gekauft?** what sort of dress did you buy?
ein *adjective* **1** one; **sie haben nur ein Kind** they've got just one child; **eines Abends** one evening; **2 einer Meinung sein** to be of the same opinion; **3 ein für alle Mal** once and for all.

einander *pronoun* each other, one another.

Einbahnstraße *die* (PL *die* Einbahnstraßen) one-way street.

Einband *der* (PL *die* Einbände) cover.

einbauen *verb* (PERF hat eingebaut) **1** to fit; **2** to install.

Einbauküche *die* (PL *die* Einbauküchen) fitted kitchen.

einbiegen ⬦*verb* (IMPERF bog ein, PERF ist eingebogen) to turn; **der Radfahrer bog langsam in die Seitenstraße ein** the cyclist turned slowly down the side street.

einbilden *verb* (PERF hat sich eingebildet) **1 sich einbilden** to imagine; **das bildest du dir nur ein** you're only imagining it; **2 Till bildet sich viel ein** Till is very conceited.

Einbildung *die* imagination; **das ist alles nur Einbildung** it's all in the mind.

einbrechen ⬦*verb* (PRES bricht ein, IMPERF brach ein, PERF ist eingebrochen) to break in; **in unserem Haus sind Diebe eingebrochen** thieves broke into our house; **bei unseren Nachbarn ist eingebrochen worden** our neighbours have been burgled.

Einbrecher *der* (PL *die* Einbrecher) burglar.

einbringen *verb* (IMPERF brachte ein, PERF hat eingebracht) to bring in; **die Ernte einbringen** to gather in the harvest.

Einbruch *der* (PL *die* **Einbrüche**)
1 burglary; **2 vor Einbruch der Dunkelheit** before it gets dark; **3 bei Einbruch der Nacht** at nightfall.

einchecken *verb* (PERF **hat eingecheckt**) **am Flughafen einchecken** to check in at the airport.

eindeutig *adjective* **1** clear; **2** definite (*proof*).

Eindruck *der* (PL *die* **Eindrücke**) impression; **einen guten Eindruck auf jemanden machen** to make a good impression on somebody.

eindrucksvoll *adjective* impressive.

eine SEE **ein, einer**.

eineinhalb *number* one and a half.

einer, eine, ein(e)s *pronoun*
1 one; **einer von uns** one of us; **wie soll das einer wissen?** how is one supposed to know?; **2** somebody; **3 kaum einer** hardly anyone; **4** you; **das macht einen müde** it makes you tired.

einerseits *adverb* on the one hand; **einerseits sagt sie, dass sie kein Geld hat, andererseits kauft sie sich dauernd neue Sachen** on the one hand she claims to have no money, on the other hand she's constantly buying new things.

eines SEE **einer**.

einfach *adjective* **1** simple; **2** easy; **3** single (*ticket, knot*).
einfach *adverb* simply.

Einfachheit *die* simplicity.

Einfahrt *die* (PL *die* **Einfahrten**)
1 entrance; **2** arrival (*of a train*); **3** slip road (*on a motorway*).

Einfall *der* (PL *die* **Einfälle**) idea.

einfallen ⋄*verb* (PRES **fällt ein**, IMPERF **fiel ein**, PERF **ist eingefallen**)
1 jemandem einfallen to occur to somebody; **2 ihr Name fällt mir nicht ein** I can't think of her name; **3 was fällt dir eigentlich ein?** what do you think you're doing?; **4 sich etwas einfallen lassen** to think of something.

Einfamilienhaus *das* (PL *die* **Einfamilienhäuser**) detached family house.

Einfluss *der* (PL *die* **Einflüsse**) influence.

einfrieren ⋄*verb* (IMPERF **fror ein**, PERF **ist eingefroren**) **1** to freeze; **2** (PERF **hat eingefroren**) to freeze (*food in the freezer*).

Einfuhr *die* (PL *die* **Einfuhren**) import.

einführen *verb* (PERF **hat eingeführt**) **1** to import; **2** to introduce.

Einführung *die* (PL *die* **Einführungen**) introduction.

Eingabe *die* input (*of data*).

Eingang *der* (PL *die* **Eingänge**) entrance.

Eingangshalle *die* (PL *die* **Eingangshallen**) hallway.

eingeben ⋄*verb* (PRES **gibt ein**, IMPERF **gab ein**, PERF **hat eingegeben**) **1** to hand in; **2** to input, to key in.

eingebildet *adjective* 1 conceited; 2 imaginary (*illness*).

Eingeborene *der/die* (PL *die* Eingeborenen) native.

eingehen ◇*verb* (IMPERF ging ein, PERF ist eingegangen) 1 to shrink (*of clothes*); 2 to die (*of plants*); 3 to arrive (*of goods*); 4 **auf etwas eingehen** to go into something; **sie ging näher darauf ein** she went into it in more detail; 5 **auf etwas nicht eingehen** to ignore something; 6 **auf etwas eingehen** to agree to something; **Oliver ist auf unseren Plan eingegangen** Oliver agreed to our plan; 7 **ein Risiko eingehen** to take a risk.

eingeschrieben *adjective* registered; **ein eingeschriebener Brief** a registered letter.

eingestellt *adjective* 1 **auf etwas eingestellt sein** to be prepared for something; 2 **fortschrittlich eingestellt sein** to be progressively minded.

eingewöhnen *verb* (PERF hat sich eingewöhnt) **sich eingewöhnen** to settle in.

eingießen ◇*verb* (IMPERF goss ein, PERF hat eingegossen) to pour.

Eingriff *der* (PL *die* Eingriffe) 1 intervention; 2 operation (*surgical*).

einheimisch *adjective* 1 native; 2 local.

Einheit *die* (PL *die* Einheiten) 1 unity; 2 unit (*of drink, soldiers*).

Einheitspreis *der* (PL *die* Einheitspreise) 1 standard price; 2 flat fare.

einholen *verb* (PERF hat eingeholt) 1 to catch up with; 2 to make up (*time, a delay*); 3 to buy; **einholen gehen** to go shopping.

einhundert *number* one hundred.

einige SEE **einiger**.

einigen *verb* (PERF hat sich geeinigt) **sich einigen** to come to an agreement; **sich auf etwas einigen** to agree on something.

einiger, einige, einiges *adjective, pronoun* 1 some; **vor einiger Zeit** some time ago; 2 several; 3 **nur einige waren noch da** there were only a few left; 4 **einiges** quite a lot; **wir haben einiges gesehen** we saw quite a lot (of things); 5 **einiges** some things; **einiges hat uns nicht gefallen** there were some things we didn't like.

einigermaßen *adverb* 1 fairly; 2 fairly well; 3 'wie geht es dir?'– 'einigermaßen' 'how are you?'– 'so-so'.

einiges SEE **einiger**.

Einigung *die* agreement.

Einkauf *der* (PL *die* Einkäufe) 1 purchase; 2 shopping; **Einkäufe machen** to do some shopping.

einkaufen *verb* (PERF hat eingekauft) 1 to buy; **ich habe vergessen Milch einzukaufen** I forgot to buy milk; 2 to shop; **wir kaufen meist im Supermarkt ein**

a
b
c
d
e
f
g
h
i
j
k
l
m
n
o
p
q
r
s
t
u
v
w
x
y
z

we usally shop at the supermarket;
einkaufen gehen to go shopping.

Einkaufsbummel der (PL die
Einkaufsbummel) shopping spree.

Einkaufswagen der (PL die
Einkaufswagen) shopping trolley.

Einkaufszentrum das (PL die
Einkaufszentren) shopping centre.

Einkommen das (PL die
Einkommen) income.

einladen ⋄verb (PRES lädt ein,
IMPERF lud ein, PERF hat
eingeladen) **1** to invite; **jemanden
zum Abendessen einladen** to
invite somebody for dinner;
2 jemanden ins Kino einladen to
take sombody to the cinema; **3** to
treat; **ich lade euch ein** I'll treat
you; **4** to load (*goods*).

Einladung die (PL die Einladungen)
invitation.

einleben verb (PERF hat sich
eingelebt) **sich einleben** to settle
down.

Einleitung die (PL die
Einleitungen) introduction.

einlösen verb (PERF hat eingelöst)
to cash.

einmal adverb **1** once (*in the past*);
es war einmal ... once upon a time
...; **2** one day (*in the future*); **3 auf
einmal** suddenly; **4 auf einmal** at
the same time; **sie kamen alle auf
einmal** they all came at the same
time; **5 nicht einmal** not even;
6 noch einmal again; **7 es geht
nun einmal nicht** it's just not
possible.

einmalig adjective **1** unique;
2 fantastic; **3** single, one-off
(*payment*).

einmischen verb (PERF hat sich
eingemischt) **sich einmischen** to
interfere.

Einmündung die (PL die
Einmündungen) **1** junction (*of
roads*); **2** confluence (*of rivers*).

einordnen verb (PERF hat
eingeordnet) **1** to put in order;
2 sich einordnen to fit in (*with
other people*); **3 sich einordnen** to
get in lane (*when driving*).

einpacken verb (PERF hat
eingepackt) **1** to pack; **2** to wrap.

einreichen verb (PERF hat
eingereicht) to hand in.

Einreise die (PL die Einreisen)
entry.

einreisen verb (PERF ist
eingereist) to enter a country; **er
reiste nach Italien ein** he entered
Italy.

einrichten verb (PERF hat
eingerichtet) **1** to furnish; **2** to set
up (*an organisation*); **3** to arrange;
**kannst du es so einrichten, dass
du vormittags da bist?** can you
arrange to be here in the morning?;
4 sich einrichten to furnish your
home; **5 sich einrichten** to
economize; **6 sich auf etwas
einrichten** to prepare for
something.

Einrichtung die (PL die
Einrichtungen) **1** furnishing;
2 furnishings; **3** setting up;

4 institution; **staatliche Einrichtungen** state institutions.

Eins *die* (PL *die* Einsen) one.

eins *number* one; **eins zu eins** one all; **es ist eins** it's one o'clock.
eins *pronoun* SEE **einer**
eins *adjective* **mir ist alles eins** it's all the same to me.

einsam *adjective* lonely.

einsammeln *verb* (PERF **hat eingesammelt**) to collect.

Einsatz *der* **1** use; **2** stake (*when betting*).

einschalten *verb* (PERF **hat eingeschaltet**) **1** to switch on (*a radio, TV*); **2 sich einschalten** to intervene.

einschlafen ◇*verb* (PRES **schläft ein**, IMPERF **schlief ein**, PERF **ist eingeschlafen**) to go to sleep.

einschließen ◇*verb* (IMPERF **schloss ein**, PERF **hat eingeschlossen**) **1** to lock in; **2** include; **3 sich einschließen** to lock yourself in.

einschließlich *preposition* (+ GEN) including; **einschließlich der Unkosten** including expenses.
einschließlich *adverb* inclusive.

einschränken *verb* (PERF **hat eingeschränkt**) **1** to restrict; **2** to cut back; **3 sich einschränken** to economize.

einschreiben ◇*verb* (IMPERF **schrieb sich ein**, PERF **hat sich eingeschrieben**) **1 sich einschreiben** to enrol (*at university*); **2 sich einschreiben** to put your name down.

Einschreiben *das* (PL *die* Einschreiben) registered letter, registered parcel; **per Einschreiben** registered.

einsehen ◇*verb* (PRES **sieht ein**, IMPERF **sah ein**, PERF **hat eingesehen**) **1** to realize; **2** to see; **das sehe ich nicht ein** I don't see why.

einseitig *adjective* one-sided.

einsenden ◇*verb* (IMPERF **sendete ein/sandte ein**, PERF **hat eingesendet/hat eingesandt**) to send in.

einsetzen *verb* (PERF **hat eingesetzt**) **1** to put in (*a missing part*) to insert; **2** to use; **während der Weltmeisterschaft wurden Sonderzüge eingesetzt** special trains were put on during the World Cup; **3** to stake (*money*); **4** to start (*of rain, snow*); **5 sich für jemanden einsetzen** to support somebody.

Einsicht *die* **1** insight; **2** sense; **3 zu der Einsicht kommen, dass** ... to come to realize that ....

einsperren *verb* (PERF **hat eingesperrt**) to lock up.

Einspruch *der* (PL *die* Einsprüche) objection.

einst *adverb* **1** once; **2** one day (*in the future*).

einstecken *verb* (PERF **hat eingesteckt**) **1** to put in (*a coin*); **2 einen Brief einstecken** to post a letter; **3** to plug in; **4 etwas einstecken** to put something in your pocket or bag, to take

a
b
c
d
e
f
g
h
i
j
k
l
m
n
o
p
q
r
s
t
u
v
w
x
y
z

something; **5** (*informal*) to take (*insults*).

einsteigen ⋄*verb* (IMPERF **stieg ein**, PERF **ist eingestiegen**) **1** to get in; **2** to get on (*a bus or train*).

einstellen *verb* (PERF **hat eingestellt**) **1** to employ (*in a job*); **2** to adjust (*a machine*); **3** to focus (*a camera*); **4** to tune into (*a radio station*); **5** to stop; **6 sich auf etwas einstellen** to prepare yourself for something; **7 sich schnell auf eine neue Situation einstellen** to adjust quickly to a new situation.

Einstellung *die* (PL *die* **Einstellungen**) **1** employment; **2** adjustment; **3** stopping; **4** take (*of a film*); **5** attitude; **seine politische Einstellung** his political views.

Einstieg *der* (PL *die* **Einstiege**) entrance.

einstürzen *verb* (PERF **ist eingestürzt**) to collapse.

einstweilen *adverb* **1** for the time being; **2** meanwhile.

eintausend *number* one thousand.

einteilen *verb* (PERF **hat eingeteilt**) **1** to divide up; **2 sich seine Zeit gut einteilen** to organize your time well.

Eintopf *der* (PL *die* **Eintöpfe**) stew.

Eintrag *der* (PL *die* **Einträge**) entry.

eintragen ⋄*verb* (PRES **trägt ein**, IMPERF **trug ein**, PERF **hat eingetragen**) **1** to enter, to write; **2 sich eintragen** to put your name down.

einträglich *adjective* profitable.

eintreffen ⋄*verb* (PRES **trifft ein**, IMPERF **traf ein**, PERF **ist eingetroffen**) **1** to arrive; **2** to come true.

eintreten ⋄*verb* (PRES **tritt ein**, IMPERF **trat ein**, PERF **ist eingetreten**) **1** to enter; **2 in einen Klub eintreten** to join a club; **3 für jemanden eintreten** to stand up for somebody.

Eintritt *der* **1** entrance; **2** admission; **'Eintritt frei'** 'admission free'.

Eintrittskarte *die* (PL *die* **Eintrittskarten**) (admission) ticket.

Eintrittspreis *der* (PL *die* **Eintrittspreise**) admission charge.

einverstanden *adjective* **1 einverstanden sein** to agree; **einverstanden!** okay!; **2 mit jemandem einverstanden sein** to approve of somebody.

Einwand *der* (PL *die* **Einwände**) objection.

Einwanderer *der* (PL *die* **Einwanderer**) immigrant.

Einwanderin *die* (PL *die* **Einwanderinnen**) immigrant.

einwandern *verb* (PERF **ist eingewandert**) to immigrate; **nach Europa einwandern** to immigrate into Europe.

Einwanderung *die* immigration.

einwärts *adverb* inwards.

einweichen *verb* (PERF **hat eingeweicht**) to soak (*washing*).

einwerfen ⋄*verb* (PRES **wirft ein**, IMPERF **warf ein**, PERF **hat**

Eisportionierer

eingeworfen) 1 to post; **2** to put in (*a coin, money*); **3** to throw in; **4** to smash.

Einwohner *der* (PL *die* **Einwohner**) inhabitant.

Einzahl *die* singular.

einzahlen *verb* (PERF **hat eingezahlt**) to pay in.

Einzel *das* (PL *die* **Einzel**) singles (*in sport*).

Einzelheit *die* (PL *die* **Einzelheiten**) detail.

Einzelkarte *die* (PL *die* **Einzelkarten**) single ticket.

Einzelkind *das* (PL *die* **Einzelkinder**) only child.

einzeln *adjective* **1** single; **2** individual; **3** odd (*sock, for example*).
einzeln *adverb* **1** individually; **2** separately, one at a time; **bitte einzeln eintreten** please enter one at a time.

Einzelne *der/die/das* (PL *die* **Einzelnen**) **1** *der/die* **Einzelne** the individual; **2 Einzelne** some; **3 ein Einzelner/eine Einzelne/ein Einzelnes** a single one; **jeder/jede/jedes Einzelne** every single one; **4 im Einzelnen** in detail; **ins Einzelne gehen** to go into detail.

Einzelzimmer *das* (PL *die* **Einzelzimmer**) single room.

einziehen ✧*verb* (IMPERF **zog ein**, PERF **hat eingezogen**) **1** to collect (*payment*); **2** to draw in (*its feelers, claws*); **3 den Kopf einziehen** to duck; **4** (PERF **ist eingezogen**) to move in; **wann zieht ihr in die neue Wohnung ein?** when are you moving into your new flat?; **5** (PERF **ist eingezogen**) to soak in.

einzig *adjective* only; **ein einziges Mal** only once.

Einzige *der/die/das* (PL *die* **Einzigen**) **1** *der/die/das* **Einzige** the only one; **2 ein Einziger/eine Einzige/ein Einziges** a single one; **kein Einziger/keine Einzige/kein Einziges** not a single one; **3 das Einzige, was mich stört** the only thing that bothers me.

Eis *das* **1** ice; **2** ice cream.

Eisbahn *die* (PL *die* **Eisbahnen**) skating rink.

Eisbär *der* (PL *die* **Eisbären**) polar bear.

Eisbecher *der* (PL *die* **Eisbecher**) ice-cream sundae.

Eisdiele *die* (PL *die* **Eisdielen**) ice-cream parlour.

Eisen *das* iron.

Eisenbahn *die* (PL *die* **Eisenbahnen**) railway.

eisern *adjective* iron.

Eishockey *das* ice hockey.

eisig *adjective* icy.

eiskalt *adjective* **1** ice-cold (*drink*); **2** freezing cold.

Eislaufen *das* ice-skating.

Eisläufer *der* (PL *die* **Eisläufer**) skater (*on ice*).

Eisläuferin *die* (PL *die* **Eisläuferinnen**) skater (*on ice*).

Eisportionierer *der* (PL *die* **Eisportionierer**) scoop.

a
b
c
d
e
f
g
h
i
j
k
l
m
n
o
p
q
r
s
t
u
v
w
x
y
z

Eiswürfel *der* (PL *die* **Eiswürfel**) ice cube.

Eiszapfen *der* (PL *die* **Eiszapfen**) icicle.

eitel *adjective* vain.

Eitelkeit *die* vanity.

Eiter *der* pus.

Eiweiß *das* **1** egg-white; **2** protein.

Ekel *der* disgust.

ekelhaft *adjective* disgusting.

ekeln *verb* (PERF **hat sich geekelt**) **sich vor etwas ekeln** to find something disgusting.

eklig *adjective* disgusting.

Ekzem *das* (PL *die* **Ekzeme**) eczema.

Elefant *der* (PL *die* **Elefanten**) elephant.

elegant *adjective* elegant, stylish.

Elektriker *der* (PL *die* **Elektriker**) electrician.

elektrisch *adjective* electrical.

Elektrizität *die* electricity.

Elektroherd *der* (PL *die* **Elektroherde**) electric cooker.

Elektronik *die* electronics.

elektronisch *adjective* electronic.

Elektrorasierer *der* (PL *die* **Elektrorasierer**) electric razor.

Elend *das* misery.

elend *adjective* **1** miserable; **2** terrible.

elf *number* eleven.

Elfe *die* (PL *die* **Elfen**) fairy.

Elfmeter *der* (PL *die* **Elfmeter**) penalty (*in soccer*).

Ellbogen *der* (PL *die* **Ellbogen**) elbow.

Eltern *plural noun* parents.

Email *das* (PL *die* **Emails**) enamel.

E-Mail *die* (PL *die* **E-Mails**) email.

empfahl SEE **empfehlen**.

Empfang *der* (PL *die* **Empfänge**) **1** reception; **2** receipt (*of goods or a letter*).

empfangen ◇*verb* (PRES **empfängt**, IMPERF **empfing**, PERF **hat empfangen**) to receive.

Empfängnisverhütung *die* contraception.

Empfangsdame *die* (PL *die* **Empfangsdamen**) receptionist.

empfehlen ◇*verb* (PRES **empfiehlt**, IMPERF **empfahl**, PERF **hat empfohlen**) to recommend.

empfindlich *adjective* **1** sensitive; **2** delicate; **3** touchy.

empfing SEE **empfangen**.

empfohlen SEE **empfehlen**.

empört *adjective* indignant.

Ende *das* (PL *die* **Enden**) **1** end; **Ende April** at the end of April; **am Ende der Straße** at the end of the road; **2 am Ende** in the end; **3** ending (*of a film, novel*); **4 zu Ende sein** to be finished, to be over; **5 Ende gut, alles gut** all's well that ends well.

enden *verb* (PERF **hat geendet**) to end.

endgültig *adjective* **1** final (*consent, decision*); **2** definite.

Endivie *die* (PL *die* **Endivien**) endive.

endlich *adverb* finally, at last; **na endlich!** at last!

endlos *adjective* endless.

Endspiel *das* (PL *die* **Endspiele**) final.

Endstation *die* (PL *die* **Endstationen**) terminus.

Endung *die* (PL *die* **Endungen**) ending.

Energie *die* energy.

energisch *adjective* energetic.

eng *adjective* **1** narrow; **2** tight; **3** close; **eng befreundet sein** to be close friends.

Engel *der* (PL *die* **Engel**) angel.

England *das* England; **aus England** from England.

Engländer *der* (PL *die* **Engländer**) Englishman.

Engländerin *die* (PL *die* **Engländerinnen**) Englishwoman.

englisch *adjective* English.

Englisch *das* English; **auf Englisch** in English.

Enkel *der* (PL *die* **Enkel**) grandson.

Enkelin *die* (PL *die* **Enkelinnen**) granddaughter.

Enkelkind *das* (PL *die* **Enkelkinder**) grandchild.

entdecken *verb* (PERF **hat entdeckt**) to discover.

Entdeckung *die* (PL *die* **Entdeckungen**) discovery.

Ente *die* (PL *die* **Enten**) duck.

entfernen *verb* (PERF **hat entfernt**) to remove.

entfernt *adjective* **1** distant; **2 zehn Kilometer entfernt** ten kilometres away.
entfernt *adverb* **entfernt verwandt sein** to be distantly related.

Entfernung *die* (PL *die* **Entfernungen**) distance.

entführen *verb* (PERF **hat entführt**) **1** to kidnap; **2** to hijack.

Entführer *der* (PL *die* **Entführer**) **1** hijacker; **2** kidnapper.

Entführerin *die* (PL *die* **Entführerinnen**) **1** hijacker; **2** kidnapper.

Entführung *die* (PL *die* **Entführungen**) **1** hijacking; **2** kidnapping.

entgegen *preposition* (+ DAT) contrary to.

entgegengesetzt *adjective* **1** opposite; **2** opposing (*views*).

entgegenkommen ✧*verb* (IMPERF **kam entgegen**, PERF **ist entgegengekommen**) **1** to come towards; **2 jemandem entgegenkommen** to come to meet somebody; **3 jemandem auf halbem Wege entgegenkommen** to meet somebody halfway; **4 jemandem freundlich entgegenkommen** to be accommodating towards somebody.

entgegenkommend *adjective* **1** obliging; **2 der entgegenkommende Verkehr** the oncoming traffic.

Entgelt *das* payment.

Enthaarungsmittel *das* (PL *die* Enthaarungsmittel) hair remover, depilatory.

enthalten ⋄*verb* (PRES **enthält**, IMPERF **enthielt**, PERF **hat enthalten**) **1** to contain; **2 sich einer Sache enthalten** to abstain from something; **sich der Stimme enthalten** to abstain; **3** (PERF **ist enthalten**) **in etwas enthalten sein** to be included in something; **im Preis enthalten** included in the price.

entkommen ⋄*verb* (IMPERF **entkam**, PERF **ist entkommen**) to escape.

entlang *preposition* (+ ACC *or* + DAT) along; **die Straße entlang** along the road; **am Fluss entlang** along the river.

entlanggehen ⋄*verb* (IMPERF **ging entlang**, PERF **ist entlanggegangen**) to walk along.

entlanglaufen ⋄*verb* (PRES **läuft entlang**, IMPERF **lief entlang**, PERF **ist entlanggelaufen**) to run along.

entlassen ⋄*verb* (PRES **entlässt**, IMPERF **entließ**, PERF **hat entlassen**) **1** to dismiss (*from a job*); **2** to discharge (*from hospital*); **3** to release (*from prison*).

Entlassung *die* (PL *die* Entlassungen) **1** dismissal; **2** discharge; **3** release.

entmutigen *verb* (PERF **hat entmutigt**) to discourage.

entschädigen *verb* (PERF **hat entschädigt**) to compensate.

Entschädigung *die* compensation.

entscheiden ⋄*verb* (IMPERF **entschied**, PERF **hat entschieden**) **1** to decide (on); **2 sich entscheiden** to decide.

entscheidend *adjective* decisive, crucial.

Entscheidung *die* (PL *die* Entscheidungen) decision.

Entschiedenheit *die* decisiveness.

entschließen ⋄*verb* (IMPERF **entschloss sich**, PERF **hat sich entschlossen**) **1 sich entschließen** to decide; **2 sich anders entschließen** to change your mind; **Karl hat sich anders entschlossen** Karl has changed his mind.

entschlossen *adjective* determined.

Entschluss *der* (PL *die* Entschlüsse) decision.

entschuldigen *verb* (PERF **hat entschuldigt**) **1** to excuse; **entschuldigen Sie bitte** excuse me; **2 sich entschuldigen** to apologize; **ich habe mich bei Michi entschuldigt** I apologized to Michi.

Entschuldigung *die* (PL *die* Entschuldigungen) **1** apology; **2 jemanden um Entschuldigung bitten** to apologize to somebody; **3 Entschuldigung!** sorry!; **4 Entschuldigung** (*with a question or request*) excuse me; **Entschuldigung, können Sie mir sagen, wie ich zum Bahnhof**

a b c d e f g h i j k l m n o p q r s t u v w x y z

komme? excuse me, could you tell me the way to the station?; **5** excuse.

Entsetzen das horror.

entsetzlich adjective **1** horrible; **2** terrible.

entsetzt adjective horrified.

entspannen verb (PERF hat sich entspannt) **1** sich entspannen to relax; **2** sich entspannen to ease (of a situation).

entspannend adjective relaxing.

entsprechen ◇verb (PRES entspricht, IMPERF entsprach, PERF hat entsprochen) **1** den Anforderungen entsprechen to meet the requirements; **2** einer Sache entsprechen to correspond to something; **3** to agree with (the truth, a description); **4** to comply with (certain standards).

entsprechend adjective **1** corresponding; **2** appropriate.
entsprechend preposition (+ DAT) in accordance with.

entstehen ◇verb (IMPERF entstand, PERF ist entstanden) **1** to develop; **2** to result (of damage).

enttäuschen verb (PERF hat enttäuscht) to disappoint.

Enttäuschung die (PL die Enttäuschungen) disappointment.

entweder conjunction either; **entweder heute oder morgen** either today or tomorrow.

entwerten verb (PERF hat entwertet) **1** to devalue; **2** to punch (a ticket in a machine found on trains, trams, buses, and on the platform; you have to punch your ticket before each journey).

Entwerter der (PL die Entwerter) ticket-punching machine (these machines are found on trains, trams, buses, and on the platform; you have to punch your ticket before each journey).

entwickeln verb (PERF hat entwickelt) **1** to develop; **2** to display (ability, a characteristic); **3** sich entwickeln to develop.

Entwicklung die (PL die Entwicklungen) **1** development; **2** developing.

Entwicklungsland das (PL die Entwicklungsländer) developing country.

Entwurf der (PL die Entwürfe) **1** design; **2** draft.

entzückend adjective delightful.

entzünden verb (PERF hat entzündet) **1** to light (a fire, match); **2** sich entzünden to become inflamed; **3** sich entzünden to ignite.

Entzündung die (PL die Entzündungen) inflammation.

Enzian der (PL die Enziane) gentian.

Epidemie die (PL die Epidemien) epidemic.

er pronoun **1** he; **2** it; **'wo ist mein Mantel?' – 'er liegt auf dem Stuhl'** 'where's my coat?' – 'it's on the chair'; **3** him (stressed); **er war es** it was him.

erben verb (PERF hat geerbt) to inherit.

a b c d e f g h i j k l m n o p q r s t u v w x y z

83

erblich *adjective* hereditary.

Erbschaft die (PL die **Erbschaften**) inheritance.

Erbse die (PL die **Erbsen**) pea.

Erdbeben das (PL die **Erdbeben**) earthquake.

Erdbeere die (PL die **Erdbeeren**) strawberry.

erbrechen *verb* (PRES **erbricht**, IMPERF **erbrach**, PERF **hat erbrochen**) 1 to brng up (*food*); 2 **sich erbrechen** to be sick.

Erde die 1 earth, soil; 2 ground; **auf der Erde** on the ground; 3 Earth; 4 earth (*for electricity*).

Erdgeschoss das (PL die **Erdgeschosse**) ground floor; **im Erdgeschoss** on the ground floor.

Erdkunde die geography.

Erdnuss die (PL die **Erdnüsse**) peanut.

ereignen *verb* (PERF **hat sich ereignet**) **sich ereignen** to happen.

Ereignis das (PL die **Ereignisse**) event.

erfahren ◇*verb* (PRES **erfährt**, IMPERF **erfuhr**, PERF **hat erfahren**) 1 to hear, to learn; 2 to experience. **erfahren** *adjective* experienced.

Erfahrung die (PL die **Erfahrungen**) experience.

erfinden ◇*verb* (IMPERF **erfand**, PERF **hat erfunden**) to invent.

Erfindung die (PL die **Erfindungen**) invention.

Erfolg der (PL die **Erfolge**) 1 success; **Erfolg haben** to be successful;

2 **Erfolg versprechend** promising; 3 **viel Erfolg!** good luck!

erfolglos *adjective* unsuccessful.

erfolgreich *adjective* successful.

erfolgversprechend SEE **Erfolg**.

erforderlich *adjective* necessary.

erforschen *verb* (PERF **hat erforscht**) 1 to explore; 2 to investigate.

erfreulicherweise *adverb* happily.

erfreut *adjective* pleased.

Erfrischung die (PL die **Erfrischungen**) refreshment.

Erfrischungsgetränk das (PL die **Erfrischungsgetränke**) soft drink.

erfüllen *verb* (PERF **hat erfüllt**) to fulfil; **sich erfüllen** to come true.

Ergebnis das (PL die **Ergebnisse**) result.

ergreifen ◇*verb* (IMPERF **ergriff**, PERF **hat ergriffen**) 1 to seize, to grab; 2 to take (*measures, an opportunity*); 3 to take up (*a job, career*); 4 to move; **die Nachricht von ihrem Tod hat uns tief ergriffen** the news of her death moved us deeply; 5 **die Flucht ergreifen** to flee.

ergreifend *adjective* moving.

erhalten ◇*verb* (PRES **erhält**, IMPERF **erhielt**, PERF **hat erhalten**) 1 to receive; 2 to preserve.

erhältlich *adjective* obtainable.

Erhaltung die 1 preservation; 2 conservation; 3 maintenance.

erheben ◇*verb* (IMPERF **erhob**, PERF **hat erhoben**) **1** to raise; **2** to charge (*a fee*); **3 Protest erheben** to protest; **4 sich erheben** to rise up (*in a rebellion*).

erheblich *adjective* considerable.

erheitern *verb* (PERF **hat erheitert**) to amuse.

erhitzen *verb* (PERF **hat erhitzt**) to heat.

erhöhen *verb* (PERF **hat erhöht**) **1** to increase; **2 sich erhöhen** to rise.

Erhöhung *die* (PL *die* **Erhöhungen**) increase.

erholen *verb* (PERF **hat sich erholt**) **1 sich erholen** to have a rest; **ich habe mich in den Ferien gut erholt** I had a good rest on holiday; **2 sich von einer Krankheit erholen** to recover from an illness.

erholsam *adjective* restful.

Erholung *die* rest; **Iris ist zur Erholung in die Berge gefahren** Iris went to the mountains for a rest.

erinnern *verb* (PERF **hat erinnert**) **1** to remind; **2 sich erinnern** to remember.

Erinnerung *die* (PL *die* **Erinnerungen**) **1** memory; **2** souvenir.

erkälten *verb* (PERF **hat sich erkältet**) **1 sich erkälten** to catch a cold; **2 erkältet sein** to have a cold; **Ben ist erkältet** Ben has a cold.

Erkältung *die* (PL *die* **Erkältungen**) cold.

erkennbar *adjective* recognizable.

erkennen ◇*verb* (IMPERF **erkannte**, PERF **hat erkannt**) **1** to recognize; **2** to realize.

erklären *verb* (PERF **hat erklärt**) **1** to explain; **2** to declare; **3 sich zu etwas bereit erklären** to agree to something.

Erklärung *die* (PL *die* **Erklärungen**) **1** explanation; **2** declaration; **3 eine öffentliche Erklärung** a public statement.

erkundigen *verb* (PERF **hat sich erkundigt**) **1 sich erkundigen** to enquire; **ich werde mich nach den Zügen erkundigen** I'm going to enquire about the trains; **2** to ask about; **Susi hat sich nach dir erkundigt** Susi was asking about you.

Erkundigung *die* (PL *die* **Erkundigungen**) enquiry.

erlauben *verb* (PERF **hat erlaubt**) **1** to allow; **jemandem etwas erlauben** to allow somebody to do something; **2 sich etwas erlauben** to allow yourself something; **3 sich alles erlauben** to do as you please; **4 erlauben Sie mal!** (*informal*) do you mind!

Erlaubnis *die* permission.

erleben *verb* (PERF **hat erlebt**) **1** to experience; **2** to have (*a disappointment, an experience*); **eine Überraschung erleben** to have a surprise; **3 er hat die Geburt seines Enkels nicht mehr erlebt** he didn't live to see the birth of his grandson.

Erlebnis *das* (PL *die* **Erlebnisse**) experience.

a
b
c
d
e
f
g
h
i
j
k
l
m
n
o
p
q
r
s
t
u
v
w
x
y
z

erledigen *verb* (PERF **hat erledigt**)
to deal with, to do.

erledigt *adjective* **1** settled;
2 (*informal*) worn out.

Erleichterung *die* relief.

erleiden ⬦*verb* (IMPERF **erlitt**, PERF
hat erlitten) to suffer.

Erlös *der* (PL *die* **Erlöse**) proceeds.

erloschen *adjective* **1** out,
extinguished; **2** extinct.

ermäßigen *verb* (PERF **hat**
ermäßigt) to reduce.

Ermäßigung *die* (PL *die*
Ermäßigungen) reduction.

ermorden *verb* (PERF **hat**
ermordet) to murder.

ermutigen *verb* (PERF **hat**
ermutigt) to encourage.

ernähren *verb* (PERF **hat ernährt**)
1 to feed; **2 sich von Nudeln**
ernähren to live on pasta; **3** to
support (*a family*).

Ernährung *die* **1** diet; **eine**
gesunde Ernährung a healthy diet;
2 nutrition.

erneuern *verb* (PERF **hat erneuert**)
to renew.

erneut *adjective* renewed.
erneut *adverb* once again.

Ernst *der* **1** seriousness; **2 im Ernst**
seriously; **3 ist das dein Ernst?** are
you serious?

ernst *adjective* serious.

ernsthaft *adjective* serious.

ernstlich *adjective* serious.

Ernte *die* (PL *die* **Ernten**) harvest; **die**
Ernte einbringen to gather in the
harvest.

ernten *verb* (PERF **hat geerntet**) to
harvest.

erobern *verb* (PERF **hat erobert**) to
conquer.

Eroberung *die* (PL *die*
Eroberungen) conquest.

eröffnen (PERF **hat eröffnet**) to
open.

Eröffnung *die* (PL *die* **Eröffnungen**)
opening.

erraten ⬦*verb* (PRES **errät**, IMPERF
erriet, PERF **hat erraten**) to guess.

erregen *verb* (PERF **hat erregt**) **1** to
arouse; **2** to cause; **sie erregte viel**
Aufsehen she caused a sensation.

Erreger *der* (PL *die* **Erreger**) germ.

Erregung *die* excitement.

erreichen *verb* (PERF **hat erreicht**)
1 to reach; **2 den Zug erreichen** to
catch the train; **3** to achieve (*a goal,
aim*); **4 Irene ist telefonisch zu**
erreichen Irene can be contacted by
phone.

erröten *verb* (PERF **ist errötet**) to
blush.

Ersatz *der* replacement, substitute.

Ersatzmann *der* (PL *die*
Ersatzmänner) substitute (*in sport*).

Ersatzmittel *das* (PL *die*
Ersatzmittel) substitute (*material,
ingredient*).

Ersatzreifen *der* (PL *die*
Ersatzreifen) spare tyre.

Ersatzteil *das* (PL *die* **Ersatzteile**)
spare part.

erschaffen *verb* (IMPERF **erschuf**, PERF **erschaffen**) to create.

erscheinen ◇*verb* (IMPERF **erschien**, PERF **ist erschienen**) to appear.

erschöpft *adjective* exhausted.

erschrecken *verb* **1** (PERF **hat erschreckt**) to scare; **2** (◇PRES **erschrickt**, IMPERF **erschrak**, PERF **ist erschrocken**) to get a fright.

erschreckend *adjective* alarming.

erschrocken *adjective* **1** frightened; **2** startled.

ersetzen *verb* (PERF **hat ersetzt**) to replace; **jemandem einen Schaden ersetzen** to compensate somebody for damages.

Ersparnisse *plural noun* savings.

erst *adverb* **1** first; **erst einmal** first of all; **2** only; **eben erst** only just; **3** not until; **erst nächste Woche** not until next week; **Oma war erst zufrieden, als die ganze Familie da war** granny was not happy until all the family were there.

erstatten *verb* (PERF **hat erstattet**) to reimburse.

Erstattung *die* (PL *die* **Erstattungen**) reimbursement.

erstaunen *verb* (PERF **hat erstaunt**) to astonish.

erstaunlich *adjective* astonishing.

erstaunt *adjective* amazed; **über etwas erstaunt sein** to be amazed about something.

Erste *der/die/das* (PL *die* **Ersten**) **1** **der/die Erste** the first (one); **das Erste** the first (thing); **2** **Dirk kam als Erster** Dirk arrived first; **Marianne ging als Erste** Marianne left first; **3** **als Erster/Erste etwas tun** to be the first to do something; **4** **als Erstes** first of all; **5** **fürs Erste** for the time being.

erstens *adverb* firstly.

erster, **erste**, **erstes** *adjective* first; **mein erstes Rad war rot** my first bike was red; **der erste April** the first of April; **erste Hilfe** first aid.

erstklassig *adjective* first-class.

erstmals *adverb* for the first time.

erteilen *verb* (PERF **hat erteilt**) to give (*advice, information*).

ertragen ◇*verb* (PRES **erträgt**, IMPERF **ertrug**, PERF **hat ertragen**) to bear.

ertrinken ◇*verb* (IMPERF **ertrank**, PERF **ist ertrunken**) to drown; **sie ertrank im See** she drowned in the lake.

erwachsen *adjective* grown-up.

Erwachsene *der/die* (PL *die* **Erwachsenen**) adult, grown-up.

Erwachsenenbildung *die* adult education.

erwähnen *verb* (PERF **hat erwähnt**) to mention.

erwarten *verb* (PERF **hat erwartet**) to expect.

Erwartung *die* (PL *die* **Erwartungen**) expectation.

a
b
c
d
e
f
g
h
i
j
k
l
m
n
o
p
q
r
s
t
u
v
w
x
y
z

erwürgen *verb* (PERF **hat erwürgt**) to strangle.

erzählen *verb* (PERF **hat erzählt**) to tell.

Erzählung *die* (PL *die* **Erzählungen**) story.

Erzeugnis *das* (PL *die* **Erzeugnisse**) product.

erziehen ⬦*verb* (IMPERF **erzog**, PERF **hat erzogen**) **1** to bring up; **2** to educate.

Erzieher *der* (PL *die* **Erzieher**) teacher.

Erzieherin *die* (PL *die* **Erzieherinnen**) teacher.

Erziehung *die* **1** upbringing; **2** education.

es *pronoun* **1** it; **es regnet** it is raining; **2 es gibt** there is, there are; **3 'wo ist das Baby?' – 'es schläft'** 'where's the baby?' – 'he's/she's asleep'.

Esel *der* (PL *die* **Esel**) donkey.

essbar *adjective* edible.

essen ⬦*verb* (PRES **isst**, IMPERF **aß**, PERF **hat gegessen**) to eat; **iss keine Bonbons** don't eat sweets.

Essen *das* **1** meal; **2** food.

Essig *der* vinegar.

Essiggurke *die* (PL *die* **Essiggurken**) gherkin.

Esskastanie *die* (PL *die* **Esskastanien**) sweet chestnut.

Esszimmer *das* (PL *die* **Esszimmer**) dining room.

Etage *die* (PL *die* **Etagen**) floor; **in der zweiten Etage** on the second floor.

Etagenbett *das* (PL *die* **Etagenbetten**) bunk beds.

ethnisch *adjective* ethnic.

Etikett *das* (PL *die* **Etikette(n)**) label.

Etui *das* (PL *die* **Etuis**) case.

etwa *adverb* **1** about; **er ist etwa so groß wie du** he's about as tall as you; **2** for example; **3 nicht etwa, dass** ... not that ...; **4 hat Klaus etwa Angst gehabt?** Klaus wasn't scared, was he?

etwas *pronoun, adverb* **1** something; **2** anything; **sonst noch etwas?** anything else?; **3** some; **etwas von dem Geld** some of the money; **noch etwas Kaffee?** (some) more coffee?; **4** a little; **nur etwas Zucker** only a little sugar; **etwas lauter singen** to sing a little louder.

EU *die* (*Europäische Union*) EU.

euch *pronoun* **1** you; **ich habe euch eingeladen** I've invited you; **2** to you; **Eva hat es euch geschenkt** Eva gave it to you; **3** (*reflexive*) yourselves.

euer *adjective* your.

Eule *die* (PL *die* **Eulen**) owl.

eurer, eure, eures *pronoun* yours.

Euro *der* (PL *die* **Euros**) euro; **ein Euro hat hundert Cent** the euro is divided into a hundred cents; **es kostet 3 Euro** it costs 3 euros.

Eurocent *der* (PL *die* **Eurocents**) cent; **50 Eurocent** 50 cents.

Euroland *das* eurozone.

Europa *das* Europe.

Europäer *der* (PL *die* Europäer)
European.

Europäerin *die* (PL *die*
Europäerinnen) European.

europäisch *adjective* European.

Eurostar *der* Eurostar; **mit dem
Eurostar fahren** to go by Eurostar.

Eurostück *das* (PL *die* Eurostücke)
one-euro coin.

evangelisch *adjective* Protestant.

eventuell *adjective* possible.
eventuell *adverb* possibly.

ewig *adjective* eternal.
ewig *adverb* forever.

Ewigkeit *die* eternity.

Examen *das* (PL *die* Examen)
examination, exam.

Exemplar *das* (PL *die* Exemplare)
1 copy; **2** specimen.

existieren *verb* (PERF **hat
existiert**) to exist.

Expedition *die* (PL *die*
Expeditionen) expedition.

explodieren *verb* (PERF **ist
explodiert**) to explode.

Explosion *die* (PL *die* Explosionen)
explosion.

Export *der* (PL *die* Exporte) export.

exportieren *verb* (PERF **hat
exportiert**) to export; **Russland
exportiert viel Öl und Holz** Russia
exports a lot of oil and timber.

extra *adverb* **1** separately; **2** extra;
3 specially; **4** (*informal*) on
purpose.

extrem *adjective* extreme.

Ff

fabelhaft *adjective* fabulous,
fantastic.

Fabrik *die* (PL *die* Fabriken) factory.

Fach *das* (PL *die* Fächer)
1 compartment; **2** drawer; **3** subject
(*at school*).

Facharzt *der* (PL *die* Fachärzte)
specialist.

Fachärztin *die* (PL *die*
Fachärztinnen) specialist.

Fachfrau *die* (PL *die* Fachfrauen)
expert.

Fachmann *der* (PL *die* Fachleute)
expert.

fade *adjective* tasteless.

Faden *der* (PL *die* Fäden) thread.

fähig *adjective* **1** capable; **2** able.

Fähigkeit *die* (PL *die* Fähigkeiten)
ability.

Fahne *die* (PL *die* Fahnen) flag.

Fahrausweis *der* (PL *die*
Fahrausweise) ticket.

Fahrbahn *die* (PL *die* Fahrbahnen)
1 carriageway; **2** road.

Fähre *die* (PL *die* Fähren) ferry.

fahren ◇*verb* (PRES **fährt**, IMPERF
fuhr, PERF **ist gefahren**) **1** to go; **mit
dem Zug nach Wien fahren** to go to
Vienna by train; **ich bin mit dem
Auto gefahren** I went by car; ; **2** to
drive; **Hanna ist sehr schnell
gefahren** Hanna drove very fast;
3 to ride (*of a cyclist*); **4** to run (*of a
train, bus*); **der Zug fährt nicht an
Sonn- und Feiertagen** the train

doesn't run on Sundays and public holidays; **5** to leave; **wann fahrt ihr?** when are you leaving?; **6 was ist in sie gefahren?** (*informal*) what's got into her?; **7** (PERF **hat gefahren**) to drive; **er hat Doris nach Hause gefahren** he drove Doris home; **ich habe das Auto in die Garage gefahren** I drove the car into the garage.

Fahrer der (PL die **Fahrer**) driver.

Fahrerflucht die hit-and-run driving; **Fahrerflucht begehen** to be involved in a hit-and-run.

Fahrerin die (PL die **Fahrerinnen**) driver.

Fahrgast der (PL die **Fahrgäste**) passenger.

Fahrkarte die (PL die **Fahrkarten**) ticket.

Fahrkartenausgabe die ticket office.

Fahrkartenautomat der (PL die **Fahrkartenautomaten**) ticket machine.

Fahrkartenschalter der (PL die **Fahrkartenschalter**) ticket office.

fahrlässig *adjective* negligent.

Fahrlehrer der (PL die **Fahrlehrer**) driving instructor.

Fahrplan der (PL die **Fahrpläne**) timetable.

Fahrpreis der (PL die **Fahrpreise**) fare.

Fahrprüfung die (PL die **Fahrprüfungen**) driving test; **die Fahrprüfung machen** to take your driving test.

Fahrrad das (PL die **Fahrräder**) bicycle.

Fahrradfahrer der (PL die **Fahrradfahrer**) cyclist.

Fahrradfahrerin die (PL die **Fahrradfahrerinnen**) cyclist.

Fahrradweg der (PL die **Fahrradwege**) cycle lane.

Fahrschein der (PL die **Fahrscheine**) ticket.

Fahrschule die (PL die **Fahrschulen**) driving school.

Fahrstuhl der (PL die **Fahrstühle**) lift.

Fahrt die (PL die **Fahrten**) **1** journey; **gute Fahrt!** have a good journey!; **2** trip; **3** drive; **4 in voller Fahrt** at full speed.

Fahrzeug das (PL die **Fahrzeuge**) vehicle.

fair *adjective* fair.

Faktor der (PL die **Faktoren**) factor.

Falke der (PL die **Falken**) falcon.

Fall der (PL die **Fälle**) **1** case; **in diesem Fall** in this case; **auf alle Fälle, auf jeden Fall** in any case; **für alle Fälle** just in case; **2 auf jeden Fall** definitely; **3 auf keinen Fall** on no account; **4** fall.

Falle die (PL die **Fallen**) trap.

fallen ⬦*verb* (PRES **fällt**, IMPERF **fiel**, PERF **ist gefallen**) **1** to fall; **2 etwas fallen lassen** to drop something; **wir haben den Plan fallen lassen** we've dropped the idea; **3 eine Bemerkung fallen lassen** to make a comment.

fällen *verb* (PERF **hat gefällt**) to fell, to cut down (*trees*).

fallenlassen SEE **fallen**.

fällig *adjective* due.

falls *conjunction* **1** if; **2** in case.

Fallschirm *der* (PL *die* **Fallschirme**) parachute.

falsch *adjective* **1** wrong; **du hast ihn falsch verstanden** you got him wrong; **2** false (*teeth, etc.*); **3** forged.

fälschen *verb* (PERF **hat gefälscht**) to forge.

Fälschung *die* (PL *die* **Fälschungen**) **1** fake; **2** forgery.

Falte *die* (PL *die* **Falten**) **1** fold; **2** crease; **3** pleat; **4** wrinkle.

falten *verb* (PERF **hat gefaltet**) to fold.

faltig *adjective* **1** wrinkled; **2** creased.

familiär *adjective* familiar.

Familie *die* (PL *die* **Familien**) family.

Familienname *der* (PL *die* **Familiennamen**) surname.

Fan *der* (PL *die* **Fans**) fan.

fand SEE **finden**.

Fantasie *die* **1** imagination; **2 Fantasien** (*plural*) fantasies.

fantasievoll *adjective* imaginative.

fangen ◇*verb* (PRES **fängt**, IMPERF **fing**, PERF **hat gefangen**) to catch.

Fantasie *die* **1** imagination; **2 Fantasien** (*plural*) fantasies.

fantasievoll *adjective* imaginative.

fantastisch *adjective* fantastic.

Farbe *die* (PL *die* **Farben**) **1** colour; **2** paint; **3** dye; **4** suit (*in playing cards*).

farbecht *adjective* colour fast.

färben *verb* (PERF **hat gefärbt**) **1** to dye; **2 sich die Haare färben** to dye your hair; **3 das Sweatshirt färbt** this sweatshirt runs.

farbenblind *adjective* colour blind.

Farbfernsehen *das* colour television.

Farbfilm *der* (PL *die* **Farbfilme**) colour film.

farbig *adjective* coloured.

farblos *adjective* colourless.

Farbstift *der* (PL *die* **Farbstifte**) coloured pencil.

Farbstoff *der* (PL *die* **Farbstoffe**) **1** dye; **2** colouring (*for food*).

Farbton *der* (PL *die* **Farbtöne**) shade.

Fasan *der* (PL *die* **Fasane**) pheasant.

Fasching *der* (PL *die* **Faschinge**) carnival.

Faser *die* (PL *die* **Fasern**) fibre.

Fass *das* (PL *die* **Fässer**) barrel; **Bier vom Fass** draught beer.

fassen *verb* (PERF **hat gefasst**) **1** to grasp; **2 einen Dieb fassen** to catch a thief; **3** to hold (*of a container*); **4** to understand; **5 nicht zu fassen** unbelievable; **6 sich fassen** to compose yourself; **7 einen Entschluss fassen** to make a decision; **8 sich kurz fassen** to be brief.

Fassung *die* (PL *die* **Fassungen**) **1** version; **2** composure;

a
b
c
d
e
f
g
h
i
j
k
l
m
n
o
p
q
r
s
t
u
v
w
x
y
z

a
b
c
d
e
f
g
h
i
j
k
l
m
n
o
p
q
r
s
t
u
v
w
x
y
z

3 jemanden aus der Fassung bringen to throw somebody, to upset somebody; **4** setting (*for gems*).

fassungslos *adjective* speechless.

Fastfood *das* fast food.

fast *adverb* **1** almost; **2 fast nie** hardly ever.

Fastenzeit *die* (PL *die* **Fastenzeiten**) Lent.

Fastnacht *die* carnival.

faul *adjective* **1** lazy; **2** rotten; **3 eine faule Ausrede** a lame excuse; **4 an der Sache ist etwas faul** (*informal*) there's something fishy about it.

faulen *verb* (PERF **ist gefault**) to rot.

faulenzen *verb* (PERF **hat gefaulenzt**) to laze about.

Faust *die* (PL *die* **Fäuste**) **1** fist; **2 auf eigene Faust** off your own bat.

Fax *das* (PL *die* **Fax(e)**) fax.

faxen *verb* (PERF **hat gefaxt**) to fax; **ich faxe Ihnen die Liste** I'll fax you the list.

Februar *der* February.

fechten ◇*verb* (PRES **ficht**, IMPERF **focht**, PERF **hat gefochten**) to fence.

Feder *die* (PL *die* **Federn**) **1** feather; **2** spring; **3** nib (*of a pen*).

Federball *der* (PL *die* **Federbälle**) **1** badminton; **2** shuttlecock.

Federhalter *der* (PL *die* **Federhalter**) fountain pen.

Federmäppchen *das* (PL *die* **Federmäppchen**) pencil case.

Fee *die* (PL *die* **Feen**) fairy.

fegen *verb* (PERF **hat gefegt**) to sweep.

fehl *adjective* **fehl am Platz** out of place.

fehlen *verb* (PERF **hat gefehlt**) **1** to be missing; **2** to be lacking; **3** to be absent (*from school*); **4 mir fehlt die Zeit** I haven't got the time; **es fehlt ihnen einfach das Geld für ein neues Auto** they simply haven't got the money for a new car; **5 was fehlt dir?** what's the matter?; **6 Rudi fehlt mir** I miss Rudi.

Fehler *der* (PL *die* **Fehler**) **1** mistake; **2** fault.

Feier *die* (PL *die* **Feiern**) **1** party; **2** celebration.

Feierabend *der* (PL *die* **Feierabende**) **1** finishing time; **2 nach Feierabend** after work.

Feierlichkeiten *plural noun* festivities.

feiern *verb* (PERF **hat gefeiert**) to celebrate.

Feiertag *der* (PL *die* **Feiertage**) **1** holiday; **ein gesetzlicher Feiertag** a public holiday; **2 am ersten Feiertag** on Christmas Day; **der zweite Feiertag** Boxing Day.

Feige *die* (PL *die* **Feigen**) fig.

feige *adjective* cowardly; **du bist feige** you're a coward.

Feigenbaum *der* (PL *die* **Feigenbäume**) fig tree.

Feigling *der* (PL *die* **Feiglinge**) coward.

Feile *die* (PL *die* **Feilen**) file.

fein *adjective* **1** fine; **2** delicate; **3** refined; **4 sich fein machen** to dress up.

Feind *der* (PL *die* **Feinde**) enemy.

feindlich *adjective* hostile.

Feld *das* (PL *die* **Felder**) **1** field; **2** pitch; **3** box (*on a form*); **4** square (*on a board game*).

Fell *das* (PL *die* **Felle**) fur, skin.

Fels *der* rock.

Felsen *der* (PL *die* **Felsen**) cliff.

feminin *adjective* feminine.

Feminist *der* (PL *die* **Feministen**) feminist.

Feministin *die* (PL *die* **Feministinnen**) feminist.

Fenster *das* (PL *die* **Fenster**) window.

Fensterladen *der* (PL *die* **Fensterläden**) shutter.

Ferien *plural noun* holidays; **Ferien haben** to be on holiday.

Ferienhaus *das* (PL *die* **Ferienhäuser**) holiday home.

fern *adjective* **1** distant; **2 sich fern halten** to keep away; **jemanden von etwas fern halten** to keep somebody away from something. **fern** *adverb* far away.

Fernbedienung *die* remote control.

Ferngespräch *das* (PL *die* **Ferngespräche**) long-distance call.

ferngesteuert *adjective* remote-controlled.

Fernglas *das* (PL *die* **Ferngläser**) binoculars.

fernhalten SEE **fern**.

Fernost *das* Far East.

Fernrohr *das* (PL *die* **Fernrohre**) telescope.

Fernsehapparat *der* (PL *die* **Fernsehapparate**) television set.

fernsehen ⬦*verb* (PRES **sieht fern**, IMPERF **sah fern**, PERF **hat ferngesehen**) to watch television.

Fernsehen *das* television; **im Fernsehen** on television.

Fernseher *der* (PL *die* **Fernseher**) television (set).

Fernsehsendung *die* (PL *die* **Fernsehsendungen**) television programme.

Fernsehturm *der* (PL *die* **Fernsehtürme**) television tower.

Fernsprecher *der* (PL *die* **Fernsprecher**) telephone.

Ferse *die* (PL *die* **Fersen**) heel.

fertig *adjective* **1** finished; **mit den Hausaufgaben fertig werden** to finish your homework; **fertig sein** to be finished; **2 mit jemandem fertig sein** (*informal*) to be through with somebody; **3 völlig fertig sein** to be completely worn out; **4 mit etwas fertig werden** to cope with something (*problems, for example*); **5** ready; **das Essen ist fertig** food's ready; **6 etwas fertig machen** (*prepare*) to get something ready; (*complete*) to finish something; **sich fertig machen** to get ready; **7 jemanden fertig machen** to wear somebody out, to wear somebody down; **der ständige Stress macht mich fertig** this constant stress is

a
b
c
d
e
f
g
h
i
j
k
l
m
n
o
p
q
r
s
t
u
v
w
x
y
z

wearing me down; **8 es fertig bringen, etwas zu tun** to bring yourself to do something; **ich bringe es einfach nicht fertig** I just can't bring myself to do it.
fertig *adverb* **fertig essen** to finish eating.

fertigbringen SEE **fertig**.

Fertiggericht *das* (PL *die* Fertiggerichte) ready-to-serve meal.

fertigmachen SEE **fertig**.

Fest *das* (PL *die* Feste) **1** party; **2** celebration; **3** festival.

fest *adjective* **1** firm; **2** fixed (*salary, address*); **3** solid; **feste Nahrung** solids; **4 fest werden** to harden.
fest *adverb* **1 fest schlafen** to be fast asleep; **2 fest befreundet sein** to be close friends; **3 fest angestellt sein** to be in permanent employment.

festbinden ⬦*verb* (IMPERF **band fest**, PERF **hat festgebunden**) to tie (up).

festhalten ⬦*verb* (PRES **hält fest**, IMPERF **hielt fest**, PERF **hat festgehalten**) **1** to hold on to; **2 sich festhalten** to hold on; **halt dich an mir fest** hold on to me.

Festigkeit *die* strength.

festlegen *verb* (PERF **hat festgelegt**) **1** to fix; **2 sich auf etwas festlegen** to commit yourself to something.

Festlegung *die* (PL *die* Festlegungen) establishment.

festlich *adjective* festive.

festmachen *verb* (PERF **hat festgemacht**) **1** to fix; **ich mache gleich einen Termin fest** I'll fix a date straight away; **2** to fasten.

Festnahme *die* (PL *die* Festnahmen) arrest.

festnehmen ⬦*verb* (PRES **nimmt fest**, IMPERF **nahm fest**, PERF **hat festgenommen**) to arrest.

Festplatte *die* (PL *die* Festplatten) hard disk.

feststehen ⬦*verb* (IMPERF **stand fest**, PERF **hat festgestanden**) to be certain; **eins steht fest, Daniel lade ich nicht mehr ein** one thing's certain, I'm not going to invite Daniel again.

feststellen *verb* (PERF **hat festgestellt**) **1** to establish; **2** to notice.

Fete *die* (PL *die* Feten) party.

Fett *das* (PL *die* Fette) **1** fat; **2** grease.

fett *adjective* **1** fat (*person*); **2** greasy, fatty (*food*); **3** bold (*type*).

fettarm *adjective* low-fat; **fettarme Milch** skimmed milk.

fettig *adjective* greasy.

Fetzen *der* (PL *die* Fetzen) **1** scrap; **2** rag.

feucht *adjective* **1** damp; **2** humid.

Feuchtigkeit *die* **1** moisture; **2** humidity.

Feuer *das* **1** fire; **2 hast du Feuer?** have you got a light?

Feuerlöscher *der* (PL *die* Feuerlöscher) fire extinguisher.

Feuermelder *der* (PL *die* Feuermelder) fire alarm.

Feuertreppe die (PL die Feuertreppen) fire escape.

Feuerwehr die (PL die Feuerwehren) fire brigade.

Feuerwehrauto das (PL die Feuerwehrautos) fire engine.

Feuerwehrmann der (PL die Feuerwehrleute) fireman.

Feuerwerk das fireworks.

Feuerzeug das (PL die Feuerzeuge) lighter.

ficht SEE **fechten**.

Fieber das (high) temperature, fever; **(hohes) Fieber haben** to have a (high) temperature.

fiel SEE **fallen**.

fies adjective (informal) nasty.

Figur die (PL die Figuren) **1** figure; **2** character.

Filiale die (PL die Filialen) branch.

Film der (PL die Filme) film.

filmen verb (PERF hat gefilmt) to film.

Filter der (PL die Filter) filter.

Filzstift der (PL die Filzstifte) felt pen.

Finale das (PL die Finale) final.

finanziell adjective financial.

finanzieren verb (PERF hat finanziert) to finance.

finden ◇verb (IMPERF fand, PERF hat gefunden) **1** to find; **2** to think; **wie findest du das?** what do you think of it?; **findest du?** do you think so?; **3 ich finde nichts dabei** I don't mind.

fing SEE **fangen**.

Finger der (PL die Finger) finger.

Fingernagel der (PL die Fingernägel) fingernail.

Finne der (PL die Finnen) Finn.

Finnin die (PL die Finninnen) Finn.

Finnland das Finland.

finster adjective **1** dark; **im Finstern** in the dark; **2** sinister.

Finsternis die darkness.

Firma die (PL die Firmen) firm, company.

Fisch der (PL die Fische) **1** fish; **2 Fische** Pisces; **Helmut ist Fisch** Helmut is Pisces.

Fischer der (PL die Fischer) fisherman.

fit adjective fit; **er hält sich durch Jogging fit** he keeps fit by jogging.

Fitnesstraining das keep fit.

fix adjective **1** quick; **2 fix und fertig** all finished, all ready; **3 ich bin fix und fertig** (informal) I'm shattered.

flach adjective **1** flat; **2** low; **3** shallow; **die Erdbeeren kommen in die flache Schüssel** the strawberries go into the shallow bowl.

Fläche die (PL die Flächen) **1** surface; **2** area.

flackern verb (PERF hat geflackert) to flicker.

Flagge die (PL die Flaggen) flag.

Flamme die (PL die Flammen) flame.

Flasche die (PL die Flaschen) bottle.

Flaschenöffner der (PL die Flaschenöffner) bottle opener.

a
b
c
d
e
f
g
h
i
j
k
l
m
n
o
p
q
r
s
t
u
v
w
x
y
z

flauschig *adjective* **1** fluffy; **2** fleecy.

Fleck *der* (PL *die* Flecken) **1** stain; **2** spot; **3 ein blauer Fleck** a bruise.

fleckig *adjective* **1** stained; **2** blotchy (*skin*).

Fledermaus *die* (PL *die* Fledermäuse) bat.

Fleisch *das* **1** meat; **2** flesh.

Fleischer *der* (PL *die* Fleischer) butcher.

Fleischerei *die* (PL *die* Fleischereien) butcher's.

Fleiß *der* hard work.

fleißig *adjective* hard-working.

flicken *verb* (PERF **hat geflickt**) to mend.

Flicken *der* (PL *die* Flicken) patch (*for mending*).

Fliege *die* (PL *die* Fliegen) **1** fly; **2** bow tie.

fliegen ⋄*verb* (IMPERF **flog**, PERF **ist geflogen**) **1** to fly; **2 ich bin geflogen** (*informal*) I fell; **3 Manfred ist geflogen** (*informal*) Manfred has been fired; **4** (PERF **hat geflogen**) to fly (*a plane*).

fliehen ⋄*verb* (IMPERF **floh**, PERF **ist geflohen**) to flee.

Fliese *die* (PL *die* Fliesen) tile.

Fließband *das* (PL *die* Fließbänder) **1** conveyor belt; **2** assembly line.

fließen ⋄*verb* (IMPERF **floss**, PERF **ist geflossen**) to flow.

fließend *adjective* **1** running; **2** fluent; **fließendes Deutsch** fluent German; **3** moving (*traffic*).

Flitterwochen *plural noun* honeymoon; **sie fahren nach Ägyten für ihre Flitterwochen** they're going to Egypt for their honeymoon.

flitzen *verb* (*informal*) (PERF **ist geflitzt**) **1** to dash; **2** to whizz.

Flocke *die* (PL *die* Flocken) flake.

flog SEE **fliegen**.

Floh *der* (PL *die* Flöhe) flee.

floh SEE **fliehen**.

Flohmarkt *der* (PL *die* Flohmärkte) flea market.

floss SEE **fließen**.

Flosse *die* (PL *die* Flossen) **1** fin; **2** flipper.

Flöte *die* (PL *die* Flöten) flute.

fluchen *verb* (PERF **hat geflucht**) to curse.

Flüchtling *der* (PL *die* Flüchtlinge) refugee.

Flug *der* (PL *die* Flüge) flight.

Flugbegleiter *der* (PL *die* Flugbegleiter) flight attendant.

Flugbegleiterin *die* (PL *die* Flugbegleiterinnen) flight attendant.

Flugblatt *das* (PL *die* Flugblätter) pamphlet.

Flugdienstleiter *der* (PL *die* Flugdienstleiter) air-traffic controller.

Flugdienstleiterin *die* (PL *die* Flugdienstleiterinnen) air-traffic controller.

Flügel *der* (PL *die* Flügel) **1** wing; **2** grand piano.

a
b
c
d
e
f
g
h
i
j
k
l
m
n
o
p
q
r
s
t
u
v
w
x
y
z

Fluggast der (PL die **Fluggäste**) (air) passenger.

Fluggesellschaft die (PL die **Fluggesellschaften**) airline.

Flughafen der (PL die **Flughäfen**) airport.

Fluglotse der (PL die **Fluglotsen**) air-traffic controller.

Fluglotsin der (PL die **Fluglotsinnen**) air-traffic controller.

Flugplatz der (PL die **Flugplätze**) 1 airport; 2 airfield.

Flugzeug das (PL die **Flugzeuge**) aeroplane; **mit dem Flugzeug fliegen** to go by air.

Fluor das fluoride.

Flur der (PL die **Flure**) 1 hall; 2 corridor.

Fluss der (PL die **Flüsse**) river.

flüssig adjective liquid.

Flüssigkeit die (PL die **Flüssigkeiten**) liquid.

flüstern verb (PERF **hat geflüstert**) to whisper.

Flut die (PL die **Fluten**) 1 high tide; **bei Flut** at high tide; 2 flood (of letters, complaints).

Flutlicht das floodlight.

focht SEE **fechten**.

Föhn der (PL die **Föhne**) hair drier.

föhnen verb (PERF **hat geföhnt**) to blow-dry.

Folge die (PL die **Folgen**) 1 consequence; 2 episode; 3 **etwas zur Folge haben** to result in something; 4 **an den Folgen eines Unfalls sterben** to die as the result of an accident.

folgen verb (PERF **ist gefolgt**) 1 to follow; **daraus folgt, dass** ... it follows that ...; **ich kann dir nicht folgen** I can't follow what you're saying; 2 (PERF **hat gefolgt**) to obey.

folgend adjective 1 following; 2 **Folgendes** the following.

Folgerung die (PL die **Folgerungen**) conclusion.

folgsam adjective obedient.

Folie die (PL die **Folien**) foil.

Folienkartoffel die (PL die **Folienkartoffeln**) jacket potato.

Folterkammer die (PL die **Folterkammern**) torture chamber.

Fön™ SEE **Föhn**.

fönen SEE **föhnen**.

fördern verb (PERF **hat gefördert**) 1 to promote; 2 to sponsor.

fordern verb (PERF **hat gefordert**) to demand.

Forderung die (PL die **Forderungen**) 1 demand; 2 claim.

Forelle die (PL die **Forellen**) trout.

Form die (PL die **Formen**) 1 shape; 2 form; **in Form sein** to be on form; 3 tin (for baking).

Format das (PL die **Formate**) format.

formatieren verb (PERF **hat formatiert**) to format.

formen verb (PERF **hat geformt**) 1 to form; 2 **sich formen** to take shape.

förmlich adjective formal.

förmlich adverb 1 formally;

a b c d e f g h i j k l m n o p q r s t u v w x y z

2 jemanden förmlich zwingen, etwas zu tun to positively force somebody to do something; **ich hätte förmlich schreien können** I really could have screamed.

Formular das (PL die **Formulare**) form.

Forscher der (PL die **Forscher**) **1** researcher, research scientist; **2** explorer.

Forschung die (PL die **Forschungen**) research.

Forst der (PL die **Forste(n)**) forest.

Förster der (PL die **Förster**) forester.

fort adverb **1** away; **2 fort sein** to have gone; **3 und so fort** and so on; **4 in einem fort** on and on.

fortbewegen verb (PERF hat **fortbewegt**) **1** to move; **2 sich fortbewegen** to move.

fortfahren ⬧verb (PRES **fährt fort**, IMPERF **fuhr fort**, PERF **ist fortgefahren**) **1** to leave; **wann fahrt ihr fort?** when are you leaving?; **2** to continue.

fortgeschritten adjective advanced.

Fortpflanzung die (PL die **Fortpflanzungen**) **1** reproduction; **2** propagation.

Fortschritt der (PL die **Fortschritte**) progress; **Fortschritte machen** to make progress.

fortsetzen verb (PERF hat **fortgesetzt**) to continue.

Fortsetzung die (PL die **Fortsetzungen**) **1** continuation; **2** instalment.

Foto das (PL die **Fotos**) photo.

Fotoapparat der (PL die **Fotoapparate**) camera.

Fotograf der (PL die **Fotografen**) photographer.

Fotografie die (PL die **Fotografien**) **1** photography; **2** photograph.

fotografieren verb (PERF hat **fotografiert**) **1** to photograph, to take a photograph of; **2** to take photographs.

Fotografin die (PL die **Fotografinnen**) photographer.

Fotokopie die (PL die **Fotokopien**) photocopy.

fotokopieren verb (PERF hat **fotokopiert**) to photocopy.

Fracht die (PL die **Frachten**) freight, cargo.

Frage die (PL die **Fragen**) question; **eine Frage stellen** to ask a question; **etwas in Frage stellen** to question something; **das kommt nicht in Frage** that's out of the question.

Fragebogen der (PL die **Fragebogen**) questionnaire.

fragen verb (PERF hat **gefragt**) **1** to ask; **2 sich fragen** to wonder.

Fragezeichen das (PL die **Fragezeichen**) question mark.

fraglich adjective doubtful.

Franken[1] der (PL die **Franken**) (Swiss) franc.

Franken[2] das Franconia.

Frankreich *das* France.

Franzose *der* (PL *die* **Franzosen**) Frenchman.

Französin *die* (PL *die* **Französinnen**) Frenchwoman.

Französisch *das* French.

französisch *adjective* French.

fraß SEE **fressen**.

Frau *die* (PL *die* **Frauen**) **1** woman; **2** wife; **3** Mrs, Ms (*'Frau' is usually used to address both married and unmarried women*).

Fräulein *das* (PL *die* **Fräulein**) **1** young lady; **2** Miss; **Fräulein Schmidt** Miss Schmidt.

frech *adjective* cheeky.

Frechheit *die* (PL *die* **Frechheiten**) **1** cheek; **2** cheeky remark.

Frechheit *die* (PL *die* **Frechheiten**) **1** cheeky remark; **2** cheekiness.

frei *adjective* **1** free; **2** freelance; **3 ist dieser Platz frei?** is this seat taken?; **4 ein freier Tag** a day off; **sich frei nehmen** to take a day off; **5 'Zimmer frei'** 'vacancies'.

Freibad *das* (PL *die* **Freibäder**) open-air swimming pool.

Freie *das* **im Freien** in the open air.

freigebig *adjective* generous.

Freiheit *die* (PL *die* **Freiheiten**) **1** freedom; **2** liberty; **sich Freiheiten erlauben** to take liberties.

freimachen *verb* (PERF **hat freigemacht**) **1** to take time off; **2 sich freimachen** to take time off.

Freistoß *der* (PL *die* **Freistöße**) free kick.

Freistunde *die* (PL *die* **Freistunden**) free period.

Freitag *der* (PL *die* **Freitage**) Friday.

freitags *adverb* on Fridays.

freiwillig *adjective* voluntary.

Freizeit *die* **1** spare time; **2** leisure.

Freizeitkleidung *die* leisure wear, casual clothes.

fremd *adjective* **1** foreign; **2** strange; **fremde Leute** strangers; **ich bin hier fremd** I'm a stranger here.

Fremde *der/die* (PL *die* **Fremden**) **1** foreigner; **2** stranger.

Fremdenverkehr *der* tourism.

Fremdenverkehrsbüro *das* (PL *die* **Fremdenverkehrsbüros**) tourist office.

Fremdenzimmer *das* (PL *die* **Fremdenzimmer**) room (to let).

Fremdsprache *die* (PL *die* **Fremdsprachen**) foreign language.

fressen ◊*verb* (PRES **frisst**, IMPERF **fraß**, PERF **hat gefressen**) to eat.

Freude *die* (PL *die* **Freuden**) **1** joy; **2** pleasure; **mit Freuden** with pleasure; **3 an etwas Freude haben** to be delighted with something; **4 jemandem eine Freude machen** to please somebody.

freuen *verb* (PERF **hat sich gefreut**) **1 sich freuen** to be pleased; **sich über etwas freuen** to be pleased about something; **2 sich auf etwas freuen** to look forward to something.

Freund der (PL die **Freunde**)
1 friend; **2** boyfriend.

Freundin die (PL die **Freundinnen**)
1 friend; **2** girlfriend.

freundlich adjective **1** friendly;
2 kind.

freundlicherweise adverb
kindly.

Freundlichkeit die friendliness.

Freundschaft die (PL die
Freundschaften) friendship; **mit
jemandem Freundschaft
schließen** to make friends with
somebody.

Frieden der peace.

Friedhof der (PL die **Friedhöfe**)
cemetery.

friedlich adjective peaceful.

frieren ◇verb (IMPERF **fror**, PERF **hat
gefroren**) **1** to be cold; **frierst du?**
are you cold?; **2 es friert** it's
freezing, it's frosty; **3** (PERF **ist
gefroren**) to freeze.

Frikadelle die (PL die **Frikadellen**)
rissole.

frisch adjective fresh; **sich frisch
machen** to freshen up.
frisch adverb freshly; **'frisch
gestrichen'** 'wet paint'.

Friseur der (PL die **Friseure**)
hairdresser.

Friseuse die (PL die **Friseusen**)
hairdresser.

frisieren verb (PERF **hat frisiert**)
1 jemanden frisieren to do
somebody's hair; **2 sich frisieren** to
do your hair.

frisst SEE **fressen**.

Frisur die (PL die **Frisuren**) hairstyle,
hairdo.

froh adjective **1** happy; **frohe
Weihnachten!** happy Christmas!;
2 über etwas froh sein to be glad
about something.

fröhlich adjective cheerful.

Fröhlichkeit die cheerfulness.

fromm adjective devout.

fror SEE **frieren**.

Frosch der (PL die **Frösche**) frog.

Frost der (PL die **Fröste**) frost.

frostig adjective frosty.

Frottee das (PL die **Frottees**)
towelling.

Frottiertuch das (PL die
Frottiertücher) towel.

Frucht die (PL die **Früchte**) fruit.

fruchtbar adjective fertile.

Fruchtsaft der (PL die **Fruchtsäfte**)
fruit juice.

früh adjective, adverb **1** early; **von
früh auf** from an early age; **2 heute
früh** this morning.

Frühe die **in aller Frühe** at the crack
of dawn.

früher adjective **1** earlier; **2** former.
früher adverb **1** earlier;
2 formerly; **3 früher war sie ganz
anders** she used to be quite
different; **das war früher ein
Blumengeschäft** it used to be a
florist's.

frühestens adverb at the earliest.

Frühjahr das (PL die **Frühjahre**)
spring; **im Frühjahr** in spring.

Frühling der (PL die Frühlinge) spring; **im Frühling** in spring.

Frühstück das (PL die Frühstücke) breakfast.

frühstücken verb (PERF hat gefrühstückt) to have breakfast.

frühzeitig adjective early.

Fuchs der (PL die Füchse) fox.

fühlen verb (PERF hat gefühlt) **1** to feel; **2 sich krank fühlen** to feel ill.

fuhr SEE **fahren**.

führen verb (PERF hat geführt) **1** to lead; **sie führt mit fünf Punkten** she is five points in the lead; **unsere Mannschaft führt** our team's winning; **2** to run (a shop or business); **3** to show round; **4** to keep (a diary, list); **5 ein Telefongespräch führen** to make a phone call.

Führer der (PL die Führer) **1** leader; **2** guide.

Führerschein der (PL die Führerscheine) driving licence; **den Führerschein machen** to take your driving test.

Führung die (PL die Führungen) **1** leadership; **2** guided tour; **3** management (of a shop); **4 in Führung** in the lead.

Führungsposition die (PL die Führungspositionen) **1** top position; **2** pole position.

füllen verb (PERF hat gefüllt) **1** to fill; **2** to stuff (a turkey, peppers); **3 sich füllen** to fill (up).

Füller der (PL die Füller) fountain pen.

Füllfederhalter der (PL die Füllfederhalter) fountain pen.

Füllung die (PL die Füllungen) filling.

Fundament das (PL die Fundamente) foundations.

Fundbüro das (PL die Fundbüros) lost property office.

fünf number five.

fünfhundert number five hundred.

Fünftel das (PL die Fünftel) fifth.

fünfter, fünfte, fünftes adjective fifth.

fünfzehn number fifteen.

fünfzig number fifty.

Funkausstellung die (PL die Funkausstellungen) radio and television exhibition.

Funke der (PL die Funken) spark.

funkeln verb (PERF hat gefunkelt) **1** to sparkle; **2** to twinkle (of a star).

funktionieren verb (PERF hat funktioniert) to work.

für preposition (+ ACC) **1** for; **2 was für ein …?** what sort of … ?; **3 für sich** by yourself; **jetzt habe ich das Haus ganz für mich** now I've got the house to myself; **4 das Für und Wider** the pros and cons.

Furcht die fear.

furchtbar adjective terrible.

fürchten verb (PERF hat gefürchtet) **1** to fear; **2 sich fürchten** to be afraid; **ich fürchte mich vor ihm** I'm afraid of him; **ich fürchte, das geht nicht** I'm afraid that's not possible.

a
b
c
d
e
f
g
h
i
j
k
l
m
n
o
p
q
r
s
t
u
v
w
x
y
z

fürchterlich *adjective* dreadful.

füreinander *adverb* for each other.

fürs = **für das**.

Fürsorge *die* **1** care; **2** welfare; **3** (*informal*) social security.

Fuß *der* (PL *die* **Füße**) **1** foot; **zu Fuß** on foot; **zu Fuß gehen** to walk; **2** base.

Fußabdruck *der* (PL *die* **Fußabdrücke**) footprint.

Fußball *der* (PL *die* **Fußbälle**) football.

Fußballplatz *der* (PL *die* **Fußballplätze**) football pitch.

Fußballspiel *das* (PL *die* **Fußballspiele**) football match.

Fußballspieler *der* (PL *die* **Fußballspieler**) footballer.

Fußboden *der* (PL *die* **Fußböden**) floor.

Fußgänger *der* (PL *die* **Fußgänger**) pedestrian.

Fußgängerzone *die* (PL *die* **Fußgängerzonen**) pedestrian precinct.

Fußweg *der* (PL *die* **Fußwege**) footpath.

Futter *das* **1** feed; **ich habe dem Hund schon Futter gegeben** I've already given the dog his food; **2** lining (*of clothes*).

füttern *verb* (PERF **hat gefüttert**) **1** to feed; **den Hund und die Katze füttern** to feed the dog and the cat; **2** to line.

Futur *das* (PL *die* **Future**) future (*tense*).

Gg

gab SEE **geben**.

Gabel *die* (PL *die* **Gabeln**) fork.

gähnen *verb* (PERF **hat gegähnt**) to yawn.

Galerie *die* (PL *die* **Galerien**) gallery.

galoppieren *verb* (PERF **ist galoppiert**) to gallop.

Gammler *der* (PL *die* **Gammler**) drop-out.

Gammlerin *die* (PL *die* **Gammlerinnen**) drop-out.

Gang *der* (PL *die* **Gänge**) **1** walk; **2** errand; **3** corridor; **4 ein Platz am Gang** an aisle seat; **5** course (*of a meal*); **6** gear (*of a car*); **7 in Gang setzen** to get going; **8 im Gange** in progress.

gängig *adjective* **1** common; **2** popular (*goods*).

Gans *die* (PL *die* **Gänse**) goose.

Gänseblümchen *das* (PL *die* **Gänseblümchen**) daisy.

Gänsehaut *die* goose pimples.

ganz *adjective* whole **1 ganz Deutschland** the whole of Germany; **2 im Großen und Ganzen** on the whole; **3 eine ganze Menge** quite a lot; **4** all; **mein ganzes Geld** all my money; **die ganzen Leute** all the people; **5 etwas wieder ganz machen** to mend something.
ganz *adverb* **1** quite; **es war ganz gut** it was quite good; **2 ganz und gar** completely; **3 ganz und gar nicht** not at all.

ganztägig *adjective, adverb* **1** full-time; **2** all-day; **ganztägig geöffnet** open all day.

ganztags *adverb* **1** full time; **2** all day.

Ganztagsschule *die* (PL *die* Ganztagsschulen) **1** all-day school; **2** all-day schooling.

gar *adjective* done, cooked.
gar *adverb* **1 gar nicht** not at all; **gar nichts** nothing; **2 oder gar** or even.

Garage *die* (PL *die* Garagen) garage.

Garantie *die* (PL *die* Garantien) guarantee.

garantieren *verb* (PERF hat garantiert) to guarantee.

Garderobe *die* (PL *die* Garderoben) cloakroom; **wir können die Mäntel an der Garderobe abgeben** we can leave the coats in the cloakroom.

Gardine *die* (PL *die* Gardinen) curtain.

Garn *das* (PL *die* Garne) thread.

Garnele *die* (PL *die* Garnelen) **1** shrimp; **2** prawn.

Garten *der* (PL *die* Gärten) garden.

Gärtner *der* (PL *die* Gärtner) gardener.

Gärtnerin *die* (PL *die* Gärtnerinnen) gardener.

Gas *das* (PL *die* Gase) **1** gas; **2 Gas geben** to accelerate.

Gasherd *der* (PL *die* Gasherde) gas cooker.

Gaspedal *das* (PL *die* Gaspedale) accelerator.

Gasse *die* (PL *die* Gassen) lane.

Gast *der* (PL *die* Gäste) **1** guest; **wir haben heute Abend Gäste** we've got guests tonight; **2 bei jemandem zu Gast sein** to be staying with somebody.

Gastarbeiter *der* (PL *die* Gastarbeiter) foreign worker, guest worker.

Gästezimmer *das* (PL *die* Gästezimmer) **1** (hotel) room; **2** spare room.

gastfreundlich *adjective* hospitable.

Gastfreundschaft *die* hospitality.

Gastgeber *der* (PL *die* Gastgeber) host.

Gastgeberin *die* (PL *die* Gastgeberinnen) host.

Gasthaus *das* (PL *die* Gasthäuser) inn.

Gasthof *der* (PL *die* Gasthöfe) inn.

Gaststätte *die* (PL *die* Gaststätten) restaurant.

Gauner *der* (PL *die* Gauner) crook.

Gebäck *das* **1** pastries; **2** biscuits.

gebären ◇*verb* (IMPERF gebar, PERF hat geboren) **1** to give birth to; **2 geboren werden** to be born.

Gebäude *das* (PL *die* Gebäude) building.

geben ◇*verb* (PRES gibt, IMPERF gab, PERF hat gegeben) **1** to give; **2** to deal (*cards*); **3** to teach (*at school*); **4 geben Sie mir bitte Frau Scheck** please put me through to Mrs Scheck; **5 es gibt** there is, there are;

a b c d e f **g** h i j k l m n o p q r s t u v w x y z

es gibt viele gute Restaurants in München there are lots of good restaurants in Munich; **was gibts** or **gibt's im Kino?** what's on at the cinema?; **was gibt es zum Mittagessen?** what are we having for lunch?; **6 was gibts** or **gibt's Neues?** what's the news?, what's new?; **7 sich geschlagen geben** to admit defeat; **8 das gibt sich wieder** it'll get better; **9 das gibts** or **gibt's doch nicht!** I don't believe it!

Gebet das (PL die Gebete) prayer.

gebeten SEE **bitten**.

Gebiet das (PL die Gebiete) **1** area; **2** field.

gebildet adjective educated.

Gebirge das (PL die Gebirge) mountain range; **im Gebirge** in the mountains.

Gebiss das (PL die Gebisse) **1** teeth; **2** false teeth, dentures.

gebissen SEE **beißen**.

geblieben SEE **bleiben**.

geboren verb SEE **gebären** **geboren** adjective **1** born; **2** née; **Frau Hahn, geborene Müller** Mrs Hahn, née Müller.

geborgen adjective safe.

geboten SEE **bieten**.

gebracht SEE **bringen**.

gebraten adjective fried.

Gebrauch der (PL die Gebräuche) **1** use; **vor Gebrauch schütteln** shake before use; **2** custom.

gebrauchen verb (PERF hat gebraucht) to use.

Gebrauchsanweisung die (PL die Gebrauchsanweisungen) instructions (for use).

gebraucht adjective used, second-hand.

Gebrauchtwagen der (PL die Gebrauchtwagen) second-hand car.

gebrochen SEE **brechen**.

Gebühr die (PL die Gebühren) fee, charge.

gebührenfrei adjective free (of charge).

gebührenpflichtig adjective **1** subject to a charge; **2 eine gebührenpflichtige Straße** a toll road.

gebunden SEE **binden**.

Geburt die (PL die Geburten) birth.

Geburtenregelung die birth control.

Geburtsdatum das (PL die Geburtsdaten) date of birth.

Geburtsort der (PL die Geburtsorte) place of birth.

Geburtstag der (PL die Geburtstage) birthday.

Geburtsurkunde die (PL die Geburtsurkunden) birth certificate.

gedacht SEE **denken**.

Gedächtnis das (PL die Gedächtnisse) memory.

Gedanke der (PL die Gedanken) **1** thought; **in Gedanken versunken sein** to be lost in thought; **2 sich Gedanken machen** to worry; **3 jemanden auf andere Gedanken**

bringen to take somebody's mind off things.

gedankenlos *adjective* thoughtless.
gedankenlos *adverb* without thinking.

Gedeck *das* (PL die **Gedecke**)
1 place setting; **2** set meal.

Gedicht *das* (PL die **Gedichte**) poem.

Geduld *die* patience.

geduldig *adjective* patient.

gedurft SEE **dürfen**.

geehrt *adjective* **1** honoured;
2 Sehr geehrte Frau Ross Dear Mrs Ross.

geeignet *adjective* **1** suitable;
2 right.

Gefahr *die* (PL die **Gefahren**)
1 danger; **außer Gefahr** out of danger; **2 auf eigene Gefahr** at your own risk; **Gefahr laufen, etwas zu tun** to run the risk of doing something.

gefährdet *adjective* at risk, endangered; **eine gefährdete Art** an endangered species.

gefährlich *adjective* dangerous.

gefallen¹ SEE **fallen**.

gefallen² ⬦*verb* (PRES **gefällt**, IMPERF **gefiel**, PERF **hat gefallen**)
1 es gefällt mir I like it; **es hat mir sehr gut gefallen** I liked it a lot;
2 sich etwas gefallen lassen to put up with something.

Gefallen¹ *der* (PL die **Gefallen**) favour.

Gefallen² *das* pleasure; **dir zu Gefallen** to please you.

Gefangene *der/die* (PL die **Gefangenen**) prisoner.

Gefängnis *das* (PL die **Gefängnisse**) prison.

Gefäß *das* (PL die **Gefäße**) container.

gefasst *adjective* **1** calm, composed; **2 auf etwas gefasst sein** to be prepared for something.

gefiel SEE **gefallen**.

geflogen SEE **fliegen**.

geflossen SEE **fließen**.

Geflügel *das* poultry.

gefochten SEE **fechten**.

gefräßig *adjective* (*informal*) greedy.

gefrieren ⬦*verb* (IMPERF **gefror**, PERF **ist gefroren**) to freeze.

Gefrierfach *das* (PL die **Gefrierfächer**) freezer (compartment).

gefroren *adjective* frozen.

Gefühl *das* (PL die **Gefühle**)
1 feeling; **2 etwas im Gefühl haben** to have a feel for something.

gefüllt *adjective* stuffed (*peppers, for example*).

gefunden SEE **finden**.

gegangen SEE **gehen**.

gegeben SEE **geben**.

gegebenenfalls *adverb* if need be.

gegen *preposition* (+ ACC) **1** against;
2 gegen die Mauer fahren to drive into the wall; **3 ein Mittel gegen Grippe** a cure for flu; **4** towards;

gegen Abend towards evening;
5 gegen vier Uhr around four
o'clock; **6** compared with; **7** versus
(*in sport*).

Gegend *die* (PL *die* **Gegenden**)
1 area; **2** neighbourhood.

gegeneinander *adverb* against
each other, against one another.

Gegenmittel *das* (PL *die*
Gegenmittel) **1** remedy; **2** antidote.

Gegensatz *der* (PL *die*
Gegensätze) **1** contrast;
2 opposite; **3 im Gegensatz zu mir**
unlike me.

gegenseitig *adjective* mutual.
gegenseitig *adverb* **sich**
gegenseitig helfen to help each
other.

Gegenstand *der* (PL *die*
Gegenstände) **1** object; **2** subject
(*in grammar or of a discussion*).

Gegenteil *das* (PL *die* **Gegenteile**)
1 opposite; **2 im Gegenteil** on the
contrary.

gegenüber *preposition* (+ DAT)
1 opposite; **Susi saß mir**
gegenüber Susi sat opposite me;
2 compared with; **3** towards;
jemandem gegenüber freundlich
sein to be friendly towards
somebody.
gegenüber *adverb* opposite;
meine Freundin wohnt gegenüber
my friend lives opposite.

Gegenwart *die* **1** present;
2 presence.

gegessen SEE **essen**.

Gegner *der* (PL *die* **Gegner**)
opponent.

Gegnerin *die* (PL *die* **Gegnerinnen**)
opponent.

gegrillt *adjective* grilled.

Gehackte *das* mince.

Gehalt *das* (PL *die* **Gehälter**) salary.

gehässig *adjective* spiteful.

geheim *adjective* secret.

Geheimnis *das* (PL *die*
Geheimnisse) secret.

geheimnisvoll *adjective*
mysterious.

gehen ◇*verb* (IMPERF **ging**, PERF **ist**
gegangen) **1** to go; **schlafen gehen**
to go to bed; **2** to walk; **3 über die**
Straße gehen to cross the road;
4 es geht ihr gut she's well; **wie**
geht es Ihnen? how are you?; **es**
geht it's not too bad; **5 das geht**
nicht that's impossible; **6 um etwas**
gehen to be about something;
worum gehts *or* **geht's hier?**
what's it all about?; **7 die Uhr geht**
falsch the clock's wrong.

Gehirn *das* (PL *die* **Gehirne**) brain.

Gehirnerschütterung *die* (PL
die **Gehirnerschütterungen**)
concussion.

gehoben SEE **heben**.

geholfen SEE **helfen**.

Gehör *das* hearing.

gehorchen *verb* (PERF **hat**
gehorcht) to obey.

gehören *verb* (PERF **hat gehört**)
1 to belong; **es gehört mir** it
belongs to me; **2 dazu gehört Mut**
that takes courage; **3 es gehört**
sich nicht it isn't done.

gehorsam *adjective* obedient.

Gehsteig *der* (PL *die* Gehsteige) pavement.

Geier *der* (PL *die* Geier) vulture.

Geige *die* (PL *die* Geigen) violin.

Geisel *die* (PL *die* Geiseln) hostage.

Geist *der* (PL *die* Geister) **1** mind; **2** ghost; **3** wit.

geistesabwesend *adjective* absent-minded.

Geisteskrankheit *die* (PL *die* Geisteskrankheiten) mental illness.

Geisteswissenschaften (*plural noun*) arts, humanities.

geistig *adjective* mental.

geistreich *adjective* witty, clever.

geizig *adjective* mean.

gekannt SEE **kennen**.

gekonnt SEE **können**.

Gel *das* (PL *die* Gele) gel.

Gelächter *das* (PL *die* Gelächter) laughter.

geladen SEE **laden**.

gelähmt *adjective* paralysed.

Gelände *das* (PL *die* Gelände) **1** ground; **2** area.

Geländer *das* (PL *die* Geländer) **1** banister(s); **2** railing(s).

gelangweilt *adjective* bored.

gelassen *verb* SEE **lassen** **gelassen** *adjective* calm.

geläufig *adjective* **1** common; **2 das ist mir nicht geläufig** I'm not familiar with it.

gelaunt *adjective* **gut gelaunt sein** to be in a good mood.

gelb *adjective* yellow.

Geld *das* (PL *die* Gelder) money.

Geldautomat *der* (PL *die* Geldautomaten) cash dispenser.

Geldbörse *die* (PL *die* Geldbörsen) purse.

Geldschein *der* (PL *die* Geldscheine) banknote.

Geldstrafe *die* (PL *die* Geldstrafen) fine.

Geldwechsel *der* **1** bureau de change; **2** currency exchange.

gelegen SEE **liegen**.

Gelegenheit *die* (PL *die* Gelegenheiten) **1** opportunity; **2** occasion.

gelegentlich *adverb* occasionally.

Gelenk *das* (PL *die* Gelenke) joint.

Geliebte *der/die* (PL *die* Geliebten) lover.

geliehen SEE **leihen**.

gelingen ◇*verb* (IMPERF **gelang**, PERF **ist gelungen**) to succeed; **es ist mir gelungen, sie zu überreden** I succeeded in persuading her.

gelten ◇*verb* (PRES **gilt**, IMPERF **galt**, PERF **hat gegolten**) **1** to be valid; **2** to apply (*of a rule*); **3 jemandem gelten** to be directed at somebody; **4 sein Wort gilt viel** his word is worth a lot; **5 das gilt nicht** that doesn't count; **6 als etwas gelten** to be regarded as something.

gelungen *verb* SEE **gelingen** **gelungen** *adjective* successful.

Gemälde *das* (PL *die* Gemälde) painting.

a
b
c
d
e
f
g
h
i
j
k
l
m
n
o
p
q
r
s
t
u
v
w
x
y
z

gemein *adjective* mean.

Gemeinde *die* (PL *die* **Gemeinden**) **1** community; **2** congregation.

gemeinsam *adjective* **1** common; **2** joint.
gemeinsam *adverb* together; **gemeinsam essen** to eat together.

Gemeinschaft *die* (PL *die* **Gemeinschaften**) community.

gemischt *adjective* mixed.

gemocht SEE **mögen**.

Gemüse *das* (PL *die* **Gemüse**) vegetables.

Gemüsehändler *der* (PL *die* **Gemüsehändler**) greengrocer.

Gemüseladen *der* (PL *die* **Gemüseläden**) greengrocer's shop.

gemusst SEE **müssen**.

gemustert *adjective* patterned.

gemütlich *adjective* **1** cosy; **2 mach es dir gemütlich** make yourself comfortable.

genannt SEE **nennen**.

genau *adjective* **1** exact; **2** accurate (*scales, description*); **3** meticulous; **4 ich weiß nichts Genaues** I don't know any details.
genau *adverb* **1** exactly; **sich etwas genau ansehen** to look at something carefully; **2 genau genommen** strictly speaking.

Genauigkeit *die* accuracy.

genauso *adverb* **1** just the same; **2 genauso gut** just as good; **genauso viel** just as much, just as many; **genauso lange** just as long.

Genehmigung *die* (PL *die* **Genehmigungen**) **1** permission; **2** permit; **3** licence.

Generation *die* (PL *die* **Generationen**) generation.

Generator *der* (PL *die* **Generatoren**) generator.

generell *adjective* general.

Genetik *die* genetics.

Genf *das* Geneva.

Genfer See *der* Lake Geneva.

genial *adjective* brilliant.

Genick *das* (PL *die* **Genicke**) (back of the) neck.

Genie *das* (PL *die* **Genies**) genius.

genießbar *adjective* edible.

genießen ◇*verb* (IMPERF **genoss**, PERF **hat genossen**) to enjoy.

genommen SEE **nehmen**.

genug *adverb* enough.

genügen *verb* (PERF **hat genügt**) to be enough.

genügend *adjective* **1** enough; **2** sufficient.

Genuss *der* (PL *die* **Genüsse**) **1** enjoyment; **2** consumption (*of alcohol*).

geöffnet *adjective* open.

Geometrie *die* geometry.

Gepäck *das* luggage.

Gepäckaufbewahrung *die* (PL *die* **Gepäckaufbewahrungen**) left-luggage office.

Gepäckausgabe *die* left-luggage office.

Gepäckträger der (PL die Gepäckträger) **1** porter; **2** roof rack; **3** carrier (on a bike).

gerade adjective **1** straight; **2 etwas gerade biegen** to straighten something; **3** upright; **4 eine gerade Zahl** an even number.
gerade adverb **1** just; **gerade erst** only just; **2 es war nicht gerade billig** it wasn't exactly cheap.

geradeaus adverb straight ahead.

geradebiegen SEE **gerade**.

gerannt SEE **rennen**.

Gerät das (PL die Geräte) **1** appliance; **2** set (TV or radio); **3** tool; **4** gadget; **5 die Geräte** apparatus (in gymnastics).

geraten ◇verb (PRES **gerät**, IMPERF **geriet**, PERF **ist geraten**) **1** to get (somewhere, the wrong side of the road etc.); **in etwas geraten** to get into something; **in Wut geraten** to get angry; **2 an den Richtigen geraten** to come to the right person; **3 gut/schlecht geraten** to turn out well/badly; **4 nach jemandem geraten** to take after somebody.

Gerätetauchen das scuba diving.

geräuchert adjective smoked.

geräumig adjective spacious.

Geräusch das (PL die Geräusche) noise.

gerecht adjective **1** just; **2** fair.

Gerechtigkeit die justice.

Gerede das gossip.

Gericht das (PL die Gerichte) **1** court; **2** dish.

gerieben SEE **reiben**.

gering adjective **1** small (amount); **2** low (value); **3** short (time, distance).

Gerippe das (PL die Gerippe) skeleton.

gerissen adjective crafty.

geritten SEE **reiten**.

gern(e) adverb **1** gladly; **2 jemanden gern haben** to like somebody; **etwas gern tun** to like doing something; **ich tanze gern** I like dancing; **ich hätte gerne einen Kaffee** I'd like a coffee; **welchen Belag hättest du gerne?** which topping would you like?; **3 ja, gern!** yes, I'd love to!; **4 das glaube ich gern** I can well believe that.

Gerste die barley.

Geruch der (PL die Gerüche) smell.

Gerücht das (PL die Gerüchte) rumour.

Gerümpel das junk.

gesalzen verb SEE **salzen**
gesalzen adjective **1** salted; **2 gesalzene Preise** (informal) steep prices.

gesamt adjective **1** whole; **2 die gesamten Kosten** the total cost; **3 die gesamten Werke** the complete works.

Gesamtschule die (PL die Gesamtschulen) comprehensive school.

gesandt SEE **senden**.

Geschäft das (PL die Geschäfte)
1 shop; 2 business; 3 deal.

Geschäftsführer der (PL die
Geschäftsführer) manager.

Geschäftsführerin die (PL die
Geschäftsführerinnen)
manageress.

Geschäftszeiten plural noun
business hours.

geschehen ◇verb (PRES
geschieht, IMPERF geschah, PERF ist
geschehen) to happen.

gescheit adjective clever.

Geschenk das (PL die Geschenke)
present, gift.

Geschichte die (PL die
Geschichten) 1 story; 2 history;
3 **mach bloß keine große
Geschichte daraus** don't make
such a thing of it.

Geschick das 1 skill; 2 fate.

geschickt adjective 1 skilful;
2 clever.

geschieden verb SEE **scheiden**
geschieden adjective divorced;
meine Eltern sind geschieden my
parents are divorced.

geschienen SEE **scheinen**.

Geschirr das 1 crockery; 2 dishes.

Geschirrspülmaschine die
(PL die Geschirrspülmaschinen)
dishwasher.

Geschirrtuch das (PL die
Geschirrtücher) tea towel.

Geschlecht das (PL die
Geschlechter) 1 sex; 2 gender.

geschlossen verb SEE **schließen**
geschlossen adjective closed.

Geschmack der (PL die
Geschmäcke) taste.

geschmacklos adjective
1 tasteless; 2 **geschmacklos sein**
to be in bad taste.

geschnitten SEE **schneiden**.

geschossen SEE **schießen**.

geschrieben SEE **schreiben**.

geschrien SEE **schreien**.

Geschwätz das talk.

geschwätzig adjective talkative.

Geschwindigkeit die (PL die
Geschwindigkeiten) speed.

**Geschwindigkeitsbeschrän-
kung** die (PL die Geschwindigkeits-
beschränkungen) speed limit.

Geschwister plural noun
brothers and sisters, siblings.

geschwommen SEE
schwimmen.

Geschwür das (PL die Geschwüre)
ulcer.

gesellig adjective sociable.

Gesellschaft die (PL die
Gesellschaften) 1 society;
2 company; **ich leiste dir
Gesellschaft** I'll keep you company;
3 party.

gesessen SEE **sitzen**.

Gesetz das (PL die Gesetze) law.

gesetzlich adjective legal; **ein
gesetzlicher Feiertag** a public
holiday.
gesetzlich adverb legally, by law.

Gesicht das (PL die Gesichter) face.

Gesichtsausdruck der (facial)
expression.

a b c d e f g h i j k l m n o p q r s t u v w x y z

gesollt SEE **sollen**.

gespannt *adjective* **1** eager; **2 auf etwas gespannt sein** to look forward eagerly to something; **auf jemanden gespannt sein** to look forward to seeing somebody; **3 ich bin gespannt, ob** ... I wonder whether ...; **4** tense; **in Südafrika ist die Lage immer noch gespannt** the situation in South Africa is still tense.

Gespenst *das* (PL *die* Gespenster) ghost.

Gespräch *das* (PL *die* Gespräche) **1** conversation; **2** call (*on the phone*).

gesprächig *adjective* talkative.

gesprochen SEE **sprechen**.

gesprungen SEE **springen**.

Gestalt *die* (PL *die* Gestalten) **1** figure; **2** form.

gestanden SEE **stehen**, **gestehen**.

Geständnis *das* (PL *die* Geständnisse) confession.

gestatten *verb* (PERF hat gestattet) **1** to permit; **2 nicht gestattet** prohibited; **3 gestatten Sie?** may I?

Geste *die* (PL *die* Gesten) gesture.

gestehen ⋄*verb* (IMPERF gestand, PERF hat gestanden) to confess.

Gestell *das* (PL *die* Gestelle) **1** rack; **2** stand; **3** frame.

gestern *adverb* **1** yesterday; **2 gestern Nacht** last night.

gestohlen SEE **stehlen**.

gestorben SEE **sterben**.

gestreift *adjective* striped.

gesund *adjective* **1** healthy; **2 wieder gesund werden** to get well again; **3 Schwimmen ist gesund** swimming is good for you.

Gesundheit *die* **1** health; **2 Gesundheit!** bless you! (*said after someone sneezes*).

gesungen SEE **singen**.

getan SEE **tun**.

Getränk *das* (PL *die* Getränke) drink.

Getränkekarte *die* (PL *die* Getränkekarten) wine list.

getrauen *verb* (PERF hat sich getraut) **sich getrauen** to dare.

Getreide *das* grain.

Getriebe *das* (PL *die* Getriebe) gearbox.

getrieben SEE **treiben**.

getroffen SEE **treffen**.

getrunken SEE **trinken**.

Getue *das* fuss.

geübt *adjective* **1** accomplished; **2 mit geübtem Auge** with a practised eye.

Gewächshaus *das* (PL *die* Gewächshäuser) greenhouse.

Gewalt *die* **1** power; **2** force; **mit Gewalt** by force; **3** violence.

gewaltig *adjective* enormous.

gewalttätig *adjective* violent.

gewann SEE **gewinnen**.

Gewebe *das* (PL *die* Gewebe) **1** fabric; **2** tissue.

Gewehr *das* (PL *die* Gewehre) rifle, gun.

a b c d e f g h i j k l m n o p q r s t u v w x y z

Gewerkschaft *die* (PL *die* Gewerkschaften) trade union.

gewesen SEE **sein**.

Gewicht *das* (PL *die* Gewichte) weight.

Gewinn *der* (PL *die* Gewinne) **1** profit; **2** winnings; **3** prize.

gewinnen ◇*verb* (IMPERF **gewann**, PERF **hat gewonnen**) **1** to win; **mit 3 zu 2 Toren gewinnen** to win by 3 goals to 2; **2** to gain (*time or influence*); **an Bedeutung gewinnen** to gain in importance.

Gewinner *der* (PL *die* Gewinner) winner.

Gewinnerin *die* (PL *die* Gewinnerinnen) winner.

gewiss *adjective* certain; **ein gewisser Herr Schmidt möchte Sie sprechen** a Mr Schmidt would like to speak to you.
gewiss *adverb* certainly; **'darf ich?' 'aber gewiss doch'** 'may I?' 'but of course'.

Gewissen *das* (PL *die* Gewissen) conscience.

gewissenhaft *adjective* conscientious.

gewissermaßen *adverb* **1** more or less; **2** as it were.

Gewitter *das* (PL *die* Gewitter) thunderstorm.

gewittrig *adjective* thundery.

gewöhnen *verb* (PERF **hat gewöhnt**) **1 jemanden an etwas gewöhnen** to get somebody used to something; **2 an etwas gewöhnt sein** to be used to something; **3 sich an etwas gewöhnen** to get used to something.

Gewohnheit *die* (PL *die* Gewohnheiten) habit.

gewöhnlich *adjective* **1** usual; **2** ordinary.
gewöhnlich *adverb* usually; **wie gewöhnlich** as usual.

gewohnt *adjective* **1** usual; **2 etwas gewohnt sein** to be used to something; **Renate ist es nicht gewohnt, früh aufzustehen** Renate isn't used to getting up early.

gewollt SEE **wollen**.

gewonnen SEE **gewinnen**.

geworden SEE **werden**.

geworfen SEE **werfen**.

Gewürz *das* (PL *die* Gewürze) spice.

gewusst SEE **wissen**.

Gezeiten *plural noun* tides.

gezogen SEE **ziehen**.

gezwungen SEE **zwingen**.

gibt SEE **geben**.

gierig *adjective* greedy.

gießen ◇*verb* (IMPERF **goss**, PERF **hat gegossen**) **1** to pour; **es gießt** it's pouring; **2** to water; **vergiss nicht, die Blumen zu gießen** don't forget to water the flowers.

Gießkanne *die* (PL *die* Gießkannen) watering can.

Gift *das* (PL *die* Gifte) poison.

giftig *adjective* **1** poisonous; **2** toxic.

Gigabyte *das* (PL *die* Gigabytes) gigabyte; **eine Festplatte mit 20 Gigabyte Speicherkapazität** a twenty gigabyte hard disk.

ging SEE **gehen**.

Gipfel der (PL die **Gipfel**) **1** peak, summit; **2 der Gipfel der Geschmacklosigkeit** the height of bad taste.

Gips der plaster.

Giraffe die (PL die **Giraffen**) giraffe.

Girokonto das (PL die **Girokonten**) current account.

Gitarre die (PL die **Gitarren**) guitar.

Gitarrist der (PL die **Gitarristen**) guitarist, guitar player.

Gitter das (PL die **Gitter**) **1** grid; **2** bars.

glänzen verb (PERF hat **geglänzt**) to shine.

glänzend adjective **1** shining; **2** brilliant; **ein glänzender Erfolg** a brilliant success.

Glas das (PL die **Gläser**) **1** glass (the material); **2** glass (for a drink); **3** jar.

Glasscheibe die (PL die **Glasscheiben**) pane (of glass).

Glasur die **1** icing; **2** glaze.

glatt adjective **1** smooth; **2** slippery; **3 eine glatte Absage** a flat refusal. **glatt** adverb **1** smoothly; **2** flatly; **etwas glatt ablehnen** to flatly reject something; **3 das ist glatt gelogen** that's a downright lie; **4 ich habe ihren Geburtstag glatt vergessen** I totally forgot about her birthday.

Glatteis das (black) ice.

Glatze die (PL die **Glatzen**) **eine Glatze haben** to be bald; **eine Glatze bekommen** to go bald.

glauben verb (PERF hat **geglaubt**) **1** to believe; **an Gott glauben** to believe in God; **2** to think; **3 nicht zu glauben!** incredible!

gleich adjective **1** same; **2** identical; **3 gleich bleibend** constant; **4 das ist mir gleich** it's all the same to me; **ganz gleich, wer anruft** no matter who calls. **gleich** adverb **1** the same; **2** equally; **3** immediately; **gleich danach** immediately afterwards; **gleich neben** right next to; **ich komme gleich** I'm coming (right away); **er ist gleich fertig** he'll be ready in a minute.

gleichartig adjective similar.

gleichberechtigt adjective equal.

Gleichberechtigung die equality.

gleichbleibend SEE **gleich**.

gleichen ◇verb (IMPERF **glich**, PERF hat **geglichen**) **1** to be like; **2 sich gleichen** to be alike.

gleichfalls adverb **1** also; **2 danke gleichfalls!** the same to you!

Gleichgewicht das balance.

gleichgültig adjective indifferent; **das ist doch gleichgültig** it's not important.

gleichwertig adjective **1** equivalent; **2** of the same value; **3** of the same standard.

gleichzeitig adverb at the same time.

a
b
c
d
e
f
g
h
i
j
k
l
m
n
o
p
q
r
s
t
u
v
w
x
y
z

Gleis *das* (PL *die* Gleise) **1** track, line; **2** platform; **Gleis vier** platform four.

glich SEE **gleichen**.

Glied *das* (PL *die* Glieder) **1** limb; **2** link.

glitschig *adjective* slippery.

glitzern *verb* (PERF **hat geglitzert**) to glitter.

global *adjective* global, general; **der globale Temperaturanstieg** global warming.

Glocke *die* (PL *die* Glocken) bell.

Glück *das* **1** luck; **viel Glück!** good luck!; **Glück haben** to be lucky; **zum Glück** luckily; **2** happiness.

glücklich *adjective* **1** lucky; **es war ein glücklicher Zufall, dass ich ihn heute in der Stadt getroffen habe** it was a lucky coincidence that I met him in town today; **2** happy.

glücklicherweise *adverb* luckily, fortunately.

Glückwunsch *der* (PL *die* Glückwünsche) congratulations; **herzlichen Glückwunsch zum Geburtstag!** happy birthday!

Glückwunschkarte *die* (PL *die* Glückwunschkarten) greetings card.

Glühbirne *die* (PL *die* Glühbirnen) light bulb.

glühen *verb* (PERF **hat geglüht**) to glow.

Gokart *der* (PL *die* Gokarts) go-kart; **Gokart gehen** to go karting.

Gold *das* gold.

golden *adjective* **1** gold; **2** golden.

Goldfisch *der* (PL *die* Goldfische) goldfish.

Golf[1] *der* (PL *die* Golfe) gulf.

Golf[2] *das* golf.

Golfplatz *der* (PL *die* Golfplätze) golf course.

Golfschläger *der* (PL *die* Golfschläger) golf club.

Golfspieler *der* (PL *die* Golfspieler) golfer.

Golfspielerin *die* (PL *die* Golfspielerinnen) golfer.

Gorilla *der* (PL *die* Gorillas) gorilla.

goss SEE **gießen**.

Gosse *die* (PL *die* Gossen) gutter (*in street*).

Gott *der* (PL *die* Götter) god.

Gottesdienst *der* (PL *die* Gottesdienste) service.

Göttin *die* (PL *die* Göttinnen) goddess.

Grab *das* (PL *die* Gräber) grave.

graben *verb* (PRES **gräbt**, IMPERF **grub**, PERF **hat gegraben**) to dig.

Grad *der* (PL *die* Grade) degree.

Grafik *die* (PL *die* Grafiken) graphics.

Gramm *das* (PL *die* Gramme) gram.

Grammatik *die* (PL *die* Grammatiken) grammar.

grammatikalisch *adjective* grammatical; **ein grammatikalischer Fehler** a grammatical error.

grantig *adjective* grumpy.

Gras das (PL die Gräser) grass.

grässlich adjective horrible.

Gräte die (PL die Gräten) (fish)bone.

gratis adverb free of charge.

gratulieren verb (PERF hat gratuliert) **1** to congratulate; **2 ich habe Gabi zum Geburtstag gratuliert** I wished Gabi happy birthday; **3 wir gratulieren!** congratulations!

grau adjective grey.

Gräuel der horror.

grauen verb (PERF hat gegraut) **mir graut es davor** I dread it.

grauenvoll adjective **1** grim; **2** horrific.

grauhaarig adjective grey-haired.

grausam adjective cruel.

Grausamkeit die cruelty.

graziös adjective graceful.

greifen ◇verb (IMPERF **griff**, PERF **hat gegriffen**) **1** to take hold of; **2** to catch; **3 nach etwas greifen** to reach for something; **4 um sich greifen** to spread (of fire).

grell adjective **1** glaring; **2** garish; **3** shrill.

Grenze die (PL die Grenzen) **1** border; **2** boundary; **3** limit.

grenzen verb (PERF hat gegrenzt) **an etwas grenzen** to border on something.

Greuel SEE **Gräuel**.

Grieche der (PL die Griechen) Greek.

Griechenland das Greece.

Griechin die (PL die Griechinnen) Greek.

griechisch adjective Greek.

Griff der (PL die Griffe) **1** grasp; **2** handle.

griff SEE **greifen**.

griffbereit adjective handy; **sie hat den Korkenzieher immer griffbereit** she always keeps the corkscrew handy.

Grill der (PL die Grills) **1** grill; **2** barbecue.

Grille die (PL die Grillen) cricket (the insect).

grillen verb (PERF hat gegrillt) **1** to grill; **2** to have a barbecue.

Grillfest das (PL die Grillfeste) barbecue.

grinsen verb (PERF hat gegrinst) to grin.

Grippe die (PL die Grippen) flu.

grob adjective **1** coarse; **2** rough; **3** rude; **4 ein grober Fehler** a bad mistake.

Groschen der (PL die Groschen) **1** groschen (one hundredth of a Schilling in the former Austrian currency) SEE **Schilling**; **2** (informal) **der Groschen ist gefallen** the penny's dropped.

groß adjective **1** big; **2** great; **Gisela hatte große Angst** Gisela was very frightened; **3** tall; **4 ein großer Buchstabe** a capital letter; **5 groß werden** to grow up; **6 die großen Ferien** the summer holidays; **7 im Großen und Ganzen** on the whole; **8 Groß und Klein** young and old.

a b c d e f g h i j k l m n o p q r s t u v w x y z

a
b
c
d
e
f
g
h
i
j
k
l
m
n
o
p
q
r
s
t
u
v
w
x
y
z

groß *adverb* **was soll man da schon groß machen?** what are you supposed to do?

großartig *adjective* great.

Großbritannien *das* Great Britain.

Großbuchstabe *der* (PL *die* Großbuchstaben) capital (letter).

Größe *die* (PL *die* Größen) **1** size; **2** height; **3** greatness.

Großeltern *plural noun* grandparents.

großenteils *adverb* largely.

Großmarkt *der* (PL *die* Großmärkte) hypermarket.

Großmutter *die* (PL *die* Großmütter) grandmother.

großschreiben ◇*verb* (IMPERF großschrieb, PERF hat großgeschrieben) **ein Wort großschreiben** to write a word with a capital.

Großstadt *die* (PL *die* Großstädte) city.

Großvater *der* (PL *die* Großväter) grandfather.

großzügig *adjective* generous.

grub SEE **graben**.

grün *adjective* **1** green; **2 im Grünen** in the country; **3 die Grünen** the Greens.

Grund *der* (PL *die* Gründe) **1** ground; **2** bottom; **3** reason; **aus diesem Grund** for this reason; **4 im Grunde genommen** basically.

gründen *verb* (PERF hat gegründet) **1** to set up, to found;

2 sich auf etwas gründen to be based on something.

Grundlage *die* (PL *die* Grundlagen) basis.

gründlich *adjective* thorough.

grundsätzlich *adjective* **1** fundamental; **2** basic.

grundsätzlich *adverb* **1** basically; **2** on principle.

Grundschule *die* (PL *die* Grundschulen) primary school.

Grundstück *das* (PL *die* Grundstücke) plot (of land).

Gruppe *die* (PL *die* Gruppen) group.

Gruß *der* (PL *die* Grüße) greeting; **einen schönen Gruß an Lars** give my regards to Lars; **mit herzlichen Grüßen** with best wishes.

grüßen *verb* (PERF hat gegrüßt) **1** to greet; **2** to say hello; **3 grüß Gott!** hello; **4 grüße Thomas von mir** give Thomas my regards; **Gisela lässt grüßen** Gisela sends her regards.

gucken *verb* (PERF hat geguckt) to look.

gültig *adjective* valid.

Gültigkeit *die* validity.

Gummi *der* (PL *die* Gummis) rubber.

Gummiband *das* (PL *die* Gummibänder) rubber band.

Gummistiefel *der* (PL *die* Gummistiefel) wellington (boot).

günstig *adjective* **1** favourable; **2** convenient.

Gurgel *die* (PL *die* Gurgeln) throat.

gurgeln *verb* (PERF hat gegurgelt) to gargle.

Gurke *die* (PL *die* **Gurken**)
1 cucumber; **2** gherkin.

Gürtel *der* (PL *die* **Gürtel**) belt.

Gürteltasche *die* (PL *die*
Gürteltaschen) bum bag.

gut *adjective* **1** good; **2 guten
Appetit!** enjoy your meal!; **3 schon
gut** that's all right; **also gut** all
right; **4 im Guten** amicably; **5 alles
Gute!** all the best!
gut *adverb* **1** well; **2 gut
schmecken** to taste good; **3 gut
zwei Stunden** a good two hours;
4 uns geht's gut we're fine; **ihm
geht es nicht gut** he's not well.

Gut *das* (PL *die* **Güter**) **1** property;
2 estate; **3** (*plural*) goods, freight.

Güte *die* **1** goodness; **du meine
Güte!** my goodness!; **2** quality.

Güterzug *der* (PL *die* **Güterzüge**)
goods train.

gutgehen SEE **gut**.

gutmütig *adjective* good-natured.

Gutschein *der* (PL *die* **Gutscheine**)
1 voucher; **2** coupon.

Gymnasium *das* (PL *die*
Gymnasien) grammar school.

Gymnastik *die* **1** gymnastics;
2 keep-fit (*exercises*).

Hh

Haar *das* (PL *die* **Haare**) **1** hair; **sich
die Haare waschen** to wash your
hair; **2 um ein Haar** (*informal*) very
nearly.

Haarbürste *die* (PL *die*
Haarbürsten) hairbrush.

haarig *adjective* hairy.

Haarschnitt *der* (PL *die*
Haarschnitte) haircut.

Haarwaschmittel *das* (PL *die*
Haarwaschmittel) shampoo.

haben ⬦*verb* (PRES **hat**, IMPERF
hatte, PERF **hat gehabt**) **1** to have
(got); **ich habe ein neues Auto** I
have (I've got) a new car; **etwas
gegen jemanden haben** to have
something against somebody;
2 (*used with another verb, like 'have'
in English, to form past tenses*) **ich
habe Werners Adresse verloren**
I've lost Werner's address; **ich habe
deine Mutter gestern angerufen** I
rang your mother yesterday;
3 Angst haben to be frightened;
Hunger haben to be hungry;
Husten haben to have a cough;
4 heute haben wir Mittwoch it's
Wednesday today; **5 die Kinder
haben Ferien** the children are on
holiday; **6 was hat sie?** what's the
matter with her?; **7 ich hätte gern
...** I'd like ...; **ich hätte ihr geholfen**
I would have helped her; **8 sich
haben** (*informal*) to make a fuss.

Habicht *der* (PL *die* **Habichte**)
hawk.

hacken *verb* (PERF **hat gehackt**)
1 to chop (up); **2** to peck (*of a bird*).

Hackfleisch *das* minced meat.

Hacksteak *das* (PL *die*
Hacksteaks) beefburger (*without
bread*).

Hafen *der* (PL *die* **Häfen**) harbour.

Haferflocken *plural noun* porridge oats.

haftbar *adjective* **für etwas haftbar sein** to be liable for something.

haften *verb* (PERF **hat gehaftet**) **1** to stick; **2 für etwas haften** to be responsible for something.

Hagel *der* hail.

hageln *verb* (PERF **hat gehagelt**) to hail.

Hagelschauer *der* (PL *die* **Hagelschauer**) hailstorm.

Hahn *der* (PL *die* **Hähne**) **1** cock; **2** tap.

Hähnchen *das* (PL *die* **Hähnchen**) chicken.

Hai *der* (PL *die* **Haie**) shark.

Haken *der* (PL *die* **Haken**) **1** hook; **2** tick; **3** catch; **da muss ein Haken dran sein** there must be a catch.

halb *adjective* half; **zum halben Preis** at half price; **halb eins** half past twelve.

Halbbruder *der* (PL *die* **Halbbrüder**) half-brother.

Halbfinale *das* (PL *die* **Halbfinale**) semi-final.

halbieren *verb* (PERF **hat halbiert**) to halve.

Halbkreis *der* (PL *die* **Halbkreise**) semicircle.

Halbpension *die* half board.

Halbschwester *die* (PL *die* **Halbschwestern**) half-sister.

halbtags *adverb* part-time.

halbwegs *adverb* **1** half-way; **2** more or less.

Halbzeit *die* (PL *die* **Halbzeiten**) **1** half; **2** half-time; **während der Halbzeit** during half-time.

half SEE **helfen**.

Hälfte *die* (PL *die* **Hälften**) half; **zur Hälfte** half.

Halle *die* (PL *die* **Hallen**) **1** hall; **2** foyer.

Hallenbad *das* (PL *die* **Hallenbäder**) indoor swimming pool.

hallo *exclamation* hello!

Hals *der* (PL *die* **Hälse**) **1** neck; **2** throat; **mir tut der Hals weh** I've got a sore throat; **3 aus vollem Hals schreien** to shout at the top of your voice; **4 Hals über Kopf** in a rush.

Halsband *das* (PL *die* **Halsbänder**) collar.

Halsschmerzen *plural noun* sore throat; **Paul hat Halsschmerzen** Paul's got a sore throat.

Halstuch *das* (PL *die* **Halstücher**) scarf.

Halt *der* **1** hold; **jetzt hat es einen besseren Halt** it holds better now; **2 Halt machen** to stop.

halt *exclamation* stop!

haltbar *adjective* **1** hard-wearing; **2** durable; **3 mindestens haltbar bis** ... best before ....

halten ⋄*verb* (PRES **hält**, IMPERF **hielt**, PERF **hat gehalten**) **1** to hold; **2** to keep; **sein Versprechen halten** to keep your promise; **warm halten**

to keep warm; **3** to stop; **der Bus hält direkt vor seiner Haustür** the bus stops right outside his door; **4** to save (*in sport*); **5** to take (*a paper, magazine*); **6 ich habe ihn für deinen Bruder gehalten** I took him for your brother; **7 viel von jemandem halten** to think a lot of somebody; **jemanden für ehrlich halten** to think somebody is honest; **8 zu jemandem halten** to stand by somebody; **9 eine Rede halten** to make a speech; **10 sich halten** to keep (*of milk, fruit, etc.*); **11 sich links/rechts halten** to keep left/right; **12 sich gut halten** to do well; **13 sich an etwas halten** to keep to something.

Haltestelle die (PL die Haltestellen) stop.

haltmachen SEE **Halt**.

Haltung die (PL die Haltungen) **1** posture; **2** attitude; **3** composure.

Hammelfleisch das mutton.

Hammer der (PL die Hämmer) hammer.

hämmern verb (PERF hat gehämmert) to hammer.

Hamster der (PL die Hamster) hamster.

Hand die (PL die Hände) hand; **jemandem die Hand geben** to shake hands with somebody.

Handarbeit die (PL die Handarbeiten) **1** handicraft; **2** hand-made article.

Handball der handball.

Handbremse die (PL die Handbremsen) handbrake; **die**

Handbremse ziehen to pull the handbrake.

Handbuch das (PL die Handbücher) manual.

Handel der **1** trade; **2** deal; **3 in den Handel kommen** to come on the market.

handeln verb (PERF hat gehandelt) **1** to trade, to deal; **2 mit jemandem handeln** to bargain with somebody; **3** to act; **4 von etwas handeln** to be about something; **5 es handelt sich um** ... it's about ...; **worum handelt es sich?** what's it about?

Handelsschule die (PL die Handelsschulen) business school, vocational college.

Handfläche die (PL die Handflächen) palm.

Handgelenk das (PL die Handgelenke) wrist.

Handgepäck das hand luggage.

handhaben verb (PERF hat gehandhabt) to handle.

Händler der (PL die Händler) dealer.

handlich adjective handy.

Handlung die (PL die Handlungen) **1** act; **2** action; **3** plot.

Handschellen (plural noun) handcuffs.

Handschrift die (PL die Handschriften) handwriting.

Handschuh der (PL die Handschuhe) glove.

Handtasche die (PL die Handtaschen) bag.

Handtrommel die (PL die Handtrommeln) tambourine.

a
b
c
d
e
f
g
h
i
j
k
l
m
n
o
p
q
r
s
t
u
v
w
x
y
z

Handtuch das (PL die **Handtücher**) towel.

Handwerker der (PL die **Handwerker**) **1** craftsman; **2** workman.

Handwerkszeug das tools.

Handy das (PL die **Handys**) mobile (phone).

Hang der (PL die **Hänge**) slope.

Hängematte die (PL die **Hängematten**) hammock.

hängen[1] verb (PERF hat gehängt) **1** to hang; **Florian hat das Bild an die Wand gehängt** Florian hung the picture on the wall; **sie hängte ihren Mantel in den Schrank** she hung her coat up in the cupboard; **2 sie haben den Wohnwagen an das Auto gehängt** they attached the caravan to the car; **3 sich an jemanden hängen** to latch on to somebody.

hängen[2] ◇verb (IMPERF **hing**, PERF **hat gehangen**) **1** to hang; **mein Bild hat immer hier gehangen** my picture used to hang here; **2 an seinen Eltern hängen** to be attached to your parents; **sie hängt sehr an ihrer Mutter** she's very attached to her mother; **3 an etwas hängen bleiben** to catch on something, to stick to something; **ich bin mit dem Ärmel am Zaun hängen geblieben** I got my sleeve caught on the fence.

hängenbleiben SEE **hängen**[2].

Hansaplast™ das plaster.

Happen der (PL die **Happen**) mouthful; **ich habe heute keinen Happen gegessen** I haven't had a bite to eat all day.

Harfe die (PL die **Harfen**) harp.

Harke die (PL die **Harken**) rake.

harmlos adjective harmless.

hart adjective **1** hard; **2** harsh.

hart gekocht adjective hard-boiled.

Häschen das (PL die **Häschen**) bunny rabbit.

Hase der (PL die **Hasen**) hare.

Haselnuss die (PL die **Haselnüsse**) hazelnut.

Hass der hatred.

hassen verb (PERF hat gehasst) to hate.

hässlich adjective **1** ugly; **sie hat ein hässliches Gesicht** she's got an ugly face; **2** nasty; **das war sehr hässlich von dir** that was very nasty of you.

hast SEE **haben**.

hastig adjective hasty.

hat, **hatte**, **hatten**, **hattest**, **hattet** SEE **haben**.

Haube die (PL die **Hauben**) **1** bonnet; **2** cap.

hauen ◇verb (PRES **haut**, IMPERF **haute**, PERF **hat gehauen**) **1** to beat; **2** to thump, to bang; **3 sich hauen** to fight; **4 jemanden übers Ohr hauen** (informal) to cheat somebody.

Haufen der (PL die **Haufen**) **1** heap; **2** crowd (of people); **3 ein Haufen** (informal) heaps of; **ein Haufen Geld** heaps of money.

haufenweise *adverb* heaps of;
Gabi hat haufenweise CDs Gabi
has heaps of CDs.

häufig *adjective* frequent.

Häufigkeit die frequency.

Hauptbahnhof der (PL die
Hauptbahnhöfe) main station.

Hauptgericht das (PL die
Hauptgerichte) main course.

Hauptrolle die (PL die Hauptrollen)
lead.

Hauptsache die (PL die
Hauptsachen) main thing.

hauptsächlich *adjective* main.
hauptsächlich *adverb* mainly.

Hauptschule die secondary
school.

Hauptstadt die (PL die
Hauptstädte) capital.

Hauptstraße die (PL die
Hauptstraßen) main road.

Hauptverkehrszeit die (PL die
Hauptverkehrszeiten) rush hour.

Hauptwort das (PL die
Hauptwörter) noun.

Haus das (PL die Häuser) **1** house;
2 nach Hause home; **zu Hause** at
home.

Hausarbeit die (PL die
Hausarbeiten) **1** housework; **die
Kinder müssen bei der Hausarbeit
helfen** the children have to help
with the housework; **2** homework.

Hausaufgaben *plural noun*
homework; **hast du deine
Hausaufgaben gemacht?** have you
done your homework?

Hausfrau die (PL die Hausfrauen)
housewife.

Haushalt der (PL die Haushalte)
1 household; **2 den Haushalt
machen** to do the housework; **im
Haushalt helfen** to help with the
housework; **3** budget.

Haushaltswarengeschäft
das (PL die Haushaltswarengeschäfte) hardware shop.

Hausmeister der (PL die
Hausmeister) caretaker.

Hausnummer die house number.

Hausschlüssel der (PL die
Hausschlüssel) front-door key.

Hausschuh der (PL die
Hausschuhe) slipper.

Haustier das (PL die Haustiere) pet.

Haustür die (PL die Haustüren)
front door.

Haut die (PL die Häute) skin; **aus der
Haut fahren** (*informal*) to go up the
wall.

Hebamme die (PL die Hebammen)
midwife.

Hebel der (PL die Hebel) lever.

heben ◇*verb* (IMPERF **hob**, PERF **hat
gehoben**) **1** to lift; **2 sich heben** to
rise.

Hecke die (PL die Hecken) hedge.

Heer das (PL die Heere) army.

Hefe die (PL die Hefen) yeast.

Heft das (PL die Hefte) **1** exercise
book; **2** issue (*of a magazine*).

heften *verb* (PERF **hat geheftet**)
1 to pin; **2** to tack (*by sewing*); **3**
clip; **4** to staple.

a
b
c
d
e
f
g
h
i
j
k
l
m
n
o
p
q
r
s
t
u
v
w
x
y
z

heftig *adjective* **1** violent; **2** heavy (*snow, rain*).

Heftklammer die (PL die Heftklammern) staple.

Heftpflaster das (PL die Heftpflaster) sticking plaster.

Heftzwecke die (PL die Heftzwecken) drawing pin.

Heide die heath.

Heidekraut das heather.

Heidelbeere die (PL die Heidelbeeren) bilberry.

heilen *verb* (PERF hat geheilt) **1** to cure; **2** to heal.

heilig *adjective* **1** holy; **2** **heilig halten** to hold sacred; **3** **der heilige Franz von Assisi** Saint Francis of Assisi.

Heiligabend der (PL die Heiligabende) Christmas Eve.

Heilige der/die (PL die Heiligen) saint.

Heilmittel das (PL die Heilmittel) remedy.

Heim das (PL die Heime) **1** home; **2** hostel.

heim *adverb* home.

Heimat die (PL die Heimaten) **1** home; **2** native land.

Heimatstadt die home town.

Heimfahrt die (PL die Heimfahrten) **1** journey home; **2** way home.

heimgehen ◇*verb* (IMPERF ging heim, PERF ist heimgegangen) to go home.

heimlich *adjective* secret. **heimlich** *adverb* secretly.

Heimspiel das (PL die Heimspiele) home game.

Heimweg der (PL die Heimwege) way home.

Heimweh das homesickness; **Heimweh haben** to be homesick.

Heirat die (PL die Heiraten) marriage.

heiraten *verb* (PERF hat geheiratet) to marry.

heiser *adjective* hoarse.

heiß *adjective* hot.

heißen ◇*verb* (IMPERF hieß, PERF hat geheißen) **1** to be called; **wie heißt du?** what's your name?; **2** to mean; **3 das heißt** that is; **4 es heißt** it is said; **5 wie heißt 'dog' auf Deutsch?** what's the German for 'dog'?

heiter *adjective* **1** bright; **2** cheerful.

heizen *verb* (PERF hat geheizt) **1** to heat (*a room*); **2** to put the heating on; **3** to have the heating on.

Heizung die heating.

hektisch *adjective* hectic.

Held der (PL die Helden) hero.

Heldin die (PL die Heldinnen) heroine.

helfen ◇*verb* (PRES hilft, IMPERF half, PERF hat geholfen) **1** to help; **Lisa hilft mir** Lisa is helping me; **2 es hilft nichts** it's no good; **3 sich zu helfen wissen** to know what to do; **ich weiß mir nicht zu helfen** I don't know what to do.

Helfer *der* (PL *die* **Helfer**) **1** helper;
2 assistant.

Helferin *die* (PL *die* **Helferinnen**)
1 helper; **2** assistant.

hell *adjective* **1** light (*colour*);
2 bright; **3 eine helle Stimme** a
clear voice; **4 helles Bier** lager;
5 da ist heller Wahnsinn (*informal*)
that's sheer madness.

hellwach *adjective* wide awake.

Helm *der* (PL *die* **Helme**) helmet.

Hemd *das* (PL *die* **Hemden**) **1** shirt;
2 vest.

Henkel *der* (PL *die* **Henkel**) handle.

Henne *die* (PL *die* **Hennen**) hen.

her *adverb* **1** here; **komm her** come
here; **2 vor jemandem her** in front
of somebody; **3 hinter etwas her
sein** to be after something; **4 von
der Farbe her** as far as the colour is
concerned; **5 wo bist du her?**
where do you come from?; **6 wo hat
Klaus das her?** where did Klaus get
it from?; **7 her damit!** (*informal*)
give it to me!; **8** ago; **das ist schon
lange her** it was a long time ago;
das ist drei Tage her it was three
days ago.

herab *adverb* down.

herablassend *adjective*
condescending.

herabsetzen *verb* (PERF **hat
herabgesetzt**) **1** to reduce; **2** to
belittle.

heran *adverb* **1 an etwas heran**
close to something, right up to
something; **bis an die Wand heran**
up to the wall; **2 immer heran!** come
closer!

herankommen ⋄*verb* (IMPERF
kam heran, PERF **ist
herangekommen**) **1** to come near;
2 herankommen an to come up to;
3 ich komme nicht heran I can't
get at it.

herauf *adverb* up.

heraufkommen ⋄*verb* (IMPERF
kam herauf, PERF **ist
heraufgekommen**) to come up.

heraus *adverb* out.

herausbekommen ⋄*verb*
(IMPERF **bekam heraus**, PERF **hat
herausbekommen**) **1** to get out;
2 to find out; **3** to solve; **4 Geld
herausbekommen** to get change.

herausbringen *verb* (IMPERF
brachte heraus, PERF **hat
herausgebracht**) **1** to publish (*a
book*); **2** to release (*an album*); **3** to
launch.

herausfinden ⋄*verb* (IMPERF **fand
heraus**, PERF **hat herausgefunden**)
1 to find out; **2** to find your way out.

herausgeben ⋄*verb* (PRES **gibt
heraus**, IMPERF **gab heraus**, PERF
hat herausgegeben) **1** to hand
over; **2** to bring out.

herauskommen ⋄*verb* (IMPERF
kam heraus, PERF **ist
herausgekommen**) to come out.

herausnehmen ⋄*verb* (PRES
nimmt heraus, IMPERF **nahm
heraus**, PERF **hat
herausgenommen**) **1** to take out;
**sie hat ihren Lippenstift aus der
Tasche herausgenommen** she took
her lipstick out of the bag; **2 sich
die Mandeln herausnehmen**

a
b
c
d
e
f
g
h
i
j
k
l
m
n
o
p
q
r
s
t
u
v
w
x
y
z

lassen to have your tonsils out; **3 es sich herausnehmen, etwas zu tun** to have the nerve to do something; **du nimmst dir zu viel heraus** you're going too far.

herausstellen verb (PERF **hat herausgestellt**) **1** to put out; **2 sich herausstellen** to turn out; **es stellte sich heraus, dass** ... it turned out that ....

herausziehen ◇verb (IMPERF **zog heraus**, PERF **hat herausgezogen**) to pull out.

herb adjective **1** sharp; **2** dry (wine).

herbei adverb over (here); **kommt herbei!** come over here!

Herberge die (PL die **Herbergen**) hostel.

Herbergsmutter die (PL die **Herbergsmütter**) warden (in a youth hostel).

Herbergsvater der (PL die **Herbergsväter**) warden (in a youth hostel).

herbringen ◇verb (IMPERF **brachte her**, PERF **hat hergebracht**) to bring (here).

Herbst der (PL die **Herbste**) autumn; **im Herbst** in autumn.

Herd der (PL die **Herde**) cooker.

Herde die (PL die **Herden**) **1** herd; **2** flock.

herein adverb in; **herein!** come in!

hereinfallen ◇verb (PRES **fällt herein**, IMPERF **fiel herein**, PERF **ist hereingefallen**) to be taken in; **auf einen Betrüger hereinfallen** to be taken in by a swindler.

hereinkommen ◇verb (IMPERF **kam herein**, PERF **ist hereingekommen**) to come in.

hereinlassen ◇verb (PRES **lässt herein**, IMPERF **ließ herein**, PERF **hat hereingelassen**) to let in; **Max lässt mich nicht ins Zimmer herein** Max won't let me into the room.

Herfahrt die (PL die **Herfahrten**) **1** journey here; **2** way here.

hergeben ◇verb (PRES **gibt her**, IMPERF **gab her**, PERF **hat hergegeben**) **1** to hand over; **gib die Tasche her!** hand over the bag!; **2** to give away; **3 sich für etwas hergeben** to get involved in something; **dazu gebe ich mich nicht her** I won't have anything to do with it.

Hering der (PL die **Heringe**) herring.

herkommen ◇verb (IMPERF **kam her**, PERF **ist hergekommen**) to come (here); **wo kommt das her?** where does it come from?

Herkunft die (PL die **Herkünfte**) **1** origin; **2** background.

Heroin das heroin.

Herr der (PL die **Herren**) **1** gentleman; **2 Herr Huber** Mr Huber; **3 Sehr geehrte Herren** Dear Sirs (in a letter); **4 meine Herren!** gentlemen!; **5** master; **6 der Herr** the Lord.

herrichten verb (PERF **hat hergerichtet**) to get ready, to prepare; **sie richtet die Betten für die Gäste her** she's getting the beds for the guests ready.

herrlich adjective marvellous.

124

herrschen *verb* (PERF **hat geherrscht**) **1** to rule; **2** to be; **es herrschte große Aufregung** there was great excitement.

herstellen *verb* (PERF **hat hergestellt**) to manufacture, to make; **in Deutschland hergestellt** made in Germany.

Herstellung *die* (PL *die* **Herstellungen**) manufacture, production.

herüber *adverb* over (here).

herum *adverb* **um … herum** round; **falsch herum** the wrong way round; **im Kreis herum** in a circle.

herumdrehen *verb* (PERF **hat herumgedreht**) **1** to turn (over or round); **2 sich herumdrehen** to turn round.

herumführen *verb* (PERF **hat herumgeführt**) to show around.

herumgehen ◇*verb* (IMPERF **ging herum**, PERF **ist herumgegangen**) **1** to go round; **2** to walk around; **im Park herumgehen** to walk around the park; **3** to pass (*of time*).

herunter *adverb* down; **die Treppe herunter** down the stairs.

herunterfallen ◇*verb* (PRES **fällt herunter**, IMPERF **fiel herunter**, PERF **ist heruntergefallen**) **1** to fall down; **2** to fall off.

herunterkommen ◇*verb* (IMPERF **kam herunter**, PERF **ist heruntergekommen**) **1** to come down; **2** (*informal*) to go to rack and ruin.

herunterlassen ◇*verb* (PRES **lässt herunter**, IMPERF **ließ herunter**, PERF **hat heruntergelassen**) to let down, to lower.

hervor *adverb* out.

hervorragend *adjective* outstanding.
hervorragend *adverb* outstandingly well.

hervorrufen ◇*verb* (IMPERF **rief hervor**, PERF **hat hervorgerufen**) to cause.

Herz *das* (PL *die* **Herzen**) **1** heart; **2** hearts (*in cards*).

Herzanfall *der* (PL *die* **Herzanfälle**) heart attack.

Herzinfarkt *der* (PL *die* **Herzinfarkte**) heart attack.

herzlich *adjective* **1** warm; **2** sincere; **3 herzlichen Dank** many thanks; **4 herzliche Grüße** best wishes; **5 herzlichen Glückwunsch!** congratulations!; **6 herzlich willkommen in Passau!** welcome to Passau!

herzlos *adjective* heartless.

Herzschlag *der* (PL *die* **Herzschläge**) **1** heartbeat; **2** heart failure; **er hat einen Herzschlag bekommen** he had a heart attack.

heterosexuell *adjective* heterosexual.

Heterosexuelle *der/die* (PL *die* **Heterosexuellen**) heterosexual.

Heu *das* hay.

heulen *verb* (PERF **hat geheult**) **1** to howl; **2** (*informal*) to cry.

a b c d e f g h i j k l m n o p q r s t u v w x y z

Heuschnupfen *der* hayfever; **ich habe Heuschnupfen** I suffer from hayfever.

heute *adverb* today; **heute Abend** this evening; **heute Morgen** this morning.

heutig *adjective* 1 today's; 2 **in der heutigen Zeit** nowadays.

heutzutage nowadays; **heutzutage sind sie häufig** they're common nowadays.

Hexe *die* (PL *die* **Hexen**) witch.

Hexenschuss *der* lumbago.

hielt SEE **halten**.

hier *adverb* here.

hierher *adverb* here; **komm sofort hierher!** come here immediately!

hierhin *adverb* here.

hiesig *adjective* local.

hieß SEE **heißen**.

Hilfe *die* (PL *die* **Hilfen**) 1 help; 2 aid.

hilflos *adjective* helpless.

hilfsbereit *adjective* helpful.

hilft SEE **helfen**.

Himbeere *die* (PL *die* **Himbeeren**) raspberry.

Himmel *der* (PL *die* **Himmel**) 1 sky; 2 heaven.

himmlisch *adjective* heavenly.

hin *adverb* 1 there; **hin und zurück** there and back; 2 **hin und wieder** now and again; 3 **hin und her** back and forth, to and fro; 4 **auf meinen Rat hin** on my advice; **auf Ihren Brief hin** in reply to your letter; 5 **wo ist Dominik hin?** where's Dominik gone?; 6 **es ist nicht mehr lange hin** it's not long to go; 7 **ich bin hin** (*informal*) I'm worn out.

hinauf *adverb* up; **die Straße hinauf** up the road.

hinaufgehen ◇*verb* (IMPERF **ging hinauf**, PERF **ist hinaufgegangen**) to go up.

hinaus *adverb* 1 out; 2 **auf Jahre hinaus** for years to come.

hinausbringen ◇*verb* (IMPERF **brachte hinaus**, PERF **hat hinausgebracht**) 1 to see out (*a person*); 2 to take out; **den Abfall hinausbringen** to take the rubbish out.

hinausgehen ◇*verb* (IMPERF **ging hinaus**, PERF **ist hinausgegangen**) 1 to go out; 2 **über etwas hinausgehen** to exceed something; 3 **das Zimmer geht nach Norden hinaus** the room faces north.

hindern *verb* (PERF **hat gehindert**) to stop; **jemanden daran hindern, etwas zu tun** to stop somebody from doing something.

Hindernis *das* (PL *die* **Hindernisse**) obstacle.

hinduistisch *adjective* Hindu.

hindurch *adverb* 1 through it/them; 2 **das ganze Jahr hindurch** throughout the year.

hinein *adverb* 1 in; 2 **in etwas hinein** into something.

hineingehen ◇*verb* (IMPERF **ging hinein**, PERF **ist hineingegangen**) 1 to go in; 2 **in etwas hineingehen** to go into something.

hinfahren ◇*verb* (PRES **fährt hin**, IMPERF **fuhr hin**, PERF **ist**

hingefahren) 1 to go/drive there;
2 (PERF **hat hingefahren**) to take/
drive there.

Hinfahrt *die* (PL *die* **Hinfahrten**)
1 journey there, way there;
2 outward journey.

hinfallen ◇*verb* (PRES **fällt hin**,
IMPERF **fiel hin**, PERF **ist hingefallen**)
to fall over.

hing SEE **hängen**.

hingehen ◇*verb* (IMPERF **ging hin**,
PERF **ist hingegangen**) **1** to go there;
wo geht ihr hin? where are you
going?; **2** to go by (*of time*).

hinken *verb* (PERF **hat/ist gehinkt**)
to limp.

hinkommen ◇*verb* (IMPERF **kam
hin**, PERF **ist hingekommen**) **1** to get
there; **2** to go; **wo kommt das Buch
hin?** where does the book go?; **3 mit
etwas hinkommen** (*informal*) to
manage (with something).

hinlegen *verb* (PERF **hat hingelegt**)
1 to put down; **leg die Zeitung
unten hin** put the paper down there;
2 sich hinlegen to lie down.

hinsetzen *verb* (PERF **hat sich
hingesetzt**) **sich hinsetzen** to sit
down; **Petra setzte sich neben ihm
hin** Petra sat down next to him.

hinten *adverb* at the back; **von
hinten** from behind.

hinter *preposition* (+ DAT *or* + ACC)
1 behind; **2 etwas hinter sich
bringen** to get something over with.

hintere SEE **hinterer**.

hintereinander *adverb* **1** one
behind the other; **2** one after the

other; **dreimal hintereinander**
three times in a row.

hinterer, hintere, hinteres
adjective **1** back; **2 am hinteren
Ende** at the far end.

Hintergrund *der* (PL *die*
Hintergründe) background.

hinterher *adverb* afterwards.

Hintern *der* (PL *die* **Hintern**) bottom.

Hinterrad *das* (PL *die* **Hinterräder**)
back wheel.

hinters = **hinter das.**

hinüber *adverb* **1** over (there),
across (there); **2 das Radio ist
hinüber** (*informal*) the radio has
had it.

hinübergehen ◇*verb* (IMPERF
ging hinüber, PERF **ist
hinübergegangen**) to go over, to go
across.

hinunter *adverb* down.

Hinweg *der* (PL *die* **Hinwege**) way
there; **auf dem Hinweg** on the way
there.

Hinweis *der* (PL *die* **Hinweise**)
1 hint; **das war ein deutlicher
Hinweis, dass er lieber allein fährt**
it was an obvious hint that he
prefers to go on his own;
2 reference; **3 Hinweise zur
Bedienung** operating instructions.

hinweisen ◇*verb* (IMPERF **wies hin**,
PERF **hat hingewiesen**) to point;
jemanden auf etwas hinweisen to
point something out to somebody.

Hirn *das* (PL *die* **Hirne**) brain.

Hirnhautentzündung *die*
meningitis.

Hirsch der (PL die **Hirsche**) **1** deer; **2** stag; **3** venison.

Hirt der (PL die **Hirten**) shepherd.

Hirtin die (PL die **Hirtinnen**) shepherd.

Historiker der (PL die **Historiker**) historian.

historisch adjective historical.

Hitze die heat.

hitzefrei adjective **hitzefrei haben** to be sent home early from school because of hot weather.

Hitzewelle die (PL die **Hitzewellen**) heatwave.

Hitzschlag der (PL die **Hitzschläge**) heatstroke.

hob SEE **heben**.

Hobby das (PL die **Hobbys**) hobby.

Hoch das (PL die **Hochs**) **1** cheer; **ein dreifaches Hoch für das Geburtstagskind** three cheers for the birthday girl/boy; **2** high (*pressure*).

hoch adjective (*with endings 'hoch' becomes 'hoher/hohe/hohes'*) **1** high; **der Zaun ist zu hoch** the fence is too high; **ein hoher Zaun** a high fence; **2** deep (*snow*); **3** great (*age, weight*).
hoch adverb **1** highly; **hoch begabt** highy gifted; **2 die Treppe hoch** up the stairs.

hochachtungsvoll adverb **Hochachtungsvoll** Yours faithfully.

hochhackig adjective high-heeled; **hochhackige Schuhe** high-heeled shoes.

Hochhaus das (PL die **Hochhäuser**) high-rise building.

hochheben ◇verb (IMPERF **hob hoch**, PERF **hat hochgehoben**) to lift up; **sie hob das Kind hoch** she lifted up the child.

hochnäsig adjective stuck-up.

Hochschule die (PL die **Hochschulen**) university, college.

Hochsprung der high jump.

höchst adverb extremely.

höchstens adverb **1** at most; **2** except perhaps.

höchster, höchste, höchstes adjective highest; **der Mount Everest ist der der höchste Berg der Welt** Mount Everest is the highest mountain in the world; **es ist höchste Zeit** it is high time.

Höchstgeschwindigkeit die maximum speed.

höchstmöglich adjective highest possible; **die höchstmögliche Geschwindigkeit** the highest possible speed.

Höchsttemperatur die (PL die **Höchsttemperaturen**) maximum temperature.

Hochzeit die (PL die **Hochzeiten**) wedding.

Hochzeitstag der (PL die **Hochzeitstage**) **1** wedding day; **2** wedding anniversary.

Hocker der (PL die **Hocker**) stool.

Hockey das hockey.

Hockeyschläger der (PL die **Hockeyschläger**) hockey stick.

Hof der (PL die **Höfe**) **1** yard; **2** farm.

hoffen *verb* (PERF **hat gehofft**) to hope; **auf etwas hoffen** to hope for something.

hoffentlich *adverb* hopefully; **hoffentlich nicht** I hope not.

Hoffnung die (PL die **Hoffnungen**) hope.

hoffnungslos *adjective* hopeless.

höflich *adjective* polite.

Höflichkeit die (PL die **Höflichkeiten**) politeness, courtesy.

Höhe die (PL die **Höhen**) **1** height; **2 das ist die Höhe!** (*informal*) that's the limit!

hoher, **hohe**, **hohes** SEE **hoch**.

höher *adjective* **1** higher; **2** deeper.

hohl *adjective* hollow.

Höhle die (PL die **Höhlen**) **1** cave; **2** den.

holen *verb* (PERF **hat geholt**) **1** to get, to fetch; **2 jemanden holen lassen** to send for somebody; **3 sich etwas holen** to get something.

Holland das Holland.

Holländer der (PL die **Holländer**) Dutchman.

Holländerin die (PL die **Holländerinnen**) Dutchwoman.

holländisch *adjective* Dutch.

Hölle die (PL die **Höllen**) hell.

Holz das (PL die **Hölzer**) wood.

Holzkohle die charcoal.

homöopathisch *adjective* homeopathic.

homosexuell *adjective* homosexual.

Homosexuelle der/die (PL die **Homosexuellen**) homosexual.

Honig der (PL die **Honige**) honey.

horchen *verb* (PERF **hat gehorcht**) **1** to listen; **2** to eavesdrop.

hören *verb* (PERF **hat gehört**) **1** to hear; **2** to listen (to); **Musik hören** to listen to music.

Hörer der (PL die **Hörer**) **1** listener; **2** receiver (*of a phone*).

Hörerin die (PL die **Hörerinnen**) listener.

Hörgerät das (PL die **Hörgeräte**) hearing aid.

Horizont der (PL die **Horizonte**) horizon.

horizontal *adjective* horizontal.

Horn das (PL die **Hörner**) horn.

Horoskop das (PL die **Horoskope**) horoscope.

Horrorfilm der (PL die **Horrorfilme**) horror film.

Hose die (PL die **Hosen**) trousers.

Hosenträger *plural noun* braces.

Hotdog das or der (PL die **Hotdogs**) hot dog.

Hotel das (PL die **Hotels**) hotel.

Hotelverzeichnis das (PL die **Hotelverzeichnisse**) list of hotels.

hübsch *adjective* **1** pretty; **2** nice.

Hubschrauber der (PL die **Hubschrauber**) helicopter.

Huf der (PL die **Hufe**) hoof.

Hufeisen das (PL die **Hufeisen**) horseshoe.

Hüfte die (PL die **Hüften**) hip.

129

a **Hügel** *der* (PL *die* Hügel) hill.

b **Huhn** *das* (PL *die* Hühner) **1** chicken; **2** hen.

c **Hummel** *die* (PL *die* Hummeln) bumble-bee.

d **Hummer** *der* (PL *die* Hummer) lobster.

e **Humor** *der* humour; **Humor haben** to have a sense of humour.

f **Hund** *der* (PL *die* Hunde) dog; **den Hund ausführen** to take the dog for a walk.

Hundehütte *die* (PL *die* Hundehütten) kennel.

j **hundemüde** *adjective* (*informal*) dog-tired.

k **Hundepension** *die* (PL *die* Hundepensionen) kennels (*for boarding*).

m **hundert** *number* a hundred, one hundred.

n **Hunger** *der* hunger; **Hunger haben** to be hungry.

o **hungrig** *adjective* hungry.

p **Hupe** *die* (PL *die* Hupen) horn.

q **hurra** *exclamation* hooray!

r **Husten** *der* cough.

s **husten** *verb* (PERF **hat gehustet**) to cough.

t **Hut** *der* (PL *die* Hüte) hat.

u **hüten** *verb* (PERF **hat gehütet**) **1** to look after (*a child, children*); **2 sich hüten** to be on your guard; **3 sich hüten, etwas zu tun** to take care not to do something.

z **Hütte** *die* (PL *die* Hütten) hut.

Hygiene *die* **1** hygiene; **2** health care.

hygienisch *adjective* hygienic.

hypnotisieren *verb* (PERF **hat hypnotisiert**) to hypnotize.

Hypothek *die* (PL *die* Hypotheken) mortgage.

hysterisch *adjective* hysterical.

Ii

ich *pronoun* I.

Icon *das* (PL *die* Icons) icon; **das Icon anklicken** to click the icon.

IC-Zug *der* (PL *die* IC-Züge) (*Intercityzug*) intercity train.

ideal *adjective* ideal.

Idee *die* (PL *die* Ideen) idea.

identifizieren *verb* (PERF **hat identifiziert**) to identify.

identisch *adjective* identical.

Idiot *der* (PL *die* Idioten) idiot.

idiotisch *adjective* idiotic.

idyllisch *adjective* idyllic.

Igel *der* (PL *die* Igel) hedgehog.

ihm *pronoun* **1** him, to him; **2** it, to it.

ihn *pronoun* **1** him; **2** it.

ihnen *pronoun* them, to them.

Ihr *adjective* your; **Ihr Sohn hat mir geschrieben** your son wrote to me.

ihr *pronoun* **1** you (*plural*); **2** her, to her; **3** (*standing for an object*) it, to it.

ihr *adjective* **1** her; **2** its; **3** their; **sie**

haben ihr Auto verkauft they sold their car.

ihrer, ihre, ihr(e)s *pronoun* **1** hers; **mein Rad ist rot, ihrs ist blau** my bike is red, hers is blue; **2** theirs; **das ist nicht ihre Katze, ihre ist schwarz** that's not their cat, theirs is black.

Ihrer, Ihre, Ihr(e)s *pronoun* yours; **mein Job ist nicht so interessant wie Ihrer** my job's not as interesting as yours.

ihretwegen *adverb* **1** for her sake; **2** for their sake; **3** because of her; **4** because of them.

Ihretwegen *adverb* **1** for your sake; **2** because of you.

Illusion *die* (PL die **Illusionen**) illusion.

Illustration *die* (PL die **Illustrationen**) illustration.

Illustrierte *die* (PL die **Illustrierten**) magazine.

im = **in dem; was läuft im Kino?** what's on at the cinema?; **im August** in August.

Imbiss *der* (PL die **Imbisse**) **1** snack; **2** snack bar.

Imbissstube *die* (PL die **Imbissstuben**) snack bar.

Imitator *der* (PL die **Imitatoren**) mimic, impressionist.

imitieren *verb* (PERF **hat imitiert**) to imitate.

immer *adverb* **1** always; **2 immer wieder** again and again; **3 immer mehr** more and more; **immer dunkler** darker and darker;

4 immer noch still; **5 immer, wenn er anruft** every time he rings; **6 wo/wer/wann immer** wherever/whoever/whenever; **7 für immer** for ever.

immerhin *adverb* at least.

immerzu *adverb* all the time.

Imperfekt *das* imperfect; **'ich schlug' steht im Imperfekt** 'ich schlug' is in the imperfect.

Impfausweis *der* (PL die **Impfausweise**) vaccination certificate.

impfen *verb* (PERF **hat geimpft**) to vaccinate.

Impfung *die* (PL die **Impfungen**) vaccination.

imponieren *verb* (PERF **hat imponiert**) to impress; **jemandem imponieren** to impress somebody.

Import *der* (PL die **Importe**) import.

Importeur *der* (PL die **Importeure**) importer.

importieren *verb* (PERF **hat importiert**) to import.

imprägniert *adjective* waterproof.

imstande *adverb* **imstande sein, etwas zu tun** to be able to do something; **er ist nicht imstande, seine Hausaufgaben allein zu machen** he's not able to do his homework on his own.

in *preposition* (+ DAT *or* + ACC) (*the dative is used when talking about position; the accusative shows movement towards something*) **1** in; **es ist in der Küche** it's in the kitchen; **2** into, in; **ich habe es in meine Tasche gesteckt** I've put it in my bag; **3 in die Schule gehen** to go to school; **4 Susi ist in der Schule** Susi is at school; **5 in diesem Jahr** this year; **6 in sein** to be in; **Rap ist in** rap is in.

inbegriffen *adjective* included; **Essen ist inbegriffen** food is included.

indem *conjunction* **1** while; **2** by.

Inder *der* (PL *die* **Inder**) Indian.

Inderin *die* (PL *die* **Inderinnen**) Indian.

Indianer *der* (PL *die* **Indianer**) (American) Indian, native American.

Indianerin *die* (PL *die* **Indianerinnen**) (American) Indian, native American.

indianisch *adjective* (American) Indian, native American.

Indien *das* India.

indisch *adjective* Indian.

indiskutabel *adjective* out of the question.

individuell *adjective* individual.

Individuum *das* (PL *die* **Individuen**) individual.

Industrie *die* (PL *die* **Industrien**) industry.

industriell *adjective* industrial.

Infektion *die* (PL *die* **Infektionen**) infection.

Infinitiv *der* (PL *die* **Infinitive**) infinitive.

infizieren *verb* (PERF **hat infiziert**) **1** to infect; **2 sich bei jemandem infizieren** to be infected by somebody.

Inflation *die* (PL *die* **Inflationen**) inflation.

infolge *preposition* (+ GEN) as a result of.

infolgedessen *adverb* consequently.

Informatik *die* computer science.

Informatiker *der* (PL *die* **Informatiker**) computer scientist.

Informatikerin *die* (PL *die* **Informatikerinnen**) computer scientist.

Information *die* (PL *die* **Informationen**) (piece of) information.

Informationsbüro *das* (PL *die* **Informationsbüros**) (tourist) information office.

informieren *verb* (PERF **hat informiert**) **1** to inform; **2 informiert sein** to be aware; **da bist du falsch informiert** you've been wrongly informed; **3 sich über etwas informieren** to find out about something; **ich habe mich darüber genau informieren lassen** I found out all about it.

Ingenieur *der* (PL *die* **Ingenieure**) engineer.

Ingenieurin *die* (PL *die* **Ingenieurinnen**) engineer.

Ingwer *der* ginger.

Inhaber der (PL die Inhaber)
1 owner (of a shop); **2** holder (of an office).

Inhaberin die (PL die Inhaberinnen)
1 owner (of a shop); **2** holder (of a position).

Inhalt der (PL die Inhalte) **1** contents; **den Inhalt der Dose mit etwas Wasser verdünnen** dilute the contents of the tin with a little water; **2** content (of a story, film); **er hat den Inhalt der Geschichte kurz für uns zusammengefasst** he gave us a quick summary of the content of the story; **3** volume; **4** area (of a rectangle, circle, etc.).

Initiative die (PL die Initiativen) initiative; **die Initiative ergreifen** to take the initiative.

inklusive preposition (+ GEN) including.
inklusive adverb inclusive.

innen adverb inside; **nach innen** inwards.

Innenstadt die (PL die Innenstädte) town centre, city centre.

Innere das **1** interior; **2** inside.

innerer, innere, inneres adjective **1** inner; **2** inside; **3** internal (injuries).

innerhalb preposition (+ GEN) **1** within; **2** during.
innerhalb adverb **innerhalb von** within.

innerlich adjective **1** internal; **2** inner.
innerlich adverb **1** internally; **2** inwardly.

ins = **in das**; **ins Theater gehen** to go to the theatre.

Insekt das (PL die Insekten) insect.

Insel die (PL die Inseln) island.

Inserat das (PL die Inserate) advertisement.

inserieren verb (PERF hat inseriert) to advertise.

insgesamt adverb in all.

Instinkt der (PL die Instinkte) instinct.

instinktiv adjective instinctive.

Instrument das (PL die Instrumente) instrument; **ein Instrument spielen** to play an instrument.

intelligent adjective intelligent.

Intelligenz die intelligence.

Intensivpflege die intensive care.

Intensivstation die (PL die Intensivstationen) intensive care unit.

Intercityzug der (PL die Intercityzüge) intercity train.

interessant adjective interesting.

Interesse das (PL die Interessen) interest; **Interesse für jemanden/ etwas haben** to be interested in somebody/something.

interessieren verb (PERF hat interessiert) **1** to interest; **2 sich für etwas interessieren** to be interested in something.

Internat das (PL die Internate) boarding school.

a
b
c
d
e
f
g
h
i
j
k
l
m
n
o
p
q
r
s
t
u
v
w
x
y
z

a **international** *adjective*
   international.

b **Internet** *das* Internet.

c **Internetcafé** *das* (PL *die*
d Internetcafés) Internet cafe; **wo
   gibt es hier ein Internetcafé?**
e where is there an Internet cafe?

f **Interview** *das* (PL *die* Interviews)
   interview.

g **inzwischen** *adverb* in the
h meantime, meanwhile.

i **Ire** *der* (PL *die* Iren) Irishman; **die Iren**
   the Irish.

j **irgend** *adverb* **1** at all; **wenn irgend
   möglich** if at all possible; **wenn du
k irgend kannst** if you could possibly
   manage it; **2 irgend so ein Idiot**
l some such idiot.

m **irgendein** *adjective* **1** some; **2** any;
n **3 irgendein anderer** someone else,
   anyone else.

o **irgendeiner, irgendeine,
p irgendein(e)s** *pronoun* **1** any
   one; **'welche möchten Sie?'** -
q **'irgendeine'** 'which one would you
   like?' - 'any one'; **2** somebody,
r someone; **3** anybody, anyone; **hat
s irgendeiner angerufen?** has
   anybody phoned?

t **irgendetwas** *pronoun*
u **1** something; **2** anything.

   irgendjemand *pronoun*
v **1** somebody; **2** anybody, anyone.

w **irgendwann** *adverb* **1** some time,
   at some time; **2** any time, at any
x time.

y **irgendwas** (*informal*) SEE
z **irgendetwas**.

irgendwie *adverb* somehow.

irgendwo *adverb* **1** somewhere;
2 anywhere.

Irin *die* (PL *die* Irinnen) Irishwoman.

irisch *adjective* Irish.

Irisch *das* Irish (*language*).

Irland *das* Ireland.

ironisch *adjective* ironic.

irre *adjective* **1** mad; **2** (*informal*)
incredible, fantastic (*party, song*).
irre *adverb* **irre gut** incredibly good.

irren *verb* (PERF **ist geirrt**) **1** to
wander (about) (*when lost*); **2** (PERF
hat sich geirrt) **sich irren** to be
mistaken, to be wrong.

irrsinnig *adjective* **1** mad;
2 (*informal*) incredible.

Irrtum *der* (PL *die* Irrtümer) mistake.

Islam *der* Islam.

isst SEE **essen**.

ist SEE **sein**.

Italien *das* Italy.

Italiener *der* (PL *die* Italiener)
Italian.

Italienerin *die* (PL *die*
Italienerinnen) Italian.

italienisch *adjective* Italian.

Jj

ja *adverb* **1** yes; **2 ich glaube ja** I
think so; **3 du kommst doch, ja?**
you'll come, won't you?; **es passt
doch, ja?** it fits, doesn't it?; **4 sag's
ihm ja nicht!** don't (you dare) tell

him, whatever you do!; **seid ja vorsichtig!** do be careful!; **5 es ist ja noch früh** it's still early; **ich kann ihn ja mal fragen, ob er mitkommen will** I could always ask him if he wants to come.

Jacht die (PL die **Jachten**) yacht.

Jacke die (PL die **Jacken**) **1** jacket; **2** cardigan.

Jackett das (PL die **Jacketts**) jacket.

Jagd die (PL die **Jagden**) **1** hunt; **2** hunting.

jagen verb (PERF **hat gejagt**) **1** to hunt; **2** to chase; **drei Polizisten jagten den Einbrecher, aber er hängte sie schnell ab** three policemen chased the burglar, but he soon shook them off; **meine Mutter hat mich aus dem Bett gejagt** (informal) my mother chased me out of bed; **3 jemanden aus dem Haus jagen** to throw somebody out of the house; **4 damit kannst du mich jagen** (informal) I can't stand that.

Jäger der (PL die **Jäger**) **1** hunter; **2** fighter (aircraft).

jäh adjective sudden.

Jahr das (PL die **Jahre**) **1** year; **in den sechzigen Jahren** in the sixties; **Kinder bis zu zwölf Jahren** children up to the age of twelve; **2 ein freiwilliges soziales Jahr (FSJ)** gap year (during which socially useful work is done for subsistence payment).

jahrelang adverb for years.

Jahrestag der (PL die **Jahrestage**) anniversary.

Jahrestag der (PL die **Jahrestage**) anniversary.

Jahreszeit die (PL die **Jahreszeiten**) season.

Jahrgang der (PL die **Jahrgänge**) **1** year; **2** vintage.

Jahrhundert das (PL die **Jahrhunderte**) century.

-jährig adjective **eine dreißigjährige Frau** a woman aged thirty; **eine zweijährige Verspätung** a two-year delay.

jährlich adjective, adverb yearly; **zweimal jährlich** twice a year.

Jahrmarkt der (PL die **Jahrmärkte**) fair.

Jahrtausend das (PL die **Jahrtausende**) millennium.

Jahrzehnt das (PL die **Jahrzehnte**) decade.

jähzornig adjective hot-tempered.

jammern verb (PERF **hat gejammert**) to moan.

Januar der January.

Japan das Japan.

Japaner der (PL die **Japaner**) Japanese.

Japanerin die (PL die **Japanerinnen**) Japanese.

japanisch adjective zu Japanese.

jawohl adverb **1** yes; **2** certainly.

je adverb **1** ever; **besser denn je** better than ever; **2** each; **sie kosten je zwanzig Euro** they are twenty euros each; **3 seit eh und je** always; **4 je nach** depending on.
je preposition (+ ACC) per.
je conjunction **1 je mehr, desto**

a
b
c
d
e
f
g
h
i
j
k
l
m
n
o
p
q
r
s
t
u
v
w
x
y
z

besser the more the better; **2 je nachdem** it depends.

Jeans *plural noun* jeans.

jede SEE **jeder**.

jedenfalls *adverb* in any case.

jeder, jede, jedes *adjective*
1 every; **jedes Mal** every time;
2 each; **3** any; **ohne jeden Grund** without any reason.
jedes *pronoun* **1** everybody, everyone; **2** each one; **3** anybody, anyone; **das kann jeder** anybody can do that.

jedermann *pronoun* everybody, everyone.

jederzeit *adverb* at any time.

jedes SEE **jeder**.

jedesmal SEE **jeder**.

jedoch *adverb* however.

jemals *adverb* ever.

jemand *pronoun* **1** somebody, someone; **jemand hat das für dich abgegeben** sombody left this for you; **2** anybody, anyone; **hat jemand angerufen?** did anybody call?

jener, jene, jenes *adjective (used in elevated language and in literature)* **1** that; **2** those *(plural)*.
jenes *pronoun* **1** that one; **2** those *(plural)*.

jenseits *preposition* (+ GEN) (on) the other side of.

Jetlag *der* jet lag.

jetzt *adverb* now.

Job *der* (PL die Jobs) job.

jobben *verb* (*informal*) (PERF **hat gejobbt**) to work.

joggen *verb* (PERF **ist gejoggt**) to jog.

Jogginganzug *der* (PL die Jogginganzüge) tracksuit.

Joghurt *der* (PL die Joghurt(s)) yoghurt.

Johannisbeere *die* (PL die Johannisbeeren) **1 rote Johannisbeeren** redcurrants; **2 schwarze Johannisbeeren** blackcurrants.

Journalist *der* (PL die Journalisten) journalist.

Journalistin *die* (PL die Journalistinnen) journalist.

Joystick *der* (PL die Joysticks) joystick *(for computer games)*.

jubeln *verb* (PERF **hat gejubelt**) **1** to cheer; **2 Beifall jubeln** to applaud.

Jubiläum *das* (PL die Jubiläen) **1** anniversary; **2** jubilee.

Jude *der* (PL die Juden) Jew.

Judentum *das* Judaism.

Jüdin *die* (PL die Jüdinnen) Jew.

jüdisch *adjective* Jewish.

Jugend *die* youth.

Jugendherberge *die* (PL die Jugendherbergen) youth hostel.

Jugendklub *der* (PL die Jugendklubs) youth club.

Jugendliche *der/die* (PL die Jugendlichen) **1** young man/woman; **2 die Jugendlichen** youth, young people.

Jugendzentrum *das* (PL die Jugendzentren) youth centre.

Jugoslawien *das* Yugoslavia.

jugoslawisch *adjective* Yugoslavian.

Juli *der* July.

jung *adjective* **1** young; **2 Jung und Alt** young and old.

Junge[1] *der* (PL *die* **Jungen**) boy.

Junge[2] *das* (PL *die* **Jungen**) young (animal).

Jungfrau *die* (PL *die* **Jungfrauen**) **1** virgin; **2** Virgo.

jüngster, jüngste, jüngstes *adjective* **1** youngest; **2** latest (*news, developments*); **3 in jüngster Zeit** recently.

Juni *der* June.

Jury *die* (PL *die* **Jurys**) **1** jury; **2** judges (*in sport*).

Juwelier *der* (PL *die* **Juweliere**) jeweller.

Jux *der* (*informal*) laugh; **aus Jux** for a laugh.

Kk

Kabel *das* (PL *die* **Kabel**) **1** cable; **2** wire.

Kabelfernsehen *das* cable television.

Kabeljau *der* (PL *die* **Kabeljaus**) cod.

Kabine *die* (PL *die* **Kabinen**) **1** cabin; **2** cubicle (*for changing*); **3** car (*of a cable car*).

Kachel *die* (PL *die* **Kacheln**) tile.

Käfer *der* (PL *die* **Käfer**) beetle.

Kaffee *der* (PL *die* **Kaffee(s)**) coffee; **zwei Kaffee mit Milch bitte** two white coffees please.

Kaffeekanne *die* (PL *die* **Kaffeekannen**) coffee-pot.

Käfig *der* (PL *die* **Käfige**) cage.

kahl *adjective* **1** bald (*head*); **2** bare (*tree, walls*).

Kahn *der* (PL *die* **Kähne**) **1** barge; **2** rowing boat.

Kaiser *der* (PL *die* **Kaiser**) emperor.

Kaiserin *die* (PL *die* **Kaiserinnen**) empress.

Kakao *der* (PL *die* **Kakao(s)**) cocoa; **zwei Kakao bitte** two cups of cocoa please.

Kakerlak *der* (PL *die* **Kakerlaken**) cockroach.

Kaktus *der* (PL *die* **Kakteen**) cactus.

Kalb *das* (PL *die* **Kälber**) **1** calf; **2** veal.

Kalbfleisch *das* veal.

Kalender *der* (PL *die* **Kalender**) **1** calendar; **2** diary.

Kalk *der* **1** lime; **2** limescale; **3** calcium.

Kalorie *die* (PL *die* **Kalorien**) calorie.

kalorienarm *adjective* low-calorie, low in calories.

kalorienreich *adjective* high-calorie, rich in calories.

kalt *adjective* cold; **ist dir kalt?** are you cold?; **stell die Heizung an, den Kindern ist kalt** put on the heating, the children are cold; **abends essen wir kalt** we have a cold meal in the evening; **den Wein kalt stellen** to chill the wine.

Kälte die **1** cold; **2** coldness; **3 fünf Grad Kälte** five degrees below zero.

kam SEE **kommen**.

Kamel das (PL die **Kamele**) camel.

Kamera die (PL die **Kameras**) camera.

Kamerad der (PL die **Kameraden**) friend.

Kameradin die (PL die **Kameradinnen**) friend.

Kameramann der (PL die **Kameramänner**) cameraman.

Kamin der (PL die **Kamine**) fireplace; **wir saßen am Kamin** we sat by the fire.

Kamm der (PL die **Kämme**) **1** comb; **2** ridge (*of a mountain*).

kämmen *verb* (PERF **hat gekämmt**) **1** to comb; **2 sich kämmen** to comb your hair.

Kammer die (PL die **Kammern**) **1** store room; **2** chamber.

Kampagne die (PL die **Kampagnen**) campaign.

Kampf der (PL die **Kämpfe**) **1** fight; **2** contest; **3** struggle.

kämpfen *verb* (PERF **hat gekämpft**) to fight.

Kanada das Canada.

Kanadier der (PL die **Kanadier**) Canadian.

Kanadierin die (PL die **Kanadierinnen**) Canadian.

kanadisch *adjective* Canadian.

Kanal der (PL die **Kanäle**) **1** canal; **2** channel (*radio, TV*); **3 der Kanal** the (English) Channel; **4** sewer, drain.

Kanalinseln *plural noun* Channel Islands.

Kanalisation die sewers, drains.

Kanarienvogel der (PL die **Kanarienvögel**) canary.

Kandidat der (PL die **Kandidaten**) candidate.

Kandidatin die (PL die **Kandidatinnen**) candidate.

Känguru das (PL die **Kängurus**) kangaroo.

Kaninchen das (PL die **Kaninchen**) rabbit.

kann SEE **können**.

Kännchen das (PL die **Kännchen**) **1** pot; **ein Kännchen Kaffee bitte** a pot of coffee please; **2** jug (*of milk*).

Kanne die (PL die **Kannen**) **1** pot (*for coffee, tea*); **2** jug (*for water*); **3** can (*for oil*); **4** churn (*for milk*); **5** watering can.

kannst SEE **können**.

kannte SEE **kennen**.

Kante die (PL die **Kanten**) edge.

Kantine die (PL die **Kantinen**) canteen; **wir essen immer in der Kantine zu Mittag** we always have lunch in the canteen.

Kanu das (PL die **Kanus**) canoe; **Kanu fahren** to go canoeing.

Kapelle die (PL die **Kapellen**) **1** chapel; **2** (brass) band.

kapieren *verb* (*informal*) (PERF **hat kapiert**) to understand; **er hat es mir schon dreimal erklärt, aber ich kapier es einfach nicht** he's already explained it to me three times, but I still don't get it.

Kapital *das* capital.

Kapitalismus *der* capitalism.

Kapitän *der* (PL *die* **Kapitäne**) captain.

Kapitel *das* (PL *die* **Kapitel**) chapter.

Kappe *die* (PL *die* **Kappen**) cap.

kaputt *adjective* **1** broken; **2 an meinem Computer ist etwas kaputt** there's something wrong with my computer; **3 ich bin kaputt** (*informal*) I'm shattered.

kaputtgehen ⋄*verb* (*informal*) (IMPERF **ging kaputt**, PERF **ist kaputtgegangen**) **1** to break; **2** to pack up; **mein Fernseher ist mitten im Fußballspiel kaputtgegangen** the television packed up in the middle of the football match; **3** to wear out (*of clothing*); **4** to break up (*of a marriage or friendship*).

kaputtmachen *verb* (*informal*) (PERF **hat kaputtgemacht**) **1** to break; **er macht alle seine Spielsachen kaputt** he breaks all his toys; **2** to ruin (*clothes, furniture*); **3** to finish off (*a person*); **die viele Arbeit macht mich ganz kaputt** all this work is wearing me out; **4 sich kaputtmachen** to wear yourself out.

Kapuze *die* (PL *die* **Kapuzen**) hood.

Karamell *der* (PL *die* **Karamells**) caramel.

Karfreitag *der* Good Friday.

Karibik *die* **die Karibik** the Caribbean.

karibisch *adjective* Caribbean.

kariert *adjective* **1** check; **ein karierter Rock** a check skirt; **2** squared (*paper*).

Karneval *der* (PL *die* **Karnevale**) carnival.

Karo *das* (PL *die* **Karos**) **1** square; **2** diamonds (*in cards*).

Karotte *die* (PL *die* **Karotten**) carrot.

Karpfen *der* (PL *die* **Karpfen**) carp.

Karriere *die* (PL *die* **Karrieren**) career; **Karriere machen** to get to the top.

Karte *die* (PL *die* **Karten**) **1** card; **ich schicke euch eine Karte aus Italien** I'll send you a card from Italy; **2** card (*for playing*); **wir haben den ganzen Abend Karten gespielt** we played cards all evening; **gute/schlechte Karten haben** to have a good/bad hand; **3** ticket; **gibt es noch Karten für das Popfestival?** can you still get tickets for the pop festival?; **4** menu; **5** map; **ich kann Oberammergau nicht auf der Karte finden** I can't find Oberammergau on the map; **6 alles auf eine Karte setzen** to put all your eggs in one basket.

Kartenspiel *das* (PL *die* **Kartenspiele**) **1** card game; **2** pack of cards.

Kartoffel *die* (PL *die* **Kartoffeln**) potato.

Kartoffelbrei *der* mashed potatoes.

Kartoffelchips *plural noun* potato crisps.

a
b
c
d
e
f
g
h
i
j
k
l
m
n
o
p
q
r
s
t
u
v
w
x
y
z

Karton der (PL die **Kartons**)
1 cardboard; 2 cardboard box.

Karussell das (PL die **Karussells**)
merry-go-round; **Karussell fahren**
to go on the merry-go-round.

Käse der cheese.

Käsekuchen der (PL die
Käsekuchen) cheesecake.

Kaserne die (PL die **Kasernen**)
barracks.

Kasse die (PL die **Kassen**) 1 till;
2 checkout; **an der Kasse zahlen**
pay at the checkout; 3 cash desk (in
a bank); 4 box-office; **Sie können
die Karten an der Kasse abholen**
you can collect the tickets from the
box office; 5 ticket office (at a sports
stadium); **Sie müssen sich an der
Kasse anstellen** you have to queue
at the ticket office; 6 health
insurance; 7 **knapp bei Kasse sein**
(informal) to be short of money; **gut
bei Kasse sein** (informal) to be in
the money.

Kassenzettel der (PL die
Kassenzettel) receipt.

Kassette die (PL die **Kassetten**)
1 cassette, tape; **ich habe den
neuen Song auf Kassette
aufgenommen** I've taped the new
song; 2 box (for money, jewellery).

Kassettenrekorder der (PL die
Kassettenrekorder) cassette
recorder.

kassieren verb (PERF hat
kassiert) 1 to collect the money;
2 to collect the fares; 3 **wie viel hat
er kassiert?** how much did he
charge you?; 4 **darf ich bei Ihnen**

kassieren? would you like to pay
now? (your bill in a restaurant);
5 (informal) to take away (a driving
licence, for example).

Kassierer der (PL die **Kassierer**)
cashier.

Kassiererin die (PL die
Kassiererinnen) cashier.

Kastanie die (PL die **Kastanien**)
chestnut.

Kasten der (PL die **Kästen**) 1 box;
2 crate; **ein Kasten Bier** a crate of
beer; 3 bin; 4 letter-box; 5 **was auf
dem Kasten haben** (informal) to be
brainy.

Katalog der (PL die **Kataloge**)
catalogue.

Katalysator der (PL die
Katalysatoren) catalytic converter.

katastrophal adjective, adverb
1 catastrophic; 2 **sie hat
katastrophal schlecht
abgeschnitten** she came out
terribly badly.

Katastrophe die (PL die
Katastrophen) catastrophe.

Kategorie die (PL die **Kategorien**)
category.

Kater der (PL die **Kater**) 1 tom-cat;
2 **einen Kater haben** (informal) to
have a hangover.

Kathedrale die (PL die
Kathedralen) cathedral.

Katholik der (PL die **Katholiken**)
Catholic.

Katholikin die (PL die
Katholikinnen) Catholic.

katholisch adjective Catholic.

Kätzchen *das* (PL *die* Kätzchen) kitten.

Katze *die* (PL *die* Katzen) cat.

kauen *verb* (PERF **hat gekaut**) to chew.

kauern *verb* (PERF **hat gekauert**) to crouch.

Kauf *der* (PL *die* Käufe) **1** purchase; **2 ein guter Kauf** a bargain; **3 etwas in Kauf nehmen** to put up with something.

kaufen *verb* (PERF **hat gekauft**) to buy.

Käufer *der* (PL *die* Käufer) buyer.

Käuferin *die* (PL *die* Käuferinnen) buyer.

Kauffrau *die* (PL *die* Kauffrauen) businesswoman.

Kaufhaus *das* (PL *die* Kaufhäuser) department store.

Kaufmann *der* (PL *die* Kaufleute) businessman.

Kaugummi *der* (PL *die* Kaugummis) chewing gum.

Kaulquappe *die* (PL *die* Kaulquappen) tadpole.

kaum *adverb* hardly, scarcely.

Kaution *die* (PL *die* Kautionen) **1** deposit; **2** bail.

Kegel *der* (PL *die* Kegel) **1** cone; **2** skittle.

Kegelbahn *die* skittle alley.

kegeln *verb* (PERF **hat gekegelt**) to play skittles.

Kehle *die* (PL *die* Kehlen) throat.

Keim *der* (PL *die* Keime) **1** shoot; **2** germ.

kein *adjective* **1** no; **auf keinen Fall** on no account; **2 ich habe keine Zeit** I haven't got any time; **er hat kein Geld** he hasn't got any money; **3 keine zehn Minuten** less than ten minutes.

keiner, keine, kein(e)s *pronoun* **1** nobody, no one; **2** none, not one; **3 von diesen Kleidern gefällt mir keins** I don't like any of these dresses; **4 keiner von beiden** neither (of them).

keinesfalls *adverb* on no account.

keineswegs *adverb* by no means.

keinmal *adverb* not once.

keins SEE **keiner**.

Keks *der* (PL *die* Kekse) biscuit.

Keller *der* (PL *die* Keller) cellar.

Kellergeschoss *das* (PL *die* Kellergeschosse) basement.

Kellner *der* (PL *die* Kellner) waiter.

Kellnerin *die* (PL *die* Kellnerinnen) waitress.

kennen ◇*verb* (IMPERF **kannte**, PERF **hat gekannt**) **1** to know; **2 kennen lernen** to get to know; **sich kennen lernen** to get to know each other; **3 kennen lernen** to meet; **ich habe Ulrike in London kennen gelernt** I met Ulrike in London; **wo habt ihr euch kennen gelernt?** where did you meet?

kennenlernen SEE **kennen**.

Kenntnis *die* (PL *die* Kenntnisse) **1** knowledge; **2 etwas zur Kenntnis nehmen** to take note of something.

Kennzeichen *das* (PL *die* Kennzeichen) **1** mark;

a
b
c
d
e
f
g
h
i
j
k
l
m
n
o
p
q
r
s
t
u
v
w
x
y
z

2 characteristic; **3** registration (number) (*of a vehicle*).

Kerl *der* (PL *die* **Kerle**) **1** bloke; **2 Eva ist ein netter Kerl** Eva's a nice girl.

Kern *der* (PL *die* **Kerne**) **1** pip; **2** stone (*of an apricot, peach*); **3** kernel (*of a nut*).

Kernenergie *die* nuclear power.

Kernkraftwerk *das* (PL *die* **Kernkraftwerke**) nuclear power station.

Kernwaffen *plural noun* nuclear weapons.

Kerze *die* (PL *die* **Kerzen**) candle.

Kerzenhalter *der* (PL *die* **Kerzenhalter**) candlestick.

Kessel *der* (PL *die* **Kessel**) **1** kettle; **2** boiler.

Kette *die* (PL *die* **Ketten**) chain.

Keule *die* (PL *die* **Keulen**) **1** club; **2** leg (*of lamb*); **3** drumstick (*of chicken*).

kichern *verb* (PERF **hat gekichert**) to giggle.

Kiefer[1] *der* (PL *die* **Kiefer**) jaw.

Kiefer[2] *die* (PL *die* **Kiefern**) pine tree.

Kiefernzapfen *der* (PL *die* **Kiefernzapfen**) cone.

Kieselstein *der* (PL *die* **Kieselsteine**) pebble.

Kilo *das* (PL *die* **Kilo(s)**) kilo.

Kilogramm *das* (PL *die* **Kilogramme**) kilogram.

Kilometer *der* (PL *die* **Kilometer**) kilometre.

Kind *das* (PL *die* **Kinder**) child.

Kindergarten *der* (PL *die* **Kindergärten**) nursery school.

Kindergeld *das* child benefit.

Kinderkrippe *die* (PL *die* **Kinderkrippen**) crèche.

kinderleicht *adjective* very easy; **das ist kinderleicht** it's child's play.

Kindertagesstätte *die* (PL *die* **Kindertagesstätten**) day nursery.

Kinderwagen *der* (PL *die* **Kinderwagen**) pram.

Kindheit *die* childhood.

kindisch *adjective* childish.

Kinn *das* (PL *die* **Kinne**) chin.

Kino *das* (PL *die* **Kinos**) cinema.

Kiosk *das* (PL *die* **Kioske**) kiosk (*for newspapers or snacks*).

kippen *verb* (PERF **hat gekippt**) **1** to tip; **2** (PERF **ist gekippt**) to topple.

Kirche *die* (PL *die* **Kirchen**) church.

Kirsche *die* (PL *die* **Kirschen**) cherry.

Kissen *das* (PL *die* **Kissen**) **1** cushion; **2** pillow.

Kiste *die* (PL *die* **Kisten**) **1** crate; **2** box.

kitzeln *verb* (PERF **hat gekitzelt**) to tickle.

kitzlig *adjective* ticklish.

Kiwi *die* (PL *die* **Kiwis**) kiwi fruit.

klagen *verb* (PERF **hat geklagt**) to complain.

Klammer *die* (PL *die* **Klammern**) **1** peg (*for washing*); **2** grip (*for hair*); **3** bracket.

Klammeraffe *die* (PL *die* **Klammeraffen**) at, @ (*in email*

a b c d e f g h i j **k** l m n o p q r s t u v w x y z

addresses); **dieter-punkt-schmidt-Klammeraffe-einfachkom-punkt-com** dieter-dot-schmidt@einfachkom-dot-com.

Klamotten *plural noun* gear (*clothes*).

Klang der (PL die **Klänge**) sound.

klang SEE **klingen**.

Klappe die (PL die **Klappen**) **1** flap; **2** clapperboard; **3** (*informal*) trap (*mouth*); **halt die Klappe!** shut up!

klappen *verb* (PERF **hat geklappt**) **1 nach vorne klappen** to tilt forward; **2 nach hinten klappen** to tip back; **3 nach oben klappen** to lift up; **4 nach unten klappen** to put down; **5** to work out; **hoffentlich klappt es** I hope it'll work out.

Klappstuhl der (PL die **Klappstühle**) folding chair.

klar *adjective* **1** clear (*water, answer*); **klar werden** to become clear; **2 jetzt ist mir alles klar** now I understand; **3 sich klar werden** to make up your mind; **4 sich über etwas im Klaren sein** to realize something. **klar** *adverb* clearly; **na klar!** (*informal*) of course!

klären *verb* (PERF **hat geklärt**) **1** to clarify; **2** to sort out; **3** to purify (*sewage*); **4 sich klären** to clear (*of the weather or the sky*); **5 sich klären** to resolve itself, to be settled.

Klarinette die (PL die **Klarinetten**) clarinet.

klarwerden SEE **klar**.

Klasse die (PL die **Klassen**) **1** class; **erster Klasse reisen** to travel first class; **2** year; **in die sechste Klasse gehen** to be in year six.

klasse *adjective* (*informal*) great, smashing.

Klassenarbeit die (PL die **Klassenarbeiten**) (written) test.

Klassenbuch das register (*kept by the teacher, it also contains notes about students' achievements*).

Klassenfahrt die (PL die **Klassenfahrten**) school trip.

Klassenkamerad der (PL die **Klassenkameraden**) class-mate.

Klassenkameradin die (PL die **Klassenkameradinnen**) class-mate.

Klassensprecher der (PL die **Klassensprecher**) class representative.

Klassensprecherin die (PL die **Klassensprecherinnen**) class representative.

Klassenzimmer das (PL die **Klassenzimmer**) classroom.

klassisch *adjective* classical.

Klatsch der gossip.

klatschen *verb* (PERF **hat geklatscht**) **1** to clap; **jemandem Beifall klatschen** to clap somebody, to applaud somebody; **2** to slap; **3** to gossip.

klauen *verb* (*informal*) (PERF **hat geklaut**) to pinch.

Klavier das (PL die **Klaviere**) piano.

kleben *verb* (PERF **hat geklebt**) **1** to stick; **2** to glue; **3 jemandem eine kleben** (*informal*) to belt somebody one.

a
b
c
d
e
f
g
h
i
j
k
l
m
n
o
p
q
r
s
t
u
v
w
x
y
z

a **klebrig** *adjective* sticky.

b **Klebstoff** *der* (PL *die* **Klebstoffe**) glue.

c **Klebstreifen** *der* (PL *die* **Klebstreifen**) sticky tape.

d **Klecks** *der* (PL *die* **Kleckse**) stain.

e **Kleid** *das* (PL *die* **Kleider**) **1** dress; **Uschi hat sich zwei neue Kleider gekauft** Uschi bought two new dresses; **2 Kleider** clothes.

Kleiderbügel *der* (PL *die* **Kleiderbügel**) coat hanger.

Kleiderschrank *der* (PL *die* **Kleiderschränke**) wardrobe.

k **Kleidung** *die* clothes, clothing.

klein *adjective* **1** small, little; **etwas klein schneiden** to cut something up small; **2** short; **Peter ist kleiner als Klaus** Peter is shorter than Klaus.

Kleingarten *der* (PL *die* **Kleingärten**) allotment (*used mainly as garden*).

Kleingeld *das* change.

Klempner *der* (PL *die* **Klempner**) plumber.

klettern *verb* (PERF **ist geklettert**) to climb.

Klick *der* (PL *die* **Klicks**) click (*with mouse*).

Klicken *das* click (*noise*).

Klient *der* (PL *die* **Klienten**) client.

Klientin *die* (PL *die* **Klientinnen**) client.

Klima *das* (PL *die* **Klimas**) climate.

Klimaanlage *die* (PL *die* **Klimaanlagen**) air conditioning.

Klinge *die* (PL *die* **Klingen**) blade.

Klingel *die* (PL *die* **Klingeln**) bell.

klingeln *verb* (PERF **hat geklingelt**) to ring; **es klingelt** there's a ring at the door.

klingen ◇*verb* (IMPERF **klang**, PERF **hat geklungen**) to sound.

Klinik *die* (PL *die* **Kliniken**) clinic.

Klinke *die* (PL *die* **Klinken**) handle.

Klippe *die* (PL *die* **Klippen**) rock.

Klo *das* (*informal*) (PL *die* **Klos**) loo.

klopfen *verb* (PERF **hat geklopft**) **1** to knock; **2** to beat.

Klosett *das* (PL *die* **Klosetts**) lavatory.

Kloß *der* (PL *die* **Klöße**) dumpling.

Kloster *das* (PL *die* **Kloster**) **1** monastery; **2** convent.

Klotz *der* (PL *die* **Klötze**) block.

Klub *der* (PL *die* **Klubs**) club.

klug *adjective* **1** clever; **2 ich werde daraus nicht klug** I don't understand it.

Klugheit *die* cleverness.

Klumpen *der* (PL *die* **Klumpen**) lump.

knabbern *verb* (PERF **hat geknabbert**) to nibble.

Knäckebrot *das* (PL *die* **Knäckebrote**) crispbread.

knacken *verb* (PERF **hat geknackt**) to crack.

Knall *der* (PL *die* **Knalle**) bang.

knallen *verb* (PERF **hat geknallt**) **1** to go bang; **2** to pop (*of a cork*); **3** to slam (*of a door*); **4** to crack (*of a whip*).

knapp *adjective* **1** scarce; **2** tight (*skirt, top*); **3 knapp bei Kasse sein** to be short of money; **4 mit knapper Mehrheit** by a narrow majority; **5** just; **eine knappe Stunde** just under an hour; **sie haben knapp verloren** they only just lost; **6 das war knapp** (*informal*) that was a close shave.

knarren *verb* (PERF **hat geknarrt**) to creak.

Knauf *der* (PL die **Knäufe**) knob.

knautschen *verb* (PERF **hat geknautscht**) **1** to crumple; **2** to crease.

kneifen ◇*verb* (IMPERF **kniff**, PERF **hat gekniffen**) **1** to pinch; **2** (*informal*) to chicken out; **sie hat mal wieder gekniffen und nichts gesagt** she's chickened out yet again and didn't say anything.

Kneipe *die* (PL die **Kneipen**) pub.

kneten *verb* (PERF **hat geknetet**) to knead.

knicken *verb* (PERF **hat geknickt**) **1** to bend; **2** to fold.

Knie *das* (PL die **Knie**) knee.

knien *verb* (PERF **hat gekniet**) **1** to kneel; **2 sich knien** to kneel down.

kniff SEE **kneifen.**

knipsen *verb* (PERF **hat geknipst**) (*to photograph*) to take a snap, to take snaps.

Knoblauch *der* garlic.

Knoblauchzehe *die* (PL die **Knoblauchzehen**) clove of garlic.

Knöchel *der* (PL die **Knöchel**) **1** ankle; **2** knuckle; **Mario hat sich beim Jogging den Knöchel verstaucht** Mario sprained his ankle when jogging.

Knochen *der* (PL die **Knochen**) bone.

Knopf *der* (PL die **Knöpfe**) button.

Knoten *der* (PL die **Knoten**) **1** knot; **2** bun (*as a hairstyle*); **3** lump.

Knüller *der* (PL die **Knüller**) scoop (*in journalism*).

knurren *verb* (PERF **hat geknurrt**) **1** to growl; **2** to rumble; **3** to grumble.

knusprig *adjective* crisp, crusty (*bread*).

Koalabär *der* (PL die **Koalabären**) koala bear.

Koch *der* (PL die **Köche**) **1** cook; **2** chef.

Kochbuch *das* (PL die **Kochbücher**) cookery book.

kochen *verb* (PERF **hat gekocht**) **1** to cook; **2** to boil; **das Wasser kocht** the water's boiling.

Köchin *die* (PL die **Köchinnen**) cook.

Kochtopf *der* (PL die **Kochtöpfe**) saucepan.

Koffer *der* (PL die **Koffer**) suitcase.

Kofferkuli *der* (PL die **Kofferkulis**) baggage trolley.

Kofferraum *der* (PL die **Kofferräume**) boot.

Kohl *der* **1** cabbage; **2** (*informal*) rubbish; **rede keinen Kohl** don't talk rubbish.

Kohle *die* (PL die **Kohlen**) coal.

a
b
c
d
e
f
g
h
i
j
k
l
m
n
o
p
q
r
s
t
u
v
w
x
y
z

a
b
c
d
e
f
g
h
i
j
k
l
m
n
o
p
q
r
s
t
u
v
w
x
y
z

Kohlrübe *die* (PL *die* **Kohlrüben**) swede.

Kokain *das* cocaine.

Kokosnuss *die* (PL *die* **Kokosnüsse**) coconut.

Kollege *der* (PL *die* **Kollegen**) colleague.

Kollegin *die* (PL *die* **Kolleginnen**) colleague.

Köln *das* Cologne.

Kölnischwasser *das* eau de cologne.

Kombination *die* (PL *die* **Kombinationen**) combination.

Komfort *der* comfort.

Komiker *der* (PL *die* **Komiker**) comedian.

komisch *adjective* funny.

Komma *das* (PL *die* **Kommas**) **1** comma; **2** decimal point; **zwei Komma fünf** two point five.

kommen ◇*verb* (IMPERF **kam**, PERF **ist gekommen**) **1** to come; **2** to get; **wie komme ich zur U-Bahn?** how do I get to the tube station?; **kommt gut nach Hause!** have a safe journey home!; **3 etwas kommen lassen** to send for something; **4 wie kommst du darauf?** what gave you that idea?; **5 hinter etwas kommen** to find out about something; **6 zur Schule kommen** to start school; **7** to go; **die Gabeln kommen in die Schublade** the forks go in the drawer; **ins Krankenhaus kommen** to go to hospital; **8 wer kommt zuerst?** who's first?; **du kommst an die Reihe** it's your turn; **9 wie kommt das?** why is that?; **10 zu**

etwas kommen to acquire something; **11 wieder zu sich kommen** to come round (*after fainting or anaesthetic*); **12 dazu kommen, etwas zu tun** to get round to doing something; **ich komme einfach nicht zum Einkaufen** I just can't get round to doing the shopping; **13 das kommt davon!** see what happens!

Kommissar *der* (PL *die* **Kommissare**) superintendent.

Kommode *die* (PL *die* **Kommoden**) chest of drawers.

Kommunismus *der* communism.

Kommunist *der* (PL *die* **Kommunisten**) communist.

Kommunistin *die* (PL *die* **Kommunistinnen**) communist.

kommunizieren *verb* (PERF **hat kommuniziert**) to communicate.

Komödie *die* (PL *die* **Komödien**) comedy.

Kompass *der* (PL *die* **Kompasse**) compass.

komplett *adjective* complete.

Kompliment *das* (PL *die* **Komplimente**) compliment.

kompliziert *adjective* complicated.

Komponist *der* (PL *die* **Komponisten**) composer.

Komponistin *die* (PL *die* **Komponistinnen**) composer.

Kompott *das* (PL *die* **Kompotte**) stewed fruit.

Kompromiss *der* (PL *die* **Kompromisse**) compromise; **einen**

Kompromiss schließen to compromise.

Konditional das (*verb tense*) conditional.

Konditorei die (PL die **Konditoreien**) patisserie, cake shop.

Kondom das (PL die **Kondome**) condom.

Konfektion die ready-made clothes.

Konferenz die (PL die **Konferenzen**) conference.

Konflikt der (PL die **Konflikte**) conflict.

König der (PL die **Könige**) king.

Königin die (PL die **Königinnen**) queen.

königlich *adjective* royal.

Königreich das (PL die **Königreiche**) kingdom.

Konjunktion die (PL die **Konjunktionen**) conjunction.

Konkurrent der (PL die **Konkurrenten**) competitor.

Konkurrentin die (PL die **Konkurrentinnen**) competitor.

Konkurrenz die competition.

können ◇*verb* (PRES **kann**, IMPERF **konnte**, PERF **hat gekonnt**) **1** can; **kann ich Ihnen helfen?** can I help you?; **kannst du Auto fahren?** can you drive?; **kannst du Deutsch?** can you speak German?; **ich konnte nicht früher kommen** I couldn't come any earlier; **das kann ich nicht** I can't do that; **2 etwas können** to be able to do something;

er wird es vor Dienstag nicht machen können he won't be able to do it before Tuesday; **3 das kann gut sein** that may well be so; **es kann sein, dass** ... it may be that ...; **4 ich kann nichts dafür** it's not my fault.

Können das ability.

Könner der (PL die **Könner**) expert.

könnt SEE **können**.

konnte, konnten, konntest, konntet SEE **können**.

Konrektor der (PL die **Konrektoren**) deputy headteacher, deputy headmaster.

Konrektorin die (PL die **Konrektorinnen**) deputy headteacher.

Konserven *plural noun* tinned food.

Konsonant der (PL die **Konsonanten**) consonant.

Konstruktion die (PL die **Konstruktionen**) construction (*in grammar*).

Konsul der (PL die **Konsuln**) consul.

Konsulat das (PL die **Konsulate**) consulate.

konsultieren *verb* (PERF **hat konsultiert**) to consult.

Kontakt der (PL die **Kontakte**) contact.

Kontaktlinse die (PL die **Kontaktlinsen**) contact lens.

Kontinent der (PL die **Kontinente**) continent.

Konto das (PL die **Konten**) account.

Kontrolle die (PL die Kontrollen) **1** check; **2** control.

Kontrolleur der (PL die Kontrolleure) inspector.

kontrollieren verb (PERF hat kontrolliert) **1** to check; **2** to control.

konzentrieren verb (PERF hat konzentriert) **1** to concentrate; **2 sich konzentrieren** to concentrate.

Konzert das (PL die Konzerte) **1** concert; **2** concerto.

Kopf der (PL die Köpfe) **1** head; **2 sich den Kopf zerbrechen** to rack your brains; **3 seinen Kopf durchsetzen** to get your own way; **4 sich den Kopf waschen** to wash your hair; **5 auf dem Kopf** upside down; **6 ein Kopf Salat** a lettuce.

köpfen verb (PERF hat geköpft) **1** to head (in football); **2** to behead.

Kopfhörer der (PL die Kopfhörer) headphones.

Kopfkissen das (PL die Kopfkissen) pillow.

Kopfsalat der (PL die Kopfsalate) lettuce.

Kopfschmerzen plural noun headache.

Kopie die (PL die Kopien) copy.

kopieren verb (PERF hat kopiert) **1** to copy; **2** to photocopy.

Kopiergerät das (PL die Kopiergeräte) photocopier.

Korb der (PL die Körbe) **1** basket; **2 jemandem einen Korb geben** to turn somebody down.

Kork der (PL die Korke) cork.

Korken der (PL die Korken) cork.

Korkenzieher der (PL die Korkenzieher) corkscrew.

Korn das (PL die Körner) **1** corn (in general); **2** grain (a seed).

Körper der (PL die Körper) body.

körperbehindert adjective disabled.

Körpergeruch der (PL die Körpergerüche) body odour.

körperlich adjective physical.

Korrektur die (PL die Korrekturen) correction.

korrigieren verb (PERF hat korrigiert) to correct.

Korsika das Corsica.

koscher adjective kosher.

Kosmetik die (PL die Kosmetika) **1** cosmetics; **2** beauty care.

Kost die food.

kostbar adjective precious.

Kosten plural noun **1** cost; **2** expenses.

kosten verb (PERF hat gekostet) **1** to cost; **2 wie viel kostet es?** how much is it?; **3** to taste.

kostenlos adjective free (of charge).

köstlich adjective **1** delicious; **2** funny.

Kostüm das (PL die Kostüme) **1** suit; **2** costume.

Kotelett das (PL die Koteletts) chop.

Krabbe die (PL die Krabben) **1** crab; **2** shrimp.

krabbeln *verb* (PERF **ist** gekrabbelt) to crawl.

Krach *der* **1** row; **2** noise; **3** crash.

krachen *verb* (PERF **hat gekracht**) **1** to crash; **2** (PERF **ist gekracht**) to crack; **er ist gegen die Mauer gekracht** he crashed into the wall.

krächzen *verb* (PERF **hat** gekrächzt) to croak.

Kraft *die* (PL **die Kräfte**) **1** strength; **er hat nicht viel Kraft** he's not very strong; **2** force; **in Kraft treten** to come into force; **3 geistige Kräfte** mental powers; **4** worker.

kräftig *adjective* **1** strong; **2** nourishing.
kräftig *adverb* **1** strongly; **2** hard; **kräftig schütteln** shake hard.

Kraftwerk *das* (PL **die Kraftwerke**) power station.

Kragen *der* (PL **die Kragen**) collar.

Krähe *die* (PL **die Krähen**) crow.

Kralle *die* (PL **die Krallen**) claw.

Kram *der* stuff; **mach deinen Kram allein!** (*informal*) do it yourself!

kramen *verb* (PERF **hat gekramt**) to rummage about.

Krampf *der* (PL **die Krämpfe**) cramp.

Kran *der* (PL **die Kräne**) crane (*machine*).

Kranich *der* (PL **die Kraniche**) crane (*bird*).

krank *adjective* ill, sick; **krank werden** to fall ill.

Kranke *der/die* (PL **die Kranken**) patient.

kränken *verb* (PERF **hat gekränkt**) to hurt.

Krankenhaus *das* (PL **die Krankenhäuser**) hospital; **sie haben ihn gestern ins Krankenhaus eingeliefert** he was taken to hospital yesterday.

Krankenkasse *die* health insurance; **bei welcher Krankenkasse sind Sie versichert?** what health insurance have you got?

Krankenpfleger *der* (PL **die Krankenpfleger**) (male) nurse.

Krankenpflegerin *die* (PL **die Krankenpflegerinnen**) nurse.

Krankenschwester *die* (PL **die Krankenschwestern**) nurse; **Ulrike ist Krankenschwester** Ulrike is a nurse.

Krankenversicherung *die* (PL **die Krankenversicherungen**) medical insurance.

Krankenwagen *der* (PL **die Krankenwagen**) ambulance.

Krankheit *die* (PL **die Krankheiten**) illness, disease.

kratzen *verb* (PERF **hat gekratzt**) to scratch.

Kratzer *der* (PL **die Kratzer**) scratch.

kraus *adjective* frizzy.

Kraut *das* (PL **die Kräuter**) **1** herb; **2** sauerkraut; **3** cabbage.

Kräutertee *der* (PL **die Kräutertees**) herbal tea.

Krawall *der* (PL **die Krawalle**) **1** riot; **2** row.

Krawatte *die* (PL **die Krawatten**) tie.

kreativ *adjective* creative.

a
b
c
d
e
f
g
h
i
j
k
l
m
n
o
p
q
r
s
t
u
v
w
x
y
z

Krebs der (PL die **Krebse**) 1 crab;
2 cancer; 3 Cancer.

Kredit der (PL die **Kredite**) 1 loan
(*by a bank*); **auf Kredit** on credit;
2 credit (*reputation*).

Kreditkarte die (PL die
Kreditkarten) credit card.

Kreide die (PL die **Kreiden**) chalk.

kreieren verb (PERF **hat kreiert**) to
create.

Kreis der (PL die **Kreise**) 1 circle;
2 district.

Kreislauf der 1 cycle;
2 circulation.

Kreuz das (PL die **Kreuze**) 1 cross;
2 (small of the) back; 3 intersection
(*of a motorway*); 4 clubs (*in cards*).

kreuzen verb (PERF **hat gekreuzt**)
1 to cross; 2 **sich kreuzen** to cross.

Kreuzfahrt die (PL die
Kreuzfahrten) 1 cruise; **eine
Kreuzfahrt machen** to go on a
cruise; 2 crusade.

Kreuzung die (PL die **Kreuzungen**)
1 crossroads; 2 cross (*of plants,
animals*).

Kreuzworträtsel das (PL die
Kreuzworträtsel) crossword
(puzzle).

kriechen ⬦verb (IMPERF **kroch**, PERF
ist gekrochen) to crawl.

Krieg der (PL die **Kriege**) war.

kriegen verb (*informal*) (PERF **hat
gekriegt**) 1 to get; 2 **ein Kind
kriegen** to have a baby.

Krimi der (PL die **Krimis**) thriller.

Kriminalroman der (PL die
Kriminalromane) crime novel.

kriminell adjective criminal.

Kriminelle der/die (PL die
Kriminellen) criminal.

Krippe die (PL die **Krippen**)
1 manger; 2 crib; 3 crèche.

Krise die (PL die **Krisen**) crisis.

Kristall[1] der (PL die **Kristalle**)
crystal.

Kristall[2] das (*glass*) crystal.

kritisch adjective critical.

kritisieren verb (PERF **hat
kritisiert**) 1 to criticize; 2 to review.

kroch SEE **kriechen**.

Krokodil das (PL die **Krokodile**)
crocodile.

Krone die (PL die **Kronen**) crown.

Kröte die (PL die **Kröten**) toad.

Krücke die (PL die **Krücken**) crutch.

Krug der (PL die **Krüge**) 1 jug; 2 mug.

Krümel der (PL die **Krümel**) crumb.

krümelig adjective crumbly.

krumm adjective 1 bent; 2 crooked.

Kruste die (PL die **Krusten**) crust.

Küche die (PL die **Küchen**)
1 kitchen; 2 cooking; **die
italienische Küche** Italian cooking;
3 **warme Küche** hot food.

Kuchen der (PL die **Kuchen**) cake.

Kuckuck der (PL die **Kuckucke**)
cuckoo.

Kugel die (PL die **Kugeln**) 1 ball;
2 bullet; 3 sphere; **wieviele Kugeln
Eis möchtest du?** how many scoops
of ice-cream would you like?

a b c d e f g h i j k l m n o p q r s t u v w x y z

Kugelschreiber *der* (PL *die* Kugelschreiber) ballpoint pen, biro.

Kuh *die* (PL *die* Kühe) cow.

kühl *adjective* cool.

kühlen *verb* (PERF hat gekühlt) **1** to cool, to chill; **2** to refrigerate.

Kühler *der* (PL *die* Kühler) radiator.

Kühlerhaube *die* (PL *die* Kühlerhauben) bonnet.

Kühlschrank *der* (PL *die* Kühlschränke) fridge.

Kühltruhe *die* (PL *die* Kühltruhen) freezer.

Küken *das* (PL *die* Küken) chick.

Kuli *der* (PL *die* Kulis) biro.

Kultur *die* (PL *die* Kulturen) **1** culture; **2** civilization.

Kulturbeutel *der* (PL *die* Kulturbeutel) toilet bag.

kulturell *adjective* cultural.

Kummer *der* **1** sorrow; **2** worry; **3** trouble.

kümmern *verb* (PERF hat gekümmert) **1** to concern; **2 sich um jemanden kümmern** to look after somebody; **sich um den Garten kümmern** to look after the garden; **3 sich darum kümmern, dass** ... to see to it that ...; **4 kümmere dich um deine eigenen Angelegenheiten** mind your own business.

Kunde *der* (PL *die* Kunden) **1** customer; **2** client.

Kundendienst *der* **1** customer services (department); **2** after-sales service.

kündigen *verb* (PERF hat gekündigt) **1** to cancel; **2** to give notice; **die Firma hat ihm gekündigt** the company gave him his notice; **3 seine Stellung kündigen** to hand in your notice.

Kundin *die* (PL *die* Kundinnen) **1** customer; **2** client.

Kundschaft *die* customers.

Kunst *die* (PL *die* Künste) **1** art; **2** skill.

Kunstausstellung *die* (PL *die* Kunstausstellungen) art exhibition.

Künstler *der* (PL *die* Künstler) artist.

Künstlerin *die* (PL *die* Künstlerinnen) artist.

künstlerisch *adjective* artistic.

künstlich *adjective* artificial.

Kunststoff *der* (PL *die* Kunststoffe) plastic.

Kunststück *das* (PL *die* Kunststücke) **1** trick; **2** feat.

Kunstwerk *das* (PL *die* Kunstwerke) work of art.

Kupfer *das* copper.

Kupplung *die* (PL *die* Kupplungen) **1** clutch (*of a car*); **2** coupling.

Kürbis *der* (PL *die* Kürbisse) pumpkin.

Kurier *der* (PL *die* Kuriere) courier (*delivery person*).

Kurierdienst *der* (PL *die* Kurierdienste) courier service.

Kurort *der* (PL *die* Kurorte) health resort.

a b c d e f g h i j **k** l m n o p q r s t u v w x y z

a

b

c

d

e

f

g

h

i

j

k

l

m

n

o

p

q

r

s

t

u

v

w

x

y

z

Kurs der (PL die Kurse) **1** course;
2 exchange rate; **3** price (*of shares*).

Kurve die (PL die Kurven) **1** curve;
2 bend.

kurz adjective **1** short; **vor kurzem** a
short time ago; **2 zu kurz kommen**
to get less than your fair share, to
come off badly.
kurz adverb **1** shortly; **2** briefly;
3 kurz gesagt in a word.

Kurzarbeit die short-time
working.

kurzärmelig adjective short-
sleeved.

kürzen verb (PERF **hat gekürzt**) **1** to
shorten; **2** to cut.

kurzfristig adjective short-term.
kurzfristig adverb at short notice.

kürzlich adverb recently.

kurzsichtig adjective short-
sighted.

Kurzwaren plural noun
haberdashery.

Kusine die (PL die Kusinen) cousin.

Kuss der (PL die Küsse) kiss.

küssen verb (PERF **hat geküsst**)
1 to kiss; **2 sich küssen** to kiss.

Küste die (PL die Küsten) coast.

Kuvert das (PL die Kuverts)
envelope.

Ll

Labor das (PL die Labors) laboratory.

Lache die (PL die Lachen) pool.

lächeln verb (PERF **hat gelächelt**)
to smile.

lachen verb (PERF **hat gelacht**) to
laugh.

lächerlich adjective ridiculous.

Lachs der (PL die Lachse) salmon.

Lack der (PL die Lacke) **1** varnish;
2 paint.

lackieren verb (PERF **hat lackiert**)
1 to varnish; **2** to spray (*with paint*).

laden ⬦verb (PRES **lädt**, IMPERF **lud**,
PERF **hat geladen**) **1** to load; **wir
haben die Möbel in den
Möbelwagen geladen** we loaded
the furniture into the removal van;
2 eine Batterie laden to charge a
battery; **3** to summon; **mein Bruder
wurde als Zeuge geladen** my
brother was summoned as a
witness.

Laden der (PL die Läden) **1** shop;
wann macht der Laden zu? when
does the shop close?; **2** shutter;
**wenn es heiß ist, lassen wir die
Läden den ganzen Tag zu** when it's
hot we keep the shutters closed all
day.

Ladendieb der (PL die Ladendiebe)
shoplifter.

Ladung die (PL die Ladungen)
1 cargo; **2** charge (*of dynamite or
shot*); **3** summons; **4** load.

lag SEE **liegen**.

Lage die (PL die Lagen) **1** situation;
**nicht in der Lage sein, etwas zu
tun** not be in a position to do
something; **2** layer.

Lager *das* (PL *die* Lager) **1** camp;
2 warehouse; **3** stock; **etwas auf
Lager haben** to have something in
stock; **4** stock-room; **5** bearing (*in a
machine*).

lagern *verb* (PERF **hat gelagert**)
1 to store; **2** to camp.

lahm *adjective* lame.

lähmen *verb* (PERF **hat gelähmt**) to
paralyse.

Lähmung *die* paralysis.

Laib *der* (PL *die* Laibe) loaf.

Laken *das* (PL *die* Laken) sheet.

Lakritze *die* liquorice.

Lamm *das* (PL *die* Lämmer) lamb.

Lampe *die* (PL *die* Lampen) lamp.

Lampenschirm *der* (PL *die*
Lampenschirme) lampshade.

Lancieren *das* launch (*of product*).

Land *das* (PL *die* Länder) **1** country;
auf dem Land in the country;
2 land; **3** state (*there are 16 Länder
in Germany*).

Landebahn *die* (PL *die*
Landebahnen) runway.

landen *verb* (PERF **ist gelandet**)
1 to land; **2 im Krankenhaus
landen** (*informal*) to end up in
hospital.

Landkarte *die* (PL *die* Landkarten)
map.

Landkreis *der* (PL *die* Landkreise)
district.

ländlich *adjective* rural.

Landschaft *die* (PL *die*
Landschaften) **1** countryside;
2 landscape.

Landschaftsschutzgebiet *das*
(PL *die* Landschaftsschutzgebiete)
conservation area.

Landstraße *die* (PL *die*
Landstraßen) country road.

landswirtschaftlich *adjective*
agricultural.

Landtag *der* state parliament.

Landwirtschaft *die* agriculture,
farming.

lang *adjective* **1** long; **seit langem**
for a long time; **2** tall.
lang *adverb* **eine Woche lang** for a
week.

langärmelig *adjective* long-sleeved.

Länge *die* (PL *die* Längen) **1** length;
2 longitude.

lange *adverb* **1** a long time; **lange
nicht** not for a long time; **2 so lange
wie möglich** as long as possible;
3 er ist lange nicht so reich he's
nowhere near as rich.

langen *verb* (PERF **hat gelangt**) **1** to
be enough; **das Geld langt nicht**
(*informal*) it's not enough money;
mir langt's (*informal*) I've had
enough; **2** to reach; **nach etwas
langen** to reach for something;
3 jemandem eine langen
(*informal*) to slap somebody's face.

Langlauf *der* cross-country (*in
skiing*).

langsam *adjective*, *adverb* slow;
**die Musik geht mir langsam auf
die Nerven** the music is slowly
getting on my nerves.

längst *adverb* **1** a long time ago;
**das habe ich schon längst
gemacht** I did it a long time ago;

a
b
c
d
e
f
g
h
i
j
k
l
m
n
o
p
q
r
s
t
u
v
w
x
y
z

2 for a long time; **er weiß es schon längst** he's known it for a long time; **3 längst nicht** nowhere near, not nearly.

längster, längste, längstes *adjective* longest; **Marion hat den längsten Aufsatz geschrieben** Marion wrote the longest essay.

langweilen *verb* (PERF **hat gelangweilt**) **1** to bore; **2 sich langweilen** to be bored.

langweilig *adjective* boring.

Lappen *der* (PL *die* **Lappen**) cloth, rag.

Laptop *der* (PL *die* **Laptops**) laptop.

Lärm *der* noise; **sich über den Lärm beschweren** to complain about the noise.

las SEE **lesen**.

Laser *der* (PL *die* **Laser**) laser.

Laserdrucker *der* (PL *die* **Laserdrucker**) laser printer.

Laseroperation *die* laser surgery.

Laserstrahl *der* (PL *die* **Laserstrahlen**) laser beam.

lassen ⬦*verb* (PRES **lässt**, IMPERF **ließ**, PERF **hat gelassen**) **1** to let; **jemanden schlafen lassen** to let somebody sleep; **lass uns jetzt gehen** let's go now; **2 jemandem etwas lassen** to let somebody have something; **3** to leave; **die Kinder zu Hause lassen** to leave the children at home; **lass mich!** leave me!; **4 jemanden warten lassen** to keep somebody waiting; **5 etwas reparieren lassen** to have something repaired; **6 lass das!** stop it!; **7 die Tür lässt sich leicht öffnen** the door opens easily; **das lässt sich alles machen** that can all be arranged.

lässig *adjective* casual.

Last *die* (PL *die* **Lasten**) **1** load; **2 jemandem zur Last fallen** to be a burden on somebody.

lästig *adjective* troublesome.

Lastwagen *der* (PL *die* **Lastwagen**) lorry, truck.

Latein *das* Latin.

Laterne *die* (PL *die* **Laternen**) **1** lantern; **2** street lamp.

Laub *das* leaves.

Lauch *der* leek(s).

Lauf *der* (PL *die* **Läufe**) **1** run; **2** course; **im Laufe der Zeit** in the course of time; **im Laufe der Jahre** over the years; **3** race; **4** barrel (*of a gun*).

Laufbahn *die* (PL *die* **Laufbahnen**) career.

laufen ⬦*verb* (PRES **läuft**, IMPERF **lief**, PERF **ist gelaufen**) **1** to run; **sie kann viel schneller laufen als ihr Bruder** she can run much faster than her brother; **2** to walk; **du kannst nach Hause laufen oder mit dem Bus fahren** you can walk home or go on the bus; **3** to be valid; **4 Ski laufen** to ski; **5** to be on (*of a film, programme, or machine*).

laufend *adjective* **1** running; **2** current (*issue, month*); **3 auf dem Laufenden sein** to be up to date; **Anita hält mich auf dem Laufenden** Anita keeps me up to date.

laufend *adverb* continually, constantly.

Läufer *der* (PL *die* **Läufer**) **1** runner; **2** rug; **3** bishop (*in chess*).

Läuferin *die* (PL *die* **Läuferinnen**) runner.

Laufmasche *die* (PL *die* **Laufmaschen**) ladder (*in your tights*).

Laufwerk *das* (PL *die* **Laufwerke**) drive (*on a computer*).

Laune *die* (PL *die* **Launen**) mood.

launisch *adjective* moody.

Laus *die* (PL *die* **Läuse**) louse.

Laut *der* (PL *die* **Laute**) sound.

laut *adjective* **1** loud; **2** noisy.
laut *adverb* **1** loudly; **2 laut lesen** to read aloud; **3 lauter stellen** to turn up.
laut *preposition* (+ GEN *or* + DAT) according to.

lauten *verb* (PERF **hat gelautet**) **1** to be; **2** to go.

läuten *verb* (PERF **hat geläutet**) to ring.

lauter *adjective* nothing but.

Lautsprecher *der* (PL *die* **Lautsprecher**) (loud)speaker.

Lautstärke *die* volume.

lauwarm *adjective* lukewarm.

Lavendel *der* lavender.

Lawine *die* (PL *die* **Lawinen**) avalanche.

Leben *das* (PL *die* **Leben**) life; **am Leben sein** to be alive; **ums Leben kommen** to lose your life.

leben *verb* (PERF **hat gelebt**) **1** to live; **2** to be alive; **3 leb wohl!** farewell!

lebend *adjective* living.

lebendig *adjective* **1** living; **2 lebendig sein** to be alive; **3** lively.

Lebensgefahr *die* mortal danger; **sein Vater ist in Lebensgefahr** his father is critically ill.

lebensgefährlich *adjective* **1** extremely dangerous; **2** critical; **lebensgefährlich verletzt** critically injured.

Lebenshaltungskosten *plural noun* cost of living.

lebenslänglich *adjective* life.
lebenslänglich *adverb* for life.

Lebenslauf *der* (PL *die* **Lebensläufe**) CV.

Lebensmittel *plural noun* food, groceries.

Lebensmittelgeschäft *das* (PL *die* **Lebensmittelgeschäfte**) grocer's (shop).

Lebensmittelvergiftung *die* (PL *die* **Lebensmittelvergiftungen**) food poisoning.

Lebensunterhalt *der* livelihood; **seinen Lebensunterhalt verdienen** to earn one's living.

Leber *die* (PL *die* **Lebern**) liver.

Leberfleck *der* (PL *die* **Leberflecke**) mole.

Leberwurst *die* liver sausage.

Lebewesen *das* (PL *die* **Lebewesen**) living being, living thing.

a
b
c
d
e
f
g
h
i
j
k
l
m
n
o
p
q
r
s
t
u
v
w
x
y
z

a
b
c
d
e
f
g
h
i
j
k
l
m
n
o
p
q
r
s
t
u
v
w
x
y
z

lebhaft *adjective* **1** lively; **2** vivid (*idea, colour*).

Lebkuchen *der* (PL *die* **Lebkuchen**) gingerbread.

leblos *adjective* lifeless.

Leck *das* (PL *die* **Lecks**) leak.

lecken *verb* (PERF **hat geleckt**) **1** to lick; **die Katze leckte ihre Jungen** the cat licked the kittens; **an etwas lecken** to lick something; **2** to leak.

lecker *adjective* delicious.

Leder *das* (PL *die* **Leder**) leather.

ledig *adjective* single.

lediglich *adverb* merely.

leer *adjective* empty; **leer machen** to empty.

leeren *verb* (PERF **hat geleert**) **1** to empty; **2 ein leeres Blatt Papier** a blank sheet of paper; **3 sich leeren** to empty.

Leerlauf *der* neutral (*gear*).

Leerung *die* (PL *die* **Leerungen**) collection.

legal *adjective* legal.

legen *verb* (PERF **hat gelegt**) **1** to put; **2** to lay; **3 sich legen** to lie down; **4 sich legen** to die down (*of a storm, noise*); **unsere Begeisterung hat sich gelegt** our enthusiasm has worn off.

leger *adjective, adverb* casual; **leger gekleidet sein** to be casually dressed.

Lehm *der* clay.

Lehne *die* (PL *die* **Lehnen**) **1** back (*of a chair*); **2** arm (*of a sofa or chair*).

lehnen *verb* (PERF **hat gelehnt**) **1** to lean; **2 sich an etwas lehnen** to lean against something.

Lehrbuch *das* (PL *die* **Lehrbücher**) textbook.

lehren *verb* (PERF **hat gelehrt**) to teach.

Lehrer *der* (PL *die* **Lehrer**) **1** teacher; **2** instructor.

Lehrerin *die* (PL *die* **Lehrerinnen**) **1** teacher; **2** instructor.

Lehrerzimmer *das* (PL *die* **Lehrerzimmer**) staffroom.

Lehrling *der* (PL *die* **Lehrlinge**) **1** apprentice; **2** trainee.

Lehrplan *der* (PL *die* **Lehrpläne**) syllabus.

Lehrstelle *die* (PL *die* **Lehrstellen**) apprenticeship, trainee post.

Leibwächter *der* (PL *die* **Leibwächter**) bodyguard.

Leiche *die* (PL *die* **Leichen**) (dead) body, corpse.

leicht *adjective* **1** light; **2** easy; **jemandem leicht fallen** to be easy for somebody; **es ist ihm nicht leicht gefallen** it wasn't easy for him; **Markus macht es sich immer leicht** Markus always takes the easy way out; **3 ein leichter Akzent** a slight accent.

Leichtathletik *die* athletics.

leichtfallen SEE **leicht**.

Leichtsinn *der* **1** carelessness; **2** recklessness.

leichtsinnig *adjective* **1** careless; **2** reckless.

Leid *das* **1** sorrow; **2** harm; **3 es tut mir Leid** I'm sorry; **Andreas tut mir Leid** I feel sorry for Andreas.

leid *adjective* **jemanden leid sein** to be fed up with somebody; **etwas leid sein** to be fed up with something.

leiden ⬦*verb* (IMPERF **litt**, PERF **hat gelitten**) **1** to suffer; **2 jemanden gut leiden können** to like somebody; **3 ich kann Erika nicht leiden** I can't stand Erika.

leider *adverb* **1** unfortunately; **2 leider ja** I'm afraid so; **leider nicht** I'm afraid not.

leihen ⬦*verb* (IMPERF **lieh**, PERF **hat geliehen**) **1** to lend; **2 sich etwas leihen** to borrow something; **ich habe mir das Buch von Alex geliehen** I borrowed the book from Alex.

Leihgabe *die* (PL die **Leihgaben**) loan (*by a bank*).

Leihwagen *der* (PL die **Leihwagen**) hire car.

Leim *der* (PL die **Leime**) glue.

Leine *die* (PL die **Leinen**) **1** rope; **2** line (*for washing*); **3** lead (*for a dog*).

Leinen *das* (PL die **Leinen**) linen.

Leinwand *die* (PL die **Leinwände**) screen (*in a cinema*).

leise *adjective* quiet.
leise *adverb* **1** quietly; **2 die Musik leiser stellen** to turn the music down.

leisten *verb* (PERF **hat geleistet**) **1** to achieve; **2 jemandem Hilfe leisten** to help somebody; **3 jemandem Gesellschaft leisten** to keep somebody company; **4 sich etwas leisten** to treat yourself to something; **5 sich etwas leisten können** to be able to afford something; **ich kann mir kein neues Auto leisten** I can't afford a new car.

Leistung *die* (PL die **Leistungen**) **1** achievement; **2** performance; **3 Leistungen** payment.

Leistungskurs *der* (PL die **Leistungskurse**) main subject.

leiten *verb* (PERF **hat geleitet**) **1** to lead; **2** to direct; **3** to manage, run (*a business*); **4** to conduct.

Leiter[1] *die* (PL die **Leitern**) ladder.

Leiter[2] *der* (PL die **Leiter**) **1** leader; **2** head; **3** manager; **4** director; **5** conductor (*of an orchestra or electricity*).

Leiterin *die* (PL die **Leiterinnen**) **1** leader; **2** head; **3** manageress; **4** director.

Leitung *die* (PL die **Leitungen**) **1** direction; **2** management; **3** (*phone*) line; **4** (*electric*) lead; **5** cable; **6** pipe; **7 unter der Leitung von** conducted by.

Leitungswasser *das* tap water.

Lektion *die* (PL die **Lektionen**) lesson.

lenken *verb* (PERF **hat gelenkt**) **1** to steer; **2** to guide; **3 den Verdacht auf jemanden lenken** to throw suspicion on somebody.

Lenkrad *das* (PL die **Lenkräder**) steering wheel.

Lenkstange *die* (PL die **Lenkstangen**) handlebars.

a
b
c
d
e
f
g
h
i
j
k
l
m
n
o
p
q
r
s
t
u
v
w
x
y
z

a

b

lernen *verb* (PERF **hat gelernt**) **1** to learn; **schwimmen lernen** to learn to swim; **2** to study.

c

lesbisch *adjective* lesbian.

d

lesen ⋄*verb* (PRES **liest**, IMPERF **las**, PERF **hat gelesen**) to read.

e

Leser *der* (PL *die* **Leser**) reader.

f

Leseratte *die* (PL *die* **Leseratten**) bookworm.

g

Leserin *die* (PL *die* **Leserinnen**) reader.

h

i

Letzte *der/die/das* (PL *die* **Letzten**) **1** **der/die Letzte** the last (one); **das Letzte** the last (thing); **2 Boris kam als Letzter** Boris arrived last.

j

k

letzte SEE **letzter**.

l

letztens *adverb* **1** recently; **2** lastly.

m

n

o

p

letzter, letzte, letztes *adjective* **1** last; **zum letzten Mal** for the last time; **das letzte Mal** the last time; **2** latest (*news, information*); **3 in letzter Zeit** recently.

q

leuchten *verb* (PERF **hat geleuchtet**) to shine.

r

Leuchter *der* (PL *die* **Leuchter**) candlestick.

s

Leuchtreklame *die* neon sign.

t

u

Leuchtturm *der* (PL *die* **Leuchttürme**) lighthouse.

v

leugnen *verb* (PERF **hat geleugnet**) to deny.

w

Leukämie *die* leukaemia.

x

Leute *plural noun* people.

y

Lexikon *das* (PL *die* **Lexika**) **1** encyclopaedia; **2** dictionary.

z

Licht *das* (PL *die* **Lichter**) light.

Lichtbild *das* (PL *die* **Lichtbilder**) photograph.

Lichtschalter *der* (PL *die* **Lichtschalter**) light switch.

Lid *das* (PL *die* **Lider**) (eye)lid.

Lidschatten *der* (PL *die* **Lidschatten**) eye shadow.

lieb *adjective* **1** dear; **liebe Gabi** dear Gabi; **2** nice; **das ist lieb von euch** that's nice of you; **3 jemanden lieb haben** to be fond of somebody; **4 es wäre mir lieber, wenn ...** I'd prefer it if ...; **5 ihr liebstes Spielzeug** her favourite toy.

Liebe *die* (PL *die* **Lieben**) love.

lieben *verb* (PERF **hat geliebt**) to love.

liebenswürdig *adjective* kind.

lieber *adverb* **1** rather; **2 lieber mögen** to like better; **3 lass das lieber** you'd better not do that; **4 ich trinke lieber Kaffee** I prefer coffee.

Liebesbrief *der* (PL *die* **Liebesbriefe**) love letter.

Liebesfilm *der* (PL *die* **Liebesfilme**) romantic film.

Liebeskummer *der* **Liebeskummer haben** to be lovesick.

liebevoll *adjective* loving.

liebhaben SEE **lieb**.

Liebling *der* (PL *die* **Lieblinge**) **1** darling; **2** favourite.

Lieblings- *prefix* favourite.

liebster, liebste, liebstes *adjective* **1** dearest; **2** favourite. **liebstes** *adverb* **am liebsten** best (of all); **ich mag Max am liebsten** I like Max best.

Lied *das* (PL *die* **Lieder**) song.

lief SEE **laufen**.

liefern *verb* (PERF **hat geliefert**) **1** to deliver; **2** to supply.

Lieferung *die* (PL *die* **Lieferungen**) delivery.

Lieferwagen *der* (PL *die* **Lieferwagen**) (delivery) van.

liegen ⋄*verb* (IMPERF **lag**, PERF **hat gelegen**) **1** to lie; **der Brief liegt auf dem Tisch** the letter is on the table; **es liegt viel Schnee** there's lots of snow; **2** to be, to be situated; **3 liegen bleiben** to stay (*in bed*); **er ist liegen geblieben** he didn't get up; **4 etwas bleibt liegen** something is left behind; **die Arbeit ist liegen geblieben** the job was left undone; **5 der Schnee bleibt liegen** the snow is settling; **6 liegen lassen** to leave; **7 es liegt mir nicht** it doesn't suit me; **8 an etwas liegen** to be due to something; **9 das liegt an ihm** it's up to him.

liegenbleiben, **liegenlassen** SEE **liegen**.

Liegestuhl *der* (PL *die* **Liegestühle**) deckchair.

Liegewagen *der* (PL *die* **Liegewagen**) couchette (car).

ließ SEE **lassen**.

liest SEE **lesen**.

Lift *der* (PL *die* **Lifte**) lift.

Liga *die* (PL *die* **Ligen**) league.

lila *adjective* **1** purple; **2** mauve.

Limo *die* (PL *die* **Limo(s)**) SEE **Limonade**.

Limonade *die* (PL *die* **Limonaden**) **1** fizzy drink; **2** lemonade.

Limone *die* (PL *die* **Limonen**) lime.

Lineal *das* (PL *die* **Lineale**) ruler.

Linie *die* (PL *die* **Linien**) **1** line; **2** route (*of a bus*); **Linie 6** number 6.

Linienflug *der* (PL *die* **Linienflüge**) scheduled flight.

Linke *die* **1** left; **zu meiner Linken** on my left; **2** left hand; **3** left side; **4 die Linke** the left (*in politics*).

linker, linke, linkes *adjective* **1** left; **2** left-wing.

links *adverb* **1** on the left; **links fahren** to drive on the left; **links abbiegen** to turn left; **nach links** left; **von links** from the left; **2 links sein** to be left-wing; **3 zwei links, zwei rechts stricken** to purl two, knit two; **4** (*clothing*) inside out.

Linkshänder *der* (PL *die* **Linkshänder**) left-hander.

Linkshänderin *die* (PL *die* **Linkshänderinnen**) left-hander.

Linse *die* (PL *die* **Linsen**) **1** lens; **2** lentil.

Lippe *die* (PL *die* **Lippen**) lip.

Lippenstift *der* (PL *die* **Lippenstifte**) lipstick.

Liste *die* (PL *die* **Listen**) list.

listig *adjective* cunning.

Liter *der* (PL *die* **Liter**) litre.

Literatur *die* literature.

litt SEE **leiden**.

a
b
c
d
e
f
g
h
i
j
k
l
m
n
o
p
q
r
s
t
u
v
w
x
y
z

Livesendung die (PL die Livesendungen) live programme.

Lizenz die (PL die Lizenzen) licence.

Lkw der (PL die Lkws) (*Lastkraftwagen*) lorry, truck.

Lob das praise.

loben verb (PERF hat gelobt) to praise.

Loch das (PL die Löcher) hole.

Locke die (PL die Locken) curl.

locken verb (PERF hat gelockt) 1 to tempt; 2 to curl.

locker adjective 1 loose; 2 slack (*rope*); 3 relaxed (*atmosphere, person*).

lockerlassen ⋄verb (PRES lässt locker, IMPERF ließ locker, PERF hat lockergelassen) **nicht lockerlassen** (*informal*) not to let up.

lockig adjective curly.

Löffel der (PL die Löffel) 1 spoon; 2 **ein Löffel Mehl** a spoonful of flour.

log SEE lügen.

Logik die logic.

logisch adjective 1 logical; 2 **ja, logisch!** yes, of course!

Lohn der (PL die Löhne) 1 wages; 2 reward.

lohnen verb (PERF hat sich gelohnt) **sich lohnen** to be worth it.

Lokal das (PL die Lokale) 1 bar; 2 restaurant.

Lokomotive die (PL die Lokomotiven) locomotive, engine.

Lorbeerblatt das (PL die Lorbeerblätter) bay leaf.

Los das (PL die Lose) 1 (lottery) ticket; 2 **das große Los ziehen** to hit the jackpot; 3 lot.

los adjective 1 **der Hund ist los** the dog is off the lead; 2 **die Schraube ist los** the screw's loose; 3 **es ist viel los** there's a lot going on; 4 **etwas los sein** to be rid of something; 5 **was ist los?** what's the matter?
los adverb 1 **los!** go on!; 2 **Achtung, fertig, los!** ready, steady, go!

losbinden ⋄verb (IMPERF band los, PERF hat losgebunden) to untie.

löschen verb (PERF hat gelöscht) 1 to put out; 2 **seinen Durst löschen** to quench your thirst; 3 to delete, to cancel; 4 to erase.

lose adjective loose.

lösen verb (PERF hat gelöst) 1 to solve; 2 to undo; 3 to buy; **eine Fahrkarte lösen** to buy a ticket; 4 to release; 5 to remove; 6 **sich lösen** to come undone; 7 **sich lösen** to be solved (*of a puzzle or mystery*); **sich von selbst lösen** to be resolved (*of a problem*); 8 **sich in Wasser lösen** to dissolve in water.

losfahren ⋄verb (PRES fährt los, IMPERF fuhr los, PERF ist losgefahren) 1 to set off; 2 to drive off.

losgehen ⋄verb (IMPERF ging los, PERF ist losgegangen) 1 to set off; 2 to start; 3 to come off (*of a button*); 4 to go off (*of a bomb*); 5 **auf jemanden losgehen** to go for somebody.

loslassen ◇*verb* (PRES **lässt los,** IMPERF **ließ los,** PERF **hat losgelassen**) **1** to let go of; **2** to let go.

Lösung *die* (PL *die* **Lösungen**) solution.

Losung *die* (PL *die* **Losungen**) **1** slogan; **2** password; **die Losung nennen** to give the password.

loswerden ◇*verb* (PRES **wird los,** IMPERF **wurde los,** PERF **ist losgeworden**) to get rid of.

Lotterie *die* (PL *die* **Lotterien**) lottery.

Lotto *das* (PL *die* **Lottos**) (national) lottery.

Löwe *der* (PL *die* **Löwen**) **1** lion; **2** Leo; **Wilhelm ist Löwe** Wilhelm's a Leo.

Loyalität *die* loyalty.

Lücke *die* (PL *die* **Lücken**) gap.

Luft *die* (PL *die* **Lüfte**) **1** air; **2 die Luft anhalten** to hold your breath; **3 in die Luft gehen** (*informal*) to blow your top; **4 jemanden wie Luft behandeln** to ignore somebody.

Luftballon *der* (PL *die* **Luftballons**) balloon.

Luftdruck *der* air pressure.

Luftmatratze *die* (PL *die* **Luftmatratzen**) air-bed.

Luftpost *die* airmail; **per Luftpost** by airmail.

Luftverschmutzung *die* air pollution.

Luftwaffe *die* air force.

Lüge *die* (PL *die* **Lügen**) lie.

lügen ◇*verb* (IMPERF **log,** PERF **hat gelogen**) to lie.

Lügner *der* (PL *die* **Lügner**) liar.

Lügnerin *die* (PL *die* **Lügnerinnen**) liar.

Lunge *die* (PL *die* **Lungen**) lungs.

Lungenentzündung *die* pneumonia.

Lupe *die* (PL *die* **Lupen**) magnifying glass.

Lust *die* **1** pleasure; **2 Lust haben, etwas zu tun** to feel like doing something; **ich habe keine Lust** I don't feel like it; **Lust auf etwas haben** to feel like something.

lustig *adjective* **1** jolly; **2** funny; **3 Dieter hat sich über mich lustig gemacht** Dieter made fun of me.

lutschen *verb* (PERF **hat gelutscht**) to suck.

Lutscher *der* (PL *die* **Lutscher**) lollipop.

Luxemburg *das* Luxembourg.

Luxus *der* luxury.

Mm

machen *verb* (PERF **hat gemacht**) **1** to make; **2** to do; **was machst du da?** what are you doing?; **3 was macht die Arbeit?** how's work?; **was macht Karin?** how's Karin?; **4 sich an die Arbeit machen** to get down to work; **5 schnell machen** to hurry; **6 das macht nichts** it doesn't matter; **7** to come to; **das**

a
b
c
d
e
f
g
h
i
j
k
l
m
n
o
p
q
r
s
t
u
v
w
x
y
z

macht fünf Euro that comes to five euros; **8 sich nichts aus etwas machen** to not be very keen on something; **Gisela macht sich nichts aus Schokolade** Gisela isn't keen on chocolate.

Macht *die* (PL *die* Mächte) power; **an die Macht kommen** to come to power.

Mädchen *das* (PL *die* Mädchen) girl.

Mädchenname *der* (PL *die* Mädchennamen) maiden name.

Made *die* (PL *die* Maden) maggot.

mag SEE **mögen**.

Magazin *das* (PL *die* Magazine) magazine.

Magen *der* (PL *die* Mägen) stomach.

Magenschmerzen *plural noun* stomach-ache.

mager *adjective* **1** thin; **2** lean; **3** low-fat.

Magie *die* magic.

Magnet *der* (PL *die* Magnete(n)) magnet.

magnetisch *adjective* magnetic.

magst SEE **mögen**.

Mahagoni *das* mahogany.

mähen *verb* (PERF **hat gemäht**) to mow; **den Rasen mähen** to mow the lawn.

mahlen ⋄*verb* (PERF **hat gemahlen**) to grind.

Mahlzeit *die* (PL *die* Mahlzeiten) meal; **Mahlzeit!** enjoy your meal!

Mai *der* May; **der Erste Mai** May Day.

Maiglöckchen *das* (PL *die* Maiglöckchen) lily of the valley.

Mais *der* maize.

Majonäse *die* mayonnaise.

Majoran *der* marjoram.

Makkaroni (*plural noun*) macaroni.

Makler *der* (PL *die* Makler) estate agent.

Makrele *die* (PL *die* Makrelen) mackerel.

Mal *das* (PL *die* Male) **1** time; **nächstes Mal** next time; **zum ersten Mal** for the first time; **2** mark; **3** mole.

mal *adverb* **1** times; **zwei mal drei** two times three; **2** by (*with measurements*); **3** sometime (*in the future*); **ich möchte mal nach Brasilien fahren** I'd like to go to Brazil sometime; **4 schon mal** ever; **5 ich war schon mal da** I've been once before; **6 nicht mal** not even; **7 komm mal her!** come here!

malen *verb* (PERF **hat gemalt**) to paint.

Maler *der* (PL *die* Maler) painter.

Malerei *die* painting.

Malerin *die* (PL *die* Malerinnen) painter.

Mallorca *das* Majorca.

Mama *die* (PL *die* Mamas) mum.

Mami *die* (PL *die* Mamis) mummy.

man *pronoun* **1** you, one; **wie macht man das?** how do you do it?; **man kann ja nie wissen** one can never tell; **2** they, people; **man sagt** they say; **3 man hat mir gesagt** I was told.

mancher, manche, manches *adjective* **1** many a; **so manchen Tag** many a day; **2 manche** (*plural*) some; **an manchen Tagen** some days. **manches** *pronoun* **1** many a person; **2 manche** (*plural*) some people; **3 manches** some things.

manchmal *adverb* sometimes.

Mandarine *die* (PL *die* Mandarinen) mandarin.

Mandel *die* (PL *die* Mandeln) **1** almond; **2** tonsil.

Mandelentzündung *die* tonsillitis.

Mangel *der* (PL *die* Mängel) **1** lack; **2** shortage; **3** defect, fault.

mangelhaft *adjective* **1** faulty; **2** unsatisfactory (*school mark*).

Manie *die* (PL *die* Manien) mania.

Manieren *plural noun* manners; **er hat keine Manieren** he's got no manners.

Mann *der* (PL *die* Männer) **1** man; **2** husband.

Männchen *das* (PL *die* Männchen) male (*animal*).

Mannequin *das* (PL *die* Mannequins) model.

männlich *adjective* **1** male; **2** manly; **3** masculine.

Mannschaft *die* (PL *die* Mannschaften) **1** team; **2** crew.

Manschette *die* (PL *die* Manschetten) cuff.

Mantel *der* (PL *die* Mäntel) coat.

Mappe *die* (PL *die* Mappen) **1** folder; **2** briefcase; **3** bag.

Märchen *das* (PL *die* Märchen) fairy tale.

Margarine *die* margarine.

Marienkäfer *der* (PL *die* Marienkäfer) ladybird.

Marine *die* (PL *die* Marinen) navy.

Mark *die* (PL *die* Mark) mark (*German currency until replaced by the euro; one hundred marks = h51.13 euros*).

Marke *die* (PL *die* Marken) **1** make, brand; **meine Mutter fährt seit Jahren die gleiche Marke** my mother has been driving the same make of car for years; **Adidas ist eine führende Marke** Adidas is a leading brand; **2** tag; **3** stamp (*for letters*); **4** coupon.

markieren *verb* (PERF **hat markiert**) **1** to mark; **2** to fake.

Markt *der* (PL *die* Märkte) market; **auf den Markt bringen** to launch (*a product*).

Marktplatz *der* (PL *die* Marktplätze) market-place.

Marmelade *die* (PL *die* Marmeladen) jam.

Marmor *der* marble.

Marokko *das* Morocco.

Marsch *der* (PL *die* Märsche) march.

März *der* March.

Masche *die* (PL *die* Maschen) **1** stitch; **2** mesh; **3** (*informal*) trick; **die Masche raushaben** to know how to do it; **das ist die neueste Masche** that's the latest thing.

Maschine *die* (PL *die* Maschinen) **1** machine; **2** plane; **3** typewriter; **Maschine schreiben** to type.

a
b
c
d
e
f
g
h
i
j
k
l
m
n
o
p
q
r
s
t
u
v
w
x
y
z

Masern *plural noun* measles.

Maske *die* (PL *die* **Masken**) mask.

maskieren *verb* (PERF **hat sich maskiert**) **1 sich maskieren** to dress up; **2 sich maskieren** to disguise yourself.

Maß[1] *das* (PL *die* **Maße**) **1** measure; **2** measurement; **3** extent; **in hohem Maße** to a high degree; **4 Maß halten** to show moderation.

Maß[2] *die* (PL *die* **Maß**) litre (of beer).

maß SEE **messen**.

Masse *die* (PL *die* **Massen**) **1** mass; **eine Masse Arbeit** masses of work; **2** crowd; **3** mixture (*in cooking*).

massenhaft *adjective* masses of.

Massenvernichtungswaffen *plural noun* weapons of mass destruction.

massieren *verb* (PERF **hat massiert**) to massage.

mäßig *adjective* moderate.

Maßnahme *die* (PL *die* **Maßnahmen**) measure.

Maßstab *der* (PL *die* **Maßstäbe**) **1** standard; **2** scale.

Mast *der* (PL *die* **Masten**) **1** mast; **2** pole; **3** pylon.

Material *das* (PL *die* **Materialien**) **1** material; **2** materials.

Mathe *die* (*informal*) maths.

Mathematik *die* mathematics.

Matratze *die* (PL *die* **Matratzen**) mattress.

Matrose *der* (PL *die* **Matrosen**) sailor.

Matsch *der* **1** mud; **2** slush.

matschig *adjective* **1** muddy; **2** slushy.

matt *adjective* **1** weak; **2** matt; **3** dull; **4 matt!** checkmate!

Matte *die* (PL *die* **Matten**) mat.

Mauer *die* (PL *die* **Mauern**) wall.

Maul *das* (PL *die* **Mäuler**) mouth; **halt's Maul!** (*informal*) shut up!

Maulkorb *der* (PL *die* **Maulkörbe**) muzzle.

Maulwurf *der* (PL *die* **Maulwürfe**) mole.

Maulwurfshügel *der* (PL *die* **Maulwurfshügel**) molehill.

Maurer *der* (PL *die* **Maurer**) bricklayer.

Maus *die* (PL *die* **Mäuse**) mouse.

Maximum *das* (PL *die* **Maxima**) maximum.

Mayonnaise *die* mayonnaise.

Mechaniker *der* (PL *die* **Mechaniker**) mechanic.

Mechanikerin *die* (PL *die* **Mechanikerinnen**) mechanic.

mechanisch *adjective* mechanical.

meckern *verb* (PERF **hat gemeckert**) **1** to bleat; **2** to grumble.

Medaille *die* (PL *die* **Medaillen**) medal.

Medien *plural noun* media.

Medikament *das* (PL *die* **Medikamente**) medicine, drug.

Medizin *die* (PL *die* **Medizinen**) medicine.

a b c d e f g h i j k l **m** n o p q r s t u v w x y z

Meer das (PL die Meere) sea.

Meeresfrüchte plural noun seafood.

Meerschweinchen das (PL die Meerschweinchen) guinea pig.

Megabyte das (PL die Megabytes) megabyte.

Mehl das flour.

mehr adverb, pronoun more; **nichts mehr** no more; **nie mehr** never again.

mehrere pronoun several.

mehreres pronoun several things.

mehrfach adjective **1** multiple, many; **2** repeated.
mehrfach adverb several times.

Mehrheit die (PL die Mehrheiten) majority.

mehrmalig adjective repeated.

mehrmals adverb several times.

Mehrwertsteuer die value added tax.

Mehrzahl die **1** majority; **2** plural.

meiden ◇verb (IMPERF **mied**, PERF **hat gemieden**) to avoid.

Meile die (PL die Meilen) mile.

mein adjective my.

meine SEE **meiner**.

meinen verb (PERF **hat gemeint**) **1** to think; **2** to mean; **es gut meinen** to mean well; **3** to say.

meiner, meine, mein(e)s pronoun mine.

meinetwegen adverb **1** for my sake; **2** because of me; **3** as far as I'm concerned; **'kann ich das Auto haben?'** – **'meinetwegen'** 'can I take the car?' – 'I don't mind'.

meins SEE **meiner**.

Meinung die (PL die Meinungen) opinion.

meist adverb **1** mostly; **2** usually.

meiste adjective, pronoun **der/die/das meiste** most; **die meisten** most; **am meisten** most, the most.

meistens adverb **1** mostly; **2** usually.

Meister der (PL die Meister) **1** master; **2** champion.

Meisterin die (PL die Meisterinnen) champion.

Meisterschaft die (PL die Meisterschaften) championship.

Meisterstück das (PL die Meisterstücke) **1** masterpiece; **2** masterstroke.

Meisterwerk das (PL die Meisterwerke) masterpiece.

melden verb (PERF **hat gemeldet**) **1** to report; **2** to register; **3 sich melden** to report, (on the phone) to answer; **Luise hat sich gemeldet** (in school) Luise put up her hand; **4 sich bei jemandem melden** to get in touch with somebody.

Melodie die (PL die Melodien) melody, tune.

Melone die (PL die Melonen) **1** melon; **2** bowler (hat).

Menge die (PL die Mengen) **1** quantity; **eine Menge Geld** a lot of money; **2** crowd; **3** set (in maths).

Mensch der (PL die Menschen) **1** human being; **2** person; **kein**

Mensch nobody; **jeder Mensch** everybody; **3 die Menschen** people; **wie viele Menschen?** how many people?; **4** *(as an exclamation)* **Mensch!** *(informal)* wow!, hey!; **Mensch, hab ich mich geärgert!** *(informal)* I was damn annoyed.

menschenleer *adjective* deserted.

Menschenverstand *der* **gesunder Menschenverstand** common sense.

Menschheit *die* mankind.

menschlich *adjective* **1** human; **2** humane.

Mentalität *die* (PL die Mentalitäten) mentality.

Menü *das* (PL die Menüs) **1** set menu *(in restaurant)*; **2** menu *(of computer program)*.

merken *verb* (PERF **hat gemerkt**) **1** to notice; **2 sich etwas merken** to remember something.

Merkmal *das* (PL die Merkmale) feature.

merkwürdig *adjective* strange, odd.

Messe *die* (PL die Messen) **1** mass; **2** trade fair.

messen ⬦*verb* (PRES **misst**, IMPERF **maß**, PERF **hat gemessen**) **1** to measure; **(bei jemandem) Fieber messen** to take somebody's temperature; **2 sich mit jemandem messen können** to be as good as somebody.

Messer *das* (PL die Messer) knife.

Messing *das* brass.

Metall *das* (PL die Metalle) metal.

Meter *der* (PL die Meter) metre.

Metermaß *das* (PL die Metermaße) tape measure.

Methode *die* (PL die Methoden) method.

metrisch *adjective* metric.

Metzger *der* (PL die Metzger) butcher.

Metzgerei *die* (PL die Metzgereien) butcher's (shop).

Mexiko *das* Mexico.

miauen *verb* (PERF **hat miaut**) to miaow.

mich *pronoun* **1** me; **2** myself.

mied SEE **meiden**.

Miete *die* (PL die Mieten) **1** rent; **zur Miete wohnen** to live in rented accommodation; **2** hire charge.

mieten *verb* (PERF **hat gemietet**) **1** to rent; **2** to hire.

Mieter *der* (PL die Mieter) tenant.

Mieterin *die* (PL die Mieterinnen) tenant.

Mietshaus *das* (PL die Mietshäuser) block of rented flats.

Mietvertrag *der* (PL die Mietverträge) lease.

Mietwagen *der* (PL die Mietwagen) hire car.

Migräne *die* (PL die Migränen) migraine.

Mikrochip *der* (PL die Mikrochips) microchip.

Mikrofon *das* (PL die Mikrofone) microphone.

Mikroskop *das* (PL *die* **Mikroskope**) microscope.

Mikrowellenherd *der* (PL *die* **Mikrowellenherde**) microwave oven.

Milch *die* milk.

Milchshake *der* (PL *die* **Milchshakes**) milk shake.

mild *adjective* mild.

Militär *das* army.

militärisch *adjective* military.

Milliarde *die* (PL *die* **Milliarden**) thousand million, billion; **zwei Milliarden Euro** two billion euros.

Millimeter *der* (PL *die* **Millimeter**) millimetre.

Million *die* (PL *die* **Millionen**) million.

Millionär *der* (PL *die* **Millionäre**) millionaire.

Millionärin *die* (PL *die* **Millionärinnen**) millionairess.

Minderheit *die* (PL *die* **Minderheiten**) minority.

minderjährig *adjective* under age.

mindestens *adverb* at least.

mindester, mindeste, mindestes *adjective* least. **mindestes** *pronoun* **1 der/die/das Mindeste** the least; **zum Mindesten** at least; **2 nicht im Mindesten** not in the least.

Mine *die* (PL *die* **Minen**) **1** mine; **2** lead (*in a pencil*); **3** refill (*for a ball-point*).

Mineralwasser *das* (PL *die* **Mineralwässer**) mineral water.

Minirock *der* (PL *die* **Miniröcke**) miniskirt.

Minister *der* (PL *die* **Minister**) minister.

Ministerin *die* (PL *die* **Ministerinnen**) minister.

Ministerium *das* (PL *die* **Ministerien**) ministry, department.

minus *adverb* minus.

Minute *die* (PL *die* **Minuten**) minute.

mir *pronoun* **1** me, to me; **2** myself.

mischen *verb* (PERF **hat gemischt**) **1** to mix; **2 die Karten mischen** to shuffle the cards; **3 sich mischen** to mix.

Mischung *die* (PL *die* **Mischungen**) **1** mixture; **2** blend.

miserabel *adjective* (*informal*) **1** hopeless; **2** dreadful.

missbilligen *verb* (PERF **hat missbilligt**) to disapprove.

Missbrauch *der* abuse.

missbrauchen *verb* (PERF **hat missbraucht**) to abuse.

Misserfolg *der* (PL *die* **Misserfolge**) failure.

Missgeschick *das* (PL *die* **Missgeschicke**) **1** misfortune; **2** mishap.

misshandeln *verb* (PRES **hat misshandelt**) to ill-treat.

misslingen ⬦*verb* (IMPERF **misslang**, PERF **ist misslungen**) to fail; **es misslang ihr** she failed.

misst SEE **messen**.

Misstrauen *das* **1** mistrust; **2** distrust.

a
b
c
d
e
f
g
h
i
j
k
l
m
n
o
p
q
r
s
t
u
v
w
x
y
z

misstrauen *verb* (PERF hat misstraut) **jemandem misstrauen** to mistrust somebody.

misstrauisch *adjective* suspicious.

Missverständnis *das* (PL *die* Missverständnisse) misunderstanding.

missverstehen ◇*verb* (IMPERF missverstand, PERF hat missverstanden) to misunderstand.

Mist *der* **1** manure; **2** (*informal*) rubbish.

Mistel *die* (PL *die* Misteln) mistletoe.

mit *preposition* (+ DAT) **1** with; **2 mit der Bahn fahren** to go by train; **mit dem Boot fahran** to go by boat; **3 mit sechs Jahren** at the age of six; **4 mit jemandem sprechen** to speak to somebody; **5 mit Bleistift** in pencil; **6 mit lauter Stimme** in a loud voice.

mit *adverb* as well, too; **warst du mit dabei?** were you there too?

Mitarbeiter *der* (PL *die* Mitarbeiter) **1** colleague; **2** employee.

Mitarbeiterin *die* (PL *die* Mitarbeiterinnen) **1** colleague; **2** employee.

mitbringen ◇*verb* (IMPERF brachte mit, PERF hat mitgebracht) to bring, to bring along; **ich bringe den Kindern Schokolade mit** I'm taking the children some chocolate.

miteinander *adverb* with each other, with one another.

Mitesser *der* (PL *die* Mitesser) blackhead.

mitfahren ◇*verb* (PRES fährt mit, IMPERF fuhr mit, PERF ist mitgefahren) **1 mit jemandem mitfahren** to go with somebody; **die Kinder fahren mit uns mit** the children are coming with us; **2 bei jemandem mitfahren** to get a lift with somebody; **jemanden mitfahren lassen** to give somebody a lift.

mitgeben ◇*verb* (PRES gibt mit, IMPERF gab mit, PERF hat mitgegeben) to give.

Mitglied *das* (PL *die* Mitglieder) member.

mithalten ◇*verb* (PRES hält mit, IMPERF hielt mit, PERF hat mitgehalten) to keep up.

mitkommen ◇*verb* (IMPERF kam mit, PERF ist mitgekommen) **1** to come too; **2** to keep up.

Mitleid *das* pity; **kein Mitleid mit jemandem haben** not to feel any sympathy for somebody.

mitmachen *verb* (PERF hat mitgemacht) **1** to join in; **hast du Lust, bei dem Spiel mitzumachen?** do you want to join in the game?; **2** to take part in; **3** to go through (*experiences, troubles*); **sie hat viel mitgemacht** she's gone through a lot.

mitnehmen ◇*verb* (PRES nimmt mit, IMPERF nahm mit, PERF hat mitgenommen) **1** to take, to take along; **Anni hat die Kinder auf den Spielplatz mitgenommen** Anni has taken the children to the

a
b
c
d
e
f
g
h
i
j
k
l
m
n
o
p
q
r
s
t
u
v
w
x
y
z

playground; **2** to give a lift to; **3** to affect (badly); **4 zum Mitnehmen** to take away.

Mitschüler der (PL die Mitschüler) schoolfriend.

Mitschülerin die (PL die Mitschülerinnen) schoolfriend.

mitsingen verb (IMPERF sang mit, PERF hat mitgesungen) to sing along.

mitspielen verb (PERF hat mitgespielt) **1** to play; **wer spielt bei dem Fußballspiel mit?** who's playing in the football match?; **willst du mitspielen?** do you want to join in?; **2 in einem Film mitspielen** to be in a film.

Mittag der (PL die Mittage) **1** midday; **2** lunch; **zu Mittag essen** to have lunch; **3** lunch-break.

Mittagessen das (PL die Mittagessen) lunch; **beim Mittagessen** at lunch.

mittags adverb **1** at lunchtime, at midday; **2 um zwölf Uhr mittags** at noon.

Mittagspause die (PL die Mittagspausen) lunch-break.

Mitte die (PL die Mitten) **1** middle; **2** centre.

Mitteilung die (PL die Mitteilungen) **1** announcement; **2** communication.

Mittel das (PL die Mittel) **1** means; **2 ein Mittel gegen Husten** a cough remedy; **3 öffentliche Mittel** public funds.

Mittelalter das Middle Ages.

Mitteleuropa das Central Europe.

mittelgroß adjective medium-sized.

mittelmäßig adjective mediocre.

Mittelmeer das Mediterranean.

Mittelpunkt der (PL die Mittelpunkte) centre; **im Mittelpunkt stehen** to be the centre of attention.

Mittelstand der middle class.

Mittelstürmer der (PL die Mittelstürmer) centre-forward.

mitten adverb **mitten in/auf** in the middle of; **mitten in der Nacht** in the middle of the night.

Mitternacht die midnight.

mittlerer, mittlere, mittleres adjective **1** middle; **2** medium (quality, size); **3** average.

mittlerweile adverb **1** meanwhile; **2** by now.

Mittwoch der (PL die Mittwoche) Wednesday.

mittwochs adverb on Wednesdays.

Mixer der (PL die Mixer) liquidizer.

Möbel plural noun furniture.

Möbelwagen der (PL die Möbelwagen) removal van.

Mobiltelefon das (PL die Mobiltelefone) mobile phone.

möbliert adjective furnished.

mochte, möchte SEE **mögen**.

Mode die (PL die Moden) fashion.

Modell das (PL die Modelle) model.

Moderator der (PL die Moderatoren) presenter (on TV).

a
b
c
d
e
f
g
h
i
j
k
l
m
n
o
p
q
r
s
t
u
v
w
x
y
z

Moderatorin die (PL die Moderatorinnen) presenter (*on TV*).

modern *adjective* modern.

modernisieren *verb* (PERF hat modernisiert) to modernize.

modisch *adjective* fashionable.

Mofa die (PL die Mofas) moped.

mogeln *verb* (PERF hat gemogelt) to cheat.

mögen ◇*verb* (PRES mag, IMPERF mochte, PERF hat gemocht) **1** to like; **ich mag ihn nicht** I don't like him; **ich möchte** I'd like; **ich möchte gern wissen** I'd like to know; **möchtest du nach Hause?** would you like to go home?; **2 lieber mögen** to prefer; **ich möchte lieber Tee** I would prefer tea; **3 etwas nicht tun mögen** not to want to do something; **ich mag nicht fragen** I don't want to ask; **ich mag nicht mehr** I've had enough; **4 das mag sein** maybe; **5 was mag das sein?** whatever can it be?

möglich *adjective* possible; **alles Mögliche** all sorts of things.

möglicherweise *adverb* possibly.

Möglichkeit die (PL die Möglichkeiten) possibility.

möglichst *adverb* if possible; **möglichst früh** as early as possible.

Möhre die (PL die Möhren) carrot.

Mokka der (PL die Mokkas) mocca.

Molekül das (PL die Moleküle) molecule.

Moment der (PL die Momente) moment; **im Moment** at the moment; **Moment (mal)!** just a moment!

momentan *adjective* **1** temporary; **2** current.
momentan *adverb* **1** temporarily; **2** at the moment.

Monat der (PL die Monate) month.

monatelang *adverb* for months.

monatlich *adjective, adverb* monthly.

Mönch der (PL die Mönche) monk.

Mond der (PL die Monde) moon.

Mondschein der moonlight; **im Mondschein** by moonlight.

Montag der (PL die Montage) Monday.

montags *adverb* on Mondays.

Moped das (PL die Mopeds) moped.

Moral die **1** moral; **2** morale; **3** morals.

moralisch *adjective* moral.

Mord der (PL die Morde) murder.

Mörder der (PL die Mörder) murderer.

Mörderin die (PL die Mörderinnen) murderer.

Morgen der (PL die Morgen) morning; **am Morgen** in the morning; **heute Morgen** this morning; **guten Morgen!** good morning!

morgen *adverb* tomorrow; **morgen Abend** tomorrow evening.

morgens *adverb* in the morning.

Moschee die (PL die Moscheen) mosque.

Mosel die (River) Moselle.

Moskau das Moscow.

Moslem der (PL die Moslems) Muslim.

moslemisch adjective Muslim.

Moslenin die (PL die Mosleninnen) Muslim.

Motiv das (PL die Motive) **1** motive; **2** motif.

Motivation die motivation.

Motor der (PL die Motoren) engine, motor.

Motorrad das (PL die Motorräder) motorcycle, motorbike.

Mousse die (PL die Mouses) mousse.

Möwe die (PL die Möwen) seagull.

Mücke die (PL die Mücken) **1** midge; **2** mosquito.

müde adjective tired.

Müdigkeit die tiredness.

Mühe die (PL die Mühen) **1** effort; **sich Mühe geben** to make an effort; **2** trouble; **machen Sie sich keine Mühe** don't go to any trouble; **3 mit Müh und Not** only just.

Mühle die (PL die Mühlen) **1** mill; **2** grinder (for coffee).

mühsam adjective laborious.

Müll der rubbish.

Müllabfuhr die refuse collection.

Mülleimer der (PL die Mülleimer) rubbish bin.

Mülltonne die (PL die Mülltonnen) dustbin.

Mumps der mumps.

München das Munich.

Mund der (PL die Münder) mouth; **halt den Mund!** (informal) shut up!

Mundharmonika die (PL die Mundharmonikas) mouth organ.

mündlich adjective oral.

Münster das (PL die Münster) cathedral.

Münze die (PL die Münzen) coin.

Münzfernsprecher der (PL die Münzfernsprecher) payphone.

murmeln verb (PERF hat gemurmelt) to mumble.

mürrisch adjective surly.

Muschel die (PL die Muscheln) **1** mussel; **2** (sea) shell; **3** mouthpiece (of a phone).

Museum das (PL die Museen) museum.

Musik die music.

Musikal das (PL die Musikals) musical.

musikalisch adjective musical.

Musiker der (PL die Musiker) musician.

Musikerin die (PL die Musikerinnen) musician.

Muskat der nutmeg.

Muskel der (PL die Muskeln) muscle.

Müsli das muesli.

muss SEE **müssen**.

müssen ◇verb (PRES **muss**, IMPERF **musste**, PERF **hat gemusst**) **1 etwas tun müssen** to have to do something; **sie muss es tun** she's got to do it, she must do it; **muss**

a
b
c
d
e
f
g
h
i
j
k
l
m
n
o
p
q
r
s
t
u
v
w
x
y
z

ich? do I have to?; **muss das sein?** is that necessary?; **2 Sie müssten es mal versuchen** you should try it; **3 sie müssen gleich hier sein** they'll be here at any moment; **4 ich muss mal** (*informal*) I need (to go to) the loo.

Muster *das* (PL *die* **Muster**) **1** pattern; **2** sample.

Mut *der* courage; **jemandem Mut machen** to encourage somebody.

mutig *adjective* courageous.

Mutter[1] *die* (PL *die* **Mütter**) mother.

Mutter[2] *die* (PL *die* **Muttern**) nut.

Muttersprache *die* (PL *die* **Muttersprachen**) mother tongue, native language.

Muttertag *der* (PL *die* **Muttertage**) Mother's Day.

Mutti *die* (PL *die* **Muttis**) mum.

Mütze *die* (PL *die* **Mützen**) cap.

MwSt. (*Mehrwertsteuer*) VAT.

Mythos *der* (PL *die* **Mythen**) myth.

Nn

na *exclamation* well; **na und?** so what?; **na gut** all right then.

Nabel *der* (PL *die* **Nabel**) navel.

nach *preposition* (+ DAT) **1** to; **nach Hause gehen** to go home; **nach oben** up; **nach hinten** back; **nach rechts abbiegen** to turn right; **2** after; **nach Ihnen** after you; **zehn nach eins** ten past one; **nach etwas greifen** to reach for something;

3 according to; **meiner Meinung nach** in my opinion.
nach *adverb* **nach und nach** bit by bit, gradually; **nach wie vor** still.

nachahmen *verb* (PERF **hat nachgeahmt**) to imitate.

Nachbar *der* (PL *die* **Nachbarn**) neighbour.

Nachbarin *die* (PL *die* **Nachbarinnen**) neighbour.

Nachbarschaft *die* neighbourhood.

nachdem *conjunction* **1** after; **2 je nachdem** it depends; **je nachdem, wie schnell du damit fertig wirst** it depends on how quicky you can finish it.

nachdenken ⬦*verb* (IMPERF **dachte nach**, PERF **hat nachgedacht**) to think; **über etwas nachdenken** to think about something; **ich habe lange über ihr Angebot nachgedacht und mich schließlich dagegen entschieden** I've thought a long time about her offer and finally decided against it.

nachdenklich *adjective* thoughtful.

nacheinander *adverb* one after the other; **die Bewerber kamen nacheinander herein** the applicants came in one after the other.

Nachfrage *die* (PL *die* **Nachfragen**) demand; **es besteht keine Nachfrage** there's no demand for it.

nachgehen ⬦*verb* (IMPERF **ging nach**, PERF **ist nachgegangen**) **1** to be slow; **meine Uhr geht nach** my watch is slow; **2 jemandem nachgehen** to follow somebody; **einer Sache nachgehen** to look into something.

nachher *adverb* afterwards; **erst gehen wir ins Kino und nachher könnten wir essen gehen** we go to the cinema first and afterwards we could go for a meal; **bis nachher!** see you later!

nachholen *verb* (PERF hat nachgeholt) **1** to catch up on; **ich hatte Grippe und muss jetzt viel Mathe nachholen** I've had flu and now I've got a lot of maths to catch up on; **2** to make up for (*something missed*); **3 eine Prüfung nachholen** to do an exam at a later date.

nachkommen ⋄*verb* (IMPERF kam nach, PERF ist nachgekommen) **1** to come later, to follow; **2 ich komme nicht nach** I can't keep up; **3 einem Versprechen nachkommen** to carry out a promise; **seinen Verpflichtungen nachkommen** to meet your commitments.

nachlassen ⋄*verb* (PRES lässt nach, IMPERF ließ nach, PERF hat nachgelassen) **1** to ease; **meine Zahnschmerzen lassen langsam nach** my toothache is getting better; **2** to let up; **sobald die Kälte nachlässt** as soon as it gets warmer; **3** to deteriorate; **4 etwas vom Preis nachlassen** to take something off the price; **jemandem zwanzig Euro nachlassen** to give somebody twenty euros off.

nachlässig *adjective* careless.

nachlaufen ⋄*verb* (PRES läuft nach, IMPERF lief nach, PERF ist nachgelaufen) **jemandem nachlaufen** to run after somebody; **Philipp läuft allen Mädchen nach** (*informal*) Philipp chases all the girls.

nachmachen *verb* (PERF hat nachgemacht) to copy.

Nachmittag *der* (PL die Nachmittage) afternoon.

nachmittags *adverb* in the afternoon.

Nachnahme *die* **per Nachnahme** cash on delivery.

Nachname *der* (PL die Nachnamen) surname.

nachprüfen *verb* (PERF hat nachgeprüft) to check; **er prüft nach, ob es stimmt** he's going to check if it is correct.

Nachricht *die* (PL die Nachrichten) **1** news; **ich warte noch immer auf eine Nachricht von ihm** I'm still waiting for news of him; **eine Nachricht hinterlassen** to leave a message; **2 die Nachrichten** the news; **das kam in den Nachrichten** it was on the news.

Nachrichtensprecher *der* (PL die Nachrichtensprecher) newsreader.

Nachrichtensprecherin *die* (PL die Nachrichtensprecherinnen) newsreader.

nachschlagen ⋄*verb* (PRES schlägt nach, IMPERF schlug nach, PERF hat nachgeschlagen) to look up.

a
b
c
d
e
f
g
h
i
j
k
l
m
n
o
p
q
r
s
t
u
v
w
x
y
z

nachsehen ◇*verb* (PRES **sieht nach**, IMPERF **sah nach**, PERF **hat nachgesehen**) **1** to check; **sieh nach, wer da ist** go and see who's there; **2** to look up; **3 jemandem etwas nachsehen** to let somebody get away with something.

nachsitzen ◇*verb* (IMPERF **saß nach**, PERF **hat nachgesessen**) to be in detention; **Jan muss nachsitzen** Jan has detention.

Nachspeise die (PL die **Nachspeisen**) dessert, pudding.

nächste SEE **nächster**.

nächstens *adverb* shortly.

nächster, nächste, nächstes *adjective* **1** next; **2** nearest; **am nächsten sein** to be nearest; **3 in nächster Nähe** close by.
nächstes *pronoun* **der/die/das Nächste** (the) next; **als Nächstes** next.

Nacht die (PL die **Nächte**) night.

Nachteil der (PL die **Nachteile**) disadvantage.

Nachtfalter der (PL die **Nachtfalter**) moth.

Nachthemd das (PL die **Nachthemden**) nightdress, nightshirt.

Nachtigall die (PL die **Nachtigallen**) nightingale.

Nachtisch der (PL die **Nachtische**) dessert, pudding.

Nachtklub der (PL die **Nachtklubs**) night club.

Nachtleben das nightlife.

nachträglich *adjective* **1** subsequent; **2** belated.
nachträglich *adverb* **1** later; **2** belatedly.

nachts *adverb* at night; **um zwei Uhr nachts** at two o'clock in the morning.

Nacken der (PL die **Nacken**) neck.

nackt *adjective* **1** naked; **2** bare.

Nacktschnecke die (PL die **Nacktschnecken**) slug.

Nadel die (PL die **Nadeln**) **1** needle; **2** pin.

Nagel der (PL die **Nägel**) nail.

Nagelbürste die (PL die **Nagelbürsten**) nailbrush.

Nagelfeile die (PL die **Nagelfeilen**) nailfile.

Nagellack der (PL die **Nagellacke**) nail varnish.

nagelneu *adjective* brand-new.

Nagelschere die (PL die **Nagelscheren**) nail scissors.

Nähe die **1** proximity; **2 in der Nähe der Kirche** near the church; **ganz in der Nähe** nearby; **3 aus der Nähe** close up.

nahe, nah *adjective, adverb* **1** near, nearby; **der Nahe Osten** the Middle East; **nahe daran sein, etwas zu tun** to nearly do something; **2** close; **nahe bei** close to; **nahe verwandt sein** to be closely related; **3 jemandem nahe legen, etwas zu tun** to urge somebody to do something; **4 nahe liegend** obvious.
nah *preposition* (+ DAT) near, close to.

nahelegen, naheliegend SEE **nahe.**

nähen *verb* (PERF **hat genäht**) **1** to sew; **2** to stitch (*a wound*).

näher *adjective* **1** closer; **2 nähere Einzelheiten** further details; **3** shorter (*way, road*).
näher *adverb* **1** closer; **näher kommen** to come closer; **2** more closely; **3 Näheres** further details.

nähern *verb* (PERF **hat sich genähert**) **sich nähern** to approach; **wir näherten uns dem Dorf** we were approaching the village.

Nähgarn *das* cotton.

nahm SEE **nehmen.**

Nähmaschine *die* (PL *die* **Nähmaschinen**) sewing machine.

Nahrung *die* food.

Naht *die* (PL *die* **Nähte**) seam.

Nahverkehrszug *der* (PL *die* **Nahverkehrszüge**) local train.

Name *der* (PL *die* **Namen**) name; **im Namen von** on behalf of; **ich rufe im Namen von Herrn und Frau Schmidt an** I'm calling on behalf of Mr and Mrs Schmidt.

nämlich *adverb* **1** because; **2** namely; **3 das war nämlich ganz anders** it was quite different actually.

nannte SEE **nennen.**

nanu *exclamation* well, well!

Narbe *die* (PL *die* **Narben**) scar.

Narr *der* (PL *die* **Narren**) fool.

Närrin *die* (PL *die* **Närrinnen**) fool.

Nase *die* (PL *die* **Nasen**) nose; **die Nase voll haben** (*informal*) to have had enough.

Nasenbluten *das* nosebleed.

Nashorn *das* (PL *die* **Nashörner**) rhinoceros.

nass *adjective* wet.

Nation *die* (PL *die* **Nationen**) nation.

Nationalhymne *die* (PL *die* **Nationalhymnen**) national anthem.

Nationalität *die* (PL *die* **Nationalitäten**) nationality.

Natur *die* **1** nature; **von Natur aus** by nature; **2 die freie Natur** the open countryside.

Naturlehrpfad *der* (PL *die* **Naturlehrpfade**) nature trail.

natürlich *adjective* natural.
natürlich *adverb* of course, naturally.

Natürlichkeit *die* naturalness.

Naturschützer *der* (PL *die* **Naturschützer**) conservationist.

Naturschützerin *der* (PL *die* **Naturschützerinnen**) conservationist.

Naturschutzgebiet *das* (PL *die* **Naturschutzgebiete**) nature reserve.

Naturwissenschaft *die* natural science.

Nebel *der* (PL *die* **Nebel**) **1** fog; **2** mist.

nebelig *adjective* SEE **neblig.**

neben *preposition* (+ DAT *or* + ACC *with movement towards a place*) **1** next to; **er hat neben mir gesessen** he sat next to me; **er hat**

sich neben mich gesetzt he sat down next to me; **2** apart from.

nebenan *adverb* next door.

nebenbei *adverb* **1** as well, at the same time; **er liest die Zeitung und hört nebenbei Musik** he reads the newspaper and listens to music at the same time; **2** on the side; **nebenbei arbeite ich noch in einem Blumengeschäft** I work in a florist's on the side; **das mache ich so nebenbei** (*informal*) that's just a sideline; **3** in passing; **nebenbei bemerkt** by the way.

nebeneinander *adverb* next to each other.

nebenhergehen ◇*verb* (IMPERF **ging nebenher**, PERF **ist nebenhergegangen**) to walk alongside.

neblig *adjective* **1** foggy; **2** misty.

necken *verb* (PERF **hat geneckt**) to tease.

Neffe *der* (PL **die Neffen**) nephew.

Negativ *das* (PL **die Negative**) negative.

negativ *adjective* negative.

nehmen ◇*verb* (PRES **nimmt**, IMPERF **nahm**, PERF **hat genommen**) **1** to take; **2 ich nehme eine Suppe** I'll have soup; **3 was nehmen Sie dafür?** how much do you want for it?; **4 jemanden zu sich nehmen** to have somebody live with you; **5 sich etwas nehmen** to take something; **nimm dir ein Stück Kuchen** help yourself to a piece of cake.

Neid *der* envy, jealousy.

neidisch *adjective* envious, jealous.

nein *adverb* no.

Nelke *die* (PL **die Nelken**) carnation.

nennen ◇*verb* (IMPERF **nannte**, PERF **hat genannt**) **1** to call; **2** to name; **3 ihr Name wurde nicht genannt** her name wasn't mentioned; **4 sich nennen** to call yourself.

Nerv *der* (PL **die Nerven**) nerve; **Gabi geht mir auf die Nerven** Gabi gets on my nerves.

nervig *adjective* nerve-wracking.

nervös *adjective* nervous.

Nervosität *die* nervousness.

Nessel *die* (PL **die Nesseln**) nettle.

Nest *das* (PL **die Nester**) **1** nest; **2** little place (*a village*).

nett *adjective* nice.

netto *adverb* net.

Netz *das* (PL **die Netze**) **1** net; **2** network; **3** string bag; **4** (*spider's*) web.

Netzkarte *die* (PL **die Netzkarten**) unlimited travel ticket (*over a transport network*).

Netzwerk *das* (PL **die Netzwerke**) network.

neu *adjective* **1** new; **wie neu** as good as new; **neue Sprachen** modern languages; **2 seit neuestem** recently; **3 die neueste Mode** the latest fashion; **das Neueste** the latest news; **das Neueste an Audioausrüstung** the latest in audio equipment; **4 das ist mir neu** that's news to me.

neu *adverb* **1** newly; **2** only just; **es**

ist neu eingetroffen it has only just come in; **3 etwas neu schreiben** to rewrite something.

neuartig *adjective* new; **ein neuartiger Flaschenöffner** a new kind of bottle opener.

neuerdings *adverb* recently.

Neugier *die* curiosity.

neugierig *adjective* curious, inquisitive.

Neuigkeit *die* (PL *die* **Neuigkeiten**) piece of news; **gibt es irgendwelche Neuigkeiten?** is there any news?

Neujahr *das* New Year, New Year's Day.

neulich *adverb* the other day.

neun *number* nine.

neunter, neunte, neuntes *adjective* ninth.

neunzehn *number* nineteen.

neunzig *number* ninety.

Neuseeland *das* New Zealand.

nicht *adverb* **1** not; **ich kann nicht** I can't; **Iris hat nicht angerufen** Iris didn't ring; **bitte nicht** please don't; **nicht!** don't!; **nicht berühren!** don't touch!; **2 'ich mag das nicht' – 'ich auch nicht'** 'I don't like it' – 'neither do I'; **3 nicht (wahr)?** isn't he/she/it?; **du kennst ihn doch, nicht?** you know him, don't you?; **4 gar nicht** not at all; **5 nicht mehr** no more.

Nichte *die* (PL *die* **Nichten**) niece.

Nichtraucher *der* (PL *die* **Nichtraucher**) non-smoker.

Nichtraucherabteil *das* (PL *die* **Nichtraucherabteile**) no-smoking compartment.

Nichtraucherin *die* (PL *die* **Nichtraucherinnen**) non-smoker.

nichts *pronoun* **1** nothing; **2 ich habe nichts gewusst** I didn't know anything; **3 nichts mehr** no more; **4 das macht nichts** it doesn't matter; **5 nichts ahnend** unsuspecting.

nichtsahnend SEE **nichts**.

Nichtschwimmerbecken *das* (PL *die* **Nichtschwimmerbecken**) shallow swimming pool (*for non-swimmers and learners*).

nicken *verb* (PERF **hat genickt**) to nod.

Nickerchen *das* (PL *die* **Nickerchen**) nap; **ein Nickerchen machen** to have a nap.

nie *adverb* never.

nieder *adjective* low.
nieder *adverb* down.

Niederlage *die* (PL *die* **Niederlagen**) defeat.

Niederlande *plural noun* **die Niederlande** the Netherlands.

Niederländer *der* (PL *die* **Niederländer**) Dutchman; **die Niederländer** the Dutch.

Niederländerin *die* (PL *die* **Niederländerinnen**) Dutchwoman.

niederländisch *adjective* Dutch.

niedlich *adjective* sweet.

niedrig *adjective* **1** low; **2** base.

niemals *adverb* never.

a
b
c
d
e
f
g
h
i
j
k
l
m
n
o
p
q
r
s
t
u
v
w
x
y
z

niemand *pronoun* nobody; **wir haben niemand** or **niemanden gesehen** we didn't see anybody.

Niere *die* (PL die **Nieren**) kidney.

nieseln *verb* (PERF **hat genieselt**) to drizzle; **es nieselt** it's drizzling.

niesen *verb* (PERF **hat geniest**) to sneeze.

Nil *der* **der Nil** the River Nile.

Nilpferd *das* (PL die **Nilpferde**) hippopotamus.

nimmt SEE **nehmen**.

nirgends, nirgendwo *adverb* nowhere.

Niveau *das* (PL die **Niveaus**) 1 level; 2 standard.

noch *adverb* 1 still; **immer noch** still; 2 even; **noch besser** even better; 3 **noch nicht** not yet; **noch nie** never; 4 **gerade noch** only just; 5 **wer war noch da?** who else was there?; **was noch?** what else?; 6 **noch einmal** again; 7 **noch ein Bier** another beer; **noch etwas Kaffee?** (would you like some) more coffee?; 8 **noch gestern** only yesterday; 9 **noch und noch Geld** loads of money.
noch *conjunction* nor; **weder … noch** neither … nor.

nochmals *adverb* again.

Nominativ *der* (PL die **Nominative**) nominative.

Nonne *die* (PL die **Nonnen**) nun.

Nordamerika *das* North America.

Nordamerikaner *der* (PL die **Nordamerikaner**) North American.

Nordamerikanerin *die* (PL die **Nordamerikanerinnen**) North American.

nordamerikanisch *adjective* North American.

Norden *der* north.

Nordirland *das* Northern Ireland.

nördlich *adjective* 1 northern; 2 northerly (*direction*).
nördlich *adverb, preposition* (+ GEN) **nördlich von Wien** to the north of Vienna; **nördlich der Stadt** north of the town.

Nordosten *der* north-east.

Nordpol *der* North Pole.

Nordsee *die* North Sea.

Nordwesten *der* north-west.

nörgeln *verb* (PERF **hat genörgelt**) to grumble.

Norm *die* (PL die **Normen**) 1 norm; 2 standard.

normal *adjective* normal.

normalerweise *adverb* normally.

Norwegen *das* Norway.

Norweger *der* (PL die **Norweger**) Norwegian.

Norwegerin *die* (PL die **Norwegerinnen**) Norwegian.

norwegisch *adjective* Norwegian.

Not *die* (PL die **Nöte**) 1 need; **zur Not** if necessary, at a pinch; **mit knapper Not** only just; 2 hardship.

Notaufnahme *die* (PL die **Notaufnahmen**) accident & emergency (*hospital department*).

Notausgang der (PL die Notausgänge) emergency exit.

Notdienst der **Notdienst haben** to be on call.

Note die (PL die Noten) **1** note; **Noten lesen** to read music; **2** mark.

Notfall der (PL die Notfälle) emergency.

notfalls adverb if need be.

notieren verb (PERF **hat notiert**) **1** to note down; **2 sich etwas notieren** to make a note of something.

nötig adjective necessary.
nötig adverb urgently.

Notiz die (PL die Notizen) **1** note; **2 keine Notiz von etwas nehmen** to take no notice of something; **3** item (in a newspaper).

Notizblock der (PL die Notizblöcke) notepad.

Notizbuch das (PL die Notizbücher) notebook.

Notlage die (PL die Notlagen) crisis.

Notruf der (PL die Notrufe) **1** emergency call; **2** emergency number.

notwendig adjective necessary.

November der November.

nüchtern adjective **1** sober; **wieder nüchtern werden** to sober up; **2 auf nüchternen Magen** on an empty stomach; **3** down-to-earth.

Nudeln plural noun **1** noodles; **2** pasta.

Null die (PL die Nullen) **1** zero, nought; **2** failure.

null number **1** nought; **unter null** below zero; **2** nil; **zwei zu null** two nil; **3** love (in tennis); **4 null Fehler haben** to have no mistakes; **ich habe null Ahnung** (informal) I haven't got a clue; **5 in null Komma nichts** (informal) in less than no time.

numerieren SEE **nummerieren**.

Nummer die (PL die Nummern) **1** number; **2** issue (of a magazine); **3** size (of clothing); **4** act; **5 auf Nummer sicher gehen** to play safe.

nummerieren verb (PERF **hat nummeriert**) to number.

Nummernschild das (PL die Nummernschilder) number plate.

nun adverb now.
nun exclamation well; **nun ja** ... well, yes ....

nur adverb **1** only; **2 was sollen wir nur tun?** what on earth are we going to do?; **sie soll es nur versuchen!** just let her try!; **3 nur zu!** go ahead!

Nürnberg das Nuremberg.

Nuss die (PL die Nüsse) nut.

Nutzen der benefit; **von Nutzen sein** to be useful.

nutzen, nützen verb (PERF **hat genutzt/genützt**) **1** to use; **etwas nutzen** to take advantage of something; **2** to be useful; **3 nichts nutzen** to be no use; **das nutzt mir nichts** that won't help me; **4 das nutzt ja doch nichts** it's pointless.

nützlich adjective useful.

nutzlos adjective useless.

a
b
c
d
e
f
g
h
i
j
k
l
m
n
o
p
q
r
s
t
u
v
w
x
y
z

Oo

ob *conjunction* **1** whether; **wissen Sie, ob heute noch ein Zug nach Freising fährt?** do you know if there is another train to Freising today?; **2 ob Alex noch anruft?** I wonder if Alex will ring; **3 und ob!** you bet!

obdachlos *adjective* homeless.

Obdachlose *der/die* (PL *die* Obdachlosen) homeless person; **die Obdachlosen** the homeless.

oben *adverb* **1** on top; **oben auf** on top of; **die Vase steht oben auf dem Schrank** the vase is on top of the cupboard; **2** at the top; **von oben bis unten** from top to bottom; **er hat uns von oben bis unten gemustert** he looked us up and down; **3** upstairs; **4 nach oben** up, upstairs; **er ist nach oben in sein Zimmer gegangen** he went up into his room; **geht der Fahrstuhl nach oben?** is the lift going up?; **hier oben** up here; **da oben** up there; **5 siehe oben** see above (*on a page*); **oben erwähnt** above mentioned; **6 oben ohne** (*informal*) topless.

obenerwähnt SEE **oben**.

Ober *der* (PL *die* Ober) waiter; **Herr Ober!** waiter!

oberer, obere, oberes *adjective* upper, top.

Oberfläche *die* (PL *die* Oberflächen) surface.

oberflächlich *adjective* superficial.

Oberhaupt *das* (PL *die* Oberhäupter) head.

Oberhemd *das* (PL *die* Oberhemden) shirt.

Oberschenkel *der* (PL *die* Oberschenkel) thigh.

Oberschule *die* (PL *die* Oberschulen) secondary school.

oberster, oberste, oberstes *adjective* top.

Oberstufe *die* (PL *die* Oberstufen) upper school.

Oberweite *die* (PL *die* Oberweiten) chest size, bust measurement.

Objekt *das* (PL *die* Objekte) object.

Objektiv *das* (PL *die* Objektive) lens.

objektiv *adjective* objective.

Oboe *die* (PL *die* Oboen) oboe; **Oboe spielen** to play the oboe.

Obst *das* fruit.

Obstbaum *der* (PL *die* Obstbäume) fruit tree.

Obstsalat *der* (PL *die* Obstsalate) fruit salad.

obszön *adjective* obscene.

obwohl *conjunction* although.

öde *adjective* **1** desolate; **2** dreary; **das ist so ein furchtbar öder Job** it's such terribly dull job.

oder *conjunction* **1** or; **2 du kennst sie doch, oder?** you know her, don't you?

Ofen *der* (PL *die* Öfen) **1** oven; **2** stove; **3** heater.

offen *adjective* **1** open; **offen haben** to be open; **Tag der offenen Tür** open day; **2** frank; **3** vacant; **eine**

offene Stelle a vacancy; **4 offen bleiben** to stay open; **5 offen bleiben** to remain open (*of a question, possibility*).
offen *adverb* **1** openly; **2** frankly; **offen gesagt** frankly.

offenbar *adjective* obvious.
offenbar *adverb* **1** apparently; **2 da hast du dich offenbar geirrt** you seem to have made a mistake; **sie hat offenbar den Zug verpasst** she must have missed the train.

offenbleiben SEE **offen**.

offensichtlich *adjective* obvious.

öffentlich *adjective* public.

Öffentlichkeit *die* public; **in aller Öffentlichkeit** in public.

offiziell *adjective* official.

Offizier *der* (PL *die* **Offiziere**) officer.

öffnen *verb* (PERF **hat geöffnet**) to open; **jemandem die Tür öffnen** to open the door for somebody.

Öffner *der* (PL *die* **Öffner**) opener.

Öffnung *die* (PL *die* **Öffnungen**) opening.

Öffnungszeiten *plural noun* opening times.

oft *adverb* often.

öfter, öfters *adverb* quite often; **ich habe ihn öfters mal getroffen** I used to meet him quite often.

ohne *preposition* (+ ACC) **1** without; **ohne mich** count me out; **2 ohne weiteres** easily; **3 oben ohne** (*informal*) topless; **4 das ist nicht ohne** (*informal*) it's not bad.
ohne *conjunction* without; **ohne zu überlegen** without thinking.

Ohnmacht *die* in **Ohnmacht fallen** to faint.

ohnmächtig *adjective*
1 unconscious; **2 ohnmächtig werden** to faint; **Gisela ist ohnmächtig** Gisela's fainted.

Ohr *das* (PL *die* **Ohren**) ear.

Ohrenschmerzen *plural noun* earache.

Ohrring *der* (PL *die* **Ohrringe**) earring.

oje *exclamation* oh dear!

Ökoladen *der* (PL *die* **Ökoläden**) health-food shop.

Ökologie *die* ecology.

ökologisch *adjective* ecological.

Oktober *der* October.

Öl *das* (PL *die* **Öle**) oil.

Ölfarbe *die* (PL *die* **Ölfarben**) oil-paint.

Ölgemälde *das* (PL *die* **Ölgemälde**) oil painting.

ölig *adjective* oily.

Olive *die* (PL *die* **Oliven**) olive.

Olivenöl *das* (PL *die* **Olivenöle**) olive oil.

Ölteppich *der* (PL *die* **Ölteppiche**) oil slick.

Olympiade *die* (PL *die* **Olympiaden**) Olympic Games; **die Olympiade findet alle vier Jahre statt** the Olympic Games take place every four years.

olympisch *adjective* Olympic.

Oma *die* (PL *die* **Omas**) granny.

Omelett *das* (PL *die* **Omeletts**) omelette.

a
b
c
d
e
f
g
h
i
j
k
l
m
n
o
p
q
r
s
t
u
v
w
x
y
z

Omi *die* (PL *die* Omis) granny.

Onkel *der* (PL *die* Onkel) uncle.

Opa *der* (PL *die* Opas) grandpa.

Oper *die* (PL *die* Opern) opera.

Operation *die* (PL *die* Operationen) operation.

Operationssaal *der* (PL *die* Operationssäle) operating theatre.

operieren *verb* (PERF hat operiert) **1** to operate on; **sich operieren lassen** to have an operation; **sie wurde am Magen operiert** she had a stomach operation; **2** to operate.

Opfer *das* (PL *die* Opfer) **1** sacrifice; **2** victim; **das Erdbeben forderte viele Opfer** the earthquake claimed many victims.

Optiker *der* (PL *die* Optiker) optician.

Optikerin *die* (PL *die* Optikerinnen) optician.

Optimist *der* (PL *die* Optimisten) optimist.

optimistisch *adjective* optimistic.

Orange *die* (PL *die* Orangen) orange.

orange *adjective* orange.

Orangensaft *der* (PL *die* Orangensäfte) orange juice.

Orchester *das* (PL *die* Orchester) orchestra.

ordentlich *adjective* **1** tidy; **2** respectable; **3** proper (*meal, job, salary*); **4 eine ordentliche Tracht Prügel** (*informal*) a good hiding. **ordentlich** *adverb* **1** tidily; **ordentlich schreiben** to write neatly; **2** respectably; **3** properly;

4 ordentlich feiern (*informal*) to have a really good celebration; **wir sind ordentlich nass geworden** (*informal*) we got soaked.

ordinär *adjective* vulgar.

ordnen *verb* (PERF hat geordnet) **1** to arrange; **2** to put in order.

Ordner *der* (PL *die* Ordner) file.

Ordnung *die* **1** order; **Ordnung halten** to keep order; **2 Ordnung machen** to tidy up; **die Wohnung in Ordnung bringen** to tidy up the flat; **3 mit der Waschmaschine ist etwas nicht in Ordnung** there's something wrong with the washing machine; **4 etwas in Ordnung bringen** to put something right; **die Waschmaschine in Ordnung bringen** to repair the washing machine; **5 in Ordnung!** okay!; **6 er ist in Ordnung** he's all right.

Organ *das* (PL *die* Organe) **1** organ; **2** (*informal*) voice.

Organisation *die* (PL *die* Organisationen) organization.

organisch *adjective* organic.

organisieren *verb* (PERF hat organisiert) **1** to organize; **2** (*informal*) to get (hold of).

Orgel *die* (PL *die* Orgeln) organ.

orientieren *verb* (PERF hat sich orientiert) **1 sich orientieren** to get your bearings; **2 sich über etwas orientieren** to inform yourself about something.

Orientierung *die* **1** orientation; **die Orientierung verlieren** to lose your bearings; **2 zu Ihrer Orientierung** for your information.

Orientierungsjahr *das* (PL *die* Orientierungsjahre) gap year.

Orientierungspunkt *der* (PL *die* Orientierungspunkte) landmark, reference point.

Orientierungsrennen *das* orienteering.

Orientierungssinn *der* sense of direction.

originell *adjective* original.

Orkan *der* (PL *die* Orkane) hurricane.

Ort *der* (PL *die* Orte) **1** place; **an Ort und Stelle** on the spot; **2** (small) town.

Orthografie, Orthographie *die* spelling.

örtlich *adjective* local.

Ortschaft *die* (PL *die* Ortschaften) village.

Ortsgespräch *das* (PL *die* Ortsgespräche) local call.

Ossi *der* (*informal*) (PL *die* Ossis) East German.

Osten *der* east.

Osterei *das* (PL *die* Ostereier) Easter egg.

Ostern *das* Easter.

Österreich *das* Austria.

Österreicher *der* (PL *die* Österreicher) Austrian.

Österreicherin *die* (PL *die* Österreicherinnen) Austrian.

österreichisch *adjective* Austrian.

östlich *adjective* **1** eastern; **2** easterly.

östlich *adverb, preposition* (+ GEN) **östlich von Wien** to the east of Vienna; **östlich der Stadt** east of the town.

Ostsee *die* Baltic (Sea).

oval *adjective* oval.

Ozean *der* (PL *die* Ozeane) ocean.

Ozon *das* ozone.

Ozonschicht *die* ozone layer.

Pp

Paar *das* (PL *die* Paare) **1** pair; **ein Paar Schuhe** a pair of shoes; **2** couple.

paar *pronoun* **ein paar** a few; **ein paar Mal** a few times; **alle paar Tage** every few days.

paarmal SEE **paar**.

paarweise *adjective* in pairs; **die Kinder stellten sich paarweise auf** the children lined up in pairs.

Päckchen *das* (PL *die* Päckchen) **1** package, packet; **2** small parcel.

packen *verb* (PERF **hat gepackt**) **1** to pack; **ich muss jetzt meinen Koffer packen** I must pack my case now; **2** to grab (hold of); **von Furcht gepackt** seized with fear.

Packung *die* (PL *die* Packungen) packet, pack.

Pädagoge *der* (PL *die* Pädagogen) **1** educationalist; **2** teacher.

pädagogisch *adjective* educational.

Paddel *das* (PL *die* Paddel) paddle.

a
b
c
d
e
f
g
h
i
j
k
l
m
n
o
p
q
r
s
t
u
v
w
x
y
z

paddeln *verb* **1** (PERF **hat gepaddelt**) to paddle (*a canoe*); **2** (PERF **ist gepaddelt**) to paddle (*along a lake, river*).

Paket *das* (PL die **Pakete**) **1** parcel; **Gabi hat mir ein Paket geschickt** Gabi sent me a parcel; **2** packet; **kaufe bitte ein Paket Waschpulver für mich** can you please buy a packet of washing powder for me.

Pakistan *das* Pakistan.

Pakistaner *der* (PL die **Pakistaner**) Pakistani.

Pakistanerin *die* (PL die **Pakistanerinnen**) Pakistani.

pakistanisch *adjective* Pakistani.

Palast *der* (PL die **Paläste**) palace.

Palme *die* (PL die **Palmen**) palm (tree).

Pampelmuse *die* (PL die **Pampelmusen**) grapefruit.

Panik *die* panic; **in Panik geraten** to panic.

Panne *die* (PL die **Pannen**) **1** breakdown; **wir haben auf dem Rückweg eine Panne gehabt** we had a breakdown on the way back; **2** mishap; **uns ist eine Panne passiert** we had a mishap.

Panzer *der* (PL die **Panzer**) tank (*military*).

Papa *der* (PL die **Papas**) daddy.

Papagei *der* (PL die **Papageien**) parrot.

Papier *das* (PL die **Papiere**) paper.

Papierkorb *der* (PL die **Papierkörbe**) waste-paper basket.

Papiertüte *die* (PL die **Papiertüten**) paper bag.

Pappe *die* (PL die **Pappen**) cardboard.

Paprika *der* (PL die **Paprikas**) **1** pepper; **2** paprika.

Papst *der* (PL die **Päpste**) pope.

Parabolantenne *die* (PL die **Parabolantennen**) satellite dish.

Paradies *das* paradise.

Paragraph *der* (PL die **Paragraphen**) **1** section; **2** clause.

parallel *adjective* parallel.

Pärchen *das* (PL die **Pärchen**) couple.

Parfüm *das* (PL die **Parfüms**) perfume.

Park *der* (PL die **Parks**) park.

Parkanlage *die* (PL die **Parkanlagen**) park.

parken *verb* (PERF **hat geparkt**) to park.

Parkett *das* (PL die **Parkette**) **1** (*in a theatre*) stalls; **2** parquet floor.

Parkhaus *das* (PL die **Parkhäuser**) multi-storey car park.

Parklücke *die* (PL die **Parklücken**) parking space.

Parkplatz *der* (PL die **Parkplätze**) **1** car park; **2** parking space.

Parkschein *der* (PL die **Parkscheine**) car-park ticket.

Parkuhr *die* (PL die **Parkuhren**) parking meter.

Parkverbot *das* '**Parkverbot**' 'no parking'; **in der Innenstadt ist**

Parkverbot you can't park in the town centre.

Parlament *das* (PL *die* **Parlamente**) parliament.

Parole *die* (PL *die* **Parolen**) slogan.

Partei *die* (PL *die* **Parteien**) **1** party; **2 für jemanden Partei ergreifen** to side with somebody.

Parterre *das* (PL *die* **Parterres**) ground floor.

Partie *die* (PL *die* **Partien**) **1** part; **2** game (*of tennis, chess*).

Partner *der* (PL *die* **Partner**) partner.

Partnerin *die* (PL *die* **Partnerinnen**) partner.

Partnerstadt *die* (PL *die* **Partnerstädte**) twin town.

Party *die* (PL *die* **Partys**) party.

Pass *der* (PL *die* **Pässe**) **1** passport; **2** pass.

Passage *die* (PL *die* **Passagen**) **1** shopping arcade; **2** passage (*of text*); **3** sequence (*of music, film*).

Passagier *der* (PL *die* **Passagiere**) passenger.

Passant *der* (PL *die* **Passanten**) passer-by.

Passantin *die* (PL *die* **Passantinnen**) passer-by.

passen (PERF **hat gepasst**) **1** to fit; **jemandem passen** to fit somebody; **2** to suit; **jemandem passen** to suit somebody; **Freitag passt mir nicht** Friday doesn't suit me; **seine Art passt mir nicht** I don't like his manner; **3 zu etwas passen** to go with something; **zu jemandem passen** to be right for somebody.

passend *adjective* **1** suitable; **2** matching.

passieren *verb* (PERF **ist passiert**) to happen.

Passiv *das* passive.

passiv *adjective* passive.

Passkontrolle *die* passport control.

Passwort *das* (PL *die* **Passwörter**) password (*in computing*); **das Passwort eingeben** to give the password.

Paste *die* (PL *die* **Pasten**) paste.

Pastete *die* (PL *die* **Pasteten**) pie.

Pate *der* (PL *die* **Paten**) godfather.

Patenkind *das* (PL *die* **Patenkinder**) godchild.

patent *adjective* capable, clever.

Patentante *die* (PL *die* **Patentanten**) godmother.

Patient *der* (PL *die* **Patienten**) patient.

Patientin *die* (PL *die* **Patientinnen**) patient.

Patin *die* (PL *die* **Patinnen**) godmother.

patschnass *adjective* soaking wet.

pauken *verb* (*informal*) (PERF **hat gepaukt**) to swot.

pauschal *adjective* all-inclusive.

Pauschalreise *die* (PL *die* **Pauschalreisen**) package tour.

Pause *die* (PL *die* **Pausen**) **1** break; **2** pause; **3** interval.

Pazifik *der* **der Pazifik** the Pacific (Ocean).

a
b
c
d
e
f
g
h
i
j
k
l
m
n
o
p
q
r
s
t
u
v
w
x
y
z

PC *der* (PL *die* **PCs**) PC.

Pech *das* **1** bad luck; **Pech haben** to be unlucky; **2** pitch.

Pedal *das* (PL *die* **Pedale**) pedal.

peinlich *adjective* **1** embarrassing; **es war mir sehr peinlich** I felt very embarrassed about it; **2** awkward; **3** meticulous.

Peitsche *die* (PL *die* **Peitschen**) whip.

Pelle *die* skin.

Pelz *der* (PL *die* **Pelze**) fur.

pendeln *verb* **1** (PERF **ist gependelt**) to commute; **2** (PERF **hat gependelt**) to swing.

Pendelverkehr *der* **1** commuter traffic; **2** shuttle service.

Pendler *der* (PL *die* **Pendler**) commuter.

penetrant *adjective* **1** overpowering (*odour, perfume*); **2** pushy (*person*).

Penis *der* (PL *die* **Penisse**) penis.

pennen *verb* (*informal*) (PERF **hat gepennt**) to sleep, to kip.

Pension *die* (PL *die* **Pensionen**) **1** guesthouse; **2 volle Pension** full board; **3** pension; **eine schöne Pension haben** to get a good pension; **in Pension gehen** to retire.

pensioniert *adjective* retired.

per *preposition* (+ ACC) **1** by; **per Luftpost** by airmail; **2** per.

Perfekt *das* (PL *die* **Perfekte**) perfect.

perfekt *adjective* perfect.

Periode *die* (PL *die* **Perioden**) period.

Perle *die* (PL *die* **Perlen**) **1** pearl; **2** bead.

Person *die* (PL *die* **Personen**) person; **für vier Personen** for four people; **ich für meine Person** personally.

Personal *das* staff, personnel.

Personalausweis *der* (PL *die* **Personalausweise**) identity card.

Personenzug *der* (PL *die* **Personenzüge**) stopping train.

persönlich *adjective* personal. **persönlich** *adverb* **1** personally; **2** in person.

Persönlichkeit *die* (PL *die* **Persönlichkeiten**) personality.

Perücke *die* (PL *die* **Perücken**) wig.

Pessimist *der* (PL *die* **Pessimisten**) pessimist.

pessimistisch *adjective* pessimistic.

Petersilie *die* parsley.

Petroleum *das* paraffin.

Pfad *der* (PL *die* **Pfade**) path.

Pfadfinder *der* (PL *die* **Pfadfinder**) (Boy) Scout.

Pfadfinderin *die* (PL *die* **Pfadfinderinnen**) (Girl) Guide.

Pfand *das* (PL *die* **Pfänder**) **1** forfeit; **2** deposit (*on a bottle*); **3** pledge.

Pfandflasche *die* (PL *die* **Pfandflaschen**) returnable bottle.

Pfanne die (PL die Pfannen) (frying) pan.

Pfannkuchen der (PL die Pfannkuchen) pancake.

Pfarrer der (PL die Pfarrer) **1** vicar; **2** priest.

Pfau der (PL die Pfauen) peacock.

Pfauhenne die (PL die Pfauhennen) peahen.

Pfeffer der pepper.

Pfefferkorn das (PL die Pfefferkörner) peppercorn.

Pfefferkuchen der gingerbread.

Pfefferminzbonbon der (PL die Pfefferminzbonbons) mint.

Pfefferminze die peppermint.

Pfeffermühle die (PL die Pfeffermühlen) peppermill.

Pfeife die (PL die Pfeifen) **1** whistle; **2** pipe.

pfeifen ◇verb (IMPERF pfiff, PERF hat gepfiffen) to whistle.

Pfeil der (PL die Pfeile) arrow.

Pfeiler der (PL die Pfeiler) **1** pillar; **2** pier.

Pfennig der (PL die Pfennige) pfennig (one hundredth of a mark in the former German currency) **ich habe keinen Pfennig mehr** I haven't got a penny left SEE **Mark**.

Pferd das (PL die Pferde) horse.

Pferderennen das (PL die Pferderennen) horse race.

Pferdeschwanz der (PL die Pferdeschwänze) ponytail.

pfiff SEE **pfeifen**.

Pfingsten das (PL die Pfingsten) Whitsun.

Pfirsich der (PL die Pfirsiche) peach.

Pflanze die (PL die Pflanzen) plant.

pflanzen verb (PERF hat gepflanzt) to plant; **pflanze mehr Bäume** plant more trees.

Pflaster das (PL die Pflaster) **1** pavement; **2** plaster.

Pflaume die (PL die Pflaumen) plum.

Pflege die **1** care; **2** nursing; **3 ein Kind in Pflege nehmen** to foster a child.

Pflegeeltern plural noun foster parents.

Pflegeheim das (PL die Pflegeheime) nursing home.

Pflegekind das (PL die Pflegekinder) foster child.

pflegeleicht adjective easy-care (fabric).

pflegen verb (PERF hat gepflegt) **1** to look after, to care for; **eine Freundschaft pflegen** to foster a friendship; **2** to nurse.

Pfleger der (PL die Pfleger) (male) nurse.

Pflicht die (PL die Pflichten) duty; **Pflicht sein** to be compulsory.

pflichtbewusst adjective conscientious.

Pflichtfach das (PL die Pflichtfächer) compulsory subject.

a
b
c
d
e
f
g
h
i
j
k
l
m
n
o
p
q
r
s
t
u
v
w
x
y
z

pflücken *verb* (PERF **hat gepflückt**) to pick.

Pflug *der* (PL *die* **Pflüge**) plough.

pflügen *verb* (PERF **hat gepflügt**) to plough.

Pforte *die* (PL *die* **Pforten**) gate.

Pförtner *der* (PL *die* **Pförtner**) porter.

Pfosten *der* (PL *die* **Pfosten**) post.

Pfote *die* (PL *die* **Pfoten**) paw.

pfui *exclamation* ugh!

Pfund *das* (PL *die* **Pfund(e)**) pound.

Pfütze *die* (PL *die* **Pfützen**) puddle.

Phantasie *die* SEE **Fantasie**.

phantasievoll *adjective* SEE **Fantasievoll**.

phantastisch *adjective* fantastic.

Philosoph *der* (PL *die* **Philosophen**) philosopher.

Philosophie *die* (PL *die* **Philosophien**) philosophy.

Photo *das* (PL *die* **Photos**) SEE **Foto**.

Phrase *die* (PL *die* **Phrasen**) 1 phrase; 2 cliché.

Physik *die* physics.

Physiker *der* (PL *die* **Physiker**) physicist.

Physikerin *die* (PL *die* **Physikerinnen**) physicist.

Pickel *der* (PL *die* **Pickel**) spot, pimple.

Picknick *das* (PL *die* **Picknicks**) picnic.

Pik *das* spades (*in cards*).

pikant *adjective* spicy.

Pille *die* (PL *die* **Pillen**) pill.

Pilot *der* (PL *die* **Piloten**) pilot.

Pilotin *die* (PL *die* **Pilotinnen**) pilot.

Pilz *der* (PL *die* **Pilze**) 1 mushroom; 2 fungus.

Pinguin *der* (PL *die* **Pinguine**) penguin.

pinkeln *verb* (*informal*) (PERF **hat gepinkelt**) to pee.

Pinnwand *die* (PL *die* **Pinnwände**) noticeboard.

Pinsel *der* (PL *die* **Pinsel**) brush.

Pinzette *die* (PL *die* **Pinzetten**) tweezers.

Pirat *der* (PL *die* **Piraten**) pirate.

Piste *die* (PL *die* **Pisten**) 1 run, piste; 2 track; 3 runway.

Pizza *die* (PL *die* **Pizzas**) pizza.

Pkw *der* (PL *die* **Pkws**) (*Personenkraftwagen*) car.

plagen *verb* (PERF **hat geplagt**) 1 to bother, to torment; 2 to pester; 3 **sich plagen** to struggle; **sich in der Schule plagen** to struggle at school; **er muss sich plagen** he has to work hard.

Plakat *das* (PL *die* **Plakate**) poster.

Plan *der* (PL *die* **Pläne**) 1 plan; 2 map.

planen *verb* (PERF **hat geplant**) to plan.

Planierraupe *die* (PL *die* **Planierraupen**) bulldozer.

planmäßig *adjective* scheduled. **planmäßig** *adverb* 1 according to plan; **alles läuft planmäßig** everything is going according to plan; **2** on schedule; **der Zug ist planmäßig abgefahren** the train left on schedule.

Plastik[1] *das* plastic.

Plastik[2] *die* (PL *die* **Plastiken**) sculpture.

Plastiktüte *die* (PL *die* **Plastiktüten**) plastic bag.

Platin *das* platinum.

platt *adjective* flat; **platt sein** (*informal*) to be flabbergasted.

plattdeutsch *adjective* low German.

Platte *die* (PL *die* **Platten**) **1** plate; **2** dish; **kalte Platte** cold meats and cheeses; **3** hotplate; **4** record; **5** board (*made of wood*); **6** slab (*made of stone*); **7** sheet (*made of metal or glass*); **8** top (*of a table*).

Plattenspieler *der* (PL *die* **Plattenspieler**) record player.

Platz *der* (PL *die* **Plätze**) **1** place; **viel Platz haben** to have a lot of room; **Platz lassen** to leave room; **auf die Plätze, fertig, los!** on your marks, get set, go!; **2** seat; **Platz nehmen** to take a seat; **3** square (*in a town*); **4** ground, pitch; **einen Spieler vom Platz stellen** to send a player off; **5** court (*for tennis*); **6** course (*for golf*).

Plätzchen *das* (PL *die* **Plätzchen**) **1** biscuit; **2** spot.

platzen *verb* (PERF **ist geplatzt**) **1** to burst; **2 der Plan ist geplatzt** (*informal*) the plan fell through; **3 vor Neugier platzen** to be bursting with curiosity.

plaudern *verb* (PERF **hat geplaudert**) to chat.

pleite *adjective* (*informal*) broke.

Plombe *die* (PL *die* **Plomben**) filling.

plombieren *verb* (PERF **hat plombiert**) to fill.

plötzlich *adjective* sudden. **plötzlich** *adverb* suddenly.

plump *adjective* **1** plump; **2** clumsy.

Plural *der* (PL *die* **Plurale**) plural.

Plus *das* **1** plus; **2** profit; **3** advantage.

plus *adverb* plus.

PLZ SEE **Postleitzahl**.

Po *der* (*informal*) (PL *die* **Pos**) bottom.

Poesie *die* poetry.

Pokal *der* (PL *die* **Pokale**) **1** cup; **2** goblet.

Pokalspiel *das* (PL *die* **Pokalspiele**) cup-tie.

Pole *der* (PL *die* **Polen**) Pole.

Polen *das* Poland.

polieren *verb* (PERF **hat poliert**) to polish.

Polin *die* (PL *die* **Polinnen**) Pole.

Politik *die* **1** politics; **2** policy.

Politiker *der* (PL *die* **Politiker**) politician.

Politikerin *die* (PL *die* **Politikerinnen**) politician.

politisch *adjective* political.

Politur *die* (PL *die* **Polituren**) polish.

Polizei *die* police.

a
b
c
d
e
f
g
h
i
j
k
l
m
n
o
p
q
r
s
t
u
v
w
x
y
z

polizeilich *adjective* police.
polizeilich *adverb* by the police;
sich polizeilich anmelden to
register with the police.

Polizeiwache *die* (PL *die*
Polizeiwachen) police station.

Polizist *der* (PL *die* *Polizisten*)
policeman.

Polizistin *die* (PL *die* *Polizistinnen*)
policewoman.

polnisch *adjective* Polish.

Pommes frites *plural noun*
chips, French fries.

Pony¹ *das* (PL *die* *Ponys*) pony.

Pony² *der* (PL *die* *Ponys*) fringe.

Popmusik *die* pop music.

poppig *adjective* bright; **Natalie
hat immer poppige Socken an**
Natalie always wears bright socks.

Porree *der* (PL *die* *Porrees*) leek;
eine Stange Porree a leek.

Portemonnaie *das* SEE
Portmonee.

Portier *der* (PL *die* *Portiers*) porter.

Portion *die* (PL *die* *Portionen*)
portion; **möchtest du eine zweite
Portion?** would you like a second
helping?

Portmonee *das* (PL *die*
Portmonees) purse.

Porto *das* postage.

Porträt *das* (PL *die* *Porträts*)
portrait.

Portugal *das* Portugal.

Portugiese *der* (PL *die*
Portugiesen) Portuguese.

Portugiesin *die* (PL *die*
Portugiesinnen) Portuguese.

portugiesisch *adjective*
Portuguese.

Posaune *die* (PL *die* *Posaunen*)
trombone.

Post *die* **1** post; **mit der Post** by post;
2 post office.

Postamt *das* (PL *die* *Postämter*)
post office.

Postbote *der* (PL *die* *Postboten*)
postman.

Poster *das* (PL *die* *Poster*) poster.

Postkarte *die* (PL *die* *Postkarten*)
postcard.

Postleitzahl *die* (PL *die*
Postleitzahlen) postcode.

Pracht *die* splendour.

prächtig *adjective* splendid.

prahlen *verb* (PERF **hat geprahlt**) to
boast.

praktisch *adjective* **1** practical;
praktische Erfahrung practical
experience; **2** handy; **3 ein
praktischer Arzt** a general
practitioner.
praktisch *adverb* **1** practically;
2 in practice.

Praline *die* (PL *die* *Pralinen*)
chocolate.

Präposition *die* (PL *die*
Präpositionen) preposition.

Präsens *das* present (tense).

Präservativ *das* (PL *die*
Präservative) condom.

Präsident *der* (PL *die* *Präsidenten*)
president.

Präsidentin *die* (PL *die* Präsidentinnen) president.

Pratikum *das* (PL *die* Praktika) practical training.

Praxis *die* (PL *die* Praxen) **1** practice; **2** practical experience; **3** surgery.

Preis *der* (PL *die* Preise) **1** price; **um keinen Preis** not at any price; **2** prize.

Preisausschreiben *das* (PL *die* Preisausschreiben) competition.

Preiselbeere *die* (PL *die* Preiselbeeren) cranberry.

preiswert *adjective* reasonable, cheap.

Prellung *die* (PL *die* Prellungen) bruise.

Premierminister *der* (PL *die* Premierminister) prime minister.

Presse *die* press.

Priester *der* (PL *die* Priester) priest.

prima *adjective* (*informal*) brilliant.

Prinz *der* (PL *die* Prinzen) prince.

Prinzessin *die* (PL *die* Prinzessinnen) princess.

Prise *die* (PL *die* Prisen) pinch; **eine Prise Salz** a pinch of salt.

privat *adjective* private.

Privileg *das* (PL *die* Privilegien) privilege.

pro *preposition* (+ ACC) per.

Probe *die* (PL *die* Proben) **1** test; **jemanden auf die Probe stellen** to test somebody; **ein Auto Probe fahren** to test-drive a car; **2** sample; **3** rehearsal.

probefahren SEE **Probe**.

probieren *verb* (PERF **hat probiert**) **1** to try; **2** to taste.

Problem *das* (PL *die* Probleme) problem.

Produkt *das* (PL *die* Produkte) product.

Produzent *der* (PL *die* Produzenten) producer.

produzieren *verb* (PERF **hat produziert**) to produce.

Profi *der* (PL *die* Profis) pro.

Profil *das* (PL *die* Profile) **1** profile; **2** tread (*of a tyre*).

Programm *das* (PL *die* Programme) **1** programme; **2** program (*in computing*); **3** channel (*on TV*).

programmieren *verb* (PERF **hat programmiert**) to program.

Programmierer *der* (PL *die* Programmierer) programmer.

Programmiererin *die* (PL *die* Programmiererinnen) programmer.

Projekt *das* (PL *die* Projekte) project.

Promille *das* (PL *die* Promille) alcohol level; **zuviel Promille haben** to be over the limit.

Pronomen *das* (PL *die* Pronomen) pronoun.

Prospekt *der* (PL *die* Prospekte) brochure.

prost *exclamation* cheers!

Protein das (PL die **Proteine**) protein.

Protest der (PL die **Proteste**) protest.

protestantisch adjective Protestant.

protestieren verb (PERF hat **protestiert**) to protest.

Protokoll das (PL die **Protokolle**) 1 minutes, transcript; 2 record (in court); 3 protocol.

protzen verb (PERF hat **geprotzt**) to show off; **Klaus protzt mit seinem neuen Auto** Klaus is showing off with his new car.

Proviant der provisions.

Prozent das (PL die **Prozente**) 1 per cent; **zehn Prozent** ten per cent; 2 **Prozente bekommen** (informal) to get a discount.

Prozentsatz der (PL die **Prozentsätze**) percentage.

Prozess der (PL die **Prozesse**) 1 court case; **einen Prozess gewinnen** to win a case; 2 trial; 3 process.

Prozession die (PL die **Prozessionen**) procession.

prüfen verb (PERF hat **geprüft**) 1 to test, to examine (at school); 2 to check; **hast du die Reifen geprüft?** have you checked the tyres?

Prüfung die (PL die **Prüfungen**) 1 examination, exam; **eine Prüfung bestehen** to pass an examination; **sie ist durch die Prüfung gefallen** she failed the exam; 2 check.

Prügel der (PL die **Prügel**) 1 stick; 2 **Prügel bekommen** to get a beating.

Prügelei die (PL die **Prügeleien**) fight.

prügeln verb (PERF hat **geprügelt**) 1 to beat; 2 **sich prügeln** to fight; **sich um etwas prügeln** to fight for something.

Psychiater der (PL die **Psychiater**) psychiatrist.

Psychiaterin die (PL die **Psychiaterinnen**) psychiatrist.

psychisch adjective psychological.

Psychologe der (PL die **Psychologen**) psychologist.

Psychologie die psychology.

Psychologin die (PL die **Psychologinnen**) psychologist.

Publikum das 1 audience, crowd; 2 public.

Pudding der (PL die **Puddinge**) 1 blancmange; 2 pudding (steamed).

Pudel der (PL die **Pudel**) poodle.

Puder der (PL die **Puder**) powder.

Puffmais der popcorn.

Pulli der (PL die **Pullis**) pullover.

Pullover der (PL die **Pullover**) pullover.

Puls der (PL die **Pulse**) pulse; **der Arzt maß meinen Puls** the doctor took my pulse.

Pult das (PL die **Pulte**) desk.

Pulver das (PL die **Pulver**) powder.

Pulverkaffee *der* instant coffee.

Pumpe *die* (PL *die* **Pumpen**) pump.

pumpen *verb* (PERF **hat gepumpt**) **1** to pump; **2** (*informal*) to lend; **jemandem Geld pumpen** to lend somebody money; **3** (*informal*) to borrow; **sich etwas pumpen** to borrow something.

Punker *der* (PL *die* **Punker**) punk.

Punkerin *die* (PL *die* **Punkerinnen**) punk.

Punkt *der* (PL *die* **Punkte**) **1** dot, spot; **Punkt sechs Uhr** at six o'clock on the dot; **2** full stop; **3** point; **nach Punkten siegen** to win on points.

pünktlich *adjective* punctual.

Puppe *die* (PL *die* **Puppen**) **1** doll; **2** puppet.

pur *adjective* **1** pure; **2 Whisky pur** neat whisky.

Purzelbaum *der* (PL *die* **Purzelbäume**) somersault.

pusten *verb* (PERF **hat gepustet**) to blow.

Pute *die* (PL *die* **Puten**) turkey.

putzen *verb* (PERF **hat geputzt**) **1** to clean; **putz dir die Zähne** clean your teeth; **putzen gehen** to work as a cleaner; **2 sich die Nase putzen** to blow your nose.

Putzfrau *die* (PL *die* **Putzfrauen**) cleaning lady, cleaner.

putzig *adjective* cute.

Puzzle *das* (PL *die* **Puzzles**) jigsaw (puzzle).

Pyjama *der* (PL *die* **Pyjamas**) pyjamas.

Pyramide *die* (PL *die* **Pyramiden**) pyramid.

Pyrenäen (*plural noun*) **die Pyrenäen** the Pyrenees.

Qq

Quadrat *das* (PL *die* **Quadrate**) square.

quadratisch *adjective* square.

Quadratmeter *der* (PL *die* **Quadratmeter**) square metre.

quaken *verb* (PERF **hat gequakt**) **1** to quack; **2** to croak (*of a frog*).

Qual *die* (PL *die* **Qualen**) **1** torment; **2** agony; **es war eine Qual, das ansehen zu müssen** it was agony to watch.

quälen *verb* (PERF **hat gequält**) **1** to torment; **2** to torture; **3** to pester; **4 sich quälen** to suffer; **5 sich mit etwas quälen** to struggle with something; **sich durch ein Buch quälen** to struggle (your way) through a book.

Quälgeist *der* (*informal*) (PL *die* **Quälgeister**) pest.

Qualifikation *die* (PL *die* **Qualifikationen**) qualification.

qualifizieren *verb* (PERF **hat qualifiziert**) **sich qualifizieren** to qualify; **sie haben sich für die dritte Runde qualifiziert** they qualified for the third round.

Qualität *die* (PL *die* **Qualitäten**) quality.

a
b
c
d
e
f
g
h
i
j
k
l
m
n
o
p
q
r
s
t
u
v
w
x
y
z

Qualle *die* (PL *die* **Quallen**) jellyfish.

Qualm *der* thick smoke.

qualmen *verb* (PERF **hat gequalmt**) to give off clouds of smoke; **sie qualmt wie ein Schlot** (*informal*) she smokes like a chimney.

Quarantäne *die* quarantine.

Quark *der* (*curd cheese*) quark.

Quartett *das* (PL *die* **Quartette**) quartet.

Quartier *das* (PL *die* **Quartiere**) **1** accommodation; **2** quarters.

quasseln *verb* (*informal*) (PERF **hat gequasselt**) to natter.

Quatsch *der* (*informal*) rubbish.

quatschen *verb* (*informal*) (PERF **hat gequatscht**) to chat.

Quelle *die* (PL *die* **Quellen**) **1** source; **2** spring.

quer *adverb* **1** across; **2** crosswise; **3** diagonally; **quer gestreift** with diagonal stripes; **4** quer durch straight through.

quergestreift SEE **quer**.

Querstraße *die* (PL *die* **Querstraßen**) side street; **die erste Querstraße rechts** the first turning on the right.

quetschen *verb* (PERF **hat gequetscht**) **1** to crush; **2** to squash; **3** ich habe mich in meine Jeans gequetscht I squeezed into my jeans.

Quetschung *die* (PL *die* **Quetschungen**) bruise.

quietschen *verb* (PERF **hat gequietscht**) to squeak.

quitt *adjective* quits.

Quittung *die* (PL *die* **Quittungen**) receipt.

Quiz *das* (PL *die* **Quiz**) quiz.

Rr

Rabatt *der* (PL *die* **Rabatte**) discount.

Rache *die* revenge.

rächen *verb* (PERF **hat gerächt**) **1** to avenge; **2** sich an jemandem rächen to take revenge on somebody; **3** das wird sich rächen you'll have to pay for it.

Rad *das* (PL *die* **Räder**) **1** wheel; **2** bike; **Julia ist mit dem Rad gekommen** Julia came by bike; **3** Rad fahren to cycle.

Radar *der* radar.

Radarschirm *der* (PL *die* **Radarschirme**) radar screen.

radeln *verb* (PERF **ist geradelt**) to cycle; **Max ist ins Dorf geradelt** Max cycled into the village.

radfahren SEE **Rad**.

Radfahrer *der* (PL *die* **Radfahrer**) cyclist.

Radfahrerin *die* (PL *die* **Radfahrerinnen**) cyclist.

Radfahrweg *der* (PL *die* **Radfahrwege**) cycle lane.

Radiergummi *der* (PL *die* **Radiergummis**) rubber.

Radieschen *das* (PL *die* **Radieschen**) radish.

Radio *das* (PL *die* **Radios**) radio.

radioaktiv *adjective* radioactive.

Radiosendung *die* (PL *die* Radiosendungen) radio broadcast.

Radler *der* (PL *die* Radler) cyclist.

Radlerin *die* (PL *die* Radlerinnen) cyclist.

Radrennen *das* **1** cycle race; **Maria hat das Radrennen gewonnen** Maria won the cycle race; **2** cycle racing.

Radweg *der* (PL *die* Radwege) cycle path.

raffiniert *adjective* crafty.

Rahm *der* cream.

Rahmen *der* (PL *die* Rahmen) **1** frame; **2** framework; **3** limits; **im Rahmen des Möglichen** within the bounds of possibility.

rahmen *verb* (PERF **hat gerahmt**) to frame (*a picture*).

Rakete *die* (PL *die* Raketen) rocket.

ran (*informal*) SEE **heran**.

Rand *der* (PL *die* Ränder) **1** edge; **2** rim; **der Rand der Tasse war angeschlagen** the rim of the cup was chipped; **3** ring, mark; **4** margin (*of a page*); **du musst einen Rand für die Korrekturen lassen** you must leave a margin for the corrections; **5** outskirts (*of a town*); **6** etwas am Rande erwähnen to mention something in passing; **7** am Rande der Pleite sein** to be on the verge of bankruptcy; **8** außer Rand und Band geraten** (*informal*) to go wild.

Randstreifen *der* (PL *die* Randstreifen) hard shoulder.

Rang *der* (PL *die* Ränge) **1** rank; **2** (*in a theatre*) circle.

rannte SEE **rennen**.

rasch *adjective* quick.

Rasen *der* (PL *die* Rasen) lawn, grass.

rasen *verb* (PERF **ist gerast**) to tear along, to rush; **gegen eine Mauer rasen** to career into a wall.

Rasenmäher *der* (PL *die* Rasenmäher) lawnmower.

Rasierapparat *der* (PL *die* Rasierapparate) **1** shaver; **2** razor.

Rasiercreme *die* (PL *die* Rasiercremes) shaving cream.

rasieren *verb* (PERF **hat rasiert**) **1** to shave; **2** sich rasieren to shave.

Rasierklinge *die* (PL *die* Rasierklingen) razor blade.

Rasierwasser *das* aftershave.

Rasse *die* (PL *die* Rassen) **1** race; **2** breed; **ich weiß nicht, was für eine Rasse unser Hund ist** I don't know what breed our dog is.

Rassenhass *der* racial hatred.

rassisch *adjective* racial.

Rassismus *der* racism.

Rassist *der* (PL *die* Rassisten) racist.

Rassistin *die* (PL *die* Rassistinnen) racist.

rassistisch *adjective* racist.

rasten *verb* (PERF **hat gerastet**) to rest.

Rastplatz *der* (PL *die* Rastplätze) picnic area (*on a motorway*).

a
b
c
d
e
f
g
h
i
j
k
l
m
n
o
p
q
r
s
t
u
v
w
x
y
z

Raststätte die (PL die **Raststätten**) services (*on a motorway*).

Rat der **1** advice; **ein Rat** a piece of advice; **jemanden zu Rate ziehen** to ask somebody's advice; **2 sich keinen Rat wissen** not to know what to do; **3** council.

Rate die (PL die **Raten**) instalment; **in monatlichen Raten abzahlen** to pay in monthly instalments.

raten ⋄*verb* (PRES **rät**, IMPERF **riet**, PERF **hat geraten**) **1 jemandem raten** to advise somebody; **was rätst du mir?** what do you advise me to do?; **2** to guess; **richtig raten** to guess right.

Rathaus das (PL die **Rathäuser**) town hall.

rationell *adjective* efficient.

ratlos *adjective* helpless; **Emma hat mich ratlos angesehen** Emma gave me a helpless look; **ratlos sein** not to know what to do.

ratsam *adjective* advisable; **es wäre ratsam, früher zu fahren** it would be advisable to leave earlier.

Ratschlag der (PL die **Ratschläge**) piece of advice, advice; **deine klugen Ratschläge kannst du dir sparen** you can keep your advice to yourself.

Rätsel das (PL die **Rätsel**) **1** puzzle; **2** mystery.

rätselhaft *adjective* mysterious.

Ratte die (PL die **Ratten**) rat.

rau *adjective* **1** rough; **2** harsh; **3 eine raue Stimme** a husky voice; **4 einen rauen Hals haben** to have a sore throat.

Raub der robbery.

Raubdruck der (PL die **Raubdrucke**) pirated edition.

Räuber der (PL die **Räuber**) robber.

Rauch der smoke.

rauchen *verb* (PERF **hat geraucht**) to smoke; **'Rauchen verboten'** 'no smoking'.

Rauchen das smoking; **passives Rauchen** passive smoking.

Raucher der (PL die **Raucher**) smoker.

Raucherin die (PL die **Raucherinnen**) smoker.

Räucherlachs der smoked salmon.

räuchern *verb* (PERF **hat geräuchert**) to smoke (*fish, meat*).

rauf (*informal*) SEE **herauf, hinauf**.

rauh *adjective* SEE **rau**.

Raum der (PL die **Räume**) **1** room; **das Haus hat sehr große Räume** the house has very big rooms; **2** space; **wir brauchen mehr Raum** we need more space; **3 die Rakete ist im Raum explodiert** the rocket exploded in space; **4** area; **im Raum Berlin** in the area of Berlin.

räumen *verb* (PERF **hat geräumt**) **1** to clear; **das Geschirr vom Tisch räumen** to clear away the dishes; **2 die Hemden in den Schrank räumen** to put the shirts in the cupboard; **seine Sachen beiseite räumen** to put your things to one side; **die Akten aus dem Schrank räumen** to take the files out of the cabinet; **3** to vacate.

Raumfahrt *die* space travel.

Raumschiff *das* (PL *die* **Raumschiffe**) space ship.

Räumungsverkauf *der* closing-down sale.

Raupe *die* (PL *die* **Raupen**) caterpillar.

raus (*informal*) SEE **heraus, hinaus**.

Rauschgift *das* (PL *die* **Rauschgifte**) drug; **Rauschgift nehmen** to take drugs.

Rauschgiftsüchtige *der/die* (PL *die* **Rauschgiftsüchtigen**) drug addict.

rauskriegen *verb* (*informal*) (PERF **hat rausgekriegt**) **1** to get out; **2 ein Geheimnis rauskriegen** to find out a secret; **3 ich kann die Aufgabe nicht rauskriegen** I can't do the exercise.

räuspern *verb* (PERF **hat sich geräuspert**) **sich räuspern** to clear your throat.

reagieren *verb* (PERF **hat reagiert**) to react.

Reaktion *die* (PL *die* **Reaktionen**) reaction.

realisieren *verb* (PERF **hat realisiert**) **1** to realize; **2** to implement.

Reality-Show *die* (PL *die* **Reality-Shows**) reality show.

Realschule *die* (PL *die* **Realschulen**) secondary school.

rebellieren *verb* (PERF **hat rebelliert**) to rebel.

Rechen *der* (PL *die* **Rechen**) rake.

Recherche *die* (PL *die* **Recherchen**) investigation.

rechnen *verb* (PERF **hat gerechnet**) **1** to do arithmetic; **Peter kann gut rechnen** Peter's good at arithmetic, Peter's good at figures; **2** to reckon; **mit etwas rechnen** to reckon with something; **3 er wird zu den besten Schauspielern gerechnet** he's reckoned to be one of the best actors; **4** to count; **jemanden zu seinen Freunden rechnen** to count somebody as a friend; **5 mit etwas rechnen** to expect something; **6 auf jemanden rechnen** to count on somebody.

Rechner *der* (PL *die* **Rechner**) **1** calculator; **2** computer.

Rechnung *die* (PL *die* **Rechnungen**) **1** bill; **2** invoice; **die Rechnung liegt bei** the invoice is enclosed; **3** calculation.

Recht *das* (PL *die* **Rechte**) **1** law; **nach deutschem Recht** under German law; **2** right; **Recht haben** to be right; **im Recht sein** to be in the right; **Recht bekommen** to be proved right; **3 jemandem Recht geben** to agree with somebody; **4 mit Recht** rightly; **du hast dich mit Recht beschwert** you were right to complain.

recht *adjective* **1** right; **jemandem recht sein** to be all right with somebody; **wenn es dir recht ist** if it's all right with you; **2 der/die Rechte** the right man/woman; **3 das Rechte** the right thing; **etwas Rechtes** something proper; **ich**

habe nichts Rechtes gegessen I haven't had a proper meal; **etwas Rechtes lernen** to learn something useful; **4** real; **ich habe keine rechte Lust** I don't really feel like it.

recht *adverb* **1** correctly; **2** quite; **recht einfach** quite simple; **3** really; **4 recht vielen Dank** many thanks; **5 das geschieht dir recht!** (it) serves you right!; **6 man kann es nicht allen recht machen** you can't please everyone.

Rechte *die* **1** right (side); **zu meiner Rechten** on my right; **2** right hand; **3 die Rechte** the right (*in politics*).

rechte SEE **rechter**.

Rechteck *das* (PL *die* **Rechtecke**) rectangle.

rechteckig *adjective* rectangular.

rechter, rechte, rechtes *adjective* **1** right; **auf der rechten Seite** on the right; **2** right-wing.

rechtfertigen *verb* **1** (PERF **hat gerechtfertigt**) to justify; **2 sich rechtfertigen** to justify yourself.

rechtlich *adjective* legal.

rechts *adverb* on the right; **nimm die dritte Abzweigung rechts** take the third turning on the right; **von rechts** from the right; **rechts abbiegen** to turn right.

Rechtsanwalt *der* (PL *die* **Rechtsanwälte**) lawyer.

Rechtsanwältin *die* (PL *die* **Rechtsanwältinnen**) lawyer.

Rechtschreibprogramm *das* (PL *die* **Rechtschreibprogramme**) spell checker.

Rechtschreibung *die* spelling.

Rechtshänder *der* (PL *die* **Rechtshänder**) **Klaus ist Rechtshänder** Klaus is right-handed.

Rechtshänderin *die* (PL *die* **Rechtshänderinnen**) **Beate ist Rechtshänderin** Beate is right-handed.

rechtzeitig *adjective* timely. **rechtzeitig** *adverb* in time; **wir sind gerade noch rechtzeitig angekommen** we got there just in time.

Redakteur *der* (PL *die* **Redakteure**) editor.

Redakteurin *die* (PL *die* **Redakteurinnen**) editor.

Rede *die* (PL *die* **Reden**) **1** speech; **eine Rede halten** to make a speech; **2 nicht der Rede wert** not worth mentioning; **davon kann keine Rede sein** it's out of the question; **jemanden zur Rede stellen** to take somebody to task.

reden *verb* (PERF **hat geredet**) **1** to talk; **2** to speak; **mit jemandem reden** to speak to somebody; **3 sie hat kein Wort geredet** she didn't say a word; **4 mir ist egal, was über mich geredet wird** I don't care what people say about me.

Redewendung *die* (PL *die* **Redewendungen**) idiom, expression.

redigieren *verb* (PERF **hat redigiert**) to edit.

redlich *adjective* honest.

Redlichkeit *die* honesty.

Redner *der* (PL *die* **Redner**) speaker.

Rednerin *die* (PL *die* **Rednerinnen**) speaker.

reduzieren *verb* (PERF **hat reduziert**) to reduce.

reflexiv *adjective* reflexive.

Reformhaus *das* (PL *die* **Reformhäuser**) health-food shop.

Regal *das* (PL *die* **Regale**) **1** shelf; **2** shelves, bookcase.

Regel *die* (PL *die* **Regeln**) **1** rule; **in der Regel** as a rule; **2** period (*menstruation*).

regelmäßig *adjective* regular.

regeln *verb* (PERF **hat geregelt**) **1** to regulate; **2** to direct (*the traffic*); **3** to settle (*a matter*); **wir haben die Sache so geregelt, dass** ... we've arranged things so that ...; **4 sich von selbst regeln** to sort itself out.

Regelung *die* (PL *die* **Regelungen**) **1** regulation; **2** settlement.

Regen *der* rain.

Regenbogen *der* (PL *die* **Regenbogen**) rainbow.

Regenmantel *der* (PL *die* **Regenmäntel**) raincoat.

Regenschirm *der* (PL *die* **Regenschirme**) umbrella.

Regenwurm *der* (PL *die* **Regenwürmer**) earthworm.

regieren *verb* (PERF **hat regiert**) **1** to govern; **2** to rule, to reign.

Regierung *die* (PL *die* **Regierungen**) **1** government; **2** reign.

Regisseur *der* (PL *die* **Regisseure**) director.

Regisseurin *die* (PL *die* **Regisseurinnen**) director.

Register *das* (PL *die* **Register**) **1** index; **2** register.

regnen *verb* (PERF **hat geregnet**) to rain.

regnerisch *adjective* rainy.

Reh *das* (PL *die* **Rehe**) deer.

reiben ✧*verb* (IMPERF **rieb**, PERF **hat gerieben**) **1** to rub; **2** to grate.

reibungslos *adjective* smooth.

reich *adjective* rich.

Reich *das* (PL *die* **Reiche**) **1** empire; **das Römische Reich** the Roman Empire; **2** kingdom, realm.

reichen *verb* (PERF **hat gereicht**) **1** to hand, to pass; **2** to be enough; **mit dem Geld reichen** to have enough money; **3 bis zu etwas reichen** to reach up to something; **er reicht seinem Vater bis zur Schulter** he comes up to his father's shoulder; **die Felder reichen bis zum Wald** the fields extend as far as go right up to the forest; **4 mir reichts!** (*informal*) I've had enough!

reichlich *adjective* **1** large; **2** ample (*space*). **reichlich** *adverb* plenty of.

Reichtum *der* (PL *die* **Reichtümer**) wealth.

Reichweite *die* **1** reach; **außer Reichweite** out of reach; **2** range.

reif *adjective* **1** ripe; **2** mature.

Reife *die* maturity; **mittlere Reife** exams taken after five years of secondary schooling.

a
b
c
d
e
f
g
h
i
j
k
l
m
n
o
p
q
r
s
t
u
v
w
x
y
z

Reifen der (PL die **Reifen**) **1** tyre; **2** hoop.

Reifendruck der tyre pressure.

Reifenpanne die (PL die **Reifenpannen**) puncture.

Reihe die (PL die **Reihen**) **1** row; **2** series; **eine Reihe von Ereignissen** a series of events; **3 der Reihe nach** in turn; **außer der Reihe** out of turn; **du bist an der Reihe** it's your turn.

Reihenfolge die (PL die **Reihenfolgen**) order; **in der richtigen Reihenfolge** in the right order.

Reihenhaus das (PL die **Reihenhäuser**) terraced house.

Reim der (PL die **Reime**) rhyme.

reimen verb (PERF **hat gereimt**) **1** to rhyme; **2 sich reimen** to rhyme.

rein¹ adjective **1** pure; **2** clean; **3** sheer (madness); **4 etwas ins Reine schreiben** to make a fair copy of something; **etwas ins Reine bringen** to sort something out. **rein** adverb **1** purely; **2** absolutely; **rein gar nichts** absolutely nothing.

rein² (informal) SEE **herein, hinein**.

reinigen verb (PERF **hat gereinigt**) to clean.

Reinigung die (PL die **Reinigungen**) **1** cleaning; **2** cleaner's.

Reis der rice.

Reise die (PL die **Reisen**) **1** journey, trip; **gute Reise!** have a good journey!; **auf meinen Reisen** on my travels; **2** voyage.

Reiseandenken das (PL die **Reiseandenken**) souvenir.

Reisebüro das (PL die **Reisebüros**) travel agency.

Reisebus der (PL die **Reisebusse**) coach.

Reiseführer der (PL die **Reiseführer**) **1** guidebook; **2** (travel) guide.

reisekrank adjective travel-sick; **reisekrank werden** to get travel-sick.

Reiseleiter der (PL die **Reiseleiter**) (travel) guide.

Reiseleiterin die (PL die **Reiseleiterinnen**) tourist guide.

reisen verb (PERF **ist gereist**) to travel.

Reisende der/die (PL die **Reisenden**) traveller.

Reisepass der (PL die **Reisepässe**) passport.

Reisescheck der (PL die **Reiseschecks**) traveller's cheque.

Reiseziel das (PL die **Reiseziele**) destination.

reißen ⬦verb (IMPERF **riss**, PERF **hat gerissen**) **1** to tear; **2** to snatch; **3** to pull; **an etwas reißen** to pull at something; **4 mit sich reißen** to sweep away; **5 etwas an sich reißen** to snatch something; **die Macht an sich reißen** to seize power; **6 Witze reißen** to crack jokes; **7 sich um etwas reißen** to fight for something; **8** (PERF **ist gerissen**) **hin und her gerissen sein** to be torn; **9** (PERF **ist gerissen**) to tear, to break.

Reißverschluss der (PL die Reißverschlüsse) zip.

Reißzwecke die (PL die Reißzwecken) drawing pin.

reiten ◇verb (IMPERF ritt, PERF ist geritten) to ride.

Reiter der (PL die Reiter) rider.

Reiterin die (PL die Reiterinnen) rider.

Reitschule die (PL die Reitschulen) riding school.

Reiz der (PL die Reize) **1** attraction, appeal; **2** charm.

reizen verb (PERF hat gereizt) **1** to appeal to, to tempt; **das reizt mich sehr** it's very tempting; **2** to annoy; **jemanden zum Zorn reizen** to provoke somebody to anger; **3** to irritate (the skin, eyes); **4** to bid (when playing cards).

reizend adjective charming.

reizvoll adjective attractive.

Reklame die (PL die Reklamen) **1** advertisement, advert; **für etwas Reklame machen** to advertise something; **2** commercial (on TV).

Rekord der (PL die Rekorde) record.

Rektor der (PL die Rektoren) **1** head (of a school); **2** vice-chancellor (of a university).

Religion die (PL die Religionen) religion.

religiös adjective religious.

Rendezvous das (PL die Rendezvous) date.

Rennbahn die (PL die Rennbahnen) racetrack.

rennen ◇verb (IMPERF rannte, PERF ist gerannt) to run.

Rennen das (PL die Rennen) race.

Rennfahrer der (PL die Rennfahrer) racing driver.

Rennwagen der (PL die Rennwagen) racing car.

renovieren verb (PERF hat renoviert) to renovate, to redecorate.

rentabel adjective profitable.

Rente die (PL die Renten) pension; **in Rente gehen** to retire.

Rentner der (PL die Rentner) pensioner.

Rentnerin die (PL die Rentnerinnen) pensioner.

Reparatur die (PL die Reparaturen) repair.

reparieren verb (PERF hat repariert) to repair.

Reportage die (PL die Reportagen) **1** report; **2** live commentary.

Reporter der (PL die Reporter) reporter.

Reporterin die (PL die Reporterinnen) reporter.

Reptil das (PL die Reptile) reptile.

Republik die (PL die Republiken) republic.

Reservat das (PL die Reservate) reservation.

Reserverad das (PL die Reserveräder) spare wheel.

reservieren verb (PERF hat reserviert) to reserve.

Reservierung die (PL die Reservierungen) reservation.

Reservoir das (PL die Reservoirs) reservoir.

Respekt der respect.

respektieren verb (PERF hat respektiert) to respect.

Rest der (PL die Reste) **1** rest, remainder; **2** left-over; **zum Mittagessen gibts die Reste** we're having the leftovers for lunch; **3 die Reste** the remains.

Restaurant das (PL die Restaurants) restaurant.

restlich adjective remaining.

restlos adjective complete.

Resultat das (PL die Resultate) result.

retten verb (PERF hat gerettet) **1** to save, to rescue; **jemandem das Leben retten** to save somebody's life; **2 sich retten** to escape.

Rettich der (PL die Rettiche) radish.

Rettung die rescue.

Rettungsboot das (PL die Rettungsboote) life boat.

Rettungsring der (PL die Rettungsringe) lifebelt.

Rettungsschwimmer der (PL die Rettungsschwimmer) lifeguard; **gibt es einen Rettungsschwimmer im Schwimmbad?** is there a lifeguard at the pool?

Rettungsschwimmerin die (PL die Rettungsschwimmerinnen) lifeguard.

Rettungswagen der (PL die Rettungswagen) ambulance.

Rezept das (PL die Rezepte) **1** prescription; **2** recipe.

Rezeption die (PL die Rezeptionen) reception; **bitte geben Sie Ihren Schlüssel an der Rezeption ab** please leave your key at reception.

R-Gespräch das (PL die R-Gespräche) reverse-charge call.

Rhabarber der rhubarb.

Rhein der Rhine.

Rheuma das rheumatism.

Rhythmus der (PL die Rhythmen) rhythm.

richten verb (PERF hat gerichtet) **1** to direct, to point (a torch, telescope, gun); **2 eine Frage an jemanden richten** to put a question to somebody; **3** to address (a letter, remarks); **4** to prepare (a meal, room); **5 sich auf etwas richten** to be directed towards something; **6 sich nach jemandem richten** to fit in with somebody's wishes; **sich nach den Vorschriften richten** to follow the rules; **7 sich nach etwas richten** to depend on something.

Richter der (PL die Richter) judge.

richtig adjective **1** right; **2 das Richtige** the right thing; **der/die Richtige** the right man/woman; **3** real, proper.
richtig adverb **1** correctly; **hast du das Formular richtig ausgefüllt?** have you filled in the form correctly?; **2** really; **3 richtig stellen** to put right; **die Uhr geht**

richtig the clock is telling the right time.

Richtlinie die (PL die Richtlinien) guideline.

Richtung die (PL die Richtungen) **1** direction; **2** trend.

rieb SEE **reiben**.

riechen ◇verb (IMPERF **roch**, PERF **hat gerochen**) **1** to smell; **2 ich kann ihn nicht riechen** (informal) I can't stand him.

rief SEE **rufen**.

Riegel der (PL die Riegel) **1** bolt; **2 ein Riegel Schokolade** a bar of chocolate.

Riemen der (PL die Riemen) strap.

Riese der (PL die Riesen) giant.

riesengroß adjective gigantic.

riesig adjective gigantic, huge; **ein riesiger Lastwagen** a gigantic lorry.

riet SEE **raten**.

Rind das (PL die Rinder) **1** ox; **2** cow; **Rinder** cattle; **3** beef.

Rinde die (PL die Rinden) **1** bark; **2** rind; **3** crust.

Rinderbraten der (PL die Rinderbraten) roast beef.

Rindfleisch das beef.

Ring der (PL die Ringe) ring.

Ringbuch das (PL die Ringbücher) ring binder.

Ringen das wrestling.

Rinne die (PL die Rinnen) **1** gutter; **2** drainpipe, channel.

Rippe die (PL die Rippen) rib.

Risiko das (PL die Risiken) risk.

riskant adjective risky.

riskieren verb (PERF **hat riskiert**) to risk, to put at risk.

Riss der (PL die Risse) **1** tear; **2** crack.

riss SEE **reißen**.

ritt SEE **reiten**.

Rivale der (PL die Rivalen) rival.

Rivalin die (PL die Rivalinnen) rival.

Robbe die (PL die Robben) seal.

Roboter der (PL die Roboter) robot.

roch SEE **riechen**.

Rock der (PL die Röcke) skirt.

Roggen der rye.

roh adjective **1** raw; **2** rough; **3** brutal.

Rohr das (PL die Rohre) **1** pipe; **2** reed; **3** cane.

Rohstoff der (PL die Rohstoffe) raw material.

Rolladen SEE **Rollladen**.

Rolle die (PL die Rollen) **1** roll; **2** reel; **3** role, part; **4 es spielt keine Rolle** it doesn't matter.

rollen verb (PERF **hat gerollt**) **1** to roll; **2** (PERF **ist gerollt**) to roll.

Roller der (PL die Roller) scooter.

Rollkragen der (PL die Rollkrägen) polo neck.

Rollladen der (PL die Rolllläden) shutter.

Rollschuh der (PL die Rollschuhe) roller-skate.

Rollschuhfahrer der (PL die Rollschuhfahrer) skater (on rollerskates).

203

Rollschuhfahrerin die (PL die Rollschuhfahrerinnen) skater (on rollerskates).

Rollschuhlaufen das roller-skating.

Rollstuhl der (PL die Rollstühle) wheelchair.

Rolltreppe die (PL die Rolltreppen) escalator.

Rom das Rome.

Roman der (PL die Romane) novel.

romantisch adjective romantic.

Römer der (PL die Römer) Roman.

Römerin die (PL die Römerinnen) Roman.

röntgen verb (PERF hat geröntgt) to X-ray.

rosa adjective pink.

Rose die (PL die Rosen) rose.

Rosenkohl der (Brussels) sprouts.

Rosine die (PL die Rosinen) raisin.

Rosmarin der rosemary.

Rosskastanie die (PL die Rosskastanien) horse-chestnut, conker.

Rost der (PL die Roste) **1** rust; **2** grate, grill.

rösten (PERF hat geröstet) **1** to roast; **2** to toast.

rosten verb (PERF ist gerostet) to rust.

rostig adjective rusty.

Röstkartoffeln plural noun roast potatoes.

rot adjective red.

Röteln plural noun German measles.

rothaarig adjective red-haired.

Rotkehlchen das (PL die Rotkehlchen) robin.

Rotkohl der red cabbage.

Rotwein der (PL die Rotweine) red wine.

Routine die routine.

rüber adverb (informal) over; **komm zu uns rüber** come over to us.

Rückblende die (PL die Rückblenden) flashback.

Rücken der (PL die Rücken) **1** back; **2** spine (of a book).

rücken verb (PERF hat gerückt) to move; **kannst du ein wenig rücken?** can you move over a bit?

Rückfahrkarte die (PL die Rückfahrkarten) return ticket; **eine Rückfahrkarte nach München** a return ticket to Munich.

Rückfahrt die return journey; **auf der Rückfahrt** on the way back.

Rückgabe die (PL die Rückgaben) return.

Rückgang der (PL die Rückgänge) decrease; **ein Rückgang in der Anzahl der Unfälle** a decrease in the number of accidents.

rückgängig adjective **etwas rückgängig machen** to cancel something.

Rückhand die backhand (in tennis).

Rückkehr die return.

Rückreise die return journey.

Rucksack *der* (PL *die* **Rucksäcke**) rucksack.

Rückseite *die* (PL *die* **Rückseiten**) back.

Rücksicht *die* consideration.

rücksichtslos *adjective*
1 inconsiderate; **ein rücksichtsloser Fahrer** a reckless driver; **2** ruthless.

rücksichtsvoll *adjective* considerate.

Rücksitz *der* (PL *die* **Rücksitze**) back seat.

rückwärts *adverb* backwards.

Rückwärtsgang *der* (PL *die* **Rückwärtsgänge**) reverse (gear).

Rückweg *der* (PL *die* **Rückwege**)
1 way back; **2** return journey.

Rückzahlung *die* (PL *die* **Rückzahlungen**) refund, repayment.

Ruder *das* (PL *die* **Ruder**) **1** oar;
2 rudder.

Ruderboot *das* (PL *die* **Ruderboote**) rowing boat.

rudern *verb* (PERF **ist gerudert**)
1 to row; **ich bin über den See gerudert** I rowed across the lake;
2 (PERF **hat gerudert**) to row; **ich habe Monika über den See gerudert** I rowed Monika across the lake.

Rudern *das* rowing; **du bist mit dem Rudern dran** it's your turn to row.

Ruf *der* (PL *die* **Rufe**) **1** call, shout;
2 reputation; **3** phone number.

rufen ✧*verb* (IMPERF **rief**, PERF **hat gerufen**) to call; **den Arzt rufen** to send for the doctor.

Rufnummer *die* (PL *die* **Rufnummern**) phone number.

Ruhe *die* **1** silence; **Ruhe bitte!** quiet please!; **2** rest; **3** peace; **jemanden in Ruhe lassen** to leave somebody in peace; **in aller Ruhe** calmly;
4 sich nicht aus der Ruhe bringen lassen to not get worked up; **5 sich zur Ruhe setzen** to retire.

ruhen *verb* (PERF **hat geruht**) to rest; **hier ruht** ... here lies ....

Ruhestand *der* **im Ruhestand** retired.

Ruhetag *der* (PL *die* **Ruhetage**) closing day; **'Dienstag Ruhetag'** 'closed on Tuesdays'.

ruhig *adjective* **1** quiet; **2** peaceful;
3 calm.
ruhig *adverb* **1** quietly; **sich ruhig verhalten** to keep quiet; **2** calmly;
ruhig bleiben to remain calm;
3 sehen Sie sich ruhig um you're welcome to look around; **du kannst es ihm ruhig sagen** it's OK, you can tell him.

Ruhm *der* fame.

Rührei *das* scrambled eggs.

rühren *verb* (PERF **hat gerührt**) **1** to move; **2** to stir; **3 sich rühren** to move; **4 an etwas rühren** to touch, to touch on.

Ruine *die* (PL *die* **Ruinen**) ruin.

ruinieren *verb* (PERF **hat ruiniert**) to ruin.

rülpsen *verb* (PERF **hat gerülpst**) to belch.

a
b
c
d
e
f
g
h
i
j
k
l
m
n
o
p
q
r
s
t
u
v
w
x
y
z

Rum *der* rum.

Rumänien *das* Romania.

rumänisch *adjective* Romanian.

Rummel *der* **1** hustle and bustle; **2** fuss; **3** fair.

Rummelplatz *der* (PL *die* Rummelplätze) fairground.

rund *adjective* round.
rund *adverb* about; **rund um** around.

Runde *die* (PL *die* Runden) **1** round; **2** lap; **3** circle, group; **4 über die Runden kommen** (*informal*) to get by.

Rundfahrt *die* (PL *die* Rundfahrten) tour.

Rundfrage *die* (PL *die* Rundfragen) poll.

Rundfunk *der* radio; **im Rundfunk** on the radio.

rundherum *adverb* all around.

Rundkurs *der* (PL *die* Rundkurse) (motor racing) circuit.

runter *adverb* (*informal*) SEE **herunter, hinunter; runter da!** get off!

runzlig *adjective* wrinkled.

Rüsche *die* (PL *die* Rüschen) frill.

Russe *der* (PL *die* Russen) Russian.

Rüssel *der* (PL *die* Rüssel) trunk.

Russin *die* (PL *die* Russinnen) Russian.

russisch *adjective* Russian.

Russland *das* Russia.

Rüstung *die* (PL *die* Rüstungen) **1** armament; **2** arms; **3** (suit of) armour.

Rutschbahn *die* (PL *die* Rutschbahnen) slide.

rutschen *verb* (PERF **ist gerutscht**) **1** to slide; **2** to slip; **3 rutsch mal!** move over!

rutschig *adjective* slippery.

rütteln *verb* (PERF **hat gerüttelt**) to shake; **an der Tür rütteln** to rattle at the door.

Ss

Saal *der* (PL *die* Säle) hall.

Saatkrähe *die* (PL *die* Saatkrähen) rook.

Sabbat *der* (PL *die* Sabbate) Sabbath.

Sache *die* (PL *die* Sachen) **1** matter; **das ist eine andere Sache** that's a different matter; **2** business; **das ist seine Sache** that's his business; **3** thing; **meine Sachen** my things (*clothing*); **sie räumt nie ihre Sachen weg** she never puts away her things; **4 zur Sache kommen** to get to the point; **5 das ist so 'ne Sache** (*informal*) it's a bit tricky.

Sachgebiet *das* (PL *die* Sachgebiete) field, area.

sachlich *adjective* **1** objective; **2** factual.

sächlich *adjective* neuter.

Sachsen *das* Saxony.

Sack *der* (PL *die* Säcke) **1** sack; **2** bag.

Sackgasse die (PL die Sackgassen) dead end, cul-de-sac.

Saft der (PL die Säfte) **1** juice; **2** sap.

saftig adjective juicy.

Säge die (PL die Sägen) saw.

Sägemehl das sawdust.

sagen verb (PERF **hat gesagt**) **1** to say; **man sagt, dass** … it's said that …; **2 was ich noch sagen wollte** by the way; **unter uns gesagt** between you and me; **3** to tell; **jemandem etwas sagen** to tell somebody something; **sag mal** tell me; **was sagen Sie dazu?** what do you think about it?; **4** to mean; **das hat nichts zu sagen** it doesn't mean anything; **5 zu jemandem Tante sagen** to call somebody aunt; **6 ihr Gesicht sagte alles** it was written all over her face.

sägen verb (PERF **hat gesägt**) to saw.

sagenhaft adjective **1** legendary; **2** (informal) brilliant.

sah SEE **sehen**.

Sahne die cream.

Saison die (PL die Saisons) season.

Saite die (PL die Saiten) string.

Sakko das (PL die Sakkos) jacket.

Salami die (PL die Salamis) salami.

Salat der (PL die Salate) **1** lettuce; **ein grüner Salat** a lettuce; **2** salad.

Salatsoße die (PL die Salatsoßen) salad dressing.

Salbe die (PL die Salben) ointment.

Salbei der sage.

salopp adjective casual, informal.

Salz das salt.

salzen verb (PERF **hat gesalzen**) to salt.

salzig adjective salty.

Salzkartoffeln plural noun boiled potatoes.

Salzwasser das **1** salt water; **2** salted water (for cooking).

Samen der (PL die Samen) **1** seed; **2** sperm, semen.

Sammelalbum das (PL die Sammelalben) scrapbook.

sammeln verb (PERF **hat gesammelt**) **1** to collect; **Martin sammelt Briefmarken** Martin collects stamps; **2** to gather; **3 sich sammeln** to gather; **seine Gedanken sammeln** to gather your thoughts.

Sammler der (PL die Sammler) collector.

Sammlerin die (PL die Sammlerinnen) collector.

Sammlung die (PL die Sammlungen) collection; **eine Sammlung für einen guten Zweck** a collection for a good cause.

Samstag der (PL die Samstage) Saturday.

samstags adverb on Saturdays.

Samt der (PL die Samte) velvet.

samt preposition (+ DAT) (together) with; **Mimi kam samt Puppen und Katze** Mimi arrived with her dolls and cat.

sämtlicher, sämtliche, sämtliches adjective all the;

a
b
c
d
e
f
g
h
i
j
k
l
m
n
o
p
q
r
s
t
u
v
w
x
y
z

meine sämtlichen Bücher all my books.

Sand *der* sand.

Sandale *die* (PL *die* **Sandalen**) sandal.

sandig *adjective* sandy.

Sandpapier *das* (PL *die* **Sandpapiere**) sandpaper.

sandte SEE **senden**.

sanft *adjective* gentle; **eine sanfte Stimme** a soft voice.

sang SEE **singen**.

Sänger *der* (PL *die* **Sänger**) singer.

Sängerin *die* (PL *die* **Sängerinnen**) singer.

sank SEE **sinken**.

Sardelle *die* (PL *die* **Sardellen**) anchovy.

Sardine *die* (PL *die* **Sardinen**) sardine.

Sarg *der* (PL *die* **Särge**) coffin.

Sarkasmus *der* sarcasm.

sarkastisch *adjective* sarcastic.

SARS *das* SARS (*the disease*).

saß SEE **sitzen**.

Satellit *der* (PL *die* **Satelliten**) satellite.

Satellitenfernsehen *das* satellite television.

satt *adjective* **1** full (up); **bist du satt geworden?** have you had enough to eat?; **sich satt essen** to eat as much as one wants; **satt machen** to be filling; **2 etwas satt haben** (*informal*) to be fed up with something.

Sattel *der* (PL *die* **Sättel**) saddle.

Satteltasche *die* (PL *die* **Satteltaschen**) saddlebag.

Satz *der* (PL *die* **Sätze**) **1** sentence; **2** set (*of things or in tennis*); **ein Satz Reifen** a set of tyres; **3** movement (*in music*); **4** rate (*of tax, interest*); **5** leap.

sauber *adjective* **1** clean; **2** neat; **3** (*informal*) fine (*expressing irony*); **4 sauber machen** to clean.

Sauberkeit *die* cleanliness, cleanness.

saubermachen SEE **sauber**.

Sauce *die* (PL *die* **Saucen**) SEE **Soße**.

sauer *adjective* **1** sour; **2** pickled; **3** acid; **saurer Regen** acid rain; **4 sauer sein** (*informal*) to be annoyed; **ich bin sauer auf Eva** I'm annoyed with Eva.

Sauerei *die* (*informal*) (PL *die* **Sauereien**) **1** mess; **2** disgrace, scandal; **3** obscenity.

Sauerstoff *der* oxygen.

saufen ◇*verb* (*informal*) (PRES **säuft**, IMPERF **soff**, PERF **hat gesoffen**) to drink, to booze.

saugen *verb* (PERF **hat gesaugt**) **1** to suck; **2** to vacuum, to hoover.

Säugetier *das* (PL *die* **Säugetiere**) mammal.

Säugling *der* (PL *die* **Säuglinge**) baby, infant.

Säule *die* (PL *die* **Säulen**) column, pillar.

Saum *der* (PL *die* **Säume**) hem.

Säure *die* (PL *die* **Säuren**) acid.

Saxofon *das* (PL *die* **Saxofone**) saxophone.

S-Bahn *die* (PL *die* **S-Bahnen**) city and suburban railway.

Scanner *der* (PL *die* **Scanner**) scanner.

schäbig *adjective* shabby.

Schach *das* chess; **Schach!** check!

Schachbrett *das* (PL *die* **Schachbretter**) chessboard.

Schachfigur *die* (PL *die* **Schachfiguren**) chess piece.

Schachtel *die* (PL *die* **Schachteln**) box.

schade *adjective* **1 schade sein** to be a pity; **schade!** (what a) pity!; **2 zu schade für jemanden sein** to be too good for somebody.

Schädel *der* (PL *die* **Schädel**) skull.

Schaden *der* (PL *die* **Schäden**) **1** damage; **2** disadvantage.

schaden *verb* (PERF **hat geschadet**) **1** to damage; **das hat seinem Ruf geschadet** it damaged his reputation; **2 jemandem schaden** to harm somebody; **3 das schadet nichts** it doesn't matter.

schädlich *adjective* harmful.

Schaf *das* (PL *die* **Schafe**) sheep.

Schäfer *der* (PL *die* **Schäfer**) shepherd.

Schäferhund *der* (PL *die* **Schäferhunde**) sheepdog.

schaffen[1] ◇*verb* (IMPERF **schuf**, PERF **hat geschaffen**) to create; **wie geschaffen für** made for.

schaffen[2] *verb* (PERF **hat geschafft**) **1** to manage; **es schaffen, etwas zu tun** to manage to do something; **2 eine Prüfung**

schaffen to pass an exam; **3 jemandem zu schaffen machen** to cause somebody trouble; **4 geschafft sein** (*informal*) to be worn out.

Schaffner *der* (PL *die* **Schaffner**) **1** conductor; **2** (ticket) inspector.

Schaffnerin *die* (PL *die* **Schaffnerinnen**) **1** conductress; **2** (ticket) inspector.

Schakal *der* (PL *die* **Schakale**) jackal.

Schal *der* (PL *die* **Schals**) scarf.

Schale *die* (PL *die* **Schalen**) **1** skin; **2** peel; **3** shell; **4** dish, bowl; **eine Schale Obst** a bowl of fruit.

schälen *verb* (PERF **hat geschält**) **1** to peel; **er hat ihr eine Orange geschält** he peeled an orange for her; **2 sich schälen** to peel; **mein Rücken schält sich** my back's peeling.

Schall *der* sound.

Schallplatte *die* (PL *die* **Schallplatten**) record.

schalten *verb* (PERF **hat geschaltet**) **1** to switch; **auf etwas schalten** to turn to something; **2** to change gear; **3 schnell schalten** (*informal*) to catch on quickly.

Schalter *der* (PL *die* **Schalter**) **1** switch; **2** counter.

Schaltjahr *das* (PL *die* **Schaltjahre**) leap year.

schämen *verb* (PERF **hat sich geschämt**) **sich schämen** to be ashamed.

a
b
c
d
e
f
g
h
i
j
k
l
m
n
o
p
q
r
s
t
u
v
w
x
y
z

Schampon das (PL die Schampons) SEE **Shampoo**.

Schande die **1** disgrace; **2** shame.

scharf adjective **1** sharp; **2** hot (food); **ein scharfer Wind** a biting wind; **3** fierce (dog, frost); **4 scharf nachdenken** to think hard; **5** (in photography) **scharf sein** to be in focus; **scharf einstellen** to focus; **6 scharf schießen** to fire live ammunition; **7 scharf auf etwas sein** (informal) to be really keen on something; **sie ist scharf auf Bernd** (informal) she fancies Bernd.

Schaschlik der (PL die Schaschliks) kebab.

Schatten der (PL die Schatten) **1** shadow; **2** shade.

schattig adjective shady.

Schatz der (PL die Schätze) **1** treasure; **2** darling.

Schätzchen das (PL die Schätzchen) darling.

schätzen verb (PERF hat geschätzt) **1** to estimate; **2** to value; **3** to reckon, to guess; **schätz mal!** guess!; **4 etwas zu schätzen wissen** to appreciate something.

Schau die (PL die Schauen) show.

schauen verb (PERF hat geschaut) **1** to look; **2** to watch; **Fernsehen schauen** to watch television.

Schauer der (PL die Schauer) shower.

Schauergeschichte die (PL die Schauergeschichten) horror story.

Schaufel die (PL die Schaufeln) **1** shovel; **2** dustpan.

Schaufenster das (PL die Schaufenster) shop window.

Schaukel die (PL die Schaukeln) swing.

schaukeln verb (PERF hat geschaukelt) to swing.

Schaukelstuhl der (PL die Schaukelstühle) rocking chair.

Schaum der **1** foam; **2** froth; **3** lather.

schäumen verb (PERF hat geschäumt) **1** to foam; **2** to froth (up).

Schauplatz der (PL die Schauplätze) scene.

Schauspiel das (PL die Schauspiele) **1** play; **2** spectacle.

Schauspieler der (PL die Schauspieler) actor.

Schauspielerin die (PL die Schauspielerinnen) actress.

Schauspielkunst die dramatic art, acting.

Scheck der (PL die Schecks) cheque.

Scheckbuch das (PL die Scheckbücher) chequebook.

Scheckkarte die (PL die Scheckkarten) cheque card.

Scheibe die (PL die Scheiben) **1** pane (of a window, car); **2** slice; **eine Scheibe Schinken** a slice of ham; **die Salami in Scheiben schneiden** to slice the salami; **du könntest dir eine Scheibe von ihr**

abschneiden (*informal*) you could take a leaf out of her book; **3** disc.

Scheibenwischer der (PL die Scheibenwischer) windscreen wiper.

scheiden ◇*verb* (IMPERF **schied**, PERF **hat geschieden**) **1** to separate; **sich scheiden lassen** to get divorced; **sie haben sich im Juli scheiden lassen** they got divorced in July; **2 geschieden sein** to be divorced.

Scheidung die (PL die Scheidungen) divorce.

Schein der (PL die Scheine) **1** light; **2** appearance; **etwas nur zum Schein machen** to only pretend to do something; **3** certificate; **4** note (*money*).

scheinbar *adverb* apparently.

scheinen ◇*verb* (IMPERF **schien**, PERF **hat geschienen**) **1** to shine; **2** to seem; **mir scheint** it seems to me.

Scheinwerfer der (PL die Scheinwerfer) **1** headlamp, headlight; **2** floodlight, spotlight.

Scheitel der (PL die Scheitel) parting (*in your hair*).

scheitern *verb* (PERF **ist gescheitert**) to fail.

Schenkel der (PL die Schenkel) thigh.

schenken *verb* (PERF **hat geschenkt**) **1** to give; **etwas geschenkt bekommen** to be given something; **2 sich etwas schenken** to give something a miss; **3 das ist ja geschenkt!** (*informal*) it's a gift!

Schere die (PL die Scheren) **1** (pair of) scissors; **2** shears; **3** claw (*of a crab*).

scheren *verb* (*informal*) (PERF **hat geschert**) to bother; **sich nicht um etwas scheren** not to care about something; **scher dich um deine eigenen Angelegenheiten!** mind your own business!; **scher dich zum Teufel!** go to hell!

Scherz der (PL die Scherze) joke.

scheu *adjective* shy.

scheuern *verb* (PERF **hat gescheuert**) **1** to scrub; **2** to rub.

Scheune die (PL die Scheunen) barn.

scheußlich *adjective* horrible.

Schi der (PL die Schi(er)) SEE **Ski**.

Schicht die (PL die Schichten) **1** layer; **2** class; **3** shift.

Schicht die (PL die Schichten) **1** stratum; **2** section; **3** shift (*in factory etc*).

schick *adjective* **1** stylish, smart; **2** (*informal*) great.

schicken *verb* (PERF **hat geschickt**) to send.

Schicksal das (PL die Schicksale) fate.

Schiebedach das (PL die Schiebedächer) sunroof.

schieben ◇*verb* (IMPERF **schob**, PERF **hat geschoben**) **1** to push; **2 etwas auf etwas schieben** to blame something for something; **die Schuld auf jemanden schieben** to put the blame on somebody.

schied SEE **scheiden**.

a
b
c
d
e
f
g
h
i
j
k
l
m
n
o
p
q
r
s
t
u
v
w
x
y
z

Schiedsrichter der (PL die Schiedsrichter) referee, umpire.

schief adjective crooked; **ein schiefer Blick** a funny look.
schief adverb **1 das Bild hängt schief** the picture is not straight;
2 schief gehen to go wrong.

Schiefer der slate.

schiefgehen SEE **schief**.

schielen verb (PERF hat geschielt) to squint.

schien SEE **scheinen**.

Schienbein das (PL die Schienbeine) shin.

Schiene die (PL die Schienen) **1** rail; **2** splint.

schießen ⋄verb (IMPERF schoss, PERF hat geschossen) **1** to shoot; **auf jemanden schießen** to shoot at somebody; **ein Tor schießen** to score a goal; **2** (PERF ist geschossen) to shoot (along); **Andrea ist in die Höhe geschossen** Andrea's shot up (has got a lot taller).

Schiff das (PL die Schiffe) ship; **ein Schiff zu Wasser lassen** to launch a ship.

Schifffahrt die (PL die Schifffahrten) boat trip.

schikanieren verb (PERF hat schikaniert) to bully.

Schikoree der SEE **Chicorée**.

Schild[1] das (PL die Schilder) **1** sign; **2** badge; **3** label.

Schild[2] der (PL die Schilde) shield.

Schildkröte die (PL die Schildkröten) **1** tortoise; **2** turtle.

Schilling der (PL die Schilling(e)) Schilling (*the currency of Austria until replaced by the euro; 100 Schillings = h7.26 euros*).

Schimmel der (PL die Schimmel) **1** mould; **2** white horse.

Schimpanse der (PL die Schimpansen) chimpanzee.

schimpfen verb (PERF hat geschimpft) **1** to tell off; **2** to grumble.

Schinken der (PL die Schinken) ham; **ein Schinkenbrötchen** a ham roll.

Schirm der (PL die Schirme) **1** umbrella; **2** sunshade; **3** shade (*of a lamp*); **4** peak (*of a cap*).

Schlaf der sleep.

Schlafanzug der (PL die Schlafanzüge) pyjamas.

Schlafcouch die (PL die Schlafcouchs) sofa bed.

schlafen ⋄verb (PRES schläft, IMPERF schlief, PERF hat geschlafen) **1** to sleep; **2** to be asleep; **das Baby schläft** the baby's asleep; **3 schlafen gehen** to go to bed.

schlaff adjective **1** slack (*rope*); **2** limp (*handshake, body*); **3** lethargic.

schläfrig adjective sleepy; **ich bin schläfrig** I'm sleepy.

Schlafsaal der (PL die Schlafsäle) dormitory.

Schlafsack der (PL die Schlafsäcke) sleeping bag.

a b c d e f g h i j k l m n o p q r s t u v w x y z

Schlafwagen *der* (PL *die* Schlafwagen) sleeper.

Schlafzimmer *das* (PL *die* Schlafzimmer) bedroom.

Schlag *der* (PL *die* Schläge) **1** blow, punch; **Schläge kriegen** to get a beating; **2** stroke; **3** (*electric*) shock; **4 Schlag auf Schlag** in quick succession; **auf einen Schlag** all at once.

schlagen ⬦*verb* (PRES **schlägt**, IMPERF **schlug**, PERF **hat geschlagen**) **1** to hit; **einen Nagel in die Wand schlagen** to knock a nail into the wall; **2** to beat; **3** to bang; **mit dem Kopf gegen etwas schlagen** to bang your head against something; **4** to strike (*of a clock*); **5** to whip (*cream*); **6 sich schlagen** to fight; **7 sich geschlagen geben** to admit defeat.

Schlager *der* (PL *die* Schlager) hit.

Schläger *der* (PL *die* Schläger) **1** racket (*in tennis*); **2** bat (*in baseball*); **3** club (*in golf*); **4** stick (*in hockey*); **5** thug.

Schlägerei *die* (PL *die* Schlägereien) fight.

Schlagsahne *die* **1** whipping cream; **2** whipped cream.

Schlagzeile *die* (PL *die* Schlagzeilen) headline.

Schlagzeug *das* (PL *die* Schlagzeuge) drums.

Schlagzeuger *der* (PL *die* Schlagzeuger) drummer.

Schlamm *der* mud.

schlampen *verb* (PERF **hat geschlampt**) to be sloppy.

Schlamperei *die* (PL *die* Schlampereien) **1** sloppiness; **2** mess.

schlampig *adjective* sloppy.

Schlange *die* (PL *die* Schlangen) **1** snake; **2** queue; **Schlange stehen** to queue.

schlank *adjective* slim.

Schlankheitskur *die* (PL *die* Schlankheitskuren) diet; **eine Schlankeitskur machen** to be on a diet.

schlapp *adjective* worn out, tired out.

schlau *adjective* **1** crafty; **2** clever; **ich werde nicht schlau daraus** I can't make head nor tail of it.

Schlauch *der* (PL *die* Schläuche) hose.

schlauchlos *adjective* tubeless.

schlecht *adjective* **1** bad; **schlecht werden** to go bad; **2 mir ist schlecht** I feel sick; **3 jemanden schlecht machen** to run somebody down.
schlecht *adverb* **1** badly; **schlecht gelaunt** in a bad mood; **2 es geht ihm schlecht** he's not well.

schleichen ⬦*verb* (IMPERF **schlich**, PERF **ist geschlichen**) **1** to creep; **2** to crawl (*in traffic*); **3 sich schleichen** to creep.

Schleife *die* (PL *die* Schleifen) **1** bow; **2** loop.

Schlepper *der* (PL *die* Schlepper) **1** tug; **2** tractor.

Schleuder *die* (PL *die* Schleudern) **1** catapult; **2** spin-dryer.

schleudern *verb* (PERF **hat geschleudert**) **1** to hurl; **2** to spin (*washing*); **3** (PERF **ist geschleudert**) to skid.

schlich SEE **schleichen**.

schlicht *adjective* plain, simple.

schlief SEE **schlafen**.

schließen ◇*verb* (IMPERF **schloss**, PERF **hat geschlossen**) **1** to close, to shut; **2** to close down; **3** to lock; **4** to conclude; **aus etwas schließen, dass** ... to conclude from something that ...; **5 einen Vertrag schließen** to enter into a contract; **6 Freundschaft mit jemandem schließen** to make friends with somebody; **7 sich schließen** to close.

Schließfach *das* (PL *die* **Schließfächer**) locker.

schließlich *adverb* **1** finally; **2** after all; **er hat sie schließlich doch eingeladen** he's invited her after all.

schlimm *adjective* bad.

schlimmstenfalls *adverb* if the worst comes to the worst.

Schlips *der* (PL *die* **Schlipse**) tie.

Schlitten *der* (PL *die* **Schlitten**) sledge; **Schlitten fahren gehen** to go sledging.

Schlittschuh *der* (PL *die* **Schlittschuhe**) skate; **Schlittschuh laufen** to skate.

Schlittschuhlaufen *das* ice-skating.

Schlitz *der* (PL *die* **Schlitze**) **1** slit; **2** flies (*in trousers*); **3** slot.

Schloss *das* (PL *die* **Schlösser**) **1** lock; **2** castle.

schloss SEE **schließen**.

Schluck *der* (PL *die* **Schlucke**) **1** mouthful; **2** gulp.

Schluckauf *der* hiccups.

schlucken *verb* (PERF **hat geschluckt**) to swallow.

schlug SEE **schlagen**.

Schlüpfer *der* (PL *die* **Schlüpfer**) knickers.

Schluss *der* (PL *die* **Schlüsse**) **1** end, ending; **zum Schluss** in the end; **Schluss machen** to stop; **mit jemandem Schluss machen** to finish with somebody; **2** conclusion.

Schlüssel *der* (PL *die* **Schlüssel**) **1** key; **2** spanner.

Schlussverkauf *der* sales.

schmal *adjective* **1** narrow; **2** thin (*face, nose*); **3** **sie ist schmäler geworden** she's lost weight.

schmecken *verb* (PERF **hat geschmeckt**) to taste; **die Suppe schmeckt gut** the soup tastes good; **das schmeckt mir nicht** I don't like it; **das Eis schmeckt nach Zitrone** the ice cream tastes of lemon.

schmeicheln *verb* (PERF **hat geschmeichelt**) to flatter; **jemandem schmeicheln** to flatter somebody.

schmeißen ◇*verb* (*informal*) (IMPERF **schmiss**, PERF **hat geschmissen**) to chuck; **mit etwas schmeißen** to chuck something.

schmelzen ◇*verb* (PRES **schmilzt**, IMPERF **schmolz**, PERF **ist**

geschmolzen) **1** to melt; **der Schnee ist geschmolzen** the snow has melted; **2** (PERF **hat geschmolzen**) to melt (*snow, ice*); **3** (PERF **hat geschmolzen**) to smelt (*ore*).

Schmerz *der* (PL **die Schmerzen**) **1** pain; **2** grief.

schmerzen *verb* (PERF **hat geschmerzt**) to hurt; **mein Kopf schmerzt** my head is aching.

schmerzhaft *adjective* painful.

schmerzlos *adjective* painless.

Schmerzmittel *das* (PL **die Schmerzmittel**) painkiller.

Schmerzschwelle *das* (PL **die Schmerzschwellen**) painthreshold.

Schmetterling *der* (PL **die Schmetterlinge**) butterfly.

schmettern *verb* (PERF **hat geschmettert**) **1** to hurl; **2** to smash (*in tennis*); **3** to blare out (*music, orders*).

schmieren *verb* (PERF **hat geschmiert**) **1** to lubricate; **2** to spread (*butter, jam*); **Brote schmieren** to spread slices of bread; **jemandem eine schmieren** (*informal*) to clout somebody; **3** to scrawl; **4** to smudge.

schmilzt SEE **schmelzen**.

Schminke *die* make-up.

schminken *verb* (PERF **hat geschminkt**) **1** to make up; **2 sich schminken** to put on make-up.

schmiss SEE **schmeißen**.

schmolz SEE **schmelzen**.

Schmuck *der* **1** jewellery; **2** decoration.

schmücken *verb* (PERF **hat geschmückt**) to decorate.

schmuggeln *verb* (PERF **hat geschmuggelt**) to smuggle.

schmusen *verb* (PERF **hat geschmust**) to cuddle; **Gabi hat mit Max geschmust** Gabi cuddled Max.

Schmutz *der* dirt.

schmutzig *adjective* dirty.

Schmutzigkeit *die* dirtiness.

Schnabel *der* (PL **die Schnäbel**) beak.

Schnalle *die* (PL **die Schnallen**) buckle.

schnallen *verb* (PERF **hat geschnallt**) **1** to fasten; **2** to buckle.

schnarchen *verb* (PERF **hat geschnarcht**) to snore.

Schnauze *die* (PL **die Schnauzen**) **1** muzzle; **eine kalte Schnauze** a cold nose; **2 die Schnauze halten** (*informal*) to keep your mouth shut.

schnäuzen (PERF **hat sich geschnäuzt**) **sich schnäuzen** to blow your nose.

Schnecke *die* (PL **die Schnecken**) snail.

Schnee *der* snow.

Schneeregen *der* sleet.

Schneesturm *der* (PL **die Schneestürme**) blizzard.

Schneewehe *die* (PL **die Schneewehen**) snow drift.

schneiden ◇*verb* (IMPERF **schnitt**, PERF **hat geschnitten**) **1** to cut;

a
b
c
d
e
f
g
h
i
j
k
l
m
n
o
p
q
r
s
t
u
v
w
x
y
z

ich kann dir die Haare schneiden
I can cut your hair; **Evi hat sich die Haare kurz schneiden lassen** Evi had her hair cut short; **in Scheiben schneiden** to slice; **2 sich schneiden** to cut yourself; **ich habe mich in den Finger geschnitten** I've cut my finger; **3 sich schneiden** to intersect; **4 Gesichter schneiden** to pull faces.

Schneider der (PL die Schneider) tailor.

Schneiderin die (PL die Schneiderinnen) dressmaker.

schneien verb (PERF hat geschneit) to snow; **es schneit** it's snowing.

schnell adjective quick, fast. **schnell** adverb quickly; **mach schnell!** hurry up!

Schnelligkeit die speed.

Schnellimbiss der (PL die Schnellimbisse) snack bar.

schnellstens adverb as quickly as possible.

Schnellzug der (PL die Schnellzüge) express (train).

schneuzen SEE **schnäuzen**.

Schnitt der (PL die Schnitte) **1** cut; **er hat einen tiefen Schnitt im Finger** he's got a deep cut in his finger; **das Kostüm hat einen sehr guten Schnitt** the suit is well cut; **2** cutting (of a film); **3 im Schnitt** on average; **4** pattern.

schnitt SEE **schneiden**.

Schnittlauch der chives.

Schnitzel das (PL die Schnitzel) **1** escalope; **2** scrap.

schnitzen verb (PERF hat geschnitzt) to carve.

Schnorchel der (PL die Schnorchel) snorkel.

schnüffeln verb (PERF hat geschnüffelt) **1** to sniff; **2** to snoop around.

Schnuller der (PL die Schnuller) dummy.

Schnupfen der (PL die Schnupfen) cold.

Schnur die (PL die Schnüre) **1** (piece of) string; **2** flex; **3** cord.

Schnurrbart der (PL die Schnurrbärte) moustache.

schnurren verb (PERF hat geschnurrt) to purr.

Schnurrhaar das (PL die Schnurrhaare) whisker.

Schnürsenkel der (PL die Schnürsenkel) shoelace.

schob SEE **schieben**.

Schock der (PL die Schocks) shock.

schockieren verb (PERF hat schockiert) to shock.

Schokolade die (PL die Schokoladen) chocolate.

schön adjective **1** beautiful; **2** nice; **schönes Wochenende!** have a nice weekend!; **3** good; **na schön** all right then; **4 schönen Dank** thank you very much; **schöne Grüße** best wishes.

schon adverb **1** already ('schon' is often not translated); **schon wieder** again; **schon oft** often; **du wirst**

schon sehen you'll see; **ja schon, aber ...** well yes, but ...; **nun geh schon!** go on then!; **2** yet; **hast du sie schon gesehen?** have you seen her yet?; **du weißt schon** you know; **3** even; **4 komm schon!** come on!; **5 schon deshalb** for that reason alone; **6 das ist schon möglich** that's quite possible; **7 er war schon mal da** he's been there before.

schonen *verb* (PERF **hat geschont**) **1** to look after; **2 sich schonen** to take things easy.

Schönheit die (PL die **Schönheiten**) beauty.

Schornstein der (PL die **Schornsteine**) chimney, funnel.

schoss SEE **schießen**.

Schoß der (PL die **Schöße**) lap.

Schotte der (PL die **Schotten**) Scot, Scotsman.

Schottin die (PL die **Schottinnen**) Scot, Scotswoman.

schottisch *adjective* Scottish.

Schottland das Scotland.

schräg *adjective* **1** diagonal; **2** sloping.
schräg *adverb* **etwas schräg halten** to tilt something; **etwas schräg stellen** to put something at an angle.

Schrank der (PL die **Schränke**) **1** cupboard; **2** wardrobe.

Schranke die (PL die **Schranken**) barrier.

Schraube die (PL die **Schrauben**) screw.

schrauben *verb* (PERF **hat geschraubt**) to screw.

Schraubenschlüssel der (PL die **Schraubenschlüssel**) spanner.

Schraubenzieher der (PL die **Schraubenzieher**) screwdriver.

Schreck der fright; **jemandem einen Schreck einjagen** to give somebody a fright; **ich habe einen Schreck bekommen** I got a fright.

schrecklich *adjective* terrible.

Schrei der (PL die **Schreie**) **1** cry, shout; **2** scream; **3 der letzte Schrei** (*informal*) the latest thing.

Schreibblock der (PL die **Schreibblöcke**) writing pad.

schreiben ◇*verb* (IMPERF **schrieb**, PERF **hat geschrieben**) **1** to write; **David hat mir einen Brief geschrieben** David wrote a letter to me; **einen Test schreiben** to do a test; **2** to spell; **wie schreibt man das?** how is it spelt?; **3** to type.

Schreibmaschine die (PL die **Schreibmaschinen**) typewriter.

Schreibpapier das writing paper.

Schreibtisch der (PL die **Schreibtische**) desk.

Schreibwaren *plural noun* stationery.

schreien ◇*verb* (IMPERF **schrie**, PERF **hat geschrien**) **1** to cry, to shout; **das Baby schreit** the baby's crying; **2** to scream; **vor Lachen schreien** to scream with laughter; **zum Schreien sein** (*informal*) to be a scream.

a
b
c
d
e
f
g
h
i
j
k
l
m
n
o
p
q
r
s
t
u
v
w
x
y
z

Schreiner der (PL die **Schreiner**) joiner.

schrie SEE **schreien**.

schrieb SEE **schreiben**.

Schrift die (PL die **Schriften**) **1** writing; **2** type; **3** script.

schriftlich adjective written. **schriftlich** adverb in writing; **das lasse ich mir schriftlich geben** I'll get that in writing; **jemanden schriftlich einladen** to send somebody a written invitation.

Schriftsteller der (PL die **Schriftsteller**) writer.

Schriftstellerin die (PL die **Schriftstellerinnen**) writer.

Schritt der (PL die **Schritte**) **1** step; **2** footstep.

schrumpfen verb (PERF **ist geschrumpft**) **1** to shrink; **2** to shrivel.

Schublade die (PL die **Schubladen**) drawer.

schubsen verb (PERF **hat geschubst**) to shove.

schüchtern adjective shy.

schuf SEE **schaffen**.

Schuh der (PL die **Schuhe**) shoe.

Schuhgröße die (PL die **Schuhgrößen**) shoe size.

Schularbeiten plural noun homework.

Schulaufgaben plural noun homework.

Schulbuch das (PL die **Schulbücher**) schoolbook.

Schuld die (PL die **Schulden**) **1** blame; **Schuld haben** to be to blame; **jemandem Schuld geben** to blame somebody; **2** fault; **es war seine Schuld** it was his fault; **3** guilt; **4** debt; **Schulden haben** to be in debt; **Schulden machen** to get into debt.

schuld adjective **schuld sein** to be to blame; **du bist schuld daran** it's your fault.

schulden verb (PERF **hat geschuldet**) to owe.

schuldig adjective **1** guilty; **2 jemandem etwas schuldig sein** to owe somebody something.

Schule die (PL die **Schulen**) school; **in die Schule gehen** to go to school.

schulen verb (PERF **hat geschult**) to train.

Schüler der (PL die **Schüler**) pupil, student.

Schülerin die (PL die **Schülerinnen**) pupil, student.

Schulferien plural noun school holidays.

schulfrei adjective **ein schulfreier Tag** a day off school; **wir haben heute schulfrei** there's no school today.

Schulfreund der (PL die **Schulfreunde**) schoolfriend.

Schulfreundin die (PL die **Schulfreundinnen**) schoolfriend.

Schulheft das (PL die **Schulhefte**) exercise book.

Schulhof der (PL die **Schulhöfe**) playground.

schwanken

Schuljahr das (PL die Schuljahre) school year.

Schulschwänzer der (PL die Schulschwänzer) truant.

Schulschwänzerin die (PL die Schulschwänzerinnen) truant.

Schulstunde die (PL die Schulstunden) period.

Schultasche die (PL die Schultaschen) schoolbag.

Schulter die (PL die Schultern) shoulder.

schummeln verb (PERF hat geschummelt) to cheat.

Schuppe die (PL die Schuppen) 1 scale; 2 Schuppen dandruff.

Schuppen der (PL die Schuppen) shed.

Schürze die (PL die Schürzen) apron.

Schuss der (PL die Schüsse) 1 shot; 2 dash (of brandy, vinegar); 3 schuss (in skiing).

Schüssel die (PL die Schüsseln) bowl, dish.

Schuster der (PL die Schuster) shoemaker.

schütteln verb (PERF hat geschüttelt) 1 to shake; 2 sich schütteln to shake yourself; sich vor Ekel schütteln to shudder.

schütten verb (PERF hat geschüttet) 1 to pour; es schüttet (informal) it's pouring (down); 2 to tip; 3 to spill.

Schutz der 1 protection; 2 shelter; 3 conservation.

Schutzbrille die (PL die Schutzbrillen) goggles.

Schütze der (PL die Schützen) 1 marksman; 2 Sagittarius; Daniel ist Schütze Daniel's Sagittarius.

schützen verb (PERF hat geschützt) 1 to protect; die meisten Cremes schützen die Haut gegen Sonnenbrand most creams protect the skin from sunburn; 2 gesetzlich geschützt registered (as a trade-mark).

Schutzhütte die (PL die Schutzhütten) 1 mountain refuge; 2 shelter.

schwach adjective 1 weak; 2 dim (light); 3 poor (performance, memory).

Schwäche die (PL die Schwächen) weakness.

schwachsinnig adjective idiotic.

Schwager der (PL die Schwäger) brother-in-law.

Schwägerin die (PL die Schwägerinnen) sister-in-law.

Schwalbe die (PL die Schwalben) swallow.

Schwamm der (PL die Schwämme) sponge.

schwamm SEE **schwimmen**.

Schwan der (PL die Schwäne) swan.

schwanger adjective pregnant.

Schwangerschaft die (PL die Schwangerschaften) pregnancy.

schwanken verb (PERF hat geschwankt) 1 to sway; 2 to fluctuate; 3 to waver; 4 (PERF ist geschwankt) to stagger.

a
b
c
d
e
f
g
h
i
j
k
l
m
n
o
p
q
r
s
t
u
v
w
x
y
z

Schwanz *der* (PL *die* Schwänze) tail.

schwänzen *verb* (PERF **hat geschwänzt**) to skip, to skive off; **die Schule schwänzen** to play truant.

Schwarm *der* (PL *die* Schwärme) swarm.

schwarz *adjective, adverb* **1** black; **schwarz gekleidet** dressed in black; **ein schwarz gestreiftes Kleid** a dress with black stripes; **das habe ich schwarz auf weiß** I have it in black and white; **2 ins Schwarze treffen** to hit the nail on the head, to score a bull's eye; **3 schwarz sehen** to be pessimistic; **4 etwas schwarz machen** to do something illegally.

Schwarze *der/die* (PL *die* Schwarzen) black.

schwarzsehen SEE **schwarz**.

Schwarzwald *der* Black Forest.

schwätzen *verb* (PERF **hat geschwätzt**) to chatter.

Schwede *der* (PL *die* Schweden) Swede.

Schweden *das* Sweden.

Schwedin *die* (PL *die* Schwedinnen) Swede.

schwedisch *adjective* Swedish.

schweigen ⬦*verb* (IMPERF **schwieg**, PERF **hat geschwiegen**) to be silent; **ganz zu schweigen von** ... not to mention ....

Schwein *das* (PL *die* Schweine) **1** pig; **2** pork; **3 du Schwein!** (*informal*) you swine!; **Schwein haben** (*informal*) to be lucky.

Schweinefleisch *das* pork.

Schweinekotelett *das* (PL *die* Schweinekoteletts) pork chop.

Schweiß *der* sweat.

Schweiz *die* **die Schweiz** Switzerland.

Schweizer *der* (PL *die* Schweizer) Swiss.

Schweizerin *die* (PL *die* Schweizerinnen) Swiss.

schweizerisch *adjective* Swiss.

Schwelle *der* (PL *die* Schwellen) threshold.

Schwellung *die* (PL *die* Schwellungen) swelling.

schwer *adjective* **1** heavy; **zwei Pfund schwer sein** to weigh two pounds; **2** difficult; **3** serious. **schwer** *adverb* **1** heavily; **2** seriously; **schwer krank** seriously ill; **3 schwer arbeiten** to work hard; **jemandem schwer fallen** to be hard for somebody; **4 sich mit etwas schwer tun** to have difficulty with something.

schwerfallen SEE **schwer**.

schwerhörig *adjective* hard of hearing.

Schwert *das* (PL *die* Schwerter) sword.

schwertun SEE **schwer**.

Schwester *die* (PL *die* Schwestern) sister.

schwieg SEE **schweigen**.

Schwiegereltern *plural noun* parents-in-law.

Schwiegermutter *die* (PL *die* Schwiegermütter) mother-in-law.

Schwiegersohn der (PL die Schwiegersöhne) son-in-law.

Schwiegertochter die (PL die Schwiegertöchter) daughter-in-law.

Schwiegervater der (PL die Schwiegerväter) father-in-law.

schwierig adjective difficult.

Schwierigkeit die (PL die Schwierigkeiten) difficulty.

Schwimmbad das (PL die Schwimmbäder) swimming baths.

schwimmen ◇verb (IMPERF schwamm, PERF ist/hat geschwommen) **1** to swim; **2** to float.

Schwimmer der (PL die Schwimmer) swimmer.

Schwimmerbecken das (PL die Schwimmbecken) swimming pool (for experienced swimmers).

Schwimmerin die (PL die Schwimmerinnen) swimmer.

Schwimmweste die (PL die Schwimmwesten) life-jacket.

schwindlig adjective dizzy; **mir ist schwindlig** I feel dizzy.

Schwips der (PL die Schwipse) **einen Schwips haben** to be tipsy.

schwitzen verb (PERF hat geschwitzt) to sweat.

schwören ◇verb (IMPERF schwor, PERF hat geschworen) to swear.

schwül adjective close.

schwul adjective gay.

Schwule der (PL die Schwulen) gay.

Schwung der (PL die Schwünge) **1** swing; **2** drive; **die Party in Schwung bringen** to get the party going.

sechs number six.

sechster, sechste, sechstes adjective sixth.

sechzehn number sixteen.

sechzig number sixty.

See[1] der (PL die Seen) lake.

See[2] die sea.

Seehund der (PL die Seehunde) seal.

seekrank adjective seasick.

Seele die (PL die Seelen) soul.

Seemann der (PL die Seeleute) seaman, sailor.

Seetang der seaweed.

Segel das (PL die Segel) sail.

Segelboot das (PL die Segelboote) sailing boat.

Segelfliegen das gliding.

Segelflugzeug das (PL die Segelflugzeuge) glider.

Segellehrer der (PL die Segellehrer) sailing instructor.

Segellehrerin die (PL die Segellehrerinnen) sailing instructor.

segeln verb (PERF ist gesegelt) to sail.

sehen ◇verb (PRES sieht, IMPERF sah, PERF hat gesehen) **1** to see; **jemanden wieder sehen** to see somebody again; **mal sehen, ob ...** let's see if ...; **2** to look; **3 eine Fernsehsendung sehen** to watch a

221

television programme; **4 gut/ schlecht sehen** to have good/bad eyesight; **5 nach jemandem sehen** to look after somebody.

sehenswert *adjective* worth seeing.

Sehenswürdigkeiten *plural noun* sights.

Sehnsucht *die* longing; **Sehnsucht nach jemandem haben** to long to see somebody.

sehr *adverb* **1** very; **sehr gut** very good; **2 danke sehr** thank you very much; **3 ich habe Karin sehr gern** I like Karin a lot; **4 Sehr geehrte Frau Huber** Dear Mrs Huber.

seid SEE **sein**.

Seide *die* (PL **die Seiden**) silk.

Seife *die* (PL **die Seifen**) soap.

Seil *das* (PL **die Seile**) **1** rope; **2** cable.

Seilbahn *die* (PL **die Seilbahnen**) cable railway.

sein[1] ◇*verb* (PRES **ist**, IMPERF **war**, PERF **ist gewesen**) **1** to be; **wir sind in der Küche** we're in the kitchen; **Rosi ist krank** Rosi is ill; **mir ist schlecht** I feel sick; **mir ist kalt/heiß** I'm cold/hot; **2 sie ist Lehrerin** she's a teacher; **3 es ist drei Uhr** it's three o'clock; **Karl ist aus München** Karl's from Munich; **es war viel zu tun** there was a lot to be done; **4 aus Seide sein** to be made of silk; **5 etwas sein lassen** to stop something; **lass das sein!** stop it!; **6 es sei denn, dass** ... unless ...; **7** (*used with certain verbs to form past tenses*) **ich bin nach Berlin gefahren** I went to Berlin; **wir sind**

kurz vor acht nach Hause gekommen we got home shortly before eight o'clock; **er ist abgeholt worden** he's been collected.

sein[2] *adjective* **1** his; **2** (*of a thing or animal*) its; **der Hund ist in seiner Hütte** the dog is in its kennel; **3** (*after the pronoun 'man'*) your, one's; **wenn man sich seine Eltern aussuchen könnte** if you could choose your parents.

seiner, seine, sein(e)s *pronoun* **1** his; **das ist nicht meine CD, das ist seine** it's not my CD, it's his; **du kannst seins nehmen** you can take his; **2** (*after the pronoun 'man'*) your own, one's own; **das Seine tun** to do one's share.

seinetwegen *adverb* **1** for his sake; **2** because of him; **3** on his account.

seinlassen SEE **sein**.

seins SEE **seiner**.

seit *preposition* (+ DAT) *conjunction* **1** since; **seit etwa einer Woche** since about a week; **seit du hier wohnst** since you've been living here; **seit wann?** since when?; **2 ich bin seit zwei Wochen hier** I've been here for two weeks; **seit einiger Zeit** for some time.

seitdem *adverb* since then; **ich habe sie seitdem nicht mehr gesehen** I haven't seen her since. **seitdem** *conjunction* since.

Seite *die* (PL **die Seiten**) **1** side; **auf der einen Seite** on the one hand; **2** page; **das steht auf Seite zwanzig** it's on page twenty.

Seitenstechen *das* stich; **ich habe Seitenstechen** I've got a stitch.

Seitenstraße *die* (PL *die* **Seitenstraßen**) side street.

seither *adverb* since then.

Sekretär *der* (PL *die* **Sekretäre**) secretary.

Sekretärin *die* (PL *die* **Sekretärinnen**) secretary.

Sekt *der* (PL *die* **Sekte**) sparkling wine.

Sekte *die* (PL *die* **Sekten**) sect.

Sekunde *die* (PL *die* **Sekunden**) second.

selbst *pronoun* **1 ich selbst** I myself; **er selbst** he himself; **wir selbst** we ourselves; **Sie selbst** you yourself, you yourselves; **2 von selbst** by itself; **3 sie schneidet sich die Haare selbst** she cuts her own hair; **4** on one's own; **ich kann es selbst machen** I can do it on my own; **5 selbst gemacht** home-made.
   selbst *adverb* even; **selbst wenn** even if.

selbständig SEE **selbstständig**.

Selbstbedienung *die* self-service.

selbstbewusst *adjective* self-confident.

Selbstbewusstsein *das* **1** self-confidence; **2** self-awareness.

selbstgemacht SEE **selbst**.

Selbstmord *der* (PL *die* **Selbstmorde**) suicide; **Selbstmord begehen** to commit suicide.

selbstsicher *adjective* self-confident.

selbstständig *adjective* **1** independent; **2** self-employed; **sich selbstständig machen** to set up on your own.

selbstverständlich *adjective* natural; **etwas für selbstverständlich halten** to take something for granted; **das ist selbstverständlich** it goes without saying.
   selbstverständlich *adverb* naturally, of course; **wir haben ihn selbstverständlich auf die Party eingeladen** of course we invited him to the party.

selten *adjective* rare.
   selten *adverb* rarely.

seltsam *adjective* strange, odd.

Semester *das* (PL *die* **Semester**) semester, term.

Semikolon *das* (PL *die* **Semikolons**) semicolon.

Semmel *die* (PL *die* **Semmeln**) roll.

senden *verb* (PERF **hat gesendet**) **1** to send; **etwas an jemanden senden** to send something to somebody; **2** to broadcast; **seine Rede wird im ersten Programm gesendet** his speech will be broadcast on channel one; **3** to transmit.

Sendung *die* (PL *die* **Sendungen**) **1** programme; **2** consignment.

Senf *der* (PL *die* **Senfe**) mustard.

Senior *der* (PL *die* **Senioren**) **1** senior; **2 Senioren** senior citizens.

a
b
c
d
e
f
g
h
i
j
k
l
m
n
o
p
q
r
s
t
u
v
w
x
y
z

senkrecht *adjective* vertical.

Sensation die (PL die Sensationen) sensation, stir.

sensationell *adjective* sensational.

sensibel *adjective* sensitive.

sentimental *adjective* sentimental.

September der September.

Sequenz die (PL die Sequenzen) sequence (*in a film*).

Serie die (PL die Serien) **1** series; **2** serial.

Service¹ das (PL die Service) set (*of china, for example*).

Service² der service; **das Essen im Hotel ist gut, aber der Service ist furchtbar** the food in the hotel is good but the service is appalling.

servieren *verb* (PERF hat serviert) to serve.

Serviette die (PL die Servietten) napkin.

Sessel der (PL die Sessel) armchair.

Sessellift der (PL die Sessellifte) chair-lift.

setzen *verb* (PERF hat gesetzt) **1** to put; **ein Komma setzen** to put a comma; **vergiss nicht, deinen Namen auf die Liste zu setzen** don't forget to put your name on the list; **2** to move (*a counter in games*); **3 auf etwas setzen** to bet on something; **auf ein Pferd setzen** to back a horse; **4 sich setzen** to sit down; **sich auf einen Stuhl setzen** to sit down on a chair.

seufzen *verb* (PERF hat geseufzt) to sigh.

Seufzer der (PL die Seufzer) sigh.

Sex der sex; **Sex mit jemandem haben** to have sex with somebody.

Sexismus der sexism.

sexistisch *adjective* sexist.

sexuell *adjective* sexual.

Shampoo das (PL die Shampoos) shampoo.

Shuttledienst der (PL die Shuttledienste) shuttle service.

sich *pronoun* **1** (*with 'er/sie/es'*) himself/herself/itself; **sie hat sich eingeschlossen** she locked herself in; **2** (*with plural 'sie'*) themselves; **3** (*with 'Sie'*) yourself, yourselves (*plural*); **4** each other, one another; **sich kennen** to know each other; **Petra und Werner lieben sich** Petra and Werner love each other; **5** (*not translated with certain verbs*) **sich freuen** to be pleased; **sich wundern** to be surprised; **6 Anita wäscht sich die Haare** Anita is washing her hair; **sich den Arm brechen** to break your arm; **7 sich gut verkaufen** to sell well; **8 von sich aus** of your own accord.

sicher *adjective* **1** safe; **2** certain; **bist du sicher?** are you sure?

sicher *adverb* **1** safely; **2** certainly, surely; **sicher!** certainly!

Sicherheit die **1** safety; **zur Sicherheit** for safety's sake; **schnallen Sie sich zur Ihrer eigenen Sicherheit an** fasten your seat belt for your own safety; **etwas in Sicherheit bringen** to rescue something; **in Sicherheit sein** to be safe; **2** security; **die Sicherheit der Arbeitsplätze** job security; **3** certainty; **mit Sicherheit!** certainly! (*as a reply*).

Sicherheitsgurt *der* (PL *die* **Sicherheitsgurte**) seatbelt.

Sicherheitsnadel *die* (PL *die* **Sicherheitsnadeln**) safety pin.

sicherlich *adverb* certainly.

sichern *verb* (PERF **hat gesichert**) to secure; **jemandem etwas sichern** to secure something for somebody.

Sicherung *die* (PL *die* **Sicherungen**) **1** fuse; **die Sicherung is durchgebrannt** the fuse has blown; **2** safeguard; **die Sicherung der Arbeitsplätze** safeguarding jobs; **3** safety catch.

Sicht *die* **1** view; **ich hatte eine gute Sicht auf den See** I had a good view of the lake; **auf lange Sicht** in the long term; **2 aus meiner Sicht** as I see it; **3** visibility; **gute/ schlechte Sicht** good/poor visibility.

sichtbar *adjective* visible.

sie *pronoun* **1** she; **2** her; **ich kenne sie** I know her; **3** it; **so eine hübsche Bluse, war sie teuer?** what a pretty blouse, was it expensive?; **4** they; **sie sind in der Küche** they're in the kitchen; **5** them; **ich habe sie gestern abgeschickt** I posted them yesterday.

Sie *pronoun* you; **kommen Sie herein!** come in!

Sieb *das* (PL *die* **Siebe**) **1** sieve; **2** strainer.

sieben *number* seven.

siebter, siebte, siebtes *adjective* seventh.

siebzehn *number* seventeen.

siebzig *number* seventy.

Siedlung *die* (PL *die* **Siedlungen**) **1** (housing) estate; **2** settlement.

Sieg *der* (PL *die* **Siege**) victory, win.

Siegel *das* (PL *die* **Siegel**) seal.

siegen *verb* (PERF **hat gesiegt**) to win.

Sieger *der* (PL *die* **Sieger**) winner.

Siegerin *die* (PL *die* **Siegerinnen**) winner.

sieht SEE **sehen**.

Silbe *die* (PL *die* **Silben**) syllable.

Silber *das* silver.

silbern *adjective* silver.

Silvester *das* New Year's Eve.

sind SEE **sein**.

Sinfonie *die* (PL *die* **Sinfonien**) symphony.

singen ◇*verb* (IMPERF **sang**, PERF **hat gesungen**) to sing.

sinken ◇*verb* (IMPERF **sank**, PERF **ist gesunken**) **1** to sink; **2** to go down.

Sinn *der* (PL *die* **Sinne**) **1** sense; **2** meaning; **3** point; **das hat keinen Sinn** there's no point.

sinnlos *adjective* pointless.

sinnvoll *adjective* **1** sensible; **2** meaningful.

Situation *die* (PL *die* **Situationen**) situation.

a
b
c
d
e
f
g
h
i
j
k
l
m
n
o
p
q
r
s
t
u
v
w
x
y
z

Sitz der (PL die **Sitze**) **1** seat; **2** fit (of clothes).

sitzen ◇verb (IMPERF **saß**, PERF **hat gesessen**) **1** to sit; **sitzen bleiben** to remain seated; **2 sitzen bleiben** to have to repeat a year, to stay down (at school); **3 er sitzt** (informal) he's in jail; **4 jemanden sitzen lassen** (informal) to leave somebody in the lurch; **5** to fit (of clothes); **der Mantel sitzt gut** the coat fits well.

Sitzplatz der (PL die **Sitzplätze**) seat.

Sitzung die (PL die **Sitzungen**) **1** meeting; **2** session.

Sizilien das Sicily.

Skandal der (PL die **Skandale**) scandal.

Skandinavien das Scandinavia.

skandinavisch adjective Scandinavian.

Skateboard der (PL die **Skateboards**) skateboard; **Skateboard fahren** to skateboard.

Skater der (PL die **Skater**) skater (on a skateboard).

Skelett das (PL die **Skelette**) skeleton.

skeptisch adjective sceptical.

Ski der (PL die **Ski(er)**) ski; **Ski fahren/laufen** to ski.

Skianzug der (PL die **Skianzüge**) ski suit.

Skibrille die (PL die **Skibrillen**) skiing goggles.

Skifahren das skiing.

Skifahrer der (PL die **Skifahrer**) skier.

Skifahrerin die (PL die **Skifahrerinnen**) skier.

Skilaufen das skiing.

Skiläufer der (PL die **Skiläufer**) skier.

Skiläuferin die (PL die **Skiläuferinnen**) skier.

Skilehrer der (PL die **Skilehrer**) ski instructor.

Skizze die (PL die **Skizzen**) sketch.

Skooter der (PL die **Skooter**) bumper car, dodgem car.

Skorpion der (PL die **Skorpione**) **1** scorpion; **2** Scorpio.

Skulptur die (PL die **Skulpturen**) sculpture.

Slip der (PL die **Slips**) briefs, pants.

Slowake der (PL die **Slowaken**) Slovak.

Slowakei die Slovakia.

Slowakin die (PL die **Slowakinnen**) Slovak.

slowakisch adjective Slovak.

Slowenien das Slovenia.

Smoking der (PL die **Smokings**) dinner jacket.

SMS die (PL die **SMS**) text message.

so adverb **1** so; **nicht so viel** not so much; **und so weiter** and so on; **2** like this, like that; **so nicht** not like that; **3** as; **so bald wie** as soon as; **4** such; **so ein Zufall!** what a coincidence!; **5 das kriegst du so** (informal) you get it for nothing; **6 so um zwanzig Euro** (informal) about twenty euros.

so conjunction **so dass** so that.

so *exclamation* right!, well!; **so?** really?

sobald *conjunction* as soon as.

Socke *die* (PL *die* **Socken**) sock.

Sofa *das* (PL *die* **Sofas**) sofa.

sofort *adverb* immediately.

sogar *adverb* even.

sogleich *adverb* at once.

Sohle *die* (PL *die* **Sohlen**) sole.

Sohn *der* (PL *die* **Söhne**) son.

Soja *die* soy.

solange *conjunction* as long as.

solch *pronoun* such; **solch einer/eine/eins** one like that, somebody like that.

solcher, solche, solches *adjective, pronoun* **1** such; **ich habe solche Angst** I'm so frightened; **2 ein solcher Mann** a man like that; **eine solche Frage** a question like that; **ein solches Haus** a house like that; **3 solche** (*plural*) those; **solche wie die** people like that.

Soldat *der* (PL *die* **Soldaten**) soldier.

solide *adjective* **1** solid; **2** respectable.

Solist *der* (PL *die* **Solisten**) soloist.

Solistin *die* (PL *die* **Solistinnen**) soloist.

sollen ⋄*verb* (PRES **soll**, IMPERF **sollte**, PERF **hat gesollt**) **1** should; **sollte es regnen** if it should rain; **2** to be supposed to; **was soll das heißen?** what's that supposed to mean?; **3 sagen Sie ihr, sie soll anrufen** tell her to ring; **4 was soll ich machen?** what shall I do?; **soll ich?** shall I?; **5 was soll's!** so what!

sollte, sollten, solltest, solltet SEE **sollen**.

Sommer *der* (PL *die* **Sommer**) summer.

sommerlich *adjective* summery, summer.

Sommersprossen *plural noun* freckles.

Sonderangebot *das* (PL *die* **Sonderangebote**) special offer; **im Sonderangebot** on special offer.

sonderbar *adjective* strange, odd.

sondern *conjunction* but; **nicht nur ..., sondern auch** ... not only ..., but also ...

Song *der* (PL *die* **Songs**) song.

Sonnabend *der* (PL *die* **Sonnabende**) Saturday.

sonnabends *adverb* on Saturdays.

Sonne *die* (PL *die* **Sonnen**) sun.

sonnen *verb* (PERF **hat sich gesonnt**) **sich sonnen** to sun yourself.

Sonnenaufgang *der* sunrise.

Sonnenbrand *der* sunburn.

Sonnenbrille *die* (PL *die* **Sonnenbrillen**) sunglasses.

Sonnencreme *die* (PL *die* **Sonnencremes**) suntan lotion.

Sonnenenergie *die* solar energy.

Sonnenmilch *die* suntan lotion.

Sonnenöl *das* suntan oil.

Sonnenschein *der* sunshine.

Sonnenstich *der* sunstroke.

sonnig *adjective* sunny.

a
b
c
d
e
f
g
h
i
j
k
l
m
n
o
p
q
r
s
t
u
v
w
x
y
z

Sonntag der (PL die **Sonntage**)
Sunday.

sonntags adverb on Sundays.

sonst adverb **1** usually; **2** else; **wer
sonst?** who else?; **was sonst?** what
else?; **3 sonst noch etwas?**
anything else?; **sonst noch
jemand?** anybody else?; **4 sonst wo**
somewhere; **es kann sonst wo sein**
it could be anywhere; **5** otherwise;
**geh jetzt, sonst verpasst du den
Bus** go now, otherwise you'll miss
the bus.

sonstwo SEE **sonst**.

sooft conjunction whenever.

Sorge die (PL die **Sorgen**) worry;
sich Sorgen machen to worry.

sorgen verb (PERF **hat gesorgt**)
1 für etwas sorgen to take care of
something; **für die Musik sorgen** to
see to the music; **für jemanden
sorgen** to look after somebody;
2 dafür sorgen, dass ... to make
sure that ...; **3 sich sorgen** to
worry; **ich sorge mich um meine
Eltern** I worry about my parents.

sorgfältig adjective careful.

Sorte die (PL die **Sorten**) **1** kind;
2 brand.

Soße die (PL die **Soßen**) **1** sauce;
2 gravy; **3** dressing.

Souvenir das (PL die **Souvenirs**)
souvenir.

soviel conjunction as far as; **soviel
ich weiß** as far as I know.
soviel adverb SEE **viel**.

soweit conjunction as far as;
soweit ich weiß, ist er in Ferien as

far as I know, he's on holiday.
soweit adverb SEE **weit**.

sowenig SEE **wenig**.

sowie conjunction **1** as well as; **2** as
soon as.

sowieso adverb anyway.

sowohl adverb **sowohl ... als auch
... both ... and ...; **sowohl er wie
auch sein Freund** both he and his
friend.

sozial adjective social.

Sozialarbeiter der (PL die
Sozialarbeiter) social worker.

Sozialarbeiterin die (PL die
Sozialarbeiterinnen) social worker.

Sozialhilfe die social security.

Sozialismus der socialism.

sozialistisch adjective socialist.

Sozialkunde die social studies.

Sozialwohnung die (PL die
Sozialwohnungen) council flat.

Soziologie die sociology.

sozusagen adverb so to speak.

Spalte die (PL die **Spalten**) **1** crack;
2 column (in text).

spalten verb (PERF **hat gespalten**)
to split.

Spaniel der (PL die **Spaniels**)
Spaniel.

Spanien das Spain.

Spanier der (PL die **Spanier**)
Spaniard.

Spanierin die (PL die
Spanierinnen) Spaniard.

spanisch adjective Spanish.

Spanisch das Spanish (language).

spann SEE **spinnen**.

spannend *adjective* exciting.

Spannung *die* (PL *die* Spannungen)
1 tension; **2** suspense (*in a film or novel, for example*); **ich erwarte seine Antwort mit Spannung** I can't wait for his answer; **3** voltage.

Sparbüchse *die* (PL *die* Sparbüchsen) money box.

sparen *verb* (PERF **hat gespart**)
1 to save; **auf etwas sparen** to save up for something; **2 sich etwas sparen** not to bother with something; **sich die Mühe sparen** to save yourself the trouble; **3 an etwas sparen** to economize on something.

Spargel *der* asparagus.

Sparkasse *die* savings bank.

sparsam *adjective* **1** economical; **2** thrifty.

Sparschwein *das* (PL *die* Sparschweine) piggy bank.

Spaß *der* (PL *die* Späße) **1** fun; **zum/ aus Spaß** for fun; **das macht Spaß** it's fun; **Segeln macht mir keinen Spaß** I don't like sailing; **2 viel Spaß!** have a good time!; **3** joke; **er macht nur Spaß** he's only joking.

spät *adjective, adverb* late; **zu spät kommen** to be late; **wie spät ist es?** what time is it?

Spaten *der* (PL *die* Spaten) spade.

später *adjective* later.

spätestens *adverb* at the latest.

Spatz *der* (PL *die* Spatzen) sparrow.

Spätzle *plural noun* noodles (*South German dish*).

spazieren *verb* (PERF **ist spaziert**)
1 to stroll; **2 spazieren gehen** to go for a walk; **hast du Lust, spazieren zu gehen?** would you like to go for a walk?

spazierengehen SEE **spazieren**.

Spaziergang *der* (PL *die* Spaziergänge) walk; **einen Spaziergang machen** to go for a walk.

Speck *der* bacon.

Speiche *die* (PL *die* Speichen) spoke.

Speicher *der* (PL *die* Speicher)
1 loft, attic; **2** memory (*in computing*).

Speicherkapazität *die* storage capacity (*on hard disk*).

speichern *verb* (PERF **hat gespeichert**) **1** to store; **2** to save (*in computing*).

Speise *die* (PL *die* Speisen) **1** food; **2** dish.

Speisekarte *die* (PL *die* Speisekarten) menu.

Speisesaal *der* (PL *die* Speisesäle)
1 dining hall; **2** dining room.

Speisewagen *der* (PL *die* Speisewagen) dining car.

Spende *die* (PL *die* Spenden) donation.

spenden *verb* (PERF **hat gespendet**) **1** to donate; **2** to give.

spendieren *verb* (PERF **hat spendiert**) **jemandem etwas spendieren** to treat somebody to something.

a
b
c
d
e
f
g
h
i
j
k
l
m
n
o
p
q
r
s
t
u
v
w
x
y
z

Sperling der (PL die Sperlinge) sparrow.

Sperre die (PL die Sperren) **1** barrier; **2** ban.

sperren verb (PERF hat gesperrt) **1** to close; **2** to block (an entrance, access); **3 den Strom sperren** to cut off the electricity; **4 einen Scheck sperren** to stop a cheque; **5 ein Tier in einen Käfig sperren** to shut an animal (up) in a cage.

spezialisieren verb (PERF hat spezialisiert) **sich spezialisieren** to specialize.

Spezialität die (PL die Spezialitäten) speciality.

speziell adjective special.

Spezies die (PL die Spezies) species.

Spiegel der (PL die Spiegel) mirror.

Spiegelbild das (PL die Spiegelbilder) reflection.

Spiegelei das (PL die Spiegeleier) fried egg.

spiegeln verb (PERF hat gespiegelt) **1** to reflect; **2 sich spiegeln** to be reflected.

Spiel das (PL die Spiele) **1** game; **2 ein Spiel Karten** a pack of cards; **3 es steht viel auf dem Spiel** there's a lot at stake.

Spielautomat der (PL die Spielautomaten) gaming machine.

spielen verb (PERF hat gespielt) **1** to play; **wir spielen morgen Fußball** we're playing football tomorrow; **2** to gamble; **3** to act; **das Stück war gut gespielt** the play

was well acted; **4 der Film spielt in Rom** the film is set in Rome.

spielend adverb easily.

Spieler der (PL die Spieler) **1** player; **2** gambler.

Spielerin die (PL die Spielerinnen) **1** player; **2** gambler.

Spielfeld das (PL die Spielfelder) pitch, field.

Spielhalle die (PL die Spielhallen) amusement arcade.

Spielplatz der (PL die Spielplätze) playground.

Spielverderber der (PL die Spielverderber) spoilsport.

Spielverderberin die (PL die Spielverderberinnen) spoilsport.

Spielwaren plural noun toys.

Spielzeug das **1** toy; **2** toys.

Spinat der spinach.

Spinne die (PL die Spinnen) spider.

spinnen ⋄verb (IMPERF spann, PERF hat gesponnen) **1** to spin; **2 du spinnst!** (informal) you're mad!

Spinnennetz das (PL die Spinnennetze) **1** spider's web; **2** cobweb.

Spion der (PL die Spione) spy.

Spionage die spying, espionage.

spionieren verb (PERF hat spioniert) to spy.

Spirituosen plural noun spirits (alcohol).

spitz adjective pointed.

Spitze die (PL die Spitzen) **1** point; **2** top; **Schalke liegt jetzt an der Spitze** Schalke is top of the league at the moment; **3** peak; **von hier kann man die schneebedeckten Spitzen sehen** you can see the snow-covered peaks from here; **4** front; **an der Spitze liegen** to be in the lead; **5** lace; **6 Spitze sein** (*informal*) to be great.

spitzen *verb* (PERF **hat gespitzt**) **1** to sharpen; **2 sich auf etwas spitzen** (*informal*) to look forward to something.

Spitzname *der* (PL *die* Spitznamen) nickname.

Splitter *der* (PL *die* Splitter) splinter.

splittern *verb* (PERF **hat/ist gesplittert**) **1** to splinter; **2** to shatter.

sponsern *verb* (PERF **hat gesponsert**) to sponsor.

Sport *der* sport.

Sportgeschäft *das* (PL *die* Sportgeschäfte) sports shop.

Sporthalle *die* (PL *die* Sporthallen) sports hall.

Sportler *der* (PL *die* Sportler) sportsman.

Sportlerin *die* (PL *die* Sportlerinnen) sportswoman.

sportlich *adjective* **1** sporting; **2** sporty.

Sportplatz *der* (PL *die* Sportplätze) sports field, sports ground.

Sportschuh *der* (PL *die* Sportschuhe) trainer.

Sportverein *der* (PL *die* Sportvereine) sports club.

Sportwagen *der* (PL *die* Sportwagen) **1** sports car; **2** pushchair.

Sportzentrum *das* (PL *die* Sportzentren) sports centre.

spotten *verb* (PERF **hat gespottet**) to mock.

sprach SEE **sprechen**.

Sprache *die* (PL *die* Sprachen) **1** language; **2** speech; **etwas zur Sprache bringen** to bring something up.

Sprachführer *der* (PL *die* Sprachführer) phrase-book.

sprachlos *adjective* speechless.

sprang SEE **springen**.

Sprechblase *die* (PL *die* Sprechblasen) speech bubble.

sprechen ⋄*verb* (PRES **spricht**, IMPERF **sprach**, PERF **hat gesprochen**) **1** to speak; **Deutsch sprechen** to speak German; **mit wem spreche ich?** who's speaking? (*on the phone*); **jemanden sprechen** to speak to somebody; **2 Frau Hahn ist nicht zu sprechen** Mrs Hahn is not available; **3** to talk; **mit jemandem über etwas sprechen** to talk to somebody about something; **4** to say (*a word, sentence*).

Sprecher *der* (PL *die* Sprecher) **1** spokesman; **2** (*on TV*) announcer; **3** (*in a film*) narrator; **4** speaker.

Sprecherin *die* (PL *die* Sprecherinnen) **1** spokeswoman; **2** (*on TV*) announcer; **3** (*in a film*) narrator; **4** speaker.

a
b
c
d
e
f
g
h
i
j
k
l
m
n
o
p
q
r
s
t
u
v
w
x
y
z

Sprechstunde die (PL die Sprechstunden) surgery.

spricht SEE **sprechen**.

Sprichwort das (PL die Sprichwörter) proverb.

springen ◇verb (IMPERF sprang, PERF ist gesprungen) 1 to jump; 2 to bounce (of a ball); 3 to dive; 4 to crack.

Spritze die (PL die Spritzen) 1 syringe; 2 injection; 3 hose.

spritzen verb (PERF hat gespritzt) 1 to inject; 2 to splash; **du hast mich nass gespritzt** you've splashed me; 3 to spray; 4 to spit (of fat); 5 (PERF ist gespritzt) to splash up.

Sprudel der (PL die Sprudel) sparkling mineral water.

sprühen verb (PERF hat gesprüht) 1 to spray; 2 to sparkle (of eyes); 3 (PERF ist gesprüht) to fly (of sparks); **die Funken sind in alle Richtungen gesprüht** sparks flew in all directions.

Sprung der (PL die Sprünge) 1 jump; 2 dive; 3 crack (in china, glass).

Sprungbrett das (PL die Sprungbretter) diving board.

spucken verb (PERF hat gespuckt) to spit.

Spülbecken das (PL die Spülbecken) sink.

spülen verb (PERF hat gespült) 1 to rinse; 2 to wash up; 3 to flush.

Spülmaschine die (PL die Spülmaschinen) dishwasher.

Spülmittel das (PL die Spülmittel) washing-up liquid.

Spültuch das (PL die Spültücher) dishcloth.

Spur die (PL die Spuren) 1 track; **auf der falschen Spur sein** to be on the wrong track; **jemandem auf die Spur kommen** to get on to somebody; 2 lane; **in der Spur bleiben** to keep in lane; 3 trail; 4 trace.

spüren verb (PERF hat gespürt) 1 to feel; 2 to sense.

Staat der (PL die Staaten) state.

staatlich adjective state; **eine staatliche Schule** a state school. **staatlich** adverb by the state.

Staatsangehörigkeit die (PL die Staatsangehörigkeiten) nationality.

stabil adjective 1 stable; 2 sturdy.

stach SEE **stechen**.

Stachel der (PL die Stacheln) 1 spine; 2 spike; 3 sting.

Stachelbeere die (PL die Stachelbeeren) gooseberry.

Stacheldraht der barbed wire.

Stadion das (PL die Stadien) stadium.

Stadium das (PL die Stadien) stage.

Stadt die (PL die Städte) town, city.

städtisch adjective 1 urban; 2 municipal.

Stadtmitte die town centre.

Stadtplan der (PL die Stadtpläne) street map.

Stadtrand der outskirts (of town); **am Stadtrand von Lübeck** on the outskirts of Lübeck.

Stadtrat der (PL die Stadträte) town or city council.

Stadtrundfahrt die (PL die Stadtrundfahrten) sightseeing tour (of a town).

Stadtteil der (PL die Stadtteile) district.

Stahl der steel.

stahl SEE **stehlen**.

Stall der (PL die Ställe) **1** stable; **2** cowshed; **3** pigsty.

Stamm der (PL die Stämme) **1** trunk; **2** tribe; **3** stem (of a word).

Stammbaum der (PL die Stammbäume) family tree.

stammen verb (PERF hat gestammt) **aus Deutschland stammen** to come from Germany.

Stammgast der (PL die Stammgäste) regular customer (in a pub or restaurant).

stand SEE **stehen**.

Stand der (PL die Stände) **1** state; **etwas auf den neuesten Stand bringen** to bring something up to date; **2** score (in a game); **3** stall (for a horse); **4** stand (in a fair); **5** level (of water, of a river).

ständig adjective constant.

Standort der (PL die Standorte) position, location; **von ihrem Standort aus konnte sie nichts sehen** she couldn't see anything from where she was standing.

Stange die (PL die Stangen) **1** bar; **2** pole.

stank SEE **stinken**.

starb SEE **sterben**.

stark adjective **1** strong; **2** heavy (rain, traffic); **3** severe (frost, pain); **4** (informal) great; **das ist stark!** that's great!

Stärke die (PL die Stärken) **1** strength; **2** starch.

starrsinnig adjective obstinate.

Start der (PL die Starts) **1** start; **2** take-off.

Startbahn die (PL die Startbahnen) runway.

starten verb (PERF ist gestartet) **1** (of a plane) to take off; **2** (PERF hat gestartet) to start, to launch (a campaign).

Station die (PL die Stationen) **1** station; **2** stop; **Station machen** to stop over; **3** ward (in hospital).

statt conjunction, preposition (+ GEN) instead of; **statt zu arbeiten** instead of working; **sie ging statt ihrer Schwester** she went instead of her sister.

stattdessen conjunction instead.

stattfinden ⋄verb (IMPERF fand statt, PERF hat stattgefunden) to take place.

Stau der (PL die Staus) **1** congestion; **2** traffic jam.

Staub der dust.

staubig adjective dusty.

a
b
c
d
e
f
g
h
i
j
k
l
m
n
o
p
q
r
s
t
u
v
w
x
y
z

staubsaugen *verb* (PERF **hat staubgesaugt**) to vacuum.

Staubsauger *der* (PL *die* **Staubsauger**) vacuum cleaner.

staunen *verb* (PERF **hat gestaunt**) to be amazed.

Steak *das* (PL *die* **Steaks**) steak.

stechen ⬦*verb* (PRES **sticht**, IMPERF **stach**, PERF **hat gestochen**) **1** to prick; **sich in den Finger stechen** to prick your finger; **2** to sting, to bite (*of an insect*); **3 mit etwas in etwas stechen** to jab something into something.

Steckbrief *der* (PL *die* **Steckbriefe**) description (*of a wanted person*).

Steckdose *die* (PL *die* **Steckdosen**) socket.

stecken *verb* (PERF **hat gesteckt**) **1** to put; **du musst die Münze in den Schlitz stecken** put the coin into the slot; **2** to pin; **3 wo steckt er?** where is he?; **4 stecken bleiben** to get stuck; **den Schlüssel stecken lassen** to leave the key in the lock.

Stecker *der* (PL *die* **Stecker**) plug.

Stecknadel *die* (PL *die* **Stecknadeln**) pin.

Steckrübe *die* (PL *die* **Steckrüben**) turnip.

stehen ⬦*verb* (IMPERF **stand**, PERF **hat gestanden**) **1** to stand; **2** to be; **es steht zwei zu zwei** the score is two all; **wie steht's?** what's the score?; **3** to have stopped (*of a clock or a machine*); **4 es steht schlecht um ihn** he's in a bad way; **na, wie**

steht's? how are you?; **5 stehen bleiben** to stop; **die Uhr ist stehen geblieben** the clock has stopped; **6 in der Zeitung steht, dass** ... it says in the paper that ...; **7 jemandem (gut) stehen** to suit somebody; **8 zu jemandem stehen** to stand by somebody; **9 sich gut stehen** to be on good terms; **10 zum Stehen kommen** to come to a standstill.

stehenbleiben SEE **stehen**.

stehlen ⬦*verb* (PRES **stiehlt**, IMPERF **stahl**, PERF **hat gestohlen**) to steal.

steif *adjective* stiff.

steigen *verb* (IMPERF **stieg**, PERF **ist gestiegen**) **1** to climb; **auf eine Leiter steigen** to climb up a ladder; **auf ein Fahrrad steigen** to get on a bike; **in den Bus steigen** to get on the bus; **2** to rise.

steil *adjective* steep.

Stein *der* (PL *die* **Steine**) stone.

Steinbock *der* (PL *die* **Steinböcke**) **1** ibex; **2** Capricorn; **Petra ist Steinbock** Petra's Capricorn.

Steinbruch *der* (PL *die* **Steinbrüche**) quarry.

Stelle *die* (PL *die* **Stellen**) **1** place, spot; **an deiner Stelle** in your place; **an dritter Stelle liegen** to be in third place; **2** job; **eine freie Stelle** a vacancy; **3** authority; **4 auf der Stelle** immediately.

stellen *verb* (PERF **hat gestellt**) **1** to put; **2** to set (*a watch, task*); **3 zur Verfügung stellen** to provide; **4 lauter stellen** to turn up; **leiser stellen** to turn down; **die Heizung**

höher stellen to turn the heating up; **5 sich krank stellen** to pretend to be ill; **6 sich stellen** to give yourself up; **7 die Kinder stellten sich an die Wand** the children stood against the wall.

Stellenanzeige die (PL die Stellenanzeigen) job advertisement.

Stellplatz der (PL die Stellplätze) pitch (*for a tent*).

Stellung die (PL die Stellungen) position.

stellvertretend *adjective*
1 acting; **2** deputy; **der stellvertretende Feuerwehrhauptmann** the deputy chief fire officer.

Stellvertreter der (PL die Stellvertreter) **1** deputy; **2** representative.

Stellvertreterin die (PL die Stellvertreterinnen) **1** deputy; **2** representative.

Stempel der (PL die Stempel) **1** stamp; **2** postmark.

stempeln *verb* (PERF hat gestempelt) to stamp.

Steppdecke die (PL die Steppdecken) quilt.

sterben ◇*verb* (PRES stirbt, IMPERF starb, PERF ist gestorben) to die.

Stereoanlage die (PL die Stereoanlagen) stereo (system).

Stern der (PL die Sterne) star.

Sternzeichen das (PL die Sternzeichen) star sign; **was ist dein Sternzeichen?** what star sign are you?

Steuer[1] das (PL die Steuer) **1** (steering) wheel; **2** helm.

Steuer[2] die (PL die Steuern) tax.

steuern *verb* (PERF hat gesteuert) **1** to steer; **2** to control; **3** (PERF ist gesteuert) to head.

Stewardess die (PL die Stewardessen) stewardess, air hostess.

Stich der (PL die Stiche) **1** prick; **2** stab; **3** sting, bite (*of an insect*); **4** stitch; **5** trick (*when playing cards*); **6** engraving; **7 jemanden im Stich lassen** to leave somebody in the lurch.

sticht SEE **stechen**.

sticken *verb* (PERF hat gestickt) to embroider.

Stickstoff der nitrogen.

Stiefbruder der (PL die Stiefbrüder) stepbrother.

Stiefel der (PL die Stiefel) boot.

Stiefkind das (PL die Stiefkinder) stepchild.

Stiefmutter die (PL die Stiefmütter) stepmother.

Stiefschwester die (PL die Stiefschwestern) stepsister.

Stiefvater der (PL die Stiefväter) stepfather.

stieg SEE **steigen**.

stiehlt SEE **stehlen**.

Stiel der (PL die Stiele) **1** handle; **2** stem.

a
b
c
d
e
f
g
h
i
j
k
l
m
n
o
p
q
r
s
t
u
v
w
x
y
z

Stier der (PL die Stiere) 1 bull; 2 Taurus; **Andrea ist Stier** Andrea's Taurus.

stieß SEE **stoßen**.

Stift der (PL die Stifte) 1 pencil; 2 crayon; 3 tack (*nail*).

Stil der (PL die Stile) style.

still *adjective* 1 quiet; 2 still.

stillen *verb* (PERF **hat gestillt**) 1 to quench; 2 to breast-feed.

stillhalten ◇*verb* (PRES **hält still**, IMPERF **hielt still**, PERF **hat stillgehalten**) to keep still.

Stimme die (PL die Stimmen) 1 voice; 2 vote.

stimmen *verb* (PERF **hat gestimmt**) 1 to be right; **stimmt das?** is that right?; 2 to vote; 3 to tune.

Stimmung die (PL die Stimmungen) 1 mood; 2 atmosphere.

stinken ◇*verb* (IMPERF **stank**, PERF **hat gestunken**) to smell, to stink.

Stipendium das (PL die Stipendien) 1 scholarship; 2 grant.

stirbt SEE **sterben**.

Stirn die (PL die Stirnen) forehead.

Stock[1] der (PL die Stöcke) stick.

Stock[2] der (PL die Stock) floor; **im ersten Stock** on the first floor.

Stockwerk das (PL die Stockwerke) floor.

Stoff der (PL die Stoffe) 1 material, fabric; 2 substance.

stöhnen *verb* (PERF **hat gestöhnt**) to groan.

stolpern *verb* (PERF **ist gestolpert**) 1 to stumble; 2 to trip; **ich bin über einen Stein gestolpert** I tripped on a stone.

stolz *adjective* proud.

stoppen *verb* (PERF **hat gestoppt**) to stop.

Stöpsel der (PL die Stöpsel) 1 plug; 2 stopper.

stören *verb* (PERF **hat gestört**) 1 to disturb; **Bitte nicht stören** please do not disturb; 2 to bother; **das stört mich nicht** that doesn't bother me; 3 **stört es Sie, wenn ich das Fenster aufmache?** do you mind if I open the window?; **der Empfang ist gestört** there's interference (*on a TV*).

Störung die (PL die Störungen) 1 disturbance, interruption; **entschuldigen Sie die Störung** I'm sorry to bother you; 2 interference; **eine technische Störung** a technical fault.

Stoß der (PL die Stöße) 1 push; 2 pile; **ein Stoß Handtücher** a pile of towels.

stoßen ◇*verb* (PRES **stößt**, IMPERF **stieß**, PERF **hat gestoßen**) 1 to push; 2 to kick; 3 **sich den Kopf stoßen** to hit your head; **ich habe mir den Kopf an dem Balken gestoßen** I hit my head on the beam; **sich stoßen** to bump yourself; 4 **sich an etwas stoßen** to object to something; 5 (PERF **ist gestoßen**) **gegen etwas stoßen** to bump into something; 6 (PERF **ist gestoßen**) **auf etwas stoßen** to come across something.

Stoßstange die (PL die Stoßstangen) bumper.

Stoßzeit die (PL die Stoßzeiten) rush hour.

stottern verb (PERF hat gestottert) to stutter.

Strafe die (PL die Strafen) **1** punishment; **2** fine; **3** penalty.

Straftat die (PL die Straftaten) crime.

Strahl der (PL die Strahlen) **1** ray, beam; **2** jet.

strahlen verb (PERF hat gestrahlt) **1** to shine; **2** to beam.

Strahlung die (PL die Strahlungen) radiation.

Strand der (PL die Strände) beach.

Straße die (PL die Straßen) street, road; **in welcher Straße ist der Supermarkt?** which street is the supermarket in?; **über die Straße gehen** to cross the road; **jemanden auf die Straße setzen** (informal) to give somebody the sack; **mein Wirt hat mich einfach auf die Straße gesetzt** (informal) my landlord just turned me out (of a flat or room).

Straßenbahn die (PL die Straßenbahnen) tram; **mit der Straßenbahn fahren** to go by tram.

Straßenraub der **1** mugging; **2** street robbery.

Straßenräuber der (PL die Straßenräuber) mugger.

Straßenüberführung die (PL die Straßenüberführungen) **1** footbrige; **2** roadbridge.

Straßenunterführung die (PL die Straßenunterführungen) **1** subway; **2** underpass.

Strauch der (PL die Sträucher) bush.

Strauß ¹ der (PL die Sträuße) bunch of flowers, bouquet.

Strauß ² der (PL die Strauße) ostrich.

Streber der (PL die Streber) swot.

Strecke die (PL die Strecken) **1** distance; **2** route; **3** line (rail).

strecken verb (PERF hat gestreckt) **1** to stretch (your arms, legs); **2** sich strecken to stretch.

Streich der (PL die Streiche) trick.

streicheln verb (PERF hat gestreichelt) to stroke.

streichen ◇verb (IMPERF strich, PERF hat gestrichen) **1** to paint; **'frisch gestrichen'** 'wet paint'; **2** to spread (with butter); **3** to delete; **4** to cancel (a flight); **5** jemandem den Kopf streichen to stroke somebody's head.

Streichholz das (PL die Streichhölzer) match.

Streifen der (PL die Streifen) **1** stripe; **2** strip.

Streik der (PL die Streiks) strike.

streiken verb (PERF hat gestreikt) to strike.

Streit der (PL die Streite) quarrel, argument.

streiten ◇verb (IMPERF stritt, PERF hat gestritten) **1** to quarrel, to argue; **2** sich streiten to quarrel, to argue.

streng adjective strict.

Stress *der* stress.

stressig *adjective* stressful.

streuen *verb* (PERF **hat gestreut**)
1 to spread; **die Straßen streuen** to grit the roads; **2** to sprinkle.

Strich *der* (PL *die* **Striche**) **1** line;
2 stroke.

strich SEE **streichen**.

Strichpunkt *der* (PL *die* **Strichpunkte**) semicolon.

stricken *verb* (PERF **hat gestrickt**) to knit.

Strickjacke *die* (PL *die* **Strickjacken**) cardigan.

stritt SEE **streiten**.

Stroh *das* straw.

Strohhalm *der* (PL *die* **Strohhalme**) straw (*for drinking*).

Strom *der* (PL *die* **Ströme**) **1** river;
2 stream (*of people or blood*); **es regnet in Strömen** it's pouring with rain; **3** current.

Stromausfall *der* (PL *die* **Stromausfälle**) power failure.

strömen *verb* (PERF **ist geströmt**) to stream.

Strömung *die* (PL *die* **Strömungen**) current.

Strudel *der* (PL *die* **Strudel**) strudel (*kind of Austrian cake*).

Strumpf *der* (PL *die* **Strümpfe**)
1 stocking; **2** sock.

Strumpfhose *die* (PL *die* **Strumpfhosen**) tights.

Stube *die* (PL *die* **Stuben**) room.

Stück *das* (PL *die* **Stücke**) **1** piece;
2 item; **ein Euro das Stück** one euro each; **3** play.

Stückchen *das* (PL *die* **Stückchen**) little piece.

Student *der* (PL *die* **Studenten**) student.

Studentin *die* (PL *die* **Studentinnen**) student.

studieren *verb* (PERF **hat studiert**) to study; **Horst studiert Mathematik** Horst is studying mathematics.

Studium *das* (PL *die* **Studien**) studies.

Stufe *die* (PL *die* **Stufen**) **1** step;
'Vorsicht Stufe' 'mind the step';
2 stage (*of development*).

Stuhl *der* (PL *die* **Stühle**) chair.

stumm *adjective* **1** dumb; **2** silent.

stumpf *adjective* **1** blunt; **2** dull;
3 ein stumpfer Winkel an obtuse angle.

Stunde *die* (PL *die* **Stunden**) **1** hour;
2 lesson.

stundenlang *adverb* for hours.

Stundenplan *der* (PL *die* **Stundenpläne**) timetable.

stündlich *adjective* hourly.

stur *adjective* stubborn.

Sturm *der* (PL *die* **Stürme**) storm.

stürmisch *adjective* stormy.

Sturz *der* (PL *die* **Stürze**) **1** fall;
2 overthrow.

a b c d e f g h i j k l m n o p q r **s** t u v w x y z

stürzen *verb* (PERF **ist gestürzt**)
1 to fall; **2** to rush (*into a room*);
3 (PERF **hat gestürzt**) to overthrow;
4 (PERF **hat sich gestürzt**) **er hat
sich aus dem Fenster gestürzt** he
threw himself out of the window;
sich auf jemanden stürzen to
pounce on somebody.

Sturzhelm *der* (PL *die* **Sturzhelme**)
crash helmet.

stützen *verb* (PERF **hat gestützt**) to
support; **sich auf jemanden
stützen** to lean on somebody.

Subjekt *das* (PL *die* **Subjekte**)
subject.

Substantiv *das* (PL *die*
Substantive) noun.

subtil *adjective* subtle.

Subvention *die* (PL *die*
Subventionen) subsidy.

subventionieren *verb* (PERF **hat
subventioniert**) to subsidize.

Suche *die* (PL *die* **Suchen**) search.

suchen *verb* (PERF **hat gesucht**)
1 to look for; **'Zimmer gesucht'**
'room wanted'; **2** to search.

süchtig *adjective* addicted.

Süchtige *der/die* (PL *die* **Süchtigen**)
addict.

Südafrika *das* South Africa.

Südamerika *das* South America.

Süden *der* south.

südlich *adjective* **1** southern;
2 southerly.
südlich *adverb*, *preposition* (+ GEN)
südlich von Wien south of Vienna;
südlich der Stadt to the south of the
town.

Südosten *der* south-east.

Südpol *der* South Pole.

Südwesten *der* south-west.

Summe *die* (PL *die* **Summen**) sum.

summen *verb* (PERF **hat gesummt**)
1 to hum; **2** to buzz.

Sünde *die* (PL *die* **Sünden**) sin.

super *adjective* (*informal*) great.

Supermarkt *der* (PL *die*
Supermärkte) supermarket.

Suppe *die* (PL *die* **Suppen**) soup.

Surfen *das* surf.

surfen *verb* (PERF **hat gesurft**) to
surf (*in the sea, on the Internet*); **im
Internet surfen** to surf the Internet.

Surfer *der* (PL *die* **Surfer**) surfer (*on
the sea and Internet*).

Surferin *die* (PL *die* **Surferinnen**)
surfer (*on the sea and Internet*).

süß *adjective* sweet.

Süßigkeit *die* (PL *die* **Süßigkeiten**)
sweet.

Sweatshirt *die* (PL *die*
Sweatshirts) sweatshirt.

symbolisch *adjective* symbolic.

sympathisch *adjective* likeable.

Symphonie *die* (PL *die*
Symphonien) SEE **Sinfonie**.

Synagoge *die* (PL *die* **Synagogen**)
synagogue.

synthetisch *adjective* synthetic.

System *das* (PL *die* **Systeme**)
system.

Szene *die* (PL *die* **Szenen**) scene.

a
b
c
d
e
f
g
h
i
j
k
l
m
n
o
p
q
r
s
t
u
v
w
x
y
z

Tt

Tabak der (PL die **Tabake**) tobacco.

Tabelle die (PL die **Tabellen**) table.

Tablett das (PL die **Tabletts**) tray.

Tablette die (PL die **Tabletten**)
tablet.

Tafel die (PL die **Tafeln**) **1** board,
blackboard; **ein Wort an die Tafel
schreiben** to write a word on the
blackboard; **2 eine Tafel
Schokolade** a bar of chocolate.

Tag der (PL die **Tage**) day; **guten Tag**
hello; **am Tag** in the daytime.

Tagebuch das (PL die **Tagebücher**)
diary.

tagelang adverb for days.

Tagesanbruch der dawn.

Tagesausflug der (PL die
Tagesausflüge) day trip.

Tageskarte die (PL die
Tageskarten) **1** today's menu;
2 day ticket.

Tageslicht das daylight.

Tageslichtprojektor der (PL die
Tageslichtprojektoren) overhead
projector.

Tagesmutter die (PL die
Tagesmütter) childminder.

Tagesschau die (PL die
Tagesschauen) news (on
television).

Tageszeitung die (PL die
Tageszeitungen) daily paper.

täglich adjective daily; **sein
täglicher Besuch** his daily visit.

täglich adverb daily; **zweimal
täglich** twice daily, twice a day.

tagsüber adverb during the day.

Taille die (PL die **Taillen**) waist.

Takt der (PL die **Takte**) **1** tact; **2** time;
im Takt in time to the music;
3 rhythm.

taktlos adjective tactless.

taktvoll adjective tactful.

Tal das (PL die **Täler**) valley.

Talent das (PL die **Talente**) talent.

Tampon der (PL die **Tampons**)
tampon.

Tang der seaweed.

Tank der (PL die **Tanks**) tank.

tanken verb (PERF **hat getankt**) to
fill up (with petrol) to get petrol.

Tanker der (PL die **Tanker**) tanker
(on sea).

Tankstelle die (PL die **Tankstellen**)
petrol station.

Tankwagen der (PL die
Tankwagen) tanker (on road).

Tankwart der (PL die **Tankwarte**)
petrol-pump attendant.

Tanne die (PL die **Tannen**) fir.

Tannenbaum der (PL die
Tannenbäume) **1** fir tree;
2 Christmas tree.

Tante die (PL die **Tanten**) aunt.

Tanz der (PL die **Tänze**) dance.

tanzen verb (PERF **hat getanzt**) to
dance.

Tänzer der (PL die **Tänzer**) dancer.

Tänzerin die (PL die **Tänzerinnen**)
dancer.

Tapete die (PL die **Tapeten**) wallpaper.

tapezieren verb (PERF **hat tapeziert**) to (wall)paper.

tapfer adjective brave.

Tapferkeit die bravery.

Tarif der (PL die **Tarife**) 1 tariff; 2 rate.

Tasche die (PL die **Taschen**) 1 bag; 2 pocket; **er hat es aus eigener Tasche bezahlt** he paid for it out of his own pocket; **Max hat mir fünf Euro aus der Tasche gezogen** (informal) Max wangled five euros out of me.

Taschenbuch das (PL die **Taschenbücher**) paperback.

Taschendieb der (PL die **Taschendiebe**) pickpocket.

Taschengeld das pocket money.

Taschenlampe die (PL die **Taschenlampen**) torch.

Taschenmesser das (PL die **Taschenmesser**) penknife.

Taschenrechner der (PL die **Taschenrechner**) pocket calculator.

Taschentuch das (PL die **Taschentücher**) handkerchief.

Tasse die (PL die **Tassen**) cup.

Tastatur die (PL die **Tastaturen**) keyboard.

Taste die (PL die **Tasten**) 1 key; 2 button (on a phone or a machine).

tasten verb (PERF **hat getastet**) 1 to feel; 2 **sich tasten** to feel your way.

Tat die (PL die **Taten**) 1 action; 2 **eine gute Tat** a good deed; 3 crime; 4 **in der Tat** indeed.

tat SEE **tun**.

Täter der (PL die **Täter**) 1 culprit; 2 offender.

Täterin die (PL die **Täterinnen**) 1 culprit; 2 offender.

tätig adjective active.

Tätigkeit die (PL die **Tätigkeiten**) 1 activity; 2 job.

Tätigkeit die (PL die **Tätigkeiten**) activity.

Tätowierung die (PL die **Tätowierungen**) tattoo.

Tatsache die (PL die **Tatsachen**) fact.

tatsächlich adjective actual. **tatsächlich** adverb 1 actually; 2 really.

Tau¹ der dew.

Tau² das (PL die **Taue**) rope.

taub adjective deaf.

Taube die (PL die **Tauben**) 1 pigeon; 2 dove.

tauchen verb (PERF **hat getaucht**) 1 to dip; 2 (PERF **hat/ist getaucht**) ('ist getaucht' is used when movement is described) to dive.

Taucher der (PL die **Taucher**) diver.

Taucherbrille die (PL die **Taucherbrillen**) diving goggles.

Taucherin die (PL die **Taucherinnen**) diver.

tauen verb (PERF **ist getaut**) 1 to melt; 2 **es taut** it's thawing.

a
b
c
d
e
f
g
h
i
j
k
l
m
n
o
p
q
r
s
t
u
v
w
x
y
z

Taufe die (PL die Taufen) christening.

taufen verb (PERF hat getauft) **1** to christen; **2** to baptize.

taugen verb (PERF hat getaugt) **nichts taugen** to be no good.

tauschen verb (PERF hat getauscht) to exchange, to swap.

tausend number a thousand.

Taxi das (PL die Taxis) taxi.

Taxifahrer der (PL die Taxifahrer) taxi driver.

Taxifahrerin die (PL die Taxifahrerinnen) taxi driver.

Taxistand der (PL die Taxistände) taxi rank.

Technik die (PL die Techniken) **1** technology; **2** technique.

Techniker der (PL die Techniker) technician.

Technikerin die (PL die Technikerinnen) technician.

technisch adjective **1** technical; **2** technological.

Technologie die technology.

technologisch adjective technological.

Teddybär der (PL die Teddybären) teddy bear.

Tee der (PL die Tee(s)) tea; **ein Tee mit Zitrone** one lemon tea; **ein Tee mit Milch** one tea with milk.

Teebeutel der (PL die Teebeutel) tea bag.

Teekanne die (PL die Teekannen) teapot.

Teelöffel der (PL die Teelöffel) teaspoon.

Teenager der (PL die Teenager) teenager.

Teich der (PL die Teiche) pond.

Teig der (PL die Teige) **1** dough; **2** pastry; **3** mixture.

Teigwaren plural noun pasta.

Teil[1] der (PL die Teile) **1** part; **der zweite Teil** the second part; **zum größten Teil** for the most part; **2 zum Teil** partly; **3** share; **mein Teil am Gewinn** my share of the profit.

Teil[2] das (PL die Teile) **1** spare part; **2** part (of a car, machine); **3** unit (of furniture).

teilen verb (PERF hat geteilt) **1** to divide; **2 sich etwas mit jemandem teilen** to share something with somebody.

teilnehmen ◇verb (PRES nimmt teil, IMPERF nahm teil, PERF hat teilgenommen) **an etwas teilnehmen** to take part in something.

Teilnehmer der (PL die Teilnehmer) **1** participant; **2** competitor.

Teilnehmerin die (PL die Teilnehmerinnen) **1** participant; **2** competitor.

teils adverb partly.

Teilung die (PL die Teilungen) division.

Teilzeitarbeit die part-time work.

Telefax das (PL die Telefax(e)) fax.

Telefon das (PL die Telefone) telephone.

Telefonanruf der (PL die Telefonanrufe) phone call.

Telefonbuch das (PL die Telefonbücher) telephone directory, phone book.

Telefongespräch das (PL die Telefongespräche) telephone call.

Telefonhörer der (PL die Telefonhörer) receiver.

telefonieren verb (PERF hat telefoniert) to telephone, to make a phone call.

telefonisch adjective telephone. **telefonisch** adverb by telephone; **er ist telefonisch nicht erreichbar** he can't be contacted by phone.

Telefonkarte die (PL die Telefonkarten) phone card.

Telefonnummer die (PL die Telefonnummern) telephone number.

Telefonzelle die (PL die Telefonzellen) phone box, call box.

Teleskop das (PL die Teleskope) telescope.

Teller der (PL die Teller) plate.

Temperatur die (PL die Temperaturen) temperature.

Tempo das (PL die Tempos) speed; **Tempo Tempo!** (*informal*) hurry up!

Tendenz die (PL die Tendenzen) **1** trend; **2** tendency.

tendieren verb (PERF hat tendiert) **zu etwas tendieren** to tend towards something.

Tennis das tennis.

Tennisplatz der (PL die Tennisplätze) tennis court.

Tennisschläger der (PL die Tennisschläger) tennis racket.

Tennisspieler der (PL die Tennisspieler) tennis player.

Tennisspielerin die (PL die Tennisspielerinnen) tennis player.

Teppich der (PL die Teppiche) **1** carpet; **2** rug.

Termin der (PL die Termine) **1** date; **einen Termin vereinbaren** to fix a date; **2** appointment; **3** der letzte **Termin** the deadline.

Terminal[1] der (PL die Terminals) terminal.

Terminal[2] das (PL die Terminals) (computer) terminal.

Terrasse die (PL die Terrassen) terrace.

Terror der terror.

Terrorismus der terrorism.

Terrorist der (PL die Terroristen) terrorist.

Terroristin die (PL die Terroristinnen) terrorist.

Tesafilm™ der Sellotape™.

Test der (PL die Tests) test; **ein Test zum Hörverständnis** a listening comprehension test.

testen verb (PERF hat getestet) to test.

teuer adjective expensive; **wie teuer?** how much?

Teufel der (PL die Teufel) devil.

Text der (PL die Texte) **1** text; **2** lyrics; **3** caption.

Textverarbeitung die word processing.

Theater das (PL die Theater) **1** theatre; **2** (*informal*) fuss.

Theaterstück das (PL die Theaterstücke) play.

Theke die (PL die Theken) **1** bar; **2** counter.

Thema das (PL die Themen) subject, topic.

Themenpark der (PL die Themenparks) theme park.

Themse die Thames.

theoretisch *adjective* theoretical. **theoretisch** *adverb* in theory.

Theorie die (PL die Theorien) theory.

Therapie die (PL die Therapien) therapy.

Thermometer das (PL die Thermometer) thermometer.

Thron der (PL die Throne) throne.

Thunfisch der (PL die Thunfische) tuna.

Thymian der thyme.

tief *adjective* **1** deep; **2** low.

Tiefe die (PL die Tiefen) depth.

Tiefgarage die (PL die Tiefgaragen) underground car park.

Tiefkühlfach das (PL die Tiefkühlfächer) freezer compartment.

Tiefkühlkost die frozen food.

Tiefkühltruhe die (PL die Tiefkühltruhen) freezer.

Tiefsttemperatur die (PL die Tiefsttemperaturen) minimum temperature.

Tier das (PL die Tiere) animal.

Tierarzt der (PL die Tierärzte) vet.

Tierärztin die (PL die Tierärztinnen) vet.

Tiergarten der (PL die Tiergärten) zoo.

Tierkreis der zodiac.

Tierpark der (PL die Tierparks) zoo.

Tiger der (PL die Tiger) tiger.

Tinte die (PL die Tinten) ink.

Tintenfisch der (PL die Tintenfische) **1** octopus; **2** squid.

Tipp der (PL die Tipps) tip.

tippen *verb* (PERF hat getippt) **1** to type; **2** to tap; **3 auf etwas tippen** to bet on something; **ich tippe auf ihn** I'm tipping him to win; **im Lotto tippen** to do the lottery.

Tisch der (PL die Tische) **1** table; **2 nach Tisch** after the meal.

Tischdecke die (PL die Tischdecken) tablecloth.

Tischler der (PL die Tischler) joiner, carpenter.

Tischtennis das table tennis.

Tischtuch das (PL die Tischtücher) tablecloth.

Titel der (PL die Titel) title.

Toast der (PL die Toasts) toast.

toben *verb* (PERF hat getobt) **1** to rage; **2** to go mad; **3** to charge about.

a b c d e f g h i j k l m n o p q r s t u v w x y z

Tochter *die* (PL *die* **Töchter**) daughter.

Tod *der* (PL *die* **Tode**) death.

Todesstrafe *die* death penalty.

tödlich *adjective* **1** fatal; **2** deadly.

todmüde *adjective* (*informal*) dead tired.

todschick *adjective* (*informal*) trendy.

Toilette *die* (PL *die* **Toiletten**) toilet; **auf die Toilette gehen** to go to the toilet.

Toilettenpapier *das* toilet paper.

toll *adjective* (*informal*) brilliant.

Tollwut *die* rabies.

Tomate *die* (PL *die* **Tomaten**) tomato.

Tomatenmark *das* tomato purée.

Ton¹ *der* (PL *die* **Töne**) **1** sound; **er hat keinen Ton gesagt** he didn't make a sound; **2 große Töne spucken** (*informal*) to talk big; **3** tone; **einen frechen Ton anschlagen** to adopt a cheeky tone; **4** note; **5** shade (*of colour*); **6** stress (*in pronunciation*).

Ton² *der* clay.

Tonband *das* (PL *die* **Tonbänder**) tape.

Tonbandgerät *das* (PL *die* **Tonbandgeräte**) tape recorder.

Tonne *die* (PL *die* **Tonnen**) **1** barrel; **2** bin (*for rubbish*); **3** tonne, ton.

Topf *der* (PL *die* **Töpfe**) **1** pot; **2** pan.

Töpferei *die* (PL *die* **Töpfereien**) pottery.

Tor *das* (PL *die* **Tore**) **1** gate; **2** goal; **mit 3 zu 2 Toren gewinnen** to win by 3 goals to 2.

Torte *die* (PL *die* **Torten**) **1** gateau; **2** cake.

Torwart *der* (PL *die* **Torwarte**) goalkeeper.

tot *adjective* dead.

total *adjective* complete.
total *adverb* completely; **du bist total verrückt** you're totally mad.

Tote *der/die* (PL *die* **Toten**) **1** dead man/woman; **die Toten** the dead; **2** fatality.

töten *verb* (PERF **hat getötet**) to kill.

totlachen *verb* (*informal*) (PERF **hat sich totgelacht**) **sich totlachen** to laugh your head off.

Tour *die* (PL *die* **Touren**) **1** tour; **2** trip; **3 auf diese Tour** (*informal*) in this way.

Tourismus *der* tourism.

Tourist *der* (PL *die* **Touristen**) tourist.

Touristeninformation *die* (PL *die* **Touristeninformationen**) **1** tourist information office; **2** tourist information.

Touristin *die* (PL *die* **Touristinnen**) tourist.

Tournee *die* (PL *die* **Tournees**) tour.

traben *verb* (PERF **ist getrabt**) to trot.

Tradition *die* (PL *die* **Traditionen**) tradition.

traditionell *adjective* traditional.

traf SEE **treffen**.

tragbar *adjective* **1** portable; **2** wearable.

tragen ◇*verb* (PRES **trägt**, IMPERF **trug**, PERF **hat getragen**) **1** to carry; **2** to wear; **sie trug ein weißes Kleid** she wore a white dress; **man trägt wieder kurz** short skirts are in fashion again; **3** to bear; **die Verantwortung für etwas tragen** to be responsible for something; **4** to support; **die Organisation trägt sich selbst** the organization is self-supporting.

Träger *der* (PL die **Träger**) **1** porter; **2** bearer (*of a name, title*); **3** strap (*of a dress*); **4** girder.

Tragetasche *die* (PL die **Tragetaschen**) carrier bag.

tragisch *adjective* tragic.

Tragödie *die* (PL die **Tragödien**) tragedy.

Trainer *der* (PL die **Trainer**) coach, trainer.

trainieren *verb* (PERF **hat trainiert**) **1** to coach; **2** to train.

Training *das* training.

Trainingsanzug *der* (PL die **Trainingsanzüge**) tracksuit.

Trainingsschuh *der* (PL die **Trainingsschuhe**) trainer (*shoe*).

Traktor *der* (PL die **Traktoren**) tractor.

trampen *verb* (PERF **ist getrampt**) to hitchhike.

Trampen *das* hitchhiking.

Tramper *der* (PL die **Tramper**) hitchhiker.

Tramperin *die* (PL die **Tramperinnen**) hitchhiker.

Träne *die* (PL die **Tränen**) tear.

trank SEE **trinken**.

Transplantation *die* (PL die **Transplantationen**) transplant.

Transport *der* (PL die **Transporte**) **1** transport; **2** consignment.

transportieren *verb* (PERF **hat transportiert**) to transport.

trat SEE **treten**.

Traube *die* (PL die **Trauben**) grape.

trauen *verb* (PERF **hat getraut**) **1** to trust; **jemandem trauen** to trust somebody; **2 sich trauen** to dare; **Ich trau mich nicht** I don't dare; **3** to marry.

Trauer *die* **1** grief; **2** mourning.

Traum *der* (PL die **Träume**) dream.

träumen *verb* (PERF **hat geträumt**) to dream.

traumhaft *adjective* fabulous.

traurig *adjective* sad.

Traurigkeit *die* sadness.

Trauung *die* (PL die **Trauungen**) wedding.

Trauzeuge *der* (PL die **Trauzeugen**) witness (*at a wedding ceremony*).

treffen ◇*verb* (PRES **trifft**, IMPERF **traf**, PERF **hat getroffen**) **1** to hit; **2** to meet; **3** to make (*arrangements, a decision*); **4 sich mit jemandem treffen** to meet somebody; **5 sich gut treffen** to be convenient; **6** (PERF **ist getroffen**) **auf etwas treffen** to meet with (*resistance, difficulties*).

Treffen das (PL die **Treffen**) meeting.

Treffer der (PL die **Treffer**) **1** hit; **2** winner; **3** goal.

Treffpunkt der (PL die **Treffpunkte**) meeting place.

treiben ⬦verb (IMPERF **trieb**, PERF **hat getrieben**) **1** to drive; **2** to do; **viel Sport treiben** to do a lot of sport; **Handel treiben** to trade; **3 jemanden zur Eile treiben** to hurry somebody up; **4 Unsinn treiben** to mess about; **5** (PERF **ist getrieben**) to drift.

Treibhaus das (PL die **Treibhäuser**) hothouse.

Treibhauseffekt der greenhouse effect.

Treibstoff der fuel.

trennen verb (PERF **hat getrennt**) **1** to separate; **2** to divide (*words, parts of a room*); **3 sich trennen** to separate; **wir haben uns getrennt** we've separated; **Jutta hat sich von ihm getrennt** Jutta has left him; **4 sich von etwas trennen** to part with something.

Trennung die (PL die **Trennungen**) **1** separation; **2** division.

Treppe die (PL die **Treppen**) stairs; **eine Treppe** a flight of stairs.

Treppenhaus das stairwell; **im Treppenhaus** on the stairs.

treten ⬦verb (PRES **tritt**, IMPERF **trat**, PERF **ist getreten**) **1** to step; **2** to tread; **3** to kick; **4 mit jemandem in Verbindung treten** to get in touch with somebody.

treu adjective faithful.

Treuekarte die (PL die **Treuekarten**) loyalty card.

Tribüne die (PL die **Tribünen**) **1** stand (*in a stadium*); **2** platform.

Trick der (PL die **Tricks**) trick.

Trickfilm der (PL die **Trickfilme**) cartoon.

trieb SEE **treiben**.

trifft SEE **treffen**.

Trimm-dich-Pfad der (PL die **Trimm-dich-Pfade**) keep-fit trail.

trimmen verb (PERF **hat getrimmt**) **1** to trim; **2 sich trimmen** to keep fit.

trinken ⬦verb (IMPERF **trank**, PERF **hat getrunken**) to drink.

Trinkgeld das (PL die **Trinkgelder**) tip.

Trinkschokolade die drinking chocolate.

Trinkwasser das drinking water.

Tritt der (PL die **Tritte**) **1** step; **2** kick.

tritt SEE **treten**.

Triumph der (PL die **Triumphe**) triumph.

trocken adjective dry.

trockenlegen verb (PERF **hat trockengelegt**) to drain (*a marsh, a pond*).

trocknen verb (PERF **hat getrocknet**) to dry.

Trockner der (PL die **Trockner**) drier.

Trödel der (*informal*) junk.

Trödelmarkt der (PL die **Trödelmärkte**) flea market.

a
b
c
d
e
f
g
h
i
j
k
l
m
n
o
p
q
r
s
t
u
v
w
x
y
z

Trommel *die* (PL *die* **Trommeln**) drum.

trommeln *verb* (PERF **hat getrommelt**) to drum.

Trompete *die* (PL *die* **Trompeten**) trumpet.

Tropen (*plural noun*) **die Tropen** the tropics.

Tropfen *der* (PL *die* **Tropfen**) drop.

tropfen *verb* (PERF **hat getropft**) to drip.

Trophäe *die* (PL *die* **Trophäen**) trophy.

tropisch *adjective* tropical.

trösten *verb* (PERF **hat getröstet**) to console, to comfort.

trotz *preposition* (+ GEN) despite, in spite of.

trotzdem *adverb* nevertheless.

trüb *adjective* **1** dull, dismal; **2** cloudy (*liquid*).

trübsinnig *adjective* gloomy.

trug SEE **tragen**.

Truhe *die* (PL *die* **Truhen**) chest.

Trümmer *plural noun* ruins.

Trumpf *der* (PL *die* **Trümpfe**) **1** trump (card); **2** trumps.

Trunkenheit *die* drunkenness; **Trunkenheit am Steuer** drink-driving.

Truppen *plural noun* troops.

Truthahn *der* (PL *die* **Truthähne**) turkey.

Tscheche *der* (PL *die* **Tschechen**) Czech.

Tschechin *die* (PL *die* **Tschechinnen**) Czech.

tschechisch *adjective* Czech.

Tschechische Republik *die* Czech Republic.

tschüss *exclamation* bye!

T-Shirt *das* (PL *die* **T-Shirts**) T-shirt.

Tube *die* (PL *die* **Tuben**) tube.

Tuberkulose *die* tuberculosis.

Tuch *das* (PL *die* **Tücher**) **1** cloth; **2** scarf.

tüchtig *adjective* **1** efficient; **2** competent.

Tüchtigkeit *die* **1** efficiency; **2** competence.

Tulpe *die* (PL *die* **Tulpen**) tulip.

Tumor *der* (PL *die* **Tumoren**) tumour.

tun ⋄*verb* (PRES **tut**, IMPERF **tat**, PERF **hat getan**) **1** to do; **das tut man nicht** it isn't done; **das tut's** (*informal*) that'll do; **2** to put; **die Butter in den Kühlschrank tun** to put the butter in the fridge; **3** to pretend; **er tut nur so** he's only pretending; **4** to act; **freundlich tun** to act friendly; **5 jemandem etwas tun** to hurt somebody; **6 mit jemandem etwas zu tun haben** to have dealings with somebody; **das hat nichts damit zu tun** it's got nothing to do with it; **7 das tut nichts** it doesn't matter; **es hat sich viel getan** lots has happened.

Tunesien *das* Tunisia.

Tunesier *der* (PL *die* **Tunesier**) Tunisian.

Tunesierin *die* (PL *die* **Tunesierinnen**) Tunisian.

tunesisch *adjective* Tunisian.

Tunfisch *der* (PL *die* **Tunfische**) tuna.

Tunnel *der* (PL *die* **Tunnel**) tunnel.

Tupfen *der* (PL *die* **Tupfen**) dot.

tupfen *verb* (PERF **hat getupft**) to dab.

Tür *die* (PL *die* **Türen**) door.

Türke *der* (PL *die* **Türken**) Turk.

Türkei *die* Turkey.

Türkin *die* (PL *die* **Türkinnen**) Turk.

türkis *adjective* turquoise.

türkisch *adjective* Turkish.

Turm *der* (PL *die* **Türme**) **1** tower; **2** steeple; **3** rook, castle (*in chess*).

Turnanzug *der* (PL *die* **Turnanzüge**) leotard.

Turnen *das* **1** gymnastics; **2** physical education, PE.

turnen *verb* (PERF **hat geturnt**) to do gymnastics.

Turnhalle *die* (PL *die* **Turnhallen**) gymnasium, gym.

Turnier *das* (PL *die* **Turniere**) tournament.

Turnschuh *der* (PL *die* **Turnschuhe**) **1** trainer; **2** gym shoe.

Turnverein *der* (PL *die* **Turnvereine**) gymnastics club.

tuscheln *verb* (PERF **hat getuschelt**) to whisper.

tut SEE **tun**.

Tüte *die* (PL *die* **Tüten**) bag.

Typ *der* (PL *die* **Typen**) **1** type; **2** (*informal*) bloke.

typisch *adjective* typical.

Uu

U-Bahn *die* (PL *die* **U-Bahnen**) underground.

übel *adjective* **1** bad; **2** mir ist übel I feel sick; **3** etwas übel nehmen to take offence at something; **jemandem etwas übel nehmen** to hold something against somebody.

Übelkeit *die* nausea.

übelnehmen SEE **übel**.

üben *verb* (PERF **hat geübt**) to practise.

über *preposition* (+ DAT, *or* + ACC *with movement towards a place*) **1** over; **über Weihnachten** over Christmas; **2** above; **er wohnt über uns** he lives above us; **fünf Grad über Null** five degrees above zero; **3** about; **über etwas schreiben** to write about something; **4** for; **ein Scheck über hundert Euro** a cheque for one hundred euros; **5** across (*a field, the street*); **6 über Frankfurt fahren** to go via Frankfurt; **7 über die Straße gehen** to cross the road.
über *adverb* **1 über und über** over and over; **2 jemandem über sein** to be better than somebody; **3 über sein** (*informal*) to be left over; **4 jemanden ist etwas über** (*informal*) somebody is fed up with something; **5 etwas über haben** (*informal*) to be fed up with something; **Nudeln habe ich über** I'm getting fed up with pasta.

überall *adverb* everywhere.

überarbeiten *verb* (PERF **hat überarbeitet**)) to revise (*a text*).

a b c d e f g h i j k l m n o p q r s **t** **u** v w x y z

Überblick *der* (PL *die* Überblicke)
**1 einen guten Überblick über
etwas haben** to have a good view of
something; **2** overall view; **den
Überblick verlieren** to lose track of
things; **3** summary.

überblicken *verb* (PERF **hat
überblickt**) **1** to overlook; **2** to
assess.

Überdosis *die* (PL *die* Überdosen)
overdose.

Überdruss *der* **bis zum
Überdruss** ad nauseam.

übereinander *adverb* **1** one on
top of the other; **2 übereinander
sprechen** to talk about each other.

übereinstimmen *verb* (PERF **hat
übereingestimmt**) to agree.

überempfindlich *adjective*
hypersensitive.

überfahren ⋄*verb* (PRES
überfährt, IMPERF **überfuhr**, PERF
hat überfahren) to run over; **das
Kind ist von einem Auto
überfahren worden** the child was
run over by a car.

Überfahrt *die* (PL *die* Überfahrten)
crossing.

Überfall *der* (PL *die* Überfälle)
1 attack; **2** raid.

überfallen ⋄*verb* (PRES **überfällt**,
IMPERF **überfiel**, PERF **hat
überfallen**) **1** to attack, to mug; **2** to
raid; **3 jemanden mit Fragen
überfallen** to bombard somebody
with questions.

überfällig *adjective* overdue.

überflüssig *adjective* superfluous.

Überführung *die* (PL *die*
Überführungen) **1** transfer;
2 flyover; **3** footbridge.

überfüllt *adjective* **1** crowded;
2 oversubscribed.

Übergang *der* (PL *die* Übergänge)
1 crossing; **2** transition.

übergeben ⋄*verb* (PRES **übergibt**,
IMPERF **übergab**, PERF **hat
übergeben**) **1** to hand over; **2 sich
übergeben** to be sick.

überhaben SEE **über**.

überhaupt *adverb* **1** in general;
2 anyway; **was will er überhaupt?**
what does he want anyway?;
3 überhaupt nicht not at all;
überhaupt nichts nothing at all;
überhaupt keine Zeit haben to
have no time at all.

überholen *verb* (PERF **hat
überholt**) **1** to overtake; **2** to
overhaul.

überholt *adjective* out-of-date.

überlassen ⋄*verb* (PRES
überlässt, IMPERF **überließ**, PERF **hat
überlassen**) **1 jemandem etwas
überlassen** to let somebody have
something; **2 etwas jemandem
überlassen** to leave something up to
somebody (*a decision, for example*);
das bleibt dir überlassen it's up to
you.

überlaufen ⋄*verb* (PRES **läuft
über**, IMPERF **lief über**, PERF **ist
übergelaufen**) to overflow.

überleben *verb* (PERF **hat
überlebt**) to survive.

überlegen[1] *verb* (PERF **hat
überlegt**) **1** to think; **sich etwas**

überlegen to think something over;
ohne zu überlegen without
thinking; **2 ich habe es mir anders
überlegt** I've changed my mind.

überlegen[2] *adjective* **1** superior;
jemandem überlegen sein to be
superior to somebody; **2** convincing
(*victory*).

überm = **über dem.**

übermäßig *adjective* excessive.

übermorgen *adverb* the day after
tomorrow.

übernächster,
übernächste,
übernächstes *adjective* next
but one; **übernächstes Jahr** the
year after next.

übernachten *verb* (PERF hat
übernachtet) to stay the night; **bei
jemandem übernachten** to stay the
night at somebody's house.

übernehmen ◇*verb* (PRES
übernimmt, IMPERF übernahm, PERF
hat übernommen) **1** to take over;
2 to take on; **3 sich übernehmen** to
take on too much.

überqueren *verb* (PERF hat
überquert) to cross.

überraschen *verb* (PERF hat
überrascht) to surprise.

Überraschung die (PL die
Überraschungen) surprise.

überreden *verb* (PERF hat
überredet) to persuade.

übers = **über das.**

Überschrift die (PL die
Überschriften) heading.

überschüssig *adjective* surplus.

überschütten *verb* (PERF hat
überschüttet) **jemanden mit
etwas überschütten** to shower
somebody with something.

Überschwemmung die (PL die
Überschwemmungen) flood.

übersehen[1] ◇*verb* (PRES
übersieht, IMPERF übersah, PERF hat
übersehen) **1** to overlook;
(*informal*) **einen Fehler übersehen**
to overlook a mistake; **2** to assess
(*consequences, damages*).

übersehen[2] ◇*verb* (PRES sieht
sich über, IMPERF sah sich über,
PERF hat sich übergesehen) **sich
etwas übersehen** (*informal*) to get
fed up of seeing something.

übersetzen *verb* (PERF hat
übersetzt) to translate.

Übersetzer der (PL die Übersetzer)
translator.

Übersetzerin die (PL die
Übersetzerinnen) translator.

Übersetzung die (PL die
Übersetzungen) translation.

Übersicht die **1** overall view;
2 summary.

überspringen ◇*verb* (IMPERF
übersprang, PERF hat
übersprungen) **1** to jump (over);
2 to skip (*a chapter*).

überstehen ◇*verb* (IMPERF
überstand, PERF hat überstanden)
1 to get over; **2** to survive.

Überstunden *plural noun*
overtime; **Überstunden machen** to
work overtime.

übertragen ◇*verb* (PRES
überträgt, IMPERF übertrug, PERF

a
b
c
d
e
f
g
h
i
j
k
l
m
n
o
p
q
r
s
t
u
v
w
x
y
z

251

hat übertragen 1 to transfer; 2 to transmit; 3 to broadcast; 4 **etwas ins Reine übertragen** to make a fair copy of something; 5 **sich auf jemanden übertragen** to communicate itself to somebody (*of enthusiasm or nervousness*).

Übertragung die (PL die Übertragungen) 1 broadcast; 2 transmission.

übertreiben ◇*verb* (IMPERF übertrieb, PERF hat übertrieben) 1 to exaggerate; 2 to overdo.

Übertreibung die (PL die Übertreibungen) exaggeration.

überwältigend *adjective* overwhelming.

überweisen ◇*verb* (IMPERF überwies, PERF hat überwiesen) 1 to transfer; 2 to refer (*a patient*).

überzeugen *verb* (PERF hat überzeugt) 1 to convince; 2 **sich selbst überzeugen** to satisfy yourself.

überzeugend *adjective* convincing.

Überzeugung die (PL die Überzeugungen) conviction.

überziehen¹ ◇*verb* (IMPERF zog über, PERF hat übergezogen) to put on (*a cardigan, jacket*).

überziehen² ◇*verb* (IMPERF überzog, PERF hat überzogen) 1 to overdraw; 2 to cover (*with icing, for example*).

üblich *adjective* usual.

U-Boot das (PL die U-Boote) submarine.

übrig *adjective* 1 remaining; 2 **übrig sein** to be left over; 3 **etwas übrig lassen** to leave something (over); 4 **uns blieb nichts anderes übrig** we had no other choice; 5 **alles Übrige** the rest; **die Übrigen** the others; 6 **im Übrigen** besides.

übrigens *adverb* by the way.

übriglassen SEE **übrig**.

Übung die (PL die Übungen) 1 exercise; 2 practice; **aus der Übung sein** to be out of practice.

Ufer das (PL die Ufer) 1 bank (*of a river*); 2 shore.

Uhr die (PL die Uhren) 1 clock; 2 watch; 3 (*in time phrases*) **es ist ein Uhr** it's one o'clock; **wie viel Uhr ist es?** what's the time?; **um sechzehn Uhr** at four o'clock (in the afternoon).

Uhrzeiger der (PL die Uhrzeiger) hand (*of a clock or watch*).

Uhrzeigersinn der **im Uhrzeigersinn** clockwise; **entgegen dem Uhrzeigersinn** anti-clockwise.

Uhrzeit die time; **jemanden nach der Uhrzeit fragen** to ask somebody the time.

ulkig *adjective* funny.

um *preposition* (+ ACC) 1 round, around; **um das Haus herum** around the house; 2 at; **um fünf Uhr** at five o'clock; 3 around (about); 4 for; **um etwas bitten** to ask for something; **um seinetwillen** for his sake; 5 **sich um jemanden sorgen** to worry about somebody; 6 by (*indicating difference*); **um vieles**

besser better by far; **um so besser** so much the better.

um *adverb* **1** about, around; **um die dreihundert Euro herum** about three hundred euros; **um Weihnachten** around Christmas; **2 um sein** (*informal*) to be over.

um *conjunction* **um zu** (in order) to; **er ist noch zu klein, um in die Schule zu gehen** he's too young to go to school.

umarmen *verb* (PERF **hat umarmt**) to hug.

Umbau *der* (PL **die Umbauten**) **1** renovation; **2** conversion.

umbinden ⋄*verb* (IMPERF **band um**, PERF **hat umgebunden**) to put on.

umblättern *verb* (PERF **hat umgeblättert**) to turn over.

umbringen ⋄*verb* (IMPERF **brachte um**, PERF **hat umgebracht**) to kill.

umdrehen *verb* (PERF **hat umgedreht**) **1** to turn (round); **2 sich umdrehen** to turn round, to turn over.

umfallen ⋄*verb* (PRES **fällt um**, IMPERF **fiel um**, PERF **ist umgefallen**) to fall down.

Umfrage *die* (PL **die Umfragen**) survey.

umgänglich *adjective* sociable.

Umgangsformen *plural noun* manners.

Umgangssprache *die* slang, colloquial language.

umgeben ⋄*verb* (PRES **umgibt**, IMPERF **umgab**, PERF **hat umgeben**) to surround.

Umgebung *die* (PL **die Umgebungen**) **1** surroundings; **2** neighbourhood.

umgehen[1] ⋄*verb* (IMPERF **ging um**, PERF **ist umgegangen**) **1** to go round (*of a rumour, an illness*); **2 mit jemandem streng umgehen** to treat somebody strictly; **3 er kann mit Geld nicht umgehen** he can't handle money; **mit seinen Sachen sorgfältig umgehen** to handle one's things carefully.

umgehen[2] ⋄*verb* (IMPERF **umging**, PERF **hat umgangen**) to avoid.

Umgehungsstraße *die* (PL **die Umgehungsstraßen**) bypass.

umgekehrt *adjective* **1** opposite; **2** reverse (*order*); **3 es war umgekehrt** it was the other way round.

umgekehrt *adverb* **1 und umgekehrt** and vice versa; **2** the other way round; **warum machst du es nicht umgekehrt?** why don't you do it the other way round?

umkehren *verb* (PERF **ist umgekehrt**) **1** to turn back; **nach zehn Minuten sind wir wieder umgekehrt** ten minutes later we turned back again; **2** to turn round (*a picture, book*); **3** to turn inside out (*a bag, for example*); **4 sie hat das ganze Zimmer umgekehrt** (*informal*) she turned the whole room upside down.

Umkleidekabine *die* (PL **die Umkleidekabinen**) changing cubicle.

Umkleideraum *der* (PL **die Umkleideräume**) changing room.

a
b
c
d
e
f
g
h
i
j
k
l
m
n
o
p
q
r
s
t
u
v
w
x
y
z

umkommen ⋄*verb* (IMPERF **kam um**, PERF **ist umgekommen**) to be killed.

Umlaut *der* (PL *die* **Umlaute**) umlaut.

umlegen *verb* (PERF **hat umgelegt**) **1** to put on (*a scarf*); **2** to transfer (*a patient, call*); **3 jemanden umlegen** (*informal*) to bump somebody off.

Umleitung *die* (PL *die* **Umleitungen**) diversion.

umrechnen *verb* (PERF **hat umgerechnet**) to convert.

Umrechnung *die* conversion.

Umrechnungskurs *der* exchange rate.

Umriss *der* (PL *die* **Umrisse**) outline.

umrühren *verb* (PERF **hat umgerührt**) to stir.

ums = **um das.**

umschalten *verb* (PERF **hat umgeschaltet**) **1** to turn over; **vom ersten aufs zweite Programm umschalten** to turn from channel one to channel two; **2 auf Rot umschalten** to change to red.

Umschlag *der* (PL *die* **Umschläge**) **1** envelope; **2** cover.

umsehen ⋄*verb* (PRES **sieht sich um**, IMPERF **sah sich um**, PERF **hat sich umgesehen**) **sich umsehen** to look round.

umso *adverb* **umso besser** all the better; **je mehr, umso besser** the more the better.

umsonst *adverb* **1** in vain; **2** free, for nothing.

Umstand *der* (PL *die* **Umstände**) **1** circumstance; **unter diesen Umständen** under these circumstances; **2 unter Umständen** possibly; **3 jemandem Umstände machen** to put somebody to trouble; **das macht gar keine Umstände** it's no trouble at all; **4 in anderen Umständen sein** to be pregnant.

umständlich *adjective* **1** laborious; **2** complicated.

umsteigen ⋄*verb* (IMPERF **stieg um**, PERF **ist umgestiegen**) to change.

umstellen¹ *verb* (PERF **hat umgestellt**) **1** to rearrange; **2** to reset; **3** to change over; **4 sich umstellen** to adjust.

umstellen² *verb* (PERF **hat umstellt**) to surround.

Umtausch *der* exchange.

umtauschen *verb* (PERF **hat umgetauscht**) to change, to exchange.

Umweg *der* (PL *die* **Umwege**) detour.

Umwelt *die* environment.

umweltfeindlich *adjective* environmentally unfriendly.

umweltfreundlich *adjective* environmentally friendly.

Umweltschützer *der* (PL *die* **Umweltschützer**) environmentalist.

Umweltschützerin die (PL die Umweltschützerinnen) environmentalist.

Umweltverschmutzung die pollution.

umwerfen ◇verb (PRES **wirft um**, IMPERF **warf um**, PERF **hat umgeworfen**) **1** to knock over; **2** to upset (*a plan*); **das hat mich umgeworfen** it's thrown me.

umwerfend adjective fantastic.

umziehen ◇verb (IMPERF **zog um**, PERF **ist umgezogen**) **1** to move; **sie ziehen nächste Woche um** they're moving next week; **2** (PERF **hat umgezogen**) to change; **3** (PERF **hat sich umgezogen**) **sich umziehen** to get changed.

Umzug der (PL die **Umzüge**) **1** move; **2** procession.

unabhängig adjective independent.

Unabhängigkeit die independence.

unangenehm adjective **1** unpleasant; **2** embarrassing (*question, situation*).

unartig adjective naughty.

unbedeutend adjective insignificant.
unbedeutend adverb slightly.

unbedingt adjective absolute.
unbedingt adverb really; **ich muss ihn unbedingt sprechen** I really must talk to him; **nicht unbedingt** not necessarily.

unbefriedigend adjective unsatisfactory.

unbefriedigt adjective unsatisfied.

unbegrenzt adjective unlimited.

unbehaglich adjective **1** uncomfortable; **2** uneasy.

unbekannt adjective unknown.

unbeliebt adjective unpopular.

unbequem adjective uncomfortable.

unbestimmt adjective **1** indefinite; **auf unbestimmte Zeit** for an indefinite period; **2** uncertain.
unbestimmt adverb vaguely; **etwas unbestimmt lassen** to leave something open.

unbewusst adjective unconscious.

und conjunction and; **und so weiter** and so on; **na und?** so what?

undankbar adjective ungrateful.

undeutlich adjective unclear.

undicht adjective leaking, leaky; **eine undichte Stelle** a leak.

uneben adjective uneven.

unehrlich adjective dishonest.

unempfindlich adjective **1** hard-wearing, easy-care; **2** immune; **gegen Kälte unempfindlich sein** not to feel the cold.

unentbehrlich adjective indispensable.

unentschieden adjective undecided; **unentschieden spielen** to draw.

unerträglich adjective unbearable.

a
b
c
d
e
f
g
h
i
j
k
l
m
n
o
p
q
r
s
t
u
v
w
x
y
z

unerwartet *adjective* unexpected.

unfähig *adjective* **1** incompetent; **2 unfähig sein, etwas zu tun** to be incapable of doing something.

unfair *adjective* unfair.

Unfall *der* (PL *die* **Unfälle**) accident.

unfreundlich *adjective* unfriendly.

Unfug *der* **1** nonsense; **2** mischief; **Unfug machen** to get up to mischief.

Ungar *der* (PL *die* **Ungarn**) Hungarian.

Ungarin *die* (PL *die* **Ungarinnen**) Hungarian.

ungarisch *adjective* Hungarian.

Ungarn *das* Hungary.

Ungeduld *die* impatience.

ungeduldig *adjective* impatient.

ungeeignet *adjective* unsuitable.

ungefähr *adjective* approximate. **ungefähr** *adverb* approximately, about.

ungefährlich *adjective* safe, harmless.

Ungeheuer *das* (PL *die* **Ungeheuer**) monster.

ungeheuer *adjective* enormous.

ungehorsam *adjective* disobedient.

ungelegen *adjective* inconvenient.

ungemütlich *adjective* uncomfortable.

ungenau *adjective* **1** inaccurate; **2** vague.

ungenießbar *adjective* **1** inedible; **2** undrinkable; **3 Bernd ist heute aber ungenießbar** (*informal*) Bernd is quite unbearable today.

ungenügend *adjective* **1** insufficient; **2** unsatisfactory (*mark at school*).

ungerade *adjective* **eine ungerade Zahl** an odd number.

ungerecht *adjective* unjust.

ungern *adverb* reluctantly.

ungeschickt *adjective* clumsy.

ungesund *adjective* unhealthy.

ungewöhnlich *adjective* unusual.

Ungeziefer *das* vermin.

ungezwungen *adjective* **1** informal; **2** natural.

unglaublich *adjective* incredible.

Unglück *das* (PL *die* **Unglücke**) **1** accident; **2** misfortune; **3** bad luck; **das bringt Unglück** that's unlucky.

unglücklich *adjective* **1** unhappy; **2** unfortunate.

unglücklicherweise *adverb* unfortunately.

unheilbar *adjective* incurable.

unheimlich *adjective* eerie. **unheimlich** *adverb* **1** eerily; **2** (*informal*) incredibly; **unheimlich viel** an incredible amount.

unhöflich *adjective* impolite.

Uniform *die* (PL *die* **Uniformen**) uniform.

uninteressant *adjective* uninteresting.

Universität *die* (PL *die* **Universitäten**) university.

Unkenntnis *die* ignorance.

unklar *adjective* unclear.

Unkosten *plural noun* expenses.

Unkraut *das* weed.

unleserlich *adjective* illegible.

unlogisch *adjective* illogical.

unmittelbar *adjective* immediate, direct.

unmodern *adjective* old-fashioned.

unmöglich *adjective* impossible.

Unmöglichkeit *die* impossibility.

unnötig *adjective* unnecessary.

unordentlich *adjective* untidy.

Unordnung *die* **1** disorder; **2** mess.

unpraktisch *adjective* impractical.

unpünktlich *adjective* unpunctual; **unpünktlich sein** to be late.

Unrecht *das* **1** wrong; **zu Unrecht** wrongly; **Unrecht haben** to be wrong; **2** **jemandem Unrecht geben** to disagree with somebody.

unrecht *adjective* wrong; **jemandem unrecht tun** to do somebody an injustice.

unregelmäßig *adjective* irregular.

unreif *adjective* **1** unripe; **2** immature.

Unruhe *die* (PL *die* **Unruhen**) **1** restlessness; **2** agitation; **3 Unruhen** unrest.

Unruhestifter *der* (PL *die* **Unruhestifter**) troublemaker.

unruhig *adjective* restless.

uns *pronoun* **1** us; **gib es uns** give it to us; **sie kommen mit uns** they're coming with us; **2** ourselves; **wir waschen uns die Hände** we are washing our hands; **3** each other; **wir kennen uns** we know each other.

unscharf *adjective* blurred, indistinct.

unschuldig *adjective* innocent.

unser *pronoun* our.

unserer, unsere, unser(e)s *pronoun* ours.

unsertwegen *adverb* **1** for our sake; **2** because of us; **3** as far as we're concerned.

unsicher *adjective* **1** uncertain; **2** insecure.
unsicher *adverb* unsteadily.

unsichtbar *adjective* invisible.

Unsinn *der* nonsense.

unsrer SEE **unserer**.

unsympathisch *adjective* unpleasant; **Tobias ist mir unsympathisch** I don't like Tobias.

unten *adverb* **1** at the bottom; **2** underneath; **3** downstairs; **hier unten** down here; **nach unten** down.

a
b
c
d
e
f
g
h
i
j
k
l
m
n
o
p
q
r
s
t
u
v
w
x
y
z

unter *preposition* (+ DAT *or* + ACC *with movement towards a place*) **1** under, below; **2** among; **unter anderem** among other things; **3 unter sich** by themselves; **unter uns gesagt** between ourselves; **4 unter der Woche** during the week.

Unterbewusstsein *das* subconscious.

unterbrechen ◇*verb* (PRES **unterbricht**, IMPERF **unterbrach**, PERF **hat unterbrochen**) to interrupt.

Unterbrechung *die* (PL *die* **Unterbrechungen**) interruption.

unterbringen ◇*verb* (IMPERF **brachte unter**, PERF **hat untergebracht**) **1** to put; **2** to put up (*a guest*).

untere SEE **unterer**.

untereinander *adverb* **1** among ourselves/yourselves/themselves; **2** one below the other.

unterer, untere, unteres *adjective* lower.

Unterführung *die* (PL *die* **Unterführungen**) subway.

untergehen ◇*verb* (IMPERF **ging unter**, PERF **ist untergegangen**) **1** to set (*of the sun*); **2** to sink, to drown; **3** to come to an end.

Untergrundbahn *die* (PL *die* **Untergrundbahnen**) underground.

unterhalb *preposition* (+ GEN) below.

unterhalten ◇*verb* (PRES **unterhält**, IMPERF **unterhielt**, PERF **hat unterhalten**) **1** to support; **2** to run (*a hotel, leisure centre*); **3** to entertain; **4 sich über etwas unterhalten** to talk about something; **5 sich unterhalten** to enjoy yourself.

unterhaltsam *adjective* entertaining.

Unterhaltung *die* (PL *die* **Unterhaltungen**) **1** conversation; **2** entertainment.

Unterhemd *das* (PL *die* **Unterhemden**) vest.

Unterhose *die* (PL *die* **Unterhosen**) underpants.

Unterkunft *die* (PL *die* **Unterkünfte**) accommodation.

Unterlagen *plural noun* documents, papers.

Untermieter *der* (PL *die* **Untermieter**) lodger.

Untermieterin *die* (PL *die* **Untermieterinnen**) lodger.

unternehmen ◇*verb* (PRES **unternimmt**, IMPERF **unternahm**, PERF **hat unternommen**) **1** to undertake; **2 nichts unternehmen** to do nothing; **was unternehmt ihr heute?** what are you doing today?

Unternehmen *das* (PL *die* **Unternehmen**) **1** enterprise; **2** concern.

Unterricht *der* **1** lessons; **heute haben wir keinen Unterricht** we've got no lessons today; **2** teaching.

unterrichten *verb* (PERF **hat unterrichtet**) **1** to teach; **2** to inform; **3 sich unterrichten** to inform yourself.

Unterrichtsfach das (PL die Unterrichtsfächer) subject.

Unterrock der (PL die Unterröcke) slip.

unterscheiden ◇verb (IMPERF unterschied, PERF hat unterschieden) **1** to distinguish, to tell apart; **2 sich unterscheiden** to differ.

Unterschied der (PL die Unterschiede) difference.

unterschiedlich adjective different; **das ist unterschiedlich** it varies.

unterschreiben ◇verb (IMPERF unterschrieb, PERF hat unterschrieben) to sign.

Unterschrift die (PL die Unterschriften) signature.

Unterseeboot (PL die Unterseeboote) submarine.

unterster, unterste, unterstes adjective bottom, lowest.

unterstreichen ◇verb (IMPERF unterstrich, PERF hat unterstrichen) to underline.

unterstützen verb (PERF hat unterstüzt) to support.

Unterstützung die support.

untersuchen verb (PERF hat untersucht) **1** to examine; **2** to investigate.

Untersuchung die (PL die Untersuchungen) **1** examination, check-up; **2** investigation.

Untertasse die (PL die Untertassen) saucer.

Untertitel der (PL die Untertitel) subtitle.

Unterwäsche die underwear.

unterwegs adverb on the way; **den ganzen Tag unterwegs sein** to be out all day.

untreu adjective **1** unfaithful; **2** disloyal.

untüchtig adjective **1** inefficient; **2** incompetent.

ununterbrochen adjective uninterrupted.

unverbleit adjective unleaded.

unvergleichlich adjective incomparable.

unverheiratet adjective unmarried.

unverkäuflich adjective not for sale; **ein unverkäufliches Muster** a free sample.

unverschämt adjective impertinent.

unverständlich adjective incomprehensible.

unverzüglich adjective promptly; **bitte antworten Sie unverzüglich** please reply promptly.

unvorsichtig adjective careless.

unwahr adjective untrue.

unwahrscheinlich adjective **1** unlikely; **2** incredible. **unwahrscheinlich** adverb (informal) incredibly; **unwahrscheinlich schön** incredibly beautiful.

Unwetter das (PL die Unwetter) storm.

unwichtig adjective unimportant.

a unzählig *adjective* countless.

b unzerbrechlich *adjective* unbreakable.

c unzertrennlich *adjective* inseparable.

d unzufrieden *adjective* dissatisfied.

f üppig *adjective* lavish.

g uralt *adjective* ancient.

h Urenkel *der* (PL *die* Urenkel) great-grandson; **die Urenkel** the great-grandchildren.

i Urenkelin *die* (PL *die* Urenkelinnen) great-granddaughter.

k Urkunde *die* (PL *die* Urkunden) certificate.

m Urlaub *der* (PL *die* Urlaube) holiday; **Urlaub haben** to be on holiday; **auf/ im Urlaub** on holiday.

n Urlauber *der* (PL *die* Urlauber) holidaymaker.

o Ursache *die* (PL *die* Ursachen) cause; **keine Ursache!** don't mention it!

p Ursprung *der* (PL *die* Ursprünge) origin.

s ursprünglich *adjective* original. ursprünglich *adverb* originally.

t Urteil *das* (PL *die* Urteile) **1** judgement; **2** opinion; **3** verdict.

u urteilen *verb* (PERF hat geurteilt) to judge.

w Urwald *der* (PL *die* Urwälder) jungle.

x USA *plural noun* USA.

z usw. (*und so weiter*) etc.

Vv

vage *adjective* vague.

Vagina *die* (PL *die* Vaginen) vagina.

Valentinskarte *die* (PL *die* Valentinskarten) valentine card.

Valentinstag *der* Valentine's Day.

Vanille *die* vanilla.

Variante *die* (PL *die* Varianten) variety.

Vase *die* (PL *die* Vasen) vase.

Vater *der* (PL *die* Väter) father.

Vaterunser *das* Lord's Prayer.

Vati *der* (PL *die* Vatis) dad.

Veganer *der* (PL *die* Veganer) vegan.

Vegetarier *der* (PL *die* Vegetarier) vegetarian.

Vegetarierin *die* (PL *die* Vegetarierinnen) vegetarian.

vegetarisch *adjective* vegetarian.

Veilchen *das* (PL *die* Veilchen) violet.

Vene *die* (PL *die* Venen) vein.

Ventil *das* (PL *die* Ventile) valve.

Ventilator *der* (PL *die* Ventilatoren) fan.

verabreden *verb* (PERF hat verabredet) **1** to arrange; **was habt ihr verabredet?** what did you arrange?; **mit jemandem verabredet sein** to have arranged to meet somebody; **Laura ist mit Frank verabredet** Laura has a date with Frank; **2 sich mit jemandem verabreden** to arrange to meet somebody; **ich habe mich mit Oliver zum Tennis verabredet** I've arranged to play tennis with Oliver.

Verabredung die (PL die Verabredungen) 1 appointment; 2 date; 3 arrangement.

verabschieden verb (PERF hat verabschiedet) 1 to say goodbye to; 2 **sich verabschieden** to say goodbye.

Verachtung die contempt.

verallgemeinern verb (PERF hat verallgemeinert) to generalize.

veralten verb (PERF ist veraltet) to become obsolete.

veränderlich adjective changeable.

verändern verb (PERF hat verändert) 1 to change; 2 **sich verändern** to change.

Veränderung die (PL die Veränderungen) change.

veranstalten verb (PERF hat veranstaltet) to organize.

Veranstalter der (PL die Veranstalter) organizer.

Veranstaltung die (PL die Veranstaltungen) event.

verantwortlich adjective responsible.

Verantwortung die responsibility.

verantwortungsbewusst adjective responsible.

verantwortungslos adjective irresponsible.

verarbeiten verb (PERF hat verarbeitet) 1 to process; **etwas zu** **etwas verarbeiten** to make something into something; 2 to digest (food, information).

Verarbeitung die 1 use; 2 digestion; 3 processing of data.

verärgern verb (PERF hat verärgert) to annoy.

Verb das (PL die Verben) verb.

Verband der (PL die Verbände) 1 association; **sich zu einem Verband zusammenschließen** to form an associaton; 2 bandage, dressing; **einen Verband anlegen** to apply a dressing.

verband SEE **verbinden**.

verbergen ⋄verb (PRES **verbirgt**, IMPERF **verbarg**, PERF hat **verborgen**) 1 to hide; 2 **sich verbergen** to hide.

verbessern verb (PERF hat verbessert) 1 to improve; 2 to correct; 3 **sich verbessern** to improve.

Verbesserung die (PL die Verbesserungen) 1 improvement; 2 correction.

verbiegen ⋄verb (IMPERF **verbog**, PERF hat **verbogen**) 1 to bend; 2 **sich verbiegen** to bend.

verbieten ⋄verb (IMPERF **verbot**, PERF hat **verboten**) 1 to forbid; **sie hat ihm verboten, das Haus zu betreten** she forbade him to enter the house; **meine Eltern verbieten mir, am Abend wegzugehen** my parents don't allow me to go out in the evening; 2 to ban.

verbilligt adjective reduced.

a b c d e f g h i j k l m n o p q r s t u v w x y z

verbinden ◇*verb* (IMPERF **verband**, PERF **hat verbunden**) **1** to connect, to join; **2** to combine; **3** to bandage, to dress (*a wound*); **jemandem die Augen verbinden** to blindfold somebody; **4** **jemanden verbinden** to put somebody through (*on the phone*); **ich verbinde** I'm putting you through.

verbindlich *adjective* **1** friendly; **2** binding (*agreement, decision*).

Verbindung *die* (PL *die* **Verbindungen**) **1** connection; **2** **gute Verbindungen haben** to have good contacts; **sich mit jemandem in Verbindung setzen** to get in touch with somebody; **3** combination; **4** **eine chemische Verbindung** a chemical compound.

verbirgt SEE **verbergen**.

verbleit *adjective* leaded.

verblüffen *verb* (PERF **hat verblüfft**) to amaze.

verbog SEE **verbiegen**.

verbogen *adjective* hidden.

Verbot *das* (PL *die* **Verbote**) ban.

verbot SEE **verbieten**.

verboten *adjective* forbidden; **'Rauchen verboten'** 'no smoking'.

verbracht, verbrachte SEE **verbringen**.

verbrannt, verbrannte SEE **verbrennen**.

Verbrauch *der* consumption.

verbrauchen *verb* (PERF **hat verbraucht**) to use, to use up; **die Waschmaschine verbraucht nicht viel Strom** the washing machine doesn't use up much electricity.

Verbraucher *der* (PL *die* **Verbraucher**) consumer.

Verbrechen *das* (PL *die* **Verbrechen**) crime.

Verbrecher *der* (PL *die* **Verbrecher**) criminal.

verbreiten *verb* (PERF **hat verbreitet**) **1** to spread; **eine Krankheit verbreiten** to spread an illness; **2** **eine Meldung über den Rundfunk verbreiten** to broadcast a message; **3** **sich verbreiten** to spread; **die Neuigkeit hat sich schnell verbreitet** the news spread quickly.

verbreitet *adjective* widespread.

verbrennen ◇*verb* (IMPERF **verbrannte**, PERF **ist verbrannt**) **1** to burn; **2** (PERF **hat verbrannt**) to burn (*rubbish, leaves*); **3** (PERF **hat verbrannt**) to cremate; **4** (PERF **hat verbrannt**) **sich die Hand verbrennen** to burn your hand.

verbringen ◇*verb* (IMPERF **verbrachte**, PERF **hat verbracht**) to spend; **wir haben schöne Ferien in Bayern verbracht** we spent a nice holiday in Bavaria.

verbunden SEE **verbinden**.

Verdacht *der* suspicion.

verdächtig *adjective* suspicious.

verdächtigen *verb* (PERF **hat verdächtigt**) to suspect.

verdammt *adjective, adverb* (*informal*) damned; **verdammt!** damn!

a b c d e f g h i j k l m n o p q r s t u v w x y z

verdarb SEE **verderben**.

Verdauung *die* digestion.

verderben ◇*verb* (PRES **verdirbt**, IMPERF **verdarb**, PERF **hat verdorben**) **1** to spoil, to ruin; **das hat mir den Abend verdorben** it ruined the evening for me; **ich habe mir den Magen verdorben** I have an upset stomach; **2 es sich mit jemandem verderben** to get into somebody's bad books; **3** (PERF **ist verdorben**) to go off; **die Milch verdirbt, wenn du sie nicht in den Kühlschrank stellst** the milk will go off if you don't put it in the fridge.

verdienen *verb* (PERF **hat verdient**) **1** to earn; **2** to deserve.

Verdienst *der* (PL *die* **Verdienste**) **1** salary; **2** achievement.

verdirbt SEE **verderben**.

verdoppeln *verb* (PERF **hat verdoppelt**) **1** to double; **2 sich verdoppeln** to double.

verdorben SEE **verderben**.

verdünnen *verb* (PERF **hat verdünnt**) to dilute.

verehren *verb* (PERF **hat verehrt**) to worship.

Verehrer *der* (PL *die* **Verehrer**) admirer.

Verehrerin *die* (PL *die* **Verehrerinnen**) admirer.

Verein *der* (PL *die* **Vereine**) **1** society; **2** organization; **3** club.

vereinbaren *verb* (PERF **hat vereinbart**) to arrange.

Vereinbarung *die* (PL *die* **Vereinbarungen**) **1** agreement; **2** arrangement.

vereinfachen *verb* (PERF **hat vereinfacht**) to simplify.

vereinigen *verb* (PERF **hat vereinigt**) to unite; **ein Land wieder vereinigen** to reunify a country.

Vereinigte Staaten *plural noun* United States.

Vereinigung *die* (PL *die* **Vereinigungen**) organization.

verfahren ◇*verb* (PRES **verfährt**, IMPERF **verfuhr**, PERF **ist verfahren**) **1** to proceed; **2 ich habe mich verfahren** I've lost my way.

verfallen ◇*verb* (PRES **verfällt**, IMPERF **verfiel**, PERF **ist verfallen**) **1** to decay; **2** to expire (*of a passport or ticket*).

Verfallsdatum *das* (PL *die* **Verfallsdaten**) use-by date.

Verfassung *die* (PL *die* **Verfassungen**) **1** constitution; **2** state (*of a person*).

verfaulen *verb* (PERF **ist verfault**) to rot.

verfiel SEE **verfallen**.

verfolgen *verb* (PERF **hat verfolgt**) **1** to follow; **2** to persecute.

Verfolgung *die* (PL *die* **Verfolgungen**) **1** pursuit, hunt; **2** persecution.

verfügbar *adjective* available.

Verfügung *die* **jemandem etwas zur Verfügung stellen** to put something at somebody's disposal;

jemandem zur Verfügung stehen to be at somebody's disposal.

verfuhr SEE **verfahren**.

verführen *verb* (PERF **hat verführt**) **1** to tempt; **2** to seduce.

Verführung die (PL die **Verführungen**) **1** temptation; **2** seduction.

vergab SEE **vergeben**.

vergangen *verb* SEE **vergehen**

vergangen *adjective* last.

Vergangenheit die **1** past; **2** past tense.

vergaß SEE **vergessen**.

vergeben ⬦*verb* (PRES **vergibt**, IMPERF **vergab**, PERF **hat vergeben**) **1** to forgive; **jemandem etwas vergeben** to forgive somebody for something; **2** to give away, to award; **3 vergeben sein** to be taken; **das Zimmer ist schon vergeben** the room's already taken.

vergeblich *adverb* in vain.

vergehen ⬦*verb* (IMPERF **verging**, PERF **ist vergangen**) to pass.

vergessen ⬦*verb* (PRES **vergisst**, IMPERF **vergaß**, PERF **hat vergessen**) to forget.

vergesslich *adjective* forgetful.

vergewaltigen *verb* (PERF **hat vergewaltigt**) to rape.

Vergewaltigung die (PL die **Vergewaltigungen**) rape.

vergibt SEE **vergeben**.

vergiften *verb* (PERF **hat vergiftet**) to poison.

verging SEE **vergehen**.

vergisst SEE **vergessen**.

Vergleich der (PL die **Vergleiche**) comparison.

vergleichen ⬦*verb* (IMPERF **verglich**, PERF **hat verglichen**) to compare.

Vergnügen das (PL die **Vergnügen**) pleasure; **viel Vergnügen!** have fun!

vergnügen *verb* (PERF **hat sich vergnügt**) **sich vergnügen** to have fun.

vergnügt *adjective* cheerful.

vergrößern *verb* (PERF **hat vergrößert**) **1** to enlarge; **2** to increase; **3** to magnify; **4** to extend (*a room, building*); **5 sich vergrößern** to expand, to grow bigger.

Vergrößerung die (PL die **Vergrößerungen**) **1** expansion; **2** enlargement (*of a photograph*).

verhaften *verb* (PERF **hat verhaftet**) to arrest; **er ist verhaftet worden** he was arrested.

verhalten ⬦*verb* (PRES **verhält sich**, IMPERF **verhielt sich**, PERF **hat sich verhalten**) **sich verhalten** to behave.

Verhalten das behaviour.

Verhältnis das (PL die **Verhältnisse**) **1** relationship; **sie hat ein gutes Verhältnis zu ihren Eltern** she has a good relationship with her parents; **2** affair; **Gabi hat ein Verhältnis mit einem verheirateten Mann** Gabi is having an affair with a married man; **3** ratio (*in maths*); **4 in keinem Verhältnis zu etwas stehen** to be

out of all proportion to something;
5 Verhältnisse conditions; **über
seine Verhältnisse leben** to live
beyond your means.

verhältnismäßig *adverb*
relatively.

verhandeln *verb* (PERF hat
verhandelt) to negotiate; **über
etwas verhandeln** to negotiate
something.

Verhandlung *die* (PL *die*
Verhandlungen) **1** negotiation;
2 hearing; **3** trial.

verhauen *verb* (PERF hat
verhauen) **1** to beat up; **2 die
Prüfung verhauen** (*informal*) to
make a mess of the exam.

verheimlichen *verb* (PERF hat
verheimlicht) to keep secret.

verheiratet *adjective* married.

verhext *adjective* bewitched.

verhielt SEE **verhalten**.

verhindern *verb* (PERF hat
verhindert) **1** to prevent;
2 verhindert sein to be unable to
make it; **Petra ist verhindert** Petra
won't be able to make it.

verhungern *verb* (PERF ist
verhungert) to starve.

Verhütungsmittel *das* (PL *die*
Verhütungsmittel) contraceptive.

verirren *verb* (PERF hat sich
verirrt) **sich verirren** to get lost.

verkam SEE **verkommen**.

Verkauf *der* (PL *die* Verkäufe) sale;
zum Verkauf for sale.

verkaufen *verb* (PERF hat
verkauft) to sell; **zu verkaufen** for
sale.

Verkäufer *der* (PL *die* Verkäufer)
1 seller; **2** sales assistant.

Verkäuferin *die* (PL *die*
Verkäuferinnen) **1** seller; **2** sales
assistant.

Verkaufsautomat *der* (PL *die*
Verkuaufsautomaten) vending
machine.

Verkehr *der* traffic.

Verkehrsampel *die* (PL *die*
Verkehrsampeln) traffic lights.

Verkehrsamt *das* (PL *die*
Verkehrsämter) tourist office.

Verkehrsinsel *die* (PL *die*
Verkehrsinseln) traffic island.

Verkehrsunfall *der* (PL *die*
Verkehrsunfälle) road accident.

Verkehrszeichen *das* (PL *die*
Verkehrszeichen) traffic sign, road
sign.

verkehrt *adjective* **1** wrong;
2 verkehrt herum inside out, the
wrong way round.

verklagen *verb* (PERF hat
verklagt) to sue.

verkleiden *verb* (PERF hat sich
verkleidet) **sich verkleiden** to dress
up.

Verkleidung *die* (PL *die*
Verkleidungen) disguise, fancy
dress.

verkommen ◇*verb* (IMPERF
verkam, PERF ist verkommen) **1** to
go off (*of food*); **2** to become

a
b
c
d
e
f
g
h
i
j
k
l
m
n
o
p
q
r
s
t
u
v
w
x
y
z

dilapidated (*of a house*); **3** to go to the bad.

verkratzt *adjective* scratched.

Verlag *der* (PL *die* **Verlage**) publisher's.

verlangen *verb* (PERF **hat verlangt**) **1** to ask for, to require; **am Telefon verlangt werden** to be wanted on the phone; **2** to demand; **3** to charge.

verlängern *verb* (PERF **hat verlängert**) **1** to extend; **2** to lengthen; **3** to renew (*a passport, driving licence*).

Verlängerung *die* (PL *die* **Verlängerungen**) **1** extension; **2** renewal; **3** extra time (*in sport*).

verlassen[1] ◇*verb* (PRES **verlässt**, IMPERF **verließ**, PERF **hat verlassen**) **1** to leave; **jemanden verlassen** to leave somebody; **2 sich auf etwas verlassen** to rely on something; **du kannst dich auf ihn verlassen** you can rely on him.

verlassen[2] *adjective* deserted.

verlaufen ◇*verb* (PRES **verläuft**, IMPERF **verlief**, PERF **ist verlaufen**) **1** to go; **es ist gut verlaufen** it went well; **2 sich verlaufen** to lose your way; **3 die Menge verlief sich schnell** the crowd quickly dispersed.

verlegen[1] *adjective* embarrassed.

verlegen[2] *verb* (PERF **hat verlegt**) **1** to mislay; **2** to postpone; **3** to publish; **4** to lay (*a carpet, cable*).

Verlegenheit *die* embarrassment.

Verleih *der* (PL *die* **Verleihe**) **1** renting out, hiring out; **2** rental firm, hire shop.

verleihen ◇*verb* (IMPERF **verlieh**, PERF **hat verliehen**) **1** to hire out; **2** to lend; **3** to award.

verlernen *verb* (PERF **hat verlernt**) to forget.

verletzen *verb* (PERF **hat verletzt**) **1** to injure; **2** to hurt; **3** to violate (*a law*); **4 sich verletzen** to hurt yourself.

Verletzte *der/die* (PL *die* **Verletzten**) **1** injured person; **2** casualty.

Verletzung *die* (PL *die* **Verletzungen**) injury.

verlieben *verb* (PERF **hat sich verliebt**) **sich verlieben** to fall in love.

verlief SEE **verlaufen**.

verlieh SEE **verleihen**.

verlieren ◇*verb* (IMPERF **verlor**, PERF **hat verloren**) to lose.

verließ SEE **verlassen**.

verloben *verb* (PERF **hat sich verlobt**) **sich verloben** to get engaged.

Verlobte *der/die* (PL *die* **Verlobten**) fiancé, fiancée.

Verlobung *die* (PL *die* **Verlobungen**) engagement.

verlocken *verb* (PERF **hat verlockt**) to tempt, to entice.

verlor, **verloren** SEE **verlieren**.

Verlosung *die* (PL *die* **Verlosungen**) prize draw.

Verlust *der* (PL *die* **Verluste**) loss.

a b c d e f g h i j k l m n o p q r s t u v w x y z

vermeiden ◇*verb* (IMPERF
vermied, PERF **hat vermieden**) to
avoid.

vermieten *verb* (PERF **hat
vermietet**) **1** to rent out, to hire out;
2 to let; **Zimmer zu vermieten**
rooms to let.

Vermieter *der* (PL die **Vermieter**)
landlord.

Vermieterin *die* (PL die
Vermieterinnen) landlady.

vermissen *verb* (PERF **hat
vermisst**) to miss.

Vermittlung *die* (PL die
Vermittlungen) **1** arrangement;
2 agency; **3** switchboard;
4 telephone exchange; **5** mediation.

Vermögen *das* (PL die **Vermögen**)
fortune; **ein Vermögen machen** to
make a fortune.

vermuten *verb* (PERF **hat
vermutet**) to suspect.

vermutlich *adjective* probable.
vermutlich *adverb* probably.

vernachlässigen *verb* (PERF **hat
vernachlässigt**) to neglect.

vernichten *verb* (PERF **hat
vernichtet**) **1** to destroy; **2** to
exterminate.

Vernunft *die* reason.

vernünftig *adjective* sensible.

verpacken *verb* (PERF **hat
verpackt**) **1** to pack; **2** to wrap up.

Verpackung *die* (PL die
Verpackungen) packaging.

verpassen *verb* (PERF **hat
verpasst**) to miss.

verpesten *verb*, (PERF **hat
verpestet**) to pollute.

Verpflegung *die* food; **Unterkunft
und Verpflegung** board and
lodging.

verpflichten *verb* (PERF **hat
verpflichtet**) **1 sich verpflichten** to
promise; **2 sich vertraglich
verpflichten** to sign a contract;
3 verpflichtet sein, etwas zu tun
to be obliged to do something;
**jemandem zu Dank verpflichtet
sein** to be obliged to somebody;
4 verpflichtend binding.

Verpflichtung *die* (PL die
Verpflichtungen) **1** obligation;
2 commitment.

verprügeln *verb* (PERF **hat
verprügelt**) to beat up.

verraten ◇*verb* (PRES **verrät**, IMPERF
verriet, PERF **hat verraten**) **1** to
betray; **2** to give away; **3** to tell;
4 sich verraten to give yourself
away.

verrechnen *verb* (PERF **hat sich
verrechnet**) **sich verrechnen** to
make a mistake.

verregnet *adjective* rainy.

verreisen *verb* (PERF **ist verreist**)
to go away; **verreist sein** to be away.

verriet SEE **verraten**.

verrosten *verb* (PERF **ist
verrostet**) to rust.

verrostet *adjective* rusty.

verrückt *adjective* mad, crazy.

Verrückte *der/die* (PL die
Verrückten) maniac.

a
b
c
d
e
f
g
h
i
j
k
l
m
n
o
p
q
r
s
t
u
v
w
x
y
z

versagen *verb* (PERF **hat versagt**) to fail.

versammeln *verb* (PERF **hat versammelt**) **1** to assemble; **2 sich versammeln** to assemble.

Versammlung *die* (PL *die* Versammlungen) meeting.

versäumen *verb* (PERF **hat versäumt**) to miss; **es versäumen, etwas zu tun** to fail to do something.

verschenken *verb* (PERF **hat verschenkt**) to give away.

verschieben ◇*verb* (IMPERF **verschob**, PERF **hat verschoben**) to postpone.

verschieden *adjective* **1** different; **2** various.

verschlafen ◇*verb* (PRES **verschläft**, IMPERF **verschlief**, PERF **hat verschlafen**) **1** to oversleep; **2** to sleep through (*the day*); **3** to miss (*a date, the train*).

verschlechtern *verb* (PERF **hat verschlechtert**) **1** to make worse; **2 sich verschlechtern** to get worse.

verschlief SEE **verschlafen**.

verschließen ◇*verb* (IMPERF **verschloss**, PERF **hat verschlossen**) **1** to close (*a tin, package*); **2** to lock (*a door, drawer*).

verschlimmern *verb* (PERF **hat verschlimmert**) **1** to make worse; **2 sich verschlimmern** to get worse.

verschloss SEE **verschließen**.

verschlucken *verb* (PERF **hat verschluckt**) **1** to swallow; **2 sich verschlucken** to choke.

Verschluss *der* (PL *die* Verschlüsse) **1** fastener, clasp; **2** top (*of a bottle*).

verschmutzen *verb* (PERF **hat verschmutzt**) to soil; **die Umwelt verschmutzen** to pollute the environment.

Verschmutzung *die* pollution.

verschob SEE **verschieben**.

verschreiben ◇*verb* (IMPERF **verschrieb**, PERF **hat verschrieben**) **1** to prescribe; **2 sich verschreiben** to make a mistake.

verschütten *verb* (PERF **hat verschüttet**) to spill.

verschwand SEE **verschwinden**.

verschwenden *verb* (PERF **hat verschwendet**) to waste.

Verschwendung *die* waste.

verschwinden ◇*verb* (IMPERF **verschwand**, PERF **ist verschwunden**) to disappear.

verschwommen *adjective* blurred.

Versehen *das* (PL *die* Versehen) oversight; **aus Versehen** by mistake.

versehentlich *adverb* by mistake.

versetzen *verb* (PERF **hat versetzt**) **1** to move, to transfer (*a person*); **2** to move up (*into the next class at school*); **3 jemanden versetzen** to stand somebody up; **4 jemandem einen Schreck versetzen** to give somebody a fright; **jemandem einen Tritt versetzen** to kick somebody; **5 sich in jemandes**

Lage versetzen to put yourself in somebody's position.

verseuchen *verb* (PERF **hat verseucht**) to contaminate.

Verseuchung die (PL die **Verseuchungen**) contamination.

versichern *verb* (PERF **hat versichert**) 1 to insure; 2 to assert; **jemandem versichern, dass** … to assure somebody that ….

Versicherung die (PL die **Versicherungen**) 1 insurance; 2 assurance.

Versicherungsgesellschaft die (PL die **Versicherungsgesell-schaften**) insurance company.

Versicherungsschein der (PL die **Versicherungsscheine**) insurance policy document.

versöhnen *verb* (PERF **hat sich versöhnt**) **sich versöhnen** to make up; **sich mit jemandem versöhnen** to make it up with somebody.

versorgen *verb* (PERF **hat versorgt**) 1 to supply; 2 to provide for; 3 to look after.

verspäten *verb* (PERF **hat sich verspätet**) **sich verspäten** to be late.

Verspätung die lateness, delay; **Verspätung haben** to be late.

versprechen ◇*verb* (PRES **verspricht**, IMPERF **versprach**, PERF **hat versprochen**) 1 to promise; 2 **sich viel von etwas versprechen** to have high hopes of something; 3 **sich versprechen** to make a slip of the tongue.

Versprechen das (PL die **Versprechen**) promise.

Verstand der 1 mind; **den Verstand verlieren** to go out of your mind; 2 reason.

verstand SEE **verstehen**.

verstanden SEE **verstehen**.

verständigen *verb* (PERF **hat verständigt**) 1 to notify; 2 **sich verständigen** to communicate, to make yourself understood; 3 **sich über etwas verständigen** to agree on something.

Verständigung die 1 communication; 2 notification.

verständlich *adjective* 1 understandable; **jemandem etwas verständlich machen** to make something clear to somebody; 2 comprehensible.

Verständnis das (PL die **Verständnisse**) 1 comprehension; 2 understanding.

Verstärker der (PL die **Verstärker**) amplifier.

verstauchen *verb* (PERF **hat verstaucht**) to sprain; **sich den Fuß verstauchen** to sprain your ankle.

Versteck das (PL die **Verstecke**) hiding place.

verstecken *verb* (PERF **hat versteckt**) 1 to hide; 2 **sich verstecken** to hide.

verstehen ◇*verb* (IMPERF **verstand**, PERF **hat verstanden**) 1 to understand; **etwas falsch verstehen** to misunderstand something; 2 **sich gut verstehen** to get on well; **3 das versteht sich von selbst** that goes without saying.

verstellbar *adjective* adjustable.

verstellen *verb* (PERF **hat verstellt**) **1** to adjust; **2** to block; **3** to disguise; **4 sich verstellen** to pretend.

verstimmt *adjective* **1** out of tune; **2** peeved; **3 ein verstimmter Magen** an upset stomach.

verstopft *adjective* constipated.

Versuch *der* (PL die **Versuche**) **1** attempt; **2** experiment.

versuchen *verb* (PERF **hat versucht**) to try.

verteidigen *verb* (PERF **hat verteidigt**) to defend.

Verteidiger *der* (PL die **Verteidiger**) **1** defender; **2** defence counsel.

Verteidigung *die* defence.

verteilen *verb* (PERF **hat verteilt**) to distribute.

Vertrag *der* (PL die **Verträge**) **1** contract; **2** treaty.

vertragen ◇*verb* (PRES **verträgt**, IMPERF **vertrug**, PERF **hat vertragen**) **1** to stand, to take; **2 ich vertrage keinen Kaffee** coffee disagrees with me; **3 sich vertragen** to get on; **sich wieder vertragen** to make it up.

vertrat SEE **vertreten**.

Vertrauen *das* trust; **im Vertrauen** in confidence.

vertrauen *verb* (PERF **hat vertraut**) to trust.

vertraulich *adjective* **1** confidential; **2** familiar.

vertreten ◇*verb* (PRES **vertritt**, IMPERF **vertrat**, PERF **hat vertreten**) **1** to stand in for; **2** to represent; **3 eine Meinung vertreten** to hold an opinion; **4 sich die Beine vertreten** to stretch your legs.

Vertreter *der* (PL die **Vertreter**) **1** representative; **2** deputy.

Vertreterin *die* (PL die **Vertreterinnen**) **1** representative; **2** deputy.

vertritt SEE **vertreten**.

vertrug SEE **vertragen**.

verunglücken *verb* (PERF **ist verunglückt**) to have an accident.

verursachen *verb* (PERF **hat verursacht**) to cause.

verurteilen *verb* (PERF **hat verurteilt**) **1** to sentence; **2** to condemn.

Verwaltung *die* (PL die **Verwaltungen**) administration.

verwandt *adjective* related.

Verwandte *der/die* (PL die **Verwandten**) relative.

Verwandtschaft *die* relatives.

verwechseln *verb* (PERF **hat verwechselt**) to mix up, to confuse; **jemanden mit jemandem verwechseln** to mistake somebody for somebody; **ich verwechsele ihn mit seinem Bruder** I mistake him for his brother.

verwenden *verb* (PERF **hat verwendet**) to use.

Verwendung *die* use.

verwickelt *adjective* complicated.

verwirren *verb* (PERF **hat verwirrt**)
1 to confuse; **2** to tangle up.

verwirrt *adjective* confused.

verwöhnen *verb* (PERF **hat
verwöhnt**) to spoil.

verwunden *verb* (PERF **hat
verwundet**) to wound.

Verwundete *der/die* (PL *die*
Verwundeten) casualty, injured
person.

Verwundung *die* (PL *die*
Verwundungen) injury, wound.

verzählen *verb* (PERF **hat sich
verzählt**) **sich verzählen** to
miscount.

Verzeichnis *das* (PL *die*
Verzeichnisse) **1** list; **2** index.

verzeihen *verb* (IMPERF **verzieh**,
PERF **hat verziehen**) to forgive;
**verzeihen Sie, können Sie mir
sagen ...?** excuse me, could you tell
me ...?

Verzeihung *die* forgiveness;
jemanden um Verzeihung bitten to
apologize to somebody; **Verzeihung!**
sorry!

verzichten *verb* (PERF **hat
verzichtet**) **1** to do without; **ich
verzichte auf deine Hilfe** I can do
without your help; **2 auf etwas
verzichten** to give up something
(*smoking or your share of
something*); to relinquish something
(*a right or privilege*).

verzieh, verziehen SEE
verzeihen.

verzögern *verb* (PERF **hat
verzögert**) **1** to delay; **2 sich
verzögern** to be delayed.

Verzögerung *die* (PL *die
Verzögerungen) delay.

verzollen *verb* (PERF **hat verzollt**)
to pay duty on; **haben Sie etwas zu
verzollen?** have you anything to
declare?

verzweifeln *verb* (PERF **ist
verzweifelt**) to despair.

verzweifelt *adjective* desperate.

Verzweiflung *die* despair.

Vetter *der* (PL *die* **Vettern**) cousin.

Video *das* (PL *die* **Videos**) video.

Videokamera *die* (PL *die*
Videokameras) video camera.

Videokassette *die* (PL *die*
Videokassetten) video cassette.

Videorekorder *der* (PL *die*
Videorekorder) video recorder.

Videospiel *das* (PL *die*
Videospiele) video game.

Videothek *die* (PL *die*
Videotheken) video shop.

Vieh *das* cattle.

viel *adjective, pronoun* **1** a lot of;
Erika hat viel Arbeit Erika's got a
lot of work; **2 viele** (*plural*) many, a
lot of; **viele Leute** many people;
3 much, a lot; **wie viel?** how much?,
how many?; **zu viel** too much; **vielen
Dank** thank you very much; **viel
Spaß!** have fun!; **viel Glück!** good
luck!; **4 das viele Geld** all that
money.

viel *adverb* **1** much, a lot; **viel
weniger** much less; **so viel wie**

möglich as much as possible; **sie redet viel** she talks a lot; **2 viel zu groß** far too big, much too big; **das dauert viel zu lange** it'll take far too long.

vielleicht *adverb* perhaps.

vielmals *adverb* **danke vielmals** thanks a lot.

vier *number* four.

Viereck *das* (PL *die* Vierecke) **1** rectangle; **2** square.

viereckig *adjective* **1** rectangular; **2** square.

vierte SEE **vierter**.

Viertel *das* (PL *die* Viertel) quarter; **es ist Viertel vor acht** it's quarter to eight.

viertel *adjective* quarter; **wir treffen uns um viertel acht** we'll meet at quarter past seven; **um drei viertel acht** at quarter to eight.

Viertelfinale *das* (PL *die* Viertelfinale) quarter finals.

Viertelstunde *die* (PL *die* Viertelstunden) quarter of an hour.

vierter, vierte, viertes *adjective* fourth.

vierzehn *number* fourteen.

vierzig *number* forty.

Villa *die* (PL *die* Villen) villa.

virtuell *adjective* virtual; **virtuelle Realität** virtual reality.

Virus *das* (PL *die* Viren) virus.

visuell *adjective* visual.

Visum *das* (PL *die* Visa) visa.

Vitamin *das* (PL *die* Vitamine) vitamin.

vitaminarm *adjective* low in vitamins.

vitaminreich *adjective* rich in vitamins.

Vogel *der* (PL *die* Vögel) bird.

Vogelbeobachter *der* (PL *die* Vogelbeobachter) birdwatcher.

Vogelbeobachterin *die* (PL *die* Vogelbeobachterinnen) birdwatcher.

Vogelscheuche *die* (PL *die* Vogelscheuchen) scarecrow.

Vokabel *die* (PL *die* Vokabeln) word; **Vokabeln** vocabulary.

Vokal *der* (PL *die* Vokale) vowel.

Volk *das* (PL *die* Völker) people.

Volkshochschule *die* adult education centre; **ein Kurs an der Volkshochschule** an adult education class.

Volkslied *das* (PL *die* Volkslieder) folk song.

Volkswirtschaft *die* economics.

voll *adjective* **1** full; **ein Korb voll Äpfel** a basket full of apples; **die volle Wahrheit** the whole truth; **2 etwas voll machen** to fill something up; **voll tanken** to fill up with petrol.
voll *adverb* **1** fully, completely; **voll und ganz** completely; **2 jemanden nicht für voll nehmen** (*informal*) not to take somebody seriously.

Volleyball *der* volleyball; **Volleyball spielen** to play volleyball.

völlig *adjective* complete.
völlig *adverb* completely.

vollkommen *adjective* **1** perfect;
2 complete.
vollkommen *adverb* completely.

Vollkornbrot *das* wholemeal
bread.

vollmachen SEE **voll**.

Vollpension *die* full board.

vollständig *adjective* complete.

volltanken SEE **voll**.

vom = **von dem**.

von *preposition* (+ DAT) **1** from; **von
heute an** from today; **von hier bis
... from here to ...; 2** of; **eine
Freundin von mir** a friend of mine;
3 about; **Peter hat mir von dem
neuen Haus erzählt** Peter told me
about the new house; **4** by; **ein
Theaterstück von Brecht** a play by
Brecht; **5 von mir aus** I don't mind.

voneinander *adverb* from each
other; **sie sind voneinander
abhängig** they depend on each
other.

vor *preposition* (+ DAT *or* + ACC *with
movement towards a place*) **1** in
front of; **2** before; **Manfred war vor
euch da** Manfred arrived before
you; **kurz vor der Ampel** shortly
before the lights; **3** with; **vor Angst
zittern** to tremble with fear; **4** (*with
clock time*) **zehn vor fünf** ten to five;
5 ago; **vor zwei Jahren** two years
ago; **6 sich vor jemandem
fürchten** to be frightened of
somebody; **7 vor allen Dingen**
above all; **8 vor sich hin summen** to
hum to yourself.
vor *adverb* forward; **vor und
zurück** backwards and forwards.

voraus *adverb* **1** ahead; **2 im
Voraus** in advance.

vorausgehen ◊*verb* (IMPERF **ging
voraus**, PERF **ist vorausgegangen**)
1 to go on ahead; **2** to precede.

voraussetzen *verb* (PERF **hat
vorausgesetzt**) **1** to take for
granted; **2** to require;
3 vorausgesetzt, dass ... provided
that ...

Voraussetzung *die* (PL *die*
Voraussetzungen) **1** condition;
2 assumption.

vorbei *adverb* **1** past; **2** over; **vorbei
sein** to be over.

vorbeifahren ◊*verb* (PRES **fährt
vorbei**, IMPERF **fuhr vorbei**, PERF **ist
vorbeigefahren**) to drive past, to
pass.

vorbeigehen ◊*verb* (IMPERF **ging
vorbei**, PERF **ist vorbeigegangen**)
1 to go past, to pass; **2** to drop in; **ich
gehe bei Anne vorbei** I'll drop in on
Anne.

vorbeikommen ◊*verb* (IMPERF
kam vorbei, PERF **ist
vorbeigekommen**) **1** to pass; **2** to
get past; **3** to drop in.

vorbereiten *verb* (PERF **hat
vorbereitet**) **1** to prepare; **2 sich
vorbereiten** to prepare.

Vorbereitung *die* (PL *die*
Vorbereitungen) preparation.

vorbeugen *verb* (PERF **hat
vorgebeugt**) **1** to prevent; **2 sich
vorbeugen** to lean forward.

Vorbild *das* (PL *die* **Vorbilder**)
example.

a
b
c
d
e
f
g
h
i
j
k
l
m
n
o
p
q
r
s
t
u
v
w
x
y
z

vorderer, vordere, vorderes *adjective* front.

Vordergrund *der* foreground; **im Vordergrund** in the foreground.

Vorderseite *die* front.

vorderster, vorderste, vorderstes *adjective* front.

Vorfahr *der* (PL *die* **Vorfahren**) ancestor.

Vorfahrt *die* right of way; **'Vorfahrt beachten/gewähren'** 'give way'.

Vorfall *der* (PL *die* **Vorfälle**) incident.

Vorführung *die* (PL *die* **Vorführungen**) **1** performance; **2** demonstration.

Vorgänger *der* (PL *die* **Vorgänger**) predecessor.

Vorgängerin *die* (PL *die* **Vorgängerinnen**) predecessor.

vorgehen ◇*verb* (IMPERF **ging vor**, PERF **ist vorgegangen**) **1** to go on ahead; **2** to go forward; **3** to proceed; **4 die Uhr geht vor** the clock is fast; **5 was geht hier vor?** what's going on here?

Vorgehensweise *die* (PL *die* **Vorgehensweisen**) policy.

vorgestern *adverb* the day before yesterday.

vorhaben ◇*verb* (PRES **hat vor**, IMPERF **hatte vor**, PERF **hat vorgehabt**) **1** to intend; **2 etwas vorhaben** to have something planned.

Vorhang *der* (PL *die* **Vorhänge**) curtain.

Vorhängeschloss *das* (PL *die* **Vorhängeschlösser**) padlock.

vorher *adverb* beforehand, before.

Vorhersage *die* (PL *die* **Vorhersagen**) **1** forecast; **2** prediction.

vorhin *adverb* just now.

voriger, vorige, voriges *adjective* last.

vorkommen ◇*verb* (IMPERF **kam vor**, PERF **ist vorgekommen**) **1** to happen; **2** to occur; **3** to come forward; **4** to come out (*from behind somewhere*); **5** to seem; **jemandem bekannt vorkommen** to seem familiar to somebody; **6 sich alt vorkommen** to feel old.

Vorlauf *der* fast forward (*on video*).

vorläufig *adjective* temporary.

vorlesen ◇*verb* (PRES **liest vor**, IMPERF **las vor**, PERF **hat vorgelesen**) **1** to read (out); **2 jemandem vorlesen** to read to somebody.

vorletzter, vorletzte, vorletztes *adjective* last but one; **vorletztes Jahr** the year before last.

Vormittag *der* (PL *die* **Vormittage**) morning.

vormittags *adverb* in the morning.

vorn *adverb* **1** at the front; **nach vorn** to the front; **2 von vorn** from the beginning; **wieder von vorn anfangen** to start again at the beginning; **da vorn** over there.

Vorname *der* (PL *die* **Vornamen**) first name.

vorne SEE **vorn**.

vornehm *adjective* **1** elegant; **2** distinguished.

vornehmen ⋄*verb* (PRES **nimmt vor**, IMPERF **nahm vor**, PERF **hat vorgenommen**) **1** to carry out; **2 sich vornehmen, etwas zu tun** to plan to do something.

Vorort *der* (PL die **Vororte**) suburb.

Vorrat *der* (PL die **Vorräte**) supply, stock.

Vorsatz *der* (PL die **Vorsätze**) intention.

Vorschau *die* **1** preview; **2** trailer (*of a film*).

Vorschlag *der* (PL die **Vorschläge**) suggestion.

vorschlagen ⋄*verb* (PRES **schlägt vor**, IMPERF **schlug vor**, PERF **hat vorgeschlagen**) to suggest.

Vorschrift *die* (PL die **Vorschriften**) **1** regulation; **2** instruction.

Vorschule *die* (PL die **Vorschulen**) infant school.

vorsehen ⋄*verb* (PRES **sieht sich vor**, IMPERF **sah sich vor**, PERF **hat sich vorgesehen**) **sich vorsehen** to be careful.

Vorsicht *die* care; **Vorsicht!** careful!, (*on a sign*) caution!

vorsichtig *adjective* careful.

vorsichtshalber *adverb* to be on the safe side.

Vorsichtsmaßnahme *die* (PL die **Vorsichtsmaßnahmen**) precaution; **Vorsichtsmaßnahmen gegen etwas ergreifen** to take precautions against something.

Vorspeise *die* (PL die **Vorspeisen**) starter.

Vorsprung *der* (PL die **Vorsprünge**) **1** ledge (*of a rock*); **2** lead (*over somebody*).

vorstellen *verb* (PERF **hat vorgestellt**) **1** to introduce; **darf ich Ihnen Herrn Schulz vorstellen?** may I introduce Mr Schulz?; **2 die Uhr vorstellen** to put the clock forward; **3 sich vorstellen** to introduce yourself; **4 sich beim Personalchef vorstellen** to go for an interview with the personnel manager; **5 sich etwas vorstellen** to imagine something; **stell dir vor!** can you imagine?

Vorstellung *die* (PL die **Vorstellungen**) **1** performance; **2** introduction; **3** interview (*for a job*); **4** idea; **5** imagination.

Vorstellungsgespräch *das* (PL die **Vorstellungsgespräche**) interview.

Vorteil *der* (PL die **Vorteile**) advantage.

Vortrag *der* (PL die **Vorträge**) talk.

vorüber *adverb* **vorüber sein** to be over.

vorübergehend *adjective* temporary.
vorübergehend *adverb* temporarily.

Vorurteil *das* (PL die **Vorurteile**) prejudice.

Vorwahl *die* (PL die **Vorwahlen**) dialling code; **wählen Sie die Vorwahl 00 44 für Großbritannien** dial 00 44 for Britain.

a b c d e f g h i j k l m n o p q r s t u v w x y z

vorwärts *adverb* forward(s).

vorwiegend *adverb* predominantly.

Vorwurf *der* (PL *die* Vorwürfe) reproach; **jemandem Vorwürfe machen** to reproach somebody.

vorzeigen *verb* (PERF **hat vorgezeigt**) to show.

vorziehen ⬦*verb* (PRES **zieht vor**, IMPERF **zog vor**, PERF **hat vorgezogen**) 1 to prefer; 2 to pull up (*a chair*); 3 **den Vorhang vorziehen** to draw the curtain.

vorzüglich *adjective* excellent.

vulgär *adjective* vulgar.

Vulkan *der* (PL *die* Vulkane) volcano.

Ww

Waage *die* (PL *die* Waagen) 1 scales; 2 Libra; **Gabi ist Waage** Gabi's Libra.

waagerecht *adjective* horizontal.

wach *adjective* awake; **wach sein** to be awake; **wach werden** to wake up.

Wache *die* (PL *die* Wachen) 1 guard; 2 (police) station.

Wachhund *der* (PL *die* Wachhunde) guard dog.

Wachs *das* wax.

wachsen ⬦*verb* (PRES **wächst**, IMPERF **wuchs**, PERF **ist gewachsen**) to grow.

Wachstum *das* growth.

wackelig *adjective* wobbly.

wackeln *verb* (PERF **hat gewackelt**) to wobble.

Wade *die* (PL *die* Waden) calf.

Waffe *die* (PL *die* Waffen) weapon.

Waffel *die* (PL *die* Waffeln) waffle.

Waffenhandel *der* arms trade.

Wagen *der* (PL *die* Wagen) 1 car; **nimmst du den Wagen?** are you going by car?; 2 carriage (*of a train*); 3 cart.

wagen *verb* (PERF **hat gewagt**) 1 to risk; 2 **es wagen, etwas zu tun** to dare to do something; **sich nicht irgendwohin wagen** not dare to go somewhere.

Wagenheber *der* (PL *die* Wagenheber) jack.

Wahl *die* (PL *die* Wahlen) 1 choice; **er hat die Wahl** it's his choice; 2 election; **die nächsten Wahlen sind im Herbst** the next election is in autumn.

wählen *verb* (PERF **hat gewählt**) 1 to choose; **zwischen zwei Möglichkeiten wählen** to choose between two possibilities; 2 **haben Sie schon gewählt?** are you ready to order? (*in a restaurant*); 3 to elect; 4 to vote, to vote for; **sie wählt immer grün** she always votes green; **wählt Schröder!** vote for Schröder; 5 to dial; **ich muss die falsche Nummer gewählt haben** I must have dialled the wrong number.

Wahlfach *das* (PL *die* Wahlfächer) optional subject, option.

Wahnsinn *der* madness.

wahnsinnig *adjective* 1 mad; **wahnsinnig werden** to go mad;

2 wahnsinnigen Durst haben to be terribly thirsty; **der Film war wahnsinnig gut** the film was incredibly good.

wahr *adjective* **1** true; **2 du kommst doch, nicht wahr?** you're coming, aren't you?

während *preposition* (+ GEN) during.
während *conjunction* **1** while; **2** whereas.

Wahrheit die (PL die Wahrheiten) truth.

Wahrsager der (PL die Wahrsager) fortune-teller.

Wahrsagerin die (PL die Wahrsagerinnen) fortune-teller.

wahrscheinlich *adjective* probable, likely.
wahrscheinlich *adverb* probably.

Währung die (PL die Währungen) currency.

Waise die (PL die Waisen) orphan; **er ist Waise** he's an orphan.

Wal der (PL die Wale) whale.

Wald der (PL die Wälder) wood, forest.

Waliser der (PL die Waliser) Welshman.

Waliserin die (PL die Waliserinnen) Welshwoman.

walisisch *adjective* Welsh.

Walkman™ der (PL die Walkmans) walkman™.

Walnuss die (PL die Walnüsse) walnut.

Wand die (PL die Wände) wall.

Wanderer der (PL die Wanderer) **1** hiker; **2** rambler.

Wanderin die (PL die Wanderinnen) **1** hiker; **2** rambler.

wandern *verb* (PERF **ist gewandert**) **1** to hike; **2** to go walking.

Wandern das hiking.

Wanderung die (PL die Wanderungen) **1** hike; **2** walking tour.

Wandteppich der (PL die Wandteppiche) tapestry.

wann *adverb* when.

Wanne die (PL die Wannen) **1** tub; **2** bath.

war SEE **sein**.

warb SEE **werben**.

Ware die (PL die Waren) **1** article; **2 Waren** goods.

waren SEE **sein**.

Warenhaus das (PL die Warenhäuser) department store.

warf SEE **werfen**.

warm *adjective* warm; **eine warme Mahlzeit** a hot meal; **das Essen warm machen** to heat up the food.

Wärme die warmth.

wärmen *verb* (PERF **hat gewärmt**) to warm, to heat.

Warndreieck das (PL die Warndreiecke) warning triangle.

warnen *verb* (PERF **hat gewarnt**) to warn; **jemanden vor etwas warnen** to warn somebody of something.

Warnung die (PL die Warnungen) warning.

a
b
c
d
e
f
g
h
i
j
k
l
m
n
o
p
q
r
s
t
u
v
w
x
y
z

warst, wart SEE **sein**.

Warteliste die (PL die Wartelisten) waiting list.

warten verb (PERF hat gewartet) **1** to wait; **auf jemanden warten** to wait for somebody; **2 auf sich warten lassen** to take your time.

Wärter der (PL die Wärter) **1** keeper; **2** attendant; **3** warder.

Warteraum der (PL die Warteräume) waiting room.

Wärterin die (PL die Wärterinnen) **1** keeper; **2** attendant; **3** warder.

Wartezeit die wait; **eine Stunde Wartezeit** an hour's wait.

Wartezimmer das (PL die Wartezimmer) waiting room.

warum adverb why.

Warze die (PL die Warzen) wart.

was pronoun **1** what; **was für ein/ eine ...?** what kind of ...?; **was für ein Fahrrad hast du?** what kind of bike do you have?; **was für ein Glück!** what luck!; **was kostet das?** how much is it?; **2** that; **alles, was wir brauchen** all (that) we need; **alles, was du willst** all (that) you want; **3** (short for 'etwas') something; **heute gibts was Gutes im Fernsehen** there's something good on television today; **4** (short for 'etwas' in questions and negatives) anything; **hast du was für mich?** have you got anything for me?

Waschbecken das (PL die Waschbecken) washbasin.

Wäsche die **1** washing; **2** underwear.

waschen ⋄verb (PRES wäscht, IMPERF wusch, PERF hat gewaschen) **1** to wash; **2 sich waschen** to have a wash; **sich die Hände waschen** to wash your hands.

Wäscheraum der (PL die Wäscheräume) laundry room.

Wäscherei die (PL die Wäschereien) laundry.

Waschlappen der (PL die Waschlappen) flannel.

Waschmaschine die (PL die Waschmaschinen) washing machine.

Waschpulver das (PL die Waschpulver) washing powder.

Waschsalon der (PL die Waschsalons) launderette.

Wasser das water.

wasserdicht adjective waterproof.

Wasserfall der (PL die Wasserfälle) waterfall.

Wasserfarbe die (PL die Wasserfarben) watercolour.

Wasserhahn der (PL die Wasserhähne) tap.

Wassermann der Aquarius; **Lisa ist Wassermann** Lisa's Aquarius.

Wassermelone die (PL die Wassermelonen) water melon.

Wasserskifahren das water-skiing.

Wassersport der water sport.

Wassertiefe die depth (of water); **Wassertiefe: 2 Meter** depth: 2 metres.

Watte *die* cotton wool.

wattiert *adjective* padded.

WC *das* (PL *die* WCs) WC, toilet.

weben *verb* (PERF **hat gewebt**) to weave.

Webseite *die* (PL *die* Webseiten) web page.

Website *die* (PL *die* Websites) web site.

Wechselkurs *der* (PL *die* Wechselkurse) exchange rate.

wechseln *verb* (PERF **hat gewechselt**) **1** to change; **kannst du mir zehn Euro wechseln?** have you got change for ten euros?; **2** to exchange (*glances, letters*).

Wechselstube *die* (PL *die* Wechselstuben) bureau de change.

wecken *verb* (PERF **hat geweckt**) to wake (up).

Wecker *der* (PL *die* Wecker) alarm clock; **Max geht mir auf den Wecker** (*informal*) Max gets on my nerves.

weder *conjunction* **weder … noch** neither … nor.

Weg *der* (PL *die* Wege) **1** way; **auf dem Weg nach Hause** on the way home; **2** path; **3 sich auf den Weg machen** to set off; **4 im Weg sein** to be in the way.

weg *adverb* **1** away; **geh weg!** go away!; **Hände weg!** hands off!; **2** gone; **der Ring ist weg** the ring's gone; **Heidi ist schon weg** Heidi's already gone.

wegen *preposition* (+ GEN) because of.

wegfahren ⬦*verb* (PRES **fährt weg**, IMPERF **fuhr weg**, PERF **ist weggefahren**) **1** to leave; **sie fahren gerade weg** they are leaving just now; **2** (PERF **hat weggefahren**) to drive away (*a car or things*).

weggehen ⬦*verb* (IMPERF **ging weg**, PERF **ist weggegangen**) **1** to go away; **2** to leave; **3** to go out; **wir gehen heute Abend weg** we're going out tonight; **4** to come out (*of a stain*).

weglassen ⬦*verb* (PRES **lässt weg**, IMPERF **ließ weg**, PERF **hat weggelassen**) **1** to let go; **2** to leave out.

weglaufen ⬦*verb* (PRES **läuft weg**, IMPERF **lief weg**, PERF **ist weggelaufen**) to run away.

weglegen *verb* (PERF **hat weggelegt**) **1** to put down; **2** to put away.

wegmachen *verb* (PERF **hat weggemacht**) to get rid of (*a stain or wart, for example*).

wegmüssen ⬦*verb* (*informal*) (PRES **muss weg**, IMPERF **musste weg**, PERF **hat weggemusst**) to have to go.

wegnehmen ⬦*verb* (PRES **nimmt weg**, IMPERF **nahm weg**, PERF **hat weggenommen**) to take away.

wegräumen *verb* (PERF **hat weggeräumt**) to clear away.

wegschicken *verb* (PERF **hat weggeschickt**) **1** to send away; **2** to send off.

wegtun ⬦*verb* (IMPERF **tat weg**, PERF **hat weggetan**) to put away.

a b c d e f g h i j k l m n o p q r s t u v w x y z

Wegweiser der (PL die **Wegweiser**) signpost.

wegwerfen ◇verb (PRES **wirft weg**, IMPERF **warf weg**, PERF **hat weggeworfen**) to throw away.

weh adjective **1** sore; **2 oh weh!** oh dear!; **3 es tut weh** it hurts.

wehen verb (PERF **hat geweht**) to blow.

Wehrdienst der military service.

wehren verb (PERF **hat sich gewehrt**) **sich wehren** to defend yourself.

wehrlos adjective defenceless.

wehtun ◇verb (PRES **tut weh**, IMPERF **tat weh**, PERF **hat wehgetan**) **1** to hurt; **mein Arm tut weh** my arm hurts; **jemandem wehtun** to hurt somebody; **2 sich wehtun** to hurt yourself.

Weibchen das (PL die **Weibchen**) female.

weiblich adjective **1** female; **2** feminine (noun).

weich adjective soft.

Weide die (PL die **Weiden**) **1** willow; **2** pasture.

weigern verb (PERF **hat sich geweigert**) **sich weigern** to refuse.

Weihnachten das (PL die **Weihnachten**) Christmas; **Frohe Weihnachten!** Merry Christmas!

Weihnachtskrippe die (PL die **Weihnachtskrippen**) Christmas crib scene.

Weihnachtslied das (PL die **Weihnachtslieder**) Christmas carol.

Weihnachtsmann der (PL die **Weihnachtsmänner**) Father Christmas.

Weihnachtstag der (PL die **Weihnachtstage**) Christmas Day; **zweiter Weihnachtstag** Boxing Day.

weil conjunction because.

Weile die while.

Wein der (PL die **Weine**) wine.

Weinberg der (PL die **Weinberge**) vineyard.

Weinbergschnecke die (PL die **Weinbergschnecken**) snail.

Weinbrand der (PL die **Weinbrände**) brandy.

weinen verb (PERF **hat geweint**) to cry.

Weinkarte die (PL die **Weinkarten**) wine list.

Weinkeller der (PL die **Weinkeller**) wine cellar.

Weinstube die (PL die **Weinstuben**) wine bar.

Weintraube die (PL die **Weintrauben**) grape.

Weise die (PL die **Weisen**) way; **auf diese Weise** in this way.

weise adjective wise.

Weisheit die (PL die **Weisheiten**) wisdom.

weiß¹ SEE **wissen**.

weiß² adjective white.

Weißwein der (PL die **Weißweine**) white wine.

weit adjective, adverb **1** wide, loose (clothes); **2** long; **eine weite Reise** a long journey; **3** far; **wie weit ist es?** how far is it?; **ist es noch weit?** is it much further?; **so weit wie möglich** as far as possible; **bei weitem** by far; **4 von weitem** from a distance; **5 ich bin so weit** I'm ready; **6 weit verbreitet** widespread; **7 zu weit gehen** to go too far.

weiten *verb* (PERF **hat sich geweitet**) **sich weiten** to stretch.

weiter *adjective, adverb* **1** further; **2** in addition; **3 etwas weiter tun** to go on doing something; **weiter nichts** nothing else; **weiter niemand** nobody else; **4 und so weiter** and so on.

weiterer, weitere, weiteres *adjective* **1** further; **2 ohne weiteres** just like that, easily; **3 bis auf weiteres** for the time being.

weiterfahren ⬦*verb* (PRES **fährt weiter**, IMPERF **fuhr weiter**, PERF **ist weitergefahren**) to go on.

weitergehen ⬦*verb* (IMPERF **ging weiter**, PERF **ist weitergegangen**) to go on.

weiterhin *adverb* **1** still; **2** in future; **3 etwas weiterhin tun** to go on doing something.

weitermachen *verb* (PERF **hat weitergemacht**) to carry on.

Weitsprung *der* long jump.

Weizen *der* wheat.

welcher, welche, welches *adjective* which; **welches Kleid?** which dress?; **um welche Zeit?** at what time?

welches *pronoun* **1** which (one);

2 some; **brauchst du Briefmarken? ich habe welche** do you need stamps? I've got some; **3** any; **hast du welche?** have you got any?

Welle *die* (PL *die* **Wellen**) wave.

Wellensittich *der* (PL *die* **Wellensittiche**) budgerigar.

wellig *adjective* wavy.

Welt *die* (PL *die* **Welten**) world; **auf der ganzen Welt** in the whole world.

Weltall *das* universe.

Weltkrieg *der* (PL *die* **Weltkriege**) world war.

Weltmeister *der* (PL *die* **Weltmeister**) world champion.

Weltmeisterin *die* (PL *die* **Weltmeisterinnen**) world champion.

Weltmeisterschaft *die* (PL *die* **Weltmeisterschaften**) **1** world championship; **2 die Weltmeisterschaft** (*football*) the World Cup.

Weltraum *der* space.

Weltreise *die* (PL *die* **Weltreisen**) world tour.

wem *pronoun* to whom; **wem hat er das Geld gegeben?** who did he give the money to?

wen *pronoun* whom, who; **wen hast du eingeladen?** who did you invite?

Wende *die* **1** change; **2** reunification (*of Germany*).

wenig *pronoun, adjective* **1** little; **zu wenig** too little, not enough; **2 wenige** few; **in wenigen Wochen** in a few weeks.

wenig *adverb* little; **so wenig wie möglich** as little as possible.

weniger *pronoun, adjective* less, fewer; **sie hat weniger Geschenke bekommen** she got fewer presents; **immer weniger Geld** less and less money; **immer weniger Häuser** fewer and fewer houses.

weniger *adverb, conjunction* less; **zehn weniger fünf** ten minus five.

wenigste SEE **wenigster**.

wenigstens *adverb* at least.

wenigster, wenigste, wenigstes *adjective, pronoun* least; **am wenigsten** least; **sein Geschenk hat mir am wenigsten gefallen** I liked his present least.

wenn *conjunction* 1 when; **wenn ich in München bin, schreibe ich dir** I'll write to you when I'm in Munich; **immer, wenn** whenever; 2 if; **wenn es regnet** if it rains; 3 **außer wenn** unless.

wer *pronoun* who.

werben ◇*verb* (PRES **wirbt**, IMPERF **warb**, PERF **hat geworben**) 1 to advertise; 2 to recruit (*members*).

Werbespot *der* (PL die **Werbespots**) commercial, advert.

Werbung *die* 1 advertising; **in der Werbung arbeiten** to work in advertising; 2 advertisement; **im Fernsehen kommt viel Werbung** there are many advertisements on television; **Werbung für etwas machen** to advertise something.

werden ◇*verb* (PRES **wird**, IMPERF **wurde**, PERF **ist geworden**) 1 to become; **Arzt werden** to become a doctor; 2 **müde werden** to get tired; **alt werden** to get old; **mir wird kalt** I'm getting cold; 3 **mir wurde schlecht** I felt sick; **blass werden** to turn pale; 4 **wach werden** to wake up; 5 (*used to form the future tense*) will, shall; **sie wird anrufen** she'll ring; **sie wird gleich da sein** she'll be here in a minute; 6 (*used to form the passive*) to be; **gerufen werden** to be called; **er wurde gefragt** he was asked; 7 (*used to form the conditional*) **sie würde kommen** she would come; **ich würde gern kommen, aber** ... I'd like to come but ....

werfen ◇*verb* (PRES **wirft**, IMPERF **warf**, PERF **hat geworfen**) to throw.

Werk *das* (PL die **Werke**) 1 work; 2 works (*a factory*).

Werken *das* handicraft.

Werkstatt *die* (PL die **Werkstätten**) workshop.

Werktag *der* (PL die **Werktage**) weekday.

werktags *adverb* on weekdays.

Werkzeug *das* (PL die **Werkzeuge**) tool.

Werkzeugkasten *der* (PL die **Werkzeugkästen**) tool box.

wert *adjective* **viel wert sein** to be worth a lot; **nichts wert sein** to be worthless.

Wert *der* (PL die **Werte**) 1 value; **im Wert von hundert Euro** worth one hundred euros; 2 **auf etwas Wert legen** to attach importance to something; 3 **es hat doch keinen Wert** there's no point.

wertlos *adjective* worthless.

wertvoll *adjective* valuable.

Wesen *das* (PL *die* **Wesen**) **1** nature, manner; **2** creature.

wesentlich *adjective* essential; **im Wesentlichen** essentially.
wesentlich *adverb* considerably.

weshalb *adverb* why.

Wespe *die* (PL *die* **Wespen**) wasp.

wessen *pronoun* whose.

Wessi *der* (*informal*) (PL *die* **Wessis**) West German.

Weste *die* (PL *die* **Westen**) waistcoat.

Westen *der* west.

Western *der* (PL *die* **Western**) western (*film*).

Westinder *der* (PL *die* **Westinder**) West Indian.

Westinderin *die* (PL *die* **Westinderinnen**) West Indian.

westlich *adjective* **1** western; **2** westerly.
westlich *adverb*, *preposition* (+ GEN) **westlich von Wien** west of Vienna; **westlich der Stadt** to the west of the town.

weswegen *adverb* why.

Wettbewerb *der* (PL *die* **Wettbewerbe**) competition, contest.

Wette *die* (PL *die* **Wetten**) bet; **mit jemandem um die Wette laufen** to race somebody.

wetten *verb* (PERF **hat gewettet**) to bet; **mit jemandem um etwas wetten** to bet somebody something.

Wetter *das* weather.

Wetterbericht *der* (PL *die* **Wetterberichte**) weather report.

Wettervorhersage *die* weather forecast.

Wettkampf *der* (PL *die* **Wettkämpfe**) contest.

Wettlauf *der* race.

wichtig *adjective* important; **das wichtigste Exportgut ist Wolle** the most important export is wool.

wickeln *verb* (PERF **hat gewickelt**) **1** to wind; **2** **ein Kind wickeln** to change a baby.

Widder *der* (PL *die* **Widder**) **1** ram; **2** Aries; **Jan ist Widder** Jan's Aries.

widerlich *adjective* disgusting.

widersprechen ◇*verb* (PRES **widerspricht**, IMPERF **widersprach**, PERF **hat widersprochen**) to contradict.

Widerspruch *der* (PL *die* **Widersprüche**) contradiction.

Widerstand *der* resistance.

widerstehen ◇*verb* (IMPERF **widerstand**, PERF **hat widerstanden**) to resist.

widmen *verb* (PERF **hat gewidmet**) **1** to dedicate; **2** to devote; **3** **sich einer Sache widmen** to devote yourself to something.

wie *adverb* **1** how; **wie geht's?** how are you?; **wie viel?** how much?, how many?; **wie viele Leute waren da?** how many people were there?; **um wie viel Uhr kommst du?** (at) what time are you coming?; **2** **wie ist Ihr Name?** what is your name?; **wie ist das Wetter?** what's the weather like?; **3 wie bitte?** sorry?

wie *conjunction* **1** as; **so schnell wie möglich** as quickly as possible; **2** like; **wie du** like you; **3 wie zum Beispiel** such as.

wieder *adverb* **1** again; **sie ist wieder da** she's back again; **2 jemanden wieder erkennen** to recognize somebody; **etwas wieder finden** to find something (again); **etwas wieder verwerten** to recycle something; **jemanden wieder beleben** to revive somebody.

wiederbekommen ◇*verb* (IMPERF **bekam wieder**, PERF **hat wiederbekommen**) to get back.

wiederbeleben *verb* (PERF **hat wiederbelebt**) SEE **wieder**.

wiedererkennen SEE **wieder**.

wiederfinden SEE **wieder**.

wiederholen *verb* (PERF **hat wiederholt**) **1** to repeat; **2** to bring back; **3** to revise (*schoolwork*); **4 sich wiederholen** to recur; **er hat sich wiederholt** he's repeated himself.

Wiederholung *die* (PL *die* **Wiederholungen**) **1** repetition; **2** repeat performance; **3** replay; **4** revision (*at school*).

Wiederhören *das* **auf Wiederhören!** (*said on the phone*) goodbye!

wiederkommen ◇*verb* (IMPERF **kam wieder**, PERF **ist wiedergekommen**) **1** to come back; **2** to come again.

Wiedersehen *das* (PL *die* **Wiedersehen**) **1** reunion; **2 auf Wiedersehen!** goodbye!

wiedersehen SEE **sehen**.

wiedervereinigen SEE **vereinigen**.

Wiedervereinigung *die* reunification.

wiederverwerten SEE **wieder**.

Wiege *die* (PL *die* **Wiegen**) cradle.

wiegen ◇*verb* (IMPERF **wog**, PERF **hat gewogen**) to weigh.

Wiegenlied *das* (PL *die* **Wiegenlieder**) lullaby.

Wien *das* Vienna.

Wiese *die* (PL *die* **Wiesen**) meadow.

wieso *adverb* why.

wieviel SEE **wie**.

wievielmal *adverb* how often.

wievielter, wievielte, wievieltes *adjective* **1** which; **2 die wievielte Querstraße ist das von hier aus?** how many roads is that from here?; **der Wievielte ist heute?** what's the date today?

wild *adjective* wild.

Wildleder *das* suede.

Wildpark *der* (PL *die* **Wildparks**) wildlife park.

Wildschwein *das* (PL *die* **Wildschweine**) wild boar.

will SEE **wollen**.

Wille *der* will; **seinen Willen durchsetzen** to get your own way.

willkommen *adjective* welcome.

willst SEE **wollen**.

Wimper die (PL die Wimpern) eyelash.

Wimperntusche die (PL die Wimperntuschen) mascara.

Wind der (PL die Winde) wind.

Windel die (PL die Windeln) nappy.

Windhund der (PL die Windhunde) greyhound.

windig adjective windy.

Windmühle die (PL die Windmühlen) windmill.

Windpark der (PL die Windparks) wind farm.

Windpocken plural noun chickenpox.

Windschutzscheibe die (PL die Windschutzscheiben) windscreen.

Windsurfen das windsurfing; **Windsurfen gehen** to go windsurfing.

Winkel der (PL die Winkel) **1** angle; **2** corner.

winken verb (PERF hat gewinkt) to wave.

Winter der (PL die Winter) winter.

winzig adjective tiny.

Wippe die (PL die Wippen) seesaw.

wir pronoun we; **wir sind es** it's us; **wir alle** all of us.

Wirbel der (PL die Wirbel) **1** whirl; **2** whirlwind; **3** whirlpool; **4** commotion.

Wirbelsäule die (PL die Wirbelsäulen) spine.

wirbt SEE **werben**.

wird SEE **werden**.

wirft SEE **werfen**.

wirken verb (PERF hat gewirkt) **1** to have an effect; **2 gegen etwas wirken** to be effective against something; **3** to seem (sad, happy).

wirklich adjective real. **wirklich** adverb really.

Wirklichkeit die reality.

wirksam adjective effective.

Wirkung die (PL die Wirkungen) effect.

wirst SEE **werden**.

Wirt der (PL die Wirte) landlord.

Wirtin die (PL die Wirtinnen) landlady.

Wirtschaft die (PL die Wirtschaften) **1** economy; **2** pub.

wirtschaftlich adjective economic.

Wirtschaftswissenschaften plural noun business studies.

Wirtshaus das (PL die Wirtshäuser) pub.

wischen verb (PERF hat gewischt) to wipe.

wissen ⬦verb (PRES weiß, IMPERF wusste, PERF hat gewusst) to know; **ich weiß, dass er in London wohnt** I know he lives in London; **ich wüsste gern** ... I'd like to know ...; **von etwas wissen** to know about something; **weißt du was?** you know what?

Wissen das knowledge.

Wissenschaft die (PL die Wissenschaften) science.

Wissenschaftler der (PL die Wissenschaftler) scientist.

a
b
c
d
e
f
g
h
i
j
k
l
m
n
o
p
q
r
s
t
u
v
w
x
y
z

Wissenschaftlerin *die* (PL *die* Wissenschaftlerinnen) scientist.

wissenschaftlich *adjective* scientific.

Witwe *die* (PL *die* Witwen) widow.

Witwer *der* (PL *die* Witwer) widower.

Witz *der* (PL *die* Witze) joke.

witzig *adjective* funny.

wo *adverb* where; **wo seid ihr gewesen?** where have you been?; **in München, wo Markus seit einem Jahr lebt** in Munich, where Markus has been living for a year; **wo immer** wherever.

wo *conjunction* **1** seeing that; **2** although; **jetzt ist sie mir böse, wo ich doch so nett zu ihr war** now she's angry with me, although I've been so nice to her.

woanders *adverb* elsewhere.

Woche *die* (PL *die* Wochen) week.

Wochenende *das* (PL *die* Wochenenden) weekend.

wochenlang *adverb* for weeks.

Wochentag *der* (PL *die* Wochentage) weekday.

wochentags *adverb* on weekdays.

wöchentlich *adjective* weekly.

wofür *adverb* what ... for; **wofür brauchst du das Geld?** what do you need the money for?

wog SEE **wiegen**.

woher *adverb* where ... from; **woher ist er?** where does he come from?; **woher weißt du das?** how do you know?

wohin *adverb* where ... (to); **wohin geht ihr?** where are you going?

Wohl *das* **1** welfare, well-being; **2 zu seinem Wohl** for his benefit; **3 zum Wohl!** cheers!

wohl *adverb* **1** well; **sich wohl fühlen** to feel well; **ich fühle mich heute nicht wohl** I don't feel well today; **2 sich wohl fühlen** to be happy; **Anni fühlt sich in London wohl** Anni is happy in London; **3 jemandem wohl tun** to do somebody good; **4** probably; **er hat den Zug wohl verpasst** he probably missed the train; **du bist wohl verrückt!** you must be mad!; **5 wohl kaum** hardly.

wohlhabend *adjective* well-off.

wohltun SEE **wohl**.

wohnen *verb* (PERF **hat gewohnt**) **1** to live; **2** to stay (*for a short time*).

Wohngemeinschaft *die* (PL *die* Wohngemeinschaften) people sharing a flat/house; **wir wohnen in einer Wohngemeinschaft** we share a flat.

wohnhaft *adjective* resident.

Wohnheim *das* (PL *die* Wohnheime) **1** hostel; **2** home (*for old people*).

Wohnmobil *das* (PL *die* Wohnmobile) motor home.

Wohnort *der* (PL *die* Wohnorte) place of residence.

Wohnsitz *der* (PL *die* Wohnsitze) place of residence.

Wohnung *die* (PL *die* Wohnungen) flat, apartment.

Wohnwagen *der* (PL *die* Wohnwagen) caravan.

Wohnzimmer *das* (PL *die* Wohnzimmer) living room.

Wolf *der* (PL *die* Wölfe) wolf.

Wolke *die* (PL *die* Wolken) cloud.

Wolkenkratzer *der* (PL *die* Wolkenkratzer) skyscraper.

wolkig *adjective* cloudy.

Wolldecke *die* (PL *die* Wolldecken) blanket.

Wolle *die* wool.

wollen ⬥*verb* (PRES **will**, IMPERF **wollte**, PERF **hat gewollt**) **1** to want; **Anne will einen Hund** Anne wants a dog; **ich will nach Hause** I want to go home; **2 sie wollte gerade gehen** she was just about to go; **3 ganz wie du willst** as you like.

womit *adverb* **1** what ... with; **womit hast du das gewaschen?** what did you wash it with?; **2** with which.

womöglich *adverb* possibly.

wonach *adverb* **1** what ... for; **wonach suchst du?** what are you looking for?; **wonach riecht es?** what does it smell of?; **2** after which, according to which; **eine Regelung, wonach wir eine Stunde mehr arbeiten müssen** a rule according to which we have to work an extra hour.

woran *adverb* what ... of **1 woran denkst du?** what are you thinking of?; **woran hast du ihn erkannt?** how did you recognize him?; **2** on which, of which; **nichts, woran man sich verletzen könnte** nothing you could hurt yourself on.

worauf *adverb* **1** what ... on, what ... for; **worauf hast du die Vase gestellt?** what did you put the vase on?; **worauf wartet ihr?** what are you waiting for?; **2** on which, for which; **das Regal, worauf das Radio steht** the shelf the radio is on; **das Einzige, worauf ich mich freue** the only thing I'm looking forward to.

woraus *adverb* **1** what ... from, what ... of; **woraus ist das?** what's it made of?; **2** from which; **es gibt nichts, woraus wir trinken können** there isn't anything we can drink out of.

worin *adverb* **1** what ... in, in what; **2** in which; **die Punkte, worin ich mit dir übereinstimme** the points I agree with you on.

Wort *das* (PL *die* Worte/Wörter) word; **mir fehlen die Worte** I'm lost for words; **ich habe heute zwanzig neue Wörter gelernt** I've learnt twenty new words today.

Wörterbuch *das* (PL *die* Wörterbücher) dictionary.

wörtlich *adjective* word for word.

Wortschatz *der* vocabulary.

Wortspiel *das* (PL *die* Wortspiele) pun.

Wortstellung *die* word order.

worüber *adverb* **1** what ... over, what ... about; **worüber lacht ihr?** what are you laughing about?; **2** over which, about which.

a
b
c
d
e
f
g
h
i
j
k
l
m
n
o
p
q
r
s
t
u
v
w
x
y
z

worum *adverb* **1** about what; **worum geht es?** what's it about?; **worum hat sie dich gebeten?** what did she ask you for?; **2** for which; **3** round which.

wovon *adverb* **1** what ... from, what ... about; **wovon redet ihr?** what are you talking about?; **2** from which, about which; **der Geruch, wovon mir schlecht geworden ist** the smell which made me feel sick.

wovor *adverb* **1** what ... of; **wovor hast du Angst?** what are you frightened of?; **2** in front of what; **3** of which; **4** in front of which; **der Turm, wovor wir stehen** the tower we are standing in front of.

wozu *adverb* **1** what ... for, why; **wozu brauchst du das?** what do you need it for?; **wozu?** what for?; **2** to which, for which; **wozu ich dir raten würde** which I would advise.

Wrack *das* (PL **die Wracks**) wreck.

Wuchs *der* growth.

wuchs SEE **wachsen**.

wund *adjective* sore.

Wunde *die* (PL **die Wunden**) wound.

Wunder *das* (PL **die Wunder**) miracle; **kein Wunder!** no wonder!

wunderbar *adjective* wonderful.

wundern *verb* (PERF **hat sich gewundert**) **sich wundern** to be surprised.

wunderschön *adjective* beautiful.

wundervoll *adjective* wonderful.

Wundschorf *der* (PL **die Wundschorfe**) scab.

Wunsch *der* (PL **die Wünsche**) wish; **auf Wunsch** on request; **haben Sie sonst noch einen Wunsch?** will there be anything else?

wünschen *verb* (PERF **hat gewünscht**) **1** to wish; **ich wünsche dir alles Gute zum Geburtstag** I wish you a happy birthday; **ich wünschte, ich könnte** ... I wish I could ...; **was wünschen Sie?** can I help you?; **2 sich etwas wünschen** to want something.

wünschenswert *adjective* desirable.

wurde, würde, wurden, würden, wurdest, würdest, wurdet, würdet SEE **werden**.

Wurf *der* (PL **die Würfe**) throw.

Würfel *der* (PL **die Würfel**) **1** dice (*in games*); **2** cube.

würfeln *verb* (PERF **hat gewürfelt**) to throw the dice.

Würfelspiel *das* (PL **die Würfelspiele**) game of dice.

Wurm *der* (PL **die Würmer**) worm.

Wurst *die* (PL **die Würste**) **1** sausage; **2 das ist mir Wurst** (*informal*) I couldn't care less.

Würstchen *das* (PL **die Würstchen**) (little) sausage.

Wurzel *die* (PL **die Wurzeln**) root.

würzen *verb* (PERF **hat gewürzt**) to season.

würzig *adjective* spicy.

wusch SEE **waschen**.

wusste SEE **wissen**.

Wüste *die* (PL *die* Wüsten) desert.

Wut *die* rage; **eine Wut auf jemanden haben** to be furious with somebody.

wütend *adjective* furious.

Xx

x-beliebig *adjective* (*informal*) any; **eine x-beliebige Zahl** any number (you like).

x-mal *adverb* (*informal*) umpteen times; **zum x-ten Mal** for the umpteenth time.

Xylophon *das* (PL *die* Xylophone) xylophone.

Yy

Yoga *das* yoga.

Ypsilon *das* (PL *die* Ypsilons) Y.

Zz

zaghaft *adjective* **1** timid; **2** tentative.

zäh *adjective* tough.

Zahl *die* (PL *die* Zahlen) **1** number; **2** figure.

zahlen *verb* (PERF **hat gezahlt**) **1** to pay; **hast du schon gezahlt?** have

you paid?; **2** to pay for; **bitte zahlen!** the bill please!

zählen *verb* (PERF **hat gezählt**) **1** to count; **auf jemanden zählen** to count on somebody; **jemanden zu seinen Freunden zählen** to count somebody among your friends; **2 zählen zu** to be one of.

Zähler *der* (PL *die* Zähler) meter.

zahlreich *adjective* numerous.

Zahlung *die* (PL *die* Zahlungen) payment.

Zählung *die* (PL *die* Zählungen) **1** count; **2** census.

zahm *adjective* tame.

Zahn *der* (PL *die* Zähne) tooth.

Zahnarzt *der* (PL *die* Zahnärzte) dentist.

Zahnärztin *die* (PL *die* Zahnärztinnen) dentist.

Zahnbürste *die* (PL *die* Zahnbürsten) toothbrush.

Zahnfleisch *das* gums.

Zahnpasta *die* (PL *die* Zahnpasten) toothpaste.

Zahnschmerzen *plural noun* toothache.

Zange *die* (PL *die* Zangen) pliers.

zanken *verb* (PERF **hat sich gezankt**) **sich zanken** to squabble.

Zapfen *der* (PL *die* Zapfen) **1** cone; **2** icicle.

zappeln *verb* (PERF **hat gezappelt**) **1** to wriggle; **2** to fidget.

zart *adjective* **1** delicate, soft; **2** gentle; **3** tender.

zärtlich *adjective* affectionate.

a
b
c
d
e
f
g
h
i
j
k
l
m
n
o
p
q
r
s
t
u
v
w
x
y
z

Zauber der **1** magic; **2** spell.

Zauberer der (PL die **Zauberer**) magician, conjurer.

Zaubererin die (PL die **Zaubererinnen**) magician, conjurer.

zauberhaft *adjective* enchanting.

zaubern *verb* (PERF **hat gezaubert**) to do magic.

Zaumzeug das (PL die **Zaumzeuge**) bridle.

Zaun der (PL die **Zäune**) fence.

z. B. (*zum Beispiel*) e.g.

Zebra das (PL die **Zebras**) zebra.

Zebrastreifen der (PL die **Zebrastreifen**) zebra crossing.

Zeh der (PL die **Zehen**) toe.

Zehe die (PL die **Zehen**) **1** toe; **2** clove (*of garlic*).

Zehenspitze die (PL die **Zehenspitzen**); **auf Zehenspitzen** on tiptoes.

zehn *number* ten.

Zehntel das (PL die **Zehntel**) tenth.

zehnter, zehnte, zehntes *adjective* tenth.

Zeichen das (PL die **Zeichen**) **1** sign; **2** signal.

Zeichentrickfilm der (PL die **Zeichentrickfilme**) cartoon film.

zeichnen *verb* (PERF **hat gezeichnet**) to draw.

Zeichnung die (PL die **Zeichnungen**) drawing.

Zeigefinger der (PL die **Zeigefinger**) index finger.

zeigen *verb* (PERF **hat gezeigt**) **1** to show; **Peter hat uns sein neues Auto gezeigt** Peter showed us his new car; **2** to point; **auf jemanden zeigen** to point at somebody; **3 sich zeigen** to appear; **4 es hat sich gezeigt, dass** ... it has become clear that ...; **es wird sich zeigen** time will tell.

Zeiger der (PL die **Zeiger**) hand.

Zeile die (PL die **Zeilen**) line.

Zeit die (PL die **Zeiten**) **1** time; **sich Zeit lassen** to take your time; **ich habe keine Zeit mehr** I haven't got any more time; **eine Zeit lang** for a time; **2 es hat Zeit** there's no hurry; **die erste Zeit** at first; **in nächster Zeit** in the near future.

Zeitalter das (PL die **Zeitalter**) age.

Zeitlang die SEE **Zeit**.

Zeitlupe die slow motion; **in Zeitlupe** in slow motion.

Zeitraum der (PL die **Zeiträume**) period.

Zeitschrift die (PL die **Zeitschriften**) magazine.

Zeitung die (PL die **Zeitungen**) newspaper.

Zeitungshändler der (PL die **Zeitungshändler**) newsagent.

Zeitverschwendung die waste of time.

zeitweise *adverb* at times.

Zelle die (PL die **Zellen**) **1** cell; **2** booth.

Zelt das (PL die **Zelte**) tent.

zelten *verb* (PERF **hat gezeltet**) to camp.

Zeltplatz *der* (PL *die* **Zeltplätze**) campsite.

Zement *der* cement.

Zentimeter *der* (PL *die* **Zentimeter**) centimetre.

Zentimetermaß *das* (PL *die* **Zentimetermaße**) tape measure.

zentral *adjective* central.

Zentrale *die* (PL *die* **Zentralen**) **1** central office, head office; **2** headquarters; **3** (telephone) exchange, switchboard.

Zentralheizung *die* central heating.

Zentrum *das* (PL *die* **Zentren**) centre.

zerbrechen ✧*verb* (PRES **zerbricht**, IMPERF **zerbrach**, PERF **hat zerbrochen**) **1** to break; **Irene hat meine Vase zerbrochen** Irene broke my vase; **2** (PERF **ist zerbrochen**) to break; **die Untertasse ist zerbrochen** the saucer broke.

zerbrechlich *adjective* fragile.

Zerbrechlichkeit *die* fragility.

Zeremonie *die* (PL *die* **Zeremonien**) ceremony.

zerfallen *verb* (PRES **zerfällt**, IMPERF **zerfiel**, PERF **ist zerfallen**) to disintegrate, to decay.

zerreißen ✧*verb* (IMPERF **zerriss**, PERF **hat zerrissen**) **1** to tear; **sie hat sich das Kleid zerrissen** she tore her dress; **2** to tear up; **Anna hat seinen Brief zerrissen** Anna tore up his letter; **3** (PERF **ist zerrissen**) to tear; **das Hemd ist in der Wäsche zerrissen** the shirt got torn in the washing.

zerschlagen ✧*verb* (PRES **zerschlägt**, IMPERF **zerschlug**, PERF **hat zerschlagen**) **1** to smash, to smash up; **2 sich zerschlagen** to fall through (*of plans*); **meine Hoffnungen haben sich zerschlagen** my hopes were dashed.

zerschneiden *verb* (IMPERF **zerschnitt**, PERF **zerschnitten**) to cut up, to cut to pieces.

zerstören *verb* (PERF **hat zerstört**) to destroy.

Zerstörung *die* destruction.

zerstreuen *verb* (PERF **hat zerstreut**) **1** to scatter; **2 jemanden zerstreuen** to entertain somebody; **3 sich zerstreuen** to take your mind off things; **4 die Menge hat sich zerstreut** the crowd's dispersed.

zerstreut *adjective* absent-minded.

Zettel *der* (PL *die* **Zettel**) **1** piece of paper; **2** note; **3** leaflet.

Zeug *das* (*informal*) **1** stuff; **2** things, gear; **3 dummes Zeug** nonsense.

Zeuge *der* (PL *die* **Zeugen**) witness.

Zeugin *die* (PL *die* **Zeuginnen**) witness.

Zeugnis *das* (PL *die* **Zeugnisse**) **1** certificate; **2** report (*at school*).

Zickzack *der* (PL *die* **Zickzacke**) zigzag; **im Zickzack laufen** to zigzag.

a
b
c
d
e
f
g
h
i
j
k
l
m
n
o
p
q
r
s
t
u
v
w
x
y
z

Ziege die (PL die Ziegen) goat.

Ziegel der (PL die Ziegel) **1** brick; **2** tile.

ziehen ⋄verb (IMPERF **zog**, PERF **hat gezogen**) **1** to pull; **an etwas ziehen** to pull on something; **einen Zahn ziehen** to pull out a tooth; **2** to draw; **einen Strich ziehen** to draw a line; **eine Niete ziehen** to draw a blank; **3 die Bremse ziehen** to put on the brakes; **4** to grow (*vegetables, flowers*); **5 sich ziehen** to run (*of a path, road*); **6** (PERF **ist gezogen**) to move; **sie sind nach Berlin gezogen** they've moved to Berlin.

Ziel das (PL die Ziele) **1** destination; **2** goal, aim; **3** finish (*in sport*).

zielen verb (PERF **hat gezielt**) to aim; **auf etwas zielen** to aim at something.

Zielscheibe die (PL die Zielscheiben) target.

zielstrebig adjective determined.

ziemlich adjective fair. **ziemlich** adverb **1** quite; **ziemlich viel** quite a lot; **2** fairly; **ihre Eltern haben ein ziemlich großes Haus** her parents have a fairly large house.

zierlich adjective dainty.

Ziffer die (PL die Ziffern) figure.

Zifferblatt das (PL die Zifferblätter) face, dial.

zig adjective (*informal*) umpteen.

Zigarette die (PL die Zigaretten) cigarette.

Zigarre die (PL die Zigarren) cigar.

Zigeuner der (PL die Zigeuner) gypsy.

Zigeunerin die (PL die Zigeunerinnen) gypsy.

Zimmer das (PL die Zimmer) room; **Zimmer mit Frühstück** bed and breakfast; **'Zimmer frei'** 'vacancies'.

Zimmermädchen das (PL die Zimmermädchen) chambermaid.

Zimt der cinnamon.

Zink das zinc.

zirka adverb about.

Zirkel der (PL die Zirkel) pair of compasses.

Zirkus der (PL die Zirkusse) circus.

zischen verb (PERF **hat gezischt**) to hiss.

Zitat das (PL die Zitate) quotation.

zitieren verb (PERF **hat zitiert**) to quote.

Zitrone die (PL die Zitronen) lemon.

Zitronensaft der (PL die Zitronensäfte) lemon juice.

zittern verb (PERF **hat gezittert**) to tremble; **vor Kälte zittern** to shiver.

Zivildienst der community service.

Zivilisation die (PL die Zivilisationen) civilization.

zog SEE **ziehen**.

zögern verb (PERF **hat gezögert**) to hesitate.

Zoll der (PL die Zölle) **1** customs; **am Zoll** at customs; **2** duty; **Zoll auf etwas bezahlen** to pay duty on something.

Zollbeamte der (PL die Zollbeamten) customs officer.

Zollbeamtin die (PL die Zollbeamtinnen) customs officer.

zollfrei adjective duty-free.

Zollkontrolle die (PL die Zollkontrollen) customs check.

Zone die (PL die Zonen) zone.

Zoo der (PL die Zoos) Zoo.

Zoomobjektiv das (PL die Zoomobjektive) zoom lens.

Zopf der (PL die Zöpfe) plait.

Zorn der anger.

zornig adjective angry.

zu preposition (+ DAT) **1** to; **ich gehe zum Arzt** I'm going to the doctor's; **zu einer Party eingeladen sein** to be invited to a party; **2 zu … hin** towards; **zum Fenster hin** towards the window; **er kam zu dieser Tür herein** he came in through this door; **3** with; **das passt nicht zu meinem Mantel** it doesn't go with my coat; **es gab Wein zum Käse** there was wine with the cheese; **4** at; **zu Weihnachten** at Christmas; **zu Hause** at home; **zu etwas werden** to turn into something; **6 zu diesem Zweck** for this purpose; **was schenkst du Karin zum Geburtstag?** what are you giving Karin for her birthday?; **zum Spaß** for fun; **zum ersten Mal** for the first time; **7 sich zu etwas äußern** to comment on something; **Papier zum Schreiben** paper to write on; **8 nett zu jemandem sein** to be nice to somebody; **9 sie waren zu zweit** there were two of them; **eine Marke**

zu achtzig Cent an 80-Cent stamp; **es steht drei zu zwei** the score is 3-2; **10 zu Fuß** on foot.

zu adverb **1** too; **zu groß** too big; **2** closed; **zu haben** to be closed; **Tür zu!** (informal) shut the door!; **3 zu sein** to be closed; **alle Läden sind zu gewesen** the shops were all closed; **4** towards (indicating direction); **5 mach zu!** (informal) hurry up!

zu conjunction to; **nichts zu essen** nothing to eat; **zu verkaufen** for sale.

zuallererst adverb first of all.

zuallerletzt adverb last of all.

Zubehör das accessories.

zubereiten verb (PERF hat zubereitet) to prepare; **sie bereitet das Essen zu** she's preparing the meal.

zubinden ◇verb (IMPERF band zu, PERF hat zugebunden) to tie, to tie up.

zubringen ◇verb (IMPERF brachte zu, PERF hat zugebracht) to spend; **sie bringt viel Zeit bei ihrem Freund zu** she spends a lot of time with her boyfriend.

Zucchini plural noun courgettes.

Zucht die (PL die Zuchten) **1** breed, species; **2** breeding (of animals); **3** breeding establishment.

züchten verb (PERF hat gezüchtet) to breed.

zucken verb (PERF hat gezuckt) to twitch.

Zucker der sugar.

Zuckerguss der icing.

a
b
c
d
e
f
g
h
i
j
k
l
m
n
o
p
q
r
s
t
u
v
w
x
y
z

zuckerkrank *adjective* diabetic.

zudecken *verb* (PERF hat zugedeckt) **1** to cover up, to cover; **2** to tuck up (*in bed*).

zueinander *adverb* **1** to one another; **lieb zueinander sein** to be nice to one another; **2** together; **zueinander passen** to go together; **zueinander halten** to stick together.

zuerst *adverb* **1** first; **2** at first.

Zufahrt *die* (PL die Zufahrten) **1** access; **2** drive(way).

Zufall *der* (PL die Zufälle) **1** chance; **durch Zufall** by chance; **2** coincidence; **so ein komischer Zufall** such a strange coincidence; **per Zufall traf ich ihn in der U-Bahn** by coincidence I met him in the tube.

zufällig *adjective* chance; **das war rein zufällig** it was purely by chance.
zufällig *adverb* by chance; **kannst du mir zufällig zehn Euro leihen?** could you lend me ten euros by any chance?

Zuflucht *die* refuge.

zufrieden *adjective* **1** content; **2** satisfied; **mit etwas zufrieden sein** to be satisfied with something.
zufrieden *adverb* **jemanden zufrieden lassen** to leave somebody in peace; **jemanden zufrieden stellen** to satisfy somebody.

zufriedenlassen, **zufriedenstellen** SEE **zufrieden**.

Zug *der* (PL die Züge) **1** train; **2** procession; **3** characteristic, trait; **4** move (*in games*); **5** swig (*when drinking*); **6** drag (*when smoking*); **7 in einem Zug** in one go.

Zugabe *die* (PL die Zugaben) **1** free gift; **2** encore.

Zugang *der* (PL die Zugänge) access.

zugeben ◇*verb* (PRES gibt zu, IMPERF gab zu, PERF hat zugegeben) **1** to add; **2** to admit.

zugehen ◇*verb* (IMPERF ging zu, PERF ist zugegangen) **1** to close, to shut; **die Tür geht nicht zu** the door won't shut; **2 auf etwas zugehen** to go towards something; **auf jemanden zugehen** to walk up to somebody; **3 jemandem zugehen** to be sent to somebody; **4 auf der Party ging es lustig zu** the party was good fun; **5 dem Ende zugehen** to be nearing the end.

zügig *adjective* quick.

zugreifen ◇*verb* (IMPERF griff zu, PERF hat zugegriffen) **1** to grab it/them; **2** to help yourself; **3** to lend a hand.

zugunsten *preposition* (+ GEN) in favour of.

zuhaben SEE **zu**.

Zuhause *das* home.

zuhören *verb* (PERF hat zugehört) to listen.

Zuhörer *der* (PL die Zuhörer) listener.

Zuhörerin *die* (PL die Zuhörerinnen) listener.

zukleben *verb* (PERF hat zugeklebt) to seal (*an envelope*).

zukommen ◇*verb* (IMPERF kam zu, PERF ist zugekommen) **1 auf jemanden zukommen** to come up to somebody; **nächstes Jahr kommt eine Menge Arbeit auf mich zu** I'm in for a lot of work next year; **2 jemandem etwas zukommen lassen** to give somebody something; **3 etwas auf sich zukommen lassen** to take things as they come.

Zukunft *die* future.

zukünftig *adjective* future.

zulassen ◇*verb* (PRES lässt zu, IMPERF ließ zu, PERF hat zugelassen) **1** to allow; **2** to register (*a car*); **3** to leave closed.

Zulassung *die* (PL die Zulassungen) **1** registration; **2** admission.

zuletzt *adverb* **1** last; **2** in the end.

zum = **zu dem; 1 etwas zum Lesen** something to read; **2 spätestens zum fünften März** by 5 March at the latest; **3 er hat es zum Fenster hinausgeworfen** he threw it out of the window.

zumachen *verb* (PERF hat zugemacht) **1** to close, to shut; **2** to fasten.

zumindest *adverb* at least.

zunächst *adverb* **1** first (of all); **2** at first.

Zunahme *die* (PL die Zunahmen) increase.

Zuname *der* (PL die Zunamen) surname.

zunehmen ◇*verb* (PRES nimmt zu, IMPERF nahm zu, PERF hat zugenommen) **1** to increase; **2** to put on weight.

Zunge *die* (PL die Zungen) tongue.

zur = **zu der.**

zurechtkommen ◇*verb* (IMPERF kam zurecht, PERF ist zurechtgekommen) to cope, to manage.

zurechtlegen *verb* (PERF hat zurechtgelegt) **1** to put out ready; **2 sich eine Ausrede zurechtlegen** to think up an excuse.

zurück *adverb* **1** back; **2 Hamburg, hin und zurück** a return to Hamburg.

zurückbekommen ◇*verb* (IMPERF bekam zurück, PERF hat zurückbekommen) to get back; **zehn Pfennig zurückbekommen** to get 10 pfennigs change.

zurückbringen ◇*verb* (IMPERF brachte zurück, PERF hat zurückgebracht) **1** to bring back; **2** to take back.

zurückfahren ◇*verb* (PRES fährt zurück, IMPERF fuhr zurück, PERF ist zurückgefahren) **1** to go back; **2** to drive back; **3** (PERF hat zurückgefahren) to drive back; **jemanden zurückfahren** to drive somebody back.

zurückgeben ◇*verb* (PRES gibt zurück, IMPERF gab zurück, PERF hat zurückgegeben) to give back.

zurückgehen ◇*verb* (IMPERF ging zurück, PERF ist zurückgegangen)

a
b
c
d
e
f
g
h
i
j
k
l
m
n
o
p
q
r
s
t
u
v
w
x
y
z

1 to go back; **zurückgehen auf** to go back to; 2 to go down; 3 to decrease.

zurückhalten ◇*verb* (PRES **hält zurück**, IMPERF **hielt zurück**, PERF **hat zurückgehalten**) 1 to hold back; 2 **sich zurückhalten** to restrain yourself.

zurückkommen ◇*verb* (IMPERF **kam zurück**, PERF **ist zurückgekommen**) 1 to come back; **nach Hause zurückkommen** to return home; 2 to get back.

zurücklassen ◇*verb* (PRES **lässt zurück**, IMPERF **ließ zurück**, PERF **hat zurückgelassen**) to leave behind.

zurücklegen *verb* (PERF **hat zurückgelegt**) 1 to put back; 2 to keep, to put aside; 3 **Geld für etwas zurücklegen** to put money by for something; 4 to cover (*a distance*); 5 **sich zurücklegen** to lie back.

zurücknehmen ◇*verb* (PRES **nimmt zurück**, IMPERF **nahm zurück**, PERF **hat zurückgenommen**) to take back.

zurückrufen ◇*verb* (IMPERF **rief zurück**, PERF **hat zurückgerufen**) to call back.

zurücktreten ◇*verb* (PRES **tritt zurück**, IMPERF **trat zurück**, PERF **ist zurückgetreten**) 1 to step back; 2 to resign.

zurückzahlen *verb* (PERF **hat zurückgezahlt**) to pay back.

zurückziehen ◇*verb* (IMPERF **zog zurück**, PERF **hat zurückgezogen**) 1 to draw back; 2 to withdraw (*an offer*); 3 **sich zurückziehen** to withdraw, to retire.

zurzeit *adverb* at the moment.

Zusage *die* (PL **die Zusagen**) acceptance.

zusammen *adverb* 1 together; **zusammen sein** to be together; 2 altogether.

Zusammenarbeit *die* co-operation.

zusammenarbeiten *verb* (PERF **hat zusammengearbeitet**) to co-operate.

zusammenbleiben ◇*verb* (IMPERF **blieb zusammen**, PERF **ist zusammengeblieben**) to stay together.

zusammenbrechen ◇*verb* (PRES **bricht zusammen**, IMPERF **brach zusammen**, PERF **ist zusammengebrochen**) to collapse.

zusammenfassen *verb* (PERF **hat zusammengefasst**) to summarize.

Zusammenfassung *die* (PL **die Zusammenfassungen**) summary.

zusammenhalten ◇*verb* (PRES **hält zusammen**, IMPERF **hielt zusammen**, PERF **hat zusammengehalten**) 1 to hold together; 2 to keep together; 3 **die Kinder haben zusammengehalten** the children stuck together.

Zusammenhang *der* (PL **die Zusammenhänge**) 1 context; 2 connection.

zusammenkommen ◇*verb* (IMPERF **kam zusammen**, PERF **ist zusammengekommen**) 1 to meet; 2 to accumulate.

Zusammenkunft *die* (PL die Zusammenkünfte) meeting.

zusammenlegen *verb* (PERF hat zusammengelegt) **1** to put together; **2** to fold up; **3** to club together.

zusammennehmen ◇*verb* (PRES **nimmt zusammen,** IMPERF **nahm zusammen,** PERF **hat zusammengenommen**) **1** to gather up; **2** to summon up, to collect; **3 sich zusammennehmen** to pull yourself together.

zusammenpassen *verb* (PERF **hat zusammengepasst**) **1** to match; **2** to be well matched (*of people*); **3** to fit together.

Zusammensein *das* get-together.

Zusammenstoß *der* (PL die Zusammenstöße) collision, crash.

zusammenstoßen ◇*verb* (PRES **stößt zusammen,** IMPERF **stieß zusammen,** PERF **ist zusammengestoßen**) to collide, to crash.

zusammenzählen *verb* (PERF **hat zusammengezählt**) to add up.

zusätzlich *adjective* additional, extra.
zusätzlich *adverb* in addition, extra.

zuschauen *verb* (PERF **hat zugeschaut**) to watch.

Zuschauer *der* (PL die Zuschauer) **1** spectator; **2** viewer; **3 die Zuschauer** the audience.

Zuschauerin *die* (PL die Zuschauerinnen) **1** spectator; **2** viewer.

Zuschlag *der* (PL die Zuschläge) **1** surcharge; **2** supplement.

Zuschuss *der* (PL die Zuschüsse) **1** contribution; **2** grant.

zusehen ◇*verb* (PRES **sieht zu,** IMPERF **sah zu,** PERF **hat zugesehen**) **1** to watch; **2 zusehen, dass** ... to see (to it) that ...

zusein SEE **zu.**

zusenden *verb* (PERF **hat zugesendet**) to send; **jemandem etwas zusenden** to send something to somebody.

Zustand *der* (PL die Zustände) **1** condition; **2** state.

zustande *adverb* **zustande bringen** to bring about; **zustande kommen** to come about.

zuständig *adjective* responsible.

Zustellung *die* (PL die Zustellungen) delivery.

zustimmen *verb* (PERF **hat zugestimmt**) to agree.

Zustimmung *die* (PL die Zustimmungen) **1** agreement; **2** approval.

zustoßen ◇*verb* (PRES **stößt zu,** IMPERF **stieß zu,** PERF **ist zugestoßen**) to happen.

Zutat *die* (PL die Zutaten) ingredient.

zutreffen ◇*verb* (PRES **trifft zu,** IMPERF **traf zu,** PERF **hat zugetroffen**) **auf etwas zutreffen** to apply to something.

Zutritt *der* entry; **Zutritt haben** to have access.

zuverlässig *adjective* reliable.

zuversichtlich *adjective* confident, optimistic.

Zuversichtlichkeit *die* confidence.

zuviel SEE **viel**.

zuvor *adverb* **1** before; **der Tag zuvor** the day before; **2** first.

zuwenig SEE **wenig**.

zuzahlen *verb* (PERF **hat zugezahlt**) to pay extra.

zuziehen ⬦*verb* (IMPERF **zog zu,** PERF **hat zugezogen**) **1** to pull tight; **2** to draw (*curtains*); **3** to call in (*an expert etc.*); **4** (PERF **ist zugezogen**) to move into an area; **5 sich eine Verletzung zuziehen** to sustain an injury; **sich eine Erkältung zuziehen** to catch a cold.

zuzüglich *preposition* (+ GEN) plus.

Zwang *der* (PL die **Zwänge**) **1** compulsion; **2** urge; **3** obligation.

zwang SEE **zwingen**.

zwängen *verb* (PERF **hat gezwängt**) to squeeze.

zwanglos *adjective* casual, informal.

zwar *adverb* **1** admittedly; **2 ich war zwar dabei, habe aber nichts gesehen** I was there, but I didn't see anything; **3 und zwar** to be exact.

Zweck *der* (PL die **Zwecke**) **1** purpose; **2** point; **es hat keinen Zweck** there's no point.

zwecklos *adjective* pointless.

zwei *number* two.

zweideutig *adjective* ambiguous.

zweifach *adjective* twice.

Zweifel *der* (PL die **Zweifel**) doubt.

zweifelhaft *adjective* **1** doubtful; **2** dubious.

zweifellos *adverb* undoubtedly.

zweifeln *verb* (PERF **hat gezweifelt**) to doubt; **an etwas zweifeln** to doubt something.

Zweig *der* (PL die **Zweige**) **1** branch; **2** twig.

zweihundert *number* two hundred.

zweimal *adverb* twice.

zweisprachig *adjective* bilingual.

zweispurig *adjective* two-track (*railway, recording, road*); **eine zweispurigen Straße** a dual carriageway.

zweit *adverb* **zu zweit** in twos; **wir sind zu zweit** there are two of us.

zweite SEE **zweiter**.

zweitens *adverb* secondly.

zweiter, zweite, zweites *adjective* second; **Mario kam als Zweiter** Mario was the second to arrive.

Zwerg *der* (PL die **Zwerge**) dwarf.

Zwiebel *die* (PL die **Zwiebeln**) **1** onion; **2** bulb.

Zwilling *der* (PL die **Zwillinge**) **1** twin; **2 Zwillinge** Gemini; **Markus ist Zwilling** Markus is Gemini.

a
b
c
d
e
f
g
h
i
j
k
l
m
n
o
p
q
r
s
t
u
v
w
x
y
z

zwingen ◇*verb* (IMPERF **zwang**, PERF hat **gezwungen**) **1** to force; **2 sich zwingen** to force yourself.

zwinkern *verb* (PERF hat gezwinkert) to wink.

zwischen *preposition* (+ DAT , or + ACC *with movement towards a place*) **1** between; **2** among (*a crowd*).

zwischendurch *adverb* **1** in between; **2** now and again.

Zwischenfall *der* (PL die Zwischenfälle) incident.

Zwischenlandung *die* (PL die Zwischenlandungen) stop-over.

Zwischenraum *der* (PL die Zwischenräume) gap, space.

Zwischenzeit *die* **in der Zwischenzeit** in the meantime.

zwo *number* two.

zwölf *number* twelve.

zwoter, **zwote**, **zwotes** *adjective* second.

a
b
c
d
e
f
g
h
i
j
k
l
m
n
o
p
q
r
s
t
u
v
w
x
y
z

VERB TABLES AND FORMS

On the following pages you will find forms for a regular German verb **machen** followed by the forms for a reflexive verb **sich waschen** and then the forms for the twelve most important irregular verbs in alphabetical order: **dürfen**, **essen**, **fahren**, **gehen**, **haben**, **kommen**, **können**, **müssen**, **sein**, **sollen**, **werden**, **wissen**.

After these are given the main forms for other irregular verbs. Note that the forms for the separable verbs such as **aufstehen** are not given as they can be looked up under the base form (**stehen**).

machen
to do *or* to make

Imperative

mach!
macht!
machen Sie!

Past participle

hat gemacht

Present

ich mache
du machst
er* macht
wir machen
ihr macht
sie machen

Perfect

ich habe gemacht
du hast gemacht
er hat gemacht
wir haben gemacht
ihr habt gemacht
sie haben gemacht

Future

ich werde machen
du wirst machen
er wird machen
wir werden machen
ihr werdet machen
sie werden machen

Present subjunctive

ich mache
du machest
er mache
wir machen
ihr machet
sie machen

Imperfect

ich machte
du machtest
er machte
wir machten
ihr machtet
sie machten

Conditional

ich würde machen
du würdest machen
er würde machen
wir würden machen
ihr würdet machen
sie würden machen

* In these tables er *should be read as* er/sie/es

2

sich waschen
to wash (oneself)

Imperative
wasch dich!
wascht euch!
waschen Sie sich!

Past participle
hat sich
gewaschen

Present
ich wasche mich
du wäschst dich
er wäscht sich
wir waschen uns
ihr wascht euch
sie waschen sich

Present subjunctive
ich wasche mich
du waschest dich
er wasche sich
wir waschen uns
ihr waschet euch
sie waschen sich

Perfect
ich habe mich gewaschen
du hast dich gewaschen
er hat sich gewaschen
wir haben uns gewaschen
ihr habt euch gewaschen
sie haben sich gewaschen

Imperfect
ich wusch mich
du wuschst dich
er wusch sich
wir wuschen uns
ihr wuscht euch
sie wuschen sich

Future
ich werde mich waschen
du wirst dich waschen
er wird sich waschen
wir werden uns waschen
ihr werdet euch waschen
sie werden sich waschen

Conditional
ich würde mich waschen
du würdest dich waschen
er würde sich waschen
wir würden uns waschen
ihr würdet euch waschen
sie würden sich waschen

dürfen
to be allowed

Imperative	Past participle
—	hat gedurft

Present
ich darf
du darfst
er darf
wir dürfen
ihr dürft
sie dürfen

Perfect
ich habe gedurft
du hast gedurft
er hat gedurft
wir haben gedurft
ihr habt gedurft
sie haben gedurft

Future
ich werde dürfen
du wirst dürfen
er wird dürfen
wir werden dürfen
ihr werdet dürfen
sie werden dürfen

Present subjunctive
ich dürfe
du dürfest
er dürfe
wir dürfen
ihr dürfet
sie dürfen

Imperfect
ich durfte
du durftest
er durfte
wir durften
ihr durftet
sie durften

Conditional
ich würde dürfen
du würdest dürfen
er würde dürfen
wir würden dürfen
ihr würdet dürfen
sie würden dürfen

Imperative	**Past participle**	**essen**
iss!	hat gegessen	to eat
esst!		
essen Sie!		

Present

ich esse
du isst
er isst
wir essen
ihr esst
sie essen

Perfect

ich habe gegessen
du hast gegessen
er hat gegessen
wir haben gegessen
ihr habt gegessen
sie haben gegessen

Future

ich werde essen
du wirst essen
er wird essen
wir werden essen
ihr werdet essen
sie werden essen

Present subjunctive

ich esse
du essest
er esse
wir essen
ihr esset
sie essen

Imperfect

ich aß
du aßest
er aß
wir aßen
ihr aßt
sie aßen

Conditional

ich würde essen
du würdest essen
er würde essen
wir würden essen
ihr würdet essen
sie würden essen

fahren
to drive or to go

Imperative
fahr!
fahrt!
fahren Sie!

Past participle
ist gefahren

Present
ich fahre
du fährst
er fährt
wir fahren
ihr fahrt
sie fahren

Perfect
ich bin gefahren
du bist gefahren
er ist gefahren
wir sind gefahren
ihr seid gefahren
sie sind gefahren

Future
ich werde fahren
du wirst fahren
er wird fahren
wir werden fahren
ihr werdet fahren
sie werden fahren

Present subjunctive
ich fahre
du fahrest
er fahre
wir fahren
ihr fahret
sie fahren

Imperfect
ich fuhr
du fuhrst
er fuhr
wir fuhren
ihr fuhrt
sie fuhren

Conditional
ich würde fahren
du würdest fahren
er würde fahren
wir würden fahren
ihr würdet fahren
sie würden fahren

Imperative

geh!
geht!
gehen Sie!

Past participle

ist gegangen

gehen
to go

Present

ich gehe
du gehst
er geht
wir gehen
ihr geht
sie gehen

Present subjunctive

ich gehe
du gehest
er gehe
wir gehen
ihr gehet
sie gehen

Perfect

ich bin gegangen
du bist gegangen
er ist gegangen
wir sind gegangen
ihr seid gegangen
sie sind gegangen

Imperfect

ich ging
du gingst
er ging
wir gingen
ihr gingt
sie gingen

Future

ich werde gehen
du wirst gehen
er wird gehen
wir werden gehen
ihr werdet gehen
sie werden gehen

Conditional

ich würde gehen
du würdest gehen
er würde gehen
wir würden gehen
ihr würdet gehen
sie würden gehen

haben
to have

Imperative	Past participle
hab!	hat gehabt
habt!	
haben Sie!	

Present

ich habe
du hast
er hat
wir haben
ihr habt
sie haben

Perfect

ich habe gehabt
du hast gehabt
er hat gehabt
wir haben gehabt
ihr habt gehabt
sie haben gehabt

Future

ich werde haben
du wirst haben
er wird haben
wir werden haben
ihr werdet haben
sie werden haben

Present subjunctive

ich habe
du habest
er habe
wir haben
ihr habet
sie haben

Imperfect

ich hatte
du hattest
er hatte
wir hatten
ihr hattet
sie hatten

Imperfect subjunctive

ich hätte
du hättest
er hätte
wir hätten
ihr hättet
sie hätten

Conditional

ich würde haben
du würdest haben
er würde haben
wir würden haben
ihr würdet haben
sie würden haben

Imperative

komm!
kommt!
kommen Sie!

Past participle

ist gekommen

kommen
to come

Present

ich komme
du kommst
er kommt
wir kommen
ihr kommt
sie kommen

Present subjunctive

ich komme
du kommest
er komme
wir kommen
ihr kommet
sie kommen

Perfect

ich bin gekommen
du bist gekommen
er ist gekommen
wir sind gekommen
ihr seid gekommen
sie sind gekommen

Imperfect

ich kam
du kamst
er kam
wir kamen
ihr kamt
sie kamen

Future

ich werde kommen
du wirst kommen
er wird kommen
wir werden kommen
ihr werdet kommen
sie werden kommen

Conditional

ich würde kommen
du würdest kommen
er würde kommen
wir würden kommen
ihr würdet kommen
sie würden kommen

können
can *or* or to be able to

Imperative	Past participle
—	hat gekonnt
	hätte können

Present
ich kann
du kannst
er kann
wir können
ihr könnt
sie können

Perfect
ich habe gekonnt
du hast gekonnt
er hat gekonnt
wir haben gekonnt
ihr habt gekonnt
sie haben gekonnt

Future
ich werde können
du wirst können
er wird können
wir werden können
ihr werdet können
sie werden können

Present subjunctive
ich könne
du könnest
er könne
wir können
ihr könnet
sie können

Imperfect
ich konnte
du konntest
er konnte
wir konnten
ihr konntet
sie konnten

Imperfect subjunctive
ich könnte
du könntest
er könnte
wir könnten
ihr könntet
sie könnten

Conditional
ich würde können
du würdest können
er würde können
wir würden können
ihr würdet können
sie würden können

Imperative	Past participle	**müssen**
—	hat gemusst	must *or* to have to
	hätte müssen	

Present

ich muss
du musst
er muss
wir müssen
ihr müsst
sie müssen

Present subjunctive

ich müsse
du müssest
er müsse
wir müssen
ihr müsset
sie müssen

Perfect

ich habe gemusst
du hast gemusst
er hat gemusst
wir haben gemusst
ihr habt gemusst
sie haben gemusst

Imperfect

ich musste
du musstest
er musste
wir mussten
ihr musstet
sie mussten

Future

ich werde müssen
du wirst müssen
er wird müssen
wir werden müssen
ihr werdet müssen
sie werden müssen

Imperfect subjunctive

ich müsste
du müsstest
er müsste
wir müssten
ihr müsstet
sie müssten

Conditional

ich würde müssen
du würdest müssen
er würde müssen
wir würden müssen
ihr würdet müssen
sie würden müssen

sein
to be

Imperative

sei!
seid!
seinen Sie!

Past participle

ist gewesen

Present

ich bin
du bist
er ist
wir sind
ihr seid
sie sind

Perfect

ich bin gewesen
du bist gewesen
er ist gewesen
wir sind gewesen
ihr seid gewesen
sie sind gewesen

Future

ich werde sein
du wirst sein
er wird sein
wir werden sein
ihr werdet sein
sie werden sein

Present subjunctive

ich sei
du seist/seiest
er sei
wir seien
ihr seiet
sie seien

Imperfect

ich war
du warst
er war
wir waren
ihr wart
sie waren

Imperfect subjunctive

ich wäre
du wärst/wärest
er wäre
wir wären
ihr wärt/wäret
sie wären

Conditional

ich würde sein
du würdest sein
er würde sein
wir würden sein
ihr würdet sein
sie würden sein

Imperative	**Past participle**	**sollen**
—	hat gesollt	should

Present

ich soll
du sollst
er soll
wir sollen
ihr sollt
sie sollen

Perfect

ich habe gesollt
du hast gesollt
er hat gesollt
wir haben gesollt
ihr habt gesollt
sie haben gesollt

Future

ich werde sollen
du wirst sollen
er wird sollen
wir werden sollen
ihr werdet sollen
sie werden sollen

Present subjunctive

ich solle
du sollest
er solle
wir sollen
ihr sollet
sie sollen

Imperfect

ich sollte
du solltest
er sollte
wir sollten
ihr solltet
sie sollten

Imperfect subjunctive

ich sollte
du solltest
er sollte
wir sollten
ihr solltet
sie sollten

Conditional

ich würde sollen
du würdest sollen
er würde sollen
wir würden sollen
ihr würdet sollen
sie würden sollen

werden
to become *or* to get

Imperative
werde!
werdet!
werden Sie!

Past participle
ist geworden

Present
ich werde
du wirst
er wird
wir werden
ihr werdet
sie werden

Perfect
ich bin geworden
du bist geworden
er ist geworden
wir sind geworden
ihr seid geworden
sie sind geworden

Future
ich werde werden
du wirst werden
er wird werden
wir werden werden
ihr werdet werden
sie werden werden

Present subjunctive
ich werde
du werdest
er werde
wir werden
ihr werdet
sie werden

Imperfect
ich wurde
du wurdest
er wurde
wir wurden
ihr wurdet
sie wurden

Conditional
ich würde werden
du würdest werden
er würde werden
wir würden werden
ihr würdet werden
sie würden werden

14

Imperative	Past participle	**wissen**
wisse!	hat gewusst	to know
wisst!		
wissen Sie!		

Present

ich weiß
du weißt
er weiß
wir wissen
ihr wisst
sie wissen

Perfect

ich habe gewusst
du hast gewusst
er hat gewusst
wir haben gewusst
ihr habt gewusst
sie haben gewusst

Future

ich werde wissen
du wirst wissen
er wird wissen
wir werden wissen
ihr werdet wissen
sie werden wissen

Present subjunctive

ich wisse
du wissest
er wisse
wir wissen
ihr wisset
sie wissen

Imperfect

ich wusste
du wusstest
er wusste
wir wussten
ihr wusstet
sie wussten

Conditional

ich würde wissen
du würdest wissen
er würde wissen
wir würden wissen
ihr würdet wissen
sie würden wissen

German irregular verb forms

This list shows the main forms of other irregular verbs.

Infinitive	Present ich, du, er/sie/es	Imperfect er/sie/es	Perfect er/sie/es
bekommen	bekomme, bekommst, bekommt	bekam	hat bekommen
bergen	berge, birgst, birgt	barg	hat geborgen
besitzen	besitze, besitzst, besitzt	besaß	hat besessen
betrügen	betrüge, betrügst, betrügt	betrog	hat betrogen
biegen	biege, biegst, biegt	bog	hat or ist gebogen
bieten	biete, bietest, bietet	bot	hat geboten
binden	binde, bindest, bindet	band	hat gebunden
bitten	bitte, bittest, bittet	bat	hat gebeten
blasen	blase, bläst, bläst	blies	hat geblasen
bleiben	bleibe, bleibst, bleibt	blieb	ist geblieben
braten	brate, brätst, brät	briet	hat gebraten
brechen	breche, brichst, bricht	brach	hat or ist gebrochen
brennen	brenne, brennst, brennt	brannte	hat gebrannt
bringen	bringe, bringst, bringt	brachte	hat gebracht
denken	denke, denkst, denkt	dachte	hat gedacht
dürfen	darf, darfst, darf	durfte	hat gedurft
einladen	lade ein, lädst ein, lädt ein	lud ein	hat eingeladen
empfangen	empfange, empfängst, empfängt	empfing	hat empfangen
empfehlen	empfehle, empfiehlst, empfiehlt	empfahl	hat empfohlen
entscheiden	entscheide, entscheidest, entscheidet	entschied	hat entschieden
erfahren	erfahre, erfährst, erfährt	erfuhr	hat erfahren

Infinitive	Present ich, du, er/sie/es	Imperfect er/sie/es	Perfect er/sie/es
erfinden	erfinde, erfindest, erfindet	erfand	hat erfunden
erschrecken	erschrecke, erschrickst, erschrickt	erschrak	ist erschrocken
ertrinken	ertrinke, ertrinkst, ertrinkt	ertrank	ist ertrunken
essen	esse, isst, isst	aß	hat gegessen
fahren	fahre, fährst, fährt	fuhr	ist *or* hat gefahren
fallen	falle, fällst, fällt	fiel	ist gefallen
fangen	fange, fängst, fängt	fing	hat gefangen
fechten	fechte, fichtst, ficht	focht	hat gefochten
finden	finde, findest, findet	fand	hat gefunden
fliegen	fliege, fliegst, fliegt	flog	ist *or* hat geflogen
fliehen	fliehe, fliehst, flieht	floh	ist geflohen
fließen	fließe, fließt, fließt	floss	ist geflossen
fressen	fresse, frisst, frisst	fraß	hat gefressen
frieren	friere, frierst, friert	fror	hat *or* ist gefroren
geben	gebe, gibst, gibt	gab	hat gegeben
gefallen	gefalle, gefällst, gefällt	gefiel	hat gefallen
gehen	gehe, gehst, geht	ging	ist gegangen
gelingen	es gelingt mir/dir/ihm, ihr, ihm	gelang	ist gelungen
gelten	gelte, giltst, gilt	galt	hat gegolten
genießen	genieße, genießt, genießt	genoss	hat genossen
geraten	gerate, gerätst, gerät	geriet	ist geraten
geschehen	es geschieht	geschah	ist geschehen
gewinnen	gewinne, gewinnst, gewinnt	gewann	hat gewonnen
gießen	gieße, gießt, gießt	goss	hat gegossen
gleichen	gleiche, gleichst, gleicht	glich	hat geglichen
graben	grabe, gräbst, gräbt	grub	hat gegraben
greifen	greife, greifst, greift	griff	hat gegriffen

Infinitive	Present ich, du, er/sie/es	Imperfect er/sie/es	Perfect er/sie/es
helfen	helfe, hilfst, hilft	half	hat geholfen
hinweisen	weise hin, weist hin, weist hin	wies hin	hat hingewiesen
kennen	kenne, kennst, kennt	kannte	hat gekannt
klingen	klinge, klingst, klingt	klang	hat geklungen
kneifen	kneife, kneifst, kneift	kniff	hat gekniffen
kommen	komme, kommst, kommt	kam	ist gekommen
können	kann, kannst, kann	konnte	hat gekonnt
kriechen	krieche, kriechst, kriecht	kroch	ist gekrochen
lassen	lasse, lässt, lässt	ließ	hat gelassen
laufen	laufe, läufst, läuft	lief	ist gelaufen
leiden	leide, leidest, leidet	litt	hat gelitten
leihen	leihe, leihst, leiht	lieh	hat geliehen
lesen	lese, liest, liest	las	hat gelesen
liegen	liege, liegst, liegt	lag	hat gelegen
lügen	lüge, lügst, lügt	log	hat gelogen
mahlen	mahle, mahlst, mahlt	mahlte	hat gemahlen
meiden	meide, meidest, meidet	mied	hat gemieden
messen	messe, mißt, mißt	maß	hat gemessen
misslingen	misslinge, misslingst, misslingt	misslang	ist misslungen
mögen	mag, magst, mag	mochte	hat gemocht
müssen	muss, musst, muss	musste	hat gemusst
nehmen	nehme, nimmst, nimmt	nahm	hat genommen
nennen	nenne, nennst, nennt	nannte	hat genannt
pfeifen	pfeife, pfeifst, pfeift	pfiff	hat gepfiffen

Infinitive	Present	Imperfect	Perfect
	ich, du, er/sie/es	er/sie/es	er/sie/es
raten	rate, rätst, rät	riet	hat geraten
reiben	reibe, reibst, reibt	rieb	hat gerieben
reißen	reiße, reißt, reißt	riss	hat or ist gerissen
reiten	reite, reitest, reitet	ritt	hat or ist geritten
rennen	renne, rennst, rennt	rannte	ist gerannt
riechen	rieche, riechst, riecht	roch	hat gerochen
rufen	rufe, rufst, ruft	rief	hat gerufen
saufen	saufe, säufst, säuft	soff	hat gesoffen
schaffen	schaffe, schaffst, schafft	schuf	hat geschaffen
scheiden	scheide, scheidest, scheidet	schied	hat or ist geschieden
scheinen	scheine, scheinst, scheint	schien	hat geschienen
schieben	schiebe, schiebst, schiebt	schob	hat geschoben
schießen	schieße, schießt, schießt	schoss	hat or ist geschossen
schlafen	schlafe, schläfst, schläft	schlief	hat geschlafen
schlagen	schlage, schlägst, schlägt	schlug	hat geschlagen
schleichen	schleiche, schleichst, schleicht	schlich	ist geschlichen
schließen	schließe, schließt, schließt	schloss	hat geschlossen
schmeißen	schmeiße, schmeißt, schmeißt	schmiss	hat geschmissen
schmelzen	schmelze, schmilzt, schmilzt	schmolz	ist geschmolzen
schneiden	schneide, schneidest, schneidet	schnitt	hat geschnitten
schreiben	schreibe, schreibst, schreibt	schrieb	hat geschrieben
schreien	schreie, schreist, schreit	schrie	hat geschrien
schweigen	schweige, schweigst, schweigt	schwieg	hat geschwiegen
schwimmen	schwimme, schwimmst, schwimmt	schwamm	ist or hat geschwommen
schwören	schwöre, schwörst, schwört	schwor	hat geschworen
sehen	sehe, siehst, sieht	sah	hat gesehen
sein	bin, bist, ist	war	ist gewesen

Infinitive	Present ich, du, er/sie/es	Imperfect er/sie/es	Perfect er/sie/es
singen	singe, singst, singt	sang	hat gesungen
sinken	sinke, sinkst, sinkt	sank	ist gesunken
sitzen	sitze, sitzt, sitzt	saß	hat gesessen
sollen	soll, sollst, soll	sollte	hat gesollt
spinnen	spinne, spinnst, spinnt	spann	hat gesponnen
springen	springe, springst, springt	sprang	ist gesprungen
stechen	steche, stichst, sticht	stach	hat gestochen
stehen	stehe, stehst, steht	stand	hat gestanden
sprechen	spreche, sprichst, spricht	sprach	hat gesprochen
stehlen	stehle, stiehlst, stiehlt	stahl	hat gestohlen
steigen	steige, steigst, steigt	stieg	ist gestiegen
sterben	sterbe, stirbst, stirbt	starb	ist gestorben
stinken	stinke, stinkst, stinkt	stank	hat gestunken
stoßen	stoße, stößt, stößt	stieß	hat *or* ist gestoßen
streichen	streiche, streichst, streicht	strich	hat gestrichen
streiten	streite, streitest, streitet	stritt	hat gestritten
tragen	trage, trägst, trägt	trug	hat getragen
treffen	treffe, triffst, trifft	traf	hat getroffen
treiben	treibe, treibst, treibt	trieb	hat getrieben
treten	trete, trittst, tritt	trat	hat *or* ist getreten
trinken	trinke, trinkst, trinkt	trank	hat getrunken
tun	tue, tust, tut	tat	hat getan
überweisen	überweise, überweist, überweist	überwies	hat überwiesen
umziehen	ziehe um, ziehst um, zieht um	zog um	ist *or* hat umgezogen
verbieten	verbiete, verbietest, verbietet	verbot	hat verboten

Infinitive	Present ich, du, er/sie/es	Imperfect er/sie/es	Perfect er/sie/es
verderben	verderbe, verdirbst, verdirbt	verdarb	hat *or* ist verdorben
vergessen	vergesse, vergißt, vergißt	vergaß	hat vergessen
verlieren	verliere, verlierst, verliert	verlor	hat verloren
verschwinden	verschwinde, verschwindest, verschwindet	verschwand	ist verschwunden
verzeihen	verzeihe, verzeihst, verzeiht	verzieh	hat verziehen
verstehen	verstehe, verstehst, versteht	verstand	hat verstanden
wachsen	wachse, wächst, wächst	wuchs	ist gewachsen
waschen	wasche, wäscht, wäscht	wusch	hat gewaschen
werben	werbe, wirbst, wirbt	warb	hat geworben
werden	werde, wirst, wird	wurde	ist geworden
werfen	werfe, wirfst, wirft	warf	hat geworfen
wiegen	wiege, wiegst, wiegt	wog	hat gewogen
wissen	weiß, weißt, weiß	wusste	hatgewusst
wollen	will, willst, will	wollte	hat gewollt
ziehen	ziehe, ziehst, zieht	zog	hat *or* ist gezogen
zwingen	zwinge, zwingst, zwingt	zwang	hat gezwungen

Aa

a *indefinite article* **1** (*before a noun which is masculine in German*) ein; **a tree** ein Baum; **2** (*before a noun which is feminine in German*) eine; **a story** eine Geschichte; **3** (*before a noun which is neuter in German*) ein; **a dress** ein Kleid; **4 not a** kein; **the party was not a success** die Party war kein Erfolg; **he didn't say a word** er hat kein Wort gesagt; **5 ten euros a metre** zehn Euro den Meter; **6 fifty kilometres an hour** fünfzig Stundenkilometer; **7 three times a day** dreimal täglich.

abandon *verb* **1** aufgeben✧ SEP; **they abandoned the plan** sie gaben den Plan auf; **2** verlassen✧; **they abandoned the city** sie verließen die Stadt.

abbey *noun* Abtei *die* (PL *die* Abteien).

abbreviation *noun* Abkürzung *die* (PL *die* Abkürzungen).

ability *noun* Fähigkeit *die* (PL *die* Fähigkeiten); **to have the ability to do something** etwas tun können.

able *adjective* fähig; **to be able to do something** etwas tun können; **she wasn't able to come** sie konnte nicht kommen.

abortion *noun* Abtreibung *die* (PL *die* Abtreibungen).

about *preposition* **1** über (+ ACC); **a film about space** ein Film über den Weltraum; **to talk about something/somebody** über etwas/ jemanden reden; **what is she** talking about? worüber redet sie?; **2** um (+ ACC); **to be about something** um etwas gehen; **what's it about?** worum geht es?; **3 to know about something** von etwas (DAT) wissen; **she didn't know about the party** sie wusste nichts von der Party; **he knows nothing about it** er weiß nichts davon; **4 to think about something/somebody** an etwas/jemanden (+ ACC) denken; **I'm thinking about you** ich denke an dich.

about *adverb* **1** (*approximately*) ungefähr; **about sixty people** ungefähr sechzig Leute; **in about a week** in ungefähr einer Woche; **2** (*when talking about time*) gegen; **about three o'clock** gegen drei Uhr; **3 to be about to do something** gerade etwas tun wollen; **I was (just) about to leave** ich wollte gerade gehen.

above *preposition* **1** über (+ DAT); **the lamp above the table** die Lampe über dem Tisch; **2 above all** vor allem.

abroad *adverb* im Ausland; **to live abroad** im Ausland leben; **to go abroad** ins Ausland fahren.

abscess *noun* Abszess *der* (PL *die* Abszesse).

abseiling *noun* Abseilen *das*.

absent *adjective* abwesend; **to be absent from school** in der Schule fehlen.

absent-minded *adjective* zerstreut.

absolute *adjective* absolut; **an absolute disaster** eine absolute Katastrophe.

absolutely *adverb* **1** wirklich; **it's absolutely dreadful** das ist wirklich furchtbar; **2** völlig; **you're absolutely right** du hast völlig Recht.

abuse *noun* **1** Missbrauch *der*; **drug abuse** Der Drogenmissbrauch; **2** (*insults*) Beschimpfungen (*plural*).
abuse *verb* **1** **to abuse somebody** jemanden missbrauchen; **2** (*to insult*) beschimpfen.

accelerate *verb* beschleunigen.

accelerator *noun* Gaspedal *das* (PL *die* Gaspedale).

accent *noun* Akzent *der* (PL *die* Akzente); **to speak with a German accent** mit deutschem Akzent sprechen.

accept *verb* annehmen✧ SEP; **he accepted the invitation** er nahm die Einladung an.

acceptable *adjective* annehmbar.

access *noun* Zugang *der*.
access *verb* **to access data** auf Daten zugreifen.

accessory *noun* **1** Zubehörteil *das*; **accessories** Zubehör *das*; **2 accessories** (*fashion items*) Accessoires (*plural*).

accident *noun* **1** Unfall *der* (PL *die* Unfälle); **to have an accident** einen Unfall haben; **road accident** *der* Verkehrsunfall; **car accident** *der* Autounfall; **2** Zufall *der* (PL *die* Zufälle); **by accident** zufällig; I

found it by accident ich habe es zufällig gefunden.

accidental *adjective* zufällig; **an accidental discovery** eine zufällige Entdeckung.

accidentally *adverb* **1** (*without meaning to*) versehentlich; **I accidentally threw it away** ich habe es versehentlich weggeworfen; **2** (*by chance*) zufällig; **I accidentally discovered that ...** ich habe zufällig herausgefunden, dass ....

accident & emergency *noun* Notaufnahme *die*.

accommodation *noun* Unterkunft *die*; **accommodation is free** Unterkunft ist kostenlos; **I'm looking for accommodation** (*when looking for a room*) ich suche ein Zimmer.

accompany *verb* begleiten; **to accompany somebody** jemanden begleiten.

according *in phrase* **according to** laut (+ DAT); **according to Sophie** laut Sophie.

accordion *noun* Akkordeon *das* (PL *die* Akkordeons).

account *noun* **1** (*in a bank, shop, or post office*) Konto *das* (PL *die* Konten); **bank account** *das* Bankkonto; **to open an account** ein Konto eröffnen; **I have fifty pounds in my account** ich habe fünfzig Pfund auf meinem Konto; **2** (*an explanation*) Darstellung *die* (PL *die* Darstellungen); **I want to hear his account of what happened** ich möchte seine Darstellung der

Ereignisse hören; **3 on account of** wegen (+ GEN); **4 to take something into account** etwas berücksichtigen.

accountant *noun* Buchhalter *der* (PL *die* Buchhalter), Buchhalterin *die* (PL *die* Buchhalterinnen); **she's an accountant** sie ist Buchhalterin.

accurate *adjective* genau.

accurately *adverb* genau.

accuse *verb* beschuldigen; **she accused me of stealing her pen** sie beschuldigte mich, ihren Kugelschreiber gestohlen zu haben.

ace *noun* Ass *das* (PL *die* Asse); **the ace of hearts** das Herzass. **ace** *adjective* klasse (*informal*); **he's an ace drummer** er spielt klasse Schlagzeug.

ache *verb* schmerzen; **my head aches** mein Kopf schmerzt.

achieve *verb* **1** leisten; **she's achieved a great deal** sie hat eine Menge geleistet; **2** erreichen (*an aim*); **he achieved what he wanted** er hat erreicht, was er wollte.

achievement *noun* Leistung *die* (PL *die* Leistungen); **it's a great achievement** das ist eine große Leistung.

acid *noun* Säure *die* (PL *die* Säuren).

acne *noun* Akne *die*.

across *preposition* **1** (*over to the other side of*) über (+ ACC); **to run across the road** über die Straße laufen; **we walked across the park** wir sind durch den Park gegangen; **2** (*on the other side of*) auf der anderen Seite (+ GEN); **he lives across the river** er wohnt auf der anderen Seite des Flusses; **3 they live across the street** sie wohnen gegenüber.

act *noun* (*deed*) Tat *die* (PL *die* Taten). **act** *verb* (*in a play or film*) spielen; **to act the part of the hero** die Rolle des Helden spielen.

action *noun* **1** Handlung *die* (PL *die* Handlungen); **2 to take action** etwas unternehmen.

action replay *noun* Wiederholung *die* (PL *die* Wiederholungen).

active *adjective* aktiv.

activity *noun* Aktivität *die* (PL *die* Aktivitäten).

actor *noun* Schauspieler *der* (PL *die* Schauspieler).

actress *noun* Schauspielerin *die* (PL *die* Schauspielerinnen).

actual *adjective* **what were his actual words?** was genau hat er gesagt?; **in actual fact** eigentlich.

actually *adverb* **1** (*in fact, as it happens*) eigentlich; **actually, I've changed my mind** ich habe mich eigentlich anders entschlossen; **2** (*really and truly*) wirklich; **did she actually say that?** hat sie das wirklich gesagt?

AD (*Anno Domini*) n. Chr. (*nach Christus*); **in 400 AD** 400 n.Chr.

ad *noun* **1** (*on TV*) Werbespot *der* (PL *die* Werbespots); **2** (*in a newspaper*) Anzeige *die* (PL *die* Anzeigen); **to put an ad in the paper** eine Anzeige in die Zeitung setzen; **the small ads** die Kleinanzeigen.

a
b
c
d
e
f
g
h
i
j
k
l
m
n
o
p
q
r
s
t
u
v
w
x
y
z

a
b
c
d
e
f
g
h
i
j
k
l
m
n
o
p
q
r
s
t
u
v
w
x
y
z

adapt *verb* **1** to adapt something (*a book or film*) etwas bearbeiten; **2** to adapt to sich anpassen SEP (+ DAT); **she's adapted to her new surroundings** sie hat sich der neuen Umgebung angepasst.

adaptor *noun* **1** Adapter *der* (PL *die* Adapter); **2** (*for two plugs*) Doppelstecker *der* (PL *die* Doppelstecker).

add *verb* **1** hinzufügen SEP; **to add an introduction to something** etwas (DAT) eine Einleitung hinzufügen; **2** dazugeben◇ SEP; **add three eggs** geben Sie drei Eier dazu.
• **to add up** zusammenzählen SEP.

addict *noun* **1** (*drug addict*) Süchtige *der/die* (PL *die* Süchtigen); **2** **she's a telly addict** sie ist fernsehsüchtig; **he's a football addict** er ist ein Fußballnarr.

addicted *adjective* **1** to become addicted to drugs drogensüchtig werden; **2** he's addicted to football Fußball ist bei ihm zur Sucht geworden; **3** I'm addicted to sweets ich bin nach Süßigkeiten süchtig.

addition *noun* **1** (*adding up*) Addition *die*; **2** in addition außerdem; **3** in addition to zusätzlich zu (+ DAT).

additional *adjective* zusätzlich.

additive *noun* Zusatz *der* (PL *die* Zusätze).

address *noun* Adresse *die* (PL *die* Adressen); **do you know his address?** weißt du seine Adresse?;

to change address die Adresse wechseln.

address book *noun* Adressbuch *das* (PL *die* Adressbücher).

adequate *adjective* angemessen.

adhesive *noun* Klebstoff *der*.
adhesive *adjective* **adhesive tape** *der* Klebstreifen.

adjective *noun* Adjektiv *das* (PL *die* Adjektive).

adjust *verb* **1** to adjust something etwas einstellen SEP; **he adjusted the set** er stellte das Gerät ein; **to adjust the distance** auf die (richtige) Entfernung einstellen; **2** to adjust to something sich an etwas (ACC) gewöhnen.

adjustable *adjective* verstellbar.

administration *noun* Verwaltung *die*.

admiration *noun* Bewunderung *die*.

admire *verb* bewundern.

admission *noun* Eintritt *der*; **'admission free'** 'Eintritt frei'.

admit *verb* **1** (*confess, concede*) zugeben◇ SEP; **she admits she lied** sie gibt zu, dass sie gelogen hat; **2** (*allow to enter*) hereinlassen◇ SEP; **to admit somebody to a restaurant** jemanden in ein Restaurant lassen; **3** to be admitted to hospital ins Krankenhaus eingeliefert werden.

adolescence *noun* Jugend *die*.

adolescent *noun* Jugendliche *der/die* (PL *die* Jugendlichen).

adopt *verb* adoptieren.

adopted *adjective* adoptiert.

adoption *noun* Adoption *die* (PL *die* Adoptionen).

adore *verb* lieben.

adult *noun* Erwachsene *der/die* (PL *die* Erwachsenen).
adult *adjective* **the adult population** Erwachsene (*plural*).

Adult Education *noun* Erwachsenenbildung *die*.

advance *noun* Fortschritt *der* (PL *die* Fortschritte); **advances in technology** technologische Fortschritte.
advance *verb* **1** (*make progress*) Fortschritte machen; **2** (*move forward*) (*of a group or an army*) vorrücken SEP (PERF *sein*).

advanced *adjective* fortgeschritten (*student, age*).

advantage *noun* **1** Vorteil *der* (PL *die* Vorteile); **there are several advantages** es gibt verschiedene Vorteile; **2 to take advantage of something** etwas ausnutzen SEP; **I always take advantage of the sales to buy myself some shoes** ich warte immer bis zum Schlussverkauf, um mir Schuhe zu kaufen; **3 to take advantage of somebody** (*unfairly*) jemanden ausnutzen SEP.

Advent *noun* Advent *der*.

adventure *noun* Abenteuer *das* (PL *die* Abenteuer).

adverb *noun* Adverb *das* (PL *die* Adverbien).

advert, advertisement *noun* **1** (*at the cinema or on television*) Werbespot *der* (PL *die* Werbespots); **2** (*in a newspaper for a job, article for sale, etc.*) Anzeige *die* (PL *die* Anzeigen); **she answered a job advertisement** sie meldete sich auf eine Stellenanzeige.

advertise *verb* **to advertise something in the newspaper** (*in the small ads*) etwas in der Zeitung inserieren; **I saw a bike advertised in the paper** ich habe ein Rad in der Zeitung inseriert gesehen.

advertising *noun* Werbung *die*.

advice *noun* Rat *der*; **to ask somebody's advice** jemanden um Rat fragen; **a piece of advice** ein Ratschlag.

advise *verb* raten◇ (+ DAT); **to advise somebody to do something** jemandem raten, etwas zu tun; **I advised him to stop** ich riet ihm anzuhalten; **I advised her not to buy the car** ich habe ihr geraten, das Auto nicht zu kaufen.

aerial *noun* Antenne *die* (PL *die* Antennen).

aerobics *noun* Aerobic *das*; **to do aerobics** Aerobic machen.

aeroplane *noun* Flugzeug *das* (PL *die* Flugzeuge).

aerosol *noun* **an aerosol can** eine Spraydose.

affair *noun* **1** Angelegenheit *die* (PL *die* Angelegenheiten); **international affairs** internationale Angelegenheiten; **current affairs** *die* Tagespolitik; **2 love affair** *das* Liebesverhältnis.

affect *verb* beeinflussen.

a

affectionate *adjective* liebevoll.

afford *verb* **to be able to afford something** sich (DAT) etwas leisten können; **we can't afford to go out much** wir können es uns nicht leisten, oft auszugehen; **I can't afford a new bike** ich kann mir kein neues Rad leisten.

afraid *adjective* **1 to be afraid of something** Angst vor etwas (DAT) haben; **she's afraid of dogs** sie hat Angst vor Hunden; **2 I'm afraid I can't help you** ich kann dir leider nicht helfen; **I'm afraid so** leider ja; **I'm afraid not** leider nicht.

Africa *noun* Afrika *das*; **to Africa** nach Afrika.

African *noun* Afrikaner *der* (PL *die* Afrikaner), Afrikanerin *die* (PL *die* Afrikanerinnen).
African *adjective* afrikanisch; **she is African** sie ist Afrikanerin.

after *preposition, adverb* **1** nach (+ DAT); **after 10 o'clock** nach zehn Uhr; **after lunch** nach dem Mittagessen; **after school** nach der Schule; **2 the day after tomorrow** übermorgen; **soon after** kurz danach; **3 to run after somebody** jemandem hinterherlaufen ◆ SEP.
after *conjunction* nachdem; **after I'd finished my homework** nachdem ich meine Hausaufgaben gemacht hatte.

after all *adverb* schließlich; **after all, she's only six** sie ist schließlich erst sechs.

afternoon *noun* **1** Nachmittag *der* (PL *die* Nachmittage); **in the afternoon** am Nachmittag; **every afternoon** jeden Nachmittag; **2 this afternoon** heute Nachmittag; **on Sunday afternoon** am Sonntagnachmittag; **3 on Saturday afternoons** samstagsnachmittags; **at four o' clock in the afternoon** um vier Uhr nachmittags.

after-shave *noun* Rasierwasser *das* (PL *die* Rasierwasser).

afterwards *adverb* danach; **shortly afterwards** kurz danach.

again *adverb* **1** wieder; **she's ill again** sie ist wieder krank; **2 I saw her again yesterday** ich habe sie gestern wieder gesehen; **3 never again!** nie wieder!; **again and again** immer wieder; **4** (*one more time*) noch einmal; **try again** versuche es noch einmal; **you should ask her again** du solltest sie noch einmal fragen.

against *preposition* gegen (+ ACC); **against the wall** gegen die Wand; **to lean against the wall** sich gegen die Wand lehnen; **I'm against the idea** ich bin gegen die Idee.

age *noun* **1** Alter *das*; **at the age of fifty** im Alter von fünfzig; **she's the same age as me** sie ist genauso alt wie ich; **to be under age** minderjährig sein; **2 I haven't seen Johnny for ages** ich habe Johnny schon ewig nicht mehr gesehen; **I haven't been to London for ages** ich bin schon ewig nicht mehr in London gewesen.

aged *adjective* alt; **a woman aged thirty** eine dreißigjährige Frau.

agent *noun* Vertreter *der* (PL *die* Vertreter), Vertreterin *die* (PL *die*

Vertreterinnen); **an estate agent** ein Immobilienmakler; **a travel agent's** ein Reisebüro.

aggressive *adjective* aggressiv.

ago *adverb* vor (+ DAT); **an hour ago** vor einer Stunde; **three days ago** vor drei Tagen; **a long time ago** vor langer Zeit; **not long ago** vor kurzem; **how long ago was it?** wie lange ist das her?

agree *verb* **1 to agree with somebody** mit jemandem gleicher Meinung sein; **I agree with Laura** ich stimme Laura zu; **2 I agree** ich bin der gleichen Meinung; **I don't agree** ich bin anderer Meinung; **3 to agree that** ... zugeben⋄ SEP, dass ...; **I agree that it's too late now** ich gebe zu, dass es jetzt zu spät ist; **4 to agree to something** mit etwas einverstanden sein; **Steve's agreed to help me** Steve hat sich einverstanden erklärt, mir zu helfen; **5 coffee doesn't agree with me** Kaffee bekommt mir nicht.

agreement *noun* **1** (*when sharing an opinion*) Übereinstimmung *die*; **2** (*contract*) Abkommen *das* (PL *die* Abkommen).

agriculture *noun* Landwirtschaft *die*.

ahead *adverb* **1 go ahead!** bitte!; **2 straight ahead** geradeaus; **keep going straight ahead until you get to the crossroads** gehen Sie immer geradeaus bis zur Kreuzung; **3 our team was ten points ahead** unsere Mannschaft hatte zehn Punkte Vorsprung; **4 ahead of time** früher

als geplant; **5 the people ahead of me** die Leute vor mir.

aid *noun* **1** Hilfe *die*; **aid to developing countries** die Entwicklungshilfe; **2 in aid of** zugunsten (+ GEN); **in aid of the homeless** zugunsten der Obdachlosen.

Aids *noun* Aids *das*; **to have Aids** Aids haben.

aim *noun* Ziel *das* (PL *die* Ziele); **their aim is to control pollution** ihr Ziel ist es, die Umweltverschmutzung unter Kontrolle zu bringen. **aim** *verb* **1 to aim to do something** beabsichtigen, etwas zu tun; **we're aiming to finish it today** wir beabsichtigen, es heute fertig zu machen; **2 the campaign is aimed at young people** die Kampagne zielt auf junge Leute ab.

air *noun* **1** Luft *die*; **in the open air** im Freien; **to go out for a breath of air** frische Luft schöpfen gehen; **2 to travel by air** fliegen⋄ (PERF *sein*).

air-conditioned *adjective* klimatisiert.

air conditioning *noun* Klimaanlage *die*.

Air Force *noun* Luftwaffe *die*.

air hostess *noun* Stewardess *die* (PL *die* Stewardessen); **she's an air hostess** sie ist Stewardess.

airline *noun* Fluggesellschaft *die* (PL *die* Fluggesellschaften).

airmail *noun* **by airmail** per Luftpost.

air pollution *noun* Luftverschmutzung *die*.

a b c d e f g h i j k l m n o p q r s t u v w x y z

airport *noun* Flughafen der (PL die Flughäfen).

alarm *noun* Alarm der (PL die Alarme); **fire alarm** der Feuermelder; **burglar alarm** die Alarmanlage.

alarm clock *noun* Wecker der (PL die Wecker).

album *noun* Album das (PL die Alben).

alcohol *noun* Alkohol der.

alcoholic *noun* Alkoholiker der (PL die Alkoholiker), Alkoholikerin die (PL die Alkoholikerinnen).
alcoholic *adjective* alkoholisch.

A levels *noun* Abitur das (*Students take 'Abitur' at about 19 years of age. You can explain A levels briefly as follows: Diese Prüfungen werden in zwei Schritten abgelegt: AS und A2. AS Prüfungen finden nach einjähriger Vorbereitungszeit statt, und umfassen normalerweise vier bis fünf Fächer. A2 Prüfungen macht man in weniger Fächern als man für die AS Prüfungen belegt hatte. AS und A2 Prüfungen werden benotet von A (beste Note) bis N (nicht bestanden). A levels stellen eine Zugangsberechtigung für die Universität dar*) SEE **Abitur**.

alien *noun* **1** (*foreigner*) Ausländer der (PL die Ausländer), Ausländerin die (PL die Ausländerinnen); **2** (*from outer space*) Außerirdische der/die (PL die Außerirdischen).

alike *adjective* **1** gleich; **2 they're all alike** sie sind alle gleich; **3 to look alike** sich (DAT) ähnlich sehen;

the two brothers look alike die beiden Brüder sehen sich ähnlich.

alive *adjective* **1 to be alive** leben; **to stay alive** am Leben bleiben; **2** (*lively*) lebendig.

all *adjective* **1** (*with a singular noun*) ganz; **all the time** die ganze Zeit; **all day** den ganzen Tag; **2** (*with a plural noun*) alle; **all the knives** alle Messer; **all our friends** alle unsere Freunde.

all *pronoun* **1** (*everything*) alles; **they've eaten it all** sie haben alles aufgegessen; **2** (*everybody*) alle; **all of us** wir alle; **they're all there** sie sind alle da; **3 not at all** gar nicht.

all *adverb* **1** ganz; **all alone** ganz allein; **2 three all** drei beide.

all along *adverb* die ganze Zeit; **I knew it all along** ich habe es die ganze Zeit gewusst.

allergic *adjective* allergisch; **to be allergic to something** gegen etwas (ACC) allergisch sein.

allow *verb* **1 to allow somebody to do something** jemandem erlauben, etwas zu tun; **the teacher allowed them to go home** der Lehrer erlaubte ihnen, nach Hause zu gehen; **2 to be allowed to** dürfen◇; **I'm not allowed to go to the cinema during the week** ich darf während der Woche nicht ins Kino gehen.

all right *adverb* **1** (*yes*) ist gut, okay (*informal*); **'come round to my house around six' – 'all right'** 'komm um sechs bei mir vorbei' – 'okay'; **2** (*fine*) in Ordnung, okay (*informal*); **is everything all right?**

ist alles okay?; **she's all right again** es geht ihr wider gut; **it's all right by me** das geht in Ordnung; **is it all right if I come later?** ist es in Ordnung, wenn ich später komme?; **3** (*not bad*) gut, okay (*informal*); **the meal was all right** das Essen war okay; **4 'how are you?' – 'I'm all right'** 'wie geht's dir?' – 'mir geht's gut'.

almost *adverb* fast; **almost every day** fast jeden Tag; **almost everybody** fast alle.

alone *adjective* **1** allein; **he lives alone** er lebt allein; **2 leave me alone!** lass mich in Ruhe!

along *preposition* **1** entlang (+ ACC, or + DAT); **there are trees all along the river** am Fluss entlang stehen Bäume; **to go for a walk along the beach** am Strand entlang spazieren gehen; **2** (*there is often no direct translation for 'along', so the sentence has to be expressed differently*) **she lives along the road from me** sie wohnt in der gleichen Straße wie ich; **I'll bring it along** ich bringe es mit.

aloud *adverb* laut; **to read something aloud** etwas vorlesen✧ SEP.

alphabet *noun* Alphabet *das* (PL *die* Alphabete).

Alps *plural noun* **the Alps** die Alpen.

already *adverb* schon; **they've already left** sie sind schon weggegangen; **it's six o'clock already** es ist schon sechs Uhr.

Alsatian *noun* Schäferhund *der* (PL *die* Schäferhunde).

also *adverb* auch; **I've also invited Karen** ich habe Karen auch eingeladen.

alter *verb* **1** ändern (*a report, a dress*); **2** (*to change*) sich verändern.

alternative *noun* **1** Alternative *die* (PL *die* Alternativen); **there are several alternatives** es gibt mehrere Alternativen; **2 we have no alternative** wir haben keine andere Wahl.
alternative *adjective* anderer/ andere/anderes (*masculine/ feminine/neuter*); **to find an alternative solution** eine andere Lösung finden.

alternative medicine *noun* Alternativmedizin *die*.

although *conjunction* obwohl; **although she's ill, she wants to help us** obwohl sie krank ist, will sie uns helfen.

altogether *adverb* **1** insgesamt; **I've spent thirty pounds altogether** insgesamt habe ich dreißig Pfund ausgegeben; **2** (*completely*) ganz; **I'm not altogether convinced** ich bin nicht ganz überzeugt.

always *adverb* immer; **I always leave at five** ich gehe immer um fünf (weg).

am *verb* SEE **be**.

a.m. *abbreviation* vormittags; **at 8 a.m.** um acht Uhr morgens.

amateur *noun* **1** Amateur *der* (PL *die* Amateure), Amateurin *die* (PL *die*

a b c d e f g h i j k l m n o p q r s t u v w x y z

Amateurinnen); **2 amateur dramatics** das Laientheater.

amaze verb erstaunen; **what amazes me is** ... was mich erstaunt, ist ....

amazed adjective erstaunt; **I was amazed to see her** ich war erstaunt, sie zu sehen.

amazing adjective **1** (terrific) fantastisch; **they've got an amazing house** sie haben ein fantastisches Haus; **2** (extraordinary) erstaunlich; **she has an amazing number of friends** sie hat erstaunlich viele Freunde.

ambition noun Ehrgeiz der.

ambitious adjective ehrgeizig.

ambulance noun Krankenwagen der (PL die Krankenwagen).

America noun Amerika das; **in America** in Amerika; **to America** nach Amerika.

American noun Amerikaner der (PL die Amerikaner), Amerikanerin die (PL die Amerikanerinnen). **American** adjective amerikanisch; **she's American** sie ist Amerikanerin.

among, amongst preposition **1** unter (+ DAT); **I found it amongst my books** ich habe es unter meinen Büchern gefunden; **amongst other things** unter anderem; **2** (between) **among yourselves** untereinander.

amount noun **1** Menge die (PL die Mengen); **a huge amount of work** eine Menge Arbeit; **2** (of money) Betrag der (PL die Beträge); **a large**

amount of money ein sehr hoher Betrag.

amount verb **1 to amount to** sich belaufen◇; **the bill amounts to five hundred euros** die Rechnung beläuft sich auf fünfhundert Euro.

amp noun (amplifier) Verstärker der (PL die Verstärker).

amplifier noun Verstärker der (PL die Verstärker).

amuse verb amüsieren.

amusement arcade noun Spielhalle die (PL die Spielhallen).

amusing adjective amüsant.

an article SEE **a**.

anaesthetic noun Narkose die (PL die Narkosen).

analyse verb analysieren.

ancestor noun Vorfahr der (PL die Vorfahren).

anchovy noun Sardelle die (PL die Sardellen).

ancient adjective **1** alt; **ancient Greece** das alte Griechenland; **2** (very old) uralt; **an ancient pair of jeans** uralte Jeans.

and conjunction **1** und; **Rosie and I** Rosie und ich; **girls and boys** Mädchen und Jungen; **2 louder and louder** immer lauter; **3 try and come** versuche zu kommen.

angel noun Engel der (PL die Engel).

anger noun Zorn der.

angle noun Winkel der (PL die Winkel).

angrily adverb wütend.

angry adjective **to be angry** böse sein; **she was angry with me** sie war böse auf mich; **to get angry** böse werden.

animal *noun* Tier *das* (PL *die* Tiere).

ankle *noun* Knöchel *der* (PL *die* Knöchel).

anniversary *noun* **1** Jahrestag *der* (PL *die* Jahrestage); **2 our wedding anniversary** unser Hochzeitstag.

announce *verb* bekanntgeben ✧ SEP; **she announced her engagement** sie gab ihre Verlobung bekannt.

annoy *verb* **to be annoyed** verärgert sein; **to get annoyed with somebody** sich über jemanden ärgern; **she got annoyed about it** sie hat sich darüber geärgert.

annoying *adjective* ärgerlich.

annual *adjective* jährlich.

anorak *noun* Anorak *der* (PL *die* Anoraks).

anorexia *noun* Magersucht *die*.

another *adjective* **1** (*additional*) noch ein/noch eine/noch ein; **would you like another cup of tea?** möchtest du noch eine Tasse Tee?; **we need another three chairs** wir brauchen noch drei Stühle; **2** (*different*) ein anderer/eine andere/ein anderes; **we saw another film** wir haben einen anderen Film gesehen; **3 in another two years** in zwei weiteren Jahren.

answer *noun* **1** Antwort *die* (PL *die* Antworten); **the right answer** die richtige Antwort; **the wrong answer** die falsche Antwort; **2 the**

answer to a problem die Lösung eines Problems.

answer *verb* **1** antworten (+ DAT); **why don't you answer him?** warum antwortest du ihm nicht?; **2** beantworten (*a letter, a question*); **he hasn't answered our letter** er hat unseren Brief nicht beantwortet.

answering machine *noun* Anrufbeantworter *der* (PL *die* Anrufbeantworter).

ant *noun* Ameise *die* (PL *die* Ameisen).

anthem *noun* **the national anthem** die Nationalhymne.

antibiotic *noun* Antibiotikum *das* (PL *die* Antibiotika).

antique *noun* **antiques** Antiquitäten (*plural*). **antique** *adjective* antik; **an antique table** ein antiker Tisch.

antique shop *noun* Antiquitätengeschäft *das* (PL *die* Antiquitätengeschäfte).

antiseptic *noun* Antiseptikum *das* (PL *die* Antiseptika).

anxious *adjective* **1** (*worried*) besorgt; **2** (*keen*) **she was anxious to see him** sie wollte ihn unbedingt sehen.

anxiously *adverb* ängstlich.

any *adjective* **1** irgendein; **if they had any plan** wenn sie irgendeinen Plan hätten; **2** (*with plural nouns*) irgendwelche; **if they had any plans** wenn sie irgendwelche Pläne hätten; **3** (*in questions 'any' is often not translated*) **have you got any stamps?** haben Sie Briefmarken?;

a
b
c
d
e
f
g
h
i
j
k
l
m
n
o
p
q
r
s
t
u
v
w
x
y
z

have we got any milk? haben wir Milch?; **4** *not any* kein; **they haven't made any plans** sie haben nichts geplant; **we haven't got any milk** wir haben keine Milch; **5** (*no matter which*) jeder beliebige/jede beliebige/jedes beliebige; **you can have any colour** du kannst jede beliebige Farbe haben.

any *pronoun* **1** (*in questions, replacing the noun*) welcher/welche/welches, (*replacing a plural noun*) welche; **I need some flour, have you got any?** ich brauche Mehl, hast du welches?; **2** *not any* keiner/keine/keins, (*replacing a plural noun*) keine; **I don't want any** ich will keins haben; **there aren't any** es gibt keine; **3** (*no matter which one*) irgendein; **'which chair can I take?' – 'take any of them'** 'welchen Stuhl kann ich nehmen?' – 'nimm irgendeinen'.

any *adverb* **1** (*in questions*) noch; **would you like any more?** möchtest du noch etwas?; **2** (*with negatives*) **I can't see him any more** ich kann ihn nicht mehr sehen.

anybody, anyone *pronoun* **1** (*in questions*) jemand; **does anybody want some tea?** möchte jemand Tee?; **is anybody in?** ist irgendjemand da?; **2** *not anybody* niemand; **there isn't anybody in the office** niemand ist im Büro; **3** (*absolutely anybody*) jeder; **anybody can do it** das kann jeder.

anyhow *adverb* SEE **anyway**.

anyone *pronoun* SEE **anybody**.

anything *pronoun* **1** (*in questions*) irgendetwas; **is there anything I can do to help?** kann ich irgendwie helfen?; **2** *not anything* nichts; **there isn't anything on the table** auf dem Tisch liegt nichts; **3** (*anything at all*) alles; **I'll do anything to help him** ich werde alles tun, um ihm zu helfen.

anyway, anyhow *adverb* **1** jedenfalls; **anyway, I'll ring you before I leave** jedenfalls ruf ich dich an, bevor ich fahre; **2** sowieso.

anywhere *adverb* **1** (*in questions*) irgendwo; **have you seen my keys anywhere?** hast du meine Schlüssel irgendwo gesehen?; **2** *not anywhere* nirgends; **I can't find my keys anywhere** ich kann meine Schlüssel nirgends finden; **3** (*to any place*) irgendwohin; **are you going anywhere tomorrow?** fahrt ihr morgen irgendwohin?; **put your cases down anywhere** stell deine Koffer irgendwohin; **4** (*in any place*) überall; **you can get that anywhere** das kann man überall kriegen.

apart *adjective, adverb* **1** (*separate*) auseinander; **they've been apart for some time** sie sind schon lange auseinander; **2** *to be two metres apart* zwei Meter auseinander liegen; **3** *apart from* außer (+ DAT); **apart from my brother everybody was there** außer meinem Bruder waren alle da.

apologize *verb* sich entschuldigen; **he apologized for his mistake** er enschuldigte sich für seinen Fehler; **he apologized to**

Sam er hat sich bei Sam entschuldigt.

apology *noun* Entschuldigung *die* (PL *die* Entschuldigungen).

apostrophe *noun* Apostroph *der* (PL *die* Apostrophe).

apparent *adjective* offensichtlich.

apparently *adverb* offensichtlich.

appeal *noun* Appell *der* (PL *die* Appelle).
appeal *verb* **1 to appeal for something** um etwas (ACC) bitten◊; **2 to appeal to somebody** sich an jemanden wenden◊; **horror films don't appeal to me** Horrorfilme sind nicht mein Geschmack.

appear *verb* **1** erscheinen◊ (PERF *sein*); **Mick appeared at breakfast** Mick erschien zum Frühstück; **2 to appear on television** im Fernsehen auftreten◊ SEP (PERF *sein*); **3** (*seem*) scheinen◊; **it appears that somebody has stolen the key** es scheint, dass jemand den Schlüssel gestohlen hat.

appendicitis *noun* Blinddarmentzündung *die*.

appetite *noun* Appetit *der*; **it'll spoil your appetite** das verdirbt dir den Appetit.

applaud *verb* Beifall klatschen.

applause *noun* Beifall *der*.

apple *noun* Apfel *der* (PL *die* Äpfel).

apple tree *noun* Apfelbaum *der* (PL *die* Apfelbäume).

applicant *noun* Bewerber *der* (PL *die* Bewerber), Bewerberin *die* (PL *die* Bewerberinnen).

application form *noun* (*for a job*) Bewerbungsformular *das* (PL *die* Bewerbungsformulare).

application *noun* Bewerbung *die* (PL *die* Bewerbungen).

apply *verb* **1 to apply for a job** sich um eine Stelle bewerben◊; **2 to apply for university** sich um einen Studienplatz bewerben◊; **3 to apply for a passport** einen Pass beantragen; **4 to apply to** zutreffen◊ SEP auf (+ ACC); **that doesn't apply to students** das trifft nicht auf Studenten zu.

appointment *noun* Termin *der* (PL *die* Termine); **to make a dental appointment** einen Zahnarzttermin vereinbaren; **I've got a hair appointment at four** ich habe um vier einen Friseurtermin.

appreciate *verb* **I appreciate your advice** ich bin dir für deinen Rat dankbar; **I'd appreciate it if you could tidy up afterwards** es wäre nett von dir, wenn du danach aufräumen würdest.

apprentice *noun* Lehrling *der* (PL *die* Lehrlinge).

apprenticeship *noun* Lehre *die* (PL *die* Lehren).

approach *verb* sich nähern (+ DAT) (PERF *sein*); **we were approaching the village** wir näherten uns dem Dorf.

approve *verb* **to approve of something** mit etwas (DAT) einverstanden sein; **they don't approve of her friends** sie lehnen ihre Freunde ab.

a
b
c
d
e
f
g
h
i
j
k
l
m
n
o
p
q
r
s
t
u
v
w
x
y
z

a
b
c
d
e
f
g
h
i
j
k
l
m
n
o
p
q
r
s
t
u
v
w
x
y
z

approximate *adjective* ungefähr.

approximately *adverb* ungefähr; **approximately fifty people** ungefähr fünfzig Personen.

apricot *noun* Aprikose *die* (PL *die* Aprikosen).

April *noun* April *der*; **in April** im April.

April Fool *noun* (*trick*) Aprilscherz *der* (PL *die* Aprilscherze); **April fool!** April, April!

April Fool's Day *noun* der erste April.

apron *noun* Schürze *die* (PL *die* Schürzen).

aquarium *noun* Aquarium *das* (PL *die* Aquarien).

Aquarius *noun* Wassermann *der*; **Sharon's Aquarius** Sharon ist Wassermann.

Arab *noun* Araber *der* (PL *die* Araber), Araberin *die* (PL *die* Araberinnen).
Arab *adjective* arabisch; **the Arab countries** die arabischen Länder.

arch *noun* Bogen *der* (PL *die* Bogen).

archaeologist *noun* Archäologe *der* (PL *die* Archäologen), Archäologin *die* (PL *die* Archäologinnen); **she's an archaeologist** sie ist Archäologin.

archaeology *noun* Archäologie *die*.

architect *noun* Architekt *der* (PL *die* Architekten), Architektin *die* (PL *die* Architektinnen); **he's an architect** er ist Architekt.

architecture *noun* Architektur *die*.

are *verb* SEE **be**.

area *noun* **1** (*part of a town, a region*) Gegend *die* (PL *die* Gegenden); **a nice area** eine nette Gegend; **in the Leeds area** in der Gegend von Leeds; **2 picnic area** *der* Picknickplatz.

argue *verb* sich streiten✧; **to argue about something** sich über etwas (ACC) streiten; **they're arguing about the result** sie streiten sich über das Ergebnis.

argument *noun* Streit *der* (PL *die* Streite); **to get into an argument with somebody** mit jemandem in Streit geraten✧; **to have an argument** sich streiten✧.

Aries *noun* Widder *der*; **Pauline's Aries** Pauline ist Widder.

arm *noun* Arm *der* (PL *die* Arme); **arm in arm** Arm in Arm; **to break your arm** sich (DAT) den Arm brechen.

armchair *noun* Sessel *der* (PL *die* Sessel).

armed *adjective* bewaffnet.

army *noun* **1** Heer *das* (PL *die* Heere); **2** (*profession*) Militär *das*; **to join the army** zum Militär gehen.

around *preposition, adverb* **1** (*with time of day*) gegen (+ ACC); **we'll be there around ten** wir werden gegen zehn da sein; **2** (*with ages or amounts*) etwa; **she's around fifteen** sie ist etwa fünfzehn; **we need around six kilos** wir brauchen etwa sechs Kilo; **3** (*with dates*) um (+ ACC *herum*); **around 10**

August um den 10. August herum; **4** (*surrounding*) um ... herum; **the countryside around Edinburgh** die Landschaft um Edinburgh herum; **5** (*near*) **is there a post office around here?** gibt es hier in der Gegend eine Post?; **is Phil around?** ist Phil da?

arrange *verb* **to arrange something** etwas vereinbaren; **we've arranged to go to the cinema on Saturday** wir haben vereinbart, am Samstag ins Kino zu gehen.

arrest *noun* **to be under arrest** verhaftet sein.
arrest *verb* verhaften.

arrival *noun* Ankunft *die* (PL *die* Ankünfte).

arrive *verb* ankommen ◊ SEP (PERF *sein*); **they arrived at 3 p.m.** sie kamen um fünfzehn Uhr an.

arrow *noun* Pfeil *der* (PL *die* Pfeile).

art *noun* **1** Kunst *die* (PL *die* Künste); **modern art** moderne Kunst; **2** (*school subject*) Kunsterziehung *die*.

artery *noun* Arterie *die* (PL *die* Arterien).

art gallery *noun* Kunstgalerie *die* (PL *die* Kunstgalerien).

article *noun* **1** (*in a newspaper or magazine*) Artikel *der* (PL *die* Artikel); **2** (*object*) Stück *das* (PL *die* Stücke).

artificial *adjective* künstlich.

artist *noun* Künstler *der* (PL *die* Künstler), Künstlerin *die* (PL *die* Künstlerinnen); **he's an artist** er ist Künstler.

artistic *adjective* künstlerisch.

art school *noun* Kunsthochschule *die* (PL *die* Kunsthochschulen).

as *conjunction, adverb* **1** wie; **as you know** wie du weißt; **as usual** wie üblich; **as I told you** wie ich dir gesagt habe; **2** (*because*) da; **as there was no bus, we took a taxi** da es keinen Bus gab, nahmen wir ein Taxi; **3 as ... as** so ...wie; **he's as tall as his brother** er ist so groß wie sein Bruder; **come as quickly as possible** komm so schnell wie möglich; **4 as much ... as** so viel ... wie; **you have as much time as I do** du hast so viel Zeit wie ich; **5 as many ... as** so viele ... wie; **we have as many problems as he does** wir haben genauso viele Probleme wie er; **6 as long as** vorausgesetzt; **we'll go tomorrow, as long as it's a nice day** wir gehen morgen, vorausgesetzt es ist schönes Wetter; **7 for as long as** solange; **you can stay for as long as you like** du kannst bleiben, solange du willst; **8 as soon as possible** so bald wie möglich; **9 to work as** arbeiten als; **he works as a waiter in the evenings** abends arbeitet er als Kellner; **as well** auch.

ash *noun* **1** Asche *die* (PL *die* Aschen); **2** (*tree*) Esche *die* (PL *die* Eschen).

ashamed *adjective* **to be ashamed of something** sich wegen etwas (DAT) schämen; **you should be ashamed of yourself!** du solltest dich schämen!

a
b
c
d
e
f
g
h
i
j
k
l
m
n
o
p
q
r
s
t
u
v
w
x
y
z

ashtray *noun* Aschenbecher der (PL die Aschenbecher).

Asia *noun* Asien das; **in Asia** in Asien.

Asian *noun* Asiate der (PL die Asiaten), Asiatin die (PL die Asiatinnen).
Asian *adjective* asiatisch.

ask *verb* 1 fragen; **to ask somebody something** jemanden nach etwas (DAT) fragen; **I asked him the way** ich fragte ihn nach dem Weg; 2 **to ask something** um etwas (ACC) bitten; **to ask somebody a favour** jemanden um einen Gefallen bitten; **to ask somebody to do something** jemanden bitten, etwas zu tun; **ask Danny to give you a hand** bitte Danny, dir zu helfen; 3 **to ask somebody a question** jemandem eine Frage stellen; **I asked him a few questions** ich habe ihm ein paar Fragen gestellt; 4 einladen✧ SEP; **they've asked us to a party** sie haben uns auf eine Party eingeladen; **Paul's asked Janie out on Friday** Paul hat Janie Freitag eingeladen; 5 **to ask for** verlangen; **how much are they asking for the car?** wieviel verlangen sie für das Auto?

asleep *adjective* **to be asleep** schlafen ✧; **the baby's asleep** das Baby schläft; **to fall asleep** einschlafen ✧ SEP (PERF *sein*).

asparagus *noun* Spargel der (PL die Spargel).

aspirin *noun* Aspirin das.

assembly *noun* (*at school*) Morgenandacht die (PL die Morgenandachten).

assess *verb* beurteilen.

assignment *noun* (*at school*) Aufgabe die (PL die Aufgaben).

assist *verb* helfen (+ DAT) .

assistance *noun* Hilfe die.

assistant *noun* 1 Helfer der (PL die Helfer), Helferin die (PL die Helferinnen); 2 (*in school*) Assistent der (PL die Assistenten), Assistentin die (PL die Assistentinnen); 3 **shop assistant** der Verkäufer, die Verkäuferin.

association *noun* Verband der (PL die Verbände).

assorted *adjective* gemischt.

assortment *noun* Auswahl die.

assume *verb* annehmen✧ SEP; **I assume** ich nehme an.

asthma *noun* Asthma das.

astrology *noun* Astrologie die.

astronaut *noun* Astronaut der (PL die Astronauten), Astronautin die (PL die Astronautinnen).

astronomy *noun* Astronomie die.

at *preposition* 1 in (+ DAT); **at school** in der Schule; **at my office** in meinem Büro; **at the supermarket** im Supermarket; 2 an (+ DAT); **at the station** am Bahnhof; **at the bus stop** an der Bushaltestelle; 3 bei (+ DAT); **at the dentist** beim Zahnarzt; **at Emma's** bei Emma; **she's at her brother's this evening** sie ist heute Abend bei ihrem Bruder; **at the hairdresser's** beim

Friseur; **4 at a party** auf einer Party; **5 at home** zu Hause; **6** (*talking about the time*) um; **at eight o'clock** um acht Uhr; **7 at night** nachts; **at Christmas** zu Weihnachten; **at the weekend** am Wochenende; **8** (*@ in e-mail addresses*) Klammeraffe *der*; **john-dot-smith@easycom-dot-com** john-punkt-smith-Klammeraffe-easycom-punkt-com; **9 at last** endlich; **she's found a job at last** sie hat endlich einen Job gefunden.

athlete *noun* Athlet *der* (PL *die* Athleten), Athletin *die* (PL *die* Athletinnen).

athletic *adjective* sportlich.

athletics *noun* Leichtathletik *die*.

Atlantic *noun* **the Atlantic (Ocean)** der Atlantik.

atlas *noun* Atlas *der* (PL *die* Atlanten).

atmosphere *noun* Atmosphäre *die* (PL *die* Atmosphären).

atom *noun* Atom *das* (PL *die* Atome).

atomic *adjective* Atom-; **an atomic bomb** eine Atombombe.

attach *verb* befestigen.

attached *adjective* (*emotionally*) **to be attached to somebody/ something** an jemandem/etwas (DAT) hängen✧.

attachment *noun* **1** (*in a letter*) Anlage *die* (PL *die* Anlagen); **2** (*in an email*) Attachment *das* (PL *die* Attachments).

attack *noun* Angriff *der* (PL *die* Angriffe).

attack *verb* **1** angreifen✧ SEP; **2** (*mug or raid*) überfallen✧.

attempt *noun* Versuch *der* (PL *die* Versuche); **at the first attempt** beim ersten Versuch. **attempt** *verb* **to attempt to do something** versuchen, etwas zu tun.

attend *verb* teilnehmen✧ SEP an (+ DAT) ; **to attend a meeting** an einer Besprechung teilnehmen; **to attend an evening class** einen Abendkurs besuchen.

attention *noun* **1** Aufmerksamkeit *die*; **to pay attention** aufpassen SEP; **I wasn't paying attention** ich habe nicht aufgepasst; **2 he wasn't paying attention to the teacher** er hörte dem Lehrer nicht zu.

attic *noun* Dachboden *der* (PL *die* Dachböden); **in the attic** auf dem Dachboden.

attitude *noun* **1** (*way of thinking*) Einstellung *die*; **2** (*way of acting*) Haltung *die*.

attract *verb* anziehen✧ SEP.

attraction *noun* **1** Anziehung *die*; **2** (*a thing that attracts*) Attraktion *die* (PL *die* Attraktionen); **the whale was a big attraction** der Wal war eine große Attraktion.

attractive *adjective* attraktiv.

au pair *noun* Aupairmädchen *das* (PL *die* Aupairmädchen); **I'm looking for a job as an au pair** ich suche eine Aupair-Stelle.

aubergine *noun* Aubergine *die* (PL *die* Auberginen).

a
b
c
d
e
f
g
h
i
j
k
l
m
n
o
p
q
r
s
t
u
v
w
x
y
z

a
b
c
d
e
f
g
h
i
j
k
l
m
n
o
p
q
r
s
t
u
v
w
x
y
z

audience *noun* Publikum *das*; **the television audience** die Fernsehzuschauer (*plural*).

August *noun* August *der*; **in August** im August.

aunt, **auntie** *noun* Tante *die* (PL *die* Tanten).

Australia *noun* Australien *das*; **to Australia** nach Australien.

Australian *noun* Australier *der* (PL *die* Australier), Australierin *die* (PL *die* Australierinnen).
Australian *adjective* australisch; **she's Australian** sie ist Australierin.

Austria *noun* Österreich *das*; **in Austria** in Österreich.

Austrian *noun* Österreicher *der* (PL *die* Österreicher), Österreicherin *die* (PL *die* Österreicherinnen).
Austrian *adjective* österreichisch; **he's Austrian** er ist Österreicher.

author *noun* Autor *der* (PL *die* Autoren), Autorin *die* (PL *die* Autorinnen).

autograph *noun* Autogramm *das* (PL *die* Autogramme).

automatic *adjective* automatisch.

automatically *adverb* automatisch.

autumn *noun* Herbst *der* (PL *die* Herbste); **in autumn** im Herbst.

available *adjective* (*on sale*) erhältlich.

average *noun* Durchschnitt *der* (PL *die* Durchschnitte); **on average** im Durchschnitt; **above average** über dem Durchschnitt.

average *adjective* durchschnittlich; **the average height** die durchschnittliche Größe.

avocado *noun* Avocado *die* (PL *die* Avocados).

avoid *verb* 1 vermeiden◇; **to avoid doing something** es vermeiden, etwas zu tun; **I avoid speaking to him** ich vermeide es, mit ihm zu reden; 2 (*keep away from somebody or a place*) meiden◇; **she avoids me** sie meidet mich.

awake *adjective* **to be awake** wach sein; **are you still awake?** bist du noch wach?

award *noun* Preis *der* (PL *die* Preise); **to win an award** einen Preis gewinnen.

aware *adjective* **to be aware of a problem** sich (DAT) eines Problems bewusst sein; **I'm aware of the danger** ich bin mir der Gefahr bewusst; **as far as I'm aware** soweit ich weiß.

away *adverb* 1 **to be away** nicht da sein; **I'll be away next week** ich bin nächste Woche nicht da; 2 **to go away** verreisen (PERF *sein*); **Laura's gone away for a week** Laura ist auf eine Woche verreist; **go away!** geh weg!; 3 **to run away** weglaufen◇ SEP (PERF *sein*); **the thieves ran away** die Diebe liefen weg; 4 **the school is two kilometres away** die Schule ist zwei Kilometer entfernt; **how far away is it?** wie weit entfernt ist es?; **not far away** nicht weit entfernt; 5 **to put something away** etwas wegräumen SEP; **I'm just putting my books away** ich räume gerade meine Bücher weg; **6 to give something away** etwas weggeben❖ SEP, (*as a present*) etwas verschenken; **she's given away all her cassettes** sie hat alle ihre Kassetten verschenkt.

away match *noun* Auswärtsspiel *das* (PL die Auswärtsspiele).

awful *adjective* furchtbar; **the film was awful** der Film war furchtbar; **I feel awful** (*ill*) ich fühle mich furchtbar; **I feel awful about it** es ist mir furchtbar unangenehm; **an awful lot of mistakes** furchtbar viele Fehler.

awkward *adjective* **1** schwierig; **it's an awkward situation** das ist eine schwierige Situation; **it's a bit awkward** das ist ein bisschen schwierig; **an awkward child** ein schwieriges Kind; **2 an awkward question** eine peinliche Frage.

axe *noun* Axt *die* (PL die Äxte).

Bb

baby *noun* Baby *das* (PL die Babys).

babysit *verb* babysitten.

babysitter *noun* Babysitter *der* (PL die Babysitter), Babysitterin *die* (PL die Babysitterinnen).

babysitting *noun* Babysitten *das*.

back *noun* **1** (*of a person or animal*) Rücken *der* (PL die Rücken); **he did it behind my back** er hat es hinter meinem Rücken getan; **2** (*of a piece of paper, cheque, or building*) Rückseite *die* (PL die Rückseiten); **on**

the back auf der Rückseite; **3 the back of your hand** der Handrücken; **4 at the back** hinten; **at the back of the room** hinten im Zimmer; **we sat at the back** wir saßen hinten; **a garden at the back of the house** ein Garten hinter dem Haus; **5** (*of a chair or sofa*) Rückenlehne *die* (PL die Rückenlehnen); **6** (*in football or hockey*) Verteidiger *der* (PL die Verteidiger), Verteidigerin *die* (PL die Verteidigerinnen); **left back** der Linksverteidiger.

back *adjective* **1 the back seat** (*of a car*) der Rücksitz; **2 the back door** die Hintertür; **the back garden** der Garten hinter dem Haus.

back *adverb* **1** zurück; **there and back** hin und zurück; **to go back** (*on foot*) zurückgehen❖ SEP (PERF *sein*) (*in a vehicle*) zurückfahren❖ SEP (PERF *sein*); **2 to come back** zurückkommen❖ SEP (PERF *sein*); **they've come back from Italy** sie sind aus Italien zurückgekommen; **I'll be back at 8 o'clock** ich bin um acht Uhr zurück; **Sue's not back yet** Sue ist noch nicht zurück; **3 to phone back** zurückrufen❖ SEP; **I'll ring back later** ich rufe dich später zurück; **4 to give something back to somebody** jemandem etwas zurückgeben❖ SEP; **give it back!** gib es zurück!

back *verb* (*bet on*) setzen auf (+ ACC).

● **to back up** (*computing*) sichern; **to back up a file** eine Sicherungskopie machen.

● **to back somebody up** jemanden unterstützen.

backache noun
Rückenschmerzen (plural).

background noun 1 (of a person)
Verhältnisse (plural); **she comes
from a poor background** sie
kommt aus ärmlichen
Verhältnissen; 2 (in a picture, view,
or situation) Hintergrund der (PL die
Hintergründe); **background noise**
Hintergrundgeräusche (plural);
3 (to events or problems)
Hintergründe (plural).

backhand noun Rückhand die.

backing noun 1 (on sticky-back
plastic, for example) Verstärkung die
(PL die Verstärkungen); 2 (moral
support) Unterstützung die; 3 (in
music) Begleitung die; **a backing
group** eine Begleitband.

backpack noun Rucksack der (PL
die Rucksäcke).
backpack verb **to go
backpacking** trampen (PERF sein).

back seat noun Rücksitz der (PL die
Rücksitze).

backstroke noun
Rückenschwimmen das.

back to front adverb verkehrt
herum; **your jumper's back to
front** du hast deinen Pullover
verkehrt herum an.

backup noun 1 (support)
Unterstützung die; 2 (in computing)
Sicherungskopie die (PL die
Sicherungskopien); **a backup disk**
eine Sicherungsdiskette.

backwards adverb 1 rückwärts;
2 **to lean backwards** sich nach
hinten lehnen; **to fall backwards**
nach hinten fallen.

bacon noun Speck der; **bacon and
eggs** Eier mit Speck.

bad adjective 1 (not good) schlecht; **a
bad idea** eine schlechte Idee; **a bad
meal** ein schlechtes Essen; **his new
film's not bad** sein neuer Film ist
nicht schlecht; **it's bad for your
health** das ist ungesund; **I'm bad at
physics** ich bin schlecht in Physik;
2 (serious) schlimm; **a bad mistake**
ein schlimmer Fehler; **a bad cold**
eine schlimme Erkältung; 3 **a bad
accident** ein schwerer Unfall;
4 (rotten) schlecht; **to go bad**
schlecht werden; 5 **a bad apple** ein
fauler Apfel; 6 **bad language**
Kraftausdrücke (plural); ★**too bad!**
schade!, so ein Pech!

badge noun Abzeichen das (PL die
Abzeichen).

badly adverb 1 (poorly) schlecht; **he
writes badly** er schreibt schlecht; **I
slept badly** ich habe schlecht
geschlafen; 2 (seriously) schwer;
they were badly injured sie waren
schwer verletzt; 3 (very much)
dringend; **to need something
badly** etwas dringend brauchen.

bad-mannered adjective **to be
bad-mannered** schlechte Manieren
haben.

badminton noun Badminton das.

bad-tempered adjective schlecht
gelaunt; **a bad-tempered old man**
ein schlecht gelaunter alter Mann.

bag *noun* **1** Tasche *die* (PL *die* Taschen); **2** (*made of paper or plastic*) Tüte *die* (PL *die* Tüten).

baggage *noun* Gepäck *das*.

bagpipes *plural noun* Dudelsack *der* (PL *die* Dudelsäke).

bags *plural noun* Gepäck *das*; **to pack your bags** (sein Gepäck) packen; ⋆ **to have bags under your eyes** Ringe unter den Augen haben (*informal*).

bake *verb* **1** backen; **to bake a cake** einen Kuchen backen; **2 I'm baking** mir ist furchtbar heiß.

baked *adjective* **1** (*fish or fruit*) überbacken; **baked apples** Bratäpfel; **2 baked potatoes** die Ofenkartoffeln.

baked beans *plural noun* Bohnen in Tomatensoße.

baker *noun* Bäcker *der* (PL *die* Bäcker); **to go to the baker's** zum Bäcker gehen.

bakery *noun* Bäckerei *die* (PL *die* Bäckereien).

balance *noun* **1** Gleichgewicht *das*; **to lose your balance** das Gleichgewicht verlieren; **2** (*in a bank account*) Kontostand *der*.

balanced *adjective* ausgeglichen.

balcony *noun* Balkon *der* (PL *die* Balkons).

bald *adjective* **1** kahl; **2** (*of a person*) kahlköpfig; **to go bald** eine Glatze bekommen.

ball *noun* **1** (*for tennis, football, or golf*) Ball *der* (PL *die* Bälle); **2** (*for billiards, croquet*) Kugel *die* (PL *die*

Kugeln); **3** (*of string or wool*) Knäuel *das* (PL *die* Knäuel).

ballet *noun* Ballett *das* (PL *die* Ballette).

ballet dancer *noun* Balletttänzer *der* (PL *die* Balletttänzer), Balletttänzerin *die* (PL *die* Balletttänzerinnen).

balloon *noun* **1** Luftballon *der* (PL *die* Luftballons); **2** (*hot-air*) Ballon *der* (PL *die* Ballons).

ballpoint (pen) *noun* Kugelschreiber *der* (PL *die* Kugelschreiber).

ban *noun* Verbot *das* (PL *die* Verbote); **a ban on smoking** ein Rauchverbot. **ban** *verb* verbieten⋄; **to ban someone from smoking** jemandem verbieten zu rauchen.

banana *noun* **1** Banane *die* (PL *die* Bananen); **2 a banana yoghurt** ein Bananenjoghurt.

band *noun* **1** (*playing music*) Band *die* (PL *die* Bands); **rock band** die Rockband; **brass band** die Blaskapelle; **2 rubber band** *das* Gummiband.

bandage *noun* Verband *der* (PL *die* Verbände). **bandage** *verb* verbinden⋄.

bang *noun* (*noise*) Knall *der* (PL *die* Knalle). **bang** *verb* **1** (*hit, knock*) schlagen⋄; **he banged his fist on the table** er schlug mit der Faust auf den Tisch; **to bang on the door** gegen die Tür schlagen; **2 I banged my head on the door** ich habe mir den Kopf an der Tür gestoßen; **3 to bang into something** gegen etwas (ACC)

343

a
b
c
d
e
f
g
h
i
j
k
l
m
n
o
p
q
r
s
t
u
v
w
x
y
z

a
b
c
d
e
f
g
h
i
j
k
l
m
n
o
p
q
r
s
t
u
v
w
x
y
z

knallen; **4** (*shut loudly*) zuknallen SEP; **he banged the door** er knallte die Tür zu.
bang *exclamation* peng!

bank *noun* **1** (*for money*) Bank *die* (PL *die* Banken); **I'm going to the bank** ich gehe auf die Bank; **2** (*of a river or lake*) Ufer *das* (PL *die* Ufer).

bank account *noun* Bankkonto *das* (PL *die* Bankkonten).

bank balance *noun* Kontostand *der* (PL *die* Kontostände).

bank card *noun* Scheckkarte *die* (PL *die* Scheckkarten).

bank holiday *noun* gesetzliche Feiertag *der* (PL *die* gesetzlichen Feiertage).

banknote *noun* Geldschein *der* (PL *die* Geldscheine).

bank statement *noun* Kontoauszug *der* (PL *die* Kontoauszüge).

bar *noun* **1** (*selling drinks*) Bar *die* (PL *die* Bars); **Janet works in a bar** Janet arbeitet in einer Bar; **2** (*counter*) Theke *die* (PL *die* Theken); **on the bar** auf der Theke; **3 a bar of chocolate** eine Tafel Schokolade; **4 a bar of soap** ein Stück Seife; **5** (*made of wood or metal*) Stange *die* (PL *die* Stangen); **an iron bar** eine Eisenstange; **6** (*in music*) Takt *der* (PL *die* Takte).

barbecue *noun* **1** (*apparatus*) Grill *der* (PL *die* Grills); **2** (*party*) Grillfest *das* (PL *die* Grillfeste).
barbecue *verb* **to barbecue a chicken** ein Hühnchen grillen;

barbecued chicken gegrilltes Hühnchen.

bare *adjective* nackt.

barefoot *adjective* **to be barefoot** barfuß sein; **to walk barefoot** barfuß gehen.

bargain *noun* (*a good buy*) gute Kauf *der* (PL *die* guten Käufe); **I got a bargain** ich habe einen guten Kauf gemacht; **it's a bargain!** das ist ein Schnäppchen!

barge *noun* Kahn *der* (PL *die* Kähne).

bark *noun* **1** (*of a tree*) Rinde *die* (PL *die* Rinden); **2** (*of a dog*) Bellen *das*.
bark *verb* bellen.

barmaid *noun* Bardame *die* (PL *die* Bardamen).

barman *noun* Barkeeper *der* (PL *die* Barkeeper).

barn *noun* Scheune *die* (PL *die* Scheunen).

barrel *noun* Fass *das* (PL *die* Fässer).

barrier *noun* Absperrung *die* (PL *die* Absperrungen).

base *noun* (*bottom part*) Fuß *der* (PL *die* Füße).

baseball *noun* Baseball *der*.

based *adjective* **1 to be based on** basieren auf (+ DAT); **the film is based on a true story** der Film basiert auf einer wahren Geschichte; **2 to be based in** wohnen in (+ DAT); **he's based in Bristol** er wohnt in Bristol.

basement *noun* Kellergeschoss *das* (PL *die* Kellergeschosse).

344

bash *noun* **1** Schlag der (PL die Schläge); **2 I'll have a bash** ich probier's mal.
bash *verb* **I bashed my head** ich habe mir den Kopf angestoßen.

basic *adjective* **1** grundlegend, Grund-; **basic knowledge** Grundkenntnisse (*plural*); **her basic salary** ihr Grundgehalt; **2 the basic problem** das Hauptproblem; **3** (*not luxurious*) einfach.

basically *adverb* **1** grundsätzlich; **it's basically all right** grundsätzlich ist es okay; **2 basically, I don't want to come** eigentlich will ich nicht kommen.

basics *plural noun* **the basics** das Wesentliche.

basin *noun* Becken das (PL die Becken).

basis *noun* **1** Basis die; **2 on a regular basis** regelmäßig.

basket *noun* Korb der (PL die Körbe); **a basket of apples** ein Korb Äpfel; **waste-paper basket** der Papierkorb.

basketball *noun* Basketball der.

bass *noun* **1** Bass der (PL die Bässe); **2 double bass** der Kontrabass.

bass guitar *noun* Bassgitarre die (PL die Bassgitarren).

bassoon *noun* Fagott das (PL die Fagotte).

bat *noun* **1** (*for games*) Schläger der (PL die Schläger); **2** (*animal*) Fledermaus die (PL die Fledermäuse).

bath *noun* **1** Bad das (PL die Bäder); **to have a bath** baden; **2** (*tub*) Badewanne die (PL die Badewannen).

bathroom *noun* Badezimmer das (PL die Badezimmer).

baths *plural noun* Badeanstalt die (PL die Badeanstalten).

bath towel *noun* Badetuch das (PL die Badetücher).

batter *noun* Teig der (PL die Teige); **fish in batter** ausgebackener Fisch.

battery *noun* Batterie die (PL die Batterien).

battle *noun* **1** (*in war*) Schlacht die (PL die Schlachten); **2** (*contest*) Kampf der (PL die Kämpfe).

Bavaria *noun* Bayern das.

bay *noun* **1** (*on coast*) Bucht die (PL die Buchten); **2** (*in bus station*) Haltebucht die (PL die Haltebuchten).

BC (*before Christ*) v.Chr. (*vor Christus*).

be *verb* **1** sein✧ (PERF *sein*); **Melanie is in the kitchen** Melanie ist in der Küche; **where is the butter?** wo ist die Butter?; **I'm tired** ich bin müde; **when we were in Germany** als wir in Deutschland waren; **2** (*with jobs and professions*) sein✧ (PERF *sein*); **she's a teacher** sie ist Lehrerin; **he's a taxi driver** er ist Taxifahrer; **3** (*in clock times, days of the week, dates, and age*) sein✧ (PERF *sein*); **it's three o'clock** es ist drei Uhr; **it's half past five** es ist halb sechs; **what day is it today?** welcher Tag ist heute?; **it's Tuesday today** heute ist Dienstag; **it's the twentieth of May** heute ist der zwanzigste Mai; **what's**

the date today? der Wievielte ist heute?; **how old are you?** wie alt bist du?; **I'm fifteen** ich bin fünfzehn; **4** (*cold, hot, ill*) sein◇ (PERF *sein*); **I'm hot** mir ist heiß; **I'm cold** mir ist kalt; **to be ill** krank sein; **5** (*weather*) sein◇ (PERF *sein*); **it's cold today** heute ist es kalt; **it's a nice day** es ist schönes Wetter; **it's raining** es regnet; **6 I'm hungry** ich habe Hunger; **she's thirsty** sie hat Durst; **7** (*saying how much something costs*) kosten; **how much are the bananas?** wie viel kosten die Bananen?; **8** (*go, come, or visit*) sein◇ (PERF *sein*); **I've never been to Berlin** ich war noch nie in Berlin gewesen; **have you been to England before?** warst du schon einmal in England?; **has the postman been?** war der Briefträger schon da?; **9** (*forming the passive*) werden◇ (PERF *sein*); **to be loved** geliebt werden; **he has been promoted** er ist befördert worden; **10 there is/are** es gibt; **is there a bank near here?** gibt es hier in der Nähe eine Bank?

beach *noun* Strand *der* (PL *die* Strände); **to go to the beach** zum Strand gehen; **on the beach** am Strand.

bead *noun* Perle *die* (PL *die* Perlen).

beak *noun* Schnabel *der* (PL *die* Schnäbel).

beam *noun* **1** (*of light*) Strahl *der* (PL *die* Strahlen); **2** (*for a roof*) Balken *der* (PL *die* Balken).

bean *noun* Bohne *die* (PL *die* Bohnen); **green beans** grüne Bohnen.

bear *noun* Bär *der* (PL *die* Bären). **bear** *verb* **1** ertragen◇; **I can't bear the idea** ich kann den Gedanken nicht ertragen; **2 to bear something in mind** an etwas (ACC) denken; **I'll bear it in mind** ich denke daran.

beard *noun* Bart *der* (PL *die* Bärte).

bearded *adjective* bärtig.

bearings *plural noun* **to get one's bearings** sich orientieren.

beast *noun* **1** (*animal*) Tier *das* (PL *die* Tiere); **2 you beast!** du Biest!

beat *noun* (*in music*) Takt *der*. **beat** *verb* **1** (*defeat*) schlagen◇; **we beat them!** wir haben sie geschlagen; **2 you can't beat a good meal** es geht doch nichts über ein gutes Essen.

● **to beat somebody up** jemanden verprügeln.

beautiful *adjective* schön.

beauty *noun* **1** Schönheit *die* (PL *die* Schönheiten); **2 the beauty of it is that** ... das Schöne daran ist, dass ....

because *conjunction* **1** weil; **because it's cold** weil es kalt ist; **2 because** of wegen (+ GEN); **because of the accident** wegen des Unfalls; **because of you** deinetwegen.

become *verb* werden◇ (PERF *sein*); **she's become a painter** sie ist Malerin geworden.

bed *noun* **1** Bett *das* (PL *die* Betten); **double bed** *das* Doppelbett; **in bed** im Bett; **to go to bed** ins Bett gehen; **2** (*flower bed*) Beet *das* (PL *die* Beete).

bedclothes *plural noun* Bettwäsche *die*.

bedding *noun* Bettzeug *das*.

bedroom *noun* Schlafzimmer *das* (PL *die* Schlafzimmer); **bedroom furniture** Schlafzimmermöbel (*plural*); **my bedroom window** mein Schlafzimmerfenster.

bedside table *noun* Nachttisch *der* (PL *die* Nachttische).

bedsit, bedsitter *noun* möblierte Zimmer *das* (PL *die* möblierten Zimmer).

bedspread *noun* Tagesdecke *die* (PL *die* Tagesdecken).

bedtime *noun* Schlafenszeit *die*; **at bedtime** vor dem Schlafengehen.

bee *noun* Biene *die* (PL *die* Bienen).

beech *noun* Buche *die* (PL *die* Buchen).

beef *noun* Rindfleisch *das*; **we had roast beef** wir haben Rinderbraten gegessen.

beefburger *noun* Hamburger *der* (PL *die* Hamburger).

beer *noun* Bier *das* (PL *die* Biere); **two beers please** zwei Bier bitte; **beer can** *die* Bierdose.

beetle *noun* Käfer *der* (PL *die* Käfer).

beetroot *noun* Rote Bete *die*.

before *preposition* **1** vor (+ DAT); **before Monday** vor Montag; **he left before me** er ist vor mir gegangen; **the day before the wedding** am Tag vor der Hochzeit; **2 the day before** am Tag zuvor; **the day before yesterday** vorgestern; **the week before** in der Woche zuvor;

3 (*already*) schon einmal; **I've seen him before somewhere** ich habe ihn schon einmal irgendwo gesehen; **I had seen the film before** ich hatte den Film schon einmal gesehen.

before *conjunction* bevor; **I closed the windows before leaving** (or **before I left**) ich habe die Fenster zugemacht, bevor ich wegging; **before the train leaves** bevor der Zug abfährt; **oh, before I forget** ... oh, bevor ich es vergesse ....

beforehand *adverb* (*ahead of time*) vorher; **phone beforehand** rufe vorher an.

beg *verb* **1** betteln; **to beg for money** um Geld betteln; **2** (*ask*) bitten◇; **he begged her not to say anything** er bat sie, nichts zu sagen; **3 I beg your pardon** entschuldigen Sie bitte.

begin *verb* anfangen◇ SEP, beginnen◇; **the meeting begins at ten** die Besprechung fängt um zehn an; **the words beginning with P** die Wörter, die mit P anfangen; **to begin to do something** anfangen, etwas zu tun; beginnen, etwas zu tun; **I'm beginning to understand why** ... ich beginne zu verstehen, warum ....

beginner *noun* Anfänger *der* (PL *die* Anfänger), Anfängerin *die* (PL *die* Anfängerinnen).

beginning *noun* Anfang *der* (PL *die* Anfänge); **at the beginning** am Anfang; **at the beginning of the holidays** am Anfang der Ferien.

behalf *noun* **on behalf of** im Namen von (+ DAT); **on behalf of Mr**

and Mrs Smith im Namen von Herrn und Frau Smith.

behave *verb* **1** sich benehmen◇; **he behaved badly** er hat sich schlecht benommen; **2 to behave oneself** sich benehmen◇; **behave yourself!** benimm dich!

behaviour *noun* Benehmen *das*.

behind *noun* Hintern *der* (*informal*) (PL *die* Hintern).

behind *preposition, adverb* **1** hinter (+ DAT, or + ACC *when there is movement towards a place*); **behind the sofa** hinter dem Sofa; **behind them** hinter ihnen; **the car behind** das Auto hinter ihnen/uns; **2 to leave something behind** (*belongings*) etwas vergessen.

beige *adjective* beige.

Belgian *noun* Belgier *der* (PL *die* Belgier), Belgierin *die* (PL *die* Belgierinnen).

Belgian *adjective* belgisch; **he's Belgian** er ist Belgier.

Belgium *noun* Belgien *das*; **to Belgium** nach Belgien.

belief *noun* Glaube *der* (PL *die* Glauben); **his political beliefs** seine politische Überzeugung.

believe *verb* **1** glauben; **I believe so** ich glaube schon; **they believed what I said** sie glaubten, was ich sagte; **I don't believe you** das glaube ich dir nicht; **2 to believe in something** an etwas (ACC) glauben; **to believe in God** an Gott glauben.

bell *noun* **1** (*in a church*) Glocke *die* (PL *die* Glocken); **2** (*on a door*) Klingel *die* (PL *die* Klingeln); **to ring the bell**

klingeln; **3** (*for a cat or toy*) Glöckchen *das* (PL *die* Glöckchen); **´that name rings a bell** der Name sagt mir etwas (*literally: says something to me*).

belong *verb* **1 to belong to** gehören (+ DAT); **that belongs to my mother** das gehört meiner Mutter; **2 to belong to a club** einem Klub angehören; **3** (*go*) gehören; **where does this vase belong?** wo gehört diese Vase hin?

belongings *plural noun* Sachen (*plural*); **all my belongings** alle meine Sachen.

below *preposition* unter (+ DAT, *or* + ACC *when there is movement towards a place*); **below the window** unter dem Fenster; **the flat below yours** die Wohnung unter dir.
below *adverb* **1** (*further down*) unten; **he called from below** er rief von unten herauf; **2 the flat below** die Wohnung darunter.

belt *noun* Gürtel *der* (PL *die* Gürtel).

bench *noun* Bank *die* (PL *die* Bänke).

bend *noun* **1** (*in a road*) Kurve *die* (PL *die* Kurven); **2** (*in a river*) Biegung *die* (PL *die* Biegungen).
bend *verb* **1** (*make a bend in*) biegen◇ (*a pipe or wire*) beugen (*your knee, arm, or head*); **2** (*curve*) eine Biegung machen; **3 to bend down** sich bücken.

beneath *preposition* unter (+ DAT).

benefit *noun* **1** Vorteil *der* (PL *die* Vorteile); **2 unemployment benefit** *die* Arbeitslosenunterstützung.

bent *adjective* verbogen.

beret *noun* Baskenmütze die (PL die Baskenmützen).

beside *preposition* (*next to*) neben (+ DAT, *or* + ACC *when there is movement towards a place*); **she was sitting beside me** sie saß neben mir; **she sat down beside me** sie hat sich neben mich gesetzt; ★ **that's beside the point** das hat nichts damit zu tun.

besides *adverb* (*anyway*) außerdem; **besides, it's too late** außerdem ist es zu spät; (*as well*) **four dogs, and six cats besides** vier Hunde und außerdem sechs Katzen.

best *adjective* 1 bester/beste/ bestes; **she's my best friend** sie ist meine beste Freundin; 2 **she's the best at tennis** im Tennis ist sie die Beste; **it's best to wait** das Beste ist zu warten.

best *adverb* am besten; **he plays best** er spielt am besten; **I like Munich best** München gefällt mir am besten; **best of all** am allerbesten; **I like grapes best** ich mag Weintrauben am liebsten; ★ **all the best!** alles Gute!; ★ **to make the best of it** das Beste daraus machen; ´**to do your best** sein Bestes tun;; **I did my best to help her** ich habe mein Bestes getan, um ihr zu helfen.

best man *noun* Trauzeuge der (PL die Trauzeugen).

bet *noun* Wette die (PL die Wetten).
bet *verb* wetten; **to bet on a horse** auf ein Pferd wetten; **I bet you he'll forget it** ich wette mit dir, dass er es vergisst.

better *adjective, adverb* 1 besser; **she's found a better flat** sie hat eine bessere Wohnung gefunden; 2 **it works better than the other one** dieser geht besser als der andere; **even better** noch besser; **it's even better than before** das ist noch besser als vorher; 3 (*less ill*) **I'm better** es geht mir besser; **he's a bit better today** es geht ihm heute ein bisschen besser; **I feel better** ich fühle mich besser; 4 **to get better** besser werden; **my German is getting better** mein Deutsch wird besser; 5 **so much the better** umso besser; **the sooner the better** je eher, desto besser.

better *adverb* **it's better to phone at once** es wäre besser, sofort anzurufen; **he'd better not go** er sollte besser nicht gehen; **I'd better go now** ich gehe jetzt besser.

better off *adjective* 1 (*richer*) besser gestellt; **they're better off than us** sie sind besser gestellt als wir; 2 (*more comfortable*) **to be better off** besser dran sein; **you'd be better off in bed** im Bett wärst du besser aufgehoben.

between *preposition* 1 zwischen (+ DAT, *or* + ACC *when there is movement towards a place*); **between London and Dover** zwischen London und Dover; **between Monday and Friday** zwischen Montag und Freitag; 2 (*sharing*) unter (+ DAT); **between ourselves** unter uns; **between the two of them** unter sich.

beyond *preposition* 1 (*in space*) jenseits (+ GEN); **beyond the border**

jenseits der Grenze; **2** (*in time*) nach (+ DAT); **beyond midnight** nach Mitternacht; **3 it's beyond me!** das ist mir unverständlich.

Bible *noun* **the Bible** die Bibel.

bicycle *noun* Fahrrad *das* (PL *die* Fahrräder); **she rides a bicycle** sie fährt Rad.

bicycle lane *noun* Fahrradweg *der* (PL *die* Fahrradwege).

big *adjective* groß; **a big house** ein großes Haus; **my big sister** meine große Schwester; **a big mistake** ein großer Fehler; **it's too big for me** das ist mir zu groß.

big toe *noun* große Zehe *die* (PL *die* großen Zehen).

bike *noun* **1** (*with pedals*) Rad *das* (PL *die* Räder); **by bike** mit dem Rad; **2** (*with motor*) Motorrad *das* (PL *die* Motorräder).

bikini *noun* Bikini *der* (PL *die* Bikinis).

bilingual *adjective* zweisprachig.

bill *noun* Rechnung *die* (PL *die* Rechnungen); **can we have the bill, please?** die Rechnung bitte.

billiards *noun* Billard *das*; **to play billiards** Billard spielen.

billion *noun* Milliarde *die* (PL *die* Milliarden), Billion *die* (PL *die* Billionen); **two billion euros** zwei Milliarden Euro.

bin *noun* Mülleimer *der* (PL *die* Mülleimer).

binoculars *plural noun* Fernglas *das* (PL *die* Ferngläser).

biochemistry *noun* Biochemie *die*.

biology *noun* Biologie *die*.

bird *noun* Vogel *der* (PL *die* Vögel).

bird sanctuary *noun* Vogelschutzgebiet *das* (PL *die* Vogelschutzgebiete).

birdwatching *noun* das Beobachten von Vögeln; **to go birdwatching** Vögel beobachten.

Biro *noun* Kugelschreiber *der* (PL *die* Kugelschreiber).

birth *noun* Geburt *die* (PL *die* Geburten).

birth certificate *noun* Geburtsurkunde *die* (PL *die* Geburtsurkunden).

birthday *noun* Geburtstag *der* (PL *die* Geburtstage); **happy birthday!** herzlichen Glückwunsch zum Geburtstag!

birthday party *noun* Geburtstagsfeier *die* (PL *die* Geburtstagsfeiern).

biscuit *noun* Keks *der* (PL *die* Kekse).

bishop *noun* **1** (*churchman*) Bischof *der* (PL *die* Bischöfe); **2** (*in chess*) Läufer *der* (PL *die* Läufer).

bit *noun* **1** (*piece*) Stückchen *das* (PL *die* Stückchen); **a bit of chocolate** ein Stückchen Schokolade; **2** (*a small amount*) **a bit of** ein bisschen; **a bit of sugar** ein bisschen Zucker; **3** (*in a book, film, etc.*) Teil *der* (PL *die* Teile); **this bit is brilliant** dieser Teil ist hervorragend; **4 a bit** ein bisschen; **a bit too early** ein bisschen zu früh; **wait a bit!** warte ein bisschen!; **5 he's a bit of a**

show-off er ist ein ziemlicher Angeber; **6 bit by bit** nach und nach.

bite *noun* **1** (*snack*) Happen *der* (PL *die* Happen); **we'll just have a bite before we go** wir essen noch einen kleinen Happen, bevor wir gehen; **2** (*from an insect*) Stich *der* (PL *die* Stiche); **mosquito bite** *der* Mückenstich; **3** (*from a dog*) Biss *der* (PL *die* Bisse).
bite *verb* **1** (*person or dog*) beißen✧; **2** (*insect*) stechen✧.

bitter *adjective* (*taste*) bitter.

black *adjective* **1** schwarz; **my black jacket** meine schwarze Jacke; **2 a black man** ein Schwarzer; **a black woman** eine Schwarze.

blackberry *noun* Brombeere *die* (PL *die* Brombeeren).

blackbird *noun* Amsel *die* (PL *die* Amseln).

blackboard *noun* Tafel *die* (PL *die* Tafeln).

blackcurrant *noun* Schwarze Johannisbeere *die* (PL *die* Schwarzen Johannisbeeren).

black pudding *noun* Blutwurst *die* (PL *die* Blutwürste).

blade *noun* Klinge *die* (PL *die* Klingen).

blame *noun* Schuld *die*; **to take the blame for something** die Schuld für etwas (ACC) auf sich (ACC) nehmen; **to put the blame on somebody** die Schuld auf jemanden schieben.
blame *verb* **to blame somebody**

for something jemandem die Schuld an etwas (DAT) geben; **they blamed him for the accident** sie haben ihm die Schuld an dem Unfall gegeben; **she is to blame for it** sie ist daran schuld; **I blame the parents** ich gebe den Eltern Schuld; **I don't blame you** ich kann es dir nicht verdenken.

blank *noun* Lücke *die* (PL *die* Lücken).
blank *adjective* **1** (*page*) leer (*tape or disk*) unbespielt; **2 blank cheque** *der* Blankoscheck.

blanket *noun* Decke *die* (PL *die* Decken).

blaze *noun* Feuer *das* (PL *die* Feuer).
blaze *verb* brennen✧.

bleach *noun* Bleichmittel *das* (PL *die* Bleichmittel).

bleed *verb* bluten; **my nose is bleeding** meine Nase blutet.

blend *verb* mischen.

blender *noun* Mixer *der* (PL *die* Mixer).

bless *verb* segnen; **bless you!** (*after a sneeze*) Gesundheit!

blind *noun* (*in a window*) Rollo *das* (PL *die* Rollos).
blind *adjective* blind.

blink *verb* (mit den Augen) blinzeln.

blister *noun* Blase *die* (PL *die* Blasen).

blizzard *noun* Schneesturm *der* (PL *die* Schneestürme).

block *noun* (*a building or buildings*) Block *der* (PL *die* Blocks); **block of flats** *der* Wohnblock; **office block**

das Bürohaus; **to drive round the block** um den Block fahren.

block *verb* **1** sperren (*an exit or a road*); **2 the sink's blocked** das Spülbecken ist verstopft.

blonde *adjective* blond.

blood *noun* Blut *das*.

blood test *noun* Blutprobe *die* (PL *die* Blutproben).

blouse *noun* Bluse *die* (PL *die* Blusen).

blow *noun* Schlag *der* (PL *die* Schläge).

blow *verb* **1** (*a person*) blasen◇; **2** (*the wind*) wehen; **3 the bomb blew the bridge to pieces** die Bombe hat die Brücke in die Luft gesprengt; **4 to blow your nose** sich (DAT) die Nase putzen.
- **to blow something out** etwas ausblasen◇ SEP.
- **to blow up** (*explode*) explodieren (PERF *sein*).
- **to blow something up** (*a tyre or balloon*) etwas aufblasen◇ SEP, (*with explosives*) etwas sprengen.

blow-dry *noun* Föhnen *das*; **a cut and blow-dry** Schneiden und Föhnen.

blue *adjective* blau; **blue eyes** blaue Augen.

blunder *noun* Fehler *der* (PL *die* Fehler).

blunt *adjective* **1** (*a knife, pencil, or scissors*) stumpf; **2** (*a person or question*) direkt.

blurred *adjective* **1** (*not distinct*) verschwommen; **2** (*photo*) unscharf.

blush *verb* erröten (PERF *sein*).

board *noun* **1** (*plank, notice board, game*) Brett *das* (PL *die* Bretter); **chess board** das Schachbrett; **2** (*blackboard*) Tafel *die* (PL *die* Tafeln); **3** (*accommodation in a hotel*) **full board** die Vollpension; **half board** die Halbpension; **board and lodging** Unterkunft und Verpflegung.

boarder *noun* (*in a school*) Internatsschüler *der* (PL *die* Internatsschüler), Internatsschülerin *die* (PL *die* Internatsschülerinnen).

board game *noun* Brettspiel *das* (PL *die* Brettspiele).

boarding *noun* (*on a plane, train*) Einsteigen *das*.

boarding card *noun* Bordkarte *die* (PL *die* Bordkarten).

boarding school *noun* Internat *das* (PL *die* Internate).

boast *verb* prahlen; **he was boasting about his new bike** er prahlte mit seinem neuen Rad.

boat *noun* **1** Boot *das* (PL *die* Boote); **rowing boat** *das* Ruderboot; **2** (*larger boat*) Schiff *das* (PL *die* Schiffe); **to go by boat** mit dem Schiff fahren.

body *noun* **1** Körper *der* (PL *die* Körper); **2** (*corpse*) Leiche *die* (PL *die* Leichen).

bodybuilding *noun* Bodybuilding *das*.

bodyguard *noun* Leibwächter *der* (PL *die* Leibwächter).

body odour *noun* Körpergeruch *der*.

boil *noun* **1 to bring the water to the boil** das Wasser zum Kochen bringen; **2** (*swelling*) Furunkel *der* (PL *die* Furunkel).
boil *verb* **1** kochen; **the water's boiling** das Wasser kocht; **to boil vegetables** Gemüse kochen; **2** (*put the kettle on*) **to boil some water** Wasser aufsetzen SEP.

● **to boil over** überkochen SEP (PERF *sein*).

boiled egg *noun* gekochte Ei *das* (PL *die* gekochten Eier).

boiled potato *noun* Salzkartoffel *die* (PL *die* Salzkartoffeln).

boiler *noun* (*for central heating*) Heizkessel *der* (PL *die* Heizkessel).

boiling *adjective* **1** (*water*) kochend; **2 it's boiling hot today** heute ist es wahnsinnig heiß.

bolt *noun* (*on a door*) Riegel *der* (PL *die* Riegel).
bolt *verb* **1** (*lock*) verriegeln; **2** (*gobble down*) runterschlingen✧ SEP (*informal*).

bomb *noun* Bombe *die* (PL *die* Bomben).
bomb *verb* bombardieren.

bombing *noun* **1** (*in war*) Bombardierung *die* (PL *die* Bombardierungen); **2** (*a terrorist attack*) Bombenattentat *das* (PL *die* Bombenattentate).

bone *noun* **1** Knochen *der* (PL *die* Knochen); **2** (*of a fish*) Gräte *die* (PL *die* Gräten).

bonfire *noun* Feuer *das* (PL *die* Feuer).

bonnet *noun* **1** (*of a car*) Kühlerhaube *die* (PL *die* Kühlerhauben); **2** (*clothing*) Haube *die* (PL *die* Hauben).

boo *verb* ausbuhen SEP; **the crowd booed the referee** die Menge buhte den Schiedsrichter aus.

book *noun* **1** Buch *das* (PL *die* Bücher); **a book about dinosaurs** ein Buch über Dinosaurier; **my biology book** mein Biologiebuch; **2** (*of stamps, tickets*) Heft *das* (PL *die* Hefte); **3 exercise book** *das* Heft; **cheque book** *das* Scheckbuch.
book *verb* **1** buchen (*holiday, flight*); **2** bestellen (*a table, theatre, or cinema tickets*); **I booked a table for 8 p.m.** ich habe einen Tisch für zwanzig Uhr bestellt.

bookcase *noun* Bücherregal *das* (PL *die* Bücherregale).

booking *noun* (*for a flight or a holiday, for example*) Buchung *die* (PL *die* Buchungen).

booking office *noun* **1** (*at a train station*) Fahrkartenschalter *der* (PL *die* Fahrkartenschalter); **2** (*in a theatre or cinema*) Kasse *die* (PL *die* Kassen).

booklet *noun* Broschüre *die* (PL *die* Broschüren).

bookshelf *noun* Bücherregal *das* (PL *die* Bücherregale).

bookshop *noun* Buchhandlung *die* (PL *die* Buchhandlungen).

boot *noun* **1** Stiefel *der* (PL *die* Stiefel); **2** (*for football, walking, climbing, or skiing*) Schuh *der* (PL *die* Schuhe); **football boots**

a
b
c
d
e
f
g
h
i
j
k
l
m
n
o
p
q
r
s
t
u
v
w
x
y
z

Fußballschuhe; **3** (*of a car*) Kofferraum *der* (PL *die* Kofferräume).

border *noun* (*between countries*) Grenze *die* (PL *die* Grenzen); **at the border** an der Grenze.

bore *noun* **1** (*a boring person*) langweilige Mensch *der* (PL *die* langweiligen Menschen); **2** (*a nuisance*) **what a bore!** wie ärgerlich!

bored *adjective* **to be bored** sich langweilen; **I'm bored** ich langweile mich.

boring *adjective* langweilig.

born *adjective* geboren; **to be born** geboren werden; **she was born in Germany** sie ist in Deutschland geboren.

borrow *verb* sich (DAT) borgen; **can I borrow your bike?** kann ich mir dein Rad borgen?; **to borrow something from somebody** sich etwas von jemandem borgen; **I borrowed some money from Dad** ich habe mir Geld von Vati geborgt.

boss *noun* Chef *der* (PL *die* Chefs), Chefin *die* (PL *die* Chefinnen).

bossy *adjective* herrisch.

both *pronoun* beide; **they both came** sie kamen beide; **both my sisters were there** meine beiden Schwestern waren da; **both of us** wir beide; **they are both sold** beide sind verkauft.
both *adverb* **both at home and at school** sowohl zu Hause als auch in der Schule; **both in summer and in winter** sowohl im Sommer als auch im Winter.

bother *noun* **1** (*minor trouble*) Ärger *der*, **I've had a lot of bother with the car** ich hatte viel Ärger mit dem Auto; **2 if it isn't too much bother** wenn es nicht zu viel Mühe macht; **it's no bother** das ist kein Problem; **the children were no bother** die Kinder waren kein Problem; **without any bother** ohne irgendwelche Schwierigkeiten.
bother *verb* **1** (*disturb*) stören; **I'm sorry to bother you** es tut mir Leid, dich zu stören; **2** (*worry*) stören; **what's bothering you?** was stört dich?; **it doesn't bother me at all** das stört mich überhaupt nicht; **3** (*take trouble*) **don't bother to write** du brauchst nicht zu schreiben; **she didn't even bother to wait** sie hat nicht einmal gewartet; **don't bother!** lass es! (*informal*); **I can't be bothered** ich habe keine Lust.

bottle *noun* Flasche *die* (PL *die* Flaschen).

bottle bank *noun* Altglascontainer *der* (PL *die* Altglascontainer).

bottle opener *noun* Flaschenöffner *der* (PL *die* Flaschenöffner).

bottom *noun* **1** (*of a bag, bottle, hole, or stretch of water*) Boden *der* (PL *die* Böden); **at the bottom of the lake** am Boden des Sees; **at the bottom of the well** auf dem Grund des Brunnens; **2** (*of a hill or building*) Fuß *der* (PL *die* Füße); **at the bottom of the tower** am Fuß des Turms; **3** (*of a garden, street, list*)

Ende *das* (PL *die* Enden); **at the bottom of the street** am Ende der Straße; **4 at the bottom of the page** unten auf der Seite; **5** (*buttocks*) Hintern *der* (*informal*) (PL *die* Hintern).

bottom *adjective* **1** unterster/unterste/unterstes; **the bottom shelf** das unterste Regalbrett; **2 the bottom flat** die Wohnung im Erdgeschoss.

bounce *verb* (*jump*) springen⋄ (PERF *sein*).

bouncer *noun* Rausschmeißer *der* (PL *die* Rausschmeißer).

bound *adjective* (*certain*) **he's bound to be late** er kommt ganz bestimmt zu spät; **that was bound to happen** das musste ja kommen.

boundary *noun* Grenze *die* (PL *die* Grenzen).

bow *noun* **1** (*in a shoelace or ribbon*) Schleife *die* (PL *die* Schleifen); **2** (*for a violin or with arrows*) Bogen *der* (PL *die* Bogen); **with bow and arrow** mit Pfeil und Bogen.

bowl *noun* **1** (*large, for salad, mixing, or washing up*) Schüssel *die* (PL *die* Schüsseln); **2** (*smaller*) Schale *die* (PL *die* Schalen).

bowler *noun* (*in cricket*) Werfer *der* (PL *die* Werfer), Werferin *die* (PL *die* Werferinnen).

bowling *noun* (*tenpin*) Bowling *das*; **to go bowling** kegeln gehen.

bow tie *noun* Fliege *die* (PL *die* Fliegen).

box *noun* **1** Schachtel *die* (PL *die* Schachteln); **a box of chocolates** eine Schachtel Pralinen; **2 cardboard box** *der* Karton; **3** (*on a form*) Kästchen *das* (PL *die* Kästchen).

boxer *noun* Boxer *der* (PL *die* Boxer).

boxing *noun* **1** Boxen *das*; **2 boxing match** *der* Boxkampf.

Boxing Day *noun* zweite Weihnachtsfeiertag *der*.

box office *noun* Kasse *die* (PL *die* Kassen).

boy *noun* Junge *der* (PL *die* Jungen); **a little boy** ein kleiner Junge.

boyfriend *noun* Freund *der* (PL *die* Freunde).

bra *noun* BH *der* (PL *die* BHs).

brace *noun* (*for teeth*) Spange *die* (PL *die* Spangen).

bracelet *noun* Armband *das* (PL *die* Armbänder).

bracket *noun* Klammer *die* (PL *die* Klammern); **in brackets** in Klammern.

brain *noun* Gehirn *das* (PL *die* Gehirne).

brainwave *noun* Geistesblitz *der* (PL *die* Geistesblitze).

brake *noun* Bremse *die* (PL *die* Bremsen).
brake *verb* bremsen.

branch *noun* **1** (*of a tree*) Ast *der* (PL *die* Äste); **2** (*of a shop*) Filiale *die* (PL *die* Filialen); **3** (*of a bank*) Zweigstelle *die* (PL *die* Zweigstellen).

brand *noun* Marke *die* (PL *die* Marken).

brand new *adjective* nagelneu.

brandy *noun* Weinbrand *der* (PL *die* Weinbrände).

a
b
c
d
e
f
g
h
i
j
k
l
m
n
o
p
q
r
s
t
u
v
w
x
y
z

a
b
c
d
e
f
g
h
i
j
k
l
m
n
o
p
q
r
s
t
u
v
w
x
y
z

brass *noun* **1** (*metal*) Messing *das*; **2** (*in an orchestra*) **the brass** die Blechbläser.

brass band *noun* Blaskapelle *die* (PL die Blaskapellen).

brave *adjective* tapfer.

bravery *noun* Tapferkeit *die*.

Brazilian *adjective* brasilianisch. **Brazilian** *noun* Brasilianer *der* (PL die Brasilianer), Brasilianerin *die* (PL die Brasilianerinnen).

bread *noun* Brot *das* (PL die Brote); **a slice of bread** eine Scheibe Brot; **a piece of bread and butter** ein Butterbrot.

break *noun* **1** (*a short rest or at school*) Pause *die* (PL die Pausen); **ten minutes' break** eine Pause von zehn Minuten; **to take a break** Pause machen; **at break** in der Pause; **2 the Christmas break** die Weihnachtsferien (*plural*).
break *verb* **1** zerbrechen◇, kaputtmachen SEP (*informal*); **he broke a glass** er hat ein Glas zerbrochen; **don't break the doll** mach die Puppe nicht kaputt; **2** (*get damaged*) zerbrechen◇ (PERF *sein*), kaputtgehen◇ SEP (*informal*) PERF *sein*); **the glass broke** das Glas zerbrach; **the eggs broke** die Eier sind kaputtgegangen; **3 to break your arm** sich (DAT) den Arm brechen; **4** brechen◇ (*rules, promise*); **to break one's promise** sein Versprechen brechen; **5 to break the record** den Rekord brechen◇; **6 to break the news that** ... melden, dass ....
● **to break down 1** (*car*) eine Panne

haben; **the car broke down** das Auto hatte eine Panne; **2** (*talks, negotiations*) scheitern (PERF *sein*).
● **to break in** einbrechen◇ SEP (PERF *sein*).
● **to break up 1** (*couple*) sich trennen; **2** (*crowd*) sich auflösen SEP; **3 we break up on Thursday** die Ferien fangen Donnerstag an.

breakdown *noun* **1** (*of a vehicle*) Panne *die* (PL die Pannen); **we had a breakdown on the motorway** wir hatten eine Panne auf der Autobahn; **2** (*in talks or negotiations*) Scheitern *das*; **3** (*a nervous collapse*) Zusammenbruch *der* (PL die Zusammenbrüche); **to have a nervous breakdown** einen Nervenzusammenbruch haben.

breakdown truck *noun* Abschleppwagen *der* (PL die Abschleppwagen).

breakfast *noun* Frühstück *das* (PL die Frühstücke); **we have breakfast at eight** wir frühstücken um acht Uhr.

break-in *noun* Einbruch *der* (PL die Einbrüche).

breast *noun* Brust *die* (PL die Brüste).

breaststroke *noun* Brustschwimmen *das*.

breath *noun* Atem *der*; **out of breath** außer Atem; **to hold your breath** den Atem anhalten; **to get your breath back** wieder zu Atem kommen; **to take a deep breath** tief einatmen.

breathe *verb* atmen.

breathing noun Atmen das

breed noun (of animal) Rasse die (PL die Rassen).

breeze noun Brise die (PL die Brisen).

brew verb 1 brauen (beer); 2 aufbrühen SEP (tea); **the tea's brewing** der Tee zieht noch.

brewery noun Brauerei die (PL die Brauereien).

brick noun Ziegel der (PL die Ziegel); **a brick wall** eine Ziegelmauer.

bride noun Braut die (PL die Bräute); **the bride and groom** das Brautpaar.

bridegroom noun Bräutigam der (PL die Bräutigame).

bridesmaid noun Brautjungfer die (PL die Brautjungfern).

bridge noun 1 (over a river) Brücke die (PL die Brücken); 2 (card game) Bridge das.

bridle noun Zaumzeug das (PL die Zaumzeuge).

brief adjective kurz.

briefcase noun Aktentasche die (PL die Aktentaschen).

briefly adverb kurz.

briefs plural noun Slip der (PL die Slips).

bright adjective 1 (colour) leuchtend; **bright green socks** leuchtend grüne Socken; 2 (eyes, sunshine) strahlend; 3 (light) hell; 4 (clever) intelligent; **she's not very bright** sie ist nicht sehr intelligent; ´**to look on the bright side** die

Sache positiv sehen (literally: to see things positively).

brilliant adjective 1 (very clever) glänzend; **he's a brilliant surgeon** er ist ein glänzender Chirurg; 2 (wonderful) toll; **the party was brilliant!** die Party war toll!

bring verb 1 mitbringen◇ SEP; **he brought a present** er brachte ein Geschenk mit; **bring your camera** bring deinen Fotoapparat mit; 2 (to a place) bringen◇; **she's bringing the children home** sie bringt die Kinder nach Hause.

● **to bring somebody up** jemanden großziehen◇ SEP; **he was brought up by his aunt** er wurde von seiner Tante großgezogen.

Britain noun Großbritannien das; **to Britain** nach Großbritannien.

British plural noun **the British** die Briten.
British adjective 1 britisch; **the British Isles** die Britischen Inseln; 2 **he's British** er ist Brite; **she's British** sie ist Britin.

broad adjective 1 (wide) breit; 2 (extensive) weit.

broad bean noun dicke Bohne die (PL die dicken Bohnen).

broadcast noun Sendung die (PL die Sendungen).
broadcast verb senden.

broccoli noun Brokkoli der (PL die Brokkolis).

brochure noun Broschüre die (PL die Broschüren).

broke adjective **to be broke** pleite sein (informal).

a
b
c
d
e
f
g
h
i
j
k
l
m
n
o
p
q
r
s
t
u
v
w
x
y
z

broken *adjective* zerbrochen, kaputt (*informal*); **the window's broken** das Fenster ist kaputt; **to have a broken leg** ein gebrochenes Bein haben.

bronchitis *noun* Bronchitis *die*.

brooch *noun* Brosche *die* (PL *die* Broschen).

broom *noun* Besen *der* (PL *die* Besen).

brother *noun* Bruder *der* (PL *die* Brüder); **my mother's brother** der Bruder meiner Mutter.

brother-in-law *noun* Schwager *der* (PL *die* Schwäger).

brown *adjective* braun; **my brown shoes** meine braunen Schuhe; **light brown** hellbraun; **dark brown** dunkelbraun; **to go brown** (*suntanned*) braun werden.

brown bread *noun* Mischbrot *das* (PL *die* Mischbrote).

bruise *noun* **1** (*on a person*) blaue Fleck *der* (PL *die* blauen Flecken); **2** (*on fruit*) Druckstelle *die* (PL *die* Druckstellen).

brush *noun* **1** (*for your hair, clothes, nails, or shoes*) Bürste *die* (PL *die* Bürsten); **my hair brush** meine Haarbürste; **2** (*for sweeping*) Besen *der* (PL *die* Besen); **3** (*for paint*) Pinsel *der* (PL *die* Pinsel).

brush *verb* **1** bürsten; **to brush your hair** sich (DAT) die Haare bürsten; **I brushed my hair** ich habe mir die Haare gebürstet; **2 to brush your teeth** sich (DAT) die Zähne putzen.

Brussels *noun* Brüssel *das*.

Brussels sprout *noun* Rosenkohl *der*; **he likes Brussels sprouts** er mag Rosenkohl.

bubble *noun* Blase *die* (PL *die* Blasen).

bubble bath *noun* Badeschaum *der*.

bucket *noun* Eimer *der* (PL *die* Eimer).

buckle *noun* Schnalle *die* (PL *die* Schnallen).

Buddhism *noun* Buddhismus *der*.

Buddhist *noun* Buddhist *der* (PL *die* Buddhisten), Buddhistin *die* (PL *die* Buddhistinnen).

budget *noun* Budget *das* (PL *die* Budgets).

budgie *noun* Wellensittich *der* (PL *die* Wellensittiche).

buffet *noun* Büffet *das* (PL *die* Büffets).

buffet car *noun* Speisewagen *der* (PL *die* Speisewagen).

bug *noun* **1** (*insect*) Wanze *die* (PL *die* Wanzen); **2** (*germ*) Bazillus *der* (PL *die* Bazillen); **a stomach bug** eine Magengrippe; **3 a computer bug** ein Programmierfehler.

build *verb* bauen.

builder *noun* Bauarbeiter *der* (PL *die* Bauarbeiter).

building *noun* Gebäude *das* (PL *die* Gebäude).

building site *noun* Baustelle *die* (PL *die* Baustellen).

building society *noun* Bausparkasse *die* (PL *die* Bausparkassen).

built-up *adjective* **1** bebaut; **2 built-up area** das Wohngebiet.

bulb *noun* **1** (*lightbulb*) Glühbirne die (PL die Glühbirnen); **2** (*flower bulb*) Blumenzwiebel die (PL die Zwiebeln).

bull *noun* Bulle der (PL die Bullen).

bulldozer *noun* Planierraupe die (PL die Planierraupen).

bullet *noun* Kugel die (PL die Kugeln).

bulletin *noun* **1** (*written*) Bulletin das (PL die Bulletins); **2** (*on TV, radio*) **news bulletin** die Kurzmeldung.

bully *noun* **1** (*in school*) Rabauke der (PL die Rabauken); **2** (*adult*) Tyrann der (PL die Tyrannen).
bully *verb* schikanieren.

bum *noun* Hintern der (*informal*) (PL die Hintern).

bump *noun* **1** (*on a surface*) Unebenheit die (PL die Unebenheiten); **there are lots of bumps in the road** die Straße ist sehr uneben; **2** (*swelling*) Beule die (PL die Beulen); **a bump on the head** eine Beule am Kopf; **3** (*jolt*) Stoß der (PL die Stöße); **4** (*noise*) Bums der (PL die Bumse).
bump *verb* **1** (*bang*) stoßen◇; **I bumped my head** ich habe mir den Kopf gestoßen; **to bump into something** gegen etwas (ACC) stoßen; **2 to bump into somebody** (*meet by chance*) jemanden zufällig treffen.

bumper *noun* Stoßstange die (PL die Stoßstangen).

bumpy *adjective* holperig.

bun *noun* **1** (*for a burger*) Brötchen das (PL die Brötchen), Semmel die (PL die Semmeln); **2** (*sweet*) süße Brötchen das (PL die süßen Brötchen).

bunch *noun* **1** (*of flowers*) Strauß der (PL die Sträuße); **2** (*of carrots, radishes*) Bund das (PL die Bunde); **a bunch of keys** ein Schlüsselbund; **3 a bunch of grapes** eine ganze Weintraube.

bundle *noun* Bündel das (PL die Bündel).

bungalow *noun* Bungalow der (PL die Bungalows).

bunk *noun* **1** (*on a boat*) Koje die (PL die Kojen); **2** (*on a train*) Bett das (PL die Betten).

bunk bed *noun* Etagenbett das (PL die Etagenbetten).

burger *noun* Hamburger der (PL die Hamburger).

burglar *noun* Einbrecher der (PL die Einbrecher), Einbrecherin die (PL die Einbrecherinnen).

burglar alarm *noun* Alarmanlage die (PL die Alarmanlagen).

burglary *noun* Einbruch der (PL die Einbrüche).

burn *noun* **1** (*on the skin*) Verbrennung die (PL die Verbrennungen); **2** (*on fabric, object*) Brandstelle die (PL die Brandstellen).
burn *verb* **1** verbrennen◇; **she burnt his letters** sie hat seine Briefe verbrannt; **2** (*fire, candle*) brennen◇; **3** (*injure*) verbrennen◇;

to burn yourself sich verbrennen; **you'll burn your fingers!** du verbrennst dir die Finger!; 4 (*cake, meat, etc.*) anbrennen✧ SEP; **Mum's burnt the cake** Mutti hat den Kuchen anbrennen lassen.

burnt *adjective* 1 (*papers, rubbish*) verbrannt; 2 (*cake, meat, etc.*) angebrannt.

burst *verb* 1 platzen lassen (*a balloon*); **the tyre has burst** der Reifen ist geplatzt; 2 **to burst out laughing** in Lachen ausbrechen✧ SEP (PERF *sein*); **to burst into tears** in Tränen ausbrechen✧ SEP (PERF *sein*); 3 **to burst into flames** in Flammen aufgehen✧ SEP (PERF *sein*).

bury *verb* 1 begraben✧ (*a dead person*); 2 vergraben✧ (*treasure or a bone*).

bus *noun* Bus *der* (PL die Busse); **on the bus** im Bus; **by bus** mit dem Bus.

bus driver *noun* Busfahrer *der* (PL die Busfahrer), Busfahrerin *die* (PL die Busfahrerinnen).

bush *noun* Busch *der* (PL die Büsche).

business *noun* 1 (*commercial dealings*) Geschäfte (*plural*); **business is bad** die Geschäfte gehen schlecht; **he's in Leeds on business** er ist geschäftlich in Leeds; 2 (*a line of business or profession*) Branche *die* (PL die Branchen); **he's in the insurance business** er ist in der Versicherungsbranche; 3 (*firm or company*) Betrieb *der* (PL die Betriebe); **small businesses** kleine Betriebe; 4 (*personal concern*)

Angelegenheit *die* (PL die Angelegenheiten); **mind your own business!** kümmere dich um deine eigenen Angelegenheiten!

businessman *noun* Geschäftsmann *der* (PL die Geschäftsleute).

business trip *noun* Geschäftsreise *die* (PL die Geschäftsreisen).

businesswoman *noun* Geschäftsfrau *die* (PL die Geschäftsfrauen).

bus pass *noun* Zeitkarte *die* (PL die Zeitkarten).

bus route *noun* Buslinie *die* (PL die Buslinien).

bus shelter *noun* Wartehäuschen *das* (PL die Wartehäuschen).

bus station *noun* Busbahnhof *der* (PL die Busbahnhöfe).

bus stop *noun* Bushaltestelle *die* (PL die Bushaltestellen).

bus ticket *noun* Busfahrkarte *die* (PL die Busfahrkarten).

busy *adjective* 1 beschäftigt; **he's busy** er ist beschäftigt; **she was busy packing** sie war mit Packen beschäftigt; 2 **to have a busy day** viel zu tun haben; 3 **the shops were busy** in den Läden war sehr viel los; 4 (*phone*) besetzt.

but *conjunction* 1 aber; **small but strong** klein aber stark; 2 (*after a negative statement*) sondern; **not Thursday but Friday** nicht Donnerstag, sondern Freitag; **not only ... but also** nicht nur ... sondern auch.

but *preposition* **1** außer (+ DAT); **everyone but Winston** alle außer Winston; **anything but that!** nur das nicht!; **2 the last but one** der/die/das Vorletzte.

butcher *noun* **1** Fleischer der (PL die Fleischer), Fleischerin die (PL die Fleischerinnen), Metzger der (PL die Metzger), Metzgerin die (PL die Metzgerinnen); **he's a butcher** er ist Fleischer, er ist Metzger; **2 the butcher's** die Fleischerei, die Metzgerei.

butter *noun* Butter die.
butter *verb* buttern.

butterfly *noun* Schmetterling der (PL die Schmetterlinge).

button *noun* Knopf der (PL die Knöpfe); **the record button** die Aufnahmetaste.

buttonhole *noun* Knopfloch das (PL die Knopflöcher).

buy *noun* Kauf der (PL die Käufe); **a bad buy** ein schlechter Kauf.
buy *verb* kaufen; **I bought the tickets** ich habe die Karten gekauft; **to buy something for somebody** jemandem etwas kaufen; **Sarah bought him a sweater** Sarah hat ihm einen Pullover gekauft.

buzz *verb* (*a fly or bee*) summen.

buzzer *noun* Summer der (PL die Summer).

by *preposition* **1** von (+ DAT); **I was bitten by a dog** ich bin von einem Hund gebissen worden; **by Mozart** von Mozart; **2 by mistake** versehentlich; **3** (*travel*) mit (+ DAT); **to come by bus** mit dem Bus kommen; **to go by train** mit dem Zug fahren; **by bike** mit dem Rad; **4** (*near*) an (+ DAT); **by the sea** am Meer; **the stop by the school** die Haltestelle an der Schule; **5** (*before*) bis; **it'll be ready by Monday** es wird bis Montag fertig sein; **I'll be back by four** ich bin bis vier Uhr zurück; **6 by now** inzwischen; **7 by yourself** ganz allein; **I was by myself in the house** ich war ganz allein im Haus; **she did it by herself** sie hat es ganz allein gemacht; **8 by the way** übrigens; **9 to go by** vorbeigehen✧ SEP (PERF *sein*).

bye *exclamation* tschüs! (*informal*).

bypass *noun* Umgehungsstraße die (PL die Umgehungsstraßen).

Cc

cab *noun* **1** Taxi das (PL die Taxis); **to call a cab** ein Taxi rufen; **2** (*on a lorry*) Führerhaus das (PL die Führerhäuser).

cabbage *noun* Kohl der.

cable *noun* Kabel das (PL die Kabel).

café *noun* Café das (PL die Cafés).

cage *noun* Käfig der (PL die Käfige).

cagoule *noun* Anorak der (PL die Anoraks).

cake *noun* Kuchen der (PL die Kuchen); **would you like a piece of cake?** möchtest du ein Stück Kuchen?

calculate *verb* berechnen.

a
b
c
d
e
f
g
h
i
j
k
l
m
n
o
p
q
r
s
t
u
v
w
x
y
z

calculation *noun* Rechnung *die* (PL *die* Rechnungen).

calculator *noun* Taschenrechner *der* (PL *die* Taschenrechner).

calendar *noun* Kalender *der* (PL *die* Kalender).

calf *noun* **1** (*animal*) Kalb *das* (PL *die* Kälber); **2** (*of your leg*) Wade *die* (PL *die* Waden).

call *noun* (*telephone*) Anruf *der* (PL *die* Anrufe); **I had several calls this morning** ich erhielt heute Morgen mehrere Anrufe; **thank you for your call** danke für deinen Anruf; **a phone call** ein Telefonanruf.

call *verb* **1** rufen◇; **to call a taxi** ein Taxi rufen; **to call the doctor** einen Arzt rufen; **they called the police** sie riefen die Polizei; **2** (*phone*) anrufen◇ SEP; **call me later** ruf mich später an; **thank you for calling** danke für deinen Anruf; **I'll call you back later** ich rufe dich später zurück; **3** nennen◇; **they've called the baby Julie** sie haben das Baby Julie genannt; **4** to be called heißen◇; **her brother is called Dan** ihr Bruder heißt Dan; **what's he called?** wie heißt er?

call box *noun* Telefonzelle *die* (PL *die* Telefonzellen).

calm *adjective* ruhig.
calm *verb* beruhigen.

● **to calm down** sich beruhigen; **he's calmed down a bit** er hat sich etwas beruhigt.

● **to calm somebody down** jemanden beruhigen; **I tried to calm her down** ich habe versucht, sie zu beruhigen.

calmly *adverb* ruhig.

calorie *noun* Kalorie *die* (PL *die* Kalorien).

camcorder *noun* Camcorder *der* (PL *die* Camcorder).

camel *noun* Kamel *das* (PL *die* Kamele).

camera *noun* **1** Fotoapparat *der* (PL *die* Fotoapparate); **2** (*film or video camera*) Kamera *die* (PL *die* Kameras).

camp *noun* Lager *das* (PL *die* Lager).
camp *verb* campen, zelten.

campaign *noun* Kampagne *die* (PL *die* Kampagnen).

camper *noun* **1** (*person*) Camper *der* (PL *die* Camper), Camperin *die* (PL *die* Camperinnen); **2** (*vehicle*) Campingbus *der* (PL *die* Campingbusse).

camper van *noun* Wohnmobil *das* (PL *die* Wohnmobile).

camping *noun* Camping *das*; **to go camping** zelten; **we're going camping in Bavaria this summer** diesen Sommer zelten wir in Bayern.

campsite *noun* Campingplatz *der* (PL *die* Campingplätze).

can[1] *noun* **1** Dose *die* (PL *die* Dosen); **a can of tomatoes** eine Dose Tomaten; **2** (*for petrol or oil*) Kanister *der* (PL *die* Kanister).

can[2] *verb* **1** können◇; **I can't be there before ten** ich kann vor zehn Uhr nicht da sein; **can you open the door, please?** kannst du die Tür bitte aufmachen?; **can I help you?** kann ich Ihnen helfen?; **they**

couldn't come sie konnten nicht kommen; **you could have told me** das hättest du mir wirklich sagen können; **I can't see him** ich kann ihn nicht sehen; **I can't remember it** ich kann mich nicht daran erinnern; **she can't drive** sich kann nicht Auto fahren; **2** (*be allowed*) dürfen✧; **you can't smoke here** Sie dürfen hier nicht rauchen.

Canada *noun* Kanada *das*; **to Canada** nach Kanada.

Canadian *noun* Kanadier *der* (PL *die* Kanadier), Kanadierin *die* (PL *die* Kanadierinnen).
Canadian *adjective* kanadisch; **he is Canadian** er ist Kanadier.

canal *noun* Kanal *der* (PL *die* Kanäle).

cancel *verb* absagen SEP; **the concert's been cancelled** das Konzert ist abgesagt worden.

cancer *noun* Krebs *der*; **to have lung cancer** Lungenkrebs haben.

Cancer *noun* Krebs *der* (PL *die* Krebse); **I'm Cancer** ich bin Krebs.

candidate *noun* Kandidat *der* (PL *die* Kandidaten), Kandidatin *die* (PL *die* Kandidatinnen).

candle *noun* Kerze *die* (PL *die* Kerzen).

candlestick *noun* Kerzenständer *der* (PL *die* Kerzenständer).

canned *adjective* in Dosen; **canned tomatoes** Tomaten in Dosen.

canoe *noun* Kanu *das* (PL *die* Kanus).

canoeing *noun* **to go canoeing** Kanu fahren✧ (PERF *sein*); **I like canoeing** ich fahre gerne Kanu.

can-opener *noun* Dosenöffner *der* (PL *die* Dosenöffner).

canteen *noun* Kantine *die* (PL *die* Kantinen).

canvas *noun* **1** (*of a tent or bag*) Segeltuch *das*; **2** (*for painting on*) Leinwand *die*.

cap *noun* **1** (*hat*) Kappe *die* (PL *die* Kappen); **baseball cap** *die* Baseballkappe; **2** (*on a bottle or tube*) Verschluss *der* (PL *die* Verschlüsse).

capable *adjective* fähig.

capital *noun* **1** (*city*) Hauptstadt *die* (PL *die* Hauptstädte); **Berlin is the capital of Germany** Berlin ist die Hauptstadt von Deutschland; **2** (*letter*) Großbuchstabe *der* (PL *die* Großbuchstaben); **in capitals** mit Großbuchstaben.

capitalism *noun* Kapitalismus *der*.

Capricorn *noun* Steinbock *der* (PL *die* Steinböcke); **Linda's Capricorn** Linda ist Steinbock.

captain *noun* Kapitän *der* (PL *die* Kapitäne).

capture *verb* festnehmen ✧ SEP.

car *noun* Auto *das* (PL *die* Autos); **to park the car** das Auto einparken; **we're going by car** wir fahren mit dem Auto; **car crash** *der* Autounfall.

caramel *noun* Karamell *der* (PL *die* Karamells).

caravan *noun* Wohnwagen *der* (PL *die* Wohnwagen).

card noun Karte die (PL die Karten); **card game** das Kartenspiel; **to have a game of cards** Karten spielen.

cardboard noun Pappe die.

cardigan noun Strickjacke die (PL die Strickjacken).

cardphone noun Kartentelefon das (PL die Kartentelefone).

care noun **1** Vorsicht die; **to take care crossing the road** beim Überqueren der Straße vorsichtig sein; **take care!** (be careful) sei vorsichtig!, (when saying goodbye) mach's gut!; **2 to take care to do something** darauf achten, dass man etwas tut; **to take care of somebody** auf jemanden aufpassen.

care verb **1 to care about something** sich für etwas (ACC) interessieren; **she cares about the environment** die Umwelt liegt ihr am Herzen; **2 she doesn't care** es ist ihr egal; **I couldn't care less!** das ist mir völlig egal!

career noun Karriere die (PL die Karrieren).

careful adjective vorsichtig; **a careful driver** ein vorsichtiger Fahrer, eine vorsichtige Fahrerin; **be careful!** sei vorsichtig!

carefully adverb **1** sorgfältig; **to read the instructions carefully** die Anweisungen sorgfältig lesen; **2** vorsichtig; **she put the vase down carefully** sie stellte die Vase vorsichtig hin; **drive carefully!** fahr vorsichtig!; **3 listen carefully!** hören Sie gut zu!

careless adjective **1 he's very careless** er ist sehr nachlässig; **this is careless work** das ist eine schlampige Arbeit; **2 a careless mistake** ein Flüchtigkeitsfehler; **3 a careless driver** ein leichtsinniger Fahrer.

car ferry noun Autofähre die (PL die Autofähren).

car hire noun Autovermietung die.

Caribbean noun **the Caribbean (islands)** die Karibik (singular).

carnation noun Nelke die (PL die Nelken).

carnival noun Karneval der (PL die Karnevale).

car park noun Parkplatz der (PL die Parkplätze), (multi-storey) Parkhaus das (PL die Parkhäuser).

carpenter noun Tischler der (PL die Tischler), Tischlerin die (PL die Tischlerinnen).

carpentry noun Tischlerhandwerk das.

carpet noun Teppich der (PL die Teppiche).

car phone noun Autotelefon das (PL die Autotelefone).

car radio noun Autoradio das (PL die Autoradios).

carriage noun (of a train) Abteil das (PL die Abteile).

carrier bag noun Tragetasche die (PL die Tragetaschen).

carrot noun Karotte die (PL die Karotten), Möhre die (PL die Möhren).

a
b
c
d
e
f
g
h
i
j
k
l
m
n
o
p
q
r
s
t
u
v
w
x
y
z

carry *verb* tragen; **she was carrying a case** sie trug einen Koffer.

• **to carry on** weitermachen SEP; **they carried on working** sie arbeiteten weiter.

carrycot *noun* Babytragetasche *die* (PL *die* Babytragetaschen).

carsick *adjective* **he gets carsick** ihm wird beim Autofahren schlecht.

carton *noun* **1** (*of cream or yoghurt*) Becher *der* (PL *die* Becher); **2** (*of milk or orange*) Tüte *die* (PL *die* Tüten).

cartoon *noun* **1** (*a film*) Zeichentrickfilm *der* (PL *die* Zeichentrickfilme); **2** (*a comic strip*) Cartoon *der* (PL *die* Cartoons); **3** (*a drawing*) Karikatur *die* (PL *die* Karikaturen).

cartridge *noun* (*for a pen*) Patrone *die* (PL *die* Patronen).

case[1] *noun* **1** (*suitcase*) Koffer *der* (PL *die* Koffer); **to pack a case** einen Koffer packen; **2** (*a large wooden box*) Kiste *die* (PL *die* Kisten); **3** (*for spectacles or small things*) Etui *das* (PL *die* Etuis).

case[2] *noun* **1** Fall *der* (PL *die* Fälle); **in that case** in dem Fall; **that's not the case** das ist nicht der Fall; **in case of fire** bei Feuer; **2 in case** falls; **in case he comes** falls er kommt; **3 just in case** für alle Fälle; **4 in any case** sowieso; **in any case, it's too late** es ist sowieso zu spät.

cash *noun* **1** (*money in general*) Geld *das*; **I haven't any cash on me** ich habe kein Geld dabei; **2** (*money rather than a cheque*) Bargeld *das*; **to**

pay in cash bar zahlen; **£50 in cash** fünfzig Pfund in bar.

cash card *noun* Bankkarte *die* (PL *die* Bankkarten).

cash desk *noun* Kasse *die* (PL *die* Kassen); **to pay at the cash desk** an der Kasse zahlen.

cash dispenser *noun* Geldautomat *der* (PL *die* Geldautomaten).

cashier *noun* Kassierer *der* (PL *die* Kassierer), Kassiererin *die* (PL *die* Kassiererinnen).

cash point *noun* Geldautomat *der* (PL *die* Geldautomaten).

cassette *noun* Kassette *die* (PL *die* Kassetten).

cassette recorder *noun* Kassettenrekorder *der* (PL *die* Kassettenrekorder).

cast *noun* (*of a play*) Besetzung *die*.

castle *noun* **1** Burg *die* (PL *die* Burgen); **2** (*in chess*) Turm *der* (PL *die* Türme).

casual *adjective* zwanglos.

casualty *noun* **1** (*in an accident*) Verletzte *der/die* (PL *die* Verletzten); **2** (*hospital department*) Unfallstation *die* (PL *die* Unfallstationen); **he's in casualty** er ist auf der Unfallstation.

cat *noun* Katze *die* (PL *die* Katzen), (*tomcat*) Kater *der* (PL *die* Kater); ★ **it's raining cats and dogs** es regnet in Strömen (*literally: it's raining in streams*).

catalogue *noun* Katalog *der* (PL *die* Kataloge).

a

b

c

d

e

f

g

h

i

j

k

l

m

n

o

p

q

r

s

t

u

v

w

x

y

z

catastrophe noun Katastrophe die (PL die Katastrophen).

catch noun 1 (on a door) Schnappriegel der (PL die Schnappriegel); 2 (a drawback) Haken der (PL die Haken); **where's the catch?** wo ist der Haken? **catch** verb 1 fangen◇; **Tom caught the ball** Tom hat den Ball gefangen; **she caught a fish** sie hat einen Fisch gefangen; **catch me!** fang mich!; 2 to catch somebody doing something jemanden bei etwas (DAT) erwischen; **he was caught stealing money** er wurde beim Geldstehlen erwischt; 3 (be in time for) noch erreichen; **did Tim catch his plane?** hat Tim sein Flugzeug noch erreicht?; 4 (become ill with) bekommen◇; **she's caught chickenpox** sie hat die Windpocken bekommen; 5 verstehen◇ (what somebody says); **I didn't catch your name** ich habe Ihren Namen nicht verstanden.

● **to catch up with somebody** jemanden einholen SEP.

category noun Kategorie die (PL die Kategorien).

catering noun 1 (trade) Gastronomie die; 2 who's doing the catering? wer liefert das Essen und die Getränke?

caterpillar noun Raupe die (PL die Raupen).

cathedral noun Kathedrale die (PL die Kathedralen); **Cologne cathedral** der Kölner Dom.

Catholic noun Katholik der (PL die Katholiken), Katholikin die (PL die Katholikinnen).
Catholic adjective katholisch.

cattle plural noun Vieh das.

cauliflower noun Blumenkohl der; **cauliflower cheese** mit Käse überbackener Blumenkohl.

cause noun 1 Ursache die (PL die Ursachen); **the cause of the accident** die Unfallursache; 2 for a good cause für eine gute Sache.
cause verb verursachen; **to cause difficulties** Schwierigkeiten verursachen.

cave noun Höhle die (PL die Höhlen).

caving noun Höhlenforschung die; **to go caving** auf Höhlenforschung gehen.

CD noun CD die (PL die CDs).

CD player noun CD-Player der (PL die CD-Player).

CD-ROM noun CD-ROM die (PL die CD-ROMs).

ceiling noun Decke die (PL die Decken); **on the ceiling** an der Decke.

celebrate verb feiern; **he's celebrating his birthday** er feiert seinen Geburtstag.

celebrity noun Berühmtheit die (PL die Berühmtheiten).

celery noun Sellerie der (PL die Sellerie).

cell noun Zelle die (PL die Zellen).

cellar noun Keller der (PL die Keller).

cello noun Cello das (PL die Cellos); **to play the cello** Cello spielen.

cement noun Zement der.

cemetery *noun* Friedhof *der* (PL *die* Friedhöfe).

cent *noun* 1 (*in euro system*) Eurocent *der* (PL *die* Eurocents), Cent *der* (PL *die* Cents); **50 cents** 50 (Euro)cent; 2 (*in dollar system*) Cent *der* (PL *die* Cents); **25 cents** 25 Cent.

centigrade *adjective* Celsius; **ten degrees centigrade** zehn Grad Celsius.

centimetre *noun* Zentimeter *der* (PL *die* Zentimeter).

central *adjective* 1 zentral; **the office is very central** das Büro ist sehr zentral gelegen; 2 **in central London** im Zentrum von London.

Central Europe *noun* Mitteleuropa *das*.

central heating *noun* Zentralheizung *die*.

centre *noun* Zentrum *das* (PL *die* Zentren); **in the centre of** im Zentrum von (+ DAT); **in the town centre** im Stadtzentrum; **a shopping centre** ein Einkaufszentrum.

century *noun* Jahrhundert *das* (PL *die* Jahrhunderte); **in the twentieth century** im zwanzigsten Jahrhundert.

cereal *noun* **breakfast cereal** Frühstücksflocken (*plural*).

ceremony *noun* Zeremonie *die* (PL *die* Zeremonien).

certain *adjective* 1 (*definite*) bestimmt; **a certain number of** eine bestimmte Zahl von (+ DAT); 2 (*confident*) sicher; **to be certain** sich (DAT) sicher sein; **are you certain of the address?** bist du sicher, dass das die richtige Adresse ist?; **I'm absolutely certain** ich bin mir ganz sicher; **to be certain that ...** sicher sein, dass ...; 3 **nobody knows for certain** niemand weiß es genau.

certainly *adverb* bestimmt; **certainly not** bestimmt nicht.

certificate *noun* 1 Bescheinigung *die* (PL *die* Bescheinigungen); 2 **birth certificate** *die* Geburtsurkunde; 3 (*at school*) Zeugnis *das* (PL *die* Zeugnisse).

chain *noun* Kette *die* (PL *die* Ketten).

chair *noun* 1 (*upright*) Stuhl *der* (PL *die* Stühle); **a kitchen chair** ein Küchenstuhl; 2 (*with arms*) Sessel *der* (PL *die* Sessel).

chair lift *noun* Sessellift *der* (PL *die* Sessellifte).

chalet *noun* 1 (*in the mountains*) Chalet *das* (PL *die* Chalets); 2 (*in a holiday camp*) Ferienhaus *das* (PL *die* Ferienhäuser).

challenge *noun* Herausforderung *die* (PL *die* Herausforderungen).

champion *noun* Meister *der* (PL *die* Meister), Meisterin *die* (PL *die* Meisterinnen); **the world slalom champion** der Weltmeister im Slalom, die Weltmeisterin im Slalom.

chance *noun* 1 (*opportunity*) Gelegenheit *die* (PL *die* Gelegenheiten); **to have the chance to do something** die Gelegenheit haben, etwas zu tun; **if you have the chance to go to New**

York wenn du die Gelegenheit hast, nach New York zu fahren; **I had no chance to speak to him** ich hatte keine Gelegenheit, mit ihm zu reden; **2** (*likelihood*) Aussicht *die* (PL *die* Aussichten); **he's got no chance of winning** er hat keine Aussicht zu gewinnen; **3** (*luck*) Zufall *der*; **by chance** zufällig; **do you have her address, by any chance?** hast du zufällig ihre Adresse?

change *noun* **1** (*from one thing to another*) Änderung *die* (PL *die* Änderungen); **a change of address** eine Adressänderung; **there's been a change of plan** der Plan ist geändert worden; **2** (*alteration*) Veränderung *die* (PL *die* Veränderungen); **they've made some changes to the house** sie haben im Haus ein paar Veränderungen vorgenommen; **a change in the weather** eine Wetterumschwung; **3** (*for the sake of variety*) **for a change, we could go to a restaurant** zur Abwechslung könnten wir in ein Restaurant gehen; **it makes a change from hamburgers** das ist mal etwas anderes als Hamburger; **a change of clothes** etwas anderes zum Anziehen; **4** (*cash*) Wechselgeld *das*; **I haven't any change** ich habe kein Wechselgeld.

change *verb* **1** (*make different*) ändern; **you can't change her** du kannst sie nicht ändern; **to change your address** seine Adresse ändern; **2** (*become different*) sich verändern; **Liz has changed a lot** Liz hat sich sehr verändert;

3 (*transform completely*) verwandeln; **the prince changed into a frog** der Prinz verwandelte sich in einen Frosch; **4** (*exchange in a shop*) umtauschen SEP; **just change it for a larger size** tauschen Sie es einfach gegen eine Nummer größer um; **5** (*change clothes*) sich umziehen◇ SEP; **Mike's just changing** Mike zieht sich gerade um; **6** (*switch from one train or bus to another*) umsteigen◇ SEP (PERF *sein*); **we changed trains at Crewe** wir stiegen in Crewe um; **7** (*switch one thing for another*) wechseln; **I want to change my job** ich möchte meinen Arbeitsplatz wechseln; **they changed places** sie haben die Plätze gewechselt; **8 to change your mind** sich anders entschließen◇.

changing room *noun* (*for sport or swimming*) Umkleideraum *der* (PL *die* Umkleideräume).

channel *noun* **1** (*on TV*) Kanal *der* (PL *die* Kanäle); **to change channels** auf einen anderen Kanal umschalten; **2 the Channel** der Ärmelkanal.

Channel Tunnel *noun* Eurotunnel *der*.

chaos *noun* Chaos *das*; **it was chaos!** das war ein Chaos!

chapel *noun* Kapelle *die* (PL *die* Kapellen).

chapter *noun* Kapitel *das* (PL *die* Kapitel); **in chapter two** im zweiten Kapitel.

character *noun* **1** (*personality*) Charakter *der*; **2** (*somebody in a* *book*) Charakter *der* (PL *die* Charaktere); **3** (*part in a play or film*) Rolle *die* (PL *die* Rollen); **the main character** die Hauptrolle.

charcoal *noun* **1** (*for burning*) Holzkohle *die*; **2** (*for drawing*) Kohle *die*.

charge *noun* **1** (*what you pay*) Gebühr *die* (PL *die* Gebühren); **a booking charge** eine Buchungsgebühr; **an extra or additional charge** eine zusätzliche Gebühr; **there's no charge** das ist kostenlos; **2 to be in charge** für etwas (ACC) verantwortlich sein; **who's in charge of the children?** wer ist für die Kinder verantwortlich?; **3 to be on a charge of theft** wegen Diebstahls angeklagt sein.
charge *verb* **1** (*ask to pay*) berechnen; **they charge us fifteen pounds an hour** sie berechnen uns fünfzehn Pfund pro Stunde; **they didn't charge for delivery** sie haben die Lieferung nicht berechnet; **we won't charge you for it** wir berechnen Ihnen nichts dafür; **2 to charge somebody with something** jemanden wegen etwas (+ GEN) anklagen SEP.

charity *noun* Wohltätigkeitsverein *der* (PL *die* Wohltätigkeitsvereine).

charming *adjective* reizend.

chart *noun* **1** (*table*) Tabelle *die* (PL *die* Tabellen); **2 the weather chart** die Wetterkarte; **3 the charts** die Hitparade.

charter flight *noun* Charterflug *der* (PL *die* Charterflüge).

chase *noun* Verfolgungsjagd *die* (PL *die* Verfolgungsjagden); **a car chase** eine Verfolgungsjagd mit dem Auto.
chase *verb* jagen.

chat *noun* Plauderei *die* (PL *die* Plaudereien); **to have a chat with somebody** mit jemandem plaudern.

chatroom *noun* Chatroom *der* (PL *die* Chatrooms).

chat show *noun* Talkshow *die* (PL *die* Talkshows).

chatter *verb* **1** (*talk*) schwatzen; **2 my teeth were chattering** ich klapperte mit den Zähnen.

cheap *adjective* billig; **cheap shoes** billige Schuhe; **that's very cheap** das ist sehr billig.

cheaply *adverb* billig; **to eat cheaply** billig essen.

cheap-rate *adjective* verbilligt; **a cheap-rate phone call** ein Gespräch zum Billigtarif.

cheat *noun* **1** Betrüger *der* (PL *die* Betrüger), Betrügerin *die* (PL *die* Betrügerinnen); **2** (*in games*) Mogler *der* (PL *die* Mogler), Moglerin *die* (PL *die* Moglerinnen).
cheat *verb* **1** betrügen◇; **2** (*in games*) mogeln.

check *noun* **1** (*in a factory or at a border control*) Kontrolle *die* (PL *die* Kontrollen); **passport check** die Passkontrolle; **2** (*in chess*) **check!** Schach!
check *verb* **1** (*make sure*) prüfen; **he checked their statements** er prüfte ihre Aussagen; **2** (*make sure by looking*) nachsehen◇ SEP; **to check the time** auf die Uhr sehen;

a
b
c
d
e
f
g
h
i
j
k
l
m
n
o
p
q
r
s
t
u
v
w
x
y
z

check they're all back sieh nach, ob alle wieder da sind; **3** (*inspect*) kontrollieren; **to check the tickets** die Fahrkarten kontrollieren.

● **to check in** sich anmelden SEP; **to check in at the airport** am Flughafen einchecken.

● **to check out** abreisen◇ SEP (PERF *sein*); **to check out of the hotel** das Hotel verlassen.

check-in *noun* Abfertigungsschalter *der* (PL die Abfertigungsschalter).

checkout *noun* Kasse *die* (PL die Kassen); **at the checkout** an der Kasse.

check-up *noun* Untersuchung *die* (PL die Untersuchungen).

cheek *noun* **1** (*part of face*) Backe *die* (PL die Backen); **2** (*nerve*) Frechheit *die*; **what a cheek!** so eine Frechheit!

cheeky *adjective* frech.

cheer *noun* **1 three cheers for Tom!** ein dreifaches Hoch auf Tom!; **2** (*when drinking*) **cheers!** prost! **cheer** *verb* (*shout hurray*) Hurra schreien◇.

● **to cheer somebody up** jemanden aufmuntern SEP; **your visits always cheer me up** deine Besuche muntern mich immer auf; **cheer up!** Kopf hoch!

cheerful *adjective* fröhlich.

cheese *noun* Käse *der*; **a cheese sandwich** ein Käsebrot.

chef *noun* Koch *der* (PL die Köche), Köchin *die* (PL die Köchinnen).

chemical *noun* Chemikalie *die* (PL die Chemikalien).

chemist *noun* **1** (*in a pharmacy*) Apotheker *der* (PL die Apotheker), Apothekerin *die* (PL die Apothekerinnen); **2 chemist's** (*dispensing*) Apotheke *die* (PL die Apotheken); **at the chemist's** in der Apotheke; **3** (*scientist*) Chemiker *der* (PL die Chemiker), Chemikerin *die* (PL die Chemikerinnen).

chemistry *noun* Chemie *die*.

cheque *noun* Scheck *der* (PL die Schecks); **to pay by cheque** mit Scheck bezahlen; **to write a cheque** einen Scheck ausstellen.

cheque book *noun* Scheckbuch *das* (PL die Scheckbücher).

cherry *noun* Kirsche *die* (PL die Kirschen).

chess *noun* Schach *das*; **to play chess** Schach spielen.

chessboard *noun* Schachbrett *das* (PL die Schachbretter).

chest *noun* **1** (*part of the body*) Brust *die* (PL die Brüste); **2** (*box*) Truhe *die* (PL die Truhen); **3 a chest of drawers** eine Kommode.

chestnut *noun* Esskastanie *die* (PL die Esskastanien).

chestnut tree *noun* **1** (*horse-chestnut*) Rosskastanie *die* (PL die Rosskastanien); **2** (*sweet chestnut*) Edelkastanie *die* (PL die Edelkastanien).

chew *verb* kauen.

chewing gum *noun* Kaugummi *der* (PL die Kaugummis).

chicken *noun* Huhn *das* (PL *die* Hühner); **roast chicken** *das* Brathähnchen; **chicken breast** *die* Hühnerbrust.

chickenpox *noun* Windpocken (*plural*).

child *noun* Kind *das* (PL *die* Kinder); **when I was a child** ... als Kind ....

childish *adjective* kindisch.

childminder *noun* Tagesmutter *die* (PL *die* Tagesmütter).

chill *noun* **1** Kälte *die*; **2 to have a chill** eine Erkältung haben.

chilled *adjective* gekühlt.

chilli *noun* Chili *der*.

chimney *noun* Schornstein *der* (PL *die* Schornsteine).

chimpanzee *noun* Schimpanse *der* (PL *die* Schimpansen).

chin *noun* Kinn *das* (PL *die* Kinne).

China *noun* China *das*.

china *noun* Porzellan *das*; **the china bowl** die Porzellanschüssel.

Chinese *noun* **1 the Chinese** (*people*) die Chinesen; **2** (*language*) Chinesisch *das*.
Chinese *adjective* **1** chinesisch; **a Chinese man** ein Chinese; **a Chinese woman** eine Chinesin; **2 to have a Chinese meal** chinesisch essen.

chip *noun* **1** (*fried potato*) **chips** Pommes frites (*plural*); **fish and chips** ausgebackener Fisch mit Pommes frites; **2** (*microchip*) Chip *der* (PL *die* Chips); **3** (*in glass or china*) angeschlagene Stelle *die* (PL *die* angeschlagenen Stellen).

chipped *adjective* angeschlagen.

chocolate *noun* **1** Schokolade *die*; **a box of chocolates** eine Schachtel Pralinen; **2 chocolate ice cream** *das* Schokoladeneis; **3 a cup of hot chocolate** eine Tasse Kakao.

choice *noun* **1** Wahl *die* (PL *die* Wahlen); **to make a good choice** eine gute Wahl treffen; **2** (*variety*) Auswahl *die*; **you have a choice of two flights** du hast zwei Flüge zur Auswahl.

choir *noun* Chor *der* (PL *die* Chöre).

choke *noun* (*on a car*) Choke *der* (PL *die* Chokes).
choke *verb* (*by yourself*) sich verschlucken; **she choked on a bone** sie hat sich an einer Gräte verschluckt.

choose *verb* **1** wählen; **you chose well** du hast gut gewählt; **it's hard to choose from all these colours** es ist schwer, unter allen diesen Farben zu wählen; **2** (*select from a group of things*) sich (DAT) aussuchen SEP; **Cathy chose the red skirt** Cathy suchte sich den roten Rock aus.

chop *noun* Kotelett *das* (PL *die* Koteletts); **a pork chop** ein Schweinekotelett.
chop *verb* hacken.

chord *noun* Akkord *der* (PL *die* Akkorde).

chorus *noun* **1** (*when you all join in the song*) Refrain *der* (PL *die* Refrains); **2** (*a group of singers*) Chor *der* (PL *die* Chöre).

Christ *noun* Christus *der*.

a
b
c
d
e
f
g
h
i
j
k
l
m
n
o
p
q
r
s
t
u
v
w
x
y
z

christening noun Taufe die (PL die Taufen).

Christian noun Christ der (PL die Christen), Christin die (PL die Christinnen).
Christian adjective christlich.

Christianity noun Christentum das.

Christian name noun Vorname der (PL die Vornamen).

Christmas noun Weihnachten das (PL die Weihnachten); **at Christmas** zu Weihnachten; **what did you get for Christmas?** was hast du zu Weihnachten bekommen?; **Happy Christmas!** Frohe Weihnachten!

Christmas card noun Weihnachtskarte die (PL die Weihnachtskarten).

Christmas carol noun Weihnachtslied das (PL die Weihnachtslieder).

Christmas cracker noun Knallbonbon der (PL die Knallbonbons).

Christmas Day noun erste Weihnachtstag der.

Christmas Eve noun Heiligabend der; **on Christmas Eve** Heiligabend.

Christmas present noun Weihnachtsgeschenk das (PL die Weihnachtsgeschenke).

Christmas tree noun Weihnachtsbaum der (PL die Weihnachtsbäume).

church noun Kirche die (PL die Kirchen); **to go to church** in die Kirche gehen.

chute noun (in a swimming pool or playground) Rutsche die (PL die Rutschen).

cider noun Apfelwein der (PL die Apfelweine).

cigar noun Zigarre die (PL die Zigarren).

cigarette noun Zigarette die (PL die Zigaretten).

cinema noun Kino das (PL die Kinos); **to go to the cinema** ins Kino gehen.

circle noun Kreis der (PL die Kreise); **to sit in a circle** im Kreis sitzen; **to go round in circles** sich im Kreis drehen.

circuit noun **1** (for athletes) Bahn die (PL die Bahnen); **2** (for cars) Rennbahn die (PL die Rennbahnen).

circumstance noun Umstand der (PL die Umstände); **under these circumstances** unter diesen Umständen.

circus noun Zirkus der (PL die Zirkusse).

citizen noun Bürger der (PL die Bürger), Bürgerin die (PL die Bürgerinnen).

city noun Stadt die (PL die Städte); **the city of Berlin** die Stadt Berlin.

city centre noun Stadtzentrum das (PL die Stadtzentren); **in the city centre** im Stadtzentrum, in der Innenstadt.

civil servant noun Beamte der (PL die Beamten), Beamtin die (PL die Beamtinnen); **she's a civil servant** sie ist Beamtin.

civilization *noun* Zivilisation *die* (PL *die* Zivilisationen).

claim *verb* behaupten; **he claims to know who** ... er behauptet zu wissen, wer ....

claim *noun* **1** (*statement*) Behauptung *die* (PL *die* Behauptungen); **2** (*for compensation*) Anspruch *der* (PL *die* Ansprüche); **to make a claim on insurance** seine Versicherungsansprüche geltend machen.

clap *verb* **1** klatschen; **everyone clapped** alle klatschten; **2 to clap your hands** in die Hände klatschen.

clarinet *noun* Klarinette *die* (PL *die* Klarinetten); **to play the clarinet** Klarinette spielen.

clash *noun* (*between two groups*) Zusammenstoß *der* (PL *die* Zusammenstöße).
clash *verb* **1** (*rival groups*) zusammenstoßen◇ SEP; **2** (*colours*) sich beißen◇; **the curtains clash with the wallpaper** die Vorhänge passen farblich nicht zur Tapete.

class *noun* **1** (*a group of students or pupils*) Klasse *die* (PL *die* Klassen); **she's in my class** sie geht in meine Klasse; **2** (*a lesson*) Stunde *die* (PL *die* Stunden); **history class** die Geschichtsstunde; **in class** im Unterricht; **3** (*category*) Klasse *die* (PL *die* Klassen); **social class** die Gesellschaftsschicht.

classic *adjective* klassisch.

classical *adjective* klassisch; **classical music** *die* klassische Musik.

classroom *noun* Klassenzimmer *das* (PL *die* Klassenzimmer).

clay *noun* Ton *der*.

clean *adjective* sauber; **a clean shirt** ein sauberes Hemd; **my hands are clean** ich habe saubere Hände.
clean *verb* **1** putzen; **I cleaned the windows** ich habe die Fenster geputzt; **2 to clean your teeth** sich (DAT) die Zähne putzen; **I'm going to clean my teeth** ich putze mir jetzt die Zähne.

cleaner *noun* **1** (*cleaning lady*) Putzfrau *die* (PL *die* Putzfrauen); **2** (*in a public place*) Reinigungskraft *die* (PL *die* Reinigungskräfte); **3 dry cleaner's** die (chemische) Reinigung.

cleaning *noun* **to do the cleaning** putzen.

cleanser *noun* **1** (*for the house*) Reinigungsmittel *das* (PL *die* Reinigungsmittel); **2** (*for your face*) Reinigungsmilch *die*.

clear *adjective* **1** (*that you can see through*) klar; **clear water** klares Wasser; **2** (*cloudless*) klar; **3** (*easy to understand*) **clear instructions** klare Anweisungen; **is that clear?** ist das klar? (*informal*); **to make something clear** etwas klar machen.
clear *verb* **1** räumen; **have you cleared your stuff out of your room?** hast du deine Sachen aus deinem Zimmer geräumt?; **2 can I clear the table?** kann ich den Tisch abräumen SEP?; **3 to clear your throat** sich räuspern.

- **to clear up 1** (*tidy up*) aufräumen SEP; **2** (*the weather*) sich aufklären SEP; **the weather's clearing up a bit** das Wetter klärt sich ein bisschen auf.

clearly *adverb* **1** (*to think, speak, or hear*) deutlich; **2** (*obviously*) eindeutig; **she was clearly better** sie war eindeutig besser.

clementine *noun* Klementine *die* (PL *die* Klementinen).

clever *adjective* **1** klug; **their children are all very clever** ihre Kinder sind alle sehr klug; **2** (*ingenious*) clever; **a clever idea** eine clevere Idee.

click *noun* **1** (*noise*) Klicken *das*; **2** (*with mouse*) Klick *der* (PL *die* Klicks); **a double click** ein Doppelklick.

click *verb* **to click on something** etwas anklicken SEP; **click on the icon twice** doppelklicken Sie das Icon!

client *noun* Klient *der* (PL *die* Klienten), Klientin *die* (PL *die* Klientinnen).

cliff *noun* Klippe *die* (PL *die* Klippen).

climate *noun* Klima *das* (PL *die* Klimata).

climb *verb* **1** (*the stairs, a hill*) hinaufgehen◇ SEP (PERF *sein*); **to climb a mountain** einen Berg besteigen◇ (PERF *sein*); **2** (*a wall, tree, or rock*) klettern (PERF *sein*), auf (+ ACC); **to climb a tree** auf einen Baum klettern.

climber *noun* Bergsteiger *der* (PL *die* Bergsteiger), Bergsteigerin *die* (PL *die* Bergsteigerinnen).

climbing *noun* Bergsteigen *das*; **they go climbing in Italy** sie gehen in Italien bergsteigen.

clinic *noun* Klinik *die* (PL *die* Kliniken).

clip *noun* **1** (*from a film*) Ausschnitt *der* (PL *die* Ausschnitte); **2** (*for your hair*) Klammer *die* (PL *die* Klammern).

cloakroom *noun* (*for coats*) Garderobe *die* (PL *die* Garderoben).

clock *noun* **1** Uhr *die* (PL *die* Uhren); **to put the clocks forward an hour** die Uhr eine Stunde vorstellen; **to put the clocks back** die Uhr zurückstellen; **2 an alarm clock** ein Wecker.

close¹ *adjective, adverb* **1** (*result*) knapp; **2** (*friend, connection*) eng; **3** (*relation or acquaintance*) nahe; **4** (*near*) in der Nähe; **the station's very close** der Bahnhof ist ganz in der Nähe; **she lives close by** sie wohnt in der Nähe; **5 close to** nahe, nah (*informal*) (+ DAT); **close to the cinema** nahe am Kino; **not very close** nicht sehr nah.

close² *noun* Ende *das*; **at the close** am Ende.
close *verb* zumachen SEP, schließen◇; **close your eyes!** mach die Augen zu!; **she closed the door** sie machte die Tür zu; **the post office closes at six** die Post macht um sechs zu, die Post schließt um sechs.

closed *adjective* geschlossen; **'closed on Mondays'** 'Montags geschlossen'.

closely *adverb* **1** (*in distance*) eng; **2** (*carefully*) genau; **to look at something closely** sich etwas genau ansehen.

closing date *noun* **the closing date for entries** (*for a competition*) der Einsendeschluss, (*for a sporting event*) der Meldeschluss.

closing time *noun* **1** Ladenschluss der; **2** (*of a pub*) Polizeistunde die.

cloth *noun* **1** (*for drying up and polishing*) Tuch das (PL die Tücher); **2** (*for the floor*) Lappen der (PL die Lappen); **3** (*fabric*) Stoff der (PL die Stoffe).

clothes *plural noun* **1** Kleider (*plural*); **2 to put your clothes on** sich anziehen◇ SEP; **to take your clothes off** sich ausziehen◇ SEP; **to change your clothes** sich umziehen◇ SEP.

clothes peg *noun* Wäscheklammer die (PL die Wäscheklammern).

clothing *noun* Kleidung die.

cloud *noun* Wolke die (PL die Wolken).

cloudy *adjective* bewölkt.

clown *noun* Clown der (PL die Clowns).

club *noun* **1** (*association, for tennis-players, golfers*) Klub der (PL die Klubs), (*for footballers*) Verein der (PL die Vereine); **a football club** ein Fußballverein; **2** (*in cards*) Kreuz das (PL die Kreuze); **the four of clubs** die Kreuz-Vier; **3** (*golfing iron*) Schläger der (PL die Schläger).

clue *noun* **1** Anhaltspunkt der (PL die Anhaltspunkte); **they have a few clues** sie haben ein paar Anhaltspunkte; **2** (*in a crossword*) Frage die (PL die Fragen); ★**I haven't a clue** ich habe keine Ahnung.

clumsy *adjective* ungeschickt.

clutch *noun* (*in a car*) Kupplung die (PL die Kupplungen).
clutch *verb* **to clutch something** etwas festhalten◇ SEP.

coach *noun* **1** (*bus*) Bus der (PL die Busse); **on the coach** im Bus; **to travel by coach** mit dem Bus fahren; **2** (*sports trainer*) Trainer der (PL die Trainer), Trainerin die (PL die Trainerinnen); **3** (*railway carriage*) Wagen der (PL die Wagen).

coach station *noun* Busbahnhof der (PL die Busbahnhöfe).

coach trip *noun* Busausflug der (PL die Busausflüge); **to go on a coach trip** einen Busausflug machen.

coal *noun* Kohle die (PL die Kohlen).

coarse *adjective* grob.

coast *noun* Küste die (PL die Küsten); **on the east coast** an der Ostküste.

coat *noun* **1** Mantel der (PL die Mäntel); **2 coat of paint** der Anstrich.

coat hanger *noun* Kleiderbügel der (PL die Kleiderbügel).

cobweb *noun* Spinnennetz das (PL die Spinnennetze).

cocaine *noun* Kokain das.

a
b
c
d
e
f
g
h
i
j
k
l
m
n
o
p
q
r
s
t
u
v
w
x
y
z

cock *noun* Hahn *der* (PL *die* Hähne).

cocoa *noun* Kakao *der*.

coconut *noun* Kokosnuss *die* (PL *die* Kokosnüsse).

cod *noun* Kabeljau *der* (PL *die* Kabeljaue).

code *noun* 1 (*in law*) Gesetzbuch *das*; **the highway code** die Straßenverkehrsordnung; 2 **the dialling code for Hull** die Vorwahl für Hull.

coffee *noun* Kaffee *der* (PL *die* Kaffees); **a cup of coffee** eine Tasse Kaffee; **a black coffee, please** einen Kaffee ohne Milch bitte; **a white coffee, please** einen Kaffee mit Milch bitte.

coffee break *noun* Kaffeepause *die* (PL *die* Kaffeepausen).

coffee cup *noun* Kaffeetasse *die* (PL *die* Kaffeetassen).

coffee machine *noun* Kaffeemaschine *die* (PL *die* Kaffeemaschinen).

coffin *noun* Sarg *der* (PL *die* Särge).

coin *noun* 1 Münze *die* (PL *die* Münzen); **she collects old coins** sie sammelt alte Münzen; 2 **a pound coin** ein Einpfundstück.

coincidence *noun* Zufall *der* (PL *die* Zufälle).

Coke *noun* Cola *die*; **two Cokes please** zwei Cola bitte.

cold *noun* 1 (*cold weather*) Kälte *die*; **to be out in the cold** draußen in der Kälte sein; 2 (*illness*) Schnupfen *der* (PL *die* Schnupfen), Erkältung *die* (PL *die* Erkältungen); **to have a cold** Schnupfen haben; **Carol's got a cold** Carol hat Schnupfen; **a bad cold** eine schlimme Erkältung.

cold *adjective* 1 kalt; **your hands are cold** du hast kalte Hände; **cold milk** kalte Milch; 2 (*weather, temperature*) **it's cold today** heute ist es kalt; 3 (*feeling*) **I'm cold** mir ist kalt.

collapse *verb* 1 (*a roof or wall*) einstürzen SEP (PERF *sein*); 2 (*a person*) zusammenbrechen◇ SEP (PERF *sein*); **he collapsed in his office** er brach in seinem Büro zusammen.

collar *noun* 1 (*on a garment*) Kragen *der* (PL *die* Kragen); 2 (*for an animal*) Halsband *das* (PL *die* Halsbänder).

colleague *noun* Kollege *der* (PL *die* Kollegen), Kollegin *die* (PL *die* Kolleginnen).

collect *verb* 1 (*as a hobby*) sammeln; **do you collect stamps?** sammelst du Briefmarken?; 2 (*fetch*) abholen SEP; **she collects the children from school** sie holt die Kinder von der Schule ab; 3 **to collect up the exercise books** die Hefte einsammeln SEP.

collection *noun* (*of stamps, CDs, money, etc.*) Sammlung *die* (PL *die* Sammlungen).

collector *noun* Sammler *der* (PL *die* Sammler), Sammlerin *die* (PL *die* Sammlerinnen).

college *noun* 1 (*for higher education*) Hochschule *die* (PL *die* Hochschulen); **to go to college**

studieren; **2** (*a school*) College *das* (PL *die* Colleges).

Cologne *noun* Köln *das*.

colour *noun* Farbe *die* (PL *die* Farben); **what colour is it?** welche Farbe hat es?; **do you have it in a different colour?** haben Sie es in einer anderen Farbe?
colour *verb* **1** (*with paints or crayons*) anmalen SEP; **to colour something red** etwas rot anmalen; **2** (*with dye*) färben.

colour blind *adjective* farbenblind.

colour film *noun* Farbfilm *der* (PL *die* Farbfilme).

colourful *adjective* bunt.

column *noun* **1** (*of a building*) Säule *die* (PL *die* Säulen); **2** (*on a page*) Spalte *die* (PL *die* Spalten).

comb *noun* Kamm *der* (PL *die* Kämme).
comb *verb* kämmen; **to comb your hair** sich (DAT) die Haare kämmen; **I'll just comb my hair** ich kämme mir nur die Haare.

come *verb* **1** kommen◇ (PERF *sein*); **come quick!** komm schnell!; **come here!** komm mal her!; **Nick came by car** Nick kam mit dem Auto; **can you come over for a coffee?** kannst du auf eine Tasse Kaffe kommen?; **did Jess come to school yesterday?** war Jess gestern in der Schule?; **2** (*arrive*) **coming!** ich komme schon!; **the bus is coming** der Bus kommt gerade; **come along!** komm schon!
• **to come back** zurückkommen◇ SEP (PERF *sein*); **he's coming back to**

collect us er kommt zurück, um uns abzuholen.
• **to come down** herunterkommen◇ SEP (PERF *sein*).
• **to come for** (*collect*) abholen SEP; **my father's coming for me** mein Vater holt mich ab.
• **to come in** hereinkommen ◇ SEP (PERF *sein*); **come in!** herein!; **she came into the kitchen** sie kam in die Küche.
• **to come off** (*a button*) abgehen ◇ SEP (PERF *sein*).
• **to come out** herauskommen ◇ SEP (PERF *sein*); **they came out when I called** als ich rief, kamen sie heraus; **the new CD's coming out soon** die neue CD kommt bald heraus.
• **to come up** heraufkommen ◇ SEP (PERF *sein*); **can you come up a moment?** kannst du eine Sekunde heraufkommen?
• **to come up to somebody** auf jemanden zukommen ◇ SEP (PERF *sein*).

comedian *noun* Komiker *der* (PL *die* Komiker), Komikerin *die* (PL *die* Komikerinnen).

comedy *noun* Komödie *die*.

comfortable *adjective* **1** bequem; **this chair's really comfortable** dieser Sessel ist wirklich bequem; **2 to feel comfortable** (*a person*) sich wohl fühlen.

comfortably *adverb* bequem.

comic *noun* (*magazine*) Comicheft *das* (PL *die* Comichefte).

comic strip *noun* Comic *der* (PL *die* Comics).

a
b
c
d
e
f
g
h
i
j
k
l
m
n
o
p
q
r
s
t
u
v
w
x
y
z

a
b
c
d
e
f
g
h
i
j
k
l
m
n
o
p
q
r
s
t
u
v
w
x
y
z

comma *noun* Komma *das* (PL *die* Kommas).

command *noun* Befehl *der* (PL *die* Befehle).

comment *noun* (*remark*) Bemerkung *die* (PL *die* Bemerkungen); **he made some rude comments about my friends** er hat ein paar unhöfliche Bemerkungen über meine Freunde gemacht.

commentary *noun* Reportage *die* (PL *die* Reportagen); **the commentary on the soccer match** die Reportage über das Fußballspiel.

commentator *noun* Reporter *der* (PL *die* Reporter), Reporterin *die* (PL *die* Reporterinnen); **sports commentator** *der* Sportreporter.

commercial *noun* Werbespot *der* (PL *die* Werbespots). **commercial** *adjective* kommerziell.

commit *verb* **1** begehen ◈ (*a crime*); **2 to commit yourself to** sich festlegen SEP: auf (+ ACC).

committee *noun* Ausschuss *der* (PL *die* Ausschüsse).

common *adjective* **1** häufig; **it's a common problem** das Problem kommt häufig vor; **2 in common** gemeinsam; **they have nothing in common** sie haben nichts gemeinsam.

common sense *noun* gesunde Menschenverstand *der*.

communicate *verb* kommunizieren.

communication *noun* Verständigung *die*.

communion *noun* (*in a Catholic church*) Kommunion *die*, (*in a Protestant church*) Abendmahl *das*.

communism *noun* Kommunismus *der*.

community *noun* Gemeinschaft *die* (PL *die* Gemeinschaften); **the European Community** die Europäische Gemeinschaft.

commute *verb* **to commute between Oxford and London** zwischen Oxford und London pendeln (PERF *sein*).

commuter *noun* Pendler *der* (PL *die* Pendler), Pendlerin *die* (PL *die* Pendlerinnen).

compact disc *noun* Compactdisc *die* (PL *die* Compactdiscs).

compact disc player *noun* Compactdisc-Player *der* (PL *die* Compactdisc-Player).

company *noun* **1** (*business*) Gesellschaft *die* (PL *die* Gesellschaften); **an airline company** eine Fluggesellschaft; **she's set up a company** sie hat eine Firma gegründet; **2** (*group*) Truppe *die* (PL *die* Truppen); **a theatre company** eine Theatertruppe; **3 to keep somebody company** jemandem Gesellschaft leisten; **the dog keeps me company** der Hund leistet mir Gesellschaft.

compare *verb* vergleichen ◈; **if you compare the German phrase with**

the English wenn man den deutschen mit dem englischen Ausdruck vergleicht; **our house is small compared with yours** verglichen mit eurem ist unser Haus klein.

compartment *noun* Abteil *das* (PL *die* Abteile).

compass *noun* Kompass *der* (PL *die* Kompasse).

compatible *adjective* **1** zueinander passend; **2** (*in computing*) kompatibel.

compete *verb* **1 to compete in something** (*race, event*) an etwas (DAT) teilnehmen✧ SEP; **2 to compete with each other** miteinander konkurrieren; **3 to compete for something** um etwas (ACC) kämpfen; **thirty people are competing for one job** dreißig Leute kämpfen um eine Stelle.

competent *adjective* fähig.

competition *noun* **1** (*a contest*) Wettbewerb *der* (PL *die* Wettbewerbe); **2** (*in a magazine*) Preisausschreiben *das* (PL *die* Preisausschreiben).

competitor *noun* Konkurrent *der* (PL *die* Konkurrenten), Konkurrentin *die* (PL *die* Konkurrentinnen).

complain *verb* sich beschweren; **we complained about the meals** wir haben uns über das Essen beschwert.

complaint *noun* Beschwerde *die* (PL *die* Beschwerden); **to make a complaint** sich beschweren; **she made a complaint to the manager about the poor service** sie beschwerte sich bei dem Geschäftsführer über den schlechten Service.

complete *adjective* **1** (*whole*) vollständig; **the complete collection** die vollständige Sammlung; **2** (*absolute*) völlig; **a complete idiot** ein völliger Idiot (*informal*).
complete *verb* (*to finish*) beenden.

completely *adverb* völlig.

complexion *noun* Teint *der* (PL *die* Teints).

complicated *adjective* kompliziert.

compliment *noun* Kompliment *das* (PL *die* Komplimente); **to pay somebody a compliment** jemandem ein Kompliment machen.

composer *noun* Komponist *der* (PL *die* Komponisten), Komponistin *die* (PL *die* Komponistinnen).

comprehension *noun* Verständnis *das*; **a comprehension test** ein Test zum Textverständnis.

comprehensive school *noun* Gesamtschule *die* (PL *die* Gesamtschulen).

compulsory *adjective* **1** obligatorisch; **2** (*at school*) **compulsory subject** *das* Pflichtfach.

computer *noun* Computer *der* (PL *die* Computer); **to work on a computer** am Computer arbeiten; **to have something on computer**

a
b
c
d
e
f
g
h
i
j
k
l
m
n
o
p
q
r
s
t
u
v
w
x
y
z

etwas im Computer gespeichert haben.

computer engineer *noun* Computertechniker *der* (PL *die* Computertechniker), Computertechnikerin *die* (PL *die* Computertechnikerinnen).

computer game *noun* Computerspiel *das* (PL *die* Computerspiele).

computer program *noun* Computerprogramm *das* (PL *die* Computerprogramme).

computer programmer *noun* Programmierer *der* (PL *die* Programmierer), Programmiererin *die* (PL *die* Programmiererinnen).

computer science *noun* Informatik *die*.

computing *noun* Informatik *die*.

concentrate *verb* sich konzentrieren; **I can't concentrate** ich kann mich nicht konzentrieren; **I was concentrating on the film** ich konzentrierte mich auf den Film.

concentration *noun* Konzentration *die*.

concern *verb* (*to affect*) betreffen◇; **this doesn't concern you** das betrifft Sie nicht; **as far as I'm concerned** was mich betrifft.

concert *noun* **1** Konzert *das* (PL *die* Konzerte); **to go to a concert** ins Konzert gehen; **2 concert ticket** *die* Konzertkarte.

conclusion *noun* Schluss *der* (PL *die* Schlüsse).

concrete *noun* Beton *der*; **the concrete floor** der Betonboden.

condemn *verb* verurteilen; **to condemn somebody to death** jemanden zum Tode verurteilen.

condition *noun* **1** Zustand *der* (PL *die* Zustände); **in good condition** in gutem Zustand; **weather conditions** *die* Wetterlage; **2** (*something you insist on*) Bedingung *die* (PL *die* Bedingungen); **on condition that you let me pay** unter der Bedingung, dass du mich zahlen lässt.

conditional *noun* Konditional *das*.

conditioner *noun* (*for your hair*) Spülung *die* (PL *die* Spülungen).

condom *noun* Kondom *das* (PL *die* Kondome).

conduct *noun* Benehmen *das*. **conduct** *verb* dirigieren (*an orchestra or a piece of music*).

conductor *noun* (*of an orchestra*) Dirigent *der* (PL *die* Dirigenten), Dirigentin *die* (PL *die* Dirigentinnen).

cone *noun* **1** (*for ice cream*) Eistüte *die* (PL *die* Eistüten); **2** (*for traffic*) Verkehrshütchen *das* (PL *die* Verkehrshütchen).

conference *noun* Konferenz *die* (PL *die* Konferenzen).

confess *verb* gestehen◇.

confession *noun* Geständnis *das* (PL *die* Geständnisse).

confidence *noun* **1** (*self-confidence*) Selbstvertrauen *das*; **to be lacking in confidence** kein Selbstvertrauen haben; **2** (*faith in somebody else*) Vertrauen *das*; **to**

have confidence in somebody jemandem vertrauen.

confident *adjective* **1** (*sure of yourself*) selbstbewusst; **2** (*sure that something will happen*) zuversichtlich.

confirm *verb* bestätigen; **he confirmed the date** er bestätigte das Datum.

confuse *verb* **1** verwirren (*a person*); **2 to confuse someone with somebody else** jemanden (mit jemandem anderem) verwechseln; **I confuse him with his brother** ich verwechsle ihn immer mit seinem Bruder.

confused *adjective* **1** wirr; **a confused story** eine wirre Geschichte; **2** durcheinander; **I'm confused about the holiday plans** ich bin mit den Ferienplänen durcheinander; **now I'm completely confused** jetzt bin ich völlig durcheinander.

confusing *adjective* verwirrend; **the instructions are confusing** die Anweisungen sind verwirrend.

confusion *noun* Verwirrung *die*.

congratulate *verb* gratulieren; **I congratulated Tim on passing his exam** ich gratulierte Tim zur bestandenen Prüfung.

congratulations *plural noun* Glückwünsche (*plural*); **congratulations on the baby!** herzlichen Glückwunsch zum Baby!

connect *verb* (*to plug in to the mains*) anschließen◇ SEP (*a dishwasher or TV, for example*).

connection *noun* **1** (*between two ideas or events*) Zusammenhang *der* (PL *die* Zusammenhänge); **there's no connection between his letter and my decision** es besteht kein Zusammenhang zwischen seinem Brief und meiner Entscheidung; **2** (*between trains, planes, on phone, and electrical*) Anschluss *der* (PL *die* Anschlüsse); **Sally missed her connection** Sally hat ihren Anschluss verpasst.

conscience *noun* Gewissen *das*; **to have a guilty conscience** ein schlechtes Gewissen haben.

conscious *adjective* bei Bewusstsein sein◇; **she is not fully conscious yet** sie ist noch nicht wieder bei vollem Bewusstsein; **I was conscious that he was a policeman** es war mir bewusst, dass er Polizist war.

conservation *noun* (*of nature*) Schutz *der*; **environmental conservation** *der* Umweltschutz.

conservative *noun* Konservative *der/die* (PL *die* Konservativen). **conservative** *adjective* konservativ.

conservatory *noun* Wintergarten *der* (PL *die* Wintergärten).

consider *verb* **1** sich (DAT) überlegen (*a suggestion or idea*) **all things considered** alles in allem; **2** (*think about (doing)*) erwägen◇; **we are considering buying a flat** wir erwägen, eine Wohnung zu kaufen.

a
b
c
d
e
f
g
h
i
j
k
l
m
n
o
p
q
r
s
t
u
v
w
x
y
z

considerate *adjective*
rücksichtsvoll.

considering *preposition* wenn
man bedenkt; **considering her age**
wenn man ihr Alter bedenkt;
considering he did it all himself
wenn man bedenkt, dass er es ganz
allein gemacht hat.

consist *verb* **to consist of**
bestehen✧ aus (+ DAT).

consonant *noun* Konsonant *der*
(PL *die* Konsonanten).

constant *adjective* ständig.

constipated *adjective* verstopft.

construct *verb* bauen.

construction *noun* **1** (*building*)
Gebäude *das* (PL *die* Gebäude); **a
construction site** eine Baustelle;
2 (*in grammar*) Konstruktion *die* (PL
die Konstruktionen).

consul *noun* Konsul *der* (PL *die*
Konsuln).

consulate *noun* Konsulat *das* (PL
die Konsulate).

consult *verb* konsultieren.

consumer *noun* Verbraucher *der*
(PL *die* Verbraucher), Verbraucherin
die (PL *die* Verbraucherinnen).

contact *noun* Kontakt *der* (PL *die*
Kontakte); **to be in contact with
somebody** mit jemandem in
Kontakt sein; **we've lost contact**
wir haben den Kontakt verloren;
**Rob has contacts in the music
business** Rob hat Kontakte zur
Musikindustrie.
contact *verb* sich in Verbindung
setzen mit (+ DAT); **I'll contact you**

tomorrow ich setze mich morgen
mit dir in Verbindung.

contact lens *noun* Kontaktlinse
die (PL *die* Kontaktlinsen).

contain *verb* enthalten✧.

container *noun* Behälter *der* (PL *die*
Behälter).

contaminate *verb* verseuchen.

contemporary *adjective*
1 (*around today*) zeitgenössisch;
2 (*modern*) modern.

contents *plural noun* Inhalt *der*;
the contents of my suitcase der
Inhalt meines Koffers.

contest *noun* Wettbewerb *der* (PL
die Wettbewerbe).

contestant *noun* Teilnehmer *der*
(PL *die* Teilnehmer), Teilnehmerin
die (PL *die* Teilnehmerinnen).

continent *noun* Kontinent *der* (PL
die Kontinente).

continue *verb* **1** fortsetzen SEP; **we
continued (with) our journey** wir
setzten unsere Reise fort; **2 to
continue to do something** etwas
weiter tun; **Jill continued talking**
Jill redete weiter; **3 'to be
continued'** 'Fortsetzung folgt'.

continuous *adjective*
ununterbrochen.

contraception *noun* Verhütung
die.

contraceptive *noun*
Verhütungsmittel *das* (PL *die*
Verhütungsmittel).

contract *noun* Vertrag *der* (PL *die*
Verträge).

contradict *verb* widersprechen✧ (+ DAT).

contradiction *noun* Widerspruch *der* (PL *die* Widersprüche).

contrary *noun* Gegenteil *das*; **on the contrary** im Gegenteil.

contrast *noun* Kontrast *der* (PL *die* Kontraste).

contribute *verb* beisteuern SEP (*money*).

contribution *noun* (*to charity or an appeal*) Spende *die* (PL *die* Spenden).

control *noun* (*of a crowd or animals*) Kontrolle *die*; **the police are in control of the situation** die Polizei hat die Situation unter Kontrolle; **keep your dogs under control** halten Sie Ihre Hunde unter Kontrolle; **everything's under control** alles ist unter Kontrolle; **to get out of control** außer Kontrolle geraten.
control *verb* **to control yourself** sich beherrschen.

convenient *adjective* **1** praktisch; **frozen food is very convenient** Tiefkühlkost ist sehr praktisch; **2 to be convenient for somebody** jemandem passen; **whenever's convenient for you** wann immer es dir passt.

conventional *adjective* konventionell.

conversation *noun* Gespräch *das* (PL *die* Gespräche).

convert *verb* **1** umwandeln SEP; **2** (*adapt a building*) umbauen SEP;

we're going to convert the garage into a workshop wir wollen die Garage zu einer Werkstatt umbauen.

convince *verb* überzeugen; **I'm convinced he's wrong** ich bin davon überzeugt, dass er sich irrt.

convincing *adjective* überzeugend.

cook *noun* Koch *der* (PL *die* Köche), Köchin *die* (PL *die* Köchinnen).
cook *verb* **1** kochen; **who's cooking tonight?** wer kocht heute Abend?; **I like cooking** ich koche gern; **to cook vegetables and pasta** Gemüse und Nudeln kochen; **cook the cabbage for five minutes** lass den Kohl fünf Minuten kochen; **2** (*prepare food or a meal*) machen; **Fran's busy cooking supper** Fran macht gerade Abendessen; **how do you cook duck?** wie macht man Ente?; **3** (*boil*) kochen, (*fry or roast*) braten✧; **the potatoes are cooking** die Kartoffeln kochen; **the sausages are cooking** die Würstchen braten.

cooker *noun* Herd *der* (PL *die* Herde); **electric cooker** *der* Elektroherd; **gas cooker** *der* Gasherd.

cookery *noun* Kochen *das*.

cookery book *noun* Kochbuch *das* (PL *die* Kochbücher).

cooking *noun* **1** (*preparing food*) Kochen *das*; **cooking is fun** Kochen macht Spaß; **who's doing the cooking?** wer kocht?; **2** (*food*) Küche *die*; **Italian cooking** die italienische Küche.

a
b
c
d
e
f
g
h
i
j
k
l
m
n
o
p
q
r
s
t
u
v
w
x
y
z

cool *noun* **1** (*coldness*) Kühle *die*;
2 (*calm*) **to lose one's cool**
durchdrehen SEP (PERF *sein*)
(*informal*); **don't lose your cool!**
dreh nicht durch!; **he kept his cool**
er blieb gelassen.
cool *adjective* **1** (*cold*) kühl; **it's
cool inside** drinnen ist es kühl;
2 (*laid back*) gelassen; **to stay cool**
gelassen bleiben (PERF *sein*).
cool *verb* abkühlen SEP (PERF *sein*).

cop *noun* Polizist *der* (PL *die*
Polizisten).

cope *verb* zurechtkommen◇ SEP
(PERF *sein*); **she copes well** sie
kommt gut zurecht; **to cope with
the children** mit den Kindern
zurechtkommen; **she's had a lot to
cope with** sie musste mit viel fertig
werden.

copy *noun* **1** (*photocopy*) Kopie *die*
(PL *die* Kopien); **2** (*of a book*)
Exemplar *das* (PL *die* Exemplare).
copy *verb* **1** (*imitate*) kopieren;
2 (*make a copy of*) abschreiben◇ SEP;
I copied (down) the address ich
habe die Adresse abgeschrieben; (*in
an exam*) **to copy from somebody**
bei jemandem abschreiben.

cord *noun* (*for a blind, for example*)
Schnur *die* (PL *die* Schnüre).

cordless telephone *noun*
schnurlose Telefon *das* (PL *die*
schnurlosen Telefone).

core *noun* (*of an apple or a pear*)
Kerngehäuse *das* (PL *die*
Kerngehäuse).

cork *noun* **1** (*in a bottle*) Korken *der*
(PL *die* Korken); **2** (*material*) Kork *der*.

corkscrew *noun* Korkenzieher
der (PL *die* Korkenzieher).

corn *noun* **1** (*wheat*) Korn *das*;
2 (*sweetcorn*) Mais *der*.

corner *noun* **1** Ecke *die* (PL *die*
Ecken); **at the corner of the street**
an der Straßenecke; **it's just round
the corner** es ist gleich um die Ecke;
2 (*of mouth*) Mundwinkel *der*; **3** (*of eye*)
Augenwinkel *der* (PL *die*
Augenwinkel); **out of the corner of
your eye** aus den Augenwinkeln
heraus; **4** (*bend in the road*) Kurve
die (PL *die* Kurven); **5** (*in football*)
Eckball *der* (PL *die* Eckbälle).

cornflakes *plural noun* die Cornflakes (*plural*) .

corpse *noun* Leiche *die* (PL *die*
Leichen).

correct *adjective* **1** richtig; **the
correct answer** die richtige
Antwort; **2 yes, that's correct** ja,
das stimmt.
correct *verb* **1** verbessern;
2 (*teacher*) korrigieren; **the teacher
has already corrected our
homework** der Lehrer hat unsere
Hausaufgaben schon korrigiert.

correction *noun* Verbesserung *die*
(PL *die* Verbesserungen).

correctly *adverb* richtig; **have
you filled in the form correctly?**
hast du das Formular richtig
ausgefüllt?

corridor *noun* Korridor *der* (PL *die*
Korridore).

cosmetics *plural noun* Kosmetik
die.

cost *noun* **1** Kosten (*plural*); **the cost of living** die Lebenshaltungskosten (*plural*); **2 the cost of a new computer** der Preis für einen neuen Computer.
cost *verb* kosten; **how much does it cost?** was kostet es?; **the tickets cost £10** die Karten kosten zehn Pfund; **it costs too much** das ist zu teuer.

costume *noun* Kostüm *das* (PL *die* Kostüme).

cosy *adjective* (*a room*) gemütlich.

cot *noun* Kinderbett *das* (PL *die* Kinderbetten).

cottage *noun* Häuschen *das* (PL *die* Häuschen).

cotton *noun* **1** (*fabric*) Baumwolle *die*; **cotton shirt** *das* Baumwollhemd; **2** (*thread*) Nähgarn *das* (PL *die* Nähgarne).

cotton wool *noun* Watte *die*.

couch *noun* Couch *die* (PL *die* Couchs).

cough *noun* Husten *der*; **a nasty cough** ein schlimmer Husten; **to have a cough** Husten haben.
cough *verb* husten.

could *verb* **1** (*the past tense of können is used to translate 'was able to'*) **I couldn't open it** ich konnte es nicht aufmachen; **they couldn't come** sie konnten nicht kommen; **she did all she could** sie hat getan, was sie konnte; **he couldn't drive** er konnte nicht Auto fahren; **she couldn't see anything** sie konnte überhaupt nichts sehen; **2** (*the past tense of dürfen is used to translate*

'was allowed to') **they couldn't smoke there** sie durften dort nicht rauchen; **3** (*might*) (*the subjunctive of können is used to translate a wish or suggestion*) **could I speak to David?** könnte ich mit David sprechen?; **you could try phoning** du könntest versuchen anzurufen; **if he could pay** wenn er zahlen könnte; **he could be right** er könnte recht haben.

council *noun* Stadtrat *der* (PL *die* Stadträte).

count *verb* **1** (*reckon up*) zählen; **I counted my money** ich habe mein Geld gezählt; **2** (*include*) mitzählen SEP; **thirty-five not counting the children** fünfunddreißig, die Kinder nicht mitgezählt.

counter *noun* **1** (*in a shop*) Ladentisch *der* (PL *die* Ladentische); **2** (*in a post office or bank*) Schalter *der* (PL *die* Schalter); **3** (*in a bar or café*) Theke *die* (PL *die* Theken); **4** (*for board games*) Spielmarke *die* (PL *die* Spielmarken).

country *noun* **1** (*Germany, etc.*) Land *das* (PL *die* Länder); **a foreign country** ein fremdes Land; **from another country** aus einem anderen Land; **2** (*not town*) Land *das*; **in the country** auf dem Land; **country road** *die* Landstraße.

country dancing *noun* Volkstanz *der*.

countryside *noun* **1** (*not town*) Land *das*; **2** (*scenery*) Landschaft *die*.

county *noun* Grafschaft *die* (PL *die* Grafschaften).

couple *noun* **1** (*a pair*) Paar *das* (PL *die* Paare); **2 a couple of** ein paar; **a couple of times** ein paar Mal; **I've got a couple of things to do** ich habe ein paar Sachen zu tun.

courage *noun* Mut *der*.

courgette *noun* Zucchini *die* (PL *die* Zucchini).

courier *noun* **1** (*for tourist group*) Reiseleiter *der* (PL *die* Reiseleiter), Reiseleiterin *die* (PL *die* Reiseleiterinnen); **2** (*delivery person*) Kurier *der* (PL *die* Kuriere); **it will be delivered by courier** es wird mit Kurierdienst gebracht.

course *noun* **1** (*lessons*) Kurs *der* (PL *die* Kurse); **computer course** der Computerkurs; **to go on a course** einen Kurs machen; **2** (*part of a meal*) Gang *der* (PL *die* Gänge); **the main course** der Hauptgang; **3 golf course** der Golfplatz; **4 of course** natürlich; **yes, of course!** ja, natürlich!; **he's forgotten, of course** er hat es natürlich vergessen.

court *noun* **1** (*for playing sports*) Platz *der* (PL *die* Plätze); **2** (*lawcourt*) Gericht *das*; **to go to court** vor Gericht gehen.

cousin *noun* Cousin *der* (PL *die* Cousins), Kusine *die* (PL *die* Kusinen); **my cousin Sonia** meine Kusine Sonia.

cover *noun* **1** (*of a book*) Einband *der* (PL *die* Einbände); **2** (*for a duvet or cushion*) Bezug *der* (PL *die* Bezüge).
cover *verb* **1** (*to cover up*) zudecken SEP; **he covered her with a blanket** er hat sie mit einer Decke zugedeckt;

2 he was covered in spots er war mit Pickeln übersät; **the room was covered in dust** das Zimmer war völlig verstaubt; **3** (*with leaves, snow, or for protection*) bedecken; **the ground was covered with snow** der Boden war mit Schnee bedeckt; **4** (*with fabric*) beziehen◇.

cow *noun* Kuh *die* (PL *die* Kühe); **mad cow disease** der Rinderwahn.

coward *noun* Feigling *der* (PL *die* Feiglinge).

cowboy *noun* Cowboy *der* (PL *die* Cowboys).

crab *noun* Krabbe *die* (PL *die* Krabben).

crack *noun* **1** (*in a glass or cup*) Sprung *der* (PL *die* Sprünge); **2** (*in wood or a wall*) Riss *der* (PL *die* Risse); **3** (*a cracking noise*) Knacks *der* (PL *die* Knackse).
crack *verb* **1** (*to make a crack in*) anschlagen◇ SEP; **2** (*to break*) zerbrechen◇; **3** (*to make a noise*) (*a twig*) knacken.

cracker *noun* **1** (*biscuit*) Cracker *der* (PL *die* Cracker); **2** (*Christmas cracker*) Knallbonbon *der* (PL *die* Knallbonbons).

craft *noun* (*at school*) Werken *das*.

cramp *noun* Krampf *der* (PL *die* Krämpfe); **to have cramp in your leg** einen Krampf im Bein haben.

crane *noun* Kran *der* (PL *die* Kräne).

crash *noun* **1** (*an accident*) Unfall *der* (PL *die* Unfälle); **car crash** der Autounfall; **2** (*a noise*) Krachen *das*.
crash *verb* **1** (*a plane*) abstürzen SEP (PERF *sein*); **the plane crashed**

das Flugzeug ist abgestürzt; **3** (*have a collision in a car*) einen Unfall haben; **3 to crash into something** gegen etwas (ACC) krachen (PERF *sein*); **the car crashed into a tree** das Auto krachte gegen einen Baum.

crash course *noun* Schnellkurs der (PL die Schnellkurse).

crash helmet *noun* Sturzhelm der (PL die Sturzhelme).

crate *noun* Kiste die (PL die Kisten).

crawl *noun* (*in swimming*) Kraulen das.
crawl *verb* **1** (*a person*) kriechen✧ (PERF *sein*), (*a baby*) krabbeln (PERF *sein*); **2** (*cars in a jam*) im Schneckentempo fahren✧ (PERF *sein*); **we were crawling along** wir fuhren im Schneckentempo.

crayon *noun* **1** (*wax*) Wachsmalstift der (PL die Wachsmalstifte); **2** (*coloured pencil*) Buntstift der (PL die Buntstifte).

craze *noun* Mode die; **the craze for rollerblades** die Inlinerwelle.

crazy *adjective* verrückt; **to be crazy for something** verrückt auf etwas (ACC) sein.

cream *noun* Sahne die; **strawberries and cream** Erdbeeren mit Sahne.

cream cheese *noun* Frischkäse der.

creased *adjective* zerknittert.

create *verb* (er)schaffen✧.

creative *adjective* kreativ.

creature *noun* Geschöpf das (PL die Geschöpfe).

crèche *noun* Kinderkrippe die (PL die Kinderkrippen).

credit *noun* Kredit der; **to buy something on credit** etwas auf Kredit kaufen.

credit card *noun* Kreditkarte die (PL die Kreditkarten).

cress *noun* Kresse die.

crew *noun* **1** (*on a ship or plane*) Besatzung die; **2 camera crew** das Kamerateam; **3** (*in water sports*) Mannschaft die (PL die Mannschaften).

crew cut *noun* Bürstenschnitt der (PL die Bürstenschnitte).

cricket *noun* **1** (*game*) Kricket das; **to play cricket** Kricket spielen; **2** (*insect*) Grille die (PL die Grillen).

cricket bat *noun* Kricketschläger der (PL die Kricketschläger).

crime *noun* **1** Verbrechen das (PL die Verbrechen); **theft is a crime** Diebstahl ist ein Verbrechen; **2** (*criminality*) Kriminalität die; **to fight crime** die Kriminalität bekämpfen.

criminal *noun* Kriminelle der/die (PL die Kriminellen).
criminal *adjective* kriminell.

crisis *noun* Krise die (PL die Krisen).

crisp *noun* Chip der (PL die Chips); **a packet of potato crisps** eine Tüte Kartoffelchips.
crisp *adjective* **1** (*biscuit*) knusprig; **2** (*apple*) knackig.

critical *adjective* **1** kritisch (*remark, medical condition*); **2** entscheidend (*moment*).

criticism *noun* Kritik *die*.

criticize *verb* kritisieren.

crocodile *noun* Krokodil *das* (PL *die* Krokodile).

crook *noun* (*criminal*) Gauner *der* (PL *die* Gauner), Gaunerin *die* (PL *die* Gaunerinnen).

crop *noun* Ernte *die*.

cross *noun* Kreuz *das* (PL *die* Kreuze).
cross *adjective* ärgerlich; **she was very cross** sie war sehr ärgerlich; **I'm cross with you** ich bin sehr ärgerlich auf dich.
cross *verb* **1** (*to cross over*) überqueren; **to cross the road** die Straße überqueren; **2 to cross your legs** die Beine übereinander schlagen❖; **3** (*to cross each other*) sich kreuzen; **the two roads cross here** die beiden Straßen kreuzen sich hier.

● **to cross out** durchstreichen❖ SEP.

cross-Channel *adjective* **a cross-Channel ferry** eine Fähre über den Ärmelkanal.

cross-country *noun* **1** Crosslauf *der*; **2 cross-country skiing** *der* Langlauf.

crossing *noun* **1** (*from one place to another*) Überquerung *die* (PL *die* Überquerungen); **2** (*a sea journey*) Überfahrt *die* (PL *die* Überfahrten); **Channel crossing** *die* Überfahrt über den Ärmelkanal; **3 pedestrian crossing** *der* Fußgängerübergang; **level crossing** *der* Bahnübergang.

crossroads *noun* Kreuzung *die* (PL *die* Kreuzungen); **at the crossroads** an der Kreuzung.

crossword *noun* Kreuzworträtsel *das* (PL *die* Kreuzworträtsel); **to do the crossword** ein Kreuzworträtsel machen.

crow *noun* Krähe *die* (PL *die* Krähen).
crow *verb* (*a cock*) krähen.

crowd *noun* **1** Menschenmenge *die* (PL *die* Menschenmengen); **in the crowd** in der Menschenmenge; **2** (*spectators*) **a crowd of five thousand** fünftausend Zuschauer (*plural*).
crowd *verb* **to crowd into** or **onto something** sich in etwas (ACC) drängen; **we all crowded into the train** wir drängten uns alle in den Zug.

crowded *adjective* überfüllt.

crown *noun* Krone *die* (PL *die* Kronen).

crude *adjective* **1** (*rough and ready*) primitiv; **2** (*vulgar*) ordinär.

cruel *adjective* grausam.

cruise *noun* Kreuzfahrt *die* (PL *die* Kreuzfahrten); **to go on a cruise** eine Kreuzfahrt machen.

crumb *noun* Krümel *der* (PL *die* Krümel).

crumpled *adjective* zerknittert.

crunchy *adjective* knusprig.

crush *verb* zerquetschen.

crust *noun* Kruste *die* (PL *die* Krusten).

crusty *adjective* knusprig.

a b c d e f g h i j k l m n o p q r s t u v w x y z

crutch *noun* Krücke *die* (PL *die* Krücken); **to be on crutches** an Krücken gehen.

cry *noun* Schrei *der* (PL *die* Schreie). **cry** *verb* **1** (*weep*) weinen; **2** (*call out*) schreien◇.

cub *noun* **1** (*animal*) Junge *das* (PL *die* Jungen); **2** (*boy scout*) Wölfling *der* (PL *die* Wölflinge).

cube *noun* Würfel *der* (PL *die* Würfel); **ice cube** *der* Eiswürfel.

cubic *adjective* (*in measurements*) Kubik-; **three cubic metres** drei Kubikmeter.

cubicle *noun* **1** (*in a changing room*) Kabine *die*; **2** (*in a public lavatory*) Toilette *die* (PL *die* Toiletten).

cuckoo *noun* Kuckuck *der* (PL *die* Kuckucke).

cucumber *noun* Gurke *die* (PL *die* Gurken).

cuddle *noun* **to give somebody a cuddle** jemanden in den Arm nehmen. **cuddle** *verb* schmusen.

cue *noun* (*billiards, pool, snooker*) Queue *das* (PL *die* Queues).

cuff *noun* (*on a shirt*) Manschette *die* (PL *die* Manschetten).

cul-de-sac *noun* Sackgasse *die* (PL *die* Sackgassen).

culture *noun* Kultur *die* (PL *die* Kulturen).

cunning *adjective* listig.

cup *noun* **1** (*for drinking*) Tasse *die* (PL *die* Tassen); **a cup of tea** eine Tasse Tee; **2** (*a trophy*) Pokal *der* (PL *die* Pokale).

cupboard *noun* Schrank *der* (PL *die* Schränke); **in the kitchen cupboard** im Küchenschrank.

cup tie *noun* Pokalspiel *das* (PL *die* Pokalspiele).

cure *noun* Heilmittel *das* (PL *die* Heilmittel). **cure** *verb* heilen.

curiosity *noun* Neugier *die*.

curious *adjective* neugierig.

curl *noun* Locke *die* (PL *die* Locken). **curl** *verb* **1** locken (*hair*); **2** (*of hair*) sich locken.

currant *noun* Korinthe *die* (PL *die* Korinthen).

currency *noun* Währung *die* (PL *die* Währungen); **the Japanese currency** die japanische Währung; **foreign currencies** Devisen (*plural*).

current *noun* **1** (*electricity*) Strom *der*; **2** (*in water or air*) Strömung *die* (PL *die* Strömungen). **current** *adjective* aktuell.

current affairs *noun* Tagespolitik *die*.

curriculum *noun* Lehrplan *der* (PL *die* Lehrpläne).

curry *noun* Curry *das*; **vegetable curry** *das* Gemüse in Currysoße.

cursor *noun* Cursor *der* (PL *die* Cursors).

curtain *noun* Vorhang *der* (PL *die* Vorhänge).

cushion *noun* Kissen *das* (PL *die* Kissen).

a b c d e f g h i j k l m n o p q r s t u v w x y z

a
b
c
d
e
f
g
h
i
j
k
l
m
n
o
p
q
r
s
t
u
v
w
x
y
z

custard *noun* Vanillesoße *die* (PL *die* Vanillesoßen).

custom *noun* Brauch *der* (PL *die* Bräuche).

customer *noun* Kunde *der* (PL *die* Kunden), Kundin *die* (PL *die* Kundinnen); **customer services** Kundendienst *der*.

customs hall *noun* Zollabfertigung *die*.

customs officer *noun* Zollbeamte *der* (PL *die* Zollbeamten), Zollbeamtin *die* (PL *die* Zollbeamtinnen).

customs *plural noun* Zoll *der*; **to go through customs** durch den Zoll gehen.

cut *noun* **1** (*injury*) Schnittwunde *die* (PL *die* Schnittwunden); **2** (*haircut*) Schnitt *der* (PL *die* Schnitte).

cut *verb* **1** schneiden✧; **can you cut the bread please?** kannst du bitte das Brot schneiden?; **you'll cut yourself!** du schneidest dich!; **Kevin's cut his finger** Kevin hat sich in den Finger geschnitten; **2 to cut the grass** den Rasen mähen; **3 to get your hair cut** sich (DAT) die Haare schneiden lassen; **I had my hair cut** ich habe mir die Haare schneiden lassen; **4 to cut prices** die Preise senken.

● **to cut down 1** fällen (*a tree*); **2 to cut down on cigarettes** seinen Zigarettenkonsum einschränken SEP.

● **to cut out something 1** etwas ausschneiden✧ SEP (*a shape, a newspaper article*); **2** etwas streichen✧ (*sugar, fatty food, holidays, for example*).

● **to cut something up** etwas klein schneiden✧ (*food*).

cutlery *noun* Besteck *das* (PL *die* Bestecke).

CV *noun* Lebenslauf *der* (PL *die* Lebensläufe).

cycle *noun* (*bike*) Rad *das* (PL *die* Räder).
cycle *verb* Rad fahren✧ (PERF *sein*); **do you like cycling?** fährst du gerne Rad?; **we cycle to school** wir fahren mit dem Rad zur Schule.

cycle lane *noun* Fahrradweg *die* (PL *die* Fahrradwege).

cycle race *noun* Radrennen *das* (PL *die* Radrennen).

cycling *noun* Radfahren *das*.

cycling shorts *noun* Radlerhose *die* (PL *die* Radlerhosen).

cyclist *noun* Radfahrer *der* (PL *die* Radfahrer), Radfahrerin *die* (PL *die* Radfahrerinnen).

Dd

dad *noun* Vati *der* (PL *die* Vatis).

daffodil *noun* Osterglocke *die* (PL *die* Osterglocken).

daily *adjective* täglich; **his daily visit** sein täglicher Besuch.
daily *adverb* täglich; **she visits him daily** sie besucht ihn täglich.

dairy products *plural noun* Milchprodukte (*plural*).

daisy *noun* Gänseblümchen *das* (PL die Gänseblümchen).

dam *noun* Damm *der* (PL die Dämme).

damage *noun* Schaden *der* (PL die Schäden); **to do a lot of damage** großen Schaden anrichten.
damage *verb* beschädigen.

damn *noun* **I don't give a damn** das ist mir piepegal (*informal*).
damn *exclamation* **damn!** verdammt!

damp *adjective* feucht.
damp *noun* Feuchtigkeit *die*.

dance *noun* Tanz *der* (PL die Tänze); **a folk dance** ein Volkstanz.
dance *verb* tanzen; **I like dancing** ich tanze gerne.

dancer *noun* Tänzer *der* (PL die Tänzer), Tänzerin *die* (PL die Tänzerinnen).

dancing class *noun* Tanzstunde *die* (PL die Tanzstunden); **to go to dancing classes** in die Tanzstunde gehen.

dancing *noun* Tanzen *das*.

dandruff *noun* Schuppen (*plural*).

danger *noun* Gefahr *die* (PL die Gefahren); **to be in danger** in Gefahr sein.

dangerous *adjective* gefährlich; **it's dangerous to drive too fast** es ist gefährlich, zu schnell zu fahren.

Danish *noun* Dänisch *das*.
Danish *adjective* dänisch; **he's Danish** er ist Däne; **she's Danish** sie ist Dänin.

dare *verb* **1** wagen; **to dare to do something** es wagen, etwas zu tun;

I didn't dare suggest it ich habe es nicht gewagt, das vorzuschlagen; **2 don't you dare tell her I'm here!** untersteh dich, ihr zu sagen, dass ich hier bin!; **3 I dare you!** du traust dich doch nicht!; **I dare you to tell him!** sag's ihm doch wenn du dich traust!

daring *adjective* gewagt; **that was a bit daring** das war etwas gewagt.

dark *noun* **in the dark** im Dunkeln; **after dark** nach Einbruch der Dunkelheit; **to be afraid of the dark** Angst im Dunkeln haben.
dark *adjective* **1** (*colour*) dunkel (*adjectives ending in -el drop the e when followed by a vowel, which means that dunkel becomes dunkler/dunkle/dunkles*); **a dark colour** eine dunkle Farbe; **it gets dark around five** es wird gegen fünf dunkel; **2 a dark blue skirt** ein dunkelblauer Rock; **she has dark brown hair** sie hat dunkelbraune Haare.

darkness *noun* Dunkelheit *die*; **in darkness** in der Dunkelheit.

darling *noun* Liebling *der* (PL die Lieblinge); **see you later, darling!** bis später, Liebling!

dart *noun* **1** Wurfpfeil *der* (PL die Wurfpfeile); **2** (*game*) **darts** Darts *das*; **to play darts** Darts spielen.

data *plural noun* Daten (*plural*).

database *noun* Datenbank *die* (PL die Datenbanken).

date *noun* **1** Datum *das* (PL die Daten); **what's the date today?** welches Datum haben wir heute?; **the date of the meeting** das Datum für das Treffen; **what date is he**

coming? wann kommt er?;
2 Termin der (PL die Termine); **the
last date for payment** der letzte
Zahlungstermin; **3 out of date**
ungültig; **my passport's out of
date** mein Pass ist ungültig;
4 (*appointment*) Verabredung die (PL
die Verabredungen); **Laura's got a
date with Frank** Laura ist mit
Frank verabredet; **5** (*fruit*) Dattel die
(PL die Datteln).

date of birth *noun* Geburtsdatum
das (PL die Geburtsdaten).

daughter *noun* Tochter die (PL die
Töchter); **Tina's daughter** Tinas
Tochter.

daughter-in-law *noun*
Schwiegertochter die (PL die
Schwiegertöchter).

dawn *noun* Morgendämmerung die
(PL die Morgendämmerungen).

day *noun* **1** Tag der (PL die Tage);
three days later drei Tage später; **a
few days ago** vor ein paar Tagen;
the day I went to London an dem
Tag, an dem ich nach London
gefahren bin; **we spent the day in
London** wir haben den Tag in
London verbracht; **it rained all day**
es hat den ganzen Tag geregnet; **the
day after** am Tag danach; **the day
after the wedding** am Tag nach der
Hochzeit; **the day before** am Tag
davor; **the day before the wedding**
am Tag vor der Hochzeit; **2 the day
after tomorrow** übermorgen; **my
sister's arriving the day after
tomorrow** meine Schwester kommt
übermorgen an; **3 the day before
yesterday** vorgestern; **my brother**

arrived the day before yesterday
mein Bruder kam vorgestern an;
4 during the day tagsüber.

dead *adjective* tot; **her father's
dead** ihr Vater ist tot.
dead *adverb* (*really*) irre
(*informal*); **he's dead nice** er ist irre
nett; **it was dead good** es war irre
gut; **it was dead easy** es war
kinderleicht; **you're dead right** du
hast völlig Recht; **she arrived dead
on time** sie kam auf die Minute
pünklich an.

dead end *noun* Sackgasse die (PL
die Sackgassen).

deadline *noun* letzte Termin der
(PL die letzten Termine).

deaf *adjective* taub.

deafening *adjective*
ohrenbetäubend.

deal *noun* **1** (*involving money*)
Geschäft das (PL die Geschäfte); **it's a
good deal** das ist ein gutes
Geschäft; **2** (*agreement*)
Vereinbarung die (PL die
Vereinbarungen); **to make a deal
with somebody** mit jemandem eine
Vereinbarung treffen; **it's a deal!**
abgemacht!; **3 a great deal of** viel; **I
don't have a great deal of time** ich
habe nicht viel Zeit.
deal *verb* (*in cards*) geben; **it's you
to deal** du gibst.

● **to deal with something** sich um
etwas (ACC) kümmern; **Linda deals
with the accounts** Linda kümmert
sich um die Buchführung; **I'll deal
with it as soon as possible** ich
kümmere mich so schnell wie
möglich darum.

dear *adjective* **1** lieb; **Dear Franz** Lieber Franz; **Dear Mr Smith** Sehr geehrter Herr Smith; **2** (*expensive*) teuer.

death *noun* Tod *der*; **after his father's death** nach dem Tod seines Vaters; **three deaths** drei Todesfälle; ★**I was bored to death** ich habe mich zu Tode gelangweilt; ★**I'm sick to death of it** ich habe es gründlich satt.

death penalty *noun* Todesstrafe *die*.

debate *noun* Debatte *die* (PL *die* Debatten).
debate *verb* debattieren.

debt *noun* (*money owed*) Schulden (*plural*); **to get into debt** in Schulden geraten.

decade *noun* Jahrzehnt *das* (PL *die* Jahrzehnte).

decaffeinated *adjective* koffeinfrei.

deceive *verb* betrügen◇.

December *noun* Dezember *der* (PL *die* Dezember); **in December** im Dezember.

decent *adjective* anständig; **a decent salary** ein anständiges Gehalt; **a decent meal** ein anständiges Essen.

decide *verb* **1** entscheiden◇; **to decide on something** sich für etwas (ACC) entscheiden; **he's decided against buying a new car** er hat sich entschieden, kein neues Auto zu kaufen; **2 to decide to do something** sich entschließen◇, etwas zu tun; **they've decided to** buy a house sie haben sich entschlossen, ein Haus zu kaufen.

decimal *adjective* Dezimal-; **decimal number** die Dezimalzahl.

decimal point *noun* Komma *das* (PL *die* Kommas).

decision *noun* Entscheidung *die* (PL *die* Entscheidungen); **to make a decision** eine Entscheidung treffen.

deckchair *noun* Liegestuhl *der* (PL *die* Liegestühle).

declare *verb* **1** erklären; **2** (*at customs*) **nothing to declare** nichts zu verzollen.

decorate *verb* **1** schmücken; **to decorate the Christmas tree** den Weihnachtsbaum schmücken; **2** (*with paint*) streichen◇, (*with wallpaper*) tapezieren; **we're decorating the kitchen this weekend** wir streichen dieses Wochenende die Küche.

decoration *noun* Verzierung *die* (PL *die* Verzierungen); **Christmas decorations** der Weihnachtsschmuck.

decrease *noun* Rückgang *der* (PL *die* Rückgänge); **a decrease in the number of accidents** ein Rückgang in der Anzahl der Unfälle.
decrease *verb* zurückgehen ◇ SEP (PERF *sein*), abnehmen ◇ SEP.

deep *adjective* tief; **a deep feeling of gratitude** ein tiefes Dankbarkeitsgefühl; **how deep is the swimming pool?** wie tief ist das Schwimmbecken?; **a hole two metres deep** ein zwei Meter tiefes Loch.

deep end *noun*
Schwimmerbecken *das* (PL *die*
Schwimmerbecken); **deep end: 2
metres** Wassertiefe: 2 Meter.

deep freeze *noun* Tiefkühltruhe
die (PL *die* Tiefkühltruhen), (*upright*)
Tiefkühlschrank *der* (PL *die*
Tiefkühlschränke).

deeply *adverb* tief.

deer *noun* **1** Hirsch *der* (PL *die*
Hirsche); **2** (*roe deer*) Reh *das* (PL *die*
Rehe).

defeat *noun* Niederlage *die* (PL *die*
Niederlagen).
defeat *verb* schlagen◇.

defence *noun* Verteidigung *die*.

defend *verb* verteidigen.

defender *noun* Verteidiger *der* (PL
die Verteidiger), Verteidigerin *die* (PL
die Verteidigerinnen).

definite *adjective* **1** eindeutig; **a
definite improvement** eine
eindeutige Besserung; **2** (*certain*)
sicher; **it's not definite yet** es ist
noch nicht sicher; **3** (*exact*) klar; **a
definite answer** eine klare Antwort.

definite article *noun*
bestimmter Artikel *der* (PL *die*
bestimmten Artikel).

definitely *adverb* **1** (*when giving
your opinion about something*)
eindeutig; **your German is
definitely better than mine**
dein Deutsch ist eindeutig besser
als meins; **2** (*without doubt*)
bestimmt; **she's definitely going
to be there** sie wird bestimmt dort
sein; **I'm definitely not coming**
ich komme ganz bestimmt nicht;

**3 'are you sure you like this one
better?'** – **'definitely!'** 'gefällt dir
diese wirklich besser?' - 'auf jeden
Fall!'

definition *noun* Definition *die* (PL
die Definitionen).

degree *noun* **1** Grad *der* (PL *die*
Grade); **thirty degrees** dreißig
Grad; **2 a university degree** ein
akademischer Grad.

delay *noun* Verspätung *die* (PL *die*
Verspätungen); **a two-hour delay**
eine zweistündige Verspätung.
delay *verb* **1** (*hold up*) aufhalten◇
SEP; **she was delayed in the office**
sie ist im Büro aufgehalten worden;
2 (*train, plane*) **to be delayed**
Verspätung haben; **the flight was
delayed by bad weather** der Flug
hatte wegen des schlechten Wetters
Verspätung; **3** (*postpone*)
aufschieben◇ SEP; **the decision has
been delayed until Thursday** die
Entscheidung wurde bis
Donnerstag aufgeschoben.

delete *verb* **1** streichen◇; **2** (*in
computing*) löschen.

deliberate *adjective* absichtlich.

deliberately *adverb* absichtlich;
she did it deliberately sie hat das
absichtlich getan.

delicate *adjective* **1** (*fabric, health*)
zart; **2** (*situation, question*) heikel;
3 (*taste, smell*) fein.

delicatessen *noun*
Feinkostgeschäft *das* (PL *die*
Feinkostgeschäfte).

delicious *adjective* köstlich.

delighted *adjective* hocherfreut; **to be delighted** begeistert sein; **they're delighted with their new flat** sie sind von ihrer neuen Wohnung begeistert; **I'm delighted that you can come** ich freue mich sehr, dass ihr kommen könnt.

deliver *verb* 1 liefern; **they're delivering the washing machine tomorrow** die Waschmaschine wird morgen geliefert; 2 (*mail, newspapers*) zustellen SEP.

delivery *noun* 1 Lieferung *die* (PL *die* Lieferungen); 2 (*of mail, newspapers*) Zustellung *die* (PL *die* Zustellungen).

demand *noun* Nachfrage *die* (PL *die* Nachfragen); **much in demand** sehr gefragt.
demand *verb* verlangen.

demo *noun* (*protest*) Demo *die* (*informal*) (PL *die* Demos).

democracy *noun* Demokratie *die* (PL *die* Demokratien).

democratic *adjective* demokratisch.

demolish *verb* abreißen ✧ SEP.

demonstrate *verb* 1 (*a machine, product, or technique*) vorführen SEP; 2 (*protest*) demonstrieren; **to demonstrate against something** gegen etwas (ACC) demonstrieren.

demonstration *noun* 1 (*of a machine, product, or technique*) Vorführung *die* (PL *die* Vorführungen); 2 (*protest*) Demonstration *die* (PL *die* Demonstrationen).

demonstrator *noun* Demonstrant *der* (PL *die* Demonstranten), Demonstrantin *die* (PL *die* Demonstrantinnen).

denim *noun* Jeansstoff *der* (PL *die* Jeansstoffe); **a denim jacket** eine Jeansjacke.

Denmark *noun* Dänemark *das*.

dental *adjective* 1 Zahn-; **dental floss** *die* Zahnseide; **dental hygiene** *die* Zahnpflege; 2 **to have a dental appointment** einen Zahnarzt Termin haben.

dental surgeon *noun* Zahnarzt *der* (PL *die* Zahnärzte), Zahnäztin *die* (PL *die* Zahnärztinnen).

dentist *noun* Zahnarzt *der* (PL *die* Zahnärzte), Zahnärztin *die* (PL *die* Zahnärztinnen); **my mum's a dentist** meine Mutter ist Zahnärztin.

deny *verb* bestreiten✧.

deodorant *noun* Deodorant *das* (PL *die* Deodorants).

depart *verb* 1 (*set out on a journey*) abreisen SEP (PERF *sein*); 2 (*train, coach*) abfahren✧ SEP (PERF *sein*); 3 (*plane*) abfliegen✧ SEP (PERF *sein*).

department *noun* 1 (*in a shop, firm, or hospital*) Abteilung *die* (PL *die* Abteilungen); **the men's department** die Herrenabteilung; 2 (*of a university*) Seminar *das* (PL *die* Seminare); **the history department** das Seminar für Geschichte; 3 (*in school*) Fachbereich *der* (PL *die* Fachbereiche).

department store *noun* Kaufhaus *das* (PL *die* Kaufhäuser).

a
b
c
d
e
f
g
h
i
j
k
l
m
n
o
p
q
r
s
t
u
v
w
x
y
z

a
b
c
d
e
f
g
h
i
j
k
l
m
n
o
p
q
r
s
t
u
v
w
x
y
z

departure noun **1** (of a person) Abreise die; **2** (of a car, train) Abfahrt die; **3** (of a plane) Abflug der.

departure lounge noun Abflughalle die (PL die Abflughallen).

depend verb **1 to depend on** abhängen⋄ SEP von (+ DAT); **it depends on the price** das hängt vom Preis ab; **it depends on what you want** das hängt davon ab, was du willst; **2 it depends** es kommt darauf an.

deposit noun **1** (when renting or hiring) Kaution die (PL die Kautionen); **2** (when booking a holiday or hotel room) Anzahlung die (PL die Anzahlungen); **to pay a deposit** eine Anzahlung leisten; **3** (on a bottle) Pfand das.

depressed adjective deprimiert.

depressing adjective deprimierend.

depth noun Tiefe die.

deputy noun Stellvertreter der (PL die Stellvertreter), Stellvertreterin die (PL die Stellvertreterinnen); **the deputy headteacher** Konrektor der (PL die Konrektoren), Konrektorin die (PL die Konrektorinnen).

describe verb beschreiben⋄.

description noun Beschreibung die (PL die Beschreibungen).

desert noun Wüste die (PL die Wüsten).

desert island noun verlassene Insel die (PL die verlassenen Inseln).

deserve verb verdienen.

design noun **1** Konstruktion die (PL die Konstruktionen); **the design of the plane** die Flugzeugkonstruktion; **2** (artistic design) Design das (PL die Designs); **modern design** modernes Design; **3** (pattern) Muster das (PL die Muster); **a floral design** ein Blumenmuster; **4** (sketch) Entwurf der (PL die Entwürfe).
design verb **1** konstruieren (a machine, plane, system); **2** entwerfen⋄ (costumes, fabric, scenery).

designer noun Designer der (PL die Designer), Designerin die (PL die Designerinnen).

desk noun **1** (in an office or at home) Schreibtisch der (PL die Schreibtische); **2** (pupil's) Pult das (PL die Pulte); **3 the reception desk** die Rezeption; **the information desk** die Auskunft.

despair noun Verzweiflung die.
despair verb **to despair of doing something** alle Hoffnung aufgeben⋄ SEP, etwas zu tun.

desperate adjective **1** verzweifelt; **a desperate attempt** ein verzweifelter Versuch; **2 to be desperate to do something** etwas dringend tun müssen; **I'm desperate to speak to you** ich muss dich dringend sprechen; **to be desperate for something** etwas dringend brauchen.

dessert noun Nachtisch der (PL die Nachtische); **what's for dessert?** was gibts zum Nachtisch?

destination *noun* Ziel das (PL die Ziele).

destroy *verb* zerstören.

destruction *noun* Zerstörung die.

detached house *noun* Einfamilienhaus das (PL die Einfamilienhäuser).

detail *noun* Einzelheit die (PL die Einzelheiten).

detailed *adjective* ausführlich.

detective *noun* **1** (*in the police*) Kriminalbeamte der (PL die Kriminalbeamten), Kriminalbeamtin die (PL die Kriminalbeamtinnen); **2 private detective** der Detektiv, die Detektivin.

detective story *noun* Detektivgeschichte die (PL die Detektivgeschichten).

detention *noun* **1** (*at school*) Nachsitzen das; **2** (*in prison*) Haft die.

detergent *noun* Waschmittel das (PL die Waschmittel).

determined *adjective* entschlossen; **he's determined to leave** er ist fest entschlossen zu gehen.

detour *noun* Umweg der (PL die Umwege).

develop *verb* **1** entwickeln; **to get a film developed** einen Film entwickeln lassen; **2** sich entwickeln; **how children develop** wie Kinder sich entwickeln.

developing country *noun* Entwicklungsland das (PL die Entwicklungsländer).

development *noun* Entwicklung die (PL die Entwicklungen).

devil *noun* Teufel der (PL die Teufel).

devoted *adjective* treu.

diabetes *noun* Zuckerkrankheit die.

diabetic *noun* Diabetiker der (PL die Diabetiker), Diabetikerin die (PL die Diabetikerinnen).
diabetic *adjective* zuckerkrank; **to be diabetic** zuckerkrank sein.

diagnosis *noun* Diagnose die (PL die Diagnosen).

diagonal *adjective* diagonal.

diagram *noun* Diagramm das (PL die Diagramme).

dial *verb* wählen; **I dialled the wrong number** ich habe die falsche Nummer gewählt; **dial 00 49 for Germany** wählen Sie die Vorwahl 00 49 für Deutschland.

dialling tone *noun* Freizeichen das.

dialogue *noun* Dialog der (PL die Dialoge).

diamond *noun* **1** Diamant der (PL die Diamanten), (*gemstone*) Brillant der (PL die Brillanten); **2** (*in cards*) Karo das; **the jack of diamonds** der Karobube; **3** (*shape*) Raute die (PL die Rauten).

diarrhoea *noun* Durchfall der.

diary *noun* **1** (*for appointments*) Terminkalender der (PL die Terminkalender); **2** Tagebuch das (PL die Tagebücher); **to keep a diary** ein Tagebuch führen.

a
b
c
d
e
f
g
h
i
j
k
l
m
n
o
p
q
r
s
t
u
v
w
x
y
z

dice *noun* Würfel *der* (PL *die* Würfel); **to throw the dice** würfeln.

dictation *noun* Diktat *das* (PL *die* Diktate).

dictionary *noun* Wörterbuch *das* (PL *die* Wörterbücher).

did *verb* SEE **do**.

die *verb* **1** sterben⋄ (PERF *sein*); **my grannie died in January** meine Oma starb im Januar; **2 to be dying to do something** darauf brennen, etwas zu tun; **I'm dying to meet her** ich brenne darauf, sie kennen zu lernen.

diesel *noun* **1** Dieselöl *das*; **2 diesel engine** *der* Dieselmotor; **diesel car** *der* Diesel.

diet *noun* **1** Ernährung *die*; **a healthy diet** eine gesunde Ernährung; **2** (*slimming or special*) Diät *die* (PL *die* Diäten); **to be on a diet** Diät machen.

difference *noun* **1** Unterschied *der* (PL *die* Unterschiede); **I can't see any difference between the two** ich erkenne keinen Unterschied zwischen den beiden; **what's the difference between ...?** was ist der Unterschied zwischen ...?; **2 it makes a difference** es ist ein Unterschied; **it makes no difference** es ist egal; **it makes no difference what I say** es ist egal, was ich sage.

different *adjective* **1** verschieden; **the two sisters are very different** die beiden Schwestern sind sehr verschieden; **2 to be different from** anders sein als; **she's very different from her sister** sie ist ganz anders

als ihre Schwester; **3** (*separate*) anderer/andere/anderes; **she reads a different book every day** sie liest jeden Tag ein anderes Buch.

difficult *adjective* schwer; **it's really difficult** es ist sehr schwer; **he finds it difficult** es fällt ihm schwer.

difficulty *noun* Schwierigkeit *die* (PL *die* Schwierigkeiten); **to have difficulty doing something** Schwierigkeiten haben, etwas zu tun; **I had difficulty finding your house** ich hatte Schwierigkeiten, dein Haus zu finden.

dig *verb* graben⋄; **to dig a hole** ein Loch graben.

digestion *noun* Verdauung *die*.

digital *adjective* digital; **digital watch** *die* Digitaluhr; **digital recording** *die* Digitalaufnahme.

dim *adjective* **1** schwach; **a dim light** ein schwaches Licht; **2** beschränkt; **she's a bit dim** sie ist ein bisschen beschränkt.

din *noun* Lärm *der*; **stop making such a din!** hör auf, so einen Lärm zu machen!

dinghy *noun* **1 sailing dinghy** *das* Dingi; **2 rubber dinghy** *das* Schlauchboot.

dining room *noun* Esszimmer *das* (PL *die* Esszimmer); **in the dining room** im Esszimmer.

dinner *noun* **1** (*evening*) Abendessen *das* (PL *die* Abendessen); **to invite somebody to dinner** jemanden zum Abendessen einladen; **2** (*midday*) Mittagessen *das* (PL *die* Mittagessen); **to have school dinner** in der Schulkantine zu Mittag essen.

dinner party *noun* Abendessen *das* (PL *die* Abendessen).

dinner time *noun* Essenszeit *die*.

dinosaur *noun* Dinosaurier *der* (PL *die* Dinosaurier).

diploma *noun* Diplom *das* (PL *die* Diplome).

direct *adjective* direkt; **a direct flight** ein Direktflug.
direct *adverb* direkt; **the bus goes direct to the airport** der Bus fährt direkt zum Flughafen.
direct *verb* **1 to direct a film or a play** bei einem Film oder einem Theaterstück Regie führen; **2** regeln (*traffic*).

direction *noun* **1** Richtung *die* (PL *die* Richtungen); **to go in the other direction** in die andere Richtung gehen; **2 to ask somebody for directions** jemanden nach dem Weg fragen; **3 directions for use** die Gebrauchsanweisung (*singular*).

directly *adverb* direkt; **directly afterwards** gleich danach.

director *noun* **1** (*of a company*) Direktor *der* (PL *die* Direktoren), Direktorin *die* (PL *die* Direktorinnen); **2** (*of a play, film*) Regisseur *der* (PL *die* Regisseure), Regisseurin *die* (PL *die* Regisseurinnen); **3** (*of a programme*) Leiter *der* (PL *die* Leiter), Leiterin *die* (PL *die* Leiterinnen).

directory *noun* Telefonbuch *das* (PL *die* Telefonbücher); **he's ex-** **directory** seine Nummer steht nicht im Telefonbuch.

dirt *noun* Schmutz *der*.

dirty *adjective* schmutzig; **my hands are dirty** ich habe schmutzige Hände; **to get something dirty** etwas schmutzig machen; **you'll get your dress dirty** du machst dir das Kleid schmutzig; **to get dirty** schmutzig werden; **the curtains get dirty quickly** die Vorhänge werden sehr schnell schmutzig.

disability *noun* Behinderung *die* (PL *die* Behinderungen); **does he have a disability?** ist er behindert?

disabled *adjective* behindert; **disabled people** Behinderte (*plural*).

disadvantage *noun* **1** Nachteil *der* (PL *die* Nachteile); **2 to be at a disadvantage** im Nachteil sein.

disagree *verb* **1 I disagree** ich bin anderer Meinung; **2 to disagree with somebody** mit jemandem nicht übereinstimmen SEP; **I disagree with James** ich stimme mit James nicht überein.

disappear *verb* verschwinden✧ (PERF *sein*).

disappearance *noun* Verschwinden *das*.

disappointed *adjective* enttäuscht; **I'm disappointed with my marks** ich bin über meine Noten enttäuscht.

disappointment *noun* Enttäuschung *die* (PL *die* Enttäuschungen).

a
b
c
d
e
f
g
h
i
j
k
l
m
n
o
p
q
r
s
t
u
v
w
x
y
z

a
b
c
d
e
f
g
h
i
j
k
l
m
n
o
p
q
r
s
t
u
v
w
x
y
z

disaster *noun* Katastrophe *die* (PL die Katastrophen); **it was a complete disaster** es war eine komplette Katastrophe.

disastrous *adjective* katastrophal.

disc *noun* **1 compact disc** *die* Compactdisc; **2 tax disc** (*for a vehicle*) *die* Steuerplakette; **3 slipped disc** *der* Bandscheibenvorfall.

discipline *noun* Disziplin *die*.

disc-jockey *noun* Diskjockey *der* (PL die Diskjockeys).

disco *noun* **1** Disko *die* (PL die Diskos); **they're having a disco** sie veranstalten eine Disko; **2** (*club*) Disko *die* (PL die Diskos); **to go to a disco** in eine Disko gehen.

discount *noun* Rabatt *der* (PL die Rabatte).

discover *verb* entdecken.

discovery *noun* Entdeckung *die* (PL die Entdeckungen).

discreet *adjective* diskret.

discrimination *noun* Diskriminierung *die*; **discrimination against women** die Diskriminierung von Frauen; **racial discrimination** die Rassendiskriminierung.

discuss *verb* **to discuss something** etwas besprechen◇; **we'll discuss the problem tomorrow** wir besprechen das Problem morgen; **I'm going to discuss it with Phil** ich werde es mit Phil besprechen.

discussion *noun* Gespräch *das* (PL die Gespräche).

disease *noun* Krankheit *die* (PL die Krankheiten).

disguise *noun* Verkleidung *die* (PL die Verkleidungen); **to be in disguise** verkleidet sein. **disguise** *verb* verkleiden; **disguised as a woman** als Frau verkleidet.

disgust *noun* Ekel *der*.

disgusted *adjective* **1** (*filled with indignation*) empört; **2** (*nauseated*) angeekelt.

disgusting *adjective* eklig.

dish *noun* **1** Schüssel *die* (PL die Schüsseln); **a large white dish** eine große weiße Schüssel; **satellite dish** die Satellitenschüssel; **2** (*type of food*) Gericht *das* (PL die Gerichte); **risotto is my favourite dish** Risotto ist mein Lieblingsgericht; **3** (*crockery*) **the dishes** das Geschirr; **to do the dishes** Geschirr spülen.

dishcloth *noun* Spültuch *das* (PL die Spültücher).

dishonest *adjective* unehrlich.

dishonesty *noun* Unehrlichkeit *die*.

dishwasher *noun* Geschirrspülmaschine *die* (PL die Geschirrspülmaschinen).

disinfect *verb* desinfizieren.

disinfectant *noun* Desinfektionsmittel *das*.

disk noun Diskette die (PL die Disketten); **floppy disk** die Diskette; **hard disk** die Festplatte.

diskdrive noun Diskettenlaufwerk das (PL die Diskettenlaufwerke).

diskette noun Diskette die (PL die Disketten).

dismiss verb entlassen◇ (an employee).

disobedient adjective ungehorsam.

display noun 1 Ausstellung die (PL die Ausstellungen); **handicrafts display** die Handarbeitsausstellung; **to be on display** ausgestellt sein; **2 window display** die Auslage; **3 firework display** das Feuerwerk.
display verb ausstellen SEP.

disposable adjective Wegwerf-; **disposable towel** das Wegwerfhandtuch.

disqualify verb disqualifizieren.

disrupt verb stören.

dissolve verb auflösen SEP.

distance noun Entfernung die (PL die Entfernungen); **from this distance** aus dieser Entfernung; **from a distance** von weitem; **in the distance** in der Ferne; **it's within walking distance** es ist zu Fuß erreichbar.

distant adjective fern.

distinct adjective deutlich.

distinctly adverb 1 deutlich; **2 it's distinctly odd** es ist äußerst komisch.

distract verb ablenken SEP.

distribute verb verteilen.

district noun 1 (of a town) Stadtteil der (PL die Stadtteile); **a poor district of Berlin** ein ärmlicher Stadtteil von Berlin; **2** (in the country) Gebiet das (PL die Gebiete).

disturb verb stören; **sorry to disturb you** Entschuldigung, dass ich störe.

dive noun Kopfsprung der (PL die Kopfsprünge).
dive verb 1 einen Kopfsprung machen; **2** (swim underwater) tauchen (PERF sein).

diver noun 1 (underwater) Taucher der (PL die Taucher), Taucherin die (PL die Taucherinnen); **2** (from a diving board) Kunstspringer der (PL die Kunstspringer), Kunstspringerin die (PL die Kunstspringerinnen).

diversion noun (of traffic) Umleitung die (PL die Umleitungen).

divide verb teilen.

diving noun 1 (underwater) Tauchen das; **2** (from a diving board) Kunstspringen das.

diving board noun Sprungbrett das (PL die Sprungbretter).

division noun 1 Teilung die (PL die Teilungen); **2** (in maths) Division die (PL die Divisionen); **3** (sports league) Liga die (PL die Ligen).

divorce noun Scheidung die (PL die Scheidungen).
divorce verb sich scheiden lassen◇; **they divorced in May** sie haben sich im Mai scheiden lassen.

divorced adjective geschieden.

a
b
c
d
e
f
g
h
i
j
k
l
m
n
o
p
q
r
s
t
u
v
w
x
y
z

a
b
c
d
e
f
g
h
i
j
k
l
m
n
o
p
q
r
s
t
u
v
w
x
y
z

DIY *noun* **1** Heimwerken *das*; **2 to do DIY** heimwerken; **3 DIY shop** *der* Baumarkt (PL *die* Baumärkte).

dizzy *adjective* **I feel dizzy** mir ist schwindlig.

DJ *noun* DJ *der* (PL *die* DJs).

do *verb* **1** tun◇, machen; **what are you doing?** was machst du?; **I'm doing my homework** ich mache meine Hausaufgaben; **what have you done with the hammer?** was hast du mit dem Hammer gemacht?; **can you do me a favour?** kannst du mir einen Gefallen tun?; **do as I say** tu was ich sage; **2** she's doing the cleaning sie putzt; **I'll do the washing up** ich wasche ab; **I must do the shopping** ich muss einkaufen gehen; **3** (*in questions*) **do you like it?** gefällt es dir?; **when does the film start?** wann fängt der Film an?; **how do you open the door?** wie macht man die Tür auf?; **do you know him?** kennst du ihn?; **4** (*in negative sentences*) **I don't like mushrooms** ich mag keine Pilze; **Rosie doesn't like spinach** Rosie mag keinen Spinat; **you didn't shut the door** du hast die Tür nicht zugemacht; **it doesn't matter** das macht nichts; **5** (*when it refers back to another verb, 'do' is not translated*) **'do you live here?' – 'yes, I do'** 'wohnst du hier?' -'ja'; **she has more money than I do** sie hat mehr Geld als ich; **'I live in Oxford' – 'so do I'** 'ich wohne in Oxford' - 'ich auch'; **'I didn't phone Gemma' – 'neither did I'** 'ich habe Gemma nicht angerufen' - 'ich auch nicht'; **6** don't you?, doesn't he?

nicht wahr?; **you know Helen, don't you?** du kennst Helen, nicht wahr?; **she left on Thursday, didn't she?** sie ist Donnerstag abgefahren, nicht wahr?; **7 that'll do** das reicht; **it'll do like that** das geht so.

● **to do something up 1** etwas zubinden◇ SEP (*shoes*); **2** etwas zumachen SEP (*a cardigan, jacket*); **3** etwas renovieren (*a house*).

● **to do without something** ohne etwas (ACC) auskommen◇ SEP (PERF *sein*); **we can do without knives** wir können ohne Messer auskommen.

doctor *noun* Arzt *der* (PL *die* Ärzte), Ärztin *die* (PL *die* Ärztinnen); **her mother's a doctor** ihre Mutter ist Ärztin.

document *noun* Dokument *das* (PL *die* Dokumente).

documentary *noun* Dokumentarfilm *der* (PL *die* Dokumentarfilme).

dodgems *plural noun* **the dodgems** Autoskooter *der* (PL *die* Autoskooter).

dog *noun* Hund *der* (PL *die* Hunde).

do-it-yourself *noun* Heimwerken *das*.

dole *noun* Arbeitslosgeld *das*; **to be on the dole** arbeitslos sein.

doll *noun* Puppe *die* (PL *die* Puppen).

dollar *noun* Dollar *der* (PL *die* Dollars).

dolphin *noun* Delfin *der* (PL *die* Delfine).

domino *noun* **1** Dominostein *der* (PL *die* Dominosteine); **2** (*game*)

dominoes Domino *das*; **to play dominoes** Domino spielen.

donkey *noun* Esel *der* (PL *die* Esel).

don't SEE **do**.

door *noun* Tür *die* (PL *die* Türen); **to open the door** die Tür aufmachen; **to shut the door** die Tür zumachen.

doorbell *noun* Türklingel *die* (PL *die* Türklingeln); **to ring the doorbell** klingeln.

dot *noun* **1** Punkt *der* (PL *die* Punkte); **at ten on the dot** Punkt zehn Uhr; **2** (*small dot on fabric*) Pünktchen *das* (PL *die* Pünktchen).

double *adjective, adverb* **1** doppelt; **a double helping** eine doppelte Portion; **double the size** doppelt so groß; **double the time** doppelt so viel Zeit; **at double the price** zum doppelten Preis; **2 double room** *das* Doppelzimmer; **3 double bed** *das* Doppelbett.

double bass *noun* Kontrabass *der* (PL *die* Kontrabässe).

double-decker bus *noun* Doppeldeckerbus *der* (PL *die* Doppeldeckerbusse).

doubles *noun* (*in tennis*) Doppel *das* (PL *die* Doppel).

doubt *noun* Zweifel *der* (PL *die* Zweifel); **there's no doubt about it** es besteht kein Zweifel daran; **I have my doubts** ich habe gewisse Zweifel.

doubt *verb* **to doubt something** etwas bezweifeln; **I doubt it** das bezweifle ich; **I doubt that** ... ich bezweifle, dass ...; **I doubt they'll buy it** ich bezweifle, dass sie es kaufen.

doubtful *adjective* **1** fraglich; **it's doubtful** es ist fraglich; **2 to be doubtful about doing something** Bedenken haben, ob man etwas tun soll; **I'm doubtful about inviting them together** ich habe Bedenken, ob ich sie zusammen einladen soll.

dough *noun* Teig *der*.

doughnut *noun* Krapfen *der* (PL *die* Krapfen).

down *adverb, preposition* **1** unten; **he's down in the cellar** er ist unten im Keller; **it's down there** es ist da unten; **2 down the road** (*nearby*) in der Nähe; **there's a chemist's just down the road** eine Apotheke ist ganz in der Nähe; **3 to go down** nach unten gehen; **I went down to open the door** ich ging nach unten, um die Tür aufzumachen; **to walk down the street** die Straße entlanggehen✧ SEP (PERF *sein*); **to run down the stairs** die Treppe runterrennen SEP (PERF *sein*) (*informal*); **4 to come down** herunterkommen✧ SEP (PERF *sein*); **she came down into the kitchen** sie kam in die Küche herunter; **5 to sit down** sich setzen; **she sat down on the chair** sie setzte sich auf den Stuhl; **6 to write something down** etwas aufschreiben✧ SEP.

downstairs *adverb* **1** unten; **she's downstairs** sie ist unten; **2** (*with movement*) nach unten; **to go downstairs** nach unten gehen; **3** im Erdgeschoss; **the flat**

a
b
c
d
e
f
g
h
i
j
k
l
m
n
o
p
q
r
s
t
u
v
w
x
y
z

403

downstairs die Wohnung im Erdgeschoss.

doze *verb* dösen.

dozen *noun* Dutzend *das* (PL *die* Dutzende).

drag *noun* **1 what a drag!** so'n Mist! (*informal*); **2 what a drag she is!** Mann, ist die langweilig! (*informal*).
drag *verb* schleppen.

dragon *noun* Drache *der* (PL *die* Drachen).

drain *noun* **1** (*outlet pipe*) Abflussrohr *das* (PL *die* Abflussrohre); **2 the drains:** Kanalisation *die* (PL *die* Kanalisationen).
drain *verb* abgießen ⬦ SEP (*vegetables*); trockenlegen SEP (*fields, land*).

drama *noun* **1** (*play*) Drama *das* (PL *die* Dramen); **he made a big drama out of it** er hat ein großes Drama daraus gemacht (*informal*); **2** (*dramatic nature*) Dramatik *die*.

dramatic *adjective* dramatisch.

draught *noun* Luftzug *der*; **there's a draught in here** hier zieht es.

draughts *noun* Damespiel *das*; **to play draughts** Dame spielen.

draw *noun* **1** (*in a match*) Unentschieden *das*; **to end in a draw** mit einem Unentschieden enden; **2** (*lottery*) Ziehung *die* (PL *die* Ziehungen).
draw *verb* **1** zeichnen; **she can draw really well** sie kann wirklich sehr gut zeichnen; **2 to draw the curtains** (*open*) die Vorhänge aufziehen ⬦ SEP, (*close*) die Vorhänge

zuziehen ⬦ SEP; **3** (*in a match*) unentschieden spielen; **we drew three all** wir haben drei zu drei unentschieden gespielt.

drawer *noun* Schublade *die* (PL *die* Schubladen).

drawing *noun* Zeichnung *die* (PL *die* Zeichnungen).

drawing pin *noun* Reißzwecke *die* (PL *die* Reißzwecken).

dreadful *adjective* furchtbar.

dreadfully *adverb* furchtbar; **I'm dreadfully late** ich habe mich furchtbar verspätet; **I'm dreadfully sorry** es tut mir furchtbar Leid.

dream *noun* Traum *der* (PL *die* Träume); **to have a dream** einen Traum haben.
dream *verb* träumen; **to dream about something** von etwas (DAT) träumen.

dress *noun* Kleid *das* (PL *die* Kleider).
dress *verb* **to dress a child** ein Kind anziehen ⬦ SEP.
● **to dress up** sich verkleiden; **to dress up as a vampire** sich als Vampir verkleiden.

dressed *adjective* **1** angezogen; **is Tom dressed yet?** ist Tom schon angezogen?; **2 she was dressed in black trousers and a yellow shirt** sie trug eine schwarze Hose und ein gelbes Hemd; **3 to get dressed** sich anziehen ⬦ SEP; **I got dressed quickly** ich zog mich schnell an.

dressing gown *noun* Morgenrock *der* (PL *die* Morgenröcke).

dressing table *noun*
Frisierkommode die (PL die
Frisierkommoden).

drier *noun* **hair drier** der Föhn;
tumble drier der Wäschetrockner.

drill *noun* Bohrer der (PL die Bohrer).

drink *noun* Getränk das (PL die
Getränke) **1 to have a drink** etwas
trinken; **would you like a drink of
water?** möchtest du etwas Wasser
trinken?; **2** (*an alcoholic drink*)
Drink der (PL die Drinks); **they've
invited us round for drinks** sie
haben uns auf einen Drink
eingeladen; **let's have a drink!**
trinken wir einen! (*informal*).
drink *verb* trinken◇; **he drank a
glass of water** er trank ein Glas
Wasser.

drive *noun* **1 to go for a drive** eine
Autofahrt machen; **2** (*in front of a
house*) Einfahrt die (PL die
Einfahrten).
drive *verb* **1** fahren◇ (PERF *sein*);
she drives very fast sie fährt sehr
schnell; **to drive a car** Auto fahren;
I'd like to learn to drive ich möchte
Autofahren lernen; **can you drive?**
kannst du Auto fahren?; **2 we drove
to Berlin** wir sind mit dem Auto
nach Berlin gefahren; **3 to drive
somebody (to a place)** jemanden
(irgendwohin) fahren (PERF *haben*);
Mum drove me to the station Mutti
hat mich zum Bahnhof gefahren; **to
drive somebody home** jemanden
nach Hause fahren; ★ **she drives me
mad!** sie macht mich verrückt!

driver *noun* **1** Fahrer der (PL die
Fahrer), Fahrerin die (PL die
Fahrerinnen); **2** (*of a locomotive*)
Lokomotivführer der (PL die
Lokomotivführer),
Lokomotivführerin die (PL die
Lokomotivführerinnen).

driving instructor *noun*
Fahrlehrer der (PL die Fahrlehrer),
Fahrlehrerin die (PL die
Fahrlehrerinnen).

driving lesson *noun* Fahrstunde
die (PL die Fahrstunden).

driving licence *noun*
Führerschein der (PL die
Führerscheine).

driving test *noun* Fahrprüfung
die; **to take your driving test** die
Fahrprüfung machen; **Jenny's
passed her driving test** Jenny hat
die Fahrprüfung bestanden.

drop *noun* Tropfen der (PL die
Tropfen).
drop *verb* **1 to drop something**
etwas fallen lassen; **I dropped my
glasses** ich habe meine Brille fallen
lassen; **2 drop it!** lass das!; **3 I'm
going to drop history next year**
nächstes Jahr lege ich Geschichte
ab; **4** absetzen SEP (*a person*); **could
you drop me at the station?**
könntest du mich am Bahnhof
absetzen?

drought *noun* Dürre die (PL die
Dürren).

drown *verb* ertrinken ◇ (PERF *sein*);
she drowned in the lake sie
ertrank im See.

drug *noun* **1** (*medicine*) Medikament
das (PL die Medikamente); **2** (*illegal*)
drugs Drogen (*plural*).

a
b
c
d
e
f
g
h
i
j
k
l
m
n
o
p
q
r
s
t
u
v
w
x
y
z

drug abuse *noun*
Drogenmissbrauch *der*.

drug addict *noun*
Drogenabhängige *der/die* (PL *die*
Drogenabhängigen).

drug addiction *noun*
Drogenabhängigkeit *die*.

drum *noun* **1** Trommel *die* (PL *die*
Trommeln); **2 drums** *das*
Schlagzeug; **to play drums**
Schlagzeug spielen.

drummer *noun* Schlagzeuger *der*
(PL *die* Schlagzeuger),
Schlagerzeugerin *die* (PL *die*
Schlagzeugerinnen).

drunk *noun* Betrunkene *der/die* (PL
die Betrunkenen).
drunk *adjective* betrunken; **to get**
drunk sich betrinken✧.

dry *adjective* trocken.
dry *verb* **1** trocknen; **to let**
something dry etwas trocknen
lassen; **to dry your hair** sich (DAT)
die Haare trocknen; **to dry the**
washing die Wäsche trocknen; **2 to**
dry your hands sich (DAT) die
Hände abtrocknen SEP; **I dried my**
feet ich trocknete mir die Füße ab;
to dry the dishes das Geschirr
abtrocknen .

dry cleaner's *noun* chemische
Reinigung *die*.

dryer *noun* SEE **drier**.

dual carriageway *noun*
zweispurige Straße *die* (PL *die*
zweispurigen Straßen).

dubbed *adjective* **a dubbed film**
ein synchronisierter Film.

duck *noun* Ente *die* (PL *die* Enten).

due *adjective, adverb* **1 to be due to**
do something etwas tun müssen;
Paul's due back soon Paul muss
bald zurück sein; **we're due to**
leave on Thursday wir müssen
Donnerstag abfahren; **2 due to**
wegen (+ GEN); **due to bad weather**
wegen schlechten Wetters.

dull *adjective* **1 dull weather** trübes
Wetter; **it's a dull day today** heute ist
ein trüber Tag; **2** (*boring*) langweilig.

dumb *adjective* **1** stumm; **2** (*stupid*)
dumm; **he asked some dumb**
questions er hat ein paar dumme
Fragen gestellt.

dump *verb* **1** abladen✧ SEP
(*rubbish*); **2** (*put down*) hinwerfen✧
SEP; **he dumped it in the rubbish** er
hat es in den Müll geworfen;
3 abschieben✧ SEP (*a person*)
(*informal*); **she's dumped her**
boyfriend sie hat ihren Freund
abgeschoben.

dungarees *plural noun* Latzhose
die (PL *die* Latzhosen).

during *preposition* während (+ GEN);
during the night während der
Nacht; **I saw her during the**
holidays ich habe sie während der
Ferien gesehen.

dusk *noun* Dämmerung *die* (PL *die*
Dämmerungen); **at dusk** bei
Einbruch der Dunkelheit.

dust *noun* Staub *der*.
dust *verb* **1** abstauben SEP
(*furniture, objects*); **2** (*in a room*)
Staub wischen; **she's dusting** sie
wischt Staub.

dustbin *noun* Mülltonne *die* (PL *die* Mülltonnen).

dustman *noun* Müllmann *der* (PL *die* Müllmänner).

dusty *adjective* staubig.

Dutch *noun* **1** (*language*) Holländisch *das*; **2 the Dutch** (*people*) die Holländer.
Dutch *adjective* holländisch; **he's Dutch** er ist Holländer; **she's Dutch** sie ist Holländerin.

duty *noun* **1** Pflicht *die* (PL *die* Pflichten); **to have a duty to do something** die Pflicht haben, etwas zu tun; **you have a duty to inform us** du hast die Pflicht, uns zu benachrichtigen; **2 to be on duty** Dienst haben; **to be on night duty** Nachtdienst haben; **I'm off duty tonight** ich habe heute Abend keinen Dienst.

duty-free *adjective* zollfrei; **duty-free shop** *der* Dutyfreeshop; **duty-free goods** zollfreie Waren (*plural*).

duvet *noun* Bettdecke *die* (PL *die* Bettedecken).

duvet cover *noun* Bettbezug *der* (PL *die* Bettbezüge).

dye *noun* Färbemittel *das* (PL *die* Färbemittel).
dye *verb* färben; **to dye your hair** sich die Haare färben; **I'm going to dye my hair black** ich werde mir die Haare schwarz färben; **I'm going to have my hair dyed pink** ich lasse mir die Haare rosa färben.

dynamic *adjective* dynamisch.

dyslexia *noun* Legasthenie *die*.

dyslexic *adjective* legasthenisch; **to be dyslexic** Legastheniker sein, Legasthenikerin sein.

Ee

each *adjective, pronoun* **1** jeder/jede/jedes; **each Sunday** jeden Sonntag; **each time** jedes Mal; **at the beginning of each year** am Anfang jedes Jahres; **we each have an invitation** jeder von uns hat eine Einladung; **my sisters each have a computer** jede meiner Schwestern hat einen Computer; **she gave us an apple each** sie hat jedem von uns einen Apfel gegeben; **each of you** jeder von euch/jede von euch; **we each got a present** jeder Einzelne hat ein Geschenk bekommen; **2 the tickets cost ten pounds each** die Karten kosten je zehn Pfund; **£5 each** (*per person*) fünf Pfund pro Person, (*per item*) fünf Pfund pro Stück.

each other *pronoun* ('*each other*' *is usually translated using a reflexive pronoun*) **they love each other** sie lieben sich; **we know each other** wir kennen uns; **do you see each other often?** seht ihr euch oft?

eagle *noun* Adler *der* (PL *die* Adler).

ear *noun* Ohr *das* (PL *die* Ohren).

earache *noun* **to have earache** Ohrenschmerzen haben.

a
b
c
d
e
f
g
h
i
j
k
l
m
n
o
p
q
r
s
t
u
v
w
x
y
z

a
b
c
d
e
f
g
h
i
j
k
l
m
n
o
p
q
r
s
t
u
v
w
x
y
z

earlier *adverb* **1** (*a while ago*) vor kurzem; **your brother phoned earlier** dein Bruder hat vor kurzem angerufen; **2** (*not as late*) früher; **we should have started earlier** wir hätten früher anfangen sollen.

early *adverb* **1** (*in the morning*) früh; **to get up early** früh aufstehen; **it's too early** es ist zu früh; **2** (*for an appointment*) **to be early** (zu) früh dran sein; **we're early, the train doesn't leave until ten** wir sind früh dran, der Zug fährt erst um zehn Uhr ab.
early *adjective* **1** (*one of the first*) **in the early months** während der ersten Monate; **I'm getting the early train** ich nehme den früheren Zug; **2 to have an early lunch** früh zu Mittag essen; **Jan's having an early night** Jan geht früh zu Bett; **3 in the early afternoon** am frühen Nachmittag; **in the early hours** in den frühen Morgenstunden.

earn *verb* verdienen; **Richard earns five pounds an hour** Richard verdient fünf Pfund die Stunde.

earring *noun* Ohrring *der* (PL *die* Ohrringe).

earth *noun* Erde *die*; **life on earth** das Leben auf der Erde; ★ **what on earth are you doing?** was in aller Welt machst du da?

earthquake *noun* Erdbeben *das* (PL *die* Erdbeben).

easily *adverb* leicht; **he's easily the best** er ist mit Abstand der Beste.

east *noun* Osten *der*; **in the east** im Osten.
east *adjective, adverb* östlich, Ost-; **the east side** die Ostseite; **an east wind** ein Ostwind; **east of Munich** östlich von München.

Easter *noun* Ostern *das* (PL *die* Ostern); **they're coming at Easter** sie kommen zu Ostern; **Happy Easter** Frohe Ostern.

Easter Day *noun* Ostersonntag *der* (PL *die* Ostersonntage).

Easter egg *noun* Osterei *das* (PL *die* Ostereier).

Eastern Europe *noun* Osteuropa *das*.

easy *adjective* leicht; **it's easy!** das ist leicht!; **it was easy to decide** die Entscheidung fiel uns leicht.

eat *verb* **1** essen✧; **he was eating a banana** er aß eine Banane; **we're going to have something to eat** wir essen jetzt etwas; **2 to eat your breakfast** frühstücken.

EC *noun* EG *die* (*Europäische Gemeinschaft*).

echo *noun* Echo *das* (PL *die* Echos).
echo *verb* wiederholen.

ecological *adjective* ökologisch.

ecology *noun* Ökologie *die*.

economical *adjective* sparsam.

economics *noun* Wirtschaftswissenschaften (*plural*).

economy *noun* Wirtschaft *die*.

edge *noun* **1** Kante *die* (PL *die* Kanten); **the edge of the table** die Tischkante; **2** (*of a road, sheet of paper, or cliff*) Rand *der* (PL *die*

Ränder); **at the edge of the forest** am Waldrand.

edible *adjective* essbar.

edit *verb* redigieren.

editor *noun* **1** (*of a newspaper or magazine*) Chefredakteur *der* (PL *die* Chefredakteure), Chefredakteurin *die* (PL *die* Chefredakteurinnen); **2** (*of a book*) Redakteur *der* (PL *die* Redakteure), Redakteurin *die* (PL *die* Redakteurinnen).

educate *verb* erziehen✧.

education *noun* Ausbildung *die*.

effect *noun* **1** Wirkung *die* (PL *die* Wirkungen); **the effect of the explosion was horrific** die Wirkung der Explosion war entsetzlich; **2 to have an effect on something** eine Auswirkung auf etwas (ACC) haben; **it had a good effect on the whole family** es hatte eine gute Auswirkung auf die ganze Familie; **3** (*in a film*) Effekt *der* (PL *die* Effekte); **special effects** die Specialeffekte.

effective *adjective* effektiv.

efficient *adjective* **1** (*person*) tüchtig; **2** (*machine or organization*) leistungsfähig.

effort *noun* **1** Mühe *die* (PL *die* Mühen); **2 to make an effort** sich bemühen; **Toya made an effort to help us** Toya hat sich bemüht, uns zu helfen; **he didn't even make the effort to apologize** er hat sich nicht einmal die Mühe gemacht, sich zu entschuldigen.

e.g. *abbreviation* z.B. (*zum Beispiel*).

egg *noun* Ei *das* (PL *die* Eier); **a fried egg** ein Spiegelei; **a hard-boiled egg** ein hart gekochtes Ei.

egg-cup *noun* Eierbecher *der* (PL *die* Eierbecher).

eggshell *noun* Eierschale *die* (PL *die* Eierschalen).

egg-white *noun* Eiweiß *das* (PL *die* Eiweiße).

egg-yolk *noun* Eigelb *das* (PL *die* Eigelbe).

eight *number* acht; **Maya's eight** Maya ist acht; **at eight o'clock** um acht Uhr.

eighteen *number* achtzehn; **Jason's eighteen** Jason ist achtzehn.

eighth *number* achter/achte/ achtes; **on the eighth of July** am achten Juli.

eighty *number* achtzig; **eighty-five** fünfundachtzig.

either *pronoun* **1** (*one or the other*) einer von beiden/eine von beiden/ eins von beiden; **take either (of them)** nimm einen von beiden/eine von beiden/eins von beiden; **I don't like either (of them)** ich mag keinen von beiden/keine von beiden/keins von beiden; **2** (*both*) beide (*plural*); **either is possible** beide sind möglich; **on either side** auf beiden Seiten.

either *conjunction* **1 either … or** entweder … oder; **either Susie or Judy** entweder Susie oder Judy; **2** (*with a negative*) **either … or** weder … noch; **he didn't ring either Sam or Emma** er hat weder Sam noch Emma angerufen; **3 I don't know them either** ich kenne sie auch nicht.

elastic *noun* Gummiband *das* (PL *die* Gummibänder).

elastic band *noun* Gummiband *das* (PL *die* Gummibänder).

elbow *noun* Ellbogen *der* (PL *die* Ellbogen).

elder *adjective* älterer/ältere/älteres; **her elder brother** ihr älterer Bruder.

elderly *adjective* alt; **the elderly** ältere Menschen (*plural*).

eldest *adjective* ältester/älteste/ältestes; **her eldest brother** ihr ältester Bruder.

elect *verb* wählen; **she has been elected** sie ist gewählt worden.

election *noun* Wahl *die* (PL *die* Wahlen); **in the election** bei den Wahlen; **to call an election** allgemeine Wahlen ausrufen SEP.

electric *adjective* elektrisch.

electrical *adjective* elektrisch, Elektro-; **electrical equipment** Elektrogeräte (*plural*).

electrician *noun* Elektriker *der* (PL *die* Elektriker), Elektrikerin *die* (PL *die* Elektrikerinnen).

electricity *noun* Strom *der*.

electronic *adjective* elektronisch.

electronics *noun* Elektronik *die*.

elegant *adjective* elegant.

elephant *noun* Elefant *der* (PL *die* Elefanten).

eleven *number* elf; **Josh is eleven** Josh ist elf; **at eleven o'clock** um elf Uhr; **a football eleven** eine Fußballelf.

eleventh *number* elfter/elfte/elftes; **the eleventh of September** der elfte September; **on the eleventh floor** im elften Stock.

else *adverb* **1** (*in addition*) sonst; **who else?** wer sonst?; **did you see anyone else?** hast du sonst noch jemanden gesehen?; **nothing else** sonst nichts; **I don't want anything else** ich will sonst nichts; **2 would you like something else?** möchten Sie sonst noch etwas?; **3** (*instead or different*) anderer/andere/anderes; **somewhere else** irgendwo anders; **everyone else** alle anderen; **somebody else** jemand anders; **something else** etwas anderes; **4 or else** sonst; **hurry up, or else we'll be late** beeil dich, sonst kommen wir zu spät.

email *noun* E-Mail *die* (PL *die* E-Mails).

embarrassed *adjective* verlegen; **he was very embarrassed** er war ganz verlegen.

embarrassing *adjective* peinlich.

embassy *noun* Botschaft *die* (PL *die* Botschaften); **the German Embassy** die Deutsche Botschaft.

emergency exit *noun* Notausgang *der* (PL *die* Notausgänge).

emergency *noun* Notfall *der* (PL *die* Notfälle).

emotion *noun* Gefühl *das* (PL *die* Gefühle).

emotional *adjective* **1** (*person*) emotional; **2** (*speech or occasion*) emotionsgeladen.

emperor *noun* Kaiser *der* (PL *die* Kaiser).

emphasize *verb* betonen; **he emphasized that it was voluntary** er betonte, dass es freiwillig war.

empire *noun* Reich *das* (PL *die* Reiche); **the Roman Empire** das Römische Reich.

employ *verb* **1** (*have working for you*) beschäftigen; **2** (*take on a worker*) einstellen SEP.

employee *noun* Angestellte *der/die* (PL *die* Angestellten).

employer *noun* Arbeitgeber *der* (PL *die* Arbeitgeber), Arbeitgeberin *die* (PL *die* Arbeitgeberinnen).

employment *noun* Arbeit *die*.

empty *adjective* leer; **an empty bottle** eine leere Flasche.
empty *verb* **1** (*empty out*) ausleeren SEP; **2** (*pour*) schütten.

enclose *verb* (*in a letter*) beilegen SEP; **please find enclosed a cheque** ein Scheck liegt bei.

encourage *verb* ermutigen; **to encourage somebody to do something** jemanden (dazu) ermutigen, etwas zu tun; **Mum encouraged me to try again** Mutti hat mich dazu ermutigt, es noch einmal zu versuchen.

encouragement *noun* Ermutigung *die* (PL *die* Ermutigungen).

encouraging *adjective* ermutigend.

encyclopedia *noun* Lexikon *das* (PL *die* Lexika).

end *noun* **1** Ende *das* (PL *die* Enden); **'The End'** 'Ende'; **at the end of the film** am Ende des Films; **by the end of the lesson** als die Stunde zu Ende war; **in the end I went home** schließlich bin ich nach Hause gegangen; **Sally's coming at the end of June** Sally kommt Ende Juni; **I read to the end of the page** ich habe die Seite zu Ende gelesen; **hold the other end** halte das andere Ende fest; **at the end of the street** am Ende der Straße; **2** (*in sports*) Spielfeldhälfte *die* (PL *die* Spielfeldhälften); **to change ends** die Seiten wechseln.
end *verb* **1** (*to put an end to*) beenden; **they've ended the strike** sie haben den Streik beendet; **2** (*to come to an end*) enden; **the day ended with a meal** der Tag endete mit einem Essen.

● **to end up 1 to end up doing something** am Ende etwas tun; **we ended up taking a taxi** am Ende haben wir ein Taxi genommen; **2 to end up somewhere** irgendwo landen (PERF *sein*) (*informal*); **Rob ended up in Berlin** Rob landete schließlich in Berlin.

endangered *adjective* gefährdet; **an endangered species** eine von Aussterben bedrohte Art.

ending *noun* **1** Ende *das* (PL *die* Enden); **2** (*in grammar*) Endung *die* (PL *die* Endungen).

a b c d e f g h i j k l m n o p q r s t u v w x y z

a
b
c
d
e
f
g
h
i
j
k
l
m
n
o
p
q
r
s
t
u
v
w
x
y
z

endless *adjective* endlos (*day or journey, for example*).

enemy *noun* Feind *der* (PL *die* Feinde); **to make enemies** sich (DAT) Feinde machen.

energetic *adjective* energiegeladen.

energy *noun* Energie *die*.

engaged *adjective* **1** (*to be married*) verlobt; **they're engaged** sie sind verlobt; **to get engaged** sich verloben; **2** (*a phone or toilet*) besetzt; **it's engaged, I'll ring later** es ist besetzt, ich rufe später an.

engagement *noun* (*to marry*) Verlobung *die* (PL *die* Verlobungen).

engagement ring *noun* Verlobungsring *der* (PL *die* Verlobungsringe).

engine *noun* **1** (*in a car*) Motor *der* (PL *die* Motoren); **2** (*pulling a train*) Lokomotive *die* (PL *die* Lokomotiven).

engineer *noun* **1** (*who comes for repairs*) Techniker *der* (PL *die* Techniker), Technikerin *die* (PL *die* Technikerinnen); **2** (*who builds roads and bridges*) Ingenieur *der* (PL *die* Ingenieure), Ingenieurin *die* (PL *die* Ingenieurinnen).

England *noun* England *das*; **I'm from England** ich bin Engländer, ich bin Engländerin.

English *noun* **1** (*the language*) Englisch *das*; **do you speak English?** sprechen Sie Englisch?; **he answered in English** er hat auf Englisch geantwortet; **2** (*the people*) **the English** die Engländer.
English *adjective* **1** (*of or from England*) englisch; **the English team** die englische Mannschaft; **he's English** er ist Engländer; **she's English** sie ist Engländerin; **2 an English lesson** eine Englischstunde; **our English teacher** unser Englischlehrer, unsere Englischlehrerin.

English Channel *noun* **the English Channel** der Ärmelkanal.

Englishman *noun* Engländer *der* (PL *die* Engländer).

Englishwoman *noun* Engländerin *die* (PL *die* Engländerinnen).

enjoy *verb* **1 did you enjoy the party?** hat dir die Party gefallen?; **we really enjoyed the concert** das Konzert hat uns wirklich gut gefallen; **2 to enjoy doing something** etwas gerne tun◇; **I enjoy reading** ich lese gerne; **do you enjoy living in York?** wohnst du gerne in York?; **3 to enjoy oneself** sich gut amüsieren; **we really enjoyed ourselves** wir haben uns richtig gut amüsiert; **enjoy yourselves!** viel Vergnügen!; **did you enjoy yourself?** hast du dich gut amüsiert?

enjoyable *adjective* nett.

enormous *adjective* riesig.

enough *adverb, adjective, pronoun* **1** genug; **there's enough for everyone** es gibt genug für alle; **big enough** groß genug; **have we got enough bread?** haben wir genug Brot?; **2 that's enough** das reicht.

412

enquire *verb* **to enquire about** sich erkundigen nach (+ DAT); **I'm going to enquire about the trains** ich werde mich nach den Zügen erkundigen.

enrol *verb* sich anmelden SEP; **I want to enrol on the course** ich möchte mich zu dem Kurs anmelden.

enter *verb* **1** (*to go inside*) gehen◇PERF *sein*) in (+ ACC) (*a room or a building*); **we all entered the church** wir gingen alle in die Kirche hinein; **2** (*in computing*) eingeben◇ SEP; **3 to enter for** sich anmelden SEP zu (+ DAT) (*an exam or a race*); **to enter for a competition** an einem Preisausschreiben teilnehmen◇ SEP.

entertain *verb* **1** (*to keep amused*) unterhalten◇; **2** (*to have people round*) Gäste haben◇; **they don't entertain much** sie haben selten Gäste.

entertainment *noun* (*fun*) Unterhaltung *die*; **there wasn't much entertainment in the evenings** abends war wenig Unterhaltung geboten.

enthusiasm *noun* Begeisterung *die*.

enthusiast *noun* **1** Enthusiast *der* (PL *die* Enthusiasten), Enthusiastin *die* (PL *die* Enthusiastinnen); **2** (*for sports*) Fan *der* (PL *die* Fans); **he's a rugby enthusiast** er ist ein Rugbyfan.

enthusiastic *adjective* begeistert.

entire *adjective* ganz; **the entire class** die ganze Klasse.

entirely *adverb* ganz.

entrance *noun* **1** (*fee*) Eintritt *der*; **2** (*way in*) Eingang *der* (PL *die* Eingänge).

entry *noun* **1** (*way in*) Eingang *der* (PL *die* Eingänge), (*for cars*) Einfahrt *die* (PL *die* Einfahrten); **2 'no entry'** 'Zutritt verboten', (*to cars*) 'Einfahrt verboten'.

entry phone *noun* Sprechanlage *die* (PL *die* Sprechanlagen).

envelope *noun* Briefumschlag *der* (PL *die* Briefumschläge).

environment *noun* Umwelt *die*.

environmental *adjective* Umwelt-; **environmental pollution** die Umweltverschmutzung.

environment-friendly *adjective* umweltfreundlich.

epidemic *noun* Epidemie *die* (PL *die* Epidemien).

epileptic *adjective* epileptisch.

episode *noun* **1** (*an event*) Episode *die* (PL *die* Episoden); **2** (*on TV or radio*) Folge *die* (PL *die* Folgen).

equal *adjective* gleich; **milk and water in equal quantities** gleich viel Milch und Wasser.
equal *verb* gleichen◇ (+ DAT).

equality *noun* Gleichberechtigung *die*.

equalize *verb* ausgleichen ◇ SEP; **they equalized in the last minute** sie haben in der letzten Minute ausgeglichen.

equally *adverb* (*to share*) gleichmäßig; **we divided it equally** wir haben es gleichmäßig verteilt.

a b c d e f g h i j k l m n o p q r s t u v w x y z

413

equator *noun* Äquator *der*.

equip *verb* ausrüsten SEP; **well equipped for the hike** für die Wanderung gut ausgerüstet; **equipped with rucksacks** mit Rucksäcken ausgerüstet.

equipment *noun* **1** (*for sport*) Ausrüstung *die* (PL *die* Ausrüstungen); **2** Ausstattung *die* (PL *die* Ausstattungen); **laboratory equipment** *die* Laborausstattung; **3** (*something needed for an activity*) Geräte (*plural*); **recording equipment** Aufnahmegeräte.

equivalent *adjective* gleichwertig; **to be equivalent to** etwas (DAT) entsprechen; **1 litre is equivalent to about 1.75 pints** ein Liter entspricht ungefähr 1,75 Pints.

error *noun* **1** (*in spelling, typing, on a computer, or in maths*) Fehler *der* (PL *die* Fehler); **spelling error** *der* Rechtschreibfehler; **2** (*wrong opinion*) Irrtum *der* (PL *die* Irrtümer).

error message *noun* Fehlermeldung *die* (PL *die* Fehlermeldungen).

escalator *noun* Rolltreppe *die* (PL *die* Rolltreppen).

escape *noun* (*from prison*) Ausbruch *der* (PL *die* Ausbrüche). **escape** *verb* **1** (*from prison*) ausbrechen◇ SEP (PERF *sein*); **2** entkommen◇ (PERF *sein*); **to escape from somebody** jemandem entkommen.

especially *adverb* besonders.

essay *noun* Aufsatz *der* (PL *die* Aufsätze); **an essay on German reunification** ein Aufsatz über die deutsche Wiedervereinigung.

essential *adjective* unbedingt erforderlich; **it's essential to reply quickly** es ist unbedingt erforderlich, sofort zu antworten.

estate *noun* **1** (*a housing estate*) Wohnsiedlung *die* (PL *die* Wohnsiedlungen); **2** (*a big house and grounds*) Landsitz *der* (PL *die* Landsitze).

estate agent *noun* Immobilienmakler *der* (PL *die* Immobilienmakler), Immobilienmaklerin *die* (PL *die* Immobilienmaklerinnen).

estate car *noun* Kombiwagen *der* (PL *die* Kombiwagen).

estimate *noun* **1** (*a quote for work*) Kostenvoranschlag *der* (PL *die* Kostenvoranschläge); **2** (*a rough guess*) Schätzung *die* (PL *die* Schätzungen). **estimate** *verb* schätzen.

etc. *abbreviation* usw. (*und so weiter*).

ethnic *adjective* ethnisch; **an ethnic minority** eine ethnische Minderheit.

EU *noun* EU *die* (*Europäische Union*).

euro *noun* Euro *der* (PL *die* Euros); **the euro is divided into 100 cents** ein Euro hat 100 Cent.

Europe *noun* Europa *das*.

European *noun* Europäer *der* (PL *die* Europäer), Europäerin *die* (PL *die*

Europäerinnen).

European *adjective* europäisch.

European Union *noun*
Europäische Union *die*.

eurozone *noun* Euroland *das*

even[1] *adverb* **1** sogar; **even Lisa is coming** sogar Lisa kommt; **2 not even** nicht einmal; **I don't like animals, not even dogs** ich mag keine Tiere, nicht einmal Hunde; **3 without even asking** ohne wenigstens zu fragen; **4 even if** selbst wenn; **even if they arrive late** selbst wenn sie spät ankommen; **5** (*with a comparison*) (sogar) noch; **even bigger** sogar noch größer; **even faster** noch schneller; **even better than** sogar noch besser als; **the song is even better than their last one** das Lied ist sogar noch besser als ihr letztes; **6 even so** trotzdem; **even so, we had a good time** trotzdem haben wir uns gut amüsiert.

even[2] *adjective* **1** (*surface or layer*) eben; **2** (*number*) gerade; **six is an even number** sechs ist eine gerade Zahl; **3** (*equal*) gleich (*distance, value*); **the score is even** die Punktzahl ist gleich; **4 to get even with somebody** es jemandem heimzahlen.

evening *noun* **1** Abend *der* (PL *die* Abende); **in the evening** am Abend; **this evening** heute Abend; **tomorrow evening** morgen Abend; **on Monday evening** am Montagabend; **every Thursday evening** jeden Donnerstagabend; **the evening before** am Abend

zuvor; **the evening meal** das Abendessen; **2 at six o'clock in the evening** um sechs Uhr abends; **the other evening** neulich abends; **I work in the evening(s)** ich arbeite abends.

evening class *noun* Abendkurs *der* (PL *die* Abendkurse).

event *noun* **1** (*a happening*) Ereignis *das* (PL *die* Ereignisse); **2** (*in athletics*) Disziplin *die* (PL *die* Disziplinen).

eventually *adverb* schließlich.

ever *adverb* **1** (*at any time*) je; **have you ever noticed that?** hast du das je bemerkt?; **more than ever** mehr denn je; **colder than ever** kälter denn je; **he drove more slowly than ever** er fuhr langsamer als je zuvor; **2 not ever** nie; **nobody ever came** es kam nie jemand; **hardly ever** fast nie; **3** (*always*) immer; **as cheerful as ever** so vergnügt wie immer; **the same as ever** so wie immer; **4 ever since** seitdem; **and it's been raining ever since** und seitdem regnet es.

every *adjective* **1** jeder/jede/jedes; **every house has a garden** jedes Haus hat einen Garten; **every day** jeden Tag; **every Monday** jeden Montag; **every time** jedes Mal; **2 every few days** alle paar Tage; **every ten kilometres** alle zehn Kilometer; **3 every one** jeder Einzelne/jede Einzelne/jedes Einzelne; **I've seen every one of his films** ich habe jeden Einzelnen seiner Filme gesehen; **4 every now and then** ab und zu.

a
b
c
d
e
f
g
h
i
j
k
l
m
n
o
p
q
r
s
t
u
v
w
x
y
z

a
b
c
d
e
f
g
h
i
j
k
l
m
n
o
p
q
r
s
t
u
v
w
x
y
z

everybody, everyone *pronoun*
1 alle (*plural*); **everybody knows that** ... alle wissen, dass ...; **everyone else** alle anderen; **2** (*each one*) jeder; **not everybody can afford it** das kann sich nicht jeder leisten.

everything *pronoun* alles; **everything is ready** es ist alles fertig; **everything's fine** es ist alles okay (*informal*); **everything else** alles andere; **he gets everything he wants** er bekommt alles, was er will.

everywhere *adverb* **1** überall; **there was dirt everywhere** überall war Dreck; **she went everywhere** sie ist überall hingegangen; **everywhere else** sonst überall; **2 everywhere she went** wohin sie auch ging.

evidently *adverb* offensichtlich.

evil *noun* Böse *das*.
evil *adjective* böse.

exact *adjective* genau; **the exact fare** das genaue Fahrgeld; **it's the exact opposite** das ist das genaue Gegenteil.

exactly *adverb* genau; **they're exactly the right age** sie sind genau im richtigen Alter; **yes, exactly!** ja, genau!

exaggerate *verb* übertreiben◇.

exaggeration *noun* Übertreibung *die* (PL *die* Übertreibungen).

exam *noun* Prüfung *die* (PL *die* Prüfungen); **history exam** *die* Geschichtsprüfung; **to sit an exam** eine Prüfung machen; **to pass an**

exam eine Prüfung bestehen; **to fail an exam** durch eine Prüfung fallen.

examination *noun* Prüfung *die* (PL *die* Prüfungen).

examine *verb* **1** (*at school or university*) prüfen; **2** (*at the doctor's*) untersuchen.

examiner *noun* Prüfer *der* (PL *die* Prüfer), Prüferin *die* (PL *die* Prüferinnen).

example *noun* Beispiel *das* (PL *die* Beispiele); **for example** zum Beispiel; **to set a good example** ein gutes Beispiel geben.

excellent *adjective* ausgezeichnet.

except *preposition* **1** außer (+ DAT); **every day except Tuesday** täglich außer Dienstag; **we play except when it rains** wir spielen, außer wenn es regnet; **except in March** außer März; **2 except for** außer (+ DAT); **except for the children** außer den Kindern.

exception *noun* Ausnahme *die* (PL *die* Ausnahmen); **without exception** ohne Ausnahme; **with the exception of** mit Ausnahme von (+ DAT).

exchange *noun* **1** Austausch *der*; **the students are coming to London on an exchange** die Schüler kommen auf einen Schüleraustausch nach London; **exchange student** *der* Austauschstudent, *die* Austauschstudentin; **an exchange of pupils** ein Schüleraustausch; **2 in exchange for his help** für seine Hilfe.

exchange *verb* umtauschen SEP;

can I exchange this shirt for a smaller one? kann ich dieses Hemd gegen ein kleineres umtauschen?

exchange rate *noun* Wechselkurs der (PL die Wechselkurse).

excite *verb* **1** (*thrill*) begeistern; **2** (*agitate*) aufregen SEP.

excited *adjective* **1** aufgeregt; **the children are excited** die Kinder sind aufgeregt; **the dogs get excited when they hear the car** die Hunde geraten in Aufregung, wenn sie das Auto hören; **2** (*annoyed or angry*) **to get excited** sich aufregen SEP.

exciting *adjective* aufregend; **a very exciting film** ein sehr aufregender Film.

exclamation mark *noun* Ausrufezeichen das (PL die Ausrufezeichen).

excursion *noun* Ausflug der (PL die Ausflüge).

excuse *noun* Entschuldigung die (PL die Entschuldigungen). **excuse** *verb* (*apologizing*) **excuse me!** Entschuldigung!

exercise *noun* **1** Übung die (PL die Übungen); **a maths exercise** eine Matheübung; **2 physical exercise** körperliche Bewegung; **to get exercise** sich Bewegung verschaffen.

exercise bike *noun* Heimtrainer der (PL die Heimtrainer).

exercise book *noun* Heft das (PL die Hefte); **my German exercise book** mein Deutschheft.

exhaust (pipe) *noun* Auspuff der (PL die Auspuffe).

exhaust fumes *noun* Abgase die (*plural*).

exhausted *adjective* erschöpft.

exhibition *noun* Ausstellung die (PL die Ausstellungen); **the Dürer exhibition** die Dürer-Ausstellung.

exist *verb* existieren.

exit *noun* **1** Ausgang der (PL die Ausgänge); **2** (*from a motorway*) Ausfahrt die (PL die Ausfahrten).

expect *verb* **1** erwarten (*guests or a baby*); **we're expecting thirty visitors** wir erwarten dreißig Besucher; **2** (*require something*) **to expect somebody to do something** von jemandem erwarten, dass er etwas tut; **3** rechnen mit (+ DAT) (*something to happen*); **I didn't expect that** damit habe ich nicht gerechnet; **I didn't expect it at all** damit habe ich überhaupt nicht gerechnet; **4** (*suppose*) glauben; **I expect she'll bring her boyfriend** ich glaube, sie bringt ihren Freund mit; **yes, I expect so** ich glaube ja.

expedition *noun* Expedition die (PL die Expeditionen).

expel *verb* **to be expelled** (*from school*) von der Schule verwiesen werden.

expensive *adjective* teuer; **those shoes are too expensive for me** diese Schuhe sind mir zu teuer; **the most expensive CDs** die teuersten CDs.

417

a
b
c
d
e
f
g
h
i
j
k
l
m
n
o
p
q
r
s
t
u
v
w
x
y
z

experience *noun* **1** Erfahrung *die* (PL *die* Erfahrungen); **2** (*an event*) Erlebnis *das* (PL *die* Erlebnisse).

experienced *adjective* erfahren.

experiment *noun* Experiment *das* (PL *die* Experimente); **to do an experiment** ein Experiment machen.

expert *noun* Experte *der* (PL *die* Experten), Expertin *die* (PL *die* Expertinnen); **he's a computer expert** er ist ein Computerexperte.

expire *verb* ablaufen✧ SEP (PERF *sein*).

expiry date *noun* Verfallsdatum *das* (PL *die* Verfallsdaten).

explain *verb* erklären.

explanation *noun* Erklärung *die* (PL *die* Erklärungen).

explode *verb* explodieren (PERF *sein*).

explore *verb* erforschen.

explosion *noun* Explosion *die* (PL *die* Explosionen).

export *noun* Export *der* (PL *die* Exporte); **the chief export is wool** das wichtigste Exportgut ist Wolle.
export *verb* exportieren; **Russia exports a lot of oil and timber** Russland exportiert viel Öl und Holz.

exposure *noun* (*of a film*) Belichtung *die*; **a 24-exposure film** ein Film mit 24 Aufnahmen.

express *noun* (*train*) Schnellzug *der* (PL *die* Schnellzüge).
express *verb* **1** ausdrücken SEP;

2 to express yourself sich ausdrücken.

expression *noun* Ausdruck *der* (PL *die* Ausdrücke).

extend *verb* **1** verlängern; **2** ausbauen SEP (*a house*).

extension *noun* **1** (*to a house*) Anbau *der* (PL *die* Anbauten); **2** (*telephone*) Apparat *der* (PL *die* Apparate); **can I have extension 2347 please?** bitte verbinden Sie mich mit Apparat 2347 (*note that in spoken German telephone numbers are usually broken down into groups of two figures*); **3** (*electrical*) Verlängerung *die* (PL *die* Verlängerungen).

extension number *noun* Apparatnummer *die* (PL *die* Apparatnummern).

exterior *adjective* äußerer/äußere/ äußeres.

extinct *adjective* **1** (*animal*) ausgestorben; **2** (*volcano*) erloschen.

extinguish *verb* **1** löschen (*a fire*); **2 to extinguish a cigarette** eine Zigarette ausmachen SEP.

extinguisher *noun* Feuerlöscher *der* (PL *die* Feuerlöscher).

extra *adjective* **1** zusätzlich, extra (*informal*) (*extra never has an ending*); **extra homework** zusätzliche Hausaufgaben; **wine is extra** Wein kostet extra; **you have to pay extra** das wird extra berechnet; **2 at no extra charge** ohne Aufschlag.

extra *adverb* **1** besonders; **he was**

extra careful er war besonders vorsichtig; **2 extra large** extragroß.

extraordinary *adjective* außerordentlich.

extra time *noun* (*in football*) Verlängerung *die* (PL *die* Verlängerungen); **to go into extra time** in die Verlängerung gehen.

extravagant *adjective* verschwenderisch (*person*).

extreme *noun* Extrem *das* (PL *die* Extreme); **to go from one extreme to another** von einem Extrem ins andere fallen.
extreme *adjective* extrem.

extremely *adverb* äußerst; **extremely fast** äußerst schnell.

eye *noun* Auge *das* (PL *die* Augen); **a girl with blue eyes** ein Mädchen mit blauen Augen; **shut your eyes!** mach die Augen zu!; ★**to keep an eye on something** auf etwas (ACC) aufpassen SEP.

eyebrow *noun* Augenbraue *die* (PL *die* Augenbrauen).

eyelash *noun* Augenwimper *die* (PL *die* Augenwimpern).

eyelid *noun* Augenlid *das* (PL *die* Augenlider).

eyeliner *noun* Eyeliner *der* (PL *die* Eyeliner).

eye shadow *noun* Lidschatten *der* (PL *die* Lidschatten).

eyesight *noun* **to have good eyesight** gute Augen haben; **to have bad eyesight** schlechte Augen haben.

Ff

fabric *noun* (*cloth*) Stoff *der* (PL *die* Stoffe).

fabulous *adjective* phantastisch.

face *noun* **1** (*of a person*) Gesicht *das* (PL *die* Gesichter); **to pull a face** eine Grimasse schneiden; **2** (*of a clock or watch*) Zifferblatt *das* (PL *die* Zifferblätter).
face *verb* **1** gegenüberstehen◇ SEP (PERF *sein*) (+ DAT); **she was facing him** sie stand ihm gegenüber; **2 the house faces the park** das Haus befindet sich gegenüber dem Park; **3** (*to stand the idea of*) verkraften; **I can't face going back** ich bringe es nicht über mich zurückzugehen; **4 to face up to something** sich etwas (DAT) stellen.

facilities *plural noun* **1 the school has good sports facilities** die Schule hat gute Sportanlagen; **2 the flat has no cooking facilities** die Wohnung hat keine Kochgelegenheit.

fact *noun* Tatsache *die* (PL *die* Tatsachen); **the fact is that ...** Tatsache ist, dass ...; **in fact** tatsächlich; **is that a fact?** Tatsache?

factory *noun* Fabrik *die* (PL *die* Fabriken).

fade *verb* **1** (*fabric*) ausbleichen◇SEP (PERF *sein*); **faded jeans** ausgeblichene Jeans; **2** (*a colour or memory*) verblassen (PERF *sein*); **the colours have faded** die Farben sind verblasst.

a
b
c
d
e
f
g
h
i
j
k
l
m
n
o
p
q
r
s
t
u
v
w
x
y
z

fail *verb* **1** nicht bestehen◇ (*a test or an exam*); **I failed my driving test** ich habe meine Fahrprüfung nicht bestanden; **2** (*in a test or an exam*) durchfallen◇ SEP (PERF *sein*); **three students failed** drei Studenten sind durchgefallen; **3 to fail to do something** etwas nicht tun; **he failed to inform us** er hat uns nicht benachrichtigt; ⋆**without fail** auf jeden Fall;; **ring me without fail** ruf mich auf jeden Fall an.

failure *noun* **1** Misserfolg *der* (PL *die* Misserfolge); **it was a terrible failure** es war ein schrecklicher Misserfolg; **2** (*of equipment*) Ausfall *der* (PL *die* Ausfälle); **a power failure** ein Stromausfall.

faint *adjective* **1** (*slight*) leicht; **a faint smell of gas** ein leichter Gasgeruch; **I haven't the faintest idea** ich habe nicht die blasseste Ahnung (*informal*); **2** (*voice or sound*) leise.
faint *verb* ohnmächtig werden; **Lisa fainted** Lisa wurde ohnmächtig.

fair *noun* Jahrmarkt *der* (PL *die* Jahrmärkte).
fair *adjective* **1** (*not unfair*) gerecht; **2** (*hair*) blond; **he's fair-haired** er ist blond; **3** (*skin*) hell; **fair-skinned** hellhäutig; **4** (*fairly good*) ganz gut (*chance, condition, or performance*); **5** (*weather*) schön; **if it's fair tomorrow** wenn es morgen schön ist.

fairground *noun* Jahrmarkt *der* (PL *die* Jahrmärkte).

fairly *adverb* (*quite*) ziemlich.

fairy *noun* Fee *die* (PL *die* Feen).

fairy tale *noun* Märchen *das* (PL *die* Märchen).

faith *noun* **1** (*trust*) Vertrauen *das*; **to have faith in somebody** Vertrauen zu jemandem haben; **2** (*religious belief*) Glaube *der* (PL *die* Glauben).

faithful *adjective* treu; **to be faithful to somebody** jemandem treu sein.

faithfully *adverb* **Yours faithfully** Hochachtungsvoll.

fake *noun* **1** Imitation *die* (PL *die* Imitationen); **the diamonds were fakes** die Brillanten waren eine Imitation; **2** (*a painting or money*) Fälschung *die* (PL *die* Fälschungen).
fake *adjective* gefälscht; **a fake passport** ein gefälschter Pass.

fall *noun* Fall *der* (PL *die* Fälle); **to have a fall** stürzen (PERF *sein*).
fall *verb* **1** fallen◇ (PERF *sein*); **mind, you'll fall** pass auf, dass du nicht hinfällst; **Tony fell off his bike** Tony ist vom Rad gefallen; **she fell down the stairs** sie ist die Treppe hinuntergefallen; **2** (*of temperature, prices*) sinken◇ (PERF *sein*).

false *adjective* falsch; **a false alarm** ein falscher Alarm.

fame *noun* Ruhm *der*.

familiar *adjective* bekannt; **his face is familiar** sein Gesicht kommt mir bekannt vor.

family *noun* Familie *die* (PL *die* Familien); **a family of six** eine sechsköpfige Familie; **Ben's one of the family** Ben gehört zur Familie; **the Morris family** Familie Morris.

famous *adjective* berühmt.

fan *noun* **1** (*a supporter*) Fan *der* (PL *die* Fans); **Will's a Chelsea fan** Will ist ein Fan von Chelsea; **2** (*electric, for cooling*) Ventilator *der* (PL *die* Ventilatoren); **3** (*hand-held*) Fächer *der* (PL *die* Fächer).

fanatic *noun* Fanatiker *der* (PL *die* Fanatiker), Fanatikerin *die* (PL *die* Fanatikerinnen).

fancy *noun* **to take somebody's fancy** jemandem gefallen◇; **the picture took his fancy** das Bild hat es ihm angetan.
fancy *adjective* (*equipment*) ausgefallen.
fancy *verb* **1** (*to want*) **(do you) fancy a coffee?** hast du Lust auf einen Kaffee?; **do you fancy going to the cinema?** hast du Lust, ins Kino zu gehen?; **2 I really fancy him** ich stehe total auf ihn; **3 (just) fancy that!** stell dir vor!; **fancy you being here!** na so was, dich hier zu treffen!

fancy dress *noun* **in fancy dress** verkleidet; **fancy-dress party** *das* Kostümfest.

fantastic *adjective* fantastisch; **really? that's fantastic!** wirklich? das ist ja fantastisch!; **a fantastic holiday** fantastische Ferien.

far *adverb, adjective* **1** weit; **it's not far** es ist nicht weit; **is it far to Carlisle?** ist es weit nach Carlisle?; **how far is it to Bristol?** wie weit ist es bis nach Bristol?; **2 he took us as far as Newport** er hat uns bis Newport mitgenommen; **3 by far** bei weitem; **the prettiest by far** bei weitem das hübscheste; **4** (*much*)

viel; **far better** viel besser; **far faster** viel schneller; **far too many people** viel zu viele Leute; **5 so far** bis jetzt; **so far everything's going well** bis jetzt läuft alles gut; **6 as far as I know** soweit ich weiß.

fare *noun* **1** (*on a bus, train, or the underground*) Fahrpreis *der* (PL *die* Fahrpreise); **2** (*on a plane*) Flugpreis *der* (PL *die* Flugpreise); **half fare** *der* halbe Fahrpreis; **full fare** *der* volle Fahrpreis.

Far East *noun* der Ferne Osten, Fernost *das*

farm *noun* Bauernhof *der* (PL *die* Bauernhöfe).

farmer *noun* Bauer *der* (PL *die* Bauern), Bäuerin *die* (PL *die* Bäuerinnen).

farming *noun* Landwirtschaft *die*.

fascinating *adjective* faszinierend.

fashion *noun* Mode *die* (PL *die* Moden); **in fashion** in Mode; **to go out of fashion** aus der Mode kommen.

fashionable *adjective* modisch.

fashion model *noun* Mannequin *das* (PL *die* Mannequins).

fashion show *noun* Modenschau *die* (PL *die* Modenschauen).

fast *adjective* **1** schnell; **a fast car** ein schnelles Auto; **2** (*of a clock or watch*) **to be fast** vorgehen◇ SEP (PERF *sein*); **my watch is fast** meine Uhr geht vor; **you're ten minutes fast** deine Uhr geht zehn Minuten vor.
fast *adverb* **1** schnell; **he swims**

fast er schwimmt schnell; **2 to be fast asleep** fest schlafen.

fast food *noun* Fastfood *das*.

fast forward *noun* Vorlauf *der*.

fat *noun* Fett *das* (PL die Fette). **fat** *adjective* **1** (*meat*) fett; **2** (*person*) dick, fett (*informal*); **a fat man** ein dicker Mann; **to get fat** fett werden (*informal*).

fatal *adjective* tödlich.

father *noun* Vater *der* (PL die Väter); **my father's office** das Büro von meinem Vater.

Father Christmas *noun* der Weihnachtsmann.

father-in-law *noun* Schwiegervater *der* (PL die Schwiegerväter).

fault *noun* **1** (*when you are responsible*) Schuld *die*; **it's Stephen's fault** Stephen ist schuld; **it's not my fault** es ist nicht meine Schuld; **2** (*in tennis*) **double fault** *der* Doppelfehler.

favour *noun* **1** (*a kindness*) Gefallen *der* (PL die Gefallen); **to do somebody a favour** jemandem einen Gefallen tun; **can you do me a favour?** kannst du mir einen Gefallen tun?; **to ask a favour of somebody** jemanden um einen Gefallen bitten; **2 to be in favour of something** für etwas (ACC) sein.

favourite *adjective* Lieblings-; **my favourite band** meine Lieblingsband.

fax *noun* Fax *das* (PL die Faxe). **fax** *verb* faxen.

fear *noun* Angst *die* (PL die Ängste). **fear** *verb* fürchten.

feather *noun* Feder *die* (PL die Federn).

feature *noun* **1** (*of your face*) Gesichtszug *der* (PL die Gesichtszüge); **to have delicate features** feine Gesichtszüge haben; **2** (*of a car or a machine*) Merkmal *das* (PL die Merkmale).

February *noun* Februar *der*; **in February** im Februar.

fed up *adjective* **1 I'm fed up** ich habe die Nase voll (*informal*); **he's fed up with her** er hat die Nase voll von ihr; **2 to be fed up with something** etwas (ACC) satt haben (*informal*); **I'm fed up with working every day** ich habe es satt, jeden Tag zu arbeiten.

feed *verb* füttern; **have you fed the dog?** hast du den Hund gefüttert?

feel *verb* **1** sich fühlen; **I don't feel well** ich fühle mich nicht gut; **2** spüren; **I didn't feel a thing** ich habe nichts gespürt; **3 I feel tired** ich bin müde; **I feel cold** mir ist kalt; **4 to feel afraid** Angst haben; **to feel thirsty** Durst haben; **5 to feel like doing something** Lust haben, etwas zu tun; **I feel like going to the cinema** ich habe Lust, ins Kino zu gehen; **6** (*touch*) fühlen; **7** (*to the touch*) sich anfühlen SEP; **to feel soft** sich weich anfühlen.

feeling *noun* **1** Gefühl *das* (PL die Gefühle); **to show your feelings** seine Gefühle zeigen; **a dizzy feeling** ein Schwindelgefühl; **I have the feeling James doesn't like me**

a
b
c
d
e
f
g
h
i
j
k
l
m
n
o
p
q
r
s
t
u
v
w
x
y
z

ich habe das Gefühl, dass James mich nicht mag; **2 to hurt somebody's feelings** jemanden verletzen.

felt-tip (pen) *noun* Filzstift *der* (PL die Filzstifte).

female *noun* (*animal*) Weibchen *das* (PL die Weibchen).
female *adjective* weiblich.

feminine *adjective* weiblich.

feminist *noun* Feministin *die* (PL die Feministinnen), Feminist *der* (PL die Feministen).
feminist *adjective* feministisch.

fence *noun* Zaun *der* (PL die Zäune).

ferry *noun* Fähre *die* (PL die Fähren).

fertilizer *noun* Dünger *der*.

festival *noun* (*of films, art, or music*) Festspiele (*plural*).

fetch *verb* **1** (*collect*) abholen SEP; **Tom's fetching the children** Tom holt die Kinder ab; **2** holen; **fetch me the other knife** hol mir das andere Messer.

fever *noun* Fieber *das*.

few *adjective, pronoun* **1** wenige; **few people know that** ... wenige Leute wissen, dass ...; **2 a few** (*several*) ein paar (*ein paar never changes*); **a few weeks** ein paar Wochen; **in a few minutes** in ein paar Minuten; **have you got any tomatoes? we want a few for the salad** haben Sie Tomaten? wir brauchen ein paar für den Salat; **3 quite a few** eine ganze Menge; **there were quite a few questions** es gab eine ganze Menge Fragen.

fewer *adjective* weniger; **there are fewer mosquitoes this year** dieses Jahr gibt es weniger Mücken.

fiancé *noun* Verlobte *der* (PL die Verlobten).

fiancée *noun* Verlobte *die* (PL die Verlobten).

field *noun* **1** (*with grass or crops*) Feld *das* (PL die Felder); **a field of wheat** ein Kornfeld; **2** (*for sport*) Spielfeld *das* (PL die Spielfelder).

fierce *adjective* **1** wild (*animal or person*); **2** heftig (*storm or battle*).

fifteen *number* fünfzehn.

fifth *number* fünfter/fünfte/fünftes; **the fifth of January** der fünfte Januar; **on the fifth floor** im fünften Stock.

fifty *number* fünfzig.

fig *noun* Feige *die* (PL die Feigen).

fight *noun* **1** (*a scuffle*) Schlägerei *die* (PL die Schlägereien); **2** (*in boxing or against illness*) Kampf *der* (PL die Kämpfe).
fight *verb* **1** (*to have a fight*) sich prügeln; **they were fighting** sie haben sich geprügelt; **2** (*to quarrel*) sich streiten◇; **they're always fighting** sie streiten sich immer; **3** (*struggle against*) kämpfen gegen (+ ACC) (*poverty or a disease*).

figure *noun* **1** (*number*) Zahl *die* (PL die Zahlen); **a four-figure number** eine vierstellige Zahl; **2** (*body shape*) Figur *die*; **good for your figure** gut für die Figur; **3** (*a person*) Gestalt *die* (PL die Gestalten).
figure *verb* **to figure something**

a
b
c
d
e
f
g
h
i
j
k
l
m
n
o
p
q
r
s
t
u
v
w
x
y
z

a
b
c
d
e
f
g
h
i
j
k
l
m
n
o
p
q
r
s
t
u
v
w
x
y
z

out etwas herausfinden✧ SEP (*the answer or reason*).

file *noun* **1** (*for records of a person or case*) Akte die (PL die Akten); **2** (*ring binder or folder*) Ordner der (PL die Ordner); **3** (*on a computer*) Datei die (PL die Dateien); **4 a nail file** eine Nagelfeile.
file *verb* **1** ablegen SEP (*documents*); **2 to file your nails** sich (DAT) die Nägel feilen.

fill *verb* **1** füllen (*a container*); **she filled my glass** sie füllte mein Glas; **2 to be filled with people** voller Menschen sein; **filled with smoke** voller Rauch.
● **to fill in** ausfüllen SEP (*a form*).

filling *noun* **1** (*of a pie*) Füllung die (PL die Füllungen); **2** (*in a tooth*) Füllung die (PL die Füllungen).

film *noun* (*in a cinema and for a camera*) Film der (PL die Filme); **shall we go and see the new film about Freud?** wollen wir uns den neuen Film über Freud ansehen?; **to make a film** einen Film drehen; **a 24-exposure colour film** ein Farbfilm mit 24 Aufnahmen.

film star *noun* Filmstar der (PL die Filmstars).

filter *noun* Filter der (PL die Filter).

filthy *adjective* dreckig.

final *noun* (*in sport*) Endspiel das (PL die Endspiele).
final *adjective* letzter/letzte/letztes; **the final instalment** die letzte Folge; **the final result** das Endergebnis.

finally *adverb* schließlich.

find *verb* finden✧; **did you find your passport?** hast du deinen Pass gefunden?; **I can't find my keys** ich kann meine Schlüssel nicht finden.
● **to find out 1** (*to enquire*) sich informieren; **I don't know, I'll find out** das weiß ich nicht, ich werde mich informieren; **2 to find something out** etwas (ACC) herausfinden✧ SEP (*the facts or an answer*); **when she found out the truth** als sie die Wahrheit herausfand.

fine *noun* Bußgeld das (PL die Bußgelder) (*for parking or speeding*).
fine *adjective* **1** (*in good health*) gut; **'how are you?'** – **'fine, thanks'** 'wie gehts?' - 'danke, gut'; **I'm fine** mir geht es gut; **2** (*convenient*) in Ordnung; **ten o'clock? yes, that's fine** zehn Uhr? ja, in Ordnung!; **Friday will be fine** Freitag geht in Ordnung; **3** (*sunny*) schön; (*weather or day*) **if it's fine** wenn es schön ist; **in fine weather** bei schönem Wetter; **4** (*not coarse or thick*) fein.

finely *adverb* fein (*chopped or grated*).

finger *noun* Finger der (PL die Finger); ⋆ **I'll keep my fingers crossed for you** ich drücke dir den Daumen.

fingernail *noun* Fingernagel der (PL die Fingernägel).

finish *noun* **1** (*end*) Schluss der (PL die Schlüsse); **2** (*in a race*) Ziel das (PL die Ziele).
finish *verb* **1** beenden (*a conversation or quarrel*); **to finish a**

discussion ein Gespräch beenden; **to be finished with something** mit etwas (DAT) fertig sein (*work or a project*); **have you finished your homework?** bist du mit den Hausaufgaben fertig?; **wait, I haven't finished!** warte, ich bin noch nicht fertig!; **2** (*to finish off*) **to finish doing something** etwas zu beenden; **have you finished (reading) the letter?** hast du den Brief zu Ende gelesen?; **he hasn't yet finished (writing) the report** er hat den Bericht noch nicht zu Ende geschrieben; **3** (*come to an end*) zu Ende sein, aus sein (*informal*) (*a meeting or performance*); **the film finishes at ten o'clock** der Film ist um zehn Uhr zu Ende; **when does school finish?** wann ist die Schule aus?

● **to finish with** (*complete your use of*) nicht mehr brauchen; **when you've finished with these clothes, give them back to me** wenn du die Sachen nicht mehr brauchst, gib sie mir zurück; **have you finished with the computer?** brauchen Sie den Computer noch?

Finland *noun* Finnland *das*.

Finnish *noun* (*the language*) Finnisch *das*.
Finnish *adjective* finnisch; **he's Finnish** er ist Finne; **she's Finnish** sie ist Finnin.

fire *noun* **1** (*in a grate*) Kaminfeuer *das* (PL *die* Kaminfeuer); **to light the fire** das Feuer im Kamin anmachen; **2** (*accidental*) Feuer *das* (PL *die* Feuer); **to catch fire** (*fabric, furnishings*) Feuer fangen; **3** (*in a building or forest*) Brand *der* (PL *die* Brände); **to set fire to a factory** eine Fabrik in Brand stecken; **4 to be on fire** brennen⋄.
fire *verb* **1** (*with a gun*) schießen⋄; **to fire at somebody** auf jemanden schießen; **2** abfeuern SEP (*a gun*).

fire alarm *noun* Feuermelder *der* (PL *die* Feuermelder).

fire brigade *noun* Feuerwehr *die*.

fire engine *noun* Feuerwehrauto *das* (PL *die* Feuerwehrautos).

fire escape *noun* Feuertreppe *die* (PL *die* Feuertreppen).

fire extinguisher *noun* Feuerlöscher *der* (PL *die* Feuerlöscher).

firefighter *noun* Feuerwehrmann *der* (PL *die* Feuerwehrleute).

fireplace *noun* Kamin *der* (PL *die* Kamine).

fire station *noun* Feuerwache *die* (PL *die* Feuerwachen).

firework *noun* Feuerwerkskörper *der* (PL *die* Feuerwerkskörper); **firework display** *das* Feuerwerk.

firm *noun* (*business*) Firma *die* (PL *die* Firmen).
firm *adjective* **1** fest; **2** (*strict*) streng.

first *adjective* erster/erste/erstes; **the first of May** der erste Mai; **for the first time** zum ersten Mal; **I was the first to arrive** ich kam als Erster/Erste an; **Susan was first** Susan war die Erste; **to come first in the 100 metres** beim Hundertmeterlauf Erster/Erste werden.

first *adverb* **1** (*to begin with*) zuerst; **first, I'm going to make some tea** zuerst mache ich Tee; **2 at first** zuerst; **at first he was shy** er war zuerst schüchtern.

first aid *noun* erste Hilfe *die*.

first class *adjective* (*ticket, carriage, or hotel*) erster Klasse (*goes after the noun*); **a first-class hotel** ein Hotel erster Klasse; **he always travels first class** er reist immer erster Klasse; **a first-class compartment** ein Erste-Klasse-Abteil.

first floor *noun* erste Stock *der*; **on the first floor** im ersten Stock.

firstly *adverb* zunächst.

first name *noun* Vorname *der* (PL die Vornamen).

fir tree *noun* Tanne *die* (PL die Tannen).

fish *noun* Fisch *der* (PL die Fische). **fish** *verb* fischen, (*with a rod*) angeln.

fish and chips *noun* ausgebackener Fisch mit Pommes frites.

fisherman *noun* Fischer *der* (PL die Fischer).

fishing *noun* Fischen *das*, (*with a rod*) Angeln *das*; **to go fishing** fischen/angeln gehen.

fishing rod *noun* Angel *die* (PL die Angeln).

fishing tackle *noun* Angelausrüstung *die*.

fist *noun* Faust *die* (PL die Fäuste).

fit *noun* **1** (*of rage*) Anfall *der* (PL die Anfälle); **your dad'll have a fit when he sees your hair** dein Vater kriegt bestimmt einen Anfall, wenn er deine Haare sieht; **2 an epileptic fit** ein epileptischer Anfall. **fit** *adjective* (*healthy*) fit; **I feel really fit** ich fühle mich richtig fit; **to keep fit** fit bleiben. **fit** *verb* **1** (*be the right size for*) (*of shoes or a garment*) passen (+ DAT); **this skirt doesn't fit me** der Rock passt mir nicht; **2** (*be able to be put into*) passen in (+ ACC); **will my cases all fit in the car?** passen meine Koffer alle in das Auto?; **the key doesn't fit in the lock** der Schlüssel passt nicht ins Schloss; **3** (*install*) einbauen SEP.

fitted carpet *noun* Teppichboden *der* (PL die Teppichböden).

fitted kitchen *noun* Einbauküche *die* (PL die Einbauküchen).

fitting room *noun* Umkleidekabine *die* (PL die Umkleidekabinen).

five *number* fünf; **it's five o'clock** es ist fünf Uhr.

fix *verb* **1** (*repair*) reparieren; **Mum's fixed the computer** Mutti hat den Computer repariert; **2** (*decide on*) festlegen◇ SEP; **to fix a date** einen Termin festlegen; **3** machen (*a meal*); **I'll fix supper** ich mache Abendessen.

fizzy *adjective* sprudelnd; **fizzy water** *das* Sprudelwasser.

flag *noun* Fahne *die* (PL die Fahnen).

flame *noun* Flamme *die* (PL *die* Flammen).

flan *noun* Torte *die* (PL *die* Torten); **fruit flan** *die* Obsttorte.

flap *verb* (*of a bird*) **to flap its wings** mit den Flügeln schlagen◇.

flash *noun* (*on a camera*) Blitz *der* (PL *die* Blitze); **flash of lightning** *der* Blitz.
flash *verb* **1** (*a light*) aufleuchten SEP, (*repeatedly*) blinken; **2 to flash by** or **past** vorbeiflitzen SEP (*informal*).

flashback *noun* Rückblende *die* (PL *die* Rückblenden).

flat *noun* Wohnung *die* (PL *die* Wohnungen); **a third-floor flat** eine Wohnung im dritten Stock.
flat *adjective* **1** flach; **flat shoes** flache Schuhe; **a flat landscape** eine flache Landschaft; **2 a flat tyre** ein platter Reifen.

flatmate *noun* Mitbewohner *der* (PL *die* Mitbewohner), Mitbewohnerin *die* (PL *die* Mitbewohnerinnen).

flatter *noun* schmeicheln (+ DAT).

flavour *noun* **1** Geschmack *der* (PL *die* Geschmäcke); **the sauce has a bitter flavour** die Soße hat einen bitteren Geschmack; **strawberry flavour** Erdbeergeschmack; **2** (*of drinks, coffee, or tea*) Aroma *das* (PL *die* Aromen).
flavour *verb* würzen; **vanilla-flavoured** mit Vanillegeschmack.

flea *noun* Floh *der* (PL *die* Flöhe).

flesh *noun* Fleisch *das*.

flex *noun* Kabel *das* (PL *die* Kabel).

flight *noun* **1** Flug *der* (PL *die* Flüge); **the flight was delayed** der Flug hatte Verspätung; **charter flight** *der* Charterflug; **the flight from Munich to London takes an hour and a half** die Flugzeit von München nach London beträgt eineinhalb Stunden; **2 flight of stairs** die Treppe.

flight attendant *noun* Flugbegleiter *der* (PL *die* Flugbegleiter), Flugbegleiterin *die* (PL *die* Flugbegleiterinnen).

flipper *noun* Flosse *die* (PL *die* Flossen).

flirt *verb* flirten.

float *verb* **1** (*on water*) treiben◇; **2** (*in the air*) schweben.

flood *noun* **1** (*of water*) Überschwemmung *die* (PL *die* Überschwemmungen); **2 to be in floods of tears** in Tränen aufgelöst sein; **3** (*of letters or complaints*) Flut *die*.
flood *verb* überschwemmen.

floodlight *noun* Flutlicht *das*.

floor *noun* **1** Boden *der* (PL *die* Böden); **your glasses are on the floor** deine Brille liegt auf dem Boden; **2 to sweep the floor** fegen; **to sweep the kitchen floor** die Küche fegen; **3** (*a storey*) Stock *der* (PL *die* Stock); **on the second floor** im zweiten Stock.

floppy disk *noun* Diskette *die* (PL *die* Disketten).

florist *noun* Blumenhändler *der* (PL *die* Blumenhändler),

a
b
c
d
e
f
g
h
i
j
k
l
m
n
o
p
q
r
s
t
u
v
w
x
y
z

Blumenhändlerin die (PL die Blumenhändlerinnen).

flour noun Mehl das.

flow verb fließen✧ (PERF sein).

flower noun Blume die (PL die Blumen); **bunch of flowers** der Blumenstrauß.
flower verb blühen.

flu noun Grippe die (PL die Grippen); **to have flu** die Grippe haben.

fluent adjective **she speaks fluent Italian** sie spricht fließend Italienisch.

fluently adverb fließend.

flute noun Flöte die (PL die Flöten); **to play the flute** Flöte spielen.

fly noun Fliege die (PL die Fliegen).
fly verb **1** fliegen✧ (PERF sein); **we flew to Berlin** wir sind nach Berlin geflogen; **2** steigen lassen (a kite); **3** fliegen✧ (PERF haben) (a plane or helicopter); **4** (to pass quickly) schnell vergehen✧ (PERF sein).

foam noun **1** (foam rubber) Schaumgummi der; **foam mattress** die Schaumgummimatratze; **2** (on a drink) Schaum der.

focus noun Brennpunkt der (PL die Brennpunkte) **to be in focus** scharf sein; **to be out of focus** unscharf sein.
focus verb scharf stellen (a camera).

fog noun Nebel der.

foggy adjective neblig.

foil noun (kitchen foil) Alufolie die.

fold noun **1** (in fabric or skin) Falte die (PL die Falten); **2** (in paper) Falz

der (PL die Falze).
fold verb falten; **to fold something up** etwas zusammenfalten SEP.

folder noun Mappe die (PL die Mappen).

follow verb **1** folgen (PERF sein) (+ DAT); **follow me!** folgen Sie mir!; **2 do you follow me?** verstehst du, was ich meine?

following adjective folgend; **the following evening** am folgenden Abend.

fond adjective **to be fond of somebody** jemanden gern haben; **I'm very fond of him** ich habe ihn sehr gern.

food noun **1** Essen das; **I have to buy some food** ich muss noch etwas zu essen einkaufen; **2 I like German food** ich mag die deutsche Küche; **3** (stocks) Lebensmittel (plural); **we bought food for the holiday** wir haben Lebensmittel für die Ferien eingekauft.

food poisoning noun Lebensmittelvergiftung.

fool noun Dummkopf der (PL die Dummköpfe).

foot noun Fuß der (PL die Füße); **Lucy came on foot** Lucy ist zu Fuß gekommen.

football noun Fußball der (PL die Fußbälle); **to play football** Fußball spielen.

footballer noun Fußballspieler der (PL die Fußballspieler), Fußballspielerin die (PL die Fußballspielerinnen).

428

footpath *noun* Fußweg *der* (PL *die* Fußwege).

footprint *noun* Fußabdruck *der* (PL *die* Fußabdrücke).

footstep *noun* Schritt *der* (PL *die* Schritte).

for *preposition* **1** für (+ ACC); **a present for my mother** ein Geschenk für meine Mutter; **what's it for?** wofür ist das?; **2** (*for a particular occasion or event*) zu (+ DAT); **sausages for lunch** Würstchen zum Mittagessen; **Sam got a bike for Christmas** Sam hat zu Weihnachten ein Rad bekommen; **what for?** wozu?; **3** (*time expressions in the past but continuing in the present*) seit (+ DAT); **I've been waiting here for an hour** (*and I'm still waiting*) ich warte hier seit einer Stunde; **my brother's been living in Berlin for three years** (*and he still lives there*) mein Bruder wohnt seit drei Jahren in Berlin; **4** (*time expressions in the past or the future*) **I studied French for six years** (*but I no longer do*) ich habe sechs Jahre lang Französisch gelernt; **I'll be away for four days** ich werde vier Tage nicht da sein; **5** (*with a price*) für (+ ACC); **I sold my bike for fifty pounds** ich habe mein Rad für fünfzig Pfund verkauft; **6 what's the German for 'bee'?** wie heißt 'bee' auf Deutsch?

forbid *verb* verbieten✧; **to forbid somebody to do something** jemandem verbieten, etwas zu tun.

forbidden *adjective* verboten.

force *noun* Kraft *die* (PL *die* Kräfte). **force** *verb* zwingen✧; **to force somebody to do something** jemanden zwingen, etwas zu tun.

forecast *noun* Vorhersage *die* (PL *die* Vorhersagen).

foreground *noun* Vordergrund *der*; **in the foreground** im Vordergrund.

forehead *noun* Stirn *die* (PL *die* Stirnen).

foreign *adjective* **1** ausländisch; **in a foreign country** im Ausland; **from a foreign country** aus dem Ausland; **2 foreign language** *die* Fremdsprache.

foreigner *noun* Ausländer *der* (PL *die* Ausländer), Ausländerin *die* (PL *die* Ausländerinnen).

forest *noun* Wald *der* (PL *die* Wälder).

forever *adverb* **1** immer; **I'd like to stay here forever** ich möchte für immer hier bleiben; **2** (*non-stop*) ständig; **he's forever asking questions** er fragt ständig.

forget *verb* vergessen✧; **to forget about something** etwas vergessen; **we've forgotten the bread** wir haben das Brot vergessen; **to forget to do something** vergessen, etwas zu tun; **I forgot to phone** ich habe vergessen anzurufen.

forgive *verb* verzeihen✧ (+ DAT); **to forgive somebody** jemandem verzeihen; **I forgave him** ich habe ihm verziehen; **to forgive somebody for doing something** jemandem verzeihen, dass er/sie etwas getan hat; **I forgave her for**

losing my ring ich habe ihr verziehen, dass sie meinen Ring verloren hat.

fork *noun* Gabel *die* (PL *die* Gabeln).

form *noun* **1** Formular *das* (PL *die* Formulare); **to fill in a form** ein Formular ausfüllen; **2** (*shape or kind*) Form *die* (PL *die* Formen); **in the form of** in Form von; **to be on form** gut in Form sein; **3** (*in school*) Klasse *die* (PL *die* Klassen).
form *verb* bilden.

formal *adjective* formell (*invitation, event*).

format *noun* Format *das* (PL *die* Formate).

former *adjective* ehemalig; **a former pupil** ein ehemaliger Schüler, eine ehemalige Schülerin.

fortnight *noun* vierzehn Tage (*plural*); **we're going to Spain for a fortnight** wir fahren vierzehn Tage nach Spanien.

fortunately *adverb* glücklicherweise.

fortune *noun* Vermögen *das* (PL *die* Vermögen); **to make a fortune** ein Vermögen machen.

forty *number* vierzig.

forward *noun* (*in sport*) Stürmer *der* (PL *die* Stürmer).
forward *adverb* (*to the front*) nach vorn; **to move forward** vorrücken SEP (PERF *sein*); **a seat further forward** ein Platz weiter vorn.

foster child *noun* Pflegekind *das* (PL *die* Pflegekinder).

foul *noun* (*in sport*) Foul *das* (PL *die* Fouls).

foul *adjective* scheußlich; **the weather's foul** das Wetter ist scheußlich.

fountain *noun* Brunnen *der* (PL *die* Brunnen).

fountain pen *noun* Füllfederhalter *der* (PL *die* Füllfederhalter).

four *number* vier; **it's four o'clock** es ist vier Uhr; ★ **on all fours** auf allen vieren.

fourteen *number* vierzehn.

fourth *number* vierter/vierte/viertes; **the fourth of July** der vierte Juli; **on the fourth floor** im vierten Stock.

fox *noun* Fuchs *der* (PL *die* Füchse).

fragile *adjective* zerbrechlich.

frame *noun* **1** Rahmen *der* (PL *die* Rahmen); **2** (*of spectacles*) Gestell *das* (PL *die* Gestelle).

franc *noun* **1** (*Swiss*) Franken *der* (PL *die* Franken); **a fifty-franc note** ein Fünfzig-Franken-Schein; **2** (*former French and Belgian currencies*) Franc *der* (PL *die* Francs).

France *noun* Frankreich *das*; **to France** nach Frankreich.

frantic *adjective* **1** (*very upset*) **to be frantic** außer sich (DAT) sein; **I was frantic with worry** ich war außer mir vor Sorge; **2** (*desperate*) fieberhaft (*effort or search*).

freckle *noun* Sommersprosse *die* (PL *die* Sommersprossen).

free *adjective* **1** (*when you don't pay*) kostenlos; **a free ride** eine kostenlose Fahrt; **a free ticket** eine

Freikarte; **2** (*without charge*) umsonst; **to do something for free** etwas umsonst machen; **3** (*not occupied*) frei; **are you free on Thursday?** haben Sie am Donnerstag Zeit?; **4 sugar-free** ohne Zucker; **lead-free** bleifrei. **free** *verb* befreien.

freedom *noun* Freiheit *die*.

free gift *noun* Werbegeschenk *das* (PL *die* Werbegeschenke).

free kick *noun* Freistoß *der* (PL *die* Freistöße).

freeze *verb* **1** (*in a freezer*) einfrieren ⬦ SEP; **to freeze raspberries** Himbeeren einfrieren; **2** (*in cold weather*) frieren ⬦; **it's freezing** es friert; **3** (*become covered with ice*) zufrieren ⬦ SEP (PERF *sein*); **the pond is frozen** der Teich ist zugefroren.

freezer *noun* Gefrierschrank *der* (PL *die* Gefrierschränke).

freezing *noun* **below freezing** unter Null; **three degrees above freezing** drei Grad über Null. **freezing** *adjective* **1 I'm freezing** ich friere sehr; **2 it's freezing outside** es ist eiskalt draußen.

French *noun* **1** (*the language*) Französisch *das*; **2** (*the people*) **the French** die Franzosen. **French** *adjective* **1** französisch; **Jean-Marc is French** Jean-Marc ist Franzose; **2** (*teacher or lesson*) Französisch-; **the French class** der Französischunterricht.

French bean *noun* grüne Bohne *die* (PL *die* grünen Bohnen).

French dressing *noun* Vinaigrette *die*.

French fries *plural noun* Pommes frites (*plural*).

Frenchman *noun* Franzose *der* (PL *die* Franzosen).

French window *noun* Terrassentür *die* (PL *die* Terrassentüren).

Frenchwoman *noun* Französin *die* (PL *die* Französinnen).

frequent *adjective* häufig.

fresh *adjective* frisch; **fresh eggs** frische Eier; **I'm going out for some fresh air** ich gehe ein bisschen frische Luft schnappen.

Friday *noun* **1** Freitag *der* (PL *die* Freitage); **next Friday** nächsten Freitag; **last Friday** letzten Freitag; **on Friday** (am) Freitag; **I'll phone you on Friday evening** ich rufe dich Freitagabend an; **every Friday** jeden Freitag; **Good Friday** Karfreitag; **2 on Fridays** freitags; **closed on Fridays** freitags geschlossen.

fridge *noun* Kühlschrank *der* (PL *die* Kühlschränke); **put it in the fridge** stell es in den Kühlschrank.

friend *noun* **1** Freund *der* (PL *die* Freunde), Freundin *die* (PL *die* Freundinnen); **a friend of mine** ein Freund von mir; **2 to make friends** sich anfreunden; **he made friends with Danny** er hat sich mit Danny angefreundet; **he is friends with Danny** er ist mit Danny befreundet.

friendly *adjective* freundlich.

a
b
c
d
e
f
g
h
i
j
k
l
m
n
o
p
q
r
s
t
u
v
w
x
y
z

friendship noun Freundschaft die (PL die Freundschaften).

fries plural noun Pommes frites (plural).

fright noun **1** Schreck der (PL die Schrecke); **to have** or **get a fright** einen Schreck bekommen; **2 you gave me a fright!** du hast mich erschreckt!

frighten verb **1** (of an explosion or shot) erschrecken; **2** (scare or threaten) **to frighten somebody** jemandem Angst machen.

frightened adjective **to be frightened** Angst haben; **Martin's frightened of snakes** Martin hat Angst vor Schlangen.

frightening adjective beängstigend.

fringe noun **1** (hairstyle) Pony der (PL die Ponys); **2** (on clothes or a curtain) Fransen (plural).

frog noun Frosch der (PL die Frösche).

from preposition **1** von (+ DAT); **ten metres from the cinema** zehn Meter vom Kino; **a letter from Tom** ein Brief von Tom; **from Monday to Friday** von Montag bis Freitag; **from now on** von jetzt an; **2** aus (+ DAT); **he comes from Dublin** er kommt aus Dublin; **the train from London** der Zug aus London; **3 from seven o'clock onwards** ab sieben Uhr; **from then on** von da ab.

front noun **1** (of a cupboard, card, or envelope) Vorderseite die (PL die Vorderseiten), (of a building) Vorderfront die (PL die Vorderfronten); **2** (of a garment or in an interior) Vorderteil das (PL die Vorderteile); **3** (at the seaside) Strandpromenade die (PL die Strandpromenaden); **4** (of a car) **to sit in (the) front** vorne sitzen; **5** (of a train or queue) vordere Ende das; **6** (of a procession or in a race) Spitze die; **7 in/at the front** vorne; **in/at the front of** vorne in (+ DAT, or + ACC with movement towards a place); **there are still seats at the front of the train** es gibt noch Plätze vorne im Zug; **we got on at the front of the train** wir sind vorne in den Zug eingestiegen; **8 in front of** vor (+ DAT, or + ACC with movement towards a place); **in front of the TV** vor dem Fernseher; **in front of me** vor mir.

front adjective **1** vorderer/vordere/vorderes; **in the front rows** in den vorderen Reihen; **2** Vorder-; **front seat** (of a car) der Vordersitz; **front wheel** das Vorderrad.

front door noun Haustür die (PL die Haustüren).

frontier noun Grenze die (PL die Grenzen).

frost noun Frost der.

frosty adjective frostig.

frown verb die Stirn runzeln; **he frowned at us** er blickte uns mit gerunzelter Stirn an.

frozen adjective (in a freezer) tiefgekühlt; **a frozen pizza** eine Tiefkühlpizza.

fruit noun **1** (a single fruit or type of fruit) Frucht die (PL die Früchte); **2** (various fruits) Obst das; **we bought cheese and fruit** wir haben Käse und Obst gekauft.

fruit juice *noun* Fruchtsaft *der* (PL die Fruchtsäfte).

fruit machine *noun* Spielautomat *der* (PL die Spielautomaten).

fruit salad *noun* Obstsalat *der* (PL die Obstsalate).

frustrated *adjective* frustriert.

fry *verb* braten◇; **we fried fish** wir haben Fisch gebraten; **fried potatoes** Bratkartoffeln; **fried egg** *das* Spiegelei.

frying pan *noun* Bratpfanne *die* (PL die Bratpfannen).

fuel *noun* (*for a car*) Kraftstoff *der*.

full *adjective* **1** voll; **the glass is full** das Glas ist voll; **I'm full** ich bin voll (*informal*); **2 full of** voller (+ GEN); **the train was full of tourists** der Zug war voller Touristen; **3 at full speed** in voller Fahrt; **4 to write something out in full** etwas voll ausschreiben.

full stop *noun* Punkt *der* (PL die Punkte).

full-time *adjective* **a full-time job** eine Ganztagsstelle.

fully *adverb* voll.

fun *noun* **1** Spaß *der*; **have fun!** viel Spaß!; **we had fun catching the ponies** die Ponys einzufangen machte uns Spaß; **skiing is fun** Skifahren macht Spaß; **I do it for fun** ich mache es aus Spaß; **2 to have fun** sich amüsieren; ★**to make fun of somebody** sich über jemanden lustig machen.

funds *plural noun* Geldmittel (*plural*).

funeral *noun* Beerdigung *die* (PL die Beerdigungen).

funfair *noun* Jahrmarkt *der* (PL die Jahrmärkte).

funny *adjective* **1** (*amusing*) lustig; **a funny story** eine lustige Geschichte; **he's so funny** er ist so witzig; **2** (*strange*) komisch; **a funny noise** ein komisches Geräusch; **that's funny, I'm sure I paid** das ist komisch, ich bin mir sicher, dass ich gezahlt habe.

fur *noun* **1** (*on an animal*) Fell *das* (PL die Felle); **2** (*for a coat*) Pelz *der* (PL die Pelze); **fur coat** *der* Pelzmantel.

furious *adjective* wütend; **she was furious with Steve** sie war wütend auf Steve.

furniture *noun* Möbel (*plural*); **to buy some furniture** Möbel kaufen; **piece of furniture** *das* Möbelstück.

further *adverb* weiter; **further than the station** weiter als der Bahnhof; **ten kilometres further on** zehn Kilometer weiter; **further off** weiter entfernt; **further forward** weiter vorn; **further back** weiter hinten.

fuse *noun* Sicherung *die* (PL die Sicherungen).

fuss *noun* Theater *das*; **to make a fuss** ein Theater machen; **to make a big fuss about the bill** ein großes Theater um die Rechnung machen.

fussy *adjective* **to be fussy about something** wählerisch in etwas (DAT) sein (*food, for example*).

future *noun* Zukunft *die*; **in future** in Zukunft.

a
b
c
d
e
f
g
h
i
j
k
l
m
n
o
p
q
r
s
t
u
v
w
x
y
z

a
b
c
d
e
f
g
h
i
j
k
l
m
n
o
p
q
r
s
t
u
v
w
x
y
z

Gg

gadget *noun* Gerät das (PL die Geräte).

gain *verb* **1** gewinnen✧; **in order to gain time** um Zeit zu gewinnen; **2** profitieren; **to gain by something** von etwas profitieren.

gale *noun* Sturm der (PL die Stürme).

gallery *noun* Galerie die (PL die Galerien).

gamble *verb* spielen (*for money*).

game *noun* **1** Spiel das (PL die Spiele); **game of chance** das Glücksspiel; **board game** das Brettspiel; **2 to have a game of cards** eine Partie Karten spielen; **3 to have a game of football** Fußball spielen; **4 games** (*at school*) Sport der.

gang *noun* Bande die (PL die Banden); **all the gang were there** die ganze Bande war da.

gap *noun* **1** (*hole*) Lücke die (PL die Lücken); **2** (*in time*) Pause die (PL die Pausen); **a two-hour gap** eine zweistündige Pause; **3 age gap** der Altersunterschied.

gap year *noun* Orientierungsjahr das (PL die Orientierungsjahre).

garage *noun* **1** (*for keeping your car*) Garage die (PL die Garagen); **2** (*for repairing cars*) Autowerkstatt die (PL die Autowerkstätten); **3** (*for petrol*) Tankstelle die (PL die Tankstellen).

garden *noun* Garten der (PL die Gärten).

gardener *noun* Gärtner der (PL die Gärtner), Gärtnerin die (PL die Gärtnerinnen).

gardening *noun* Gartenarbeit die.

garlic *noun* Knoblauch der.

garment *noun* Kleidungsstück das (PL die Kleidungsstücke).

gas *noun* Gas das.

gas cooker *noun* Gasherd der (PL die Gasherde).

gas fire *noun* Gasofen der (PL die Gasöfen).

gas meter *noun* Gaszähler der (PL die Gaszähler).

gate *noun* **1** (*in garden*) Pforte die (PL die Pforten); **2** (*in field*) Gatter das (PL die Gatter); **3** (*at an airport*) Flugsteig der (PL die Flugsteige).

gather *verb* **1** (*of people*) sich versammeln; **2** sammeln (*fruit, vegetables, flowers*); **3 as far as I can gather** soweit ich weiß.

gay *adjective* (*homosexual*) schwul (*informal*).

gaze *verb* **to gaze at something** etwas anstarren SEP.

GCSEs *noun plural* (*You can explain GCSEs briefly as follows: Dies sind Prüfungen, die im Alter von ca 16 Jahren in bis zu 12 Fächern abgelegt werden. Sie werden von A* (beste Note) bis N (nicht bestanden) benotet. Viele Schüler und Schülerinnen machen nach den GCSEs weiter und legen die A-level Prüfungen ab*) SEE **A levels**.

gear lever *noun* Schalthebel der (PL die Schalthebel).

gear *noun* **1** (*in a car*) Gang *der* (PL die Gänge); **to change gear** schalten; **2** (*equipment*) Ausrüstung *die*; **camping gear** die Campingausrüstung; **3** (*things*) Sachen (*plural*); **I've left all my gear at Gary's** ich habe alle meine Sachen bei Gary gelassen.

gel *noun* Gel *das* (PL die Gele).

Gemini *noun* Zwillinge (*plural*); **Steph's Gemini** Steph ist Zwilling.

gender *noun* (*of a word*) Geschlecht *das* (PL die Geschlechter); **what is the gender of 'Haus'?** welches Geschlecht hat 'Haus'?

general *noun* General *der* (PL die Generäle).
general *adjective* allgemein; **in general** im Allgemeinen; **the general election** die allgemeinen Wahlen.

general knowledge *noun* Allgemeinwissen *das*.

generally *adverb* im Allgemeinen.

generation *noun* Generation *die* (PL die Generationen).

generator *noun* Generator *der* (PL die Generatoren).

generous *adjective* großzügig.

genetics *noun* Genetik *die*.

Geneva *noun* Genf *das*; **Lake Geneva** der Genfer See.

genius *noun* Genie *das* (PL die Genies); **Lisa, you're a genius!** Lisa, du bis ein Genie!

gentle *adjective* sanft.

gentleman *noun* Herr *der* (PL die Herren); **ladies and gentlemen!** meine Damen und Herren!

gently *adverb* sanft.

gents *noun* (*lavatory*) Herrentoilette *die* (PL die Herrentoiletten); (*on a sign*) **'Gents'** 'Herren'; **where's the gents?** wo ist die Herrentoilette?

genuine *adjective* **1** (*real, authentic*) echt; **a genuine diamond** ein echter Brillant; **2** aufrichtig (*person*); **she's very genuine** sie ist sehr aufrichtig.

geography *noun* Geographie *die*, (*at school*) Erdkunde *die*.

germ *noun* **1** Keim *der* (PL die Keime); **2** (*causing a cold*) **germs** Bazillen (*plural*).

German *noun* **1** (*person*) Deutsche *der/die* (PL die Deutschen); **2** (*language*) Deutsch *das*; **in German** auf Deutsch.
German *adjective* deutsch; **he is German** er ist Deutscher; **she is German** sie ist Deutsche; **our German teacher** unser Deutschlehrer, unsere Deutschlehrerin.

Germany *noun* Deutschland *das*; **to Germany** nach Deutschland; **from Germany** aus Deutschland.

get *verb* **1** (*obtain, receive*) bekommen◇, kriegen (*informal*); **I got a bike for my birthday** ich habe ein Rad zum Geburtstag bekommen; **Fred got the job** Fred hat die Stelle bekommen; **she got a shock** sie hat einen Schreck gekriegt; **I got a good mark for my**

German homework ich habe auf meine Deutschhausaufgaben eine gute Note bekommen; **2 he's got lots of money** er hat viel Geld; **she's got long hair** sie hat lange Haare; **I've got a headache** ich habe Kopfschmerzen; **3** (*fetch*) holen; **I'll get some bread** ich hole Brot; **I'll get your bag for you** ich hole dir deine Tasche; **4 to have got to do something** etwas tun müssen◇; **I've got to phone before midday** ich muss vor Mittag anrufen; **5 to get (to) somewhere** irgendwo ankommen◇ SEP (PERF *sein*); **when I got to London** als ich in London ankam; **we got here this morning** wir sind heute Morgen angekommen; **what time did they get there?** wann sind sie angekommen?; **6** (*become*) werden◇ (PERF *sein*); **it's getting late** es wird spät; **it's getting dark** es wird dunkel; **7 to get something done** etwas machen lassen◇; **I'm getting my hair cut today** ich lasse mir heute die Haare schneiden.

● **to get back** zurückkommen◇ SEP (PERF *sein*); **Mum gets back at six** Mutti kommt um sechs zurück.

● **to get something back** etwas zurückbekommen◇ SEP, etwas zurückkriegen SEP (*informal*); **did you get your books back?** hast du deine Bücher zurückbekommen?

● **to get into something** (*a vehicle*) in etwas (ACC) einsteigen◇ SEP (PERF *sein*); **he got into the car** er ist ins Auto eingestiegen.

● **to get off something** (*a vehicle*) aus etwas (DAT) aussteigen◇ SEP (PERF

sein); **I got off the train at Banbury** ich bin in Banbury aus dem Zug ausgestiegen.

● **to get on: how's Amanda getting on?** wie gehts Amanda?

● **to get on something** (*a vehicle*) in etwas (ACC) einsteigen◇ SEP (PERF *sein*); **she got on the train at Reading** sie ist in Reading in den Zug eingestiegen.

● **to get on with somebody** sich mit jemandem verstehen◇; **she doesn't get on with her brother** sie versteht sich nicht mit ihrem Bruder.

● **to get out of something** (*a vehicle*) aus etwas (DAT) aussteigen◇ SEP (PERF *sein*); **Laura got out of the car** Laura ist aus dem Auto ausgestiegen.

● **to get together** sich wieder sehen◇ SEP; **we must get together soon** wir müssen uns bald mal wieder sehen.

● **to get up** aufstehen◇ SEP (PERF *sein*); **I get up at seven** ich stehe um sieben auf.

ghost *noun* Geist *der* (PL *die* Geister).

giant *noun* Riese *der* (PL *die* Riesen). **giant** *adjective* riesig; **a giant lorry** ein riesiger Lastwagen.

gift *noun* **1** Geschenk *das* (PL *die* Geschenke); **a Christmas gift** ein Weihnachtsgeschenk; **2** Begabung *die*; **to have a gift for something** für etwas (ACC) begabt sein; **Jo has a real gift for languages** Jo ist wirklich sprachbegabt.

gigabyte *noun* Gigabyte *das* (PL *die* Gigabytes); **a fifty gigabyte hard**

disk eine Festplatte mit fünfzig Gigabyte Speicherkapazität.

gigantic *adjective* riesig.

gin *noun* Gin der (PL die Gins).

ginger *noun* Ingwer der (PL die Ingwer).

gipsy *noun* Zigeuner der (PL die Zigeuner), Zigeunerin die (PL die Zigeunerinnen).

giraffe *noun* Giraffe die (PL die Giraffen).

girl *noun* Mädchen das (PL die Mädchen); **three boys and four girls** drei Jungen und vier Mädchen; **when I was a little girl I had** ... als kleines Mädchen hatte ich ....

girlfriend *noun* Freundin die (PL die Freundinnen).

give *verb* **1** geben✧; **to give something to somebody** jemandem etwas geben; **I'll give you my address** ich gebe dir meine Adresse; **give me the key** gib mir den Schlüssel; **Yasmin's dad gave her the money** Yasmins Vater hat ihr das Geld gegeben; **2** (*give as a gift*) schenken; **to give somebody a present** jemandem etwas schenken.

● **to give something away** etwas weggeben✧ SEP; **she's given away all her books** sie hat alle ihre Bücher weggegeben.

● **to give something back to somebody** jemandem etwas zurückgeben✧ SEP; **I gave her back the keys** ich habe ihr die Schlüssel zurückgegeben.

● **to give in** nachgeben✧ SEP; **my mum said no but she gave in in the end** meine Mutti hat nein gesagt, aber schließlich hat sie nachgegeben.

● **to give up** aufgeben✧ SEP; **I give up!** ich gebe auf!

● **to give up doing something** etwas aufgeben✧SEP; **she's given up smoking** sie hat das Rauchen aufgegeben.

glad *adjective* froh; **I'm glad to hear he's better** ich bin froh, dass es ihm besser geht; **I'm glad to be back** ich bin froh, dass ich wieder zurück bin.

glass *noun* Glas das (PL die Gläser); **a glass of water** ein Glas Wasser; **a glass table** ein Glastisch.

glasses *plural noun* Brille die (PL die Brillen); **to wear glasses** eine Brille tragen.

glider *noun* Segelflugzeug das (PL die Segelflugzeuge).

global warming *noun* globale Temperaturanstieg der.

glove *noun* Handschuh der (PL die Handschuhe); **a pair of gloves** ein Paar Handschuhe.

glove compartment *noun* Handschuhfach das (PL die Handschuhfächer).

glue *noun* Klebstoff der (PL die Klebstoffe).

go *noun* **1** (*in a game*) **whose go is it?** wer ist dran?; **it's my go** ich bin dran; **2 to have a go at doing something** versuchen, etwas zu tun; **I'll have a go at mending it** ich versuche, es zu reparieren.

go *verb* **1** (*on foot*) gehen✧ (PERF sein); **to go to school** in die Schule gehen; **Mark's gone to the**

dentist's Mark ist zum Zahnarzt gegangen; **to go shopping** einkaufen gehen; **2** (*in a vehicle*) fahren⬦ (PERF *sein*); **we're going to London** wir fahren nach London; **we're planning to go early** wir wollen früh losfahren; **to go on holiday** in die Ferien fahren; **3** (*by plane*) fliegen⬦ (PERF *sein*); **4 to go for a walk** spazieren gehen⬦ SEP (PERF *sein*); **5** (*with another verb*) **I'm going to do it** ich werde es tun; **I'm going to make some tea** ich mache Tee; **he was going to phone you** er wollte dich anrufen; **6** (*leave*) gehen⬦ (PERF *sein*); **Pauline's already gone** Pauline ist schon gegangen; **7** (*on a journey*) abfahren⬦ SEP (PERF *sein*); **when does the train go?** wann fährt der Zug ab?; **8** (*turn out*) verlaufen⬦ (PERF *sein*) (*event*); **how did your evening go?** wie ist dein Abend verlaufen?; **the party went well** die Party war gut.

● **to go away 1** weggehen⬦ SEP (PERF *sein*); **go away!** geh weg!; **2** (*on holiday*) verreisen (PERF *sein*).

● **to go back 1** zurückgehen⬦ SEP (PERF *sein*); **I'm going back to Germany in March** ich werde im März nach Deutschland zurückkehren; **I'm not going back there again!** ich gehe da nicht wieder zurück!; **2 I went back home** ich bin nach Hause gegangen.

● **to go down 1** hinuntergehen⬦ SEP (PERF *sein*); **she's gone down to the kitchen** sie ist in die Küche hinuntergegangen; **to go down the stairs** die Treppe hinuntergehen;

2 (*price, temperature*) fallen⬦ (PERF *sein*); **3** (*tyre, balloon, airbed*) Luft verlieren⬦.

● **to go in** hineingehen⬦ SEP (PERF *sein*); **he went in and shut the door** er ist hineingegangen und hat die Tür zugemacht.

● **to go into 1** (*person*) gehen in (+ ACC) PERF *sein*); **Fran went into the kitchen** Fran ging in die Küche; **2** (*object*) passen in (+ ACC); **this book won't go into my bag** dieses Buch passt nicht in meine Tasche.

● **to go off 1** (*bomb*) explodieren (PERF *sein*); **2** (*alarm clock*) klingeln; **my alarm clock went off at six** mein Wecker hat um sechs geklingelt; **3** (*fire or burglar alarm*) losgehen⬦ SEP (PERF *sein*); **the fire alarm went off** der Feuermelder ging los.

● **to go on 1 what's going on?** was ist los?; **2 to go on doing something** weiter etwas tun; **she went on talking** sie hat weitergeredet; **3 to go on about something** stundenlang von etwas (DAT) reden; **he's always going on about his dog** er redet stundenlang von seinem Hund.

● **to go out 1** (*for an evening*) ausgehen⬦ SEP, weggehen⬦ SEP (PERF *sein*) (*informal*); **we're going out tonight** wir gehen heute Abend aus; **2** (*leave*) **she went out of the kitchen** sie ist aus der Küche gegangen; **3 to be going out with somebody** mit jemandem gehen⬦ (PERF *sein*) (*informal*); **she's going out with my brother** sie geht mit meinem Bruder; **4** (*light, fire*) ausgehen◇ SEP (PERF *sein*); **the light went out** das Licht ist ausgegangen.

● **to go past something** an etwas (DAT) vorbeigehen◇ SEP; **we went past your house** wir sind an eurem Haus vorbeigegangen.

● **to go round: to go round to somebody's house** jemanden besuchen; **we went round to Fred's last night** wir haben gestern Abend Fred besucht.

● **to go round something 1** um etwas (ACC) herumgehen◇ SEP (PERF *sein*) (*building, park, garden*); **2** besichtigen (*museum, monument*).

● **to go through 1 the train goes through Cologne** der Zug fährt durch Köln; **2 to go through a room** durch ein Zimmer gehen; **3** (*search*) durchsuchen.

● **to go up 1** (*person*) hinaufgehen◇ SEP (PERF *sein*); **she's gone up to her room** sie ist in ihr Zimmer hinaufgegangen; **to go up the stairs** die Treppe hinaufgehen; **2** (*prices*) steigen◇ (PERF *sein*); **the price of petrol has gone up** die Benzinpreise sind gestiegen.

goal *noun* Tor *das* (PL die Tore); **to score a goal** ein Tor schießen; **to win by 3 goals to 2** mit 3 zu 2 Toren gewinnen.

goalkeeper *noun* Torwart *der* (PL die Torwarte), Torfrau *die* (PL die Torfrauen).

goat *noun* Ziege *die* (PL die Ziegen).

God *noun* Gott *der*; **to believe in God** an Gott glauben.

god *noun* Gott *der* (PL die Götter).

godchild *noun* Patenkind *das* (PL die Patenkinder).

goddaughter *noun* Patentochter *die* (PL die Patentöchter).

goddess *noun* Göttin *die* (PL die Göttinnen).

godfather *noun* Pate *der* (PL die Paten).

godmother *noun* Patin *die* (PL die Patinnen).

godson *noun* Patensohn *der* (PL die Patensöhne).

goggles *plural noun* Schutzbrille *die* (PL die Schutzbrillen); **swimming goggles** Schwimmbrille *die* (PL die Schwimmbrillen); **skiing goggles** Skibrille *die* (PL die Skibrillen).

gold *noun* Gold *das*; **a gold bracelet** ein Goldarmband.

goldfish *noun* Goldfisch *der* (PL die Goldfische).

golf *noun* Golf *das*; **to play golf** Golf spielen.

golf club *noun* **1** (*place*) Golfklub *der* (PL die Golfklubs); **2** (*iron*) Golfschläger *der* (PL die Golfschläger).

golf course *noun* Golfplatz *der* (PL die Golfplätze).

golfer *noun* Golfspieler *der* (PL die Golfspieler), Golfspielerin *die* (PL die Golfspielerinnen).

good *adjective* **1** gut; **she's a good teacher** sie ist eine gute Lehrerin; **the cherries are very good** die Kirschen sind sehr gut; **2 to be good for you** gesund sein; **tomatoes are good for you**

a
b
c
d
e
f
g
h
i
j
k
l
m
n
o
p
q
r
s
t
u
v
w
x
y
z

Tomaten sind gesund; **3 good at** gut in (+ DAT); **she's good at maths** sie ist gut in Mathe; **he's good at drawing** er kann gut zeichnen; **4** (*well-behaved*) brav; **be good!** sei brav!; **5** (*kind*) nett; **she's been very good to me** sie ist sehr nett zu mir gewesen; **6 for good** endgültig; **I've stopped smoking for good** ich habe das Rauchen endgültig aufgegeben.

good afternoon *exclamation* guten Tag!

goodbye *exclamation* auf Wiedersehen!

good evening *exclamation* guten Abend!

Good Friday *noun* Karfreitag *der* (PL *die* Karfreitage).

good-looking *adjective* gut aussehend.

good morning *exclamation* guten Morgen!

goodness *exclamation* meine Güte!; **for goodness sake!** um Himmels willen!

good night *exclamation* gute Nacht!

goods *plural noun* Waren (*plural*).

goods train *noun* Güterzug *der* (PL *die* Güterzüge).

goose *noun* Gans *die* (PL *die* Gänse).

gorgeous *adjective* herrlich; **it's a gorgeous day** es ist ein herrlicher Tag.

gorilla *noun* Gorilla *der* (PL *die* Gorillas).

gosh *exclamation* Mensch!

gossip *noun* **1** (*person*) Klatschbase *die* (PL *die* Klatschbasen); **2** (*scandal*) Klatsch *der*.
gossip *verb* klatschen.

government *noun* Regierung *die* (PL *die* Regierungen).

grab *verb* **1** packen; **she grabbed my arm** sie packte mich am Arm; **2 to grab something from somebody** jemandem etwas (ACC) entreißen⋄; **he grabbed the book from me** er hat mir das Buch entrissen.

grade *noun* (*mark*) Note *die* (PL *die* Noten); **to get good grades** gute Noten bekommen.

gradual *adjective* allmählich.

gradually *adverb* allmählich; **the weather got gradually better** das Wetter wurde allmählich besser.

graffiti *plural noun* Graffiti (*plural*).

grain *noun* Korn *das* (PL *die* Körner).

gram *noun* Gramm *das*; **100 grams of salami** hundert Gramm Salami.

grammar *noun* Grammatik *die*.

grammar school *noun* Gymnasium *das* (PL *die* Gymnasien).

grammatical *adjective* grammatikalisch; **a grammatical error** eine Grammatikfehler.

gran *noun* Oma *die* (PL *die* Omas).

grandchildren *plural noun* Enkelkinder (*plural*).

granddad *noun* Opa *der* (PL *die* Opas).

granddaughter *noun* Enkelin *die* (PL *die* Enkelinnen).

grandfather *noun* Großvater *der* (PL *die* Großväter).

grandma *noun* Oma *die* (PL *die* Omas).

grandmother *noun* Großmutter *die* (PL *die* Großmütter).

grandpa *noun* Opa *der* (PL *die* Opas).

grandparents *plural noun* Großeltern (*plural*).

grandson *noun* Enkel *der* (PL *die* Enkel).

granny *noun* Omi *die* (PL *die* Omis).

grape *noun* Weintraube *die* (PL *die* Weintrauben); **a grape** eine Weintraube; **to buy some grapes** Weintrauben kaufen; **do you like grapes?** magst du Weintrauben?; **a bunch of grapes** eine ganze Weintraube.

grapefruit *noun* Grapefruit *die* (PL *die* Grapefruits).

graph *noun* Grafik *die* (PL *die* Grafiken).

grasp *verb* festhalten⋄ SEP.

grass *noun* 1 Gras *das*; **to lie on the grass** im Gras liegen; 2 (*lawn*) Rasen *der* (PL *die* Rasen); **to cut the grass** den Rasen mähen.

grasshopper *noun* Heuschrecke *die* (PL *die* Heuschrecken).

grate *verb* reiben⋄; **grated cheese** geriebener Käse.

grateful *adjective* dankbar; **to be grateful to somebody** jemandem dankbar sein.

grater *noun* Reibe *die* (PL *die* Reiben).

grave *noun* Grab *das* (PL *die* Gräber).

graveyard *noun* Friedhof *der* (PL *die* Friedhöfe).

gravy *noun* Soße *die* (PL *die* Soßen).

grease *noun* Fett *das*.

greasy *adjective* 1 fettig; **to have greasy skin** fettige Haut haben; 2 (*food*) fett.

great *adjective* 1 groß; **a great poet** ein großer Dichter; 2 (*terrific*) großartig; **it was a great party** das war eine großartige Party; **great!** großartig!, prima! (*informal*); 3 **a great deal of** sehr viel; **a great many** sehr viele.

Great Britain *noun* Großbritannien *das*.

Greece *noun* Griechenland *das*.

greedy *adjective* gierig, (*with food*) gefräßig.

Greek *noun* 1 (*person*) Grieche *der* (PL *die* Griechen), Griechin *die* (PL *die* Griechinnen); 2 (*language*) Griechisch *das*.
Greek *adjective* griechisch; **she's Greek** sie ist Griechin.

green *noun* 1 (*colour*) Grün *das*; **a pale green** ein Hellgrün; 2 **the Greens** (*ecologists*) die Grünen.
green *adjective* 1 grün; **a green door** eine grüne Tür; 2 **the Green Party** die Grünen (*plural*).

greengrocer *noun* Obst- und Gemüsehändler *der* (PL *die* Obst- und Gemüsehändler).

greenhouse *noun* Gewächshaus *das* (PL *die* Gewächshäuser).

greenhouse effect *noun* Treibhauseffekt *der*.

a
b
c
d
e
f
g
h
i
j
k
l
m
n
o
p
q
r
s
t
u
v
w
x
y
z

greetings *plural noun* Grüße (*plural*); **Season's Greetings** fröhliche Weihnachten und ein glückliches neues Jahr.

greetings card *noun* Glückwunschkarte *die* (PL *die* Glückwunschkarten).

grey *adjective* grau.

greyhound *noun* Windhund *der* (PL *die* Windhunde).

grid *noun* 1 (*grating*) Gitter *das* (PL *die* Gitter); 2 (*network*) Netz *das* (PL *die* Netze).

grief *noun* Trauer *die*.

grill *noun* Grill *der* (PL *die* Grills). **grill** *verb* grillen; **I'm going to grill the sausages** ich grille die Würstchen.

grim *adjective* grauenvoll.

grin *verb* grinsen.

grind *verb* mahlen.

grip *verb* (*hold on to*) festhalten✧ SEP.

groan *noun* Stöhnen *das*. **groan** *verb* stöhnen.

grocer *noun* Lebensmittelhändler *der* (PL *die* Lebensmittelhändler).

groceries *plural noun* Lebensmittel (*plural*).

grocer's *noun* Lebensmittelgeschäft *das* (PL *die* Lebensmittelgeschäfte).

groom *noun* Bräutigam *der* (PL *die* Bräutigame); **the bride and groom** das Brautpaar.

gross *adjective* 1 **a gross injustice** eine schreiende Ungerechtigkeit; 2 grob; **a gross error** ein grober Fehler; 3 (*disgusting*) ekelhaft; **the**

food was gross! das Essen war ekelhaft!

ground *noun* 1 Boden *der*; **to sit on the ground** auf dem Boden sitzen; 2 (*for sport*) Sportplatz *der* (PL *die* Sportplätze); **football ground** *der* Fußballplatz.
ground *adjective* gemahlen; **ground coffee** gemahlener Kaffee.

ground floor *noun* Erdgeschoss *das*; **they live on the ground floor** sie wohnen im Erdgeschoss.

group *noun* Gruppe *die* (PL *die* Gruppen).

grow *verb* (*get bigger*) 1 wachsen✧ (PERF *sein*); **your hair grows very quickly** deine Haare wachsen sehr schnell; **my little sister's grown quite a bit this year** meine kleine Schwester ist dieses Jahr ein ganzes Stück gewachsen; **the number of students is still growing** die Zahl der Studenten wächst noch; 2 anbauen SEP (*fruit, vegetables*); 3 **to grow a beard** sich (DAT) einen Bart wachsen lassen; 4 (*become*) werden✧ (PERF *sein*); **to grow old** alt werden.
● **to grow up** 1 erwachsen werden; **the children are growing up** die Kinder werden erwachsen; 2 aufwachsen✧ SEP (PERF *sein*); **she grew up in Scotland** sie ist in Schottland aufgewachsen.

growl *verb* knurren.

grown-up *noun* Erwachsene *der/die* (PL *die* Erwachsenen).

growth *noun* Wachstum *das*.

grudge *noun* **to bear a grudge against somebody** etwas gegen jemanden haben; **she bears me a grudge** sie hat etwas gegen mich.

grumble *verb* **1** murren; **he's always grumbling** er murrt immer; **2 to grumble about something** sich über etwas (ACC) beklagen; **what's she grumbling about?** worüber beklagt sie sich?

guarantee *noun* Garantie die (PL die Garantien); **a year's guarantee** ein Jahr Garantie.
guarantee *verb* garantieren.

guard *noun* **1 prison guard** der Gefängniswärter, die Gefängniswärterin; **2** (*on a train*) Zugführer der (PL die Zugführer), Zugführerin die (PL die Zugführerinnen); **3 security guard** der Wächter, die Wächterin.
guard *verb* bewachen.

guard dog *noun* Wachhund der (PL die Wachhunde).

guess *noun* **have a guess!** rate mal!; **it's a good guess** gut geraten.
guess *verb* **1** raten✧; **guess who I saw last night** rate mal, wen ich gestern Abend gesehen habe; **2** (*guess something correctly*) es erraten✧; **you'll never guess!** du errätst es nie!

guest *noun* Gast der (PL die Gäste); **we've got guests coming tonight** wir haben heute Abend Gäste; **a paying guest** ein zahlender Gast.

guide *noun* **1** (*person*) Führer der (PL die Führer), Führerin die (PL die Führerinnen); **2** (*book*) Reiseführer der (PL die Reiseführer); **3** (*girl guide*) Pfadfinderin die (PL die Pfadfinderinnen).

guidebook *noun* **1** Reiseführer der (PL die Reiseführer); **2** (*to a museum or monument*) Handbuch das (PL die Handbücher).

guide dog *noun* Blindenhund der (PL die Blindenhunde).

guideline *noun* Richtlinie die (PL die Richtlinien).

guilty *adjective* **1** schuldig; **2 to feel guilty** ein schlechtes Gewissen haben; **I felt guilty about the noise** ich hatte ein schlechtes Gewissen wegen des Lärms.

guinea pig *noun* **1** (*pet*) Meerschweinchen das (PL die Meerschweinchen); **2** (*in an experiment*) Versuchskaninchen das (PL die Versuchskaninchen).

guitar *noun* Gitarre die (PL die Gitarren); **to play the guitar** Gitarre spielen.

gum *noun* **1** (*in your mouth*) Zahnfleisch das; **2** (*chewing gum*) Kaugummi der (PL die Kaugummi).

gun *noun* **1** Pistole die (PL die Pistolen); **2** (*rifle*) Gewehr das (PL die Gewehre).

gutter *noun* **1** (*in the street*) Rinnstein der (PL die Rinnsteine); **2** (*on roof edge*) Dachrinne die (PL die Dachrinnen).

guy *noun* Typ der (PL die Typen) (*informal*); **he's a nice guy** er ist ein netter Typ; **that guy from Newcastle** der Typ aus Newcastle.

gym *noun* **1** (*school lesson*) Turnen das; **2** (*building*) Turnhalle die (PL die Turnhallen); **3** (*health club*) Fitnesscenter das (PL die

Fitnesscenter); **to go to the gym** ins Fitnesscenter gehen.

gym shoe *noun* Turnschuh *der* (PL *die* Turnschuhe).

gymnasium *noun* Turnhalle *die* (PL *die* Turnhallen).

gymnast *noun* Turner *der* (PL *die* Turner), Turnerin *die* (PL *die* Turnerinnen).

gymnastics *noun* Turnen *das*.

Hh

habit *noun* Gewohnheit *die* (PL *die* Gewohnheiten); **it's a bad habit** es ist eine schlechte Gewohnheit.

haddock *noun* Schellfisch *der*; **smoked haddock** geräucherter Schellfisch.

hail *noun* Hagel *der*.

hailstone *noun* Hagelkorn *das* (PL *die* Hagelkörner).

hailstorm *noun* Hagelschauer *der* (PL *die* Hagelschauer).

hair *noun* **1** Haare (*plural*); **to comb your hair** sich (DAT) die Haare kämmen; **to wash your hair** sich (DAT) die Haare waschen; **to have your hair cut** sich (DAT) die Haare schneiden lassen; **she's had her hair cut** sie hat sich die Haare schneiden lassen; **2 a hair** ein Haar.

hairbrush *noun* Haarbürste *die* (PL *die* Haarbürsten).

haircut *noun* **1** Haarschnitt *der* (PL *die* Haarschnitte); **2 to have a**

haircut sich (DAT) die Haare schneiden lassen.

hairdresser *noun* Friseur *der* (PL *die* Friseure), Friseurin *die* (PL *die* Friseurinnen); **at the hairdresser's** beim Friseur.

hair drier *noun* Föhn *der* (PL *die* Föhne).

hair gel *noun* Haargel *das* (PL *die* Haargele).

hairgrip *noun* Haarklemme *die* (PL *die* Haarklemmen).

hairslide *noun* Haarspange *die* (PL *die* Haarspangen).

hairspray *noun* Haarspray *das* (PL *die* Haarsprays).

hairstyle *noun* Frisur *die* (PL *die* Frisuren).

hairy *adjective* behaart.

half *noun* **1** Hälfte *die* (PL *die* Hälften); **half of** die Hälfte von (+ DAT); **I gave him half of the money** ich habe ihm die Hälfte von dem Geld gegeben; **half of it** die Hälfte davon; **2 half an apple** ein halber Apfel; **3 to cut something in half** etwas halbieren; **4** (*as a fraction*) halb; **three and a half** dreieinhalb; **5** (*in time*) halb; **half an hour** eine halbe Stunde; **an hour and a half** anderthalb Stunden; **it's half past three** es ist halb vier (*literally: half on the way to four*); **6** (*in weights and measures*) halb; **half a litre** ein halber Liter.

half hour *noun* halbe Stunde *die*; **every half hour** jede halbe Stunde.

half price *adjective, adverb* zum halben Preis; **half-price CDs** CDs zum halben Preis.

half-time *noun* Halbzeit die; **at half-time the score is 0-0** zur Halbzeit steht es null zu null.

halfway *adverb* **1** auf halbem Weg; **halfway to Frankfurt** auf halbem Weg nach Frankfurt; **2 to be halfway through doing something** mit etwas halb fertig sein; **I'm halfway through my homework** ich bin mit meinen Hausaufgaben halb fertig.

hall *noun* **1** (*in a house*) Diele die (PL die Dielen); **2** (*public*) Saal der (PL die Säle); **village hall** der Gemeindesaal; **concert hall** der Konzertsaal.

Hallowe'en *noun* der Tag vor Allerheiligen (*in Germany there are no particular customs for this date*).

ham *noun* Schinken der; **a ham sandwich** ein Schinkenbrot.

hamburger *noun* Hamburger der (PL die Hamburger).

hammer *noun* Hammer der (PL die Hammer).

hamster *noun* Hamster der (PL die Hamster).

hand *noun* **1** Hand die (PL die Hände); **to have something in your hand** etwas in der Hand haben; **to hold somebody's hand** jemandes Hand halten; **2 to give somebody a hand** jemandem helfen◇; **can you give me a hand to move the table into the corner?** kannst du mir helfen, den Tisch in die Ecke zu rücken?; **do you need a hand?** kann ich dir helfen?; **3 on the other hand** ... andererseits ...; **4** (*of a watch or clock*) Zeiger der (PL die Zeiger); **the hour hand** der Stundenzeiger.

hand *verb* **to hand something to somebody** jemandem etwas geben◇; **I handed him the keys** ich gab ihm die Schlüssel.

● **to hand something in** etwas abgeben◇ SEP; **hand in your homework** gebt eure Hausaufgaben ab.

● **to hand something out** etwas austeilen SEP.

handbag *noun* Handtasche die (PL die Handtaschen).

handcuffs *plural noun* Handschellen (*plural*).

handful *noun* **a handful of** eine Hand voll.

handicapped *adjective* behindert.

handkerchief *noun* Taschentuch das (PL die Taschentücher).

handle *noun* **1** (*of a door, drawer, bag, or knife*) Griff der (PL die Griffe); **2** (*on a cup, jug, or basket*) Henkel der (PL die Henkel); **3** (*of a frying pan or broom*) Stiel der (PL die Stiele).

handle *verb* **1** erledigen; **Gina handles the correspondence** Gina erledigt die Korrespondenz; **2** umgehen◇ SEP (PERF *sein*) mit; **she's good at handling people** sie kann gut mit Menschen umgehen; **3** fertig werden ◇PERF *sein*) mit; **he can't handle problems** er kann mit Problemen nicht fertig werden.

handlebars *plural noun* Lenkstange die (PL die Lenkstangen).

hand luggage *noun* Handgepäck das.

handmade *adjective* handgemacht.

handsome *adjective* gut aussehend; **he's a handsome guy** er ist ein gut aussehender Typ.

handwriting *noun* Handschrift die (PL die Handschriften).

handy *adjective* 1 praktisch; **this little knife's very handy** dieses kleine Messer ist sehr praktisch; 2 griffbereit; **I always keep a notebook handy** ich habe immer ein kleines Notizbuch griffbereit.

hang *verb* 1 hängen◇; **there was a mirror hanging on the wall** an der Wand hing ein Spiegel; 2 aufhängen SEP; **to hang a mirror on the wall** einen Spiegel an der Wand aufhängen.

● **to hang around** rumhängen◇ SEP (PERF *sein*) (*informal*); **we were hanging around outside the cinema** wir haben vor dem Kino rumgehangen.

● **to hang on** warten; **hang on a second!** warten Sie einen Moment!

● **to hang up** (*on the phone*) auflegen SEP; **she hung up on me** sie hat einfach aufgelegt.

● **to hang something up** etwas aufhängen SEP.

hang-gliding *noun* Drachenfliegen das; **to go hang-gliding** Drachenfliegen gehen.

hangover *noun* Kater der (PL die Kater).

happen *verb* 1 passieren (PERF *sein*); **what happened?** was ist passiert?; **it happened in June** es ist im Juni passiert; 2 **what's**

happened to Jill? was ist mit Jill los?; 3 **what's happened to the can-opener?** wo ist der Dosenöffner?; 4 **if you happen to see him** wenn du ihn zufällig triffst; **Leila happened to be there** Leila war zufällig da.

happily *adverb* 1 glücklich; 2 (*willingly*) gerne; **I'll happily do it for you** ich tu es gerne für dich.

happiness *noun* Glück das.

happy *adjective* glücklich; **a happy child** ein glückliches Kind; **Happy Birthday** herzlichen Glückwunsch zum Geburtstag.

harbour *noun* Hafen der (PL die Häfen).

hard *adjective* 1 hart; 2 (*difficult*) schwer; **a hard question** eine schwere Frage; **it's hard to say** es ist schwer zu sagen.
hard *adverb* 1 **to work hard** hart arbeiten; 2 **to try hard** sich sehr bemühen.

hard disk *noun* Festplatte die (PL die Festplatten).

hardly *adverb* 1 kaum; **I can hardly hear him** ich kann ihn kaum hören; **there was hardly anybody there** es war kaum jemand da; **we've got hardly any milk** wir haben kaum Milch; **hardly anything** kaum etwas; **he ate hardly anything** er hat kaum etwas gegessen; 2 **hardly ever** fast nie; **I hardly ever see him** ich sehe ihn fast nie.

hard up *adjective* **to be hard up** knapp bei Kasse sein.

hare *noun* Hase der (PL die Hasen).

harm *noun* **it won't do any harm** es kann nichts schaden.

harm *verb* **1 to harm somebody** jemandem etwas tun; **they didn't harm him** sie haben ihm nichts getan; **2** schaden (+ DAT) (*health, environment, reputation*); **a cup of coffee won't harm you** eine Tasse Kaffee schadet nicht.

harmful *adjective* schädlich.

harmless *adjective* unschädlich.

harvest *noun* Ernte die (PL die Ernten); **to get the harvest in** die Ernte einbringen.

hat *noun* Hut der (PL die Hüte).

hate *verb* hassen; **I hate geography** ich hasse Erdkunde.

hatred *noun* Hass der.

have *verb* **1** haben✧; **Anna has three brothers** Anna hat drei Brüder; **how many sisters do you have?** wie viele Schwestern hast du?; **2 what have you got in your hand?** was hast du in der Hand?; **he has (got) flu** er hat die Grippe; **3** (*to form past tenses, some verbs in German take 'haben' and others 'sein'*) **I've finished** ich bin fertig; **have you seen the film?** hast du den Film gesehen?; **Rosie hasn't arrived yet** Rosie ist noch nicht angekommen; **4 to have to do something** etwas tun müssen✧; **I have to phone my mum** ich muss meine Mutter anrufen; **5** (*'have' is often translated by a more specific German verb*) **we had a coffee** wir haben einen Kaffee getrunken; **what will you have?** was nehmen

Sie?; **I'll have an omelette** ich nehme ein Omelett; **I'm going to have a shower** ich dusche jetzt; **to have lunch** zu Mittag essen; **to have dinner** (*in the evening*) zu Abend essen; **6** (*get*) bekommen✧; **Emma had a letter from Sam yesterday** gestern bekam Emma einen Brief von Sam; **she had a baby** sie hat ein Baby bekommen; **7 to have something done** etwas machen lassen✧; **I'm going to have my hair cut** ich lasse mir die Haare schneiden; **8 to have on** (*be wearing*) anhaben✧ SEP; **to have nothing on** nichts anhaben.

hawk *noun* Habicht der (PL die Habichte).

hay *noun* Heu das.

hay fever *noun* Heuschnupfen der.

hazelnut *noun* Haselnuss die (PL die Haselnüsse).

he *pronoun* er; **he lives in Manchester** er wohnt in Manchester.

head *noun* **1** Kopf der (PL die Köpfe); **he shook his head** er schüttelte den Kopf; **2** (*of a school*) Direktor der (PL die Direktoren), Direktorin die (PL die Direktorinnen); **3** (*of a firm*) Chef der (PL die Chefs), Chefin die (PL die Chefinnen); **4** (*when tossing a coin*) **'heads or tails?'** 'Kopf oder Zahl?'

● **to head for something** auf etwas (ACC) zusteuern SEP (PERF *sein*); **Liz headed for the door** Liz steuerte auf die Tür zu.

a
b
c
d
e
f
g
h
i
j
k
l
m
n
o
p
q
r
s
t
u
v
w
x
y
z

headache *noun* Kopfschmerzen (*plural*); **I've got a headache** ich habe Kopfschmerzen.

headlight *noun* Scheinwerfer *der* (PL *die* Scheinwerfer).

headline *noun* Schlagzeile *die* (PL *die* Schlagzeilen).

headmaster *noun* Direktor *der* (PL *die* Direktoren).

headmistress *noun* Direktorin *die* (PL *die* Direktorinnen).

headphones *noun* Kopfhörer *der* (PL *die* Kopfhörer).

headteacher *noun* Direktor *der* (PL *die* Direktoren), Direktorin *die* (PL *die* Direktorinnen).

health *noun* Gesundheit *die*.

health centre *noun* Ärztezentrum *das* (PL *die* Ärztezentren).

healthy *adjective* gesund.

heap *noun* Haufen *der* (PL *die* Haufen); **I've got heaps of work** ich habe einen Haufen Arbeit (*informal*).

hear *verb* hören; **I can't hear anything** ich kann überhaupt nichts hören; **I hear you've bought a dog** ich habe gehört, dass ihr einen Hund gekauft habt.

● **to hear about something** von etwas (DAT) hören; **have you heard about the concert?** hast du von dem Konzert gehört?

● **to hear from somebody** von jemandem hören.

hearing aid *noun* Hörgerät *das* (PL *die* Hörgeräte).

heart *noun* **1** Herz *das* (PL *die* Herzen); **2 to learn something by heart** etwas auswendig lernen; **3** (*in cards*) Herz *das*; **the jack of hearts** der Herzbube.

heart attack *noun* Herzinfarkt *der* (PL *die* Herzinfarkte).

heat *noun* Hitze *die*.

heat *verb* **1 to heat something** etwas heiß machen; **I'll go and heat the soup** ich mache die Suppe heiß; **2 the soup's heating** die Suppe wird warm; **3** heizen (*a room*).

● **to heat something up** etwas aufwärmen SEP; **I'm heating the sauce up** ich wärme die Soße auf.

heater *noun* Heizgerät *das* (PL *die* Heizgeräte).

heather *noun* Heidekraut *das*.

heating *noun* Heizung *die*.

heatwave *noun* Hitzewelle *die* (PL *die* Hitzewellen).

heaven *noun* Himmel *der*.

heavy *adjective* **1** schwer; **my rucksack's really heavy** mein Rucksack ist sehr schwer; **2** (*busy*) **I've got a heavy day tomorrow** ich habe morgen viel zu tun; **3** (*in quantity*) stark; **heavy rain** starker Regen.

hectic *adjective* hektisch; **a hectic day** ein hektischer Tag.

hedge *noun* Hecke *die* (PL *die* Hecken).

hedgehog *noun* Igel *der* (PL *die* Igel).

heel *noun* **1** (*of foot or sock*) Ferse *die* (PL *die* Fersen); **2** (*of a shoe*) Absatz *der* (PL *die* Absätze).

height *noun* **1** (*of a person*) Größe die; **what height are you?** wie groß bist du?; **2** (*of a building, mountain*) Höhe die; **what height is it?** wie hoch ist es?

helicopter *noun* Hubschrauber der (PL die Hubschrauber).

hell *noun* Hölle die; **hell!** verdammt! (*informal*).

hello *exclamation* **1** (*polite*) guten Tag!; **2** (*informal, and on the phone*) hallo!

helmet *noun* Helm der (PL die Helme).

help *noun* Hilfe die; **do you need any help?** kann ich dir helfen?, (*in a shop*) kann ich Ihnen behilflich sein?

help *verb* **1** helfen✧ (+ DAT); **to help somebody (to) do something** jemandem helfen, etwas zu tun; **can you help me lay the table?** kannst du mir helfen, den Tisch zu decken?; **2 to help yourself to something** sich (DAT) etwas nehmen✧; **help yourself to vegetables** nimm dir Gemüse; **help yourself!** greif zu!; **3 help!** Hilfe!; **4** he can't help it er kann nichts dafür.

helper *noun* Helfer der (PL die Helfer), Helferin die (PL die Helferinnen).

helpful *adjective* (*person*) hilfsbereit.

helping *noun* Portion die (PL die Portionen); **would you like a second helping?** möchtest du eine zweite Portion?

hem *noun* Saum der (PL die Säume).

hen *noun* Henne die (PL die Hennen).

her *pronoun* (*in German this pronoun changes according to the function it has in the sentence or the preposition it follows*) **1** (*as a direct object in the accusative*) sie; **I know her** ich kenne sie; **I saw her last week** ich habe sie letzte Woche gesehen; **2** (*after prepositions* + ACC) sie; **without her** ohne sie; **we've heard a lot about her** wir haben viel über sie gehört; **3** (*as an indirect object or after verbs that take the dative*) ihr; **I gave her my address** ich habe ihr meine Adresse gegeben; **we helped her** wir haben ihr geholfen; **4** (*after prepositions* + DAT) ihr; **with her** mit ihr; **5** (*in comparisons*) sie; **he's older than her** er ist älter als sie; **6** (*in the nominative*) sie; **it was her** sie war es.

her *adjective* **1** (*before a masculine noun*) ihr; **her brother** ihr Bruder; **2** (*before a feminine noun*) ihre; **her sister** ihre Schwester; **3** (*before a neuter noun*) ihr; **her house** ihr Haus; **4** (*before a plural noun*) ihre; **her children** ihre Kinder; **5** (*with parts of the body*) der/die/das, die (*plural*) ; **she had a glass in her hand** sie hatte ein Glas in der Hand; **she's washing her hands** sie wäscht sich die Hände.

herb *noun* Kraut das (PL die Kräuter).

herd *noun* (*of cattle, goats*) Herde die (PL die Herden).

here *adverb* **1** (*in or at this place*) hier; **not far from here** nicht weit von hier; **here's my address** hier ist

meine Adresse; **I want to stay here**
ich möchte hier bleiben; **2** (*to this
place*) hierher; **when Peter came
here** als Peter hierher kam; **3 here
they are!** da sind sie!; **Tom isn't
here at the moment** Tom ist im
Moment nicht da.

hero *noun* Held *der* (PL *die* Helden).

heroin *noun* Heroin *das*.

heroine *noun* Heldin *die* (PL *die*
Heldinnen).

herring *noun* Hering *der* (PL *die*
Heringe).

hers *pronoun* **1** (*for a masculine
noun*) ihrer; **my coat is blue and
hers is red** mein Mantel ist blau
und ihrer ist rot; **I took my hat and
she took hers** ich nahm meinen
Hut und sie nahm ihren; **2** (*for a
feminine noun*) ihre; **I gave Ann my
address and she gave me hers** ich
habe Ann meine Adresse gegeben
und sie hat mir ihre gegeben; **3** (*for
a neuter noun*) ihr(e)s; **my bike is
new but hers is old** mein Rad ist
neu, aber ihrs ist alt; **4** (*for
masculine/ feminine/neuter plural
nouns*) ihre; **I showed Emma my
photos and she showed me hers**
ich habe Emma meine Fotos gezeigt
und sie hat mir ihre gezeigt; **5 the
CDs are hers** die CDs gehören ihr;
it's hers das gehört ihr.

herself *pronoun* **1** (*reflexive*) sich;
she's hurt herself sie hat sich
wehgetan; **2** (*stressing something*)
selbst; **she said it herself** sie hat es
selbst gesagt; **3 she did it by
herself** sie hat es ganz allein
gemacht.

hesitate *verb* zögern.

heterosexual *adjective*
heterosexuell.

heterosexual *noun*
Heterosexuelle *der/die* (PL *die*
Heterosexuellen).

hi *exclamation* hallo!

hiccups *plural noun* **to have the
hiccups** einen Schluckauf haben.

hidden *adjective* verborgen.

hide *verb* **1** sich verstecken; **she hid
behind the door** sie hat sich hinter
der Tür versteckt; **2 to hide
something** etwas verstecken.

hi-fi *noun* Hi-Fi-Anlage *die* (PL *die* Hi-
Fi-Anlagen).

high *adjective* **1** hoch; **how high is
the wall?** wie hoch ist die Mauer?;
the wall is two metres high die
Mauer ist zwei Meter hoch; **the
shelf is too high** das Regal ist zu
hoch; (*the adjective 'hoch' loses its c
when it has an ending, becoming
hoher/hohe/hohes*) **a high tower** ein
hoher Turm; **a high wall** eine hohe
Mauer; **at high speed** mit hoher
Geschwindigkeit; **a high voice** eine
hohe Stimme; **2 high winds** starker
Wind.

high *adverb* hoch.

**Highers, Advanced
Highers** *noun plural* Abitur *das*
((*Students take 'Abitur' at about 19
years of age. You can explain Highers
briefly as follows: Highers werden im
vorletzten Jahr der Sekundarstufe in
bis zu fünf Fächern abgelegt.
Manche Schüler legen zusätzlich
Advanced Highers in ihrem letzten
Schuljahr ab. Advanced Highers*

werden in bis zu drei Fächern, die bereits für Highers belegt wurden, abgelegt. Beide Qualifikationen werden von A bis C benotet und sind Hochschulzugangsberechtigungen) SEE **Abitur**.

high-heeled *adjective* hochhackig.

high jump *noun* Hochsprung der.

hijack *verb* **to hijack a plane** ein Flugzeug entführen.

hijacker *noun* Entführer der (PL die Entführer).

hijacking *noun* Entführung die (PL die Entführungen).

hike *noun* Wanderung die (PL die Wanderungen).

hiker *noun* Wanderer der (PL die Wanderer), Wanderin die (PL die Wanderinnen).

hiking *noun* Wandern das

hilarious *adjective* lustig.

hill *noun* **1** (*large hill*) Berg der (PL die Berge); **you can see the hills** man kann die Berge sehen; **2** (*smaller*) Hügel der (PL die Hügel); **to walk up the hill** den Hügel hinaufgehen; **3** (*hillside*) Hang der (PL die Hänge); **the house on the hill** das Haus am Hang.

him *pronoun* (*in German this pronoun changes according to the function it has in the sentence or the preposition it follows*) **1** (*as a direct object in the accusative*) ihn; **I know him** ich kenne ihn; **I saw him last week** ich habe ihn letzte Woche gesehen; **2** (*after prepositions* + ACC) ihn; **he fought against him** er hat

gegen ihn gekämpft; **without him** ohne ihn; **3** (*as an indirect object or after verbs that take the dative*) ihm; **I gave him my address** ich habe ihm meine Adresse gegeben; **you must help him** du musst ihm helfen; **4** (*after prepositions* + DAT) ihm; **with him** mit ihm; **5** (*in comparisons*) er; **she's older than him** sie ist älter als er; **6** (*in the nominative*) er; **it was him** er war es.

himself *pronoun* **1** (*reflexive*) sich; **he's hurt himself** er hat sich wehgetan; **2** (*stressing something*) selbst; **he said it himself** er hat es selbst gesagt; **3 he did it by himself** er hat es ganz allein gemacht.

Hindu *adjective* hinduistisch.

hip *noun* Hüfte die (PL die Hüften).

hippie *noun* Hippie der (PL die Hippies).

hippopotamus *noun* Nilpferd das (PL die Nilpferde).

hire *noun* **1** Vermietung die; **car hire** die Autovermietung; **2 for hire** zu vermieten.
hire *verb* mieten.

his *adjective* **1** (*before a masculine noun*) sein; **his brother** sein Bruder; **2** (*before a feminine noun*) seine; **his sister** seine Schwester; **3** (*before a neuter noun*) sein; **his house** sein Haus; **4** (*before a plural noun*) seine; **his children** seine Kinder; **5** (*with parts of the body*) der/die/das, die (*plural*); **he had a glass in his hand** er hatte ein Glas in der Hand; **he's washing his hands** er wäscht sich (DAT) die Hände.

his *pronoun* **1** (*for a masculine*

noun) seiner; **my hat is red and his is blue** mein Hut ist rot und seiner ist blau; **2** (*for a feminine noun*) seine; **I gave him my address and he gave me his** ich habe ihm meine Adresse gegeben und er hat mir seine gegeben; **3** (*for a neuter noun*) sein(e)s; **my book is new but his is old** mein Buch ist neu, aber seins ist alt; **4** (*for masculine/feminine/ neuter plural nouns*) seine; **I've invited my parents and Steve's invited his** ich habe meine Eltern eingeladen und Steve hat seine eingeladen; **5 the green car's his** das grüne Auto gehört ihm; **it's his** das gehört ihm.

historic *adjective* historisch.

history *noun* Geschichte *die*.

hit *noun* **1** (*song*) Hit *der* (PL die Hits); **their latest hit** ihr neuester Hit; **2** (*success*) Erfolg *der* (PL die Erfolge); **the film is a huge hit** der Film ist ein großer Erfolg.
hit *verb* **1** treffen◇; **to hit the ball** den Ball treffen; **2 to hit your head on something** sich (DAT) den Kopf an etwas (DAT) stoßen; **I hit my head on the door** ich habe mir den Kopf an der Tür gestoßen; **3** prallen gegen (+ ACC) (PERF *sein*); **the car hit a wall** das Auto ist gegen eine Wand geprallt; **4 to be hit by a car** von einem Auto angefahren werden.

hitch *noun* Problem *das* (PL die Probleme); **there's been a slight hitch** ein kleines Problem ist aufgetaucht.
hitch *verb* **to hitch a lift** per Anhalter fahren◇ (PERF *sein*).

hitchhike *verb* per Anhalter fahren◇ (PERF *sein*); **we hitchhiked to Heidelberg** wir sind per Anhalter nach Heidelberg gefahren.

hitchhiker *noun* Anhalter *der* (PL die Anhalter), Anhalterin *die* (PL die Anhalterinnen).

hitchhiking *noun* Trampen *das*.

HIV-negative *adjective* HIV-negativ.

HIV-positive *adjective* HIV-positiv.

hobby *noun* Hobby *das* (PL die Hobbys).

hockey *noun* Hockey *das*.

hockey stick *noun* Hockeyschläger *der* (PL die Hockeyschläger).

hold *verb* **1** halten◇; **to hold something in your hand** etwas in der Hand halten; **can you hold the torch?** kannst du die Taschenlampe halten?; **2** (*be able to contain*) fassen; **the jug holds a litre** der Krug fasst einen Liter; **3 to hold a meeting** eine Versammlung abhalten◇ SEP; **4 can you hold the line, please?** bleiben Sie bitte am Apparat; **5 hold on!** (*wait*) warten Sie! (*on the phone*) bleiben Sie am Apparat.
● **to hold on to something** (*to stop yourself from falling*) sich an etwas (DAT) festhalten◇ SEP.
● **to hold somebody up** (*delay*) jemanden aufhalten◇ SEP; **I was held up at the dentist's** ich bin beim Zahnarzt aufgehalten worden.
● **to hold something up** (*raise*) etwas hochhalten◇ SEP.

hold-up *noun* **1** Verzögerung die (PL die Verzögerungen); **2** (*traffic jam*) Stau der (PL die Staus); **3** (*robbery*) Überfall der (PL die Überfälle).

hole *noun* Loch das (PL die Löcher).

holiday *noun* **1** Ferien (*plural*) Urlaub der (PL die Urlaube) (*students, schoolchildren, and families usually have 'Ferien'; people in paid employment usually have 'Urlaub'*); **where are you going for your holiday?** wo fahrt ihr in den Ferien hin?; **have a good holiday!** schöne Ferien!, schönen Urlaub!; **to be away on holiday** auf Urlaub sein, in den Ferien sein; **to go on holiday** in Urlaub fahren, in die Ferien fahren; **the school holidays** die Schulferien; **2** (*day off work*) freie Tag der (PL die freien Tage); **I'm taking two days' holiday next week** ich nehme mir nächste Woche zwei Tage frei; **3 public holiday** der Feiertag; **Monday's a holiday** Montag ist ein Feiertag.

holiday home *noun* Ferienhaus das (PL die Ferienhäuser).

Holland *noun* Holland das.

hollow *adjective* hohl.

holy *adjective* heilig.

home *noun* **1 I was at home** ich war zu Hause; **to stay at home** zu Hause bleiben; **2 make yourself at home** mach es dir bequem.
home *adverb* **1** (*to home*) nach Hause; **Susie's gone home** Susie ist nach Hause gegangen; **on my way home** auf dem Weg nach Hause; **to get home** nach Hause kommen; **we got home at midnight** wir sind um

Mitternacht nach Hause gekommen; **2** (*at home*) zu Hause; **I'll be home in the afternoon** ich bin am Nachmittag zu Hause.

homeless *adjective* obdachlos; **the homeless** die Obdachlosen.

homemade *adjective* selbst gemacht; **homemade biscuits** selbst gebackene Kekse.

homeopathic *adjective* homöopathisch.

homesick *adjective* **to be homesick** Heimweh haben.

homework *noun* Hausaufgaben (*plural*); **I did my homework** ich habe meine Hausaufgaben gemacht; **my German homework** meine Deutschhausaufgaben.

homosexual *adjective* homosexuell.
homosexual *noun* Homosexuelle der/die (PL die Homosexuellen).

honest *adjective* ehrlich.

honestly *adverb* ehrlich.

honesty *noun* Ehrlichkeit die.

honey *noun* Honig der (PL die Honige).

honeymoon *noun* Flitterwochen die (*plural*); **they're going to Italy on their honeymoon** sie fahren nach Italien in die Flitterwochen.

honour *noun* Ehre die.

hood *noun* **1** Kapuze die (PL die Kapuzen); **2** (*on a car*) Verdeck das (PL die Verdecke).

hook *noun* **1** Haken der (PL die Haken); **2 to take the phone off**

the **hook** das Telefon aushängen SEP.

hooligan *noun* Hooligan der (PL die Hooligans).

hooray *exclamation* hurra!

Hoover *noun* Staubsauger der (PL die Staubsauger).

hoover *verb* saugen; **I hoovered my bedroom** ich habe mein Schlafzimmer gesaugt.

hope *noun* Hoffnung die (PL die Hoffnungen); **to give up hope** die Hoffnung aufgeben.

hope *verb* **1** hoffen; **we hope you'll be able to come** wir hoffen, ihr könnt kommen; **I'm hoping to see you on Friday** ich hoffe, dich am Freitag zu sehen; **2 I hope so** hoffentlich; **I hope not** hoffentlich nicht.

hopefully *adverb* hoffentlich; **hopefully, the film won't have started** hoffentlich hat der Film noch nicht angefangen.

hopeless *adjective* miserabel (*informal*); **I'm hopeless at geography** ich bin miserabel in Erdkunde.

horizontal *adjective* horizontal, waagrecht; **the flag has three horizontal bars** die Flagge hat drei waagrechte Streifen.

horn *noun* **1** (*of an animal, instrument*) Horn das (PL die Hörner); **2** (*of a car*) Hupe die (PL die Hupen).

horoscope *noun* Horoskop das (PL die Horoskope).

horrible *adjective* **1** furchtbar; **the weather was horrible** das Wetter

war furchtbar; **2** (*person*) gemein; **she's really horrible** sie ist richtig gemein; **he was really horrible to me** er war richtig gemein zu mir.

horror *noun* Entsetzen das.

horror film *noun* Horrorfilm der (PL die Horrorfilme).

horse *noun* Pferd das (PL die Pferde).

horse chestnut *noun* (*tree and nut*) Rosskastanie die (PL die Rosskastanien).

horseshoe *noun* Hufeisen das (PL die Hufeisen).

hose *noun* Schlauch der (PL die Schläuche).

hosepipe *noun* Schlauch der (PL die Schläuche).

hospital *noun* Krankenhaus das (PL die Krankenhäuser); **in hospital** im Krankenhaus; **to be taken into hospital** ins Krankenhaus kommen.

hospitality *noun* Gastfreundschaft die.

host *noun* **1** Gastgeber der (PL die Gastgeber); **2** (*on a TV programme*) Moderator der (PL die Moderatoren).

hostage *noun* Geisel die (PL die Geiseln).

hostel *noun* **youth hostel** die Jugendherberge.

hostess *noun* **1** Gastgeberin die (PL die Gastgeberinnen); **2** (*on a TV programme*) Moderatorin die (PL die Moderatorinnen); **3 air hostess** die Stewardess.

hot *adjective* **1** heiß; **be careful, the plates are hot** sei vorsichtig, die Teller sind heiß; **it's hot today**

heute ist es heiß; **2** (*person*) **I'm very hot** mir ist sehr heiß; **3** (*spicy*) scharf; **the curry's too hot for me** das Curry ist mir zu scharf; **4 a hot meal** ein warmes Essen.

hot dog *noun* Hotdog *das* (or) *der* (PL *die* Hotdogs).

hotel *noun* Hotel *das* (PL *die* Hotels).

hour *noun* Stunde *die* (PL *die* Stunden); **two hours later** zwei Stunden später; **we waited for two hours** wir haben zwei Stunden lang gewartet; **I've been waiting for hours** ich warte schon seit Stunden; **two hours ago** vor zwei Stunden; **to be paid by the hour** pro Stunde bezahlt werden; **every hour** jede Stunde; **half an hour** eine halbe Stunde; **a quarter of an hour** eine Viertelstunde; **an hour and a half** anderthalb Stunden.

house *noun* **1** Haus *das* (PL *die* Häuser); **2 at somebody's house** bei jemandem; **I'm at Judy's house** ich bin bei Judy; **I'm going to Sid's house tonight** ich gehe heute Abend zu Sid; **I phoned from Jill's house** ich habe von Jill aus angerufen.

housewife *noun* Hausfrau *die* (PL *die* Hausfrauen).

housework *noun* Hausarbeit *die*; **he does the housework** er macht den Haushalt (*informal*).

hovercraft *noun* Luftkissenfahrzeug *das* (PL *die* Luftkissenfahrzeuge).

how *adverb* **1** wie; **how did you do it?** wie hast du das gemacht?; **how are you?** wie geht es dir?; **how**

many? wie viele?; **how many brothers do you have?** wie viele Brüder hast du?; **how old are you?** wie alt bist du?; **how far is it?** wie weit ist es?; **how far is it to York?** wie weit ist es bis York?; **how long will it take?** wie lange dauert es?; **how long have you known her?** wie lange kennst du sie?; **2 how much?** wie viel?; **how much money do you have?** wie viel Geld hast du?; **how much is it?** wie viel kostet das?

however *adverb* **1** jedoch; **2** (*in questions*) **however did she do it?** wie hat sie das nur gemacht?; **3 however famous he is** wie berühmt er auch sein mag.

hug *noun* **to give somebody a hug** jemanden umarmen; **she gave me a hug** sie hat mich umarmt.

huge *adjective* riesig.

hum *verb* summen.

human *adjective* menschlich.

human being *noun* Mensch *der* (PL *die* Menschen).

humour *noun* Humor *der*; **to have a sense of humour** Humor haben.

hundred *number* hundert; **two hundred** zweihundert; **two hundred and ten** zweihundertzehn; **a hundred people** hundert Menschen; **about a hundred** um die hundert; **hundreds of people** hunderte von Menschen.

Hungary *noun* Ungarn *das*.

hunger *noun* Hunger *der*.

a
b
c
d
e
f
g
h
i
j
k
l
m
n
o
p
q
r
s
t
u
v
w
x
y
z

455

a
b
c
d
e
f
g
h
i
j
k
l
m
n
o
p
q
r
s
t
u
v
w
x
y
z

hungry *adjective* **to be hungry** Hunger haben; **I'm hungry** ich habe Hunger.

hunt *verb* **1** jagen (*an animal*); **2** suchen (*a person*).

hunting *noun* Jagd *die*; **fox-hunting** *die* Fuchsjagd.

hurry *noun* **to be in a hurry** es eilig haben; **I'm in a hurry** ich habe es eilig; **there's no hurry** es eilt nicht. **hurry** *verb* **1** sich beeilen; **I must hurry** ich muss mich beeilen; **hurry up!** beeil dich!; **2** he hurried home er ging schnell nach Hause.

hurt *verb* **1** **to hurt somebody** jemandem wehtun◇ SEP; **you're hurting me!** du tust mir weh!; **that hurts!** das tut weh!; **2 my arm hurts** der Arm tut mir weh; **3 to hurt yourself** sich (DAT) wehtun◇ SEP; **did you hurt yourself?** hast du dir wehgetan? **hurt** *adjective* **1** (*in an accident*) verletzt; **three people were hurt** drei Menschen wurden verletzt; **2** (*in feelings*) gekränkt; **she felt hurt** sie fühlte sich gekränkt.

husband *noun* Ehemann *der* (PL *die* Ehemänner).

hygienic *adjective* hygienisch.

hymn *noun* Kirchenlied *das* (PL *die* Kirchenlieder).

hypermarket *noun* Großmarkt *der* (PL *die* Großmärkte).

hyphen *noun* Bindestrich *der* (PL *die* Bindestriche).

Ii

I *pronoun* ich; **I have two sisters** ich habe zwei Schwestern.

ice *noun* Eis *das*.

ice cream *noun* Eis *das*; **two chocolate ice creams** zwei Schokoladeneis.

ice hockey *noun* Eishockey *das*.

ice rink *noun* Eisbahn *die* (PL *die* Eisbahnen).

ice-skating *noun* **to go ice-skating** Schlittschuh laufen◇ (PERF *sein*).

icy *adjective* **1** vereist (*road*); **2** (*very cold*) eiskalt.

idea *noun* **1** Idee *die* (PL *die* Ideen); **what a good idea!** was für eine gute Idee!; **2 I've no idea** ich habe keine Ahnung.

ideal *adjective* ideal.

identical *adjective* identisch.

identification *noun* **1** Identifizierung *die*; **2** (*proof of identity*) Ausweispapiere (*plural*).

identity card *noun* Personalausweis *der* (PL *die* Personalausweise).

idiot *noun* Idiot *der* (PL *die* Idioten).

idiotic *adjective* idiotisch.

i.e. *abbreviation* d. h. (*das heißt*).

if *conjunction* **1** wenn; **if it rains** wenn es regnet; **if I won the lottery** wenn ich in der Lotterie gewinnen sollte; **if not** wenn nicht; **if only** wenn nur; **if only you'd told me** wenn du mir das nur gesagt hättest; **2 even if**

selbst wenn; **even if it snows** selbst wenn es schneit; **3 if I were you** an deiner Stelle; **4** (*whether*) ob; **I wonder if he'll come** ich bin gespannt, ob er kommt; **as if** als ob.

ignore *verb* **1** ignorieren; **2** überhören (*what somebody says*).

ill *adjective* krank; **to fall ill, to be taken ill** krank werden; **I feel ill** ich fühle mich krank.

illegal *adjective* illegal.

illness *noun* Krankheit *die* (PL *die* Krankheiten).

illusion *noun* Illusion *die* (PL *die* Illusionen).

illustration *noun* Illustration *die* (PL *die* Illustrationen).

image *noun* Bild *das* (PL *die* Bilder); ★ **he's the spitting image of his father** er ist das Ebenbild seines Vaters.

imagination *noun* Phantasie *die*.

imaginative *adjective* phantasievoll.

imagine *verb* sich (DAT) vorstellen; **imagine that you're very rich** stell dir vor, du bist sehr reich; **you can't imagine how hard it was** du kannst dir nicht vorstellen, wie schwer es war.

imitate *verb* nachahmen SEP.

immediate *adjective* **1** (*without delay*) unmittelbar; **2 the immediate family** die engste Familie.

immediately *adverb* **1** sofort; **I rang them immediately** ich habe sie sofort angerufen; **2 immediately**

before unmittelbar davor; **immediately after** unmittelbar danach.

immigrant *noun* Einwanderer *der* (PL *die* Einwanderer), Einwanderin *die* (PL *die* Einwanderinnen).

immigration *noun* Einwanderung *die*.

impatience *noun* Ungeduld *die*.

impatient *adjective* **1** ungeduldig; **2 to be impatient with somebody** ungeduldig mit jemandem sein.

impatiently *adverb* ungeduldig.

imperfect *noun* (*verb tense*) Imperfekt *das*; **"ich schlug" is in the imperfect** "ich schlug" steht im Imperfekt.

import *noun* Import *der* (PL *die* Importe). **import** *verb* importieren.

importance *noun* Wichtigkeit *die*.

important *adjective* wichtig.

impossible *adjective* unmöglich; **it's impossible to find a telephone** es ist unmöglich, ein Telefon zu finden.

impressed *adjective* beeindruckt; **to be impressed by something** von etwas (DAT) beeindruckt sein.

impression *noun* Eindruck *der* (PL *die* Eindrücke); **to make a good impression on somebody** einen guten Eindruck auf jemanden machen; **I got the impression he was hiding something** ich hatte den Eindruck, dass er etwas verheimlichte.

a
b
c
d
e
f
g
h
i
j
k
l
m
n
o
p
q
r
s
t
u
v
w
x
y
z

impressive *adjective*
eindrucksvoll.

improve *verb* **1 to improve
something** etwas verbessern; **2** (*get
better*) besser werden; **the weather
is improving** das Wetter wird
besser.

improvement *noun*
Verbesserung *die* (PL *die*
Verbesserungen).

in *preposition* **1** in (+ DAT *or, with
movement into,* + ACC); **it is in my
pocket** es ist in meiner Tasche;
(*with movement*) **he put it in his
pocket** er hat es in die Tasche
gesteckt; **she sat in the sun** sie saß
in der Sonne; **I read it in the
newspaper** ich habe es in der
Zeitung gelesen; **in Oxford** in
Oxford; **in Germany** in
Deutschland; **2 the biggest city in
the world** die größte Stadt der Welt;
a house in the country ein Haus
auf dem Land; **in the street** auf der
Straße; **3** (*wearing and with colours*)
in (+ DAT); **the girl in the pink shirt**
das Mädchen im rosa Hemd; **4 in
German** auf Deutsch; **5** (*time
expressions*) in (+ DAT); **in May** im
Mai; **in 1994** (im Jahre) 1994; **in
winter** im Winter; **in summer** im
Sommer; **in the night** in der Nacht;
I'll phone you in ten minutes ich
rufe dich in zehn Minuten an; **she
was ready in five minutes** sie war
in fünf Minuten fertig; **6 in the
morning** am Morgen; **at eight in
the morning** um acht Uhr morgens;
7 (*among people or in literature*) bei
(+ DAT); **it's rare in children** das ist
selten bei Kindern; **in Shakespeare**
bei Shakespeare; **in the army** beim
Militär; **8 in time** rechtzeitig.

in *adverb* **1** (*inside*) hinein-, herein-,
rein- (*informal*) (*Herein-, hinein-,
and rein- form prefixes to separable
verbs. 'Herein-' is used with verbs like
kommen, which have the sense of
moving towards the speaker. 'Hinein-
' is used with verbs like gehen, which
have the sense of going away from the
speaker. The informal 'rein-' can be
used with either movement*); **to come
in** hereinkommen◇ SEP (PERF *sein*);
to go in hineingehen◇ SEP (PERF
sein); **he was not allowed to go
into the room** er durfte nicht ins
Zimmer reingehen; **to run in**
reinlaufen◇ SEP (PERF *sein*)
(*informal*); **2 to be in** da sein;
Mick's not in at the moment Mick
ist im Moment nicht da; **3** (*at home*)
zu Hause; **4** (*indoors*) drinnen; **in
here** hier drinnen; **in there** da
drinnen.

include *verb* einschließen◇ SEP;
service is included in the price die
Bedienung ist im Preis inbegriffen.

including *preposition*
1 einschließlich (+ GEN); **everyone,
including the children** alle,
einschließlich der Kinder; **£50
including postage** fünfzig Pfund
einschließlich Porto; **including
Sundays** einschließlich sonntags;
2 not including Sundays außer
sonntags.

income *noun* Einkommen *das* (PL
die Einkommen).

income tax *noun*
Einkommensteuer *die* (PL *die*
Einkommensteuern).

increase *noun* Erhöhung *die* (PL *die*
Erhöhungen) (*in price, for example*).
increase *verb* **1** steigen✧ (PERF
sein); **the price has increased by
£10** der Preis ist um zehn Pfund
gestiegen; **2** erhöhen (*salary*).

incredible *adjective* unglaublich.

incredibly *adverb* (*very*)
unglaublich; **the film's incredibly
boring** der Film ist unglaublich
langweilig.

indeed *adverb* **1** (*to emphasize*)
wirklich; **she's very pleased
indeed** sie hat sich wirklich sehr
gefreut; **2** (*certainly*) natürlich; **'can
you hear the radio?' – 'indeed I
can!'** 'kannst du das Radio hören?' -
'ja, natürlich!'; **3 thank you very
much indeed** vielen herzlichen
Dank.

indefinite article *noun*
unbestimmte Artikel *der* (PL *die*
umbestimmten Artikel).

independence *noun*
Unabhängigkeit *die*.

independent *adjective*
unabhängig; **independent school**
die Privatschule.

index *noun* Register *das* (PL *die*
Register).

India *noun* Indien *das*.

Indian *noun* **1** Inder *der* (PL *die*
Inder), Inderin *die* (PL *die*
Inderinnen); **2** (*a Native American*)
Indianer *der* (PL *die* Indianer),
Indianerin *die* (PL *die*

Indianerinnen).
Indian *adjective* **1** indisch; **he's
Indian** er ist Inder; **2** (*Native
American*) indianisch; **she's Indian**
sie ist Indianerin.

indicate *verb* **1** zeigen auf (+ ACC)
(*a person or a thing*); **2** (*of a car or
driver*) blinken.

indigestion *noun*
Magenverstimmung *die* (PL *die*
Magenverstimmungen).

individual *noun* Einzelne *der/die*
(PL *die* Einzelnen).
individual *adjective* **1** einzeln
(*serving, contribution*); **2 individual
tuition** *der* Einzelunterricht.

indoor *adjective* **an indoor
swimming pool** ein Hallenbad;
indoor games Spiele im Haus, (*in
sports*) Hallenspiele.

indoors *adverb* drinnen; **it's
cooler indoors** drinnen ist es
kühler; **to go indoors** ins Haus
gehen.

industrial *adjective* industriell.

industrial estate *noun*
Industriegebiet *das* (PL *die*
Industriegebiete).

industry *noun* Industrie *die* (PL *die*
Industrien); **the car industry** die
Autoindustrie.

inefficient *adjective* uneffektiv.

inevitable *adjective*
unvermeidlich.

inevitably *adverb* zwangsläufig.

inexperienced *adjective*
unerfahren.

a
b
c
d
e
f
g
h
i
j
k
l
m
n
o
p
q
r
s
t
u
v
w
x
y
z

infant school *noun* Vorschule *die* (PL *die* Vorschulen).

infection *noun* Infektion *die* (PL *die* Infektionen); **eye infection** *die* Augeninfektion; **throat infection** *die* Halsentzündung.

infectious *adjective* ansteckend.

infinitive *noun* Infinitiv *der* (PL *die* Infinitive).

inflammable *adjective* leicht entflammbar.

inflatable *adjective* **inflatable mattress** *die* Luftmatratze; **inflatable boat** *das* Schlauchboot.

inflate *verb* aufblasen ⋄ SEP (*a mattress or boat*).

inflation *noun* Inflation *die* (PL *die* Inflationen).

influence *noun* Einfluss *der* (PL *die* Einflüsse); **to be a good influence on somebody** einen guten Einfluss auf jemanden haben.
influence *verb* beeinflussen.

inform *verb* informieren; **to inform somebody of something** jemanden über etwas (ACC) informieren.

informal *adjective* **1** zwanglos (*meal or event*); **2** ungezwungen (*language, tone*).

information *noun* Auskunft *die*; **where can I get information about flights to Berlin?** wo kann ich Auskunft über Flüge nach Berlin bekommen?

information desk, **information office** *noun* Auskunftsbüro *das* (PL *die* Auskunftsbüros).

information technology *noun* Informatik *die*.

ingredient *noun* Zutat *die* (PL *die* Zutaten).

inhabitant *noun* Einwohner *der* (PL *die* Einwohner), Einwohnerin *die* (PL *die* Einwohnerinnen).

initials *plural noun* Initialen (*plural*).

initiative *noun* Initiative *die* (PL *die* Initiativen); **you must use your initiative** du musst die Initiative ergreifen.

injection *noun* Spritze *die* (PL *die* Spritzen).

injure *verb* verletzen.

injury *noun* Verletzung *die* (PL *die* Verletzungen).

ink *noun* Tinte *die* (PL *die* Tinten).

in-laws *noun* Schwiegereltern (*plural*).

inner *adjective* inner.

innocent *adjective* unschuldig.

insane *adjective* **1** geisteskrank; **2** (*foolish*) wahnsinnig.

insect *noun* Insekt *das* (PL *die* Insekten); **insect bite** *der* Insektenstich.

insect repellent *noun* Insektenvertilgungsmittel *das*.

inside *noun* **on the inside** innen; **the inside of the oven is black** innen ist der Herd schwarz.
inside *preposition* in (+ DAT, *or, with movement towards a place*, + ACC); **inside the cinema** im Kino; **to go inside (the house)** ins Haus gehen.
inside *adverb* drinnen; **she's**

inside, I think ich glaube, sie ist drinnen.

inside out *adjective, adverb* (*clothing*) links.

insist *verb* darauf bestehen◇; **if you insist** wenn du darauf bestehst; **to insist on doing something** darauf bestehen, etwas zu tun; **he insists on paying** er besteht darauf zu zahlen; **to insist that** ... darauf bestehen, dass ...; **Ruth insisted I was wrong** Ruth hat darauf bestanden, dass ich Unrecht hatte.

inspector *noun* **1** (*on a bus or train*) Kontrolleur *der* (PL die Kontrolleure), Kontrolleurin *die* (PL die Kontrolleurinnen); **2** (*in the police*) Kommissar *der* (PL die Kommissare), Kommissarin *die* (PL die Kommissarinnen).

install *verb* installieren.

instalment *noun* (*of a story or serial*) Folge *die* (PL die Folgen).

instance *noun* **for instance** zum Beispiel.

instant *noun* Augenblick *der* (PL die Augenblicke); **come here this instant!** komm sofort her! **instant** *adjective* **1** Instant- (*coffee, tea*); **2** (*immediate*) sofortig.

instantly *adverb* sofort.

instead *adverb* **1 Ted couldn't come, so I came instead (of him)** Ted konnte nicht kommen, also bin ich an seiner Stelle gekommen; **2 instead of** statt (+ GEN *or* + DAT); **he bought a bike instead of a car** statt eines Autos hat er ein Fahrrad gekauft; **instead of cake I had**

cheese statt Kuchen habe ich Käse genommen; **instead of playing tennis we went swimming** statt Tennis zu spielen, sind wir schwimmen gegangen.

instinct *noun* Instinkt *der* (PL die Instinkte).

institute *noun* Institut *das* (PL die Institute).

instructions *plural noun* Anweisung *die* (PL die Anweisungen); **follow the instructions on the packet** befolgen Sie die Anweisung auf der Packung; **'instructions for use'** 'Gebrauchsanweisung'.

instructor *noun* Lehrer *der* (PL die Lehrer), Lehrerin *die* (PL die Lehrerinnen); **my skiing instructor** mein Skilehrer.

instrument *noun* Instrument *das* (PL die Instrumente); **to play an instrument** ein Instrument spielen.

insulin *noun* Insulin *das*.

insult *noun* Beleidigung *die* (PL die Beleidigungen).
insult *verb* beleidigen.

insurance *noun* Versicherung *die* (PL die Versicherungen); **travel insurance** *die* Reiseversicherung; **do you have holiday medical insurance?** bist du urlaubskrankenversichert?

intelligence *noun* Intelligenz *die*.

intelligent *adjective* intelligent.

intend *verb* beabsichtigen; **as I intended** wie beabsichtigt; **to intend to do something** beabsichtigen, etwas zu tun; **we intend to spend the night in Rome**

wir beabsichtigen, in Rom zu übernachten.

intensive care *noun* Intensivpflege *die*; **he's now in intensive care** er ist jetzt auf der Intensivstation.

intention *noun* Absicht *die* (PL *die* Absichten); **I have no intention of paying** ich habe nicht die Absicht zu zahlen.

interest *noun* **1** Interesse *das* (PL *die* Interessen); **to have lots of interests** viele Interessen haben; **he has an interest in jazz** er hat Interesse an Jazz; **2** (*financial*) Zinsen (*plural*).
interest *verb* interessieren; **that doesn't interest me** das interessiert mich nicht.

interested *adjective* **to be interested in something** sich für etwas (ACC) interessieren; **Sean's interested in cooking** Sean interessiert sich für Kochen.

interesting *adjective* interessant.

interfere *verb* **1 to interfere with something** (*to fiddle with it*) sich (DAT) an etwas (DAT) zu schaffen machen; **don't interfere with my computer!** mach dir nicht an meinem Computer zu schaffen!; **2 to interfere in something** sich in etwas (ACC) einmischen SEP (*somebody else's affairs*).

interior designer *noun* Innenarchitekt *der* (PL *die* Innenarchitekten), Innenarchitektin *die* (PL *die* Innenarchitektinnen).

international *adjective* international.

Internet *noun* Internet *das*; **on the Internet** im Internet.

Internet cafe *noun* Internetcafé *das* (PL *die* Internetcafés); **where is there an Internet cafe?** wo gibt es hier ein Internetcafé?

interpret *verb* (*act as an interpreter*) dolmetschen.

interpreter *noun* Dometscher *der* (PL *die* Dolmetscher), Dolmetscherin *die* (PL *die* Dometscherinnen).

interrupt *verb* unterbrechen✧.

interruption *noun* Unterbrechung *die* (PL *die* Unterbrechungen).

interval *noun* (*in a play or concert*) Pause *die* (PL *die* Pausen).

interview *noun* **1** (*for a job*) Vorstellungsgespräch *das* (PL *die* Vorstellungsgespräche); **to go for an interview** sich vorstellen SEP; **2** (*in a newspaper, on TV, or radio*) Interview *das* (PL *die* Interviews).
interview *verb* interviewen (*on TV, radio*).

interviewer *noun* Interviewer *der* (PL *die* Interviewer), Interviewerin *die* (PL *die* Interviewerinnen).

into *preposition* **1** in (+ ACC); **he's gone into the garden** er ist in den Garten gegangen; **I put the ball into the bag** ich habe den Ball in die Tasche getan; **we all got into the car** wir sind alle ins Auto gestiegen; **to go into town** in die Stadt gehen; **to get into bed** ins Bett gehen; **to translate into German** ins

Deutsche übersetzen; **to change pounds into euros** Pfund in Euro wechseln; **2** (*against*) gegen (+ ACC); **he drove into the wall** er ist gegen die Wand gefahren; **3 to be into jazz** auf Jazz abfahren✧ SEP (PERF *sein*) (*informal*).

introduce *verb* vorstellen SEP; **she introduced me to her brother** sie hat mich ihrem Bruder vorgestellt; **she introduced her brother to me** sie hat mir ihren Bruder vorgestellt; **can I introduce you to my mother?** darf ich Sie meiner Mutter vorstellen?

introduction *noun* (*in a book*) Einleitung *die* (PL *die* Einleitungen).

invade *verb* einfallen✧ SEP in (PERF *sein*) (+ ACC).

invalid *noun* Kranke *der/die* (PL *die* Kranken).

invent *verb* erfinden✧.

invention *noun* Erfindung *die* (PL *die* Erfindungen).

inverted commas *plural noun* Anführungszeichen (*plural*); **in inverted commas** in Anführungszeichen.

investigation *noun* Untersuchung *die* (PL *die* Untersuchungen); **an investigation into the incident** eine Untersuchung des Vorfalls.

invisible *adjective* unsichtbar.

invitation *noun* Einladung *die* (PL *die* Einladungen); **an invitation to dinner** eine Einladung zum Abendessen.

invite *verb* einladen✧ SEP; **Kirsty invited me to lunch** Kirsty hat mich zum Mittagessen eingeladen; **he's invited me out on Tuesday** er hat mich eingeladen, Dienstag mit ihm auszugehen; **they invited us round** sie haben uns zu sich eingeladen.

inviting *adjective* verlockend.

involve *verb* **1** erfordern; **it involves a lot of time** es erfordert viel Zeit; **2** (*include*) beteiligen; **the game will involve everybody** alle können sich an dem Spiel beteiligen; **to be involved in something** an etwas (DAT) beteiligt sein; **I am involved in the new project** ich bin an dem neuen Projekt beteiligt; **3** (*implicate*) verwickeln; **to get involved in something** in etwas (ACC) verwickelt werden; **two cars were involved in the accident** zwei Autos waren in den Unfall verwickelt; **4 to get involved with somebody** sich mit jemandem einlassen✧ SEP.

Iran *noun* Iran *der*.

Iraq *noun* Irak *der*.

Ireland *noun* Irland *das*; **the Republic of Ireland** die Republik Irland.

Irish *noun* **1** (*the language*) Irisch *das*; **2** (*the people*) **the Irish** die Iren. **Irish** *adjective* irisch; **he's Irish** er ist Ire; **she's Irish** sie ist Irin.

Irishman *noun* Ire *der* (PL *die* Iren).

Irish Sea *noun* Irische See *die*.

Irishwoman *noun* Irin *die* (PL *die* Irinnen).

a
b
c
d
e
f
g
h
i
j
k
l
m
n
o
p
q
r
s
t
u
v
w
x
y
z

iron noun 1 (for clothes) Bügeleisen das (PL die Bügeleisen); 2 (the metal) Eisen das.
iron verb bügeln.

ironing noun Bügeln das; **to do the ironing** bügeln.

ironing board noun Bügelbrett das (PL die Bügelbretter).

ironmonger's noun Haushaltswarengeschäft das (PL die Haushaltswarengeschäfte).

irregular adjective unregelmäßig.

irritable adjective reizbar.

irritate verb ärgern.

irritating adjective ärgerlich.

Islam noun Islam der.

Islamic adjective islamisch.

island noun Insel die (PL die Inseln).

isolated adjective 1 (remote) abgelegen; 2 (single) einzeln; **isolated cases** Einzelfälle.

Israel noun Israel das.

Israeli noun Israeli der/die (PL die Iraelis).
Israeli adjective israelisch.

issue noun 1 (something you discuss) Frage die (PL die Fragen); **a political issue** eine politische Frage; 2 (of a magazine) Ausgabe die (PL die Ausgaben).
issue verb (hand out) ausgeben✧ SEP.

it pronoun 1 (as the subject) er (standing for a masculine noun), sie (standing for a feminine noun), es (standing for a neuter noun); **'where's my key?' – 'it's in the kitchen'** 'wo ist mein Schlüssel?' –

'er ist in der Küche'; **'where's my bag?'– 'it's in the living-room'** 'wo ist meine Tasche?' – 'sie ist im Wohnzimmer'; **'how old is your car?' – 'it's five years old'** 'wie alt ist dein Auto?' – 'es ist fünf Jahre alt'; 2 (as the direct object, in the accusative) ihn (standing for a masculine noun), sie (standing for a feminine noun), es (standing for a neuter noun); **'where's your umbrella?' –'I've lost it'** 'wo ist dein Regenschirm?'– 'ich habe ihn verloren'; **'have you seen my bag?' -'I saw it in the kitchen'** 'hast du meine Tasche gesehen?' - 'ich habe sie in der Küche gesehen'; **'have you read his new book?' - 'I've just bought it'** 'hast du sein neues Buch gelesen?' - 'ich habe es gerade gekauft'; 3 **to it** ihm (masculine), ihr (feminine), ihm (neuter); 4 **yes, it's true** ja, das stimmt; **it doesn't matter** das macht nichts; 5 **who is it?** wer ist da?; **it's me** ich bins; **what is it?** was ist los?; 6 **it's raining** es regnet; **it's Monday** es ist Montag; **it's two o'clock** es ist zwei Uhr; 7 **of it** davon; 8 **out of it** daraus.

Italian noun 1 (the language) Italienisch das; 2 (person) Italiener der (PL die Italiener), Italienerin die (PL die Italienerinnen).
Italian adjective 1 italienisch; **Italian food** die italienische Küche; 2 **my Italian class** mein Italienischunterricht.

italics noun Kursivschrift die; **in italics** kursiv.

Italy noun Italien das.

itch *verb* **1 my back's itching** mein Rücken juckt; **2 this jumper itches** dieser Pullover kratzt.

item *noun* **1** Gegenstand *der* (PL *die* Gegenstände); **2** (*for sale in a shop*) Artikel *der* (PL *die* Artikel).

its *adjective* **1** sein (*for a masculine noun*), ihr (*for a feminine noun*), sein (*for a neuter noun*); **the dog has lost its collar** der Hund hat sein Halsband verloren; **the cat's in its basket** die Katze ist in ihrem Korb; **the horse is brown and its mane is black** das Pferd ist braun und seine Mähne ist schwarz; **2** (*for a plural noun*) seine (*standing for a feminine noun*), (*standing for a masculine noun*) ihre, seine (*standing for a neuter noun*); **its toys** seine Spielsachen, ihre Spielsachen.

itself *pronoun* **1** (*reflexive*) sich; **the cat's washing itself** die Katze putzt sich; **2 he left the dog by itself** er hat den Hund allein gelassen.

ivy *noun* Efeu *der*.

Jj

jack *noun* **1** (*in cards*) Bube *der* (PL *die* Buben); **the jack of clubs** der Kreuzbube; **2** (*for a car*) Wagenheber *der* (PL *die* Wagenheber).

jacket *noun* Jacke *die* (PL *die* Jacken).

jacket potatoes *noun* in der Schale gebackenen Kartoffeln.

jackpot *noun* Jackpot *der* (PL *die* Jackpots); **to win the jackpot** den Hauptgewinn bekommen; **to hit the jackpot** das große Los ziehen.

jam *noun* **1** Marmelade *die* (PL *die* Marmeladen); **raspberry jam** die Himbeermarmelade; **2 traffic jam** der Stau.

January *noun* Januar *der*; **in January** im Januar.

Japan *noun* Japan *das*.

Japanese *noun* **1** (*the language*) Japanisch *das*; **2** (*person*) Japaner *der* (PL *die* Japaner), Japanerin *die* (PL *die* Japanerinnen); **the Japanese** die Japaner.
Japanese *adjective* japanisch.

jar *noun* **1** (*small*) Glas *das* (PL *die* Gläser); **a jar of jam** ein Glas Marmelade; **2** (*large*) Topf *der* (PL *die* Töpfe).

javelin *noun* Speer *der* (PL *die* Speere).

jaw *noun* Kiefer *der* (PL *die* Kiefer).

jazz *noun* Jazz *der*.

jealous *adjective* eifersüchtig; **to be jealous of somebody** eifersüchtig auf jemanden sein.

jeans *plural noun* Jeans (*plural*); **my jeans** meine Jeans; **a pair of jeans** ein Paar Jeans.

jelly *noun* **1** Gelee *das* (PL *die* Gelees); **2** (*dessert*) Götterspeise *die* (PL *die* Götterspeisen).

jellyfish *noun* Qualle *die* (PL *die* Quallen).

a
b
c
d
e
f
g
h
i
j
k
l
m
n
o
p
q
r
s
t
u
v
w
x
y
z

jersey noun **1** (jumper) Pullover der (PL die Pullover); **2** (for football) Trikot das (PL die Trikots).

Jesus noun Jesus der; **Jesus Christ** Jesus Christus.

jet noun (a plane) Jet der (PL die Jets).

jet lag noun Jetlag der.

Jew noun Jude der (PL die Juden), Jüdin die (PL die Jüdinnen).

jewel noun Edelstein der (PL die Edelsteine).

jeweller noun Juwelier der (PL die Juweliere).

jeweller's noun Juweliergeschäft das.

jewellery noun Schmuck der.

Jewish adjective jüdisch.

jigsaw noun Puzzlespiel das (PL die Puzzlespiele).

job noun **1** (paid work) Stelle die (PL die Stellen), Job der (PL die Jobs) (informal); **a job as a secretary** eine Stelle als Sekretärin; **2** (a task) Arbeit die (PL die Arbeiten); **it's not an easy job** das ist keine leichte Arbeit; **3 she made a good job of it** sie hat es gut gemacht.

jobless adjective arbeitslos.

jog verb joggen✧ (PERF sein).

join verb **1** (become a member of) beitreten✧ SEP (+ DAT) (PERF sein); **I've joined the tennis club** ich bin dem Tennisklub beigetreten; **2** (to meet up with) treffen✧; **I'll join you later** ich treffe euch später.

● **to join in 1** mitmachen SEP; **Kylie never joins in** Kylie macht nie mit; **2 to join in something** bei etwas

(DAT) mitmachen SEP; **won't you join in the game?** willst du bei dem Spiel nicht mitmachen?

joint noun **1** (of meat) Braten der (PL die Braten); **a joint of beef** ein Rinderbraten; **2** (in your body) Gelenk das (PL die Gelenke).

joke noun Witz der (PL die Witze); **to tell a joke** einen Witz erzählen. **joke** verb Witze machen; **you must be joking!** du machst wohl Witze!

joker noun (in cards) Joker der (PL die Joker).

journalism noun Journalismus der.

journalist noun Journalist der (PL die Journalisten), Journalistin die (PL die Journalistinnen); **Sean's a journalist** Sean ist Journalist.

journey noun **1** (a long one) Reise die (PL die Reisen); **on our journey to Italy** auf unserer Reise nach Italien; **2** (shorter; to work or school) Fahrt die (PL die Fahrten); **bus journey** die Busfahrt.

joy noun Freude die (PL die Freuden).

joystick noun (for computer games) Joystick der (PL die Joysticks).

Judaism noun Judentum das.

judge noun **1** (in court) Richter der (PL die Richter); **2** (in sporting events) Schiedsrichter der (PL die Schiedsrichter); **3** (in a competition) Preisrichter der (PL die Preisrichter). **judge** verb schätzen (time or distance).

judo noun Judo das; **he does judo** er macht Judo.

jug noun Krug der (PL die Krüge).

juice *noun* Saft *der*; **two orange juices please** zwei Orangensaft bitte.

juicy *adjective* saftig.

jukebox *noun* Jukebox *die* (PL *die* Jukeboxes).

July *noun* Juli *der*; **in July** im Juli.

jumble sale *noun* Basar *der* (PL *die* Basare).

jump *noun* Sprung *der* (PL *die* Sprünge); **parachute jump** *der* Fallschirmsprung.
jump *verb* springen◇ (PERF *sein*).

jumper *noun* Pullover *der* (PL *die* Pullover).

junction *noun* **1** (*of roads*) Kreuzung *die* (PL *die* Kreuzungen); **2** (*on railway*) Gleisanschluss *der* (PL *die* Gleisanschlüsse).

June *noun* Juni *der*; **in June** im Juni.

jungle *noun* Dschungel *der*.

junior *adjective* jünger; **junior school** *die* Grundschule; **the juniors** (*at primary school*) die Grundschüler, die Grundschülerinnen.

junk *noun* Trödel *der*.

junk food *noun* ungesunde Essen *das*.

just *adverb* **1** (*very recently*) gerade; **to have just done something** gerade etwas getan haben; **Tom has just arrived** Tom ist gerade angekommen; **2 to be just doing something** gerade dabei sein, etwas zu tun; **I'm just doing the food** ich bin gerade dabei, Essen zu machen; **3 just before midday** kurz vor

Mittag; **just after 4 o'clock** kurz nach vier Uhr; **4** (*only*) nur; **just for fun** nur zum Vergnügen; **he's just a child** er ist doch nur ein Kind; **just me and Justine are coming** nur ich und Justine kommen; **5 just a minute!** einen Moment!; **6 just coming!** ich komme schon!; **7** (*exactly*) **just as** genauso wie. **he's got just as many friends** er hat genauso viele Freunde.

justice *noun* Gerechtigkeit *die*.

Kk

kangaroo *noun* Känguru *das* (PL *die* Kängurus).

karate *noun* Karate *das*.

karting *noun* Gokarten *das*; **to go go-karting** Gokarten gehen.

kebab *noun* Kebab *der* (PL *die* Kebabs).

keen *adjective* **1** (*enthusiastic or committed*) begeistert; **he's a keen photographer** er ist ein begeisterter Fotograf; **you don't seem too keen** du scheinst nicht gerade begeistert zu sein; **2 to be keen on** mögen◇; **I'm not keen on fish** ich mag Fisch nicht; **3 to be keen on doing** (or **to do**) **something** etwas gerne tun.

keep *verb* **1** behalten◇; **you can keep the book** du kannst das Buch behalten; **to keep a secret** ein Geheimnis für sich behalten; **2 will you keep my seat?** können Sie meinen Platz freihalten?; **3 to keep**

somebody waiting jemanden
warten lassen; **4** (*store*)
aufbewahren SEP; **can I keep my
watch in your desk?** kann ich
meine Uhr in deinem Schreibtisch
aufbewahren?; **where do you keep
saucepans?** wo sind die Töpfe?;
5 (*not throw away*) aufheben◇ SEP;
I kept all his letters ich habe alle
seine Briefe aufgehoben; **6 to keep
on doing something** etwas weiter
tun; **she kept on talking** sie hat
weitergeredet; **keep straight on**
weiter geradeaus gehen; **7 to keep
on doing something** (*time after
time*) dauernd etwas tun; **he keeps
on ringing me up** er ruft mich
dauernd an; **8** (*maintain*) halten◇;
to keep the food warm das Essen
warm halten; **to keep a promise**
ein Versprechen halten; **9** (*stay*)
bleiben◇ (PERF *sein*); **to keep calm**
ruhig bleiben; **to keep out of the
sun** im Schatten bleiben.

kennel *noun* **1** (*for one dog*)
Hundehütte die (PL die
Hundehütten); **2** (*for boarding*)
kennels Hundepension die (PL die
Hundepensionen).

kerb *noun* Randstein der.

kettle *noun* Kessel der (PL die
Kessel); **to put the kettle on** Wasser
aufsetzen.

key *noun* **1** (*for a lock*) Schlüssel der
(PL die Schlüssel); **bunch of keys** der
Schlüsselbund; **2** (*on a piano or
keyboard*) Taste die.

keyboard *noun* (*for a computer*)
Tastatur die (PL die Tastaturen).

keyring *noun* Schlüsselring der (PL
die Schlüsselringe).

kick *noun* **1** (*from a person or a
horse*) Tritt der (PL die Tritte); **to give
somebody a kick** jemandem einen
Tritt geben; **2** (*in football*) Schuss
der (PL die Schüsse); ★**to get a kick
out of doing something** etwas
leidenschaftlich gerne tun.
kick *verb* **1 to kick somebody**
jemandem einen Tritt geben; **2 to
kick the ball** den Ball schießen.

● **to kick off** anstoßen◇ SEP.

kick-off *noun* Anstoß der.

kid *noun* (*child*) Kind das (PL die
Kinder); **Dad's looking after the
kids** Vati passt auf die Kinder auf.

kidnap *verb* entführen.

kidnapper *noun* Entführer der (PL
die Entführer), Entführerin die (PL die
Entführerinnen).

kidney *noun* Niere die (PL die
Nieren).

kill *verb* **1** töten (*an animal*);
2 (*murder*) umbringen◇ SEP; **he
killed the girl** er brachte das
Mädchen um; **3 she was killed in a
car accident** sie kam bei einem
Autounfall ums Leben.

killer *noun* Mörder der (PL die
Mörder), Mörderin die (PL die
Mörderinnen).

kilo *noun* Kilo das (PL die Kilo); **a kilo
of sugar** ein Kilo Zucker; **two euros
a kilo** zwei Euro das Kilo.

kilogram *noun* Kilogramm das (PL
die Kilogram).

kilometre *noun* Kilometer *der* (PL *die* Kilometer).

kilt *noun* Kilt *der* (PL *die* Kilts).

kind *noun* **1** Art *die* (PL *die* Arten); **this kind of book** diese Art Buch; **all kinds of people** alle möglichen Leute; **2** (*brand*) Sorte *die* (PL *die* Sorten).
kind *adjective* nett; **she was very kind to me** sie war sehr nett zu mir.

kindness *noun* Freundlichkeit *die*.

king *noun* König *der* (PL *die* Könige); **the king of hearts** der Herzkönig.

kingdom *noun* Königreich *das* (PL *die* Königreiche); **the United Kingdom** das Vereinigte Königreich.

kiosk *noun* **1** (*for newspapers or snacks*) Kiosk *das* (PL *die* Kioske); **2** (*for a phone*) Telefonzelle *die* (PL *die* Telefonzellen).

kipper *noun* Räucherhering *der* (PL *die* Räucherheringe).

kiss *noun* Kuss *der* (PL *die* Küsse); **to give somebody a kiss** jemandem einen Kuss geben.
kiss *verb* küssen; **kiss me!** küss mich!; **we kissed each other** wir haben uns geküsst.

kit *noun* **1** (*of tools*) Werkzeug *das*; **2** (*in a box*) **a tool kit** ein Werkzeugkasten; **3** (*clothes*) Sachen (*plural*); **where's my football kit?** wo sind meine Fußballsachen?; **4** (*for making a model, a piece of furniture, etc.*) Bausatz *der* (PL *die* Bausätze).

kitchen *noun* Küche *die* (PL *die* Küchen); **the kitchen table** der Küchentisch.

kitchen foil *noun* Alufolie *die*.

kitchen roll *noun* Küchenrolle *die* (PL *die* Küchenrollen).

kite *noun* Drachen *der*; **to fly a kite** einen Drachen steigen lassen.

kitten *noun* Kätzchen *das* (PL *die* Kätzchen).

kiwi fruit *noun* Kiwi *die* (PL *die* Kiwis).

knee *noun* Knie *das* (PL *die* Knie); **on (your) hands and knees** auf allen vieren.

kneel *verb* knien◇; **to kneel (down)** sich hinknien SEP.

knickers *plural noun* Schlüpfer *der* (PL *die* Schlüpfer); **two pairs of knickers** zwei Schlüpfer.

knife *noun* Messer *das* (PL *die* Messer).
knife *verb* einstechen◇ SEP auf (+ ACC), (*kill*) erstechen◇.

knight *noun* (*in chess*) Springer *der* (PL *die* Springer).

knit *verb* stricken.

knitting *noun* Strickerei *die*.

knob *noun* **1** (*on a door or walking stick*) Knauf *der* (PL *die* Knäufe); **2** (*control on a radio or machine*) Knopf *der* (PL *die* Knöpfe); **3 knob of butter** das kleine Stückchen Butter.

knock *noun* Schlag *der* (PL *die* Schläge); **a knock on the head** ein Schlag auf den Kopf; **a knock at the door** ein Klopfen an der Tür.
knock *verb* **1** (*to bang*) stoßen◇; **I knocked my arm on the table** ich

habe mir den Arm am Tisch gestoßen; **2 to knock on something** an etwas (ACC) klopfen.

● **to knock down 1** (*in a traffic accident*) anfahren✧ SEP (*a person*); **2** (*to demolish*) abreißen✧ SEP (*an old building*).

● **to knock out 1** (*to make unconscious*) bewusstlos schlagen✧; **2** (*in sport, to eliminate*) k.o. schlagen✧.

knot *noun* Knoten der (PL die Knoten); **to tie a knot** einen Knoten machen.

know *verb* **1** (*know a fact*) wissen✧; **do you know where Tim is?** weißt du, wo Tim ist?; **I know they've moved house** ich weiß, dass sie umgezogen sind; **yes, I know** ja, weiß ich; **you never know!** man kann nie wissen!; **I know how to get to town** ich weiß, wie man in die Stadt kommt; **2** (*be personally acquainted with*) kennen✧; **do you know the Jacksons?** kennst du die Jacksons?; **all the people I know** alle Leute, die ich kenne; **I don't know his mother** ich kenne seine Mutter nicht; **3 to know how to do something** wissen, wie man etwas macht; **Steve knows how to make potato salad** Steve kann Kartoffelsalat machen; **Liz knows how to mend it** Liz kann es reparieren; **4 to know about** Bescheid wissen über (+ ACC) (*items in the news*); **5 to know about** sich auskennen✧ SEP mit (*machines, cars, etc.*); **Lindy knows about computers** Lindy kennt sich mit

Computern aus; **6 to get to know somebody** jemanden kennen lernen.

knowledge *noun* Wissen das.

Koran *noun* Koran der.

kosher *adjective* koscher.

Ll

lab *noun* Labor das (PL die Labors).

label *noun* Etikett das (PL die Etikette).

laboratory *noun* Labor das (PL die Labors).

lace *noun* **1** (*for a shoe*) Schnürsenkel der (PL die Schnürsenkel); **to tie your laces** sich (DAT) die Schnürsenkel binden; **2** (*fabric or trimming*) Spitze die.

ladder *noun* **1** (*for climbing*) Leiter die (PL die Leitern); **2** (*in your tights*) Laufmasche die (PL die Laufmaschen).

ladies *noun* (*lavatory*) Damentoilette die (PL die Damentoiletten); (*on a sign*) **'Ladies'** 'Damen'.

lady *noun* Dame die (PL die Damen); **ladies and gentlemen** meine Damen und Herren.

ladybird *noun* Marienkäfer der (PL die Marienkäfer).

lager *noun* helle Bier das (PL die hellen Biere), Helle das (PL die Hellen) (*informal*); **a lager, please** ein Helles bitte.

laid-back *adjective* gelassen.

lake *noun* See der (PL die Seen); **Lake Geneva** der Genfer See.

landlady *noun* **1** (*of a house or room*) Vermieterin *die* (PL *die* Vermieterinnen); **2** (*of a pub*) Gastwirtin *die* (PL *die* Gastwirtinnen).

landlord *noun* **1** (*of a house or room*) Vermieter *der* (PL *die* Vermieter); **2** (*of a pub*) Gastwirt *der* (PL *die* Gastwirte).

lane *noun* **1** (*small road*) Weg *der* (PL *die* Wege); **2** (*of a motorway*) Spur *die* (PL *die* Spuren).

language *noun* **1** (*German, Italian, etc.*) Sprache *die* (PL *die* Sprachen); **foreign language** *die* Fremdsprache; **2** (*way of speaking*) Ausdrucksweise *die*; **bad language** Kraftausdrücke (*plural*).

lap *noun* **1** Schoß *der* (PL *die* Schöße); **2** (*in races*) Runde *die* (PL *die* Runden).

laptop *noun* Laptop *der* (PL *die* Laptops).

larder *noun* Speisekammer *die* (PL *die* Speisekammern).

large *adjective* groß.

laser *noun* Laser *der* (PL *die* Laser).

laser beam *noun* Laserstrahl *der* (PL *die* Laserstrahlen).

laser printer *noun* Laserdrucker *der* (PL *die* Laserdrucker).

laser surgery *noun* Laseroperation *die* (PL *die* Laseroperationen).

last *adjective* letzter/letzte/letztes; **last week** letzte Woche; **for the last time** zum letzten Mal; **last night** gestern Nacht.

last *adverb* **1** (*in final position*) als Letzter/als Letzte/als Letztes; **Rob arrived last** Rob kam als Letzter an; **2 at last!** endlich!; **3** (*most recently*) zuletzt; **I last saw him in May** ich habe ihn zuletzt im Mai gesehen.

last *verb* dauern; **the film lasted two hours** der Film dauerte zwei Stunden.

late *adjective, adverb* **1** spät; **I'm late** ich bin spät dran; **we were five minutes late** wir haben uns fünf Minuten verspätet; **they arrived late** sie sind zu spät angekommen; **to be late for something** zu spät zu etwas (DAT) kommen; **we were late for the party** wir kamen zu spät zur Party; **2 to be late** (*of a bus or train*) Verspätung haben; **the train was an hour late** der Zug hatte eine Stunde Verspätung; **3** (*late in the day*) spät; **we got up late** wir sind spät aufgestanden; **the chemist is open late** die Apotheke hat bis spät auf; **late last night** gestern spät in der Nacht; **too late!** zu spät!

lately *adverb* in letzter Zeit.

later *adverb* später; **I'll explain later** ich erkläre es später; **see you later!** bis später!

latest *adjective* **1** neuester/neueste/neuestes; **the latest news** die neuesten Nachrichten; **the latest in audio equipment** das Neueste an Audioausrüstung; **2 at the latest** spätestens.

Latin *noun* Latein *das*.

laugh *noun* Lachen *das*; **to do something for a laugh** etwas aus Spaß machen.

laugh *verb* **1** lachen; **everybody**

a
b
c
d
e
f
g
h
i
j
k
l
m
n
o
p
q
r
s
t
u
v
w
x
y
z

laughed alle haben gelacht; **to laugh about something** über etwas (ACC) lachen; **2 to laugh at somebody** jemanden auslachen SEP; **they'll only laugh at me** sie lachen mich bestimmt aus.

launch *noun* **1** (*of a ship*) Stapellauf der; **2** (*of a product*) Einführung die; **3** (*of a spacecraft*) Abschuss der. **launch** *verb* **1** auf den Markt bringen◇ (*a product*); **2** ins All schiessen◇ (*a spacecraft*); **3** zu Wasser lassen ◇ (*a ship*).

launderette *noun* Waschsalon der (PL die Waschsalons).

lavatory *noun* Toilette die (PL die Toiletten); **to go to the lavatory** auf die Toilette gehen.

lavender *noun* Lavendel der.

law *noun* **1** Gesetz das (PL die Gesetze); **to break the law** gegen das Gesetz verstoßen; **2 it's against the law** das ist verboten; **3** (*subject of study*) Jura die (*no plural*).

lawn *noun* Rasen der (PL die Rasen).

lawnmower *noun* Rasenmäher der (PL die Rasenmäher).

lawyer *noun* Rechtsanwalt der (PL die Rechtsanwälte), Rechtsanwältin die (PL die Rechtsanwältinnen).

lay *verb* **1** (*put*) legen; **she laid the cards on the table** sie legte die Karten auf den Tisch; **2 to lay the table** den Tisch decken.

lay-by *noun* Parkplatz der (PL die Parkplätze).

layer *noun* Schicht die (PL die Schichten).

lazy *adjective* faul.

lead[1] *noun* **1** (*when you are ahead*) Führung die; **to be in the lead** in Führung liegen; **Baxter's in the lead** Baxter liegt in Führung; **to take the lead** in Führung gehen; **2** (*electric*) Kabel das (PL die Kabel); **3** (*for a dog*) Leine die (PL die Leinen); **on a lead** an der Leine; **4** (*role*) Hauptrolle die (PL die Hauptrollen); **5** (*an actor*) Hauptdarsteller der (PL die Hauptdarsteller), Hauptdarstellerin die (PL die Hauptdarstellerinnen). **lead** *verb* **1** führen; **the path leads to the sea** der Weg führt zum Meer; **to lead by three points** mit drei Punkten führen; **2 to lead the way** vorangehen◇ SEP (PERF *sein*); **3 to lead to something** zu etwas (DAT) führen (*an accident or problems, for example*).

lead[2] *noun* (*metal*) Blei das.

lead singer *noun* Leadsänger der (PL die Leadsänger), Leadsängerin die (PL die Leadsängerinnen).

leader *noun* **1** (*of a political party*) Vorsitzende der/die (PL die Vorsitzenden); **2** (*of an expedition or group*) Leiter der (PL die Leiter), Leiterin die (PL die Leiterinnen); **3** (*in a competition*) Erste der/die (PL die Ersten); **4** (*of a gang*) Anführer der (PL die Anführer), Anführerin die (PL die Anführerinnen).

leaf *noun* Blatt das (PL die Blätter).

leaflet *noun* **1** (*with instructions*) Merkblatt das (PL die Merkblätter); **2** (*for advertising*) Reklameblatt das (PL die Reklameblätter).

leak *noun* **1** (*in a roof, tent*) undichte Stelle *die* (PL *die* undichten Stellen); **2** gas leak *die* undichte Gasleitung; **3** (*in a boat*) Leck *das* (PL *die* Lecks).
leak *verb* (*bottle or roof*) undicht sein.

lean *adjective* (*meat*) mager.
lean *verb* **1** to lean on something sich an etwas (ACC) lehnen; **he leaned against the door** er hat sich gegen die Tür gelehnt; **2** sich lehnen; **she was leaning out of the window** sie lehnte sich aus dem Fenster; **3** to lean forward sich vorbeugen SEP.

leap year *noun* Schaltjahr *das* (PL *die* Schaltjahre).

learn *verb* lernen; **to learn German** Deutsch lernen; **to learn (how) to drive** Autofahren lernen.

learner *noun* **1** Lerner *der* (PL *die* Lerner); **to be a fast learner** schnell lernen; **2** (*beginner*) Anfänger *der* (PL *die* Anfänger), Anfängerin *die* (PL *die* Anfängerinnen).

least *adjective, pronoun*
1 wenigster/wenigste/wenigstes; **to have least time** am wenigsten Zeit haben; **Tony has the least money** Tony hat das wenigste Geld; **2** (*the slightest*) geringster/geringste/geringstes; **I haven't the least idea** ich habe nicht die geringste Ahnung.
least *adverb* **1** am wenigsten; **I like the blue shirt least** ich mag das blaue Hemd am wenigsten; **2** the least expensive hotel das billigste Hotel; **3** at least (*at a minimum*)

mindestens; **at least twenty people** mindestens zwanzig Leute; **4** at least (*at any rate*) wenigstens; **she's a teacher, at least I think she is** sie ist Lehrerin, glaube ich wenigstens.

leather *noun* Leder *das*; **leather jacket** *die* Lederjacke.

leave *noun* Urlaub *der*; **three days' leave** drei Tage Urlaub.
leave *verb* **1** (*go away*) gehen◇ (PERF *sein*), (*by car*) fahren◇ SEP (PERF *sein*), (*a train or bus*) abfahren◇ SEP (PERF *sein*); **they're leaving tomorrow evening** sie fahren morgen Abend; **we left at six** wir sind um sechs Uhr gegangen; **the train leaves Munich at ten** der Zug fährt um zehn Uhr von München ab; **2** (*go away from or go out of*) verlassen◇; **I left the office at five** ich habe das Büro um fünf verlassen; **he left his wife** er hat seine Frau verlassen; **3** (*deposit or allow to remain in the same state*) lassen◇; **you can leave your coats in the hall** Sie können Ihre Mäntel in der Diele lassen; **to leave the door open** die Tür offen lassen; **leave it until tomorrow** lass es bis morgen; **4** to leave somebody something jemandem etwas hinterlassen◇ (*a message or money*); **he didn't leave a message** er hat keine Nachricht hinterlassen; **5** (*not do*) stehen lassen◇; **leave the washing up** lass den Abwasch stehen; **6** (*forget*) vergessen◇; **he left his umbrella on the train** er hat seinen Regenschirm im Zug vergessen; **7** be left übrig sein (PERF *sein*); **there are two pancakes left**

zwei Pfannkuchen sind noch übrig; **I don't have any money left** ich habe kein Geld mehr übrig; **we have ten minutes left** wir haben noch zehn Minuten Zeit.

lecture *noun* **1** (*at university*) Vorlesung *die* (PL *die* Vorlesungen); **2** (*public*) Vortrag *der* (PL *die* Vorträge).

leek *noun* Lauch *der*.

left *noun* **on the left** links; **to drive on the left** links fahren; **on my left** links von mir.
left *adverb* links; **turn left at the church** an der Kirche links abbiegen.
left *adjective* linker/linke/linkes; **his left foot** sein linker Fuß.

left-click *noun* Klick *der* (mit der linken Maustaste).
left-click *verb* **left-click the icon** das Icon mit der linken Maustaste anklicken.

left-hand *adjective* **the left-hand side** die linke Seite.

left-handed *adjective* linkshändig.

left-luggage office *noun* Gepäckaufbewahrung *die* (PL *die* Gepäckaufbewahrungen).

leg *noun* **1** Bein *das* (PL *die* Beine); **my left leg** mein linkes Bein; **to break your leg** sich (DAT) das Bein brechen; **2** (*in cooking*) Keule *die* (PL *die* Keulen); **leg of lamb** die Lammkeule; ★ **to pull somebody's leg** jemanden auf den Arm nehmen.

legal *adjective* gesetzlich.

leggings *plural noun* Leggings (*plural*).

leisure *noun* Freizeit *die*; **in my leisure time** in meiner Freizeit.

lemon *noun* Zitrone *die* (PL *die* Zitronen).

lemonade *noun* Limonade *die* (PL *die* Limonaden).

lemon juice *noun* Zitronensaft *der*.

lend *verb* leihen◇; **to lend something to somebody** jemandem etwas leihen; **I lent Judy my bike** ich habe Judy mein Rad geliehen; **will you lend it to me?** kannst du es mir leihen?

length *noun* Länge *die* (PL *die* Längen).

lens *noun* **1** (*in a camera*) Objektiv *das* (PL *die* Objektive); **2** (*in spectacles*) Brillenglas *das* (PL *die* Brillengläser); **3 contact lenses** Kontaktlinsen.

Lent *noun* Fastenzeit *die*.

lentil *noun* Linse *die* (PL *die* Linsen).

Leo *noun* Löwe *der* (PL *die* Löwen) **I'm a Leo** ich bin Löwe.

leotard *noun* Turnanzug *der* (PL *die* Turnanzüge).

lesbian *adjective* lesbisch.

less *pronoun, adjective, adverb* weniger (*'weniger' never changes*); **Ben eats less** Ben isst weniger; **less time** weniger Zeit; **less than** weniger als; **less than three hours** weniger als drei Stunden; **you spent less than me** du hast weniger als ich ausgegeben; **less and less** immer weniger.

lesson *noun* (*class*) Stunde *die* (PL *die* Stunden); **German lesson** die

Deutschstunde; **driving lesson** *die* Fahrstunde.

let¹ *verb* **1** (*allow*) lassen◇; **to let somebody do something** jemanden etwas tun lassen; **she lets me drive her car** sie lässt mich mit ihrem Auto fahren; **the police let us through** die Polizei hat uns durchgelassen; **let me in** lass mich hinein; **2** (*as a suggestion or a command*) **let's go!** gehen wir!; **let's not talk about it** reden wir nicht mehr darüber; **let's eat out** essen wir im Restaurant.

● **to let off 1** abfeuern◇ (*fireworks*); **2** (*to excuse from*) befreien von (+ DAT) (*homework*).

let² *verb* (*to rent out*) vermieten; **'flat to let'** 'Wohnung zu vermieten'.

letter box *noun* Briefkasten *der* (PL die Briefkästen).

letter *noun* **1** Brief *der* (PL die Briefe); **a letter for you from Delia** ein Brief für dich von Delia; **2** (*of the alphabet*) Buchstabe *der* (PL die Buchstaben).

lettuce *noun* Salat *der*; **two lettuces** zwei Salatköpfe.

leukaemia *noun* Leukämie *die*.

level *noun* Höhe *die*; **at eye level** in Augenhöhe.

level *adjective* **1** eben (*ground or floor*); **2** (*horizontal*) waagerecht (*shelf*); **3** (*at the same height*) auf gleicher Höhe; **to be level with the ground** auf gleicher Höhe mit dem Boden sein.

level crossing *noun* Bahnübergang *der* (PL die Bahnübergänge).

lever *noun* Hebel *der* (PL die Hebel).

liar *noun* Lügner *der* (PL die Lügner), Lügnerin *die* (PL die Lügnerinnen).

liberal *adjective* **1** tolerant; **2** (*in politics*) liberal; **the Liberal Democrats** die Liberaldemokraten.

Libra *noun* Waage *die*; **Sean's Libra** Sean ist Waage.

librarian *noun* Bibliothekar *der* (PL die Bibliothekare), Bibliothekarin *die* (PL die Bibliothekarinnen).

library *noun* Bibliothek *die* (PL die Bibliotheken); **public library** *die* öffentliche Bücherei.

licence *noun* **1** (*for a TV*) Genehmigung *die* (PL die Genehmigungen); **2** (*driving licence*) Führerschein *der* (PL die Führerscheine).

lick *verb* lecken.

lid *noun* Deckel *der* (PL die Deckel).

lie *noun* Lüge *die* (PL die Lügen); **to tell a lie** (or **lies**) lügen◇.
lie *verb* **1** (*to be stretched out*) liegen◇; **he's lying on the sofa** er liegt auf dem Sofa; **my coat lay on the bed** mein Mantel lag auf dem Bett; **2 to lie down** (*for a rest*) sich hinlegen SEP; **I'm going to lie down for a little** ich lege mich ein bisschen hin; **3** (*tell lies*) lügen◇.

lie-in *noun* **to have a lie-in** ausschlafen◇ SEP.

life *noun* Leben *das* (PL die Leben); **all her life** ihr ganzes Leben lang; **full of life** voller Leben; **that's life!** so ist das Leben!

lifeboat *noun* Rettungsboot *das* (PL die Rettungsboote).

lifeguard *noun*
Rettungsschwimmer *der* (PL *die*
Rettungsschwimmer),
Rettungsschwimmerin *die* (PL *die*
Rettungsschwimmerinnen); **is
there a lifeguard at the pool?** gibt
es einen Bademeister im
Schwimmbad?

life jacket *noun* Schwimmweste
die (PL *die* Schwimmwesten).

life-style *noun* Lebensstil *der* (PL *die*
Lebensstile).

lift *noun* **1** Aufzug *der* (PL *die*
Aufzüge); **let's take the lift** fahren
wir mit dem Aufzug; **2** (*a ride*) **to
give somebody a lift to the station**
jemanden mit zum Bahnhof
mitnehmen◇ SEP; **Khaled's giving
me a lift** Khaled nimmt mich mit;
would you like a lift? möchtest du
mitfahren?
lift *verb* hochheben◇ SEP; **he lifted
the box** er hob die Kiste hoch.

light *noun* **1** Licht *das*; **will you turn
the light on?** kannst du das Licht
anmachen?; **to turn off the light** das
Licht ausmachen; **are your lights
on?** hast du das Licht an?; **2** (*in the
street*) Straßenlampe *die* (PL *die*
Straßenlampen); **3** (*a lamp*) Lampe
die (PL *die* Lampen); **4 traffic lights**
die Ampel (*singular*); **the lights are
green** die Ampel ist grün; **5** (*for a
cigarette*) **have you got a light?** hast
du Feuer?
light *adjective* **1** (*not dark*) hell; **a
light blue dress** ein hellblaues
Kleid; **it gets light at six** es wird um
sechs hell; **2** (*not heavy*) leicht; **a
light coat** ein leichter Mantel; **a**

light breeze eine leichte Brise.
light *verb* **1** anzünden SEP (*the fire,
a match, the gas*); **we lit a fire** wir
zündeten ein Feuer an; **2 to light a
cigarette** sich (DAT) eine Zigarette
anzünden.

light bulb *noun* Glühbirne *die* (PL
die Glühbirnen).

lighter *noun* Feuerzeug *das* (PL *die*
Feuerzeuge).

lighthouse *noun* Leuchtturm *der*
(PL *die* Leuchttürme).

lightning *noun* Blitz *der*, **flash of
lightning** *der* Blitz; **to be struck by
lightning** vom Blitz getroffen
werden.

like¹ *preposition, conjunction* **1** wie;
like me wie ich; **like a duck** wie
eine Ente; **like I said** wie gesagt;
what's it like? wie ist es?; **what was
the weather like?** wie war das
Wetter?; **2 like this/that** so;
3 ähnlich (+ DAT); **to look like
somebody** jemandem ähnlich
sehen; **Cindy looks like her father**
Cindy sieht ihrem Vater ähnlich.

like² *verb* **1** mögen◇; **I like
vegetables** ich mag Gemüse; **I don't
like meat** ich mag kein Fleisch; **I
like Dürer best** ich mag Dürer am
liebsten; **2 to like doing something**
etwas gerne tun; **Mum likes
reading** Mutti liest gerne; **3 I would
like ...** ich möchte gerne ...; **would
you like a coffee?** möchten Sie
einen Kaffee?; **what would you like
to eat?** was möchten Sie essen?;
yes, if you like ja, wenn du willst;
4 I like the dress das Kleid gefällt

mir; **how do you like it?** wie gefällt es dir?

likely *adjective* wahrscheinlich; **she's likely to phone** wahrscheinlich ruft sie an.

lime *noun* Kalk *der*.

limit *noun* Grenze *die* (PL *die* Grenzen); **speed limit** *die* Geschwindigkeitsbeschränkung.

limp *noun* **to have a limp** hinken.

line *noun* **1** Linie *die* (PL *die* Linien); **a straight line** eine gerade Linie; **to draw a line** eine Linie ziehen; **2** (*in writing*) Zeile *die* (PL *die* Zeilen); **six lines of text** sechs Zeilen Text; **3** (*railway*) Bahnlinie *die* (PL *die* Bahnlinien) (*from one place to another*); **on the line** (*the track*) auf der Strecke; **4** (*a queue of people or cars*) Schlange *die* (PL *die* Schlangen); **to stand in line** Schlange stehen; **5** (*telephone*) Leitung *die* (PL *die* Leitungen); **the line's bad** die Verbindung ist schlecht; **hold the line, please** bitte bleiben Sie am Apparat.

line *verb* füttern (*a coat*).

linen *noun* Leinen *das*; **a linen jacket** eine Leinenjacke.

lining *noun* Futter *das* (PL *die* Futter).

link *noun* Verbindung *die* (PL *die* Verbindungen); **what's the link between the two?** was für eine Verbindung besteht zwischen den beiden?

link *verb* verbinden◇ (*two places*); **the two towns are linked by a railway line** die beiden Städte sind durch eine Bahnlinie miteinander verbunden.

lion *noun* Löwe *der* (PL *die* Löwen).

lip *noun* Lippe *die* (PL *die* Lippen).

lip-read *verb* von den Lippen lesen◇.

lipstick *noun* Lippenstift *der* (PL *die* Lippenstifte).

liquid *noun* Flüssigkeit *die* (PL *die* Flüssigkeiten).
liquid *adjective* flüssig.

liquidizer *noun* Mixer *der* (PL *die* Mixer).

list *noun* Liste *die* (PL *die* Listen).

listen *verb* **1** zuhören SEP; **I wasn't listening** ich habe nicht zugehört; **to listen to somebody** jemandem zuhören; **you're not listening to me** du hörst mir nicht zu; **2 to listen to something** etwas (ACC) hören; **to listen to the radio** Radio hören.

listener *noun* (*to the radio*) Hörer *der* (PL *die* Hörer), Hörerin *die* (PL *die* Hörerinnen).

literature *noun* Literatur *die* (PL *die* Literaturen).

litre *noun* Liter *der* (PL *die* Liter); **a litre of milk** ein Liter Milch.

litter *noun* (*rubbish*) Abfall *der*.

litter bin *noun* Abfalleimer *der* (PL *die* Abfalleimer).

little *adjective, pronoun* **1** (*small*) klein; **a little boy** ein kleiner Junge; **a little break** eine kleine Pause; **2** (*not much*) wenig; **we have very little time** wir haben sehr wenig Zeit; **3 a little** ein wenig; **we have a little left** wir haben ein wenig übrig; **4 just a little, please** nur ein bisschen, bitte; **it's a little late** es ist

a
b
c
d
e
f
g
h
i
j
k
l
m
n
o
p
q
r
s
t
u
v
w
x
y
z

ein bisschen spät; **a little more** ein bisschen mehr; **a little less** ein bisschen weniger; ★ **little by little** nach und nach.

little finger *noun* kleine Finger der (PL die kleinen Finger).

live[1] *verb* **1** (*in a house or town*) wohnen; **she lives in York** sie wohnt in York; **we live in a flat** wir wohnen in einer Wohnung; **2** (*be or stay alive, spend one's life*) leben; **we're living in the country now** wir leben jetzt auf dem Land; **they live on fruit** sie leben von Obst; **they live apart** sie leben getrennt.

live[2] *adjective, adverb* **1** live (*broadcast*); **a live programme** eine Livesendung; **live music** die Livemusik; **a broadcast live from Wembley** eine Liveübertragung aus Wembley; **to broadcast a concert live** ein Konzert live senden; **2** (*alive*) lebend.

lively *adjective* lebhaft.

liver *noun* Leber die (PL die Lebern).

living *noun* Lebensunterhalt der; **to earn a living** sich (DAT) seinen Lebensunterhalt verdienen.

living room *noun* Wohnzimmer das (PL die Wohnzimmer).

lizard *noun* Eidechse die (PL die Eidechsen).

load *noun* **1** (*on a lorry*) Ladung die (PL die Ladungen); **a (lorry-)load of bricks** eine Ladung Ziegelsteine; **2 a bus-load of tourists** ein Bus voll Touristen; **3 loads of** massenhaft (*informal*); **loads of tourists** massenhaft Touristen;

they've got loads of money sie haben einen Haufen Geld (*informal*).
load *verb* **1** beladen✧ (*a vehicle*); **2 to load a camera** einen Film einlegen SEP.

loaf *noun* Brot das (PL die Brote); **a loaf of white bread** ein Weißbrot.

loan *noun* **1** (*from a person*) Leihgabe die (PL die Leihgaben); **2** (*by a bank*) Kredit der (PL die Kredite).
loan *verb* leihen ✧.

loathe *verb* hassen; **I loathe getting up early** ich hasse es, früh aufzustehen.

local *noun* **1** (*a pub*) Stammkneipe die (PL die Stammkneipen); **2 the locals** (*people*) die Einheimischen.
local *adjective* **1** hiesig; **the local library** die hiesige Bücherei; **2 local newspaper** die Lokalzeitung.

lock *noun* Schloss das (PL die Schlösser).
lock *verb* abschließen✧ SEP (*a door, room, or bicycle*); **have you locked the door?** hast du abgeschlossen?

lodger *noun* Untermieter der (PL die Untermieter), Untermieterin die (PL die Untermieterinnen).

loft *noun* Dachboden der (PL die Dachböden).

log *noun* **1** Baumstamm der (PL die Baumstämme); **2** (*as firewood*) Holzscheit das (PL die Holzscheite); **a log fire** ein offenes Feuer.

lollipop *noun* Lutscher der (PL die Lutscher).

London *noun* London das.

Londoner *noun* Londoner *der* (PL *die* Londoner), Londonerin *die* (PL *die* Londonerinnen).

lonely *adjective* einsam; **to feel lonely** sich einsam fühlen.

long *adjective, adverb* **1** lang; **a long film** ein langer Film; **a long day** ein langer Tag; **it's five metres long** es ist fünf Meter lang; **the film is an hour long** der Film dauert eine Stunde; **2 a long time** lange; **he stayed for a long time** er ist lange geblieben; **I've been here for a long time** ich bin schon lange hier; **a long time ago** vor langer Zeit; **this won't take long** das dauert nicht lange; **3 how long?** wie lange?; **how long have you been here?** wie lange sind Sie schon hier?; **long ago** vor langer Zeit; **4 a long way** weit; **it's a long way to the cinema** bis zum Kino ist es weit; **5 all night long** die ganze Nacht; **6 no longer** nicht mehr; **he doesn't work here any longer** er arbeitet nicht mehr hier.

long *verb* **to long to do something** sich danach sehnen, etwas zu tun; **I'm longing to see you** ich sehne mich danach, dich zu sehen.

long-distance call *noun* (*within the country*) Ferngespräch *das* (PL *die* Ferngespräche).

long jump *noun* Weitsprung *der*.

longlife milk *noun* H-Milch *die*.

loo *noun* Klo *das* (PL *die* Klos) (*informal*).

look *noun* **1** (*a glance*) Blick *der* (PL *die* Blicke); **to take a look at somebody** einen Blick auf

jemanden werfen; **2** (*a tour*) **to have a look at the school** sich (DAT) die Schule ansehen; **to have a look round the town** sich (DAT) die Stadt ansehen; **3 to have a look for** suchen.

look *verb* **1** sehen◇; **to look out of the window** aus dem Fenster sehen; **I wasn't looking** ich habe nicht hingesehen; **2 to look at** ansehen◇ SEP; **he looked at the girl** er hat das Mädchen angesehen; **to look at something** sich (DAT) etwas ansehen; **I'm looking at the photos** ich sehe mir die Fotos an; **3** (*to seem*) aussehen◇ SEP; **she looks sad** sie sieht traurig aus; **the salad looks delicious** der Salat sieht köstlich aus; **to look like** aussehen wie; **what does the house look like?** wie sieht das Haus aus?; **4** (*resemble*) **to look like somebody** jemandem ähnlich sehen; **she looks like her aunt** sie sieht ihrer Tante ähnlich; **they look like each other** sie sehen sich ähnlich.

● **to look after 1** sich kümmern um (+ ACC); **Dad's looking after the children** Vati kümmert sich um die Kinder; **2** aufpassen SEP auf (+ ACC) (*luggage*).

● **to look for** suchen; **I'm looking for my keys** ich suche meine Schlüssel.

● **to look forward to** sich freuen auf (+ ACC) (*a party or a trip, for example*).

● **to look out** (*to be careful*) aufpassen SEP; **look out, it's hot!** pass auf, das ist heiß!

● **to look up** nachschlagen◇ SEP (*in a dictionary or directory*); **he's**

a
b
c
d
e
f
g
h
i
j
k
l
m
n
o
p
q
r
s
t
u
v
w
x
y
z

479

a

b

c

d

e

f

g

h

i

j

k

l

m

n

o

p

q

r

s

t

u

v

w

x

y

z

looking it up in the dictionary er schlägt es im Wörterbuch nach.

loose *adjective* **1** (*screw or knot*) locker; **2** (*garment*) weit; **3 loose change** das Kleingeld; ★ **I'm at a loose end** ich habe nichts zu tun.

lorry *noun* Lastwagen der (PL die Lastwagen).

lorry driver *noun* Lastwagenfahrer der (PL die Lastwagenfahrer), Lastwagenfahrerin die (PL die Lastwagenfahrerinnen).

lose *verb* **1** verlieren◇; **we lost** wir haben verloren; **we lost the match** wir haben das Spiel verloren; **Sam's lost his watch** Sam hat seine Uhr verloren; **2 to get lost** sich verlaufen◇; **we got lost in the woods** wir haben uns im Wald verlaufen; **3 to lose weight** abnehmen◇ SEP.

loss *noun* Verlust der (PL die Verluste).

lost property *noun* Fundsachen (*plural*).

lot *noun* **1 a lot** viel; **Wilbur eats a lot** Wilbur isst viel; **I spent a lot** ich habe viel ausgegeben; **he's a lot better** es geht ihm viel besser; **a lot of** viel; **a lot of coffee** viel Kaffee; **2** (*many*) **a lot of** viele; **a lot of books** viele Bücher; **3 lots of** eine Menge (*informal*); **lots of people** eine Menge Leute.

lottery *noun* Lotterie die (PL die Lotterien); **to win the lottery** in der Lotterie gewinnen.

loud *adjective* **1** laut; **in a loud voice** mit lauter Stimme; **2 to say something out loud** etwas laut sagen.

loudly *adverb* laut.

loudspeaker *noun* Lautsprecher der (PL die Lautsprecher).

lounge *noun* **1** (*in a house*) Wohnzimmer das (PL die Wohnzimmer); **2** (*in a hotel or an airport*) Halle die (PL die Hallen); **departure lounge** die Abflughalle.

love *noun* **1** Liebe die; **for love** aus Liebe; **2 to be in love with somebody** in jemanden verliebt sein; **she's in love with Jake** sie ist in Jake verliebt; **3 Gina sends her love** Gina lässt grüßen; **with love from Charlie** herzliche Grüße von Charlie; **4** (*in tennis*) null.
love *verb* **1** lieben (*a person*); **I love you** ich liebe dich; **2** sehr gerne mögen◇ (*a place or food*); **she loves London** sie mag London sehr gerne; **Wayne loves chocolate** Wayne mag Schokolade sehr gerne; **3 to love doing something** etwas sehr gerne tun; **I love dancing** ich tanze sehr gerne; **4 I'd love to come** ich würde sehr gerne kommen.

lovely *adjective* schön; **a lovely dress** ein schönes Kleid; **we had lovely weather** wir hatten schönes Wetter; **we had a lovely day** der Tag war sehr schön.

low *adjective* **1** niedrig; **a low table** ein niedriger Tisch; **at a low price** zu einem niedrigen Preis; **2** (*not loud*) leise; **in a low voice** mit leiser Stimme.

lower *adjective* (*not as high*) tiefer.
lower *verb* senken.

loyalty *noun* Loyalität die (PL die Loyalitäten).

loyalty card *noun* Treuekarte die (PL die Treuekarten).

luck *noun* 1 Glück das; **good luck!** viel Glück!; **with a bit of luck** wenn wir Glück haben; 2 **bad luck!** so ein Pech!

luckily *adverb* zum Glück; **luckily for them** zu ihrem Glück.

lucky *adjective* 1 **to be lucky** Glück haben; **we were lucky** wir haben Glück gehabt; 2 **to be lucky** (*bringing luck*) Glück bringen; **it's supposed to be lucky** es soll Glück bringen; **my lucky number** meine Glückszahl.

luggage *noun* Gepäck das; **my luggage is in the boot** mein Gepäck ist im Kofferraum.

lump *noun* 1 Klumpen der (PL die Klumpen); 2 (*of sugar or butter*) Stück das (PL die Stücke).

lunch *noun* Mittagessen das (PL die Mittagessen); **to have lunch** zu Mittag essen; **we had lunch in Oxford** wir haben in Oxford zu Mittag gegessen.

lunch break *noun* Mittagspause die (PL die Mittagspausen).

lunch hour, lunch time *noun* Mittagszeit die.

lung *noun* Lungenflügel der; **lungs** die Lunge (*singular*).

luxurious *adjective* luxuriös.

lyrics *plural noun* Text der.

Mm

mac *noun* Regenmantel der (PL die Regenmäntel).

macaroni *noun* Makkaroni (*plural*).

machine *noun* 1 Maschine die (PL die Maschinen); 2 (*a slot machine*) Automat der (PL die Automaten).

machinery *noun* die Maschinen (*plural*).

mackerel *noun* Makrele die (PL die Makrelen).

mad *adjective* 1 verrückt; **she's completely mad!** sie ist total verrückt!; 2 (*angry*) wütend; **to be mad at somebody** wütend auf jemanden sein; 3 **to be mad about something** ganz verrückt auf etwas (ACC) sein; **she's mad about horses** sie ist ganz verrückt auf Pferde.

madman *noun* Verrückte der (PL die Verrückten).

madness *noun* Wahnsinn der.

magazine *noun* Zeitschrift die (PL die Zeitschriften), (*with mostly photos*) Magazin das (PL die Magazine).

magic *noun* Zauber der, (*conjuring tricks*) Zauberei die.
magic *adjective* 1 Zauber-; **magic wand** der Zauberstab; 2 (*great*) super (*informal*).

magician *noun* 1 (*wizard*) Zauberer der (PL die Zauberer); 2 (*conjurer*) Zauberkünstler der (PL die Zauberkünstler).

a
b
c
d
e
f
g
h
i
j
k
l
m
n
o
p
q
r
s
t
u
v
w
x
y
z

a **magnificent** *adjective* wundervoll.

b **magnifying glass** *noun* Lupe die (PL die Lupen).

c **maiden name** *noun* Mädchenname der (PL die Mädchennamen).

d **mail** *noun* Post die.

f **mail order** *noun* Bestellung per Post die; **to buy something by mail order** etwas bei einem Versandhaus bestellen; **mail order catalogue** der Versandhauskatalog.

h **main** *adjective* Haupt-; **main entrance** der Haupteingang.

i **main course** *noun* Hauptgericht das (PL die Hauptgerichte).

j **mainly** *adverb* hauptsächlich.

k **main road** *noun* Hauptstraße die (PL die Hauptstraßen).

l **maize** *noun* Mais der

m **major** *adjective* 1 (*important*) groß; 2 (*serious*) schwer; **a major accident** ein schwerer Unfall.

n **Majorca** *noun* Mallorca das.

o **majority** *noun* Mehrheit die.

p **make** *noun* Marke die (PL die Marken); **the make of a car** die Automarke.

q **make** *verb* 1 machen; **to make a meal** Essen machen; **I made breakfast** ich habe Frühstück gemacht; **she made her bed** sie hat ihr Bett gemacht; **to make somebody happy** jemanden glücklich machen; **it makes you tired** das macht einen müde; 2 herstellen SEP; **they make**

computers sie stellen Computer her; **'made in Germany'** 'in Deutschland hergestellt'; 3 **he made me wait** er ließ mich warten; **she makes me laugh** sie bringt mich zum Lachen; 4 verdienen; **he makes forty pounds a day** er verdient vierzig Pfund pro Tag; **to make a living** seinen Lebensunterhalt verdienen; 5 (*force*) zwingen◇; **to make somebody do something** jemanden zwingen, etwas zu tun; **she made him give the money back** sie hat ihn gezwungen, das Geld zurückzugeben; 6 (*the verb 'make' is often translated by a more specific verb*) **to make a cake** einen Kuchen backen; **to make a phone call** telefonieren; **to make a dress** ein Kleid nähen; 7 **to make friends with somebody** sich mit jemandem anfreunden SEP; 8 **I can't make it tonight** ich kann heute Abend nicht kommen; 9 **two and three make five** zwei und drei ist fünf.

● **to make something up** 1 etwas erfinden◇; **she made up an excuse** sie hat eine Ausrede erfunden; 2 **to make it up** (*after a quarrel*) sich versöhnen; **they've made it up again** sie haben sich wieder versöhnt.

make-up *noun* 1 Make-up das; **I don't wear make-up** ich trage kein Make-up; 2 **to put on your make-up** sich schminken; **Jo's putting on her make-up** Jo schminkt sich.

male *adjective* 1 männlich; **male voice** die Männerstimme; 2 **male animal** das Männchen; **male rat** das

Rattenmännchen; **3 male student**
der Student.

male chauvinist *noun*
Chauvinist der (PL die Chauvinisten).

man *noun* **1** Mann der (PL die
Männer); **an old man** ein alter
Mann; **2** (*the human race*) der
Mensch.

manage *verb* **1** leiten (*a business,
team*); **she manages a travel
agency** sie leitet ein Reisebüro;
2 (*cope*) zurechtkommen✧ SEP (PERF
sein); **I can manage** ich komme
schon zurecht; **3 to manage to do
something** es schaffen, etwas zu
tun; **he managed to push the door
open** er hat es geschafft, die Tür
aufzustoßen; **I didn't manage to
get in touch with her** ich habe es
nicht geschafft, sie zu erreichen.

management *noun*
1 Management das (PL die
Managements); **management
course** der Managementkurs;
2 Leitung die.

manager *noun* **1** (*of a company or
bank*) Direktor der (PL die
Direktoren), Direktorin die (PL die
Direktorinnen); **2** (*of a shop or
restaurant*) Geschäftsführer der (PL
die Geschäftsführer),
Geschäftsführerin die (PL die
Geschäftsführerinnen); **3** (*in
football*) Trainer der (PL die Trainer),
Managerin die (PL die
Managerinnen), Trainerin die (PL die
Trainerinnen); **4** (*in entertainment*)
Manager der (PL die Manager),
Managerin die (PL die
Managerinnen).

manageress *noun* (*of a shop or
restaurant*) Geschäftsführerin die
(PL die Geschäftsführerinnen).

mania *noun* Manie die (PL die
Manien).

maniac *noun* Wahnsinnige der/die
(PL die Wahnsinnigen); **she drives
like a maniac** sie fährt wie eine
Wahnsinnige.

man-made *adjective* **man-made
fibre** die Kunstfaser.

manner *noun* **1 in a manner of
speaking** mehr oder weniger;
2 manners Manieren (*plural*); **to
have good manners** gute Manieren
haben; **it's bad manners to talk
like that** es gehört sich nicht, so zu
reden.

mantelpiece *noun* Kaminsims
der (PL die Kaminsimse).

manual *noun* Handbuch das (PL die
Handbücher).

manufacture *verb* herstellen SEP.

manufacturer *noun* Hersteller
der (PL die Hersteller).

many *adjective, pronoun* **1** viele;
does she have many friends? hat
sie viele Freunde?; **we didn't see
many people** wir haben nicht viele
Leute gesehen; **not many** nicht
viele; **many of them forgot** viele
haben es vergessen; **there were too
many people** es waren zu viele
(Leute) da; **how many?** wie viele?;
how many were there? wie viele
waren da?; **how many sisters have
you got?** wie viele Schwestern hast
du?; **how many are there left?** wie
viele sind übrig geblieben?; **I've**

a
b
c
d
e
f
g
h
i
j
k
l
m
n
o
p
q
r
s
t
u
v
w
x
y
z

a
b
c
d
e
f
g
h
i
j
k
l
m
n
o
p
q
r
s
t
u
v
w
x
y
z

never had so many presents ich habe noch nie so viele Geschenke bekommen; **2** (*a lot*) **so many** so viel; **I have so many things to do** ich habe so viel zu tun; **3** (*as much as*) **as many as** so viel wie; **take as many as you like** nimm so viel wie du willst; **4** (*too much*) **that's far too many** das ist viel zu viel.

map *noun* **1** Karte *die* (PL *die* Karten); **2** (*of a town*) Stadtplan (PL *die* Stadtpläne).

marathon *noun* Marathonlauf *der* (PL *die* Marathonläufe).

marble *noun* **1** Marmor *der*; **2** (*for playing*) Murmel *die* (PL *die* Murmeln); **to play marbles** Murmeln spielen.

march *noun* Marsch *der* (PL *die* Märsche).

march *verb* marschieren (PERF *sein*).

March *noun* März *der*; **in March** im März.

mare *noun* Stute *die* (PL *die* Stuten).

margarine *noun* Margarine *die*.

margin *noun* Rand *der* (PL *die* Ränder).

marijuana *noun* Marihuana *das*.

mark *noun* **1** (*at school*) Note *die* (PL *die* Noten); **I got a good mark in German** ich habe eine gute Note in Deutsch bekommen; **2** (*stain*) Fleck *der* (PL *die* Flecke); **3** (*German currency until replaced by the euro; one hundred marks = 51.13 euros*) Mark *die* (PL *die* Mark)

mark *verb* **1** korrigieren; **the teacher marks our homework** die

Lehrerin korrigiert unsere Hausaufgaben; **2** (*in sports*) decken.

market *noun* Markt *der* (PL *die* Märkte).

marketing *noun* Marketing *das*.

marmalade *noun* Orangenmarmelade *die*.

maroon *adjective* kastanienbraun.

marriage *noun* **1** Ehe *die*; **2** (*wedding*) Hochzeit *die* (PL *die* Hochzeiten).

married *adjective* **1** verheiratet; **they've been married for twenty years** sie sind seit zwanzig Jahren verheiratet; **2 married couple** *das* Ehepaar.

marry *verb* **1 to marry somebody** jemanden heiraten; **she married a Frenchman** sie hat einen Franzosen geheiratet; **2 to get married** heiraten; **they got married in July** sie haben im Juli geheiratet.

marvellous *adjective* wunderbar.

marzipan *noun* Marzipan *das*.

mascara *noun* Wimperntusche *die*.

masculine *noun* (*in German and other grammars*) männlich.

mash *verb* stampfen.

mashed potatoes *plural noun* Kartoffelbrei *der* (*singular*).

mask *noun* Maske *die* (PL *die* Masken).

mass *noun* **1 a mass of** eine Menge; **2 masses of** massenhaft (*informal*); **they've got masses of money** sie haben massenhaft Geld; **there's masses left over** es ist massenhaft übrig geblieben;

3 (*religious*) Messe *die* (PL *die* Messen); **to go to mass** zur Messe gehen.

massage *noun* Massage *die* (PL *die* Massagen).

massive *adjective* riesig.

master *verb* **1** meistern; **2 to master a language** eine Sprache beherrschen.

masterpiece *noun* Meisterwerk *das* (PL *die* Meisterwerke).

mat *noun* **1** (*doormat*) Matte *die* (PL *die* Matten); **2** (*to put under a hot dish*) Untersetzer *der* (PL *die* Untersetzer); **3 table mat** *das* Platzdeckchen.

match *noun* **1** (*for lighting*) Streichholz *das* (PL *die* Streichhölzer); **box of matches** *die* Streichholzschachtel; **2** (*in sports*) Spiel *das* (PL *die* Spiele); **football match** *das* Fußballspiel; **to watch the match** das Spiel sehen; **to win the match** das Spiel gewinnen; **to lose the match** das Spiel verlieren. **match** *verb* passen zu (+ DAT); **the jacket matches the skirt** die Jacke passt zu dem Rock.

mate *noun* Freund *der* (PL *die* Freunde); **I'm going to the pub with my mates** ich gehe mit meinen Freunden in die Kneipe.

material *noun* **1** (*fabric, also information*) Stoff *der* (PL *die* Stoffe); **2** (*substance*) Material *das* (PL *die* Materialien).

mathematics *noun* Mathematik *die*.

maths *noun* Mathe *die* (*informal*); **I like maths** ich mag Mathe gerne; **Anna's good at maths** Anna ist gut in Mathe.

matter *noun* **what's the matter?** was ist los?
matter *verb* **1 that's what matters most** das ist am wichtigsten; **it matters a lot to me** es ist mir sehr wichtig; **does it really matter?** ist das wirklich so wichtig?; **2 it doesn't matter** es macht nichts; **it doesn't matter if it rains** es macht nichts, wenn es regnet; **3 you can write it in German or English, it doesn't matter** du kannst es auf Deutsch oder Englisch schreiben, das ist egal; **4 to matter to somebody** jemandem etwas ausmachen SEP; **does it matter to you if I leave earlier?** macht es dir etwas aus, wenn ich früher gehe?

mattress *noun* Matratze *die* (PL *die* Matratzen).

maximum *noun* Maximum *das* (PL *die* Maxima); **the maximum number/speed possible is 200** die Höchstzahl/Höchstgeschwindigkeit ist 200.
maximum *adjective* maximal; **the maximum temperature** die Höchsttemperatur; **she got the maximum points** sie erreichte die Höchstpunktzahl.

may *verb* **1 she may be ill** vielleicht ist sie krank; **we may go to Spain** wir fahren vielleicht nach Spanien; **2** (*expressing permission*) dürfen❖; **may I close the door?** darf ich die Tür zumachen?

a
b
c
d
e
f
g
h
i
j
k
l
m
n
o
p
q
r
s
t
u
v
w
x
y
z

a
b
c
d
e
f
g
h
i
j
k
l
m
n
o
p
q
r
s
t
u
v
w
x
y
z

May noun Mai der; **in May** im Mai.

maybe adverb vielleicht; **maybe they've got lost** vielleicht haben sie sich verlaufen.

May Day noun der Erste Mai.

mayonnaise noun Majonäse die.

mayor noun Bürgermeister der (PL die Bürgermeister), Bürgermeisterin die (PL die Bürgermeisterinnen).

me pronoun (in German this pronoun changes according to the function it has in the sentence or the preposition it follows) **1** (as a direct object in the accusative) mich; **she knows me** sie kennt mich; **2** (after a preposition that takes the accusative) mich; **they left without me** sie sind ohne mich losgefahren; **wait for me!** warte auf mich!; **3** (as an indirect object or following a verb that takes the dative) mir; **can you give me your address?** kannst du mir deine Adresse geben?; **he helped me** er hat mir geholfen; **4** (after a preposition that takes the dative) mir; **she never talks to me** sie redet nie mit mir; **5** (in comparisons) **than me** als ich; **she's older than me** sie ist älter als ich; **6** (in the nominative) ich; **it's me** ich bin's; **not me** ich nicht.

meadow noun Wiese die (PL die Wiesen).

meal noun **1** Essen das (PL die Essen); **to cook a meal** Essen kochen; **2 to go for a meal** essen gehen.

mean verb **1** (signify) bedeuten; **what does that mean?** was

bedeutet das?; **2** (intend to say) meinen; **3 what do you mean?** was meinst du?; **that's not what I meant** das habe ich nicht gemeint; **4 to mean to do something** etwas tun wollen; **I meant to phone my mother** ich wollte meine Mutter anrufen; **5 to be meant to do something** etwas tun sollen; **she was meant to be here at six** sie sollte um sechs hier sein.

mean adjective **1** (with money) geizig; **2** (unkind) gemein; **she's really mean to her brother** sie ist richtig gemein zu ihrem Bruder; **what a mean thing to do!** das ist gemein!

meaning noun Bedeutung die (PL die Bedeutungen).

means noun **1** Mittel das (PL die Mittel); **means of transport** das Verkehrsmittel; **2 a means of** eine Möglichkeit; **a means of earning money** eine Möglichkeit, Geld zu verdienen; **3 by means of** mit Hilfe (+ GEN); **4 by all means!** selbstverständlich!

meantime adverb **for the meantime** einstweilen; **in the meantime** in der Zwischenzeit.

meanwhile adverb in der Zwischenzeit; **meanwhile she was waiting at the station** in der Zwischenzeit wartete sie am Bahnhof.

measles noun Masern (plural).

measure verb messen✧.

measurements plural noun Maße (plural); **the measurements**

of the room die Maße des Zimmers; **my measurements** meine Maße.

meat *noun* Fleisch *das*; **I don't like meat** ich mag kein Fleisch.

mechanic *noun* Mechaniker *der* (PL *die* Mechaniker), Mechanikerin *die* (PL *die* Mechanikerinnen).

mechanical *adjective* mechanisch.

medal *noun* Medaille *die* (PL *die* Medaillen); **the gold medal** die Goldmedaille.

media *noun* **the media** die Medien (*plural*).

medical *noun* **1** ärztliche Untersuchung *die* (PL *die* ärztlichen Untersuchungen); **2 to have a medical** sich untersuchen lassen. **medical** *adjective* **1** medizinisch; **2** ärztlich (*examination, treatment*).

medicine *noun* **1** (*drug*) Medikament *das* (PL *die* Medikamente); **2** (*subject of study*) Medizin *die*; **she's studying medicine** sie studiert Medizin; **3 alternative medicine** die Alternativmedizin.

Mediterranean *noun* **the Mediterranean (Sea)** das Mittelmeer.

medium *adjective* mittlerer/ mittlere/mittleres.

medium-sized *adjective* mittelgroß.

meet *verb* **1** (*by chance*) treffen✧; **I met Rosie at the baker's** ich habe Rosie beim Bäcker getroffen; **2** (*by appointment*) sich treffen mit (+ DAT); **I'll meet you outside the cinema**

ich treffe mich mit dir vor dem Kino; **3** sich treffen; **we're meeting at six** wir treffen uns um sechs; **4** (*get to know*) kennen lernen; **I met a German girl last week** ich habe letzte Woche eine Deutsche kennen gelernt; **5 I've never met Oskar** ich kenne Oskar nicht; **6** (*off a train or bus, for example*) abholen SEP; **my dad's meeting me at the station** mein Vater holt mich vom Bahnhof ab.

meeting *noun* **1** (*by arrangement*) Treffen *das* (PL *die* Treffen); **2** (*in business*) Besprechung *die* (PL *die* Besprechungen); **she's in a meeting** sie ist in einer Besprechung; **3** (*by chance, in sports*) Begegnung *die* (PL *die* Begegnungen).

megabyte *noun* Megabyte *das* (PL *die* Megabytes).

melon *noun* Melone *die* (PL *die* Melonen).

melt *verb* **1** schmelzen✧ (PERF *sein*); **the snow has melted** der Schnee ist geschmolzen; **2** (*in cookery*) zerlassen✧ (*butter, fat*); **melt the butter in a saucepan** Butter im Topf zerlassen.

member *noun* Mitglied *das* (PL *die* Mitglieder).

Member of Parliament *noun* Abgeordnete *der/die* (PL *die* Abgeordneten).

membership *noun* Mitgliedschaft *die*.

membership card *noun* Mitgliedskarte *die* (PL *die* Mitgliedskarten).

a

membership fee *noun*
Mitgliedsbeitrag *der* (PL *die*
Mitgliedsbeiträge).

b

c

memorial *noun* Denkmal *das* (PL
die Denkmäler); **a war memorial** ein
Kriegsdenkmal.

d

e

memorize *verb* **to memorize
something** etwas auswendig
lernen.

f

g

memory *noun* **1** (*of a person*)
Gedächtnis *das*; **you have a good
memory** du hast ein gutes
Gedächtnis; **2** (*of the past*)
Erinnerung *die* (PL *die*
Erinnerungen); **I have good
memories of our stay in Italy** ich
habe schöne Erinnerungen an
unseren Urlaub in Italien; **3** (*of a
computer*) Speicher *der*.

h

i

j

k

l

mend *verb* **1** reparieren; **2** (*by
sewing*) ausbessern SEP.

m

meningitis *noun*
Hirnhautentzündung *die*.

n

o

mental *adjective* **1** geistig;
2 mental illness die
Geisteskrankheit; **mental hospital**
die psychiatrische Klinik.

p

q

r

mention *verb* erwähnen.

s

menu *noun* **1** (*in a restaurant*)
Speisekarte *die* (PL *die* Speisekarten);
is there a set menu? gibt es ein
Menü?; **2** (*in computing*) Menü *das*
(PL *die* Menüs).

t

u

v

meringue *noun* Baiser *das* (PL *die*
Baisers).

w

x

merit *noun* **1** Verdienst *das* (PL *die*
Verdienste); **2** (*good feature or
advantage*) Vorzug *der* (PL *die*
Vorzüge).

y

z

merry *adjective* **1** fröhlich; **Merry
Christmas** fröhliche Weihnachten;
2 (*from drinking*) angeheitert.

merry-go-round *noun* Karussell
das (PL *die* Karussells).

mess *noun* **1** Durcheinander *das*;
**my papers are in a complete
mess** meine Unterlagen sind ein
einziges Durcheinander; **what a
mess!** was für ein Durcheinander!;
2 to make a mess Unordnung
machen; **3 to clear up the mess**
aufräumen SEP.

● **to mess about** herumalbern SEP;
stop messing about! hör auf
herumzualbern!

● **to mess about with something**
mit etwas (DAT) herumspielen SEP;
**it's dangerous to mess about with
matches** es ist gefährlich, mit
Streichhölzern herumzuspielen.

● **to mess something up 1** etwas
durcheinander bringen✧; **you've
messed up all my papers** Sie
haben meine Unterlagen völlig
durcheinander gebracht; **2** (*make
dirty*) etwas schmutzig machen;
3 (*botch*) etwas verpfuschen.

message *noun* **1** Nachricht *die* (PL
die Nachrichten); **a telephone
message** eine telefonische
Nachricht; **2 to give somebody a
message** jemandem etwas
ausrichten SEP.

messy *adjective* **1** (*dirty*) **it's a
messy job** das ist eine schnutzige
Arbeit; **2 he's a messy eater** er
bekleckert sich beim Essen; **3 her
writing's really messy** sie hat eine
furchtbare Schrift; **4** (*untidy*) **she's**

488

very messy sie ist sehr unordentlich.

metal *noun* Metall *das* (PL *die* Metalle).

meter *noun* **1** (*electricity, gas, taxi*) Zähler *der* (PL *die* Zähler); **to read the meter** den Zähler ablesen ◇ SEP; **2 parking meter** *die* Parkuhr.

method *noun* Methode *die* (PL *die* Methoden).

Methodist *noun* Methodist *der* (PL *die* Methodisten), Methodistin *die* (PL *die* Methodistinnen).

metre *noun* Meter *der* (PL *die* Meter).

metric *adjective* metrisch.

microchip *noun* Mikrochip *der* (PL *die* Mikrochips).

microphone *noun* Mikrofon *das* (PL *die* Mikrofone).

microscope *noun* Mikroskop *das* (PL *die* Mikroskope).

microwave (oven) *noun* Mikrowellenherd *der* (PL *die* Mikrowellenherde).

midday *noun* Mittag *der*; **at midday** mittags.

middle *noun* **1** Mitte *die*; **in the middle of the room** in der Mitte des Zimmers; **in the middle of June** Mitte Juni; **in the middle of the night** mitten in der Nacht; **2 to be in the middle of doing something** gerade dabei sein, etwas zu tun; **when she phoned I was in the middle of washing my hair** als sie anrief, war ich gerade dabei, mir die Haare zu waschen.

middle-aged *adjective* mittleren Alters; **a middle-aged lady** eine Dame mittleren Alters.

middle-class *adjective* der Mittelschicht; **a middle-class family** eine Familie der Mittelschicht.

Middle-East *noun* **the Middle East** der Nahe Osten.

midge *noun* Mücke *die* (PL *die* Mücken).

midnight *noun* Mitternacht *die*; **at midnight** um Mitternacht.

Midsummer's Day *noun* Sommersonnenwende *die*.

might *verb* **1** 'are you going to phone him?' — 'I might' 'rufst du ihn an?' — 'vielleicht'; **I might invite Jo** vielleicht lade ich Jo ein; **he might have forgotten** vielleicht hat er es vergessen; **2 she might be right** sie könnte Recht haben.

migraine *noun* Migräne *die*.

mike *noun* (*microphone*) Mikro *das* (PL *die* Mikros) (*informal*).

mild *adjective* mild.

mile *noun* **1** Meile *die* (PL *die* Meilen) (*Germans use kilometres for distances; to convert miles to kilometres, multiply by 8 and divide by 5*); **it's ten miles to Oxford** es sind sechzehn Kilometer bis Oxford; **2 it's miles better** das ist viel besser.

military *adjective* militärisch.

milk *noun* Milch *die*; **full-cream milk** *die* Vollmilch; **skimmed milk** *die* Magermilch; **semi-skimmed milk**

a

die fettarme Milch.
milk *verb* melken.

b

milk chocolate *noun*
Milchschokolade *die.*

c

d

milkman *noun* Milchmann *der* (PL
die Milchmänner).

e

milk shake *noun* Milchshake *der*
(PL *die* Milchshakes).

f

millennium *noun* Jahrtausend *das*
(PL *die* Jahrtausende).

g

h

millimetre *noun* Millimeter *der* (PL
die Millimeter).

i

million *noun* Million *die* (PL *die*
Millionen); **a million people** eine
Million Menschen; **two million
people** zwei Millionen Menschen.

j

k

millionaire *noun* Millionär *der* (PL
die Millionäre), Millionärin *die* (PL *die*
Millionärinnen).

l

m

mimic *verb* nachmachen SEP.

n

mince *noun* Hackfleisch *das.*

o

mind *noun* **1** Sinn *der;* **it never
crossed my mind to ask them for
help** es kam mir überhaupt nicht in
den Sinn, sie um Hilfe zu bitten;
2 Meinung *die;* **to change your
mind** seine Meinung ändern; **I've
changed my mind** ich habe meine
Meinung geändert; **3 to make up
your mind to do something** sich
entschließen◊, etwas zu tun; **I can't
make up my mind which dress to
wear** ich kann mich nicht
entschließen, welches Kleid ich
anziehe; **4 I've made up my mind**
ich habe mich entschieden.
mind *verb* **1** aufpassen SEP auf
(+ ACC); **can you mind my bag for
me?** können Sie auf meine

p

q

r

s

t

u

v

w

x

y

z

Handtasche aufpassen?; **could you
mind the baby for ten minutes?**
könntest du zehn Minuten auf das
Baby aufpassen?; **2 do you mind
closing the door?** würden Sie bitte
die Tür zumachen?; **3 do you mind
if ...?** würde es Ihnen etwas
ausmachen SEP, wenn ...?; **do you
mind if I open the window?** würde
es Ihnen etwas ausmachen, wenn
ich das Fenster aufmache?; **I don't
mind** es macht mir nichts aus; **I
don't mind the heat** die Hitze
macht mir nichts aus; **4 never mind**
macht nichts.

mine[1] *noun* Bergwerk *das* (PL *die*
Bergwerke); **coal mine** *das*
Kohlenbergwerk.

mine[2] *pronoun* **1** (*for a masculine
noun*) mein; **she took her coat and
I took mine** sie hat ihren Mantel
genommen und ich habe meinen
genommen; **2** (*for a feminine noun*)
meine; **she gave me her address
and I gave her mine** sie hat mir
ihre Adresse gegeben und ich habe
ihr meine gegeben; **3** (*for a neuter
noun*) meins; **her dress is red and
mine is blue** ihr Kleid ist rot und
meins ist blau; **4** (*for masculine/
feminine/neuter plural nouns*)
meine; **she showed me her photos
and I showed her mine** sie hat mir
ihre Fotos gezeigt und ich habe
meine gezeigt; **5 a friend of mine**
ein Freund von mir; **it's mine** das
gehört mir.

miner *noun* Bergarbeiter *der* (PL *die*
Bergarbeiter).

mineral water *noun* Mineralwasser *das*.

miniature *noun* Miniatur *die* (PL die Miniaturen)
miniature *adjective* Miniatur-; **miniature model** Miniaturmodell *das*.

minibus *noun* Kleinbus *der* (PL die Kleinbusse).

minimum *noun* Minimum *das* (PL die Minima); **a minimum of** ein Minimum von.
minimum *adjective* Mindest-; **the minimum age** das Mindestalter; **minimum wage** *der* Mindestlohn.

miniskirt *noun* Minirock *der* (PL die Miniröcke).

minister *noun* **1** (*in government*) Minister *der* (PL die Minister), Ministerin *die* (PL die Ministerinnen); **2** (*of a church*) Geistliche *der/die* (PL die Geistlichen).

ministry *noun* Ministerium *das* (PL die Ministerien).

minor *adjective* kleiner.

minority *noun* Minderheit *die* (PL die Minderheiten).

mint *noun* **1** (*herb*) Minze *die* (PL die Minzen); **2** (*sweet*) Pfefferminzbonbon *der* (PL die Pfefferminzbonbons).

minus *preposition* minus (+ GEN); **seven minus three is four** sieben minus drei ist vier; **it was minus ten this morning** es war minus zehn heute Morgen.

minute¹ *noun* **1** Minute *die* (PL die Minuten); **I'll be ready in two minutes** ich bin in zwei Minuten

fertig; **it's five minutes' walk from here** es ist fünf Minuten zu Fuß von hier; **2** Moment *der;* **just a minute!** einen Moment bitte!; **3 in a minute** gleich.

minute² *adjective* winzig; **the bedrooms are minute** die Schlafzimmer sind winzig.

miracle *noun* Wunder *das* (PL die Wunder).

mirror *noun* Spiegel *der* (PL die Spiegel); **he looked at himself in the mirror** er hat sich im Spiegel betrachtet.

misbehave *verb* sich schlecht benehmen◇.

miserable *adjective* **1** elend; **he was miserable without her** ohne sie fühlte er sich elend; **2 I feel really miserable today** ich fühle mich heute richtig elend; **3** mies; **it's miserable weather** das Wetter ist mies; **she gets paid a miserable salary** sie bekommt ein mieses Gehalt.

Miss *noun* Fräulein *das*; **Miss Jones** Fräulein Jones, Frau Jones (*adult women are usually addressed as 'Frau', whether or not they are married*).

miss *verb* **1** verpassen; **she missed her train** sie hat ihren Zug verpasst; **I missed the film** ich habe den Film verpasst; **to miss an opportunity** eine Gelegenheit verpassen; **2** nicht treffen◇; **the stone missed me** der Stein hat mich nicht getroffen; **the ball missed the goal** der Schuss ging am Tor vorbei; **missed!** nicht getroffen!; **3** versäumen; **he's**

a
b
c
d
e
f
g
h
i
j
k
l
m
n
o
p
q
r
s
t
u
v
w
x
y
z

missed his classes er hat den Unterricht versäumt; **4** vermissen (*a person or thing*); **I miss you** ich vermisse dich; **she's missing her sister** sie vermisst ihre Schwester; **I miss England** ich vermisse England.

missing *adjective* **1** fehlend; **she's found the missing pieces** sie hat die fehlenden Teile gefunden; **the missing link** das fehlende Glied; **2 to be missing** fehlen; **there's a plate missing** ein Teller fehlt; **there are three forks missing** drei Gabeln fehlen; **3 to go missing** verschwinden✧ (PERF *sein*); **several things have gone missing lately** mehrere Sachen sind kürzlich verschwunden; **4 three children are missing** drei Kinder werden vermisst.

missionary *noun* Missionar *der* (PL *die* Missionare), Missionarin *die* (PL *die* Missionarinnen).

mist *noun* Nebel *der*.

mistake *noun* **1** Fehler *der* (PL *die* Fehler); **spelling mistake** *der* Rechtschreibfehler; **you've made lots of mistakes** du hast viele Fehler gemacht; **2 to make a mistake** (*be mistaken*) sich irren; **sorry, I made a mistake** Entschuldigung, ich habe mich geirrt; **3 by mistake** aus Versehen. **mistake** *verb* **I mistook you for your brother** ich habe dich mit deinem Bruder verwechselt.

mistaken *adjective* **to be mistaken** sich täuschen; **you're mistaken** du täuschst dich.

mistletoe *noun* Mistel *die* (PL *die* Misteln).

misty *adjective* dunstig; **a misty morning** ein dunstiger Morgen.

misunderstand *verb* missverstehen✧; **I misunderstood** ich habe es missverstanden.

misunderstanding *noun* Missverständnis *das* (PL *die* Missverständnisse); **there's been a misunderstanding** da liegt ein Missverständnis vor.

mix *noun* Mischung *die* (PL *die* Mischungen); **a good mix** eine gute Mischung; **cake mix** *die* Backmischung. **mix** *verb* **1** vermischen; **mix the ingredients together** die Zutaten vermischen; **mix the cream into the sauce** die Sahne in die Soße rühren; **2 to mix with** verkehren mit (+ DAT); **she mixes with lots of interesting people** sie verkehrt mit vielen interessanten Leuten.

● **to mix up 1** durcheinander bringen✧; **you've mixed up all the papers** du hast alle Unterlagen durcheinander gebracht; **you've got it all mixed up** du hast alles durcheinander gebracht; **2** (*confuse*) verwechseln; **I get him mixed up with his brother** ich verwechsle ihn mit seinem Bruder.

mixed *adjective* **1** bunt; **a mixed programme** ein buntes Programm; **2** gemischt; **a mixed salad** ein gemischter Salat.

mixture *noun* Mischung *die* (PL *die* Mischungen); **it's a mixture of jazz**

and rock es ist eine Mischung aus Jazz und Rock.

moan verb (complain) jammern; **stop moaning!** hör auf zu jammern!

mobile home noun Wohnwagen der (PL die Wohnwagen).

mobile phone noun Handy das (PL die Handys).

mock noun (mock exam) Übungsprüfung die (PL die Übungsprüfungen).
mock verb sich lustig machen über (+ ACC); **stop mocking me** hör auf, dich über mich lustig zu machen.

model noun 1 Modell das (PL die Modelle); **his car is the latest model** sein Auto ist das neueste Modell; **a model of Westminster Abbey** ein Modell von der Westminsterabtei; 2 (fashion model) Mannequin das (PL die Mannequins); **she's a model** sie ist Fotomodell.

model aeroplane noun Modellflugzeug das (PL die Modellflugzeuge).

model railway noun Modelleisenbahn die (PL die Modelleisenbahnen).

modem noun Modem der (PL die Modems).

modern adjective modern.

modernize verb modernisieren.

modern languages noun neuere Sprachen (plural).

modest adjective bescheiden.

modify verb abändern SEP.

moisture noun Feuchtigkeit die.

moisturizer noun Feuchtigkeitscreme die.

mole noun 1 (animal) Maulwurf der (PL die Maulwürfe); 2 (on the skin) Leberfleck der (PL die Leberflecke).

molecule noun Molekül das (PL die Moleküle).

molehill noun Maulwurfshügel der (PL die Maulwurfshügel).

moment noun 1 Moment der (PL die Momente); **at any moment** jeden Moment; **at the moment** im Moment, im Augenblick; **at the right moment** im richtigen Moment; 2 Augenblick der (PL die Augenblicke); **wait a moment!** einen Augenblick!; 3 **he'll be ready in a moment** er ist gleich fertig.

monarchy noun Monarchie die.

monastery noun Kloster das (PL die Klöster).

Monday noun 1 Montag der; **on Monday** am Montag; **I'm going to see him on Monday** ich sehe ihn am Montag; **see you on Monday!** bis Montag!; **every Monday** jeden Montag; **last Monday** letzten Montag; **next Monday** nächsten Montag; 2 **on Mondays** montags; **the museum is closed on Mondays** das Museum ist montags geschlossen.

money noun Geld das; **I don't have enough money** ich habe nicht genug Geld; **to make money** Geld verdienen.

money box noun Sparbüchse die (PL die Sparbüchsen).

a
b
c
d
e
f
g
h
i
j
k
l
m
n
o
p
q
r
s
t
u
v
w
x
y
z

a

b

c

d

e

f

g

h

i

j

k

l

m

n

o

p

q

r

s

t

u

v

w

x

y

z

monitor *noun* (*of a computer*) Monitor *der* (PL *die* Monitoren).

monk *noun* Mönch *der* (PL *die* Mönche).

monkey *noun* Affe *der* (PL *die* Affen).

monotonous *adjective* eintönig.

monster *noun* Ungeheuer *das* (PL *die* Ungeheuer).

month *noun* Monat *der*; **in the month of May** im Mai; **this month** diesen Monat; **next month** nächsten Monat; **last month** letzten Monat; **for three months** drei Monate lang; **every month** jeden Monat; **every three months** alle drei Monate; **in two months' time** in zwei Monaten; **at the end of the month** am Monatsende.

monthly *adjective* monatlich; **monthly payment** *die* monatliche Zahlung; **monthly ticket** *die* Monatskarte.

monument *noun* Denkmal *das* (PL *die* Denkmäler).

mood *noun* 1 Laune *die* (PL *die* Launen); **to be in a good mood** gute Laune haben; **to be in a bad mood** schlechte Laune haben; **2 I'm not in the mood** ich habe keine Lust dazu; **I'm not in the mood for working** ich habe keine Lust zum Arbeiten.

moon *noun* Mond *der* (PL *die* Monde); **by the light of the moon** im Mondschein; ★ **to be over the moon** im siebten Himmel sein (*literally: to be in seventh heaven*).

moonlight *noun* Mondschein *der*; **by moonlight** im Mondschein.

moped *noun* Moped *das* (PL *die* Mopeds).

moral *noun* Moral *die*; **the moral of the story** die Moral der Geschichte. **moral** *adjective* moralisch.

morals *noun* Moral *die*.

more *adverb* 1 (*followed by an adjective*) (*in German the ending '-er' is added to the adjective to show the comparative*) **more interesting** interessanter; **the book's more interesting than the film** das Buch ist interessanter als der Film; **more difficult** schwieriger; **more slowly** langsamer; **more easily** einfacher; **books are getting more and more expensive** Bücher werden immer teurer; **2 not any more** (*no longer*) nicht mehr; **she doesn't live here any more** sie wohnt nicht mehr hier.

more *adjective* 1 mehr (*'mehr' never changes*); **more friends** mehr Freunde; **more ... than** mehr ... als; **they have more money than we do** sie haben mehr Geld als wir; **2 no more** kein; **there's no more milk** es ist keine Milch mehr da; **3** (*of something you have already*) noch; **would you like some more cake?** möchtest du noch etwas Kuchen?; **a few more glasses** noch ein paar Gläser.

more *pronoun* 1 mehr; **he eats more than me** er isst mehr als ich; **no more, thank you** nichts mehr, danke; **2** (*of something you have already*) noch; **we need three more** wir brauchen noch drei; **any more?** noch etwas?; **3 more and more** immer mehr; **it takes more and**

more time es beansprucht immer mehr Zeit; **4 more or less** mehr oder weniger; **it's more or less finished** es ist mehr oder weniger fertig.

morning *noun* **1** Morgen *der* (PL *die* Morgen); **in the morning** am Morgen; **this morning** heute Morgen; **tomorrow morning** morgen früh; **yesterday morning** gestern Morgen; **on Friday morning** am Freitagmorgen; **2 in the morning** (*regularly*) morgens; **she doesn't work in the morning** sie arbeitet morgens nicht; **on Friday mornings** freitagmorgens; **at six o'clock in the morning** um sechs Uhr morgens; **3** (*as opposed to afternoon*) Vormittag *der* (PL *die* Vormittage); **I spent the whole morning waiting for him** ich habe den ganzen Vormittag auf ihn gewartet.

Moscow *noun* Moskau *das*.

Moslem *noun* Moslem *der* (PL *die* Moslems), Moslemin *die* (PL *die* Mosleminnen).

mosque *noun* Moschee *die* (PL *die* Moscheen).

mosquito *noun* Mücke *die* (PL *die* Mücken); **mosquito bite** *der* Mückenstich.

most *adjective, pronoun* **1** (*followed by a plural noun*) die meisten; **most children like chocolate** die meister Kinder mögen Schokolade; **most of my friends** die meisten meinen Freunden; **2** (*followed by a singular noun*) der meiste/die meiste/das meiste; **they've eaten most of the** ice-cream sie haben das meiste Eis gegessen; **3 the most** (*followed by a noun or a verb*) am meisten; **I've got the most time** ich habe am meisten Zeit; **4 most of the time** die meiste Zeit; **most of them** die meisten.

most *adverb* **1** (*followed by an adjective*) (*in German the ending '-(e)st' is added to the adjective to show the superlative*) **the most interesting film** der interessanteste Film; **the most exciting story** die spannendste Geschichte; **the most boring book** das langweiligste Buch; **2** am meisten; **the noise bothers me most** der Lärm stört mich am meisten; **3** (*very*) höchst; **it's most unlikely** es ist höchst unwahrscheinlich.

moth *noun* **1** Nachtfalter *der* (PL *die* Nachtfalter); **2** (*clothes moth*) Motte *die* (PL *die* Motten).

mother *noun* Mutter *die* (PL *die* Mütter); **Kate's mother** Kates Mutter.

mother-in-law *noun* Schwiegermutter *die* (PL *die* Schwiegermütter).

Mother's Day *noun* Muttertag *der* (PL *die* Muttertage).

motivation *noun* Motivation *die*.

motor *noun* Motor *der* (PL *die* Motoren).

motorbike *noun* Motorrad *das* (PL *die* Motorräder).

motorcyclist *noun* Motorradfahrer *der* (PL *die* Motorradfahrer), Motorradfahrerin *die* (PL *die* Motorradfahrerinnen).

a
b
c
d
e
f
g
h
i
j
k
l
m
n
o
p
q
r
s
t
u
v
w
x
y
z

motorist *noun* Autofahrer *der* (PL die Autofahrer), Autofahrerin *die* (PL die Autofahrerinnen).

motor racing *noun* Autorennsport *der*.

motorway *noun* Autobahn *die* (PL die Autobahnen).

mouldy *adjective* schimmelig.

mountain *noun* Berg *der* (PL die Berge); **in the mountains** in den Bergen.

mountain bike *noun* Mountainbike *das* (PL die Mountainbikes).

mountaineer *noun* Bergsteiger *der* (PL die Bergsteiger), Bergsteigerin *die* (PL die Bergsteigerinnen).

mountaineering *noun* Bergsteigen *das*; **to go mountaineering** Bergsteigen gehen.

mountainous *adjective* gebirgig.

mouse *noun* Maus *die* (PL die Mäuse) (*also for a computer*).

mousse *noun* Mousse *die* (PL die Mousses).

moustache *noun* Schnurrbart *der* (PL die Schnurrbärte).

mouth *noun* **1** (*of a person*) Mund *der* (PL die Münder); **2** (*of an animal*) Maul *das* (PL die Mäuler); **3** (*of a river*) Mündung *die* (PL die Mündungen).

mouthful *noun* (*food*) Bissen *der* (PL die Bissen) (*informal*).

mouth organ *noun* Mundharmonika *die* (PL die Mundharmonikas); **to play the mouth organ** Mundharmonika spielen.

move *noun* **1** (*to a different house*) Umzug *der* (PL die Umzüge); **2** (*in a game*) Zug *der* (PL die Züge); **your move!** du bist am Zug!

move *verb* **1** sich bewegen; **she didn't move** sie hat sich nicht bewegt; **2 to move up** vorrücken SEP (PERF *sein*); **move up a bit** rücken Sie etwas vor; **3** wegnehmen◇ SEP; **can you move your bag, please?** können Sie Ihre Handtasche bitte wegnehmen?; **4 to move something somewhere else** etwas woandershin stellen; **I've moved the chest into the cellar** ich habe die Truhe in den Keller gestellt; **5** (*car*) fahren◇ (PERF *sein*); **6** (*traffic*) vorwärtskommen◇ SEP (PERF *sein*); **7** (*driver*) wegfahren◇ SEP; **could you move your car, please?** würden Sie bitte Ihr Auto wegfahren?; **8 to move forward** (*person*) vorrücken SEP (PERF *sein*) (*vehicle*) vorwärts fahren◇ (PERF *sein*); **9** (*move house*) umziehen◇ SEP (PERF *sein*); **we're moving on Tuesday** wir ziehen am Dienstag um; **they've moved to London** sie sind nach London umgezogen.

● **to move away** wegziehen SEP (PERF *sein*).

● **to move in** einziehen SEP (PERF *sein*); **she's moving in with friends** sie zieht bei Freunden ein.

● **to move out** ausziehen SEP (PERF *sein*); **we're moving out next week** wir ziehen nächste Woche aus.

movement *noun* Bewegung *die* (PL die Bewegungen).

movie *noun* Film *der* (PL die Filme); **to go to the movies** ins Kino gehen.

moving *adjective* **1** fahrend; **a moving car** ein fahrendes Auto; **2** (*emotionally*) ergreifend.

mow *verb* mähen.

mower *noun* Rasenmäher *der* (PL die Rasenmäher).

MP *noun* Abgeordnete *der/die* (PL die Abgeordneten).

Mr *noun* Herr *der*; (*in an address*) **Mr Angus Brown** Herrn Angus Brown; (*in a letter*) **Dear Mr Brown** Sehr geehrter Herr Brown.

Mrs *noun* Frau *die*; **Mrs Mary Hendry** Frau Mary Hendry; (*in a letter*) **Dear Mrs Hendry** Sehr geehrte Frau Hendry.

Ms *noun* Frau *die* (there is no direct equivalent to 'Ms' in German, but 'Frau' may be used whether the woman is married or not).

much *adjective, adverb, pronoun* **1** viel; **she doesn't eat much for breakfast** sie isst nicht viel zum Frühstück; **much more** viel mehr; **much quicker** viel schneller; **we don't have much time** wir haben nicht viel Zeit; **2 not much** nicht viel; **'do you have a lot of work?'** – **'no, not much'** 'hast du viel Arbeit?' – ' nein, nicht viel'; **3 so much** so viel; **I have so much to do** ich habe so viel zu tun; **you shouldn't have given me so much** du hättest mir nicht so viel geben sollen; **4 as much as** so viel; **take as much as you like** nimm so viel du willst; **5 too much** zu viel; **she gets too much money from her parents** sie bekommt zu viel Geld von ihren Eltern; **that's far too much** das ist viel zu viel; **6 how much?** wie viel?; **how much is it?** wie viel kostet es?; **how much do you want?** wie viel möchten Sie?; **how much money do you need?** wie viel Geld brauchst du?; **7** (*greatly*) sehr; **he loved her very much** er hat sie sehr geliebt; **too much** zu sehr; **so much** (so) sehr; **we liked it so much** es hat uns sehr gefallen; **8** (*often*) oft; **I don't watch television much** ich sehe nicht oft fern; **we don't go out much** wir gehen nicht oft aus; **9 thank you very much** vielen Dank.

mud *noun* Schlamm *der*.

muddle *noun* **1** Durcheinander *das*; **2 to be in a muddle** durcheinander sein.

mug *noun* Becher *der* (PL die Becher); **a mug of milk** ein Becher Milch. **mug** *verb* **to mug somebody** jemanden überfallen◇; **to be mugged** überfallen werden.

mugging *noun* Straßenraub *der*.

multiplication *noun* Multiplikation *die*.

multiply *verb* multiplizieren; **six multiplied by four** sechs multipliziert mit vier.

mum, mummy *noun* Mutti *die* (PL die Muttis); **Tom's mum** Toms Mutti; **I'll ask my mum** ich frage Mutti.

mumps *noun* Mumps *der*.

a
b
c
d
e
f
g
h
i
j
k
l
m
n
o
p
q
r
s
t
u
v
w
x
y
z

a

b

c

d

e

f

g

h

i

j

k

l

m

n

o

p

q

r

s

t

u

v

w

x

y

z

Munich *noun* München *das*.

murder *noun* Mord *der* (PL *die* Morde).
murder *verb* ermorden.

murderer *noun* Mörder *der* (PL *die* Mörder), Mörderin *die* (PL *die* Mörderinnen).

muscle *noun* Muskel *der* (PL *die* Muskeln).

muscular *adjective* muskulös.

museum *noun* Museum *das* (PL *die* Museen); **to go to the museum** ins Museum gehen.

mushroom *noun* Pilz *der* (PL *die* Pilze), Champignon *der* (PL *die* Champignons); **mushroom salad** *der* Champignonsalat.

music *noun* Musik *die*; **pop music** *die* Popmusik; **classical music** *die* klassische Musik.

musical *noun* Musical *das* (PL *die* Musicals).
musical *adjective* **1** **musical instrument** *das* Musikinstrument; **2** **they're a very musical family** sie sind eine sehr musikalische Familie.

musician *noun* Musiker *der* (PL *die* Musiker), Musikerin *die* (PL *die* Musikerinnen).

Muslim *noun* Muslem *der* (PL *die* Muslim), Muslimin *die* (PL *die* Musliminnen).

mussel *noun* Muschel *die* (PL *die* Muscheln).

must *verb* **1** müssen✧; **we must leave now** wir müssen jetzt gehen; **you must learn the vocabulary** du musst die Vokabeln lernen; **2** (*with*

a negative) dürfen✧; **you mustn't do that** das darfst du nicht tun; **3** (*expressing probability*) müssen✧; **you must be tired** ihr müsst müde sein; **it must be five o'clock** es muss fünf Uhr sein; **he must have forgotten** er muss es vergessen haben.

mustard *noun* Senf *der* (PL *die* Senfe).

mutter *verb* murmeln.

my *adjective* **1** (*before a masculine noun*) mein; **my brother** mein Bruder; **they don't like my dog** sie mögen meinen Hund nicht; **2** (*before a feminine noun*) meine; **my sister** meine Schwester; **3** (*before a neuter noun*) mein; **that's my new car** das ist mein neues Auto; **we can go in my car** wir können mit meinem Auto fahren; **4** (*before masculine/ feminine/neuter plural nouns*) meine; **my children** meine Kinder; **5** (*with parts of the body*) der/die/ das; **I had a glass in my hand** ich hatte ein Glas in der Hand; **I'm washing my hands** ich wasche mir die Hände.

myself *pronoun* **1** (*reflexive and after a preposition taking the accusative*) mich; **I've cut myself** ich habe mich geschnitten; **I've addressed the letter to myself** ich habe den Brief an mich adressiert; **2** (*reflexive and after a preposition taking the dative*) mir; **I've hurt myself** ich habe mir wehgetan; **I said to myself** ich habe mir gesagt; **3** (*stressing something*) selbst; **I said**

it myself ich habe es selbst gesagt; **4 by myself** allein.

mysterious *adjective* rätselhaft.

mystery *noun* **1** Rätsel *das* (PL *die* Rätsel); **2** (*book*) Krimi *der* (PL *die* Krimis) (*informal*).

myth *noun* Mythos *der* (PL *die* Mythen).

mythology *noun* Mythologie *die* (PL *die* Mythologien).

Nn

nail *noun* (*on your finger or toe, also metal*) Nagel *der* (PL *die* Nägel). **nail** *verb* nageln.

nailbrush *noun* Nagelbürste *die* (PL *die* Nagelbürsten).

nailfile *noun* Nagelfeile *die* (PL *die* Nagelfeilen).

nail polish *noun* Nagellack *der*.

nail polish remover *noun* Nagellackentferner *der*.

naked *adjective* nackt.

name *noun* **1** Name *der* (PL *die* Namen); **I've forgotten her name** ich habe ihren Namen vergessen; **what's your name?** wie heißt du?; **my name's Joy** ich heiße Joy; **2** (*of a book or film*) Titel *der* (PL *die* Titel).

napkin *noun* Serviette *die* (PL *die* Servietten).

nappy *noun* Windel *die* (PL *die* Windeln).

narrow *adjective* schmal; **a narrow street** eine schmale Straße.

nasty *adjective* **1** (*mean*) gemein; **that was a nasty thing to do** das war gemein; **2** (*unpleasant, bad*) scheußlich; **that's a nasty job** das ist eine scheußliche Arbeit; **a nasty smell** ein scheußlicher Geruch.

nation *noun* Nation *die* (PL *die* Nationen).

national *adjective* national.

national anthem *noun* Nationalhymne *die* (PL *die* Nationalhymnen).

nationality *noun* Nationalität *die* (PL *die* Nationalitäten).

national park *noun* Nationalpark *der* (PL *die* Nationalparks).

natural *adjective* natürlich.

naturally *adverb* natürlich.

nature *noun* Natur *die*.

nature reserve *noun* Naturschutzgebiet *das* (PL *die* Naturschutzgebiete).

naughty *adjective* unartig.

navy *noun* Marine *die*; **my uncle's in the navy** mein Onkel ist bei der Marine.

navy-blue *adjective* marineblau.

near *adjective* **1** nah(e); **2** (*the superlative of nah(e) is der/die/das nächste*) **the nearest park** der nächste Park; **the nearest bank** die nächste Bank; **the nearest shop** das nächste Geschäft.

near *preposition* nahe an (+ DAT); **near (to) the station** nahe am Bahnhof.

near *adverb* **1** nah(e) (*in spoken*

German 'nah' is more common); **they live quite near** sie wohnen ganz nah; **2 to come nearer** näher kommen.

nearby adverb nahe gelegen; **there's a park nearby** hier in der Nähe ist ein Park.

nearly adverb fast; **nearly empty** fast leer.

neat adjective **1** (well organized, tidy) ordentlich; **a neat room** ein ordentliches Zimmer; **2** adrett (clothes or the way you look).

necessarily adverb **not necessarily** nicht unbedingt.

necessary adjective nötig; **if necessary** falls nötig.

neck noun **1** (of a person) Hals der (PL die Hälse); **2** (of a garment) Kragen der (PL die Kragen).

necklace noun Halskette die (PL die Halsketten).

need noun **there's no need, I've already done it** das ist nicht nötig, ich habe es schon gemacht; **there's no need to wait** du brauchst nicht zu warten.

need verb **1** brauchen; **we need bread** wir brauchen Brot; **everything you need** alles, was man braucht; **2** (to have to) müssen◇; **I need to go to the bank** ich muss zur Bank gehen; **3** (with a negative) **you needn't wait** du brauchst nicht zu warten.

needle noun Nadel die (PL die Nadeln).

negative noun (of a photo) Negativ das (PL die Negative).

neglected adjective vernachlässigt.

neighbour noun Nachbar der (PL die Nachbarn), Nachbarin die (PL die Nachbarinnen); **we're going round to the neighbours'** wir besuchen die Nachbarn.

neighbourhood noun Nachbarschaft die; **in our neighbourhood** in unserer Nachbarschaft.

neither conjunction **1 neither … nor** weder … noch; **I have neither the time nor the money** ich habe weder die Zeit noch das Geld; **2 neither do I** ich auch nicht; **'I don't like fish' – 'neither do I'** 'ich mag keinen Fisch' – 'ich auch nicht'; **'I didn't like the film' – 'neither did Kirsty'** 'mir hat der Film nicht gefallen' – 'Kirsty hat er auch nicht gefallen'.

neither pronoun keiner von beiden/keine von beiden/keins von beiden; **'which do you like?' – 'neither'** 'welches gefällt dir?' – 'keins von beiden'.

nephew noun Neffe der (PL die Neffen).

nerve noun **1** Nerv der (PL die Nerven); **2 to lose your nerve** die Nerven verlieren; **you've got a nerve!** du hast Nerven! (informal); **3 what a nerve!** so eine Frechheit! ★**he gets on my nerves** er geht mir auf die Nerven (informal).

nervous adjective **1** (afraid) ängstlich; **to feel nervous about something** Angst vor etwas (DAT) haben; **2** (*highly strung*) nervös (*person*).

nest *noun* Nest *das* (PL die Nester).

net *noun* Netz *das* (PL die Netze).

Netherlands *noun* Niederlande (*plural*); **in the Netherlands** in den Niederlanden.

nettle *noun* Nessel *die* (PL die Nesseln).

network *noun* Netzwerk *das* (PL die Netzwerke).

neutral *noun* (*neutral gear*) Leerlauf *der*; **to be in neutral** im Leerlauf sein.
neutral *adjective* neutral.

never *adverb* **1** nie; **Ben never smokes** Ben raucht nie; **I've never told him** ich habe es ihm nie gesagt; **never again** nie wieder; **2** noch nie; **'have you ever been to Spain?' – 'no, never'** 'warst du schon mal in Spanien?' – 'nein, noch nie'; **3 never mind** macht nichts.

new *adjective* neu; **have you seen their new house?** hast du ihr neues Haus gesehen?

news *noun* **1** (*new information*) Nachricht *die* (PL die Nachrichten); **I've got good news** ich habe gute Nachrichten; **2 a piece of news** eine Neuigkeit; **any news?** was gibt es Neues?; **3** (*on TV or the radio*) Nachrichten (*plural*); **we saw it on the news** wir haben es in den Nachrichten gesehen.

newsagent *noun* Zeitungshändler *der* (PL die Zeitungshändler).

newspaper *noun* Zeitung *die* (PL die Zeitungen).

newsreader *noun* Nachrichtensprecher *der* (PL die Nachrichtensprecher), Nachrichtensprecherin *die* (PL die Nachrichtensprecherinnen).

New Year *noun* Neujahr *das*; **Happy New Year!** ein gutes neues Jahr!

New Year's Day *noun* Neujahr *das*.

New Year's Eve *noun* Silvester *der*.

New Zealand *noun* Neuseeland *das*.

next *adjective* **1** nächster/nächste/nächstes; **the next train leaves at ten** der nächste Zug fährt um zehn ab; **next week** nächste Woche; **next Thursday** nächsten Donnerstag; **next year** nächstes Jahr; **next time I see you** nächstes Mal, wenn ich dich sehe; **2** (*following*) **next please!** der Nächste bitte/die Nächste bitte; **the next thing** das Nächste; **the next day** am nächsten Tag; **the letter arrived the next day** der Brief kam am nächsten Tag an; **3 the week after next** übernächste Woche; **4** (*next-door*) nebenan; **I'm in the next room** ich bin nebenan.
next *adverb* **1** (*afterwards*) danach; **what did he say next?** was hat er danach gesagt?; **2** (*now*) als Nächstes; **what shall we do next?** was machen wir als Nächstes?; **3 next to** neben (+ DAT, *or* + ACC *with movement towards a place*); **the house next to the baker's** das Haus

a
b
c
d
e
f
g
h
i
j
k
l
m
n
o
p
q
r
s
t
u
v
w
x
y
z

a

b　　neben dem Bäcker; **I sat down next to her** ich habe mich neben sie gesetzt.

c

d　　**next door** *adverb* nebenan; **they live next door** sie wohnen nebenan; **the girl next door** das Mädchen von nebenan.

e

f　　**nice** *adjective* **1** (*pleasant*) schön; **we had a nice evening** wir haben einen schönen Abend verbracht; **Brighton's a nice town** Brighton ist eine schöne Stadt; **we had nice weather** wir hatten schönes Wetter; **2 to have a nice time** sich amüsieren; **have a nice day!** viel Spaß!; **3** (*attractive to look at*) hübsch; **that's a nice dress** das ist ein hübsches Kleid; **4** (*kind, friendly*) nett (*person*); **she's really nice** sie ist wirklich nett; **5 to be nice to somebody** nett zu jemandem sein; **she's been very nice to me** sie war sehr nett zu mir; **6** (*tasting good*) gut; **it tastes nice** es schmeckt gut.

g

h

i

j

k

l

m

n

o

p　　**nickname** *noun* Spitzname *der* (PL *die* Spitznamen).

q

r　　**niece** *noun* Nichte *die* (PL *die* Nichten).

s

t　　**night** *noun* **1** (*after bedtime*) Nacht *die* (PL *die* Nächte); **during the night** während der Nacht; **Sunday night** Sonntag Nacht; **it's cold at night** nachts ist es kalt; **to stay the night** über Nacht bleiben; **I stayed the night at Emma's** ich habe bei Emma übernachtet; **2** (*before you go to bed*) Abend *der* (PL *die* Abende); **what are you doing tonight?** was macht ihr heute Abend?; **one night**

u

v

w

x

y

z

eines Abends; **tomorrow night** morgen Abend; **I met Greg last night** ich habe Greg gestern Abend getroffen; **on Friday night** am Freitagabend; **see you tonight!** bis heute Abend!

night club *noun* Nachtklub *der* (PL die Nachtklubs).

nightie *noun* Nachthemd *das* (PL *die* Nachthemden).

nightmare *noun* Albtraum *der* (PL die Albträume).

nil *noun* (*in sport*) null; **they won four-nil** sie haben vier zu null gewonnen.

nine *number* neun.

nineteen *number* neunzehn.

ninety *number* neunzig.

ninth *number* neunter/neunte/neuntes; **on the ninth floor** im neunten Stock; **on the ninth of June** am neunten Juni.

no *adverb* nein; **I said no** ich habe nein gesagt; **no thank you** nein danke.
　　no *adjective* **1** kein; **we've got no bread** wir haben kein Brot; **no problem!** kein Problem!; **2** (*on a notice*) **'no smoking'** 'Rauchen verboten'; **'no parking'** 'Parken verboten'.

nobody *pronoun* niemand; **'who's there?' – 'nobody'** 'wer ist da?' - 'niemand'; **there's nobody in the kitchen** es ist niemand in der Küche; **nobody was at home** niemand war zu Hause.

nod *verb* nicken; **he nodded in agreement** er hat zustimmend genickt.

noise *noun* Lärm *der*; **to make a noise** Lärm machen.

noise pollution *noun* Lärmbelästigung *die*

noisy *adjective* laut.

none *pronoun* **1** (*not one*) keiner/ keine/keins; **none of us** keiner von uns/ keine von uns; **'how many students failed the exam?' – 'none'** 'wie viele Schüler sind durch die Prüfung gefallen?' – 'keine'; **none of the boys knows him** keiner der Jungen kennt ihn; **2 there's none left** es ist nichts mehr übrig.

nonsense *noun* Unsinn *der*; **to talk nonsense** Unsinn reden; **nonsense!** Unsinn!

non-smoker *noun* Nichtraucher *der* (PL *die* Nichtraucher) Nichtraucherin *die* (PL *die* Nichtraucherinnen).

non-stop *adjective* durchgehend (*train*), Nonstop- (*flight*). **non-stop** *adverb* ununterbrochen; **she talks non-stop** sie redet ununterbrochen.

noodles *plural noun* Nudeln *die* (*plural*).

noon *noun* Mittag *der*; **at (twelve) noon** um zwölf (Uhr mittags).

no-one *pronoun* niemand; **'who's there?' – 'no-one'** 'wer ist da?' – ' niemand'; **there's no-one in the kitchen** es ist niemand in der Küche; **no-one was at home** niemand war zu Hause.

nor *conjunction* **1 neither ...nor** weder ...noch; **I have neither the time nor the money** ich habe weder die Zeit noch das Geld; **2 nor do I** ich auch nicht; **'I don't like fish' – 'nor do I'** 'ich mag keinen Fisch' - 'ich auch nicht'; **nor do we** wir auch nicht.

normal *adjective* normal.

normally *adverb* **1** (*usually*) normalerweise; **2** (*in a normal way*) normal.

north *noun* Norden *der*; **in the north** im Norden. **north** *adjective* nördlich, Nord-; **the north side** die Nordseite; **north wind** *der* Nordwind. **north** *adverb* **1** (*towards the north*) nach Norden; **to travel north** nach Norden fahren; **2 north of London** nördlich von London.

North America *noun* Nordamerika *das*.

North American *noun* Nordamerikaner *der* (PL *die* Nordamerikaner), Nordamerikanerin *die* (PL *die* Nordamerikanerinnen). **North American** *adjective* nordamerikanisch.

northeast *noun* Nordosten *der*. **northeast** *adjective* **in northeast England** in Nordostengland.

Northern Ireland *noun* Nordirland *das*.

North Pole *noun* Nordpol *der*.

a
b
c
d
e
f
g
h
i
j
k
l
m
n
o
p
q
r
s
t
u
v
w
x
y
z

a
b
c
d
e
f
g
h
i
j
k
l
m
n
o
p
q
r
s
t
u
v
w
x
y
z

North Sea *noun* **the North Sea**
die Nordsee.

northwest *noun* Nordwesten *der*.
northwest *adjective* **in northwest
England** in Nordwestengland.

Norway *noun* Norwegen *das*.

Norwegian *noun* **1** (*person*)
Norweger *der* (PL die Norweger),
Norwegerin *die* (PL die
Norwegerinnen); **2** (*language*)
Norwegisch *das*.
Norwegian *adjective* norwegisch.

nose *noun* Nase *die* (PL die Nasen); **to
blow your nose** sich (DAT) die Nase
putzen.

not *adverb* **1** nicht; **not on Sundays**
sonntags nicht; **not all alone!** nicht
ganz allein!; **not bad** nicht schlecht;
not at all überhaupt nicht; **not yet**
noch nicht; **Sam didn't phone** Sam
hat nicht angerufen; **I hope not**
hoffentlich nicht; **2 not a** kein/
keine; **he's not a specialist** er ist
kein Fachmann; **not a bit** kein
bisschen.

note *noun* **1** (*a short letter*) Zettel *der*
(PL die Zettel), (*informal*) Brief *der* (PL
die Briefe); **2** (*in a class*) Notiz *die* (PL
die Notizen); **to take notes** sich
(DAT) Notizen machen; **3** (*a
banknote*) Schein *der* (PL die Scheine);
a ten-pound note ein
Zehnpfundschein; **4** (*in music*) Note
die (PL die Noten).

notebook *noun* Notizbuch *das* (PL
die Notizbücher).

notepad *noun* Notizblock *der* (PL die
Notizblöcke).

nothing *pronoun* nichts; **'what did
you say?' – 'nothing'** 'was hast du
gesagt?' – 'nichts'; **nothing special**
nichts Besonderes; **nothing new**
nichts Neues; **I saw nothing** ich
habe nichts gesehen; **there's
nothing left** es ist nichts mehr
übrig.

notice *noun* **1** (*a sign*) Schild *das* (PL
die Schilder); **2** (*an advertisement*)
Anzeige *die* (PL die Anzeigen);
3 (*advance warning*) Ankündigung
die; **4 don't take any notice of her**
nimm keine Notiz von ihr; **5 at
short notice** kurzfristig.
notice *verb* bemerken; **I didn't
notice anything** ich habe nichts
bemerkt.

notice board *noun*
Anschlagbrett *das* (PL die
Anschlagbretter).

nought *noun* Null *die* (PL die Nullen).

noun *noun* Substantiv *das* (PL die
Substantive).

novel *noun* Roman *der* (PL die
Romane).

novelist *noun* Romanautor *der* (PL
die Romanautoren), Romanautorin
die (PL die Romanautorinnen).

November *noun* November *der;* **in
November** im November.

now *adverb* **1** jetzt; **where is he
now?** wo ist er jetzt?; **from now on**
von jetzt an; **2 he left just now** er ist
gerade eben gegangen; **I saw her
just now in the corridor** ich habe
sie gerade eben im Gang gesehen;
3 do it right now! mach es sofort!;
4 now and then hin und wieder.

nowadays *adverb* heutzutage; **nowadays they are quite common** heutzutage sind sie ziemlich häufig.

nowhere *adjective* nirgends; **there's nowhere to park** man kann nirgends parken.

nuclear *adjective* Kern-; **nuclear power** *die* Kernenergie; **nuclear power station** *das* Kernkraftwerk.

nude *noun* **in the nude** nackt. **nude** *adjective* nackt.

nuisance *noun* **it's a nuisance** das ist ärgerlich; **what a nuisance!** wie ärgerlich!

numb *adjective* **1** (*with cold*) gefühllos; **2** (*emotionally*) benommen.

number plate *noun* Nummernschild *das* (PL *die* Nummernschilder).

number *noun* **1** (*of a house, telephone, or account*) Nummer *die* (PL *die* Nummern); **I live at number five** ich wohne in der Nummer fünf; **my new phone number** meine neue Telefonnummer; **2** (*a written figure*) Zahl *die* (PL *die* Zahlen); **3** (*amount*) Anzahl *die*; **the number of visitors** die Anzahl der Besucher.

nun *noun* Nonne *die* (PL *die* Nonnen).

nurse *noun* **1** (*female*) Krankenschwester *die* (PL *die* Krankenschwestern); **Janet's a nurse** Janet ist Krankenschwester; **2** (*male*) Krankenpfleger *der* (PL *die* Krankenpfleger).

nursery *noun* **1** (*for children*) Kindertagesstätte *die* (PL *die* Kindertagesstätten); **2** (*for plants*) Gärtnerei *die* (PL *die* Gärtnereien).

nursery school *noun* Kindergarten *der* (PL *die* Kindergärten).

nut *noun* **1** Nuss *die* (PL *die* Nüsse); **2** (*for a bolt*) Mutter *die* (PL *die* Muttern).

nylon *noun* Nylon *das*.

Oo

oak *noun* Eiche *die* (PL *die* Eichen).

oar *noun* Ruder *das* (PL *die* Ruder).

oats *noun* Hafer *der*; **porridge oats** Haferflocken (*plural*).

obedient *adjective* gehorsam.

obey *verb* **1** gehorchen (+ DAT); **to obey somebody** jemandem gehorchen; **2 to obey the rules** sich an die Vorschriften halten◊.

object *noun* **1** (*thing*) Gegenstand *der* (PL *die* Gegenstände); **2** (*aim*) Zweck *der*; **3** (*in grammar*) Objekt *das* (PL *die* Objekte). **object** *verb* etwas dagegen haben◊; **if you don't object** wenn Sie nichts dagegen haben.

objection *noun* Einwand *der* (PL *die* Einwände).

oboe *noun* Oboe *die* (PL *die* Oboen); **to play the oboe** Oboe spielen.

obscene *adjective* obszön.

observe *verb* beobachten.

obsessed *adjective* besessen; **she's really obsessed with her**

a

diet sie ist von ihrer Schlankheitskur ganz besessen.

b

c

obstacle *noun* Hindernis *das* (PL die Hindernisse).

obstinate *adjective* starrsinnig.

d

obtain *verb* erhalten✧.

e

obvious *adjective* eindeutig.

f

g

h

obviously *adverb* **1** (*of course*) natürlich; **2** (*looking at something*) offensichtlich; **the house is obviously empty** das Haus steht offensichtlich leer.

i

j

k

occasion *noun* Gelegenheit *die* (PL die Gelegenheiten); **on special occasions** zu besonderen Gelegenheiten.

l

occasionally *adverb* gelegentlich.

m

n

occupation *noun* Beruf *der* (PL die Berufe).

o

occupied *adjective* **1** (*taken*) besetzt; **the seat is occupied** der Platz ist besetzt; **2** (*lived in*) bewohnt.

p

q

r

s

t

u

occur *verb* **1 to occur to somebody** jemandem einfallen✧ SEP (PERF *sein*); **it occurs to me that** ... mir fällt ein, dass ...; **2 it never occurred to me** darauf wäre ich nie gekommen; **3** (*happen*) sich ereignen.

v

ocean *noun* Ozean *der* (PL die Ozeane).

w

x

o'clock *adverb* **at ten o'clock** um zehn Uhr; **it's three o'clock** es ist drei Uhr.

y

z

October *noun* Oktober *der*; **in October** im Oktober.

octopus *noun* Tintenfisch *der* (PL die Tintenfische).

odd *adjective* **1** (*strange*) komisch; **that's odd, I'm sure I heard the bell** das ist komisch, ich habe es bestimmt klingeln gehört; **2** (*number*) ungerade; **three is an odd number** drei ist eine ungerade Zahl; **3 the odd one out** die Ausnahme.

odds and ends *plural noun* Kleinkram *der*.

of *preposition* **1** von (+ DAT); (*instead of translating 'of' with 'von', the genitive case can be used*) **the parents of the children** die Eltern von den Kindern, die Eltern der Kinder; **the name of the flower** der Name der Blume; **it's very kind of you** das ist sehr nett von Ihnen; **2** (*with quantities 'of' is not translated*) **a kilo of tomatoes** ein Kilo Tomaten; **a bottle of milk** eine Flasche Milch; **the three of us** wir drei; **3 of it/them** davon (*things*); **of them** von ihnen (*people*); **how many of them didn't pay?** wie viele von ihnen haben nicht gezahlt?; **Ray has four cars but he's selling three of them** Ray hat vier Autos, aber er verkauft drei davon; **half of it** die Hälfte davon; **we ate a lot of it** wir haben viel davon gegessen; **4 the sixth of June** der sechste Juni; **5 made of** aus; **a bracelet made of silver** ein Armband aus Silber.

off *adverb, adjective, preposition* **1** (*switched off*) aus; **is the telly off?** ist der Fernseher aus?; **to turn off**

the lights das Licht ausmachen SEP; **2** (*electricity, water, gas*) abgestellt; **the gas and electricity were off** Gas und Strom waren abgestellt; **to turn off the tap** den Wasserhahn zudrehen SEP; **3 to be off** (*to leave*) gehen✧ (PERF *sein*), (*in a vehicle*) fahren✧ (PERF *sein*); **I must be off** ich muss gehen; **4 on my day off** an meinem freien Tag; **to take three days off work** sich (DAT) drei Tage frei nehmen; **we were given two days off school** wir hatten zwei Tage schulfrei; **to be off sick** wegen Krankheit fehlen; **Maya's off school today** Maya fehlt heute in der Schule; **5** (*cancelled*) abgesagt; **the match is off** das Spiel ist abgesagt worden; **6 '20% off shoes'** 'Schuhe 20% reduziert'.

offence *noun* **1** (*crime*) Straftat *die* (PL *die* Straftaten); **2 to take offence** beleidigt sein; **he takes offence easily** er ist schnell beleidigt.

offer *noun* **1** Angebot *das* (PL *die* Angebote); **job offer** *das* Stellenangebot; **2 on special offer** im Sonderangebot.
offer *verb* anbieten✧ SEP (*a present, a reward, or a job*); **he offered her a chair** er bot ihr einen Stuhl an; **to offer to do something** anbieten, etwas zu tun; **he offered to drive me to the station** er hat angeboten, mich zum Bahnhof zu fahren.

office *noun* Büro *das* (PL *die* Büros); **he's still at the office** er ist noch im Büro.

office block *noun* Bürohaus *das* (PL *die* Bürohäuser).

officer *noun* Offizier *der* (PL *die* Offiziere).

official *adjective* offiziell.

off-licence *noun* Wein- und Spirituosenhandlung *die* (PL *die* Wein- und Spirituosenhandlungen).

often *adverb* **1** oft; **he's often late** er kommt oft zu spät; **how often?** wie oft?; **2 more often** öfter; **couldn't you come more often?** könntest du nicht öfter kommen?

oil *noun* **1** (*crude oil*) Öl *das*; **2 olive oil** *das* Olivenöl; **suntan oil** *das* Sonnenöl.

oil slick *noun* Ölteppich *der* (PL *die* Ölteppiche).

ointment *noun* Salbe *die* (PL *die* Salben).

okay *adjective* **1** okay (*informal*); **tomorrow at ten, okay?** morgen um zehn, okay?; **is it okay if I don't come till Friday?** ist es okay, wenn ich erst Freitag komme?; **2** (*person*) in Ordnung; **Daisy's okay** Daisy ist in Ordnung; **3** (*nothing special, not ill*) ganz gut; **the film was okay** der Film war ganz gut; **I've been ill but I'm okay now** ich war krank, aber jetzt geht es mir ganz gut; **'how are you?' – 'okay'** 'wie geht's?' – 'ganz gut'; **4 it's okay by me** mir ist es recht.

old *adjective* **1** (*not young, not new, previous*) alt; **an old man** ein alter Mann; **an old lady** eine alte Dame; **an old tree** ein alter Baum; **old people** alte Leute; **bring some old clothes** bring ein paar alte Sachen mit; **I've only got their old address** ich habe nur ihre alte Adresse;

a
b
c
d
e
f
g
h
i
j
k
l
m
n
o
p
q
r
s
t
u
v
w
x
y
z

2 (*talking about age*) **how old are you?** wie alt bist du?; **James is ten years old** James ist zehn Jahre alt; **3 a two-year-old child** ein zweijähriges Kind; **4 my older sister** meine ältere Schwester; **she's older than me** sie ist älter als ich; **he's a year older than me** er ist ein Jahr älter als ich.

old age noun Alter das.

old age pensioner noun Rentner der (PL die Rentner), Rentnerin die (PL die Rentnerinnen).

old-fashioned noun altmodisch.

olive noun Olive die (PL die Oliven).

olive oil noun Olivenöl das (PL die Olivenöle).

Olympic Games, Olympics plural noun Olympische Spiele (plural).

omelette noun Omelett das (PL die Omelette); **a cheese omelette** ein Käseomelett.

on preposition **1** auf (+ DAT, or + ACC with movement towards a place); **it's on the desk** es ist auf dem Schreibtisch; **2** (attached to) an (+ DAT, or + ACC with movement towards a place); **on the wall** an der Wand; **3 on the beach** am Strand; **on the right/left** rechts/links; **4** (in expressions of time) **on March 21st** am 21. März; **he's arriving on Tuesday** er kommt am Dienstag an; **it's shut on Sundays** es ist sonntags geschlossen; **on rainy days** an Regentagen; **5** (for buses, trains, etc.) **to go on the bus** mit dem Bus fahren; **I met Jackie on the train** ich habe Jackie im Zug getroffen;

let's go on our bikes fahren wir mit dem Rad; **6 on TV** im Fernsehen; **on the radio** im Radio; **on video** auf Video; **7 on holiday** in den Ferien. **on** adjective **1** (switched on) **to be on** an sein; **the lights are on** das Licht ist an; **is the radio on?** ist das Radio an?; **2** (happening) **what's on TV?** was gibts im Fernsehen?; **what's on this week at the cinema?** was läuft diese Woche im Kino?

once adverb **1** einmal; **I've tried once already** ich habe es schon einmal versucht; **try once more** versuch es noch einmal; **once a day** einmal täglich; **once upon a time ...** es war einmal ...; **2 more than once** mehrmals; **3 at once** (immediately) sofort; **the doctor came at once** der Arzt kam sofort; **4 at once** (at the same time) gleichzeitig; **I can't do two things at once** ich kann nicht zwei Sachen gleichzeitig machen.

one number (when counting) eins, (with a noun) ein; **one son** ein Sohn; **one apple** ein Apfel; **if you want a biro I've got one** falls du einen Kugelschreiber brauchst, habe ich einen; **at one o'clock** um ein Uhr. **one** pronoun **1** einer/eine/eins; **I saw the photos, can I have one of them?** ich habe die Fotos gesehen, kann ich eins davon haben?; **2 this one** dieser/diese/dieses; **I'd prefer that bike, but this one's cheaper** ich würde lieber das Rad haben, aber dieses ist billiger; **3 that one** der da/die da/das da; **'which video?' – 'that one'** 'welches Video?' – 'das da'; **4 which one?**

welcher/welche/welches?; **'my foot's hurting'** – **'which one?'** 'mir tut der Fuß weh' – 'welcher?'; **'she borrowed a skirt from me'** – **'which one?'** 'sie hat sich einen Rock von mir geliehen' – 'welchen?'; **5** (*you*) man; **one never knows** man kann nie wissen.

one's *adjective* sein/seine/sein; **one pays for one's car** man zahlt für sein Auto.

oneself *pronoun* **1** (*reflexive*) sich; **to wash oneself** sich waschen; **2** (*stressing something*) selbst; **one has to do everything oneself** man muss alles selbst machen.

one-way street *noun* Einbahnstraße die (PL die Einbahnstraßen).

onion *noun* Zwiebel die (PL die Zwiebeln).

only *adjective* **1** einziger/einzige/einziges; **the only free seat** der einzige freie Platz; **the only thing you could do** das Einzige, was du machen könntest; **2 an only child** ein Einzelkind.

only *adverb, conjunction* **1** nur; **they've only got two bedrooms** sie haben nur zwei Schlafzimmer; **Anne's only free on Fridays** Anne hat nur freitags Zeit; **there are only three left** es sind nur noch drei übrig; **I'd walk, only it's raining** ich würde zu Fuß gehen, nur regnet es; **2** (*very recently*) gerade erst; **he's only just got the message** er hat die Nachricht gerade erst bekommen; **3** (*barely*) gerade noch; **we've only just made it on time** wir sind gerade noch rechtzeitig angekommen.

onto *preposition* auf (+ ACC).

open *noun* **in the open** im Freien. **open** *adjective* **1** offen; **the door's open** die Tür ist offen; **the baker's is not open** die Bäckerei ist nicht geöffnet; **2 in the open air** im Freien.

open *verb* **1** aufmachen SEP; **can you open the door for me?** kannst du mir die Tür aufmachen?; **the bank opens at nine** die Bank macht um neun auf; **2** (*open up*) sich öffnen; **the door opened slowly** die Tür öffnete sich langsam.

opera *noun* Oper die (PL die Opern).

operate *verb* **1** (*medically*) operieren; **will they have to operate (on him/her)?** werden sie ihn/sie operieren müssen?; **2** bedienen (*a machine*).

operation *noun* **1** Operation die (PL die Operationen); **2 to have an operation** operiert werden.

opinion *noun* Meinung die (PL die Meinungen); **in my opinion** meiner Meinung nach.

opinion poll *noun* Meinungsumfrage die (PL die Meinungsumfragen).

opponent *noun* Gegner der (PL die Gegner), Gegnerin die (PL die Gegnerinnen).

opportunity *noun* Gelegenheit die (PL die Gelegenheiten); **to have the opportunity of doing something** die Gelegenheit haben, etwas zu tun.

a
b
c
d
e
f
g
h
i
j
k
l
m
n
o
p
q
r
s
t
u
v
w
x
y
z

opposite *noun* Gegenteil *das* (PL *die* Gegenteile); **no, quite the opposite** nein, ganz im Gegenteil.

opposite *adjective*
1 entgegengesetzt (*direction*); **she went off in the opposite direction** sie ging in die entgegengesetzte Richtung; **2** (*facing*) gegenüberliegend; **in the house opposite** im gegenüberliegenden Haus.

opposite *adverb* gegenüber; **they live opposite** sie wohnen gegenüber.

opposite *preposition* gegenüber (+ DAT); **opposite the station** gegenüber dem Bahnhof.

optician *noun* Optiker *der* (PL *die* Optiker), Optikerin *die* (PL *die* Optikerinnen).

optimistic *adjective* zuversichtlich, optimistisch.

option *noun* Wahl *die*; **we have no option** wir haben keine andere Wahl.

optional *adjective* auf Wunsch erhältlich; **optional subject** *das* Wahlfach.

or *conjunction* **1** oder; **English or German?** Englisch oder Deutsch?; **today or Tuesday?** heute oder Dienstag?; **2** (*in negatives*) noch; **I don't have a cat or a dog** ich habe weder eine Katze noch einen Hund; **not in June or July** weder im Juni noch im Juli; **3** (*or else*) sonst; **phone Mum, or she'll worry** ruf Mutti an, sonst macht sie sich Sorgen.

oral *noun* (*an exam*) Mündliche *das* (*informal*); **my German oral** meine mündliche Deutschprüfung.

orange *noun* (*the fruit*) Orange *die* (PL *die* Orangen); **orange juice** *der* Orangensaft.

orange *adjective* orange ('*orange*' *never changes*); **my orange socks** meine orange Socken.

orchestra *noun* Orchester *das* (PL *die* Orchester).

order *noun* **1** (*sequence*) Reihenfolge *die* (PL *die* Reihenfolgen); **in the right order** in der richtigen Reihenfolge; **in the wrong order** in der falschen Reihenfolge; **in alphabetical order** in alphabetischer Reihenfolge; **2** (*in a restaurant, café, or shop*) Bestellung *die* (PL *die* Bestellungen); **3 'out of order'** 'außer Betrieb'; **4 in order to do something** um etwas zu tun.

order *verb* **1** (*in a restaurant or a shop*) bestellen; **we ordered soup** wir haben Suppe bestellt; **have you ordered?** haben Sie schon bestellt?; **2** bestellen (*a taxi*).

ordinary *adjective* normal.

organ *noun* **1** (*the instrument*) Orgel *die* (PL *die* Orgeln); **2** (*of the body*) Organ *das* (PL *die* Organe).

organic *adjective* Bio- (*food*); **organic food** *die* Biokost.

organization *noun* Organisation *die* (PL *die* Organisationen).

organize *verb* **1** organisieren; **2** veranstalten (*a conference or festival*).

orienteering *noun*
Orientierungslauf *der*

original *adjective* **1** ursprünglich;
the original plan was better der
ursprüngliche Plan war besser;
2 originell; **it's a really original
novel** das ist ein wirklich
origineller Roman.

originally *adverb* ursprünglich;
originally we wanted to go by car
ursprünglich wollten wir mit dem
Auto fahren.

orphan *noun* Waise *die* (PL *die*
Waisen); **he is an orphan** er ist
Waise.

ostrich *noun* Strauß *der* (PL *die*
Strauße).

other *adjective* **1** anderer/andere/
anderes; **we took the other road**
wir haben die andere Straße
genommen; **where are the others?**
wo sind die anderen?; **the other two
cars** die anderen beiden Autos;
2 give me the other one gib mir
den anderen/die andere/das andere
(*the translation of 'the other one'
depends on the gender of the noun it
refers to*); **3 the other day** neulich;
4 every other week jede zweite
Woche; **5 somebody or other**
irgendjemand; **something or other**
irgendetwas; **somewhere or other**
irgendwo; **6 any other questions?**
sonst noch Fragen?

otherwise *adverb, conjunction*
sonst.

ought *verb* (*'ought' is usually
translated by the subjunctive of
'sollen'*) **I ought to go** ich sollte
eigentlich gehen; **they ought to**

have known the address** sie hätten
die Adresse kennen sollen; **you
oughtn't to have any problems** du
solltest keine Probleme haben.

our *adjective* **1** (*before a masculine
noun*) unser; **our father** unser
Vater; **2** (*before a feminine noun*)
unsere; **our mother** unsere Mutter;
3 (*before a neuter noun*) unser; **our
house** unser Haus; **4** (*before
masculine/feminine/neuter plural
nouns*) unsere; **our parents** unsere
Eltern; **5** (*with parts of the body*)
der/die/das (*plural: die*) ; **we'll go
and wash our hands** wir waschen
uns die Hände.

ours *pronoun* **1** (*for a masculine
noun*) unserer; **their garden's
bigger than ours** ihr Garten ist
größer als unserer; **2** (*for a feminine
noun*) unsere; **their kitchen is
smaller than ours** ihre Küche ist
kleiner als unsere; **3** (*for a neuter
noun*) unseres; **their child is
younger than ours** ihr Kind ist
jünger als unseres; **4** (*for plural
nouns*) unsere; **they've invited their
friends and we've invited ours** sie
haben ihre Freunde eingeladen und
wir haben unsere eingeladen; **5 the
green car is ours** das grüne Auto
gehört uns; **it's ours** es gehört uns; **a
friend of ours** ein Freund von uns.

ourselves *pronoun* **1** (*reflexive*)
uns; **we introduced ourselves** wir
haben uns vorgestellt; **2** (*for
emphasis*) selbst; **in the end we did
it ourselves** schließlich haben wir
es selbst gemacht.

out *adverb* **1** (*outside*) draußen; **it's cold out there** es ist kalt da draußen; **they're out in the garden** sie sind draußen im Garten; **2 to go out** hinausgehen◇ SEP (PERF *sein*), rausgehen◇ SEP (PERF *sein*) (*informal*); **to go out shopping** einkaufen gehen; **3 get out!** raus! (*informal*); **4 the ball is out** der Ball ist aus; **5** (*absent*) **to be out** nicht da sein; **Mr Barnes is out** Herr Barnes ist nicht da; **6 to go out** (*for an evening or to the theatre or cinema*) ausgehen◇ SEP (PERF *sein*), weggehen◇ SEP (PERF *sein*) (*informal*); **are you going out this evening?** gehst du heute Abend weg?; **to be going out with somebody** mit jemandem gehen; **Alison's going out with Danny now** Alison geht jetzt mit Danny; **7 to ask somebody out** jemanden einladen◇ SEP; **he's asked me out** er hat mich eingeladen; **8** (*light, fire*) **are all the lights out?** ist das Licht aus?

out *preposition* **out of** aus (+ DAT); **to go out of the room** aus dem Zimmer gehen; **he threw it out of the window** er hat es aus dem Fenster geworfen; **to drink out of a glass** aus einem Glas trinken; **she took the photo out of her bag** sie hat das Foto aus der Tasche genommen.

outdoor *adjective* (*activity or sport*) im Freien; **outdoor games** Spiele im Freien.

outdoors *adverb* draußen; **to go outdoors** nach draußen gehen.

outing *noun* Ausflug der (PL die Ausflüge); **to go on an outing** einen Ausflug machen.

outline *noun* (*of an object*) Umriss der (PL die Umrisse).

out-of-date *adjective* **1** (*no longer valid*) ungültig; **my passport's out of date** mein Pass ist ungültig; **2** (*old-fashioned*) altmodisch (*clothes, music*).

outside *noun* Außenseite die; **it's blue on the outside** außen ist es blau.
outside *adjective* Außen-.
outside *adverb* draußen; **it's cold outside** es ist kalt draußen.
outside *preposition* vor (+ DAT); **I'll meet you outside the cinema** ich treffe mich vor dem Kino mit dir.

outskirts *plural noun* Stadtrand der; **on the outskirts of Lübeck** am Stadtrand von Lübeck.

oven *noun* Ofen der (PL die Öfen); **to put something in the oven** etwas in den Ofen tun.

over *preposition* **1** (*above*) über (+ DAT); **there's a mirror over the sink** über dem Waschbecken hängt ein Spiegel; **2** (*involving movement*) über (+ ACC); **he threw the ball over the wall** er hat den Ball über die Mauer geworfen; **3 over here** hier drüben; **the food is over here** das Essen ist hier drüben; **4 over there** da drüben; **she's over there** sie ist da drüben; **5** (*more than*) über; **it will cost over a hundred pounds** es wird über hundert Pfund kosten; **he's over sixty** er ist über sechzig; **6** (*during*) über (+ ACC); **over**

Christmas über Weihnachten; **over the weekend** übers Wochenende; **7** (*finished*) zu Ende; **when the meeting's over** wenn die Besprechung zu Ende ist; **it's all over** es ist vorbei; **8 over the phone** am Telefon; **to ask someone over** jemanden einladen◇ SEP; **to come over** herüberkommen◇ SEP; **come over on Saturday** komm am Samstag zu uns herüber; **9 all over the place** überall; **I've been looking for it all over** ich habe überall danach gesucht.

overdose *noun* Überdosis *die* (PL *die* Überdosen).

overtake *verb* überholen.

overtime *noun* **to work overtime** Überstunden machen.

overweight *adjective* **to be overweight** Übergewicht haben.

owe *verb* schulden; **I owe him ten pounds** ich schulde ihm zehn Pfund.

owing *adjective* **1** (*outstanding*) ausstehend; **there's five pounds owing** fünf Pfund stehen aus; **2 owing to** wegen (+ GEN); **owing to the snow** wegen des Schnees.

owl *noun* Eule *die* (PL *die* Eulen).

own *adjective* **1** eigen; **my own computer** mein eigener Computer; **I've got my own room** ich habe mein eigenes Zimmer; **2 on your own** allein; **Annie did it on her own** Annie hat es allein gemacht.
own *verb* besitzen◇.

owner *noun* Besitzer *der* (PL *die* Besitzer), Besitzerin *die* (PL *die* Besitzerinnen).

oxygen *noun* Sauerstoff *der*.

oyster *noun* Auster *die* (PL *die* Austern).

ozone layer *noun* Ozonschicht *die*.

Pp

pace *noun* **1** (*a step*) Schritt *der* (PL *die* Schritte); **2** (*the speed you walk at*) Tempo *das* (PL *die* Tempos).

Pacific *noun* **the Pacific (Ocean)** der Pazifik.

pack *noun* **1** Packung *die* (PL *die* Packungen); **2 pack of cards** das Kartenspiel.
pack *verb* **1** packen (*your case*); **I haven't packed yet** ich habe noch nicht gepackt; **I'll pack my case tonight** ich packe meinen Koffer heute Abend; **2** einpacken SEP (*clothes, shoes, etc.*); **have you packed my red shirt?** hast du mein rotes Hemd eingepackt?

package *noun* Paket *das* (PL *die* Pakete).

package holiday *noun* Pauschalurlaub *der* (PL *die* Pauschalurlaube).

packed lunch *noun* Lunchpaket *das* (PL *die* Lunchpakete).

packet *noun* **1** Päckchen *das* (PL *die* Päckchen); **a packet of tea** ein Päckchen Tee; **2** (*box*) Schachtel *die*

a
b
c
d
e
f
g
h
i
j
k
l
m
n
o
p
q
r
s
t
u
v
w
x
y
z

(PL *die* Schachteln); **3** (*bag*) Tüte *die* (PL *die* Tüten); **a packet of crisps** eine Tüte Chips.

pad *noun* (*of paper*) Block *der* (PL *die* Blöcke).

paddle *noun* (*for a canoe*) Paddel *das* (PL *die* Paddel).
paddle *verb* **1** (*at the seaside*) plauschen (PERF *sein*); **to go paddling** plauschen gehen; **2** (*a canoe*) paddeln.

padlock *noun* Vorhängeschloss *das* (PL *die* Vorhängeschlösser).

page *noun* Seite *die* (PL *die* Seiten); **on page seven** auf Seite sieben.

pain *noun* Schmerz *der* (PL *die* Schmerzen); **to be in pain** Schmerzen haben; **I've got a pain in my leg** ich habe Schmerzen im Bein; ★**Eric's a real pain (in the neck)** Eric geht einem richtig auf den Wecker (*informal*).

painful *adjective* schmerzhaft.

painkiller *noun* Schmerzmittel *das* (PL *die* Schmerzmittel).

paint *noun* Farbe *die* (PL *die* Farben); **'wet paint'** 'frisch gestrichen'.
paint *verb* malen (*a picture*), streichen◇ (*a room*); **to paint a room pink** ein Zimmer rosa streichen.

paintbrush *noun* Pinsel *der* (PL *die* Pinsel).

painter *noun* Maler *der* (PL *die* Maler), Malerin *die* (PL *die* Malerinnen).

painting *noun* (*picture*) Gemälde *das* (PL *die* Gemälde); **a painting by Picasso** ein Gemälde von Picasso.

pair *noun* **1** Paar *das* (PL *die* Paare); **a pair of socks** ein Paar Socken; **2 a pair of scissors** eine Schere; **3 a pair of trousers** eine Hose; **a pair of knickers** eine Unterhose; **4 to work in pairs** paarweise arbeiten.

Pakistan *noun* Pakistan *das*.

palace *noun* Palast *der* (PL *die* Paläste).

pale *adjective* blass; **to turn pale** blass werden; **pale green** zartgrün.

palm *noun* **1** (*of your hand*) Handfläche *die* (PL *die* Handflächen); **2** (*a palm tree*) Palme *die* (PL *die* Palmen).

pan *noun* **1** (*saucepan*) Topf *der* (PL *die* Töpfe); **a pan of water** ein Topf Wasser; **2** (*frying-pan*) Pfanne *die* (PL *die* Pfannen).

pancake *noun* Pfannkuchen *der* (PL *die* Pfannkuchen).

panel *noun* **1** (*for a discussion*) Diskussionsrunde *die*, (*for a quiz*) Rateteam *das*; **2** (*a piece of wood*) Tafel *die* (PL *die* Tafeln).

panic *noun* Panik *die*.
panic *verb* in Panik geraten◇; **don't panic!** keine Panik!

pantomime *noun* Märchenvorstellung *die* (PL *die* Märchenvorstellungen).

pants *plural noun* Unterhose *die* (PL *die* Unterhosen).

paper *noun* **1** Papier *das*; **a sheet of paper** ein Blatt Papier; **2 paper hanky** ein Papiertaschentuch; **3 paper cup** *der* Pappbecher; **4** (*newspaper*) Zeitung *die* (PL *die* Zeitungen); **it was in the paper** es

stand in der Zeitung; **5 papers**
(*documents*) Unterlagen (*plural*).

paperback *noun* Taschenbuch
das (PL *die* Taschenbücher).

paperclip *noun* Büroklammer *die*
(PL *die* Büroklammern).

paper towel *noun*
Papierhandtuch *das* (PL *die*
Papierhandtücher).

parachute *noun* Fallschirm *der*
(PL *die* Fallschirme).

parade *noun* Umzug *der* (PL *die*
Umzüge).

paraffin *noun* Petroleum *das* .

paragraph *noun* Absatz *der* (PL *die*
Absätze); **'new paragraph'** 'Absatz'.

parallel *adjective* parallel.

paralysed *adjective* gelähmt.

parcel *noun* Paket *das* (PL *die*
Pakete).

pardon *noun* **I beg your pardon** (*as
an apology*) Entschuldigung!;
pardon? wie bitte?

parent *noun* Elternteil *der*; **parents**
Eltern (*plural*); **my parents live in
Germany** meine Eltern wohnen in
Deutschland; **parents' evening** *der*
Elternabend.

park *noun* **1** Park *der* (PL *die* Parks);
theme park *der* (thematische)
Freizeitpark; **2 car park** *der*
Parkplatz.
park *verb* **1** parken; **you can park
outside the house** du kannst vor
dem Haus parken; **2 to find
somewhere to park** einen
Parkplatz finden.

parking *noun* Parken *das*; **'no
parking'** 'Parken verboten'.

parking meter *noun* Parkuhr *die*
(PL *die* Parkuhren).

parking space *noun* Parklücke
die (PL *die* Parklücken).

parking ticket *noun* Strafzettel
der (PL *die* Strafzettel).

parliament *noun* Parlament *das*
(PL *die* Parlamente).

parrot *noun* Papagei *der* (PL *die*
Papageien).

parsley *noun* Petersilie *die*.

part *noun* **1** Teil *der* (PL *die* Teile);
part of the garden Teil des Gartens;
the last part of the book der letzte
Teil des Buches; **2 that's part of
your job** das gehört dazu; **3 to take
part in something** an etwas (DAT)
teilnehmen❖ SEP; **4** (*spare part*) Teil
das (PL *die* Teile) (*for a machine or an
engine*); **5** (*a role in a play*) Rolle *die*
(PL *die* Rollen).

particular *adjective* besonderer/
besondere/besonderes; **nothing in
particular** nichts Besonderes.

particularly *adverb* besonders;
not particularly interesting nicht
besonders interessant.

parting *noun* **1** (*in your hair*)
Scheitel *der* (PL *die* Scheitel);
2 (*departure*) Abschied. *der* (PL *die*
Abschiede).

partly *adverb* teilweise.

partner *noun* Partner *der* (PL *die*
Partner), Partnerin *die* (PL *die*
Partnerinnen).

a
b
c
d
e
f
g
h
i
j
k
l
m
n
o
p
q
r
s
t
u
v
w
x
y
z

a
b
c
d
e
f
g
h
i
j
k
l
m
n
o
p
q
r
s
t
u
v
w
x
y
z

part-time *adjective* Teilzeit-; **part-time work** die Teilzeitarbeit.
part-time *adverb* **to work part-time** Teilzeit arbeiten.

party *noun* 1 (*small, private*) Party die (PL die Partys), Feier die (PL die Feiern); **a Christmas party** eine Weihnachtsfeier; **to have a birthday party** eine Geburtstagsparty machen; 2 (*more formal, in the evening*) Gesellschaft die (PL die Gesellschaften); **we've been invited to a party at the Smiths' house** wir sind zu einer Gesellschaft bei Smiths eingeladen worden; 3 (*group*) Gruppe die (PL die Gruppen); **a party of schoolchildren** eine Gruppe Schulkinder; 4 (*in politics*) Partei die (PL die Parteien).

party game *noun* Gesellschaftsspiel das (PL die Gesellschaftsspiele).

pass *noun* 1 (*to let you in*) Ausweis der (PL die Ausweise); 2 **bus pass** die Buskarte; 3 (*over the mountains*) Pass der (PL die Pässe); 4 (*in an exam*) **to get a pass in maths** die Mathematikprüfung bestehen.
pass *verb* 1 (*walk past*) vorbeigehen◇ SEP (PERF *sein*) an (+ DAT) (*a place or building*); **we passed your house** wir sind an deinem Haus vorbeigegangen; 2 (*drive past*) vorbeifahren◇ SEP (PERF *sein*) an (+ DAT) (*a place or building*); 3 (*overtake*) überholen (*a car*); 4 (*give*) reichen; **could you pass me the sugar please?** könnten Sie mir bitte den Zucker reichen?; 5 (*time*) vergehen◇ (PERF *sein*); **the time passed slowly** die Zeit verging langsam; 6 bestehen◇ (*an exam*); **to pass an exam** eine Prüfung bestehen; **did you pass in German?** hast du die Deutschprüfung bestanden?

passage *noun* 1 (*corridor*) Gang der (PL die Gänge); 2 (*a piece of text*) Passage. die (PL die Passagen).

passenger *noun* 1 (*in a plane or ship*) Passagier der (PL die Passagiere); 2 (*in a train or bus*) Fahrgast der (PL die Fahrgäste); 3 (*in a car*) Mitfahrer der (PL die Mitfahrer).

passive *noun* Passiv das,
passive *adjective* passiv.

Passover *noun* Passah das.

passport *noun* Reisepass der (PL die Reisepässe), Pass der (PL die Pässe).

password *noun* 1 (*to gain entry*) Kennwort das (PL die Kennwörter); 2 (*for access to data*) Passwort das (PL die Passwörter); **to give the password** das Passwort eingeben.

past *noun* Vergangenheit die; **in the past** in der Vergangenheit.
past *adjective* 1 (*recent*) letzter/ letzte/letztes; **in the past few weeks** in den letzten paar Wochen; 2 (*over*) vorbei; **winter is past** der Winter ist vorbei.
past *preposition, adverb* 1 **to walk past something** an etwas (DAT) vorbeigehen◇ SEP (PERF *sein*); **we went past the school** wir sind an der Schule vorbeigegangen; **to go past** vorbeifahren◇ (PERF *sein*); 2 (*after*) nach (+ DAT); **it's just past the post office** es ist kurz nach der

Post; **3** (*talking about time*) **ten past six** zehn nach sechs; **half past four** halb fünf; **a quarter past two** Viertel nach zwei.

pasta *noun* Nudeln (*plural*); **I don't like pasta** ich mag keine Nudeln.

pastry *noun* **1** (*for baking*) Teig *der*; **2** (*cake*) Gebäck *das*.

patch *noun* **1** (*for mending*) Flicken *der* (PL die Flicken); **2** (*of snow or ice*) Stelle *die* (PL die Stellen); **3** (*of blue sky*) Stückchen *das* (PL die Stückchen).

path *noun* Weg *der* (PL die Wege), (*very narrow*) Pfad *der* (PL die Pfade).

pathetic *adjective* (*useless, hopeless*) jämmerlich.

patience *noun* **1** Geduld *die*; **2** (*card game*) Patience *die*.

patient *noun* Patient *der* (PL die Patienten), Patientin *die* (PL die Patientinnen).
patient *adjective* geduldig.

patiently *adverb* geduldig.

patio *noun* Terrasse *die* (PL die Terrassen).

pattern *noun* **1** (*on wallpaper or fabric*) Muster *das* (PL die Muster); **2** (*dressmaking, knitting*) Schnitt *der* (PL die Schnitte).

pause *noun* Pause *die* (PL die Pausen).

pavement *noun* Bürgersteig *der* (PL die Bürgersteige); **on the pavement** auf dem Bürgersteig.

paw *noun* Pfote *die* (PL die Pfoten).

pawn *noun* (*in chess*) Bauer *der* (PL die Bauern).

pay *noun* (*wage*) Lohn *der* (PL die Löhne), (*salary*) Gehalt *das* (PL die Gehälter).
pay *verb* **1** zahlen; **I'm paying** ich zahle; **to pay cash** bar zahlen; **to pay by credit card** mit Kreditkarte zahlen; **they pay £8 an hour** sie zahlen acht Pfund die Stunde; **to pay by cheque** mit Scheck zahlen; **2** bezahlen (*'bezahlen' is used when you pay a person, a bill or for something*); **to pay for something** etwas bezahlen; **Tony paid for the drinks** Tony hat die Getränke bezahlt; **it's all paid for** es ist alles bezahlt; **3 to pay somebody back** (*money*) jemandem Geld zurückzahlen SEP; **4 to pay attention** aufpassen SEP; **5 to pay a visit to somebody** jemanden besuchen.

pay phone *noun* Münzfernsprecher *der* (PL die Münzfernsprecher).

payment *noun* **1** Bezahlung *die* (*of sum, bill, debt, or fine*); **2** Zahlung *die* (PL die Zahlungen) (*of interest, tax, or fee*).

PC *noun* (*computer*) PC *der* (PL die PC).

pea *noun* Erbse *die* (PL die Erbsen).

peace *noun* Frieden *der*.

peaceful *adjective* friedlich.

peach *noun* Pfirsich *der* (PL die Pfirsiche).

peacock *noun* Pfau *der* (PL die Pfauen).

peak period (*for holidays*) Hauptferienzeit *die* (PL die Hauptferienzeiten).

a
b
c
d
e
f
g
h
i
j
k
l
m
n
o
p
q
r
s
t
u
v
w
x
y
z

peak rate noun (for phoning) Höchsttarif der (PL die Höchsttarife).

peak time noun (for traffic) Stoßzeit die (PL die Stoßzeiten).

peanut noun Erdnuss die (PL die Erdnüsse).

peanut butter noun Erdnussbutter die.

pear noun Birne die (PL die Birnen).

pearl noun Perle die (PL die Perlen).

pebble noun Kieselstein der (PL die Kieselsteine).

peculiar adjective komisch.

pedal noun Pedal das (PL die Pedale). pedal verb (on a bike) **to pedal off** (mit dem Rad) wegfahren◇ (PERF sein).

pedestrian noun Fußgänger der (PL die Fußgänger), Fußgängerin die (PL die Fußgängerinnen).

pedestrian crossing noun Fußgängerüberweg der (PL die Fußgängerüberwege).

pedestrian precinct noun Fußgängerzone die (PL die Fußgängerzonen).

pee noun **to have a pee** pinkeln (informal).

peel noun Schale die (PL die Schalen). peel verb schälen (fruit, vegetables).

peg noun **1** (hook) Haken der (PL die Haken); **2 clothes peg** die Wäscheklammer (PL die Wäscheklammern); **3** (for a tent) Hering der (PL die Heringe).

pen noun (ball-point) Kugelschreiber der (PL die Kugelschreiber); **felt pen** der Filzstift.

penalty noun **1** (a fine) Geldstrafe die (PL die Geldstrafen); **2** (in football) Elfmeter der (PL die Elfmeter).

pence plural noun Pence (plural).

pencil noun Bleistift der (PL die Bleistifte); **to write in pencil** mit Bleistift schreiben.

pencil case noun Federmäppchen das (PL die Federmäppchen).

pencil sharpener noun Bleistiftanspitzer der (PL die Bleistiftanspitzer).

penfriend noun Brieffreund der (PL die Brieffreunde), Brieffreundin die (PL die Brieffreundinnen); **my German pen-friend is called Heidi** meine deutsche Brieffreundin heißt Heidi.

penguin noun Pinguin der (PL die Pinguine).

penis noun Penis der (PL die Penisse).

penknife noun Taschenmesser das (PL die Taschenmesser).

penny noun Penny der (PL die Pence).

pension noun Rente die (PL die Renten).

pensioner noun Rentner der (PL die Rentner), Rentnerin die (PL die Rentnerinnen).

people plural noun **1** Leute (plural), Menschen (plural) ('Menschen' is used in a more formal context); **most people round here** die meisten Leute hier; **several people** verschiedene Leute; **nice**

people nette Leute; **all the people in the world** alle Menschen auf der Welt; **a crowd of people** eine Menschenmenge; **2** (*when you're counting them*) Personen (*plural*); **for ten people** für zehn Personen; **how many people have you invited?** wie viele Personen hast du eingeladen?; **3 people say that** ... man sagt, dass ....

pepper *noun* **1** (*spice*) Pfeffer *der*; **2** (*vegetable*) Paprikaschote *die* (PL *die* Paprikaschoten).

peppermill *noun* Pfeffermühle *die* (PL *die* Pfeffermühlen).

peppermint *noun* (*plant*) Pfefferminze *die*; **peppermint tea** *der* Pfefferminztee.

per *preposition* pro (+ ACC); **ten pounds per person** zehn Pfund pro Person.

per cent *adverb* Prozent *das*; **sixty per cent of students** sechzig Prozent der Studenten.

percentage *noun* Prozentsatz *der* (PL *die* Prozentsätze).

percussion *noun* Schlagzeug *das*; **to play percussion** Schlagzeug spielen.

perfect *adjective* **1** perfekt; **she speaks perfect English** sie spricht perfekt Englisch; **2** (*ideal*) herrlich (*day or weather*).

perfectly *adverb* **1** (*absolutely*) vollkommen; **2** (*faultlessly*) perfekt.

perform *verb* **1** spielen (*a piece of music or a part*); **2** singen⬦ (*a song*); **3 to perform a play** ein Theaterstück aufführen SEP.

performance *noun* **1** (*playing or acting*) Darstellung *die* (PL *die* Darstellungen); **his performance as Hamlet** seine Darstellung des Hamlet; **2** (*show or film*) Vorstellung *die* (PL *die* Vorstellungen); **the performance starts at eight** die Vorstellung fängt um acht Uhr an; **3** (*of a play or opera*) Aufführung *die* (PL *die* Aufführungen).

performer *noun* Künstler *der* (PL *die* Künstler), Künstlerin *die* (PL *die* Künstlerinnen).

perfume *noun* Parfüm *das* (PL *die* Parfüme).

perhaps *adverb* vielleicht; **perhaps he's missed the train** vielleicht hat er den Zug verpasst.

period *noun* **1** (*length of time*) Zeit *die* (PL *die* Zeiten); **trial period** die Probezeit; **2** (*a portion of time*) Zeitraum *der*; **a two-year period** ein Zeitraum von zwei Jahren; **3** (*in school*) Stunde *die* (PL *die* Stunden); **4** (*menstruation*) Periode *die* (PL *die* Perioden).

perm *noun* Dauerwelle *die* (PL *die* Dauerwellen).

permanent *adjective* **1** ständig; **2** fest (*job or address, for example*).

permanently *adverb* **1** dauernd; **2 to be permanently employed** fest angestellt sein.

permission *noun* Erlaubnis *die*; **to get permission to do something** Erlaubnis zu etwas (DAT) erhalten.

permit *noun* Genehmigung *die* (PL *die* Genehmigungen).

permit *verb* **1** erlauben; **to permit**

a b c d e f g h i j k l m n o **p** q r s t u v w x y z

519

somebody to do something jemandem erlauben, etwas zu tun; **smoking is not permitted** Rauchen ist nicht gestattet; **2 weather permitting** bei entsprechendem Wetter.

person *noun* **1** Person *die* (PL *die* Personen); **there's still room for one more person** wir haben noch Platz für eine Person; **2 in person** persönlich.

personal *adjective* persönlich.

personality *noun* Persönlichkeit *die* (PL *die* Persönlichkeiten).

personally *adverb* persönlich; **personally, I'm against it** ich persönlich bin dagegen.

perspiration *noun* Schweiß *der*.

persuade *verb* überreden; **to persuade somebody to come** jemanden überreden zu kommen.

pessimistic *adjective* pessimistisch.

pest *noun* **1** (*greenfly, for example*) Schädling *der* (PL *die* Schädlinge); **2** (*annoying person*) Nervensäge *die* (PL *die* Nervensägen) (*informal*).

pet *noun* **1** Haustier *das* (PL *die* Haustiere); **do you have a pet?** habt ihr Haustiere?; **a pet dog** ein Hund; **2 Julie is teacher's pet** Julie ist der Liebling des Lehrers.

petrol *noun* Benzin *das* (PL *die* Benzine); **to fill up with petrol** tanken; **to run out of petrol** kein Benzin mehr haben.

petrol station *noun* Tankstelle *die* (PL *die* Tankstellen).

pharmacy *noun* Apotheke *die* (PL *die* Apotheken).

pheasant *noun* Fasan *der* (PL *die* Fasane).

philosophy *noun* Philosophie *die* (PL *die* Philosophien).

phone *noun* Telefon *das* (PL *die* Telefone); **she's on the phone** sie telefoniert; **I was on the phone to Sophie** ich habe mit Sophie telefoniert; **you can book by phone** du kannst telefonisch buchen. **phone** *verb* **1** telefonieren; **while I was phoning** während ich telefonierte; **2 to phone somebody** jemanden anrufen✧ SEP; **I'll phone you tonight** ich rufe dich heute Abend an.

phone book *noun* Telefonbuch *das* (PL *die* Telefonbücher).

phone box *noun* Telefonzelle *die* (PL *die* Telefonzellen).

phone call *noun* **1** Anruf *der* (PL *die* Anrufe); **to get a phone call** einen Anruf erhalten; **2 to make a phone call** ein Telefongespräch führen; **phone calls are free** Telefongespräche sind gebührenfrei.

phone card *noun* Telefonkarte *die* (PL *die* Telefonkarten).

phone number *noun* Telefonnummer *die* (PL *die* Telefonnummern).

photo *noun* Foto *das* (PL *die* Fotos); **to take a photo** ein Foto machen; **to take a photo of somebody** ein Foto von jemandem machen.

photocopier *noun* Fotokopiergerät *das* (PL *die* Fotokopiergeräte).

photocopy *noun* Fotokopie *die* (PL *die* Fotokopien).

photocopy *verb* fotokopieren.

photograph *noun* Fotografie *die* (PL *die* Fotografien); **to take a photograph** ein Foto machen.

photograph *verb* fotografieren.

photographer *noun* Fotograf *der* (PL *die* Fotografen), Fotografin *die* (PL *die* Fotografinnen).

photography *noun* Fotografie *die*.

phrase *noun* Phrase *die* (PL *die* Phrasen); **an idiomatic phrase** eine Redewendung.

phrase-book *noun* Sprachführer *der* (PL *die* Sprachführer).

physical *adjective* körperlich.

physics *noun* Physik *die*.

physiotherapist *noun* Physiotherapeut *der* (PL *die* Physiotherapeuten), Physiotherapeutin *die* (PL *die* Physiotherapeutinnen).

physiotherapy *noun* Physiotherapie *die*.

piano *noun* Klavier *das* (PL *die* Klaviere); **to play the piano** Klavier spielen; **piano lesson** die Klavierstunde.

pick *noun* **to take your pick** sich (DAT) etwas aussuchen SEP.

pick *verb* **1** (*to select*) wählen; **he picked his words carefully** er wählte seine Worte mit Bedacht; **2** (*choose for oneself*) sich (DAT) aussuchen SEP; **pick any book** such

dir irgendein Buch aus; **3 to pick a team** eine Mannschaft aufstellen; **4** pflücken (*fruit*); **to pick strawberries** Erdbeeren pflücken.

● **to pick up 1** (*lift*) (in die Hand) nehmen◇; **he picked up the papers** er nahm die Unterlagen; **2** (*collect*) abholen SEP; **I'll pick you up at six** ich hole dich um sechs Uhr ab; **I'll pick up the keys tomorrow** ich hole die Schlüssel morgen ab.

pickpocket *noun* Taschendieb *der* (PL *die* Taschendiebe).

picnic *noun* Picknick *das* (PL *die* Picknicke); **to have a picnic** ein Picknick machen.

picture *noun* **1** Bild *das* (PL *die* Bilder); **2 to go to the pictures** (*the cinema*) ins Kino gehen.

pie *noun* **1** (*sweet*) Kuchen *der* (PL *die* Kuchen); **apple pie** der Apfelkuchen; **2** (*savoury*) Pastete *die* (PL *die* Pasteten).

piece *noun* **1** (*a bit*) Stück *das* (PL *die* Stücke); **a big piece of cheese** ein großes Stück Käse; **2** (*that you fit together*) Teil *das* (PL *die* Teile); **the pieces of a jigsaw** die Teile von einem Puzzle; **to take something to pieces** etwas in Einzelteile zerlegen; **3 piece of furniture** das Möbelstück; **a piece of information** eine Information; **a piece of luck** ein Glücksfall; **4** (*coin*) Stück *das* (PL *die* Stücke); **a five-pence piece** ein Fünf-Pence-Stück.

pierce *verb* **1** durchstechen◇ SEP; **2 to have pierced ears** Löcher in den Ohrläppchen haben.

pig *noun* Schwein *das* (PL *die* Schweine).

pigeon *noun* Taube *die* (PL *die* Tauben).

piggy bank *noun* Sparschwein *das* (PL *die* Sparschweine).

pigtail *noun* Zopf *der* (PL *die* Zöpfe).

pile *noun* 1 (*a neat stack*) Stapel *der* (PL *die* Stapel); **a pile of plates** ein Stapel Teller; 2 (*a heap*) Haufen *der* (PL *die* Haufen).

● **to pile something up** (*neatly*) etwas aufstapeln SEP, (*in a heap*) etwas auftürmen SEP.

pill *noun* Pille *die* (PL *die* Pillen).

pillar *noun* Säule *die* (PL *die* Säulen).

pillow *noun* Kopfkissen *das* (PL *die* Kopfkissen).

pilot *noun* Pilot *der* (PL *die* Piloten), Pilotin *die* (PL *die* Pilotinnen).

pimple *noun* Pickel *der* (PL *die* Pickel).

pin *noun* 1 (*for sewing*) Stecknadel *die* (PL *die* Stecknadeln); 2 **a three-pin plug** ein dreipoliger Stecker.

● **to pin up** 1 hochstecken SEP (*a hem*); 2 anschlagen✧ SEP (*a notice*).

PIN *noun* (*personal identification number*) Geheimnummer *die*.

pinball *noun* Flippern *das*; **to play pinball** flippern; **pinball machine** *der* Flipper.

pinch *noun* (*of salt, for example*) Prise *die* (PL *die* Prisen).

pinch *verb* 1 kneifen✧; **she pinched my arm** sie hat mich in den Arm gekniffen; 2 (*to steal*) klauen;

somebody's pinched my bike jemand hat mein Rad geklaut.

pine *noun* Kiefer *die* (PL *die* Kiefern); **pine furniture** Kiefernmöbel (*plural*).

pineapple *noun* Ananas *die* (PL *die* Ananas).

pine cone *noun* Kiefernzapfen *der* (PL *die* Kiefernzapfen).

ping-pong *noun* Tischtennis *das*; **to play ping-pong** Tischtennis spielen.

pink *adjective* rosa (*'rosa' never changes*); **pink hats** rosa Hüte.

pip *noun* (*in a fruit*) Kern *der* (PL *die* Kerne).

pipe *noun* 1 (*for gas or water*) Rohr *das* (PL *die* Rohre); 2 (*for smoking*) Pfeife *die* (PL *die* Pfeifen); **he smokes a pipe** er raucht Pfeife.

pirate *noun* Pirat *der* (PL *die* Piraten).

Pisces *noun* Fische (*plural*); **Amanda is Pisces** Amanda ist Fisch.

pitch *noun* Platz *der* (PL *die* Plätze); **football pitch** *der* Fußballplatz.

pitch *verb* **to pitch a tent** ein Zelt aufstellen SEP.

pity *noun* 1 (*feeling sorry for somebody*) Mitleid *das*; 2 **what a pity!** wie schade!; **it would be a pity to miss the beginning** es wäre schade, den Anfang zu verpassen.

pity *verb* **to pity somebody** jemanden bemitleiden.

pizza *noun* Pizza *die* (PL *die* Pizzas).

place *noun* 1 (Ort *der* (PL *die* Orte); **Salzburg is a wonderful place**

Salzburg ist ein sehr schöner Ort; **in place** an Ort und Stelle; **2 all over the place** überall; **3** (*a space*) Platz *der* (PL *die* Plätze); **a place for the car** ein Platz für das Auto; **is there a place for me?** ist Platz für mich?; **will you keep my place?** kannst du mir den Platz freihalten?; **to change places** die Plätze tauschen; **4** (*spot*) Stelle *die* (PL *die* Stellen); **this is a good place to stop** das ist eine gute Stelle zum Halten; **5** (*in a race*) Platz *der* (PL *die* Plätze); **to gain first place** den ersten Platz belegen; **6 at your place** bei dir; **we'll go round to Zafir's place** wir gehen zu Zafir; **7 to take place** stattfinden ⋄ SEP; **the competition will take place at four** der Wettbewerb findet um vier Uhr statt.

place *verb* (*upright*) stellen, (*lying flat*) legen.

plain *noun* Ebene *die* (PL *die* Ebenen).

plain *adjective* **1** einfach; **plain food** einfaches Essen; **2** (*unflavoured*) Natur-; **plain yoghurt** *der* Naturjoghurt; **3** (*not patterned*) einfarbig; **plain curtains** einfarbige Vorhänge.

plait *noun* Zopf *der* (PL *die* Zöpfe).

plan *noun* Plan *der* (PL *die* Pläne); **we've made plans for the summer** wir haben Pläne für den Sommer gemacht; **to go according to plan** nach Plan gehen; **everything went according to plan** alles ging nach Plan.

plan *verb* **1 to plan to do something** etwas vorhaben ⋄ SEP; **we're planning to leave at eight** wir haben vor, um acht abzufahren; **2** (*make plans for, organize, design*) planen; **she's planning a trip to Italy** sie plant eine Reise nach Italien.

plane *noun* Flugzeug *das* (PL *die* Flugzeuge); **we went by plane** wir sind geflogen.

planet *noun* Planet *der* (PL *die* Planeten).

plant *noun* Pflanze *die* (PL *die* Pflanzen); **a house plant** eine Topfpflanze.
plant *verb* pflanzen.

plaster *noun* **1** (*sticking plaster*) Pflaster *das* (PL *die* Pflaster); **2** (*for walls*) Verputz *der*; **3** Gips *der*; **to have your leg in plaster** das Bein in Gips haben.

plastic *noun* Plastik *das*; **plastic bag** *die* Plastiktüte.

plate *noun* Teller *der* (PL *die* Teller).

platform *noun* **1** (*in a station*) Bahnsteig *der* (PL *die* Bahnsteige); **2 the train is arriving at platform six** der Zug fährt auf Gleis sechs ein; **3** (*for lecturing or performing*) Podium *das* (PL *die* Podien).

play *noun* (*in the theatre*) Stück *das* (PL *die* Stücke); **television play** *das* Fernsehspiel; **we are putting on a play by Brecht at school** wir führen ein Stück von Brecht in der Schule auf.

play *verb* **1** spielen; **the children are playing with a ball** die Kinder spielen Ball; **they play the piano and the guitar** sie spielen Klavier und Gitarre; **who's playing Hamlet?** wer spielt Hamlet?; **to play tennis** Tennis spielen; **they were**

a
b
c
d
e
f
g
h
i
j
k
l
m
n
o
p
q
r
s
t
u
v
w
x
y
z

playing cards sie haben Karten gespielt; **2** (*in sport*) **to play somebody** gegen jemanden spielen; **Italy are playing Germany** Italien spielt gegen Deutschland; **3** spielen (*a tape, CD, or record*); **play your new CD** spiel mal deine neue CD.

player *noun* **1** Spieler *der* (PL *die* Spieler), Spielerin *die* (PL *die* Spielerinnen); **football player** *der* Fußballspieler; **2** (*in the theatre*) Schauspieler *der* (PL *die* Schauspieler), Schauspielerin *die* (PL *die* Schauspielerinnen).

playground *noun* Spielplatz *der* (PL *die* Spielplätze); **school playground** *der* Schulhof.

playgroup *noun* Spielgruppe *die* (PL *die* Spielgruppen).

playing field *noun* Sportplatz *der* (PL *die* Sportplätze).

pleasant *adjective* angenehm.

please *adverb* bitte; **two coffees, please** zwei Kaffee bitte; **could you turn the TV off, please?** könntest du bitte den Fernseher ausmachen?

pleased *adjective* **1** erfreut; **I'm really pleased!** das freut mich wirklich!; **2 she was pleased with her present** sie hat sich über ihr Geschenk gefreut; **3 pleased to meet you!** freut mich!

pleasure *noun* **1** (*amusement*) Vergnügen *das*; **2** (*joy*) Freude *die*; **to get a lot of pleasure out of something** viel Freude an etwas (DAT) haben.

plenty *pronoun* **1** (*lots*) viel; **he's got plenty of money** er hat viel

Geld; **2** (*enough*) genug; **that's plenty!** das ist genug!; **we've got plenty of time left** wir haben noch genug Zeit.

plot *noun* (*of a film or novel*) Handlung *die*.

plough *noun* Pflug *der* (PL *die* Pflüge)
plough *verb* pflügen.

plug *noun* **1** (*electrical*) Stecker *der* (PL *die* Stecker); **2** (*in a bath or sink*) Stöpsel *der* (PL *die* Stöpsel); **to pull out the plug** den Stöpsel herausziehen.

plum *noun* Pflaume *die* (PL *die* Pflaumen); **plum tart** *der* Pflaumenkuchen.

plumber *noun* Installateur *der* (PL *die* Installateure).

plural *noun* Mehrzahl *die* Plural *der*; **in the plural** in der Mehrzahl, im Plural.

plus *preposition* plus (+ DAT); **three children plus a baby** drei Kinder und ein Baby.

p.m. *abbreviation* nachmittags (*for times up to 6 p.m.*), abends (*for times after 6 p.m.*); **at two p.m.** um zwei Uhr nachmittags, um vierzehn Uhr; **at nine p.m.** um neun Uhr abends, um einundzwanzig Uhr (*in German you usually express times after midday in terms of the 24-hour clock*).

pocket *noun* Tasche *die* (PL *die* Taschen).

pocket money *noun* Taschengeld *das*.

poem *noun* Gedicht *das* (PL *die* Gedichte).

poet *noun* Dichter der (PL die Dichter), Dichterin die (PL die Dichterinnen).

poetry *noun* Dichtung die.

point *noun* 1 (*tip*) Spitze die (PL die Spitzen); **the point of a nail** die Spitze eines Nagels; 2 (*a tiny mark or dot*) Punkt der (PL die Punkte); 3 (*in time*) Zeitpunkt der (PL die Zeitpunkte); **at that point** zu diesem Zeitpunkt; **to be on the point of doing something** gerade etwas tun wollen; 4 **that's not the point** darum geht es nicht; **there's no point phoning, he's out** es hat keinen Sinn anzurufen, er ist nicht da; **what's the point?** wozu?; 5 **that's a good point!** das stimmt!; **the point is ...** es geht darum ...; 6 **point of view** der Standpunkt; **from my point of view** von meinem Standpunkt aus; 7 **her strong point** ihre Stärke; 8 (*in scoring*) Punkt der (PL die Punkte); **to win by fifteen points** mit fünfzehn Punkten Vorsprung gewinnen; 9 (*in decimals*) 6 **point 4** sechs Komma vier (*in German, a comma is used for the decimal point*).
point *verb* 1 hinweisen⬦ SEP auf (+ ACC); **a notice pointing to the station** ein Schild, das in Richtung Bahnhof zeigt; 2 (*with your finger*) zeigen auf (+ ACC); **he pointed at Tom** er zeigte auf Tom.

pointless *adjective* sinnlos; **it's pointless to keep on ringing** es ist sinnlos, dauernd zu klingeln.

poison *noun* Gift das (PL die Gifte).
poison *verb* vergiften.

poisonous *adjective* giftig.

Poland *noun* Polen das.

polar bear *noun* Eisbär der (PL die Eisbären).

pole *noun* 1 (*for a tent*) Stange die (PL die Stangen); 2 (*for skiing*) Stock der (PL die Stöcke); 3 **the North Pole** der Nordpol.

Pole *noun* (*a Polish person*) Pole der (PL die Polen), Polin die (PL die Polinnen).

police *noun* **the police** die Polizei; **the police are coming** die Polizei kommt.

police car *noun* Streifenwagen der (PL die Streifenwagen).

policeman *noun* Polizist der (PL die Polizisten).

police station *noun* Polizeiwache die (PL die Polizeiwachen).

policewoman *noun* Polizistin die (PL die Polizistinnen).

policy *noun* 1 (*plan of action*) Vorgehensweise die (PL die Vorgehensweisen); **the policy on immigration** die Einwanderungspolitik; 2 (*document*) Versicherungsschein der (PL die Versicherungsscheine).

polish *noun* 1 (*for furniture*) Politur die; 2 (*for shoes*) Schuhcreme die; 3 (*for the floor*) Bohnerwachs das.
polish *verb* 1 polieren (*furniture, silver*); 2 **to polish your shoes** seine Schuhe putzen.

Polish *noun* (*language*) Polnisch das.
Polish *adjective* polnisch.

a
b
c
d
e
f
g
h
i
j
k
l
m
n
o
p
q
r
s
t
u
v
w
x
y
z

polite *adjective* höflich; **to be polite to somebody** höflich zu jemandem sein.

political *adjective* politisch.

politician *noun* Politiker *der* (PL *die* Politiker), Politikerin *die* (PL *die* Politikerinnen).

politics *noun* Politik *die*.

pollen *noun* Pollen *der*; **the pollen count for today is** ... die Pollenzahl heute ist ....

polluted *adjective* verschmutzt.

pollution *noun* Umweltverschmutzung *die*.

polo-necked *adjective* Rollkragen-; **a polo-necked jumper** ein Rollkragenpullover.

pond *noun* Teich *der* (PL *die* Teiche).

pony *noun* Pony *das* (PL *die* Ponys).

ponytail *noun* Pferdeschwanz *der* (PL *die* Pferdeschwänze).

poodle *noun* Pudel *der* (PL *die* Pudel).

pool *noun* 1 (*swimming pool*) Schwimmbecken *das* (PL *die* Schwimmbecken); 2 (*pond*) Tümpel *der* (PL *die* Tümpel); 3 (*puddle*) Lache *die* (PL *die* Lachen); 4 (*game*) Poolbillard *das*; 5 **the football pools** das Toto; **to do the pools** Toto spielen.

poor *adjective* 1 arm; **a poor country** ein armes Land; **a poor family** eine arme Familie; 2 **poor Tanya's failed her exam** die arme Tanya ist durch die Prüfung gefallen; 3 (*bad*) schlecht; **that's a poor result** das ist ein schlechtes Ergebnis; **the weather was pretty poor** das Wetter war ziemlich schlecht.

pop *noun* Popmusik *die*; **pop concert** das Popkonzert; **pop star** *der* Popstar; **pop song** *der* Popsong.

● **to pop into: I'll just pop into the bank** ich gehe kurz auf die Bank.

popcorn *noun* Popcorn *das*.

pope *noun* Papst *der* (PL *die* Päpste).

poppy *noun* Mohn *der*.

popular *adjective* beliebt.

population *noun* Bevölkerung *die*.

porch *noun* Vorbau *der* (PL *die* Vorbauten).

pork *noun* Schweinefleisch *das*; **pork chop** das Schweinekotelett.

porridge *noun* Haferbrei *der*.

port *noun* 1 Hafen *der* (PL *die* Häfen); 2 (*wine*) Portwein *der* (PL *die* Portweine).

porter *noun* 1 (*at a station or an airport*) Gepäckträger *der* (PL *die* Gepäckträger); 2 (*in a hotel*) Portier *der* (PL *die* Portiers).

portion *noun* (*of food*) Portion *die* (PL *die* Portionen).

portrait *noun* Porträt *das* (PL *die* Porträts).

Portugal *noun* Portugal *das*.

Portuguese *noun* 1 (*language*) Portugiesisch *das*; 2 (*a person*) Portugiese *der* (PL *die* Portugiesen), Portugiesin *die* (PL *die* Portugiesinnen).
Portuguese *adjective* portugiesisch.

posh *adjective* vornehm; **a posh area** eine vornehme Gegend.

position noun 1 Platz der (PL die Plätze); 2 (*situation*) Lage die (PL die Lagen); 3 (*status, job*) Stellung die (PL die Stellungen).

positive adjective 1 (*sure*) sicher; **I'm positive he's left** ich bin mir sicher, dass er gegangen ist; 2 (*enthusiastic*) positiv; **her reaction was very positive** ihre Reaktion war sehr positiv.

possess verb besitzen◇.

possessions plural noun Sachen (*plural*); **all my possessions are in the flat** alle meine Sachen sind in der Wohnung.

possibility noun Möglichkeit die (PL die Möglichkeiten).

possible adjective möglich; **it's possible** es ist gut möglich; **if possible** wenn möglich; **as quickly as possible** so schnell wie möglich.

possibly adverb 1 (*maybe*) möglicherweise; **'will you be at home at midday?' – 'possibly'** 'bist du mittags zu Hause?' – 'möglicherweise'; 2 **how can you possibly believe that?** wie kannst du das nur glauben?; **I can't possibly arrive before Thursday** ich kann unmöglich vor Donnerstag ankommen.

post noun 1 Post die; **to send something by post** etwas per Post schicken; (*letters*) **is there any post for me?** ist Post für mich gekommen?; 2 (*a pole*) Pfosten der (PL die Pfosten); 3 (*a job*) Stelle die (PL die Stellen).

post verb **to post a letter** einen Brief abschicken SEP.

postbox noun Briefkasten der (PL die Briefkästen).

postcard noun Postkarte die (PL die Postkarten).

postcode noun Postleitzahl die (PL die Postleitzahlen).

poster noun 1 (*for decoration*) Poster das (PL die Poster); **I've bought an Oasis poster** ich habe ein Poster von Oasis gekauft; 2 (*advertising*) Plakat das (PL die Plakate); **I saw a poster for the concert** ich habe ein Plakat für das Konzert gesehen.

postman noun Briefträger der (PL die Briefträger).

post office noun Post die; **the post office is on the right** die Post ist auf der rechten Seite.

postpone verb verschieben◇; **we've postponed the meeting until next week** wir haben die Besprechung auf nächste Woche verschoben.

postwoman noun Briefträgerin die (PL die Briefträgerinnen).

pot noun 1 (*jar*) Topf der (PL die Töpfe); **a pot of honey** ein Topf Honig; 2 (*teapot*) Kanne die (PL die Kannen); 3 **the pots and pans** die Töpfe und Pfannen.

potato noun Kartoffel die (PL die Kartoffeln); **fried potatoes** Bratkartoffeln (*plural*); **mashed potatoes** der Kartoffelbrei.

potato crisps plural noun Kartoffelchips (*plural*).

pottery noun 1 (*craft*) Töpferei die; 2 (*objects*) Töpferwaren (*plural*).

pound *noun* **1** (*money*) Pfund *das* (PL die Pfunde); **fourteen pounds** vierzehn Pfund; **1,6 euros to the pound** 1,6 Euro für ein Pfund; **a five pound note** ein Fünfpfundschein; **2** (*in weight*) Pfund *das*; **two pounds of apples** zwei Pfund Äpfel.

pour *verb* **1** gießen◇ (*liquid*); **he poured milk into the pan** er hat Milch in den Topf gegossen; **2** eingießen◇ SEP (*a drink*); **to pour the tea** den Tee eingießen; **I poured him a drink** ich habe ihm etwas zu trinken eingeschenkt; **3** (*with rain*) **it's pouring** es gießt.

poverty *noun* Armut *die*.

powder *noun* **1** Pulver *das* (PL die Pulver); **2** (*for face or body*) Puder *der* (PL die Puder).

power *noun* **1** (*electricity*) Strom *der*; **a power cut** eine Stromsperre; **2** (*energy*) Energie *die*; **nuclear power** die Kernenergie; **3** (*strength*) Kraft *die*; **4** (*over other people*) Macht *die*; **to be in power** an der Macht sein.

power point *noun* Steckdose *die* (PL die Steckdosen).

power station *noun* Kraftwerk *das* (PL die Kraftwerke).

powerful *adjective* (*strong*) stark, (*influential*) mächtig.

practical *adjective* praktisch.

practically *adverb* fast.

practice *noun* **1** (*for sport*) Training *das*; **hockey practice** das Hockeytraining; **2** Übung *die*; **to do your piano practice** Klavier üben;

to be out of practice aus der Übung sein.

practise *verb* **1** üben (*an instrument, exercise, or skill*); **to practise the piano** Klavier üben; **2** anwenden SEP (*a language*); **a week in Berlin to practise my German** eine Woche in Berlin, um mein Deutsch anzuwenden; **3** (*in sport*) trainieren; **the team practises on Wednesday** die Mannschaft trainiert mittwochs.

praise *verb* loben; **to praise somebody for something** jemanden für etwas (ACC) loben.

pram *noun* Kinderwagen *der* (PL die Kinderwagen).

prawn *noun* Garnele *die* (PL die Garnelen).

pray *verb* beten.

prayer *noun* Gebet *das* (PL die Gebete).

precaution *noun* Vorsichtsmaßnahme *die* (PL die Vorsichtsmaßnahmen); **to take precautions against something** Vorsichtsmaßnahmen gegen (+ ACC) etwas ergreifen.

precinct *noun* **shopping precinct** *das* Einkaufszentrum; **pedestrian precinct** die Fußgängerzone.

precisely *adverb* genau; **at eleven o'clock precisely** um genau elf Uhr.

prefer *verb* **1** vorziehen◇ SEP; **I prefer Anna to her sister** ich mag Anna lieber als ihre Schwester; **2 to prefer to do something** etwas lieber tun; **I prefer to stay at home** ich bleibe lieber zu Hause.

pregnant *adjective* schwanger.

prejudice *noun* Vorurteil *das* (PL *die* Vorurteile); **to fight against racial prejudice** gegen Rassenvorurteile ankämpfen.

prejudiced *adjective* **to be prejudiced** voreingenommen sein.

prep *noun* Hausaufgaben (*plural*); **my English prep** meine Englischhausaufgaben.

prep school *noun* private Grundschule *die*.

preparation *noun* Vorbereitung *die* (PL *die* Vorbereitungen); **in preparation for something** in Vorbereitung auf etwas (ACC); **our preparations for Christmas** unsere Weihnachtsvorbereitungen.

prepare *verb* 1 vorbereiten SEP; **to prepare somebody for something** jemanden auf etwas (ACC) vorbereiten; 2 **to be prepared for the worst** sich auf das Schlimmste gefasst machen.

prepared *adjective* bereit; **I'm prepared to pay half** ich bin bereit, die Hälfte zu zahlen.

preposition *noun* Präposition *die* (PL *die* Präpositionen).

prescription *noun* Rezept *das* (PL *die* Rezepte); **on prescription** auf Rezept.

presence *noun* Anwesenheit *die*; **he admitted it in my presence** er gab es in meiner Anwesenheit zu.

present *noun* 1 (*a gift*) Geschenk *das* (PL *die* Geschenke); **to give**

somebody a present jemandem ein Geschenk machen; 2 (*the time now*) Gegenwart *die*; **in the present (tense)** im Präsens; 3 **that's all for the present** das ist vorläufig alles.

present *adjective* 1 (*attending*) anwesend; **Mr Blair is not present** Herr Blair ist nicht anwesend; **to be present at something** bei etwas (DAT) anwesend sein; **fifty people were present at the funeral** fünfzig Personen waren bei der Beerdigung anwesend; 2 (*existing now*) gegenwärtig; **the present situation** die gegenwärtige Lage; 3 **at the present time** zur Zeit.

present *verb* 1 überreichen (*a prize*); 2 (*introduce*) vorstellen SEP; 3 (*on TV, radio*) moderieren (*a programme*).

presenter *noun* (*on TV*) Moderator *der* (PL *die* Moderatoren), Moderatorin *die* (PL *die* Moderatorinnen).

presently *adverb* 1 (*now*) momentan; 2 (*soon*) bald.

president *noun* Präsident *der* (PL *die* Präsidenten), Präsidentin *die* (PL *die* Präsidentinnen).

press *noun* **the press** die Presse.

press *verb* 1 (*to push*) drücken; **press here!** hier drücken!; 2 drücken auf (+ ACC) (*a button or switch*); **she pressed the button** sie hat auf den Knopf gedrückt.

press conference *noun* Pressekonferenz *die* (PL *die* Pressekonferenzen).

a

b
pressure *noun* Druck *der*; **to put pressure on somebody** jemanden unter Druck setzen.

c

d
pressure gauge *noun* Druckluftmesser *der* (PL *die* Druckluftmesser).

e

f
pressure group *noun* Interessengruppe *die* (PL *die* Interessengruppen).

g

h
pretend *verb* **to pretend that** ... so tun, als ob ...; **he's pretending not to hear** er tut so, als ob er nicht hört.

i

j
pretty *adjective* hübsch; **a pretty dress** ein hübsches Kleid.
pretty *adverb* ziemlich; **it was pretty silly** das war ziemlich blöd.

k

l

m

n
prevent *verb* **to prevent somebody from doing something** jemanden daran hindern, etwas zu tun; **there's nothing to prevent you from leaving** niemand kann dich daran hindern zu gehen.

o

p

q
previous *adjective* **1** (*earlier*) früher (*years, opportunity, or job*); **2** (*immediately preceding*) vorig; **on the previous Tuesday** am vorigen Dienstag.

r

s

t
price *noun* Preis *der* (PL *die* Preise); **the price per kilo** der Preis pro Kilo; **CDs have gone up in price** CDs sind im Preis gestiegen; **what is the price of this?** was kostet das?

u

v
price list *noun* Preisliste *die* (PL *die* Preislisten).

w
price ticket *noun* Preisschild *das* (PL *die* Preisschilder).

x
prick *verb* stechen◇; **to prick your finger** sich in den Finger stechen.

y

z
pride *noun* Stolz *der*.

priest *noun* Priester *der* (PL *die* Priester).

primary school *noun* Grundschule *die* (PL *die* Grundschulen).

primary (school) teacher *noun* Grundschullehrer *der* (PL *die* Grundschullehrer), Grundschullehrerin *die* (PL *die* Grundschullehrerinnen).

prime minister *noun* Premierminister *der* (PL *die* Premierminister), Premierministerin *die* (PL *die* Premierministerinnen).

prince *noun* Prinz *der* (PL *die* Prinzen).

princess *noun* Prinzessin *die* (PL *die* Prinzessinnen).

principal *noun* (*of a college*) Direktor *der* (PL *die* Direktoren), Direktorin *die* (PL *die* Direktorinnen).
principal *adjective* (*main*) Haupt-.

principle *noun* Prinzip *das* (PL *die* Prinzipien); **on principle** im Prinzip; **that's true in principle** im Prinzip stimmt das.

print *noun* **1** (*letters*) Druck *der*; **in small print** klein gedruckt; **2** (*a photo*) Abzug *der* (PL *die* Abzüge); **colour print** *der* Farbabzug.

printer *noun* (*for a computer*) Drucker *der* (PL *die* Drucker).

print-out *noun* Ausdruck *der* (PL *die* Ausdrucke).

prison *noun* Gefängnis *das* (PL *die* Gefängnisse); **in prison** im Gefängnis.

prisoner *noun* Gefangene der/die (PL die Gefangenen).

private *adjective* **1** Privat-, privat; **private school** die Privatschule; **private property** das Privateigentum; **to have private lessons** Privatstunden nehmen; **2 in private** privat.

prize *noun* Preis der (PL die Preise); **to win a prize** einen Preis gewinnen.

prize-giving *noun* Preisverleihung die (PL die Preisverleihungen).

prizewinner *noun* Gewinner der (PL die Gewinner), Gewinnerin die (PL die Gewinnerinnen).

probable *adjective* wahrscheinlich.

probably *adverb* wahrscheinlich.

problem *noun* Problem das (PL die Probleme); **it's a serious problem** das ist ein ernstes Problem; **no problem!** kein Problem!

process *noun* **1** Prozess der (PL die Prozesse); **2 to be in the process of doing something** dabei sein, etwas zu tun.

procession *noun* **1** (*in parade*) Umzug der (PL die Umzüge); **2** (*at religious festival*) Prozession die (PL die Prozessionen).

produce *noun* (*food*) Erzeugnisse (*plural*).

produce *verb* **1** herstellen SEP (*goods, food*); **2** vorzeigen SEP (*a ticket, document*); **I produced my passport** ich habe meinen Pass vorgezeigt; **3** erzeugen (*interest, tension*); **it produces heat** es erzeugt Wärme; **4 to produce a film** einen Film produzieren; **5 to produce a play** ein Theaterstück inszenieren.

producer *noun* (*of a film or programme*) Produzent der (PL die Produzenten).

product *noun* Produkt das (PL die Produkte).

production *noun* **1** (*of a film or an opera*) Produktion die (PL die Produktionen); **2** (*of a play*) Inszenierung die (PL die Inszenierungen); **a new production of Hamlet** eine neue Inszenierung von Hamlet; **3** (*by a factory*) Produktion die.

profession *noun* Beruf der (PL die Berufe).

professional *noun* **1** (*a trained person*) Fachmann der (PL die Fachleute); **2** (*in sport*) Profi der (PL die Profis).
professional *adjective* **1** professionell (*work, sportsman*); **a professional footballer** ein professioneller Fußballer; **2** beruflich (*career, success*); **she's a professional singer** sie ist Sängerin von Beruf.

professor *noun* Professor der (PL die Professoren), Professorin die (PL die Professorinnen).

profile *noun* Profil das (PL die Profile).

profit *noun* Gewinn der (PL die Gewinne).

profitable *adjective* rentabel.

a
b
c
d
e
f
g
h
i
j
k
l
m
n
o
p
q
r
s
t
u
v
w
x
y
z

a

b

c

d

e

f

g

h

i

j

k

l

m

n

o

p

q

r

s

t

u

v

w

x

y

z

program *noun* **computer program** das Programm.

programme *noun* **1** (*for a play or an event*) Programm das (PL die Programme); **2** (*on TV or radio*) Sendung die (PL die Sendungen).

programmer *noun* Programmierer der (PL die Programmierer), Programmiererin die (PL die Programmiererinnen).

progress *noun* **1** Fortschritt der (PL die Fortschritte); **to make progress** Fortschritte machen; **2 to be in progress** im Gange sein.

project *noun* **1** (*at school*) Arbeit die (PL die Arbeiten); **2** (*a plan*) Projekt das (PL die Projekte); **a project to build a bridge** ein Brückenbauprojekt.

promise *noun* Versprechen das (PL die Versprechen); **to make somebody a promise** jemandem ein Versprechen geben; **to keep a promise** ein Versprechen halten; **it's a promise!** versprochen! **promise** *verb* **to promise something** etwas versprechen◊; **I've promised to ring my mother** ich habe versprochen, meine Mutter anzurufen.

promote *verb* **to be promoted** (*in football*) aufsteigen◊ SEP (PERF *sein*), (*at work*) befördert werden.

promotion *noun* **1** Beförderung die; **2** (*in football*) Aufstieg der; **3** (*in advertising*) Werbung die.

promptly *adverb* **1** (*at once*) sofort; **he promptly fell off again** er fiel sofort wieder herunter; **2** (*quickly*) schnell; **please reply promptly**

bitte antworten Sie unverzüglich; **3** (*puntually*) pünktlich; **they left promptly at five o'clock** sie fuhren pünktlich um 5 Uhr ab.

pronoun *noun* Pronomen das (PL die Pronomen).

pronounce *verb* aussprechen◊ SEP; **you don't pronounce the 'c'** das 'c' spricht man nicht aus.

pronunciation *noun* Aussprache die.

proof *noun* Beweis der (PL die Beweise); **there's no proof that** ... es gibt keine Beweise dafür, dass ....

propaganda *noun* Propaganda die.

propeller *noun* Propeller der (PL die Propeller).

proper *adjective* **1** (*correct, real, genuine*) richtig; **the proper answer** die richtige Antwort; **he's not a proper doctor** er ist kein richtiger Arzt; **2** (*decent*) anständig; **I need a proper meal** ich brauche ein anständiges Essen; **3 in its proper place** an den richtigen Ort.

properly *adverb* **1** richtig; **2** (*decent*) anständig.

property *noun* **1** (*your belongings*) Eigentum das; **2** (*land, premises*) Besitz der, **'private property'** 'Privatbesitz'; **3** (*house*) Haus das (PL die Häuser).

propose *verb* **1** (*suggest*) vorschlagen◊ SEP; **2** (*marriage*) **he proposed to her** er hat ihr einen Heiratsantrag gemacht.

protect *verb* schützen; **to protect somebody from something** jemanden vor etwas (DAT) schützen.

protection *noun* Schutz *der*.

protein *noun* Protein *das* (PL die Proteine).

protest *noun* **1** Beschwerde *die* (PL die Beschwerden); **to make a protest** eine Beschwerde einlegen SEP; **2** (*disapproval*) Protest *der* (PL die Proteste); **in protest against something** aus Protest gegen etwas (ACC).
protest *verb* protestieren; **to protest about something** gegen etwas (ACC) protestieren.

protest march *noun* Protestmarsch *der* (PL die Protestmärsche).

Protestant *noun* Protestant *der* (PL die Protestanten), Protestantin *die* (PL die Protestantinnen).
Protestant *adjective* protestantisch.

proud *adjective* stolz; **to be proud about something** stolz auf etwas (ACC) sein.

prove *verb* beweisen✧.

proverb *noun* Sprichwort *das* (PL die Sprichwörter).

provide *verb* zur Verfügung stellen.

provided, providing *conjunction* vorausgesetzt; **provided it doesn't rain** vorausgesetzt, es regnet nicht.

prune *noun* Backpflaume *die* (PL die Backpflaumen).

psychiatrist *noun* Psychiater *der* (PL die Psychiater), Psychiaterin *die* (PL die Psychiaterinnen).

psychological *adjective* psychologisch.

psychologist *noun* Psychologe *der* (PL die Psychologen), Psychologin *die* (PL die Psychologinnen).

psychology *noun* Psychologie *die*.

PTO *abbreviation* b.w. (*bitte wenden*).

pub *noun* Kneipe *die* (PL die Kneipen) (*informal*).

public *noun* **the public** die Öffentlichkeit; **in public** in aller Öffentlichkeit.
public *adjective* öffentlich.

public holiday *noun* gesetzliche Feiertag *der* (PL die gesetzlichen Feiertage); **January 1st is a public holiday** der erste Januar ist ein gesetzlicher Feiertag.

publicity *noun* **1** Publicity *die*; **2** (*advertising*) Werbung *die*.

public school *noun* Privatschule *die* (PL die Privatschulen).

public transport *noun* öffentliche Verkehrsmittel (*plural*).

publish *verb* veröffentlichen.

publisher *noun* **1** Verleger *der* (PL die Verleger), Verlegerin *die* (PL die Verlegerinnen); **2** (*company*) Verlag *der* (PL die Verlage).

pudding *noun* (*dessert*) Nachtisch *der* (PL die Nachtische); **for pudding we've got strawberries** zum Nachtisch gibt es Erdbeeren.

puddle *noun* Pfütze *die* (PL die Pfützen).

puff noun (of smoke) Wölkchen das (PL die Wölkchen).

puff pastry noun Blätterteig der.

pull verb 1 ziehen⋄; **to pull a cart** einen Wagen ziehen; 2 ziehen an (+ DAT); **to pull a rope** an einem Seil ziehen; **he pulled a letter out of his pocket** er hat einen Brief aus der Tasche gezogen; ★**he's pulling your leg!** er nimmt dich auf den Arm (literally: he's picking you up in his arms).

• **to pull down 1** herunterziehen⋄ SEP; **2** (demolish) abreißen⋄ SEP (a building).

• **to pull in** (at the roadside) an den Straßenrand fahren⋄ (PERF sein).

pullover noun Pullover der (PL die Pullover).

pulse noun Puls der; **the doctor took my pulse** der Arzt maß meinen Puls.

pump noun Pumpe die (PL die Pumpen); **bicycle pump** die Fahrradpumpe.
pump verb pumpen.

• **to pump up** aufpumpen SEP.

pumpkin noun Kürbis der (PL die Kürbisse).

punch noun 1 (in boxing) Faustschlag der (PL die Faustschläge); 2 (drink) Bowle die (PL die Bowlen).
punch verb 1 **he punched me in the stomach** er hat mich in den Magen geboxt; 2 lochen (a ticket).

punctual adjective pünktlich.

punctuation noun Zeichensetzung die.

punctuation mark noun Satzzeichen das (PL die Satzzeichen).

puncture noun (flat tyre) Reifenpanne die (PL die Reifenpannen).

punish verb bestrafen.

punishment noun Strafe die (PL die Strafen).

pupil noun Schüler der (PL die Schüler), Schülerin die (PL die Schülerinnen).

puppet noun Puppe die (PL die Puppen).

puppy noun junge Hund der (PL die jungen Hunde); **a boxer puppy** ein junger Boxer.

pure adjective rein.

purple adjective lila ('lila' never changes).

purpose noun 1 Zweck der (PL die Zwecke); **what's the purpose of it?** was hat das für einen Zweck?; 2 **on purpose** absichtlich; **she did it on purpose** das hat sie absichtlich getan; **he closed the door on purpose** er hat die Tür absichtlich zugemacht.

purr verb schnurren.

purse noun Portemonee das (PL die Portemonees).

push noun **to give something a push** etwas schieben⋄.
push verb 1 schubsen; **he pushed me** er hat mich geschubst; 2 (to press) drücken auf (+ ACC) (a bell or button); 3 **to push somebody to do something** jemanden zu etwas drängen; **his teacher is pushing him to sit the exam** sein Lehrer

drängt ihn, die Prüfung zu machen; **4 to push your way through the crowd** sich durch die Menge drängeln.

- **to push something away** etwas wegschieben◇ SEP; **she pushed her plate away** sie schob ihren Teller weg.

pushchair noun Sportwagen der (PL die Sportwagen).

put verb **1** (place generally) tun◇; **put some milk in your tea** tu etwas Milch in den Tee; **you can put the butter in the fridge** du kannst die Butter in den Kühlschrank tun; **2** (lay flat) legen; **she put the pencil on the desk** sie hat den Bleistift auf den Schreibtisch gelegt; **3** (place upright) stellen; **where did you put my bag?** wo hast du meine Handtasche hingestellt?; **4** (write) schreiben◇; **put your address here** schreiben Sie Ihre Adresse hierhin.

- **to put away** wegräumen SEP; **put away your things** räume deine Sachen weg.

- **to put back 1** zurücktun SEP, zurücklegen SEP, zurückstellen SEP (the translation of 'put back' depends on the way it is done: if it's placed lying down, use 'zurücklegen', if placed upright use 'zurückstellen' and if it could be either, use 'zurücktun'); **I put it back in the drawer** ich habe es in die Schublade zurückgetan; **2** (postpone) verschieben◇; **the meeting has been put back until Thursday** die Besprechung ist auf Donnerstag verschoben worden.

- **to put down** (lying down) hinlegen SEP, (upright) hinstellen SEP; **where**

can I put the vase down? wo kann ich die Vase hinstellen?

- **to put off 1** (postpone) verschieben◇; **he's put off my lesson till Thursday** er hat meine Stunde auf Donnerstag verschoben; **2** (turn off) ausmachen SEP; **don't forget to put off the lights** vergiss nicht, das Licht auszumachen; **3 to put somebody off something** jemandem die Lust an etwas (DAT) verderben◇; **it really put me off my food** das hat mir wirklich den Appetit verdorben; **4 to put somebody off doing something** jemanden davon abbringen◇ SEP, etwas zu tun; **don't be put off** lass dich nicht davon abbringen.

- **to put on 1** anziehen◇ SEP (clothes); **I'll just put my shoes on** ich ziehe nur schnell meine Schuhe an; **2** auflegen SEP (a CD or record); **I'm putting on Oasis** ich lege Oasis auf; **3** (switch on) anmachen SEP (a light or the heating); **could you put the lamp on?** kannst du die Lampe anmachen?

- **to put out 1** (put outside) nach draußen tun◇, raustun◇ SEP (informal); **have you put the rubbish out?** hast du den Müll rausgebracht?; **2** ausmachen SEP (a light or cigarette); **I've put the lights out** ich habe das Licht ausgemacht; **3 to put out your hand** die Hand ausstrecken SEP.

- **to put up 1** heben◇ (your hand); **2** aufhängen SEP (a picture or poster); **I've put up some posters in my room** ich habe ein paar Poster in meinem Zimmer aufgehängt;

a
b
c
d
e
f
g
h
i
j
k
l
m
n
o
p
q
r
s
t
u
v
w
x
y
z

3 anschlagen◇ SEP (*a notice*);
4 erhöhen (*the price*); **they've put up the fare** sie haben den Fahrpreis erhöht; **5** (*for the night*) **friends put me up** ich habe bei Freunden übernachtet; **can you put me up on Friday?** kann ich Freitag bei euch übernachten?

• **to put up with something** etwas aushalten◇ SEP; **I don't know how she puts up with it** ich weiß nicht, wie sie das aushält.

puzzle *noun* (*jigsaw*) Puzzle *das* (PL die Puzzles).

puzzled *adjective* verdutzt.

pyjamas *plural noun* Schlafanzug *der* (PL die Schlafanzüge); **a pair of pyjamas** ein Schlafanzug; **where are my pyjamas?** wo ist mein Schlafanzug?

Qq

qualification *noun* **1** (*ability, experience*) Qualifikation *die* (PL die Qualifikationen); **2** (*on paper*) Zeugnis *das* (PL die Zeugnisse).

qualified *adjective* **1** ausgebildet; **she's a qualified ski instructor** sie ist eine ausgebildete Skilehrerin; **2** (*having a degree or a diploma*) Diplom-; **a qualified engineer** ein Diplomingenieur.

qualify *verb* **1** (*to be eligible*) berechtigt sein; **we don't qualify for a reduction** wir bekommen keine Ermäßigung; **2** (*in sport*) sich qualifizieren; **they qualified for the**

third round sie haben sich für die dritte Runde qualifiziert.

quality *noun* Qualität *die*; **good quality products** Waren von guter Qualität.

quantity *noun* Menge *die* (PL die Mengen).

quarrel *noun* Streit *der* (PL die Streite); **to have a quarrel** Streit haben.
quarrel *verb* sich streiten◇; **they're always quarrelling** sie streiten sich dauernd.

quarry *noun* Steinbruch *der* (PL die Steinbrüche).

quarter *noun* **1** Viertel *das* (PL die Viertel); **a quarter of the price** ein Viertel des Preises; **three quarters of the class** drei Viertel der Klasse; **it's a quarter past ten** es ist Viertel nach zehn; **it's a quarter to ten** es ist Viertel vor zehn; **2 we meet at quarter to eight** wir treffen uns um Viertel vor acht; **3 a quarter of an hour** eine Viertelstunde; **4 three quarters of an hour** eine Dreiviertelstunde; **5 an hour and a quarter** eineinviertel Stunden.

quarter finals *noun* Viertelfinale *das* (PL die Viertelfinale).

queen *noun* **1** Königin *die* (PL die Königinnen); **2** (*in chess, cards*) Dame *die* (PL die Damen).

query *noun* Frage *die* (PL die Fragen); **are there any queries?** gibt es irgendwelche Fragen?

question *noun* Frage *die* (PL die Fragen); **to ask somebody a question** jemandem eine Frage stellen; **I asked her a question** ich habe ihr eine Frage gestellt; **it's out of the question** das kommt nicht in Frage.

question *verb* befragen (*a person*).

question mark *noun* Fragezeichen *das* (PL *die* Fragezeichen).

questionnaire *noun* Fragebogen *der* (PL *die* Fragebögen).

queue *noun* (*of people, cars*) Schlange *die* (PL *die* Schlangen); **to stand in a queue** Schlange stehen; **a queue of cars** eine Autoschlange.

quick *adjective* schnell; **to have a quick lunch** schnell etwas zu Mittag essen; **it's quicker on the motorway** auf der Autobahn geht es schneller; **to have a quick look at something** sich (DAT) etwas schnell ansehen; **be quick!** mach schnell!

quickly *adverb* schnell; **I'll just quickly phone my mother** ich rufe nur schnell meine Mutter an.

quiet *adjective* 1 (*silent*) still; **to keep quiet** still sein; **please keep quiet** sei bitte still; 2 (*not loud*) leise; **the children are very quiet** die Kinder sind ganz leise; **in a quiet voice** mit leiser Stimme; 3 (*peaceful*) ruhig; **a quiet street** eine ruhige Straße.

quietly *adverb* 1 (*speak, move*) leise; **he got up quietly** er ist leise aufgestanden; 2 (*read or play*) ruhig; **to sit quietly** ruhig sitzen.

quilt *noun* Steppdecke *die* (PL *die* Steppdecken).

quite *adverb* 1 (*fairly*) ziemlich; **it's quite cold outside** es ist ziemlich kalt draußen; **quite often** ziemlich oft; **quite a few** ziemlich viele; **quite a few of our friends came** ziemlich viele unserer Freunde sind gekommen; **quite a few people** ziemlich viele Leute; **that's quite a good idea** das ist eine ganz gute Idee; 2 (*completely*) völlig; **it was quite amazing** es war einfach fantastisch; **not quite** nicht ganz; **she's not quite ready** sie ist noch nicht ganz fertig; 3 genau; **I don't quite know what he wants** ich weiß nicht genau, was er will; **quite!** genau!

quiz *noun* Quiz *das* (PL *die* Quiz).

quotation *noun* (*from a book*) Zitat *das* (PL *die* Zitate).

quotation marks *plural noun* Anführungszeichen (*plural*); **in quotation marks** in Anführungszeichen.

quote *noun* 1 (*from a book*) Zitat *das* (PL *die* Zitate); 2 (*estimate*) Kostenvoranschlag *der* (PL *die* Kostenvoranschläge).
quote *verb* zitieren.

Rr

rabbi *noun* Rabbi *der* (PL *die* Rabbis).

rabbit *noun* Kaninchen *das* (PL *die* Kaninchen).

rabies *noun* Tollwut *die*.

race *noun* 1 (*a sports event*) Rennen *das* (PL *die* Rennen); **cycle race** *das* Radrennen; 2 **to have a race** (*running*) um die Wette laufen◇ (PERF *sein*), (*swimming*) um die Wette schwimmen◇ (PERF *sein*); 3 (*an*

a

ethnic group) Rasse die (PL die Rassen).

b

racetrack *noun* Rennbahn die (PL die Rennbahnen).

c

d

racial *adjective* rassisch, Rassen-; **racial discrimination** die Rassendiskriminierung.

e

f

racing car *noun* Rennwagen der (PL die Rennwagen), Rennfahrerin die (PL die Rennfahrerinnen).

g

h

racing driver *noun* Rennfahrer der (PL die Rennfahrer).

i

racism *noun* Rassismus der.

j

k

racist *noun* Rassist der (PL die Rassisten), Rassistin die (PL die Rassistinnen).
racist *adjective* rassistisch.

l

m

n

racket *noun* 1 (*for tennis*) Schläger der (PL die Schläger); **my tennis racket** mein Tennisschläger; 2 (*noise*) Krach der.

o

p

radiation *noun* Strahlung die (PL die Strahlungen).

q

radiator *noun* Heizkörper der (PL die Heizkörper).

r

s

t

radio *noun* Radio das (PL die Radios); **to listen to the radio** Radio hören; **to hear something on the radio** etwas im Radio hören.

u

radioactive *adjective* radioaktiv.

v

radio-controlled *adjective* ferngesteuert.

w

x

radio station *noun* Rundfunkstation die (PL die Rundfunkstationen).

y

z

radish *noun* Radieschen das (PL die Radieschen).

rag *noun* Lumpen der (PL die Lumpen).

rage *noun* Wut die; **to fly into a rage** in Wut geraten◇ (PERF *sein*); **she's in a rage** sie ist wütend; ★ **it's all the rage** das ist der letzte Schrei (*literally: it's the last scream*).

rail *noun* 1 (*for a train*) Schiene die (PL die Schienen); 2 (*the railway*) **to go by rail** mit der Bahn fahren; 3 (*on a balcony, bridge, or stairs*) Geländer das (PL die Geländer).

rail card *noun* Bahnpass der (PL die Bahnpässe).

railing(s) *noun* Geländer das (PL die Geländer).

railway *noun* 1 (*the system*) Bahn die; **the railways** die Bahn; 2 **railway line** (*from one place to another*) die Bahnstrecke; 3 **on the railway line** (*the track*) auf dem Gleis.

railway carriage *noun* Eisenbahnwagen der (PL die Eisenbahnwagen).

railway station *noun* Bahnhof der (PL die Bahnhöfe).

rain *noun* Regen der; **in the rain** im Regen.
rain *verb* regnen; **it's raining** es regnet; **it's going to rain** es wird regnen.

rainbow *noun* Regenbogen der (PL die Regenbogen).

raincoat *noun* Regenmantel der (PL die Regenmäntel).

rainy *adjective* regnerisch.

raise *verb* 1 (*lift up*) hochheben◇ SEP; 2 (*increase*) erhöhen (*prices*);

3 to raise money for something
Geld für etwas aufbringen◇ SEP.

raisin *noun* Rosine *die* (PL *die* Rosinen).

rake *noun* Rechen *der* (PL *die* Rechen).

rally *noun* **1** (*a meeting*) Versammlung *die* (PL *die* Versammlungen); **2** (*for cars*) Rallye *die* (PL *die* Rallyes); **3** (*in tennis*) Ballwechsel *der* (PL *die* Ballwechsel).

rambler *noun* Wanderer *der* (PL *die* Wanderer), Wanderin *die* (PL *die* Wanderinnen).

rambling *noun* Wandern *das*.

range *noun* **1** (*a choice*) Auswahl *die*; **a wide range of travel brochures** eine große Auswahl an Reiseprospekten; **2 a range of subjects** verschiedene Fächer; **in a range of colours** in verschiedenen Farben; **3 a computer in this price range** ein Computer in dieser Preislage; **that's out of my price range** das kann ich mir nicht leisten.

rap *noun* Rap *der* (*music*).

rape *noun* Vergewaltigung *die* (PL *die* Vergewaltigungen).
rape *verb* vergewaltigen.

rare *adjective* **1** selten; **a rare bird** ein seltener Vogel; **2** englisch gebraten (*steak*).

rarely *adverb* selten.

rash *noun* Ausschlag *der* (PL *die* Ausschläge).
rash *adjective* voreilig.

raspberry *noun* Himbeere *die* (PL *die* Himbeeren); **raspberry jam** *die* Himbeermarmelade.

rat *noun* Ratte *die* (PL *die* Ratten).

rate *noun* **1** (*a charge*) Gebühren (*plural*); **postage rates** Postgebühren; **2 are there special rates for children?** gibt es Sonderpreise für Kinder?; **at reduced rates** zu ermäßigten Preisen; **3 rate of exchange** *der* Wechselkurs; **4 rate of pay** *der* Lohnsatz; **5** (*a level*) Rate *die* (PL *die* Raten); **a high cancellation rate** eine hohe Absagerate; **6 at any rate** auf jeden Fall.

rather *adverb* **1** lieber; **I'd rather wait** ich warte lieber; **I'd rather you didn't go** es wäre mir lieber, wenn du nicht gingest; **2** ziemlich; **I'm rather busy** ich habe ziemlich viel zu tun; **I've got rather a lot of shopping to do** ich muss noch ziemlich viel einkaufen; **3 rather than** eher als; **in summer rather than winter** eher im Sommer als im Winter.

rave *noun* (*party*) Fete *die* (PL *die* Feten) (*informal*).

raw *adjective* roh.

razor *noun* Rasierapparat *der* (PL *die* Rasierapparate).

razor blade *noun* Rasierklinge *die* (PL *die* Rasierklingen).

RE *noun* Religionsunterricht *der*.

reach *noun* Reichweite *die*; **out of reach** außer Reichweite; **within reach** leicht erreichbar; **to be within easy reach of Munich** von München aus leicht erreichbar sein.
reach *verb* **1** ankommen◇ SEP (PERF *sein*) an (+ DAT) a place or point, ankommen◇ SEP (PERF *sein*) in (+ DAT)

a
b
c
d
e

(*a town or country*); **when you reach the station** wenn du am Bahnhof ankommst; **2** kommen◇ (PERF *sein*) zu (+ DAT) (*an agreement, a conclusion*); **to reach a decision** zu einer Entscheidung kommen; **3 to reach for something** nach etwas (DAT) greifen◇.

f **react** *verb* reagieren.

g **reaction** *noun* Reaktion *die* (PL *die* Reaktionen).

h
i
j
k
l

read *verb* **1** lesen◇; **what are you reading at the moment?** was liest du zur Zeit?; **I'm reading a detective novel** ich lese einen Krimi; **2 to read out** vorlesen◇ SEP; **he read out the list to the students** er hat die Liste den Studenten vorgelesen.

m
n
o

reading *noun* **1** (*action*) Lesen *das*; **2** (*reading matter*) Lektüre *die*; **some easy reading for the holidays** eine leichte Lektüre für die Ferien.

p
q
r
s
t
u
v
w
x
y
z

ready *adjective* **1** fertig; **supper's not ready yet** das Essen ist noch nicht fertig; **we are not quite ready** wir sind noch nicht ganz fertig; **are you ready to leave?** seid ihr fertig?, (*on a journey*) seid ihr reisefertig?; **to get ready** sich fertig machen; **I'm getting ready to play tennis** ich mache mich zum Tennisspielen fertig; **I was getting ready for bed** ich war gerade dabei, ins Bett zu gehen; **2 to get something ready** (*complete*) etwas fertig machen, etwas vorbereiten SEP (*a room or food*); **I'll get your room ready** ich bereite dein Zimmer vor.

real *adjective* **1** (*genuine*) echt; **it's a real diamond** das ist ein echter Brillant; **he's a real coward** er ist ein echter Feigling; **2** (*true*) richtig; **is that her real name?** ist das ihr richtiger Name?; **3** (*not imagined*) wirklich; **it's a real pity you can't come** es ist wirklich schade, dass du nicht kommen kannst.

realistic *adjective* realistisch.

reality *noun* Wirklichkeit *die*; **a reality show** eine Reality-Show.

realize *verb* wissen◇; **I hadn't realized** das wusste ich nicht; **I didn't realize he was French** ich wusste nicht, dass er Franzose ist; **do you realize what time it is?** weißt du, wie viel Uhr es ist?

really *adverb* **1** wirklich; **the film was really good** der Film war wirklich gut; **really?** wirklich?; **2 not really** eigentlich nicht.

reason *noun* Grund *der* (PL *die* Gründe); **for that reason** aus diesem Grund; **the reason why I phoned** der Grund meines Anrufs.

reasonable *adjective* vernünftig.

receipt *noun* Quittung *die* (PL *die* Quittungen).

receive *verb* erhalten◇.

receiver *noun* Hörer *der* (PL *die* Hörer); **to pick up the receiver** den Hörer abnehmen◇ SEP.

recent *adjective* **1** kürzlich erfolgter/kürzlich erfolgte/ kürzlich erfolgtes; **the recent closure** die kürzlich erfolgte Schließung; **2 in recent years** in den letzten Jahren.

recently *adverb* **1** (*at a time not long ago*) kürzlich; **2** (*over the recent period*) in letzter Zeit.

reception *noun* **1** Rezeption *die* (PL die Rezeptionen); **he's waiting at reception** er wartet an der Rezeption; **2** Empfang *der* (PL die Empfänge); **a big wedding reception** ein großer Hochzeitsempfang; **3 to get a good reception** gut aufgenommen werden.

receptionist *noun* **1** Empfangsdame *die* (PL die Empfangsdamen); **2** (*in a doctor's surgery*) Sprechstundenhilfe *die* (PL die Sprechstundenhilfen).

recipe *noun* Rezept *das* (PL die Rezepte).

reckon *verb* glauben; **I reckon it's a good idea** ich glaube, das ist eine gute Idee.

recognize *verb* erkennen❖.

recommend *verb* empfehlen❖; **can you recommend a dentist?** kannst du mir einen Zahnarzt empfehlen?; **I recommend the fish soup** ich empfehle die Fischsuppe.

record *noun* **1** Rekord *der* (PL die Rekorde); **it's a world record** das ist ein Weltrekord; **record sales** Verkaufsrekorde; **2** (*of events*) Aufzeichnung *die* (PL die Aufzeichnungen); **on record** aufgezeichnet; **to keep a record of something** über etwas Buch führen; **3** (*music*) Platte *die* (PL die Platten); **a Miles Davis record** eine Platte von Miles Davis; **4 records** (*office files*) Unterlagen (*plural*); **I'll just check**

your records ich prüfe nur Ihre Unterlagen.

record *verb* (*on tape*) aufnehmen❖ SEP; **I'm recording it on cassette** ich nehme es auf Kassette auf.

recorder *noun* **1** Blockflöte *die* (PL die Blockflöten); **to play the recorder** Blockflöte spielen; **2 cassette recorder** *der* Kassettenrekorder; **video recorder** *der* Videorekorder.

recording *noun* (*on tape or CD*) Aufnahme *die* (PL die Aufnahmen), (*on video*) Aufzeichnung *die* (PL die Aufzeichnungen).

record player *noun* Plattenspieler *der* (PL die Plattenspieler).

recover *verb* sich erholen; **she's recovered now** sie hat sich wieder erholt.

recovery *noun* (*from an illness*) Erholung *die*; **to make a good recovery** sich gut erholen.

rectangle *noun* Rechteck *das* (PL die Rechtecke).

rectangular *adjective* rechteckig.

recycle *verb* recyceln.

red *adjective* rot; **a red car** ein rotes Auto; **to go red** rot werden; **to have red hair** rote Haare haben.

Red Cross *noun* **the Red Cross** das Rote Kreuz.

redcurrant *noun* Johannisbeere *die* (PL die Johannisbeeren); **redcurrant jelly** *das* Johannisbeergelee.

redecorate *verb* (*with paint*) neu streichen❖, (*with wallpaper*) neu

a
b
c
d
e
f
g
h
i
j
k
l
m
n
o
p
q
r
s
t
u
v
w
x
y
z

tapezieren; **they've redecorated the kitchen** sie haben die Küche neu gestrichen.

redo *verb* noch einmal machen.

reduce *verb* **1 to reduce prices** die Preise herabsetzen SEP; **2 to reduce speed** die Geschwindigkeit verringern.

reduction *noun* **1** (*in price*) Ermäßigung *die* (PL *die* Ermäßigungen); **2** (*in speed or number*) Reduzierung *die*.

redundant *adjective* **to be made redundant** entlassen werden.

referee *noun* (*in sport*) Schiedsrichter *der* (PL *die* Schiedsrichter), Schiedsrichterin *die* (PL *die* Schiedsrichterinnen).

reference *noun* Referenz *die* (PL *die* Referenzen); (*for a job*) **she gave me a good reference** sie hat mir eine gute Referenz gegeben.

reference book *noun* Nachschlagewerk *das* (PL *die* Nachschlagewerke).

refill *verb* nachfüllen SEP.

reflect *verb* spiegeln; **to be reflected** sich spiegeln.

reflection *noun* **1** (*in a mirror or on water*) Spiegelung *die* (PL *die* Spiegelungen); **to see your reflection in the mirror** sich im Spiegel sehen; **2** (*thought*) Überlegung *die*; **on reflection** nach nochmaliger Überlegung.

reflexive *adjective* **a reflexive verb** ein reflexives Verb.

refreshing *adjective* erfrischend.

refreshment *noun* Erfrischung *die* (PL *die* Erfrischungen).

refrigerator *noun* Kühlschrank *der* (PL *die* Kühlschränke).

refuge *noun* Zuflucht *die*; **a mountain refuge** eine Schutzhütte; **to take refuge in** sich flüchten in (+ DAT).

refugee *noun* Flüchtling *der* (PL *die* Flüchtlinge).

refund *noun* Rückzahlung *die* (PL *die* Rückzahlungen).
refund *verb* zurückerstatten SEP.

refusal *noun* **1** Weigerung *die* (PL *die* Weigerungen); **2** (*for a job*) Absage *die* (PL *die* Absagen); **to get a refusal** eine Absage bekommen.

refuse *noun* (*rubbish*) Abfall *der*.
refuse *verb* sich weigern; **I refused** ich habe mich geweigert; **he refuses to help** er weigert sich zu helfen.

regards *plural noun* Grüße (*plural*); **regards to your parents** viele Grüße an deine Eltern; **Nat sends his regards** Nat lässt grüßen.

reggae *noun* Reggae *der*.

region *noun* Gebiet *das* (PL *die* Gebiete).

regional *adjective* regional.

register *noun* (*in school*) Anwesenheitsliste *die* (PL *die* Anwesenheitslisten).
register *verb* **1** eintragen✧ SEP (*a name*); **2** (*report*) anmelden SEP.

registered letter *noun* Einschreiben *das* (PL *die* Einschreiben).

registration number *noun*
Autonummer *die* (PL *die*
Autonummern).

regret *verb* bedauern.

regular *adjective* regelmäßig;
regular visits regelmäßige
Besuche.

regularly *adverb* regelmäßig.

regulation *noun* Vorschrift *die* (PL
die Vorschriften).

rehearsal *noun* Probe *die* (PL *die*
Proben).

rehearse *verb* proben.

reheat *verb* aufwärmen SEP.

reject *verb* ablehnen SEP.

related *adjective* verwandt; **we're
not related** wir sind nicht
verwandt.

relation *noun* Verwandte *der/die* (PL
die Verwandten).

relationship *noun* Beziehung *die*
(PL *die* Beziehungen); **I have a good
relationship with my parents** ich
habe eine gute Beziehung zu meinen
Eltern.

relative *noun* Verwandte *der/die* (PL
die Verwandten).

relatively *adverb* relativ.

relax *verb* entspannen; **I'm going to
relax and watch telly tonight**
heute Abend entspanne ich und
sehe fern.

relaxed *adjective* entspannt.

relaxing *adjective* entspannend.

relay race *noun* Staffel *die* (PL *die*
Staffeln).

release *noun* (*a film, CD, or book*)
1 Neuerscheinung *die* (PL *die*
Neuerscheinungen); **this week's
new releases** die neuen Filme der
Woche; **2** (*of a prisoner or hostage*)
Freilassung *die* (PL *die*
Freilassungen).
release *verb* **1** herausbringen◇ SEP
(*a record, film, or video*);
2 freilassen◇ SEP (*a person*).

reliable *adjective* zuverlässig.

relief *noun* Erleichterung *die*; **what
a relief!** da bin ich aber erleichtert!

relieve *verb* stillen (*pain*).

relieved *adjective* erleichtert; **I
was relieved to hear you'd arrived**
ich war erleichtert zu hören, dass du
angekommen bist.

religion *noun* Religion *die* (PL *die*
Religionen).

religious *adjective* religiös.

rely *verb* **1** (*trust*) **to rely on
somebody** sich auf jemanden
verlassen◇; **I'm relying on your
help for Saturday** ich verlasse mich
darauf, dass du mir am Samstag
hilfst; **2** (*be dependent on*) **to rely on**
angewiesen sein auf (+ ACC).

remain *verb* (*be left over*) übrig
bleiben◇ (PERF *sein*); (*stay*) bleiben◇
(PERF *sein*).

remark *noun* Bemerkung *die* (PL *die*
Bemerkungen); **to make remarks
about something** Bemerkungen
über etwas (ACC) machen.

remarkable *adjective*
bemerkenswert.

remarkably *adverb*
bemerkenswert.

a b c d e f g h i j k l m n o p q r s t u v w x y z

remember *verb* **1** sich erinnern an (+ ACC) (*a person or an occasion*); **I don't remember** daran kann ich mich nicht erinnern; **do you remember the holiday in Italy?** erinnerst du dich noch an die Ferien in Italien?; **2 I can't remember his number** seine Nummer fällt mir nicht ein; **3 to remember to do something** daran denken✧, etwas zu tun; **remember to lock the door** denk daran abzuschließen; **I remembered to bring the CDs** ich habe daran gedacht, die CDs mitzubringen.

remind *verb* **1** erinnern; **to remind somebody to do something** jemanden daran erinnern, etwas zu tun; **remind your mother to pick me up** erinnere deine Mutter daran, mich abzuholen; **he reminds me of my brother** er erinnert mich an meinen Bruder; **2 oh, that reminds me ...** dabei fällt mir ein ....

remote *adjective* abgelegen.

remote control *noun* **1** (*for a car or plane*) Fernsteuerung *die* (PL die Fernsteuerungen); **2** (*for TV or video*) Fernbedienung *die* (PL die Fernbedienungen).

remove *verb* **1** entfernen (*a stain, mark, or obstacle*); **2** ausziehen✧ SEP (*clothes*).

renew *verb* verlängern (*a passport or licence*).

rent *noun* Miete *die* (PL die Mieten).
rent *verb* mieten; **Simon's rented a flat** Simon hat eine Wohnung gemietet.

reorganize *verb* umorganisieren.

repair *noun* Reparatur *die* (PL die Reparaturen).
repair *verb* reparieren; **to get something repaired** etwas reparieren lassen; **we've had the television repaired** wir haben unseren Fernseher reparieren lassen.

repay *verb* zurückzahlen SEP.

repeat *noun* Wiederholung *die* (PL die Wiederholungen).
repeat *verb* wiederholen.

repeatedly *adverb* wiederholt.

repetitive *adjective* eintönig.

replace *verb* ersetzen.

reply *noun* Antwort *die* (PL die Antworten); **I didn't get a reply to my letter** ich habe keine Antwort auf meinen Brief bekommen; **there's no reply** niemand antwortet.
reply *verb* antworten; **I still haven't replied to the letter** ich habe immer noch nicht auf den Brief geantwortet.

report *noun* **1** (*of an event*) Bericht *der* (PL die Berichte); **2** (*school report*) Zeugnis *das* (PL die Zeugnisse).
report *verb* **1** melden (*a problem or an accident*); **we've reported the theft** wir haben den Diebstahl gemeldet; **2** sich melden; **I had to report to reception** ich musste mich an der Rezeption melden; **3** (*in the news*) berichten; **to report on the strike** über den Streik berichten.

reporter *noun* Reporter *der* (PL die Reporter), Reporterin *die* (PL die Reporterinnen).

represent *verb* **1** darstellen SEP (*a word, a thing, an idea*); **2** vertreten◇ (*a group or company*).

representative *noun* Vertreter *der* (PL *die* Vertreter), Vertreterin *die* (PL *die* Vertreterinnen).

reproduction *noun* **1** (*process*) Fortpflanzung *die* (PL *die* Fortpflanzungen); **2** (*of sound etc*) Wiedergabe *die* ; **3** (*copy*) Reproduktion. *die* (PL *die* Reproduktionen).

republic *noun* Republik *die* (PL *die* Republiken).

reputation *noun* **1** Ruf *der*; **to have a good reputation** einen guten Ruf haben; **2 she has a reputation for honesty** sie gilt als ehrlich.

request *noun* Bitte *die* (PL *die* Bitten); **at my mother's request** auf Bitte meiner Mutter.
request *verb* bitten◇; **to request something** um etwas (ACC) bitten.

rescue *noun* Rettung *die*; **rescue operation** *die* Rettungsaktion; **to come to somebody's rescue** jemandem zu Hilfe kommen.
rescue *verb* retten; **they rescued the dog** sie haben den Hund gerettet.

rescue party *noun* Rettungsmannschaft *die* (PL *die* Rettungsmannschaften).

research *noun* **1** Forschung *die*; **for research into Aids** für die Aidsforschung; **2 to do research** forschen.
research *verb* **to research into something** etwas erforschen.

resemblance *noun* Ähnlichkeit *die* (PL *die* Ähnlichkeiten).

reservation *noun* (*a booking*) Reservierung *die* (PL *die* Reservierungen); **to make a reservation (for a room)** (ein Zimmer) reservieren lassen.

reserve *noun* **1** Reserve *die* (PL *die* Reserven); **we have a few in reserve** wir haben ein paar in Reserve; **2 nature reserve** *das* Naturschutzgebiet; **3** (*for a match*) Reservespieler *der* (PL *die* Reservespieler), Reservespielerin *die* (PL *die* Reservespielerinnen).
reserve *verb* reservieren; **this table is reserved** dieser Tisch ist reserviert.

reservoir *noun* Reservoir *das* (PL *die* Reservoirs).

resident *noun* Bewohner *der* (PL *die* Bewohner), Bewohnerin *die* (PL *die* Bewohnerinnen).

residential *adjective* Wohn-; **a residential area** eine Wohngegend.

resign *verb* **1** (*from your job*) kündigen; **2** (*from an official post*) zurücktreten◇ SEP.

resignation *noun* **1** Kündigung *die* (PL *die* Kündigungen); **2** (*from an official post*) Rücktritt *der*.

resist *verb* widerstehen◇ (+ DAT) (*an offer or temptation*).

resit *verb* wiederholen (*an exam*).

resort *noun* **1** (*for holidays*) **holiday resort** *der* Urlaubsort; **ski resort** *der* Wintersportort; **seaside resort** *das* Seebad; **2 as a last resort** als letzter Ausweg.

respect *noun* Respekt *der*.
respect *verb* respektieren.

respectable *adjective* anständig.

responsibility *noun*
Verantwortung *die* (PL *die*
Verantwortungen).

responsible *adjective*
1 verantwortlich; **he was
responsible for the accident** er
war für den Unfall verantwortlich;
**I'm responsible for booking the
rooms** ich bin für die
Zimmerreservierung
verantwortlich; **2** (*reliable*)
verantwortungsbewusst; **he's not
very responsible** er ist nicht sehr
verantwortungsbewusst.

rest *noun* **1 the rest** der Rest; **the
rest of the day** der Rest des Tages;
the rest of the bread der Brotrest,
der Rest von dem Brot; **2** (*the others*)
the rest die Übrigen; **the rest have
gone home** die Übrigen sind nach
Hause gegangen; **3** Erholung *die*;
**he's going to the mountains for a
rest** er fährt zur Erholung ins
Gebirge; **ten days' rest** zehn Tage
Erholung; **to have a rest** sich
ausruhen SEP; **4** (*a short break*)
Pause *die* (PL *die* Pausen); **to stop for
a rest** eine Pause machen.
rest *verb* (*have a rest*) sich
ausruhen SEP.

restaurant *noun* Restaurant *das*
(PL *die* Restaurants).

restful *adjective* erholsam.

restless *adjective* unruhig.

restrain *verb* zurückhalten◇ SEP.

result *noun* **1** Ergebnis *das* (PL *die*
Ergebnisse); **the exam results** die
Prüfungsergebnisse; **2 as a result**
infolgedessen; **as a result we
missed the train** infolgedessen
haben wir den Zug verpasst.

retire *verb* **1** (*from work*) in den
Ruhestand gehen◇, (*civil servant,
teacher, soldier*) in Pension gehen◇;
she retires in June sie geht im Juni
in Pension; **2 to be retired** im
Ruhestand sein◇.

retirement *noun* Ruhestand *der*;
since his retirement seitdem er in
den Ruhestand gegangen ist.

return *noun* **1** (*coming back*)
Rückkehr *die*; **the return journey**
die Rückreise; **2 by return of post**
postwendend; **3 in return for** für; **in
return for his help** für seine Hilfe;
4 in return dafür; ★ **many happy
returns!** herzlichen Glückwunsch
zum Geburtstag.
return *verb* **1** (*come back*)
zurückkommen◇ SEP (PERF *sein*); **he
returned ten minutes later** er kam
zehn Minuten später zurück; **to
return from holiday** aus den Ferien
zurückkommen; **2** (*go back*)
zurückgehen◇ SEP (PERF *sein*), (*drive*)
zurückfahren◇ SEP (PERF *sein*); **we
are planning to return in the
evening** wir wollen am Abend
zurückfahren; **3** (*to give back*)
zurückgeben◇ SEP; **Gemma's never
returned the video** Gemma hat das
Video nie zurückgegeben.

return fare *noun* Preis für eine
Rückfahrkarte *der*, (*for a flight*) Preis
für einen Rückflugschein *der*.

return ticket *noun* Rückfahrkarte *die* (PL *die* Rückfahrkarten); (*for a flight*) Rückflugticket *das* (PL *die* Rückflugtickets).

reveal *verb* enthüllen.

reverse *verb* 1 (*in a car*) rückwärts fahren◇ (PERF *sein*); 2 **to reverse the charges** ein R-Gespräch führen.

review *noun* (*of a book, play, or film*) Kritik *die* (PL *die* Kritiken). **review** *verb* rezensieren (*a book, play, or film*).

revise *verb* 1 lernen (*for an exam*); **Tessa's busy revising for her exams** Tessa lernt jetzt für ihre Prüfung; 2 wiederholen; **to revise maths** Mathe wiederholen.

revision *noun* Wiederholung *die*.

revive *verb* 1 (*a person*) wiederbeleben SEP; 2 (*to recover*) sich erholen.

revolting *adjective* eklig.

revolution *noun* Revolution *die* (PL *die* Revolutionen).

reward *noun* Belohnung *die* (PL *die* Belohnungen). **reward** *verb* belohnen.

rewind *verb* zurückspulen SEP (*a cassette or video*).

rhinoceros *noun* Nashorn *das* (PL *die* Nashörner).

rhubarb *noun* Rhabarber *der*.

rhyme *noun* Reim *der* (PL *die* Reime).

rhythm *noun* Rhythmus *der* (PL *die* Rhythmen).

rib *noun* Rippe *die* (PL *die* Rippen).

ribbon *noun* Band *das* (PL *die* Bänder).

rice *noun* Reis *der*; **rice pudding** *der* Milchreis.

rich *adjective* 1 reich; **they are very rich** sie sind sehr reich; 2 **the rich** die Reichen.

rid *adjective* **to get rid of something** etwas loswerden◇ SEP (PERF *sein*) (*informal*); **we got rid of the car** wir sind das Auto losgeworden.

riddle *noun* Rätsel *das* (PL *die* Rätsel).

ride *noun* Fahrt *die* (PL *die* Fahrten); **to go for a ride (on a bike)** eine Fahrt machen; **to go for a ride (on a horse)** reiten gehen◇ (PERF *sein*). **ride** *verb* 1 **to ride a bike** Rad fahren◇ (PERF *sein*); **can you ride a bike?** kannst du Rad fahren?; **I've never ridden a bike** ich bin noch nie Rad gefahren; 2 **to ride (a horse)** reiten◇ (PERF *sein*); **I've never ridden a horse** ich bin noch nie auf einem Pferd geritten.

rider *noun* 1 (*on a horse*) Reiter *der* (PL *die* Reiter), Reiterin *die* (PL *die* Reiterinnen); 2 (*on a bike*) Radler *der* (PL *die* Radler), Radlerin *die* (PL *die* Radlerinnen); 3 (*on a motorbike*) Fahrer *der* (PL *die* Fahrer), Fahrerin *die* (PL *die* Fahrerinnen).

ridiculous *adjective* lächerlich.

riding *noun* Reiten *das*; **to go riding** reiten gehen◇.

riding school *noun* Reitschule *die* (PL *die* Reitschulen).

rifle *noun* Gewehr *das* (PL *die* Gewehre).

a
b
c
d
e
f
g
h
i
j
k
l
m
n
o
p
q
r
s
t
u
v
w
x
y
z

right *noun* **1** (*not left*) rechte Seite *die*; **on the right** auf der rechten Seite; **on my right** rechts von mir; **2** (*to do something*) Recht *das* (PL *die* Rechte); **to have the right to something** ein Recht auf etwas (ACC) haben; **the right to work** das Recht auf Arbeit; **you have no right to say that** du hast kein Recht, das zu sagen.

right *adjective* **1** (*not left*) rechter/rechte/rechtes; **my right hand** meine rechte Hand; **2** (*correct*) richtig; **the right answer** die richtige Antwort; **is this the right address?** ist das die richtige Adresse?; **3 to be right** (*of a person*) Recht haben; **you see, I was right** siehst du, ich hatte Recht; **4 you were right not to say anything** du hattest Recht, nichts zu sagen; **5 the clock is right** die Uhr geht richtig; **6 yes, that's right** ja, das stimmt; **is that right?** stimmt das?

right *adverb* **1** (*direction*) rechts; **turn right at the lights** biege an der Ampel rechts ab; **2** (*correctly*) richtig; **you're not doing it right** du machst das nicht richtig; **3** (*completely*) ganz; **right at the bottom** ganz unten; **right at the beginning** ganz am Anfang; **4** (*exactly*) genau; **right in the middle** genau in der Mitte; **5 right now** sofort; **6** (*okay*) gut; **right, let's go** gut, gehen wir.

right-click *noun* Klick *der* mit der rechten Maustaste (PL *die* Klicks mit der rechten Maustaste).

right-hand *adjective* **on the right-hand side** rechts.

right-handed *adjective* rechtshändig.

ring *noun* **1** (*on the phone*) **to give somebody a ring** jemanden anrufen✧ SEP; **2** (*for your finger*) Ring *der* (PL *die* Ringe); **3** (*circle*) Kreis *der* (PL *die* Kreise); **4 there was a ring at the door** es hat geklingelt.

ring *verb* **1** (*a bell or phone*) klingeln; **the phone rang** das Telefon klingelte; **2** (*phone*) anrufen✧ SEP; **I'll ring you tomorrow** ich rufe dich morgen an; **3 to ring for a taxi** ein Taxi rufen.

● **to ring back** zurückrufen✧ SEP; **I'll ring you back later** ich rufe dich später zurück.

● **to ring off** auflegen SEP.

ring road *noun* Ringstraße *die* (PL *die* Ringstraßen).

rinse *verb* spülen.

riot *noun* Aufstand *der* (PL *die* Aufstände).

rioting *noun* Unruhen (*plural*).

rip *verb* zerreißen✧.

ripe *adjective* reif; **are the tomatoes ripe?** sind die Tomaten reif?

rip-off *noun* **it's a rip-off** das ist Nepp (*informal*).

rise *noun* **1** Anstieg *der*; **a rise in temperature** ein Temperaturanstieg; **2 pay rise** *die* Gehaltserhöhung.

rise *verb* **1** (*the sun*) aufgehen✧ SEP (PERF *sein*); **2** (*prices*) steigen✧ (PERF *sein*).

risk *noun* Risiko *das* (PL *die* Risiken); **to take a risk** ein Risiko eingehen.

risk *verb* riskieren; **he risks losing**

his job er riskiert es, seine Stelle zu verlieren.

river *noun* Fluss *der* (PL *die* Flüsse).

road *noun* **1** Straße *die* (PL *die* Straßen); **the road to London** die Straße nach London; **2 the baker's is on the other side of the road** die Bäckerei ist auf der anderen Straßenseite; **3 across the road** gegenüber; **they live across the road from us** sie wohnen bei uns gegenüber.

road accident *noun* Verkehrsunfall *der* (PL *die* Verkehrsunfälle).

road map *noun* Straßenkarte *die* (PL *die* Straßenkarten).

roadside *noun* **by the roadside** am Straßenrand.

road sign *noun* Straßenschild *das* (PL *die* Straßenschilder).

roadworks *plural noun* Straßenarbeiten (*plural*).

roast *noun* Braten *der* (PL *die* Braten).
roast *adjective* gebraten; **roast potatoes** Bratkartoffeln; **roast beef** *der* Rinderbraten.

rob *verb* **1** berauben (*a person*); **2** ausrauben SEP (*a bank*).

robber *noun* Räuber *der* (PL *die* Räuber).

robbery *noun* Raub *der* (PL *die* Raube); **bank robbery** *der* Bankraub.

robot *noun* Roboter *der* (PL *die* Roboter).

rock climbing *noun* Klettern *das*; **to go rock climbing** (zum) Klettern gehen.

rock *noun* **1** (*a big stone*) Felsen *der* (PL *die* Felsen); **2** (*the material*) Fels *der*; **3** (*music*) Rock *der*; **rock band** *die* Rockband; **to dance rock and roll** Rock 'n' Roll tanzen.

rocket *noun* Rakete *die* (PL *die* Raketen).

rock music *noun* Rockmusik *die*.

rock star *noun* Rockstar *der* (PL *die* Rockstars).

rocky *adjective* felsig.

rod *noun* **a fishing rod** eine Angel.

role *noun* Rolle *die* (PL *die* Rollen); **to play the role of Hamlet** die Rolle des Hamlet spielen.

roll *noun* **1** Rolle *die* (PL *die* Rollen); **a roll of film** eine Rolle Film; **a toilet roll** eine Rolle Toilettenpapier; **2 bread roll** *das* Brötchen, *die* Semmel (*South German*).
roll *verb* rollen (PERF *sein*).

roller *noun* **1** (*for hair*) Lockenwickler *der* (PL *die* Lockenwickler); **2** (*for paint*) Rolle *die* (PL *die* Rollen).

rollerblades *plural noun* Inlineskates (*plural*), Inliners (*plural*).

rollercoaster *noun* Achterbahn *die* (PL *die* Achterbahnen).

roller skates *plural noun* Rollschuhe (*plural*).

Roman Catholic *adjective* römisch-katholisch.

a
b
c
d
e
f
g
h
i
j
k
l
m
n
o
p
q
r
s
t
u
v
w
x
y
z

549

romantic *adjective* romantisch.

roof *noun* Dach *das* (PL die Dächer).

roof rack *noun* Gepäckträger *der* (PL die Gepäckträger).

rook *noun* 1 (*in chess*) Turm *der* (PL die Türme); 2 (*bird*) Saatkrähe *die* (PL die Saatkrähen).

room *noun* 1 Zimmer *das* (PL die Zimmer); **she's in the other room** sie ist im anderen Zimmer; **a three-room flat** eine Dreizimmerwohnung; 2 (*space*) Platz *der*; **enough room for two** genug Platz für zwei; **very little room** wenig Platz; **to make room** Platz machen.

root *noun* Wurzel *die* (PL die Wurzeln).

rope *noun* Seil *das* (PL die Seile).

rose *noun* Rose *die* (PL die Rosen).

rot *verb* verfaulen (PERF sein).

rotten *adjective* verfault.

rough *adjective* 1 (*scratchy*) rau; 2 (*vague*) grob (*plan or estimate*); 3 **a rough idea** eine vage Vorstellung; 4 (*stormy*) stürmisch; **a rough sea** eine stürmische See; 5 (*difficult*) **to have a rough time** es schwer haben; 6 **to sleep rough** im Freien schlafen.

roughly *adverb* (*approximately*) ungefähr; **roughly ten per cent** ungefähr zehn Prozent; **it takes roughly three hours** es dauert ungefähr drei Stunden.

round *noun* Runde *die* (PL die Runden); **a round of talks** eine Gesprächsrunde; **a round of drinks** eine Runde.

round *adjective* rund; **a round table** ein runder Tisch.

round *preposition* 1 um (+ ACC); **round the city** um die Stadt; **round my arm** um meinen Arm; **they were sitting round the table** sie haben um den Tisch gesessen; **it's just round the corner** es ist gleich um die Ecke; 2 **to go round a museum** ein Museum besuchen.

round *adverb* 1 **to go round to somebody's house** jemanden besuchen (+ DAT); 2 **to invite somebody round** jemanden zu sich (DAT) einladen⋄ SEP; **we invited Sally round for lunch** wir haben Sally zum Mittagessen eingeladen; 3 **to look round the shops** sich in den Geschäften umsehen⋄ SEP; 4 **all the year round** das ganze Jahr hindurch.

roundabout *noun* 1 (*for traffic*) Kreisverkehr *der*; 2 (*in a fairground*) Karussell *das* (PL die Karussells).

route *noun* 1 (*that you plan*) Route *die* (PL die Routen); **the best route is via Calais** die beste Route führt über Calais; 2 **bus route** *die* Buslinie.

routine *noun* Routine *die* (PL die Routinen).

row¹ *noun* 1 Reihe *die* (PL die Reihen); **in the front row** in der ersten Reihe; **in the back row** in der letzten Reihe; 2 **in a row** hintereinander; **four times in a row** viermal hintereinander.

row *verb* (*in a boat*) rudern (PERF sein), (*a boat, a person*) rudern (PERF haben); **we rowed across the lake**

wir sind über den See gerudert; **he rowed us across the lake** er hat uns über den See gerudert.

row[2] *noun* **1** (*a quarrel*) Krach *der* (*informal*) (PL *die* Kräche); **to have a row** Krach haben; **they've had a row** sie haben Krach gehabt; **I had a row with my parents** ich habe Krach mit meinen Eltern gehabt; **2** (*noise*) Krach *der*; **they were making a terrible row** sie haben einen furchtbaren Krach gemacht.

rowing *noun* Rudern *das*; **to go rowing** rudern gehen.

rowing boat *noun* Ruderboot *das* (PL *die* Ruderboote).

royal *adjective* königlich; **the royal family** die königliche Familie.

rub *verb* reiben✧; **to rub your eyes** sich (DAT) die Augen reiben.

● **to rub something out** etwas ausradieren SEP.

rubber *noun* **1** (*an eraser*) Radiergummi *der* (PL *die* Radiergummis); **2** (*material*) Gummi *der*; **rubber soles** Gummisohlen.

rubbish *noun* **1** (*for the bin*) Müll *der*; **2** (*nonsense*) Quatsch *der* (*informal*); **you're talking rubbish!** du redest Quatsch.

rubbish *adjective* schlecht; **the film was rubbish** der Film war schlecht; **they're a rubbish band** sie sind eine lausige Band.

rubbish bin *noun* Mülleimer *der* (PL *die* Mülleimer).

rucksack *noun* Rucksack *der* (PL *die* Rucksäcke).

rude *adjective* **1** unhöflich; **that's rude** das ist unhöflich; **2** unanständig; **a rude joke** ein unanständiger Witz.

rug *noun* **1** Teppich *der* (PL *die* Teppiche); **2** (*a blanket*) Decke *die* (PL *die* Decken).

rugby *noun* Rugby *das*.

ruin *noun* (*remains*) Ruine *die* (PL *die* Ruinen); **in ruins** in Trümmern.
ruin *verb* **1** ruinieren; **you'll ruin your jacket** du ruinierst dir die Jacke; **2** verderben✧ (*day, holiday*); **it ruined my evening** das hat mir den Abend verdorben.

rule *noun* **1** Regel *die* (PL *die* Regeln); **the rules of the game** die Spielregeln; **as a rule** in der Regel; **2** (*administrative*) Vorschrift *die* (PL *die* Vorschriften); **according to the school rules** nach den Schulvorschriften.

ruler *noun* Lineal *das* (PL *die* Lineale); **I've lost my ruler** ich habe mein Lineal verloren.

rum *noun* Rum *der*.

rumour *noun* Gerücht *das* (PL *die* Gerüchte).

run *noun* **1** (*in games, sport, and for fitness*) Lauf *der* (PL *die* Läufe); **to go for a run** laufen gehen (PERF *sein*), joggen gehen (PERF *sein*); **2** (*of a play*) Laufzeit *die*; **3** (*in skiing*) Abfahrt *die* (PL *die* Abfahrten); **4 in the long run** auf lange Sicht.
run *verb* **1** laufen✧ (PERF *sein*); **I ran**

a
b
c
d
e
f
g
h
i
j
k
l
m
n
o
p
q
r
s
t
u
v
w
x
y
z

ten kilometres ich bin zehn Kilometer gelaufen; **he ran across the pitch** er ist über das Spielfeld gelaufen; **2** (*run fast*) rennen◊ (PERF *sein*); **Kitty ran for the bus** Kitty rannte, um den Bus zu kriegen; **3** (*drive*) fahren◊; **I'll run you home later** ich fahre dich später nach Hause; **4** (*organize*) veranstalten (*a course or competition*); **who's running this competition?** wer veranstaltet diesen Wettbewerb?; **5** (*manage*) leiten (*a business*); **she's been running the firm for years** sie leitet die Firma schon seit Jahren; **to run a shop** ein Geschäft leiten; **6** (*a train or a bus*) fahren◊ (PERF *sein*); **the buses don't run on Sundays** sonntags fahren keine Busse; **7 to run a bath** ein Bad einlaufen lassen.

● **to run away** weglaufen◊ SEP (PERF *sein*).

● **to run into something** gegen etwas (ACC) fahren◊ (PERF *sein*); **the car ran into a tree** das Auto ist gegen einen Baum gefahren.

● **to run out of something: we've run out of bread** wir haben kein Brot mehr; **I'm running out of money** ich habe kaum noch Geld.

● **to run somebody over** jemanden überfahren◊; **he nearly got run over** er ist beinahe überfahren worden.

runner *noun* Läufer *der* (PL *die* Läufer), Läuferin *die* (PL *die* Läuferinnen).

runner-up *noun* Zweite *der/die* (PL *die* Zweiten).

running *noun* (*for exercise*) Laufen *das*; Jogging *das*.
running *adjective* **1 running water** fließendes Wasser; **2 three days running** drei Tage hintereinander; **to win three times running** dreimal hintereinander gewinnen.

runway *noun* **1** (*for take-off*) Startbahn *die* (PL *die* Startbahnen); **2** (*for landing*) Landebahn *die* (PL *die* Landebahnen).

rush *noun* (*a hurry*) **to be in a rush** in Eile sein; **sorry, I'm in a rush** Entschuldigung, ich bin in Eile.
rush *verb* **1** (*hurry*) sich beeilen; **I must rush!** ich muss mich beeilen; **2** (*run*) hetzen (PERF *sein*); **she rushed out** sie stürmte raus (*informal*); **3 Louise was rushed to hospital** Louise ist schnellstens ins Krankenhaus gebracht worden.

rush hour *noun* Stoßzeit *die* (PL *die* Stoßzeiten); **in the rush hour** während der Stoßzeit.

Russia *noun* Russland *das*.

Russian *noun* **1** (*a person*) Russe *der* (PL *die* Russen), Russin *die* (PL *die* Russinnen); **2** (*the language*) Russisch *das*.
Russian *adjective* russisch; **he's Russian** er ist Russe.

rust *noun* Rost *der*.

rusty *adjective* rostig.

rye *noun* Roggen *der*.

Ss

Sabbath *noun* **1** (*Jewish*) Sabbat der (PL die Sabbate); **2** (*Christian*) Sonntag der (PL die Sonntage).

sack *noun* **1** Sack der (PL die Säcke); **2 to get the sack** rausgeschmissen werden (*informal*).
sack *verb* **to sack somebody** jemanden rausschmeißen❖ SEP (*informal*).

sad *adjective* traurig.

saddle *noun* Sattel der (PL die Sättel).

saddlebag *noun* Satteltasche die (PL die Satteltaschen).

sadly *adverb* **1** traurig; **she looked at me sadly** sie hat mich traurig angesehen; **2** (*unfortunately*) leider.

safe *adjective* **1** (*out of danger*) sicher; **to feel safe from something** sich vor etwas (DAT) sicher fühlen; **2 she's safe** sie ist in Sicherheit; **3** (*not dangerous*) ungefährlich; **the path is safe** der Weg ist ungefährlich; **it's not safe** das ist gefährlich.

safety *noun* Sicherheit die.

safety belt *noun* Sicherheitsgurt der (PL die Sicherheitsgurte).

safety pin *noun* Sicherheitsnadel die (PL die Sicherheitsnadeln).

Sagittarius *noun* Schütze der; **Kylie's Sagittarius** Kylie ist Schütze.

sail *noun* Segel das (PL die Segel).

sailing *noun* Segeln das; **to go sailing** segeln.

sailing boat *noun* Segelboot das (PL die Segelboote).

sailor *noun* Seemann der (PL die Seeleute).

saint *noun* Heilige der/die (PL die Heiligen).

sake *noun* **1 for your mother's sake** deiner Mutter zuliebe; **2 for heaven's sake** um Gottes willen.

salad *noun* Salat der (PL die Salate); **tomato salad** der Tomatensalat.

salad dressing *noun* Salatsoße die (PL die Salatsoßen).

salami *noun* Salami die (PL die Salamis).

salary *noun* Gehalt das (PL die Gehälter).

sale *noun* **1** (*selling*) Verkauf der (PL die Verkäufe); **the sale of the house** der Verkauf des Hauses; **'for sale'** 'zu verkaufen'; **2 the sales** der Ausverkauf; **I bought it in the sales** ich habe es im Ausverkauf gekauft.

sales assistant *noun* Verkäufer der (PL die Verkäufer), Verkäuferin die (PL die Verkäuferinnen).

salesman *noun* Verkäufer der (PL die Verkäufer).

saleswoman *noun* Verkäuferin die (PL die Verkäuferinnen).

salmon *noun* Lachs der (PL die Lachse).

salt *noun* Salz das.

salty *adjective* salzig.

same *adjective* **the same** der gleiche/die gleiche/das gleiche; **she said the same thing** sie hat das gleiche gesagt; **her birthday's the**

a
b
c
d
e
f
g
h
i
j
k
l
m
n
o
p
q
r
s
t
u
v
w
x
y
z

same day as mine sie hat am gleichen Tag Geburtstag wie ich; **at the same time** zur gleichen Zeit; **their car's the same as ours** sie haben das gleiche Auto wie wir.

same *adverb* **1 the same** gleich; **the two bikes look the same** die beiden Fahrräder sehen gleich aus; **2 all the same** trotzdem.

sample *noun* Muster *das* (PL *die* Muster); **a free sample** ein unverkäufliches Muster, eine Warenprobe.

sand *noun* Sand *der*.

sandal *noun* Sandale *die* (PL *die* Sandalen); **a pair of sandals** ein Paar Sandalen.

sandpaper *noun* Sandpapier *das* (PL *die* Sandpapiere).

sandwich *noun* Sandwich *das* (PL *die* Sandwichs), belegte Brot *das* (PL *die* belegten Brote); **ham sandwich** *das* Schinkenbrot.

sanitary towel *noun* Damenbinde *die* (PL *die* Damenbinden).

Santa Claus *noun* der Weihnachtsmann.

sarcastic *adjective* sarkastisch.

sardine *noun* Sardine *die* (PL *die* Sardinen).

SARS *noun* SARS *das*.

satchel *noun* Ranzen *der* (PL *die* Ranzen).

satellite *noun* Satellit *der* (PL *die* Satelliten).

satellite dish *noun* Satellitenschüssel *die* (PL *die* Satellitenschüsseln).

satellite television *noun* Satellitenfernsehen *das*.

satisfactory *adjective* befriedigend.

satisfied *adjective* zufrieden.

satisfy *verb* befriedigen.

satisfying *adjective* **1** befriedigend; **2 a satisfying meal** ein sättigendes Essen.

Saturday *noun* **1** Samstag *der* (PL *die* Samstage), Sonnabend *der* (*North German*) (PL *die* Sonnabende); **on Saturday** am Sonnabend/am Samstag; **I'm going out on Saturday** ich gehe Sonnabend aus; **see you on Saturday!** bis Samstag!; **every Saturday** jeden Samstag; **last Saturday** vorigen Sonnabend; **next Saturday** nächsten Sonnabend; **2 on Saturdays** samstags, sonnabends (*North German*); **the museum is closed on Saturdays** das Museum ist sonnabends/ samstags geschlossen; **to have a Saturday job** sonnabends/samstags arbeiten.

sauce *noun* Soße *die* (PL *die* Soßen).

saucepan *noun* Kochtopf *der* (PL *die* Kochtöpfe).

saucer *noun* Untertasse *die* (PL *die* Untertassen).

sausage *noun* Wurst *die* (PL *die* Würste).

save *verb* **1** retten (*life*); **to save somebody's life** jemandem das Leben retten; **the doctors saved**

his life die Ärzte haben ihm das Leben gerettet; **2** sparen (*money*); **I've saved £60** ich habe sechzig Pfund gespart; **I cycle to school to save money** ich fahre mit dem Rad zur Schule, um Geld zu sparen; **we'll take a taxi to save time** um Zeit zu sparen, nehmen wir ein Taxi; **3** (*on a computer*) speichern; **4** (*stop*) abwehren SEP (*a shot*); **to save a penalty** einen Elfmeter abwehren.

● **to save up** sparen; **I'm saving up for a car** ich spare auf ein Auto.

savings *plural noun* Ersparnisse (*plural*).

savoury *adjective* (*not sweet*) pikant.

saw *noun* Säge *die* (PL *die* Sägen).

sax *noun* Saxophon *das* (PL *die* Saxophone).

saxophone *noun* Saxophon *das* (PL *die* Saxophone); **to play the saxophone** Saxophon spielen.

say *verb* **1** sagen; **what did you say?** was hast du gesagt?; **she says she's tired** sie sagt, dass sie müde ist; **he said to wait here** er hat gesagt, wir sollen hier warten; **they say** man sagt; **2 to say something again** etwas wiederholen; **3 that's to say** das heißt.

saying *noun* Redensart *die* (PL *die* Redensarten); **it's just a saying** das ist so eine Redensart; **as the saying goes** wie man so sagt.

scab *noun* Wundschorf *der* (PL *die* Wundschorfe).

scale *noun* **1** (*of a map or model*) Maßstab *der* (PL *die* Maßstäbe);

2 (*extent*) Ausmaß *das* (PL *die* Ausmaße); **the scale of the disaster** das Ausmaß der Katastrophe; **3** (*in music*) Tonleiter *die* (PL *die* Tonleitern).

scales *noun* Waage *die* (PL *die* Waagen); **bathroom scales** die Personenwaage.

scandal *noun* **1** Skandal *der* (PL *die* Skandale); **2** (*gossip*) Klatsch *der* (*informal*).

Scandinavia *noun* Skandinavien *das*.

Scandinavian *adjective* skandinavisch.

scanner *noun* Scanner *der* (PL *die* Scanner).

scar *noun* Narbe *die* (PL *die* Narben).

scarce *adjective* knapp.

scare *noun* **1** Schrecken *der* (PL *die* Schrecken); **to give somebody a scare** jemandem einen Schrecken einjagen SEP; **2** (*general alarm*) Panik *die* (PL *die* Paniken); **to cause a scare** eine Panik auslösen; **3 bomb scare** die Bombendrohung. **scare** *verb* **to scare somebody** jemanden erschrecken; **you scared me!** du hast mich erschreckt!

scarecrow *noun* Vogelscheuche *die* (PL *die* Vogelscheuchen).

scared *adjective* **1 to be scared** Angst haben; **I'm scared** ich habe Angst; **to be scared of something** vor etwas (DAT) Angst haben; **he's scared of dogs** er hat vor Hunden Angst; **2 to be scared of doing something** sich nicht trauen, etwas zu tun; **I'm scared of telling him**

the truth ich traue mich nicht, ihm die Wahrheit zu sagen.

scarf *noun* **1** (*silky*) Tuch *das* (PL die Tücher); **2** (*long, warm*) Schal *der* (PL die Schals).

scary *adjective* unheimlich.

scene *noun* **1** (*of an incident or event*) Schauplatz *der* (PL die Schauplätze); **to be on the scene** am Schauplatz sein; **the scene of the crime** der Tatort; **2** (*world*) **the music scene** die Musikszene; **on the fashion scene** in der Modewelt; **3** (*argument*) Szene *die* (PL die Szenen); **to make a scene** eine Szene machen.

scenery *noun* **1** (*landscape*) Landschaft *die*; **2** (*in the theatre*) Bühnenbild *das*.

schedule *noun* Programm *das* (PL die Programme).

scheduled flight *noun* Linienflug *der* (PL die Linienflüge).

scheme *noun* Projekt *das* (PL die Projekte).

scholarship *noun* Stipendium *das* (PL die Stipendien).

school *noun* Schule *die* (PL die Schulen); **at school** in der Schule; **to go to school** zur Schule gehen.

schoolbook *noun* Schulbuch *das* (PL die Schulbücher).

schoolboy *noun* Schüler *der* (PL die Schüler).

schoolchildren *plural noun* Schulkinder (*plural*).

schoolfriend *noun* Schulfreund *der* (PL die Schulfreunde),

Schulfreundin *die* (PL die Schulfreundinnen).

schoolgirl *noun* Schülerin *die* (PL die Schülerinnen).

science *noun* Wissenschaft *die* (PL die Wissenschaften).

science fiction *noun* Sciencefiction *die*.

scientific *adjective* wissenschaftlich.

scientist *noun* Wissenschaftler *der* (PL die Wissenschaftler), Wissenschaftlerin *die* (PL die Wissenschaftlerinnen).

scissors *plural noun* Schere *die* (PL die Scheren); **a pair of scissors** eine Schere.

scoop *noun* **1** (*implement*) Eisportionierer *der* (PL die Eisportionierer); **2** (*quantity*) Eiskugel *die* (PL die Eiskugeln); **how many scoops would you like?** wieviele Kugeln Eis möchtest du?; **3** (*in journalism*) Knüller *der* (PL die Knüller).

scooter *noun* **1** (*motor scooter*) Motorroller *der* (PL die Motorroller); **2** (*for a child*) Roller *der* (PL die Roller).

score *noun* Spielstand *der* (PL die Spielstände); **the score was three two** es stand drei zu zwei. **score** *verb* **1** **to score a goal** ein Tor schießen◇; **2** **to score three points** drei Punkte erzielen; **3** (*keep score*) zählen.

Scorpio *noun* Skorpion *der*; **Neil is Scorpio** Neil ist Skorpion.

a b c d e f g h i j k l m n o p q r **s** t u v w x y z

Scot noun Schotte der (PL die Schotten), Schottin die (PL die Schottinnen); **the Scots** die Schotten.

Scotland noun Schottland das; **from Scotland** aus Schottland; **Pauline's from Scotland** Pauline kommt aus Schottland; **to Scotland** nach Schottland.

Scots adjective schottisch.

Scotsman noun Schotte der (PL die Schotten).

Scotswoman noun Schottin die (PL die Schottinnen).

Scottish adjective schottisch; **he's Scottish** er ist Schotte.

scout noun Pfadfinder der (PL die Pfadfinder).

scrambled eggs noun Rührei das.

scrap noun Stück das (PL die Stücke); **a scrap of paper** ein Stück Papier.

scrapbook noun Sammelalbum das (PL die Sammelalben).

scrape verb 1 schaben (potatoes or carrots); 2 (remove dirt or paint) abkratzen SEP; 3 (damage) schrammen.

scratch noun (on your skin or a surface) Kratzer der (PL die Kratzer); ´**to start from scratch** von vorn anfangen◇ SEP.
scratch verb (scratch yourself) sich kratzen; **to scratch your head** sich am Kopf kratzen.

scream noun Schrei der (PL die Schreie).
scream verb schreien◇.

screen noun 1 Bildschirm der (PL die Bildschirme) (of a TV or computer); **on the screen** auf dem Bildschirm; 2 (in the cinema) Leinwand die (PL die Leinwände).

screw noun Schraube die (PL die Schrauben).
screw verb schrauben.

screwdriver noun Schraubenzieher der (PL die Schraubenzieher).

scribble verb kritzeln.

scrub verb scheuern (a saucepan or the floor); **to scrub your nails** sich (DAT) die Nägel bürsten.

scuba diving noun Gerätetauchen das.

sculptor noun Bildhauer der (PL die Bildhauer), Bildhauerin die (PL die Bildhauerinnen); **Rebecca's a sculptor** Rebecca ist Bildhauerin.

sculpture noun Skulptur die (PL die Skulpturen).

sea noun Meer das (PL die Meere), See die; **by the sea** am Meer, an der See.

seafood noun Meeresfrüchte (plural); **I love seafood** ich esse Meeresfrüchte sehr gern.

seagull noun Möwe die (PL die Möwen).

seal noun (animal) Robbe die (PL die Robben), Seehund der (PL die Seehunde).
seal verb zukleben SEP (an envelope).

search verb 1 absuchen SEP; **I've searched my desk but I can't find the letter** ich habe meinen Schreibtisch abgesucht, aber ich

kann den Brief nicht finden;
2 durchsuchen; **they searched the building for him** sie haben das Gebäude nach ihm durchsucht;
3 suchen; **to search for something** nach etwas (DAT) suchen; **I've been searching everywhere for my scissors** ich habe überall nach meiner Schere gesucht.

seashell noun Muschel die (PL die Muscheln).

seasick adjective **to be seasick** seekrank sein.

seaside noun **at the seaside** am Meer.

season noun **1** Jahreszeit die (PL die Jahreszeiten); **the four seasons** die vier Jahreszeiten; **2** (period of social or sporting activity) Saison die (PL die Saisons); **the tennis season** die Tennissaison; **off-season prices** Preise außerhalb der Saison; **3 strawberries are not in season at the moment** jetzt ist nicht die richtige Zeit für Erdbeeren.

season ticket noun Dauerkarte die (PL die Dauerkarten).

seat noun **1** Sitz der (PL die Sitze); **the front seat** (in a car) der Vordersitz; **the back seat** der Rücksitz; **take a seat** nehmen Sie Platz (formal), setz dich (informal); **2** (on a bus, in the theatre, etc.) Platz der (PL die Plätze); **to book a seat** einen Platz reservieren; **can you keep my seat?** kannst du mir meinen Platz freihalten?

seatbelt noun Sicherheitsgurt der (PL die Sicherheitsgurte).

seaweed noun Tang der.

second noun Sekunde die (PL die Sekunden); **can you wait a second?** kannst du eine Sekunde warten?
second adjective **1** zweiter/ zweite/zweites; **for the second time** zum zweiten Mal; **2 the second of July** der zweite Juli.

secondary school noun
1 weiterführende Schule die (PL die weiterführenden Schulen) (Germans define the type of secondary school); **2** Gymnasium das (PL die Gymnasien) (grammar school, from age 10 to 19 when Abitur is taken); **3** Realschule die (PL die Realschulen) (from age 10 to 16, less academic than a Gymnasium).

secondhand adjective, adverb gebraucht; **a secondhand bike** ein gebrauchtes Fahrrad; **secondhand car** der Gebrauchtwagen; **I bought it secondhand** ich habe es gebraucht gekauft.

secondly adverb zweitens.

secret noun Geheimnis das (PL die Geheimnisse); **to tell somebody a secret** jemandem ein Geheimnis verraten; **in secret** heimlich.
secret adjective geheim; **a secret plan** ein geheimer Plan; **to keep something secret** etwas geheim halten.

secretary noun Sekretär der (PL die Sekretäre), Sekretärin die (PL die Sekretärinnen); **the secretary's office** das Sekretariat.

secretly adverb heimlich.

sect noun Sekte die (PL die Sekten).

section noun Teil der (PL die Teile).

security *noun* Sicherheit *die*.

security guard *noun* Wächter *der* (PL *die* Wächter), Wächterin *die* (PL *die* Wächterinnen).

see *verb* 1 sehen✧; **I saw Lindy yesterday** ich habe Lindy gestern gesehen; **have you seen the film?** hast du den Film gesehen?; **I can't see anything** ich kann überhaupt nichts sehen; **2 to go and see** nachsehen✧ SEP; **I'll go and see** ich sehe nach; **3** (*visit*) besuchen; **why don't you come and see us in the summer?** warum besucht ihr uns nicht im Sommer?; **4 to see somebody home** jemanden nach Hause begleiten; **5 see you!** tschüs! (*informal*); **see you on Saturday!** bis Samstag!; **see you soon!** bis bald!

• **to see to something** sich um etwas (ACC) kümmern; **Jo's seeing to the drinks** Jo kümmert sich um die Getränke.

seed *noun* Samen *der* (PL *die* Samen).

seem *verb* 1 scheinen✧; **his story seems odd to me** seine Geschichte kommt mir komisch vor; **he seems shy** er scheint schüchtern zu sein; **the museum seems to be closed** das Museum scheint geschlossen zu sein; **2 it seems (that)** ... anscheinend ...; **it seems he's left** anscheinend ist er weggegangen; **it seems that there are problems** anscheinend gibt es Probleme.

seesaw *noun* Wippe *die* (PL *die* Wippen).

select *verb* auswählen SEP.

self-confidence *noun* Selbstbewusstsein *das*; **she doesn't have much self-confidence** sie hat sehr wenig Selbstbewusstsein.

self-employed *adjective* **to be self-employed** selbstständig sein; **my parents are self-employed** meine Eltern sind selbstständig.

selfish *adjective* egoistisch.

self-service *adjective* **a self-service restaurant** ein Selbstbedienungsrestaurant.

sell *verb* 1 verkaufen; **to sell something to somebody** jemandem etwas verkaufen; **I sold him my bike** ich habe ihm mein Rad verkauft; **the house sold for a million** das Haus wurde für eine Million verkauft; **2 the concert's sold out** das Konzert ist ausverkauft; **the tickets sold out very quickly** die Karten waren schnell ausverkauft.

sell-by date *noun* Verfallsdatum *das* (PL *die* Verfallsdaten).

Sellotape™ *noun* Tesafilm *der*. **sellotape** *verb* **to sellotape something** etwas mit Tesafilm kleben.

semi *noun* Doppelhaushälfte *die* (PL *die* Doppelhaushälften).

semicircle *noun* Halbkreis *der* (PL *die* Halbkreise).

semicolon *noun* Strichpunkt *der* (PL *die* Strichpunkte).

semi-detached house *noun* Doppelhaushälfte *die* (PL *die* Doppelhaushälften).

semi-final *noun* Halbfinale *das* (PL die Halbfinale).

send *verb* schicken; **to send something to somebody** jemandem etwas schicken; **I sent her a present for her birthday** ich habe ihr zum Geburtstag ein Geschenk geschickt.

● **to send somebody back** jemanden zurückschicken SEP.

● **to send something back** etwas zurückschicken SEP.

sender *noun* Absender *der* (PL die Absender).

senior citizen *noun* Senior *der* (PL die Senioren), Seniorin *die* (PL die Seniorinnen).

sensation *noun* **1** (*feeling*) Gefühl *das* ; **2** (*impact*) Sensation *die* (PL die Sensationen); **she caused a sensation** sie erregte viel Aufsehen.

sensational *adjective* sensationell.

sense *noun* **1** (*common sense*) Verstand *der*; **2** (*faculty*) Sinn *der* (PL die Sinne); **sense of smell** *der* Geruchssinn; **sense of touch** *der* Tastsinn; **to have a sense of humour** Humor haben; **she has no sense of humour** sie hat keinen Sinn für Humor; **3** (*meaning*) Sinn *der*; **this sentence makes no sense** dieser Satz ergibt keinen Sinn; **it doesn't make sense to do that** es ist Unsinn, das zu machen; **it makes sense to collect her first** es ist sinnvoll, sie erst abzuholen.

sensible *adjective* vernünftig; **be sensible** sei vernünftig; **that's a sensible suggestion** das ist ein vernünftiger Vorschlag.

sensitive *adjective* empfindlich; **for sensitive skin** für empfindliche Haut.

sentence *noun* **1** (*words*) Satz *der* (PL die Sätze); **2** (*prison*) Strafe *die* (PL die Strafen); **the death sentence** die Todesstrafe.

sentence *verb* verurteilen; **to be sentenced to death** zum Tode verurteilt werden; **to sentence somebody to a year in prison** jemanden zu einem Jahr Gefängnis verurteilen.

sentimental *adjective* sentimental.

separate *adjective* **1** extra (*'extra' never has an ending*); **a separate pile** ein extra Stapel; **she wrote it on a separate sheet of paper** sie hat es auf ein anderes Blatt Papier geschrieben; **the drinks are separate** die Getränke gehen extra; **2** (*different*) verschieden; **two separate problems** zwei verschiedene Probleme; **3 they have separate rooms** sie haben getrennte Zimmer.

separate *verb* **1** trennen; **2** (*a couple*) sich trennen.

separately *adverb* **1** extra; **2** getrennt; **they live separately** sie leben getrennt.

separation *noun* Trennung *die* (PL die Trennungen).

September *noun* September *der*; **in September** im September.

sequel *noun* Folge *die* (PL die Folgen).

sequence *noun* **1** (*series*) Reihe die (PL die Reihen); **a sequence of events** eine Reihe von Ereignissen; **in sequence** in der richtigen Reihenfolge; **2** (*in a film*) Sequenz die (PL die Sequenzen).

sergeant *noun* **1** (*in the police*) Polizeimeister der (PL die Polizeimeister), Polizeimeisterin die (PL die Polizeimeisterinnen); **2** (*in the army*) Feldwebel der (PL die Feldwebel).

serial *noun* **1** Fortsetzungsgeschichte die (PL die Fortsetzungsgeschichten); **2** (*on TV or radio*) Serie die (PL die Serien).

series *noun* Serie die (PL die Serien); **television series** die Fernsehserie.

serious *adjective* **1** ernst; **a serious discussion** eine ernste Unterhaltung; **to be serious about something** etwas ernst nehmen; **are you serious?** ist das dein Ernst?; **2** schwer (*accident or mistake*).

seriously *adverb* **1** im Ernst; **seriously, I have to go now** im Ernst, ich muss jetzt gehen; **seriously?** im Ernst?; **2 to take somebody seriously** jemanden ernst nehmen; **3** (*gravely*) schwer; **she is seriously ill** sie ist schwer krank.

servant *noun* Bedienstete der / die (PL die Bediensteten).

serve *noun* (*in tennis*) Aufschlag der (PL die Aufschläge); **it's my serve** ich habe Aufschlag.
serve *verb* **1** (*in tennis*) aufschlagen◇ SEP; **Becker is serving** Becker schlägt auf; **2** servieren; **can you serve the vegetables, please?** können Sie bitte das Gemüse servieren? ⋆ **it serves him right** das geschieht ihm recht.

service *noun* **1** (*in a restaurant, shop, etc.*) Bedienung die; **service is included** inklusive Bedienung; **2** (*from a company or firm to a customer*) Service der; **3 the emergency services** der Notdienst; **4** (*church service*) Gottesdienst der (PL die Gottesdienste); **5** (*of a car or machine*) Wartung die (PL die Wartungen).

service area *noun* Raststätte die (PL die Raststätten).

service charge *noun* Bedienung die; **there is no service charge** die Bedienung wird nicht extra berechnet.

service station *noun* Tankstelle die (PL die Tankstellen).

serviette *noun* Serviette die (PL die Servietten).

session *noun* Sitzung die (PL die Sitzungen).

set *noun* **1** (*for playing a game*) Spiel das (PL die Spiele); **chess set** das Schachspiel; **2 train set** die Spielzeugeisenbahn; **3** (*in tennis*) Satz der (PL die Sätze).
set *adjective* **1** fest (*hours, habits*); **a set date** ein festes Datum; **at a set time** zu einer festgesetzten Zeit; **2 set menu** das Menü.
set *verb* **1** festlegen SEP (*a date, time*); **2** aufstellen SEP (*a record*);

a
b
c
d
e
f
g
h
i
j
k
l
m
n
o
p
q
r
s
t
u
v
w
x
y
z

a
b
c
d
e
f
g
h
i
j
k
l
m
n
o
p
q
r
s
t
u
v
w
x
y
z

3 to set the table den Tisch decken; **to set an alarm clock** einen Wecker stellen; **I've set my alarm for seven** ich habe meinen Wecker auf sieben gestellt; **4 to set your watch** seine Uhr richtig stellen; **5** (*sun*) untergehen✧ SEP.

● **to set off** aufbrechen✧ SEP (PERF *sein*); **we're setting off at ten** wir brechen um zehn auf; **they set off for Vienna yesterday** sie sind gestern nach Wien aufgebrochen.

● **to set off something 1** etwas auslösen SEP (*an alarm, reaction*); **2** etwas abbrennen✧ SEP (*a firework*); **3** etwas explodieren lassen (*a bomb*).

● **to set out** aufbrechen✧ SEP (PERF *sein*); **they set out for Hamburg at ten** sie sind um zehn nach Hamburg aufgebrochen.

settee *noun* Sofa *das* (PL *die* Sofas).

settle *verb* **1** bezahlen (*a bill*); **2** lösen (*a problem*); **3** beilegen SEP (*an argument*).

seven *number* sieben; **Rosie's seven** Rosie ist sieben.

seventeen *number* siebzehn; **I'm seventeen** ich bin siebzehn.

seventh *adjective* siebter/siebte/siebtes; **on the seventh floor** im siebten Stock; **the seventh of July** der siebte Juli.

seventies *plural noun* **the seventies** die Siebzigerjahre; **in the seventies** in den Siebzigerjahren.

seventieth *adjective* siebzigster/siebzigste/siebzigstes; **it's her seventieth birthday** es ist ihr siebzigster Geburtstag.

seventy *number* siebzig; **my granny's seventy** meine Oma ist siebzig.

several *adjective, pronoun* **1** mehrere; **I've read several of her novels** ich habe mehrere ihrer Romane gelesen; **2 I've seen her several times** ich habe sie mehrmals gesehen.

sew *verb* nähen.

sewing *noun* Nähen *das*; **I like sewing** ich nähe gern.

sewing machine *noun* Nähmaschine *die* (PL *die* Nähmaschinen).

sex *noun* **1** (*gender*) Geschlecht *das* (PL *die* Geschlechter); **2** (*intercourse*) Sex *der*; **to have sex with someone** mit jemandem Sex haben.

sex education *noun* Aufklärungsunterricht *der*.

sexism *noun* Sexismus *der*.

sexist *adjective* sexistisch; **sexist remarks** sexistische Bemerkungen.

sexual *adjective* sexuell.

sexual harassment *noun* sexuelle Belästigung *die*.

sexuality *noun* Sexualität *die*.

sexy *adjective* sexy.

shabby *adjective* schäbig.

shade *noun* **1** Ton *der* (PL *die* Töne); **a shade of green** ein Grünton; **2** Schatten *der*; **in the shade** im Schatten.

shadow *noun* Schatten *der* (PL *die* Schatten).

shake *verb* **1** (*tremble*) zittern; **I was shaking with fear** ich zitterte vor Angst; **2 to shake something** etwas schütteln; **to shake your head** (*meaning no*) den Kopf schütteln; **3 to shake hands with somebody** jemandem die Hand geben◇; **she shook hands with me** sie hat mir die Hand gegeben; **we shook hands** wir gaben uns die Hand.

shaken *adjective* erschüttert; **I was shaken by the news** die Nachricht hat mich erschüttert.

shall *verb* **shall I come with you?** soll ich mitkommen?; **shall we stop now?** sollen wir jetzt aufhören?

shallow *adjective* flach; **stay in the shallow end of the pool** bleib am flachen Ende des Beckens.

shambles *noun* Chaos *das*; **it was a total shambles!** es war ein völliges Chaos!

shame *noun* **1** Schande *die*; **the shame of it!** was für eine Schande!; **2 what a shame!** wie schade!; **it's a shame she can't come** schade, dass sie nicht kommen kann.

shampoo *noun* Shampoo *das* (PL *die* Shampoos); **I bought some shampoo** ich habe Shampoo gekauft.

shamrock *noun* Klee *der*.

shandy *noun* Radler *der* (PL *die* Radler) (*South German*), Alsterwasser *das* (PL *die* Alsterwasser) (*North German*).

shape *noun* Form *die* (PL *die* Formen).

share *noun* **1** Anteil *der* (PL *die* Anteile); **your share of the money** dein Anteil am Geld; **he paid his share** er hat seinen Anteil gezahlt; **2** (*in a company*) Aktie *die* (PL *die* Aktien).

share *verb* teilen; **I'm sharing a room with Lucy** ich teile ein Zimmer mit Lucy.

shark *noun* Hai *der* (PL *die* Haie), Haifisch *der* (PL *die* Haifische).

sharp *adjective* **1** (*knife*) scharf; **this knife isn't very sharp** dieses Messer ist nicht sehr scharf; **2** (*pointed*) spitz; **a sharp pencil** ein spitzer Bleistift; **3 a sharp bend** eine scharfe Kurve; **4** (*clever*) clever.

shave *verb* **1** (*have a shave*) sich rasieren; **2 to shave your legs** sich (DAT) die Beine rasieren; **3 to shave off your beard** den Bart abrasieren SEP.

shaver *noun* Rasierapparat *der* (PL *die* Rasierapparate); **electric shaver** *der* Elektrorasierer.

shaving cream *noun* Rasiercreme *die* (PL *die* Rasiercremes).

shaving foam *noun* Rasierschaum *der*.

she *pronoun* sie; **she's a student** sie ist Studentin; **she's a very good teacher** sie ist eine sehr gute Lehrerin.

shed *noun* Schuppen *der* (PL *die* Schuppen).

sheep *noun* Schaf *das* (PL *die* Schafe).

sheepdog *noun* Schäferhund *der* (PL *die* Schäferhunde).

sheer *adjective* rein; **it's sheer stupidity** das ist reine Dummheit.

sheet *noun* **1** (*for a bed*) Laken *das* (PL *die* Laken); **2 a sheet of paper** ein Blatt Papier; **a blank sheet** ein leeres Blatt; **3** (*of glass or metal*) Platte *die* (PL *die* Platten); ★**to be as white as a sheet** leichenblass sein.

shelf *noun* **1** (*in the home or a shop*) Regal *das* (PL *die* Regale); **a set of shelves** ein Regal; **2** (*in an oven*) Schiene *die* (PL *die* Schienen).

shell *noun* **1** (*of an egg or a nut*) Schale *die* (PL *die* Schalen); **2** (*seashell*) Muschel *die* (PL *die* Muscheln).

shellfish *noun* **1** Schalentier *das* (PL *die* Schalentiere); **2** (*in cookery*) Meeresfrüchte (*plural*).

shelter *noun* Schutz *der*; **in the shelter of** im Schutz (+ GEN); **to take shelter from the rain** sich unterstellen SEP.

shepherd *noun* Schäfer *der* (PL *die* Schäfer).

sherry *noun* Sherry *der* (PL *die* Sherrys).

Shetland Islands *noun* Shetlandinseln (*plural*).

shield *noun* Schild *der* (PL *die* Schilde).

shift *noun* Schicht *die* (PL *die* Schichten); **the night shift** die Nachtschicht; **to be on night shift** Nachtschicht haben.
shift *verb* **to shift something** etwas verrücken.

shifty *adjective* verschlagen; **he looks shifty** er sieht verschlagen aus; **a shifty-looking guy** ein verschlagener Typ.

shin *noun* Schienbein *das* (PL *die* Schienbeine).

shine *verb* scheinen✧; **the sun is shining** die Sonne scheint.

shiny *adjective* glänzend.

ship *noun* Schiff *das* (PL *die* Schiffe).

shipyard *noun* Werft *die* (PL *die* Werften).

shirt *noun* **1** (*man's*) Hemd *das* (PL *die* Hemden); **2** (*woman's*) Bluse *die* (PL *die* Blusen).

shiver *verb* zittern.

shock *noun* **1** Schock *der* (PL *die* Schocks); **to get a shock** einen Schock bekommen; **it gave me a shock** das hat mir einen Schock versetzt; **2 electric shock** *der* elektrische Schlag.
shock *verb* (*upset*) erschüttern (*cause scandal*) schockieren.

shocked *adjective* schockiert.

shocking *adjective* schockierend.

shoe *noun* Schuh *der* (PL *die* Schuhe); **a pair of shoes** ein Paar Schuhe.

shoelace *noun* Schnürsenkel *der* (PL *die* Schnürsenkel).

shoe polish *noun* Schuhcreme *die* (PL *die* Schuhcremes).

shoe shop *noun* Schuhgeschäft *das* (PL *die* Schuhgeschäfte).

shoot *verb* **1** (*fire*) schießen✧; **to shoot at somebody** auf jemanden schießen; **she shot him in the leg** sie hat ihm ins Bein geschossen; **he was shot in the arm** er wurde am Arm getroffen; **2** (*kill, execute*) erschießen✧; **he was shot by terrorists** er wurde von Terroristen erschossen; **3** (*in football, hockey*) schießen◇; **4 to shoot a film** einen Film drehen.

shop *noun* Geschäft *das* (PL *die* Geschäfte), Laden *der* (PL *die* Läden); **shoe shop** *das* Schuhgeschäft; **to go round the shops** einen Einkaufsbummel machen.

shop assistant *noun* Verkäufer *der* (PL *die* Verkäufer), Verkäuferin *die* (PL *die* Verkäuferinnen).

shopkeeper *noun* Ladenbesitzer *der* (PL *die* Ladenbesitzer), Ladenbesitzerin *die* (PL *die* Ladenbesitzerinnen).

shoplifter *noun* Ladendieb *der* (PL *die* Ladendiebe), Ladendiebin *die* (PL *die* Ladendiebinnen).

shoplifting *noun* Ladendiebstahl *der*.

shopping *noun* **1** Einkäufe (*plural*); **can you put the shopping away?** kannst du die Einkäufe wegräumen?; **2** (*activity*) Einkaufen *das*; **shopping is fun** Einkaufen macht Spaß; **to go shopping** einkaufen gehen◇.

shopping trolley *noun* Einkaufswagen *der* (PL *die* Einkaufswagen).

shop window *noun* Schaufenster *das* (PL *die* Schaufenster).

short *adjective* **1** kurz; **a short dress** ein kurzes Kleid; **she has short hair** sie hat kurze Haare; **2 a short break** eine kurze Pause; **to go for a short walk** einen kurzen Spaziergang machen; **it's a short walk from the bus stop** es ist nicht weit zu Fuß von der Bushaltestelle; **3 to be short of something** knapp mit etwas (DAT) sein; **we're a bit short of money at the moment** wir sind im Moment etwas knapp bei Kasse; **we're getting short of time** die Zeit wird uns knapp.

shortage *noun* Mangel *der*.

shortbread *noun* Buttergebäck *das*.

shortcrust pastry *noun* Mürbeteig *der*.

short cut *noun* Abkürzung *die* (PL *die* Abkürzungen).

shortly *adverb* gleich; **shortly before I left** kurz bevor ich ging; **shortly after** kurz danach.

shorts *plural noun* Shorts (*plural*); **a pair of shorts** ein Paar Shorts; **my red shorts** meine roten Shorts.

short-sighted *adjective* kurzsichtig; **I'm short-sighted** ich bin kurzsichtig.

shot *noun* **1** (*from a gun*) Schuss *der* (PL *die* Schüsse); **2** (*a photo*) Aufnahme *die* (PL *die* Aufnahmen).

should *verb* **1** sollen◇ (*'should' is usually translated by the imperfect subjunctive of 'sollen'*); **you should ask Simon** du solltest Simon fragen; **the potatoes should be ready now** die Kartoffeln sollten jetzt fertig sein; **2** (*'should have' is translated by 'hätte sollen'*) **you should have told me** du hättest es mir sagen sollen; **I shouldn't have stayed** ich hätte nicht bleiben sollen; **you shouldn't have said that** das hättest du nicht sagen sollen; **3** (*'should' meaning* *'would' is translated by 'würde'*) **I should forget it if I were you** an deiner Stelle würde ich es vergessen; **4 I should think** ich würde sagen; **I should think he's forgotten** ich würde sagen, er hat's vergessen; **5 this should be enough** das müsste eigentlich reichen.

shoulder *noun* Schulter *die* (PL *die* Schultern).

shoulder bag *noun* Umhängetasche *die* (PL *die* Umhängetaschen).

shout *noun* Schrei *der* (PL *die* Schreie).
shout *verb* **1** schreien❖; **stop shouting!** hör auf zu schreien!; **2** (*call*) rufen❖; **he shouted at us to come back** er rief uns zu, wir sollten zurückkommen.

shovel *noun* Schaufel *die* (PL *die* Schaufeln).

show *noun* **1** (*on stage*) Show *die* (PL *die* Shows); **we went to see a show** wir haben eine Show gesehen; **2** (*on TV, radio*) Sendung *die* (PL *die* Sendungen); **3** (*exhibition*) Ausstellung *die* (PL *die* Ausstellungen); **fashion show** *die* Modenschau.
show *verb* **1** zeigen; **to show something to somebody** jemandem etwas zeigen; **I'll show you my photos** ich zeige dir meine Fotos; **to show somebody how something works** jemandem zeigen, wie etwas funktioniert; **he showed me how to make pancakes** er hat mir gezeigt, wie

man Pfannkuchen macht; **2 it shows!** das sieht man!
● **to show off** angeben❖ SEP.

shower *noun* **1** (*in a bathroom*) Dusche *die* (PL *die* Duschen); **to have a shower** duschen; **2** (*of rain*) Schauer *der* (PL *die* Schauer).

show-jumping *noun* Springreiten *das*.

show-off *noun* Angeber *der* (PL *die* Angeber), Angeberin *die* (PL *die* Angeberinnen).

shriek *verb* kreischen.

shrimp *noun* Krabbe *die* (PL *die* Krabben).

shrink *verb* **1** schrumpfen (PERF *sein*); **2** (*clothes*) einlaufen❖ SEP (PERF *sein*); **my sweater has shrunk** mein Pullover ist eingelaufen.

Shrove Tuesday *noun* Fastnachtsdienstag *der*.

shrug *verb* **to shrug your shoulders** mit den Achseln zucken.

shuffle *verb* **to shuffle the cards** die Karten mischen.

shut *adjective* zu; **the shops are shut** die Geschäfte haben zu.
shut *verb* zumachen SEP; **can you shut the door please?** kannst du die Tür bitte zumachen?; **the shops shut at six** die Geschäfte machen um sechs zu.
● **to shut up** den Mund halten❖ (*informal*); **shut up!** halt den Mund!

shuttlecock *noun* Federball *der* (PL *die* Federbälle).

shuttle service *noun* Pendelverkehr *der*; **there's a shuttle**

service from the airport es gibt einen Shuttledienst vom Flughafen.

shy *adjective* schüchtern.

shyness *noun* Schüchternheit *die*.

Sicily *noun* Sizilien *das*.

sick *adjective* **1** (*ill*) krank; **2 to be sick** (*vomit*) sich übergeben◇; **I was sick several times** ich habe mich mehrmals übergeben; **3 I feel sick** mir ist schlecht; **4** übel; **a sick joke** ein übler Witz; **5 to be sick of something** etwas satt haben; **I'm sick of staying at home every day** ich habe es satt, jeden Tag zu Hause zu sitzen.

sickness *noun* Krankheit *die* (PL *die* Krankheiten).

side *noun* **1** Seite *die* (PL *die* Seiten); **on the other side of the street** auf der anderen Straßenseite; **on the wrong side** auf der falschen Seite; **I'm on your side** (*I agree with you*) ich bin auf deiner Seite; **2** (*edge*) Rand *der* (PL *die* Ränder) (*of a pool, river*); **at the side of the road** am Straßenrand; **3** (*team*) Mannschaft *die* (PL *die* Mannschaften); **the winning side** die siegreiche Mannschaft; **she plays on our side** sie spielt bei uns mit; **4 to take sides** Partei ergreifen◇; **he always takes sides against her** er ergreift immer gegen sie Partei; **5 side by side** nebeneinander.

sideboard *noun* Anrichte *die* (PL *die* Anrichten).

sideburns *noun* Koteletten (*plural*).

side-effect *noun* Nebenwirkung *die* (PL *die* Nebenwirkungen).

side street *noun* Seitenstraße *die* (PL *die* Seitenstraßen).

sieve *noun* Sieb *das* (PL *die* Siebe).

sigh *noun* Seufzer *der* (PL *die* Seufzer). **sigh** *verb* seufzen.

sight *noun* **1** Anblick *der*; **it was a marvellous sight** es war ein herrlicher Anblick; **2 at first sight** auf den ersten Blick; **3** (*eyesight*) **to have poor sight** schlechte Augen haben; **to know somebody by sight** jemanden vom Sehen kennen; **out of sight** außer Sicht; **to lose sight of somebody** jemanden aus den Augen verlieren; **4 the sights** die Sehenswürdigkeiten; **to see the sights** die Sehenswürdigkeiten besichtigen.

sightseeing *noun* Sightseeing *das*; **to do some sightseeing** einige Sehenswürdigkeiten besichtigen.

sign *noun* **1** (*notice*) Schild *das* (PL *die* Schilder); **there's a sign on the door** da ist ein Schild an der Tür; **2** (*trace, indication*) Zeichen *das* (PL *die* Zeichen); **3** (*of the zodiac*) Sternzeichen *das* (PL *die* Sternzeichen); **what sign are you?** was für ein Sternzeichen bist du? **sign** *verb* **1** unterschreiben◇; **to sign a cheque** einen Scheck unterschreiben; **2** (*using sign language*) sich durch Zeichensprache verständigen.

● **to sign on** sich arbeitslos melden.

signal *noun* Signal *das* (PL *die* Signale).

a
b
c
d
e
f
g
h
i
j
k
l
m
n
o
p
q
r
s
t
u
v
w
x
y
z

signature *noun* Unterschrift *die* (PL *die* Unterschriften).

significant *adjective* bedeutend.

sign language *noun* Zeichensprache *die* (PL *die* Zeichensprachen).

signpost *noun* Wegweiser *der* (PL *die* Wegweiser).

silence *noun* Stille *die*.

silent *adjective* still.

silk *noun* Seide *die*.
silk *adjective* Seiden-; **a silk blouse** eine Seidenbluse.

silky *adjective* seidig.

silly *adjective* dumm; **it was a really silly thing to do** das war wirklich dumm.

silver *noun* Silber *das*.
silver *adjective* Silber-; **a silver medal** eine Silbermedaille.

similar *adjective* ähnlich; **it looks similar to my old bike** es sieht so ähnlich wie mein altes Rad aus.

similarity *noun* Ähnlichkeit *die* (PL *die* Ähnlichkeiten).

simple *adjective* einfach.

simply *adverb* einfach.

sin *noun* Sünde *die* (PL *die* Sünden).

since *preposition* **1** seit (+ DAT) (*notice that German uses the present tense for an action starting in the past and still going on in the present*); **I have been in Berlin since Saturday** ich bin seit Samstag in Berlin; **since when?** seit wann?; **2** (*with a negative the perfect tense is used*) **I haven't seen her since Monday** ich habe sie seit Montag nicht gesehen.

since *conjunction* **1** seit; **since I have known him** seit ich ihn kenne; **since I've been learning German** seitdem ich Deutsch lerne; **2** (*because*) da; **since it was raining, the match was cancelled** da es regnete, wurde das Spiel abgesagt.
since *adverb* seitdem; **I haven't seen him since** ich habe ihn seitdem nicht mehr gesehen.

sincere *adjective* aufrichtig.

sincerely *adverb* **Yours sincerely** Mit freundlichen Grüßen.

sing *verb* singen✧.

singer *noun* Sänger *der* (PL *die* Sänger), Sängerin *die* (PL *die* Sängerinnen).

singing *noun* **1** Singen *das*; **a singing lesson** eine Singstunde; **2 I like singing** ich singe gern.

single *noun* **1** (*ticket*) einfache Fahrkarte *die* (PL *die* einfachen Fahrkarten); **a single to Munich, please** eine einfache Fahrkarte nach München bitte; **2** (*record, CD*) Single *die* (PL *die* Singles).
single *adjective* **1** (*not married*) allein stehend; **a single woman** eine allein stehende Frau, (*on forms*) ledig; **2** (*just one*) einzig; **I haven't had a single reply** ich habe keine einzige Antwort bekommen; **3 not a single one** kein Einziger/keine Einzige/kein Einziges; **4 single room** *das* Einzelzimmer; **single bed** *das* Einzelbett.

single parent *noun* allein Erziehende *der/die* (PL *die* allein Erziehenden); **she's a single**

parent sie ist allein erziehende Mutter; **a single-parent family** eine Einelternfamilie.

singles *plural noun (in tennis)* Einzel *das* (PL *die* Einzel); **the women's singles** das Dameneinzel; **the men's singles** das Herreneinzel.

singular *noun* Einzahl *die*; **in the singular** in der Einzahl.

sink *noun* Spülbecken *das* (PL *die* Spülbecken).
sink *verb* sinken⋄ (PERF *sein*).

sir *noun* Herr *der* (PL *die* Herren); *(in German,' Sir' is usually not translated)* **would you like another one, sir?** möchten Sie noch eins?; **yes, sir** ja, mein Herr.

sister *noun* Schwester *die* (PL *die* Schwestern); **my sister's ten** meine Schwester ist zehn.

sister-in-law *noun* Schwägerin *die* (PL *die* Schwägerinnen).

sit *verb* 1 *(to sit down)* sich setzen; **you can sit on the sofa** ihr könnt euch aufs Sofa setzen; **sit on the floor** setz dich auf den Boden; 2 *(to be sitting)* sitzen⋄; **Leila was sitting on the sofa** Leila saß auf dem Sofa; **to sit on the floor** auf dem Boden sitzen; 3 **to sit an exam** eine Prüfung machen.

● **to sit down** sich setzen; **he sat down on the chair** er setzte sich auf den Stuhl; **do sit down** setzen Sie sich.

sitcom *noun* Situationskomödie *die* (PL *die* Situationskomödien).

site *noun* 1 **building site** die Baustelle; 2 **camping site** *der* Campingplatz; 3 **archaeolological site** die archäologische Stätte.

sitting room *noun* Wohnzimmer *das* (PL *die* Wohnzimmer).

situated *adjective* **to be situated** sich befinden⋄; **the house is situated in a small village** das Haus befindet sich in einem kleinen Dorf.

situation *noun* 1 *(location)* Lage *die* (PL *die* Lagen); 2 *(circumstances)* Situation *die* (PL *die* Situationen).

six *number* sechs; **Harry's six** Harry ist sechs.

sixteen *number* sechzehn; **Alice is sixteen** Alice ist sechzehn.

sixth *adjective* sechster/sechste/ sechstes; **on the sixth floor** im sechsten Stock; **on the sixth of July** am sechsten Juli.

sixty *number* sechzig; **she's sixty** sie ist sechzig.

size *noun* 1 Größe *die* (PL *die* Größen); **it depends on the size of the house** es kommt auf die Größe des Hauses an; 2 **what size is the window?** wie groß ist das Fenster?; 3 *(in clothes)* Größe *die* (PL *die* Größen); **what size do you take?** welche Größe haben Sie?; 4 *(of shoes)* Schuhgröße *die* (PL *die* Schuhgrößen); **I take a size thirty-eight** ich habe Schuhgröße achtunddreißig.

skate *noun* 1 *(an ice skate)* Schlittschuh *der* (PL *die* Schlittschuhe); 2 *(a roller skate)*

a b c d e f g h i j k l m n o p q r s t u v w x y z

Rollschuh *der* (PL die Rollschuhe).
skate *verb* **1** (*ice-skate*)
Schlittschuh laufen◇ (PERF *sein*);
2 (*roller-skate*) Rollschuh laufen◇
(PERF *sein*).

skateboard *noun* Skateboard *das*
(PL die Skateboards).

skateboarding *noun*
Skateboardfahren *das*; **to go
skateboarding** Skateboard fahren◇
(PERF *sein*).

skater *noun* **1** (*on rollerskates*)
Rollschuhfahrer *der* (PL die
Rollschuhfahrer),
Rollschuhfahrerin *die* (PL die
Rollschuhfahrerinnen); **2** (*on ice*)
Eisläufer *der* (PL die Eisläufer),
Eisläuferin *die* (PL die
Eisläuferinnen); **3** (*on a skateboard*)
Skater *der* (PL die Skater).

skating *noun* **1** (*on ice*)
Schlittschuhlaufen *das*; **to go
skating** Schlittschuh laufen◇ (PERF
sein); **2** (*roller-skating*)
Rollschuhlaufen *das*; **to go roller-
skating** Rollschuh laufen◇ (PERF
sein).

skating rink *noun* **1** (*ice rink*)
Eisbahn *die* (PL die Eisbahnen); **2** (*for
roller-skating*) Rollschuhbahn *die* (PL
die Rollschuhbahnen).

skeleton *noun* Skelett *das* (PL die
Skelette).

sketch *noun* **1** Skizze *die* (PL die
Skizzen); **2** (*comedy routine*) Sketch
der (PL die Sketche).

ski *noun* Ski *der* (PL die Skier).
ski *verb* Ski fahren◇ (PERF *sein*); **he
can ski** er kann Ski fahren.

ski boot *noun* Skistiefel *der* (PL die
Skistiefel).

skid *verb* schleudern (PERF *sein*); **the
car skidded** das Auto kam ins
Schleudern.

skier *noun* Skifahrer *der* (PL die
Skifahrer), Skifahrerin *die* (PL die
Skifahrerinnen).

skiing *noun* Skifahren *das*; **to go
skiing** Ski fahren◇ (PERF *sein*).

ski lift *noun* Skilift *der* (PL die
Skilifte).

ski suit *noun* Skianzug *der* (PL die
Skianzüge).

skimmed milk *noun* fettarme
Milch *die*.

skin *noun* Haut *die* (PL die Häute).

skinhead *noun* Skinhead *der* (PL die
Skinheads).

skinny *adjective* dünn.

skip *noun* (*for rubbish*) Container
der (PL die Container).
skip *verb* **1** auslassen◇ SEP (*a meal,
part of a book*); **I skipped a few
chapters** ich ließ ein paar Kapitel
aus; **2 to skip a lesson** ein Stunde
schwänzen (*informal*).

skirt *noun* Rock *der* (PL die Röcke); **a
long skirt** ein langer Rock; **a tight
skirt** ein enger Rock; **a mini-skirt**
ein Minirock.

skittles *plural noun* Kegeln *das*.

skull *noun* Schädel *der* (PL die
Schädel).

sky *noun* Himmel *der* (PL die
Himmel).

skyscraper *noun* Wolkenkratzer
der (PL die Wolkenkratzer).

a
b
c
d
e
f
g
h
i
j
k
l
m
n
o
p
q
r
s
t
u
v
w
x
y
z

slam *verb* zuknallen SEP; **she slammed the door** sie hat die Tür zugeknallt; **the door slammed** die Tür ist zugeknallt.

slang *noun* Slang der (PL die Slangs).

slap *noun* Klaps der (PL die Klapse), (*in the face*) Ohrfeige die (PL die Ohrfeigen).
slap *verb* **to slap somebody** (*across the face*) jemanden ohrfeigen, (*on the bottom*) jemandem einen Klaps geben.

sledge *noun* Schlitten der (PL die Schlitten).

sledging *noun* **to go sledging** Schlitten fahren◇ (PERF *sein*).

sleep *noun* Schlaf der; **you need more sleep** du brauchst mehr Schlaf; **I had a good sleep** ich habe gut geschlafen; **to go to sleep** einschlafen◇ SEP (PERF *sein*); **he's gone back to sleep** er ist wieder eingeschlafen.
sleep *verb* schlafen◇; **she's sleeping** sie schläft.

sleeping bag *noun* Schlafsack der (PL die Schlafsäcke).

sleeping pill *noun* Schlaftablette die (PL die Schlaftabletten).

sleepy *adjective* **to be sleepy** schläfrig sein; **he was getting sleepy** er wurde schläfrig.

sleet *noun* Schneeregen der.

sleeve *noun* Ärmel der (PL die Ärmel); **a long-sleeved jumper** ein Pullover mit langen Ärmeln; **a short-sleeved shirt** ein Hemd mit kurzen Ärmeln; **to roll up your sleeves** die Ärmel hochkrempeln.

slice *noun* Scheibe die (PL die Scheiben); **a slice of bread** eine Scheibe Brot.
slice *verb* **to slice something** etwas in Scheiben schneiden◇.

slide *noun* 1 (*photo*) Dia das (PL die Dias); 2 (*hairslide*) Haarspange die (PL die Haarspangen); 3 (*for sliding down*) Rutschbahn die (PL die Rutschbahnen).

slight *adjective* klein; **there is a slight problem** es gibt ein kleines Problem.

slightly *adverb* etwas.

slim *adjective* schlank.
slim *verb* abnehmen◇ SEP; **I'm slimming** ich mache eine Schlankheitskur.

sling *noun* Schlinge die (PL die Schlingen); **to have your arm in a sling** den Arm in der Schlinge haben.

slip *noun* 1 (*mistake*) Fehler der (PL die Fehler); 2 (*petticoat*) Unterrock der (PL die Unterröcke).
slip *verb* 1 (*slide*) ausrutschen SEP (PERF *sein*); 2 **it slipped my mind** es ist mir entfallen.
● **to slip up** einen Fehler machen.

slipper *noun* Hausschuh der (PL die Hausschuhe).

slippery *adjective* glatt.

slope *noun* Hang der (PL die Hänge).

slot *noun* Schlitz der (PL die Schlitze).

slot machine *noun* 1 (*vending machine*) Automat der (PL die Automaten); 2 (*games machine*) Spielautomat der (PL die Spielautomaten).

a
b
c
d
e
f
g
h
i
j
k
l
m
n
o
p
q
r
s
t
u
v
w
x
y
z

a
b
c
d
e
f
g
h
i
j
k
l
m
n
o
p
q
r
s
t
u
v
w
x
y
z

slow *adjective* **1** langsam; **the service is a bit slow** die Bedienung ist etwas langsam; **2** (*of a clock or watch*) **to be slow** nachgehen✧ SEP (PERF *sein*); **my watch is slow** meine Uhr geht nach.

● **to slow down** langsamer werden.

slowly *adverb* langsam; **he got up slowly** er ist langsam aufgestanden; **can you speak more slowly, please?** können Sie bitte etwas langsamer sprechen?

slug *noun* Nacktschnecke die (PL die Nacktschnecken).

sly *adjective* gerissen (*a person*); ★ **on the sly** heimlich.

smack *noun* Klaps der (PL die Klapse).
smack *verb* **to smack somebody** jemandem einen Klaps geben✧.

small *adjective* klein; **a small dog** ein kleiner Hund.

smart *adjective* **1** (*well-dressed, posh*) elegant; **a smart restaurant** ein elegantes Restaurant; **2** (*clever*) clever.

smash *noun* (*collision*) Zusammenstoß der (PL die Zusammenstöße).
smash *verb* **1** (*break*) zerschlagen✧; **they smashed a window pane** sie haben eine Fensterscheibe zerschlagen; **2** (*get broken*) zerbrechen✧ (PERF *sein*); **the plate smashed** der Teller ist zerbrochen.

smashing *adjective* klasse (*informal*).

smell *noun* Geruch der (PL die Gerüche); **a nasty smell** ein scheußlicher Geruch; **a smell of gas** ein Gasgeruch.
smell *verb* **1** riechen✧; **I can't smell anything** ich kann nichts riechen; **to smell of perfume** nach Parfüm riechen; **2** (*smell bad*) stinken✧; **the drains smell** der Abfluss stinkt.

smelly *adjective* **1** stinkend; **her smelly dog** ihr stinkender Hund; **2 to be smelly** stinken✧.

smile *noun* Lächeln das.
smile *verb* lächeln; **to smile at somebody** jemanden anlächeln SEP.

smoke *noun* Rauch der.
smoke *verb* rauchen; **she doesn't smoke** sie raucht nicht.

smoked *adjective* geräuchert; **smoked salmon** Räucherlachs der

smoker *noun* Raucher der (PL die Raucher), Raucherin die (PL die Raucherinnen).

smoking *noun* 'no smoking' 'Rauchen verboten'; **to give up smoking** mit dem Rauchen aufhören.

smooth *adjective* **1** glatt; **a smooth surface** eine glatte Oberfläche; **2** (*person*) aalglatt.

smug *adjective* selbstgefällig.

smuggle *verb* **to smuggle something** etwas schmuggeln.

smuggler *noun* **1** Schmuggler der (PL die Schmuggler), Schmugglerin die (PL die Schmugglerinnen); **2 drugs smuggler** der Drogenschmuggler.

snack *noun* Snack der (PL die Snacks).

snail *noun* Schnecke die (PL die Schnecken).

snake *noun* Schlange die (PL die Schlangen).

snap *noun* (*card game*) Schnippschnapp das (PL die Schnippschnapp).
snap *verb* **1** (*break*) brechen✧ (PERF sein); **2 to snap something** etwas zerbrechen✧; **3 to snap your fingers** mit den Fingern schnalzen.

snapshot *noun* Schnappschuss der (PL die Schnappschüsse).

snarl *verb* knurren.

snatch *verb* **1** entreißen✧; **to snatch something from somebody** jemandem etwas entreißen; **she had her bag snatched** man hat ihr die Handtasche entrissen; **2 he snatched it out of my hand** er hat es mir aus der Hand gerissen.

sneak *verb* **1 to sneak in** sich hineinschleichen✧ SEP; **to sneak out** sich hinausschleichen✧ SEP; **2 to sneak on somebody** jemanden verpetzen (*informal*).

sneeze *verb* niesen.

sniff *verb* schnüffeln.

snob *noun* Snob der (PL die Snobs).

snobbery *noun* Snobismus der.

snooker *noun* Snooker das.

snooze *verb* Nickerchen das (PL die Nickerchen); **to have a snooze** ein Nickerchen machen.

snore *verb* schnarchen.

snow *noun* Schnee der.
snow *verb* schneien; **it's snowing** es schneit.

snowball *noun* Schneeball der (PL die Schneebälle).

snow drift *noun* Schneewehe die (PL die Schneewehen).

snowman *noun* Schneemann der (PL die Schneemänner).

so *conjunction, adverb* **1** so; **he's so lazy** er ist so faul; **not so** nicht so; **our house is a bit like yours, but not so big** unser Haus ist so ähnlich wie eures, aber nicht so groß; **2 so much** so sehr; **I hate it so much** ich hasse es so sehr; **3 so much** so viel; **I have so much work** ich habe so viel Arbeit; **4 so many** so viele; **we've got so many problems** wir haben so viele Probleme; **5** (*therefore*) also; **he got up late, so he missed his train** er ist zu spät aufgestanden und hat deshalb den Zug verpasst; **so what shall we do?** also, was machen wir?; **6 so what?** na und?; **7** (*also*) **so do I, so did I** ich auch; **'I live in Leeds'– 'so do I'** 'ich wohne in Leeds' - 'ich auch'; **I liked the film and so did he** ich fand den Film gut und er auch; **so am I** ich auch; **so do we** wir auch; **8 I think so** ich glaube schon; **9 I hope so** hoffentlich.

soak *verb* einweichen SEP.

soaked *adjective* patschnass; **★ to be soaked to the skin** patschnass sein.

soap *noun* **1** Seife, die (PL die Seifen); **2** (*soap opera*) Seifenoper die (PL die Seifenopern).

a
b
c
d
e
f
g
h
i
j
k
l
m
n
o
p
q
r
s
t
u
v
w
x
y
z

soap powder *noun* Seifenpulver *das*.

sober *adjective* nüchtern.

● **to sober up** nüchtern werden◇ (PERF *sein*).

soccer *noun* Fußball *der*.

social *adjective* 1 sozial; **social problems** soziale Probleme; 2 gesellschaftlich (*engagement, ambition*); **social engagements** gesellschaftliche Verpflichtungen; **social class** *die* gesellschaftliche Schicht; 3 (*sociable*) gesellig (*evening, person*).

socialism *noun* Sozialismus *der*.

socialist *noun* Sozialist *der* (PL *die* Sozialisten), Sozialistin *die* (PL *die* Sozialistinnen).

social security *noun* 1 Sozialhilfe *die*; **to be on social security** Sozialhilfe bekommen; 2 (*the system*) Sozialversicherung *die*.

social worker *noun* Sozialarbeiter *der* (PL *die* Sozialarbeiter), Sozialarbeiterin *die* (PL *die* Sozialarbeiterinnen).

society *noun* Gesellschaft *die* (PL *die* Gesellschaften).

sociology *noun* Soziologie *die*.

sock *noun* Socke *die* (PL *die* Socken); **a pair of socks** ein Paar Socken.

socket *noun* (*power point*) Steckdose *die* (PL *die* Steckdosen).

sofa *noun* Sofa *das* (PL *die* Sofas).

sofa bed *noun* Schlafcouch *die* (PL *die* Schlafcouchs).

soft *adjective* 1 weich; 2 **a soft option** eine bequeme Lösung; ★ **to have a soft spot for somebody** eine Schwäche für jemanden haben.

soft drink *noun* alkoholfreie Getränk *das* (PL *die* alkoholfreien Getränke).

soft toy *noun* Stofftier *das* (PL *die* Stofftiere).

software *noun* Software *die*.

soil *noun* Erde *die*.

solar energy *noun* Sonnenenergie *die*.

soldier *noun* Soldat *der* (PL *die* Soldaten).

solicitor *noun* 1 (*dealing with lawsuits*) Rechtsanwalt *der* (PL *die* Rechtsanwälte), Rechtsanwältin *die* (PL *die* Rechtsanwältinnen); 2 (*dealing with property or documents*) Notar *der* (PL *die* Notare), Notarin *die* (PL *die* Notarinnen).

solid *adjective* 1 (*not flimsy*) stabil; **a solid structure** ein stabiler Bau; 2 massiv; **a table made of solid oak** ein Tisch aus massiver Eiche; **solid silver** massives Silber.

solo *noun* Solo *das* (PL *die* Solos); **guitar solo** *das* Gitarrensolo. **solo** *adjective* Solo-; **a solo act** eine Solonummer. **solo** *adverb* solo.

soloist *noun* Solist *der* (PL *die* Solisten), Solistin *die* (PL *die* Solistinnen).

solution *noun* Lösung *die* (PL *die* Lösungen).

solve *verb* lösen.

some *adjective, adverb* **1** (*followed by a singular noun*) etwas; **would you like some salad?** möchtest du etwas Salat?; **can you lend me some money?** kannst du mir etwas Geld leihen?; **have you got some bread?** (*some is often not translated*) hast du Brot?; **2** (*followed by a plural noun*) (*a few*) ein paar; **I've bought some apples** ich habe ein paar Äpfel gekauft; **3** (*followed by a plural noun*) (*a certain number but not all*) einige; **some of his films are too violent** einige von seinen Filmen sind zu brutal; **4** (*referring to something that has been mentioned*) **'would you like tea?' — 'thanks, I've got some'** 'möchten Sie Tee?' — 'nein danke, ich habe schon welchen'; **he's eaten some of it** er hat etwas davon gegessen; **I'd like some** ich möchte etwas; (*with a plural noun*) ich möchte welche; **5** (*certain people or things*) manche; **some people think he's right** manche Leute glauben, dass er Recht hat; **6 some day** eines Tages.

somebody, **someone** *pronoun* jemand; **there's somebody in the garden** da ist jemand im Garten.

somehow *adverb* irgendwie; **I've got to finish this essay somehow** ich muss diesen Aufsatz irgendwie fertig schreiben.

something *pronoun* **1** etwas; **there's something I've got to tell you** ich muss dir etwas erzählen; **something new** etwas Neues; **something interesting** etwas Interessantes; **there's something wrong** irgendetwas stimmt nicht;

2 their house is really something! ihr Haus ist einfach Klasse!

sometime *adverb* irgendwann; **give me a ring sometime next week** ruf mich irgendwann nächste Woche an.

sometimes *adverb* manchmal; **I sometimes take the train** manchmal fahre ich mit der Bahn.

somewhere *adverb* **1** (*in a place*) irgendwo; **I've left my bag somewhere here** ich habe meine Handtasche hier irgendwo liegen lassen; **2** (*to a place*) irgendwohin; **I'd like to go somewhere warm** ich möchte irgendwohin fahren, wo es warm ist.

son *noun* Sohn *der* (PL *die* Söhne).

song *noun* Lied *das* (PL *die* Lieder).

son-in-law *noun* Schwiegersohn *der* (PL *die* Schwiegersöhne).

soon *adverb* **1** bald; **we'll soon be on holiday** wir haben bald Ferien; **see you soon!** bis bald!; **2 as soon as she arrives** sobald sie ankommt; **as soon as possible** so bald wie möglich; **3 it's too soon** es ist zu früh.

sooner *adverb* **1** früher; **we should have started sooner** wir hätten früher anfangen sollen; **sooner or later** früher oder später; **2 I'd sooner wait** ich würde lieber warten.

soprano *noun* Sopran *der* (PL *die* Soprane).

sore *noun* wunde Stelle *die* (PL *die* wunden Stellen).

sore *adjective* **1** (*inflamed*) wund;

a b c d e f g h i j k l m n o p q r **s** t u v w x y z

to have a sore throat Halsschmerzen haben; **2 he has a sore leg** ihm tut das Bein weh; **my arm's sore** mir tut der Arm weh; ´**it's a sore point** das ist ein wunder Punkt.

sorry *adjective* **1 I'm really sorry** es tut mir wirklich Leid; **sorry to disturb you** es tut mir Leid, dass ich dich störe; **I'm sorry I forgot your birthday** es tut mir Leid, dass ich deinen Geburtstag vergessen habe; **I'm sorry, we're closing** es tut mir Leid, aber wir machen jetzt zu; **2 sorry!** Entschuldigung!; **3 sorry?** wie bitte?; **4 I feel sorry for him** er tut mir Leid.

sort *noun* Art *die* (PL *die* Arten); **a sort of dance music** eine Art Tanzmusik; **what sort of car have you got?** was für ein Auto hast du?; **all sorts of people** alle möglichen Leute; **for all sorts of reasons** aus allen möglichen Gründen.

● **to sort something out 1** Ordnung schaffen◇ in (+ DAT) (*papers, desk, room, possessions*); **I must sort out my room tonight** ich muss heute Abend in meinem Zimmer Ordnung schaffen; **2** klären (*a problem, arrangement*); **Liz is sorting it out** Liz klärt es.

so-so *adjective* so lala (*informal*); **'how was the film?'— 'so-so'** 'wie war der Film?'— 'mittelmäßig'.

soul *noun* **1** Seele *die* (PL *die* Seelen); **2** (*music*) Soul *der*.

sound *noun* **1** (*noise*) Geräusch *das* (PL *die* Geräusche); **2** (*of voices, laughter, bell*) Klang *der*; **the sound**

of her voice der Klang ihrer Stimme; **I can hear the sound of voices** ich kann Stimmen hören; **3 without a sound** lautlos; **4** (*volume*) Lautstärke *die*; **to turn the sound down** leiser stellen.

sound *verb* **1 it sounds easy** es hört sich einfach an; **2 it sounds as if she's happy** sie scheint glücklich zu sein.

sound asleep *adverb* **to be sound asleep** fest schlafen◇.

sound effect *noun* Geräuscheffekt *der* (PL *die* Geräuscheffekte).

soundtrack *noun* Soundtrack *der* (PL *die* Soundtracks).

soup *noun* Suppe *die* (PL *die* Suppen); **mushroom soup** *die* Pilzsuppe.

soup plate *noun* Suppenteller *der* (PL *die* Suppenteller).

soup spoon *noun* Suppenlöffel *der* (PL *die* Suppenlöffel).

sour *adjective* sauer.

south *noun* Süden *der*; **in the south** im Süden.

south *adjective* Süd-, südlich; **the south side** die Südseite; **south wind** *der* Südwind.

south *adverb* **south of Berlin** südlich von Berlin; **they went south** sie sind nach Süden gefahren.

South Africa *noun* Südafrika *das*.

South America *noun* Südamerika *das*.

southeast *noun* Südosten *der*.

southeast *adjective* **in southeast England** in Südostengland.

South Pole *noun* Südpol *der*.

southwest *noun* Südwesten *der*.
southwest *adjective* **in southwest England** in Südwestengland.

souvenir *noun* Souvenir *das* (PL die Souvenirs).

soya *noun* Soja *die*.

space *noun* **1** (*room*) Platz *der*; **there's enough space** es ist genug Platz; **we've got enough space for two** wir haben genug Platz für zwei; **2** (*gap*) Zwischenraum *der* (PL die Zwischenräume); **to leave a large space between lines** viel Platz zwischen den Zeilen lassen; **3** (*parking*) **space** die Parklücke; **4** (*outer space*) Weltraum *der*, **in space** im Weltraum.

spacecraft *noun* Raumschiff *das* (PL die Raumschiffe).

spade *noun* **1** Spaten *der* (PL die Spaten); **2** (*in cards*) Pik *das*; **the queen of spades** die Pikdame.

Spain *noun* Spanien *das*; **from Spain** aus Spanien; **to Spain** nach Spanien.

Spaniard *noun* Spanier *der* (PL die Spanier), Spanierin *die* (PL die Spanierinnen).

spaniel *noun* Spaniel *der* (PL die Spaniels).

Spanish *noun* **1** (*language*) Spanisch *das*; **I'm learning Spanish** ich lerne Spanisch; **2 the Spanish** (*people*) die Spanier.
Spanish *adjective* spanisch; **Pedro is Spanish** Pedro ist Spanier.

spanner *noun* Schraubenschlüssel *der* (PL die Schraubenschlüssel).

spare *adjective* Extra-; **we have a spare ticket** wir haben eine Karte übrig.
spare *verb* **to have time to spare** Zeit haben; **can you spare a moment?** hast du einen Moment Zeit?

spare part *noun* Ersatzteil *das* (PL die Ersatzteile).

spare room *noun* Gästezimmer *das* (PL die Gästezimmer).

spare time *noun* Freizeit *die*; **in my spare time** in meiner Freizeit.

spare wheel *noun* Reserverad *das* (PL die Reserveräder).

sparkling *adjective* **sparkling mineral water** Mineralwasser mit Kohlensäure; **sparkling wine** der Schaumwein.

sparrow *noun* Spatz *der* (PL die Spatzen).

speak *verb* **1** sprechen✧; **do you speak German?** sprechen Sie Deutsch?; **spoken German** gesprochenes Deutsch; **to speak to somebody about something** mit jemandem über etwas (ACC) sprechen; **she's speaking to Mike about it** sie spricht mit Mike darüber; **2 who's speaking?** (*on the phone*) wer ist am Apparat?

speaker *noun* **1** (*on a music system*) Lautsprecher *der* (PL die Lautsprecher); **2** (*at a public lecture*) Redner *der* (PL die Redner), Rednerin *die* (PL die Rednerinnen).

special *adjective* **1** besonderer/besondere/besonderes; **on special occasions** bei besonderen

Anlässen; **2 special offer** das Sonderangebot.

specialist noun Fachmann der (PL die Fachleute), Fachfrau die (PL die Fachfrauen).

specialize verb sich spezialisieren auf (+ ACC); **to specialize in I'm specializing in business studies** ich spezialisiere mich auf Wirtschaftswissenschaften.

specially adverb **1** besonders; **not specially** nicht besonders; **it's specially good for babies** es ist besonders gut für Babys; **2** (specifically) speziell; **I made this cake specially for you** ich habe diesen Kuchen speziell für dich gebacken.

species noun Art die (PL die Arten).

spectacles noun Brille die (PL die Brillen).

spectacular adjective spektakulär.

spectator noun Zuschauer der (PL die Zuschauer), Zuschauerin die (PL die Zuschauerinnen).

speech noun Rede die (PL die Reden); **to make a speech** eine Rede halten.

speechless adjective sprachlos; **to be speechless: she was speechless with rage** sie war sprachlos vor Wut.

speed noun **1** Geschwindigkeit die (PL die Geschwindigkeiten); **at top speed** mit Höchstgeschwindigkeit; **what speed was he doing?** wie schnell ist er gefahren?; **2** (gear)

Gang der (PL die Gänge); **a twelve-speed bike** ein Rad mit zwölf Gängen.

● **to speed up 1** beschleunigen (a car); **2** (of a person, car) schneller werden.

speeding noun zu schnelle Fahren das; **he was fined for speeding** er hat wegen zu schnellen Fahrens ein Bußgeld bekommen.

speed limit noun Geschwindigkeitsbeschränkung die.

spell noun **1** (of time) Weile die; **for a spell** eine Weile; **2 cold spell** die Kälteperiode; **sunny spells** sonnige Abschnitte.
spell verb **1** (in writing) schreiben◇; **how do you spell it?** wie schreibt man das?; **how do you spell your surname?** wie schreibt man Ihren Nachnamen?; **2** (out loud) buchstabieren.

spell checker noun Rechtschreibprogramm das (PL die Rechtschreibprogramme).

spelling noun Rechtschreibung die; **spelling mistake** der Rechtschreibfehler.

spend verb **1** ausgeben◇ SEP (money); **I've spent all my money** ich habe mein ganzes Geld ausgegeben; **2** verbringen◇ (time); **we spent three days in Munich** wir haben drei Tage in München verbracht; **she spends her time reading** sie verbringt ihre Zeit mit Lesen.

spice noun Gewürz das (PL die Gewürze).

spicy *adjective* scharf; **he doesn't like spicy food** er mag kein scharfes Essen.

spider *noun* Spinne *die* (PL *die* Spinnen).

spill *verb* verschütten; **I've spilled my wine on the carpet** ich habe meinen Wein auf dem Teppich verschüttet.

spinach *noun* Spinat *der*.

spine *noun* Wirbelsäule *die* (PL *die* Wirbelsäulen).

spire *noun* Kirchturm *der* (PL *die* Kirchtürme).

spirit *noun* **1** (*energy*) Energie *die*; **2 in the right spirit** mit der richtigen Einstellung.

spirits *noun* **1** (*alcohol*) Spirituosen (*plural*); **2 to be in good spirits** guter Laune sein.

spit *verb* **1** spucken; **2 to spit something out** etwas ausspucken SEP; **spit it out!** spuck es aus!

spite *noun* **1 in spite of** trotz (+ GEN); **we decided to go in spite of the rain** wir beschlossen trotz des Regens zu gehen; **2** (*nastiness*) Boshaftigkeit *die*; **to do something out of spite** etwas aus Boshaftigkeit tun.

spiteful *adjective* gehässig.

splash *noun* **1** (*noise*) Platsch *der*; **2 splash of colour** der Farbfleck. **splash** *verb* bespritzen.

splendid *adjective* herrlich.

splinter *noun* Splitter *der* (PL *die* Splitter).

split *verb* **1** (*with an axe or a knife*) spalten; **to split wood** Holz spalten; **2** (*come apart*) zerreißen◇ (PERF *sein*); **the lining has split** das Futter ist zerrissen; **3** (*divide up*) teilen; **they split the money between them** sie haben das Geld untereinander geteilt.

● **to split up 1** (*a group or crowd*) sich auflösen SEP; **2** (*a couple*) sich trennen; **she's split up with her husband** sie hat sich von ihrem Mann getrennt; **she's split up with Sam** sie hat mit Sam Schluss gemacht (*informal*).

spoil *verb* verderben◇; **it completely spoiled our evening** das hat uns den Abend völlig verdorben; **to spoil somebody's fun** jemandem den Spaß verderben.

spoiled *adjective* verwöhnt; **a spoiled child** ein verwöhntes Kind.

spoilsport *noun* Spielverderber *der* (PL *die* Spielverderber), Spielverderberin *die* (PL *die* Spielverderberinnen).

spoke *noun* (*of a wheel*) Speiche *die* (PL *die* Speichen).

spokesman *noun* Sprecher *der* (PL *die* Sprecher).

spokeswoman *noun* Sprecherin *die* (PL *die* Sprecherinnen).

sponge *noun* Schwamm *der* (PL *die* Schwämme).

sponge cake *noun* Rührkuchen *der* (PL *die* Rührkuchen).

sponsor *noun* Sponsor *der* (PL *die* Sponsoren). **sponsor** *verb* sponsern.

a
b
c
d
e
f
g
h
i
j
k
l
m
n
o
p
q
r
s
t
u
v
w
x
y
z

spooky *adjective* gruselig; **a spooky story** eine gruselige Geschichte.

spoon *noun* Löffel der (PL die Löffel); **a spoon of sugar** ein Löffel Zucker; **soup spoon** der Suppenlöffel; **teaspoon** der Teelöffel.

spoonful *noun* Löffel der (PL die Löffel).

sport *noun* **1** Sport der; **to be good at sport** gut im Sport sein; **my favourite sport** mein Lieblingssport; **2** (*in games*) **to be a good sport** ein guter Verlierer sein.

sports bag *noun* Sporttasche die (PL die Sporttaschen).

sports car *noun* Sportwagen der (PL die Sportwagen).

sports centre *noun* Sportzentrum das (PL die Sportzentren).

sports club *noun* Sportverein der (PL die Sportvereine).

sportsman *noun* Sportler der (PL die Sportler).

sportswear *noun* Sportbekleidung die.

sportswoman *noun* Sportlerin die (PL die Sportlerinnen).

sporty *adjective* sportlich; **she's very sporty** sie ist sehr sportlich.

spot *noun* **1** (*pattern in fabric*) Punkt der (PL die Punkte); **a red shirt with black spots** ein rotes Hemd mit schwarzen Punkten; **2** (*on your skin*) Pickel der (PL die Pickel); **I've got spots** ich habe Pickel; **to be covered in spots** völlig verpickelt sein; **3** (*stain*) Fleck der (PL die Flecke); **you've got a spot on your shirt** du hast einen Fleck auf dem Hemd; **4** (*spotlight*) Scheinwerfer der (PL die Scheinwerfer); (*in the home*) Spot der (PL die Spots); **5 on the spot** (*immediately*) auf der Stelle; **we'll do it for you on the spot** wir machen es Ihnen auf der Stelle; **6** (*at hand*) **on the spot** zur Stelle; **7** (*at the same place*) **on the spot** an Ort und Stelle.

spot *verb* entdecken; **he spotted his friend in the crowd** er entdeckte seinen Freund in der Menge.

spotlight *noun* **1** Scheinwerfer der (PL die Scheinwerfer); **2** (*in the home*) Spot der (PL die Spots).

spotty *adjective* (*pimply*) pickelig.

spouse *noun* **1** (*male*) Ehemann der (PL die Ehemänner); **2** (*female*) Ehefrau die (PL die Ehefrauen).

sprain *noun* Verstauchung die (PL die Verstauchungen).
sprain *verb* **to sprain your ankle** sich (DAT) den Fuß verstauchen.

spray *noun* (*spray can*) Spray das (PL die Sprays).
spray *verb* sprühen.

spread *noun* Brotaufstrich der; **cheese spread** der Streichkäse.
spread *verb* **1** (*of news or a disease*) sich verbreiten; **2** streichen◇ (*butter, jam, glue*).

spreadsheet *noun* (*on a computer*) Tabellenkalkulation die.

spring *noun* **1** (*the season*) Frühling der (PL die Frühlinge); **in the spring** im Frühling; **spring flowers** Frühlingsblumen; **2** (*made of metal*)

Feder *die* (PL *die* Federn); **3** (*providing water*) Quelle *die* (PL *die* Quellen).

springtime *noun* Frühjahr *das*; **in springtime** im Frühjahr.

spring water *noun* Quellwasser *das*.

sprint *noun* Sprint *der* (PL *die* Sprints).
sprint *verb* rennen⬦ (PERF *sein*).

sprinter *noun* Sprinter *der* (PL *die* Sprinter), Sprinterin *die* (PL *die* Sprinterinnen).

sprout *noun* (*Brussels sprout*) Rosenkohl *der*; **he likes sprouts** er mag Rosenkohl.

spy *noun* Spion *der* (PL *die* Spione), Spionin *die* (PL *die* Spioninnen).
spy *verb* **to spy on somebody** jemandem nachspionieren SEP; **he's spying on me** er spioniert mir nach.

squabble *verb* sich zanken.

square *noun* **1** (*shape*) Quadrat *das* (PL *die* Quadrate); **2** (*in a town or village*) Platz *der* (PL *die* Plätze); **the village square** der Dorfplatz.
square *adjective* quadratisch; **a square box** eine viereckige Schachtel; **three square metres** drei Quadratmeter; **the room is four metres square** das Zimmer ist vier mal vier Meter; ★**to go back to square one** noch einmal von vorn anfangen.

squash *noun* **1** (*drink*) Saft *der*; **orange squash** der Orangensaft; **2** (*sport*) Squash *das*.
squash *verb* zerquetschen.

squeak *verb* **1** (*door, hinge*) quietschen; **2** (*person, animal*) quieken.

squeeze *verb* **1** drücken; **to squeeze somebody's hand** jemandem die Hand drücken; **2** drücken (*toothpaste*).

squirrel *noun* Eichhörnchen *das* (PL *die* Eichhörnchen).

stab *verb* stechen⬦; **to stab somebody** (*kill*) jemanden erstechen⬦.

stable *noun* Stall *der* (PL *die* Ställe).
stable *adjective* stabil.

stack *noun* **1** Stapel *der* (PL *die* Stapel); **2 stacks of** ein Haufen; **she's got stacks of CDs** sie hat einen Haufen CDs.

stadium *noun* Stadion *das* (PL *die* Stadien).

staff *noun* **1** (*of a company*) Personal *das*; **2** (*in a school*) Lehrkräfte (*plural*).

stage *noun* **1** (*for a performance*) Bühne *die* (PL *die* Bühnen); **on stage** auf der Bühne; **2** (*phase*) Phase *die* (PL *die* Phasen); **at this stage of the project** in dieser Phase des Projekts; **at this stage it's hard to say** im Augenblick ist es schwer zu sagen.

staggered *adjective* (*amazed*) verblüfft.

stain *noun* Fleck *der* (PL *die* Flecke).
stain *verb* beflecken.

stainless steel *noun* Edelstahl *der*; **a stainless steel sink** ein Spülbecken aus Edelstahl.

a
b
c
d
e
f
g
h
i
j
k
l
m
n
o
p
q
r
s
t
u
v
w
x
y
z

stair *noun* **1** (*step*) Stufe die (PL die Stufen); **2 the stairs** die Treppe (*singular*); **I met her on the stairs** ich habe sie auf der Treppe getroffen.

staircase *noun* Treppe die (PL die Treppen).

stale *adjective* alt.

stalemate *noun* (*in chess*) Patt das (PL die Patts).

stall *noun* **1** (*at a market or fair*) Stand der (PL die Stände); **2** (*in a theatre*) **the stalls** das Parkett.

stammer *noun* **to have a stammer** stottern.

stamp *noun* Briefmarke die (PL die Briefmarken).
stamp *verb* **1** frankieren (*a letter*); **2 to stamp your foot** mit dem Fuß aufstampfen.

stamp album *noun* Briefmarkenalbum das (PL die Briefmarkenalben).

stamp collection *noun* Briefmarkensammlung die (PL die Briefmarkensammlungen).

stand[1] *verb* **1** stehen⬦; **several people were standing** viele Leute standen; **we stood outside the cinema** wir haben vor dem Kino gestanden; **2** (*bear*) aussstehen⬦ SEP; **I can't stand her** ich kann sie nicht ausstehen; **I can't stand waiting** ich kann es nicht ausstehen, wenn man warten muss; **3** (*keep going*) aushalten⬦ SEP; **I can't stand it any longer** ich halte es nicht mehr aus.
stand *noun* (*in a stadium*) Tribüne die (PL die Tribünen).

● **to stand for something** (*be short for*) bedeuten; **UN stands for United Nations** UN bedeutet United Nations.

● **stand up** aufstehen⬦ SEP (PERF *sein*); **everybody stood up** alle standen auf.

stand[2] *noun* **1** (*in a stadium*) Tribüne die (PL die Tribünen); **2** (*in fair*) Stand der (PL die Stände).

standard *noun* **1** (*level*) Niveau das; **of high standard** von hohem Niveau; **2 standard of living** der Lebensstandard; **3 she sets herself high standards** sie stellt hohe Ansprüche an sich selbst.
standard *adjective* normal; **the standard size** die Normalgröße.

Standard grades *noun plural* (*You can explain Standard grades as follows: Diese Prüfungen werden im Alter von ca 16 Jahren in sechs oder sieben Fächern abgelegt. Sie werden von 1 (beste Note) bis 7 (Kurs abgeschlossen) benotet. Viele Schüler machen nach Standard Grades weiter, und legen Highers und Advanced Highers ab*) SEE **Highers**.

staple *noun* Heftklammer die (PL die Heftklammern).
staple *verb* heften; **to staple the pages together** die Seiten zusammenheften.

stapler *noun* Hefter der (PL die Hefter).

star *noun* **1** (*in the sky*) Stern der (PL die Sterne); **2** (*person*) Star der (PL die Stars); **he's a film star** er ist ein Filmstar.
star *verb* **to star in a film** in einem

Film die Hauptrolle spielen; **starring** ... in der Hauptrolle ....

stare *verb* **1** starren; **what are you staring at?** was starrst du so?; **2 to stare at somebody** jemanden anstarren SEP; **he's staring at the wall** er starrt die Wand an.

start *noun* **1** Anfang *der*; **at the start** am Anfang; **at the start of the film** am Anfang des Films; **from the start** von Anfang an; **we knew from the start that it was dangerous** wir wussten von Anfang an, dass es gefährlich war; **2 to make a start on something** mit etwas (DAT) anfangen◇ SEP; **I've made a start on my homework** ich habe mit meinen Hausaufgaben angefangen; **3** (*of a race*) Start *der* (PL die Starts).

start *verb* **1** anfangen◇ SEP; **the film starts at eight** der Film fängt um acht an; **I've started the book** ich habe das Buch angefangen; **to start doing something** anfangen, etwas zu tun; **I've started learning Spanish** ich habe angefangen, Spanisch zu lernen; **to start crying** anfangen zu weinen; **2 to start a business** ein Geschäft gründen; **3 to start a car** ein Auto starten; **she started the car** sie hat das Auto gestartet; **4 the car won't start** das Auto springt nicht an.

starter *noun* (*first course*) Vorspeise *die* (PL die Vorspeisen).

starve *verb* verhungern; **I'm starving!** ich bin schon am Verhungern!

state *noun* **1** Zustand *der* (PL die Zustände); **the house is in a very bad state** das Haus ist in einem sehr schlechten Zustand; **2** (*country*) Staat *der* (PL die Staaten); **the state** der Staat; **3 the States** (*USA*) die Staaten; **they live in the States** sie leben in den Staaten.

state *verb* **1** erklären (*intention, reason*); **2** angeben◇ SEP (*an address, income, a reason*).

stately home *noun* herrschaftliche Anwesen *das* (PL die herrschaftlichen Anwesen).

statement *noun* Erklärung *die* (PL die Erklärungen).

station *noun* **1** Bahnhof *der* (PL die Bahnhöfe); **at the railway station** am Bahnhof; **bus station** der Busbahnhof; **2 police station** die Polizeiwache; **3 radio station** der Rundfunksender.

stationer's *noun* Schreibwarengeschäft *das* (PL die Schreibwarengeschäfte).

statistics *noun* (*subject*) Statistik *die*; **the statistics** (*figures*) die Statistik.

statue *noun* Statue *die* (PL die Statuen).

stay *noun* Aufenthalt *der* (PL die Aufenthalte); **our stay in Cologne** unser Aufenthalt in Köln; **enjoy your stay!** einen schönen Aufenthalt!

stay *verb* **1** bleiben◇ (PERF *sein*); **I'll stay here** ich bleibe hier; **how long are you staying?** wie lange bleibst du?; **2** (*spend the night*) **you can**

stay with us du kannst bei uns übernachten; **to stay the night with friends** bei Freunden übernachten; **3** (*be temporarily lodged*) wohnen; **where are you staying ?** wo wohnst du?; **I'm staying in a hotel** ich wohne im Hotel; **4** (*be on a visit*) sein✧ (PERF *sein*); **I'm going to stay with my sister this weekend** ich bin am Wochenende bei meiner Schwester; **I stayed in Munich for a couple of days** ich war ein paar Tage in München.

● **to stay in** zu Hause bleiben✧ (PERF *sein*); **I'm staying in tonight** heute Abend bleibe ich zu Hause.

steady *adjective* **1** fest; **a steady job** eine feste Stelle; **2** gleichmäßig; **at a steady pace** mit gleichmäßiger Geschwindigkeit; **3** (*hand, voice*) ruhig; **to hold something steady** etwas ruhig halten; **4** (*dependable*) zuverlässig.

steak *noun* Steak *das* (PL *die* Steaks); **steak and chips** Steak mit Pommes frites.

steal *verb* stehlen✧.

steam *noun* Dampf *der*.

steel *noun* Stahl *der*.

steep *adjective* steil; **a steep slope** ein steiler Hang.

steeple *noun* (*spire*) Kirchturm *der* (PL *die* Kirchtürme).

steering wheel *noun* Lenkrad *das* (PL *die* Lenkräder).

step *noun* **1** Schritt *der* (PL *die* Schritte); **to take a step forwards** einen Schritt nach vorn machen; **to take a step backwards** einen

Schritt zurück machen; **2** (*stair*) Stufe *die* (PL *die* Stufen).

● **to step back** zurücktreten✧ SEP (PERF *sein*).

● **to step forward** vortreten✧ SEP (PERF *sein*).

stepbrother *noun* Stiefbruder *der* (PL *die* Stiefbrüder).

stepdaughter *noun* Stieftochter *die* (PL *die* Stieftöchter).

stepfather *noun* Stiefvater *der* (PL *die* Stiefväter).

stepladder *noun* Trittleiter *die* (PL *die* Trittleitern).

stepmother *noun* Stiefmutter *die* (PL *die* Stiefmütter).

stepsister *noun* Stiefschwester *die* (PL *die* Stiefschwestern).

stepson *noun* Stiefsohn *der* (PL *die* Stiefsöhne).

stereo *noun* Stereoanlage *die* (PL *die* Stereoanlagen).

sterling *noun* Sterling *der*; **in sterling** in Pfund (Sterling).

stew *noun* Eintopf *der* (PL *die* Eintöpfe).

steward *noun* Steward *der* (PL *die* Stewards).

stewardess *noun* Stewardess *die* (PL *die* Stewardessen).

stick *noun* **1** Stock *der* (PL *die* Stöcke); **2 hockey stick** *der* Hockeyschläger.
stick *verb* **1** (*with glue*) kleben; **2** (*put*) tun✧; **stick them on my desk** tu sie auf meinen Schreibtisch.

sticker *noun* Aufkleber *der* (PL *die* Aufkleber).

sticky tape *noun* Klebestreifen der.

sticky *adjective* **1** klebrig; **I've got sticky hands** ich habe klebrige Hände; **2 a sticky label** ein Aufkleber.

stiff *adjective* **1** steif; **to feel stiff** steif sein, (*after exercise*) Muskelkater haben; **to have a stiff neck** einen steifen Hals haben; **2 to be bored stiff** sich zu Tode langweilen; **3 to be scared stiff** furchtbare Angst haben.

still *adjective* **1 sit still!** sitz still!; **keep still!** halt still!; **2 still mineral water** Mineralwasser ohne Kohlensäure.

still *adverb* **1** noch; **do you still live in London?** wohnst du noch in London?; **I've still not finished** ich bin immer noch nicht fertig; **he's still working** er arbeitet noch; **2** (*nevertheless*) trotzdem; **I told her not to, but she still did it** ich habe es ihr verboten, aber sie hat es trotzdem gemacht; **3 better still** noch besser.

sting *noun* Stich der (PL die Stiche).
sting *verb* stechen◊.

stink *noun* Gestank der.
stink *verb* stinken◊; **it stinks of fish in here** es stinkt hier nach Fisch.

stir *verb* rühren.

stitch *noun* **1** (*in sewing, surgical*) Stich der (PL die Stiche); **2** (*in knitting*) Masche die (PL die Maschen); **3** (*pain*) Seitenstechen das.

stock *noun* **1** (*in a shop*) Warenbestand der; **to have something in stock** etwas auf Lager haben; **to be out of stock** ausverkauft sein; **2** (*supply*) Vorrat der (PL die Vorräte); **I always have a stock of pencils** ich habe immer einen Bleistiftvorrat; **3** (*for cooking*) Brühe die; **chicken stock** die Hühnerbrühe.

stock *verb* (*in a shop*) führen; **they don't stock books** sie führen keine Bücher.

stock cube *noun* Brühwürfel der (PL die Brühwürfel).

stock exchange *noun* Börse die (PL die Börsen).

stocking *noun* Strumpf der (PL die Strümpfe).

stomach *noun* Magen der (PL die Mägen).

stomach-ache *noun* Magenschmerzen (*plural*); **to have stomach-ache** Magenschmerzen haben.

stone *noun* Stein der (PL die Steine); **stone wall** die Steinmauer.

stool *noun* Hocker der (PL die Hocker).

stop *noun* Haltestelle die (PL die Haltestellen); **bus stop** die Bushaltestelle.

stop *verb* **1** halten◊; **does the train stop in Stuttgart?** hält der Zug in Stuttgart?; **2 to stop somebody/something** jemanden/etwas anhalten◊ SEP; **the police stopped the car** die Polizei hielt den Wagen an; **3** (*cease*) aufhören SEP; **the noise has stopped** der Lärm hat

a
b
c
d
e
f
g
h
i
j
k
l
m
n
o
p
q
r
s
t
u
v
w
x
y
z

aufgehört; **to stop doing something** aufhören, etwas zu tun; **he's stopped smoking** er hat aufgehört zu rauchen; **she never stops asking questions** sie hört nie auf, Fragen zu stellen; **stop it!** hör auf!; **4 to stop somebody doing something** jemanden daran hindern, etwas zu tun; **I can't stop her ringing him** ich kann sie nicht daran hindern, ihn anzurufen; **5** (*prevent*) verhindern (*an accident, a crime*).

stopwatch noun Stoppuhr die (PL die Stoppuhren).

store noun (*shop*) Geschäft das (PL die Geschäfte); **department store** das Kaufhaus.

store verb **1** aufbewahren SEP, (*in a warehouse*) lagern; **2** (*on a computer*) speichern.

storey noun Stockwerk das (PL die Stockwerke); **a four-storey house** ein vierstöckiges Haus.

storm noun **1** Sturm der (PL die Stürme); **2** (*thunderstorm*) Gewitter das (PL die Gewitter).

stormy adjective stürmisch.

story noun Geschichte die (PL die Geschichten); **to tell a story** eine Geschichte erzählen.

stove noun (*cooker*) Herd der (PL die Herde).

straight adjective **1** gerade; **a straight line** eine gerade Linie; **2 to have straight hair** glatte Haare haben.
  straight adverb **1** (*in direction*) **straight ahead** geradeaus; **to go straight ahead** geradeaus gehen;

2 (*immediately, directly*) sofort; **straight away** sofort; **he went straight to the doctor's** er ging sofort zum Arzt.

straightforward adjective einfach.

strain noun Stress der; **the strain of the last few weeks** der Stress in den letzten Wochen; **to be a strain** anstrengend sein.
  strain verb **1** zerren (*a muscle*); **2** verrenken (*your arm, back*); **he's strained his back** er hat sich (DAT) den Rücken verrenkt.

strange adjective seltsam; **his strange behaviour** sein seltsames Verhalten.

stranger noun Fremde der/die (PL die Fremden).

strangle verb erwürgen.

strap noun **1** (*on a case, bag, camera*) Riemen der (PL die Riemen); **2** (*on a garment*) Träger der (PL die Träger); **3** (*of a watch*) Armband das (PL die Armbänder).

strapless adjective trägerlos.

straw noun **1** (*for drinking*) Strohhalm der (PL die Strohhalme); **2** (*the material*) Stroh das; **straw hat** der Strohhut.

strawberry noun Erdbeere die (PL die Erdbeeren); **strawberry jam** die Erdbeermarmelade.

stray adjective **a stray dog** ein streunender Hund.

stream noun Bach der (PL die Bäche).

street noun Straße die (PL die Straßen); **I met Simon in the street**

ich habe Simon auf der Straße getroffen.

streetlamp *noun* Straßenlaterne *die* (PL *die* Straßenlaternen).

street map *noun* Stadtplan *der* (PL *die* Stadtpläne).

streetwise *adjective* gewieft.

strength *noun* Kraft *die* (PL *die* Kräfte).

stress *noun* Stress *der*.
stress *verb* betonen; **to stress the importance of something** die Wichtigkeit von etwas betonen.

stretch *verb* **1** (*garment, shoes*) sich dehnen; **this jumper has stretched** der Pullover hat sich gedehnt; **2 to stretch your legs** sich (DAT) die Beine vertreten◈.

stretcher *noun* Trage *die* (PL *die* Tragen).

stretchy *adjective* elastisch.

strict *adjective* streng.

strike *noun* Streik *der* (PL *die* Streiks); **to go on strike** in den Streik treten◈ (PERF *sein*); **to be/go on strike** streiken.
strike *verb* **1** (*hit*) schlagen◈; **the clock struck six** die Uhr schlug sechs; **2** (*be/go on strike*) streiken.

striker *noun* **1** (*in football*) Stürmer *der* (PL *die* Stürmer), Stürmerin *die* (PL *die* Stürmerinnen); **2** (*person on strike*) Streikende *der/die* (PL *die* Streikenden).

string *noun* **1** (*for tying*) Schnur *die* (PL *die* Schnüre); **2** (*on a musical instrument*) Saite *die* (PL *die* Saiten).

strip *noun* Streifen *der* (PL *die* Streifen).
strip *verb* **1** (*undress*) sich ausziehen◈ SEP; **2** (*remove paint from*) abbeizen SEP.

strip cartoon *noun* Comicstrip *der* (PL *die* Comicstrips).

stripe *noun* Streifen *der* (PL *die* Streifen).

striped *adjective* gestreift.

stroke *noun* **1** (*style of swimming*) Stil *der* (PL *die* Stile); **2** (*medical*) Schlaganfall *der* (PL *die* Schlaganfälle); **to have a stroke** einen Schlaganfall bekommen; ★**a stroke of luck** ein Glücksfall; **to have a stroke of luck** Glück haben.
stroke *verb* streicheln.

strong *adjective* **1** (*person, drink, feeling*) stark; **2** (*sturdy*) stabil (*furniture*); **strong shoes** feste Schuhe.

strongly *adverb* **1** (*believe, oppose*) fest; **2** (*support*) nachdrücklich; **3** (*advise, recommend*) dringend; **4 she smelt strongly of garlic** sie hat stark nach Knoblauch gerochen.

struggle *noun* Kampf *der* (PL *die* Kämpfe); **the struggle for freedom** der Kampf für die Freiheit; **it's been a struggle** es war ein Kampf.
struggle *verb* **1** (*to obtain something*) kämpfen; **to struggle to do something** kämpfen, um etwas zu tun; **she struggled for a place** sie kämpfte um einen Platz; **2** (*physically, in order to escape or reach something*) sich wehren; **3** (*have difficulty in doing something*) sich abmühen SEP; **they**

a
b
c
d
e
f
g
h
i
j
k
l
m
n
o
p
q
r
s
t
u
v
w
x
y
z

a
b
c
d
e
f
g
h
i
j
k
l
m
n
o
p
q
r
s
t
u
v
w
x
y
z

are struggling to pay the rent sie mühen sich ab, ihre Miete zu zahlen; **he's struggling with his homework** er müht sich mit seinen Hausaufgaben ab.

stub noun **cigarette stub** die Kippe.
● **to stub out** ausdrücken SEP.

stubborn adjective stur.

stuck adjective **1** (jammed) **it's stuck** es klemmt; **the drawer's stuck** die Schublade klemmt; **2 to get stuck** (person) stecken bleiben✧ (in a lift, traffic jam, or place).

stud noun **1** (on clothes) Niete die (PL die Nieten); **2** (on a boot) Stollen der (PL die Stollen); **3** (earring) Ohrstecker der (PL die Ohrstecker).

student noun **1** (at college or university) Student der (PL die Studenten), Studentin die (PL die Studentinnen); **2** (at school) Schüler der (PL die Schüler), Schülerin die (PL die Schülerinnen).

studio noun **1** (film, TV) Studio das (PL die Studios); **2** (artist's) Atelier das (PL die Ateliers).

study verb **1** lernen; **he's busy studying for his exams** er lernt fleißig für seine Prüfung; **2** studieren; **she's studying medicine** sie studiert Medizin.

stuff noun (things, personal belongings) Zeug das (informal); **we can put all that stuff in the attic** wir können das ganze Zeug auf den Dachboden bringen; **you can leave your stuff at my house** du kannst dein Zeug bei mir lassen.
stuff verb **1** (shove) stopfen; **she stuffed some things into a**

suitcase sie hat ein paar Sachen in einen Koffer gestopft; **2** füllen (vegetables, turkey); **stuffed peppers** gefüllte Paprikaschoten.

stuffing noun (in cooking) Füllung die (PL die Füllungen).

stuffy adjective (airless) stickig.

stumble verb stolpern (PERF sein).

stunned adjective sprachlos.

stunning adjective toll (informal).

stunt noun (in a film) Stunt der (PL die Stunts).

stuntman noun Stuntman der (PL die Stuntmen).

stupid adjective dumm; **that was really stupid** das war wirklich dumm; **I did something stupid** ich habe etwas Blödes gemacht.

stutter noun **to have a stutter** stottern.
stutter verb stottern.

style noun **1** Stil der (PL die Stile); **style of living** der Lebensstil; **he has his own style** er hat seinen eigenen Stil; **2** (fashion) Mode die; **it's the latest style** das ist die neueste Mode.

subject noun **1** Thema das (PL die Themen); **the subject of my talk** das Thema meiner Rede; **2** (at school) Fach das (PL die Fächer); **my favourite subject is biology** mein Lieblingsfach ist Biologie.

submarine noun Unterseeboot das (PL die Unterseeboote), U-Boot das (PL die U-Boote).

subscription noun Abonnement das (PL die Abonnements); **to take**

out a subscription to a magazine eine Zeitschrift abonnieren.

subsidize *verb* subventionieren.

subsidy *noun* Subvention *die* (PL *die* Subventionen).

substance *noun* Substanz *die* (PL *die* Substanzen).

substitute *noun* (*in sport*) Ersatzspieler *der* (PL *die* Ersatzspieler), Ersatzspielerin *die* (PL *die* Ersatzspielerinnen). **substitute** *verb* ersetzen.

subtitled *adjective* mit Untertiteln.

subtitles *plural noun* Untertitel (*plural*).

subtle *adjective* subtil.

subtract *verb* abziehen◇ SEP.

suburb *noun* Vorort *der* (PL *die* Vororte); **a suburb of Edinburgh** ein Vorort von Edinburgh; **in the suburbs of London** in den Londoner Vororten.

suburban *adjective* Vorort-; **a suburban train** ein Vorortzug.

subway *noun* (*underpass*) Unterführung *die* (PL *die* Unterführungen).

succeed *verb* gelingen◇ (PERF *sein*); **we've succeeded in contacting her** es ist uns gelungen, sie zu erreichen.

success *noun* Erfolg *der* (PL *die* Erfolge); **a great success** ein großer Erfolg.

successful *adjective* **1** erfolgreich; **he's a successful writer** er ist ein erfolgreicher

Schriftsteller; **2 to be successful in doing something** etwas mit Erfolg tun.

successfully *adverb* mit Erfolg.

such *adjective, adverb* **1** so; **they're such nice people** das sind so nette Leute; **I've had such a busy day** ich habe so einen hektischen Tag gehabt; **it's such a long way** es ist so weit; **it's such a pity** es ist so schade; **2 such a lot of** (*followed by a singular noun*) so viel; **they've got such a lot of money** sie haben so viel Geld; **3 such a lot of** (*followed by a plural noun*) so viele; **she's got such a lot of problems** sie hat so viele Probleme; **4 such as** wie; **in big cities such as Glasgow** in großen Städten wie Glasgow; **5 there's no such thing** so etwas gibt es nicht.

suck *verb* lutschen; **to suck your thumb** am Daumen lutschen.

sudden *adjective* plötzlich; ★**all of a sudden** plötzlich.

suddenly *adverb* plötzlich; **he suddenly started to laugh** plötzlich hat er angefangen zu lachen; **suddenly the light went out** plötzlich ging das Licht aus.

suede *noun* Wildleder *das*; **suede jacket** *die* Wildlederjacke.

suffer *verb* leiden◇; **to suffer from asthma** an Asthma leiden.

sufficiently *adverb* genug.

sugar *noun* Zucker *der*; **do you take sugar?** nimmst du Zucker?

suggest *verb* vorschlagen◇ SEP; **he suggested I should speak to you**

about it er hat vorgeschlagen, dass ich mit dir darüber sprechen soll.

suggestion *noun* Vorschlag *der* (PL *die* Vorschläge); **to make a suggestion** einen Vorschlag machen.

suicide *noun* Selbstmord *der* (PL *die* Selbstmorde); **to commit suicide** Selbstmord begehen.

suit *noun* **1** (*man's*) Anzug *der* (PL *die* Anzüge); **2** (*woman's*) Kostüm *das* (PL *die* Kostüme).
suit *verb* **1** (*be convenient*) passen (+ DAT); **does Monday suit you?** passt Ihnen Montag?; **2** (*look good on*) stehen◇ (+ DAT); **hats suit her** ihr stehen Hüte.

suitable *adjective* **1** geeignet; **to be suitable for something** für etwas geeignet sein; **it's suitable for children** es ist für Kinder geeignet; **2** (*convenient*) passend; **at a suitable time** zur passenden Zeit; **Saturday is the most suitable day for me** Samstag passt mir am besten; **3** (*for a social occasion*) angemessen (*clothes*).

suitcase *noun* Koffer *der* (PL *die* Koffer).

sulk *verb* schmollen.

sum *noun* **1** Summe *die* (PL *die* Summen); **a sum of money** eine Geldsumme; **2** (*calculation*) Rechenaufgabe *die* (PL *die* Rechenaufgaben).

● **to sum up** zusammenfassen SEP.

summarize *verb* zusammenfassen SEP.

summary *noun* Zusammenfassung *die* (PL *die* Zusammenfassungen).

summer *noun* Sommer *der* (PL *die* Sommer); **in summer** im Sommer; **summer clothes** *die* Sommerkleidung; **the summer holidays** die Sommerferien.

summertime *noun* Sommer *der*; **in summertime** im Sommer.

summit *noun* Gipfel *der* (PL *die* Gipfel).

sun *noun* Sonne *die* (PL *die* Sonnen); **in the sun** in der Sonne.

sunbathe *verb* sich sonnen.

sunblock *noun* Sunblocker *der* (PL *die* Sunblocker).

sunburn *noun* Sonnenbrand *der* (PL *die* Sonnenbrände).

sunburned *adjective* **to get sunburned** einen Sonnenbrand bekommen.

Sunday *noun* **1** Sonntag *der* (PL *die* Sonntage); **on Sunday** am Sonntag; **I'm going to the cinema on Sunday** ich gehe (am) Sonntag ins Kino; **see you on Sunday!** bis Sonntag!; **every Sunday** jeden Sonntag; **last Sunday** vorigen Sonntag; **next Sunday** nächsten Sonntag; **2 on Sundays** sonntags; **the museum is closed on Sundays** das Museum ist sonntags geschlossen.

sunflower *noun* Sonnenblume *die* (PL *die* Sonnenblumen); **sunflower oil** *das* Sonnenblumenöl.

sunglasses *plural noun* Sonnenbrille die (PL die Sonnenbrillen).

sunlight *noun* Sonnenlicht das.

sunny *adjective* sonnig; **a sunny day** ein sonniger Tag; **sunny intervals** sonnige Abschnitte.

sunrise *noun* Sonnenaufgang der (PL die Sonnenaufgänge).

sunroof *noun* Schiebedach das (PL die Schiebedächer).

sunscreen *noun* Sonnenschutzcreme die (PL die Sonnenschutzcremes).

sunset *noun* Sonnenuntergang der (PL die Sonnenuntergänge).

sunshine *noun* Sonnenschein der.

sunstroke *noun* Sonnenstich der (PL die Sonnenstiche); **to get sunstroke** einen Sonnenstich bekommen.

suntan *noun* Bräune die; **to have a suntan** braun sein; **to get a suntan** braun werden.

suntan lotion *noun* Sonnenmilch die.

suntan oil *noun* Sonnenöl das.

super *adjective* klasse (*informal*) (*'klasse' never changes*); **we had a super time** es war wirklich klasse.

supermarket *noun* Supermarkt der (PL die Supermärkte).

supernatural *adjective* übernatürlich.

superstitious *adjective* abergläubisch.

supervise *verb* beaufsichtigen.

supervisor *noun* Aufseher der (PL die Aufseher), Aufseherin die (PL die Aufseherinnen).

supper *noun* Abendessen das (PL die Abendessen); **I had supper at Sandy's** ich war bei Sandy zum Abendessen.

supplement *noun* **1** (*to newspaper*) Beilage die (PL die Beilagen); **2** (*to fare*) Zuschlag der (PL die Zuschläge).

supplies *plural noun* Vorrat der (PL die Vorräte).

supply *noun* **1** (*stock*) Vorrat der (PL die Vorräte); **2 to be in short supply** knapp sein.
supply *verb* **1** stellen; **the school supplies the books** die Schule stellt die Bücher; **2** (*deliver*) liefern; **to supply somebody with something** jemandem etwas liefern.

supply teacher *noun* Aushilfslehrer der (PL die Aushilfslehrer), Aushilfslehrerin die (PL die Aushilfslehrerinnen).

support *noun* Unterstützung die; **in support** zur Unterstützung.
support *verb* **1** (*back up*) unterstützen; **her teachers have really supported her** die Lehrer haben sie sehr unterstützt; **to support somebody financially** jemanden finanziell unterstützen; **2 Will supports Chelsea** Will ist ein Chelsea-Fan; **what team do you support?** für welche Mannschaft bist du?; **3** (*keep, provide for*) ernähren; **to support a family** eine Familie ernähren.

supporter *noun* **1** Fan *der* (PL *die* Fans); **she's a Manchester United supporter** sie ist ein Manchester-United-Fan; **2** (*of a party or cause*) Anhänger *der* (PL *die* Anhänger), Anhängerin *die* (PL *die* Anhängerinnen).

suppose *verb* annehmen⋄ SEP; **I suppose she's forgotten** ich nehme an, sie hat es vergessen.

supposed *adjective* **to be supposed to do something** etwas tun sollen; **you were supposed to be here at six** du solltest um sechs hier sein.

sure *adjective* **1** sicher; **are you sure?** bist du sicher?; **are you sure you saw her?** bis du sicher, dass du sie gesehen hast?; **2 sure!** klar!

surely *adverb* doch sicherlich; **surely she hasn't forgotten** sie hat es doch sicherlich nicht vergessen.

surf *noun* Surfen *das*,
surf *verb* **to surf the Net/Web** im Internet surfen.

surface *noun* Oberfläche *die* (PL *die* Oberflächen).

surfboard *noun* Surfbrett *das* (PL *die* Surfbretter).

surfer *noun* (*on the sea and Internet*) Surfer *der* (PL *die* Surfer), Surferin *die* (PL *die* Surferinnen).

surfing *noun* Surfen *das*.

surgeon *noun* Chirurg *der* (PL *die* Chirurgen), Chirurgin *die* (PL *die* Chirurginnen).

surgery *noun* **1 to have surgery** operiert werden; **2** (*doctor's*) Praxis *die* (PL *die* Praxen); **the dentist's**

surgery die Zahnarztpraxis; **3** (*surgery hours*) Sprechstunde *die*.

surname *noun* Nachname *der* (PL *die* Nachnamen).

surprise *noun* Überraschung *die* (PL *die* Überraschungen); **what a surprise!** was für eine Überraschung!

surprised *adjective* überrascht; **I was surprised to see her** ich war überrascht, sie zu sehen.

surprising *adjective* überraschend.

surround *verb* umgeben; **surrounded by** umgeben von (+ DAT); **she was surrounded by friends** sie war von Freunden umgeben.

survey *noun* Umfrage *die* (PL *die* Umfragen).

survive *verb* überleben.

survivor *noun* Überlebende *der/die* (PL *die* Überlebenden).

suspect *noun* Verdächtige *der/die* (PL *die* Verdächtigen).
suspect *adjective* verdächtig.
suspect *verb* verdächtigen.

suspend *verb* **1 to be suspended** (*from school*) vom Unterricht ausgeschlossen werden; **2** (*from a team*) sperren; **to suspend a player for four weeks** einen Spieler für vier Wochen sperren.

suspense *noun* Spannung *die*.

suspicious *adjective*
1 misstrauisch; **to be suspicious of somebody** jemandem misstrauen;
2 (*suspicious looking*) verdächtig.

swallow *noun* (*bird*) Schwalbe *die* (PL *die* Schwalben).
swallow *verb* schlucken.

swan *noun* Schwan *der* (PL *die* Schwäne).

swap *verb* tauschen; **do you want to swap?** willst du tauschen?; **he swapped his bike for a computer** er hat sein Rad gegen einen Computer getauscht; **we swapped seats** wir tauschten die Plätze.

swear *verb* (*use bad language*) fluchen.

swearword *noun* Kraftausdruck *der* (PL *die* Kraftausdrücke).

sweat *noun* Schweiß *der*.
sweat *verb* schwitzen.

sweater *noun* Pullover *der* (PL *die* Pullover).

Swede *noun* Schwede *der* (PL *die* Schweden), Schwedin *die* (PL *die* Schwedinnen).

swede *noun* Kohlrübe *die* (PL *die* Kohlrüben).

Sweden *noun* Schweden *das*; **from Sweden** aus Schweden; **to Sweden** nach Schweden.

Swedish *noun* (*the language*) Schwedisch *das*.
Swedish *adjective* schwedisch; **he's Swedish** er ist Schwede; **she's Swedish** sie ist Schwedin.

sweep *verb* fegen.

sweet *noun* **1** Bonbon *der* (PL *die* Bonbons); **2** (*dessert*) Nachtisch *der* (PL *die* Nachtische).
sweet *adjective* **1** süß; **I try not to eat sweet things** ich versuche nichts Süßes zu essen; **she looks really sweet in that hat** mit dem Hut sieht sie richtig süß aus; **2** (*kind*) lieb; **she's a really sweet person** sie ist wirklich ein sehr lieber Mensch; **how sweet of him** wie lieb von ihm.

sweetcorn *noun* Mais *der*.

swell *verb* (*part of the body*) anschwellen⋄ SEP (PERF *sein*).

swelling *noun* Schwellung *die* (PL *die* Schwellungen).

swim *noun* **to go for a swim** schwimmen gehen⋄ (PERF *sein*).
swim *verb* schwimmen⋄ (PERF *sein*); **can he swim?** kann er schwimmen?; **to swim across a lake** an die gegenüberliegende Seite des Sees schwimmen.

swimmer *noun* Schwimmer *der* (PL *die* Schwimmer), Schwimmerin *die* (PL *die* Schwimmerinnen); **she's a strong swimmer** sie ist eine gute Schwimmerin.

swimming *noun* Schwimmen *das*; **to go swimming** schwimmen gehen⋄.

swimming cap *noun* Badekappe *die* (PL *die* Badekappen).

swimming costume *noun* Badeanzug *der* (PL *die* Badeanzüge).

swimming pool *noun* Schwimmbecken *das* (PL *die* Schwimmbecken).

swimming trunks *noun* Badehose *die* (PL *die* Badehosen).

swimsuit *noun* Badeanzug *der* (PL *die* Badeanzüge).

swindle *noun* Betrug *der* (PL *die* Betrüge); **what a swindle!** was für

a b c d e f g h i j k l m n o p q r **s** t u v w x y z

ein Betrug!
swindle *verb* betrügen.

swing *noun* Schaukel *die* (PL *die* Schaukeln).

Swiss *noun* (*person*) Schweizer *der* (PL *die* Schweizer), Schweizerin *die* (PL *die* Schweizerinnen); **the Swiss** die Schweizer.
Swiss *adjective* schweizerisch; **she is Swiss** sie ist Schweizerin.

switch *noun* (*for a light, radio, etc.*) Schalter *der* (PL *die* Schalter).
switch *verb* (*change*) wechseln; **to switch places** die Plätze wechseln.
• **to switch something off** etwas ausschalten SEP.
• **to switch something on** etwas anschalten SEP.

Switzerland *noun* die Schweiz; **from Switzerland** aus der Schweiz; **in Switzerland** in der Schweiz; **to Switzerland** in die Schweiz.

swollen *adjective* geschwollen.

swop *verb* SEE **swap**.

sword *noun* Schwert *das* (PL *die* Schwerter).

syllabus *noun* Lehrplan *der* (PL *die* Lehrpläne); **to be on the syllabus** auf dem Lehrplan stehen.

symbol *noun* Symbol *das* (PL *die* Symbole).

symbolic *adjective* symbolisch.

sympathetic *adjective* verständnisvoll.

sympathize *verb* **to sympathize with somebody** mit jemandem mitfühlen SEP; **I sympathize with you** ich kann mit Ihnen mitfühlen.

sympathy *noun* Mitleid *das*.

symphony *noun* Sinfonie *die* (PL *die* Sinfonien).

symptom *noun* Symptom *das* (PL *die* Symptome).

synagogue *noun* Synagoge *die* (PL *die* Synagogen).

synthesizer *noun* Synthesizer *der* (PL *die* Synthesizer).

synthetic *adjective* synthetisch.

syringe *noun* Spritze *die* (PL *die* Spritzen).

system *noun* System *das* (PL *die* Systeme).

Tt

table *noun* Tisch *der* (PL *die* Tische); **to lay the table** den Tisch decken; **to clear the table** den Tisch abräumen SEP.

tablecloth *noun* Tischdecke *die* (PL *die* Tischdecken).

tablespoon *noun* Esslöffel *der* (PL *die* Esslöffel); **a tablespoon of flour** ein Esslöffel Mehl.

table tennis *noun* Tischtennis *das*.

tablet *noun* Tablette *die* (PL *die* Tabletten).

tackle *verb* **1** (*in football or hockey*) angreifen◇ SEP; **2** angehen◇ SEP (PERF *sein*) (*a job or a problem*).

tact *noun* Takt *der*.

tactful *adjective* taktvoll; **that wasn't very tactful** das war nicht sehr taktvoll.

tadpole *noun* Kaulquappe *die* (PL *die* Kaulquappen).

tail *noun* **1** Schwanz *der* (PL *die* Schwänze); **2 'heads or tails?'** — **'tails'** 'Kopf oder Zahl?'— 'Zahl'.

take *verb* **1** nehmen⬧; **he took a sweet** er nahm einen Bonbon; **take my hand** nimm meine Hand; **I took the bus** ich habe den Bus genommen; **do you take sugar?** nimmst du Zucker?; **2** (*with time*) dauern; **it takes two hours** es dauert zwei Stunden; **3** (*react to*) aufnehmen⬧ SEP; **he took the news calmly** er hat die Nachricht gelassen aufgenommen; **4** (*take to a place*) bringen⬧; **I'm taking Jake to my parents** ich bringe Jake zu meinen Eltern; **I must take the car to the garage** ich muss das Auto in die Werkstatt bringen; **to take somebody home** jemanden nach Hause bringen; **5 to take something up(stairs)** etwas hinaufbringen⬧ SEP; **could you take the towels up?** könntest du die Handtücher heraufbringen?; **6 to take something down(stairs)** etwas hinunterbringen⬧ SEP; **Cheryl's taken the cups down** Cheryl hat die Tassen heruntergebracht; **7** (*carry with you*) mitnehmen⬧ SEP; **she's taken some of the files home** sie hat einige der Akten mit nach Hause genommen; **I'm taking my Walkman** ich nehme meinen Walkman mit; **I'll take him next time** nächstes Mal nehme ich ihn mit; **8** nehmen⬧ SEP (*a credit card or a cheque*); **do you take cheques?**

nehmen Sie Schecks?; **9** machen (*an exam, a holiday, or a photo*); **she's taking her driving test tomorrow** sie macht morgen ihre Fahrprüfung; **to take a holiday** Ferien machen; **10** (*need*) brauchen; **it takes a lot of courage** dazu braucht man viel Mut; **it takes me at least two hours to read it** ich brauche mindestens zwei Stunden, um es zu lesen; **11** haben⬧ (*clothes size*); **what size do you take?** welche Größe haben Sie?

● **to take something apart** etwas auseinander nehmen⬧.

● **to take something back** etwas zurückbringen⬧ SEP.

● **to take off 1** (*plane*) abfliegen⬧ SEP (PERF *sein*); **2** ausziehen⬧ SEP (*clothes, shoes*); **take your jacket off** zieh die Jacke aus; **to take your clothes off** sich ausziehen; **3** abziehen⬧ SEP (*money*); **he took five pounds off the price** er hat fünf Pfund vom Preis abgezogen.

● **to take out something** (*from a bag or pocket*) etwas herausnehmen⬧ SEP; **Eric took out his wallet** Eric nahm seine Brieftasche heraus.

● **to take somebody out** jemanden ausführen SEP; **to take somebody out for a meal** jemanden zum Essen in ein Restaurant einladen⬧ SEP.

takeaway *noun* **1** (*meal*) Essen zum Mitnehmen *das* (PL *die* Essen zum Mitnehmen); **an Indian takeaway** ein indisches Essen zum Mitnehmen; **2** (*where you buy it*) Restaurant mit Straßenverkauf *das* (PL *die* Restaurants mit Straßenverkauf).

a

take-off *noun* (*of a plane*) Abflug der (PL die Abflüge).

b

talent *noun* Talent das (PL die Talente); **to have a talent for painting** ein Talent zum Malen haben.

c

d

talented *adjective* talentiert; **he's really talented** er ist wirklich talentiert.

e

f

talk *noun* 1 (*a chat*) Gespräch das (PL die Gespräche); **we had a serious talk about it** wir hatten ein ernstes Gespräch darüber; 2 Vortrag der (PL die Vorträge); **she's giving a talk on Hungary** sie hält einen Vortrag über Ungarn.

g

h

i

j

k

talk *verb* 1 reden; **to talk to somebody** mit jemandem reden; **we talked about football** wir haben über Fußball geredet; **what's he talking about?** wovon redet er?; **we'll talk about it later** darüber reden wir später; **they're always talking** sie reden immer; 2 **to talk to somebody on the phone** mit jemandem telefonieren.

l

m

n

o

p

q

tall *adjective* 1 groß; **she's very tall** sie ist sehr groß; **I'm 1.7 metres tall** ich bin ein Meter siebzig groß; 2 hoch (*building or tree*).

r

s

tame *adjective* zahm.

t

tampon *noun* Tampon der (PL die Tampons).

u

v

tan *noun* Bräune die; **to have a tan** braun sein; **to get a tan** braun werden.

w

x

tank *noun* 1 (*for petrol or water*) Tank der (PL die Tanks); 2 (*for fish*) Aquarium das (PL die Aquarien);

y

z

3 (*military*) Panzer der (PL die Panzer).

tanker *noun* 1 (*on sea*) Tanker der (PL die Tanker); 2 (*on the road*) Tankwagen der (PL die Tankwagen).

tanned *adjective* braun.

tap *noun* Wasserhahn der (PL die Wasserhähne); **to turn on the tap** den Wasserhahn aufdrehen SEP; **to turn off the tap** den Wasserhahn zudrehen SEP; **the hot tap** der Warmwasserhahn.

tap *verb* klopfen; **to tap on the door** an die Tür klopfen.

tap-dancing *noun* Stepptanzen das.

tape *noun* 1 Kassette die (PL die Kassetten); **my tape of the Stones** meine Kassette von den Stones; **I've got it on tape** ich habe es auf Kassette; 2 **sticky tape** der Klebestreifen.

tape *verb* aufnehmen ◇ SEP; **I want to tape the film** ich will den Film aufnehmen.

tape measure *noun* Metermaß das (PL die Metermaße).

tape recorder *noun* Tonbandgerät das (PL die Tonbandgeräte).

tapestry *noun* Wandteppich der (PL die Wandteppiche).

target *noun* Ziel das (PL die Ziele).

tart *noun* Kuchen der (PL die Kuchen); **apple tart** der Apfelkuchen.

tartan *adjective* Schotten-; **a tartan skirt** ein Schottenrock.

task *noun* Aufgabe die (PL die Aufgaben).

taste *noun* **1** Geschmack der (PL die Geschmäcke); **a taste of onions** ein Zwiebelgeschmack; **she's got no taste** sie hat keinen Geschmack; **2 in bad taste** geschmacklos.

taste *verb* **1** schmecken; **the soup tastes horrible** die Suppe schmeckt furchtbar; **2 to taste of something** nach etwas (DAT) schmecken; **it tastes of garlic** es schmeckt nach Knoblauch; **3** (*try a little*) probieren; **do you want to taste?** möchtest du mal probieren?

tasty *adjective* schmackhaft.

tattoo *noun* Tätowierung die (PL die Tätowierungen); **he's got a tattoo on his arm** er hat eine Tätowierung am Arm.

Taurus *noun* Stier der; **Josephine's Taurus** Josephine ist (ein) Stier.

tax *noun* Steuer die (PL die Steuern) (*on goods, income*).

taxi *noun* Taxi das (PL die Taxis); **to go by taxi** mit dem Taxi fahren; **to take a taxi** ein Taxi nehmen.

taxi driver *noun* Taxifahrer der (PL die Taxifahrer), Taxifahrerin die (PL die Taxifahrerinnen).

taxi rank *noun* Taxistand der (PL die Taxistände).

tea *noun* **1** Tee der (PL die Tees); **a cup of tea** eine Tasse Tee; **to have tea** Tee trinken; **2** (*evening meal*) Abendessen das (PL die Abendessen).

teabag *noun* Teebeutel der (PL die Teebeutel).

teach *verb* **1** beibringen◊ SEP; **she's teaching me to drive** sie bringt mir das Autofahren bei; **2 to teach yourself something** sich (DAT) etwas beibringen◊ SEP; **I taught myself Italian** ich habe mir Italienisch beigebracht; **3 that'll teach you!** das wird dir eine Lehre sein!; **4** unterrichten; **her mum teaches maths** ihre Mutter unterrichtet Mathematik.

teacher *noun* Lehrer der (PL die Lehrer), Lehrerin die (PL die Lehrerinnen).

teaching *noun* Unterrichten das.

team *noun* Mannschaft die (PL die Mannschaften); **football team** die Fußballmannschaft.

teapot *noun* Teekanne die (PL die Teekannen).

tear[1] *noun* (*a rip*) Riss der (PL die Risse).

tear *verb* **1** zerreißen◊; **she tore up my letter** sie hat meinen Brief zerrissen; **2** reißen◊ (PERF *sein*); **the net has torn** das Netz ist gerissen; **be careful, it tears easily** sei vorsichtig, es reißt leicht.

tear[2] *noun* (*when you cry*) Träne die (PL die Tränen); **to be in tears** in Tränen aufgelöst sein; **to burst into tears** in Tränen ausbrechen.

tease *verb* **1** necken (*a person*); **2** quälen (*an animal*).

teaspoon *noun* Teelöffel der (PL die Teelöffel); **a teaspoon of vinegar** ein Teelöffel Essig.

teatime *noun* (*evening meal*) Abendessenszeit die; **it's teatime!** es gibt Abendessen!

tea towel *noun* Geschirrtuch das (PL die Geschirrtücher).

a b c d e f g h i j k l m n o p q r s t u v w x y z

technical *adjective* technisch.

technical college *noun*
Fachhochschule *die* (PL *die*
Fachhochschulen).

technician *noun* Techniker *der* (PL
die Techniker), Technikerin *die* (PL
die Technikerinnen).

technique *noun* Technik *die* (PL *die*
Techniken).

techno *noun* (*music*) Techno *der*.

technological *adjective*
technologisch.

technology *noun* **1** Technologie
die; **2 information technology** *die*
Informatik.

teddy bear *noun* Teddybär *der* (PL
die Teddybären).

teenage *adjective* **1** Teenage-;
2 they have a teenage son sie
haben einen Sohn im Teenageralter;
3 (*films, magazines, etc.*) für
Teenager; **a teenage magazine**
eine Jugendzeitschrift.

teenager *noun* Teenager *der* (PL *die*
Teenager); **a group of teenagers**
eine Gruppe von Teenagern.

teens *plural noun* **the teens** die
Teenagerjahre; **he's in his teens** er
ist ein Teenager.

tee-shirt *noun* T-Shirt *das* (PL *die* T-
Shirts).

telephone *noun* Telefon *das* (PL *die*
Telefone); **on the telephone** am
Telefon.

telephone *verb* anrufen◇ SEP; **I'll
telephone the bank** ich rufe die
Bank an.

telephone box *noun*
Telefonzelle *die* (PL *die* Telefonzellen).

telephone call *noun*
Telefongespräch *das* (PL *die*
Telefongespräche).

telephone directory *noun*
Telefonbuch *das* (PL *die*
Telefonbücher).

telephone number *noun*
Telefonnummer *die* (PL *die*
Telefonnummern).

telescope *noun* Fernrohr *das* (PL
die Fernrohre), Teleskop *das* (PL *die*
Teleskope).

televise *verb* im Fernsehen
übertragen◇; **they're televising the
match** sie übertragen das Spiel im
Fernsehen.

television *noun* **1** Fernsehen *das*; **I
saw it on television** ich habe es im
Fernsehen gesehen; **2 to watch
television** fernsehen◇ SEP; **I'm
watching television** ich sehe fern.

television programme *noun*
Fernsehsendung *die* (PL *die*
Fernsehsendungen).

tell *verb* **1** sagen; **to tell somebody
something** jemandem etwas sagen;
if she asks, tell her sag's ihr, wenn
sie fragt; **2 to tell somebody to do
something** jemandem sagen, er/sie
soll etwas tun; **he told me to do it
myself** er hat mir gesagt, ich soll es
selbst machen; **she told me not to
wait** sie sagte ich solle nicht warten;
3 (*explain*) **can you tell me how to
do it?** kannst du mir sagen, wie man
das macht?; **4** erzählen (*a story*); **tell
me about your holiday** erzähl mir
von deinen Ferien; **5** (*to see*) sehen◇;

you can tell it's old man sieht, dass
es alt ist; **I can't tell them apart** ich
kann sie nicht unterscheiden.

telly *noun* **1** (*set*) Fernseher *der* (PL
die Fernseher); **2 to watch telly**
fernsehen✧ SEP; **I saw her on telly**
ich habe sie im Fernsehen gesehen.

temp *noun* Aushilfskraft *die* (PL *die*
Aushilfskräfte).

temper *noun* **to lose your temper**
wütend werden.

temperature *noun* **1** Temperatur
die (PL *die* Temperaturen); **what is
the temperature?** wie viel Grad
sind es?; **2 to have a temperature**
Fieber haben.

temporary *adjective*
vorübergehend.

temptation *noun* Versuchung *die*
(PL *die* Versuchungen).

tempted *adjective* versucht; **I'm
really tempted to come** ich würde
am liebsten kommen.

tempting *adjective* verlockend.

ten *number* zehn; **Harry's ten** Harry
ist zehn.

tend *verb* **to tend to do something**
dazu neigen, etwas zu tun.

tender *adjective* **1** (*loving*) zärtlich;
2 (*painful*) empfindlich.

tennis *noun* Tennis *das*; **to play
tennis** Tennis spielen.

tennis ball *noun* Tennisball *der* (PL
die Tennisbälle).

tennis court *noun* Tennisplatz
der (PL *die* Tennisplätze).

tennis player *noun*
Tennisspieler *der* (PL *die*

Tennisspieler), Tennisspielerin *die*
(PL *die* Tennisspielerinnen).

tennis racket *noun*
Tennisschläger *der* (PL *die*
Tennisschläger).

tenor *noun* Tenor *der* (PL *die* Tenöre).

tenpin bowling *noun* Bowling
das.

tense *noun* Zeit *die*; **the present
tense** das Präsens; **in the future
tense** im Futur.
tense *adjective* gespannt.

tent *noun* Zelt *das* (PL *die* Zelte).

tenth *number* zehnter/zehnte/
zehntes; **on the tenth floor** im
zehnten Stock; **the tenth of April**
der zehnte April.

term *noun* (*in school*) Halbjahr *das*
(PL *die* Halbjahre), (*at university*)
Semester *das* (PL *die* Semester).

terminal *noun* **1** (*at an airport*)
Terminal *der* (PL *die* Terminals);
2 bus terminal *die* Endstation;
3 (*computer terminal*) Terminal *das*
(PL *die* Terminals).

terrace *noun* **1** (*outside a house*)
Terrasse *die* (PL *die* Terrassen);
2 (*row of houses*) Häuserreihe *die* (PL
die Häuserreihen); **3 the terraces**
(*at a stadium*) die Ränge (*plural*).

terrible *adjective* furchtbar.

terribly *adverb* **1** (*very*) sehr; **not
terribly clean** nicht sehr sauber;
2 (*badly*) furchtbar; **I played
terribly** ich habe furchtbar gespielt.

terrific *adjective* **1** irre (*informal*);
a terrific amount eine irre Menge;
2 terrific! super! (*informal*).

a b c d e f g h i j k l m n o p q r s t u v w x y z

a
b
c
d
e
f
g
h
i
j
k
l
m
n
o
p
q
r
s
t
u
v
w
x
y
z

terrified *adjective* verängstigt; **to be terrified** furchtbare Angst haben.

terrorism *noun* Terrorismus *der*.

terrorist *noun* Terrorist *der* (PL *die* Terroristen), Terroristin *die* (PL *die* Terroristinnen).

test *noun* **1** (*in school*) Klassenarbeit *die* (PL *die* Klassenarbeiten); **we've got a maths test tomorrow** wir schreiben morgen eine Mathearbeit; **2** (*medical check, trial*) Test *der* (PL *die* Tests); **eye test** *der* Sehtest; **blood test** *die* Blutprobe; **3 driving test** *die* Fahrprüfung; **she's taking her driving test on Friday** sie macht am Freitag ihre Fahrprüfung; **he passed his driving test** er hat seine Fahrprüfung bestanden.
test *verb* (*in school*) prüfen; **can you test me?** kannst du mich abfragen?

test tube *noun* Reagenzglas *das* (PL *die* Reagenzgläser).

text *noun* Text *der* (PL *die* Texte).

textbook *noun* Lehrbuch *das* (PL *die* Lehrbücher).

text message *noun* SMS *die* (PL *die* SMS).

Thames *noun* **the Thames** die Themse.

than *conjunction* als; **they have more money than we do** sie haben mehr Geld als wir; **more than forty** mehr als vierzig; **more than thirty years** mehr als dreißig Jahre.

thank *verb* **1 to thank somebody for something** sich bei jemandem für etwas (ACC) bedanken; **2 thank you** danke; **thank you for looking after the children** danke, dass du auf die Kinder aufgepasst hast.

thanks *plural noun* **1** Dank *der*; **thanks a lot!** vielen Dank!; **many thanks** vielen Dank; **2 no thanks** nein danke; **thanks for your letter** danke für deinen Brief; **3 thanks to** dank (+ DAT); **it was thanks to him that we made it** dank ihm haben wir es geschafft.

thank you *adverb* danke; **thank you very much for the cheque** herzlichen Dank für den Scheck; **no thank you** nein danke; **a thank-you letter** ein Dankbrief.

that *adjective* **1** dieser/diese/dieses; **that boy** dieser Junge; **that woman** diese Frau; **that house** dieses Haus; **2 that one** der da/die da/das da; **'which cake would you like?' – 'that one, please'** 'welchen Kuchen möchten Sie?' - 'den da, bitte'; **I like all the dresses but I'm going to buy that one** mir gefallen alle Kleider, aber ich kaufe das da.
that *adverb* so; **it's not that easy** es ist nicht so einfach.
that *pronoun* **1** das; **what's that?** was ist das?; **who's that?** wer ist das?; **where's that?** wo ist das?; **is that Mandy?** ist das Mandy?; **2** das; **did you see that?** hast du das gesehen?; **that's my bedroom** das ist mein Schlafzimmer; **3** (*in relative clauses*) der/die/das (*depending on the gender of the noun 'that' refers to*); **the train that's leaving now** der

Zug, der jetzt abfährt; **the flower that I picked** die Blume, die ich gepflückt habe; **the car that's red** das Auto, das rot ist.

that *conjunction* dass; **I knew that he was lying** ich wußte, dass er log.

the *definite article* **1** der/die/das (*the article changes according to the gender of the noun*); (*before a masculine noun*) **the dog** der Hund; (*before a feminine noun*) **the cat** die Katze; (*before a neuter noun*) **the car** das Auto; **2** (*before all plural nouns*) die; **the windows** die Fenster.

theatre *noun* Theater *das* (PL *die* Theater); **to go to the theatre** ins Theater gehen.

theft *noun* Diebstahl *der* (PL *die* Diebstähle).

their *adjective* ihr, (*plural*) ihre; **their son** ihr Sohn; **their daughter** ihre Tochter; **their car** ihr Auto; **their presents** ihre Geschenke.

theirs *pronoun* **1** ihrer (*when standing for a masculine noun*); **our garden's smaller than theirs** unser Garten ist kleiner als ihrer; **2** ihre (*when standing for a feminine noun*); **your flat is bigger than theirs** deine Wohnung ist größer als ihre; **3** ihrs (*when standing for a neuter noun*); **our car was cheaper than theirs** unser Auto war billiger als ihrs; **4** ihre (*when standing for a plural noun*); **our children are older than theirs** unsere Kinder sind älter als ihre; **5 the yellow car's theirs** das gelbe Auto gehört ihnen; **it's theirs** das gehört ihnen.

them *pronoun* **1** (*as a direct object in the accusative*) sie; **I know them** ich kenne sie; **I don't know them** ich kenne sie nicht; **2** (*after prepositions* + ACC) sie; **it's for them** das ist für sie; **3** (*as an indirect object or following a verb that takes the dative*) ihnen; **I told them a story** ich habe ihnen eine Geschichte erzählt; **4** (*to them*) ihnen; **I gave them my address** ich habe ihnen meine Adresse gegeben; **5** (*after prepositions* + DAT) ihnen; **I'll go with them** ich gehe mit ihnen mit; **6** (*in comparisons*) **he's older than them** er ist älter als sie.

theme *noun* Thema *das* (PL *die* Themen).

theme park *noun* Themenpark *der* (PL *die* Themenparks).

themselves *pronoun* **1** sich; **they enjoyed themselves** sie haben sich amüsiert; **2** (*for emphasis*) selbst; **the boys can do it themselves** die Jungen können es selbst machen.

then *adverb* **1** (*next*) dann; **I get up and then I make the bed** ich stehe auf und dann mache ich das Bett; **I went to the post office and then the bank** ich bin zur Post und dann auf die Bank gegangen; **2** (*at that time*) damals; **we were living in York then** wir haben damals in York gewohnt; **3** (*in that case*) dann; **then why worry?** warum machst du dir dann Sorgen?; **4 since then** seitdem; **5 from then on** von da an.

theory *noun* **1** Theorie *die* (PL *die* Theorien); **2 in theory** theoretisch.

a
b
c
d
e
f
g
h
i
j
k
l
m
n
o
p
q
r
s
t
u
v
w
x
y
z

there *adverb* **1** (*in a fixed location*) da; **up there** da oben; **down there** da unten; **in there** da drin; **stay there** bleib da; **2** *over there* da drüben; **she's over there with Mark** sie ist da drüben mit Mark; **3** (*with movement to a place*) dahin; **put it there** leg es dahin; **we're going there on Tuesday** wir fahren am Dienstag dahin; **4** (*further away*) dort; **I've seen photos of Oxford but I've never been there** ich habe Fotos von Oxford gesehen, aber ich war noch nie dort; **5 there is** (*there exists*) da ist, es ist; **there's a cat in the garden** da ist eine Katze im Garten; **there's enough bread** es ist genug Brot da; **no, there's not enough** nein, es ist nicht genug da; **6 there is** es gibt; **there's only one hospital in this town** in dieser Stadt gibt es nur ein Krankenhaus; **7 there are** da sind, es sind; **there were lots of people in town** es waren viele Leute in der Stadt; **8 there are** (*there exist*) es gibt; **there are lots of museums here** es gibt hier viele Museen; **9** (*when drawing attention*) da; **there they are!** da sind sie!; **there's the bus coming!** da kommt der Bus!

therefore *adverb* deshalb.

thermometer *noun* Thermometer *das* (PL *die* Thermometer).

these *adjective* diese; **these glasses** diese Gläser.
these *pronoun* die; **these are cheaper** die sind billiger.

they *pronoun* **1** sie; **'where are the knives?'** – **'they're in the drawer'** 'wo sind die Messer?' - 'sie sind in der Schublade'; **2** man; **they say** man sagt.

thick *adjective* dick; **a thick layer of butter** eine dicke Schicht Butter.

thief *noun* Dieb *der* (PL *die* Diebe), Diebin *die* (PL *die* Diebinnen).

thigh *noun* Oberschenkel *der* (PL *die* Oberschenkel).

thin *adjective* dünn.

thing *noun* **1** (*an object*) Ding *das* (PL *die* Dinge); **they have lots of nice things** sie haben viele schöne Dinge; **she told me some strange things** sie hat mir ein paar seltsame Dinge erzählt; **that thing next to the hammer** das Ding da neben dem Hammer; **2 things** (*belongings*) Sachen (*plural*); **you can leave your things in my room** du kannst deine Sachen in meinem Zimmer lassen; **3 the best thing to do is** ... am besten wäre es ...; **4** (*subject, affair*) Sache *die* (PL *die* Sachen); **the thing is, I've lost her address** die Sache ist die, ich habe ihre Adresse verloren; **5 how are things?** wie geht's?

think *verb* **1** (*believe*) glauben; **do you think they'll come?** glaubst du, sie kommen?; **no, I don't think so** nein, ich glaube nicht; **I think so** ich glaube schon; **I think he's already paid** ich glaube, er hat schon gezahlt; **2** denken✧; **I'm thinking about you** ich denke an dich; **what are you thinking about?** woran denkst du?; **3 what do you think of**

that? was halten Sie davon?; **I don't think much of her proposal** ich halte nicht viel von ihrem Vorschlag; **4 what do you think of my new jacket?** wie findest du meine neue Jacke?; **5** (*remember*) **to think to do something** daran denken, etwas zu tun; **he didn't think of locking the door** er hat nicht daran gedacht, die Tür abzuschließen; **6** (*to think carefully*) nachdenken✧ SEP; **he thought for a moment** er hat einen Moment lang nachgedacht; **think about it!** denk darüber nach!; **7 I've thought it over carefully** ich habe es mir genau überlegt; **8** (*imagine*) sich (DAT) vorstellen SEP; **just think, we'll soon be in Spain!** stell dir nur vor, bald sind wir in Spanien!; **I never thought it would be like this** so habe ich es nie vorgestellt, dass es so sein würde.

third *noun* Drittel *das* (PL *die* Drittel); **a third of the population** ein Drittel der Bevölkerung.
third *adjective* dritter/dritte/ drittes; **on the third floor** im dritten Stock; **on the third of March** am dritten März.

thirdly *adverb* drittens.

Third World *noun* Dritte Welt *die*.

thirst *noun* Durst *der*.

thirsty *adjective* durstig; **to be thirsty** Durst haben; **I'm thirsty** ich habe Durst; **we were all thirsty** wir hatten alle Durst.

thirteen *number* dreizehn; **Ahmed's thirteen** Ahmed ist dreizehn.

thirty *number* dreißig.

this *adjective* **1** dieser/diese/dieses; **this boy** dieser Junge; **this flower** diese Blume; **this car** dieses Auto; **at the end of this week** Ende dieser Woche; **2 this morning** heute Morgen; **this evening** heute Abend; **this afternoon** heute Nachmittag; **3 this one** der/die/das, (*with more emphasis*) dieser/diese/dieses; **if you need a pen you can have this one** wenn du einen Kugelschreiber brauchst, kannst du den haben; **I'll take this one** ich nehme diesen.
this *pronoun* **1** das; **can you hold this?** kannst du das festhalten?; **what's this?** was ist das?; **2 this is my sister Carla** (*in introductions*) das ist meine Schwester Carla; **3 this is Tracy speaking** (*on the phone*) hier spricht Tracy.

thistle *noun* Distel *die* (PL *die* Disteln).

thorn *noun* Dorn *der* (PL *die* Dornen).

those *adjective* diese; **those books** diese Bücher.
those *pronoun* die da; **if you need more knives you can take those** wenn du mehr Messer brauchst, kannst du die da nehmen.

though *conjunction* obwohl; **though it's cold** obwohl es kalt ist.
though *adverb* dennoch; **it was a good idea, though** es war dennoch eine gute Idee.

thought *noun* Gedanke *der* (PL *die* Gedanken).

thousand *number* **1** tausend; **a thousand** eintausend; **three thousand** dreitausend;

a
b
c
d
e
f
g
h
i
j
k
l
m
n
o
p
q
r
s
t
u
v
w
x
y
z

a
b
c
d
e
f
g
h
i
j
k
l
m
n
o
p
q
r
s
t
u
v
w
x
y
z

2 thousands of Tausende von; **there were thousands of tourists in Venice** Tausende von Touristen waren in Venedig.

thread *noun* Faden *der* (PL *die* Fäden).

thread *verb* einfädeln (*a needle*).

threat *noun* Drohung *die* (PL *die* Drohungen); **is that a threat?** soll das eine Drohung sein?

threaten *verb* drohen (+ DAT); **he threatened her** er hat ihr gedroht; **to threaten to do something** damit drohen, etwas zu tun.

three *number* drei; **Oskar's three** Oskar ist drei.

three-quarters *noun* drei Viertel *die*.

three-quarters *adverb* **three-quarters full** drei viertel voll.

thrilled *adjective* **to be thrilled** sich wahnsinnig freuen.

thriller *noun* Thriller *der* (PL *die* Thriller).

thrilling *adjective* spannend.

throat *noun* Hals *der* (PL *die* Hälse); **to have a sore throat** Halsschmerzen haben.

through *preposition* **1** (*across, via*) durch (+ ACC); **through the forest** durch den Wald; **the train goes through Leeds** der Zug fährt durch Leeds; **through the window** durch das Fenster; **2 to let somebody through** jemanden durchlassen⋄ SEP; **the police let us through** die Polizei ließ uns durch; **3 I know them through my cousin** ich kenne sie über meinen Vetter.

throw *verb* **1** werfen⋄; **I threw the letter in the bin** ich habe den Brief in den Mülleimer geworfen; **2 to throw something to somebody** jemandem etwas zuwerfen⋄ SEP; **throw me the ball** wirf mir den Ball zu; **to throw something at somebody** etwas nach jemandem werfen.

● **to throw something away** etwas wegwerfen⋄ SEP; **I'm throwing away the old newspapers** ich werfe die alten Zeitungen weg.

● **to throw somebody out** jemanden rauswerfen⋄ SEP.

● **to throw something out** etwas wegwerfen⋄ SEP (*rubbish*).

thumb *noun* Daumen *der* (PL *die* Daumen).

thump *verb* schlagen ⋄, auf (+ ACC); **he thumped the radio to see if it would work** er schlug auf das Radio, um zu sehen ob es dann funktionierte.

thunder *noun* Donner *der*; **peal of thunder** *der* Donnerschlag.

thunderstorm *noun* Gewitter *das* (PL *die* Gewitter).

thundery *adjective* gewittrig.

Thursday *noun* **1** Donnerstag *der* (PL *die* Donnerstage); **on Thursday** (am) Donnerstag; **I'm leaving on Thursday** ich fahre am Donnerstag ab; **see you on Thursday** bis Donnerstag; **every Thursday** jeden Donnerstag; **last Thursday** vorigen Donnerstag; **next Thursday** nächsten Donnerstag; **2 on Thursdays** donnerstags; **the museum is closed on Thursdays**

das Museum ist donnerstags geschlossen.

thyme *noun* Thymian *der*.

tick *verb* **1** (*clock, watch*) ticken; **2** (*on paper*) abhaken SEP.

ticket *noun* **1** (*for an exhibition, theatre, or cinema*) Karte *die* (PL *die* Karten); **two tickets for the concert** zwei Karten für das Konzert; **2** (*for the underground, a bus, or a train*) Fahrkarte *die* (PL *die* Fahrkarten); **a plane ticket** ein Flugschein, ein Ticket; **3** (*for left luggage, parking*) Zettel *der* (PL *die* Zettel); **4** (*for a lottery or raffle*) Los *das* (PL *die* Lose); **5 parking ticket** *der* Strafzettel.

ticket inspector *noun* Schaffner *der* (PL *die* Schaffner), Schaffnerin *die* (PL *die* Schaffnerinnen).

ticket office *noun* (*at a station*) Fahrkartenschalter *der* (PL *die* Fahrkartenschalter).

tickle *verb* kitzeln.

tide *noun* **1** (*high*) Flut *die* (Fluten); **at high tide** bei Flut; **2** (*low*) Ebbe *die* (PL *die* Ebben); **the tide is out** es ist Ebbe.

tidy *adjective* ordentlich.
tidy *verb* aufräumen SEP; **I'll tidy (up) the kitchen** ich räume die Küche auf.

tie *noun* **1** (*necktie*) Krawatte *die* (PL *die* Krawatten); **2** (*in a match*) Unentschieden *das*.
tie *verb* **1** binden◊; **to tie your shoelaces** sich (DAT) die Schnürsenkel binden; **2 to tie a**

knot in something einen Knoten in etwas (ACC) machen; **3** (*in a match*) **we tied two all** wir haben zwei zu zwei gespielt.

tiger *noun* Tiger *der* (PL *die* Tiger).

tight *adjective* (*close-fitting*) eng; **the skirt's a bit tight** der Rock ist etwas eng; **these shoes are too tight** diese Schuhe sind zu eng; **she was wearing tight jeans** sie hatte enge Jeans an.

tighten *verb* anziehen◊ SEP (*a screw, knot*); **he tightened his belt** er schnallte seinen Gürtel enger; **he tightened his grip** er griff fester zu.

tightly *adverb* fest.

tights *plural noun* Strumpfhose *die* (PL *die* Strumpfhosen); **a pair of purple tights** eine lila Strumpfhose.

tile *noun* **1** (*on a floor*) Fliese *die* (PL *die* Fliesen); **2** (*on a wall*) Kachel *die* (PL *die* Kacheln); **3** (*on a roof*) Ziegel *der* (PL *die* Ziegel).

till[1] *preposition, conjunction* **1** bis; **they're staying till Sunday** sie bleiben bis Sonntag; **till then** bis dann; **till now** bis jetzt; **2** (*when 'till' is followed by a noun it is usually translated as 'bis zu'* + DAT) **till the evening** bis zum Abend; **3 not till** erst; **she won't be back till ten** sie kommt erst um zehn zurück; **we won't know till Monday** wir werden erst am Montag Bescheid wissen.

till[2] *noun* Kasse *die* (PL *die* Kassen); **please pay at the till** bitte zahlen Sie an der Kasse.

time *noun* **1** (*on the clock*) Zeit *die*; **it's time for breakfast** es ist Zeit

605

a b c d e f g h i j k l m n o p q r s t u v w x y z

zum Frühstücken; **2 what time is it?** wie viel Uhr ist es?; **at what time does it start?** um wie viel Uhr fängt es an?; **ten o'clock German time** zehn Uhr, deutsche Zeit; **3 on time** pünktlich; **4** (*an amount of time*) Zeit *die*; **we've got lots of time** wir haben viel Zeit; **I haven't got time now** ich habe jetzt keine Zeit; **there's no time left to do it** dafür bleibt keine Zeit mehr; **from time to time** von Zeit zu Zeit; **for a long time** lange; **5** (*moment*) Moment *der* (PL *die* Momente); **this isn't a good time to discuss it** das ist kein guter Moment, um darüber zu sprechen; **at the right time** im richtigen Moment; **for the time being** im Moment; **any time now** jeden Moment; **6 at times** manchmal; **7** (*in a series*) Mal *das* (PL *die* Male); **eight times** achtmal; **for the first time** zum ersten Mal; **the first time I saw you** das erste Mal, als ich dich sah; **three times a year** dreimal jährlich; **8 three times two is six** drei mal zwei ist sechs; **9 to have a good time** sich amüsieren; **we had a really good time** wir haben uns richtig gut amüsiert; **have a good time!** viel Vergnügen!

timetable *noun* **1** (*in school*) Stundenplan *der* (PL *die* Stundenpläne); **2** (*for trains or buses*) Fahrplan *der* (PL *die* Fahrpläne); **bus timetable** *der* Busfahrplan.

tin *noun* Dose *die* (PL *die* Dosen); **a tin of tomatoes** eine Dose Tomaten.

tinned *adjective* in Dosen; **tinned peas** Erbsen in Dosen.

tin opener *noun* Dosenöffner *der* (PL *die* Dosenöffner).

tiny *adjective* winzig.

tip *noun* **1** (*end*) Spitze *die* (PL *die* Spitzen); **2** (*money*) Trinkgeld *das*; **3** (*useful hint*) Tipp *der* (PL *die* Tipps) (*informal*).
tip *verb* (*give money*) ein Trinkgeld geben◇ (+ DAT); **we tipped the waiter** wir haben dem Kellner ein Trinkgeld gegeben.

tiptoe *noun* **on tiptoe** auf Zehenspitzen.

tired *adjective* **1** müde; **I'm tired** ich bin müde; **you look tired** du siehst müde aus; **2 to be tired of something** etwas satt haben; **I'm tired of London** ich habe London satt; **I'm tired of watching TV every evening** ich habe es satt, jeden Abend fernzusehen.

tiring *adjective* ermüdend.

tissue *noun* (*a paper hanky*) Papiertaschentuch *das* (PL *die* Papiertaschentücher).

tissue paper *noun* Seidenpapier *das*.

title *noun* Titel *der* (PL *die* Titel).

to *preposition* **1** (*to a country or town*) nach; **to go to London** nach London fahren; **the motorway to Italy** die Autobahn nach Italien; **they're going to Switzerland** sie fahren in die Schweiz; **2** (*to the cinema, theatre, school, office*) in (+ ACC); **I'm going to school** ich gehe in die Schule; **she's gone to the office** sie ist ins Büro gegangen; **we want to go to town** wir wollen in die Stadt gehen; **3** (*to a wedding, party, university, the toilet*) auf (+ ACC); **she's gone to the toilet** sie ist auf die Toilette gegangen; **4** (*addressed or attached to*) an (+ ACC); **a letter to my parents** ein Brief an meine Eltern; **5 give the book to her** gib ihr das Buch; **he said to me that** ... er hat mir gesagt, dass ...; **6** (*to somebody's house, a particular place, or person*) zu (+ DAT); **I went round to Paul's house** ich bin zu Paul nach Hause gegangen; **we're going to the Browns' for supper** wir gehen zu Browns zum Abendessen; **I'm going to the dentist tomorrow** morgen gehe ich zum Zahnarzt; **7** (*talking about the time*) **it's ten to nine** es ist zehn vor neun; **from eight to ten** von acht bis zehn; **from Monday to Friday** von Montag bis Freitag; **8** (*in order to*) um ... zu (+ *infinitive*); **he gave me some money to buy a sandwich** er hat mir Geld gegeben, um ein Sandwich zu kaufen; **9** (*in verbal phrases with the infinitive*) zu; **I have nothing to do** ich habe nichts zu tun; **have you got something to eat?** hast du etwas zu essen?

toast *noun* **1** Toast der (PL die Toasts); **two slices of toast** zwei Scheiben Toast; **2** (*to your health*) Toast der (PL die Toasts); **to drink a toast to somebody** auf jemanden trinken.

toaster *noun* Toaster der (PL die Toaster).

tobacco *noun* Tabak der.

tobacconist's *noun* Tabakladen der (PL die Tabakläden).

today *adverb* heute; **today's her birthday** sie hat heute Geburtstag.

toe *noun* Zeh der (PL die Zehen).

toffee *noun* Karamell der.

together *adverb* **1** zusammen; **we did it together** wir haben es zusammen gemacht; **2** (*at the same time*) gleichzeitig; **they all left together** sie sind alle gleichzeitig weggegangen.

toilet *noun* Toilette die (PL die Toiletten); **she's gone to the toilet** sie ist auf die Toilette gegangen.

toilet paper *noun* Toilettenpapier das.

toilet roll *noun* Rolle Toilettenpapier die (PL die Rollen Toilettenpapier).

token *noun* **1** (*for a machine or game*) Marke die (PL die Marken); **2** (*voucher*) Gutschein der (PL die Gutscheine); **gift token** der Geschenkgutschein.

tolerant *adjective* tolerant.

toll *noun* **1** (*payment*) Gebühr die (PL die Gebühren); **2** (*number*) Zahl die; **the death toll has risen to 25** die Zahl der Todesopfer ist jetzt bei 25.

tomato *noun* Tomate die (PL die Tomaten); **tomato salad** der Tomatensalat; **tomato sauce** die Tomatensoße.

tomorrow *adverb* **1** morgen; **I'll do it tomorrow** ich mache es morgen; **tomorrow afternoon** morgen Nachmittag; **tomorrow morning** morgen früh; **tomorrow**

a
b
c
d
e
f
g
h
i
j
k
l
m
n
o
p
q
r
s
t
u
v
w
x
y
z

night morgen Abend; **2 the day after tomorrow** übermorgen.

tone *noun* (*on an answerphone, of a voice, or letter*) Ton *der* (PL *die* Töne).

tongue *noun* Zunge *die* (PL *die* Zungen); **to stick your tongue out at somebody** jemandem die Zunge herausstrecken; ★ **it's on the tip of my tongue** es liegt mir auf der Zunge.

tonic *noun* Tonic *das* (PL *die* Tonics); **a gin and tonic** ein Gin Tonic.

tonight *adverb* **1** (*this evening*) heute Abend; **I'm going out with my friends tonight** ich gehe heute Abend mit meinen Freunden weg; **2** (*after bedtime*) heute Nacht.

tonsillitis *noun* Mandelentzündung *die*; **Ahlem's got tonsillitis** Ahlem hat eine Mandelentzündung.

too *adverb* **1** zu; **it's too expensive** es ist zu teuer; **too often** zu oft; **2 too much** zu viel; **I've spent too much** ich habe zu viel ausgegeben; **too many** zu viele; **3** (*as well*) auch; **Karen's coming too** Karen kommt auch; **me too!** ich auch!

tool *noun* Werkzeug *das* (PL *die* Werkzeuge).

tool box *noun* Werkzeugkasten *der* (PL *die* Werkzeugkästen).

tool kit *noun* Werkzeug *das*.

tooth *noun* Zahn *der* (PL *die* Zähne); **to brush your teeth** sich (DAT) die Zähne putzen.

toothache *noun* Zahnschmerzen (*plural*).

toothbrush *noun* Zahnbürste *die* (PL *die* Zahnbürsten).

toothpaste *noun* Zahnpasta *die* (PL *die* Zahnpasten).

top *noun* **1** (*highest part*) Spitze *die* (PL *die* Spitzen); (*of a tree*); **2 at the top of** oben auf (+ DAT); **at the top of the ladder** oben auf der Leiter; **it's on top of the chest of drawers** es liegt oben auf der Kommode; **3 at the top** oben; **there are four rooms at the top** oben sind vier Zimmer; **from top to bottom** von oben bis unten; **4** (*of a container, jar, or box*) Deckel *der* (PL *die* Deckel); **5** (*of a mountain*) Gipfel *der* (PL *die* Gipfel); **6** (*a lid*) Kappe *die* (PL *die* Kappen) (*of a pen*), Verschluss *der* (PL *die* Verschlüsse) (*of a bottle*); **7** (*of a garment*) Oberteil *das* (PL *die* Oberteile); **8** (*in sport*) **the top of the table** die Tabellenspitze; ★ **and on top of all that** obendrein; ★ **it was a bit over the top** es war leicht übertrieben.

top *adjective* oberster/oberste/oberstes (*step or floor*); **on the top floor** im obersten Stockwerk.

topic *noun* Thema *das* (PL *die* Themen).

topping *noun* Belag *der* (PL *die* Beläge); **which topping would you like?** welchen Belag hättest du gerne?

torch *noun* Taschenlampe *die* (PL *die* Taschenlampen).

torn *adjective* zerrissen.

tortoise *noun* Schildkröte *die* (PL *die* Schildkröten).

torture *noun* **1** Folter die (PL die Foltern); **2 the exam was torture** die Prüfung war die Hölle (*informal*).
torture *verb* quälen.

Tory *noun* Konservative der/die (PL die Konservativen).

total *noun* **1** (*number*) Gesamtzahl die (PL die Gesamtzahlen); **2** (*result of addition*) Summe die (PL die Summen).
total *adjective* gesamt.

totally *adverb* völlig.

touch *noun* **1** (*contact*) **to get in touch with somebody** sich mit jemandem in Verbindung setzen; **to stay in touch with somebody** mit jemandem Kontakt halten; **2 we've lost touch** wir haben keinen Kontakt mehr; **I've lost touch with Peter** ich habe keinen Kontakt mehr zu Peter; **3** (*a little bit*) **a touch of salt** eine Spur Salz; **it was a touch embarrassing** es war ein bisschen peinlich.
touch *verb* **1** berühren; **2** (*get hold of*) anfassen SEP; **don't touch that** fass das nicht an.

touched *adjective* gerührt.

touching *adjective* rührend.

tough *adjective* **1** hart; **she's had a tough time** sie hat eine harte Zeit hinter sich; **a tough guy** ein harter Kerl; **2** zäh; **the meat's tough** das Fleisch ist zäh; **3** fest (*material, shoes, etc.*); **4 tough luck!** Pech!; **tough, you're too late** so'n Pech, du bist zu spät dran.

tour *noun* **1** Besichtigung die (PL die Besichtigungen); **a tour of the city** eine Stadtbesichtigung; **we did a tour of the castle** wir haben das Schloss besichtigt; **2 guided tour** die Führung; **3 package tour** die Pauschalreise; **4** (*by a band or theatre group*) Tournee die (PL die Tournees); **to go on tour** auf Tournee gehen.
tour *verb* (*performer*) auf Tournee sein◇ (PERF *sein*); **they're touring America** sie sind auf Tournee in Amerika.

tour guide *noun* Reiseleiter der (PL die Reiseleiter), Reiseleiterin die (PL die Reiseleiterinnen).

tourism *noun* Tourismus der.

tourist *noun* Tourist der (PL die Touristen), Touristin die (PL die Touristinnen).

tourist information office *noun* Fremdenverkehrsbüro das (PL die Fremdenverkehrsbüros).

tournament *noun* Turnier das (PL die Turniere); **tennis tournament** das Tennisturnier.

tow *verb* **to be towed away** abgeschlept werden◇ (PERF *sein*).

towards *preposition* zu (+ DAT); **she went off towards the lake** sie ist zum See gegangen; **to come towards somebody** auf jemanden zukommen◇ SEP (PERF *sein*).

towel *noun* Handtuch das (PL die Handtücher).

tower *noun* Turm der (PL die Türme).

tower block *noun* Hochhaus das (PL die Hochhäuser).

town *noun* Stadt die (PL die Städte); **to go into town** in die Stadt gehen.

town centre *noun* Stadtmitte die (PL die Stadtmitten).

town hall *noun* Rathaus das (PL die Rathäuser).

toy *noun* Spielzeug das.

toyshop *noun* Spielzeuggeschäft das (PL die Spielzeuggeschäfte).

trace *noun* Spur die (PL die Spuren); **there was no trace of the thieves** es fehlte jede Spur von den Dieben. **trace** *verb* 1 (*find*) finden⬦; 2 (*follow*) verfolgen; 3 (*copy*) durchpausen SEP.

tracing paper *noun* Pauspapier das.

track *noun* 1 (*for sport*) Bahn die (PL die Bahnen); **cycling track** die Radrennbahn; **racing track** (*for cars*) die Rennstrecke; 2 (*a path*) Weg der (PL die Wege); 3 (*song*) Stück das (PL die Stücke); **this is my favourite track** das ist mein Lieblingsstück.

track suit *noun* Trainingsanzug der (PL die Trainingsanzüge).

tractor *noun* Traktor der (PL die Traktoren).

trade *noun* 1 (*a profession*) Gewerbe das; 2 (*skill, craft*) Handwerk das; **to learn a trade** ein Handwerk erlernen.

trade union *noun* Gewerkschaft die (PL die Gewerkschaften).

tradition *noun* Tradition die (PL die Traditionen).

traditional *adjective* traditionell.

traffic *noun* Verkehr der.

traffic island *noun* Verkehrsinsel die (PL die Verkehrsinseln).

traffic jam *noun* Stau der (PL die Staus).

traffic lights *plural noun* Ampel die (PL die Ampeln).

traffic warden *noun* Verkehrsüberwacher der (PL die Verkehrsüberwacher), Politesse die (PL die Politessen).

tragedy *noun* Tragödie die (PL die Tragödien).

tragic *adjective* tragisch.

trail *noun* (*a path*) Pfad der (PL die Pfade); **a nature trail** ein Naturlehrpfad.

trailer *noun* Anhänger der (PL die Anhänger).

train *noun* Zug der (PL die Züge); **he's coming by train** er kommt mit dem Zug; **I met her on the train** ich habe sie im Zug getroffen; **the train for York** der Zug nach York. **train** *verb* 1 (*for a career*) ausbilden SEP; 2 **she's training to be a nurse** sie macht eine Ausbidung zur Krankenschwester; 3 (*in sport*) trainieren; **the team trains on Wednesdays** die Mannschaft trainiert mittwochs.

trainee *noun* Auszubildende der/die (PL die Auszubildenden).

trainer *noun* 1 (*of an athlete or horse*) Trainer der (PL die Trainer), Trainerin die (PL die Trainerinnen); 2 **trainers** Turnschuhe (*plural*).

training *noun* **1** (*for a career*) Ausbildung *die*; **2** (*for sport*) Training *das*.

train ticket *noun* Zugfahrkarte *die* (PL *die* Zugfahrkarten).

train timetable *noun* Bahnfahrplan *der* (PL *die* Bahnfahrpläne).

tram *noun* Straßenbahn *die* (PL *die* Straßenbahnen).

tramp *noun* Landstreicher *der* (PL *die* Landstreicher), Landstreicherin *die* (PL *die* Landstreicherinnen).

transfer *noun* Abziehbild *das* (PL *die* Abziehbilder).

transform *verb* verwandeln.

transistor *noun* Transistor *der* (PL *die* Transistoren).

translate *verb* übersetzen; **to translate something into German** etwas ins Deutsche übersetzen.

translation *noun* Übersetzung *die* (PL *die* Übersetzungen).

translator *noun* Übersetzer *der* (PL *die* Übersetzer), Übersetzerin *die* (PL *die* Übersetzerinnen).

transparent *adjective* durchsichtig.

transplant *noun* Transplantation *die* (PL *die* Transplantationen).

transport *noun* Transport *der* (PL *die* Transporte); **the transport of goods** der Warentransport; **public transport** öffentliche Verkehrsmittel (*plural*).

trap *noun* Falle *die* (PL *die* Fallen).

travel *noun* Reisen *das*; **foreign travel** Auslandsreisen (*plural*). **travel** *verb* reisen (PERF *sein*).

travel agency *noun* Reisebüro *das* (PL *die* Reisebüros).

travel agent's *noun* Reisebüro *das* (PL *die* Reisebüros).

traveller *noun* **1** Reisende *der/die* (PL *die* Reisenden); **2** (*gypsy*) Zigeuner *der* (PL *die* Zigeuner), Zigeunerin *die* (PL *die* Zigeunerinnen).

traveller's cheque *noun* Reisescheck *der* (PL *die* Reiseschecks).

travel-sick *adjective* reisekrank; **I get travel-sick** ich werde reisekrank.

tray *noun* Tablett *das* (PL *die* Tabletts).

tread *verb* **to tread on something** auf etwas (ACC) treten✧ (PERF *sein*); **she trod on my foot** sie ist mir auf den Fuß getreten.

treasure *noun* Schatz *der* (PL *die* Schätze).

treat *noun* **1 I took them to the circus as a treat** ich habe ihnen eine besondere Freude gemacht und sie in den Zirkus eingeladen; **2** (*food*) Leckerbissen *der* (PL *die* Leckerbissen). **treat** *verb* **1** behandeln; **he treats his dog well** er behandelt seinen Hund gut; **the doctor who treated you** der Arzt, der dich behandelt hat; **2 to treat somebody to something** jemandem etwas

a
b
c
d
e
f
g
h
i
j
k
l
m
n
o
p
q
r
s
t
u
v
w
x
y
z

a
b
c
d
e
f
g
h
i
j
k
l
m
n
o
p
q
r
s
t
u
v
w
x
y
z

spendieren; **I'll treat you to an ice cream** ich spendiere euch ein Eis.

treatment *noun* Behandlung *die* (PL *die* Behandlungen).

tree *noun* Baum *der* (PL *die* Bäume).

tremble *verb* zittern.

trend *noun* **1** (*a fashion*) Trend *der* (PL *die* Trends); **2** (*a tendency*) Tendenz *die* (PL *die* Tendenzen).

trendy *adjective* modern.

trial *noun* (*in court*) Prozess *der* (PL *die* Prozesse).

triangle *noun* Dreieck *das* (PL *die* Dreiecke).

trick *noun* **1** (*a joke*) Streich *der* (PL *die* Streiche); **to play a trick on somebody** jemandem einen Streich spielen; **2** (*a knack or by a conjuror*) Trick *der* (PL *die* Tricks); **there must be a trick to it** da muss ein Trick dabei sein.

trick *verb* hereinlegen SEP; **he tricked me!** er hat mich hereingelegt!

tricky *adjective* verzwickt; **it's a tricky situation** das ist eine verzwickte Situation.

tricycle *noun* Dreirad *das* (PL *die* Dreiräder).

trim *verb* schneiden✧ (*hair*).

trip *noun* **1** Reise *die* (PL *die* Reisen); **a trip to Florida** eine Reise nach Florida; **he's going on a business trip** er macht eine Geschäftsreise; **2** (*a day out*) Ausflug *der* (PL *die* Ausflüge); **a day trip to France** ein Tagesausflug nach Frankreich.

trip *verb* (*to stumble*) stolpern (PERF *sein*); **Nicky tripped over a stone** Nicky ist über einen Stein gestolpert.

triumph *noun* Triumph *der* (PL *die* Triumphe).

trolley *noun* **1** (*for shopping*) Einkaufswagen *der* (PL *die* Einkaufswagen); **2** (*for luggage*) Kofferkuli *der* (PL *die* Kofferkulis).

trombone *noun* Posaune *die* (PL *die* Posaunen).

troops *plural noun* Truppen (*plural*).

trophy *noun* Trophäe *die* (PL *die* Trophäen), (*in competitions*) Pokal *der* (PL *die* Pokale).

trot *verb* traben (PERF *sein*).

trouble *noun* **1** (*general difficulties*) Ärger *der*; **to make trouble** Ärger machen; **to get into trouble** Ärger bekommen; **we had trouble with the travel agency** wir hatten Ärger mit dem Reisebüro; **2** (*problem*) Problem *das* (PL *die* Probleme); **the trouble is, I've lost his phone number** das Problem ist, dass ich seine Telefonnummer verloren habe; **Steph's in trouble** Steph hat Probleme; **what's the trouble?** was ist los?; **it's no trouble!** das ist kein Problem; **3** (*difficulty, effort*) Mühe *die*; **to have trouble doing something** Mühe haben, etwas zu tun; **I had trouble finding a seat** ich hatte Mühe, einen Platz zu finden; **it's not worth the trouble** das ist nicht der Mühe wert.

trousers *plural noun* Hose *die* (PL *die* Hosen); **my old trousers** meine alte Hose; **a new pair of trousers** eine neue Hose.

trout *noun* Forelle *die* (PL *die* Forellen).

truant *noun* Schulschwänzer *der* (PL *die* Schulschwänzer), Schulschwänzerin *die* (PL *die* Schulschwänzerinnen); **she's playing truant** sie schwänzt die Schule.

truck *noun* Lastwagen *der* (PL *die* Lastwagen).

true *adjective* **1** wahr; **a true story** eine wahre Geschichte; **2 is that true?** stimmt das?; **it's true she's absent-minded** das stimmt, sie ist sehr vergesslich.

trump *noun* Trumpf *der* (PL *die* Trümpfe); **hearts are trumps** Herz ist Trumpf.

trumpet *noun* Trompete *die* (PL *die* Trompeten).

trunk *noun* **1** (*of a tree*) Stamm *der* (PL *die* Stämme); **2** (*of an elephant*) Rüssel *der* (PL *die* Rüssel).

trunks *plural noun* **swimming trunks** Badehose *die* (PL *die* Badehosen).

trust *noun* Vertrauen *das*.
trust *verb* **1** (*believe*) **to trust somebody** jemandem vertrauen; **2** (*rely on*) **you can trust him** man kann sich auf ihn verlassen.

truth *noun* Wahrheit *die*.

try *noun* Versuch *der* (PL *die* Versuche); **it's my first try** es ist mein erster Versuch; **to have a try** es versuchen; **give it a try!** versuch's doch mal!
try *verb* **1** versuchen; **to try to do something** versuchen, etwas zu

tun; **I'm trying to open the door** ich versuche, die Tür aufzumachen; **2** (*taste*) probieren.

• **to try something on** etwas anprobieren SEP (*a garment*).

T-shirt *noun* T-Shirt *das* (PL *die* T-Shirts).

tube *noun* **1** Tube *die* (PL *die* Tuben); **2** (*the Underground*) **the Tube** die U-Bahn.

tuberculosis *noun* Tuberkulose *die*.

Tuesday *noun* **1** Dienstag *der* (PL *die* Dienstage); **on Tuesday** (am) Dienstag; **I'm going to the cinema on Tuesday** ich gehe Dienstag ins Kino; **see you on Tuesday!** bis Dienstag!; **every Tuesday** jeden Dienstag; **last Tuesday** vorigen Dienstag; **next Tuesday** nächsten Dienstag; **2 on Tuesdays** dienstags; **the museum is closed on Tuesdays** das Museum ist dienstags geschlossen.

tuition *noun* **1** Unterricht *der*; **piano tuition** *der* Klavierunterricht; **2 extra tuition** Nachhilfestunden (*plural*).

tulip *noun* Tulpe *die* (PL *die* Tulpen).

tumble-drier *noun* Wäschetrockner *der* (PL *die* Wäschetrockner).

tumbler *noun* Becherglas *das* (PL *die* Bechergläser).

tuna *noun* Thunfisch *der*.

tune *noun* Melodie *die* (PL *die* Melodien).

a
b
c
d
e
f
g
h
i
j
k
l
m
n
o
p
q
r
s
t
u
v
w
x
y
z

tunnel *noun* Tunnel *der* (PL *die* Tunnel); **the Channel Tunnel** der Eurotunnel.

turkey *noun* Pute *die* (PL *die* Puten).

Turkey *noun* die Türkei; **from Turkey** aus der Türkei; **in Turkey** in der Türkei; **to Turkey** in die Türkei.

Turkish *noun* (*language*) Türkisch *das*.

Turkish *adjective* türkisch; **he is Turkish** er ist Türke; **she is Turkish** sie ist Türkin.

turn *noun* **1** (*in a game*) **it's your turn** du bist an der Reihe; **whose turn is it?** wer ist an der Reihe?; **it's Jane's turn** Jane ist an der Reihe; **2 to take turns** sich abwechseln; **to take it in turns to do something** abwechselnd etwas tun; **3** (*in a road*) Kurve *die* (PL *die* Kurven); **to take a right/left turn** nach rechts/ links abbiegen.

turn *verb* **1** drehen; **turn the key to the right** dreh den Schlüssel nach rechts; **turn your chair round** dreh deinen Stuhl herum; **2** (*person, car*) abbiegen✧ SEP (PERF *sein*); **turn left at the next set of lights** biegen Sie an der nächsten Ampel links ab; **3** (*become*) werden✧ (PERF *sein*); **she turned red** sie wurde rot.

● **to turn back** umkehren SEP (PERF *sein*).

● **to turn off 1** (*from a road*) abbiegen✧ SEP (PERF *sein*); **2** (*switch off*) ausmachen SEP (*a light, an oven, a TV, or radio*), zudrehen SEP (*a tap*), abstellen SEP (*gas, electricity, or water*), ausschalten SEP (*an engine*).

● **to turn on** anmachen SEP (*a TV, radio, or light*), aufdrehen SEP (*a tap*), anschalten SEP (*an oven*), anlassen✧ SEP (*an engine*).

● **to turn out 1 to turn out well** gut ausgehen✧ SEP (PERF *sein*); **the discussions turned out badly** die Gespräche sind schlecht ausgegangen; **it all turned out all right in the end** am Ende ging alles gut aus; **2 it turned out that I was right** es stellte sich heraus, dass ich Recht hatte.

● **to turn up 1** (*to arrive*) aufkreuzen SEP (PERF *sein*); **they turned up an hour later** sie sind eine Stunde später aufgekreuzt; **2** (*to make louder*) lauter machen.

turning *noun* Abzweigung *die* (PL *die* Abzweigungen); **take the third turning on the right** nimm die dritte Abzweigung rechts.

turnip *noun* Steckrübe *die* (PL *die* Steckrüben).

turquoise *adjective* türkis.

turtle *noun* Schildkröte *die* (PL *die* Schildkröten).

TV *noun* Fernsehen *das*; **I saw her on TV** ich habe sie im Fernsehen gesehen.

tweezers *noun* Pinzette *die* (PL *die* Pinzetten).

twelfth *number* zwölfter/zwölfte/ zwölftes; **on the twelfth floor** im zwölften Stock; **the twelfth of May** der zwölfte Mai.

twelve *number* **1** zwölf; **Tara's twelve** Tara ist zwölf; **2 at twelve o'clock** um zwölf Uhr.

Uu

twenty *number* zwanzig; **Marie's twenty** Marie ist zwanzig; **twenty-one** einundzwanzig.

twice *adverb* **1** zweimal; **I've asked him twice** ich habe ihn zweimal gefragt; **twice a day** zweimal täglich; **2 twice as much** doppelt so viel.

twig *noun* Zweig *der* (PL die Zweige).

twin *noun* Zwilling *der* (PL die Zwillinge); **Helen and Tim are twins** Helen und Tim sind Zwillinge; **her twin sister** ihre Zwillingsschwester.
twin *verb* **Richmond is twinned with Konstanz** Richmond und Konstanz sind Partnerstädte.

twist *verb* **1** (*bend out of shape*) verbiegen◇; **2** verdrehen (*words, meaning*); **3 to twist your ankle** sich den Knöchel verrenken.

two *number* zwei; **Ben's two** Ben ist zwei; **two by two** zu zweit.

type *noun* Art *die*; **what type of computer is it?** welche Art Computer ist es?
type *verb* (*on a typewriter*) Schreibmaschine schreiben◇, tippen (*informal*); **I'm learning to type** ich lerne Schreibmaschine schreiben; **I'm just typing some letters** ich tippe gerade ein paar Briefe.

typewriter *noun* Schreibmaschine *die* (PL die Schreibmaschinen).

typical *adjective* typisch.

tyre *noun* Reifen *der* (PL die Reifen).

ugly *adjective* hässlich.

UK *noun* (*United Kingdom*) Vereinigte Königreich *das*.

ulcer *noun* Geschwür *das* (PL die Geschwüre).

Ulster *noun* Ulster; **from Ulster** aus Ulster, aus Nordirland.

umbrella *noun* Regenschirm *der* (PL die Regenschirme).

umpire *noun* Schiedsrichter *der* (PL die Schiedsrichter), Schiedsrichterin *die* (PL die Schiedsrichterinnen).

UN *noun* (*United Nations*) UN (*plural*).

unable *adjective* **to be unable to do something** etwas nicht tun können; **he's unable to come** er kann nicht kommen.

unavoidable *adjective* unvermeidlich.

unbearable *adjective* unerträglich.

unbelievable *adjective* unglaublich.

uncertain *adjective* **1** (*not sure*) **to be uncertain whether** ... sich (DAT) nicht sicher sein, ob ...; **2** (*unpredictable*) ungewiss (*future or result*).

uncle *noun* Onkel *der* (PL die Onkel).

uncomfortable *adjective* **1** unbequem (*shoes, chair, or journey*); **2** unangenehm (*situation, heat*).

a
b
c
d
e
f
g
h
i
j
k
l
m
n
o
p
q
r
s
t
u
v
w
x
y
z

unconscious *adjective* (*out cold*) bewusstlos.

under *preposition* **1** (*underneath*) unter (+ DAT, *or* + ACC *when there is movement towards a place*); **the dog's under the bed** der Hund ist unter dem Bett; **the ball rolled under the bed** der Ball ist unter das Bett gerollt; **2 under there** da drunter; **perhaps it's under there** vielleicht ist es da drunter; **3** (*less than*) unter (+ DAT); **under £20** unter zwanzig Pfund; **children under five** Kinder unter fünf.

under-age *adjective* **to be under-age** minderjährig sein.

underclothes *plural noun* Unterwäsche *die*.

undercooked *adjective* nicht gar.

underestimate *verb* unterschätzen.

underground *noun* (*railway*) U-Bahn *die* (PL *die* U-Bahnen); **I saw her on the underground** ich habe sie in der U-Bahn gesehen; **shall we go by underground?** fahren wir mit der U-Bahn?
underground *adjective* unterirdisch (*cave*); **underground car park** *die* Tiefgarage.

underline *verb* unterstreichen❖.

underneath *preposition* unter (+ DAT, *or* + ACC *when there is movement towards a place*); **it's underneath the newspaper** es ist unter der Zeitung; **I put it underneath the newspaper** ich habe es unter die Zeitung gelegt.
underneath *adverb* darunter;

check underneath sieh darunter nach.

underpants *plural noun* Unterhose *die* (PL *die* Unterhosen); **my underpants** meine Unterhose.

underpass *noun* Unterführung *die* (PL *die* Unterführungen).

understand *verb* verstehen❖; **do you understand?** verstehst du?; **I couldn't understand what he was saying** ich konnte ihn nicht verstehen; **I can't understand why she doesn't want to see him** ich kann nicht verstehen, warum sie ihn nicht sehen will.

understandable *adjective* **that's understandable** das ist verständlich.

understanding *noun* Verständnis *das*.
understanding *adjective* verständnisvoll.

underwear *noun* Unterwäsche *die*.

undo *verb* aufmachen SEP.

undone *adjective* **to come undone** aufgehen❖ SEP (PERF *sein*).

undress *verb* **to get undressed** sich ausziehen❖ SEP.

unemployed *noun* **the unemployed** die Arbeitslosen (*plural*).
unemployed *adjective* arbeitslos.

unemployment *noun* Arbeitslosigkeit *die*.

uneven *adjective* uneben (*surface*); **her pulse is uneven** ihr Puls ist unregelmäßig; **your writing is very uneven** deine Schrift ist sehr ungleichmäßig; **the icing is uneven** diese Kuchenglasur ist nicht glatt.

unexpected *adjective* unerwartet.

unexpectedly *adverb* (*to happen, arrive*) überraschend.

unfair *adjective* unfair; **it's unfair on young people** es ist jungen Leuten gegenüber unfair.

unfashionable *adjective* unmodern.

unfasten *verb* aufmachen SEP.

unfit *adjective* nicht fit; **I'm terribly unfit** ich bin nicht sehr fit.

unfold *verb* **1** (*a map*) ausbreiten SEP; **2** (*to develop*) spielen; **the story unfolds in Africa** die Geschichte spielt in Afrika.

unfortunate *adjective* unglücklich.

unfortunately *adverb* leider.

unfriendly *adjective* unfreundlich.

ungrateful *adjective* undankbar.

unhappy *adjective* **1** unglücklich; **2** (*not satisfied*) unzufrieden; **to be unhappy about something** mit etwas unzufrieden sein.

unhealthy *adjective* ungesund.

uniform *noun* Uniform die (PL die Uniformen).

union *noun* (*trade union*) Gewerkschaft die (PL die Gewerkschaften).

Union Jack *noun* **the Union Jack** die britische Nationalflagge.

unique *adjective* einzigartig.

unit *noun* **1** (*for measuring, for example*) Einheit die (PL die Einheiten); **2** (*in a kitchen*) Einbauschrank der (PL die Einbauschränke); **3** (*a department*) Abteilung die (PL die Abteilungen); **the research unit** die Forschungsabteilung.

United Kingdom *noun* Vereinigte Königreich das.

United Nations *noun* Vereinte Nationen (*plural*).

United States (of America) *plural noun* Vereinigte Staaten (von Amerika) (*plural*).

universe *noun* Universum das, Weltall das.

university *noun* Universität die (PL die Universitäten); **to go to university** auf die Universität gehen.

unkind *adjective* unfreundlich.

unknown *adjective* unbekannt.

unleaded petrol *noun* bleifreie Benzin das.

unless *conjunction* es sei denn; **unless he does it** es sei denn, er macht es; **unless you write** es sei denn, du schreibst.

unlike *adjective* **1** im Gegensatz zu (+ DAT); **unlike me, she hates dogs** im Gegensatz zu mir hasst sie Hunde; **2 it's unlike her to be late** es sieht ihr gar nicht ähnlich, zu spät zu kommen.

unlikely *adjective* unwahrscheinlich.

unlimited *adjective* unbegrenzt.

a
b
c
d
e
f
g
h
i
j
k
l
m
n
o
p
q
r
s
t
u
v
w
x
y
z

unload *verb* **1** ausladen⬦ SEP
(*luggage, car*); **2** entladen⬦ (*lorry*).

unlock *verb* aufschließen⬦ SEP.

unlucky *adjective* **1 to be unlucky**
(*person*) Pech haben; **I was unlucky,
the shop was shut** ich hatte Pech,
das Geschäft war zu; **2** (*bringing
bad luck*) Unglücks-; **thirteen is an
unlucky number** dreizehn ist eine
Unglückszahl; **it's unlucky** es bringt
Unglück.

unmarried *adjective* ledig.

unnecessary *adjective* unnötig.

unpack *verb* auspacken SEP; **I'm
just unpacking my rucksack** ich
packe gerade meinen Rucksack aus;
**I'll just unpack and then come
down** ich packe nur noch aus und
dann komme ich runter.

unpaid *adjective* unbezahlt.

unpleasant *adjective*
unangenehm.

unplug *verb* **to unplug the lamp**
den Stecker der Lampe
herausziehen⬦ SEP.

unpopular *adjective* unbeliebt.

unreasonable *adjective*
uneinsichtig; **he's being really
unreasonable** er ist so
uneinsichtig.

unrecognizable *adjective* nicht
wieder zu erkennen.

unreliable *adjective*
unzuverlässig; **he's unreliable** er ist
unzuverlässig.

unsafe *adjective* gefährlich (*wiring,
for example*).

unsatisfactory *adjective*
unbefriedigend.

unscrew *verb* aufschrauben SEP.

unshaven *adjective* unrasiert.

unsuccessful *adjective*
1 erfolglos; **an unsuccessful
attempt** ein erfolgloser Versuch;
2 to be unsuccessful keinen Erfolg
haben; **I tried, but I was
unsuccessful** ich habe es versucht,
aber ich hatte keinen Erfolg.

unsuitable *adjective* unpassend.

untidy *adjective* unordentlich; **the
house is always untidy** das Haus
ist immer unordentlich.

until *preposition, conjunction* **1** bis;
until Monday bis Montag; **until now**
bis jetzt; **until then** bis dahin;
2 (*when 'until' is followed by a noun
it is usually translated as 'bis zu'*
+ DAT) **until the tenth** bis zum
Zehnten; **until the morning** bis zum
Morgen; **3 not until** erst; **not until
September** erst im September; **it
won't be finished until Friday** es
wird erst Freitag fertig sein.

unusual *adjective* ungewöhnlich;
an unusual face ein
ungewöhnliches Gesicht.

unwilling *adjective* **to be
unwilling to do something** etwas
nicht tun wollen.

unwrap *verb* auspacken SEP.

up *preposition, adverb* **1** (*out of bed*)
to be up auf sein⬦ (PERF *sein*); **Liz
isn't up yet** Liz ist noch nicht auf; **I
was up late last night** ich war
gestern bis spät auf; **2 to get up**
aufstehen⬦ SEP (PERF *sein*); **we got**

up at six wir sind um sechs aufgestanden; **3** (*higher up*) auf (+ DAT, *or* + ACC *when there is movement towards a place*); **up on the roof** auf dem Dach; **4 up here** hier oben; **up there** da oben; **to go up** (*upstairs*) nach oben gehen; **I went up** ich bin nach oben gegangen; **5 to go up the road** die Straße entlanggehen⋄ SEP (PERF *sein*); **it's further up the road** es ist weiter die Straße entlang; **6 to go up the hill** (*on foot*) hinaufgehen⋄ SEP (PERF *sein*), (*in a vehicle*) hinauffahren⋄ SEP (PERF *sein*); (*in spoken German the prefix 'rauf-' is most common*) **does the bus go up the hill?** fährt der Bus den Berg rauf?; **7 to come up** heraufkommen⋄ SEP (PERF *sein*), raufkommen⋄ SEP (PERF *sein*) (*informal*); **8** (*wrong*) **what's up?** was ist los? (*informal*); **what's up with him?** was ist mit ihm los?; **9 up to** bis; **up to here** bis hier; **up to last week** bis zur letzten Woche; **10 she came up to me** sie kam auf mich zu; **11 what's she up to?** was hat sie vor?; **12 it's up to you** (*it's for you to decide*) das hängt von dir ab; (*it concerns only you*) das ist deine Sache; ★ **time's up!** die Zeit ist um.

up-date *noun* Aktualisierung *die* (PL *die* Aktualisierungen); **here's an up-date on our plans** dies ist der neueste Stand unserer Pläne.
up-date *verb* **1** (*to revise*) überarbeiten (*timetables, information*); **2** (*to modernize*) auf den neuesten Stand bringen ⋄ (*styles, furnishings*).

upheaval *noun* Unruhe *die* (PL *die* Unruhen).

upper-class *adjective* der Oberschicht; **an upper-class family** eine Familie der Oberschicht.

upright *adjective* aufrecht; **put it upright** stell es aufrecht; **to stand upright** aufrecht stehen.

upset *noun* **stomach upset** *die* Magenverstimmung.
upset *adjective* **1** (*annoyed*) ärgerlich; **he's upset** er ist ärgerlich; **2** (*distressed*) bestürzt, (*sad*) betrübt.
upset *verb* **to upset somebody** (*hurt*) jemanden kränken, (*annoy*) jemanden ärgern.

upside down *adjective* verkehrt herum.

upstairs *adverb* **1** oben; **Mum's upstairs** Mutti ist oben; **2** (*with movement*) nach oben; **to go upstairs** nach oben gehen.

up-to-date *adjective* **1** (*in fashion*) modern; **2** (*information*) aktuell.

upwards *adjective* nach oben.

urgent *adjective* dringend.

us *pronoun* uns; **she knows us** sie kennt uns; **they saw us** sie haben uns gesehen; **with us** mit uns.

US *noun* USA (*plural*).

USA *noun* USA (*plural*).

use *noun* **1** Gebrauch *der*; **instructions for use** *die* Gebrauchsanweisung (*singular*); **2 it's no use** es hat keinen Zweck; **it's no use phoning** es hat keinen Zweck anzurufen.
use *verb* benutzen; **we used the**

a
b
c
d
e
f
g
h
i
j
k
l
m
n
o
p
q
r
s
t
u
v
w
x
y
z

dictionary wir haben das Wörterbuch benutzt; **to use something to do something** etwas zu etwas (DAT) benutzen; **I used a towel to dry myself** ich habe ein Handtuch zum Abtrocknen benutzt.

● **to use up 1** aufbrauchen SEP (*food*); **2** verbrauchen (*money*).

used *adjective* **1 to be used to something** an etwas (ACC) gewöhnt sein; **I'm used to cats** ich bin an Katzen gewöhnt; **I'm not used to it!** das bin ich nicht gewohnt!; **I'm not used to eating in restaurants** ich bin nicht daran gewöhnt, in Restaurants zu essen; **2 to get used to something** sich an etwas (ACC) gewöhnen; **you'll soon get used to the new car** du wirst dich schnell an das neue Auto gewöhnen; **I've got used to living here** ich habe mich daran gewöhnt, hier zu wohnen; **you'll get used to it** du wirst dich schon daran gewöhnen.

used *verb* **they used to live in the country** sie haben früher auf dem Land gewohnt; **she used to smoke** sie hat früher geraucht.

useful *adjective* nützlich.

useless *adjective* **1** unbrauchbar; **this knife's useless** dieses Messer ist unbrauchbar; **you're completely useless!** du bist wirklich zu nichts zu gebrauchen!; **2** nutzlos (*advice, information, or facts, for example*); **useless knowledge** nutzloses Wissen; **3** (*pointless*) zwecklos.

user *noun* Benutzer der (PL die Benutzer), Benutzerin die (PL die Benutzerinnen).

user-friendly *adjective* benutzerfreundlich.

usual *adjective* **1** üblich; **it's the usual problem** es ist das übliche Problem; **as usual** wie üblich; **2 it's colder than usual** es ist kälter als gewöhnlich.

usually *adjective* normalerweise; **I usually leave at eight** normalerweise gehe ich um acht weg.

Vv

vacancy *noun* **1** (*in a hotel*) 'vacancies' 'Zimmer frei'; 'no vacancies' 'belegt'; **2 job vacancy** die freie Stelle.

vacant *adjective* frei.

vaccinate *noun* impfen.

vaccination *noun* Impfung die (PL die Impfungen).

vacuum *verb* saugen; **I'm going to vacuum my room** ich sauge mein Zimmer.

vacuum cleaner *noun* Staubsauger der (PL die Staubsauger).

vagina *noun* Vagina die (PL die Vaginen).

vague *adjective* vage.

vain *adjective* eitel; **in vain** vergeblich.

valentine card *noun*
Valentinskarte *die* (PL *die*
Valentinskarten).

Valentine's Day *noun*
Valentinstag *der* (PL *die*
Valentinstage).

valid *adjective* gültig.

valley *noun* Tal *das* (PL *die* Täler).

valuable *adjective* wertvoll.

value *noun* Wert *der* (PL *die* Werte).
value *verb* schätzen.

van *noun* Lieferwagen *der* (PL *die*
Lieferwagen).

vandal *noun* Rowdy *der* (PL *die*
Rowdys).

vandalism *noun* Vandalismus *der*.

vandalize *verb* mutwillig
zerstören.

vanilla *noun* Vanille *die*; **vanilla ice
cream** *das* Vanilleeis.

vanish *verb* verschwinden✧ (PERF
sein).

variety *noun* **1** Abwechslung *die* (*in
a routine, diet, or style*); **for the sake
of variety** zur Abwechslung;
2 (*kind*) Sorte *die* (PL *die* Sorten); **a
new variety of apple** eine neue
Apfelsorte; **3** (*assortment*) Auswahl
die.

various *adjective* verschieden;
there are various ways of doing it
man kann es auf verschiedene Art
und Weise machen.

vary *verb* **1** (*become different*) sich
ändern; **2 it varies a lot** es ist sehr
unterschiedlich; **3** (*make different*)
ändern (*a programme or method*).

vase *noun* Vase *die* (PL *die* Vasen).

VAT *noun* Mehrwertsteuer *die*.

VCR *noun* Videorekorder *der* (PL *die*
Videorekorder).

VDU *noun* Bildschirm *der* (PL *die*
Bildschirme).

veal *noun* Kalbfleisch *das*.

vegan *noun* Veganer *der* (PL *die*
Veganer), Veganerin *die* (PL *die*
Veganerinnen).

vegetable *noun* Gemüse *das*;
fresh vegetables frisches Gemüse.

vegetarian *noun* Vegetarier *der*
(PL *die* Vegetarier), Vegetarierin *die*
(PL *die* Vegetarierinnen).
vegetarian *adjective* vegetarisch.

vehicle *noun* Fahrzeug *das* (PL *die*
Fahrzeuge).

vein *noun* Vene *die* (PL *die* Venen).

velvet *noun* Samt *der*.

vending machine *noun*
Automat *der* (PL *die* Automaten).

verb *noun* Verb *das* (PL *die* Verben).

verdict *noun* Urteil *das* (PL *die*
Urteile).

verge *noun* **1** (*roadside*) Bankett *das*
(PL *die* Banketten); **2 to be on the
verge of doing something** im
Begriff sein, etwas zu tun; **I was on
the verge of leaving** ich war im
Begriff zu gehen.

version *noun* Version *die* (PL *die*
Versionen).

versus *preposition* gegen (+ ACC);
Arsenal versus Chelsea Arsenal
gegen Chelsea.

vertical *adjective* senkrecht.

a
b
c
d
e
f
g
h
i
j
k
l
m
n
o
p
q
r
s
t
u
v
w
x
y
z

very *adverb* sehr; **it's very difficult** es ist sehr schwer; **very much** sehr viel; **very little** sehr wenig.
very *adjective* **1 the very person I need!** genau der Mann, den ich brauche, genau die Frau, die ich brauche; **the very thing he's looking for** genau das, was er sucht; **in the very middle** genau in der Mitte; **2 at the very end** ganz am Ende; **at the very front** ganz vorne.

vest *noun* Unterhemd *das* (PL *die* Unterhemden).

vet *noun* Tierarzt *der* (PL *die* Tierärzte), Tierärztin *die* (PL *die* Tierärztinnen); **she's a vet** sie ist Tierärztin.

via *preposition* über (+ ACC); **we're going to Frankfurt via Brussels** wir fahren über Brüssel nach Frankfurt.

vicar *noun* Pfarrer *der* (PL *die* Pfarrer).

vicious *adjective* **1** bösartig (*dog*); **2** brutal (*attack*).

victim *noun* Opfer *das* (PL *die* Opfer).

victory *noun* Sieg *der* (PL *die* Siege).

video *noun* **1** (*film, cassette*) Video *das* (PL *die* Videos); **to watch a video** ein Video ansehen; **I've got it on video** ich habe es auf Video; **it's out on video** das gibts als Video; **2** (*video recorder*) Videorekorder *der* (PL *die* Videorekorder).
video *verb* aufzeichnen SEP; **I'll video it for you** ich zeichne es für dich auf.

video camera *noun* Videokamera *die* (PL *die* Videokameras).

video cassette *noun* Videokassette *die* (PL *die* Videokassetten).

video game *noun* Videospiel *das* (PL *die* Videospiele).

video recorder *noun* Videorekorder *der* (PL *die* Videorekorder).

video shop *noun* Videothek *die* (PL *die* Videotheken).

Vienna *noun* Wien *das*; **to Vienna** nach Wien.

view *noun* **1** Aussicht *die*; **a room with a view of the lake** ein Zimmer mit Aussicht auf den See; **2** (*opinion*) Meinung *die* (PL *die* Meinungen); **in my view** meiner Meinung nach; **point of view** *der* Standpunkt.

viewer *noun* Zuschauer *der* (PL *die* Zuschauer), Zuschauerin *die* (PL *die* Zuschauerinnen).

vile *adjective* ekelhaft.

villa *noun* Villa *die* (PL *die* Villen).

village *noun* Dorf *das* (PL *die* Dörfer).

vine *noun* Weinrebe *die* (PL *die* Weinreben).

vinegar *noun* Essig *der*.

vineyard *noun* Weinberg *der* (PL *die* Weinberge).

violence *noun* Gewalt *die*.

violent *adjective* **1** gewalttätig (*person, film, behaviour*); **2** heftig (*jolt, punch*).

violin *noun* Geige die (PL die Geigen); **to play the violin** Geige spielen.

violinist *noun* Geiger der (PL die Geiger), Geigerin die (PL die Geigerinnen).

virgin *noun* Jungfrau die (PL die Jungfrauen).

Virgo *noun* Jungfrau die; **Robert's Virgo** Robert ist Jungfrau.

virtual reality *noun* virtuelle Realität die.

virus *noun* (*in medicine and IT*) Virus der (PL die Viren); **anti-virus software** Antivirenprogramm das (PL die Antivirenprogramme).

visa *noun* Visum das (PL die Visa).

visible *adjective* sichtbar.

visit *noun* Besuch der (PL die Besuche); **I was in Berlin on a visit to friends** ich war in Berlin bei Freunden zu Besuch; **my last visit to Germany** mein letzter Deutschlandbesuch.
visit *verb* 1 besuchen (*a person*); 2 besichtigen (*a building, town*).

visitor *noun* 1 Besucher der (PL die Besucher), Besucherin die (PL die Besucherinnen); **2 we've got visitors tonight** wir haben heute Abend Besuch; **3** (*in a hotel*) Gast der (PL die Gäste).

visual *adjective* visuell.

vital *adjective* unbedingt erforderlich; **it's vital to book** man muss unbedingt buchen.

vitamin *noun* Vitamin das (PL die Vitamine).

vivid *adjective* lebhaft (*colours, memory*); **to have a vivid imagination** eine lebhafte Phantasie haben.

vocabulary *noun* Wortschatz der.

vocational *adjective* beruflich.

vodka *noun* Wodka der (PL die Wodkas).

voice *noun* Stimme die (PL die Stimmen).

volcano *noun* Vulkan der (PL die Vulkane).

volleyball *noun* Volleyball der; **to play volleyball** Volleyball spielen.

volume *noun* 1 Lautstärke die; **could you turn down the volume?** könntest du etwas leiser stellen?; **2** (*book*) Band der (PL die Bände).

voluntary *adjective* 1 freiwillig; **a voluntary worker** ein freiwilliger Helfer, eine freiwillige Helferin; **2 to do voluntary work** für einen wohltätigen Zweck arbeiten.

volunteer *noun* Freiwillige der/die (PL die Freiwilligen).
volunteer *verb* **to volunteer to do something** sich bereit erklären, etwas zu tun.

vomit *verb* sich übergeben ⋄.

vote *verb* wählen; **to vote for somebody** jemanden wählen; **she always votes Green** sie wählt immer die Grünen.

voucher *noun* Gutschein der (PL die Gutscheine).

vowel *noun* Vokal der (PL die Vokale).

vulgar *adjective* vulgär.

Ww

waffle *noun* Waffel die (PL die Waffeln).

wage(s) *noun* Lohn der (PL die Löhne).

waist *noun* Taille die (PL die Taillen).

waistcoat *noun* Weste die (PL die Westen).

waist measurement *noun* Taillenweite die.

wait *noun* Wartezeit die; **an hour's wait** eine Stunde Wartezeit.
wait *verb* **1** warten; **they're waiting in the car** sie warten im Auto; **she kept me waiting** sie hat mich warten lassen; **2 to wait for somebody** auf jemanden warten; **wait for me** warte auf mich; **to wait for something** auf etwas (ACC) warten; **we waited for a taxi** wir haben auf ein Taxi gewartet; **3 to wait for somebody to do something** darauf warten, dass jemand etwas tut; **I'm waiting for him to ring** ich warte darauf, dass er anruft; **4 I can't wait to open it** ich kann's kaum erwarten, es aufzumachen.

waiter *noun* Kellner der (PL die Kellner); **waiter!** Herr Ober!

waiting list *noun* Warteliste die (PL die Wartelisten).

waiting room *noun* Wartezimmer das (PL die Wartezimmer), (*at a station*) Warteraum der (PL die Warteräume).

waitress *noun* Kellnerin die (PL die Kellnerinnen); **waitress!** Fräulein!

wake *verb* **1** wecken (*somebody*); **Jess woke me at six** Jess hat mich um sechs geweckt; **2** aufwachen SEP (PERF *sein*); **I woke (up) at six** ich bin um sechs aufgewacht; **wake up!** wach auf!

Wales *noun* Wales das; **from Wales** aus Wales; **to Wales** nach Wales.

walk *noun* **1** Spaziergang der (PL die Spaziergänge); **to go for walk** einen Spaziergang machen; **we'll go for a little walk round the village** wir machen einen kleinen Spaziergang durchs Dorf; **2 to take the dog for a walk** mit dem Hund spazieren gehen◇ (PERF *sein*); **3 it's about five minutes' walk from here** es ist ungefähr fünf Minuten zu Fuß von hier.
walk *verb* **1** (*go, not run*) gehen◇ (PERF *sein*); **he walks very slowly** er geht sehr langsam; **I'll walk to the bus stop with you** ich gehe mit dir zur Bushaltestelle; **2** (*on foot rather than by car or bus*) zu Fuß gehen◇ (PERF *sein*); **it's not far, we can walk** es ist nicht weit, wir können zu Fuß gehen; **3** (*walk around*) spazieren gehen◇ (PERF *sein*); **we walked around the old town** wir sind in der Altstadt spazieren gegangen; **4** (*move on foot*) laufen◇ (PERF *sein*); **to learn to walk** laufen lernen; **the child can't walk yet** das Kind kann noch nicht laufen.

walking distance *noun* **to be within walking distance** zu Fuß zu erreichen sein; **it's within walking**

distance of the sea man kann das Meer zu Fuß erreichen.

walking *noun* (*hiking*) Wandern *das*; **to go walking** wandern (PERF *sein*).

walkman *noun* Walkman *der* (PL *die* Walkmen).

wall *noun* **1** (*inside a building*) Wand *die* (PL *die* Wände); **there's a picture on every wall** an jeder Wand hängt ein Bild; **2** (*outside*) Mauer *die* (PL *die* Mauern).

wallet *noun* Brieftasche *die* (PL *die* Brieftaschen).

wallpaper *noun* Tapete *die* (PL *die* Tapeten).

walnut *noun* Walnuss *die* (PL *die* Walnüsse).

wander *verb* **to wander around town** durch die Stadt bummeln (PERF *sein*); **to wander off** weggehen◇ SEP (PERF *sein*).

want *verb* **1** wollen◇; **do you want to come?** willst du mitkommen?; **what do you want to do?** was willst du machen?; **I don't want to bother him** ich will ihn nicht stören; **2** (*more polite*) mögen◇ (*'ich möchte' is much politer than 'ich will'*); **do you want some more coffee?** möchtest du noch Kaffee?; **I want two pounds of apples please** ich möchte gern zwei Pfund Äpfel (*'möchte gern' is particularly used when shopping*).

war *noun* Krieg *der* (PL *die* Kriege).

ward *noun* Station *die* (PL *die* Stationen).

wardrobe *noun* Kleiderschrank *der* (PL *die* Kleiderschränke).

warm *adjective* **1** warm; **a warm coat** ein warmer Mantel; **it's warm today** heute ist es warm; **I'll keep your dinner warm** ich halte dir das Essen warm; **it's warm inside** drinnen ist es warm; **I am warm** mir ist warm; **2** (*friendly*) herzlich; **a warm welcome** ein herzlicher Empfang.

warm *verb* wärmen; **to warm the plates** die Teller wärmen.

● **to warm up 1** (*weather*) warm werden; **2** (*an athlete*) sich aufwärmen SEP; **3** (*to heat up*) aufwärmen SEP; **I'll warm the soup up for you** ich wärme dir die Suppe auf.

warmth *noun* Wärme *die*.

warn *verb* **1** warnen; **I warn you, it's expensive** ich warne dich, es ist teuer; **to warn somebody not to do something** jemanden davor warnen, etwas zu tun; **she warned me not to let him drive** sie hat mich davor gewarnt, ihn fahren zu lassen; **2** **he warned me to lock the car** er hat mich ermahnt, das Auto abzuschließen.

warning *noun* Warnung *die* (PL *die* Warnungen).

wart *noun* Warze *die* (PL *die* Warzen).

wash *noun* **to give something a wash** etwas waschen◇; **to have a wash** sich waschen.

wash *verb* **1** waschen◇; **I've washed your jeans** ich habe deine Jeans gewaschen; **2** (*have a wash*) sich waschen◇; **to get washed** sich

a
b
c
d
e
f
g
h
i
j
k
l
m
n
o
p
q
r
s
t
u
v
w
x
y
z

waschen; **3 to wash your hands** sich (DAT) die Hände waschen; **I washed my hands** ich habe mir die Hände gewaschen; **to wash your hair** sich (DAT) die Haare waschen; **4 to wash the dishes** abwaschen◊ SEP.

● **to wash up** abwaschen◊ SEP.

washbasin *noun* Waschbecken *das* (PL *die* Waschbecken).

washing *noun* Wäsche *die*; **to do the washing** Wäsche waschen.

washing machine *noun* Waschmaschine *die* (PL *die* Waschmaschinen).

washing powder *noun* Waschpulver *das*.

washing-up liquid *noun* Spülmittel *das* (PL *die* Spülmittel).

washing-up *noun* Abwasch *der*; **to do the washing-up** den Abwasch machen.

wasp *noun* Wespe *die* (PL *die* Wespen).

waste *noun* Verschwendung *die*; **it's a waste of time** das ist eine Zeitverschwendung.
waste *verb* verschwenden.

waste-bin *noun* Mülltonne *die* (PL *die* Mülltonnen).

waste-paper basket *noun* Papierkorb *der* (PL *die* Papierkörbe).

watch *noun* Uhr *die* (PL *die* Uhren); **my watch is fast** meine Uhr geht vor; **my watch is slow** meine Uhr geht nach.
watch *verb* **1** (*to look at*) sich (DAT) ansehen◊ SEP; **I was watching a film** ich habe mir einen Film

angesehen; **2 to watch TV** fernsehen◊ SEP; **3** (*keep a check on, look after*) achten auf (+ ACC); **watch the children** achte auf die Kinder; **4** (*to be careful*) aufpassen SEP; **watch you don't spill it** pass auf, dass du es nicht verschüttest; **watch out!** pass auf!; **5** (*observe*) beobachten; **they were being watched** sie wurden beobachtet.

water *noun* Wasser *das*.
water *verb* gießen◊ (*plants*).

waterfall *noun* Wasserfall *der* (PL *die* Wasserfälle).

watering can *noun* Gießkanne *die* (PL *die* Gießkannen).

water melon *noun* Wassermelone *die* (PL *die* Wassermelonen).

waterproof *adjective* wasserdicht.

water-skiing *noun* Wasserskifahren *das*; **to go water-skiing** Wasserski fahren◊.

water sports *plural noun* Wassersport *der*.

wave *noun* **1** (*in the sea*) Welle *die* (PL *die* Wellen); **2** (*with your hand*) **to give somebody a wave** jemandem zuwinken SEP; **she gave him a wave from the bus** sie winkte ihm vom Bus zu.
wave *verb* **1** (*with your hand*) winken; **2** (*flap*) schwenken (*a flag, for example*).

wax *noun* Wachs *das*.

way *noun* **1** (*a route or road*) Weg *der* (PL *die* Wege); **the way to town** der Weg in die Stadt; **we asked the way**

to the station wir haben gefragt, wie man zum Bahnhof kommt; **on the way back** auf dem Rückweg; **on the way** unterwegs; **to be in the way** im Weg sein; **to be in somebody's way** jemandem im Weg sein; **to get out of the way** aus dem Weg gehen; **2 to lose your way** sich verlaufen✧, (*in a car*) sich verfahren✧; **3 'way in'** 'Eingang'; **'way out'** 'Ausgang'; **4** (*direction*) Richtung *die* (PL *die* Richtungen); **which way did he go?** in welche Richtung ist er gegangen?; **this way** in diese Richtung; **5** (*side*) **the right way up** richtig herum; **the wrong way round** falsch herum; **the other way round** andersherum; **6** (*distance*) **it's a long way** es ist weit weg; **we still had a little way to go** wir mussten noch ein kleines Stück gehen; **7** (*manner*) Art und Weise *die*; **my way of learning German** meine Art und Weise, Deutsch zu lernen; **he does it his way** er macht es auf seine Art und Weise; **I've done it the wrong way** ich habe es falsch gemacht; **in a way** in gewisser Weise; **8 no way!** auf keinen Fall!; **9 by the way** übrigens.

we *pronoun* wir; **we're going to the cinema tonight** wir gehen heute Abend ins Kino.

weak *adjective* **1** (*feeble*) schwach; **in a weak voice** mit schwacher Stimme; **2** dünn (*coffee or tea*).

wealthy *adjective* reich.

weapon *noun* Waffe *die* (PL *die* Waffen); **weapons of mass destruction** Massenvernichtungswaffen *die* (*plural*).

wear *noun* **children's wear** *die* Kinderkleidung; **sports wear** *die* Sportkleidung.
wear *verb* tragen✧, anhaben✧ SEP (*informal*); **she often wears red** sie trägt oft Rot; **Tamsin's wearing her jeans** Tamsin hat ihre Jeans an.

weather *noun* **1** Wetter *das*; **what's the weather like?** wie ist das Wetter?; **in fine weather** bei schönem Wetter; **the weather is terrible** das Wetter ist furchtbar; **2 in wet weather** wenn es regnet; **the weather was cold** es war kalt.

weather forecast *noun* Wettervorhersage *die*; **the weather forecast says it will rain** der Wettervorhersage zufolge soll es regnen.

web *noun* **1** (*spider's*) Spinnennetz *das* (PL *die* Spinnennetze); **2 the Web** Netz *das*.

web page *noun* Webseite *die* (PL *die* Webseiten).

web site *noun* Website *die* (PL *die* Websites).

wedding *noun* Hochzeit *die* (PL *die* Hochzeiten).

Wednesday *noun* **1** Mittwoch *der* (PL *die* Mittwoche); **on Wednesday** (am) Mittwoch; **I'm going to the cinema on Wednesday** ich gehe Mittwoch ins Kino; **see you on Wednesday!** bis Mittwoch!; **every Wednesday** jeden Mittwoch; **last Wednesday** vorigen Mittwoch; **next Wednesday** nächsten Mittwoch; **2 on Wednesdays** mittwochs; **the**

a
b
c
d
e
f
g
h
i
j
k
l
m
n
o
p
q
r
s
t
u
v
w
x
y
z

museum is closed on **Wednesdays** das Museum ist mittwochs geschlossen.

weed *noun* Unkraut *das*.

week *noun* Woche *die* (PL *die* Wochen); **last week** vorige Woche; **next week** nächste Woche; **this week** diese Woche; **for weeks** wochenlang; **a week today** heute in einer Woche; **in three weeks' time** in drei Wochen.

weekday *noun* **on weekdays** wochentags.

weekend *noun* Wochenende *das* (PL *die* Wochenenden); **last weekend** voriges Wochenende; **next weekend** nächstes Wochenende; **they're coming for the weekend** sie kommen übers Wochenende; **I'll do it at the weekend** ich mache es am Wochenende; **have a nice weekend!** (ein) schönes Wochenende!

weigh *verb* 1 wiegen◇; **to weigh something** etwas wiegen; **to weigh yourself** sich wiegen; 2 **how much do you weigh?** wie viel wiegst du?; **I weigh 50 kilos** ich wiege fünfzig Kilo.

weight *noun* 1 Gewicht *das* (PL *die* Gewichte); 2 **to put on weight** zunehmen◇ SEP; 3 **to lose weight** abnehmen◇ SEP.

weird *adjective* seltsam.

welcome *noun* 1 **they gave us a warm welcome** sie haben uns herzlich empfangen; 2 **welcome to Oxford!** herzlich willkommen in Oxford!

welcome *adjective* willkommen;

you're welcome any time du bist immer willkommen; **'thank you!' – 'you're welcome!'** 'danke!' - 'bitte!'.

welcome *verb* begrüßen; **to welcome somebody** jemanden begrüßen.

well[1] *adverb* 1 **to be well** gesund sein; **I'm very well, thank you** danke, es geht mir gut; **get well soon!** gute Besserung!; 2 gut; **Terry played well** Terry hat gut gespielt; **it's well paid** es wird gut bezahlt; **well done!** gut gemacht!; 3 **as well** auch; **Kevin's coming as well** Kevin kommt auch; 4 na ja; **well, never mind** na ja, macht nichts; 5 gut; **it may well be that** … es ist gut möglich, dass …; **very well then, you can go** also gut, du kannst gehen.

well[2] *noun* Brunnen *der* (PL *die* Brunnen).

well-behaved *adjective* artig.

well-done *adjective* durchgebraten (*steak*).

wellington (boot) *noun* Gummistiefel *der* (PL *die* Gummistiefel).

well-known *adjective* bekannt.

well-off *adjective* wohlhabend.

Welsh *noun* 1 **the Welsh** (*people*) die Waliser (*plural*); 2 (*language*) Walisisch *das*.
Welsh *adjective* walisisch; **he's Welsh** er ist Waliser; **she's Welsh** sie ist Waliserin.

Welshman *noun* Waliser *der* (PL *die* Waliser).

Welshwoman *noun* Waliserin *die* (PL *die* Waliserinnen).

west *noun* Westen *der*; **in the west** im Westen.
west *adjective* West-; **the west side** die Westseite; **west wind** *der* Westwind; **west of** westlich von; **it's west of Munich** es liegt westlich von München.
west *adverb* nach Westen.

western *noun* (*film*) Western *der* (PL *die* Western).

West Indian *noun* Westinder *der* (PL *die* Westinder), Westinderin *die* (PL *die* Westinderinnen).
West Indian *adjective* westindisch.

West Indies *plural noun* die Westindischen Inseln (*plural*); **in the West Indies** auf den Westindischen Inseln.

wet *adjective* **1** nass; **we got wet** wir sind nass geworden; **2 a wet day** ein regnerischer Tag.

whale *noun* Wal *der* (PL *die* Wale).

what *pronoun, adjective* **1** (*in questions*) was; **what did you say?** was hast du gesagt?; **what's she doing?** was macht sie?; **what did you buy?** was hast du gekauft?; **what is it?** was ist das?; **what's the matter?** was ist los?; **what's happened?** was ist passiert?; **what?** was?; **2 what's your address?** wie ist Ihre Adresse?; **what's her name?** wie heißt sie?; **what was it like?** wie war's?; **3** (*asking for an amount*) wie viel; **at what time?** um wie viel Uhr?; **4** (*that which*) was (*relative pronoun*); **she told me what had happened** sie hat mir gesagt, was passiert ist; **do what I tell you** tu, was ich dir sage; **5** (*which*) welcher/welche/welches; **what country is it in?** in welchem Land ist es?; **what colour is it?** welche Farbe hat es?; **what make is it?** welche Marke ist es?; **6 what for?** wozu?

wheat *noun* Weizen *der*.

wheel *noun* Rad *das* (PL *die* Räder); **the spare wheel** das Reserverad; **the steering wheel** das Lenkrad.

wheelbarrow *noun* Schubkarre *die* (PL *die* Schubkarren).

wheelchair *noun* Rollstuhl *der* (PL *die* Rollstühle).

when *adverb* wann; **when is she arriving?** wann kommt sie an?; **when's your birthday?** wann hast du Geburtstag?
when *conjunction* **1** (*with the past*) als; **I was out shopping when you rang** ich war beim Einkaufen, als du anriefst; **2** (*with the present or future*) wenn; **when she comes I'll ring** wenn sie kommt, rufe ich an.

where *adverb, conjunction* wo; **where do you live?** wo wohnst du?; **where are you going?** wo gehst du hin?; **I don't know where they live** ich weiß nicht, wo sie wohnen.

whether *conjunction* ob; **I don't know whether he's back** ich weiß nicht, ob er schon zurück ist.

which *adjective, pronoun* **1** welcher/welche/welches; **which CD did you buy?** welche CD hast du gekauft?; **2 which (one)** welcher/welche/welches (*depending on the*

a
b
c
d
e
f
g
h
i
j
k
l
m
n
o
p
q
r
s
t
u
v
w
x
y
z

gender of the noun the question refers back to); **'I met your brother'** – **'which one?'** 'ich habe deinen Bruder getroffen' - 'welchen?'; **'I met your sister'** – **'which one?'** 'ich habe deine Schwester getroffen' - 'welche?'; **'have you seen my book?'** -**'which one?'** 'hast du mein Buch gesehen?' - 'welches?'; **3** (*relative pronoun*) der/die/das (*depending on the gender of the noun 'which' refers to*), (*plural*) die; **the film which is showing now** der Film, der gerade läuft; **the lamp which is on the table** die Lampe, die auf dem Tisch steht; **the book which I lent you** das Buch, das ich dir geliehen habe; **the books which I've read** die Bücher, die ich gelesen habe.

while *noun* **for a while** eine Weile; **she worked here for a while** sie hat eine Weile hier gearbeitet; **after a while** nach einer Weile.

while *conjunction* während; **you can make some coffee while I'm finishing my homework** du kannst Kaffee kochen, während ich meine Hausaufgaben fertig mache.

whip *noun* Peitsche *die* (PL *die* Peitschen).
whip *verb* schlagen✧ (*cream*);
whipped cream *die* Schlagsahne.

whisker *noun* Schnurrhaar *das* (PL *die* Schnurrhaare).

whisky *noun* Whisky *der* (PL *die* Whiskys).

whisper *noun* Flüstern *das*; **in a whisper** im Flüsterton.
whisper *verb* flüstern.

whistle *noun* Pfeife *die* (PL *die* Pfeifen).
whistle *verb* pfeifen✧.

white *noun* Weiß *das*; **egg white** *das* Eiweiß.
white *adjective* weiß; **a white shirt** ein weißes Hemd.

white coffee *noun* Kaffee mit Milch *der* (PL *die* Kaffees mit Milch).

Whitsun *noun* Pfingsten *das* (PL *die* Pfingsten).

who *pronoun* **1** (*in questions*) wer; **who wants some chocolate?** wer möchte Schokolade?; **2** (*in the accusative*) wen; **who did you ring?** wen hast du angerufen?; **3** (*in the dative*) wem; **who did you give it to?** wem hast du es gegeben?; **4** (*relative pronoun*) der/die/das (*depending on the gender of the noun 'who' refers to*), (*plural*) die; **my boy friend who lives in Liverpool** mein Freund, der in Liverpool wohnt; **my girl friend who lives in Berlin** meine Freundin, die in Berlin wohnt; **the child who's staying with us** das Kind, das bei uns wohnt; **the friends who are coming to see us tonight** die Freunde, die heute Abend zu Besuch kommen.

whole *noun* **the whole of the class** die ganze Klasse; **the whole of Germany** ganz Deutschland; **on the whole** im Großen und Ganzen.
whole *adjective* ganz; **the whole family** die ganze Familie; **the whole morning** den ganzen Morgen; **the whole time** die ganze Zeit; **the whole world** die ganze Welt.

a b c d e f g h i j k l m n o p q r s t u v **w** x y z

wholemeal *adjective* Vollkorn-; **wholemeal bread** *das* Vollkornbrot.

whom *pronoun* **1** den/die/das, (*plural*) die; **the man whom I saw** der Mann, den ich sah; **the woman whom I saw** die Frau, die ich sah; **the child whom I saw** das Kind, das ich sah; **2** (*in the dative*) dem/der/dem, (*plural*) denen; **the girl to whom I wrote** das Mädchen, dem ich geschrieben habe; **3** (*in questions*) wen; **whom did you see?** wen haben Sie gesehen?; **4 to whom did you give it?** wem haben Sie es gegeben?

whose *pronoun, adjective* **1** (*in questions*) wessen; **whose is this jacket?** wessen Jacke ist das?; **whose shoes are these?** wessen Schuhe sind das?; **2 whose is it?** wem gehört das?; **I know whose it is** ich weiß, wem es gehört; **3** (*as a relative pronoun*) dessen/deren/dessen (*depending on the gender of the noun 'whose' refers to*), (*plural*) deren; **the man whose car I'm buying** der Mann, dessen Auto ich kaufe; **the woman whose bag I found** die Frau, deren Tasche ich gefunden habe; **the girl whose sister I know** das Mädchen, dessen Schwester ich kenne; **the people whose children he teaches** die Leute, deren Kinder er unterrichtet.

why *adverb* **1** warum; **why did she phone?** warum hat sie angerufen?; **why not?** warum nicht?; **2 that's why I don't want to come** deswegen will ich nicht kommen.

wicked *adjective* **1** (*bad*) böse; **2** (*brilliant*) geil (*informal*).

wide *adjective* **1** breit; **it's a very wide road** es ist eine sehr breite Straße; **the shelf is 30 cm wide** das Regal ist dreißig Zentimeter breit; **wide screen** *das* Breitbild; **2** groß; **a wide range** eine große Auswahl. **wide** *adverb* **the door was wide open** die Tür stand weit offen.

wide awake *adjective* hellwach.

widow *noun* Witwe *die* (PL *die* Witwen).

widower *noun* Witwer *der* (PL *die* Witwer).

width *noun* Breite *die*.

wife *noun* Ehefrau *die* (PL *die* Ehefrauen).

wig *noun* Perücke *die* (PL *die* Perücken).

wild *adjective* **1** wild; **wild animals** wilde Tiere; **2** (*crazy*) verrückt (*idea, party, person*); **3 to be wild about something** scharf auf etwas (ACC) sein.

wildlife *noun* Tierwelt *die*; **a programme on wildlife in Africa** eine Sendung über die afrikanische Tierwelt.

wildlife park *noun* Wildpark *der* (PL *die* Wildparks).

will *verb* **1** (*in German the present tense is often used to express future actions and intentions*) **I'll wait for you at the bus stop** ich warte an der Bushaltestelle auf dich; **he'll be pleased to help you** er hilft dir gern; **that won't be a problem** das ist kein Problem; **I'll phone them at**

a b c d e f g h i j k l m n o p q r s t u v w x y z

once ich rufe sie sofort an; **2** (*the German future tense is used when firm intention is stressed, when referring to the more distant future and when some doubt about the future is expressed*) werden◇; **he will definitely come** er wird ganz bestimmt kommen; **she'll probably ring before leaving** sie wird wahrscheinlich anrufen, bevor sie geht; **3** (*in questions and requests*) **will you have some more tea?** möchten Sie noch Tee?; **will you help me?** hilfst du mir?; **'will you write to me?' — 'of course I will!'** 'schreibst du mir?' — 'ja, natürlich'; **'he won't like it' — 'yes he will'** 'es wird ihm nicht gefallen' — 'doch'; **4** wollen◇; **he won't help us** er will uns nicht helfen; **the car won't start** das Auto will nicht anspringen.

willing *adjective* **to be willing to do something** bereit sein, etwas zu tun; **I'm willing to pay half** ich bin bereit, die Hälfte zu zahlen.

willingly *adverb* gern.

willow *noun* Weide die (PL die Weiden).

win *noun* Sieg der (PL die Siege); **our win over Everton** unser Sieg über Everton.
win *verb* **1** gewinnen◇; **we won!** wir haben gewonnen!; **2 to win a prize** einen Preis bekommen.

wind[1] *noun* Wind der (PL die Winde).

wind[2] *verb* **1** wickeln (*a wire or rope, for example*); **2** aufziehen◇ SEP (*a clock*).

wind farm *noun* Windpark der (PL die Windparks).

wind instrument *noun* Blasinstrument das (PL die Blasinstrumente).

window *noun* **1** Fenster das (PL die Fenster); **to look out of the window** aus dem Fenster sehen; **2** (*in a shop*) Schaufenster das (PL die Schaufenster).

windscreen *noun* Windschutzscheibe die (PL die Windschutzscheiben).

windscreen wiper *noun* Scheibenwischer der (PL die Scheibenwischer).

windsurfing *noun* Windsurfen das; **to go windsurfing** windsurfen gehen.

windy *adjective* windig; **it's windy today** heute ist es windig.

wine *noun* Wein der (PL die Weine); **a glass of white wine** ein Glas Weißwein.

wing *noun* Flügel der (PL die Flügel).

wink *verb* **to wink at somebody** jemandem zuzwinkern SEP.

winner *noun* Sieger der (PL die Sieger), Siegerin die (PL die Siegerinnen).

winning *adjective* siegreich.

winnings *plural noun* Gewinn der.

winter *noun* Winter der (PL die Winter); **in winter** im Winter.

wipe *verb* 1 abwischen SEP; **I'll just wipe the table** ich wische schnell den Tisch ab; **to wipe your nose** sich (DAT) die Nase abwischen; 2 **to wipe the floor** den Boden wischen; 3 **to wipe your feet** sich (DAT) die Schuhe abtreten SEP.

• **to wipe up** abtrocknen SEP (*dishes*).

wire *noun* Draht der (PL die Drähte); **electric wire** die Leitung.

wise *adjective* weise.

wish *noun* 1 Wunsch der (PL die Wünsche); **to make a wish** sich (DAT) etwas wünschen; **make a wish!** wünsch dir was!; 2 **best wishes on your birthday** alles Gute zum Geburtstag; 3 (*in a letter*) **with best wishes** mit freundlichen Grüßen.
wish *verb* 1 **I wish she were here** ich wünschte, sie wäre hier; 2 **to wish for something** sich (DAT) etwas wünschen; 3 **to wish somebody a happy Christmas** jemandem frohe Weihnachten wünschen; **I wished him happy birthday** ich habe ihm alles Gute zum Geburtstag gewünscht.

wit *noun* Geist der.

with *preposition* 1 mit (+ DAT); **with me** mit mir; **with pleasure** mit Vergnügen; **he went on holiday with his friends** er ist mit seinen Freunden in die Ferien gefahren; **a girl with red hair** ein Mädchen mit roten Haaren; 2 (*at the house of*) bei (+ ACC); **we're staying the night with friends** wir übernachten bei Freunden; 3 vor (+ DAT); **to shiver with cold** vor Kälte zittern; **to**

tremble with fear vor Angst zittern; 4 **I haven't got any money with me** ich habe kein Geld dabei.

without *preposition* ohne (+ ACC); **without you** ohne dich; **without a sweater** ohne einen Pullover; **without knowing** ohne zu wissen.

witness *noun* Zeuge der (PL die Zeugen), Zeugin die (PL die Zeuginnen).

witty *adjective* geistreich.

wolf *noun* Wolf der (PL die Wölfe).

woman *noun* Frau die (PL die Frauen); **a woman friend** eine Freundin; **a woman doctor** eine Ärztin.

wonder *noun* Wunder das (PL die Wunder); **it's no wonder you're tired** es ist kein Wunder, dass du müde bist.
wonder *verb* 1 sich fragen; **I wonder why she did that** ich frage mich, warum sie das getan hat; 2 **I wonder who?** wer wohl?; **I wonder where Jake is** wo Jake wohl ist?; 3 (*in polite requests*) **I wonder if you could tell me ...?** könnten Sie mir vielleicht sagen ...?

wonderful *adjective* wunderbar.

wood *noun* Holz das; **the lamp is made of wood** die Lampe ist aus Holz.

wooden *adjective* Holz-, hölzern; **wooden toys** das Holzspielzeug.

woodwork *noun* (*craft*) Tischlerei die.

wool *noun* Wolle die.

a
b
c
d
e
f
g
h
i
j
k
l
m
n
o
p
q
r
s
t
u
v
w
x
y
z

633

word *noun* **1** Wort *das* (PL *die* Wörter) (*the plural 'Wörter' is used when the words are unrelated*); **a long word** ein langes Wort; **what's the German word for 'window'?** wie heißt 'window' auf Deutsch?; **I've learned ten German words today** ich habe heute zehn deutsche Wörter gelernt; **words in the dictionary** Wörter im Wörterbuch; **2** Wort *das* (PL *die* Worte) (*the plural 'Worte' is used when the words are connected in a text or conversation*); **he wanted to say a few words** er wollte ein paar Worte sagen; **in other words** mit anderen Worten; **to have a word with somebody** mit jemandem sprechen; **3** (*promise*) Wort *das*; **to keep your word** sein Wort halten; **he broke his word** er hat sein Wort gebrochen; **4 the words of a song** der Text von einem Lied.

word processing *noun* Textverarbeitung *die*.

word processor *noun* Textverarbeitungssystem *das* (PL *die* Textverarbeitungssysteme).

work *noun* Arbeit *die*; **I enjoy my work** meine Arbeit macht mir Spaß; **she's looking for work** sie sucht Arbeit; **I've got some work to do** ich habe noch etwas Arbeit; **he's out of work** er hat keine Arbeit; **to be off work** nicht arbeiten; **Ben's off work** (*sick*) Ben ist krank; **to go to work on the tube** mit der U-Bahn zur Arbeit fahren.
work *verb* **1** arbeiten; **she works in an office** sie arbeitet in einem Büro; **Mum works as a dentist** Mutti ist Zahnärztin; **he works part-time** er arbeitet halbtags; **2** (*to operate*) sich auskennen ◇ SEP mit; **can you work the video?** kennst du dich mit dem Videorekorder aus?; **3** (*function*) funktionieren; **the washing machine's not working** die Waschmaschine funktioniert nicht; **4** (*a plan or idea*) klappen; **that worked really well** das hat prima geklappt.

● **to work out 1** (*understand*) verstehen ◇; **I can't work out why** ich kann nicht verstehen, warum; **2** (*exercise*) trainieren; **3** (*to go well*) klappen; **4** (*calculate*) ausrechnen SEP (*a sum*); **I'll work out how much it would cost** ich rechne aus, wie viel es kosten würde; **5** (*solve*) lösen (*a problem*).

worker *noun* Arbeiter *der* (PL *die* Arbeiter), Arbeiterin *die* (PL *die* Arbeiterinnen).

work experience *noun* Praktikum *das* (PL *die* Praktika); **to do work experience** ein Praktikum machen.

working-class *adjective* der Arbeiterschicht; **a working-class family** eine Familie der Arbeiterschicht.

work of art *noun* Kunstwerk *das* (PL *die* Kunstwerke).

workshop *noun* Werkstatt *die* (PL *die* Werkstätten).

world *noun* Welt *die*; **the biggest tree in the world** der größte Baum der Welt; **all over the world** auf der ganzen Welt; **the Western world** die westliche Welt.

World Cup *noun* **the World Cup** die Weltmeisterschaft.

world war *noun* Weltkrieg *der* (PL *die* Weltkriege); **the Second World War** der Zweite Weltkrieg.

worm *noun* Wurm *der* (PL *die* Würmer).

worn out *adjective* **1** (*person*) erschöpft; **2** (*clothes or shoes*) abgetragen.

worried *adjective* **1** besorgt; **his worried parents** seine besorgten Eltern; **2 to be worried about somebody** sich (DAT) um jemanden Sorgen machen; **we're worried about Susan** wir machen uns um Susan Sorgen.

worry *noun* Sorge *die* (PL *die* Sorgen). **worry** *verb* sich (DAT) Sorgen machen; **don't worry!** keine Sorge!; **don't worry about it** mach dir darum keine Sorgen.

worrying *adjective* beunruhigend.

worse *adjective* **1** (*more unpleasant*) schlimmer (*problem, pain, illness*); **things couldn't be worse** es kann nicht schlimmer kommen; **2** (*less good*) schlechter; **it was even worse than the last time** es war noch schlechter als letztes Mal; **to get worse** schlechter werden; **the weather's getting worse** das Wetter wird schlechter; **she's getting worse** (*in health*) es geht ihr schlechter.

worst *adjective* **1** (*most unpleasant*) schlimmster/schlimmste/schlimmstes; **the worst** der/die/das schlimmste; **it was the worst day of my life** es war der schlimmste

Tag meines Lebens; **if the worst comes to the worst** wenn es zum Schlimmsten kommt; **2** (*least good*) schlechtester/schlechteste/schlechtestes; **it's his worst film** das ist sein schlechtester Film; **French is my worst subject** in Französisch bin ich am schlechtesten.

worth *adjective* **to be worth** wert sein; **how much is it worth?** wie viel ist es wert?; **it's worth buying** das lohnt sich zu kaufen; **it's worth it** das lohnt sich; **it's not worth it** es lohnt sich nicht.

would *verb* **1 would you like something to eat?** möchtest du etwas essen?; **what would you like?** was möchten Sie?; **2 I wouldn't do it** ich würde das nicht machen; **I would buy it, but I haven't got any money at the moment** ich würde es kaufen, aber ich habe zur Zeit kein Geld; **I'd like to go to the cinema** ich würde gern ins Kino gehen; **she said she'd help us** sie hat gesagt, sie würde uns helfen; **3 that would be a good idea** das wäre ein gute Idee; **if we had asked her she would have helped us** wenn wir sie gefragt hätten, hätte sie uns geholfen; **4 he wouldn't answer** er wollte nicht antworten; **the car wouldn't start** das Auto wollte nicht anspringen.

wound *noun* Wunde *die* (PL *die* Wunden). **wound** *verb* verwunden.

wrap *verb* einwickeln SEP; **I'm going to wrap (up) my presents** ich wickele meine Geschenke ein; **could you wrap it for me please?** können Sie es bitte in Geschenkpapier einwickeln?

wrapping paper *noun* Geschenkpapier *das*.

wreck *noun* **1** Wrack *das* (PL *die* Wracks); **2 I feel a wreck** ich bin völlig kaputt.
wreck *verb* **1** zerstören (*a building or machinery*); **2** kaputtfahren◇ SEP (*a car*); **3** verderben◇ (*a party, holidays*); **it completely wrecked my evening** das hat mir den Abend völlig verdorben; **4** zunichte machen (*plans*).

wrestler *noun* Ringer *der* (PL *die* Ringer), Ringerin *die* (PL *die* Ringerinnen).

wrestling *noun* Ringen *das*.

wrist *noun* Handgelenk *das* (PL *die* Handgelenke).

write *verb* schreiben◇; **to write to somebody** jemandem schreiben; **I'll write her a letter** ich schreibe ihr einen Brief; **to write to a firm** an eine Firma schreiben.

• **to write down** aufschreiben◇ SEP; **I wrote down her name** ich schrieb ihren Namen auf; **she wrote it down for me** sie hat es mir aufgeschrieben.

writer *noun* Schriftsteller *der* (PL *die* Schriftsteller), Schriftstellerin *die* (PL *die* Schriftstellerinnen).

writing *noun* Schrift *die*.

wrong *adjective* **1** (*not correct*) falsch; **the wrong answer** die falsche Antwort; **it's the wrong address** das ist die falsche Adresse; **2 you've got the wrong number** Sie haben sich verwählt; **3 to be wrong** (*be mistaken*) sich irren; **I must have been wrong** ich muss mich geirrt haben; **4** (*out of order*) **to be wrong** nicht stimmen; **there's something wrong** etwas stimmt nicht; **5** (*dishonest*) nicht richtig; **it's wrong to make him pay for it** es ist nicht richtig, dass er dafür zahlen muss; **he's wrong** er hat Unrecht; **you're quite wrong there, cars pollute the environment** da haben Sie aber Unrecht, Autos verschmutzen die Umwelt; **6 what's wrong?** was ist los?
wrong *adverb* **1** (*false*) falsch; **he's got it wrong** er hat es falsch gemacht; **2 to go wrong** (*break*) kaputtgehen◇ SEP (PERF *sein*) (*informal*); **3 to go wrong** schief gehen◇ (*plan*).

Xx

xerox *noun* Fotokopie *die* (PL *die* Fotokopien).
xerox *verb* fotokopieren.

X-ray *noun* Röntgenaufnahme *die* (PL *die* Röntgenaufnahmen); **to have an X-ray** geröntgt werden◇ (PERF *sein*).
X-ray *verb* röntgen; **they X-rayed her ankle** sie haben ihren Knöchel geröntgt.

Yy

yacht *noun* **1** (*sailing boat*)
Segelboot *das* (PL *die* Segelboote);
2 (*large luxury boat*) Jacht *die* (PL *die*
Jachten).

yawn *verb* gähnen.

year *noun* **1** Jahr *das* (PL *die* Jahre);
six years ago vor sechs Jahren; **the
whole year** das ganze Jahr; **2 they
lived in Moscow for years** sie
haben jahrelang in Moskau
gewohnt; **3 to be seventeen years
old** siebzehn Jahre alt sein; **a two-
year-old child** ein zweijähriges
Kind; **4** (*in school*) Klasse *die* (PL *die*
Klassen) (*in German secondary
schools the years go from the 'fünfte
Klasse to the 'dreizehnte Klasse'*); **I'm
in Year 10** (*in Britain*) ich gehe in
die zehnte Klasse; **he'll be in Year
11** (*in Britain*) er kommt in die elfte
Klasse.

yell *verb* schreien✧.

yellow *adjective* gelb.

yes *adverb* **1** ja; **yes please** ja bitte;
'is Tom in his room?' – 'yes, he is'
'ist Tom im Zimmer?' - 'ja';
2 (*answering a negative*) doch; **'you
don't want to come with us, do
you?' – ' yes, I do!'** 'du willst nicht
mitkommen?' - 'doch!'; **'you haven't
finished, have you?' – 'yes, I have'**
'Sie sind noch nicht fertig, oder?' -
'doch!'.

yesterday *adverb* **1** gestern; **I saw
her yesterday** ich habe sie gestern
gesehen; **yesterday afternoon**
gestern Nachmittag; **yesterday**
morning gestern früh; **2 the day
before yesterday** vorgestern.

yet *adverb* **1 not yet** noch nicht; **it's
not ready yet** es ist noch nicht
fertig; **2** (*in questions*) schon; **has
she mentioned it yet?** hat sie es
schon erwähnt?

yoghurt *noun* Joghurt *der* (PL *die*
Joghurt).

yolk *noun* Eigelb *das* (PL *die* Eigelbe).

you *pronoun* **1** (*as the subject of the
sentence and in comparisons*) du
(*familiar form, singular*), Sie (*polite
form, singular and plural*); (*'du' is
the familiar way of talking to family
members, close friends, and people of
your own age; 'Sie' is more polite*) **do
you want to go to the cinema
tonight?** möchtest du heute Abend
ins Kino gehen?; **can you tell me
where the station is, please?**
können Sie mir bitte sagen, wo der
Bahnhof ist?; **he's older than you** er
ist älter als du, er ist älter als Sie;
2 (*the object form of 'du' and 'Sie', in
the dative*) dir (*familiar form,
singular*), Ihnen (*polite form,
singular and plural*); **I'll lend you
my bike** ich leihe dir mein Rad; **I'll
write to you** ich schreibe Ihnen; **I'll
come with you** ich komme mit
Ihnen mit; **3** (*the object form of 'du'
and 'Sie', in the accusative*) dich
(*familiar form, singular*), Sie (*polite
form, singular and plural*); **I saw
you** ich habe dich gesehen, ich habe
Sie gesehen; **4** (*as the subject of the
sentence*) ihr (*familiar form, plural*);
do you all want to come? wollt ihr
alle kommen?; **5** (*the object form, in*

a
b
c
d
e
f
g
h
i
j
k
l
m
n
o
p
q
r
s
t
u
v
w
x
y
z

a
b
c
d
e
f
g
h
i
j
k
l
m
n
o
p
q
r
s
t
u
v
w
x
y
z

the accusative and the dative) euch; **I'll invite you all!** ich lade euch alle ein!; **I'll give it to you later** ich gebe es euch später.

young *adjective* jung; **young people** junge Leute; **he's younger than me** er ist jünger als ich; **Tessa's two years younger than me** Tessa ist zwei Jahre jünger als ich.

your *adjective* **1** *(familiar form, singular)* dein *(this is the familiar way of talking to family members, close friends, and people of your own age; 'Ihr' is more polite);* **I met your brother** ich habe deinen Bruder getroffen; **I met your sister** ich habe deine Schwester getroffen; **I drove your car** ich bin mit deinem Auto gefahren; **I know your brothers** ich kenne deine Brüder; **2** *(familiar form, plural)* euer; **your brother** euer Bruder; **your sister** eure Schwester; **your car** euer Auto; **your friends are waiting downstairs** eure Freunde warten unten; **3** *(polite form, singular and plural)* Ihr; **your brother** Ihr Bruder; **your sister** Ihre Schwester; **your car is in the garage** Ihr Auto ist in der Garage; **you can all bring your friends** Sie können alle Ihre Freunde mitbringen.

yours *pronoun* **1** *(familiar form, singular)* deiner/deine/deins *(this is the familiar way of talking to family members, close friends, and people of your own age, 'Ihrer/Ihre/Ihrs' is more polite);* **my brother's younger than yours** mein Bruder ist jünger als deiner; **my sister is older than yours** meine Schwester ist älter als

deine; **I enjoyed that book - is it yours?** das Buch hat mir gefallen - ist es deins?; **my shoes are more expensive than yours** meine Schuhe sind teurer als deine; **2** *(familiar form, plural)* euer/eure/ eures; **my children are younger than yours** meine Kinder sind jünger als eure; **3** *(polite form, singular and plural)* Ihrer/Ihre/ Ihrs; **his father must be older than yours** sein Vater muss älter als Ihrer sein; **4 she's a friend of yours** sie ist eine Freundin von Ihnen; **these books are yours** diese Bücher gehören Ihnen; **5** *(in letters)* **Yours sincerely** Mit freundlichen Grüßen.

yourself *pronoun* **1** *(when translated by a reflexive verb in German)* dich, *(formal)* sich; **ask yourself** frage dich, fragen Sie sich; **2** *(as a reflexive dative pronoun)* dir, *(formal)* sich; **did you hurt yourself?** hast du dir wehgetan?, haben Sie sich wehgetan?; **3** *(for emphasis)* selbst; **did you do it yourself?** hast du es selbst gemacht?; **4 all by yourself** ganz allein.

yourselves *pronoun* **1** euch, *(formal)* sich; **make yourselves comfortable** macht es euch gemütlich, machen Sie es sich gemütlich; **2** *(for emphasis)* selbst; **did you do it yourselves?** habt ihr es selbst gemacht?; **3 by yourselves** allein.

youth *noun* **1** (*stage in life*) Jugend
die; **2** (*young people*) die
Jugendlichen; **today's youth** die
Jugend von heute; **3** (*young male*)
Jugendliche *der* (PL *die*
Jugendlichen).

youth hostel *noun*
Jugendherberge *die* (PL *die*
Jugendherbergen).

Yugoslavia *noun* Jugoslawien *das*;
in the former Yugoslavia im
ehemaligen Jugoslawien.

Zz

zany *adjective* verrückt.

zebra *noun* Zebra *das* (PL *die* Zebras).

zebra crossing *noun*
Zebrastreifen *der* (PL *die*
Zebrastreifen).

zero *noun* Null *die* (PL *die* Nullen).

zigzag *verb* **1** im Zickzack laufen◇
(PERF *sein*); **2** (*in a car*) im Zickzack
fahren◇ (PERF *sein*).

zip *noun* Reißverschluss *der* (PL *die*
Reißverschlüsse).

zodiac *noun* Tierkreis *der*; **the
signs of the zodiac** die
Sternzeichen (*plural*).

zone *noun* Zone *die* (PL *die* Zonen).

zoo *noun* Zoo *der* (PL *die* Zoos).

zoom lens *noun* Zoomobjektiv *das*
(PL *die* Zoomobjektive).

a
b
c
d
e
f
g
h
i
j
k
l
m
n
o
p
q
r
s
t
u
v
w
x
y
z

GERMAN LIFE AND CULTURE

The year in Germany

Neujahr
New Year's Day, a public holiday.

Id-al-Fitr
The date of this Muslim festival varies from year to year. It is celebrated mainly by the Turkish population, the largest Muslim group in Germany.

Heilige Drei Könige
Feast of the Three Kings: 6th January. This and some other days are public holidays only in Roman Catholic parts of Germany.

Valentinstag
St Valentine's Day: 14th February. The custom of people sending a special message to someone they love is growing in Germany.

Fastnacht
Carnival, celebrated in February or March with fancy dress parties, and elaborate processions in cities like Mainz and Köln. In Bavaria, *Fastnacht* is called *Fasching*.

Ostern
Easter. Children hunt for chocolate eggs in the garden, and many families decorate their dining room with intricately painted eggs. Good Friday *(Karfreitag)* and Easter Monday *(Ostermontag)* are both public holidays.

der 1. Mai
1st May: a public holiday.

Christi Himmelfahrt
Ascension Day, a public holiday at the end of May.

Pfingstmontag
Whit Monday. A public holiday, usually at the beginning of June.

Tag der Deutschen Einheit
3rd October. A public holiday that commemorates the reuniting of East and West Germany in 1989.

Reformationstag
Reformation Day, 31st October. A public holiday in the Protestant parts of Germany.

Allerheiligen
1st November: All Saints Day. A public holiday in most Roman Catholic parts of Germany.

Sankt Nikolaus
6th December. On the night before St Nicholas' day, children put a shoe outside their bedroom. In the morning, it is filled with chocolates, nuts and maybe a small present.

Heiligabend
Christmas Eve: 24th December. Most families have a real Christmas tree, and put their presents under it. The main celebration is in the evening. People exchange presents and often light real candles on the tree. Many later go to midnight mass.

Weihnachtstag
Christmas Day: 25th December. People often have a lie-in after the celebrations of the night before. They have a big midday meal, and often visit family. The 26th December is a public holiday, too.

Silvester
31st December. It is traditional to see the New Year in with fireworks.

Food and drink

Apfelstrudel
This apple pie, originally from Austria, has a very thin pastry.

Bäckerei
A baker's shop, which usually sells many different types of bread, e.g. some with whole cereal seeds. They also sell rolls, called *Brötchen* in the north of Germany, and *Semmel* in the south.

Brezeln
Salted rolls in the shape of an 8, they are a speciality of the south of Germany.

Café
A German café serves coffee, cakes and small meals. Coffee and hot chocolate are sold by the cup *(Tasse)* or the pot *(Kännchen)*.

chips
Crisps. Chips, French fries, are called *Pommes frites*.

Eis
Ice cream. Flavours may include e.g.
- Kirsch *(cherry),*
- Pistazzien *(pistachio nut),*
- Stracciatella *(vanilla with chocolate chips)*,
- Zitrone *(lemon),*
and many others.

Emmental
A Swiss cheese.

Kalb
Veal, the meat from a calf, is widely available in Germany.

Käsefondue
Cheese fondue. It is made from cheese melted in white wine, and is eaten by dipping bread into a communal pot.

Konditorei
A cake shop, which will sell a wide range of cakes *(Kuchen)* and gateaux *(Torten)*.

Milch
Milk. Full cream milk is called *Vollmilch*. *Buttermilch*, similar to a runny yoghurt, is widely available.

Sauerkraut
Sauerkraut is boiled, pickled cabbage. It is often eaten with sausages.

Schwarzwälderkirschtorte
Black Forest Gateau, made with chocolate, cherries, and fresh whipped cream.

Spezi
A refreshing drink made from lemonade and cola.

Stollen
A rich bread-like cake, often enhanced with marzipan, and eaten at Christmas.

Türkische Spezialitäten
Turkish specialities. There are many Turkish restaurants and shops, as Turks are one of the largest ethnic groups in Germany.

Wurst
Sausage. Germany has a huge range of sausages which can be boiled *(Bockwurst)*, fried or grilled *(Bratwurst)*, or served cold like salami.

Life at School

Abitur

The end-of-school exam taken by pupils who have stayed at school to the age of 18 or 19.

Gymnasium

Grammar school. At the age of 10, pupils move from primary school *(Grundschule)* to one of four types of secondary school, depending on their ability at school:
- *Gymnasium* which requires the most academic work,
- *Realschule* or *Hauptschule*, in which work is a bit easier,
- *Sonderschule*, for pupils with learning difficulties.

There are only very few comprehensive schools *(Gesamtschulen)* in Germany.

hitzefrei

"heat free". In many schools, pupils are sent home early if the thermometer reaches 27° C.

Klasse

As most German pupils begin school when they are six, they are usually in Klasse 6 at the age of 11:

Klasse 6 = *Year 7*

Klasse 7 = *Year 8*

Klasse 8 = *Year 9*

Klasse 9 = *Year 10*

Noten

School marks. There is a set system of marks from 1 – 6 throughout Germany:

Note 1 is the best mark,
Note 6 is the lowest.
Pupils with too many low marks can be required to repeat a year *(sitzen bleiben)* instead of going on to a higher class.

die Schulferien

German school holidays can vary considerably from year to year, because different parts of Germany have their summer holidays at different times, in an effort to reduce traffic jams at peak holiday periods. There may be:
- one or two weeks in October / November
- two weeks at Christmas
- one or two weeks in February
- two weeks at Easter
- a week at Whitsun
- six or seven weeks in summer
The overall length of school holidays is much as in Britain.

Schultag

School day. The German school day is usually from 8.00 a.m. to 1 p.m. for younger pupils, with older pupils often having afternoon classes on one or more afternoons a week.

Wandertag

Trip day: a day on which school classes go on class trips. It is often the pupils who suggest where they should go.

On holiday in Germany

die Alpen

The Alps cover much of Austria and Switzerland, and stretch along the southern border of Germany. They are a popular holiday area in both summer and winter. The highest points in the three countries are:

Germany: *Zugspitze* 2964m
Austria: *Groß Glockner* 3797m
Switzerland: *Monte Rosa* 4634m

Autobahn

Motorway. Germany has an impressive network of free motorways. Motorway services are called *Raststätte* or *Autohof*.

Bayern

Bavaria, Germany's biggest *Land*, or province, is in the south, with the Alps along its southern border. Its capital is Munich. Bavaria is famous for its big wooden farmhouses and its many local beers.

Brandenburger Tor

This gateway, built in 1791, is Berlin's most famous landmark, and it is where Berliners celebrated the reunification of Germany in 1989.

Berliner Mauer

The Berlin Wall. East Germany *(DDR)* was separated from West Germany, and governed by a Communist government, from 1948 to 1989. In Berlin, the Communists built a wall around West Berlin, to prevent people from East Germany fleeing to the West. The wall was taken down after the two parts of Germany were re-united in 1989.

Donau

River Danube, which begins in Germany and reaches the Black Sea in Romania. Barges bring freight to and from Eastern Europe into Austria and Germany. A canal connects the Danube to the Rhine.

Fremdenzimmer

You see this sign outside houses which offer Bed & Breakfast accommodation. Holiday flats have the sign *Ferienwohnung*.

Hauptbahnhof

In towns which have several railway stations, the main railway station is nearly always called the *Hauptbahnhof*.

ICE

InterCity Express. These are Germany's fastest trains. You pay a supplement to travel in them, and have to book a seat.

Liechtenstein

A tiny country of 160 km^2 bordering Switzerland. It has its own government and issues its own stamps, but uses Swiss francs.

Neuschwanstein

The ultimate fairy-tale castle, *Neuschwanstein* was built in a dramatic Alpine setting to the orders of King Ludwig II of Bavaria. It was completed after his death in 1886.

Oktoberfest

A popular festival in Munich, with fun fairs and beer tents. It actually begins in September.

Ostsee
Baltic Sea. With large sandy beaches, this is a popular holiday area, especially as it is within easy reach of Berlin.

Rathaus
Town hall. It is often a grand building in the main square.

Reichstag
Built in 1894, the Reichstag was the seat of the German parliament. Destroyed by fire in 1933, it was rebuilt following the reunification of Germany in 1989, and the German parliament now sits there again.

Rhein
River Rhine. It cuts through the hills in a deep valley, with vines on the hillsides and castles on the tops. Barges carry goods to and from Holland, France, etc

Skiferien
Skiing holidays. Switzerland, Austria and Germany have established ski resorts, and winter sports are popular in all three countries.

Straßenbahn
Tram. Many German cities have trams as well as buses. Buy your tickets from the machine at the stop (it's cheaper than from the driver) and cancel them once you are on the tram. The same tickets can be used on buses and underground trains, too.

Südtirol
South Tyrol. Part of Italy, in the Alps, where people speak both German and Italian.

U-Bahn
Underground trains. The trains serving the suburbs are called *S-Bahn*.

Weihnachtsmarkt
Christmas market. Decorated with greenery and smelling of mulled wine and roast chestnuts, these markets are a beautiful setting for buying Christmas gifts.

Wien
Vienna, the capital of Austria. Known for its music, its museums and cafes, the white horses in the Spanish Riding School and the *Riesenrad*, an enormous Ferris wheel built in 1897.

Life in Germany

Biergarten
'Beer gardens' are common especially in the south of Germany, where people of all generations relax on summer afternoons and evenings. Coffee, cake, soft drinks, and small meals can be ordered, as well as beer.

Bundestag
The German 'House of Commons'. Members of Parliament (*Abgeordnete*) are elected every four years.

Feiertag
Public holiday. Germany has more public holidays than most countries in Europe, but if a public holiday falls on a Saturday or Sunday, it's 'lost', i.e. the following Monday is a working day as usual.

Freibad
Outdoor swimming pool. These are very popular, as summers are hot. People often swim in lakes, too.

Hochdeutsch
High German, or 'standard German', as spoken e.g. on TV. Each area of German, Austria and German-speaking Switzerland has its own – often quite marked – dialect.

Kaffee und Kuchen
When, in mid-afternoon, Germans, Swiss and Austrians say it's time for 'coffee', they often mean it's time for a slice of cake as well. All three countries are justifiably famous for their mouth-watering cakes.

Kanton
Switzerland is divided into 26 provinces called *Kantonen*.

Kanzler
The German prime minister is called the *Kanzler* (Chancellor).

Land
Germany is divided into 16 provinces, each called a Land. The largest is Bavaria (*Bayern*), the Land with the largest population is *Nordrhein-Westfalen*. Three cities are *Länder* in their own right: Berlin, Hamburg, and Bremen.

Marktplatz
At the centre of most towns is the 'market square', often lined with gabled houses.

Olympia-Stadion
A big stadium in Munich, home to the football team, *Bayern München*.

Personalausweis
Identity card, which can be used instead of a passport for travel within the EU.

Postleitzahl
Postcode. German postcodes have five figures and no letters.

Republik
Germany is a republic, with a president (*Präsident*) at its head.

Did you know...?

★ that you can be fined if you cross the road when the traffic light *(Ampel)* is red for pedestrians?

★ that a *Berliner* is a doughnut, a *Bitburger* a beer, a *Homburger* a hat, a *Wiener* a sausage, and a *Hamburger*, of course, a hamburger?

★ that German letter boxes *(Briefkasten)* are yellow?

★ that cars from Switzerland have the letters *CH* and stamps have the name *Helvetia*?

★ that, in Austria, potatoes are often called *Erdäpfel* (apples of the earth) and tomatoes *Paradeiser* (fruits of paradise)?

★ that more people in the EU *(Europäische Union)* have German as their mother tongue than English, French, or any other language?

★ that the wooden beams of half-timbered houses *(Fachwerkhäuser)* are red, not black, because they used to be preserved with bull's blood?

★ that people who live in the south of Germany get more public holidays *(Feiertage)* than those who live in the north?

★ that Germany's biggest airport *(Flughafen)* is Frankfurt, and its busiest seaport is Hamburg?

★ that the usual way of greeting people is:
Guten Tag in northern Germany,
Grüß Gott in southern Germany,
Grüezi in Switzerland,
Servus in Austria,
but you can also say *Hallo* everywhere?

★ that the biggest city in Switzerland is Zürich, but the capital city *(Hauptstadt)* is Bern?

★ that the name *Köln* comes from the Roman word 'colonia', because the city was a Roman colony?

★ that Switzerland's most famous mountain, the *Matterhorn* (4478m), is not its highest; the highest is the *Monte Rosa* (4634m)?

★ that until 1918, Austria *(Österreich)* was at the centre of an empire that included Hungary, Slovakia, Czech Republic, and parts of Poland, Ukraine and Italy?

★ that officers in the German police *(Polizei)* wear a green uniform and are armed?

★ that a minority of Swiss people speak *Romansch*, a language derived from Latin?

★ that to travel on Swiss or Austrian motorways, you have to buy a sticker called a *Vignette*, and display the sticker on the car windscreen?

NUMBERS

null	0	einundzwanzig	21
eins	1	zweiundzwanzig	22
zwei	2	dreiundzwanzig	23
drei	3	vierundzwanzig	24
vier	4	fünfundzwanzig	25
fünf	5	sechsundzwanzig	26
sechs	6	siebenundzwanzig	27
sieben	7	achtundzwanzig	28
acht	8	neunundzwanzig	29
neun	9		
zehn	10	dreißig	30
elf	11	vierzig	40
zwölf	12	fünfzig	50
dreizehn	13	sechzig	60
vierzehn	14	siebzig	70
fünfzehn	15	achtzig	80
sechzehn	16	neunzig	90
siebzehn	17		
achtzehn	18	hundert	100
neunzehn	19	tausend	1000
zwanzig	20	eine Million	1 000 000

DATES

am ersten Januar	on January 1st
der erste Januar	the 1st of January
zweite (2.)	2nd
dritte (3.)	3rd
vierte (4.)	4th
fünfte	5th
sechste	6th
siebte	7th
achte	8th
neunte	9th
zehnte	10th
elfte	11th
zwölfte	12th
dreizehnte	13th
vierzehnte	14th
fünfzehnte	15th
sechzehnte	16th
siebzehnte	17th
achtzehnte	18th
neunzehnte	19th
zwanzigste	20th
einundzwanzigste	21st
dreißigste	30th

IMPORTANT DATES

Feiertag	public holiday
Fasching/Fastnacht	carnival time
Heiligabend	Christmas Eve
Karfreitag	Good Friday
Maifeiertag	May Day
Neujahr	New Year
Ostern	Easter
Pfingsten	Whitsun
Silvester	New Year's Eve
Weihnachten	Christmas
1.Weihnachtstag	Christmas Day
2. Weihnachtstag	Boxing Day

DAYS

Montag	Monday
Dienstag	Tuesday
Mittwoch	Wednesday
Donnerstag	Thursday
Freitag	Friday
Samstag/Sonnabend	Saturday
Sonntag	Sunday

MONTHS

Januar	January
Februar	February
März	March
April	April
Mai	May
Juni	June
Juli	July
August	August
September	September
Oktober	October
November	November
Dezember	December

SEASONS

der Winter	winter
der Frühiing	spring
der Sommer	summer
der Herbst	autumn

Deutschland

DEUTSCHLAND

Bundesland

Baden-Württemberg

Bayern

Berlin

Brandenburg

Bremen

Hamburg

Hessen

Mecklenburg-Vorpommern

Niedersachsen

Nordrhein-Westfalen

Rheinland-Pfalz

Saarland

Sachsen

Sachsen-Anhalt

Schleswig-Holstein

Thüringen

GERMANY

State

Baden-Württemberg

Bavaria

Berlin

Brandenburg

Bremen

Hamburg

Hessen

Mecklenburg-West Pomerania

Lower Saxony

North Rhine-Westphalia

Rhineland-Palatinate

Saarland

Saxony

Saxony-Anhalt

Schleswig- Holstein

Thuringia

Europa

EUROPA	EUROPE
Land	**Country**
Albanien	Albania
Andorra	Andorra
Belgien	Belgium
Bosnien-Herzogowina	Bosnia-Herzegovina
Bulgarien	Bulgaria
Dänemark	Denmark
Deutschland	Germany
Estland	Estonia
Finnland	Finland
Frankreich	France
Griechenland	Greece
Großbritannien	United Kingdom; Great Britain
England	England
Nordirland	Northern Ireland
Schottland	Scotland
Wales	Wales
Kroatien	Croatia
Island	Iceland
Italien	Italy
Jugoslawien	Yugoslavia
Lettland	Latvia
Liechtenstein	Liechtenstein
Litauen	Lithuania
Luxemburg	Luxembourg

EUROPA

Land

Mazedonien (Ehmalige Jugoslawische Republik Mazedonien)	FYROM (Former Yugoslav Republic of Macedonia)
Monaco	Monaco
Moldawien	Moldavia
Niederlande	Netherlands
Norwegen	Norway
Österreich	Austria
Polen	Poland
Portugal	Portugal
Republik Irland	Republic of Ireland
Rumänien	Romania
Russland	Russia
San Marino	San Marino
Schweden	Sweden
Schweiz	Switzerland
Slowakei	Slovakia
Slowenien	Slovenia
Spanien	Spain
Tschechische Republik	Czech Republic
Türkei	Turkey
Ukraine	Ukraine
Ungarn	Hungary
Weißrussland	Belarus

EUROPE

Country

List of new German spellings

New	Old
(heute, gestern etc.) Abend	(heute, gestern etc.) abend
Abflussrohr	Abflußrohr
Abschlussprüfung	Abschlußprüfung
Anlass	Anlaß
Anschluss	Anschluß
Ass	As
auf sein	aufsein
auseinander halten	auseinanderhalten
auseinander nehmen	auseinandernehmen
aus sein	aussein
Bass	Baß
Beschluss	Beschluß
bewusst	bewußt
bewusstlos	bewußtlos
Bewusstsein	Bewußtsein
Biss	Biß
bisschen	bißchen
blass	blaß
bleiben lassen	bleibenlassen
Brennnessel	Brennessel
dabei sein	dabeisein
da sein	dasein
dass	daß
durcheinander bringen	durcheinanderbringen
Einfluss	Einfluß
Entschluss	Entschluß
Erdgeschoss	Erdgeschoß
essbar	eßbar
Esszimmer	Eßzimmer
fallen lassen	fallenlassen
Fass	Faß
fertig bringen	fertigbringen

New	Old
fertig machen	fertigmachen
Fitnesstraining	Fitneßtraining
Fluss	Fluß
Föhn	Fön
föhnen	fönen
Gebiss	Gebiß
Genuss	Genuß
gewiss	gewiß
goss	goß
grässlich	gräßlich
großschreiben	groß schreiben
gut gehen	gutgehen
Halt machen	haltmachen
Hass	Haß
hässlich	häßlich
Imbiss	Imbiß
isst	ißt
irgendetwas	irgend etwas
irgendjemand	irgend jemand
Känguru	Känguruh
Karamell	Karamel
kennen lernen	kennenlernen
klein schneiden	kleinschneiden
Kompass	Kompaß
Kompromiss	Kompromiß
Kuss	Kuß
Leid tun	leid tun
liegen lassen	liegenlassen
missbilligen	mißbilligen
Missbrauch	Mißbrauch
missbrauchen	mißbrauchen
Missgeschick	Mißgeschick
misshandeln	mißhandeln
misslingen	mißlingen

New	Old
misstrauisch	mißtrauisch
Missverständnis	Mißverständnis
missverstehen	mißverstehen
muss	muß
müssten	müßten
nahe liegend	naheliegend
nass	naß
nummerieren	numerieren
Nuss	Nuß
offen bleiben	offenbleiben
Pass	Paß
Passkontrolle	Paßkontrolle
Passwort	Paßwort
pflichtbewusst	pflichtbewußt
Prozess	Prozeß
Rad fahren	radfahren
rau	rauh
Recht (haben etc.)	recht (haben etc.)
Reißverschluss	Reißverschluß
richtig stellen	richtigstellen
Riss	Riß
Rollladen	Rolladen
Russland	Rußland
sauber machen	saubermachen
schief gehen	schiefgehen
Schifffahrt	Schiffahrt
schlecht gehen	schlechtgehen
Schloss	Schloß
Schluss	Schluß
schnäuzen	schneuzen
Schuss	Schuß
schwer fallen	schwerfallen
sein lassen	seinlassen
sitzen bleiben	sitzenbleiben

New	Old
so viel (wie möglich etc.)	soviel (wie möglich etc.)
so weit (wie möglich etc.)	soweit (wie möglich etc.)
spazieren gehen	spazierengehen
stecken bleiben	steckenbleiben
stecken lassen	steckenlassen
Stewardess	Stewardeß
Stress	Streß
Telefon	Telephon
Tipp	Tip
tschüss	tschüs
übel nehmen	übelnehmen
übrig lassen	übriglassen
umso	um so
unbewusst	unbewußt
vergesslich	vergeßlich
vergisst	vergißt
Verschluss	Verschluß
(im) Voraus	(im) voraus
wie viel	wieviel
wusste	wußte
zurzeit	zur Zeit
zusammen sein	zusammensein
zu viel	zuviel
zu wenig	zuwenig